The Praetorship in the
Roman Republic

The Praetorship in the Roman Republic

Volume II

T. COREY BRENNAN

OXFORD
UNIVERSITY PRESS

2000

#41503761
OLC

OXFORD
UNIVERSITY PRESS

Oxford New York
Athens Auckland   Bangkok   Bogotá   Buenos Aires   Calcutta
Cape Town   Chennai   Dar es Salaam   Delhi   Florence   Hong Kong   Istanbul
Karachi   Kuala Lumpur   Madrid   Melbourne   Mexico City   Mumbai
Nairobi   Paris   São Paulo   Singapore   Taipei   Tokyo   Toronto   Warsaw

and associated companies in
Berlin Ibadan

Copyright © 2000 by Oxford University Press, Inc.

Published by Oxford University Press, Inc.
198 Madison Avenue, New York, New York 10016

Oxford is a registered trademark of Oxford University Press.

Library of Congress Cataloging-in-Publication Data
Brennan, T. Corey
    The praetorship in the Roman republic / T. Corey Brennan.
    p.   cm.
    Includes bibliographical references and indexes.
    ISBN 0–19–511459–0 (v. 1); ISBN 0–19–511460–4 (v. 2)
      1. Rome—History—Republic, 265–30 B.C.   2. Praetors—
    Rome.   3. Rome—Officials and employees.   4. Rome—
    Provinces—Administration.   I. Title.
    DG83.5.P6B74   2000
    937'.02—dc21   99-35017

1 3 5 7 9 8 6 4 2
Printed in the United States of America
on acid-free paper

Contents

VOLUME II

The Praetorship in the
Roman Republic

General Developments in the Praetorship, 122–82

This chapter and the next attempt to trace further additions to the Roman administrative system in the period after C. Gracchus' consequential reform of 122 B.C. that introduced a *provincia repetundarum*. Following the structure of chapter 9, in chapters 10 and 11 (the latter covering the years 81–50) discussion of the annexation of new territorial *provinciae* precedes permanent developments in the city. Then, in each of these two chapters comes an examination of special assignments in the spheres *militiae* and *domi*. Chapter 12 examines further select aspects of the city *provinciae*, while chapters 13–15 round off coverage of the various territorial provinces down to the year 50 B.C. At the end of chapter 15, I have summed up the principal ways in which the Senate staffed the various *provinciae* in the period 122–50 B.C. This is a sequel to the survey at 9.4.1–4 that treats this same question for the period down to 122 B.C. Commands in the permanent territorial *provinciae* discussed in chapters 10–11 and 13–15 are set out in tabular form in Appendices A.5, A.6, and A.7.

10.1 Roman Cilicia: Formation and Early Commands

The annexation of Cilicia as a Roman *provincia*, self-contained as an administrative unit, has its origins in a special command of the late second century. A praetor of 102, M. Antonius, received a commission against the maritime pirates in that region, with the rank of *pro consule* from the start (Cicero is explicit on that point).[1] We are well informed on the details of Antonius' late winter transit from Greece to Cilicia, how he crossed first to Pamphylia and, when the weather permitted, had a *legatus pro praetore* bring the bulk of the fleet behind him.[2] It is a useful episode to know about, for it is the first ironclad instance we have of a praetorian commander personally delegating his (enhanced) *imperium* to a subordinate (see 15.3.4). Antonius evidently then managed to clear the Cilician waters of pirates, but for that we have only a few bald statements by epitomators.[3] His exploits earned him a triumph in later 100,[4] and the consulship for 99.

Soon after Antonius' military success, the Senate decided to set up a new praetorian *provincia*, "Cilicia," specifically to combat piracy. The institution of this new
province is announced on an epigraphic document from Cnidus—a substantial
fragment, published in 1974 and re-edited in 1992, of a previously known law. The
date of this "Law on Praetorian Provinces" (*Lex de provinciis praetoriis*) is (probably) late 101. In the Cnidus inscription (as we have it), a consul of the following year
is instructed to write a general letter to various peoples and states announcing that
Cilicia has been made a "praetorian province" (ἐπαρχεία στρατηγική), expressly so
that Romans and Rome's friends "might be able to sail the sea in safety." Even after
the publication of this document, some have doubted whether Cilicia was in fact
organized at this time.[5] Though this is the first instance of the adjective στρατηγική
in a Roman document, later usage shows that the phrase we find here must indeed
mean "provincia praetoria."[6] In other words, the Romans wanted to announce that
Cilicia would have the same form of government as Asia—which, indeed, with the
exception of Q. Mucius Scaevola in 94 (14.5.4), was a "praetorian province" down
to the war with Mithridates, and then, after its "restoration" for 68 (14.6.5) down to
the end of our period.

Indeed, the broad outlines of praetorian *fasti* for Cilicia can be reconstructed
for the 90s and 80s, which points toward a properly organized and administered
praetorian *provincia* dating from the time of the Cnidus law. G. V. Sumner rightly
noted that "the first praetor of Cilicia under the terms of our law would most likely be a praetor of 100 going out in that year or as promagistrate in 99."[7] However,
the first named commander for the Roman province (probably the second or third
regular "governor" in Cilicia) is L. Cornelius Sulla, *pr. urb.* 97, who received the
provincia as a promagistrate—almost certainly *pro consule*, like governors for
Macedonia and Asia[8]—in 96. Elsewhere, I have suggested for Sulla the possibility
of an extended command in Cilicia (with duties *ex S.C.* in Cappadocia) spanning
the years 96 into 93 or even through 93 into early 92.[9] This long term in the east, I
have argued, accounts at least in part for Sulla's delay in reaching the consulship
(only for 88). The precise length of Sulla's command depends on whether L.
Gellius (*pr. per.* 94) proceeded "pro consule ex praetura"[10] to Cicilia or Asia for 93
(14.5.5). Even if we place Gellius in Cilicia, Sulla will have had a full three years
in the *provincia*.

A praetor Q. Oppius is attested in the *provincia* starting in 89. He was a supporting commander[11] in the disastrous campaign of that year which saw the *legatus* M.' Aquillius defeated in Cappadocia (14.5.9). In early 88, Oppius—who
certainly had the title "pro consule"—found himself hemmed in at Laodiceia in
Phrygia.[12] The town eventually surrendered Oppius to Mithridates, who ostentatiously paraded the praetor as his prisoner until Sulla secured his release in 85.[13]
Afterward, Oppius still styled himself as a praetor with enhanced *imperium*.[14]
Perhaps it was on Sulla's encouragement, as Badian[15] has suggested; or he may
have been entitled to it in any case. But I should think that the bronze coin issue
Q. OPPIVS PR., which—if M. Crawford is correct—borrows from the iconography
of the first-century coinage of Laodiceia, dates from the early part of Oppius' command; it is hard to see why Oppius would want to commemorate the town once it
had betrayed him. Badian, however, postulates that the types on Oppius' coins

strongly show Sullan influence; if so, the issue obviously belongs to the time after his release from captivity.[16]

One individual case remains to be discussed, which might shed light on Sulla's arrangement for Cilicia in the latter half of the 80s. An L. Lentulus *praetor* presided (apparently) over a panel of jurors ("iudices") in or after the praetorship of Q. Metellus Pius,[17] that is, 89 or (more likely) 88 (10.5.5). He is likely to be identical with the *pro consule* L. Cornelius L.f. Lentulus of an inscription that lists a Rhodian's embassies to Sulla and various known members of Sulla's staff in the east.[18] Broughton, citing these sources, suggests the Sullan L. Cornelius Lentulus was "proconsul . . . probably in Asia."[19] But it is hard to see when he could have held that rank there. We shall see (14.5.9) that Sulla left the *provincia* to L. Licinius Murena, and even when Murena unexpectedly went triumph hunting in Pontus, it is the *pro quaestore* L. Lucullus who is found holding Asia. It seems to make the most sense to regard L. Cornelius Lentulus as a praetor of 88 who received the *provincia* of Cilicia *ex praetura* as the intended successor of Q. Oppius, only taking up the assignment in 85 or later, perhaps after helping Sulla with his arrangements for Asia. If so, this Lentulus will have had to remain there for quite a long time, perhaps even down until the arrival of Cn. Cornelius Dolabella (*pr.* 81) for the year 80 (14.6.1).

In brief, given the general quality of our sources for the early first century, the fact that we can posit three or four praetorian commanders (counting the putative praetor of the Cnidus law) in a distant eastern territory in the years 100–89 suggests a policy of regular succession, and an annual vote on what to do, and thus a regular praetorian *provincia*.[20] This reconstruction is all the more compelling if L. Cornelius Lentulus indeed received Cilicia as *pro consule* (like Oppius) in the praetorian sortition for 87.

10.2 The Gauls in the Period before Sulla

10.2.1 *Consular Commands in Gallia Cisalpina down through 95*

We have seen that after 198, the Senate tried its hardest to keep praetorian commanders out of Cisalpine Gaul and Liguria (8.3.5). In the last three quarters of the second century there is just one exception to this policy, the "Oppius" who fought against Gauls as *praetor* or *pro praetore* in 146 (8.6.1). The rest of the individuals known to be active in Gallia Cisalpina (i.e., as a special military *provincia*) in these years are consular in rank. We have two or three names, clustered together in the first half of the teens. Q. Marcius Rex (*cos.* 118) triumphed over the Ligurian Stoeni—a "people situated at the base of the Alps"—on 3 December 117, so after a command of almost two years. An "L. Caicilius Q.f. pro cos." set a boundary by *senatus consultum* between the territory of Patavium and Ateste. The filiation allows either an identification with the *cos.* 142 L. Caecilius Calvus or the *cos.* 117 L. Caecilius Metellus Diadematus. Since Q. Marcius Rex was demonstrably in Cisalpina for most of 117, here L. Calvus—and thus a date of (probably) 141—seems marginally the more reasonable choice. Our notices of military activity in

Cisalpina for this period end with M. Aemilius Scaurus (*cos.* 115), who subdued some Gallic and Ligurian tribesmen and managed to triumph "de Galleis Karneis" between 27 November and 31 December of his year of office.[21] But there were doubtless other consuls active in this area whom we do not hear about because they did not triumph.[22]

Twenty years later, L. Licinius Crassus (*cos.* 95) tried to match Scaurus' feat. After being hailed "imperator" in his consulship while fighting some undistinguished Alpine tribes, he returned to Rome and prevailed on the Senate to grant him a triumph. Nevertheless, his colleague and erstwhile political ally Q. Mucius Scaevola most surprisingly vetoed the *senatus consultum*.[23] Scaevola had sought to establish himself as Crassus' moral superior even during their consular campaign.[24] But this veto of the triumph vote—a brutal use of his full consular power—does come as a surprise. Mommsen could find no parallel of a consul acting against his colleague in this way for the later Republic.[25]

If we take Valerius Maximus at his word, it would seem that Crassus headed back into the field for at least another year after his failed triumph bid. This author tells how Crassus included his hereditary enemy and potential prosecutor C. Papirius Carbo in his provincial judicial *consilium*, "when he held the *provincia* of Gaul *ex consulatu*." This should be evidence for prorogation into 94, whether in Cisalpina as before or (as Badian suggests) Gallia Cisalpina with Transalpina.[26] Of course, "Gallia" in Latin authors can stand for either province.[27] As it happens, Valerius never uses the phrase "ex consulatu" (or "ex praetura," "ex magistratu," or the like) elsewhere, which suggests that here he is reflecting (at least ultimately) a good Republican source. Yet he might simply be in error. Imperial authors were personally familiar with only promagisterial military commissions, and might be liable to make the slip.[28]

10.2.2 *Consular Commands in Gallia Transalpina down through 95*

Before taking the story of Gallia Cisalpina any further, we should touch on developments concerning Transalpine Gaul, where also praetors played no discernible role. In the latter half of the 120s, the Romans did send a string of consular commanders to undertake some major campaigns in the area east of the Rhône. The series starts with the *cos.* 125 M. Fulvius Flaccus, who was followed in this theater by C. Sextius Calvinus (*cos.* 124), Cn. Domitius Ahenobarbus (*cos.* 122), and Q. Fabius Maximus (*cos.* 121, the future "Allobrogicus"). The *cos.* 125 M. Flaccus and the *cos.* 124 C. Calvinus had at least two full years of *imperium* in Gaul, each triumphing "de Ligurib(us) Vocontieis Salluveisq(ue)" in 123 and 122 respectively.[29] In neither case is the precise month of the triumph preserved, so the exact length of their commands cannot be determined. But it does appear that for a good part of 124 there were two consular commanders in the same military *provincia* fighting exactly the same enemies (to judge from the triumphal lists).[30]

It is a mistake to think (as many have, and still do) that Cn. Domitius (*cos.* 122)—with or without Q. Fabius (*cos.* 121)—organized Gallia Transalpina as a proper *provincia.*[31] More than thirty years ago, Badian showed that our sources offer no justification for that notion, and no new evidence has emerged to dent his arguments, which need not be repeated in full here.[32] True, it does seem fairly certain that Cn. Domitius Ahenobarbus fortified a site at Narbo in a preliminary way before his departure from Gaul, in this case to protect his Via Domitia. Yet the triumphal *Fasti* cannot be taken as evidence that he lingered long after Fabius' return to do so, much less organize a province. Of course, a full Roman colony was to follow at Narbo just a few years later.[33]

All the same, a brief overview of Domitius' Gallic command might be useful, not least since it also shows the Senate's tightening control on the triumph. Cn. Domitius Ahenobarbus as *cos.* 122 was continuing his predecessors' campaign against the Salluvii, whose king soon brought the Allobroges and the Arverni into the war. It was quite likely in this year that Domitius won a victory at Vindalium—to be situated ten kilometers northeast of Avignon—against (probably) both the latter tribes. This battle must have earned Domitius his title "imperator," attested on a milestone from a military road he built during this command to secure the link with Spain. At any rate, after Vindalium he staged an ostentatious triumph-like display, in which he paraded through his military *provincia* on an elephant, with his troops in procession behind.[34]

Yet Gaul was declared consular again for 121. One author calls its recipient, the *cos.* 121 Q. Fabius Maximus, the "successor" of Domitius Ahenobarbus. But Ahenobarbus managed to remain in Gaul all through that year and certainly into the next, alongside Fabius. It is Q. Fabius who is universally credited with a decisive victory on 8 August 121 against the Allobroges and Arverni at the confluence of the Isère and Rhône. Yet Domitius did his best to grab for himself as much of the *gloria* as accrued from that military success. He saw fit to capture Bituitus, leader of the Arverni, while the Gallic chieftain was en route to give satisfaction at Rome. Domitius was incensed that Bituitus had persuaded his tribe and the Allobroges to surrender to Fabius. The Senate is said to have disapproved of this act, yet hypocritically accepted Bituitus as a prisoner all the same.[35]

The Senate allowed both Cn. Domitius and Q. Fabius to triumph on their return to Rome. The triumphal *Fasti* preserve no year for either of these triumphs. But they show that Fabius—though as *cos.* 121 junior to Domitius—triumphed first as *pro consule*, over the Allobroges and (significantly) "Bituitus king of the Arverni," and received the *agnomen* "Allobrogicus." Domitius' triumph was simply "de Galleis Arv[e]rneis."[36] And that despite the likelihood that he had won his own major victory against both Allobroges and Arverni, was hailed "imperator" first, and (technically) captured Bituitus.

The order of triumphs is the opposite of what we would expect, since it violates the accepted practice of having the senior of two paired "imperatores" triumph first.[37] Some even have taken it as proof that Domitius stayed on longer in Gaul than Fabius.[38] Yet there is an alternative explanation: Domitius had more difficulty than Fabius winning a triumph from the Senate. The wording of their respective entries in the triumphal lists does suggest that the Senate here was trying to privilege Q. Fabius Maximus over the assertive Domitius. One notes in particular that the Senate granted a triumphal *agnomen* to Fabius alone. Domitius' unofficial "triumph" no doubt irritated many, to judge from the reaction to a Roman commander who tried the same thing in Sardinia (though without the elephant) about a decade and a half later (13.1.1). We are also explicitly told that Domitius' capture of Bituitus offended the Senate, though only to a certain extent.

In the absence of any positive evidence to the contrary, we should assume that the two commanders returned at or nearly at the same time. Degrassi's suggestion of the year 120 for these two triumphs seems entirely reasonable. That terminal date would still give Cn. Domitius Ahenobarbus (as *cos.* 122) one of the longest commands in Gaul for the last quarter of the second century. M. Fulvius Flaccus (*cos.* 125) and C. Sextius Calvinus (*cos.* 124) are the only other men for that period known to hold a military *provincia* in Gaul for a comparable span, in each case between two and three full years. After Domitius, there are no commands in this theater known to exceed even two years until the late 90s.

To return to the main question under investigation: Badian's strongest proof that Gallia Transalpina was not organized as a proper province in this era comes from the fact that there are no known commanders in the *provincia* between ca. 119 and the German invasion. The first Roman commander to meet the Cimbri and Teutones in the field was the *cos.* 113 Cn. Papirius Carbo, not in Gaul but in Noricum—a major disaster which led to Carbo's prosecution on his return to Rome.[39] After defeating Carbo, these tribes started to move west, joining the Helvetian Tigurini to their numbers. But "Gallia" comes up in neither the consular sortition for 111, when the *provinciae* were "Italia" and "Numidia," nor 110, when the consuls were allotted "Numidia" and "Macedonia."[40] We know almost nothing of what the praetors were doing in those two years, but it seems unlikely that one of them had "Gallia" as his *provincia*. "No governor is recorded as receiving the first onslaught of the Germans," observes Badian. Indeed, when the German tribes first entered Gaul proper, they fought against Gauls.[41] The eventual Roman response, once the Germans seemed a real threat to Italy, was to dispatch against them a series of consuls in their year of office. Again, Badian:

> M. Junius Silanus as consul (109) and proconsul and L. Cassius Longinus as consul (107) fought against the Germans and their Gallic allies and were defeated. Q. Servilius Caepio as consul captured Tolosa and its famous treasure (106), and as proconsul was defeated at Arausio, together with the consul Cn. Mallius Maximus (105). Finally Marius took over (104) and remained in charge, as consul, until victory [fighting with Q. Lutatius Catulus, *cos.* 102 and *pro consule* 101].[42]

One might add (for the purposes of this study) that in this war *legati*—some quite senior—filled the most important subordinate roles. L. Calpurnius Piso Caesoninus (*cos.* 112) and C. Popillius Laenas (quite likely a *praetorius*) served as legates under L. Cassius Longinus in 107, as did M. Aurelius Scaurus (*cos. suff.* 108) under Cn. Mallius Maximus in 105.[43] Marius as *cos.* III 103, when returning to Rome to hold the elections for 102, left M.' Aquillius (the future *cos.* 101) in charge of his forces in Gaul. At this point, Aquillius surely had reached the praetorship, and was serving under Marius as a praetorian *legatus*.[44] Aquillius even might have received delegated *imperium*. But we find no actual praetors, in office or prorogued, taking part in any of these campaigns. This must have been deliberate policy.

10.2.3 *The Transformation of the Gauls into Regular* Provinciae

Only after the Cimbric Wars, when the threat posed by Gallic hordes from the north became fully apparent, does the Senate seem to have made Gallia Transalpina a regular *provincia*. We cannot specify a precise date, but it comes no later than the mid-90s.[45] The first known possible commander is L. Licinius Crassus, *cos.* 95; that depends on how we interpret Valerius Maximus' notice of his "ex consulatu" command in "Gallia" discussed above. However, C. Coelius Caldus (*cos.* 94) seems reasonably certain. Badian persuasively has identified him with the "C. Caelius" or "C. Coelius" of the Livian *Periocha* 73 found fighting the Salluvii in 90. That of course would mean he was prorogued three times even before the start of the Social War. Yet Badian further shows that the presence of a *legatus* P. Coelius at Placentia in 87 suggests the *cos.* 94 still had his command at that time, with charge of Cisalpina as well. So C. Caldus had to hold a joint *provincia* for upwards of eight years.[46] Even allowing for the effects of the Social War, the Roman administrative system quite plainly was too overstretched at this point to accommodate properly Transalpine Gaul as a new territorial *provincia*—and possibly Cisalpina alongside it.[47]

As Badian demonstrated, there are good parallels for such extended commands in distant theaters precisely around this time. Most notably, C. Sentius (*pr.* 94) went to Macedonia *ex praetura* for 93, and remained there at least into 87 (14.1.3). And C. Valerius Flaccus (*cos.* 93) had a command in Spain which may have included both *provinciae* until his return to Rome to triumph in 81 or 80 (13.3.2). Indeed, by the mid-80s Flaccus had to take over responsibility for not just Spain, but also Transalpine Gaul. Though he is found at Contrebia in Celtiberia in 87, he may have been in Gaul as early as 85, and is positively attested there in 83.[48] Flaccus clearly did some fighting against Gauls, since his triumph a few years later is said to have been "ex Celtiberia et Gal[lia]."[49]

So, down to Sulla, we can identify with fair certainty just two consular commanders who held Gallia Transalpina after its establishment, sometime by the mid-90s, as a regular *provincia*. The first secure incumbent, the *cos.* 94 C. Coelius Caldus, received it (as far as we can tell) in combination with Cisalpine Gaul; eventually (and quite irregularly) C. Valerius Flaccus (*cos.* 93) succeeded Coelius in Transalpina, where he remained until after Sulla's victory. Thanks to these extraordinarily long tenures, the creation of "Gallia Transalpina" probably had only a small indirect effect on the length of praetorian commands in overseas *provinciae* in the late 90s and 80s.

There is no sign that Gallia Cisalpina had its own governor in the years 87–82.[50] However, in the *Bellum Sullanum* we do find some Marians active in that area—P. Albinovanus, C. Coelius Antipater, Flavius Fimbria—who may be praetors or *praetorii* (discussed below in 10.5.6). Of these, P. Albinovanus was quite possibly a praetor. Yet even if so, it must be remembered he operated in Cisalpina during a civil war. His presence there of course tells us nothing about its routine administration.

10.3 Nonannexations in the Period before Sulla

10.3.1 *The Roman Reaction to the Bequest of Cyrene,* 96 B.C.

In 96, the kingdom of Cyrene was bequeathed to the Roman people by king Ptolemy Apion. The Senate's reaction to this gift was to decree that the cities of that kingdom should be "free."[51] The Roman administrative system, already over-stretched, was far less able to accommodate the addition of this *provincia* than it had been when it was first offered, by the will of Ptolemy Euergetes II in 154 (9.1.1). It was not essential to place Cyrene under permanent administration: it was not a particularly rich land (except for its silphium, which could be "annexed" without any responsibility for administration), nor was it threatening to Roman interests. When Rome backed off the second time from any administrative responsibility for Apion's kingdom, Cyrene soon slipped into anarchy. The organization of Cyrene as a proper *provincia* came only in the 60s, under Pompey (11.4).

It has been thought that C. Claudius Pulcher (*cos.* 92) had Cyrene as a special consular or proconsular *provincia*. An inscription of Cyrene honors C. Pulcher as "*euergetes* and patron" and gives him the title (in Dorian dialect) στραταγὸς ὕπατος Ῥωμαίων.[52] However, caution is necessary. C. Pulcher need not have been gover-nor of Cyrene but merely may have performed a service of some sort to earn its patronage.[53] And that service might have come even after the year 92. A Delian dedication to M. Antonius (*cos.* 99) from this general period also terms him στρατη-γὸς ὕπατος, but in addition τιμητής (he was censor in 97) as well as patron.[54] So C. Claudius Pulcher was not necessarily a consul in office, but just of consular rank, when the Cyreneans honored him in this way. Again, the nature of his service is uncertain. What is clear is that not long after C. Pulcher's consulship Cyrene was a mess. The *pro quaestore* L. Lucullus needed to restore order there during his Mediterranean circuit of 86, including suppressing a significant Jewish revolt. Lucullus even drew up laws on the request of the Cyreneans.[55]

10.3.2 *Rome's "Inheritance" of Egypt*

Egypt, a fantastically wealthy kingdom, was a different matter. In late 88 or early 87, Ptolemy X Alexander I (reigning since 107) conditionally bequeathed his kingdom to Rome, but only because he had been expelled from his throne. To regain his kingdom from his older brother (Ptolemy IX Soter II), he badly needed a loan from Roman financiers; the bequest was to serve as security.[56] Ptolemy X died before he could achieve his aim. Thereupon the Senate—now under the Cinnan govern-ment—moved to send *legati* to enter upon the "inheritance" in some way, only to have its *senatus consultum* vetoed by a tribune.[57] Even in these times, political con-siderations—that is, the question of what commander ultimately was to annex and organize this acquisition—will have played a large part in the tribunician veto of the senatorial decision to annex the land, as they did in the struggles over the "Egyptian question" in the 60s and 50s; military considerations, too, since Ptolemy IX was not going to give up his newly recovered kingdom without a fight.

But it is not too much to suggest that in this case the tribune or tribunes who interceded against the *senatus consultum* to enter upon Egypt as an inheritance in fact acted much like the tribunes of the late third and early second centuries, as guardians of constitutional propriety. Egypt, if annexed and transformed into a praetorian *provincia*, would have required a regular governor. Long commands in the lucrative province of Egypt would be no more acceptable than continued pro-rogation in Asia (which we shall see in 14.5.8 was eschewed at this time). But the Roman administrative system, which still stood at six praetors, at this point simply could not stand another praetorian *provincia* which had to be placed regularly (if not annually) in the sortition. The addition in 88 or 87 of Egypt as a *provincia* would have been enough to bring down the entire system of provincial govern-ment—or even the Republic itself. In the face of the veto, the consuls (so it appears) decided on a more limited measure, sending *legati* to collect money the Egyptian king had deposited at Tyre, which he had been using as a base in the struggle to recover his kingdom.[58]

10.4 *Quaestiones Perpetuae* down to 81

10.4.1 *Early Expansion of the* Quaestio *System*

A short passage in Cicero's *Brutus* unfortunately is our sole explicit source for the early development of the *quaestio perpetua* in Rome.[59] And here Cicero merely says that the institution of the permanent extortion court (dated to 149 B.C.), com-bined with the introduction in 137 of the secret ballot to popular trials ("iudicia populi"), gave rise to an increased number of individual trials ("plura fieri iudicia coeperunt") during the oratorical career of C. Papirius Carbo (*cos.* 120, who died in 119). Cicero in this passage implies nothing about other *quaestiones perpetuae* coming into formation after the *lex Calpurnia de repetundis* and before the 120s, though many have taken him to do so. However, he does state clearly that starting in 137 *iudicia populi* grew more frequent.

Paradoxically, the rise in the number of trials before the People and Plebs might have facilitated the expansion also of the *quaestio* system. The procedure in a popular trial had always been cumbersome, especially when it involved a capital charge before the *comitia centuriata* (see 5.6.1). And from the perspective of the senatorial establishment, popular trials in general—despite the fact that in capital cases a praetor was in charge of scheduling and voting—had a certain notoriety for capriciousness, lawlessness, and violence.[60] Comparisons were inevitable with the *quaestio perpetua*, especially once it was reinvented by C. Gracchus (discussed in 9.2.2). The praetor who had the Gracchan extortion court as his *provincia*[61] was obliged to supervise in a careful manner practically all aspects of each trial. But his power went only so far. In pronouncing the verdict the praetor was bound by the vote of his "consilium" of (equestrian) jurors. It was not tribes or centuries but a rel-atively small number of elite *iudices* who had the real power of decision. That in itself made possible the introduction of charges that rested on finer legal points. In sum, despite its complexity and its limitations, the Gracchan *quaestio* held out the prospect of a much more efficient, controlled, and orderly process than the trial *apud populum*.

As far as we can tell, the Gracchan *repetundae* court in its early years did not yield a spectacular number of convictions.[62] Yet it is clear that this *quaestio* before long inspired the establishment of other standing courts on the same basic model, each constituted by an individual law to punish a particular crime.[63] The criminal *quaestio* which tried the crime of *ambitus* was established within seven years of Gracchus' reform.[64] There are three trials on that charge known in 116 alone, in connection with the praetorian and consular elections for 115,[65] and three or four more in the years down to 81 B.C.[66]

By the end of the century, there was definitely also a third standing court. L. Appuleius Saturninus as *tribunus plebis* in 103 (but conceivably during his second tribunate in 100) invented the formal crime of *maiestas*—that is, "maiestas minuta populi Romani" ("diminution of the majesty of the Roman people")—and set up a permanent *quaestio* to try cases under his own *lex Appuleia*. The court finds it first certain attestation in 96 B.C.[67]

Maiestas was a hazy charge, not easily distinguished from *perduellio*—or various other capital crimes.[68] It is perfectly conceivable that commanders were accused of having infringed the "maiestas" of the state in *perduellio* trials long before Saturninus' time.[69] The charge of "dimunition" was certainly at work in other types of trials. One notes that the *tr. pl.* Cn. Domitius Ahenobarbus in 104 prosecuted the *pontifex maximus* M. Aemilius Scaurus on the grounds that through his agency "the rites of the Roman People were diminished" ("sacra populi Romani deminuta esse").[70]

Yet the direct stimulus for Saturninus' judicial measure must have been the shoddy record of the Roman *nobiles* in the Cimbric Wars, and the difficulty of calling them to account for their actions. In 107 or 106, the tribune C. Coelius Caldus managed to prosecute successfully before the People for *perduellio* a noble *legatus*, C. Popillius Laenas. After a major Roman defeat (10.2.2), C. Laenas had concluded a disgraceful peace with the Tigurini. But before bringing Laenas to trial, Coelius first had to push through a law extending the secret ballot to trials for *perduellio*.[71] Subsequent prosecutions were no easier. In a popular trial of 104 the tribune Cn. Domitius spectacularly failed to convict M. Iunius Silanus for his inept fighting as *cos.* 109 against the Cimbri.[72] Two difficult trials of 104 and 103 will have provided further impetus for Saturninus' judicial measure, as E. S. Gruen rightly explains:

> The prosecution of [the *cos.* 106 Q. Servilius] Caepio and [the *cos.* 105 Cn.] Mallius before the people . . . had not been an easy matter. The convictions were secured only through *seditio*, a display of violence and illegal neglect of tribunician *intercessio*. Comitial trials were still a somewhat risky and troublesome business. It would be practical and efficient to set up more permanenent machinery dealing with acts that diminished Rome's dignity and increased her peril. . . . [I]n a word, the *lex Appuleia* made permanent the temporary court of the *lex*

Mamilia.[73]

A fourth standing court to deal with poisoning, "de veneficiis," had come into existence shortly after the year 99 B.C. We do not have the details of the trials under that charge in the period before Sulla, but we do have the name of the individual who administered the *quaestio* in that year. Trials for murder ("inter sicarios") were also heard in a permanent court by the year 85 B.C. But apparently that stopped operating effectively for a time in the last years of the 80s.[74] Finally, a (noncapital) *peculatus* court—concerned with the embezzlement of public monies, including the diversion of sacred funds and (perhaps) misappropriation of booty—was definitely in operation previous to Sulla's reforms, quite probably by 85, but certainly by 83.[75]

10.4.2 *Praetors as Presidents of the Criminal* Quaestiones

Hard evidence on the praetors who administered the *quaestiones* in this period is not plentiful. (We are told, however, that all the regular courts in Rome were suspended at the start of the Social War; they stayed close for most if not all of 90 and perhaps into 89.)[76] For only about one-sixth of the forty-odd *quaestio* trials attested for the period between C. Gracchus and Sulla do we find even mention of the president of the court. Our sources when describing the trials of this period (or the post-Sullan era) are much more likely to take note of the jurors.[77] This is natural, since they are the ones making the legal decision. Lawyers showed the same emphasis in the actual trials. For instance, in Cicero's defense of Sex. Roscius in the *quaestio inter sicarios* of 80 B.C.—our earliest surviving speech from a permanent court—he addresses the presiding praetor just twice (once together with the jurors) near the beginning of the speech, and appeals to him obliquely once near the end.[78] The *iudices*, however, are addressed dozens of times.[79] Cicero maintains that relative emphasis throughout his extant forensic speeches. Still, it is clear that the court president played an essential role[80] and could exert a tremendous indirect influence on the verdict.[81]

The first individual to be named in the role of president of a post-Gracchan standing court is Q. Fabius Maximus (Eburnus, the future *cos.* 116). As praetor in 119 (surely), he presided over the *quaestio* in which the young L. Crassus successfully prosecuted the Gracchan *IIIvir a.d.a.* C. Papirius Carbo (*cos.* 120). Q. Fabius is said to have dismissed the court when Crassus found himself too nervous to speak—our earliest example of the praetor using his discretionary powers to affect the course of a trial. (Many more are to follow.)[82] In regard to this trial, Valerius Maximus[83] tells the story of how Crassus in preparing his prosecution refused to accept a letter-case (*scrinium*) of incriminating materials offered to him by a slave of "Cn." Carbo. Alexander[84] thinks this anecdote "suggests a crime in which records would be crucial, such as extortion." Yet it is equally possible that the *scrinium* contained documents bearing on Carbo's "role" in the death of Scipio Aemilianus, for which he was widely blamed, with even Cicero considering him complicit. As it happens, we know that Crassus raised this issue against Carbo in the actual trial.[85] The exact technical charge (which would help determine Fabius' city *provincia*) remains unknown. But the fact Carbo chose suicide after his condemnation shows it must have been capital in scope.

We have to wait more than a decade and a half for another possible court president. There is an outside chance that L. Licinius Lucullus (*pr.* 104), who as a city praetor had to put down a slave revolt at Capua, and then was prorogued and dispatched to Sicily after the outbreak of its Second Slave War, had a standing *quaestio* in 104.[86] Yet the peregrine praetorship is the obvious *provincia*, to gather from Lucullus' mobility during his actual magistracy.[87] Our first absolutely secure court president for whom we have a name, *provincia*, and a date is C. Claudius Pulcher (*aed. cur.* 99, *pr.* 95, and *cos.* 92), identified as "pr. repetundis" in his *elogium*. Cicero provides the date of his praetorship—and the additional information that the Senate charged this individual while praetor with drafting laws for Sicilian Halaesa. It should be noted that in the earliest instance where we have detailed information on the president of a permanent *quaestio* we see that praetor picking up additional tasks.[88]

10.4.3 *Introduction of the* Iudex Quaestionis

Evidently not all standing *quaestiones*—even in this period—were regularly entrusted to praetors. The *elogium* of C. Claudius Pulcher reveals that between his aedileship and praetorship he served as *iudex quaestionis* of a standing criminal court—in this case, *de veneficiis*. So that expedient had been introduced by the start of the first century.[89] P. Antistius, an *aedilicius* killed by the Marian government in 82, was the (openly partisan) president of the court that tried Cn. Pompeius, probably *de peculatu*, ca. 85 B.C. And M. Fannius (*aed. pl.* 86 and a future *pr.* 80) was *iudex quaestionis* over the court *inter sicarios*, probably in 85.[90]

The development of the *iudex quaestionis* was a natural and necessary one, now that the system of permanent *quaestiones* was expanding beyond state offences like *repetundae*, *ambitus*, and *maiestas* to embrace also private crimes such as poisoning and murder. It probably is no accident that the first *iudex quaestionis* known to us comes attached to the *quaestio de veneficiis*. The law that introduced this standing court might even have invented the position of *iudex quaestionis* to staff it. By the year 100 B.C., six praetors had to cover (in theory) the urban and peregrine jurisdictions, at least three standing *quaestiones* and all the overseas *provinciae* (now including Cilicia). The advantages of bringing the defendant on a murder charge before a *quaestio* as opposed to the *comitia centuriata* were obvious. Since the praetors had reached their practical limit a new quasi-magistracy was devised. The *iudex quaestionis* swore not *in leges* (like a magistrate) but *in legem*, to obey the law which had established the court in which he presided. He was given all the powers he needed to conduct a criminal trial, and magisterial attributes and insignia as well.[91] But a firm boundary was placed around those powers. In the immediate post-Sullan period, we see that the *iudex quaestionis* came under the supervision of the urban praetor and—unlike an actual magistrate of the Roman People with *imperium*—

could be removed from his position and even prosecuted during his term of presidency.[92]

How was an individual *iudex quaestionis* created? Mommsen[93] speculated that either the praetor who had received a particular *quaestio* named him, or "more probably" that this position routinely followed the aedileship, on the analogy of the *ex praetura* and *ex consulatu* commands that appear in this general era. Greenidge thought that appointment by the praetor to whom the relevant *quaestio* had come was positively unlikely. "The functions of this *iudex* do not resemble those of subordinate jurisdiction," he argued. "Besides conducting the trial from the *sortitio* of the *iudices* onward to the finding of the sentence, he seems . . . to have had the capacity of determining what cases were within the competence of the court."[94] That last point is hardy decisive: any *quaesitor* (see 10.4.4) seems to have had the power to accept or refuse prosecutions that came before him. Yet Greenidge seems to be correct on the praetor, at least for this era. The notion that before 81 B.C. praetors in their annual sortition ever drew lots for the courts "inter sicarios," "de veneficiis," and "peculatus"—in addition to other, more established *provinciae*—and then delegated the judicial responsibilities to subordinates seems most improbable. Since the urban praetor soon (by the mid-70s) appears to have had some vicarious responsibility for the performance of a *iudex quaestionis*, chances are that it was he who always saw to their election or (more likely) selection from the ex-aediles. We can suppose that at the beginning of each year the *praetor urbanus* allotted these *iudices* to the various minor standing courts, where they were to stay put.[95]

10.4.4 *Some Unnamed Court Presidents*

Our sources for three trials of this period refer to the court president without offering a name. The most difficult case has to do with a story Cicero in the *De Oratore* tells of L. Marcius Philippus (*cos. cand.* 93, *cos.* 91). In a trial administered by a "quaesitor," Philippus when allowed to cross-examine a witness tossed off a quip that inadvertently made one of the jurors look ridiculous.[96] The term "quaesitor" can be used of a *iudex quaestionis* or special court president but also a praetor.[97] Can we tell what type of trial this was? Alexander links the passage on the cross-examination with some other examples of Philippus' humor in court, including a taunt at Q. Catulus (*cos.* 102) that also backfired. When Philippus asked Catulus (literally, "whelp") during cross-examination, "What are you barking at?" he got the answer, "I see a thief." On the basis of these passages, Alexander suggests (following a suggestion of Münzer) that Philippus was prosecuted *de repetundis* following a praetorian command. Alexander even tentatively ventures "Africa" as the *provincia* and 95 (without query) as the date of his trial.[98]

Service in a territorial *provincia* naturally might give rise to accusations of thievery.[99] But one obviously need not be a praetorian governor to attract the charge.[100] According to Florus,[101] Philippus was prosecuted for *ambitus* (i.e., in connection with one of his bids for the consulship), which conceivably might have provided the context for the exchange with Catulus. Simple *peculatus* is another possibility. As for "Africa," the young Q. Hortensius is known to have spoken in the Senate on behalf of the province (perhaps representing a legation) in the year 95.[102]

True, this is the year after the date by which Philippus must have held the praetor-ship. But that is very different from knowing for certain Philippus was praetor then, or that the case of Africa (whatever the details) resulted in a *quaestio* procedure. So the "quaesitor" in this case must remain in obscurity.

There are two additional unnamed presidents for the *quaestiones* in this era. Orosius mentions in passing that a praetor presided over the *repetundae* trial of P. Rutilius Rufus in 92 B.C., and controlled who spoke. And a praetor apparently was the magistrate in charge when Q. Sosius as a defendant—probably *de peculatu*—admitted setting fire to the Capitoline *tabularium* (to destroy the evidence of thefts from the *res publica?*) in 83 B.C.[103] That latter item is a helpful piece of informa-tion; above, we have seen the possibility that *peculatus* might also fall to a *iudex quaestionis* (P. Antistius, ca. 85). In post-Sullan practice, certainly the more politi-cally important courts (*repetundae, maiestas, ambitus*) are entrusted to praetors if at all possible.[104] One reason was public order. It soon appeared that *quaestio* pro-ceedings too could dissolve into lawlessness, as reports on the violence at the trial of Servilius Augur (late 90s) demonstrate.[105]

10.4.5 *Decline of the* Iudicia Populi

By the 90s, the praetorship had been pushed quite deep into the business of admin-istering Rome's criminal law. How were the *iudicia populi* faring in comparison? For the period 137 down to 82, our record shows about two dozen individual trials before the People.[106] For the same years, we have sixteen reported prosecutions (certain or probable) in the *quaestio repetundarum* alone.[107] It does appear that after C. Gracchus the *quaestiones* quickly grew in importance, at the expense of the *iudicia populi* conducted (for all purposes) by tribunes and aediles. Indeed, one notes that fully one-quarter of the *iudicia populi* belong to the years 87 and 86. The Cinnan government immediately on coming to power used these *iudicia* as one of its principal instruments to purge the political opposition.[108] Sometimes it omitted proper procedure altogether.[109] The abuses of this era apparently went a long way toward discrediting those *iudicia*, at least in the eyes of Sulla (see further 11.1.3).

Even before Sulla's reforms, *iudicia populi* were probably well on their way toward taking a secondary role in the administration of Roman criminal law. A tell-tale sign of the ascendancy of permanent *quaestiones* is that in the first century some tribunes of the Plebs prefer to take defendants before a praetor than before the People. There is a possible instance in 97 or 96, when M. Duronius (either trib-une or *tribunicius*) prosecuted the censor M. Antonius (*cos.* 99) on a charge of *ambitus*. Another comes (possibly) in 73, if that is the date when C. Licinius Macer accused C. Rabirius of various religious offenses. But there Sulla's restrictions on the tribunate might have been a factor.[110]

We find a certain example of this phenomenon shortly after 70 B.C., when C. Carbo successfully prosecuted P. Oppius, who had served as quaestor of M. Cotta (*cos.* 74) in Bithynia. The charge was probably *maiestas*. Carbo received consular *ornamenta* as a reward for Oppius' conviction, which no doubt helped his climb to curule office. Soon (by 61) Carbo himself was governing Bithynia as a praetorian commander.[111] After the Oppius trial it is not uncommon for acting tribunes to prosecute in a permanent court—some perhaps prompted by the prospect of advancement in rank. There are instances attempted or realized in 66 (*de peculatu*), 59 (in the post-Sullan court *de vi*), possibly 58 (*inter sicarios*), then 57 (*de vi*), and 54 (two tribunician prosecutions *de repetundis*, possibly one *de ambitu*).[112] And that was notwithstanding the fact that in the 60s and 50s the alternative of popular *iudicia* always existed.[113] Yet there is not a single known example of a successful prosecution before the Plebs from these two decades.[114] That dismal record in itself goes some way toward explaining the inexorable expansion of the *quaestio* system.

10.5 Special Praetorian *Provinciae* outside Rome

10.5.1 *Special Praetorian Commands outside Italy*

We know only two possible instances of praetorian commands in special *provinciae* outside Italy in the period 122–82 B.C. The first concerns the *cos.* 117 L. Caecilius Metellus (Diadematus), so praetor by 120 under the *leges annales*, who might have had "Illyria" as his praetorian *provincia*. But the argument for it is highly conjectural. According to Appian,[115] L. (Aurelius) Cotta (*cos.* 119) and a "Metellus" inflicted an illusory defeat on the Segestani of Illyria. Who is this "Metellus"? Broughton identifies him with the *cos.* 119 L. Metellus Delmaticus, and postulates that he had stopped by to help his consular colleague Cotta at the time of his own command against the Dalmatians.[116] This is not impossible: the example of the *pro consule* C. Cosconius in the mid-70s shows the reverse scenario, that a commander for Illyria might be active in Dalmatia.[117]

However, M. G. Morgan argues that Delmaticus fought just Dalmatians; indeed, that is the only people who appear in his entry in the triumphal *Fasti*.[118] On Morgan's interpretation, L. Cotta campaigned against the Segestani with a different Metellus—L. Metellus Diademetus—in the capacity of a (praetorian) *legatus*. Now, this is precisely the relationship I have suggested (8.6.1) for the consul C. Sempronius Tuditanus and his subordinate Ti. Latinius Pandusa in this same theater in 129. But it would be odd for Diademetus, in the year his brother was consul, to serve as a *legatus* under that man's consular colleague. If we really are to identify Appian's "Metellus" with L. Metellus Diademetus, it seems preferable to assume he was already fighting in Illyria as, say, *pr.* 120, and continued to serve as *pro praetore* in 119 under the consul L. Cotta.[119]

No further praetorian commands for "Illyria" are attested for this period.[120] The one other special *provincia* is "Cilicia," allotted to the *pr.* 102 M. Antonius. As we have seen in 10.1, Antonius received enhanced *imperium* for the commission and triumphed from the *provincia* on his return to Italy in 100.

10.5.2 *The Outbreak of the Social War, 91 B.C.*

The era of the Social and Civil Wars saw any number of special praetorian *provinciae* declared within Italy. The process perhaps started even before the death of the tribune of the Plebs M. Livius Drusus in midautumn of the year 91,[121] which struck a severe blow to the hopes of the various Italian peoples for Roman citizenship. Not long afterward, in late 91, the people of Asculum set off the Social War by killing Q. Servilius, a "praetor" with enhanced *imperium* who evidently held a command for some time in the Picentine district. They also murdered his *legatus* Fonteius and all the Roman citizens in their town.[122]

There are plenty of precedents for granting consular *imperium* to a praetor during his year of office, but not for service in Italy. It is with good reason that Appian for instance found Servilius' presence as *pro consule* around Asculum so confusing.[123] One wonders whether the praetor had the Picentes as his formal *provincia*: that would have been enormously provocative to the Italians, especially since both consuls also remained in Italy that troubled year. And it seems unlikely that Servilius at the time was en route to a territorial province, though rough parallels for this type of "additional" *negotium* do exist.[124] No one foresaw extreme danger early in the year.

An easier alternative is that the political situation in Rome was so potentially explosive in 91—including not just the program of the tribune M. Drusus, but also actual fighting between adherents of Marius and Sulla[125]—that the consuls dared not stray far from the city, and the Senate created a special command *pro consule* for one or more of the praetors to watch events in Italy in their stead. Appian in fact implies this interpretation in his (admittedly confused) account; one notes also that Florus and Orosius each consider Q. Servilius a "legatus"—perhaps slight support that his was a special assignment.[126] Yet whatever the exact nature of Q. Servilius' *provincia*, the Senate's primary motive naturally would have been for his twelve axes to intimidate dissident elements in this area.

There may have been more Roman officials stationed in trouble spots in Italy in the year 91, as Appian positively suggests.[127] For a start, the *Periocha* of Livy Book 72 summarizes the story of how in (apparently) late 91 a Ser. Galba (no title) became a prisoner of the Lucanians but managed to gain his freedom. Broughton observes that "Galba's position in Lucania at the outbreak of the Social War . . . seems similar to that of Q. Servilius at Asculum," that is, a commander with *imperium*.[128] But since the epitomator does not even hint at what his position was, we have to allow for other possibilities, for example, that he was one of the "spies" Appian says were sent out to individual Italian localities[129] in the year 91. Some have ventured to identify this man with the Roman officer who scored a victory in the next year over the Paeligni, but there are less adventurous options.[130] His probable presence at Asculum in late 89 does suggest praetorian status (see 10.5.4).

Other praetors that year may have been assigned special *provinciae* elsewhere in Italy in an effort to curb dissent: one remembers the situation of 190, when Etruria and Apulia were assigned as special praetorian *provinciae* (8.4.1). Consider L. Postumius, a "praetor" in command at Nola in early 90 who lost the town—and his life—to Samnites.[131] Münzer suggests L. Postumius was an Albinus, and reasonably posits 91 as the date of his praetorship.[132] If true, his position at Nola might have been genuinely analogous to that of Q. Servilius in the territory of Asculum. But the possibility always remains open that this Postumius was merely a *legatus* who had received a special grant of *imperium* in the emergency posed by the outbreak of the Social War.

Two additional candidates for special commands in Italy in 91 are Cn. Pompeius Strabo and L. Porcius Cato, the consuls of 89. Orosius reports that at a very early stage in the Social War the Senate sent Cn. Pompeius "praetor" against the Picentes, at whose hands he suffered a defeat. Orosius implies that this rout came before the Samnites chose Papius Mutilus as their leader, or the Marsi selected Agamemnon.[133] That detail makes it hard to square with Appian's report of Pompeius' initial defeat and then success in 90 near Mount Falernus in Picenum against three well-coordinated Italian armies.[134] It is perhaps best to postulate two separate actions. The first (Orosius' defeat) is best dated to late 91 or early 90, and indeed may have been the Senate's immediate response to the murder of the *pro consule* Q. Servilius with his legate and the ensuing massacre of Roman citizens at Asculum. The second—from which Pompeius soon rebounded—dates to a point later in 90, when Pompeius was serving as *legatus* under the consul P. Rutilius Lupus, who (as we shall see) had the chief northern command that year.[135]

The title "praetor," however, in Orosius is puzzling. As *cos.* 89, we would expect Cn. Strabo to have reached the praetorship by 92. But "praetor" of course often stands for "pro praetore," in even the best sources. Since it is hard to see what a prorogued praetor would be doing in Italy in late 91 (even given the example of Q. Servilius above), we might assume that Pompeius was a *praetorius* who had received a special grant of *imperium* when news of the Asculum massacre reached Rome. Yet an alternative perhaps worth considering is that Cn. Pompeius Strabo was in fact praetor in 91, and that his cheering successes as *legatus* in 90—which the Livian tradition counts as a major turning point in the war[136]—prompted the Senate to grant him a waiver from the *leges annales* so that he could run for *cos.* 89.

There is a possible parallel in the career of Cn. Strabo's consular colleague of 89, L. Porcius Cato. Under the *leges annales*, this man should have reached the praetorship by 92. However, the Livian tradition reports that he as "praetor" defeated the Etruscans in battle in what must be the year 90.[137] Again, the most natural conclusion is that L. Cato was a *praetorius* who had received a special grant of *imperium* for that year. But it is just possible that he was a *pr.* 91 who received a dispensation in the emergency to stand for *cos.* 89.

10.5.3 *Praetorian Commands against the Italians in 90*

Italian preparations moved swiftly in late 91.[138] Diodorus gives the most detail on the united Italian war government. It was based in the territory of the Paeligni at Corfinium—now renamed "Italica"—and directed by a Senate of 500. In many ways, the Italian command system mirrored that of Rome—as Diodorus noticed.[139] The Marsian Q. Poppedius Silo and the Samnite C. Papius Mutilus were the first "consuls." "Dividing all Italy into two parts they [sc. the Italians] designated these as consular provinces and districts." Poppedius received a northern command, and had six "praetors" (στρατηγοί) under him. C. Mutilus had a large southern region, also with six "praetors."[140] The Italians had double the number of praetors in the Roman system, so as to represent the main constituent groups fighting. They were obviously much more concerned about winning the war and preserving unity than any untoward political effects!

The Romans mirrored the disposition of the chief Italian commanders. In 90, the command in the northern portion of Italy was held by the consul P. Rutilius Lupus; his consular colleague L. Iulius Caesar directed operations in the south. In 89, the consuls Cn. Pompeius Strabo and L. Porcius Cato divided up the northern and southern regions of Italy. During these years, we can assume that few praetors—or recent ex-praetors—could be spared to take a command in the overseas *provinciae*. We are told that all *iudicia* were suspended at the outbreak of the Social War. That surely included the standing *quaestiones* administered by praetors, with the notable exception of the special Varian court (discussed in 10.6.2).[141] (It is frustrating that we cannot tell whether a praetor was placed in charge of this *quaestio*.) One major reason for the declaration of this virtual *iustitium* was doubtless to free the city praetors (perhaps even the urban praetor) for potential military action. Praetors in their year of office had been employed before in this capacity (in 125), and were to be used in two similar emergencies in the post-Sullan period.[142] In mid- or late 90, some of the courts (and standing *quaestiones*?) may have been reopened, probably after the successes of L. Iulius Caesar against the Samnites. At the latest, they resumed operation following the victory (late in the year 89) of Cn. Pompeius Strabo at Asculum, when the emergency was officially declared over.[143] The background to the affair of A. Sempronius Asellio, the *praetor urbanus* of 89 who was killed (early in the year) for his stand on usury (12.1.1), implies that some normal legal procedure had resumed in the city.[144]

So what did the praetors of 90 and 89 do against the Italian rebels? It is difficult to ascertain the structure of the subordinate commands, especially since our sources are often unclear as to what individuals served as praetors, prorogued praetors, *privati cum imperio*, or simply *legati* in this conflict. What is apparent is that, once the war started in earnest, the consuls who held the chief command in 90 and 89 entrusted much of the serious fighting not to praetors but to experienced *legati* of consular or praetorian rank.[145] Cicero offers an important summary list of some of the men the Senate sent into the field: C. Marius (*cos.* I 107, VI 100), Q. Lutatius Catulus (*cos.* 102), T. Didius (*cos.* 98), P. Licinius Crassus (*cos.* 97)—every one of them a *triumphator*—and the *praetorii* L. Cornelius Sulla (*pr.* 97), M. Caecilius Cornutus, and L. Cornelius Cinna.[146] No praetors who definitely can be assigned to the year 90 are found in a major command. One possible member of that college, L. Calpurnius Piso Caesoninus, according to Cicero was "in charge of manufacturing arms" during the Social War.[147] However, in 89, once the worst of the crisis had passed, the Senate seems to have allowed praetors more latitude in the field.

Some of the subordinate officers of the year 90 apparently had *imperium*. First, the northern theater, and the *legati* of the consul P. Rutilius Lupus. Appian says those *legati* included C. Marius, Cn. Pompeius Strabo, C. "Perpenna," Q. Servilius Caepio, and a Valerius Messalla. Marius was of course of consular rank, and the other four were probably *praetorii*.[148] At least some of these men certainly had been given *imperium*. For Cn. Pompeius—who (we have seen) had an important semi-independent command in Picenum—and C. Perperna, we cannot tell. Appian simply tells us that Perperna had received a large force of ten thousand men. When he lost four thousand of these troops in battle at the hands of the Italic leader P. Praesentaeus (Praesentius?), Rutilius removed him from his command (στρατηγία) and transferred what remained of his force to his senior *legatus* C. Marius.[149] Yet Marius had consular *imperium*—surely enhanced from an original grant of praetorian *imperium*—by the time he took charge of Perperna's army. This emerges from a notice pertaining to events later in 90, after P. Rutilius Lupus had been killed in action on 11 June.[150] The Senate decided not to replace this fallen consul, since the state of the emergency did not allow his colleague L. Iulius Caesar to return to Rome. So the *legatus* Q. Caepio received command of part of the consular army by *senatus consultum*,[151] and had his *imperium*, according to the report of the *Periocha*, "made equal to that of Marius."[152] The formulation of Livy's epitomator most naturally suggests that Marius was a *pro consule* at that time in 90 and that Q. Caepio had preexisting praetorian *imperium* raised to the consular level. Whatever the level of Caepio's power, it was shortlived: he soon fell into an ambush and was killed.

This theater shows two further grants of *imperium*, each connected with special arrangements in late 90 for the siege of Asculum. The *cos.* 91 Sex. Iulius Caesar was sent with a special grant of consular *imperium*—a true *privatus cum imperio*—to take over the siege of Asculum from Cn. Pompeius Strabo after the death of the Picentine leader Vidacilius. (Our source for this, Appian, is understandably confused.) In transit, Sex. Caesar ran into an enemy force as it was changing camp, and scored a major victory. He then sat down for a siege of Asculum, only soon to die of disease (winter 90/89). But before his death this *privatus* managed to appoint a C. Baebius as *pro praetore*.[153] Baebius will have held the command at Asculum until relieved by the *cos.* 89 Cn. Pompeius Strabo. The handover seems to come only well into the year, for Strabo on taking office first conducted some campaigns against the Marsi and other tribes of central Italy.[154]

To turn briefly to the south: The *cos.* 90 L. Iulius Caesar is said to have had as his *legati* a P. (Cornelius) Lentulus, T. Didius, P. Licinius Crassus, L. Cornelius Sulla, and (M. Claudius) Marcellus.[155] That group includes two *consulares*; at least one—perhaps all three—of the others had reached the praetorship.[156] The one certain *praetorius* is of course L. Cornelius Sulla, who assisted his enemy C. Marius in a victory over the Marsians that year.[157] It is conceivable that Sulla had *imperium* at that time, just like Marius (and probably others). However, the direct evidence is quite slim. Eutropius (erroneously) says that the Social War was fought for a "quadrennium" (?92–89) with heavy loss. "Finally, in the fifth year, it met its resolution through L. Cornelius Sulla 'consul,' when earlier in this same war he strenuously had done a great deal, but as 'praetor'."[158] At any rate, we shall see Sulla probably held *imperium* the next year.

10.5.4 *Praetorian Commands against the Italians in 89*

In 89, one or two praetors possibly remained in the city alongside the *praetor urbanus* A. Sempronius Asellio to look after civil affairs. But the crisis—and the murder of the urban praetor early in the year, soon after he issued his edict—surely prevented any commanders from setting out to overseas *provinciae*. As noted above, in this year the northern command was held by Cn. Pompeius Strabo, now consul; the chief command in the south by his colleague L. Porcius Cato. We are exceptionally well informed on Cn. Strabo's staff, thanks to a major inscription detailing the members of his military *consilium* at Asculum on 18 November 89, following the capture of the city, a little more than a month before his triumph *de Asculaneis Picentibus*.[159] First place is held by L. Gellius, a *pr.* 94 who subsequently had served as *pro consule* in an eastern province (Asia or Cilicia). Second in the *consilium* is a Cn. Octavius Q.f.—probably also a *praetorius*. He is generally (and reasonably) identified with the Cn. Octavius Ruso who served as quaestor in 105 in the war against Jugurtha; but the *cos.* 87 is another real possibility.[160] Third place is wholly lost: perhaps the praetorian M. Caecilius Cornutus (see 10.5.3) belongs here. Then in fourth place on Strabo's staff is [——]cius C.f. Ani. Cichorius may be right in identifying him with the Ser. Sulpicius Galba taken captive and then released in Lucania at the start of the war. In 89, Ser. Galba is positively attested as a *legatus* of Strabo, active against the Marrucini, Vestini and (later) Marsi.[161] Cichorius also plausibly suggested an identification with the *legatus* "Galba" who fought under Sulla at the battle of Chaeronea in 86 alongside the *praetorius* L. Hortensius[162]—and thus not unlikely to be a *praetorius* himself. Next in order in the *consilium* is a L. Iunius L.f. Gal.—probably Brutus Damasippus, the *pr.* 82—so there is no absolute guarantee that the individual in third place in this list was a praetor or *praetorius* already in 89.[163]

In the southern theater, the *cos.* L. Porcius Cato defeated the Marsi several times in battle. But it was still early in the year when he lost his life in a mutiny near Lacus Fucinus.[164] No suffect was elected. It is just possible that, after the death of this consul, his *legatus* L. Cornelius Sulla received a special grant of consular *imperium*.[165] We have seen that in the similar circumstances of the previous year, after the death of the consul P. Rutilius Lupus, the command in the north was divided between two of his *legati*, both probably now *pro consulibus*. There are a few bits of evidence which seem to point toward a special grant of consular *imperium* for Sulla in 89. We have seen (10.5.3) that Eutropius seems to think he had a praetorian command in the Social War. Note also that A. Postumius Albinus— probably to be identified with the *cos.* 99—is said to have served as his *legatus* in 89 in charge of a fleet.[166] However, Valerius Maximus, in repeating a story told by Cicero of Sulla at Nola (in 89?), says that Sulla was "consul sociali bello."[167] Orosius also terms him "consul" in 89.[168]

Salmon[169] dismisses the reports of Valerius Maximus and Orosius: "Sulla was a *legatus* in 89, apparently of the consul Porcius Cato. For that matter it would have indeed been surprising if he had held higher rank than the two consulars serving in the south, A. Postumius Albinus and T. Didius, of whom the latter at least had had important military experience." But this argument of Salmon's, not conclusive in itself, glosses over the fact that Sulla is specifically said to have had A. Postumius Albinus as a *legatus* under him in this year and that T. Didius was killed 11 June 89.[170] Sulla was at least *pro praetore*. Indeed, it is just possible that Sulla may have started off the year endowed with a special grant of praetorian *imperium*, and was later elevated to the rank of *pro consule* in the crisis that followed the deaths of L.

Porcius Cato and Didius in the field. Broughton suspected a special grant of *imperium* to Sulla: "[T]he independence and prominence of Sulla's activities, with Legates in turn under his command [the reference is to A. Postumius Albinus], indicate that after the death of the consul he received a command similar to those of Marius and Caepio in 90."[171]

But there seems to have been a tradition (from Livy?) that it was Sulla as consul (i.e., 88) who ended the Social War. Some of these reports (Orosius in particular) may go back to that. Yet Eutropius, who makes Sulla "praetor" (i.e., *pro praetore*), is the most credible in light of attested practise for this war. He should probably be accepted.

The death of the consul L. Porcius Cato might also explain why we see a praetor in office, C. Cosconius, by the end of the year taking on major responsibilities in the southern theater. A successful commander, Cosconius is termed στρατηγός in late 89 or early 88[172] when he reduced the territory of a series of towns in Apulia (including Venusia) and that of the Pediculi.[173] Diodorus strongly implies Cosconius was an actual praetor of the year 89: notice of his dispatch against the Italians follows just after that of the consuls Cn. Strabo and L. Porcius Cato. And Appian has a pr. 88 succeed Cosconius in his στρατηγία (10.5.5). The "Lucanus" who fought with Cosconius against Samnites will have been his *legatus*.[174] C. Cosconius is almost certainly to be identified with the homonym who was *pro consule* in Illyricum in the first half of the 70s (11.8.1), thanks to an iterated praetorship.[175]

Cosconius was probably not the only praetor of 89 active against the Italians in the south. Florus reports the successes of a certain "Carbo" against the Lucanians; this man should be Cn. Papirius Carbo, the future *cos.* 85, III 82. Carbo was *tribunus plebis* in 92 and almost certainly praetor in 89, as Broughton suggests.[176] Cn. Carbo perhaps fought in coordination with the *legatus* A. Gabinius. Quaestor in 102 under the praetor M. Antonius in his Cilician pirate command,[177] Gabinius was quite possibly a *praetorius* by the late 90s. In the Social War, he apparently had an independent or semi-independent command against the Marsi; after successes in Lucania in (apparently) late 89, he fell while besieging an enemy camp.[178]

10.5.5 Praetorian Commands against the Italians in 88 and 87

As the war very much wound down in the year 88, the Senate seems to have allowed praetors an even wider role. Here the most important figure is Q. Caecilius Metellus Pius. Said by the *Periocha* to have won some important successes over the Marsi as a *legatus* in (apparently) late 89,[179] he was colleague in the praetorship with Ap. Claudius Pulcher and P. Gabinius, (surely) also with a Brutus and a Servilius, and perhaps with L. Cornelius Lentulus as well.[180] A word about their respective fortunes: As praetors, Metellus Pius, Ap. Pulcher, and Gabinius all registered over a sixty-day period the *professiones* of those Italians who were eligible for Roman citizenship under the *lex Plautia Papiria*.[181] Scholars have offered a date of either 89 or (as Badian has argued) 88 for that *collegium*.[182] Broughton favors 89, but the *Periocha* passage on Metellus Pius' legateship certainly seems to support

Badian's arguments for the later date. In fact, those victories as *legatus* might have won Metellus the praetorship, perhaps even by special dispensation.[183]

Unfortunately, nothing further is known of the activities of Metellus' colleague Gabinius as praetor or as prorogued praetor.[184] L. Cornelius Lentulus might have received the *provincia* of Cilicia *ex praetura*, only taking up the assignment in 85 or later (10.1). Yet a chance reference reveals that Appius Pulcher still had *imperium* in Italy in 87 (see below). Metellus himself saw a good deal of fighting in what must be 88: he is said by Appian to have succeeded (the *pr.* 89) C. Cosconius in his command in Apulia.[185] That need not count against service in the city early that same year. Indeed, perhaps one reason why the Plautian-Papirian law stipulated that registration of new citizens take place within a narrow "sixty-day" period was precisely to allow (at the least) Metellus and Appius to take the field. Appian goes on in the same passage to credit Q. Metellus with the final defeat of the Marsic leader Poppedius Silo in Apulia. Other sources differ somewhat from Appian in this.[186] Yet whatever the precise nature of his achievements, there should be no doubt that Q. Metellus indeed had an independent command in the south in 88.

The same might be true of Metellus' colleague Ap. Claudius Pulcher. In 87, Sulla, before departing for the east, placed Appius in command of a legion that was besieging Nola, which the consul Cinna later was to corrupt and win over.[187] Broughton[188] suggests that Ap. Pulcher was "probably *pro praetore*" by Sulla's delegation at the time. Rather, Appius probably had been prorogued from his praetorship. One notes that even after he lost his army he still held *imperium*, which took a popular vote to abrogate.[189] It is perfectly possible he was fighting Italians in the south in 88.

Metellus' other two known colleagues simply came to a bad end. Plutarch reports that in 88 the Senate dispatched "two of the praetors"—a Brutus and a Servilius—to forbid the consul Sulla's advance on Rome. Sulla's troops came close to killing them, but ultimately just stripped these praetors of their magisterial insignia and sent them insulted and disgraced back to the city.[190] Appian adds that Sulla, on entering Rome, outlawed a dozen of his enemies, including a "Iunius Brutus," generally held to be identical with the praetor in office at the time.[191] The interdicted Brutus fled to Spain, only to return the next year to rally around C. Marius at Telamon in Etruria.[192]

Broughton (following Münzer) identifies the praetor and the outlaw with the M. Brutus who served under the *cos.* III Cn. Carbo during his flight to Sicily in 82 (13.1.4).[193] But caution is necessary. The fact that no "Servilius" shows up in any of our detailed sources on the Marian exiles of 88[194] suggests the possibility that the victorious Sulla did not go so far as to declare those two praetors public enemies. (His *maius imperium* will have been enough to make what remained of their magistracy ineffectual.) In that case, the "Iunius Brutus" he interdicted will have been L. Iunius Brutus Damasippus, the *legatus* under Cn. Strabo in 89 (as noted above, of sufficient rank to be listed fifth in the epigraphic record of his *consilium*) who turns up as one of the chief Marians in the Civil War and indeed plays a particularly vicious role as *pr.* 82. (Whether the Brutus who was *pr.* 88 is to be identified with Carbo's subordinate in 82 remains anyone's guess.)

At any rate, Q. Metellus Pius is found still fighting Samnites in 87[195] before a series of events during the Bellum Octavianum compelled him to withdraw from Italy to Africa.[196] When Metellus reappears in Italy in 83, he is termed "pro consule."[197] Assuming that Q. Metellus Pius based his claim on an official enhancement of *imperium*, the grant can have come either during his praetorship in 88, or at the time of his prorogation into the following year—or perhaps even when the Senate so desperately was requesting his help against the Cinnans in mid-87.[198] By the time Pius quit Italy, he also had probably been hailed as *imperator*.[199]

10.5.6 *Praetorian Commands in the Civil War: The Marians*

To move now to the Civil War: Sulla's open rebellion in 84 and the certain prospect of his return to Italy—which came in spring 83—and the fighting that followed down through 82 surely meant that most potential Marian commanders were detained in Italy for these years. At the start of 83, the praetorian provinces of Sicily (13.1.4) and Africa (14.3.3) were probably not administrative priorities for the Marian government, since reliable men already held them. The commander for Gallia Transalpina was not openly hostile (13.3.2); Macedonia and Asia were very much outside the government's control. From this point, the only Marian praetors or ex-praetors positively known to set out for a *provincia* are Q. Sertorius (*pr.* by 83), who went to Hispania Citerior in late 83 (see below), and Q. Antonius Balbus, who took up Sardinia as *pr.* 82 (13.1.1). In the emergency, we can suppose that almost all other praetors (and quaestors) for 83 and 82 will have remained in Italy to resist Sulla.[200] Yet once again, the actual campaigning was very much a consular affair—regardless of individual competence. The consuls L. Cornelius Scipio Asiaticus and C. Norbanus and (in Cisalpine Gaul) the *pro consule* Cn. Papirius Carbo (*cos.* II 84) conducted—or were expected to conduct—the main fighting in 83. In the next year, the chief command went to Cn. Papirius Carbo as *cos.* III 82 and to the young (twenty-six- or twenty-seven-year-old) C. Marius as *cos.* 82. Hard evidence that actual praetors and praetorian commanders took the field against Sulla is not all that plentiful, though demonstrably some did.[201]

Q. Sertorius appears in Italy in early 83 as a (temporary) subordinate of the *cos.* L. Scipio at Teanum Sidicinum. When Scipio sent Sertorius during an armistice as an envoy to his consular colleague C. Norbanus, the praetor made an entirely unexpected diversion and took Suessa in Campania. This was a serious infraction of the truce, which Sulla is said (by Appian) to have blamed not on Sertorius, but on his superior L. Scipio. Appian also tells us that by this time Sertorius had "long" been chosen to hold a praetorian command in Spain. Apparently, the government did not plan for him to linger so long in Italy. Sertorius finally set out for Hispania Citerior in late 83; Plutarch gives him the (expected) rank of *pro consule*.[202]

Sertorius almost certainly conducted all those activities in Italy in 83 with consular *imperium*. As it happens, he is the only certain Marian praetorian commander with *imperium* we find for that year. However, three men—C. Carrinas, a "Cloelius," and (L. Iunius) Brutus Damasippus—are termed "enemy generals" (στρατηγοὶ πολέμιοι) by Plutarch in early 83. Plutarch is describing the unsuccessful attempt of these Marians to crush the young Pompey while he was still gathering forces in Picenum to aid Sulla; Pompey ended up routing all three. Diodorus also mentions the incident, but offers only the name of "Iunius Brutus."[203] Given the plural στρατηγοί (not to mention the adjective πολέμιοι), there is no reason to think that Plutarch is trying to be technically precise and all three were indeed "praetores."[204] In Plutarch, the plural στρατηγοί can mean simply "military commanders," with no implication of praetorian rank.[205] Another argument against the notion that the government had dispatched actual "praetores" is that Diodorus emphasizes it did not yet see Pompey as a serious threat. Yet each of these Marian officers should be examined individually.

On balance, Broughton is probably right to make C. Carrinas *legatus* for 83 and, following Orosius, a praetor of the Marian government at the time Sulla executed him in late 82 ("Carrinatem praetorem Sylla iugulavit").[206] For 82, Appian and some epitomators in the Livian tradition have a lot to say about Carrinas' movements against the Sullan forces, apparently with one legion.[207] Yet that Orosius passage is the most specific source on his status, with the evidence of Appian at least consistent with a praetorship in 82.[208] As for Plutarch's "Cloelius," he is perhaps to be identified with T. Cloulius, a quaestor of 98 B.C. (by M. Crawford's dating).[209] Another solution makes him the C. (Coelius) Antipater—quite conceivably a son of the historian L. Coelius Antipater—who was murdered in 82 B.C. (see below).[210] But whether he was an actual praetor in 83 is most uncertain.

Finally, L. Iunius Brutus Damasippus: his status in 83 is no more certain than that of the other στρατηγοὶ πολέμιοι, Carrinas and "Cloelius." But in 82, when Damasippus, on the consul Marius' written orders, perpetrated his notorious massacre at a Senate meeting—with his victims including Q. Mucius Scaevola, *cos.* 95 and at the time *pontifex maximus*—he definitely was a praetor. Appian even describes him as "being praetor of the city" (στρατηγῶν τῆς πόλεως).[211] Now, T. J. Luce[212] is right to point out that in Appian's terminology that does not inevitably mean he was an urban praetor.[213] Yet in this instance the *provincia urbana* looks likely. To carry out his gruesome plan, the young Marius had to choose a magistrate who was able to convoke the Senate without suspicion. The fact that Damasippus later is found in the field with two legions[214] has no bearing on his *provincia*. It only shows the extent of the military emergency for his faction.

So L. Iunius Brutus Damasippus is a certain example of a praetor holding a command in 82. M. Marius Gratidianus completed two praetorships and was an ex-praetor—perhaps even praetor—at the time Sulla had him tortured and killed in 82 (10.5.8). But he does not appear in any accounts of the fighting.[215] There are several possible praetors or *praetorii* from the Marian faction—P. Albinovanus, C. Coelius Antipater, Flavius Fimbria—who do show up in Cisalpine Gaul during the fighting of that year. P. Albinovanus was a hardcore supporter of the elder C. Marius who appears in Cisalpina commanding a legion of Lucanian *auxilia* for the government against Sullan forces. But he openly crossed to Sulla after hosting a dinner where he treacherously murdered two officers of C. Norbanus (*cos.* 83)— C. Antipater and Flavius Fimbria, both termed στρατηγοί—as well as (unnamed) στρατηγοί of the *cos.* III Cn. Papirius Carbo.[216] In Appian, the term στρατηγός usually denotes a holder of *imperium*. But (like Plutarch) this author also applies it to mere *legati*[217] or, in the plural, to a miscellaneous ensemble of commanders and *legati*.[218] So the precise status of Antipater and Fimbria must remain uncertain, as well as the identity and status of Carbo's στρατηγοί.[219] Albinovanus, however, does seem likely to be a praetor or *praetorius*, to judge from his military command. Indeed, he must have had some standing to be able to assemble and ensnare all those high-ranking officers at once. And a Ciceronian scholiast identifies him as the individual who actually handed Ariminum to Sulla.[220]

Two last officers from this faction remain to be discussed. C. Marcius Censorinus (who had a number of important military responsibilities in the year 82) and an "Albinus" show up in a very mixed list of Marian στρατηγοί who fought at the Colline Gate in 82.[221] There is an A. (Postumius) Albinus *monetalis* who is dated provisionally to 96 by Crawford; Censorinus was *monetalis* (by Crawford's dating) in 88 B.C.[222] Praetorian status is entirely conceivable at least for Albinus, but must remain quite uncertain given the nature of the evidence.

10.5.7 *Praetorian Commands in the Civil War: The Sullans*

For the war against the Marians, Sulla organized his force under *legati*, and allowed them the capability to fight independently.[223] Yet the most prominent of these were by and large not his veteran commanders (he had left most of those to hold major positions in the east) but recent volunteers to Sulla's cause.

The *pr.* 88 Q. Metellus Pius (now back from Africa) presented himself to Sulla soon after the latter's landing in Italy. Sulla recognized Metellus' claim to hold consular *imperium* (i.e., from his Italian command of years previous) and made him his principal subordinate. About that time, the young Cn. Pompeius seems to have claimed the title *pro praetore* for himself. Plutarch implies as much.[224] Pompey set up a tribunal, first in the town of Auximum and then elsewhere in Picenum, issued edicts, conducted a levy, appointed centurions—in short, he acted deliberately and conspicuously as a praetor. He even sent Sulla "dispatches."[225] If Pompey made an assertive claim to the title of "praetor," this might provide the background to Sulla's hailing him as "imperator" in that year.[226] Sulla's appellation probably had a touch of irony at the time it was delivered. But, just as Sulla recognized the claim of Q. Caecilius Metellus to consular *imperium*, it is conceivable he confirmed Cn. Pompeius as "praetor," perhaps by giving Pompey a grant of delegated *imperium* to legitimize his status. Pompey along with Q. Metellus Pius, the young M. Licinius Crassus (who returned from Spain to meet Sulla), and a "Servilius" are all termed στρατηγοί by Plutarch for 82.[227] That particular passage probably is derived from Sulla's autobiography. Yet again, the use here should be nontechnical, especially since it describes a group—two of whom are demonstrably not praetors!

In later 82, after Sulla's victory and the posting of the proscription list, Pompey was dispatched to Sicily against the Marian commander M. Perperna Veiento. For this task, he received a special grant of praetorian *imperium*. After Pompey had recovered Sicily, Sulla gave him a commission to dislodge a Marian commander from Africa. Pompey even triumphed *pro praetore* in (surely) 81 (13.1.4). Sulla really had no choice but to send out a *privatus* with a special grant of *imperium* to accomplish this task. We cannot recover the mechanism by which Pompey received his grant of praetorian *imperium*. The most probable method is the procedure we have suspected so many times in the Hannibalic period, a *senatus consultum* followed by a special *lex de imperio*: Pompey would not have been able to triumph if his *imperium* merely had come to him by delegation. The scope and importance of Pompey's assignment might be taken to justify a consular command. But even in these chaotic times, a command *pro consule* was evidently out of the question for a *privatus* who was still only of equestrian status.

Before sending Pompey to Sicily, L. Sulla tried to get the Marian governor M. Perperna Veiento to betray the *provincia* to him, but was refused (13.1.4). In this conflict, Sulla did manage to persuade some other praetors and ex-praetors to cross over to him from the Marian party. We have seen that was probably the status of the P. Albinovanus who betrayed Ariminum. Some he even put to work. One good candidate for this category is P. Cornelius Cethegus. A patrician noble, he was one of the "Mariani" forced to flee Rome in 88. At the time, Marius obviously held him in high trust,[228] and it is virtually certain he later reached a praetorship under the Marian government. However, in 83 Cethegus went over to Sulla, and appears serving under him at Praeneste in 82.[229] Q. Lucretius Afella—the man who actually took Praeneste for Sulla—is explicitly called a "praetor of the Marian faction" by Velleius. He evidently crossed too, and received a reasonably important military position.[230]

In this conflict, Sulla took his help from where he could get it.[231] After the victory, in late 82 he still required capable subordinates. Pockets of resistance remained, most notably at Volaterrae, which had to be subjected to a siege (the town evidently fell only in 80). Furthermore, Appian says that Sulla's στρατηγοί visited various cities in Italy and established garrisons at suspected places. And Sulla conducted wideranging *quaestiones* in Italy in late 82 (doubtless beyond), also targeting individual communities for punishment.[232] An example of the phenomenon of using ex-Marians even at this stage might be C. Papirius Carbo. A notice in Granius Licinianus reports Roman military action in (apparently) 79 against the people of Volaterrae for their earlier murder of the *praetorius* Carbo, "whom Sulla had placed in charge" of the town, that is, at some point after it was captured in (apparently) 80.[233] This man is reasonably identified with the *tr. pl.* 89 C. Carbo, brother of the *cos.* 85, III 82.[234] "As he supported Sulla he could hardly have attained the office [of praetor] before 81": thus Broughton,[235] tentatively assigning C. Carbo to a praetorship in that year. But C. Carbo is much more likely to have reached the praetorship under the government where his brother played so important a role than in 81 (where, as will be seen from 11.1.1, there is no room in the *fasti*) or 80 (which is a bit tight for the chronology, given the details Licinianus provides).

10.5.8 *The Social and Civil Wars: Innovations and Exemptions*

The Social War was a time of real precedent-making. As we have seen (10.5.2), Appian mentions that Q. Servilius (*pr.* 91) had a command at Asculum *pro consule*, and others like him were stationed throughout Italy. That comes from the preliminaries of the war: Servilius (and perhaps the unnamed others) seem to have been acting literally "pro consule," in place of a consul. At any rate, there is no previous example of a praetor in his year of office having consular *imperium* in Italy. It is unlikely that praetors who fought in the Social War were invested with consular *imperium* as a matter of course. Indeed, the actual record suggests that the Senate tried to keep praetors out of the central action until the real danger had passed.

True, I have suggested that the Senate after the Asculum disaster sent praetors of 91 into the field: Cn. Pompeius Strabo to Picenum, probably L. Postumius to Nola, and perhaps L. Porcius Cato to Etruria. Yet the one possible *pr.* 90 known to have served in the war, L. Calpurnius Piso Caesoninus, is said to have manufactured arms. And Cn. Pompeius Strabo does not seem to have been prorogued into 90, but made a *legatus* (though probably holding praetorian *imperium*) of the consul P. Rutilius Lupus.[236] Perhaps the same was true of L. Porcius Cato in Etruria, about whom we are less well informed.

We do see praetors fighting in the south of Italy in 89 (C. Cosconius, Cn. Papirius Carbo) and 88 (Q. Metellus Pius, possibly Ap. Claudius Pulcher). However, to do the main fighting in this war the Senate used consuls, aided not by praetors but by consulars as well as praetorians serving as legates. The Senate (I would suggest) appointed C. Marius, Q. Servilius Caepio, Cn. Pompeius Strabo, L. Cornelius Sulla, and doubtless some others as *legati pro praetore*, with *imperium* officially conferred throughout their tenure.[237] In some cases (Marius, Caepio, perhaps Sulla), the Senate saw fit to raise their rank to *pro consule* to compensate for consuls who had fallen in the war. In one instance, the Senate obtained an outright grant of consular *imperium* for a *privatus* to undertake a specific task, namely the *cos.* 91 Sex. Iulius Caesar, sent to Asculum in late 90. Infirmity in turn forced Sex. Caesar to delegate (praetorian) *imperium* to a subordinate. But there are plenty of precedents for that last type of appointment.

There is good reason to believe that the outbreak of the Social War also occasioned the partial suspension of the *leges annales*. That was a traditional emergency measure seen in the Hannibalic War and (surely) as recently as the Cimbric Wars, when C. Marius (*cos.* 107) received five additional continual consulships in the years 104–100.[238] I do think the evidence suggests that Cn. Pompeius Strabo and L. Porcius Cato were praetors of 91, who were elected to the consulship for 89, that is, within the minimum interval. A suspension of normal electoral rules would certainly help explain the attempt of C. Iulius Caesar Strabo—brother of the *cos.* 90, and curule aedile that same year—to win an exemption altogether from the praetorship so as to stand for the consulship of 88. Our sources imply that Caesar Strabo, who wanted the Mithridatic command, had a *senatus consultum* to back him and almost got his request. But two tribunes of 88, P. Antistius and P. Sulpicius Rufus, opposed the (popular) vote of exemption, first using legal methods, with Sulpicius later quashing it by turning to force, so as to be able to hand the Mithridatic war to the *privatus* C. Marius.[239]

Of course, more electoral irregularities soon followed. Cn. Pompeius Strabo (*cos.* 89) wanted a second consulship to fight Mithridates.[240] C. Marius and L. Cornelius Cinna (*cos.* 87) had themselves elected *coss.* VII and II respectively for

86—indeed, it is said, before the *comitia* were finished. There was a rumor current that Sulla had finished the war against Mithridates and was returning to Italy. That was the background to Marius' election to his seventh consulship, according to Plutarch.[241] We can presume an emergency suspension of electoral rules provided the formal justification for his colleague Cinna's *continuatio*. And once passed in reponse to the Sullan emergency, the decree was not rescinded. That gave legal cover to the *continuatio* in the consular colleges of 85 and 84, and (despite protests) the election of the younger C. Marius to the consulship for 82.[242] That there was a decree of some sort seems reasonably certain. Even in this era, the tribunes had not abandoned their traditional role as guardians of constitutional propriety,[243] and so surely will have insisted on one.

The suspension of rules in at least the *regnum Cinnanum* applied not just to consuls. M. Marius Gratidianus was apparently *tr. pl.* 87 but just possibly in 86, and then praetor twice by the time Sulla murdered him in 82.[244] Sumner suggests on the basis of his tribunate that Gratidianus held the praetorship for the first time probably for 85.[245] Sumner's placement of Gratidianus' second praetorship in 82 is convincing: "[H]e had hoped for the consulship of 82, but this was pre-empted by the illegal election of the younger Marius. So Gratidianus received his second praetorship . . . as a consolation prize," surely by special arrangement.[246]

This era of exemptions came to a screeching halt upon Sulla's victory in late 82. Q. Lucretius Afella took Praeneste for Sulla in that year, only to lose his life when he sought a consulship of 81 "against Sulla's will."[247] Sumner may be right in his provisional suggestion that Afella ("born ca. 130–124") had been literally a "Marianarum . . . partium praetor" who crossed sides (thus Velleius), against Appian's assertion that he wanted "to be consul while still an equestrian, before he had been quaestor and praetor."[248] Appian here may be simply extrapolating from his own knowledge of Sulla's measures on the *cursus honorum*.[249] This author may be no more accurate on Afella than on those other constitutional points. Cicero certainly implies Afella reached a magistracy of some sort.[250] And so we might accept Sumner's tentative reconstruction, that Afella was praetor in 83 or 82; Sulla was objecting to his failure to comply with the *biennium* between praetorship and consulship (a regulation of the *lex Annalis* unknown to Appian).

10.6 Special *Provinciae* in the City of Rome

10.6.1 *L. Cassius Ravilla and the Trial of the Vestals in 113*

For most of the second half of the second century B.C., on the few occasions when extraordinary *quaestiones* were declared, they customarily fell to to one or both consuls of the year.[251] That changed in 113, when L. Cassius Longinus Ravilla (*cos.* 127) received a special appointment by the People to inquire into the case of three Vestals tried on a charge of *incestum* in mid-December of the previous year. The *pontifex maximus* L. Caecilius Metellus Delmaticus and the college of *pontifices*— the traditional authorities for such cases—had condemned just one of the three priestesses.[252] Cassius Ravilla's appointment must be reconstructed from a number of different sources, with Asconius providing the fullest notice of the commission. There is a reasonable chance that it involved an extraordinary grant of praetorian *imperium*.

A *tribunus plebis* of 113, Sex. Peducaeus, challenged (probably immediately) the decision of the *pontifices*.[253] A plebiscite must have followed to move for a retrial: Cicero[254] in fact speaks of a "rogatio Peducaea." Allowing for the *trinum nundinum* (however computed), Peducaeus' bill can have become law no sooner than mid-January 113. We can assume that this plebiscite provided for the removal of the *pontifices* from further involvement in the case and, in their stead, the establishment of a special prosecutor to retry the Vestals. Once the law established the position, an election was held by the People to fill it. Asconius explicitly states that "populus . . . Cassium creavit" to conduct a judicial investigation of Marcia and Licinia.

Asconius then relates that Cassius was perceived to have employed excessive severity when "he condemned both these and in addition many other women." Dio seems to confirm Asconius on the point that many individuals other than the Vestals Marcia and Licinia were punished. And Valerius Maximus tells us that M. Antonius (the future *cos.* 99)—though a quaestor about to sail to his *provincia* of Asia—waived the immunity he had under a *lex Memmia* and returned from Brundisium to defend himself in Cassius Ravilla's *quaestio*. That last item helps establish the chronology. L. Cassius Ravilla must have had his appointment by early spring of 113 (as we would in any case expect), when magistrates would be on their way to overseas provinces. Valerius also mentions jurors ("iudices") in connection with Antonius' trial, which should be an accurate detail. If accepted, it shows precisely how much impact the form of the *quaestio perpetua* already had in Rome, just a decade after its reform by C. Gracchus. Some authorities have suggested that the court was staffed by equestrians: perhaps, but in that case Ravilla—who came out of this *quaestio* with a personal reputation for extreme severity—must have been allowed to pick them himself.[255] These "Cassiani iudices" later became a byword for moral strictness.[256]

To carry out his sweeping judicial tasks, L. Cassius Ravilla must have been voted special powers, perhaps even (praetorian) *imperium*, at the time of his election. In fact, Valerius Maximus terms L. Cassius "praetor" in describing how Antonius was haled before his tribunal in 113. Münzer (without argument) dismissed the title as an error on Valerius' part.[257] But it is perfectly likely to be correct (i.e., if understood as "pro praetore"). Ravilla's status as a senior consular, the circumstances of his appointment (plebiscite followed by popular "election" in a time of hysteria) and the far-reaching nature of his *quaestio*—which included the prosecution of at least one magistrate in office—all tend to support the (sole) title we are given for his position.

To be sure, a special vote of *imperium* to an individual to act within the city has little in the way of precedent. Livy reports instances of such a grant during the acute emergency of 211 when Hannibal attacked Rome (5.2.1 with Additional Note V). Q. Marcius Rex (*pr. urb.* 144) needed some sort of arrangement to complete his famous aqueduct as *pro praetore* in 143 (8.6.2). After L. Cassius Ravilla in 113, there is no indication that any *privatus* in this period (i.e. down to 81) received *imperium* to see to judicial responsibilities in Rome.

10.6.2 *Other Special* Quaestiones

In 111, the *tribunus plebis* C. Memmius tried to set up a process to prosecute M. Aemilius Scaurus (*cos.* 115) and other Romans who allegedly had taken bribes ("pecuniae captae") from Jugurtha. First, Memmius passed a bill that dispatched a certain L. Cassius Longinus, while still *pr.* 111, to bring Jugurtha to the city. We are told the tribune had positively agitated for Cassius' appointment. Was he the son of L. Cassius Ravilla? Modest support comes from Sallust's notice that this praetor Cassius had an exceptionally high reputation at the time of his commission.[258] Next, Memmius planned to make Jugurtha give public testimony against the individuals he was planning to indict. But a tribunician colleague put a stop to this scheme as soon as Jugurtha was brought before a *contio*.

Gruen argues that "if judicial proceedings were to come to fruition . . . the formal charge contemplated was clearly *perduellio*."[259] Who is to say? It is just possible that C. Memmius had passed or was going to pass a *rogatio* appointing the *pr.* 111 L. Cassius Longinus to administer the trial with jurors, on the model of the Cassian *quaestio* of 113. The advantage of using a praetor of the year was that he already had *imperium*. Yet without Jugurtha's testimony, Memmius must have known—whatever the precise form of prosecution he intended—that there was no point in continuing.

However, the inept Roman leadership in the first years of the actual Jugurthine War paved the way for the successful establishment of such a *quaestio*. To try those suspected of making accommodations with Jugurtha, the *tr. pl.* 109 C. Mamilius Limetanus provided for the election of three *quaesitores* who would simultaneously run capital courts staffed by (probably) equestrian *iudices*. The identity of just one of the *quaesitores* is known—the *cos.* 115 M. Aemilius Scaurus, who despite his status appeared as an advocate in another one of the three courts.[260] The structure of the Mamilian inquisition certainly does not seem far removed from Cassius Ravilla's *incestum* court of 113. There is no indication, however, in our (admittedly skimpy) sources on the procedure that the *quaesitores* of the *lex Mamilia* had special grants of *imperium*. The fact that there were three of them makes it most unlikely.

This *quaestio*—with its multiple courts, obviously aiming at fast results—certainly achieved its object. The juries in the constituent courts saw to the condemnation of four consulars—L. Opimius (*cos.* 121), C. Porcius Cato (*cos.* 114), (apparently) L. Calpurnius Bestia (*cos.* 111), and Sp. Postumius Albinus (*cos.* 110)—and the priest (*sacerdos*) C. Sulpicius Galba.[261] Cicero adds that Galba was the first priest ever condemned in a *iudicium publicum*, and that he "fell in his *cursus*" ("cecidit in cursu").[262] Konrad interprets Cicero to suggest that "most likely, Galba had been aiming at the praetorship (or even the consulship?) of 108."[263] Or a consulship for the following year? G. Farney[264] argues that it was precisely the unexpected and unprecedented condemnation of this priest that prompted C. Marius to think he had a chance among the consular candidates of 108 for 107. But if

Cicero means the *cursus* that C. Galba failed to complete was his "cursus forensis,"[265] we need not think he was a candidate for anything at the time of his trial under the Mamilian law. All the same, Galba seems not unlikely to have been of praetorian status at the time of his condemnation.[266]

We have notice of a handful of additional special *quaestiones* in the years down to Sulla, but in each case the administrative details are lacking. A *quaestio* was established at Rome to investigate the disappearance of the gold of Tolosa: Q. Servilius Caepio as *cos.* 106 had robbed the Volcae Tectosages of their sacred treasure, but failed to convey it safely to the city. The *quaestio* was evidently a major affair that saw a number of convictions. But no source mentions its structure.[167] The Constantinian epitomator of Diodorus relates that in 101 B.C., L. Appuleius Saturninus was prosecuted in a great public trial on a capital charge, namely, that he had violated the immunity of Mithridates' envoys to the Senate. Yet a large popular demonstration at his trial prompted senators (i.e., acting as *iudices*) to acquit him. Alexander regards this as a special *quaestio*, which may well be correct. But the excerptor of Diodorus gives no hint who presided.[268] The consular *lex Licinia Mucia* of 95 B.C. provided that Italians who were illegally acting as Roman citizens should each be reduced to the legal status of their own towns, and set up a *quaestio* to enforce it. Cicero terms that *quaestio* "very severe" ("acerrima"). Yet neither he nor any other source mentions the mechanics.[269]

Finally, after the outbreak of the Social War—and the suspension of all regular *iudicia*—the *tr. pl.* 90 Q. Varius passed, over the opposition of his colleagues, a law establishing a special *quaestio* with equestrian jurors to try those nobles suspected of helping the allies "by their aid or advice" ("ope consiliove"). For a time, the court to hear this vague charge (as Cicero tells us) was the only one functioning in Rome. Yet in early 89, the optimates took over the Varian court as their own, reconstituting it (through a tribunician *lex Plotia*) now with senators, *equites*, and even some individuals (exceptionally) *de plebe* as the jurors. For the first (i.e., anti-Optimate) phase of the Varian *quaestio*, we know of eight or nine individual trials threatened or realized, and after the reform of 89 B.C. two more. However, no source indicates who presided in any of these instances.[270]

It was probably not a praetor. Varius, when introducing his law, surely could not count on any praetor of 90 to be available continuously in Rome to run his ambitious court. In the military emergency, every city praetor was liable to be sent into the field: the Senate had suspended the regular *iudicia* for that very reason. At the time when the tribune Plotius passed his bill (very late 90 or early 89 B.C.), the regular courts may or may not have reopened but the military situation still remained quite dangerous.

The *quaestio* had run effectively—indeed, all too effectively[271]—in 90 B.C. Plotius in his reform probably kept Varius' basic structure in place, merely changing the composition of the *iudices*, so as to ensure the right type of verdicts. If a praetor was not presiding in 90 B.C. (as seems likely), the same probably goes for 89 B.C. as well.

General Developments in
the Praetorship, 81–50

11.1 The Sullan Reforms

On 29 and 30 January 81, L. Cornelius Sulla formally entered Rome in triumph. Or, rather, re-entered. Sulla had taken the city almost three full months previously, through his victory over the Marians and their Italian allies at the Colline Gate. Not long afterward, he had excused himself from Rome. The idea was to exacerbate the constitutional crisis; at this point both consuls of 82 were dead. On Sulla's request, the Senate did the only thing it could do, which was to select an *interrex*, with the expectation that this magistrate would hold consular elections. In a letter, Sulla offered the Senate an alternative, to revive the dictatorship (last seen in 202 B.C.), and suggested that it choose him for the position. The *interrex* L. Valerius Flaccus obliged, passing a law that set in motion the appointment of Sulla as dictator, technically "rei publicae constituendae causa" and (against precedent) for an indeterminate time. The new dictator reciprocated by appointing Flaccus as his *magister equitum*, though in his case for a fixed term.

It was as dictator that Sulla celebrated his late January triumph, not of course for the civil warfare of 83–82, but for his earlier victory over Mithridates. The two-day celebration was meant to underline that fact. Sulla surely wanted to evoke the three-day triumphs of T. Quinctius Flamininus in 194 and L. Aemilius Paullus in 167 for their grand eastern commands against respectively Philip V and Perseus of Macedon. After this splendid re-entry—the first triumph by a dictator since that of the great M. Valerius Corvus in 301 B.C.—Sulla set out on an ambitious legislative program to reform (among other things) Roman administrative practice.

In the next year or two—to register only the Cornelian laws of close relevance to this study—Sulla increased the number of praetors, regulated anew the *cursus honorum*, restructured the *quaestio* system, provided that consuls and praetors could stay in Rome during their actual magistracy and take up territorial provinces *ex magistratu*, and introduced a comprehensive law regulating the activities of commanders outside Rome. There is no reason to think discussion of these measures was encouraged. In the city, the dictator retained the twenty-four lictors that he had *militiae* (and thus on the days of his triumph) throughout his tenure of this formidable office—a frightening precedent that was long remembered.[1]

11.1.1 *Sulla's Increase in the Number of Praetors*

No direct source survives describing Sulla's reorganization of the praetorship. We are left to our own devices regarding how he changed this magistracy, and must piece together what we can from later (sometimes very late) literary sources. Let us start with a point of chronology. Regular magistrates—including consuls—were elected by Sulla for 81 B.C., but we do not know precisely when.[2] Cicero's *Pro Quinctio* offers a terminus for the praetorian elections. He tells us that one Sex. Naevius decided to sue for a judgment debt eighteen months after last calling P. Quinctius into court at Rome (for 13 September 83), and approached the city praetor Cn. Cornelius Dolabella to do so.[3] That means there were praetors in Rome in mid-March of 81.

Why did Naevius wait those eighteen months? The civil warfare of 83 and 82 is of course a large part of it. As for 81, there is some reason to believe the praetors entered office late and when Naevius petitioned the praetor Dolabella in March it was at his first opportunity. In a Senate session of 27 March 81, we find that it is not a quaestor but (surprisingly) a *pro quaestore* who is ordered to give the customary diplomatic gifts to an embassy from Caria. On the face of it, the presence of a prorogued magistrate in the city suggests that there were not enough quaestors to go around.[4] Indeed, under the *Lex Cornelia de XX quaestoribus* Sulla raised the number of quaestors, starting for the year 80.[5] Yet, given the importance of the two *quaestores urbani*—who had the oldest and most demanding quaestorian province—a better explanation is that on 27 March 81, elections for minor magistrates had not yet taken place.[6]

It is entirely possible that before holding the elections for curule magistrates, Sulla—in February or even early March of 81—introduced his law to increase the number of praetors. A reasonable estimate gives us more than six for that year. C. Annius (13.4.2) and M. Minucius Thermus (14.6.1) went respectively to Spain and Asia as praetorian commanders in what must be 81. Sex. Nonius Sufenas (12.1.1) is said to have held the first *Ludi Victoriae Sullanae*, and so is nearly certain to have been praetor that same year. Cn. Cornelius Dolabella, later *pro praetore* for Cilicia in 80 (15.1.1), is definite, as is M. Aemilius Lepidus (*cos.* 78, and thus *pr.* by 81), who shows up as governor of Sicily for 80 (13.2.2). On the analogy of these last two men—not to mention Cn. Cornelius Dolabella (*cos.* 81, *pro cos.* Macedonia for 80, as we shall see in 14.2.1)—we can reasonably (though not definitely) assume C. Claudius Nero, found as *pro consule* in Asia succeeding M. Thermus by early 80, also received his command *ex praetura* from a praetorship in 81 (14.6.1). Nero brings the number of certain or probable praetors for the year to six. And two more individuals readily present themselves: Q. Lutatius Catulus (*cos.* 78) almost surely reached the praetorship in 81, while one must also account for Mam. Aemilius Lepidus Livianus, a consular candidate by 78.[7]

The college of praetors had been expanded to six in 197, but never beyond that number. One does not have to look too hard to see why Sulla took his major step of lifting that numerical cap. By the late 90s, there were at least a dozen regular *provinciae* to be staffed. The territorial provinces were Sicily, Sardinia, Hispania Citerior and Ulterior, Macedonia, Asia, Africa, and Cilicia, along with Gallia Transalpina and Gallia Cisalpina (which already in the 90s appear to be two separate commands). Then there were the praetorian *provinciae* in the city, three or more of which—the urban and peregrine jurisdictions and the various criminal courts—ideally should have been allotted anew to praetors separately in the sortition each and every year. Badian was the first to demonstrate in detail how the steady accretion of new *provinciae* coupled with the emergency conditions of the Social and Civil Wars brought the administrative system to a virtual halt in the latter half of the 90s and 80s.[8] I would add that one of the early victims was Sulla himself. After a successful urban praetorship of 97, he had to stay in his promagisterial *provincia* of Cilicia for perhaps four years (10.1). So the dictator had firsthand experience of what it was like to be stuck in a distant *provincia* for a long period of time.

In chapters 10 and 13–14 passim, and in 15.3.1–3, I offer some subsidiary observations to Badian's sketch. In short, the wretched state of the territorial provinces at the conclusion of civil warfare practically demanded an immediate increase in the number of commanders with *imperium*. At the time of Sulla's late-January 81 triumph, a junior *legatus* had been holding Sicily for some months (13.1.4). Another Sullan *legatus* (an ex-consul of 91) was in charge of Sardinia—a Marian praetor lost his life there in 82 (13.1.4)—and the rebel Q. Sertorius (*pr.* by 83) had taken effective control of both the Spains (13.3.2). One of Sulla's subordinates from his eastern command must have been in charge of Macedonia since early in 83 B.C. (14.1.4). Another of Sulla's officers (probably the *pr.* 88 L. Cornelius Lentulus) had been in Cilicia even longer (10.1). The *privatus cum imperio* Pompey was in Africa, yet he was soon to leave the *provincia*, against Sulla's orders (14.3.3). In Asia, the praetorian commander L. Licinius Murena had stirred up an unauthorized war with Mithridates, and needed to be recalled (14.5.9). The Roman commander in Transalpine Gaul was a consul of 93, now starting his thirteenth continuous year of *imperium* (10.2.3).

So there were good practical reasons in early 81 why Sulla might introduce legislation to increase the number of praetors, delaying the curule elections until that law saw passage. Unfortunately, the suggestion of this date must remain a hypothesis. Just a few sources (all Imperial) mention this legislation, and then only indirectly. Speaking of the reforms of Augustus, Velleius Paterculus states, "he scaled the *imperium* of magistrates back to the old level, except that to the eight praetors two were added." Since C. Iulius Caesar had raised the number to ten, and then successively up to sixteen, the "old level" (*pristinus modus*) should be the late Republican—that is, Sullan—total.[9] Velleius should have known what he was talking about. He and his brother held the praetorship in A.D. 15, and he had some information about the history of the office (see immediately below). And Dio Cassius adds confirmation to Velleius' statement when he reports that in 47 B.C., Julius Caesar decided, in order to reward more senators, to increase the number of praetors for the coming year beyond the legal number to ten.[10] As it happens, the unreliable epitomator of Pomponius erroneously anticipates this Caesarian total by ascribing ten praetors to Sulla. We already have seen (3.1.2) how little stock one can place in this late source.[11] Plainly, there were eight praetors elected for the year 57 B.C.,[12] and thus for every other year between Sulla's dictatorship and Caesar's later reforms.[13]

An immediate effect of increasing the number of praetors was that it lessened the prestige of the office. Velleius implies as much. He boasts that the Roman people granted his great-grandfather Minatius Magius (of Aeclanum) citizenship for oustanding service in the Social War, and raised two of his sons to the praetorship, "when six were still being elected."[14] Eight praetors also meant that Sulla had to move the consular and praetorian elections in the centuriate assembly back from (so it seems) November to a point after 9 July. Apparently, the election of the two additional magistrates significantly prolonged the proceedings and thus required additional daylight![15]

More serious was the issue of *ambitus*. Sulla surely knew that to introduce two new praetors at once for a total of eight would directly cause increased competition in the consular elections. That was the reason why the Senate let the number of praetors stand at six for so long, and precisely a century previous even tried reducing the number to four in alternate years (7.2.4). For Sulla suddenly to reduce the odds of a praetor eventually reaching the consulship from one in three to one in four was one of the high costs of his political settlement.[16] The dictator did introduce new legislation to mitigate the effects of intensified electoral competition, specifically a *lex Cornelia de ambitu* that banned those convicted under the statute from seeking office for ten years.[17] Sulla's law is the first named legislation in our record for this crime since the *lex Cornelia Baebia* of 181, though the Livian *Periocha* reports a *lex de ambitu* in 159 B.C., and some statute must have set up the standing *quaestio* for this crime (10.4.1) by 116 B.C.

Sulla's particular measure on procuring election had no real deterrent effect. That can be inferred—with all due caution—from the great number of *ambitus* and related trials in the 60s and (especially) 50s. Numerically most of those known have to do with consular candidacy.[18] Indeed, from Cicero one sometimes gets the impression that the only elections that attracted serious attention were the consular ones.[19] Yet our record implies that heightened competition for the consulship apparently had a trickle-down effect on those for lower magistracies. References to prosecutions of praetorian candidates for *ambitus* are frequent enough, and spread fairly evenly throughout our period.[20]

A much sounder indication of the impact of Sulla's legislation on the eight praetors is the series of additional anti-*ambitus* measures—including three consular laws, each with progressively stricter penalties and an ever-wider scope—that start in the early 60s and continue to the end of our period. In the latter half of the 50s, city praetors even found themselves staffing a permanent *quaestio de sodaliciis*—set up to counter associations that practiced electoral bribery and intimidation (11.7.7)—alongside the regular *quaestio de ambitu*.[21] Yet perhaps the best indicator of all is the frequently delayed and disrupted consular elections of the last generation of the Republic.[22] Again, praetorian *comitia* were fully part of the problem. For instance, abuses in the (delayed) elections for 55 B.C. were serious enough for some partisans of the praetorian candidate M. Porcius Cato to propose—on the late date of 11 February in that year—that the praetors designate should not enter office immediately but be required to wait 60 days, so as to allow time for prosecutors to come forward.[23]

11.1.2 *Sulla's Legislation on the* Cursus Honorum

Alongside Sulla's change in the number of praetors and his new legislation on *ambitus*, we find reregulation of the *cursus*. Indeed, it is worth suggesting that his legislation on these matters fell precisely in that order. For this he had as a precedent the legislative program of the *lex Cornelia Baebia* of 181 followed by the *lex Villia Annalis* of 180 (see 7.2.5).[24] Age requirements for the praetorship and consulship had been in force since the early second century, and had been codified into law as early as L. Villius' tribunician law of 180 B.C. Sulla stipulated a minimum age of thirty for the quaestorship (which he made a compulsory first step), and restipulated those for the praetorship (thirty-nine) and consulship (forty-two). Other offices were outside the *cursus*, but the aedileship (curule or plebeian), if held, went before the praetorship. Sulla also maintained the two-year interval between the praetorship and the consulship, required since the early second century. The main innovation, so it seems, was the stipulation that those desiring a political career start with the quaestorship. Yet, even before Sulla, omission of this office was extremely rare.[25] Appian says he also forbade iteration of the same office within ten years.[26] The evidence is ambiguous whether that particular provision extended to the praetorship.[27]

So why this legislation? Sulla's widening of the political pyramid—with twenty quaestors and eight praetors, but just two consuls at the top—in itself necessitated a reformulation of the rules. And the previous decade had seen the formation of some unwanted precedents. I have argued (10.5.8) that at the outbreak of the Social War there was a partial suspension of the *leges annales* by traditional emergency measures. Some unusual careers resulted, most prominently (I have suggested) those of the ex-praetors Cn. Pompeius Strabo and L. Porcius Cato, who appear to have reached the consulship of 89 B.C. within the expected *biennium*. That gave a sense of entitlement to those who followed, culminating in all sorts of exemptions under the Cinnan government. Sulla had broadcast his intentions already in 82 B.C., when he had his subordinate Q. Lucretius Afella—who had strong support among the People[28]—killed for seeking a consulship in contravention of *leges annales* then on the books. Afella had seen the past irregularities and assumed he would benefit under Sulla's new government. There were surely many others like him: the strengthened *cursus* legislation was meant in part as a message to Sulla's own supporters. In the event, dispensation was given to Pompey (*cos.* I 70) to allow him to hold the consulship without having been praetor or quaestor. But no others that we know of obtained this kind of waiver.

How well did Sulla's enforced *cursus* work? There is no sense discussing progress from the quaestorship to the praetorship in any period, since we have so few firm dates for the former office. We are a bit better informed on the tribunate. Yet that office was always outside the *cursus*—and under Sulla's original settlement a political dead end, with tribunes debarred from holding higher magistracies. Once that provision was rescinded in the year 75, we find a fair number of the ex-tribunes who reach the praetorship doing so in quick order. Almost half the individuals for whom we have secure dates of tribunate and praetorship show intervals between the two magistracies of just one or two years,[29] a bit more if they also hold an aedileship.[30] However, it turns out that at no point in these decades do we have an instance of an ex-tribune being elected praetor more than eight years after his tenure of the lower office.[31] Those patterns suggest that politically ambitious men who held a tribunate tried to do so when they were not far under the qualifying age for praetorian candidacy. The idea must have been to make a bid for the praetorship while public memories of one's tribunate were still fresh. Failure to win quick election to a praetorship surely made an ex-tribune's career more difficult, and more than one or two *repulsae* were probably fatal, despite the availability of eight praetorian places each year. Though real comparative evidence for the pre-Sullan period is lacking, the impression one gets is that then ex-tribunes were not in quite such a hurry to reach the praetorship.[32] As for ex-aediles who win the praetorship in the post-Sullan era, the overwhelming majority do so at short intervals, that is, after a *biennium* or sometimes even a single year.[33] Let us postpone interpretation of that feature for a moment.

Movement from the praetorship to consulship in the later Republic is frustratingly hard to quantify. There are just thirty-seven instances where we have a reasonably firm date for a praetor who went on to hold the consulship in the period 166 down to 79 B.C. (Remember there were notionally 176 consular places to be filled over those years.) And of those individuals, one man's consulship (P. Cornelius Lentulus, *pr.* 165 and *cos.* 162) falls in an era that saw unrestricted consular iteration, another received his in the period of Marius' ascendancy (Q. Lutatius Catulus, *pr.* by 109 and elected *cos.* 102 B.C. after three *repulsae*),[34] and a half-dozen belong to either the Civil War (86–82) or the period when Sulla controlled elections (81–79). When examining post-Sullan conditions, these particular instances really cannot be used for comparison.[35] However, matters dramatically improve for the consuls of the years 78–49 B.C., where we have the dates of praetorship for roughly half (thirty-four in all) of the consuls.

Keeping those caveats in mind, in the period down to the Social War seventeen or eighteen of the twenty-nine consuls in our (tiny) sample are certain to have progressed from praetorship to consulship within three or four years.[36] In other words, about two-thirds of the ex-praetors who were elected consul reached the higher office at or just above the minimum interval. The dozen remaining individuals show a range of up to nine years.[37] In fact, L. Cornelius Sulla (*pr.* 97) had to wait precisely that long before winning his first consulship for 88, the longest known interval since (perhaps) L. Mummius, *pr.* 155 and *cos.* 146—longer even than the interval shown by the new man C. Marius (*pr.* 115, *cos.* I 107). I have suggested (7.2.5) that the experience of M. Baebius Tamphilus (*pr.* 192, *cos.* 181)—who, like his brother (*pr.* 199, *cos.* 182), had an exceptionally difficult time making it to the consulship—had something to do with his zeal for reforming the political system of his day. No doubt personal factors also partly motivated Sulla's legislation on the *cursus honorum*.

But back to the results of Sulla's overhaul: of the consuls of the years 78 down to 50, the proportion of those reaching that office at or just over the minimum interval after praetorship (i.e. three or four years) is over two-thirds—twenty-five of the thirty-five men for whom we have the requisite dates. And fully twenty of those ex-praetors gained the consulship precisely after a *biennium*.[38] It would seem that Sulla's increase in the number of praetors had no real effect at all on the speed at which one might win the consulship—until we look at the other ten individuals in our sample. Let us exclude L. Gellius—*pr.* 94 and finally elected *cos.* for the year 72 after an amazing interval of twenty-two years—as a casualty of the unusual conditions of the Social and Civil Wars. We find that four of these men have to wait five or six years for a consulship.[39] The rest show enormous intervals—waits of nine to fourteen years—between praetorship and consulship, a situation reminiscent of the decade before the passage of the *lex Villia Annalis* of 180 B.C. (7.2.5).

Simply put, Sulla's additions to the number of praetors and reform of the *cursus* evidently created a "winner takes all" atmosphere at the curule elections. Overall, our statistics for the last three decades of the Republic suggest that consular candidates who were defeated on their first try were unlikely to reach the office at all. The reappearance of consular iteration in the latter half of the 50s (Crassus and Pompey as *coss.* II 55 and Pompey as *cos.* III 52) will only have intensified the competition. Yet sometimes sheer persistence might pay off. The outstanding example in this era is Ser. Sulpicius Rufus, jurist and *pr.* 65. He was an unsuccessful candidate (at a minimum) for 62 and probably 58, but finally won the consulship for 51.[40] One might add that the overheated atmosphere of the consular elections in this period seems to have raised the temperature also of the praetorian ones—for no good reason, since Sulla had expanded the college of praetors. All the same, an examination of known careers suggests that ex-tribunes and (especially) ex-aediles had to win one of the eight places quickly or run a real risk of being shut out forever. The large number of *ambitus* trials in the later Republic that stem from praetorian elections goes some way toward confirming this picture.

11.1.3 *Institutionalization of Ex Magistratu Commands*

A major Sullan development was that it was henceforth understood that both consuls and all praetors should normally remain in Rome for the year of their actual magistracy. While in Rome, praetors were to staff the urban and peregrine jurisdictions (see 12.2.1) and the various criminal courts; the consuls had no set *provinciae* in the city. Then, following the year of office, these magistrates were to govern a territorial *provincia*. Our record suggests that Sulla on taking control of the state had already decided on this system: note Cn. Cornelius (Cn.f.) Dolabella, praetor in the city (probably *urbanus*) in 81 and then promagistrate in Cilicia in 80 (15.1.1), and also M. Aemilius Lepidus and C. Claudius Nero, who received Sicily (13.2.2) and Asia (14.6.1) respectively (probably) *ex magistratu*. But the dictator had to make allowances from the very start, thanks to the emergency posed by Sertorius in Spain and the necessity—apparently around this same time—of recalling L. Murena from Asia. Those situations caused the praetors C. Annius to be sent to Spain (13.4.2) and (probably) M. Thermus to go to Asia (14.6.1) in their magisterial year of

81. In the next year, L. Fufidius and M. Domitius Calvinus also had to take up *provinciae* (the two Spains) during the term of their actual magistracy (13.4.2).

Under the Sullan system, with (probably) ten regular territorial *provinciae* and two consuls and eight praetors to go around, it was theoretically possible that each of these *provinciae* be governed by a magistrate for one year only. What is more, the necessity of declaring the occasional special *provincia* would not place too great a strain on the administrative machinery. Yet oddly Sulla decided that the *lex Sempronia* of 123 (9.3.2) was still to fix the consular territorial *provinciae*. The Senate now had to decide eighteen or more months in advance (assuming July elections) where a given consular pair was needed.[41] "It is indeed amazing that Sulla himself did not see the shortsightedness of forcing the *lex Sempronia* to operate under such altered conditions," observed N. J. Woodhead in a full-length study of the workings of this law. "He apparently did not take into consideration the acquisition of new provinces nor the possibility that within a few years Rome would become *the* place to be, and, that therefore some potential promagistrates would refuse the opportunity to accept a *provincia* or govern a territorial province."[42] We shall take up this latter point below. Suffice it to say for now that one year after Sulla's death the *Bellum Lepidanum* forced the Sempronian arrangements for the consuls of 78 (i.e., for 77) to be abandoned. But that was an accident, in response to a crisis. Various types of exceptions followed in 74 (a year in which both consuls contrived that they be sent to fight an eastern war), 68 (the *cos.* Q. Marcius Rex received Lucullus' command in Cilicia), 67 (the *lex Gabinia* was passed, withdrawing Bithynia/Pontus from Lucullus), 59 (*lex Vatinia*), 58 (*lex Clodia*), and 55 (*lex Trebonia*). Sulla did not stipulate when a consul was to leave Rome to take up his province. Sometimes it was as early as November in one's year of office. Others delayed their departure for some months into the next year. But only as consuls could they go through the full departure ceremonies; promagistrates were debarred from doing so.[43]

As for the praetors, the Sullan system featured a process of sortition whereby the *designati*—apparently soon after their election—were allotted the urban and peregrine praetorships and various criminal *quaestiones*.[44] Sortition of the territorial provinces that ex-praetors would hold apparently came whenever the Senate got around to it. Sometimes we find sortition of promagisterial provinces during the year of the magistracy. At other times it falls early in the year in which the relevant promagistrates were to take up their command (up to mid-March). Evidently Sulla did not establish an administrative calendar to be followed.[45]

The practice of a city praetor proceeding in the year after his magistracy to hold a command in a regular territorial *provincia* was in itself not new. Even if we leave aside various wartime expedients of the late third and second centuries (discussed in 9.4.2), it receives certain attestation already in the last quarter of the second century. C. Marius served as a city praetor in 115, and after his praetorship held Hispania Ulterior as a *provincia* (13.3.1). Plutarch says Marius received that *provincia* by lot,[46] which implies—unless the author is anachronistic in this detail—that he was not the only ex-praetor to take up an overseas command in this year. And it is certain that after Marius at least five city praetors down to the time of the Social War—including Sulla himself as *pr. urb.* 97—proceeded to overseas commands (mostly though not invariably in eastern provinces) *ex praetura*.[47] In the 90s, we have some indication that the Romans had started using *ex consulatu* commands, too.[48] What was consequential about Sulla's reform is that by generalizing this practice to cover all consuls and praetors he completed a process that had begun a full century earlier with the introduction of the *lex Baebia* (7.2.4) and taken firm hold with the annexation of Macedonia and Africa in 146 (9.3.1)—the institutionalization of the promagistracy. But there is no trace of a *lex Cornelia* on this matter, and (as H. F. Pelham showed long ago) it is unlikely that there was one. Here Sullla merely had to validate the emerging *mos maiorum* through indirect means, namely, by increasing the number of praetors so that there were just as many holders of *imperium* as territorial *provinciae*.[49]

11.1.4 *Implications of Keeping Eight Praetors in the City*

What were all those city praetors supposed to do during their magistracy? We have seen (10.4.1–4) that even previous to Sulla's victory there were at least six *quaestiones perpetuae* functioning in Rome—*repetundae, ambitus, maiestas, peculatus, de veneficiis,* and *inter sicarios*. Sulla kept all these in place, merged the administration of the latter two, and introduced at least one additional court (*de testamentis*) (11.7.1–5). In theory, the increase in praetors from six to eight and institutional acceptance of the scheme by which all remained for a year in Rome ensured that there would be one praetor for each of the two "civil" jurisdictions and six for a corresponding number of permanent courts. But later practice soon shows that the system presupposed continued use of the *iudex quaestionis* (10.4.3) to cover the courts that praetors could not. So here, too, Sulla was institutionalizing what was previously an ad hoc provision.

Sulla clearly meant for the system of permanent *quaestiones*—now to be staffed by senatorial juries—to take over most capital prosecutions.[50] In his reforms, he might have positively stripped tribunes of their power to prosecute, at least for capital offenses.[51] *Iudicia populi* of that sort were a prominent feature of the Cinnan regime (10.4.5), aimed at Sulla and his adherents. Yet no such trials are attested in the 70s. However, in the year 74 we do find the *tribunus plebis* L. Quinctius prosecuting two men in popular trials for pecuniary penalties.[52] Either Sulla left that right intact, or it was restored, perhaps in 75, the year when a consular law permitted tribunes to hold higher magistracies. The former seems the more likely possibility: Quinctius may have been exploiting a loophole that previous (that is, pre-75) tribunes had been too cowed to try.[53]

So now there were notionally to be ten holders of *imperium* in the city for the duration of each and every year. Through this arangement, Sulla ran the risk of turning the consuls and praetors into a sort of glorified tribunate.[54] Praetors would suffer the greatest relative loss in prestige, since henceforth at all normal times there was at least one holder of *imperium maius* in the city. This meant, for instance, that the urban praetor was now effectively debarred from serving as Senate president (12.4.1).[55] Nor did any praetor stand much chance of getting legislation passed if either consuls or tribunes were unwilling (12.4.3). Of course, by putting so many magistrates in the city Sulla also heightened the danger of future conflict between consuls and praetors,[56] between members of the same praetorian college,[57] and between praetors and lower magistrates.[58]

On the most basic level, in such a crowded atmosphere, with newly circumscribed powers—and with the consulship now significantly harder to obtain—the temptation for an individual praetor to grandstand would be huge. The year 85 had featured a spectacular example of noncooperation between city magistrates in which a renegade praetor won popular adulation by representing a laboriously drafted joint praetorian and tribunician measure as his own.[59] Granted, even after Sulla, collegiality among praetors still meant something.[60] And we occasionally find examples of carefully concerted action by a praetorian college.[61] Yet overall, Sulla's reform set the stage for even more of that type of popularity hunting—or worse. For instance, we soon find praetors looking for political advancement by throwing themselves behind tribunician bills in a particularly ostentatious manner (the outstanding example is Cicero's support of the *lex Manilia* in 66)—or even personally promulgating legislation that they knew was unlikely to pass, simply to make a political point (12.4.3). A common scenario is for two or more praetors to team up to push a particular political program.[62] Sometimes praetors group up on a larger scale, such as when the praetorian college of 54 split in dispute over the triumph of C. Pomptinus (*pr.* 63) (12.4.3, 15.2.3). Others set out on their own path to exploit the negative power of their office. The praetors Ap. Claudius Pulcher in 57 and C. Claudius Pulcher in 56 apparently devoted the bulk of their terms to supporting their brother P. Clodius, resorting even to violence in the city.[63] Violent agitation by city praetors was not an exclusively post-Sullan problem, as the example of C. Glaucia in 100 (see below) goes to show. However, by the end of our period it is safe to say the increase in number of praetors and their restriction to Rome made the city significantly less safe in general.[64]

When it comes to disruptive behavior in the city, the *pr.* II 63 P. Cornelius Lentulus Sura is in a class by himself. Praetor in 74 and consul for 71, Lentulus was expelled from the Senate in 70 B.C.[65] He re-entered the Senate (surely) through the quaestorship and in 63 was praetor for a second time. His city *provincia* in 63 is unspecified, but he apparently was notorious for doing little of the requisite work.[66]

Many sources—including Cicero himself—identify him as the chief subordinate in Catiline's conspiracy, responsible for the urban part of the uprising.[67] When the consul Cicero and Lentulus' own praetorian colleagues L. Flaccus and C. Pomptinus arrested the Allobrogian envoys on their way out of Rome on the night of 2/3 December, Lentulus was detected.

In the days that followed, the precedent Cicero plainly was trying to avoid was that of 100 B.C. In that year, C. Marius saw the *tribunus plebis* Saturninus and the praetor C. Glaucia killed in the Curia while they were still wearing their magisterial *insignia*.[68] In this case, the consul did not let Lentulus' praetorian colleagues touch him. Rather, Cicero personally escorted this conspirator—"because he was a praetor" (thus Sallust)—by the hand to a Senate meeting at the temple of Concord to give testimony. The duty of L. Flaccus (who was *pr. urb.*) was merely to bring to the meeting the incriminating dossier of letters seized from the Allobroges.[69] On hearing various testimony, the Senate voted that Lentulus abdicate his office and be placed under arrest.[70] Plutarch says that Lentulus did so right there in the Senate, by renouncing his office on oath—Dio confirms that feature, expected in any case from the verb *abdicare*—and taking off his *toga praetexta* to put on clothes of mourning. This is a valuable notice on the mechanics of abdicating one's office. Other instances suggest that Lentulus also will have sent away his lictors.[71] (Perhaps the praetor calculated that cooperation would save his life.) Then Lentulus was handed over to an aedile, P. Cornelius Lentulus Spinther, for custody.[72] In this year, we find the city praetors housing the other leading defendants in the Catilinarian conspiracy.[74] Cicero and the Senate must have thought that charging one of the praetors of 63 with Lentulus' incarceration was inappropriate because of their (now former) collegial status.

Soon Cicero obtained the Senate's vote that Lentulus and eight of his fellow conspirators should not face life imprisonment and confiscation of property,[74] but a sentence of death.[75] As Cicero paraphrases it, the *senatus consultum* specified that Lentulus—unlike the praetor Glaucia in 100 B.C.—was fully a *privatus* and his abdication indeed removed all *religio* from his punishment.[76] Thus, the consul had Lentulus and the others put to death—without allowing them to exercise their traditional right of appeal to the People. Cicero himself handed over Lentulus to the executioners, and city praetors saw to the other conspirators.[77] In various passages, Cicero shows clear relief that in the crisis Lentulus' praetorian colleagues all came down on the appropriate side.[78] The *invidia* for all the executions fell squarely on Cicero, not least because he had presided over the Senate meeting which voted for the death sentence.[79]

11.1.5 *Generalization of Consular* Imperium *and New Restraints for Provincial Commanders*

No triumphs *pro praetore* are attested after the time of Sulla's dictatorship. The last such triumphs are those of P. Servilius Vatia in 88 (13.1.1), and then Cn. Pompeius in (surely) 81 as a *privatus* of equestrian rank (14.3.3); L. Licinius Murena in 81 probably also triumphed from Asia *pro praetore* (14.1.4). The evidence of the triumphal *fasti* is just one indication that Sulla generalized grants of consular *imperium* (long seen in the Spains, and then Macedonia, Asia, and Cilicia) to all provincial commanders. Henceforth praetorian commanders for Sicily, Sardinia, Africa and the Gauls were to set out for those provinces—as well as the eastern ones—*pro consule*.[80] Other than one exception, which I argue (15.1.1) we can ascribe to Sulla's own personal pique, good counterexamples are lacking.[81]

There must have been a rationale for this generalization of consular *imperium* over and above a simple desire for symmetry. Now, at some point praetors—even *privati*—with enhanced (i.e., consular) *imperium* could start making men *pro praetore*. This was obviously a major development. Indeed, it may help explain the decision to institutionalize grants of consular *imperium* to praetorian commanders for distant provinces like the Spains, Macedonia, Asia, and Cilicia. There, regular succession of proper governors was difficult to maintain, and *legati* might find themselves holding down a large *provincia* for a long period of time. Delegation of *imperium* allowed magistrates to get home in a timely fashion without sending a message of neglect to the (often bellicose) provincials.

The earliest evidence I can find for the practice of "praetorian delegation" has to do with the orator M. Antonius, attested as *quaestor pro praetore* in the *provincia* of Asia in (probably) 113/112 B.C. (14.5.2). A praetor *pro consule*—the standard rank at all times for governors of Asia—either had left him in charge of the province, or had delegated him *imperium* for some special task.[82] Soon after Antonius, this type of delegation by praetors is reasonably well attested, both before and after Sulla took the step of generalizing consular *imperium* for promagistrates in all the territorial provinces (see 15.3).

At the same time as he was extending consular *imperium*, Sulla was also quite concerned to regulate the behavior of Rome's promagistrates as commanders. To do so, he introduced an elaborate law *de maiestate*—spelling out in detail what he meant by that fuzzy charge—which remained in effect down to the end of the free Republic, even alongside Caesar's extraordinarily comprehensive *lex de repetundis* of 59 B.C.[83] Cicero in the *In Pisonem* of 55 B.C. provides a good summary of the more gratuitous abuses that the Cornelian and Julian legislation attempted to stem. He is assailing A. Gabinius, *cos.* 58 and afterward commander in Syria, who had marched out of his *provincia* to reinstate Ptolemy Auletes in Egypt:[84]

> I say nothing now of his leaving his *provincia*, of his leading his army out of it, of his waging war on his own account, of his entering a king's realm without the orders of the Roman People or Senate, conduct expressly forbidden by numerous ancient laws, and in particular by the law of Cornelius against *maiestas* and that of Julius against extortion.

The mention of "numerous ancient laws" ("plurimae leges veteres") shows what we would in any case suspect. There was a long tradition of legislation on provincial administration before Sulla's *maiestas* law and the extortion law of Caesar. Our information is too deficient to trace the development of this tradition in real detail. Restrictions on the activities of commanders in their military *provinciae* are attested by ca. 170 (5.4.4, 8.5.3). By the year 100, we know for a fact that there existed a small forest of regulation concerning administration in the territorial provinces. We owe that knowledge to the epigraphic *Lex de provinciis praetoriis* from Knidos that dates to the year 101 or 100. Most relevant for our purposes here, it spells our some limitations under a *lex Porcia*—apparently new—on the movements of the commander and his staff outside the *provincia* (10.1, 14.1.2).

However, the *lex Cornelia de maiestate* of 81 really marks a watershed in the history of this type of restrictive legislation. The time was ripe for a major law, especially after the rule bending of the Social War and near chaos of the 80s. No doubt a good part of Sulla's achievement was to codify in one law the mishmash of *senatus consulta* and *leges*—some demonstrably containing rather minute regulations—that had cropped up over the previous century (or more). But he must have introduced some innovations, too. What details we can expressly assign to the law mostly have to do with ensuring orderly succession in the provinces, essential for the smooth working of his administrative system. For instance, Sulla's law demanded that a promagistrate spend at least one full year in his territorial *provincia*. That must be new, since we know that one governor of Asia of the mid-90s left his province after a mere nine months, with no personal repercussions for his quick departure (14.5.4). And under Sulla's law, a commander had to quit the *provincia* thirty days after succession. Before that law, some were presumably hanging on for more than a month.[85]

One of the most significant things about Sulla in general was the scale on which he sought to transform the restraints of *mos maiorum* into positive law.[86] Those provisions on succession nicely illustrate the point. Yet in the decades after Sulla we find others who are even more pessimistic of a Roman magistrate's capacity for self-restraint. Cicero's letters to his brother Quintus as governor of Asia in 60 and 59 are a mine of information on the formal and informal rules that now restricted a magistrate in his *provincia* (14.6.7). The end result of the process was the hyperdetailed *lex Iulia de repetundis* of 59 B.C., so comprehensive (and so severe) that it remained in effect all the way to the days of Justinian.[87]

11.1.6 *The Right to Refuse Territorial* Provinciae

As *cos.* II 80, L. Cornelius Sulla was allotted but never took up Cisalpine Gaul *ex consulatu*.[88] Our sources note that a number of consuls in the later Republic followed Sulla's lead and turned down the chance to take up a territorial *provincia*.[89] For praetors, it seems over time to have grown quite common. By chance, we know that at least three of the eight members of the praetorian college of 66 declined an *ex praetura* command. One of these—C. Antonius (the future *cos.* 63)—after his praetorship refused a *provincia* of his own, (apparently) in order to serve as a *legatus* under Pompey in the east for the year 65 (12.1.3)![90]

All of our instances of consuls waiving a province[91] are subsequent to Sulla's scheme of 81 under which he aimed to send out provincial commanders *ex magistratu*. For the praetors, there is but one (relevant?) case between the year 166 B.C. (when Livy breaks off) and the Sullan legislation: a second-century Cn. Cornelius Scipio whom the Senate formally pronounced (*decrevit*) as unfit for Spain, offering as its reason, "because he did not know how to act properly" ("quod recte facere nesciret"). Valerius Maximus says by incurring the Senate's wrath he (paradoxically) was as good as condemned for *repetundae*.

Indeed, it is reasonable to suppose that, before Sulla, a magistrate who wanted to decline the *provincia* that had come to him in the sortition needed to offer a specific and compelling excuse to the Senate, which might make him confirm the veracity of that excuse by oath. Livy attests that procedure for 176 B.C. In that year, three praetors begged off having to go to their allotted territorial *provinciae*. One made his case on purely administrative grounds, arguing that there were two commanders with *imperium* in his *provincia* and supersession of one of them would disrupt the ongoing campaign. The Senate accepted his rationale. The other two, however, alleged religious impediments, and the Senate made each of them swear an oath in a *contio*.[92] The case of the Cn. Scipio, who could not go to Spain, suggests that the requirement of a formal excuse was still in effect in the latter half of the second century.[93] Indeed, we do not hear of any individuals even in the post-Sullan period refusing their magisterial *provinciae*. If praetors were easily capable of refusing to take on, say, the *quaestio repetundarum* or the *ambitus* court, we might expect at least one such instance to show up in our detailed sources for the late Republic, which are always interested in disruptive behavior. So the requirement of a formal declaration very probably remained in place.

Promagisterial *provinciae* were different. Once Sulla, by his validation of blanket *ex magistratu* commands, definitively dissociated the promagistracy from the magistracy, consuls and praetors seem to have taken the decision not to proceed to a territorial *provincia* quite lightly.[94] All ex-consuls and ex-praetors must have had to participate in the promagisterial sortition.[95] Yet a number of sources for this period describe the refusal of a *provincia* even as a positive attribute, reflecting one's moral worth. The only oath known from this era in this context is one Velleius reports for Pompey as consul in 70, "when he quite laudably had sworn—and kept—an oath that he would not proceed to any *provincia* from that magistracy." This statement implies that some magistrates who announced they would not take a territorial *provincia* apparently went back on their word.[96] One motivation for this type of volte-face will have been the fact that to remain in Rome made one liable to prosecution.[97]

The year 63 offers us our closest look at the procedure of turning down a promagisterial *provincia*.[98] Under the Sempronian law, the *provinciae* for the consuls of that year were to be Macedonia and Cisalpine Gaul. Immediately on entering office on 1 January 63, Cicero declared in the Senate that "if the *res publica* continues in its present state, and unless some danger arises which he cannot honorably avoid meeting, he will not proceed into a *provincia*."[99] As it happens, Cicero had exchanged his proper *provincia* of Macedonia with that of his consular colleague. He describes this act in various ways, including "exchanging his province" ("provinciam Galliam cum Antonio commutavi"), "neglecting it" ("provinciam ornatam . . . neglexi") and "laying it down" ("instructam ornatamque a senatu provinciam deposui").[100] Later that year, Cicero called a *contio* to announce formally that he indeed was turning down his promagisterial province of Cisalpine Gaul, again describing this act as "deponere provinciam."[101] The fact that Cicero can describe both his exchange with Antonius and his eventual refusal of Cisalpine Gaul as "deponere provinciam" suggests that it was no more of a technical term than "neglegere provinciam," "contemnere provinciam," or the like.

We can only guess at the actual procedure. In the late Republic, the magistrate who did not want a command *ex praetura* or *ex consulatu* must have made a public declaration, perhaps even sworn an oath. The purpose was not to ratify that he had a legitimate impediment, but simply that he would not take up the *provincia*. Velleius' description of the oath of Pompey in 70 suggests as much. So does the case of Cicero. Cicero's stated reason for turning down Cisalpine Gaul was merely that he wanted to preserve independence of action to deal with domestic threats, and not run the risk of being hobbled by tribunes who might seek to veto arrangements for his military *provincia*.[102] Cicero counted those two speeches among the most important of his consulship. Since the habit of turning down promagisterial *provinciae* had grown so frequent, it is not too much to suppose that by this point the public speech of refusal had developed into a genre all its own. The praetor L. Lucceius in 67 may have struck a typical note, who Dio says "was unwilling to govern Sardinia after he had been allotted it, hating the enterprise on account of the many individuals who were acting in an unhealthy fashion among the (provincial) peoples."[103] One has to allow for the possibility that Lucceius simply did not like the unhealthy *provincia* he had drawn, and that his moral reservations might have evaporated had he received Sicily or Asia.

11.1.7 *The* Lex Pompeia de Provinciis *of 52*

In 53 B.C., the delay in curule elections caused an interregnum that was to stretch into July or August. In the resulting chaos, Dio Cassius[104] tells us all the tribunes provocatively suggested that instead of the election of consuls there should be a reinstitution of the consular tribunes (not seen since 367 B.C.), "in order that there might be more magistrates." No one paid any attention to this particular proposal, says Dio. So the tribunes instead trotted out an old and controversial suggestion, that Pompey be declared dictator.[105] Pompey (then *pro cos.* outside Rome) deliberately had been keeping his distance from the city for some time, much as Sulla did at the end of 82.[106] When he eventually showed up, he refused the dictatorship and took measures that the consular elections be held.

The proposal to bring back the consular tribunes had its serious side. What the tribunes were trying to address was the bottleneck caused by Sulla's system of eight praetors but only two consuls, and the *ambitus* and electoral violence that came with it. The consuls finally elected for 53—Cn. Domitius Calvinus and M. Valerius Messalla Rufus—tried another tack, namely, to scrap the *lex Sempronia de provinciis consularibus* and the Sullan system of *ex magistratu* commands. Frustrated with their inability to conduct elections for 52 (Calvinus was even wounded in a melee), "they passed a decree that no one, either as an ex-praetor or as an ex-consul, should take up an overseas command until five years had passed." Dio (our only source for this *senatus consultum*) explicitly counts it as an anti-*ambitus* measure.[107] The basic idea was to remove the protection from prosecution that a promagisterial command had always afforded. It also aimed to disabuse men of the expectation that they might immediately recoup their electoral expenses in a territorial province. There existed a stereotype (11.1.6) that individuals who refused a territorial *provincia* were more honest than those who took one up. That in part might have informed the consuls' scheme.[108]

It was Pompey who, as sole *cos.* III in 52, actualized this reform, drawing at least broadly on the *senatus consultum* of 53. The fact this new system functioned properly only for 51/50 and then came completely crashing down in 49 B.C. makes discussion of its content and effects difficult.[109] What is certain is that Pompey legally mandated an interval between magistracy and promagistracy for ex-consuls and ex-praetors, perhaps of five years.[110] He also, for all practical purposes, got rid of the Sullan loophole that allowed the refusal of consular and praetorian *provinciae*.[111] Recent patterns had been none too salutary. Just three of the consuls of the previous four years (56–53) are known to have accepted a territorial *provincia*—Cn. Pompeius and M. Licinius Crassus in 55 and Ap. Claudius Pulcher in 54. Four of the remaining five consuls are certain not to have taken one.[112] As usual, we are less well informed on the praetors. But, after one possible instance of a *pr.* 56 declining a territorial province, we find two members of the praetorian college of 55 and one of 54 who definitely refused a *provincia*, followed by a possible case of 53.[113]

To rectify this problem, Pompey's law had a retrospective effect. It appears that all able ex-praetors and ex-consuls who previously had turned down a province were to be eligible for service—whether they liked it or not. In the first year of the law's operation (51 B.C.), a *senatus consultum* named ten men (so it appears) who were to draw lots for an equal number of *provinciae* that needed filling, two consular and eight praetorian.[114] So we see M. Tullius Cicero (*cos.* 63) and M. Calpurnius Bibulus (*cos.* 59)—presumably the two most senior eligible and capable *consulares*—sent to Cilicia and Syria respectively. A Q. Voconius Naso, probably praetor before 60, apparently was expected to have a province under that law for 49.[115] These three "Pompeian" commanders—the only ones for whom we have a date of magistracy, however approximate—are each quite senior. However, the law seems to have contained a provision that waived the minimum interval (whatever it was) between magistracy and promagistracy if the number of eligible commanders ever came up short.[116]

Two other features of the Pompeian law deserve mention. As we would expect, the People had to pass a special *lex de imperio* for the eligible ex-magistrates to take their provinces.[117] For a possible precedent, note Ap. Claudius Pulcher (*cos.* 79), who fell ill at Tarentum in 78 on the way to Macedonia, returned to Rome until 78/77 (acting there as *interrex*), and only later took up his consular *provincia* (14.2.2). He, too, must have needed such a law. And Pompey's measure stipulated that praetorian commanders were to have merely praetorian *imperium*, whatever the province; ex-consuls naturally had consular *imperium*.[118] Significantly, we now find in the provinces for the first time in the history of the Republic men who are *pro praetore* delegating *imperium* at their own level.[119]

Pompey's law clearly aimed at restoring one-year commands in the territorial provinces. Yet there is no good reason to think that a term of precisely one year was the statutory maximum for the exercise of official duties in one's *provincia*.[120] True, in Cicero's letters from Cilicia he often interprets the *senatus consultum* that pressed him into service in that way—but represents it only as an absolute mandate as the end of his term approaches. It is absurd to think that Pompey and the Senate wanted commanders out of their provinces after precisely 365 days, whether they were in the midst of the campaigning season or not. Once back in Italy, Cicero grudgingly admits (once he sees the dark political clouds on the near horizon) that he was eligible to stay in his *provincia* until the Senate superseded him.[121]

Even under this new system the Senate positively had to expect to prorogue some commanders. The number of available ex-magistrates on average will have been less than ten, since ex-praetors were of course free to stand for the consulship during the statutory interval. Meanwhile, by 52 there were fourteen territorial *provinciae* to be staffed: the ten pre-Sullan ones and also the later additions of Bithynia/Pontus, Crete, Cyrene, and Syria. Let us now turn to the question of how each of these new provinces had been added.

11.2 Bithynia/Pontus

The kingdom of Bithynia came to Rome as an inheritance from king Nicomedes IV in either (late) 75 or 74. As we shall see in 14.6.2, the Senate charged a praetorian governor of Asia, M. Iunius Iuncus, to organize Bithynia into a Roman *provincia* sometime after early 74. That work was soon cut short. The threat of war from the Pontic king Mithridates VI Eupator seemed so pressing that both consuls of 74 were sent to the east, L. Licinius Lucullus to a joint *provincia* of Cilicia with Asia, M. Aurelius Cotta to protect Bithynia. Mithridates was to attack Nicomedes' former kingdom in the spring of 73, sparking the wideranging Third Mithridatic War.

M. Iuncus no doubt yielded Bithynia to Cotta as soon as he arrived, perhaps still within the year 74, and returned to Asia and then Rome. No praetorian commander is found in the Bithynian or Pontic theatre for the next dozen or so years.[122] M. Aurelius Cotta fought in the east until (probably) late 71. On Cotta's departure the entire eastern command devolved upon his consular colleague L. Lucullus. In 70, Lucullus had made enough headway to receive from the Senate "decem legati" to help him in the organization of some of Mithridates' former possessions. But his hope of finishing the war proved illusory. Lucullus found himself superseded in Cilicia in 67 by Q. Marcius Rex (*cos.* 68) and then in Bithynia and Pontus by the *cos.* 67 M.' Acilius Glabrio. Finally, in 66 the *tribunus plebis* C. Manilius handed over responsibility for the whole Mithridatic War to the *privatus* Cn. Pompeius (still with a grant of consular *imperium* from his pirate war). Pompey remained in the east down into late 62 B.C.

Having expelled Mithridates from his kingdom, in late 65 and early 64 Pompey made first steps toward the disposition of Pontic territory before leaving Amisus for Syria in spring of 64.[123] Pompey was still in Syria when he heard of Mithridates' death, in early (i.e., spring) 62. He quickly rushed back to Amisus and finished his organization of (western) Pontus, attaching the territory of eleven individual cities to Bithynia to form a new Roman *provincia*.[124] After issuing donatives to his troops at Amisus, in the spring or summer of that year Pompey proceeded to Ephesus. And not long afterward (following Pompey's personal pilgrimages to Mytilene and Rhodes) his army embarked for the sea voyage home.[125] So the organization of Bithynia/Pontus was the capstone of Pompey's real business in the east.

The first regular governor that we can place in this new *provincia* is C. Papirius Carbo. He was a *tribunus plebis* who was granted consular insignia ca. 70–67 for his successful prosecution of one P. Oppius, a quaestor for Bithynia under M. Cotta (*cos.* 74) during the Third Mithridatic War. Dio notes the irony that Carbo himself later became governor of Bithynia.[126] We have here a good example of the *sors opportuna*!

His tenure can be fixed with some precision. Carbo issued bronze coins in the new *provincia* which (when bearing dates) show the years 222–224 of the Bithynian era.[127] That provincial era commences in 282/281, with each new year starting probably in September at the autumnal equinox, like the Macedonian calendar.[128] So the year 222 can be provisionally identified as spanning late September 61 to late September 60; 223 corresponding to that same period in 60/59; and 224 corresponding to 59/58. His coins offer no title, but the formula ΕΠΙ ΓΑΙΟΥ ΠΑΠΙΡΙΟΥ | ΚΑΡΒΩΝΟΣ[129] and length of time C. Carbo had charge of the *provincia* make it certain (if there is any doubt) that he was a praetorian commander.

The *provincia* of Syria—also newly created by Pompey—received a *pr.* 62, L. Marcius Philippus, to govern it *ex praetura* for 61 (11.5.2). We might expect that Bithynia/Pontus had a praetorian commander for 61, too. Was C. Carbo the first ex-praetor to receive it? Broughton implies as much: he lists Carbo as *pr.* 62, without query,[130] though no activities in the city are attested for him in that year. Yet the fact that Carbo's coins start in Bithynian year "222" allows for the possibility he was *pr.* 61 and arrived in his eastern command only in 60. The bulk of this governor's minting belongs to "224" = 59/58, which suggests[131] that he spent a good deal of 58 in the province. In the final analysis, Carbo's specific background as prosecutor seems to have done him little good in his *provincia*: he himself was condemned on his return from Bithynia/Pontus.[132]

So it seems C. Papirius Carbo spent at least three years in his *provincia*, from 60 through 58. The arrangements for the crucial year 61 must remain a mystery. Perhaps the Senate gave Bithynia/Pontus less immediate attention than Syria, or sent a praetorian commander for 61 whose name has fallen out of our record. The alternative is that Carbo was in Bithynia/Pontus already in 61, but minted only a small number of coins showing "Year 221" of the Bithynian provincial era (hence their disappearance), or none at all.

The direct successor of C. Carbo will have been the patron of Lucretius (and as *tr. pl.* 66, the enemy of the Luculli),[133] C. Memmius. He was praetor in 58, perhaps even *praetor urbanus* (see 12.1.3). So he had Bithynia *ex praetura* for 57—as it happens, with the poets Catullus and Cinna in his *cohors*.[134] In contrast to Carbo's repeated prorogations, Memmius' command lasted just a single year (see below). However, while in the *provincia* that short time he (apparently) earned an impera-torial acclamation.[135] What enemy he found to fight we do not know; at any rate, there was to be no triumph. Memmius either was turned down by the Senate or waived his claim.[136] C. Caecilius Cornutus must have succeeded C. Memmius for 56. Cornutus was *pr.* 57, in which capacity he aided in securing Cicero's recall from exile.[137] All we know of his provincial command is the bronze coin issue he mint-ed at Amisus, ΕΠΙ ΓΑΙΟΥ ΚΑΙΚΙΛΙΟΥ | ΚΟΡΝΟΥΤΟΥ. Unfortunately it is undated, and there are no further facts known of Cornutus' career, so we cannot guess the length of his tenure.[138] The commands of his predecessors C. Papirius Carbo (three or perhaps four years in Bithynia/Pontus) and C. Memmius (supersession after just one year) show that there is no use guessing how long the Senate made him stay.

There is silence until the arrival of P. Silius, attested as *pro praetore* in Bithynia in 51 and at least the early part of 50.[139] Silius must have been a commander of the *provincia* under the *lex Pompeia*, as the rank suggests. (The date of his actual prae-torship, however, is quite unknown.) How long he remained in the east is another question. Silius backed Cicero's request to the Senate for a *supplicatio* later in 50,[140] but it need not have been in person in Rome. We do have a possible candi-date for Silius' successor: A. Plautius (or Plotius), a curule aedile in 55 or 54.[141] In 51, Cicero, soon after entering his promagisterial *provincia* of Cilicia, remarks to

Atticus on the irony of his holding assizes at Laodiceia while Plotius pronounces on law ("ius . . . cum Romae . . . dicat") at Rome.[142] On the basis of this passage, Broughton reckoned that Plotius was urban praetor in this year.[143] Broughton's supposition regarding the city *provincia* finds support in Cicero's own usage elsewhere,[144] but some caution is necessary.[145] However, a praetorship for Plautius in 51 seems certain. This man was apparently in charge of Bithynia around the time of Pharsalus in 48.[146] So it is at least possible that he went there directly *ex praetura*, to succeed P. Silius after a single year's command.

11.3 Crete

11.3.1 *The Pirate Command of M. Antonius*

The story of Crete as a Roman *provincia* probably should begin with M. Antonius "Creticus." Son of the M. Antonius who triumphed from a praetorian command in Cilicia (10.1), as *pr.* 74 he received his own special command to suppress piracy, one that extended over a large part of the Mediterranean.[147] The consul M. Aurelius Cotta was the one who pushed through this commission. Pirates were an endemic problem, which Rome had done not all that much to address in the previous twenty-five years,[148] except of course in the area of Cilicia. Those based in Spain had been helping Sertorius for a few years.[149] And Mithridates in his first war with Rome had made effective use of pirates. With fresh hostilities imminent, he might be expected to do so again. "Once the new war had broken out," explains A. M. Ward, "the Senate would have found it imperative to combat piracy in the Mediterranean with a major command that does not seem to have been foreseen in 75."[159]

Precisely how the Senate defined the territorial bounds of M. Antonius' command is uncertain. Almost all our information comes from Ciceronian scholiasts, who are under the impression that Antonius had the entire "ora maritima" under Roman control.[151] Yet it appears certain that for this commission Antonius received enhanced *imperium*.[152] That is what his father had in his special Cilician command as *pr.* 102 (10.1), and indeed what all post-Sullan praetorian commanders had who took up overseas *provinciae*. Cicero in the *Verrines* makes it seem as though M. Antonius received "infinitum imperium."[153] But in no way should we take Cicero literally on this. It is a jibe, aimed not at the quality of *imperium* Antonius received, but rather at the vague *fines* of his *provincia* (14.2.5).

To operate in his massive province M. Antonius made wide use of independent *legati* and *praefecti*. Some were active for long stretches of time at great distances from their superior. An inscription from Gytheum records that six named subordinates passed through that town alone in the years (apparently) 74/73–73/72. Three of these subordinates (C. Iulius Caesar, P. Autronius Paetus, Fulvius) are explicitly termed *legati*; another one, Q. Ancharius, is elsewhere attested as *pro quaestore*. During this time M. Antonius was still operating in the west.[154] But there is no indication that any of them had been delegated *imperium*.

Antonius himself was to have more than three years of *imperium*, which culminated in an overconfident invasion of Crete.[155] Cretan mercenaries had been serving under Mithridates, Appian tells us (and Memnon confirms). However, Appian says Antonius' main point of contention with the people of this island was their noncooperation in his war against the pirates; in this, too, were the Cretans thought to be gratifying Mithridates.[156] Antonius first made diplomatic efforts, but when his embassy failed he launched (almost certainly in 71) an invasion of the island with the forces he had available. The Cretans under Lasthenes of Cnossus and Panares promptly handed Antonius a humiliating defeat at sea.[157] But the prospect of open war with the Romans apparently had an effect, since Diodorus says Antonius managed to get the Cretans to observe a "peace."[158] We are not told the terms; at a minimum, the Cretans must have agreed to drop their aid to Mithridates and the pirates in return for a cessation of hostilities. Though the praetor soon died of disease—tellingly, on the island itself[159]—the agreement he struck outlasted his death, which came probably in 71 and certainly before the autumn of 70. However. the Senate took no steps to ratify formally Antonius' agreement with the people of Crete.

That Antonius had been sent specifically against Crete seems to have been the contemporary perception in mainland Greece, to judge from the evidence of an inscription from Epidaurus.[160] It was somewhat of a misperception. At first, Antonius operated in the west, along the coasts of Liguria, Spain, and Sicily. Cicero complains of his harsh exactions in Sicily during autumn 74.[161] Meanwhile, Antonius also had his *legati* in Old Greece make equally severe requisitions for the projected campaign in eastern waters. No doubt Antonius had his eye on Crete from the start, out of a desire to equal the achievements that earned his father a triumph: after all, Crete was thought second only to Cilicia in number of pirates.[162] His legates perhaps even made their exactions in the name of a "Cretan war": when Antonius visited Epidaurus he certainly seems to have represented himself as "commander against the Cretans." Yet he very likely did not turn his full attention toward that island until late 72, and his invasion in 71 (as we have seen) was by no means inevitable. Crete, long soft on piracy and an old source of mercenaries, was a nuisance, especially given Rome's recent interest in exploiting Cyrene.[163] At no point, however, can the Senate have charged Antonius to turn Crete into a *provincia*.

11.3.2 *Q. Caecilius Metellus and the Annexation of Crete*

Yet perhaps as early as the year 70 the Senate did make the decision (at least in principle) to annex Crete. It declared the island a military *provincia* for one of the consuls of 69, apparently under the Sempronian law. When the *cos.* Q. Hortensius turned it down, it fell to his colleague Q. Caecilius Metellus.[164] Q. Metellus probably set out for the war only *ex consulatu*, for 68.[165] He obviously planned to fight a major campaign.[166]

Velleius and Eutropius say Metellus finished the war in three years' time.[167] It seems, however, that the subjugation of the island was already quite advanced in late 67.[168] The Cretans sent a message to Pompey—who under the Gabinian law had *imperium* equal to that of any *pro consule* over the coasts of the Mediterranean and for fifty miles inland—and offered to surrender instead to him. Plutarch says when they made their appeal, the Cretans alleged their island was part of his command: "It everywhere fell within the territorial limit from the sea" granted to Pompey under the Gabinian law.[169] Pompey went so far as to command (by letter) Metellus to withdraw from the island. He also wrote to cities in Crete to ignore the consular commander, and sent his *legatus* L. Octavius (though with no troops) to take them over until he himself could arrive. Metellus, however, refused to recognize Pompey's right to intervene in this way, and wrote back to tell him so.[170] The episode shows clearly that Pompey had no overriding "imperium maius" under the Gabinian law (as has sometimes been thought). At issue was not the respective quality of each man's *imperium*, but the question whether the relevant cities of Crete fell within the territorial boundaries of Pompey's special *provincia*. Technical questions aside, Pompey's interference as a *privatus cum imperio* with a consul in his consular province does seem quite provocative.

Metellus held firm, despite obstruction from Pompey's *legatus* L. Octavius. Octavius, though called στρατηγός in Plutarch,[171] apparently was not one of the *legati pro praetore* Pompey had received under the Gabinian law. Eventually Pompey sent one of those, namely L. Cornelius Sisenna (*pr.* 78), who brought across an armed force from his station in mainland Greece. But Sisenna soon fell ill and died, and Pompey lost interest now that he had received the Mithridatic command.[172] So, in the end, it was Metellus who was responsible (in 66 and perhaps 65) for the annexation of Crete and its organization as a Roman *provincia*.[173] We do not know when Metellus returned to Rome. In October 63, it appears from Sallust that he had been waiting long outside the city for a triumph. He finally got that honor (probably in 62) and with it the Senate's vote of the *agnomen* "Creticus." Yet, even at Metellus' actual triumph, Pompey used a friendly tribune to press a claim on the most prominent Cretan captives.[174]

By 65 the annexation of Crete was an accomplished fact. From that point, however, we have no real clues how Rome administered its new possession, except that it was counted a distinct praetorian *provincia*, separate from Cyrene, for the year 51 and indeed for some time past the end of our period.[175]

11.4 Cyrene

An item from the Fleury manuscript of Sallust *Histories* Book II, covering events from (surely) the year 75, describes how the Senate decided to send a "quaestor" to Cyrene:

> And P. [Cornelius] Lentulus Marcellinus on the motion of the same speaker (*eodem auctore*) was sent as quaestor to the new *provincia* of Cyrene, although this *provincia*—given to us by the will of the dead king Apion—needed to be controlled by an *imperium* more prudent that that of a young man (*adulescens*), and in a less greedy fashion than that one (*ille*) [sc. in particular]. Moreover <in this year there blazed forth rivalries> of the different orders.[176]

Sallust in this passage mentions *imperium*, but in a nontechnical sense. If the quaestor P. Marcellinus had it (as is likely), it naturally will have been at the praetorian level. There is no indication, however, that he was actually a "governor." The severe grain shortage of the year 75 must form the background to this quaestor's commission, as many have noted.[177] Badian persuasively has argued that his primary task was to collect money, especially through the organization of the royal lands.

Why a quaestor? "The reason was evidently the Senate's unwillingness to appoint a senior man with a dangerous *imperium* for the task."[178] To leave such a person on his own in that still-unorganized Roman possession must have seemed too politically and militarily risky. A praetorian or consular commander was apt to go off triumph hunting. But above all it was dangerous for the public finances. A well-connected senior magistrate might feel bold enough to keep a substantial portion of the royal wealth for himself—for example, to cover (whether prospectively or retrospectively) his own electoral expenses—and not worry too much about the consequences of being haled into court on his return before a jury of his peers.

P. Marcellinus appears to have remained in Cyrene down to late 74 or early 73, when he evidently returned to Rome with his money.[179] No other Roman official is known to be active in the area until the year 67, when Cn. Lentulus Marcellinus (the future *cos.* 56) turns up in Cyrene. Presumably brother of the quaestor P. Marcellinus, he is epigraphically attested as a *legatus pro praetore* under Pompey in his pirate command. Indeed, a substantial series of inscriptions commemorates Cn. Marcellinus' visit to Cyrene, including the record of his judgment in a dispute between two local cities. J. M. Reynolds has shown that this inscription and his other honors from the Cyrenaeans demonstrate that there was no Roman commander in their land at the time.[180] All the same, Reynolds relies on the Sallust *Histories* fragment to argue for annexation in 75/74, and suggests that by 67, administration had "broken down."[181] Badian, however, must be right in his conclusion that Cyrene was not yet a *provincia*.[182] Yet Pompey must soon have had it organized.[183] We find M. Iuventius Laterensis (the future *pr.* 51) there as *pro quaestore* in 63. It is impossible to tell from Cicero's brief notices of Laterensis' position whether he was serving under a praetorian governor or himself had sole charge.[184]

There is a chance that L. Caecilius Rufus, *pr. urb.* 57, had to go to Cyrene as *pro consule* in 56, but that is by process of elimination, not positive evidence.[185] However, Cyrene was definitely counted among the praetorian *provinciae* in October 51.[186] We might even be able to supply the name of a contemporary governor, one Cn. Tremelius Scrofa. A member of an established praetorian family, Tremelius was a quaestor or *pro quaestore* in 71 and senator by 70.[187] Though attested at Rome shortly before mid-May 51,[188] he is commonly thought to be a (praetorian) commander in the east that year. In February 50, Tremelius Scrofa is listed among eastern governors and said to have an unpromising appointment. Cicero had written by mid-October 50 to ask Scrofa along with the commander for Bithynia to support his bid for a triumph.[189] Broughton[190] reasonably suggests that Scrofa held the praetorship before 57, and received an *ex praetura* command under the provisions of the *lex Pompeia* of 52. For his *provincia*, Broughton initially suggested "perhaps Macedonia," later (following Shackleton Bailey) "probably Crete and Cyrene." Since M. Nonius does seem the better candidate for Macedonia (14.2.6), we can place Scrofa with some confidence in Cyrene—the only regular commander in our *fasti* for the province.[191]

11.5 Syria

11.5.1 *Pompey's Annexation of Syria*

In 83 B.C. (probably), Tigranes II of Armenia occupied Seleucid Syria—that is, Coele Syria and Phoenicia—which had been a divided kingdom for most of the previous three decades, owing to the rivalries of Antiochus VIII Grypus (125–113 then 111–96 B.C.), his cousin (and brother) Antiochus IX Cyzicenus (113–95 B.C.), and their own sons. After holding Syria for fourteen years (perhaps more), Tigranes had to abandon that territory in 69 B.C. to defend his own kingdom against the *pro consule* L. Licinius Lucullus. For the Syrian throne, Lucullus promptly recognized the claims of Antiochus XIII Asiaticus, a grandson of Antiochus Cyzicenus. (A few years earlier the Roman Senate had granted Asiaticus, while an exile, the title of "friend and ally.") Yet Asiaticus had difficulty maintaining his position in a country now destabilized by Arab dynasts, and lost the throne after only about a year. Grypus' grandson Philip II Barypous managed to establish himself in Antiochus' place for a time (67/66–66/65), in part thanks to a large sum paid to the *pro consule* for Cilicia Q. Marcius Rex (*cos.* 68). Yet with Arab support Asiaticus was able once again to take up his rule in 66/65.[192]

Pompey, during his pirate command of 67, already had one of his *legati pro praetore*, Q. Metellus Nepos, take responsibility for a district that included the waters off Phoenicia. Before he moved against Mithridates in 66, he took care that part of his fleet continued to patrol that coast.[193] In that same year, Pompey managed to defeat Mithridates and (by autumn) obtain the surrender of Tigranes. Not long afterward, his legates Q. Metellus Nepos and L. Lollius (another *legatus pro praetore* who had fought pirates in the eastern Aegean) were conducting land operations well into the interior of western Syria Phoenice. By late 66 or early 65 (surely), his legates moved against Damascus, which Tigranes had relinquished on his evacuation of Syria and (apparently) Arabs had seized in the interim. Immediately after its capture, Pompey's quaestor M. Aemilius Scaurus arrived in the city. He promptly embroiled himself in the dynastic disputes of the brothers Aristobulus II and Hyrcanus II—the rival Hasamonean claimants for the throne of Judaea—aiming to turn a profit for himself. A. Gabinius (who as *tr. pl.* 67 gave Pompey his pirate command and was now a trusted *legatus* in the east) soon joined Scaurus in this enterprise. Other areas of Syria felt the Roman presence too. In early 64, the praetorian legate (and *triumphator*) L. Afranius, fresh from a successful semi-independent command in Gordyene, was sent to clear Arabs out of northwest Syria, in the region of Mt. Amanus.[194]

In spring 64, Pompey himself arrived in Syria. Our sources make out that Pompey's goal was to launch an expedition against the Nabataean Arabs and their king Aretas III. His actions reveal a far more ambitious plan. Immediately upon setting foot in Syria, Pompey deposed Antiochus XIII Asiaticus. He then proceeded to annex and organize Seleucid Syria as a Roman *provincia*. No ancient source spells out the motive more fully than Justin, who reports that Pompey wanted to protect Seleucid Syria from the brigandage of Jews and Arabs. That might be enough to explain Pompey's decision. The sorry state of the house of Seleucus and the obvious helplessness of the current ruler Antiochus Asiaticus raised the prospect of even more chaotic local conditions. Control of piracy was also at issue. A new "Pompeian" era replaced the Seleucid, reckoned from autumn 66—the date of Tigranes' surrender. That dating, combined with the military movements outlined above, point toward the conclusion (generally accepted) that Pompey had resolved on the annexation of Syria from the start of his campaign against Mithridates.[195]

After wintering at (probably) Antioch in 64/63, Pompey subjugated a series of dynasts in Lebanon and started his campaign against the Nabataeans.[196] But resistance from Aristobulus triggered a series of events that culminated in a three-month siege of Jerusalem and a massacre on the Temple mount, followed by Pompey's establishment of a large portion of Palestine as a taxpaying protectorate. News of the death of Mithridates brought Pompey hurriedly back to Pontus, in early 62 B.C. On his departure he placed the *pro quaestore* M. Aemilius Scaurus in command of Syria *pro praetore* with two legions, evidently with orders to complete the projected campaign against Aretas and the Nabataeans.[197] Scaurus duly marched against Petra. But before causing any harm to the enemy he accepted a hefty bribe (300 talents) to call off the war, to Aretas' great relief.[198] We do not hear of Pompey's reaction. Whether this is what he had in mind when he delegated *imperium* to Scaurus seems dubious.

11.5.2 *Syria as a Praetorian* Provincia, 61–58 B.C.

Appian[199] reports that Pompey's quaestor Scaurus was superseded in Syria by (L.) Marcius Philippus, who in turn had as his successor (Cn.) Lentulus Marcellinus. Appian implies that Philippus and Marcellinus (later colleagues as *coss.* 56) went to Syria *ex praetura* (ἄμφω στρατηγικοὺς κατὰ ἀξίωσιν) and states that each held the *provincia* for two whole years. Each of these commanders, says Appian, spent the whole of his tenure driving off the neighboring Arabs who harassed this new Roman possession. Because of the military situation, Syria subsequently was entrusted to ex-consuls.

That brief notice unfortunately is our only source on the praetorian administration of Syria. The details Appian does provide seem solid. Two consecutive two-year *ex praetura* commands (i.e., 61–60 and 59–58) should be accurate, for A. Gabinius (*cos.* 58) received the *provincia* for 57 and remained—despite some talk of superseding him with a praetor (14.2.5)—down through 55 B.C.[200] And for the rest of our period Syria indeed remained consular, at least in theory. M. Licinius Crassus (*cos.* 55) succeeded Gabinius, and was supposed to have the province for five years under the *lex Trebonia*. Yet Crassus was killed not far into his second year of command at Carrhae (9 June 53) while campaigning against the Parthians. Crassus' quaestor C. Cassius Longinus escaped this military disaster and returned to take charge of his superior's province; whoever Crassus had left in charge of Roman Syria must have been junior indeed. Though only *pro quaestore*,[201] Cassius then had to act as commander-in-chief in Syria all through 52 and far down into 51 B.C. After Crassus' death it seems no one wanted the province because of the Parthian danger.[202] In 51, M. Calpurnius Bibulus (*cos.* 59)—he was *pro cos.* for Syria under the *lex Pompeia*—arrived only sometime after 20 September, shortly after Cassius saved the province from a significant Parthian invasion. M. Bibulus departed from the province by early December 50. We hear that he left a certain Veiento in charge.[203] If Bibulus made him *pro praetore* (as seems likely), Veiento will be the only subconsular known to hold *imperium* in Syria after the arrival of A. Gabinius in 57 B.C.

Looking back past those ambitious consular commands, the presence of those two praetorian commanders in the early years of this armed and financially promising *provincia*[204] seems an anomaly. How did Syria stay praetorian for four straight years? It is somewhat understandable why the Senate acted so quickly and ordained that one of the outgoing praetors of 62 should draw Syria in the sortition for 61 B.C. By the time L. Marcius Philippus arrived in Syria as its first regular governor, M. Aemilius Scaurus had marked at least one full year there as *pro praetore*.[205] And during that time he had reduced the Nabataean threat to Syria (his one stated responsibility) not a whit. Appian speaks of the first two praetorian commanders having to defend Syria against Arabs over the next four years. The *pro cos.* Gabinius suffered a humiliating cavalry defeat—surely at the hands of Arabs—immediately upon his arrival in the province in 57 B.C. Further losses soon followed.[206] A major campaign was delayed until 55 B.C.[207] The precise motivation for declaring Syria praetorian in late 62 or early 61 escapes us. But the Senate's decision was a consequential one, since it of course gave immediate de facto recognition to Pompey's arrangements in this area before any official vote on his *acta*.

We know that Cicero had to scotch plans to make that province consular (i.e., by suspension of the *lex Sempronia*) for 60. The *cos.* 61 M. Pupius Piso Frugi Calpurnianus had tried to make the Syrian command his own, perhaps starting already when he was *designatus*. In a letter to Atticus (June 61), Cicero claims the Senate almost granted Pupius his wish but that he "wrested" the province from the consul. In other words, Cicero successfully fought to have L. Philippus extended in his promagistracy for a second year.[208] Personal politics will have played their role here. Cicero had a low opinion of Pupius Piso as consul;[209] for instance, in that letter to Atticus he boasts that he has foiled Pupius in all his designs. Yet it may be that Cicero (and others) also had legitimate fears what Pupius might get up to if he had Syria as a military arena. Praetor by 71, Pupius' *ex praetura* lot had been Hispania Ulterior. By energetically hunting for enemies in this now war-weary province, he scraped up enough for a triumph, awarded in 69 B.C.—but on return met criticism for his methods (13.4.6). Six years of service under Pompey in the east were to follow, starting with a position as a *legatus pro praetore* in the Propontis region against the pirates and continuing down through the siege of Jerusalem in 63 B.C. In the consular elections for 61, Pompey threw his full *auctoritas* behind this experienced legate, even asking for the *comitia* to be delayed so that he could canvass for Pupius in person.[210] Given that background, if the Senate allowed Pupius to return to Syria *ex consulatu*, there was no telling (especially given Pompey's backing) how long it might be before it could get him out.

The consuls of 60 had to draw the Gallic *provinciae* in an emergency sortition already in March of their year of office (15.2.3). So that is how Syria remained praetorian for the year 59 B.C., falling to a new commander, the *pr.* 60 Cn. Cornelius Lentulus Marcellinus. He is attested as a *legatus pro praetore* under Pompey against the pirates in the year 67; perhaps he had just recently returned from the east.[211] For political reasons alone there was no real question of making Syria consular for 58.[212] Hence the prorogation of Marcellinus, who had earned a good reputation in his first year as governor in Syria.[213] Cn. Marcellinus positively celebrated his good fortune at receiving this grand *provincia* with a splendid gold stater provincial issue. Crawford tentatively dates this coin to 59 B.C.[214] Yet it is perhaps best placed in 58, that is, the same year the commander for Asia had received permission to mint in his *provincia* (14.6.8).

11.5.3 *Syria under Its Consular Commanders*

For 57 B.C., the consular *provinciae* under the Sempronian law were Macedonia and Cilicia. Syria was supposed to remain praetorian. But the *cos.* 58 A. Gabinius managed to swap Cilicia for Syria (15.1.2). The tribune P. Clodius passed a law to grant the province to him *extra ordinem* with special powers—including what Cicero calls "infinitum imperium," apparently the right to choose precisely the provincial boundaries (*fines*) he desired. Specifically, Clodius may have introduced into his law the formulation that occurs a few years later in the *lex Trebonia* of 55, when M. Crassus got as his *provincia* "Syria and the neighboring lands."[215] The Nabataean Arabs offered a suitable pretext for this proviso.

Like Pupius Piso, Gabinius had seen long service under Pompey in the east. Indeed, Gabinius' tribunician law of 67 on the pirates is what placed Pompey in a position in 66 B.C. to take over the Mithridatic command. In 65, we find Gabinius engaged in a semi-independent campaign that took him across the Euphrates and as far as the Tigris. In 64 and 63, he played a leading role in Pompey's efforts to bring Judaea under Roman control—accruing (it is said) 300 talents for himself in the process.[216] As consul, Gabinius was evidently anxious to get back to the east, but this time in a position of much greater power.

Once in place, Gabinius immediately changed the system of tax collection in Syria and Judaea, to the relief of provincials and consternation of *publicani*. (Cicero argues it was all for his own benefit.) There was some fighting, apparently against Arabs (none too successful). And he had to face down a major Jewish revolt led by Alexander, the son of Aristobulus, and institute a political and administrative reorganization of Judaea. Gabinius' troops must have hailed him as *imperator*. However, the Senate (on 15 May 56) refused this commander a *supplicatio*: Cicero says that no commander had suffered this indignity since the praetor T. Albucius' tenure in Sardinia at the end of the second century B.C. (13.1.1).[217] Apparently there had been an attempt to recall Gabinius and his consular colleague Piso in 57, that is, to hand Syria and Macedonia to other commanders for 56. That failed, as did efforts—led by the *publicani* and spearheaded by Cicero—to defeat Gabinius' prorogation into 55 B.C.[218] It was no easy task in this era to dislodge a well-connected consular commander from a distant *provincia*.

The events of 57 show that Gabinius had plenty to keep him busy in his province of Syria. Yet what he really had his mind on—probably from the start—was a Parthian war. Dio suggests as much,[219] and the concern during his consulship to get "infinitum imperium" confirms it. The rest of the story is well known.

In 56 or 55 B.C., Gabinius even went so far as to cross the Euphrates.[220] Then Ptolemy XII Auletes appeared on the scene, and bribed Gabinius (allegedly with 50,000 talents) to restore him to the throne in Alexandria. In spring 55, Gabinius actually marched into Egypt to do so, leaving his province proper to his stepson Cornelius Sisenna, a junior *legatus*, and unnamed others. These could not even protect Syria from pirates.[221]

Nor did Gabinius' successor, the *cos.* II 55 M. Licinius Crassus, take much interest in this *provincia* except as a springboard for a full-scale (unauthorized) invasion of Parthia. Under a tribunician law passed *ex S.C.* the consular *provinciae* were to be "Syria and the neighboring lands" and the Spains, each for five years. Efforts to mitigate the open hostility toward their extraordinary commands fell flat. The *tribunus plebis* C. Ateius in particular resorted to a whole range of obstructive tactics—culminating in public imprecations—to obstruct Crassus in setting out from the city for his (ultimately disastrous) Parthian campaign in November 55 B.C.[221] Whatever fears anyone might have harbored of M. Pupius Piso back in the year 61 will now have seemed quaint.

11.6 Resistance to the Annexation of Egypt

Surely the most significant episode in the Egyptian dynastic struggles of 88/87 B.C., is the testament of Ptolemy X. While at a political disadvantage, this monarch agreed to bequeath Egypt to the Roman People as security for a large loan. He soon died, before he was able to win back the kingdom from his elder brother Ptolemy IX. Despite internal problems, Ptolemy IX remained on the throne down to his own death in late December 81; an external challenge from Rome came to nought when a tribunician veto blocked the Cinnan Senate's resolution to move to accept Egypt as its "hereditas" (10.3.2). In 80, the Senate, now under Sullan control, had an excellent opportunity to take up the "hereditas" of Ptolemy X. Instead, Sulla established that man's son, Ptolemy XI Alexander II, as joint ruler with his step-mother (and wife) Cleopatra Berenice. Within three weeks, the king murdered his queen, only to lose his own life for that act at the hands of the Alexandrians. So by June 80 Egypt had no rulers.[223] "This surely must have shown anyone who would look," observes Badian,[224] "that the Ptolemies were no longer able to hold their kingdom and that annexation could hardly be escaped (not to mention the affront to Roman *auctoritas* that was implied in the murder of a king installed by Sulla)." Yet Sulla chose to overlook all that and allow a young illegitimate son of Ptolemy IX—Ptolemy XII "Auletes"—to rise to the throne. The Romans did stop short of granting Auletes official recognition. But they also gave the cold shoulder to rival claimants.[225]

There matters rested for a while, until the early months of the year 65 saw an open attempt to annex Egypt as a tributary province on the basis of the testament of Ptolemy X. The most visible proponent of this scheme was the censor M. Licinius Crassus, against the objections of his colleague Q. Lutatius Catulus. Apparently, a plebiscite was to create a special command (with *imperium*) to annex Egypt as a Roman province. The proposed plebiscite may have stipulated the selection of specifically a subpraetorian for the task, along the lines of what we have seen for Cyrene in 75 and later shall see for Cyprus in 58 (11.4, 11.8.4). For Suetonius tells us the curule aedile C. Iulius Caesar campaigned hard for the commission, with the backing of several tribunes—and we can assume with the support of the censor Crassus. The optimates stoutly opposed this legislation, which they ultimately defeated. However, the squabble over Egypt led the censors to abdicate before attending to any of the proper business of the magistracy, including the compilation of the senatorial album.[226]

Shockwaves from the affair still reverberated two years later in Rome. In January 63, Cicero evokes this dispute to attack a provision of the Rullan land bill that gave a board of X*viri* the right to sell foreign dominions that had come into Roman possession since 88 B.C., including (it is claimed) Egypt. Cicero portrays Rullus' bill (among other things) as a backdoor attempt to decide the question of the testament—against the Roman People and in favor of Ptolemy Auletes, Cicero predicts in a speech to the People. Evidently at this time the notion of annexation had strong popular support.[227]

Meanwhile, the Egyptians sought to avoid it, opposing efforts by their king to forge closer links with the Romans. In 63, when Auletes sent Pompey a large force of cavalry to aid his campaign in Judaea, the Alexandrians demonstrated their disapproval. Appian says that Auletes in turn invited Pompey into his kingdom to suppress sedition. Pompey declined, "whether fearing the greatness of a kingdom that was still prosperous, or guarding against the envy of his enemies, or at the bidding of oracles, or for other considerations."[228] Appian's mention of "envy" comes closest to the mark. Given the dispute in Rome of 65 B.C., had Pompey marched into Egypt he would have thrown all his hard-won arrangements in the east into jeopardy, including his annexation of Syria as a Roman province.

It was Julius Caesar as consul in 59 who resolved the question of the "hereditas"—after the payment of an enormous bribe (6,000 talents) by Auletes. Caesar passed a law to recognize this man as king, with the status of "friend and ally" of the Roman People.[229] Yet in a year's time the Alexandrians forced Auletes to leave his kingdom. The king had been squeezing his subjects hard for money. But what was particularly infuriating to the Egyptians, we are told, was the fact that Auletes meekly acquiesced in Rome's grabbing Cyprus from his own brother in 58.

Auletes was soon in Rome using money to find a commander to effect his restoration. We find various schemes proposed. In late 57, the Senate voted that the consul P. Cornelius Lentulus Spinther—who was about to take up Cilicia as promagistrate—have the restoration of the Egyptian king as part of his *provincia*. The measure was promptly vetoed. A religious objection also presented itself, when C. Cato (a new tribune of 56) illegally publicized a Sibylline oracle that prohibited the use of an army to help the king. When C. Cato fiercely and effectively opposed other proposals, Auletes eventually decided to dispense with the Senate and tribunes and approach directly A. Gabinius, the *pro consule* for Syria. Gabinius invaded Egypt in spring 55 B.C., reinstalled Auletes, and left behind a substantial garrison force to support him (11.5.3).

Gabinius was condemned *de repetundis* on his return to Rome in 54 B.C. However, the Roman garrison remained, down to the death of Auletes in 51 and beyond, when his eldest surviving daughter, Cleopatra VI, took the throne.[230] The

Senate must have decided that it was far preferable to prop up the Ptolemaic regime than to allow this particular annexation debate to resurface in Rome. Nor did the Romans tamper with other wealthy kingdoms during the rest of this period.[231]

11.7 Standing *Quaestiones* in the Post-Sullan Period

11.7.1 Quaestio Repetundarum

The *repetundae* court is easily the best attested of the permanent *quaestiones* in the post-Sullan era.[232] We have the names of at least nine of the individuals who presided over this *quaestio* in the years 80–50 B.C. Our first information is for the second half of the 70s. A Ciceronian scholiast reports that a Terentius Varro on return from Asia was accused *de repetundis* before the praetor L. Furius and then brought to trial before P. Cornelius Lentulus Sura (*pr.* 74), only to be scandalously acquitted (see 14.6.1). Broughton places both L. Furius and P. Lentulus Sura in the *provincia repetundarum*, for the years 75 and 74 respectively. However, since provincial offenses might be prosecuted in more than one *quaestio*, it is possible that Furius was a colleague of Sura—whose *provincia* is nowhere explicitly said to be *repetundarum*—in 74. Q. Hortensius was *pr. rep.* 72.[233]

Three (perhaps four) praetors are attested in this court for the five-year period 70–66 B.C. The praetor M.' Acilius Glabrio definitely had the *provincia repetundarum* in 70, followed by the praetor M. Caecilius Metellus in 69.[234] Sometime not long after the passage of the *lex Aurelia* of 70—which placed alongside senators also *equites* and "tribuni aerarii" as jurors in the courts (12.4.3)—an unnamed "quaesitor" heard M. Tullius Cicero defend M. Fonteius, who had served as a praetorian commander in Transalpine Gaul in the mid-70s, on a charge of extortion. The term "quaesitor" can denote a range of statuses, praetor among them; the date is one of the years 69–67.[235] Cicero himself as praetor had the *provincia repetundarum* in 66.[236] Though that *quaestio* was his primary responsibility, it is instructive to note he spoke in a *contio* to sway the decision in an upcoming case *de peculatu* and argued a case in the *quaestio de veneficiis* in addition to backing the Manilian law on Pompey's command in the east.[237]

In the year 59, we know of two major trials *de repetundis*—apparently with two different praetors in charge. Cn. Cornelius Lentulus Clodianus presumably was praetor when he presided in April over the trial of C. Antonius (*cos.* 63, then *pro cos.* in Macedonia).[238] Yet, later that year, Cicero when defending L. Valerius Flaccus (*pr.* 63, then *pro cos.* in Asia) for extortion, addressed one T. Vettius Sabinus, implying he was shortly about to take up a praetorian command in Africa.[239] Perhaps the *quaestio repetundarum* involved more than one praetor in this year. The alternative is that T. Vettius, though praetor, heard the Flaccus case as juror.[240] Magistrates in office are attested to have had a *vacatio* from serving on juries as late as for the year 69, but they apparently lost that privilege, perhaps as early as 64.[241] In 56, while praetor, Cn. Domitius Calvinus (who had the *ambitus* court) and his colleague Q. Ancharius sat as jurors in the trial of P. Sestius *de vi*.[242]

We shall see that a couple of other possible instances of praetors sitting as jurors crop up in the 50s.

Ap. Claudius Pulcher almost certainly was *praetor repetundarum* for 57. The *provincia* is a reasonable inference from a letter to Atticus where Cicero voices deep concern that his brother Quintus (*pr.* 62, then *pro cos.* in Asia) on return to Rome might face prosecution in a *quaestio* run by (the then praetor designate) Appius.[243] But one ought to remember that Cicero, for all his worrying about Quintus' possible prosecution for that Asian command,[244] never spells out the precise charge he feared his brother might face.

The next attested holder of the *provincia reptundarum* is M. Porcius Cato. An unsuccessful candidate for *pr.* 55, as *pr. repetundis* in 54 Cato presided over the prosecution of M. Aemilius Scaurus (*pr.* 56) for extortion in his Sardinian command as well as the *calumnia* trial or trials that followed Scaurus' acquittal. And Cato was the magistrate who presided at the *repetundae* trial in which A. Gabinius (*cos.* 58) was condemned.[245] Notwithstanding his *provincia*, Cato seems also to have had responsibilities in the area of civil law.[246]

It is possible that while praetor Cato also sat as a juror in the court that saw the acquittal of A. Gabinius (*cos.* 58) *de maiestate* by a thin margin of votes.[247] Cicero in a letter of 24 October 54 remarks that among the jurors in that case there sat two "praetorii," Cn. Domitius Calvinus (i.e., the *pr.* 56) and a "Cato" ("de iudicibus duo praetorii sederunt, Domitius Calvinus . . . et Cato"), the latter individual being the first to announce the result of the voting to Pompey (who energetically had backed Gabinius).[248] Now, Linderski identifies this "Cato" with C. Porcius Cato (*tr. pl.* 56), making him *pr.* 55 and thus a *praetorius* in 54—a solution which Broughton deemed "very probable" despite the lack of interval between tribunate and praetorship, which finds no good parallel for this era.[249]

But if Cicero's wording in this passage is merely a circumlocution for "iudices praetorii"—which seems at least a possibility—a solution presents itself. Cicero might mean only to say that there were two jurors in the trial of praetorian status— as it happens, one an ex-praetor and the other a praetor in office.[250] We have seen that a sitting praetor might have to serve as a juror in this era.

There is a different sort of practical problem. Linderski[251] speaks of the "utmost improbability of Cato Uticensis having jubilantly informed Pompeius of Gabinius' acquittal." But Cicero says nothing of the spirit of this announcement, simply that when the jurors' votes were counted Cato disengaged himself from the crowd and was the first to tell Pompey ("Pompeio primus nuntiavit"), who at the time as *pro consule* could not cross within the *pomerium*. It was precisely as *praetor repetundis*, I suggest, that Cato wanted to be the first to announce to Pompey news of the (narrow) vote that acquitted Gabinius of *maiestas*. His aim was not to cheer but to deflate the mood of Gabinius' foremost adherent by also predicting that man's imminent condemnation in his own extortion court, where the process had already started.[252] *Nuntiare* is elsewhere used of this sort of prediction.[253] Cicero himself, when he heard of Gabinius' acquittal for *maiestas*, expressed almost as his first thought that he still risked condemnation especially for extortion, which of course is precisely what happened.[254]

One other magistrate is known to have supervised the *repetundae* court in our period: M. Iuvenius Laterensis, praetor in 51.[255] So in every instance where we can check for the years following Sulla's dictatorship it is a praetor who presides in an extortion trial. We can assume with some confidence the same is true in the cases *de repetundis* for which there is no mention of the court president.[256]

11.7.2 *The* Ambitus *Court*

There are about three dozen trials on the charge of *ambitus* attested for the post-Sullan period that are certain or at least seem probable.[257] But information as to who presided in these cases is scrappy. In 66, the famous jurist C. Aquillius Gallus definitely had the *ambitus* court as his *provincia*. He was hearing a prosecution on this charge at the same time A. Cluentius Habitus was on trial for poisoning, as Cicero tells us.[258] Despite this evidence, in none of the other *ambitus* cases known to have been prosecuted in the year 66[259] is Aquillius positively attested as president. That probably just shows how little interest our sources have in the presiding magistrate in such trials. Additional hard information on Aquillius' praetorship is lacking. Now, he is lauded by Cicero in the *De Natura Deorum* (dramatic date 77 or 76) and *De Officiis* for creating a useful formula on deliberate fraud ("de dolo malo"): but as jurist or praetor? Perhaps as praetor—despite his *provincia*—to judge from Cicero's statements that he "produced" ("protulit," "protulerat") a process on this crime.[260] Cicero elsewhere uses the verb *proferre* of a praetor introducing innovations in his edict.[261] That interpretation, however, requires us to think Cicero is anachronistic in bringing up Aquillius' formula *de dolo* in the *De Natura Deorum*, for a time that he himself remembered as an adult.[262] The legal authority C. Aquillius, who, as *iudex* with a distinguished *consilium*, judged against a female plaintiff in a sordid civil case, must be the same individual as our praetor. Yet, against a suggestion by Alexander, that particular incident should be dissociated from his praetorship in 66.[263]

P. Clodius Pulcher is said to have defended a Cornelius Lentulus on a charge of *ambitus* before jurors and a praetor, despite the fact that this man had joined two other Lentuli in accusing Clodius of *incestum* in 61. But we have no date for the trial, nor details on the court president—except of course the important fact that it was a praetor.[264] We do get a revealing notice on the management of this court for late in the year 59 B.C. Cicero says that C. Porcius Cato (a future *tr. pl.* 56) could not get access to the "praetors" to submit his *postulatio* for the prosecution of A. Gabinius (then *cos. des.* 58) on an *ambitus* charge. C. Cato finally gave up and in a *contio* denounced Pompey, apparently for intervening secretly on behalf of Gabinius. Cicero's statement that the "praetors" refused to make themselves available to Cato would suggest that more than one had competence in cases *de ambitu* in that year.[265]

In 56, the praetor Cn. Domitius Calvinus had *ambitus* as his city *provincia*.[266] As noted (11.7.1), while praetor he and his colleague Q. Ancharius sat as jurors in the trial of P. Sestius *de vi*. This praetor is also likely to be identical with the Cn. Domitius who (evidently) presided over the prosecution of Caelius *de vi* in this same year:[267] no other individual by that name and of the requisite status is available. If true, the combination of jurisdictions is noteworthy—especially since it is somewhat at odds with what we have observed regarding the *praetores* of 59 B.C. The *ambitus* court must have had a certain seasonality, with the busiest stretches corresponding to the time immediately before and after curule elections.[268] Most of the *ambitus* cases we have down to 54 (when the electoral calendar becomes quite wayward) indeed suggest this pattern.[269] But accusations for *ambitus* could come in at any time—even against individuals who had won an office and held it.[270] That might have limited how far the Senate could reassign the praetor who had *ambitus* to other tasks.

Alexander[271] entertains the existence of a "Cn. Domitius" who presided as *iudex quaestionis* over Caelius' *vis* trial of 56, and then as praetor when Caelius was prosecuted by Servius Pola in 54. But Cicero's observation that "Domitius did not have the requisite number of jurors" ("Domitius ad numerum iudices non habuit") is surely a witticism and not a factual statement on the legal procedure in this case.[272] Here the "Domitius" in question is not a praetor or *quaesitor* (the two solutions offered by Broughton),[273] but none other than the *cos.* 54 L. Domitius Ahenobarbus.[274] That is clear from what immediately follows in this text, where Cicero reports that this consul had lambasted the equestrian order for their lax judicial verdicts. L. Domitius obviously had a keen interest in the outcome of various trials of the year—but especially, so it appears, that of Caelius. As it happens, in a letter to Cicero in the year 50, Caelius himself groups together L. Domitius and Servius Pola, counting both as expected legal adversaries.[275] Additional hostile references to L. Ahenobarbus by Caelius are not hard to find.[276] So the mysterious "Domitius" (= *RE* 11) who twice crops up in connection with Caelius' legal troubles should be regarded as a phantom.

In early spring 52, the senior *praetorius* A. Manlius Torquatus (*pr.* by 69) as "quaesitor" saw to the conviction (on 9 April) of T. Annius Milo under the *lex Pompeia de ambitu*. The *cos.* III Pompey had taken the *vis* and *ambitus* courts under his protection that year. Torquatus in this case was a special president, one of several attested for 52. Like the *consularis* L. Domitius Ahenobarbus (*cos.* 54), who at the time presided over the *quaestio de vi*, Torquatus probably owed his position to a popular vote (11.9.3).[277]

11.7.3 *The Maiestas Court*

Prosecutions for *maiestas* seem to have been rare in this period. Just over half a dozen are attested, including those merely threatened. The bulk belong to the 70s and first half of the 60s, though in most of those cases we have no information as to who presided.[278] It seems unlikely that the supervision of *maiestas* trials was a full-time occupation for any magistrate. Consider L. Cassius Longinus, the first named president of this court. As praetor in 66, Cassius was slated to preside over the trial of C. Cornelius (*tr. pl.* 67).[279] Asconius in his report of this *maiestas* trial (never held as such) reveals that Cassius, in addition to his *quaestio*, had responsibilities—or at least could plead responsibilities—in public grain matters. This chance notice confirms what in any case we might expect: that a praetor attached to this court—indeed, any permanent *quaestio*—might have a range of duties.[280]

C. Cornelius was tried again for *maiestas* in 65, with the praetor Q. Gallius presiding.[281] When C. Manilius (*tr. pl.* 67) also was to be prosecuted on that charge in 65, it appears the praetor C. Attius Celsus urged Cicero "with his utmost influence" ("maxima contentione") to defend the ex-tribune.[282] Alexander (like many others) believes that Attius actually presided over that trial.[283] But Cicero's usage elsewhere of *contentio* shows that one can be said to "exert influence" in backing a defendant without having any formal connection to the trial.[284] Cicero apparently supported Manilius in a *contio*, but whether he in fact obliged the praetor Attius by speaking at the ex-tribune's actual trial is most uncertain.[285] In any case, it appears from Asconius that Manilius' violent behavior during the proceedings—which were presumably under the presidency of Q. Gallius—prompted the Senate to have the two consuls of 65 offer extra military security for the trial. Manilius fled and was condemned in his absence.[286]

After Manilius' dramatic prosecution we have to wait more than a decade for the next attestation of a *maiestas* case. In 54, C. Alfius Flavus presided at the trial of Cn. Plancius under the new (55 B.C.) *lex Licinia de sodaliciis*. Later that year he also issued the edict that summoned A. Gabinius (*cos.* 58) to trial *de maiestate*, and presided at the *quaestio* itself. For both trials Cicero calls Alfius simply "quaesitor."[287] What was his precise status? C. Alfius Flavus was *tr. pl.* 59 and then, despite (apparently) Caesar's support, unsuccessful candidate for the praetorship of 56.[288] The term *quaesitor* can be used of a *iudex quaestionis* or praetor (10.4.4). The fact that Alfius was a plausible contender for the praetorship already in 56 certainly suggests that he had reached the office when he issued that edict in 54 for Gabinius to appear in the *maiestas* court. (We have seen above that the praetor M. Porcius Cato perhaps sat as juror at that trial.) Indeed, we can assume that the court *de maiestate* was Alfius' formal praetorian *provincia*. His presidency in the case of Plancius shows only that praetors shared the responsibility for trials brought under the *lex Licinia de sodaliciis*, at least in this year.

There is just one additional trial for *maiestas* known for this period—that of Ap. Claudius Pulcher (*cos.* 54, then *pro cos.* in Cilicia), who was acquitted of the charge in early 50 B.C.—but there the presiding magistrate is unknown.[289]

11.7.4 *The* Quaestio inter Sicarios et de Veneficiis

Surely the busiest court of all was the one Sulla created to try cases "inter sicarios et de veneficiis."[290] This encompassed "open crimes and routine bloodshed," and much else besides—including murder and armed robbery (even carrying a weapon with those intentions), poisoning, arson, offering false testimony in a capital case, and judicial bribery.[291] The sheer range of possible charges (some mundane) and the fact that the victim's rank was inconsequential must have made for a steady flow of cases. One also suspects that prosecutions were more readily launched on flimsy evidence in this court than in other permanent *quaestiones*.[292]

Ulpian quotes from the *lex Cornelia* that established this *quaestio*: "praetor iudexve quaestionis, cui sorte obvenerit quaestio de sicariis" ("the praetor or *iudex quaestionis* to whom the murder court shall have fallen by lot"). So, it appears from the start Sulla envisaged the possibility that a *iudex quaestionis* might take over this court—or more precisely, take part in the sortition of its constituent divisions.[293] Indeed, that is what we find in actual practice.

True, in 80 the trial of Cicero's client Sex. Roscius in the *quaestio inter sicarios* took place under the presidency of a praetor, M. Fannius.[294] Fannius had been *iudex quaestionis* over this same court, probably in 85—another nice example of a *sors opportuna*. Cicero alleges that the case of Sex. Roscius was the first murder trial in Rome for some time.[295] That might explain why a praetor—indeed, this particular praetor—presided over the *quaestio inter sicarios* in this instance. In later practice, where we can check, it is always a *iudex quaestionis* who is in charge of trials *inter sicarios* or *de veneficiis*. In 74, the *iudex quaestionis* C. Iunius is known to have heard three trials *de veneficiis*. Each of those resulted in conviction. Iunius, however, found himself condemned and fined—still within the year 74—for violating certain technicalities of his court.[296] The *quaestio* was split between three *iudices* in 66 B.C., the ex-aediles M. Plaetorius and C. Flaminius serving *inter sicarios* and Q. Voconius Naso *de veneficiis*. The arrangement—known to us completely by chance—gives some indication of the volume of activity in this *quaestio*, and may well be typical.[297] And in 64 B.C., C. Iulius Caesar (*aed. cur.* 65) as *iudex quaestionis* heard a series of trials *inter sicarios*.[298] It seems likely that the purpose of the Pompey's law on parricides (probably in his consulship of 55 or 52 B.C.) was to subdivide the work of this court further.[299]

11.7.5 *Sullan Courts for* Peculatus *and Additional Crimes*

Cicero has C. Aurelius Cotta (*cos.* 75) in the *De Natura Deorum* characterize the *peculatus* court as one the "quotidian" *quaestiones* like those *inter sicarios*, *de veneficiis*, and *de testamentis*. In the *Pro Murena*, Cicero portrays this noncapital *quaestio* as one of the grimmer lots that a praetor can receive.[300] We have seen (10.4.2) that a praetor apparently was the magistrate in charge in our one definite *peculatus* case of the pre-Sullan era, that of the burning of the Capitoline *tabularium* in 83 B.C.[301] And for the later period, the two presidents whom we can identify are both praetors, C. Orchivius in 66 and the famous jurisconsult Ser. Sulpicius Rufus in 65.[302] Yet this is a very small sample, with the two post-Sullan presidents falling in consecutive years. There is too little evidence to support Kunkel's suggestion that praetorian presidency was the rule.[303] Only a handful of *peculatus* cases are attested for this era (none with president specified). Most precede these two praetors of the mid-60s. Indeed, there are no probable instances after the year 64 B.C., which makes generalization impossible.[304] As for the *quaestio* established to hear trials under the *lex Cornelia testamentaria nummaria* on forgery, not a single secure trial—not to mention president of the court—is known for this period.[305]

11.7.6 *Post-Sullan* Quaestiones *I:* De Vi

It was inevitable that additional criminal *quaestiones* would spring up in the decades after Sulla engineered his grand reform. The first might have been introduced in the very year of Sulla's death. The *cos.* 78 Q. Lutatius Catulus passed a law to punish violence against the state (the *lex Lutatia de vi*), and, for all we know, set up a standing court to implement it. Before too long, Catulus' provision was superseded by a (presumably tribunician) *lex Plautia de vi*. The date is uncertain, but it probably falls in 70 or afterward and must predate the year 63, when a capital *quaestio de vi* was demonstrably in operation. The *lex Plautia* remained in effect to the end of this period, even alongside the sharper law *de vi* Pompey passed as *cos.* III in 52 B.C.[306]

In the first two trials under the *lex Plautia* for which the court president is indicated (one of 62 and another of 59 B.C.), it is clearly a *iudex quaestionis* who is in charge.[307] Our next real information is for the year 56.[308] Notwithstanding Mommsen's strong reservations, it is a common and reasonable inference that the praetor M. Aemilius Scaurus was president of the *quaestio* that tried P. Sestius *de vi*, in a process stretching from 10 February to 14 March of that year.[309] But we also know that the praetors Cn. Domitius Calvinus (who had "ambitus" as his formal *provincia*) and Q. Ancharius were merely jurors in this case.[310] This raises the possibility that Scaurus had merely the same status. Yet caution is necessary. The praetor Cn. Domitius Calvinus himself seems to have been the magistrate presiding over the famous prosecution of M. Caelius Rufus in early April 56. The notion that the "Cn. Domitius" Cicero addresses in his defense of Caelius was a different person than the *pr.* 56 seems hard to swallow.[311]

Three subsequent presidents for trials *de vi* are attested. Yet they all crop up in the exceptional year 52 B.C., and cannot be used toward reconstructing what was the previous regular practice. T. Annius Milo was prosecuted and convicted for the murder of Clodius first in a special *quaestio* under the new *lex Pompeia de vi*, with the People electing L. Domitius Ahenobarbus (*cos.* 54) from among the consulars as "quaesitor" for that case. Milo then (in absence) was tried before a "quaesitor" L. Fabius—surely under the *lex Plautia*—and simultaneously before the senior *praetorius* A. Manlius Torquatus for *ambitus*, and the *aedilicius* or aedile M. Favonius *de sodaliciis* (each is termed "quaesitor"). Milo was condemned on all counts. There was a double trial *de vi* also for Milo's adherent M. Saufeius. However, here the result was double acquittals, first (ca. 12 April) under the Pompeian law, and then again under the Plautian law "before the *quaesitor* Considius" ("apud Considium quaesitorem").[312]

L. Fabius and Considius apparently had split the cases that came into the *quaestio* of the *lex Plautia*. A good number of trials *de vi* are registered for the years 52 and 51 B.C., so subdivision of tasks—even to hear cases under just one of two concurrent laws *de vi*—should not surprise us.[313] The arrangement of the *quaestio inter sicarios et de veneficiis* in 66 into three divisions (each under a *iudex quaestionis*) offers a good parallel. The precise status of Considius (not readily identifiable) and L. Fabius (otherwise unknown) has to remain uncertain. In the circumstances, either *quaesitor* can have been of praetorian rank, like the A. Torquatus who tried Milo for *ambitus*, or subpraetorian, as Favonius was when he heard Milo's case *de sodaliciis*. It even is technically possible (though unlikely) that one or both of these mysterious court presidents held the praetorship in 52 B.C.[314]

11.7.7 *Post-Sullan* Quaestiones II: *The* Lex Papia *and* Lex Licinia de Sodaliciis

Two additional standing criminal courts appear in our record for the post-Sullan period, that of the *lex Papia* (65 B.C.) on claims to citizenship and another established by the *lex Licinia* (55 B.C.), a measure aimed primarily at the *sodalitates*, associations within the tribes that often bribed and intimidated voters for the benefit of individual candidates. First, the *lex Papia*: A *tribunus plebis* of 65, C. Papius, passed this law *ex S.C.* to penalize foreigners who illicitly claimed Roman citizen rights. The Papian law provided for a *quaestio* where individuals or even whole communities might lay charges. Details on the actual law are few, and not always consistent (especially on the penalty)—despite the existence of two Ciceronian speeches from this court, the *Pro Archia* and the *Pro Balbo*. Four trials are known: the prosecution of Archias in 62 B.C., that of a certain M. Cassius (by 56, prosecuted by the city of Messana), the trial of L. Cornelius Balbus in 56, and that of a freedman and *accensus* of A. Gabinius (*cos.* 58) who was condemned under the Papian law in late October 54. So it is clear that the *lex Papia*—unlike the *lex Licinia Mucia* of 95—remained in effect for some time.[315] For only the first of the Papian trials do we have an indication of the court president: a praetor presided in the case of Archias, said by a scholiast to have been Q. Tullius Cicero (*pr.* 62).[316] However, in his *Pro Balbo* of 56, Cicero in passing implies that a *iudex quaestionis* also might see to this court.[317] We do not know how the Papian president was officially styled.

It was M. Licinius Crassus, as *cos.* II in 55, who was ultimately responsible for the measure *de sodaliciis*. The immediate origins of this law go back in a way to 64, when a *senatus consultum* suppressed certain *collegia* (social clubs and religious guilds, with mostly freedmen and slaves as members) that were perceived to have been formed against the state. In 58, P. Clodius Pulcher as tribune restored those *collegia* and allowed new ones to be organized. The *sodalitates* were a different matter—and an awkward problem for any reformer, since they were so effective at securing votes by means fair or foul. As Linderski has demonstrated in detail, in his legislation the consul Crassus was largely following a *senatus consultum* moved by Q. Hortensius (*cos.* 69) in early 56.

It was perhaps obstruction by Caesar, Pompey and Crassus that prevented this *senatus consultum* from being voted into law for the rest of 56. Yet violence seriously delayed the elections for 55: Pompey and Crassus were elected to the consulship only after the year had started, under the presidency of an *interrex*. On taking office Crassus himself decided to take the credit for curbing the electoral *sodalitates* by pushing through a law based on Hortensius' *senatus consultum*, down to the detail of a jury to be named by the accuser (not appointed by lot). However, Crassus' law differed from the *senatus consultum* (so it seems) in that it did not order the outright dispersal of the *sodalitates*. Instead, it made their members who practiced actual violence and bribery liable to prosecution. Candidates, too, could face trial on that charge. Exile (in its most extreme form, with *aqua et igni interdictio*) was to be the penalty.[318]

Five trials *de sodaliciis* are known in the years that followed the tough *lex Licinia* of 55 B.C. The first three date to 54: C. Messius (a plebeian aedile of 55, tried after being acquitted twice on other charges), P. Vatinius (*pr.* 55), and Cn. Plancius (*aed. cur.* 55). Cicero defended each of these individuals, helping to secure an acquittal in certainly the latter two cases. Then T. Annius Milo (*pr.* 55 and consular candidate for 52) was tried and convicted *in absentia* on that charge in 52. And in 51, M. Valerius Messalla Rufus (*cos.* 53), after being acquitted in a trial under the Pompeian law *de ambitu* for offenses related to his election to the consulship two years previously, was condemned in the Licinian court and exiled.[319]

For three of the five trials *de sodaliciis*—C. Messius and Cn. Plancius in 54 and T. Milo in 52—there is some information on the supervision of the court. By his edict, the praetor P. Servilius Vatia Isauricus called back the ex-aedile C. Messius from a legateship under Caesar in Gaul to stand trial under the *lex Licinia*. Alexander is probably right to assume that Servilius then presided as praetor over the actual *quaestio*; naturally, a praetor might summon a defendant he intended personally to try.[320] However, Servilius' colleague C. Alfius Flavus certainly presided over the prosecution of Cn. Plancius *de sodaliciis* in the year 54, as well as conducting the *maiestas* trial of A. Gabinius (*cos.* 58).[321] The appearance of M. Favonius (aedile 53 or 52) as "quaesitor" in the trial of T. Annius Milo in 52 gets us no further than the other "quaesitores" of that extraordinary year in disengaging previous practice.[322] But the instances of 54, combined with the evidence of the years 52 and 51, should remove serious doubts that the *lex Licinia* established a new standing court. In the absence of any real conflicting evidence, we must also assume that the consul M. Licinius Crassus fully intended that his *quaestio* be staffed by praetors.[323] The idea of a designated "praetor de sodaliciis" seems dubious. Rather, the involvement of both C. Alvius Flavus (who apparently had *maiestas* as his lot) and P. Servilius Vatia in the same *quaestio* in 54 shows that reponsibility for the Licinian court impinged on more than one city praetorian *provincia*. As for how the presidency of that *quaestio* was decided, we know too little to say.

11.8 Special Praetorian *Provinciae* outside Rome, 81–50

11.8.1 *Praetorian Commands in Illyria*

It did not take long after Sulla's settlement for the Senate to declare a special praetorian military *provincia* overseas, sending C. Cosconius to Illyricum, probably *ex praetura* for 78. (We have seen in 10.5.1 there are only two known examples of such *provinciae* outside Italy in the previous fifty years.) This man was surely identical with the C. Cosconius who fought successfully in the Social War as (apparently) *pr.* 89 (10.5.4). His Illyrian command culminated in his capture of Salonae in Dalmatia after two years of campaigning.[324] Broughton reasonably suggests he was *pr.* II 79, and that his promagistracy "probably began in 78 and ended in 76."[325] All we can say for certain is that his subordinate M. Atilius Bulbus was back in Rome to serve as a juror in the notorious trial of Oppianicus in 74, only later to be condemned *de maiestate* for his previous conduct under Cosconius.[326]

A word about the second praetorship: If really *pr.* 89 and II 79 (as seems probable), the example of Cosconius *prima facie* would suggest that Sulla's statutory "ten-year interval" for iterating the various magistracies (thus Appian)[327] was based on inclusive reckoning. But Sulla was very much in personal control of the elections for 79, and so there is no telling from this particular example how the rules worked. Perhaps Sulla backed Cosconius for this unusual iteration of the office, as he is said to have "nominated" the consuls for 79.[328] An alternative (and perhaps more plausible) explanation is that Appian is inaccurate, and Sulla never forbade iteration of the praetorship: note P. Varinius, a praetor of 73 who returns as *pr.* II in 66.[329] In any case, by iterating the praetorship Cosconius obviously was trying to reposition himself for a consular bid under Sulla's newly stabilized system. However, he never made it to the higher office.

Illyria apparently comes up at least once more as a praetorian *provincia* in this period. Cicero pestered the *pro cos.* L. Culleolus to exert his official influence on the people of Byllis (southeast of Apollonia) to pay back a loan to L. Lucceius in which Pompey also had an interest.[330] Culleolus is much more likely to have held Illyricum than the other possibilities that have been suggested, Macedonia (where there is really no room in the *fasti* for the relevant time span, i.e., the 60s and 50s) and Cisalpine Gaul (technically possible but very rarely praetorian). He probably served in Illyricum not long before the Senate saw fit to attach it to the consul Caesar's massive promagisterial *provincia*, but by 59 at the latest. The fact that there were three legions at Aquileia in late 59 suggests something was afoot in Illyria precisely at this time.[331] Shackleton Bailey dates Culleolus' command to "ca. 61–60," which seems about right.[332] It must be emphasized that the command of L. Culleolus is known quite by chance. The Senate may well have allotted "Illyria" one or more times between the time of C. Cosconius and the praetorship of Culleolus in the late 60s.

11.8.2 *Pompey's Special Commands and His* Legati

Neither of the consuls of 77 were interested in taking command in Spain alongside the *pro cos.* Q. Metellus Pius in the difficult civil war against Sertorius. A debate followed on who should be sent instead. Finally on the motion of L. Philippus (*cos.* 91), the Senate gave the charge not to a praetor, but to a *privatus*—the equestrian Cn. Pompeius, who had served Sulla so successfully in Sicily and Africa a few years previously (13.1.4, 14.3.3), and had fought in early 77 as a *legatus pro praetore* in the Lepidan War (see 11.8.5). Once the Senate decided upon the *privatus* Pompey, it seems there was fresh debate on whether Pompey should serve as an *adiutor* to Pius or as his cocommander (i.e., what grade of *imperium* he should receive) and perhaps also whether he should have his own *provincia*. In the event, Pompey received Hispania Citerior as his own and consular *imperium* to hold it.[333] (There was of course a distant precedent for this sort of command, namely the *privati* who in the period 210–198 [7.1.3–6] had proceeded to Spain with enhanced *imperium*.) The Senate must also have voted him a set number of quaestors and *legati*.[334]

In this decision, the real factor was Pompey's proven military competence. In early 75, the Senate again chose not to use a praetor for an important overseas task, but for a negative reason. In a financial crisis it sent a quaestor with (probably) a special grant of praetorian *imperium* to exploit the former royal estates in Cyrene. The position was deliberately devised so as to involve the minimum status and power required for the job (11.4).

After C. Cosconius, *pr.* II in Illyria (11.8.1), the next known special praetorian *provincia* outside Italy is the one assigned to the *pr.* 74 M. Antonius (discussed in 11.3.1). Antonius' command, despite its ultimate failure, was a clear source for the pirate commission the *privatus* Pompey received in 67 under the tribunician *lex Gabinia*. Velleius in fact tells us as much.[335] But the Gabinian law went much further. It guaranteed Pompey consular *imperium* for three years. In addition, it entitled Pompey not just to appoint a large number of legates, but also to delegate each of them praetorian *imperium*.[336] Some of these subordinates were quite senior. Among the thirteen reliably transmitted names, we find two *consulares* and three or four known *praetorii*.[337] Pompey set up those legates with both land and sea forces in independent quasi *provinciae*, where they were to stay put.[338] Here one thinks of the consular and praetorian *legati* meant to serve under the consuls during the Social War, at least some of whom demonstrably had received *imperium* not for ad hoc tasks but officially conferred throughout their tenure (10.5.3).

This aspect of the *lex Gabinia* evidently had tremendous popular appeal.[339] And the legates of 67 were obviously effective, since they helped Pompey sweep the seas within just forty days. Plutarch even states that the pirates took pains to escape these legates so as to surrender to Pompey himself.[340] Pompey retained at least some of these *legati* to play a military role beyond the pirate command.[341] Hence we see Pompey (surely) ordering his legate L. Cornelius Sisenna to take his military force out of Greece to interfere with the command of Q. Caecilius Metellus in Crete (cf. 11.3.2), or the *legati* L. Lollius and Q. Caecilius Metellus Nepos to conduct land operations against Damascus in 66/65. The tenure of some of these *legati* may have lasted as long as that of Pompey himself.[342]

Interference by special commanders in overseas praetorian *provinciae* was quickly becoming a hallmark of the age. The trend starts with the special *provincia* of M. Antonius in 74 and continues through Pompey's extraordinary commands of 67 and 66 under the Gabinian and Manilian laws. Possibly relevant is a case of 65, when the Senate dispatched Cn. Calpurnius Piso as a *quaestor pro praetore* to Hispania Citerior (13.4.7). In 57, when Pompey received a special grain command *pro consule* for five years, he was voted the right also to appoint (at least) fifteen senatorial *legati* to help him in his task, to be distributed throughout the Mediterranean. The name of only one of these *legati*—Q. Tullius Cicero (*pr.* 62)— has come down to us (see 13.2.8 for his service in Sardinia). Whether he or the others had *imperium* is unknown. Pompey himself sailed to the grain-producing provinces of Sicily, Sardinia, and Africa.[343] Though each of the praetorian incumbents in those provinces had technically the same level of *imperium* as Pompey (i.e., *pro consule*), it seems unlikely that at this point any of them would try to stand up to him or his *legati*.[344]

11.8.3 *The Rullan* Xviri

We can view the land bill promulgated by the *tribunus plebis* P. Servilius Rullus at the start of 63 as another example of the phenomenon of interference in praetorian *provinciae*. The consul Cicero's three speeches *De Lege Agraria* (mostly extant) provide a wealth of detail on the measure—and much that is patently distorted and tendentious. Cicero is particularly eager to highlight the contradictions in the drafting of this complex law, no doubt because Rullus clearly took special precautions against technical objections to the implementation of its provisions.[345] The bill came to nothing, thanks to the efforts of Cicero and one of Rullus' tribunician colleagues (who threatened a veto).[346]

For his *lex agraria*, it does appear that Rullus had proposed to create a commission of Xviri who were to have the status of magistrates and with it *auspicia* and (praetorian) *imperium*—all confirmed by a *lex curiata*—for five years.[347] Rullus wanted to give his Xviri the power to purchase, adjudicate, confiscate and assign *ager publicus*, and institute or supplement colonies in Italy and the provinces.[348] That made for a considerable commission: Plutarch even alleges that Cicero's consular colleague C. Antonius wanted to receive one of the positions. Plutarch also sees a link with the ex-Sullan tribunes—who had been banned from higher magistracies but were now seeking office—and the establishment of Rullus' Xviri. Perhaps Rullus (who is said to have had his own Sullan connections) partly intended this as a magistracy to which they could aspire.[349]

The establishment of a board of ten with judicial powers to implement important agrarian legislation goes back at least as far as the legislation of *tr. pl.* II 100 L. Saturninus; the appointment of Xviri without judicial powers to make viritane assignments much further still.[350] Yet the main model for Rullus, implies Cicero, was Ti. Gracchus and the far-ranging IIIviri *agris iudicandis assignandis* he instituted with *auspicia* for his agrarian program as *tr. pl.* 133.[351] Whether the Gracchan IIIviri had *imperium* is unclear. For that aspect of Rullus' law, however, one finds an old precedent in the two commissions of IIIviri granted *imperium* "for three years" in the years 193–191, ostensibly to found colonies in south Italy (8.4.1). We owe our knowledge of that colonial commission to a chance notice in Livy; there might have been others in the second century (and beyond).

Cicero complains that despite selection by only part of the Plebs (seventeen of the thirty-five tribes), the passage of a *lex curiata* gave the Xviri full magisterial prerogatives. While in office, they had a magistrate's freedom from prosecution; in addition, they could simultaneously hold other magistracies. Cicero says they also were to have all the trappings of a commander, including publicly funded lictors and 200 equestrian "finitores" (each with his own attendants), and the right to entertainment in foreign communities. Cicero says the Xviri also had the power to delegate their responsibilities (though apparently not their *imperium*, which was praetorian) to a quaestor. Indeed, Cicero (with considerable hyperbole) makes out that the power of the Rullan *Xviri* was "infinitum."[352] One eye-opening criticism of the bill is Cicero's implication that Rullus' *Xviri* would not lose their *auspicia* upon entering the city.[353] Cicero only mentions that feature in passing, and it very likely is a distortion. It is hard to believe that Rullus hoped—or wanted—to give his agrarian commission *imperium* both *domi* and *militiae* for five years. So when Cicero says the *Xviri* could be "at Rome" ("Romae") when they chose, we should take this as "ad urbem," that is, near the city but outside the *pomerium*.[354] Yet Rullus clearly did permit his *Xviri* cumulation with proper magistracies, so problems were in the making.

11.8.4 *The Clodian Law on the Organization of Cyprus*

In 58 B.C., another plebeian tribune—P. Clodius Pulcher—hit upon a scheme to raise money for an extravagant grain law. Badian[355] has fully elucidated the background and implementation of Clodius' plan, which makes extensive discussion unnecessary here. The public treasury had been exhausted by Caesar's ambitious consular legislation in the previous year. Clodius' solution on how to fund his domestic program was to seize the kingdom of Cyprus from its ruler Ptolemy, perhaps on the pretext that the king had aided pirates. Faced with the prospect of public bankruptcy, the Senate really had no choice but to acquiesce in Clodius' intrusion in the sphere of foreign policy.[356] Clodius' law annexing Cyprus was passed before April. The Senate must have decided by that time to try to annex Cyprus in an orderly fashion and to place it under the administration of the governor for Cilicia. Clodius for his part assigned by *privilegium* that *provincia*—now suddenly important—to the friendly *cos.* 58 A. Gabinius.

Yet Clodius and his backers (Caesar, Pompey, Crassus) soon had second thoughts. The reason for annexing Cyprus, after all, was to get its wealth into the Roman treasury. So rather than use a consular commander (with consular-sized debts), Clodius instead revived the precedent seen in the exploitation of the Cyrenaean royal estates in 75. To collect Ptolemy's wealth, a position was created *extra ordinem* involving the minimum status and power appropriate to the task. We are told that many were eager for the commission. The man Clodius had settled on to fill it was the upright tribunician M. Porcius Cato.[357] In April 58, by a *privilegium*, Clodius had Cato appointed as *pro quaestore pro praetore* to annex (but not organize) Cyprus and to liquidate the royal property in the island. Cato was given a small staff of a quaestor and two scribes to assist him, and no doubt an armed force; Cicero says Cato had the power of making war to secure the royal money if need be.[358] Under the terms of another one of Clodius' laws—a further example of his interference with foreign affairs—Cato also was to restore some exiles to Byzantium. As for Gabinius, Clodius gave him the *provincia* of Syria (allegedly with enhanced boundaries) as a consolation prize.

The suicide of king Ptolemy—soon after hearing Rome had decided on annexation of Cyprus—made fighting unnecessary.[359] By personally auctioning the royal property, Cato netted the Roman treasury nearly seven thousand talents. He returned to Rome in 56 to an enthusiastic reception, says Valerius Maximus, by the consuls, magistrates, the Senate—indeed the whole Roman People. Cato capital-ized on the attention his commission attracted by having the Cypriot wealth carried in a triumph-like display through the Forum.[360] But he declined all special honors.

Here Valerius Maximus is the most precise. The Senate wanted to vote Cato a special dispensation,

> so that his candidacy might be accepted *extra ordinem* at the praetorian elections (*ut praetoriis comitiis extra ordinem ratio eius haberetur*). But he did not allow this to happen, maintaining that it was unjust that what was allowed no other [sc. of the candidates?] be decreed to himself, and lest any innovation be introduced in his own case, he considered it better to try electoral chance than to enjoy a gift of the Senate (*ac ne quid in persona sua nouaretur, campestrem experiri temeritatem quam curiae beneficio uti satius esse duxit*).

Our Greek sources tell a somewhat different story. Plutarch has Cato decline the Senate's award of an "extraordinary praetorship" (στρατηγίαν ἐξαίρετον) and with it the right of watching games in the *toga praetexta*. Dio reports that the the the consuls moved that Cato be given a praetorship, "though it did not yet belong to him in accordance with the laws" (στρατηγίαν . . . καίπερ μηδέπω ἐκ τῶν νόμων προσήκουσαν). Cato himself defeated the measure by speaking against it, but later (says Dio) was suspected of having put the consuls up to making the motion in the first place.[361]

Mommsen preferred the account of Valerius Maximus and suggested that Cato—who was born in 95 B.C., and thus no doubt perfectly eligible in 56 to seek a praetorship for 55—arrived back from Cyprus so late that he missed the opportunity to make his *professio* in person for the upcoming elections (which in the event were delayed until February 55).[362] However, H. E. Russell, in a 1950 specialized study of extraordinary advancement of rank in the Republic, dismissed the Valerius Maximus passage as a minority view. She followed L. Lange's interpretation of the Greek sources, "that Cato received the *ornamenta praetoria* and the right of wearing the *toga praetexta* and that he refused the honor because he intended to seek the actual praetorship," that is, in 55 for 54 (which he won).[363]

Yet the versions of Valerius Maximus, Plutarch, and Dio are not necessarily incompatible. It is perfectly possible in the atmosphere of the moment that the grateful Senate offered Cato first the dispensation from the *professio* and then, when it was refused, praetorian *ornamenta*. (It does not seem possible, pace Dio, that the Senate wanted to simply give Cato a praetorship.) The phrase "ac ne quid in persona sua nouaretur" in the Valerius Maximus passage does seem to introduce a new point. And Cato's stated preference "campestrem experiri temeritatem quam curiae beneficio uti" is fully consonant with the refusal of insignia for the motive Lange and Russell suggest. Indeed, making that phrase refer to the *professio* dispensation seems to give less satisfactory sense.

Strabo reports that Cyprus at this point became a "praetorian province," as it was in his own time.[364] That is not strictly accurate. Rather, the Senate after Cato's return in 56 joined Cyprus to the *provincia* of Cilicia, as it had been planning to do for at least two years. P. Cornelius Lentulus Spinther (*cos.* 57)—the first *pro consule* for the enhanced "Cilicia"—organized Cyprus. However, for the rest of the decade the island was to be administered in a minimalist fashion. Two consular commanders followed Spinther's tenure in his province of Cilicia, Ap. Claudius Pulcher (*cos.* 54, *pro cos.* 53–51) and M. Tullius Cicero (*pro cos.* 51/50). Neither of these men set foot on the island. That was no doubt fine by the Cypriots: for winter 51/50 the island was willing to pay Cicero a fabulous sum to avoid receiving a Roman camp. The only certain thing we know Appius did regarding Cyprus was to allow the *negotiator* M. Scaptius to have an appointment of prefect of cavalry to collect certain private debts from the town of Salamis. Cicero had to order Scaptius off the island, in response to a petition from the Cyprians. He tried also to restore order to Cyprus in other respects, delegating the litigation of Roman citizens there to a *praefectus* Q. Volusius. Yet the first actual quaestor to make it to Cyprus was probably for 49 B.C., after Cicero's departure from Cilicia. In the end, Caesar decided that administering Cyprus was more trouble than it was worth, and promised to restore the island to Ptolemaic rule in 47 B.C., just a decade after annexation.[365]

11.8.5 *The* Bellum Lepidanum

It remains to examine special praetorian *provinciae* declared within Italy in the post-Sullan period. The first ones probably belong to the year 77. That year opened without curule magistrates, thanks to the agitation of the *cos.* 78 M. Aemilius Lepidus, now *pro cos.* for the two Gauls. According to Sallust, L. Marcius Philippus (*cos.* 91) successfully urged passage of a *senatus consultum ultimum* against Lepidus, which specified that the *interrex* Ap. Claudius Pulcher and Q. Lutatius Catulus (*cos.* 78, and now *pro cos.*) and others who had *imperium*—probably the praetors of 78 who were now *ex magistratu* and waiting to go to their provinces—should come to the defense of the city and the state.[366] Somehow at this time also the *privatus* Cn. Pompeius received an army to fight Lepidus and his supporters. He doubtless had a special grant of (praetorian) *imperium* to go with it; otherwise his elevation to *pro consule* to combat Sertorius later in 77 (13.4.3) is hard to explain.[367]

But where would this *imperium* come from? Pompey does not fall under any of the categories set out in the *senatus consultum ultimum* as reported by Sallust. N. Criniti's explanation is the easiest, that the *pro consule* Q. Catulus gave Pompey *imperium* by delegation. Indeed, Florus thinks that in the first battle against Lepidus, near the Campus Martius, Pompey fought under Catulus. Yet that apparently is an error. At the time, Pompey probably was besieging Lepidus' *legatus* M. Iunius Brutus at Mutina in Cisalpina, a lengthy operation in which Pompey finally forced Brutus to surrender—and then treacherously had him killed. But when Catulus at Cosa again defeated Lepidus (and thus drove him out of Italy to Sardinia), Pompey returned from Gaul to assist the *pro consule*. And there is no reason to doubt Plutarch's report that when the *bellum Lepidanum* came to an end in Italy, it was Catulus who ordered Pompey to disband his army. Later tradition accused Pompey of trying to steal Catulus' thunder. Pompey's status at this point was doubtless Catulus' *legatus pro praetore.*[368]

The fighting against Lepidus in Italy was soon over—we never learn what any of those individuals *cum imperio* did except for Catulus and Pompey—and our sources shift their attention to the special commission Pompey received *pro consule* to face Sertorius in Spain.

11.8.6 *The War against Spartacus: Opening Stages*

A major slave war that broke out in Italy later in the 70s taxed Rome's command structure to a far greater extent. Here (as elsewhere in this work) my main concern is with chronology, and the titulature and prosopography of the praetorian commanders involved. At Vesuvius, Spartacus and a small group of his fellow gladiators—still at a total strength of just seventy-four[369]—scored their first success in the field by tricking and defeating a "Clodius" or "Claudius" when he marched against them with a small force before autumn of 73.[370] His name and title vary in our sources, even within the same basic tradition. The Livian *Periocha* calls him "Claudius Pulcher" and (apparently) makes him a *legatus* of a praetor "P. Varenus" (i.e., Varinius, on whom see below). For Florus, he is the *dux* "Clodius Glaber," whereas Orosius makes him "Clodius praetor." Frontinus has simply "Clodius" with no title, noting he had "a few cohorts." Plutarch is the most detailed: he relates that a "Clodius στρατηγός" was sent from Rome to fight the slaves with three thousand soldiers. Appian seems quite confused. In his narrative of the Slave War, a "Varinius Glaber" is first sent against Spartacus and then a "P. Valerius," each having only tumultuary forces. Here Münzer must be right, that Appian has combined the names of two Roman commanders into the single name "Varinius Glaber" and substituted the name "P. Valerius" for "Varinius."[371]

What can one conclude from all this? Broughton suggests that our "Clodius" is indeed *pr.* 73 and son or brother of the *praetorius* C. Claudius C.f. Arn. Glaber who is listed second in an epigraphically preserved senatorial *consilium* of mid-October 73.[372] Since the *pr.* 75 C. Sacerdos has (surely) fourth rank in the *consilium*, that C. Glaber must have reached the praetorship by 75 or earlier. I tentatively accept Broughton's view here. But the rarity of the name (no other Claudii Glabri are known to have reached a magistracy in the Republic) invites the suspicion that the title "legatus" in the *Periocha* is accurate, and that it was the praetorian C. Glaber who fought at Vesuvius with an advance force at some point before he sat in that October *consilium*.[373] In the year 133, a significant slave uprising at Minturnae and Sinuessa had led to two senior ex-consuls receiving special grants of *imperium* to put it down (8.6.2), which would provide a precedent of sorts for the alternative suggested here.

A praetor P. Varinius of 73—there is no doubt about his name, office, and date—was the next after Claudius Glaber to fight Spartacus and his forces (now significantly larger). Varinius apparently had enhanced *imperium*.[374] Yet he suffered a series of losses against the gladiators, evidently in the area of Campania and Lucania. A relatively detailed story for this man emerges from our sources,[375] with Plutarch's *Crassus* providing a basic framework and Sallust's *Histories* adding many welcome particulars. First, Varinius' *legatus* Furius was routed with three thousand soldiers, and perhaps other subordinates too.[376] Then a certain (L.) Cossinius lost his camp—and his life—to the slaves. Plutarch says he had been sent with a large force to help Varinius as "adviser and cocommander."[377] Cossinius very likely is no more than Varinius' most favored *legatus*, not a praetor of the year.[378] But that he had a grant of delegated *imperium* is quite conceivable, given that Plutarch describes him as συνάρχων with Varinius (*pro cos.*, according to Frontinus) and implies he had his own camp. Finally, Varinius found himself stymied in a series of encounters that spanned the late summer and autumn, in the end losing his camp, horse, and lictors to the gladiators.[379] Despite the title *pro consule* that we find in Frontinus, there is no reason to accept Broughton's suggestion that Varinius had been prorogued into 72.[380] Several praetors seem to have received enhanced *imperium* to act in Italy at the start and then conclusion of the Social War (10.5.2 and 10.5.5). In the year 73, the Senate might have allowed such a grant to Varinius as praetor.

11.8.7 The War against Spartacus in 72 and 71

The war against Spartacus was declared consular for 72. Both L. Gellius and Cn. Cornelius Lentulus Clodianus had it as their *provincia*, and the *cos.* 73 C. Cassius Longinus (now *pro cos.* in Gallia Cisalpina) joined them in attempting to put down the slave revolt. The Senate made use of praetorian commanders, too. One praetor of 73, Q. Arrius, had been expected even late in that year to succeed C. Verres in Sicily for 72. Instead, he fought the gladiators as a prorogued praetor under the command of the *cos.* L. Gellius.[381] According to the Livian *Periocha*, Arrius initially scored a great success in Apulia against the slave leader Crixus, whom he killed along with twenty thousand of his men. Other authors attribute Arrius' victory to his superior alone; the same goes for a later defeat Arrius and Gellius suffered at the hands of Spartacus. These examples show how readily our sources can ignore even important praetorian commands.[382] Indeed, it would be odd if in 72 Gellius' consular colleague Cn. Lentulus Clodianus did not also have a subordinate in a position analogous to that of Arrius when fighting the slaves: one notes that the *pro consule* C. Cassius Longinus in Gallia Cisalpina evidently was fighting in close connection to a praetor (or prorogued praetor) Cn. Manlius.[383]

A series of disasters in central and north Italy soon showed up the shallowness of the Roman leadership and led to the appointment of a praetor or *praetorius*, M. Licinius Crassus, to the chief command.[384] Here the Livian *Periocha* provides the chronological framework.[385] First, Spartacus defeated the consul Cn. Lentulus Clodianus — and apparently his *legati* — in the Appennines. Spartacus then routed the consul L. Gellius and praetor Q. Arrius, or both consuls together.[386] The real turning point, however, seems to have been the slaves' victory over the *pro consule* C. Cassius Longinus at Mutina (not mentioned by Appian), which came at the same time (or slightly before) the renegades' defeat of the praetor Cn. Manlius. Orosius even says that the *pro consule* was killed in battle.[387]

Appian alone has the slaves score an additional success in Picenum against the *coss.* 72,[388] which leads (in his version) to the "election" of Crassus as praetor. More plausible are the Livian epitomator, Orosius and Plutarch, who consider the defeat of the *pro consule* Cassius Longinus to have triggered the appointment of Crassus to the principal command. It was at this point, Plutarch says, that the Senate ordered the consuls of the year not to fight any longer and chose Crassus to conduct the war (Κράσσον . . . τοῦ πολέμου στρατηγὸν εἵλετο). The Senate authorized an additional levy, gave Crassus the consuls' legions (thus Orosius)—and surely (if it had not done so already) saw to the raising of his *imperium* to the consular level.[389] This vote of enhanced *imperium* may be the basis for Appian's story of a dramatic praetorian "election" of 72, which simply makes no sense. An alternative is that Appian is garbling an account of a special election granting *imperium*, such as that seen in 88 B.C., when Marius was chosen to replace Sulla for the Mithridatic command.[390] In general, Appian's account of fighting against Spartacus in 72 is quite outside the mainstream tradition. He has distorted the chronology of the war by giving the consuls of that year one defeat too many (i.e., Picenum), and furthermore will put all of Crassus' campaigning into the year 71.[391] Yet Crassus must have been in the field by November 72 with prorogation into 71.[392] For the Senate to privilege a praetor or *praetorius* over a consul (rather, two consuls) in this way has few direct precedents. (The most recent one available is the dispatch of C. Laelius against Viriathus for 144 B.C.)

Around the time the Senate was deciding on prorogations (i.e., late 72 or early 71), Crassus asked that it summon M. Lucullus (*cos.* 73) from Thrace and the *pro cos.* Pompey from Spain. But he soon regretted that, says Plutarch.[393] Appian adds that "the Romans in the city" actually voted that Pompey conduct the war in addition to Crassus. Yet Crassus hurriedly finished the conflict (in spring 71) before either of those commanders could fully steal his thunder.[394] Mopping-up operations, however, took some time. A year after Crassus' decisive victory over Spartacus, the Senate called on C. Verres (*pr.* 74) as he returned from his Sicilian governorship to fight against a small slave band at Valentia and (apparently) Tempsa (13.2.3). The Senate surely utilized other commanders (including praetors and ex-praetors) in this way in the years 71 and 70, and indeed for some time beyond. By chance we know that the Senate gave C. Octavius (*pr.* 61) a task *extra ordinem* on his way to Macedonia as *pro consule* in early 60, namely to take action against some runaway slaves—leftovers from Spartacus' revolt and adherents of Catiline—who had occupied an area around Thurii (14.2.4).

For his successes against the slaves, M. Licinius Crassus was elected consul for the year 70. But the date of his praetorship and his status as commander against Spartacus in 72 and 71 pose a vexed problem. Badian and I. Shatzman take Appian at his word that he reached the consulship according to the *leges annales*, and so make him *pr.* 73.[395] On this interpretation, after the defeat of both consuls in 72 he received as a *privatus* a special grant of consular[396] *imperium* to take the chief command in their stead.

A praetorship for Crassus in the year 73 is certainly the easiest solution, and it is the one I adopt here. But Crassus need not have been a *privatus* in the year 72. Surely it is more likely that, as in the case of Q. Arrius (*pr.* 73), the Senate had Crassus prorogued and assigned to special duties in Italy. (It is hard to believe that any praetor of 73 could decline an *ex praetura* command and then revert to the status of a *privatus* in the emergency.) Perhaps the reason that we do not hear of any special assignment for Crassus is that in early 72 he saw service in a theater less challenging than that of Arrius. That praetor, after all, managed to fight in major engagements against both Crixus (whom the *Periocha* says he killed in battle with twenty thousand of his men) and Spartacus—and still barely made it into our sources for 72. If Crassus had as his *ex praetura* assignment garrison duty or the like in Italy, his *imperium* is likely to have stayed at the praetorian level so as to avoid conflict with the three consular commanders (i.e., the prorogued *cos.* 73 and the two *coss.* 72) then active in the peninsula against the slaves.

An alternative solution is that Crassus was a praetor of 72, who had his *imperium* raised later in that year, and then after prorogation into 71 stood for the consulship of 70 by special dispensation. Appian only vouches for the fact that Crassus was praetor before consul; it is not clear whether he knew that Sulla also stipulated an interval of a *biennium* between the two offices.[397] The Senate obviously indulged in a great deal of rule bending in 71. That can be seen not just from its own dispensation to Pompey to stand for consul and also to triumph (for the second time) as an *eques*, but also the fact that it caved into Crassus' request for a *triumphator's* crown to grace his *ovatio* over the slaves.[398]

11.8.8 *Protection of the Italian Coast against Pirates*

When piracy had started to threaten the actual shores of Italy in the late 70s or early 60s, it appears that the initial Roman response was to send out "fleets and στρατη-γοί" piecemeal. Quaestors and *legati* doubtless played a large role in these operations, but so did some holders of *imperium*.[399] Cicero says that a praetor stationed at Caieta proved ineffective against the pirates who had raided that harbor, despite his large number of ships. Worse, pirates captured and sank a consul's fleet at Ostia.[400] Those Roman commanders who did manage to engage the pirates at sea regularly came off the worse for it, including a Sicilian praetor (unnamed) off the coast of that *provincia*.[401]

Eventually, the pirates were bold enough to launch raids on the interior of the Italian mainland. One low point for Rome was when they kidnapped, apparently at Misenum, the sister of the pirate-fighting *pr.* 74, M. Antonius "Creticus."[402] (The sources on that incident emphasize that the woman's father—M. Antonius, *cos.* 99—ironically had once triumphed over the pirates of Cilicia.) But the indisputable nadir seems to have been the capture of two praetors, Sextilius and "Bellinus" (i.e., a Bellienus), with their full insignia of office—including lictors and attendants. Only Plutarch gives the praetors' names (also implying that they were seized on land),[403] but the incident was obviously a well-known one. Cicero clearly refers to it in his oration *De Lege Manilia* of 66, stating that "praetors" were captured and "twelve axes" came into the possession of pirates. Appian, in reporting pirate raids on Etruria and the coast of Brundisium, also notes the loss of two praetors with their insignia.[404] It is perfectly possible that Sextilius and Bellienus had special *provinciae* in precisely these two areas: we need not assume they were captured together. But the sources do suggest they belong to the same year, one not long before the *lex Gabinia* of 67 that gave Pompey his sweeping command against the pirates. At any rate, Cicero's reference to "twelve axes" shows that they were praetors in office, wielding praetorian (i.e., unenhanced) *imperium*. The creation of Pompey's *legati pro praetore* in 67 and their effectiveness against the pirates probably eliminated the need for such special praetorian commands.

11.8.9 *Catilinarian Conspiracy and Aftermath*

The next special praetorian commands come up in the context of the Catilinarian conspiracy of 63. Under the *senatus consultum ultimum* of 21 October, the *cos.* 69 Q. Metellus Creticus and the *cos.* 68 Q. Marcius Rex—both still with *imperium* outside the walls of Rome, waiting for the Senate's vote of a triumph—were dispatched respectively to Apulia and the area around Faesulae in Etruria. (Here the year 100 provided a good precedent, in that the *S.C.U.* charged the *pr.* 102 and would-be *triumphator ex Cilicia* M. Antonius with protecting the city from external attack by Saturninus' supporters.)[405] Meanwhile, the city praetor Q. Pompeius Rufus was sent to Capua and his colleague Q. Caecilius Metellus Celer to the *ager Gallicus* and *ager Picenus*. Each praetor had authority to levy troops to meet the emergency. For Metellus, Cicero saw to the passage of a *senatus consultum* that raised his *imperium* still during his year of office and allowed him to take up his promagisterial province of Gallia Cisalpina (and its three legions) early. Special judicial powers were to follow (15.2.5).

In 62, the Senate again sent some city praetors into the field, this time to punish various allies who (it is alleged) quietly had supported Catiline but then "stirred themselves up out of fear of punishment." M. Calpurnius Bibulus was sent among the Paeligni while Q. Tullius Cicero was dispatched to Bruttium.[406] There is no reliable source on what Quintus' city *provincia* was. He is said by a scholiast to have been the praetor who presided in the case of Archias, tried under the *lex Papia*.[407] Even if true, there is no reason to believe Quintus was urban praetor; his colleague C. Iulius Caesar seems a better candidate for that position.[408] As praetor, Bibulus evidently was also active politically in the city.[409] We can presume that both received their special assignments early in their year of office, while the embers of revolt were still hot. They then will have returned to Rome to see to their civil obligations.

The instances of P. Varinius in 73 and then Q. Caecilius Metellus Celer a decade later suggest that the Senate had grown used to the idea—first seen in the Social War—of enhancing the *imperium* of praetors in office to deal with major emergencies within Italy. However mopping-up operations like those of 62 probably required no such special measures. The *pr.* 61 C. Octavius did hold the rank of *pro consule* in early 60 when he rounded up some fugitive slaves in the area of Thurii (the last such action recorded in Italy for our period). But that of course is incidental. The Senate had assigned him the task *extra ordinem* on his way to his proper *provincia* of Macedonia.

11.9 Special *Provinciae* in the City

11.9.1 *The Use of* Quaestiones extra Ordinem *in the Late Republic*

Special *quaestiones* were not a particularly important attribute of the stormy last generation of the Republic until near its very end. By 80 B.C., the number of standing *quaestiones* (which crept only upward in the 60s and 50s) and the range of crimes they encompassed made proposals for the establishment of ad hoc courts harder to justify than in previous eras. To be sure, in this period we find extraordinary *quaestiones* set up in the years 73 (prosecution of the Vestals Licinia and Fabia for *incestum*) and 61 (trial of the quaestor P. Clodius Pulcher for violating the rites of the Bona Dea). Those procedures—to be discussed below—were to punish offenses against the public religion, for which the Roman criminal law never had any regular machinery. Proposals for special *quaestiones* on more terrestrial matters usually do not come to anything. In 74, indignation at the corrupt *iudex quaestionis* C. Iunius was so great that even after he was condemned to a fine in a *iudicium populi*, the Senate decided that there should be a consular bill establishing a *quaestio extraordinaria* to investigate his behavior. But the measure ground to a halt in 73, thanks especially to a tearful plea by the young son of Iunius in some public assembly.[410] Late in 61 B.C., a *senatus consultum* ordained that a *quaestio* be established to investigate the jurors in the Bona Dea trial for corruption, but (apparently) the opposition of the *equites* ensured that the measure never came to a vote.[411] Cicero claims that in 59 B.C., the *tribunus plebis* P. Vatinius promulgated a bill to establish a special *quaestio* to investigate some leading Romans on charges of conspiracy, with the informer L. Vettius and (it was hoped) others as witnesses—but when his proposal failed had Vettius killed in prison.[412] Some other unsuccessful attempts to set up a special court to try political crimes may find the faintest echo in our sources.[413] Yet we have to wait until the violent year 52 B.C. to see such special courts actualized, in the areas of *vis* and *ambitus* by Pompey as (sole) consul. And even then the extraordinary *quaestio de vi* was attacked as superfluous.[414]

11.9.2 *Trials for Religious Offenses in 73 and 61*

The small size of this sample makes generalization about the administration of *quaestiones extra ordinem* in this era difficult indeed. First, let us look at the religious trials. In the year 73 (the date is certain), the Vestal Virgins Fabia and Licinia each stood trial on a charge of *incestum* and were acquitted. The procedure is not attested. But when M. Licinius Crassus was found innocent of *incestum* with Licinia, it was (according to Plutarch) by a panel of jurors. It stands to reason that the Vestals had the same form of trial. Alexander assumes that these cases were all heard "apud pontifices," as indeed had been traditional as late as 114 B.C. However, Plutarch's reference to δικασταί at the trial of Crassus suggests that the Romans here were following the precedent of the Peducaean law of 113—an extraordinary secular *quaestio* staffed by *iudices* and a president (I would argue) with *imperium* (10.6.1).[415] There is no use speculating what type of magistrate (consul, praetor, or special *quaesitor*) presided in this series of trials. What does seem likely is that the president handpicked the jury himself, as I have suggested L. Cassius Ravilla did as *quaesitor* under the Peducaean law. But these were no "Cassiani iudices." They seem to have acquitted all the defendants who came before them, including

Crassus—who offered as a pretext for his overintimate relations with Licinia that he wanted to do her out of a piece of property she owned.

Support for the hypothesis of handpicking comes from the heated debate over the form of the next major religious trial in Rome, the prosecution of the quaestor P. Clodius Pulcher in 61 B.C. for intruding (in early December 62) in the rites of the Bona Dea, a ceremony restricted to women. Clodius' presence caused the Vestals to have to repeat the *sacra*; when consulted by the Senate, the Vestals and the college of *pontifices* decreed that indeed a religious violation had occurred.[416] A *senatus consultum* followed (by 25 January 61), which stated that the consuls—M. Pupius Piso and M. Valerius Messalla—were to promulgate a bill setting up a special *quaestio* to investigate the matter. The *senatus consultum* also spelled out the form that trial was to take. Three details of this *senatus consultum* are of immediate interest to us here. It stipulated that the *quaestio* was to be run "no differently than that concerning *incestum*." A praetor was to preside over the court. And this magistrate personally was to select the jurors he was to use as his judicial *consilium* in the trial. This method of selecting *iudices* finds no parallel in other known Republican *quaestiones*: surely the *incestum* trials of 113 and 73 B.C. suggested it, on which the Bona Dea *quaestio* was based.[417] "The object in proposing this mode of selection," observes Greenidge of the Clodius trial, "was clearly to ensure a conviction on the pretence of securing the purity of the court."[418] Not necessarily. While L. Cassius Ravilla's *quaestio* of 113 did result in the condemnation of two Vestals and (we are told) many other women, that of 73 saw nothing but acquittals. There is no telling what the attitude of the presiding magistrate was toward Clodius in 61. But if allowed to choose the jury according to (what I argue to be) the "Peducaean" system, the praetor would have enormous power to shape the course of this trial in whatever direction he wanted it to go.

It was precisely this technical point of jury selection that caused a furious row to erupt, thanks to the dogged efforts of a single tribune, Q. Fufius Calenus, who wanted the jurors to be chosen by the procedure (probably now long standard for *quaestiones*) of the lot. This *tribunus plebis*, backed discreetly by the consul Pupius Piso and openly by Q. Hortensius (*cos.* 69), eventually forced the consular bill to be dropped and his own voted into law instead. Fufius' *rogatio*, says Cicero, contained exactly the same terms as that of the consuls, except on the central issue of how the jurors were to be picked.[419] No one seems to have made any noises about a praetor presiding over this special *quaestio*. Both consuls were available, but apparently neither wanted the *invidia* that this trial of a powerful *nobilis* was bound to generate, whatever its outcome.[420] So they let it devolve on a praetor (not necessarily the *pr. urb.*), who had to take the task. No source bothers to mention the praetor's role in the actual trial, other than Cicero's observation that he was unexpectedly favorable to the prosecution in the preliminary proceedings.[421] Before proceeding to a vote, the jurors requested a bodyguard from the Senate, raising expectations that they would condemn Clodius[422]—but then acquitted him all the same. Bribery (of all sorts) was suspected, but later in the year when an investigation—by another special *quaestio*—was mooted, the opposition of the *equites* put paid to the notion.[423]

11.9.3   *Pompey's Special* Quaestiones *of* 52

Let us turn briefly to the *leges Pompeiae* of 52 B.C. Those aimed in the short term at remedying the grave public disorder stirred up during the consular elections for that year. But they were clearly intended to serve as a launching pad for more lasting improvements to the system of *quaestiones*. Pompey referred the question of legislation *de vi* and *de ambitu* to the Senate three days after entering office (on the 24th day of the intercalary month) as sole consul elected by an *interrex*. One of the two laws that Pompey later passed *ex S.C.*[424] set up—over the wishes of some senior senators—a special *quaestio de vi* to try the consular candidate T. Annius Milo and others, especially for the murder of P. Clodius on 18 January and the acts of violence in the city that followed. The other measure was a new *lex de ambitu*. That, too, probably set up a *quaestio extra ordinem* to deal with the problems that arose from the *comitia* for 52 (see below). But it appears the law was retrospective beyond the most recent elections. Gruen makes a convincing case that henceforth the Pompeian law was to be the operative statute for that crime also in the regular *ambitus* court.[425]

Pompey provided that the courts constituted by these two laws run under some identical rules. In particular, he shortened the proceedings to (apparently) five days total, shifting the focus to the presentation of testimony, doing away with character witnesses, and placing a strict cap on the time allotted to the speeches of orators. Dio says these procedural reforms "and others" were applied to all the courts; there is no real evidence that gainsays him.[426] Pompey, in order to stem bribery, not only devised a "just-in-time" scheme for the selection of jurors, but also dissociated one group of *iudices* from another within a single trial.[427]

The one aspect of these courts that almost all our sources comment on are the armed guards Pompey introduced in some cases to offer "protection" to the proceedings. This was not a formal provision of the *leges Pompeiae*. Rather, it arose out of the circumstances of the first major trial of the year 52, the prosecution of Milo in the extraordinary *quaestio de vi*, when the defendant requested a "praesidium" from the court president who in turn asked the consul Pompey.[428] Pompey complied in a heavy-handed way, and extended this feature to other trials *de vi* and *de ambitu* that year.[429] To be sure, by the late 50s violence was practically part and parcel of the various *quaestiones perpetuae*.[430] And already in the mid-60s we have seen the placement of armed soldiers around a judicial court in Rome.[431] Yet certainly in the Milo trial of 52 B.C., our sources are virtually unanimous that Pompey's aim in ringing the court with a substantial military force was not so much to guard the process as to intimidate the jurors into voting for condemnation.

To return to Pompey's actual measure establishing an extraordinary *quaestio de vi*. Under this law, the People were to elect a president, selected from among the *consulares*. (We can assume that *imperium* went with the job, especially given the likely precedent of L. Cassius Ravilla in 113 B.C.) The *comitia* for this special post followed immediately upon the passage of Pompey's law. Cicero implies that Pompey himself nominated the man who was the People's choice, the ex-consul of 54 B.C., L. Domitius Ahenobarbus. The consul no doubt also held the relevant electoral assembly and got Domitius his *imperium*.[432]

We next find Milo indicted in four different courts: in the special *quaestio de vi* and also *de ambitu, de sodaliciis,* and in the standard (i.e., Plautian) *quaestio de vi.* The first two of these procedures started on 4 April, and Milo was condemned *de vi* on 8 April and (in absence) *de ambitu* the next day; condemnations *in absentia* on the remaining two charges shortly followed. Thanks especially to Asconius, we can identify the presidents of all four of these *quaestiones.* The *consularis* L. Domitius Ahenobarbus of course had the extraordinary *quaestio de vi.* A senior *praetorius,* A. Manlius Torquatus (*pr.* by 69)—termed "quaesitor"—heard the *ambitus* charge. Another "quaesitor," M. Favonius (aedile 53 or 52), presided over the trial *de sodaliciis,* and the "quaesitor" L. Fabius (rank unknown) had the Plautian *quaestio de vi.*[433]

Even before Milo was indicted on these various charges, the praetors for 52 should have entered office.[434] Where were they now? Though the first trials under the recent law *de sodaliciis* (introduced in 55) had come before praetors, it was as an overload. And so the presence of an aedile or ex-aedile as president in this instance need not surprise. As for the court that heard charges under the Plautian *lex de vi,* in past practice either a *iudex quaestionis* or praetor might preside. A later Plautian trial *de vi* of 52—that of Milo's adherent M. Saufeius "apud Considium quaesitorem"—shows that L. Fabius shared responsibility for this *quaestio* with at least one other individual (equally hard to identify). Whether Fabius and this Considius were subpraetorian (like Favonius), praetors, or ex-praetors is unknown.

However, *ambitus* had always been a praetorian court—indeed, a city *provincia.* The presence of a senior praetorian rather than a praetor in office at Milo's trial for this crime shows that Pompey had made some special arrangement to add extra *auctoritas* to the *quaestio de ambitu,* surely along the lines of the *lex Pompeia de vi* that set up a special court with an elected consular president. The *lex Pompeia de ambitu* must have stipulated that a "quaesitor" be chosen by the People from among the ex-praetors to hear the case of Milo and perhaps others in a *quaestio extra ordinem* under the new procedures outlined above. The same *comitia* will have elected L. Domitius Ahenobarbus and A. Torquatus, and both should have had *imperium.*

We hear of additional trials in 52 B.C. before the special *quaestio de vi* (still running in late 52 or even early 51),[435] the regular Plautian *vis* court,[436] a court operating under the *lex Pompeia de ambitu* (also down to the end of the year),[437] an unspecified *quaestio* under a *lex Pompeia,*[438] and an unnamed capital court.[439] In only one case—the mysterious Considius in the standard *quaestio de vi*—do we get a reference to the presiding magistrate. So much that we should like to know escapes us, other than one key detail: the extraordinary *quaestio de vi* continued at least down to the end of 52, presumably under L. Domitius Ahenobarbus, but did not supplant the ordinary *quaestio de vi.*[440] Perhaps Pompey's *lex de ambitu* ordained a similar parallel process for the year 52. The "quaesitor" A. Torquatus might have supervised a special *quaestio* that concentrated on abuses in the most recent consular elections (i.e., for 53 and 52) while one or more praetors in a regular court simultaneously heard other *ambitus* cases, conceivably under the same procedures. Yet that must remain a guess, since we cannot tell what (if anything) was happening in the standard *quaestio de ambitu* that year.

One assumes that for the longer term Pompey meant only to improve the existing system of *quaestiones*, not replace praetors with special *quaesitores*.[441] The trouble is that for the year 51 B.C., we have no information on who presided in the various trials known *de ambitu* (four), *de sodaliciis* (one) and *de vi* (two), nor in the one attested *ambitus* case of 50 B.C.[442] Yet the fact that we find the praetor M. Iuventius Laterensis presiding in a series of trials *de repetundis* in 51 should show that Pompey left the basic structure of the other praetorian criminal courts unaltered.[443]

The City Praetorships, 122–50

12.1 The *Provincia Urbana*

Fully three-quarters of the urban praetors of the years 122–82 B.C. are lost to us. There are just seven or so individuals who definitely or almost certainly can be placed in this *provincia* during these years, and another three or four for whom a case can be made. After Sulla, matters improve significantly. For that period, only about one-third of the urban praetors have gone missing. We are particularly well informed on the urban province in the 70s and reasonably so for the next decade as well. But then, starting in the 50s (somewhat surprisingly), the quality of our information becomes noticeably worse. I should note that direct attestation of this *provincia*—or any other city province—is not all that common for this entire period. Too often, an individual's tenure of the urban jurisdiction has to be inferred from the nature of his activities. The holding of the *Ludi Apollinares* is of course a reliable indicator. The superintendency of unnamed "games" perhaps is not, since, starting in 81 B.C., a praetor (not the urban one) had responsibility for the *Ludi Victoriae Sullanae*.[1] Even presidency of the Senate (really found only in the pre-Sullan period) is somewhat slippery. But it seems positively poor methodology to infer that a praetor had the urban *provincia* merely from his reported activity in the sphere of the civil law. The range and volume of the legal matters that might come to a praetor's attention in this period was stupefying, as Cicero explicitly tells us.[2] It is surely preferable to leave preconceptions at the door when investigating how such responsibilities were handled, especially since the praetorship is such a spottily attested office.

12.1.1 *Urban Praetors down through 81*

It would be good to have a date for the *pr. urb.* C. Caninius who adjudged a property at Ostia to the Roman People. We can assume he visited the town in either the late second or early first century B.C., but greater precision is impossible.[3] An "M.

Marcius praetor" probably had the urban jurisdiction sometime in the period ca. 125–110 (5.6.1). C. Licinius Getha was possibly *praetor urbanus* ca. 120 B.C., as was probably C. Caecilius Metellus Caprarius ca. 116.[4] M. Livius Drusus (the future *cos.* 112) was definitely urban praetor. As such, he granted an action on a consensual contract (*mandatum*) to which one of the parties had died—against the precedent another urban praetor had set eight years previously.[5] The *praetor urbanus* for the year 105 was L. [——]onius L.f. He could be, for example, a Cosconius, Duronius, Pomponius, Scribonius, or Sempronius. The stone is long lost, and hence the size of lacuna to be filled is uncertain.[6] And that is the sum of our knowledge of the urban praetorship for the last two decades of the second century.

For five of the years 100 through 89 B.C., we can attach a name to the *provincia urbana*. After a defeat in the praetorian elections for 98, L. Cornelius Sulla won the office for the next year (through bribery, it was alleged at the time). He received the urban province, followed by an *ex praetura* command in Cilicia. In his praetorian games—that is, the *Ludi Apollinares*—Sulla had Mauretanian javelin throwers hunt down a hundred maned (African) lions, all provided by his friend king Bocchus. No one had ever staged a lion-hunting spectacle on this scale in Rome, as Pliny explicitly tells us. Seneca adds the item that Sulla was the first to let lions run unfettered in the Circus. Sulla's games were emulated and (inevitably) topped in a later era by Pompey and Caesar. But Sulla's Apolline Games must significantly have raised the standard for subsequent urban praetors.[7] C. Valerius Flaccus was definitely urban praetor, and took up Asia when prorogued *pro consule*. The date of C. Flaccus' praetorship is very likely 96, but conceivably 98 or a bit earlier (14.5.5). For the year 94, C. Sentius Saturninus is epigraphically attested as *praetor urbanus*. Like Sulla and C. Flaccus, Sentius was sent *ex praetura* to the East, in this case to Macedonia.[8]

No promagisterial province is attested for the *praetor urbanus* of the year 91, Q. Pompeius Rufus. The outbreak of the Social War surely kept all the city praetors of 91 from taking up an overseas *ex praetura* command. As it happens, Q. Pompeius is the first *praetor urbanus* of this period whom we can see actually at work in the domain of civil law. Cicero in the *De Oratore* records the particulars of a civil suit for repayment of debt that came before this praetor in late summer of 91. When the plaintiff claimed in the *intentio* of the procedural formula a bigger amount than was due to him, the advocate for the defendant did not plead that the plaintiff had overclaimed—which, if proven, would have banished the case forever. Rather, the lawyer ineptly asked Pompeius to insert an inappropriate saving clause (*exceptio*) in the formula, that the claim should be limited to the amount due at the time when it was pressed. The case is of considerable interest for the development of formulary procedure—at the time of the dramatic date of this dialogue (91 B.C.), the *exceptio* in question is said to be "old and familiar"—and also for the description of the praetor's court. For Cicero has L. Licinius Crassus (*cos.* 95) say he was present at this stage of the trial, seated on the tribunal of Pompeius (termed Crassus' "familiaris") as a member of the praetor's advisory *consilium*. The presence of expert jurists in the *consilium* is found already in the 120s B.C. By this time it was no doubt entirely common. However, what does come as a surprise, even given the stated personal connection between Crassus and the praetor, is that a consular saw fit to sit in Pompeius' *consilium*. Consulars do not seem to have considered it appropriate to attend praetors as *legati* in a territorial province and serve in their *consilium* there. City and provincial practice must have differed. To sit on the tribunal of a praetor in Rome probably was thought not to matter all that much to a consular's *dignitas*. It obviously required much less investment of time and energy than to pack off to an overseas *provincia* for a year or (often) more.[9]

Q. Pompeius' other known action is deeply traditional in character. Valerius Maximus says that this praetor excluded the spendthrift son of Q. Fabius Maximus Allobrogicus (*cos.* 121) from the administration of his father's property, though he had been instituted as heir. Though Valerius does not say so, Q. Pompeius probably followed this interdiction by appointing a relative as *curator* for the prodigal Fabius—a safeguard that finds inclusion in the XII Tables.[10]

The next known urban praetor lost his life for the demagogic way he revived an obsolete measure during the debt crisis caused by the Social War. On taking office, the *pr. urb.* 89 A. Sempronius Asellio attempted to persuade creditors at Rome to give relief to their debtors who could not meet their obligations because of war conditions. When this failed, Asellio (as best we can tell) decided to grant to debtors haled into his court a certain *exceptio* under an archaic law that forbade lending at interest, and allowed such cases to proceed to the stage *apud iudicem* to be decided. If this reconstruction is accurate, the praetor's intention in granting this prejudicial *exceptio* (perhaps announced in his edict) was probably to compel the creditors to agree voluntarily to offer debt relief. Asellio's program to allay debt misery lasted not quite a month—specifically, to 27 Jan., the foundation day of the temple of Castor and Pollux in Rome and the religious rite that attended it in the Forum. As urban practor, Asellio evidently had responsibility for offering the requisite sacrifice to the Castores that day. Meanwhile, the *tr. pl.* L. Cassius had stirred up members of the crowd that attended the ceremony (many no doubt *equites*, who had the twins as their patrons). Someone pelted the praetor with a stone in the course of the ceremony. When the praetor fled, the mob chased him down—some even searching for him in the atrium of the Vestals—and ripped him apart. Despite the Senate's efforts to punish the crime, no informers came forward.[11] That a suffect was elected to replace Asellio (it certainly was early enough in the year) is conceivable but unfortunately irrecoverable.

The praetors P. Burrenus, L. Iunius Brutus Damasippus, and Cn. Cornelius Dolabella have to be mentioned together, though they held office in 83, 82, and 81 B.C. respectively, with Dolabella reaching the magistracy under Sulla's new system. When a Sex. Naevius wanted *missio in possessionem* against the property of his business partner P. Quinctius, he prevailed on the praetor P. Burrenus—with whom he had personal ties—for the grant. Burrenus gave him *missio* according to the terms of his edict, backing Naevius with his official powers.

Burrenus' political ascendancy apparently had shocked the *nobiles*—even in the political atmosphere of the day. Matters rapidly degenerated further. In the chaotic year 82 B.C., it is highly probable that L. Damasippus was urban praetor, and in that capacity convened a Senate meeting so as to have an opportunity to butcher some politically dangerous *nobiles*, including the *pontifex maximus* Q. Mucius Scaevola (*cos.* 95). But he also spent much of the year in the field, and met his death on 1 November in the battle against Sulla at the Colline Gate.

After Sulla's victory, Sex. Naevius decided to pursue further litigation. In March 81 (see 11.1.1), Naevius approached the praetor Cn. Cornelius Dolabella, again to make a claim against Quinctius. But instead of allowing the case to proceed to a proper *iudicium*, Dolabella unexpectedly compelled Quinctius to accept—on what Cicero describes as quite prejudicial terms—a *sponsio* with Naevius on the dispute. That is the occasion of the *Pro Quinctio* of 81 B.C. There Cicero, with as much tact as he can muster, characterizes Dolabella's decision on the *sponsio* as a bad innovation, perhaps even implying that it went against his edict. (The praetor's object evidently was to establish a powerful *praeiudicium* against Quinctius.) Cicero devotes the bulk of his speech to attacking Naevius' conduct in the whole affair, and arguing that in 83, the edictal provisions on *missio in possessionem* were inappropriate to Quinctius' situation in the first instance. But for all his detailed narrative, Cicero never mentions what jurisdictions the praetors Burrenus and Dolabella held.[12]

Broughton makes Burrenus *praetor urbanus* for 83, though he queries that *provincia* for Dolabella in 81.[13] A stray reference to Dolabella's praetorship elsewhere shows him making yet another contentious decision in a civil law case, which at least is consistent with an urban praetorship.[14] Expected under the Sullan system to take up a territorial *provincia* after his magistracy, Dolabella drew Cilicia. However, there is good reason to think Sulla first tried to deprive him of the province, and then allowed him to hold it merely "pro praetore"—in contrast to all other praetorian governors, who were to have consular *imperium* (15.1.1). Fifteen years earlier, Sulla himself had followed up a year in the urban jurisdiction with a long promagistracy in Cilicia. Just possibly, it was Dolabella's arbitrary general behavior as praetor that piqued Sulla enough to retaliate in this way early in 80 B.C. In a year's time, Sulla would be less concerned about potentially bad precedents for his new system (11.1.6).

12.1.2 *Urban Praetors after Sulla down to 67*

Cn. Octavius (*cos.* 76) must have been praetor by 79. B. Frier speculated that he might have introduced the *formula Octaviana* and so was *pr. urbanus* previously in 79 B.C.[15] Yet even if Frier's guess is correct on the identity of the author, there is no reason to think he must have been in the *provincia urbana*.[16] Move forward to the year 78 B.C. In mid-May of that year L. Cornelius Sisenna is epigraphically attested as *praetor urbanus et inter peregrinos*.[17] It is of course striking to see these two *provinciae* combined when no major foreign wars other than that with Sertorius were in progress or even in the works, and just a few years after Sulla had introduced provisions for eight "city" praetors. The decision to give both the urban and peregrine *provinciae* to one man may well date to the time of the sortition for 78. If so, the best explanation would be that "Sulla's new regime of *quaestiones perpetuae* brought a shortage of praetors in its wake."[18] In other words, the Senate had not yet realized that it was overly optimistic to expect praetors to superintend all the

courts, including minor ones. But would it really collapse the two oldest praetorian *provinciae* to supply a praetor for, say, the *quaestio inter sicarios et de veneficiis*?
Rather, perhaps Sisenna at first was only *praetor urbanus* for the year, though soon
picking up a second *provincia* when an emergency demanded the presence of the
peregrine praetor in the field. The attack of the Faesulani against Sullan veteran
colonies might provide such a context: the Senate considered the incident serious
enough eventually to send both consuls of 78 into Etruria during their year of
office.[19]

A single episode from L. Sisenna's city praetorship has come down to us.
Cicero in a fragment of the *Pro Cornelio* alludes to a ruling in which Sisenna—
characterized as "excessively unconstrained in making a present of his legal decisions" ("nimis in gratificando iure liber")—went against his own edict and refused
to grant *possessio* of the property of a certain Cn. Cornelius to the worthy and noble
adulescens P. Scipio (later *cos.* 52). Though further details are lacking, it is likely
that this was an inheritance case. A. Lintott offers a plausible reconstruction, that
Cn. Cornelius "might well have been a freedman and client of the Scipionic family" and "P. Scipio could have been seeking the rights of a patron of his family,
when one of their freedmen had died intestate." As for Sisenna's departure from his
own edict, "a tempting speculation is that Sisenna had done this to gratify another
powerful man who had been named in the freedman's will."[20] Sisenna probably
had Sicily as an *ex praetura* province (13.2.2).

We can identify with reasonable certainty six of the next eight holders of the
urban jurisdiction. Half these cases stem solely from a single section of Valerius
Maximus, on testaments that were overturned ("de testamentis quae scissa sunt").
The other half we owe to Cicero's *Verrines*. Cn. Aufidius Orestes (the future *cos.* 71)
received the urban *provincia* for 77.[21] Valerius Maximus reports that Orestes
upheld a freedman's will which instituted as heir Genucius, a castrated priest of the
Magna Mater. When the freedman's (excluded) patron appealed to the *cos.* Mam.
Lepidus, the consul is said to have "abrogated" the praetor's jurisdiction ("praetori-
am iurisdictionem abrogavit") with his own *decretum*. A *senatus consultum* followed that backed the consul's decision and (apparently) barred the eunuch from
asking other praetors for relief: "The Senate provided that the obscene presence of
Genucius not pollute under the pretext of legal business the tribunals of magistrates" ("prouisum est ne obscena Genucii praesentia . . . tribunalia magistratuum
sub specie petiti iuris polluerentur"). One suspects from Valerius' report of this *senatus consultum* that the consul did not actually forbid the praetor Orestes to exercise his *provincia*, but merely overruled his ruling on Genucius. The verb *abrogare*
is sometimes used in a loose rhetorical sense in Valerius. But if Valerius is to be
taken at his word and the consul did use his full *maius imperium* to check all of the
praetor's legal activities, one wonders how Cn. Orestes managed to overcome the
ignominy of such "abrogation" to win the consulship for 71 B.C.[22]

An urban praetorship for C. Licinius Sacerdos in 75 is never explicitly indicated in our sources. Yet the evidence on Sacerdos' particular civil law activities (such
as it is) implies that he preceded C. Verres (*pr.* 74) in the urban jurisdiction.
Furthermore, Sacerdos and his praetorian colleague M. Caesius assisted the consuls of the year in the massive task of repairing temples in Rome, but apparently did

not have enough time to inspect all those in need of maintenance; the next year
the urban praetor Verres and his colleague P. Coelius took up the task. That provides some further support for the *provincia*.[23] He was also Verres' predecessor as
pro consule in Sicily (13.2.2).

C. Verres, as noted, is definite for 74.[24] In the *Verrines* (esp. *actio* II.1), Cicero
describes a fairly broad range of Verres' activities in the urban province. For one
thing, Cicero attacks the way Verres allegedly profited from improperly setting certain public contacts.[25] He briefly alludes to the praetor's failure to provide for badly
needed road repair in Rome.[26] Perhaps related is the passing charge that Verres
swindled money from the public treasury.[27] Just one detailed example is offered,
but at great length—the praetor's abuse of the maintenance contract for the temple of Castor and Pollux. This was not a regular duty that came with his *provincia*.
As noted above, the consuls of the year 75 originally had responsibility for temple
repairs in Rome. The task proved so big that it devolved upon the praetor C.
Sacerdos and his colleague M. Caesius, and thence to Verres and his colleague P.
Caelius. (Caelius' role is mentioned just once, and then allowed to fade into the
background.)[28]

One reason why Cicero singles out this episode must be the irony of the situation. As we have seen for 89 B.C., the urban praetor was the magistrate charged
with celebrating the January ceremony for Castor and Pollux on the anniversary of
their temple. Note that in the *exordium* of the *Verrines*, Cicero strives to add pathos
to a long, dramatic prayer by invoking as a group Hercules, the Magna Mater, and
the Dioscuri—deities whose cult came under the supervision of the *praetor
urbanus* (see 5.5.2) and whose rites suffered through Verres' negligence.[29] But most
of all Cicero here wants to foreshadow Verres' even more heinous exploitation of
the power of granting contracts when promagistrate in Sicily.[30] Significantly, one
aspect of Verres' *provincia* about which Cicero has nothing to say is the performance of the Apolline Games. Verres' *ludi* must have been a success.

Some valuable items do emerge in the *Verrines* regarding this praetor's supervision of criminal law in Rome—again paving the way for Sicilian charges to come.
As *praetor urbanus*, Verres had ultimate responsibility for assigning *iudices* to particular cases in the standing *quaestiones*.[31] What is surprising is that he also conducted his own criminal *iudicia*. For instance, Verres presided at the trial of the *tr.
pl.* 75 Q. Opimius, who was prosecuted for exercising his veto in contravention of
the Cornelian law. Cicero says Verres' behavior in this case—Opimius was briskly
condemned to a substantial fine in three hours—led to calls to abandon this type
of public *iudicium*. But whether they led to anything is unclear.[32] Cicero also says
in passing that Verres while urban praetor administered corporal punishment to a
member of the Plebs. Whatever the substance of that precise charge, the basic incident perhaps involved another criminal *iudicium*.[33]

Verres' irregular edict and his crooked judicial decisions in civil law are perhaps Cicero's major concern in his disquisition on the urban praetorship.[34] Verres'
edict, it is said, undercut those of his predecessors, in particular by changing the
customary (praetorian) order of succession and by settling for low standards of proof
in inheritance cases. And the innovations Verres introduced were for his own personal profit.[35] Four inheritance cases are singled out to illustrate these contentions,

and to introduce proof of additional irregularities.[36] Some general themes emerge from these cases. Verres' knavery started even while *praetor designatus*, the time when he drafted his edict.[37] There his "innovations" conflicted inappropriately both with statute and with the precedents set by previous praetors. When actually hearing cases at law in the city, Verres freely departed from his own edict to gratify certain individuals, especially when there was the prospect of his own personal gain. Later, Verres did not even bother to carry over some of those innovations to his provincial edict. Nor did subsequent urban praetors accept his modifications.[38] Cicero implicitly raises the specter of the *pr. urb.* 89 A. Sempronius Asellio by pointing up instances where Verres himself narrowly escaped lynching for the way he administered the law.[39] The main "safety valve" that year, suggests Cicero, was Verres' praetorian colleague L. Calpurnius Piso. (Not so incidentally, Piso was a juror at the *repetundae* trial that occasioned the *Verrines*—hence the praise.) Cicero says that for litigants, Piso provided a much-needed safe haven ("perfugium") from the corrupt and largely inaccessible *pr. urb.* Verres. Indeed, according to Cicero, Piso filled many *codices* with instances in which he "vetoed" decisions by Verres because they were in contravention of that praetor's own edict ("multos codices implevit earum rerum in quibus ita intercessit, quod iste aliter atque ut edixerat decrevisset").[40]

A scholiast on the *Verrines* passage seems puzzled yet takes this talk of veto literally. So have many modern scholars.[41] But could "intercessit" here mean merely "intervene"[42] and not actually "veto"? Note that Cicero in the relevant passage does not use the verb *intercedere* with the dative of the person or thing vetoed, but employs a construction that finds no exact parallel in our sources.[43] As it happens, for the later Republic we have no instance of a praetor in the city using his *imperium* to veto his colleague's actions in the realm of civil law.

Litigants are known to have used a variety of informal avenues to work their will on a praetor.[44] Those who did not like a praetor's procedural decisions in the last resort customarily appealed to a tribune of the Plebs. That happened most notoriously in 89, but apparently on plenty of other occasions, too.[45] In one case from the year 77 we do, however, find an appeal to a consul, who by virtue of his *maius imperium* overrode the decision of a *praetor urbanus*—Cn. Aufidius Orestes—in an inheritance case (discussed above). Of course, in the various territorial provinces it was not uncommon for a new governor to rescind his predecessor's decisions. Cicero in the *Verrines* has much to say on how Verres flouted all sorts of weighty precedents in his provincial command (too many instances to list) and how his successor L. Metellus then spent the early part of his command in Sicily undoing Verres' rulings and arrangements.[46] Additional instances come readily to hand.[47] All the same, when the successor to a province overturned the actions of the *decessor* it was viewed as a serious affront.[48]

For these reasons—to return to Verres and the year 74—it seems hard to believe that the praetor L. Calpurnius Piso was employing the full power of his *imperium* and actually vetoing multiple decisions that his (well-connected) colleague in the urban *provincia* handed out. What seems more likely is that Verres was refusing to grant some actions for circumstances that reasonably met the terms of his own edict. (A praetor's decision to allow or not allow an action might legitimately be called a *decretum*.)[49] But when the same plaintiffs petitioned his colleague Piso, that man did grant the requested *iudicia* to individuals "without trouble, without bother, without expense, even without legal representation" ("sine labore, sine molestia, sine impensa, etiam sine patrono"). Verres, it is implied, had put up all sorts of impediments for those who had not bribed him.

It might have been somewhat common in this era for a petitioner who had been rebuffed at one praetor's tribunal to try his luck at another's. Valerius Maximus, in relating the episode of the *pr. urb.* 77 Cn. Aufidius Orestes, notes that a *senatus consultum* sought to prevent a disgruntled eunuch from attempting this very thing.[50] But in general once a praetor—especially the urban praetor—had refused on technical grounds an application for an action, his colleagues surely would be reluctant to undercut his *dignitas* by granting that same action. To sum up: when the praetor Piso "intercessit" in Verres' civil law cases, he probably did nothing more than to accept the petitions his colleague had refused. That was indeed a provocative intervention, though Cicero in his description is disingenuous in making it sound like an actual veto.

Again, Cicero's main aim in all these broadsides on Verres' urban praetorship is to make the charges he levels against the promagistracy in Sicily appear more credible.[51] In treating the city magistracy, Cicero quite transparently has chosen to probe specifically those areas where he thinks he can find continuity with Verres' later behavior as *pro consule*. It should not be imagined that we have here a comprehensive sketch of the activities of a *praetor urbanus*. However, one criticism of Verres that Cicero fails to make is that he had cheated in the sortition for his city (or promagisterial) *provincia*.[52] The omission is striking, considering the sheer number of accusations that Cicero flings at his target, including that he had bought that very praetorship[53] and that the praetor's mistress Chelidon was the one really in control during his magistracy, functioning as his main jurisconsult.[54] Had he chosen to raise it, Cicero could have made the cheating charge stick. After all, Verres was (in all likelihood) the third urban praetor in five years to go to Sicily after his magistracy. No obvious explanation presents itself. It is possible, however, that aspersions on the integrity of one praetor's *sors* were an aspersion on the *sortes* of his whole college, and so were avoided.[55]

Let us turn to Verres' successors in the urban *provincia*. In either 73 or 72, Q. Caecilius Metellus (the future *cos.* 69) as urban praetor refused to grant possession to a pimp of property that he claimed under the terms of a will.[56] Then it must be C. Calpurnius Piso (later *cos.* 67) who was the "praetor urbis" said by Valerius Maximus to void the terms of another will.[57] As the story goes, Calpurnius as praetor allowed a Terentius to take possession of the property of a deceased natural son who had disinherited him; Calpurnius also prohibited the named heirs from taking further legal action. An M. Mummius most likely had the *provincia urbana* in 70.[58] So the Calpurnius incident should date to 72 or 71—probably the latter year, as Broughton[59] has it.

A praetor "Metellus" granted the action "damnum vi hominibus armatis coactisve datum" in a dispute over possession of some land near Thurii, and presided in the case for which Cicero wrote his *Pro Tullio*.[60] This particular action on "damnum" had been invented by M. Terentius Varro Lucullus while *praetor inter peregrinos* in 76.[61] The "Metellus" in question may be Q. Caecilius Metellus, whom we have seen was urban praetor in 73 or 72. The alternative is that he is to be identified with the *pr.* 71 L. Metellus, Verres' successor in Sicily and the future *cos.* 68. L. Metellus' city *provincia* is uncertain, but in it he definitely posted an edict, which Cicero says incorporated the *formula Octaviana*, at that time a recent innovation.[62] L. Metellus need not have been urban praetor: after all, the *iudicium* he granted on "damnum" was the creation of a peregrine praetor. The *Pro Tullio* probably can be squared with 71 B.C., the year of L. Metellus' praetorship. If the date is correct, the trial surely took place later in the year.[63]

P. Cornelius Dolabella was the praetor who presided over the *sponsio*, known from Cicero's *Pro Caecina*, of A. Caecina versus Sex. Aebutius in 69 or 68. Broughton argues that "he was praetor urbanus, since he granted the interdict *de vi hominibus armatis* to Caecina."[64] But Cicero never specifies his city *provincia*. Dolabella went *ex praetura* to Asia (14.6.5).

Next, the case of M. Iunius: When a certain D. Matrinius, who had been disgraced by the censors of 70, later sought the position of *scriba aedilicius*, Cicero successfully pleaded his case before a sworn board consisting of the *praetores* M. Iunius and Q. Publicius and the curule aediles M. Plaetorius and C. Flaminius.[65] Plaetorius and Flaminius are both found as *iudices* presiding over the *quaestio de sicariis* in 66.[66] In this period, ex-aediles seem invariably to have held the position of *iudex quaestionis*, where we can check, in the year following their magistracy (10.4.3). So the year of that hearing (and thus the praetorship of Iunius and Publicius) should be 67, as Broughton and M. Crawford hold.[67] If (as seems likely) Iunius is the same man as the "M. Iunius praetor" who ordered the restoration of a painting in the temple of Apollo by Aristides of Thebes in time for his *Ludi Apollinares*,[68] he was *praetor urbanus*.[69] It is revealing that Iunius and a praetorian colleague—as well as both curule aediles—had to make themselves available (and take an oath) to hear the case of D. Matrinius. It was not a disciplinary process, as Mommsen believed, and still less a trial, as Alexander has it. Rather, it was a "job interview," to see whether Matrinius was worthy to buy a place in a high-ranking (though not the highest) scribal *decuria*.[70] The process may have been a long one, since there will have been other wealthy applicants for this position in addition to Matrinius. We hear very little about the city praetors' responsibilities for miscellaneous chores of this type, so it is a most welcome chance reference. We can safely assume that a board consisting of the *praetor urbanus*, another praetor, and the curule aediles also selected quaestorian *scribae*, who held the top position. It is an open question how much responsibility these higher magistrates had for filling vacancies in lesser scribal *decuriae*.

12.1.3 *Urban Praetors after the* Lex Cornelia

In 67, the tribune C. Cornelius passed a law compelling praetors to follow their own edicts ("ut praetores ex edictis suis perpetuis ius dicerent").[71] Asconius says that many (i.e. in the senatorial establishment) opposed the *lex Cornelia*, but did not dare to speak openly against it. Indeed, Frier argues the law served a wide purpose, namely, to regulate "the whole standard for administering private law. . . . [I]t was surely a step in the process that led to the decline of the praetorian creativity and the fossilization of the Edict."[72] Other scholars have posited alternative motives that are similarly elaborate.[73] Yet the law surely did not attempt to dictate the actual composition of the individual edicts. Its aim (probably) was only to prevent ad hoc (or better, ad hominem) deviations. Praetors make plenty of those in our record for the late 80s and 70s (12.1.2), prompted by both favoritism and spite. The persistence of that type of behavior—which as we have seen led to intervention by a consul on at least one occasion (in 77 B.C.)—is probably enough to explain the passage of this tribunician law. The real point at issue was a social one, namely, to stop praetors' flagrant abuses for personal reasons—hence the opposition by the senatorial elite, who had the most to gain from the status quo. The main legal effect of the *lex Cornelia* was one of public law, in that it cut into the praetors' exercise of their *imperium*.

We are unusually well informed on the disposition of the various city *provinciae* for the year 66—thanks largely to one passing statement in the *Pro Cluentio* by the *pr. repetundarum* M. Tullius Cicero.[74] However, neither Cicero nor any other source tells us who was urban praetor this year. Now, the praetorian *provincia* of C. Antonius—Cicero's colleague in both the praetorship and consulship[75]—is not directly attested, though like Verres and his Chelidon, Antonius is said to have openly kept a mistress at home while praetor.[76] Was Antonius also *praetor urbanus*? That is what Broughton suggests, reckoning that his famously expensive games— which impressed even Cicero—were the *Ludi Apollinares*.[77] The sources on Antonius' games offer no real specifics on whether they belonged to an (unattested) aedileship or his praetorship. However, there is hardly room for an aedileship in his *cursus*: Antonius found himself expelled from the Senate in 70, only to re-enter (surely) through a tribunate of the Plebs in 68, and then went on to be elected praetor for 66. And Cicero in the *Pro Murena* implies that he found Antonius' games worrying precisely in the context of the consular elections for 63.[78] Broughton must be correct that C. Antonius gave his games as praetor. In fact, Pliny implies that L. Licinius Murena—definitely *pr. urb.* 65—directly emulated Antonius' games.[79] They probably had the same *provincia*.

After his praetorship, Antonius evidently took up a lucrative *legatio*, just possibly under Pompey in the east.[80] It is a pity that we do not know more, for (assuming it is true) it shows something about contemporary attitudes toward provincial administration that a praetor would choose to be a *legatus* in another commander's *provincia* than to receive one for his own. Antonius must have been looking simply for the best way to pay off his debts, especially from those games—in which he seems to have overcompensated for his less-than-resplendent past.

A word about the *pr.* 65 L. Licinius Murena and the urban *provincia*: In November 63, Cicero defended L. Murena (who had an *ex praetura* command in Transalpine Gaul and was now *cos. des.* 62) against a charge of *ambitus* brought by Murena's praetorian colleague and disappointed competitor for the consulship, Ser. Sulpicius Rufus. At one point in his speech, Cicero contrasts his client's praetorian "sors iuris dicundi" to Rufus' *peculatus* court. Cicero says that the friends of Ser. Sulpicius Rufus—a noted jurist—were hoping that he would draw the urban lot:[81]

Here [i.e., the urban jurisdiction] the magnitude of the task brings glory, the bestowal of fair treatment (*aequitas*) wins influence. In this *sors* the wise praetor, such as Murena was, avoids offense by the impartiality of his decisions (*aequabilitas decernendi*), and adds goodwill by gentleness of hearing (*lenitas audiendi* [sc. cases]). It is an illustrious *provincia* and one suited for the consulship, in which the commendation that comes from fairness, integrity, and accessibility (*aequitas, integritas, facilitas*) finally is topped off by the pleasure of games.

Elsewhere, Cicero has occasion to remark on the overarching importance of this complex *provincia*.[82] Yet in the *Pro Flacco* he also portrays the urban praetorship as a breeding ground for mistrust, suspicion and personal feuds.[83] The administration of civil law strikes one as the tricky part. Here the personality of the praetor was crucial. In other contexts,[84] Cicero highlights precisely the same qualities as in the above passage—fairness and impartiality,[85] tactful judiciousness,[86] mildness,[87] integrity,[88] and accessibility[89]—as essential characteristics in any praetor who administers civil law, whether in Rome or in the provinces.[90] For Cicero, other positive attributes in a praetor in the civil sphere are a reputation for seriousness, conscientiousness, the observation of appropriate precedent, and the right sort of severity.[91] Singled out as particular evils (besides plain turpitude) are open favoritism, arbitrariness, and harshness or cruelty.[92]

Praetors faced scrutiny for the quality of their administration of the law.[93] So one would imagine technical knowledge of the law was surely a plus. But it comes up quite rarely in Cicero's various descriptions of ideal praetorian attributes.[94] In the *Pro Murena*, Cicero even denies that it was all that important.[95] In truth, the system of sortition meant that even a civil law expert had (theoretically) a one in eight chance of landing the urban jurisdiction. In 66 B.C., the great jurist C. Aquillius Gallus had the *ambitus* court while the significantly less gifted C. Antonius apparently received the *provincia urbana*. For 65, the erudite Ser. Sulpicius Rufus drew the dire *quaestio peculatus*, while another expert, P. Orbius, had some other (nonurban) *provincia*.[96] The standard of legal knowledge of their praetorian colleagues in 65 might have been quite low. Not quite a dozen years after Murena's praetorship, Caesar was to claim that before the arrival of the jurist Trebatius Testa in Gaul (spring 54 B.C.), not a single man on his staff was capable of drawing up a contract promising court appearance (*vadimonium*).[97] This is quite surprising, since there was at least one ex-praetor on Caesar's staff at the time, T. Labienus (*pr.* by 59, on whom see 15.2.4). Labienus is not known to have been *praetor urbanus*. But he was a potential recipient of the *sors*.

To return to our *Pro Murena* passage: Here, of course, Cicero is trying to show how the inherent advantages of the urban praetorship and his client's personal attributes resulted in election to a consulship without need of unfair practices. Cicero's statement in this speech cannot be considered an objective description of the nature of the *provincia*—any more than a passage in the *Pro Flacco* where, for a different rhetorical purpose, he expatiates on all the enemies an urban praetor stood to make. But the record does seem to support his claim that the urban jurisdiction is "one suited for the consulship." Fully half the praetors who have come up so far in our survey of the urban *provincia* for this era eventually reached the higher office.[98] Of those who did not progress to the consulship, almost half of those cases were affected by major external factors such as the *regnum Cinnanum* and the Civil Wars, death, or judicial condemnation.[99]

Following Murena, three of the four next known or probable urban praetors also reached the consulship. The *elogium* of M. Valerius Messalla Niger preserves the detail that he was urban praetor (and contains no indication that a promagistracy followed). Messalla was *cos.* 61 and later censor in 55; the date of the praetorship is not attested, but is almost certain to have been 64 B.C.[100] L. Valerius Flaccus followed as *praetor urbanus* for the year 63. Pretty much all we know of Flaccus' activities is that he aided in the arrest of the Allobrogian envoys on the night of 2–3 December, seized some incriminating materials, and held them overnight. Following his year in office, Flaccus went *pro consule* to Asia, where he made a mess of the province.[101] He is the one urban praetor in this group who did not progress to higher office: his trial for *repetundae* in 59 B.C., though ending in acquittal, probably wrecked his chances for the consulship.[102] There is no indication that subsequently he made much of an effort to reach it. In 57, he went off to Macedonia as a *legatus* of L. Calpurnius Piso (*cos.* 58) and returned only in summer 55.[103]

In 63 B.C., the rites of the Bona Dea were held in the consul Cicero's house on 3 December. A year later, they took place in that of the praetor C. Iulius Caesar.[104] Shackleton Bailey's suggestion that Caesar was *praetor urbanus* for 62 must surely be right.[105] In earlier (pre-Sullan) days, the home of the urban praetor is likely to have been the regular location for the rites in the (frequent) absence of the consuls from the city.[106] In December 62, the location of the consuls is unknown, but they should have been in Rome. It is natural that they would have allowed the responsibility for the Bona Dea to devolve upon the praetor Caesar, especially since he was (after 63) *pontifex maximus*. In this year Caesar is said to *ius dicere*,[107] but that in itself is inconclusive regarding his precise *provincia*. He of course reached the consulship for 59 after an *ex praetura* command in Further Spain.

The praetor allotted the urban jurisdiction for 61 is unknown. But as praetor that year, C. Octavius—the father of Augustus—had haled to court certain ex-magistrates "who had decided unjustly" and as private citizens flouted their own decisions, and also Sullani who had stolen property forcibly ("per vim et metum") but which he now made them return. The *provincia* cannot be ascertained, but Cicero's general description certainly suggests activities in a civil law court rather than a permanent *quaestio*. Octavius received an *ex praetura* command in Macedonia (14.2.4).[108] For 60, the urban praetor definitely was P. Cornelius Lentulus Spinther. Through the consul Caesar's connivance in 59, he received Hispania Citerior as his promagisterial province, and returned to win election for the consulship of 57.[109]

There are just two firmly attested urban praetors for the 50s, who show up in our record of 57 and 50 B.C. However, we may be able to account for the *provincia* in two or three additional years of this decade. As praetor in 58, C. Memmius issued an edict that P. Vatinius appear to stand trial for an alleged violation while *tr. pl.* 59 of the *lex Licinia Iunia*. That was a recent law (of 62) which set down rules for the proper deposit of proposed legislation in the *aerarium*.[110] We would assume the praetor also had formal responsibility for the trial, which most likely was not to take place in a *quaestio perpetua*. The scope of the law and the fact that the procedure of the trial itself soon came into dispute suggests rather a special *iudicium publicum*, which probably stipulated a fine as penalty. The prosecution of another ex-tribune—Q. Opimius, before the urban praetor C. Verres in 74 (12.1.2)—offers a ready parallel for the case of Vatinius.[111] We should at least allow for the possibility that Memmius, like Verres, was *praetor urbanus*. As praetor, Memmius (with his colleague L. Domitius Ahenobarbus) made one or more anti-Caesarian *relationes* in the Senate,[112] but that is immaterial to his *provincia*. A promagistracy in Bithynia (for 57)—with the poets Catullus and Cinna in his *cohors*—is not disputed. No consulship followed. Though hailed "imperator" in Bithynia, Memmius' tumultuous campaign for *cos.* 53 led to his condemnation *de ambitu* in 52 (11.2).

The disposition of the *provincia urbana* for the rest of the decade requires only brief discussion. L. Caecilius Rufus was definitely urban praetor for 57, and as such refused access in court to those who had taken possession of the property of Cicero, now in exile. L. Rufus held an overseas *provincia* (precisely which one is unknown) for 56.[113] Broughton reasonably regards a Fonteius as *praetor urbanus* for 54.[114] The next two years are a blank for this *provincia*, but in the prolonged *interregnum* of 53 B.C.—there were no curule elections until July—Dio tells us the tribunes of the Plebs contrived that they hold the *Ludi Apollinares*.[115] For 51 B.C., an A. Plautius or Plotius (*aed. cur.* probably in 55) might have had the title of urban praetor (11.2). Finally, C. Titius Rufus was urban praetor for 50 B.C.[116] None of these four men— L. Caecilius Rufus, Fonteius, A. Plautius, C. Rufus—reached the consulship. The main explanation for that is surely not any qualitative change in the status of the urban jurisdiction among the praetorian *provinciae* during the 50s, but rather the disturbed electoral conditions of the years 53 and 52 and the civil war that erupted in 49 B.C.

12.2 Other City *Provinciae*, 122–50

12.2.1 *Praetors* Inter Peregrinos

We can account for the *provincia peregrina* in just four years in this period, two before Sulla's reforms and two in the decade that followed. In 105, the peregrine jurisdiction was independently allotted to an unknown praetor; all that remains of his name in the relevant document is his filiation (he was son of a certain "Publius").[117] It now appears that L. Gellius as peregrine praetor in 94 was charged by the Senate with roadbuilding in Apulia; so he was not in Rome hearing law cases that entire year. After his magistracy, Gellius took up Cilicia or Asia *pro consule*.[118] And we have seen that L. Cornelius Sisenna as *pr.* 78 had both the urban and peregrine jurisdiction (12.1.2), probably from the beginning of the year but perhaps picking up the second *provincia* through the "mandatory" process. Finally, there is M. Terentius Varro Lucullus (the future *cos.* 73) in 76. His date and *provincia* are certain, for Asconius relates how a lawsuit involving C. Antonius (the future *cos.* 63) came *in ius* before the praetor M. Lucullus "qui ius inter peregrinos dicebat." This suit—in which Greeks were calling Antonius to account for some previous predations in Achaea—was partly responsible for Antonius' expulsion from the Senate "six years" later, in 70.[119]

Cicero tells how M. Lucullus as praetor introduced an innovation into his edict regarding crimes by armed bands of slaves.[120] Were it not for Asconius, one would be tempted to infer from Cicero's long discussion of Lucullus and his measure that he was *praetor urbanus,* from the talk of this praetor's skilled ability to *ius dicere* and the like.[121] The example of M. Lucullus goes to show how little can be taken for granted in reading even our most detailed and reliable source for the late Republic. Cicero never identifies this praetor's *provincia*—or in fact specifically mentions the peregrine jurisdiction anywhere else in his voluminous writings.

12.2.2 *Some City Praetors in Unspecified* Provinciae

We find several praetors for this period engaged in civil law activities for whom no *provincia* is specified in our sources. First, P. Decius Subulo, who, after taking on the Optimates in various ways as *tr. pl.* 120 (and escaping condemnation the next year), held the praetorship for 115. The author of the *De Viris Illustribus* (our only source on this man's praetorship) relates that when Decius refused the consul M. Aemilius Scaurus' order to rise in his presence, the consul had the praetor's magisterial robe torn and curule chair broken. The consul then by edict barred anyone from approaching Decius in civil law matters ("ne quis ad eum in ius iret, edixit"). Scaurus' behavior in this instance probably reflects pent-up class hostility at Decius the person. But Decius might have been up to something as praetor that we do not know about. The important general point that emerges from this episode is that it presupposes another praetor could step in to exercise Decius' jurisdiction.[122]

A related episode, again known only from the *De Viris Illustribus,* involves C. Servilius Glaucia during his tumultuous year as praetor in 100 B.C. The *tr. pl.* Saturninus, it is said, "to appear more 'popular,' smashed the curule chair of the praetor Glaucia, because in administering justice he had diverted part of the People" (sc. from some *contio* or assembly).[123] On this passage, Broughton[124] suggests "the order of notices [sc. in the sketch of Saturninus in the *Vir. Ill.*] implies that the incident occurred during [Saturninus'] first tribunate," and so quite tentatively postulates that another Glaucia was a (city) praetor for 103 (though not excluding that the man in question is the *pr.* 100). The suggestion of a second "Glaucia" for 103 is unnecessary. A glance at the sketches of other lives in the *De Viris Illustribus* shows that this author does not always care about preserving the relative chronology of the events he mentions.[125] Though the political background to this particular anecdote is murky, it should remain attached to the year 100—incidentally indicating that Glaucia's *provincia* included responsibilities in the civil law. He certainly was meant to be in the city all year (cf. 14.1.1).

An L. Sentius (Saturninus) while city praetor issued an edictal prohibition on the dumping of corpses and refuse apparently within 200 meters outside the Servian wall.[126] The conditions of each of the years 90 through 87 are particularly consistent with such a regulation for Rome, but there is no real possibility of anything approaching certainty on the date. The year 82, however, does seem a firm terminus for the date of L. Sentius' praetorship.[127]

In 12.1.1–3 I have discussed the cases of P. Burrenus (*pr.* 83), Cn. Cornelius Dolabella (*pr.* 81), Cn. Octavius (*pr.* by 79), L. Calpurnius Piso Frugi (*pr.* 74), L. Caecilius Metellus (*pr.* 71), P. Cornelius Dolabella (*pr.* 69 or 68), and C. Octavius (*pr.* 61). Of these, L. Piso Frugi was definitely, and L. Metellus is likely, not to have been urban praetor. Add M. Curtius Peducaenus, praetor in 50 B.C. Though not *praetor urbanus*—C. Titius Rufus had this *provincia* that year—Peducaenus presided over a civil suit between two brothers, one trying to block the other from selling a jointly owned estate. And Cicero reveals that he had an edict. That Peducaenus was *praetor inter peregrinos* (as Shackleton Bailey suggests) is a good guess but no more.[128]

Another case from this general period requires more extended discussion. In Dio's narrative of the year 67—a year for which the urban praetor was almost certainly M. Iunius (12.1.2)—we find two stories about a city praetor "L. Lucullus."[129] When the *cos.* M.' Acilius Glabrio smashed "Lucullus'" curule chair for not rising in his presence, the praetor—and his praetorian colleagues—from then on gave their judgments standing. (The consul evidently did not go so far as to prohibit the praetor from acting in his *provincia*.) And "Lucullus" turned down an *ex praetura* command for Sardinia, alleging the general state of corruption in the provinces (see 11.1.6).

Broughton rightly adopts M. Hölzl's old correction of Dio's text from "L. Lucullus" to "L. Lucceius," that is, the unsuccessful consular candidate for the year 59.[130] However, M. Dondin and J. M. David offer a transposition and reinterpretation of the Dio passage which seems extremely forced. They reject Hölzl's emendation and place the chair-smashing incident in L. Lucullus' praetorship of 78 B.C. so as to give M.' Glabrio (*cos.* 67) a tribunate. Dondin elsewhere offers this as a fact.[131] But Dio's city praetor "L. Lucullus" cannot be the *cos.* 74 B.C., for Cicero[132] explicitly tells us that Lucullus' praetorship in 78 was followed directly by a command in Africa. The anecdote is best left in the year 67, as the conflict between a consul and praetor.

The response of the praetor and his colleagues to Acilius' violence—to give legal decisions while standing—does call out for comment. Dio's ὀρθοστάδην should correspond to the technical legal term "de plano." If so, we should remember that "the magistrate could have done little *de plano* in the exercise of contentious jurisdiction."[133] And that, I suggest, was the point of the praetors' coordinated demonstration: to effect a work "slowdown" in protest of Acilius' inappropriate and insulting show of consular power. I do not see any basis for Broughton's notion that Lucceius was peregrine praetor.[134]

12.2.3 *The Workload of Praetors Allotted Criminal* Quaestiones

I have discussed the evidence for the allotment of the criminal courts in the pre- and post-Sullan periods in 10.4.1–4 and 11.7.1–7 respectively. It would be interesting to know (but seems hard to reckon) how busy the praetors were who had these courts as their *provinciae*. When it comes to the major courts—*repetundae, ambitus, maiestas*, where praetors seem regularly to have presided—there are only a few years for which we have notice of three or more trials in the same *quaestio*.[135]

However, it must be emphasized that counting the number of trials attested for a given *quaestio* over the period of a year gets us only so far. For instance, there is just one trial *inter sicarios et de veneficiis* (namely, that of A. Cluentius) that comes up in our sources for 66 B.C., yet by chance we know from a passage in the *Pro Cluentio* that in this year three *iudices quaestionis* were needed to staff the combined murder and poisoning court.[136] We do have lots of evidence showing that the Forum in the later Republic might host simultaneous criminal *quaestiones*, suggesting that the competent magistrates sometimes genuinely had their hands full.[137] Most informative is that same passage in the *Pro Cluentio*, where the praetor Cicero indicates that at the same time as the present trial *de veneficiis* under a *iudex quaestionis*, there was a process *de ambitu* in session under presidency of a praetor—but showing that *repetundarum* (his own court) and *peculatus* were in recess. Elsewhere, Cicero indicates there were quieter times in the judicial calendar, namely, the months between September and January.[138]

Information on the actual length of trials run by praetors is particularly rare, except that we know a fair number of prosecutions in each of the *quaestiones* were broken off once started.[139] Greenidge has set out in detail with admirable lucidity the evidence for the course of a trial in a permanent *quaestio*.[140] There is no need here to recount all the responsibilities the presiding praetor had from the time he accepted an accusation to the point he found and implemented the sentence. There is, however, the basic fact that once a praetor decided to accept a prosecution he had to allow by law at least ten days before assembling the full court; when the charge was *repetundae*, longer intervals came into play.[141] That gives us a baseline from which to calculate. Examples of fully completed trials for which we have actual dates amount to precisely three, all from the mid-50s. In the trial of P. Sestius *de vi* (apparently) before the praetor M. Aemilius Scaurus in 56, the whole process took a little less than five weeks, with the praetor accepting the request to prosecute (*postulatio*) on 10 February and verdict on 14 March. When M. Aemilius Scaurus himself was prosecuted *de repetundis* in 54, he was indicted on 6 July and acquitted sometime before 2 September. In this case, a process lasting anything up to seven weeks is possible, but the exact length is unknown. That was a very quick *repetundae* process: the prosecutors had received an interval of thirty days to gather evidence, but in the end decided not to travel to Sardinia, the province where Scaurus had his praetorian command. Asconius' narrative of this case shows also that the interval between *postulatio* and trial in itself offered opportunities for further charges and countercharges, which naturally required the presiding praetor to remain vigilant throughout. Finally, the *postulatio* of A. Gabinius (*cos.* 58) for *maiestas* in 54 took place by 20 Sept., and the verdict of acquittal came in on 23 October.[142]

To hazard some conclusions: When trials before a praetor ran to completion, four or five weeks might have been the norm from *postulatio* to verdict in trials—except for *repetundae*. Extortion cases will have taken substantially longer to resolve, owing especially to the need for prosecutors to gather evidence abroad and the peculiar form of the trial, with the compulsory adjournment known as *comperendinatio*.[143] The provision of the *Lex Acilia repetundarum* that stipulated 1 September as a deadline for initiating prosecution reflects this basic reality.[144] An extortion trial spanning three months was evidently not unusual.[145] So it stands to reason that the *praetor repetundarum* and (probably) the praetor who presided over the busy *ambitus* court had few extended respites from their taxing *quaestiones*. Yet, as it happens, when we have detailed information on individual praetors who had the *quaestio repetundarum*—M. Tullius Cicero (66), Ap. Claudius Pulcher (who almost certainly had this *provincia* in 57), M. Porcius Cato (54)—we find them involved in all sorts of activities outside their court (11.7.1). Indeed, Ap. Claudius Pulcher seems to have spent the bulk of his praetorship—even allowing for the strong negative bias of our main source, which is of course Cicero—away from his court and working on behalf of his brother Clodius, tribune in the previous year.[146] (No *repetundae* trials are recorded for 57.)

The praetors who drew *peculatus* and *maiestas* are unlikely in principle to have been as occupied, to judge not so much by the (low) number of attested trials as by the nature of the respective crimes. The court *inter sicarios et de veneficiis* and the later *quaestio de vi* saw the most activity in sheer number of cases—but there presidency by a praetor seems to have been the exception. Even in an individual court, the volume of trials surely varied year by year. And several *quaestiones* probably had a certain seasonality, *ambitus* for one (see 11.7.2).

Occasionally we find a praetorian president of a criminal court engaged in legal activities (broadly defined) outside his individual *quaestio*. Whether C. Aquillius Gallus introduced his formula "de dolo malo" while *praetor* for *ambitus* in 66 is dubious. Yet M. Porcius Cato seems to have had responsibilities in the area of civil law. Asconius, while describing his controversial warm-weather garb as president of the *quaestio repetundarum* in 54, adds that Cato dressed that way "also" when he went to the forum to *ius dicere*.[147]

Fairly certain is presidency of more than one court, a phenomenon found by the 50s. More than one praetor evidently had competence in cases *de ambitu* in 59. Cn. Domitius Calvinus (*pr.* for *ambitus* in 56) apparently presided over the prosecution of Caelius *de vi* in this same year. A *praetor* for *maiestas*, C. Alfius Flavus, definitely presided in a trial under the *lex Licinia de sodaliciis* in 54. Another demand was jury service in a colleague's *quaestio*. Cn. Domitius Calvinus (*pr.* for *ambitus* in 56) and perhaps M. Aemilius Scaurus (who as *pr.* heard a case *de vi*) were jurors in the trial of P. Sestius *de vi* in the latter part of February and the first weeks of March that year. And I have argued that, while *praetor repetundarum*, M. Porcius Cato sat as a juror in an important *maiestas* trial of 54.

I might point out that the titulature of the magistrates who presided over the various *quaestiones* is vague and poorly attested. Only in the case of the extortion court does our evidence give us a notion of the official full name of the lot—in this case, apparently *ut de pecuniis repetundis quaereret*—and an indication that the *quaestio* gave rise to a title ("praetor repetundis" or "repetundarum").[148] It might not simply be chance that we hear nothing of a "praetor ambitus" or "praetor maiestatis" designated as such, even though the corresponding tasks came up consistently (so far as we can tell) in the praetorian sortition. It is always worth remembering that an individual *lex* created and governed each individual *quaestio* and also prescribed who might preside. In the Gracchan extortion law (9.2.2), we hear only of the "pr(aetor), quei ex h(ac) l(ege) quaeret" and the like; contrast the formulation of the Cornelian law (11.7.4): "praetor iudexve quaestionis, cui sorte obvenerit quaestio de sicariis." If the Romans in the laws that instituted each of the post-Gracchan *quaestiones* left the matter of presidency noncommittal (as Sulla did in his law), it is little wonder that the praetors who received these courts did not themselves make a strong identification with the names on their *sortes*. To press the hypothesis further: perhaps it is this very feature that in time made possible shared praetorian presidency of a given court within the span of a single year—presumably *ex S.C.*—despite its allotment in the sortition.

12.2.4 *Further Attributes of the* Quaestio *System*

Praetors might try to affect the outcome of a case tried before one of their praetorian colleagues. Cicero as *praetor repetundarum* 66 spoke in a *contio* about a case pending in the *peculatus* court. He also argued a case in the *quaestio de veneficiis* that year. Interference also took unofficial or even extralegal forms. Plutarch says that Cicero, when prosecuting Verres in 70 B.C., was worried about the "praetors" who favored the defendant—possibly those in the city as well as his successor Metellus in Sicily. As *pr.* 57, Ap. Claudius Pulcher used a variety of techniques (including slave gangs) to help stymie an attempted prosecution of his brother P. Clodius under the *lex Plautia de vi*, a case that potentially might have come before a praetor.[149] Praetors might try to sway the course of popular trials, too. The outstanding example is Q. Caecilius Metellus Celer, who as *pr.* 63 managed to terminate the (now archaic) *perduellio* procedure of C. Rabirius for the murder of Saturninus thirty-seven years earlier by raising a (vastly more archaic) flag of military emergency on the Janiculum.[150]

There is nothing particularly remarkable about Cicero's activities outside his court in 66. We have plenty of instances where acting magistrates appear as advocates in criminal trials, from censors and consuls down to tribunes.[151] Advocacy was just one avenue for infuencing what went on in the permanent courts. The tribunes could not save a defendant from having to plead his case.[152] But they intervened in a whole host of other ways.[153] Consuls involved themselves more rarely. The consuls of 65 aided in the protection of the *maiestas* court during one particular trial (11.7.3). Building partly on that precedent as well as on that of the extraordinary Bona Dea trial of 61, Pompey as *cos.* III 52 carried through a massive intervention in the judicial process *de ambitu* and *de vi*, introducing armed guards (11.9.3).

What does seem unusual is how the *cos.* Q. Caecilius Metellus Nepos used his *maius imperium* against the urban praetor (i.e., L. Caecilius Rufus) in December 57 B.C. Nepos' object was to forestall a trial of his half-brother Clodius *de vi*. Dio says the primary responsibility for alloting *iudices* to that court lay in the hands of quaestors. However, those of 57 had gone out of office on the legal day (4 Dec.), and none yet had been elected to take their place. The question of what to do with the *iudicia* came up for discussion at a session of the Senate convened (sometime between 10 and 16 Dec.) by P. Rutilius Lupus, a new tribune of 56 and supporter of Pompey. In response to a *relatio* by another (pro-Optimate) tribune L. Racilius, the consul *designatus* Cn. Lentulus Marcellinus had suggested that the praetor see to the task of assigning a jury himself. But the consul Nepos positively forbade Rufus—a strong supporter of Cicero and enemy of Clodius—to do so.[154] There are a number of times when we see a benign form of *maius imperium* at work in the city. Cicero himself is careful to detail the routine orders he gave as consul to various city praetors in the Catilinarian crisis of 63 (see 12.4.1). But this episode of 57 has no real parallel—except perhaps the confrontations of the consul M. Aemilius Scaurus and praetor P. Decius in 115, Mam. Lepidus and Cn. Orestes in 77, and M.' Acilius Glabrio versus L. Lucceius in 67.

A few sources, scattered throughout this period, indicate how praetorian activity in the sphere of criminal law might go beyond the standing *quaestiones*. Under the *Lex de provinciis praetoriis* of 101 B.C., it is a praetor who is to constitute the *iudicium* which hears infractions of that law.[155] We have already noted (12.1.2) that Verres as *praetor urbanus* had responsibility for holding a *iudicium publicum* in which an ex-tribune was condemned to a fine, and perhaps other criminal trials as well. As praetor in 58, C. Memmius seems to have supervised another type of *iudicium*, in which violations of the *lex Licinia Iunia* were prosecuted. Consider also Memmius' colleague L. Flavius, a staunch adherent of Pompey both as *tr. pl.* 60 and as praetor in 58.[156] Flavius' duties in the city in 58 apparently extended to summary criminal jurisdiction. Asconius[157] reports how a dagger allegedly fell from the cloak of Clodius' "slave" (also called "freedman") Damio on 11 August, and was brought to the *cos.* A. Gabinius as evidence of a plot against the life of Pompey. The next substantive item Asconius reports is that a week later Damio was unsuccessful in his appeal to the tribunes against Flavius. But he does not describe what the praetor had ruled.[158] In view of Damio's low social status, the praetor (on instructions from the consul) simply may have taken cognizance of the case and decided to hand the man over to the *IIIviri capitales* for execution. That the praetor's decision involved a severe penalty seems likely. Asconius' account implies that Damio in his appeal to the tribunes went so far as to wound one member of the college who proved unsympathetic, and who promptly vetoed any further action by his tribunician colleagues. That will have sealed Damio's fate.

There is another possible case of such praetorian activity in criminal law for 50 B.C. In that year, M. Livius Drusus Claudianus (ironically, as Caelius notes) presided over the court for violations of the *lex Scantinia*, a law penalizing acts of homosexuality involving freeborn males.[159] Broughton supplies identification and name, listing him (following Münzer) as "Praetor or Iudex." Alexander offers that "iudicium apud Drusum fieri" ("a trial is taking place before Drusus") "could refer to either a praetor or juror, probably the former."[160] Yet, pace Alexander, Caelius' wording surely excludes that Drusus was a juror.[161] In any case, one notes (assuming the identification by Broughton is correct) that M. Livius Drusus Claudianus— adopted in infancy by the *tr. pl.* 91 and himself father of Livia Drusilla—by the year 50 was several years beyond the requisite minimum age for the praetorship.[162]

12.3 Interrelationship of the City *Provinciae*

12.3.1 *The Source Problem*

It seems worthwhile to speculate on some of the ways praetors in Rome interacted with each other once there were more than two city *provinciae*. Yet, first, it is impor-

tant to outline the source problem. For only a handful of years following the institution of the *praetor repetundis* in 122 down to 81 B.C. can we posit more than one
praetor in Rome for the year: 115 (two praetors in unspecified *provinciae*, with possibly an urban praetor as well), 105 (urban and peregrine praetors), 104 (apparently
at least two),[163] 100 (just one named praetor, but evidently more than two in the city
in the run-up to the consular elections for 99),[164] and 94 (urban and peregrine
praetors, but the latter not for the entire year). In 88, Cicero implies that at least
three praetors—Q. Metellus Pius, Ap. Pulcher, and P. Gabinius—were in the city
at the time when Archias made his *professio* for citizenship under the *lex Plautia
Papiria*. That same year, an L. Cornelius Lentulus *praetor* presided (apparently)
over a panel of *iudices*; Q. Metellus Pius brought a suspicious item in the citizenship records to his notice.[165] We do not know when Archias approached the praetor Metellus, but it probably was early in the year (10.5.5). In 85 (probably), the
edict of the praetor M. Marius Gratidianus on the testing of coinage for forgery and
debasement is said to have anticipated a joint declaration of the tribunes and his
collegium praetorium on that matter.[166] But we do not know what time of the year
this was (it may have been early), or how many praetors were actually there.

   Our information does not improve all that substantially even for the period
after Sulla set up a system in which each year all eight praetors could potentially
remain in Rome. Despite the evidence of Cicero, for half the years 81–50 B.C. we
can positively place no more than two members of a given praetorian college in the
city.[167] The years for which we have fuller information (three or more city praetors
specified as such) are 74, 70, 67–65, 63–62, 59–56, and 54. Yet, even here, notices
on the precise *provinciae* are in short supply.

   For instance, in 74, when C. Verres was *praetor urbanus*, though we have the
names of three (perhaps four) of his colleagues, the only other *provincia* we can
account for is *repetundarum*—and even the arrangement of that is problematic
(11.7.1). In 70, we can identify three city praetors, and (probably) two of their *provinciae* (again, *urbana* and *repetundarum*); in 67, four or five city praetors but at most
just one *provincia* (the urban one). We have references to seven, perhaps all eight,
of the city praetors for the year 63, but the urban *provincia* is the only one to which
we can attach a name (L. Valerius Flaccus). There are four attested city praetors for
the year 58, but we know nothing about what *provinciae* they received. All eight of
the city praetors are definitely known for 57—the only year in the whole post-Sullan
period for which we have this information—but merely two of their *provinciae*,
urban and *repetundarum*. And of the three known city praetors of 56, one is known
to have had *ambitus*; another (M. Aemilius Scaurus) is found in the court *de vi*, but
whether that had come to him in the sortition is most uncertain.

   There are merely three years in the period 81–50 B.C. for which we know the
disposition of three or more of the city *provinciae*. For 66, we can account for five
of the six known praetors of the year, in the urban *provincia* and then *repetundarum*, *ambitus*, *maiestas* and *peculatus*. The evidence for this year shows particularly well how a praetor attached to a permanent *quaestio* might have a range of
duties (11.7.1, 12.2.4). Above, I have outlined some of the praetor Cicero's activities
that took him beyond his allotted *repetundae* court in that year. His colleague L.
Cassius Longinus had *maiestas* as his city province, but in addition to this *quaestio*

had responsibilities—or at least could plead responsibilities—in public grain matters (11.7.3). Four city praetors are attested for 65, and three *provinciae*—the urban
jurisdiction, and then *maiestas* and *peculatus*. There we are less well informed on
the interplay between *provinciae*, except that the praetor C. Attius Celsus took an
active interest in the plight of a defendant being tried in his colleague Q. Gallius'
maiestas court (11.7.3). Finally, five city praetors crop up in our sources for the year
54, three of them having as provinces *urbana, repetundarum*, and *maiestas*. There
it appears that the praetor for *maiestas* heard trials also under the *lex Licinia de
sodaliciis* (11.7.7). And the *praetor repetundarum*—M. Porcius Cato—is found far
beyond his *quaestio*. It seems he sat as a juror in the *maiestas* court (11.7.3) and also
heard civil law cases in the Forum (12.2.4). What is more, he joined forces with the
praetor P. Servilius Isauricus in opposing one of their colleagues, Ser. Sulpicius
Galba, over the question of the long-delayed triumph of the *pr.* 63 C. Pomptinus
(15.2.3). Cato even devised a scheme in which he became the holder of securities
from the tribunician candidates for good conduct in the elections for 53—though,
in that, he was perceived to be overstretching his authority.[168] In short, even what
little we do know of the various city *provinciae* shows that the system allowed for—
and sometimes positively demanded—considerable fluidity of roles. Precisely how
much fluidity is another question, to which we can now turn.

12.3.2 *Interrelationship of the Urban and Peregrine Praetors*

Given the limitations of our evidence, we only have enough information for some
broad hypotheses on how the city *provinciae* were supposed to relate to each other.
Our consideration of the data for the period 218–166 B.C. (5.6.2) showed that when
the city praetors acted together, if tasks were divided, this was done by consideration of location (*ratione loci*), not substance or subject matter (*ratione materiae*).
The peregrine praetor traditionally seems to have had few formal responsibilities in
the city and more de facto mobility than the urban praetor. This is why he occasionally received different sorts of tasks from the urban praetor.

The same administrative principle must have been at work when it came to
legal affairs. Now, the first epigraphic mention of the peregrine praetor, in the
Gracchan *Lex repetundarum*, is not particularly informative on his competency.
There the peregrine praetor only constitutes the first panel under the new law,
which may seem a natural choice for a legal procedure which chiefly affected (so
Cicero says) *peregrini*. All subsequent references, once the court is functioning, are
to the *praetor repetundis* presiding over it.[169]

Virtually every later piece of evidence we have on the legal activities of the
peregrine praetor, both before and after Sulla and then down into the reign of
Augustus, shows him dealing with matters involving Roman citizens. The men
offered the citizenship by the *lex Plautia Papiria* of 89 or 88 could profess before
any praetor,[170] and thus before the *praetor inter peregrinos*. M. Licinius Lucullus,
peregrine praetor in 76, accepted a civil suit against the young C. Antonius,
launched by Greeks; he also introduced a formula into his edict meant to curb the
violence of gangs in (Roman) Italy. The *Lex de Gallia Cisalpina* (generally dated

between 49 and 42) seems to have specified that the peregrine praetor have juris-diction over the Roman citizens of that region.[171] In the so-called "Lex Iulia municipalis," individuals—evidently from Rome as well as Heraclea—were to make *professiones* to the consul, or, in his absence, respectively the urban praetor, the peregrine praetor, or a tribune of the Plebs, as available.[172] We have two Augustan measures which gave the *praetor inter cives et peregrinos* jurisisdiction over water supply issues: one comes from the (citizen) colony of Venafrum in Campania, the other relates to Rome itself.[173] We also know that under the Augustan *lex Iulia de iudiciis privatis* the peregrine praetor was to hear cases under the *legis actio* procedure.[174]

Watson[175] lists most of the actual *leges* cited above (but not the *lex Plautia Papiria*), commenting (somewhat surprisingly), "no doubt they are all, to a greater or lesser extent, exceptional cases." In Watson's view, they tell us nothing about the ordinary jurisdiction of the two city praetors, "but they do show that the boundaries of jurisdiction were not absolutely fixed by the status of the parties." Watson holds that the peregrine praetor indeed "had a separate primary area of responsibility," based (so it seems) on subject matter: "the status of parties in the actions, whether citizens or not, is irrelevant." Indeed, for Watson "this matter of the exact jurisdiction exercised by the two praetors is . . . not of great importance for the history of legal development once the scope of their respective edicts is established." Watson argues that the edict of the peregrine praetor—its existence is confirmed for the late Republic[176]—contained "only the clauses which could not apply to citizens (and not those which could apply to peregrines and citizens alike)."

There is an obvious snag, namely Lucullus' "iudicium de hominibus armatis coactisve." Here Watson suggests that this clause must have been issued in the urban praetor's edict, with the initiative for its insertion coming from the peregrine praetor Lucullus. The same case is made for the *edictum de dolo* of C. Aquillius Gallus (11.7.2), which Watson (overconfidently) argues he must have introduced as *praetor de ambitu* in 66.[177] "Though the urban edict was the responsibility of the urban praetor . . . he could in normal times expect the active co-operation of the other praetors. . . . [T]heir part in framing the edict would be open and recognized."

Watson's general interpretation has had a certain amount of influence.[178] It is also unlikely to be right. To make his hypothesis work, Watson has to explain away the best piece of evidence we have on the historical development of the *edictum perpetuum*, M. Lucullus' *iudicium* of 76. I also do not see how the content of the praetors' edicts can be irrelevant to their actual legal activities. A full examination of the problem of the individual praetorian edicts takes us beyond the scope of this work. In the next section I will simply sketch a provisional (and quite general) alter-nate interpretation.

12.3.3 *How Many City Praetors Posted Annual Edicts?*

The peregrine praetor, like the urban praetor, was in origin primarily a military magistrate. During the last years of the First Punic War, the *praetor inter peregrinos* was responsible for the defense of Italy. Soon, he was sent as the chief Roman commander to the new *provincia* of Sicily; after 227, he used Rome as his base. The peregrine praetor was no different in conception than the urban praetor or the (later) provincial praetors. In sum, all praetors, including those in the overseas *provinciae*, could hear cases at law—evidently regardless of the citizen status of the litigants—using or (if necessary) adapting existing civil law procedures.[179] The provision of the *lex Plautia Papiria* that a *professio* for citizenship could be made before any praetor shows that just a few years before Sulla's reforms something of this "collegial" aspect of the praetorship remained. In the post-Sullan period, the case of the *pr. urb.* Cn. Aufidius Orestes in 77 implies that an individual might petition a series of city praetors in the hope of being granted such and such an action.

In all instances where a suit actually came to trial, the judgment of a praetor's court was final, unless another competent magistrate happened to use his *intercessio* to overturn a decision. For the later Republic, we do not have a single secure instance of a praetor in the city using his *imperium* in that way. When Cicero says the praetor Piso "*intercessit*" in Verres' civil law cases, he probably did nothing more than to accept the petitions his colleague had refused (12.1.2). Litigants who did not like a praetor's actual decision customarily appealed to a tribune of the Plebs, and sometimes to a consul. However, it always remained theoretically possible for an individual city praetor to have his legal actions vetoed by a praetorian colleague.[180]

We know the peregrine praetor had (at least at the end of the Republic) an edict separate from that of the urban praetor (it is explicitly mentioned in the *Lex de Gallia Cisalpina*); the edicts of provincial commanders are of course amply attested.[181] Did the praetors in charge of the standing *quaestiones* also post their own edicts? A passage of Dio on the *lex Cornelia* of 67 B.C. might be taken to imply it.[182] But if that were really the case, it would be most surprising if, in the atmosphere of the late Republic, praetors did not at times issue competitive *edicta perpetua* to make a political point or to further their own careers. (It surely follows that the praetor who issued an edict would hear cases under it.) Separate edicts are conceivable for two praetors, who could keep an eye (and if necessary, threaten a check) on each other's actions in the administration of law. But if there were more than two full edicts, anarchy would almost certainly result.

Now Watson, who advocates a model in which each of the praetors might contribute to a "collegial" edict issued by the *praetor urbanus*, argues that "when later praetors were allotted to particular *quaestiones perpetuae*, they would (apparently) have far less to do than either the urban praetor or peregrine praetor, and yet they too were of equal rank."[183] But on this point our sources are almost universally silent. We have seen how long a case *repetundarum* or *ambitus* could take. There were not many that could be squeezed into a year. The other praetors in charge of standing courts must be presumed to have been busy too, with cases we cannot expect to hear much about. We have seen that C. Aquillius Gallus (*pr. de ambitu* 66) probably devised his *iudicium de dolo* a decade before his praetorship, so that does not help. Our conclusion must be that if an individual allotted a *quaestio perpetua* invented (as *praetor designatus* or *praetor*) a formula which found its way into the *edictum perpetuum*, that was by and large incidental to his status as magistrate. He can just as well have composed a formula as a jurist (as Aquillius seems to have done).

And so we are left with the two edicts of the urban and peregrine praetors. Naturally, each of these praetors would have to post an *edictum perpetuum* announcing the principles according to which he would exercise his jurisdiction, and our evidence suggests that the peregrine praetor as well as the *praetor urbanus* did just that. In 67, the tribune C. Cornelius passed a law compelling praetors to follow their own edicts ("ut praetores ex edictis suis perpetuis ius dicerent") (12.1.3). The plurals are significant. The *lex Cornelia* must have applied to both relevant city praetors, perhaps as well as praetorian governors in the various *provinciae*. Note perhaps also Cicero's statement in his Cilician edict, that in matters where he has not made specific provision, he would base his decisions on the "edicta urbana."[184]

In the late Republic, each praetor had full power to introduce and adopt innovations as he saw fit: consider C. Verres, *pr. urb.* 74. Sometimes (unlike Verres) his edict might influence those of other magistrates. In 76, the peregrine praetor M. Licinius Lucullus picked up on the praetor Octavius' *actio* on *metus* (ca. 80), and issued his own edict on robbery with violence. Lucullus' measure was meant to apply to Roman citizens in Italy; like the *formula Octaviana*, it also carried a heavy fourfold penalty. Within seven years, Lucullus' *iudicium* had passed into the edict of the *praetor urbanus*.[185] For provincial governors, the edict which Q. Mucius Scaevola (*cos.* 95) used in Asia provided a standard for fairness (see 14.5.4). After his tenure, a *senatus consultum* set it as a model for governors who received that *provincia*. A Sicilian governor emulated it almost immediately in his *provincia* (13.1.4); some forty years later, Cicero drew many features from it in composing his own edict as *pro consule* for Cilicia in 51–50.[186]

We do not have enough information to understand the relationship of the different *edicta* to each other, but a few things seem reasonably certain. Gaius tells us that the fullest edicts were those of the "two praetors," the *praetor urbanus* and the peregrine praetor,[287] as we would expect. In the late Republic, these praetors must have been hearing the bulk—though apparently not all—of the cases in private law. The edict of the *praetor urbanus*—surely the most important, in view of his general primacy—may have served as a convenient model for that of the peregrine praetor. Their praetorian colleagues in the city presumably by custom used one of these edicts or the other in hearing civil law cases. However, one has to admit it is most difficult to see how any praetor could be forced to adopt a particular edict lock, stock, and barrel. Remember the resentment Asconius reports against the *lex Cornelia* of 67. And that law did not attempt to dictate the actual composition of the individual edicts (12.1.3).

In order to coordinate the administration of justice, the Senate may have suggested guidelines for the relevant city and overseas *provincia*, as we know it did for the province of Asia after Scaevola. But the examples of M. Lucullus and C. Verres show that each praetor was free to innovate in the composition of his edict—though admittedly both these examples come before the *lex Cornelia*. Cross-fertilization naturally arose between the edicts of the two city praetors, as well as between *edicta* promulgated in different *provinciae*.[188] We do not hear of the innovations of provincial governors making their way into the city edicts (though there is no reason to think that was impossible). In the Republic, the difficulty of imposing strong central controls meant that, at any given time, the edicts in each praetorian *provin-*

cia may have looked quite dissimilar (the Empire would be a different matter). Given these circumstances, we perhaps should not find it entirely surprising that in the Augustan age, the jurist M. Antistius Labeo could write at least thirty books on the legal aspects of the peregrine praetor.[189]

12.4 Nonlegal Tasks of the Various City Praetors

There are three basic areas that fall under this rubric where we have enough information for discussion: movements of praetors outside the city, and praetorian activity in the Senate and legislative assemblies. Our sources tell us almost nothing about what type of elections praetors presided over in this period,[190] so on that particular point discussion is fruitless beyond what we have noted in 5.4.7. In 5.5.2 and 12.1.1–3, I have assembled the most important notices relevant to the city praetors in the spheres of religion (including games) and setting public contracts. Observations on the unofficial activities of city praetors during their term of office are scattered throughout chapters 10–11 and the present chapter—a rich subject that deserves closer attention than what I can provide here.

12.4.1 *City Praetors in the Sphere* Militiae

We have just a few known instances where a city praetor is dispatched outside the city to undertake a certain administrative task, all apparently pre-Sullan: the *pr. urb.* C. Caninius Rebilus (date unknown, but probably before 81 B.C.), who went to Ostia to adjudge the status of a piece of land "de senatus sententia" (12.1.1); L. Cassius Longinus, *pr.* 111, sent by plebiscite to bring Jugurtha to Rome under safe conduct (10.6.2); and L. Gellius, charged "de senatus sententia" with roadbuilding in Apulia as peregrine praetor in 94 (12.2.1). Yet the basic capability of the praetor to function as a commander in the field can be seen throughout our period, largely irrespective of city *provincia*.

As praetor in (surely) 104, L. Licinius Lucullus—father of the *coss.* 74 and 73— had to leave the city to put down a well-organized slave revolt at Capua. Suppressing slaves was a traditional praetorian responsibility (5.3.1), though in 133 major revolts at Minturnae and Sinuessa led to two consulars receiving special commands (8.6.2). Diodorus says Lucullus was "one of the praetors in the city" (τῶν γὰρ κατὰ πόλιν στρατηγῶν . . . ἕνα). And so Broughton (following Münzer) makes him "*pr. urbanus* or *peregrinus*." We know that there was both an urban and peregrine praetor in the city in 105 (12.1.1, 12.2.1), so it is a good guess. But *praetor repetundis* is also possible (see 10.4.2). Even before this revolt, there had been stirrings at Nuceria and a significant rising (two hundred slaves) at Capua. But the Romans evidently stopped short of stationing a praetor in the south: with a Cimbric invasion looming, flexibility was needed.[191] Lucullus' success in the special task so impressed the Senate that for the next year it had him take up Sicily—now beset by an even more dangerous slave revolt—as a promagisterial *provincia*.

In 91, the Senate created a special command *pro consule* for one or more of the praetors to watch for dissident activity in Italy. The murder of one of these commanders at Asculum sparked Rome's gravest military crisis since the Second Punic

War. All regular *iudicia* were immediately suspended, and remained so for some time to come. Before the end of the year, several praetors or praetorian command-ers were in place in various trouble spots in Italy: certainly Cn. Pompeius Strabo in Picenum, probably L. Postumius at Nola, and perhaps L. Porcius Cato in Etruria. Whether any of these men had a city *provincia* in 91 is irrecoverable, but entirely possible. But then, despite the *iustitium*, no praetor that we can confidently assign to the year 90 shows up in the field. For the principal fighting in this year—and also the next—the Senate used the two consuls. They in turn had experienced ex-con-suls and ex-praetors serving under them as legates, at least some receiving special grants of *imperium*. Where were the praetors? Our one possible *pr.* 90—L. Calpurnius Piso Caesoninus—is said to have manufactured arms (10.5.2–3). In the absence of the consuls, praetors might also have looked to the defense of the city.[192]

The circumstances in which the *pr. urb.* 89 A. Sempronius Asellio met his death in the Forum (12.1.1) imply that some normal legal procedure had resumed by late January of that year. By then, the worst of the emergency had passed. Indeed, the contentious suits which Asellio allowed under his edict suggests that he meant to remain in the city for some time and was not expecting to see military action. Another sign of Rome's growing confidence—somewhat paradoxically—is that soon the Senate allowed praetors something other than ancillary tasks. By year's end, the praetors C. Cosconius and Cn. Papirius Carbo fought in the south-ern theater, in part to compensate for the death (not too far into 89) of the *cos.* L. Porcius Cato. In 88, that same area is where we find Q. Metellus Pius, and possibly Ap. Claudius Pulcher. Yet at least two of their colleagues (a Brutus and a Servilius) remained in or near the city somewhat into the year. When the Senate needed someone with sufficient *auctoritas* to forbid the consul Sulla from marching on Rome, those praetors were available for the commission (10.5.4–5).

Five years later, Sulla posed a much greater threat. In the civil warfare of 83 and (esp.) 82, most of the Marian praetors will have remained in Italy to resist this outlawed commander. The fact that in 82, the putative urban praetor L. Iunius Brutus Damasippus is found taking such a prominent role in the field, suggests that other holders of city *provinciae* under the Government had their own military responsibilities (10.5.6).

After Sulla increased the number of praetors to eight and provided the possi-bility that they all hold city *provinciae*, we might reasonably expect to see even more city praetors venturing outside Rome on special commissions. As it happens, the only instances attested all have to do with military commands, by and large prompted by acute emergencies. The year 78 may offer one such case (12.1.2). I have hypothesized that the peregrine praetor handed his jurisdiction to the *praetor urbanus* and then set out to restore order in Etruria. If so, the two consuls of 78 later superseded that (nameless) praetor in Etruria. Yet no actual praetors of 77 are known to have taken part in the fighting against Lepidus, or the mopping-up oper-ations that followed (11.8.5).

Nor did they come into the one other great military decision of that year. When each of the consuls of 77 refused to go to Spain to join the *pro cos.* Q. Metellus Pius in fighting Sertorius, the Senate turned not to a praetor, but to a *pri-vatus*—the equestrian *triumphator* Cn. Pompeius. Just recently, a praetorian commander had suffered a major defeat when he tried to cross from his *provincia* of Transalpine Gaul into Spain (13.4.2). That may be one reason why the Senate turned first to the experienced Pompey before looking for a suitable individual in the praetorian college of 77. Two years later, we find the Senate positively skipping over the city praetors when it needed to send someone to exploit efficiently the former royal estates in Cyrene (11.4). In 58, the *tr. pl.* P. Clodius had M. Porcius Cato appointed as *pro quaestore pro praetore* for a roughly analogous task involving Cyprus (11.8.4, 15.1.2).

But that is pushing us too far ahead in our story. Some way into the year 74 B.C., through the agency of the consul M. Aurelius Cotta, the praetor M. Antonius took up a special command to suppress piracy throughout the Mediterranean. Family background helps explain the choice of this particular praetor (11.3.1). One suspects that Cotta would have secured the pirate command for himself had he failed in his machinations to join his consular colleague L. Lucullus in fighting Mithridates.

In 73 and 72, a number of praetors in their year of office had to be sent to quell the slave revolt of Spartacus in Italy (11.8.6–7). Yet when the rebellion first came to the Senate's notice, it seems that it tried to spare the city praetors. The Claudius Glaber who first fought (and failed) against the slaves was perhaps a *praetorius* rather than a praetor in 73. The next Roman commander to take the field that year, P. Varinius, was definitely a praetor—indeed, he apparently received a grant of enhanced *imperium* for the commission. Varinius fought in coordination with a *privatus*, L. Cossinius, who himself quite likely had *imperium*. Despite Varinius' protracted troubles against Spartacus, there is no indication that the Senate sent one of his praetorian colleagues to help him out. Troops certainly seem to have been in short supply. Both Claudius Glaber and—notwithstanding the grand title "pro consule"—Varinius are said to have fought Spartacus with nothing more than tumultuary forces.[193] For the years 72 and 71, there is not a word in our sources on what the city praetors were up to in the emergency, but surely some must have had duties outside Rome. The Senate's unusual decision of 72 to privilege M. Crassus over two consuls suggests that he already had done something in the field against the slaves—if not as praetor, then as prorogued praetor—to merit its attention.

Details are sketchy, but it appears that in the early 60s, city praetors aided the consuls in protecting the shores of Italy against the pirates—none too successfully, as it turned out. Cicero tells how a (nameless) consul ineffectively manned a fleet at Ostia, while in the same or a different year a praetor (also anonymous) made poor use of his substantial naval force at Caieta. In an unknown year, but probably shortly before 67 B.C., the pirates managed to capture two praetors in office. So they had been freed (at least temporarily) of their routine duties in the city (11.8.8).

Under the *senatus consultum ultimum* against Catiline of late October 63 B.C., two city praetors (but no more) were to take the field: Q. Pompeius Rufus went to Capua and (with enhanced *imperium*) his colleague Q. Caecilius Metellus Celer to the *ager Gallicus* and *ager Picenus* (15.2.5). To secure Apulia and the area around Faesulae in Etruria, the Senate used not praetors but Q. Metellus Creticus (*cos.* 69) and Q. Marcius Rex (*cos.* 68), at that time both long waiting with *imperium* outside the walls of Rome for the Senate's vote of a triumph. The consul C. Antonius took up the chief command in Etruria, while his colleague Cicero took charge of the defense of Rome, where he is found issuing detailed orders to the remaining city praetors—except of course the conspirator P. Cornelius Lentulus Sura (on whom see 11.1.4)—to expedite resolution of the affair.[194]

In 62, the Senate again sent two city praetors into the field, this time to punish various allies—the Paeligni and Bruttii are named—who (it is alleged) discreetly had supported Catiline but had now come alive in revolt (11.8.9). Yet the next year, when the Senate saw the necessity for further police action (now in the area of Thurii), it decided to give the task *extra ordinem* to a *pr.* 61 who was in transit to his promagisterial province of Macedonia.

This survey certainly suggests that throughout the period 122–50 B.C., the Senate exercised considerable restraint in sending city praetors outside Rome, whether for administrative or military purposes. Our sources are massively deficient when it comes to reporting the activities of all praetors, especially those based in Rome. But it does seem noteworthy that a maximum of two city praetors are found operating outside Rome in any given year, and that in a few instances we can see the Senate applying alternative solutions so as not to use more. The relatively well-attested year 63 B.C. is particularly illuminating in this respect. Within two decades, we learn from Cicero of a legal restriction that limited the absence of at least the urban praetor from Rome to ten days, though dispensation could be granted.[195] The "laws" Cicero cites on that matter might have come into effect at the time of Sulla's reform,[196] or even earlier: the only known urban praetor to have been away that long in the period under discussion is L. Iunius Brutus Damasippus in the extraordinary year 82 B.C. Yet the way Cicero reports these "laws" leaves open the possibility that they (whatever their date of passage) applied to any city praetor. The main point of that legislation might have been to set limits on absences for personal reasons.[197]

As far as we can tell, in this period praetors or praetorian commanders only seldom are involved with a levy in Italy (earlier practice is explored in 5.5.1). In 72 B.C., M. Licinius Crassus was allowed to hold one after the Senate gave him the chief command against Spartacus. We know by chance that L. Licinius Murena, *pr. urb.* 65 and then *pro cos.* 64, conducted a levy in Umbria en route to his promagisterial province of Cisalpine Gaul. The *prr.* 63 Q. Pompeius Rufus and Q. Metellus Celer each had power to levy troops in the Catilinarian crisis.[198] Furthermore, Dio relates that the *cos.* 63 Cicero ordered the praetors to administer a special *sacramentum* in the city right after the attempt to free the conspirator (and *pr.* II 63) P. Cornelius Lentulus Sura.[199] If true, Cicero's primary aim surely was not to meet some practical necessity but to whip up popular feeling against the Catilinarians before the Senate was to decide their fate. In this period, the responsibility for levies in Italy regularly falls to consuls (or the equivalent), with their *legati* or quaestors usually doing the actual work.[200] Of course, notices of levies by praetorian commanders in the territorial *provinciae* are common. Sometimes these commanders are reported to have sent the troops they mustered elsewhere.[201] In the provinces, we find even a well-connected *privatus* pulling off an unofficial levy.[202]

12.4.2 *Praetors as Senate President*

There is every reason to suppose that the urban praetor had plenty of opportunity to preside over the Senate in the period between the tribunates of C. Gracchus and the dictatorship of Sulla. For many years we know that both consuls had *provinciae* that took them far from Rome.[203] In their absence, the *praetor urbanus* will have served as president of the Senate, just as he did in better attested earlier periods (5.4). Yet—as Mommsen noticed (1.5.1)—Sulla, by providing that the consuls remain in Rome during their actual magistracy, practically closed the door on praetorian presidency. True, in the years 81–50 B.C., sometimes both consuls had to proceed into the field to meet emergencies. That happened evidently in 78, and certainly in 72 (until the Senate chose to recall them). A few other consuls decided to leave early for their promagisterial *provinciae*, in November or (early) December of their year of office (possibly 74, and securely attested for 67, 63, 58, and 55). But the only year in which both consuls definitely are known to have taken that step is 58 B.C., when L. Calpurnius Piso and A. Gabinius departed respectively for Macedonia and Syria before 10 Dec..[204] Neither Sulla nor anyone else in the Republic directly touched the praetor's right to convene the Senate.[205] All the same, it is clear that the Sullan system severely reduced the likelihood that an urban praetor—much less a *praetor inter peregrinos*—might find himself as head of the Senate, especially for an extended period. Over time this new state of affairs must have eroded some of the prestige of the praetorship in general. Note that the consuls, together with the holders of the urban and peregrine jurisdictions, date the headings of *senatus consulta* of 105, 94, and (shortly after Sulla's dictatorship) 78 B.C. However, already by 73 B.C. the two senior praetors have dropped out of the dating formula, and do not reappear in that context in the Republic.[206]

Unfortunately, specific documentation of actual practice is egregiously lacking for this entire period. We do have three Senate meetings where neither a consul nor praetor presided. It seems that at some point in the year 123 B.C., perhaps one or both consuls, but certainly the urban praetor (followed by all other praetors then in the city), stepped aside to allow the tribune C. Gracchus to convene at least one session of the Senate. Plutarch says Gracchus introduced a *relatio* aimed at the prorogued praetor Q. Fabius Maximus (the future Allobrogicus) in Spain, who had exacted an excessive amount of grain from his province to send to Rome. Plutarch adds that the tribune's proposal—to sell the grain and reimburse the provincials—had the full support of the Senate. Yet apparently no consul or praetor wanted to take responsibility for the *senatus consultum* that overturned an action by this highborn praetorian commander (7.3.3). There is a further example of tribunician presidency for 91 B.C., but in much different circumstances. On 13 September of that year, the *tr. pl.* M. Livius Drusus convened the Senate to introduce a *relatio* censuring the consul L. Marcius Philippus. The consul obviously was not going to chair such a session himself; it is just possible Drusus even had him in jail at that time. It is perfectly conceivable that Philippus might have taken the step of forbidding any praetor from calling the Senate and accepting this hostile *relatio*, or other proposals by Drusus.[207] Finally, late in 57 B.C., a new *tribunus plebis* (i.e., of 56), P.

Rutilius Lupus, convened the Senate and launched an attack on the agrarian legislation of Caesar's consulship. At that session another new tribune, L. Racilius,
brought up the question of Clodius' trial *de vi*. We can suppose the consul Q.
Caecilius Metellus Nepos (Clodius' half-brother) was unwilling to preside at such
a meeting. He might also have ordered the urban praetor L. Caecilius Rufus—who
shared the political sympathies of these tribunes—not to act. For, immediately following this session, we find Nepos using his *maius imperium* against the praetor to
save Clodius from coming to trial (12.2.4).

Positive notices of praetorian presidency for the pre-Sullan era are skimpy. C.
Licinius Getha (*cos.* 116) presided at a Senate meeting discussing arrangements for
adding Phrygia to the Roman province of Asia, possibly as praetor ca. 120 B.C. A
quite fragmentary letter with *senatus consultum* records that a P. Sextilius *praetor*
gave a meeting of the Senate (apparently) to an embassy from Triccala in Thessaly;
he may be either pre- or post-Gracchan.[208] The one solid example we do have of a
praetor convening the Senate in this period is L. Iunius Brutus Damasippus in 82
B.C. Acting on the orders of the consul C. Marius, Damasippus—who was almost
certainly *praetor urbanus*—used the Senate meeting as a ruse to trap and slaughter
some prominent senators thought to be at odds with his political faction (10.5.6). It
is ironic that the savage L. Damasippus turns out to be the last praetor known to
convene the Senate down to the end of our period.

On occasion, praetors in office might speak during Senate sessions.[209] And
obviously, praetors might attempt to influence the Senate's policies in other, more
informal ways.[210] However, our sources offer few instances of praetorian *relationes*
under consular presidency in this or any period.[211] Livy contains only a few explicit examples, and after his account breaks off for us there is nothing until the mid-
60s B.C. The *pr. repetundarum* M. Tullius Cicero, in his *de lege Manilia* of 66,
expressed the hope that the consuls would bring before the Senate a measure allowing A. Gabinius—*tr. pl.* 67 and now under threat of prosecution—to serve as a *legatus* under Pompey in the east. "If they hesitate or are unwilling," predicts Cicero,
"I declare I shall introduce the proposal myself . . . nor shall I heed anything short
of a veto (*intercessio*)." Whether Cicero had to make good on his promise is
unknown.[212] Starting early in 58, the praetors C. Memmius and L. Domitius
Ahenobarbus made or threatened to make *relationes* calling into question the legal-
ity of Caesar's *acta* as consul.[213] In 54, the *pr. repetundarum* M. Porcius Cato persuaded the Senate to pass an (unpopular) *senatus consultum* that the magistrates
elect should submit accounts of election before a sworn court—even if they had
not been accused of *ambitus*.[214] And that is all we have in our record. In contrast,
for the years 67–50, we find about two dozen tribunician *relationes*.[215]

One notes that each of the attested praetorian *relationes* has to do with deeply
contentious political issues—which is precisely why our sources mention them.
Before Sulla placed the Senate under (in essence) year-round consular presidency,
in the absence of the consuls the various city praetors surely brought up for discussion all sorts of consequential legislation. And for the post-Sullan period, there must
have been many praetorian *relationes* on routine matters that have not come to our
attention. Despite the doubts of Willems, from time to time praetors will have
asked the Senate for advice regarding rules of private law or criminal procedure in

particular.[216] Yet it is not hard to see why in the later Republic consuls and tribunes proved to be more important than praetors for introducing political legislation in the Senate. A praetorian *relatio* came to a dead halt if one of the consuls chose to use his *imperium* or a tribune (with or without a consul's encouragement) interposed a veto. The praetor Cicero allows for those possibilities when announcing his plan to push for Gabinius' legateship. The ever present prospect of interference over time had a chilling effect on praetorian initiatives. According to Dio, at some point praetors lost their right to make a *relatio* under consular presidency, but pressured Augustus to restore that prerogative in 9 B.C.[217] The fact that we have a praetorian *relatio* as late as 54 B.C. suggests that such a prohibition (if one really existed) came only after our period.

12.4.3 *Praetorian Presidency of Legislative and* *Electoral* Comitia

When one looks at praetorian presidency of legislative *comitia*, some of the same general tendencies that impact praetorian *relationes* reemerge. Most significantly, consuls and tribunes at all times were more important than praetors for putting bills to a popular vote. Consuls had precedence over praetors as regards the *ius agendi cum populo*,[218] and it is natural that they not let praetors take the credit for important or politically useful acts of legislation. For a praetor to try to treat with the People independently was in practical terms quite difficult, since there was always the possibility that consuls, fellow praetors, or tribunes might choose to interfere.

A glance at the material collected in G. Rotondi's *Leges Publicae Populi Romanae* will show that no ready distinctions can be drawn between the substance of "consular," "praetorian," or "tribunician" laws.[219] However, consular laws—especially those proposed by both colleagues—had the most prestige. Sometimes, the Senate prompted the consuls to pass a law precisely to forestall more extreme tribunician legislation on the same matter.[220] If the Senate used the urban praetor or any of his colleagues in this manner, we do not hear of it. It does seem that praetorian laws became somewhat more common after Sulla. That of course is partly due to the quantity of our sources for the late Republic, but is probably also a consequence of the dictator's decision to allow the possibility of eight praetors in the city. And of course in both the pre- and post-Sullan eras there were doubtless a number of praetorian laws on routine matters that have not come to our attention.

Our first positive evidence for a praetor of any period successfully having the People pass a *rogatio* under his presidency comes just at the cusp of the first century B.C. W. Blümel's text of the Cnidus copy of the *Lex de provinciis praetoriis* shows that, as praetor, "on the (?)fifth day before the Feralia" (i.e., 17 Feb.), M. Porcius Cato passed a law that contained provisions circumscribing the conduct of a commander outside his *provincia*. The casual manner in which the Cnidus inscription gives the date of Cato's measure suggests that it came in the same year as the law itself, which is very likely 101 B.C. At least one of the consuls should still have been in the city at that time of the year. M. Cato's *provincia* is unknown. But the fact that this praetor is found in the city seeing to legislation in mid-February does not preclude the possibility that even within this same year he later set out to a territorial *provincia*.[221] Another instance of praetorian legislation is found a few years later. In (probably) 96 B.C., the *pr. urb.* C. Valerius Flaccus brought a bill "de senatus sententia" before the People to give Roman citizenship to one Calliphana, a priestess of Ceres from (federated) Velia.[222] And it may be that the L. Calpurnius Piso, who in 90 passed one law "ex senati consulto" to add two new tribes and another to grant citizenship to soldiers *virtutis causa*, did so as praetor.[223]

The evidence for the post-Sullan period is rather more plentiful. In the latter part of the year 70 B.C., the praetor L. Aurelius Cotta carried an important law on the status of *iudices* for both the standing *quaestiones* and civil cases. Henceforth, not just senators, as under Sulla's reforms, but also two other "ordines"—the *equites* (sc. *equo publico*) and "tribuni aerarii" (individuals who met the equestrian property qualification)—were to constitute the *album* of jurors, in equal proportions, 300 from each class.[224] The aim, as Cicero tells us, was to produce stricter criminal courts that were less liable to corruption.[225] The system of the *lex Aurelia* was to remain in force, with minor modifications, down to the end of our period.

Cotta—who was almost certainly not urban praetor that year (see 12.1.2)—promulgated his law after the first *actio* of the *Verrines*, though the People had not yet voted on it at the (fictional) time of *actio* II (i.e., October).[226] The measure is said to have had strong popular support. However, in the Senate itself many understandably were less keen: throughout the *Verrines* Cicero plays on fears that Cotta's law will be passed.[227] At one point in the speech Cicero says that the praetor was "daily" auspicating ("qui cotidie templum tenet"). At that point there obviously was no *senatus consultum*. So Cicero most likely means that Cotta was holding auspicated *contiones* on his bill.[228] It was not that he was trying to proceed to a legislative assembly without a *senatus consultum* and others were obnuntiating against him. As in the Senate, praetors needed the cooperation of both consuls and tribunes to get anything done. In time (says Plutarch), the consul Pompey "allowed" the measure to pass—he evidently did not want to attach his own name to it—and the tribunes declined to use their veto.[229]

A possible case from the early 60s involving L. Quinctius requires some discussion. A *novus homo*, he was *tr. pl.* in 74 and then cut a flamboyant figure in his praetorship.[230] Sallust reports that L. Lucullus tried to hold on to his great eastern command against Mithridates and Tigranes by bribing this praetor. But all the same, according to Plutarch, it was Quinctius who especially persuaded the people to send "successors" to Lucullus' *provincia* and also to relieve many of his troops from service. Plutarch does not say that Quinctius actually moved those bills: he simply may have spoken persuasively in their favor, as the praetor Cicero did for the *lex Manilia* on Pompey's command in 66. (Lucullus' bribe obviously was meant to make him do the opposite.) As for the date, Plutarch's account suggests that Quinctius was praetor either during or after the time of Lucullus' "failure of fortune" in fall 68.[231] Indeed, it may be that the bill which L. Quinctius backed so persuasively was the (tribunician) *lex Gabinia* of 67, which handed Bithynia and Pontus to the *cos.* M.' Acilius Glabrio. (Plutarch mentions neither that Gabinian law nor the consul Acilius in the *Lucullus*.) Broughton implies as much, but all the same wavers merely between making Quinctius *pr.* 69 or 68.[232] Lucullus definitely received the order to dismiss his troops in 67, and so I cautiously date also Quinctius' praetorship to that year—but give him no legislation.[233]

The *tr. pl.* 63 P. Servilius Rullus in his stillborn land bill had a provision that a praetor—the first (*primus*) or last (*postremus*) elected in that year's college—carry a *lex de imperio* in the Curiate Assembly for the ten members of the agrarian commission.[234] Instructions to the consul who was elected first—and thus would have priority of action on entering office—were standard.[235] And election to first place in a praetorian college was obviously an honor, just as last place was to be avoided.[236] Was Rullus' provision a clumsy adaptation of consular procedure? Cicero certainly regards this part of Rullus' law (like many others of the tribune's planks) as a perverse innovation. But his paraphrase of it is brief and very likely tendentious. So there is really no telling what Rullus was up to. Cicero in passing reveals that consuls were normally responsible for passing curiate laws, though (perhaps significantly) he does not attack the *lex agraria* for flouting order of precedence in the Curiate Assembly.[237] It is not out of the question that Rullus' provision on the passage of the curiate law did mention the consuls, and the praetors merely as a default. But it is conceivable that since the X*viri* were to have an extraordinary grant of *imperium*, the promulgator of the bill came up with an extraordinary procedure.

The next actual example of a praetorian *rogatio* comes in 62 B.C. Immediately upon entering office, the praetor (probably *urbanus*) C. Iulius Caesar tried to transfer the honor of rededicating the temple of Jupiter Optimus Maximus from Q. Catulus (*cos.* 78) to Pompey by popular vote. Caesar soon abandoned that attempt when he saw that the Optimates were ready to use force against him. But then he sought to help the *tr. pl.* Q. Metellus Nepos push through two other (tribunician) bills that favored Pompey. One was to allow Pompey to stand for election to the consulship *in absentia*, another to give him the chief command against the Catilinarians. That second bill included the detail that the *pro cos.* Pompey would be allowed to retain his *imperium* within the *pomerium*—which the *tr. pl.* M. Porcius Cato vehemently opposed. The measures led to vetoes from Metellus' tribunician colleagues and eventually a *senatus consultum ultimum* and (for a time) suspension of both tribune and praetor from office.[238]

After Caesar's city activities in 62 B.C., we find praetorian laws (actual or contemplated) mentioned with some regularity, indeed for four of the next six years. At the very start of 61, relates Cicero, there was talk that Pompey was going to press (sc. in the Senate) for the succession of C. Antonius (*cos.* 63) in his promagisterial *provincia* of Macedonia. At the same time, it appeared a praetor might put a motion before the People for Antonius' recall. Perhaps that bill was merely threatened (it certainly was never passed). The (anonymous) praetor's object will have been to dissuade the Senate from proroguing Antonius. At the time Cicero heard those rumors, the Senate had not made arrangements for the various territorial *provinciae*—nor would it until mid-March.[239] In 60, Q. Caecilius Metellus Nepos—now praetor—passed a law that abolished customs dues in Italian ports. Dio (our only detailed source) asserts that the measure was extremely popular, "but the senators were angry at the praetor who passed it . . . and wished to strike his name from the law to inscribe another in his place," to no avail.[240] Perhaps Metellus Nepos proposed the bill without a *senatus consultum*. Yet what seems more likely is that there was a *senatus consultum*, providing that a different magistrate (but surely a praetor) bring the law to a vote, and Nepos rushed to take the credit himself. One would think that the Senate's natural choice was P. Cornelius Lentulus Spinther, urban praetor in that year—and soon to be Nepos' colleague as *cos*. 57. In 59—a year in which we do not know who had the urban jurisdiction—it was a praetor who saw to the passage of a resolution that further refined the arrangements of the *lex Aurelia iudiciaria*. Q. Fufius Calenus passed a law aiming (surely) to stem judicial bribery, that each of the three classes who constituted the juries in the various *quaestiones* were to cast their votes separately.[241] In 57, a measure to restore Cicero from exile was promulgated by the *pr. urb*. L. Caecilius Rufus. In this, he had the support of six colleagues from his college;[242] Clodius' brother Ap. Claudius Pulcher was the odd praetor out. Indeed, Appius busied himself by holding some anti-Cicero *contiones*.[243] L. Rufus' measure—like some analogous tribunician bills regarding Cicero's return—never came to a formal vote. The seven praetors and eight tribunes who backed Cicero subsumed their proposals in a major consular resolution, which the *cos*. P. Cornelius Lentulus Spinther brought before the Centuriate Assembly on 4 August of that year.[244]

Our last recorded instance of praetorian legislation for this period comes in October of the year 54 B.C. The praetor Ser. Sulpicius Galba (almost certainly not urban praetor) secretly—and quite illegally—presided in a predawn vote that allowed his old commander C. Pomptinus (*pr*. 63 and then *pro cos*. in Transalpine Gaul) to have *imperium* in the city to triumph, after years of waiting outside the *pomerium* (15.2.3).

Our survey has not yielded much that is surprising. The *lex Porcia* of (apparently) February 101 B.C. and then all the post-Sullan praetorian measures discussed above show that a praetor can propose a law while one or both consuls are in the city. That the urban praetor continued to have precedence among praetors in bringing a *rogatio* before the People throughout this entire period is suggested especially by the case of C. Valerius Flaccus in (probably) 96 and L. Caecilius Rufus in 57. The number of praetorian *rogationes* moved by individuals who were certainly or almost certainly not in the urban jurisdiction is small: L. Aurelius Cotta in 70, and then the irregular cases of Q. Caecilius Metellus Nepos in 60 (who is said to have stolen the honor of passing a popular law from someone else) and Ser. Galba in 54. But that a praetorian legislator might hold any of the *provinciae* is clear. The Rullan law of 63 B.C. even wanted to choose a praetorian *rogator* for the Curiate Assembly on the basis of electoral order.

What is interesting is that at least a few of the praetorian bills come off not so much as serious legislation, but rather as statements of personal political attitude: C. Iulius Caesar's proposal regarding the Capitoline temple in 62 B.C. and the anonymous praetor who threatened to strip C. Antonius of his command in 61. Both these praetors moved into action immediately upon entering office; Caesar appears to have held a *contio* on the matter, which was no doubt at all times a common form of political expression for the city praetors, regardless of *provincia*.[245] One also notes that some praetors (L. Quinctius in presumably 67, M. Tullius Cicero in 66, C. Iulius Caesar in 62) chose to put their main energy behind pending tribunician bills, probably because they had a greater chance of success. But by the year 57, it appears that a praetor was capable of obnuntiating against a tribune at a plebeian legislative assembly. Such a report, if the magistrate chose not just to "watch the sky" (as this one did) but to announce an adverse omen in person to the tribune who presided over the *concilium plebis*, will have been binding. So, by the late Republic, praetors apparently had acquired at least in theory some degree of negative power over the main source of the state's legislation. Cicero describes this kind of obnuntiation as a major step; one wonders how often it was employed.[246]

It is useful to keep all this in mind when reading the *Pro Milone*. Cicero devotes a fair bit of this speech to a hypothetical scenario in which P. Clodius Pulcher survives to kill the consular candidate Milo and then himself wins the praetorship for 52, with his political allies gaining the consulship. Clodius' main weapon, says Cicero, would have been an ambitious legislative program, which the Senate would be powerless to stop. Details are sparse, except for an alleged law (found among those "already engraved at his home") by which Clodius "would have made us over to our slaves"—indeed "made our slaves his own freedmen"— and thus destroyed the *res publica*. Asconius rightly understands "slaves" as *libertini* and takes Cicero to mean that Clodius intended to revive the common proposal to distribute freedmen in all thirty-five of the tribes. Cicero's implication, of course, is that once Clodius had in one stroke made himself the *patronus* of Rome's freedmen and packed the *comitia tributa* with his new clients, he was in a position to pass the (unspecified) legislation he wished. That is all we get in the *Pro Milone*, except Cicero adds that Sex. Cloelius, freedman of the deceased praetorian candidate, had saved the portfolio of supposed bills and had aimed to hand them over to a compliant tribune for enactment.[247] That last item shows what we have already observed, that there was nothing particularly distinctive about the content of praetorian laws in themselves. In truth, Cicero's economy of detail and strained hyperbole in describing Clodius' hypothetical praetorship in the *Pro Milone* demonstrates, if anything, how little real positive power praetors had in the area of legislation.[248]

Sicily, Sardinia, and the Spains, 122–50

13.1 Pre-Sullan Sicily and Sardinia

13.1.1 Sardinia down to the Time of Sulla

The picture of Sardinia for these years is reasonably clear: prolonged fighting which was serious enough to prompt some consular commands, and little concern on the part of the Senate for regular succession in the province. We have seen (9.3.3) that the *cos.* 126 L. Aurelius Orestes enjoyed—if that is the word—almost five years of *imperium* in this pestilent *provincia*, celebrating a triumph on 8 December 122. The next known commander for Sardinia, M. Caecilius Metellus (*cos.* 115), stayed almost as long, for he triumphed on 15 July 111. His brother C. Metellus Caprarius (*cos.* 113 for Macedonia, and succeeded by a *cos.* 112) apparently spent a good part of 112 and the first half of 111 outside Rome, waiting for Marcus so that they could triumph together. In the event, that is what they did—both entering the city on 15 July—though Eutropius detracts something from the glory of the occasion by noting that the news of the Cimbric invasion of Italy also arrived that day.[1]

We cannot tell when the Epicurean T. Albucius, the next known holder of Sardinia, drew the *provincia* in the praetorian sortition or how long he stayed. But his command is certain to have lasted more than one year, for Cicero says Albucius as *pro praetore* successfully fought with the aid of one auxiliary cohort against "petty bandits clad in skins."[2] On this basis, relates Cicero, Albucius asked the Senate for a *supplicatio*. To make this request, Albucius must have been acclaimed as "imperator." He surely hoped also for a triumph to follow, as it had for his predecessors the consuls L. Orestes and M. Metellus. Yet Albucius did not gain his request, and not just because his achievements were so slim. Cicero is explicit that Albucius had offended the Senate by staging—even before his petition for the *supplicatio*—his own triumphlike celebration in Sardinia.[3]

On his return, Albucius was brought to trial (probably in 105) and, despite having some support from Sardinian witnesses, was convicted, which led to an exile in

Athens. A member of his own staff (the quaestor Cn. Pompeius Strabo) had even sought to prosecute him, but was rejected in the *divinatio* for that trial. In the event it was C. Iulius Caesar Vopiscus who spoke, we are told, "pro Sardis": the charge was apparently *repetundae*. Perhaps Albucius plundered the Sardinians specifically to meet the cost of his celebrations.[4] One wonders whether he would have faced trial and condemnation if he had just plundered and not so provocatively celebrated in his province.

We would expect that later commanders for Sardinia—and other provinces—will have been careful in how they commemorated their victories as a result of Albucius' experience. As it happens, though we hear plenty about camp celebrations and the like, no commander seems to have staged a comparable "provincial triumph" after this time.[5] But Albucius may not have closed the door on praetorian triumphs from Sardinia. That emerges from the case of P. Servilius Vatia (the future *cos.* 79 "Isauricus"), who triumphed *pro praetore* from an unknown *provincia* on 21 October 88.[6] Sardinia seems quite likely to have been his *provincia*, by process of elimination. Badian suggests as the date of Servilius' praetorship a year perhaps as early as 92 or even 93, and so upwards of four years in Sardinia. That type of repeated prorogation would be not at all unusual for this low-ranking *provincia*, and might be positively expected in the pressured years of the Social War.[7]

13.1.2 *Sicily 122–105*

"From this province many have been condemned who were praetors there: two alone have been acquitted." So Cicero claims of Sicily in his *Verrines* of 70 B.C.[8] Unfortunately, from the pre-Sullan period there is not much evidence on those trials, nor on the commanders who held the *provincia* except for the period of the Second Slave War (ca. 104–99). We have precisely three possible items having to do with the praetors who governed Sicily in the years 122–105. C. Porcius Cato (the future *cos.* 114) as praetor had his baggage retained by the people of Messana. C. Cato must have harmed the town in some way; perhaps he stole something that the Mamertines hoped to find and recover. But we do not hear of prosecution in Rome for his acts in Sicily. M. Papirius Carbo—brother of the *coss.* 120 and 113—was less lucky. He was condemned for (apparently) *repetundae* or *peculatus* after service in Sicily. This Carbo was likely—but not certain—to have been praetor; if so, probably sometime ca. 114.[9] And when Sicily served as a staging area for the war against Jugurtha in 111 and (no doubt) subsequent years, praetors for Sicily must have played a part. But firm details are virtually lacking.[10]

13.1.3 *The Second Sicilian Slave War*

The Second Slave War—which was to involve freedmen as well as slaves—broke out in Sicily when the Romans had scarcely vanquished Jugurtha and were scrambling to meet the threat from the Cimbri in the north. As it happened, the Senate had no legions to send to Sicily—or elsewhere, save for the Gallic front.[11] There was a shortage of capable generals, too: three separate praetorian commanders had to fight and fail against the slaves before the Senate could manage to declare Sicily a consular *provincia* for 101.

The first of those praetorian commanders was P. Licinius Nerva, *praetor* or *pro praetore* for Sicily in what must be 104. Diodorus seems our best source on the background to the rebellion.[12] According to this author, a general *senatus consultum* had charged governors in the provinces to investigate cases of wrongful enslavement of citizens from allied states. Nerva set up a tribunal at Syracuse to hear claims, but pressure from local elites made him abandon his project. (Dio tells a different story, in which Nerva initiated and then aborted an investigation into cruelty by masters against their slaves.) In Diodorus' account, the slaves who approached or had hoped to approach the praetor at Syracuse gathered at the sanctuary of the Palici (near Menaeum in the interior, famous as a spot for oath-taking) and decided on revolt. Here one remembers the divine authority that Demeter of Henna provided for the rebel slaves of the 130s (6.3.1); the Palici were to fulfill a corresponding purpose for the slaves in the course of this later war.[13]

The Romans evidently had taken some standing precautions as a result of their experience in the First Slave War. By chance we hear that Henna had a garrison of six hundred troops at the start of the conflict; other potential trouble spots may have been similarly provisioned. At any rate, Nerva had enough wherewithal to score an initial success against the slaves. But before long he managed to lose "most of his soldiers," even previous to a major defeat before Morgantina at the hands of the slave leader Salvius. When western Sicily saw a separate slave revolt under a certain Athenion, Diodorus relates that the urban population of Sicily found itself confined behind its city walls—themselves none too secure, thanks to dangers from slaves within—and the Roman system of justice in the province ground to a halt. Soon Salvius—who was now calling himself "Tryphon"—obtained the cooperation of Athenion and his forces. Salvius even started building (surely in winter 104/103) a palace with forum at Triocala (probably near Agrigentum), forging for himself an identity that combined the trappings of a Hellenistic king with those of a Roman holder of *imperium*—lictors included.[14]

The ineffective Nerva found himself superseded in 103. His successor was L. Licinius Lucullus, a city praetor of the previous year who had been effective in quashing a slave revolt at Capua (12.4.1). Lucullus arrived in Sicily with a force of (apparently) sixteen thousand men, mostly Roman and Italians, with a sprinkling of foreign *auxilia*. He scored a major success against the slaves before the town of Scirthaea, reportedly killing half of the rebel force of forty thousand (but not their two leaders) and deeply denting their morale. But Lucullus failed in his attempt to capture the palace complex at Triocala.[15]

We do not know precisely what prompted the Senate to create this *ex praetura* command for Sicily, since the arrangements for none of the other standing territorial *provinciae* for 103 are known. It does seem as if the Senate was unwilling to entrust the war to one of the new praetors of the year, and so it chose a modestly experienced commander to take up Sicily *extra sortem*[16] instead. This was in essence a compromise that spared Marius' consular colleague L. Aurelius Orestes from having to serve in this theater during the Cimbric emergency. (As it happens, Orestes was to die in office before the elections for 102.)[17]

Lucullus' command against the Sicilian slaves lasted only this single year. Lucullus' failure to take Triocola apparently surprised the Senate: we are told that it gave rise to suspicions of incompetence or bribery. (Florus asserts he even had his camp captured by the slaves.) There was also a perception, says Diodorus, that Lucullus was trying to expand the war. What is certain is that Lucullus was hoping to be prorogued for 102 so as to get full credit for actually finishing the fighting. When he learned that a C. Servilius—evidently a mere praetor of 102—was cross-ing the strait to supersede him, Lucullus disbanded his army and burned his own camp and military equipment. The object was specifically to deprive Servilius of the resources needed for quashing the rebellion.[18] The spiteful ploy had its effect. Though Salvius "Tryphon" died in the year 102, Athenion succeeded to his com-mand and started storming cities in Sicily and inflicting actual defeats on the Romans. The slaves also captured the praetor Servilius' camp. The upshot was that Servilius achieved nothing and the Senate—apparently buoyed by Marius' victory over the Cimbri at Aquae Sextiae that year—finally took the step of declaring Sicily consular, for M.' Aquillius in 101.[19]

Aquillius found the state of agriculture in this grain-producing *provincia* in such bad shape that he had to lend grain to the various Sicilian cities. But in his first year of fighting, Aquillius scored a major victory in which he killed Athenion. Like Perperna at Henna in 132 (6.3.1), he also used a food shortage to advantage by starving out what pockets of rebel slaves remained. There were still major battles in 100, but Sicily was calm enough for veteran settlements to be conceivable for the island. Aquillius returned to Rome in 99 to celebrate an *ovatio* (perhaps after being turned down for a full triumph).[20] He would be the last consular commander to hold Sicily as a *provincia* in the period down to 49 B.C.

The Second Slave War gave Rome a nasty scare at a time when it was trying to contain an even more dangerous enemy on Italy's northern front. As it happens, the three commanders who followed P. Licinius Nerva in Sicily were all prosecuted, and the two praetors among them were found guilty. (Here at last is some light on Cicero's assertion that by 70, "many" Sicilian praetors had been condemned.) Trials in which a series of commanders from one *provincia* faced prosecution were very much a phenomenon of this general era.[21] But this series marks somewhat of a departure, since each of the Sicilian generals was tried in a permanent *quaestio*. This convenient way to attack military commanders evidently had come into its own.

L. Lucullus, after his return, was successfully prosecuted for (apparently) *repetundae* by another Servilius, a relative of his successor who held an augurate. At that trial, even Lucullus' brother-in-law Q. Caecilius Metellus Numidicus (*cos.* 109, *ces.* 102) refused to speak on his behalf. But Numidicus' stated reason was not Lucullus' conduct in the war or on supersession, but his avoidance of a *iudicium* at some previous time (10.4.2). Diodorus does, however, suggest that the failure at Triocala was what helped secure Lucullus' condemnation and exile.[22] There was clearly general dissatisfaction with the conduct of the war, for next the praetor C. Servilius himself was tried and condemned after his own supersession. One of his own quaestors even tried to prosecute him, but was rejected in the *divinatio*.[23] The charge is unknown, but we may guess it was *repetundae*.[24] And finally, in the year

97, Aquillius—though he had ended the rebellion—only narrowly escaped condemnation and exile on a technical charge of *repetundae*. Cicero tells us that the prosecutor, L. Fufius, was careful in preparing his case, implying that he brought it on behalf of the Sicilian provincials; Aquillius owed his acquittal to an emotional defense and the jurors' respect for his war record. Aquillius' trial saw a grab bag of accusations, including many allegations of *avaritia*.[25] One suspects that that particular charge—which quite likely arose at least partly from his loan of grain to the Sicilian cities—probably had some factual basis, to judge from his subsequent behavior as a *legatus* in Asia at the end of this decade.

13.1.4 *Sicily between the Slave War and Sulla*

Conditions after the war remained outwardly stable for some time, thanks especially, so it appears, to the Sicilian praetors' harsh enforcement of edictal provisions banning slaves from carrying weapons. That emerges especially from an anecdote widely told of the praetor L. Domitius Ahenobarbus (the future *cos.* 94), who crucified a shepherd merely for spearing a great boar.[26] That praetor and his immediate successors may have been just as severe in their other dealings with the Sicilians. One notes that in 95, when the citizens of Halaesa sought to resolve a controversy on how to choose their senators, they turned not to the Sicilian commander who was on the spot—as we might expect—but directly to the Roman Senate. In the event, it was the *pr. repetundis* C. Claudius Pulcher with a *consilium* of members of the Claudii Marcelli (patrons of Sicily since the Second Punic War) who saw to the matter and gave them new regulations.[27]

By the mid-90s when the *provincia* fell to the praetor L. Sempronius Asellio, it is said by Diodorus to have been "ruined."[28] But Asellio ambitiously tried to do for Sicily what Q. Mucius Scaevola had done for the province of Asia (14.5.4), with some success. He chose as the chief members of his *consilium* his friend (and *legatus*) C. Longus as well as a Syracusan *eques* "Publius"—the latter man no doubt to serve as an expert on local conditions—and then ostentatiously arranged for these men to stay near him in neighboring houses as he worked out his provincial edict.

Normal practice seems to have been for a governor to arrive in his *provincia* with his edict already prepared,[29] perhaps because one relied on the urban edicts as a model.[30] The really important innovation of Scaevola may have been that he was the first to draft his edict with the specific needs of *provincia* in mind. Asellio obviously was trying to do the same. Of his specific measures Diodorus tells us little, except that he "banished sycophancy from the forum" and, breaking with precedent, appointed himself the tutor of children and women who needed a guardian. (What were they supposed to do when he left?) He also conducted his own investigations, which Diodorus says was unusual. It may well have been: Cicero, when commander in Cilicia, could readily urge another governor to investigate various problems in person, but did not see the need to do it himself.[31] Cn. Domitius Ahenobarbus and L. Sempronius Asellio are the only praetors of the 90s specifically attested for Sicily before the period of the Social War. Neither can be firmly dated, and we are in the dark how long each had to stay in the *provincia* before finding a successor. However, in the years of the Social and Civil Wars we can be reasonably sure that Sicily had no more than two or three commanders. Only two are known: C. Norbanus (the future *cos.* 83) and M. Perperna.

Cicero says that C. Norbanus (who apparently held the quaestorship in 101) was praetor in Sicily "when all Italy was ablaze with the war of the allies," and so certainly by 90 and perhaps even already a year or two earlier. One of his duties evidently was to feed and outfit the Roman armies that were fighting the Italians as well as to supply Rome itself with grain. Norbanus seems to have been effective in this chore, as well as in the crucial task of preventing another slave uprising on the island. (Cicero strongly implies that there was a danger.) There were other challenges too. In the year 88—interestingly enough, in view of his future career— Norbanus or at least his western quaestor took aggressive measures to keep Marius and Marians off the island. And in 87, Diodorus reports a detachment of Italian rebel forces invested Rhegium, with an eye toward crossing the strait and taking control of the rich island province; Norbanus had to cross to Italy to forestall the attempt and rescue the people of Rhegium. To judge from what was happening in other *provinciae*, it is conceivable Norbanus had to stay put in Sicily for a few years beyond 87. One possible opportunity for his return was when the *coss.* 85 Cinna and Carbo recalled ships from Sicily to guard the coast of Italy against Sulla's impending invasion.[32] But Norbanus' own consulship of 83 provides the only secure *terminus*.

M. Perperna Veiento is quite likely to have directly succeeded C. Norbanus in Sicily in, say, 85 or 84. The Marian government clearly had handpicked this commander, the grandson of a hero of the First Slave War. He receives positive attestation first for 82, when we are told Sulla tried to win him over from the Marian side; Perperna in turn threatened that he would cross out of his *provincia* to rescue the younger Marius at Praeneste.[33] It is just possible, however, that a different man succeeded Norbanus and Perperna succeeded him, taking up the command only for 82. The example of Sardinia shows that even in the crisis of that year the Marian government might send praetors out to govern overseas *provinciae*: it was apparently as *pr.* 82 that Q. Antonius Balbus (the only commander attested for that *provincia* in this era) was driven from the island by Sulla's *legatus* L. Marcius Philippus (the former *cos.* 91) and killed.[34]

Perperna apparently gave little thought to the routine administration of Sicily. His rule is described as harsh, though he seems to have treated Messana and Thermae well (both towns remained pro-Marian even after Perperna's departure from the island). His chief concern was keeping a firm grip on Sicily for his faction and providing a safe haven there for Marians such as Cn. Papirius Carbo (*cos.* III 82) once they had fled Italy in defeat. Naturally, Sulla after his victory at the Colline Gate in late 82 made Perperna one of his principal targets. After posting his proscription list, he commissioned Pompey to fight him *cum imperio* "with a large force." For all his previous bluster, Perperna quickly abandoned the *provincia*. (He would resurface again only in 77, as a Lepidan and then Sertorian [13.4.3].) So Pompey was able to take Sicily—and with it, Carbo and his fleet—without actual fighting.[35]

At this point, "Sicily had been without law courts for a long time."[36] Indeed, the nature of Pompey's reported activities in the *provincia* make it clear that

Perperna (perhaps also Norbanus) had culpably deferred a good deal of basic administration. The result was that the young Pompey had to act as de facto praetor for the island. Diodorus reports that the Sicilians gave high marks to Pompey for his settlement of public disputes and matters of private contract. Cicero cites Pompey in a list of Sicilian governors who fairly obtained a high price in the auction of grain tithes. Plutarch praises Pompey's kind treatment of the Sicilian cities as well as the discipline of his soldiers and staff, whom he effectively kept from plundering on their journeys—but also reports how Pompey dispensed with legal fine points at the independent-minded federated city of Messana. Confirmation of Pompey's high reputation in the *provincia* comes years later, in 71 B.C.: when the Sicilians wanted to complain in Rome of the governor Verres, they decided to send envoys to their old patrons the Claudii Marcelli then Pompey (at the time *cos. des.*), "and other *necessarii* of the province."

The punishment of the Marians and their supporters had to be Pompey's principal concern. We hear of summary executions of Sulla's Roman political enemies. But Pompey had the consul Carbo brought before his tribunal, and gave the order for his death in a quasi-legal setting.[38] There were criminal trials of individual Sicilians, too. Plutarch tells us that Sthenius of Thermae managed to deflect Pompey from punishing his town by taking personal responsibility for its past political attitude. By chance, Cicero reports that Sthenius stood trial before Pompey on grounds of treason, but was acquitted.[39] There must have been other trials of this sort that we do not hear about. It was while he was in the midst of such activities that Pompey received a letter from Sulla (now dictator) and a *senatus consultum* ordering him to proceed to Africa against the Marian refugee Cn. Domitius. Pompey left his sister's husband (C.) Memmius as ἄρχων of Sicily—he will not have been able to delegate him *imperium*—and sailed at once to Utica.[40] Now, Sardinia at this time (late 82 or early 81) will also have been held by a legate, albeit one of consular status (i.e., L. Marcius Philippus). These *provinciae* must have been genuinely settled so as not to need proper commanders. Yet the danger to Sicily from its slaves in this disturbed era remained very real, as can be seen from the attempts by fugitives to cross over from Italy to Sicily to raise revolt in 87 and then again in 72.[41]

13.2 Sicily and Sardinia in the Post-Sullan Period

13.2.1 *Cicero's* Verrines *as a Source*

The principal and in many cases sole source for the Sicilian praetors of the decade 80–70 is Cicero's *Verrines*. This speech offers a satisfying amount of information on most individual governors of this era, and a mine of detail on C. Verres (*pr.* 74, promagistrate 73–71) and to a lesser extent L. Caecilius Metellus (*pr.* 71, promagistrate 70). Yet one must of course always be alert to Cicero's rhetorical purpose in his depiction of each of these governors. Cicero's object, simply put, was to secure Verres' condemnation; he introduces other praetors of this period mainly to offer parallels and contrasts to Verres' administration. Against Verres himself, Cicero's arguments seem overwhelming in their cumulative effect.

But there are some visible weaknesses. Much of the case is circumstantial, as Cicero admits both explicitly and implicitly. For instance, a tremendous amount hinges on Verres' relationship to his subordinates. Verres, in his defense, evidently sought to establish that if there was any wrongdoing, it was the fault of his underlings, and that he could not be held responsible for their actions. Cicero clearly considers this a miserable defense for a praetor. In the *Verrines*, Cicero seeks to prove that Verres fully knew what his subordinates were up to—even minor functionaries connected with the collection of grain[42]—and had vicarious responsibility for all the staff under his command. It was a recognized principle (indeed, by 100 B.C., a law) that a commander was liable for the public actions of his *comites*.[43] That must be one reason why in the *Verrines* Cicero is so eager to show that a wide assortment of knaves were members of Verres' official entourage, and as such his judicial *consilia*.[44]

There is much more. Throughout the speech, Cicero tries to prove that any rascals found in the field during Verres' government were working as the praetor's "go-betweens." And any legal proceedings those underlings faced are prejudicial, Cicero argues, to Verres' own case. Moreover, Verres' innovations, whether in the provincial edict or in general administration, are deemed suspicious in themselves. So are judicial reversals, whether of a predecessor or subordinate. The composition of his judicial *consilia* offers another glimpse into his character. His (or his underlings') failure to keep or preserve records is a sign of corruption. That Verres created personal enemies in the province is still another indication of criminality. The result of all this is that at many points Cicero's portrait of the praetor appoaches caricature. There is just one grudging positive admission that not all of Sicily's grievances in this period were a result of Verres' presence.[45]

13.2.2 *Commanders in Sicily down to Verres*

The first praetorian commander for Sicily under Sulla's new government was M. Aemilius Lepidus, the future *cos.* 78 (who caused so much trouble for Rome in that year and in 77). Lepidus had his own old family ties to the *provincia*: two M. Aemilii Lepidi—father and son—were praetors for Sicily in 218 and 191 respectively. As *cos.* 78, this M. Aemilius Lepidus must have been praetor by 81. There is no record of activities in a city praetorian *provincia* for this man. But the fact that his command is Sicily is said to have lasted only one year before C. Marcellus (surely *pr.* 80) came to succeed him[46] suggests that Lepidus was *pr.* 81 and held Sicily *ex praetura* in 80, as we would expect under the Sullan system. That meant Pompey's delegatee Memmius spent all of 81 (and probably a bit of 80) in the *provincia*.

Lepidus is said by Cicero to have been a harsh governor, though he did not exploit the province as much as he might have.[47] On his return (i.e., in 79) he was brought to trial by two Caecilii Metelli, Nepos and Celer (future *coss.* 60 and 57), but the case was dropped after some initial proceedings: the personal standing (*gratia*) of Aemilius among the People is said to have been too strong.[48] By the time of the *Verrines*, Lepidus' status as a villain—and a dead one at that—allowed Cicero to sketch as dark a picture as he wanted about his tenure as praetor in Sicily. Despite his "ruinous" command, we see that M. Lepidus had enough popular support to escape prosecution, and he was elected consul for 78. At the least, as a praetorian governor he must have been effective in getting grain to Rome.

Cicero specifically says C. Marcellus was *pro consule* in Sicily, succeeding *ex praetura* M. Aemilius Lepidus for 79 (and very probably 78).[49] It is a wonderful instance of the "sors opportuna" that a member of the Claudii Marcelli—the most established Roman patrons of Sicily—gets the *provincia* precisely for this year, since the province is said to have needed "reviving" after Lepidus' tenure, short as it was.[50] At this point Sulla was still very much in charge of consular elections,[51] and presumably could influence lower elections and arrangements for *provinciae* as well. So we can legitimately suspect some manipulation of the lot in this case.

The title "pro consule" deserves comment. After Sulla, it was the expected (11.1.5) rank for governors of each of the territorial provinces. Yet Cicero never uses it of C. Verres.[52] There is no apparent reason why all the post-Sullan governors of Sicily should not have had the same rank. The explanation is not constitutional, but rhetorical: C. Claudius Marcellus was a member of the senatorial jury in Verres' trial, and, as such, needed flattery.[53] This status as juror may at least partly inform also Cicero's depiction of Claudius Marcellus as a good governor. For all his "reviving" of the province, this man as praetor also had to exact an emergency tithe—perhaps for the war against Sertorius in Spain. But he did so fairly, we are told.[54] Marcellus probably had to stay in the province for two years: no one is known to have been sent *ex praetura* to Sicily for 78.

L. Cornelius Sisenna (the historian and *pr. urb. et per.* 78) quite probably drew Sicily as his promagisterial province for 77. An inscription (now long lost) recorded honors from Halaesa to a man who may be L. Sisenna.[55] Good circumstantial support for a Sicilian governorship comes from Cicero's statement that Sthenius of Thermae played host to the series Cn. Pompeius (*pro pr.* 82), C. Marcellus (*pr.* 80), L. Sisenna, and C. Verres (*pr.* 74). And Sisenna is said to have been a friend of the *eques* Cn. Calidius, who in his home in Sicily entertained "many holders of *potestas* and *imperium*."[56] Sisenna seems to have been one of Verres' supporters,[57] which may explain why Cicero chooses to say nothing about his actual command.

Sisenna can have spent no more than one year in the *provincia*. Sex. Peducaeus (*pr.* 77) is attested there for 76 and 75, with Cicero joining him as quaestor in the second of these years. This man, says Cicero, had the reputation as the most honest Sicilian praetor up to that time ("innocentissimam . . . praeturam").[58] Now, in assessing this statement one must allow for the fact he was Cicero's commanding officer[59]—but also for the possibility that he positively required some defending. Cicero tells how Verres had prohibited the Syracusan Senate from passing a decree of support for Peducaeus when they heard "some trouble (*negotium*) had been stirred up for him." The decree was ratified only after Verres' departure in the year 70, when Cicero says Peducaeus no longer needed it.[60] The mention of a "negotium" (a word which Cicero quite often uses of a legal case),[61] as well as Cicero's emphasis on Peducaeus and his praetorship as "innocentissimus" (in the superlative, regularly found in sympathetic descriptions of defendants),[62] suggests that at some point in the period 73–71 Peducaeus faced possible or actual prosecution. One principal complaint will have been in connection with grain matters. Peducaeus held Sicily for a *biennium*: in 76 we are told that grain was cheap, in 75 it was extremely expensive ("in summa caritate"). The grain shortage of the year 75 featured prominently in Sallust's *Histories*.[63] Concern extended also to other agricultural products. Peducaeus, however, used the grain shortage to his personal financial advantage: Cicero clearly admits it, and then takes pains to demonstrate that there might be a respectable precedent for this type of profiteering.[64]

Precedent or not, Peducaeus' successor C. Licinius Sacerdos (*pr.* 75, promagistrate in Sicily for 74) eschewed this particular path to self-enrichment. Though the first thing Sacerdos did on arrival in his province was to order grain for his *cella*, the manner of his requisitions for maintenance is said to have been scrupulously fair. When the Sicilian communities asked to pay Sacerdos money instead of grain—the harvest for the year 74 had not yet been reaped—he "commuted" their payments at a rate well under the market price. Yet the good fortune of the province was to prove shortlived. Later that year, M. Antonius (*pr.* 74 and the future Creticus) spent one month in Sicily as part of his special pirate command. Antonius grossly distorted Sacerdos' precedent, says Cicero, by assessing Sicilian communities for cash at the governor's rate in the post-harvest season, "when they would have given him grain for nothing." And Verres (who succeeded Sacerdos in 73) would in turn cite Antonius as a precedent, we are told, when seeking to justify his own still more open abuses.[65] Henceforth, the real danger, explains Cicero in 70, was that Verres might serve as a precedent for others.[66]

Cicero terms Sacerdos (like Peducaeus) "innocentissimus,"[67] but does not give us too many details of other aspects of his administration. The most substantial thing we find is a legal decision by Sacerdos in a capital case that Verres overturned, despite the fact that the two governors had continuity in the local members of their judicial *consilia*.[68] Verres also apparently reversed a ruling in a trial for *iniuria* from Sacerdos' year involving one P. Naevius Turpio as defendant. But that was not as consequential as that capital case, especially since the decision was probably made by a subordinate of Sacerdos', not the praetor himself.[69] If Cicero is accurate on Sacerdos' method of requisitioning grain (see above) and his general noninterference in civil matters,[70] it does suggest that he cared how he was viewed in his *provincia*. Yet that is about as far as one can go with the facts given.

Verres, on the other hand, in his promagistracy clearly looked toward Rome. It seems to have been a special point of pride for Verres that he sold the grain tithes at a higher price than his predecessor, and was effective in getting cash profits as well as actual grain to the city of Rome in all three years of his promagistracy, while a slave war was raging for most of that time in Italy, and major campaigns were under way in both west (against Sertorius) and east (versus Mithridates). Verres' aim, we are told, was to win the esteem of the urban Plebs—and its support for a consular bid.[71] Cicero has much to say on the irresponsibility of this mode of popularity seeking. He also claims that in one district alone Verres stole as much money and twice as much grain as he sent on to Rome.[72]

Cicero's audience in the *Verrines* may have needed some convincing—since Verres evidently had delivered the goods. There was obviously deep anxiety at Rome about the grain supply down into 73, when the consuls M. Terentius Varro Lucullus and C. Cassius Longinus passed their *lex frumentaria*. (Sulla had ended such distributions.)[73] By chance, we hear that in the year 70, Sosippus of Agrigentum had a large audience (including the consul Pompey) when he gave a speech in Rome on the seemingly unpromising subject of the *aestimatio* of Sicilian grain.[74] Given this charged atmosphere, it is conceivable that Verres, if he had been even moderately successful in denting the grain supply problem, might have been elected consul on his return from Sicily. Cicero says the *pr.* 81 M. Aemilius Lepidus "ruined" his *provincia*; but he knew perfectly well that Lepidus still went on to win the consulship in the minimum possible interval. So the *Verrines* had to portray Verres as substantially worse than Lepidus for Rome's food supply.[75] Had Verres escaped condemnation, his prospects would seem excellent for 68, thanks in particular to the support of Hortensius, who defended Verres in his *repetundae* trial as *cos. des.* 69.

We do not know precisely when Sacerdos left the *provincia*, but he was back in Rome certainly by mid-October 73, having spent just one year in Sicily.[76] It is likely that Sacerdos left before the *pr urb.* 74 C. Verres' arrival, just as Verres (as we shall see below) left before his own successor's arrival. It was planned that Verres have a similar term as that of Sacerdos, with supersession after one year, in early 72.[77] But his expected successor Q. Arrius (*pr.* 73) was reassigned—evidently quite soon before he was due to depart for Sicily—to the war against Spartacus. Arrius never made it to the island (11.8.7); Verres was to spend not just 72 but also 71 in Sicily, a total of three years in the *provincia*.[78]

13.2.3 *The Chronology of Verres' Command*

Cicero boasts that he can offer a detailed chronology of Verres' whole career.[79] Yet from the *Verrines* themselves it is difficult to get even a basic sense of the timeline of Verres' Sicilian command, and the most comprehensive study of that problem to date is unsatisfactory in some major respects.[80] The general effect Cicero seeks to create is one of utter consistency in Verres' character. Unlike other governors, Cicero asserts, Verres was not corrupted by his province—he came to Sicily that way.[81] It is not quite possible for us to trace development in Verres' extended promagistracy, since most of the material Cicero adduces in his attack is shorn of chronological indicators. But we do get just enough to be able to piece together some counterarguments to Cicero's polemical tour de force.

For Cicero, the story starts in 74, right after Verres drew Sicily as his *ex praetura* province. It was then, says Cicero, that Verres started developing his designs on the *provincia*. That included earmarking the legal cases he would take up, since he had the expectation of just a one-year command.[82] Elsewhere Cicero remarks that he had "budgeted the three years of his praetorship"—the first year for his own gain, the second for his (inevitably necessary) legal defense team, and the third ("the richest year") for the jurors who would hear his case[83]—but that is blatantly tendentious, and no doubt meant to be at least partly humorous.

Verres' departure for Sicily must have been early in 73,[84] though we get no particulars of the chronology. What Cicero is eager to emphasize is that Verres, after his departure, vitiated his military *auspicia* by returning—repeatedly—back across the *pomerium* to make nocturnal visits to his mistress Chelidon.[85] The allegation in itself implies that Verres, in making his defense, set great store by his military exploits in his *provincia* and on his return home.[86] Cicero elsewhere confirms it.[87]

To 73 belongs first of all Verres' alleged interference in the estate of Dio of Halaesa, whose will he had heard about when he was still "ad urbem" (that is, when he was just departing from Rome).[88] Another event to be placed in early 73 is Verres' attempt to steal a famous statue of Diana at Segesta.[89] So it appears he did get to the western portion of the island quite early in his command. At some point that same year, Verres is said to have allowed his first *in absentia* capital case to be tried. The victim was one Diodorus of the island of Melita; Verres coveted some cups that man owned.[90] The case is of symbolic importance, since Melita does represent very much the furthest reach of the province. Cicero also says that the farmers of Sicily were already hurting in Verres' first year.[91]

Later in 73 is the matter of Heraclius, an elderly native of Syracuse with "no patrons other than the Marcelli," who came into a large inheritance that fell into dispute. It is said to have been the only Syracusan case personally tried by Verres.[92] The allegation that he delegated the rest of his legal work there to a quaestor is in itself meant to be damning, since it was obviously a perverse distortion of normal practice: Syracuse, after all, was the most important city in the *provincia*. "Soon after" the affair of Heraclius—and so in late 73 or early 72—came that of Epicrates of Bidis (near Syracuse), which involved another inheritance claim.[93]

When Verres' first year came to its end, Cicero says that all of his staff decamped except for the *legatus* P. Tadius.[94] We do not know who replaced them, since no other ranking subordinate is attested for the next year.[95] In fact, for 72 we get little in the way of dated items except for a few court cases. Cicero says that in that year, Verres himself heard an inheritance dispute (we are not told where) involving two brothers of Agyrium.[96] By midway in that year, he certainly had visited Panhormus, on the northern coast of the western portion of the island. There he jailed one Apollonius for allegedly having allowed a slave conspiracy; the man was to spend eighteen months in prison. Verres never paid any heed to public entreaties on behalf of this prisoner, though he is said to have visited the town several times in the period.[97]

The statement that Verres made multiple trips to Panhormus in 72 and 71 is in fact an interesting slip on Cicero's part, since elsewhere he portrays Verres as quite idle in general.[98] Verres spent his winters at Hiero's *regia* in Syracuse; in spring, he traveled the *provincia*, but in a litter "like the kings of Bithynia"; during the summer, he set up camp at Syracuse and focused on adulterous liasons when he should have been touring the *provincia*, administering law and keeping Sicily's shores free of pirates. In the *Verrines*, Cicero provides just enough details of Verres' movements in the *provincia* to make his specific charges of criminality credible without undercutting this (obviously exaggerated) portrayal of sloth (see Additional Note XIV).

The only other case definitely to be assigned to the year 72 was the prosecution of the wealthy and well-connected Sthenius of Thermae by one of his fellow citizens: Cicero implies that affair marked a real turning point in Verres' (material) fortunes.[99] Under the *lex Rupilia*, Sthenius was entitled to a trial under the laws of Thermae. Yet, contrary to the provisions of his own edict, Verres pronounced that he personally would investigate the charge. So Sthenius fled to Rome, running the risk of sailing in "winter"—to be precise, October of 72. Sthenius was adjudged guilty of the forgery charge, and on 1 December, Verres pronounced Sthenius guilty *in absentia* of a capital crime as well.[100] Cicero says that the Senate applied substantial pressure on Verres to let up in this case,[101] but apparently there was not enough to generate a specific *senatus consultum* on Sthenius or still less Verres' supersession (for which he was now quite due). Besides some grain issues,[102] there are no additional items that one can firmly place in this year.

Though we have seen that Cicero explains the factors behind Verres' first prorogation (in 73 for 72), he conspicuously omits to mention how the Senate came to its decision to extend his command also for 71. (Given Spartacus' war it probably had no choice.) However, it is this final year in the *provincia* that receives the bulk of datable material. Here there is just one (possible) legal case, that of a certain P. Gavius of Consa, who escaped from imprisonment in the quarries of Syracuse only to divulge foolishly at Messana—which was friendly to Verres—his plan to proceed to Rome to anticipate the governor's return. But for this, the date of 71, though likely, is not positively required.[103] For that year, however, it is secure that his subordinates P. Caesetius and P. Tadius captured a pirate ship, when Verres himself was in his so-called summer headquarters at Syracuse.[104]

In 71, Verres also suspended the traditional quinquennial elections in each of the sixty-five recognized Sicilian *civitates* for two local *censores*. The praetor had introduced a system of direct appointment by himself in its stead, which led (we are told) to unsatisfactory censors and a census to match.[105] It is part of a series of Verres' administrative "reforms"—at least one other of which also dates to this final year[106]—that Cicero attacks. Now, each of Verres' new 130 censors allegedly was asked to contribute—as an *ordo*—toward a statue of the praetor costing 156,000 sesterces. This same year, the farmers of Sicily also had to contribute to the cost of some gilded equestrian statues of Verres to be placed in Rome. The praetor was evidently on a drive to collect honorific statues in this year; Cicero asserts that Verres thought they would help shield him against prosecution on his return.[107] The interpretation Cicero offers may be true, but it is not inevitable:[108] Verres may also have thought those statues, as well as other related measures[109] useful for a future consular bid. The emergency grain edicts he is said to have issued in 71 (aiming for shipment by 1 August) certainly seem to have had that purpose in mind, though again Cicero puts them in the worst possible light.[110]

Cicero alleges that in 71, Verres did not care in what state he left agriculture on the island.[111] A series of detailed (but sometimes contradictory) arguments with examples cited from throughout the *provincia* for this year are offered to lend substance to this charge.[112] And in this year, Cicero emphasizes that Verres gave his low-level subordinates particularly free rein.[113]

The various ways Verres is said to have profited from Sicilian grain—both tithed and requisitioned—are too complex for exposition here.[114] One crucial aspect for Verres' exploitation of the tithe was his collusion with the *decumani*, which Cicero says was "an open secret" that led to two *sponsiones* on the topic.[115] In general, the activities of Verres' alleged satellites and cronies in grain matters constitute a good portion of Cicero's case against the praetor.[116]

It was the resulting agricultural crisis, Cicero asserts, that drove Sicilian communities and *negotiatores* alike to send deputations of complaint—despite possible retaliation by Verres—to Sicily's foremost patrons in Rome as well as the consuls of 71. One demand evidently was that L. Metellus (*pr.* 71) succeed to the Sicilian command as soon as possible.[117] Cicero says that Metellus was the first governor ever, while still in Rome, to write a letter to the Sicilian communities to plough and sow their land; in the same letter (apparently), he promised he would comply with the *lex Hieronica*.[118]

Verres evidently had claimed to have prevented slaves from attacking Sicily, and to have quashed any incipient revolt in the *provincia*. Cicero himself implies that there was a very real fear of a slave war in Sicily during the crisis years 73–71. Yet one notes that Cicero has very little to say about the most serious event in this theater, the fierce fighting around Rhegium that spilled onto eastern Sicily in 71. Cicero does mention that Crassus (no date given, but surely in early 71) had to break down a pontoon bridge by which the slaves had aimed to cross to Messana, and faults Verres for taking inadequate precautions on the Sicilian side.[119] Yet a fragment from Sallust's *Histories* shows that Verres was not totally negligent in his defense of the island.[120] Furthermore, Plutarch for 71 tells also how Spartacus in making an attempt to cross to Sicily came close to landing two thousand men—not a small force—on the island, in a deliberate attempt to resuscitate the embers that still glowed from the second Slave War. The plan might have been realized, Plutarch implies, had not the pirates who had agreed to transport the slaves across the strait cheated Spartacus and sailed off.[121] Cicero is silent on this incident. In truth, the Roman Senate must have been aware of the danger to Sicily when the slave war in Italy moved to the south in late 72. It stands to reason that Verres had some military competence in order to be prorogued for the year 71. Cicero instead wants to make out that Verres exacerbated the slave crisis. For instance, at Lilybaeum, Verres is said to have investigated with a *consilium*—a rare instance of its proper use in the *Verrines*—a conspiracy among slaves belonging to one Leonides of Triocala. Verres, on the advice of his *consilium*, personally pronounced the slaves guilty, and condemned them to crucifixion—only later to be bribed to release them from the cross.[122] Cicero says he showed the same susceptibility to bribery when he learned of slave conspiracies elsewhere. But alternately, Verres would frame slaves so as to squeeze their masters for money.[123] The charge that a praetor was open to bribery by slave masters is paralleled earlier in this period, in Diodorus' description of the buildup to the second Sicilian Slave War.[124] Cicero's description of how Verres handled the affair of Triocala—which, of course, was the site of Athenion's palace in that rebellion (13.1.3)—is a not-so-subtle attempt to evoke the terror of those times. Verres must also have personally taken some military action against pirates during his three years in Sicily, though Cicero utterly denies it.[125] The one military encounter of this type that Cicero does mention is how pirates (very likely in the year 71) defeated a ragtag Sicilian allied fleet and then sailed with four ships into the harbor of Syracuse and back out again. More must have happened, since Cicero reports—in a quite different portion of the *Verrines*—that Verres gave out military decorations to three Romans and several Sicilians for action against pirates in the harbor. The epilogue was that Verres, after sham legal proceedings, took savage reprisals on the Sicilian naval commanders he held responsible.[126]

There may have been a factual stratum to the story of the trial: Cicero says that two captains survived and were present in Rome to testify against Verres. But Cicero's tale of the raid on Syracuse certainly seems to suppress some key facts. Orosius also alludes to this incident, yet he speaks of the defeat of an actual Roman fleet, which enabled the archpirate Pyrganio (the name is not found in the *Verrines*) to take the harbor of Syracuse. Pyrganio, says Orosius, then terrorized the island at large, and remained active after Verres' departure in 70 (providing additional confirmation for 71 as the date of the pirate raid on Syracuse).[127] A comparison of these two accounts, combined with Cicero's offhand notice that some individuals were decorated for fighting in the harbor raid, certainly suggests that Cicero in general sought to downplay the seriousness of this incident and the extent of Roman (as opposed to Sicilian) involvement. If it was Verres who commanded the fleet that met the pirates in that raid (as certainly seems possible), that would run counter to Cicero's frequent assertion that the praetor had completely abdicated all naval responsibilities.

By Cicero's account, Verres "fled" Syracuse before leaving the *provincia* for good (i.e., in early 70), without meeting his successor.[128] His two quaestors remained—we are not told whether with or without *imperium*—to manage the *provincia* in the transition between commanders.[129] Staff members such as his *accensus* Timarchides also lingered, but for purely sinister purposes, it is alleged. Verres' transit back through Italy was marred, says Cicero, by two particularly damning incidents: Verres' refusal to fight against a small slave band at Valentia, and the Senate's reluctance to have him fight against some fugitives at Tempsa. What finally happened in that latter instance is not clear: Verres in fact may have taken some military action. Cicero intimates that Verres hoped for a triumph on his return for fighting against the pirates, but that is probably a joke. (Crassus in 71 got only an *ovatio* for his efforts against Spartacus in a full-blown slave war.) One traditional honor did come his way. It is true, Cicero argues, that a company of *publicani* publicly met and thanked Verres *en route* to Rome. But Verres in turn asked the *societas* to expunge records that might later prove harmful to him, and it complied. The manner in which Verres deposited his accounts was also suspicious, despite the availability of a recent precedent.[130] Cicero indicted him for *repetundae* directly after his return.

13.2.4 *Cicero's Prosecution of Verres*

The immediate factors motivating Cicero in this prosecution must have been his previous service as quaestor in Sicily and his oratorical rivalry with (the significantly senior) Q. Hortensius, and—not unconnected—his desire to acquire Verres' praetorian speaking place in the Senate (a reward, as L. R. Taylor has shown, of the post-Sullan extortion court). In the *Verrines* Cicero is keen to represent himself as an established *patronus* of the island, though it appears there was a counterclaim that Cicero in fact had not been asked for his advocacy. For his part, Cicero (somewhat disingenuously) claims that his links with Sthenius of Thermae—a *hospes* of

Verres whom the praetor had violated—would in themselves offer enough motive for his prosecution.[131] Now, Cicero was aedile designate for 69 at the time of this trial. Surely the overarching factor in Cicero's elaborate attack on Verres was to pave the way for his own praetorship.

Cicero's first challenge was to secure the right to prosecute Verres. His competition in the *divinatio* was Verres' ex-quaestor (from 73) Q. Caecilius Niger, a native of Sicily. Caecilius, Cicero argued in the speech from the *divinatio*, had no business prosecuting his former superior. What is more, Caecilius was in fact on friendly terms with Verres, and was complicit in his thefts: his prosecution would be a sham for which the Sicilians would refuse to appear to testify. Plus, Cicero was generally more able than Caecilius.[132] Cicero won his bid to prosecute, and applied amazing energy to the task. Cicero was determined to have Verres brought to trial in the year 70, before his advocate Hortensius entered the consulship and the brother of the current Sicilian praetor took charge of the *repetundae* court as praetor.[133] Granted 110 days to collect evidence, Cicero set off for Sicily while it was still winter, and there managed to collect what he required in a mere 50 days on the island.[134]

Verres for his part, says Cicero, immediately promised a bribery agent a large sum of money to corrupt the jury in his forthcoming trial. He even, it is alleged, started plotting against Cicero's life (a traditional charge). Cicero makes out that the shameless behavior Verres exhibited in Sicily continued in the city. Verres allegedly even kept some Sicilian pirates at home, until Cicero, under the authority of the *pr. repetundis* M.' Acilius Glabrio, confiscated them, apparently in summer 70.[135]

Roman extortion trials in general allowed a tremendously wide range of charges,[136] yet Cicero's prosecution of Verres is an extreme example of the genre. Blanket accusations abound in the *Verrines*.[137] But there is a reasonably comprehensive list of detailed charges at the beginning of *actio* I.[138] Verres manipulated law (most importantly, the *lex Rupilia*) by his *imperium*, and extorted countless sums of money from Sicily's farmers by a series of perversely novel regulations that broke with Hieronic law. He treated Rome's allies like enemies, and allowed Roman citizens to suffer capital punishment. Under Verres, the guiltiest criminals bribed their way to acquittal, whereas the honest found themselves prosecuted in absence and exiled. Military affairs were a disaster: pirates and brigands were able to attack fortified ports and cities, Sicilian soldiers and sailors starved to death, and fleets were ruined. Verres robbed the public artwork that kings and Rome's own generals gave or restored to Sicily's cities. He also looted the sanctuaries of the island's gods of every notable image. Finally, he corrupted the wives and children of the island.

Cicero in the course of the *Verrines* offers detailed support for each of these charges—a summary is impossible here—with the exception of the corruption of children. (He seems to have brought up this allegation at the start of his speech purely for shock value.) And we, of course, get some items that Cicero does not list here, many clustered in the second half of *actio* II.2 (which may indicate that section indeed belongs to a later stratum of composition). Cumulatively, Verres' predations netted him a tidy sum: in all, Verres is said to have stolen 4 million sesterces from the *provincia*.[139] The trial resolved itself probably early in October 70, with Verres' condemnation when he failed to appear at the second *actio*.[140]

13.2.5 Cicero and the Sicilian Commander
L. Caecilius Metellus

Cicero in the *Verrines* offers a transparently partisan account also of the activities of Verres' successor L. Caecilius Metellus (*pr.* 71) in the province. The first month or so of Metellus' government, explains Cicero, was devoted largely to damage control.[141] The general impression Cicero seeks to establish in his narrative is one of (necessarily) wideranging activism. Metellus travelled to Sicily with two of Verres' eminent victims in tow, who had fled to Rome as suppliants two years previously. The new governor immediately set himself to reinstating them at, respectively, Syracuse and nearby Bidis. He secured reparations for another victim at Drepanum, and overturned judicial measures Verres had taken at Agrigentum, Panhormus, and Lilybaeum in the west. He even annulled Verres' census of 71—no easy thing to do—and returned to a system of elections for local Sicilian *censores*.[142] Then there was the problem of the statues. At least one representation of Verres had been knocked down (at Tyndaris) directly upon Metellus' arrival in the province; Cicero says he had to issue an emergency edict to prevent other cities from following suit. The Senate of Centuripa, we are told, defied him all the same.[143]

The most pressing concern, however, was the agriculture of Sicily. The new commander is said to have made a provincewide effort to remedy the harm Verres and his satellite, the *decumanus* Apronius, had inflicted on farming. One of Metellus' first actions was to requisition grain from Messana, which Verres improperly had exempted from that obligation. Metellus also wrote a policy letter at some point in 70 to the consuls, the praetor (apparently *urbanus*) M. Mummius, and the urban quaestors, which Cicero cites and (somewhat tendentiously) explicates as implictly critical of Verres. Yet not all of Metellus' early actions in the *provincia* square with this picture of highminded concern. He refused to entertain charges against Apronius under the "formula Octaviana"—a provision he had both in his city and provincial edict—on the grounds that it would constitute a *praeiudicium* in Verres' upcoming case.[144]

Two days after Cicero arrived in Sicily to conduct investigations for his prosecution of Verres, we are told Metellus' zeal for reform came to a dead stop. It was Verres, says Cicero, who corrupted his successor through a go-between; at this point Metellus had not been in his *provincia* a month.[145] Metellus set up all sorts of impediments to Cicero's work as prosecutor.[146] So did his quaestors—as well as those of Verres, who were still tarrying on the island.[147] Cicero tried, all the same, to avail himself of the power of the praetor by calling several of Verres' confederates—including Apronius—into Metellus' court to give evidence.[148] Yet, here and elsewhere, Cicero faced stiff resistance. For instance, it was only through Cicero's perseverance and a forceful appeal to the authority granted to him by the *praetor repetundis* that Metellus allowed him a document of the Syracusan senate pertinent to Verres' case.[149] Cicero gained access to evidence through some unofficial channels, too.[150] Metellus, however, was highly effective, says Cicero, in retaining some witnesses important for the prosecution—including the two prominent victims of Verres who had spent the years 72 and 71 as suppliants in Rome.[151]

What Cicero does not mention is any military activity by Metellus against the pirates. But that is primarily what the Livian tradition knew about Metellus' service in Sicily, and it seems to place his successful fighting against them firmly in the year 70. As we have seen above, Orosius is explicit that when Metellus arrived in the *provincia*, the archpirate Pyrganio, who had already defeated a Roman fleet and raided the harbor of Syracuse, was now plundering the island. However, Metellus, says Orosius, defeated him on land and sea and "soon" forced him to withdraw from Sicily.[152] So evidently not all of Metellus' energies after his first month in the *provincia* were devoted to foiling Cicero's prosecution of Verres.

Appian speaks of the pirates defeating an unnamed praetor for Sicily off the coast of the island, some time in the period before the *lex Gabinia* of 67. Florus reports (in this case plausibly) that pirates in this general period also raided Sicilian shores.[153] One wonders whether these passages refer to Verres in 71, or Metellus at some point after his initial victory of 70 (but before he returned to Rome, probably after just one year in the *provincia*, to win the consulship for 68), or an unknown praetorian commander of the period 69–67. It is impossible to say, since so little is known of the arrangements for Sicily for some years after Metellus' tenure.

13.2.6 *Praetorian Commands in Sicily after 70*

In (probably) the early 60s, C. Vergilius Balbus (a future *pr.* 62) served in Sicily as "pro quaestore," so in all likelihood for at least two years.[154] We can infer that Balbus' superior commander also found himself prorogued in the *provincia*. The pirates were no doubt still harassing the island during this time. When Pompey received his pirate command under the Gabinian law of 67, he charged two of his *legati pro praetore* with responsibility for Sicilian waters. But each took that task up as part of a very large territory, which extended quite far east.[155]

It is yet another good instance of the *sors opportuna* that later C. Vergilius Balbus as praetor in 62 drew Sicily as his *ex praetura* province; he is the first praetor for Sicily after L. Metellus who is known by name. P. Clodius Pulcher was Balbus' quaestor for 61, returning to Rome well before June 60.[156] C. Balbus himself had to remain for three, perhaps four full years: he was still in the *provincia* when Cicero went into exile in early 58 (he prohibited him from setting foot on the island).[157]

The long command is not atypical of this period. We shall see that Q. Pompeius Rufus (*pr.* 63) had Africa as his province from 62 to perhaps 59; his praetorian colleague C. Pomptinus received Gallia Transalpina through the year 60; Q. Tullius Cicero was (like Balbus) *pr.* 62 and, after receiving Asia, was prorogued through 59; the praetor C. Papirius Carbo was in Bithynia/Pontus by 61 or 60 and certainly seems to have stayed through 58; and Cn. Cornelius Lentulus Marcellinus had Syria for both 59 and 58. The necessity of staffing the new provinces of Bithynia and Syria explains this phenomenon in part. And Illyricum had to be declared a special *provincia* around this time and entrusted to the praetor L. Culleolus (11.8.1). But a significant proportion of consuls and perhaps also some praetors must have been declining promagisterial *provinciae* (see 11.1.6). We positively know this to be true of Cicero as *cos.* 63 and Bibulus as *cos.* 59; indeed, none of the consuls of the years 62 through 60 can be shown to have reached a territorial *provincia*. Praetors had more reason to take up a province, and where we can check (e.g., the well-attested colleges of 63 and 57), most seem to have done so in these years. But the *pr.* ca. 61 Q. Voconius Naso almost certainly did not (see Additional Note XV); if we had better evidence, we would surely find other examples. That combination of factors—the newly created provinces, the necessity of special praetorian *provinciae*, and the refusal of promagisterial commands—will have forced the Senate to keep the commanders of even rich (and thus corrupting) provinces such as Sicily and Asia in their assignments for such long spans. And as it happens, in the years 61–59—after the return of Pompey from the east and before Caesar's great Gallic command—there were no "big" multiprovince commands in process that might take pressure off the larger administrative system (see further 15.3). However, we cannot tell whether the praetors for Sicily subsequent to C. Vergilius Balbus had a similar experience of repeated prorogation, since no real details of the arrangements for the rest of the 50s are known.[158]

13.2.7 *Praetorian Commands in Sardinia*
of the 70s and 60s

The only informative source on Sardinia in this general period is the *Pro Scauro*, Cicero's defense for the *pr.* 56 M. Aemilius Scaurus, who was tried for *repetundae* on his return from this province in late June of the year 54. The speech, however, is one of Cicero's most "lawyerly," and the portions that have come down to us (it is not entirely extant) are quite sparing of historical and administrative detail. The tactic was deliberate: the ancient sources on the trial are quite clear that Scaurus' command needed all the defending it could get. One result is that for Sardinia in the period after Sulla down to 50, we can posit precisely four commanders with praetorian *imperium*—only two of whom appear to have been actual praetors.

First, the problem of Valerius Triarius in 77: Asconius tells us that the father of P. Valerius Triarius, prosecutor in the *Pro Scauro* case, fought M. Aemilius Lepidus (*cos.* 78) when he fled in defeat from Italy to Sardinia in 77, and adds that he later served as a *legatus* in the Third Mithridatic War. A late source—but one that seems reliable on the "bellum Lepidanum"—gives this Triarius the rank of "pro praetore" in Sardinia, and states that he fought repeated battles against Lepidus by which he effectively countered his designs on the island. Neither source offers a *praenomen* for the Sardinian commander, but if he is to be identified with the later *legatus* in the east, it is "Gaius."[159]

Broughton may well be right to consider Triarius not a praetor of 78 (as he once tentatively suggested), but to identify him with the (Valerius) Triarius who was *quaestor urbanus* in 81 and to place him in Sardinia in 77, "preferably as a *legatus pro praetore*."[160] If C. Triarius was indeed a mere *legatus* holding the *provincia* with delegated *imperium* in an interval between proper praetorian commanders, it would help explain why M. Lepidus, after his setbacks in Italy in 77, thought

Sardinia a reasonable place to regroup and replenish his forces and to make life difficult for Rome.[161] Now, we happen to know that through Triarius' agency a Sardinian was granted Roman citizenship and became a "Valerius." This need not imply that C. Triarius was praetor for Sardinia. Cicero's wording allows the possibility that a superior made the actual grant to gratify Triarius.[162]

The next known commander with *imperium* active in the *provincia* of Sardinia is not a problem, but neither is he a praetor. In 67, a P. Atilius served as a *legatus pro praetore* under Pompey in his pirate command, and had responsibility for the waters around Sardinia and Corsica, evidently as part of a much larger territory (extending as far south as "Libya," according to Appian).[163] Nothing is known of his activities. And Dio, in his narrative of the year 67,[164] says that a city praetor "L. Lucullus" (as seen in 11.1.6, surely an L. Lucceius) turned down an *ex praetura* command for Sardinia (i.e., for 66), alleging the general state of corruption in Rome's provinces. His refusal to serve will have meant the prorogation of whatever commander was in Sardinia, or governance by a *legatus* in default.

13.2.8 *Praetorian Commands in Sardinia of the 50s*

It is only a decade later that we start to get any solid information on the Roman administration of this province. Beginning in the fall of 57, Q. Tullius Cicero (*pr.* 62) served on Sardinia as a *legatus* under Pompey in his role as grain commissioner. Pompey joined him there briefly after the conference at Luca in April 56, and Quintus himself returned to Italy in June. Though several of Quintus' letters to his brother are extant, there is very little in them on the details of his work on the island, and nothing implying the simultaneous presence of a praetor in the *provincia*.[165] There should have been one, since we know that it came up in the *ex praetura* sortition for 56, when it fell to the *pr.* 57 Ap. Claudius Pulcher. His tenure will have been a short one. Ap. Pulcher is attested at Luca in 56, and had M. Aemilius Scaurus (*pr.* 56) as a successor for 55; in that year, Appius managed to win a consulship for 54.[166] We hear nothing of what Ap. Pulcher actually did in Sardinia. As it happens, Appius' command is never mentioned in the *Pro Scauro*, though there is extensive discussion in this speech of this man as *cos.* 54.

Scaurus was the son of the famous *cos.* 115 M. Aemilius Scaurus and Caecilia Metella, the future wife of Sulla. In the year 58, he had an expensive curule aedileship that apparently led to his near-bankruptcy.[167] But Scaurus' splendid aedicilican games evidently made the right impression: he was elected to the praetorship in the minimum interval, for the year 56. Little is known of Scaurus' activities in his city *provincia* (it was probably not the *quaestio de vi*, as is commonly supposed)[168] or — more surprisingly — of his one year *ex praetura* command in Sardinia, even though Cicero wrote a speech to defend it. A few items emerge from other sources. It does appear from Asconius that Scaurus either personally or through subordinates functioned in Corsica as well as the island of Sardinia. Asconius also says that Scaurus was thought to have acted in his province with little self-restraint and a lot of arrogance — though in other respects he behaved quite unlike his father![169] Valerius Maximus[170] tells a tale that implies there were not 120 people there that Scaurus did not rob. The basic charge of rapacity rings true. Scaurus had to recoup the expenses of that aedileship, and that was just for a start. We are told that when Scaurus returned to Rome on 29 June 54, he did so as a declared candidate for the consulship of 53.[171]

M. Scaurus opened his consular campaign by immediately (and successfully) defending C. Porcius Cato, who had found himself on trial for his activities as *tr. pl.* 56.[172] But only about a week after his return from Sardinia, Scaurus too was indicted, on 6 July, for *repetundae* before the praetor M. Porcius Cato.[173] Scaurus' principal prosecutor was the young P. Valerius Triarius, son of the *pro pr.* who (as we have seen) held Sardinia during the *bellum Lepidanum*. Triarius and his *subscriptores* were granted thirty days to investigate in Sardinia and Corsica. But Asconius says that they did not dare budge from Rome. According to Asconius, what they feared was that "Scaurus with the money he had stolen from allies would buy the consulship and—just as his father had done[174]—would enter into a magistracy before he could be tried, and plunder once again other provinces before rendering an account for his earlier governance."[175] The prosecutors no doubt said that openly at Scaurus' trial: the argument (which may have been literally true) brings up a major contemporary concern. The protection afforded by a consulship and a subsequent command is precisely what the *senatus consultum* of 53 and the *lex Pompeia* of 52 (11.1.7) sought to eliminate by stipulating an interval between magistracy and promagistracy.

Scaurus for his part, it is said, particularly feared the close personal connection of the prosecutor and *pr. repetundis* M. Cato. And he found Cato resistant to actual bribery.[176] What Scaurus did count on to secure acquittal, says Asconius, was his own father's name and—unrealistically—a marriage connection with Pompey, *cos.* II 55, and in 54 *pro cos.* outside the *pomerium*. (Scaurus had married Mucia Tertia after Pompey in 61 had taken the serious step of dismissing her for unchastity.) Cicero, in the run-up to the trial, reckoned Scaurus' chief assets would be the fame of his aedileship and the weight of his father's memory among the rural folk,[177] who evidently were expected to show up in some numbers to take in the proceedings. But Cicero thought it especially important for Scaurus to have the status of *consul designatus* when put on trial.[178] That was not to be.

Scaurus' trial did not start until late August, and was over quickly, by 2 September.[179] Scaurus did have six defenders (including three *consulares*), which Asconius considered a high number. There were also nine consular character witnesses, but most in absence, including Pompey. Scaurus' half-brother Faustus Sulla, a quaestor in that year (Asconius still terms him "adulescens"), was considered particularly effective in his eulogy.[180] Earlier Faustus no doubt had tried to influence the trial in other ways.[181]

Cicero's speech *Pro Scauro* does allow us to reconstruct a few of the accusations. Grain abuses were alleged, which Cicero belittles.[182] Cicero also takes up and dismisses the charges brought by some individual (pointedly obscure) Sardinians: the family of Bostar of Nora, whose estate Scaurus was said to have confiscated, and a certain Aris, whose wife reportedly had committed suicide because of the praetor's unwanted attention. Cicero makes out that these folk are Carthaginian liars.[183] Indeed, a large portion of the extant speech is taken up with attacks on the ethnicity and consequent lack of integrity of the Sardinian witnesses.[184] Cicero adduces the cases of the praetors for Sardinia, T. Albucius (*pr.* ca. 107) and Megabocchus (otherwise unknown), who were condemned, despite eulogies, by impartial witnesses and untampered documents: the witnesses in the present trial, he alleges, have been bribed.[185] We also get a disquisition on the history of Phoenician treachery. Cicero asks the pardon of his Sardinian friends for that, but throws in some even more hostile material by the end of the speech.[186] All the same, it is emphasized that the great mass of the people in the province had no complaint against Scaurus.[187]

Another theme is that the consul Ap. Claudius Pulcher was hostile to Scaurus for his own personal reasons. As direct predecessor of Scaurus in that *provincia*, he wanted to see him disgraced. Cicero does not elaborate, perhaps because his audience will have taken such rivalry for granted. Comparisons between successive commanders in the same province were inevitable.[188] Sometimes, the departing commander would even take practical measures to bring about his successor's failure.[189] But Cicero implies the central issue for Appius was that Scaurus would be an effective competitor for the consulship against his brother C. Claudius (*pr.* 56, and at the time still *pro cos.* in Asia). And so Appius, Cicero hints darkly, had made some sort of promises to Sardinian "barbarians."[190]

Scaurus' own speech—delivered in the traditional rags, with many tears and talk of his father and that curule aedileship—is said by Asconius to have greatly moved the jurors. He was easily acquitted by each of the three "Aurelian" judicial *ordines*.[191] Scaurus' defense was evidently highly effective also with the audience at that trial. Cicero, backed by a popular uprising, succeeded in getting the *pr. repetundis* M. Cato to admit a *calumnia* charge against Scaurus' accusers. Yet all were acquitted when tried, which is a bit surprising, since the jury was apparently the same.[192] P. Valerius Triarius prosecuted Scaurus again in 54, but for *ambitus* in connection with his consular bid. He somehow escaped, only to meet conviction and exile on an *ambitus* charge in (so it seems) the second half of 53.[193]

Scaurus is the last praetor attested for Sardinia in our period. Now, Broughton[194] tentatively identifies M. Aurelius Cotta provisionally as praetor in 55 or 54, and suggests he governed Sardinia in 50 (evidently *ex praetura*, after an interval as under the *lex Pompeia* of 52) as well as part of 49. The evidence for a praetorship is limited to two items. First, in spring 49 Caesar sent Q. Valerius Orca (*pr.* 57) as *legatus* with one legion and C. Scribonius Curio (*tr. pl.* 50) *pro praetore* with two legions to take Sardinia (with its grain) and Sicily respectively.[195] We are told M. Cotta fled from his post in Sardinia even before Caesar's *legatus* arrived in the *provincia*, as did M. Cato (*pr.* 54), whom the Senate had sent earlier that year to Sicily: Caesar's men took control of Sicily and Sardinia "vacant of their *imperia*."[196] Now, all three of the other instances in the *Bellum Civile* of "imperia" (in the plural) are derisive.[197] These passages, coupled with the fact that Caesar sent a *legatus* (evidently without *imperium*) against M. Cotta, suggest that Cotta's command was likely to have been an *ad hoc* appointment rather than a proper praetorian governorship.

The second item is even less substantial. Cicero[198] mentions that in late 54, Pompey was encouraging a certain "Gutta" in his candidacy for the consulship of 52, with talk of bringing in Caesar as a backer as well. Long ago, J. Hoffa conjectured that "Cotta" should be read for the name.[199] But the probability of the emendation is greatly diminished if the Sardinian commander of 49 was no more than a *legatus*—as Caesar indeed implies.

13.3 Pre-Sullan Spain

13.3.1 *Praetorian Commands in the Spains, 122–100*

Our first datable item for Spain in this period is an important one for the general history of Roman administration. Plutarch says that C. Marius, after his praetorship in the city (in 115), received by lot Hispania Ulterior. This is the first certain attestation of a city praetor proceeding in the year after his magistracy to hold a command in a regular territorial *provincia*.[200] Now, one must keep in mind that this is a chance reference, concerning a well-known Roman commander; Plutarch offers no special comment on the procedure. The Senate may have sent other praetors in this fashion to provinces before Marius.[201] One good possibility is C. Laelius, *pr.* 145, who apparently (see 7.3.1) took up an *ex praetura* command for Citerior for 144. In Laelius' case, however, there is no telling whether he had spent the year of his praetorship in the city or in some (non-Spanish) territorial *provincia*. When it comes to Marius' commission for 114, we know too little of what was happening in the other *provinciae* that year to see why this type of arrangement was needed.[202] Of course, soon after Marius, the practice of *ex praetura* commands grew common (15.3.2), and was de facto institutionalized for all praetors by L. Cornelius Sulla as dictator in his reforms of 81.

Once in Ulterior, Marius is said to have relieved the *provincia* of brigandage, "although the province was still wild and banditry was considered an honorable profession."[203] The only other detail of his command is that he requisitioned grain for his *cella*.[204] Exactly how long he had to stay is uncertain. The next known holder of the *provincia* is the praetor L. Calpurnius Piso Frugi, who can have arrived in either 113 or 112.[205] He is said by Appian, in a severe summary portion of his *Iberica*—unfortunately, our only continuous source on Spanish affairs in this era—to have been succeeded by Ser. Sulpicius Galba.[206] Galba was later *cos.* 108, and so must have been praetor by 111, which provides a terminus.

Appian[207] says that Piso Frugi was sent in response to revolts. He certainly had to do some fighting: for a start, Cicero describes how this praetor had to order a replacement for his (senatorial) ring, which he had damaged in battle. What happened is that Piso had a craftsman weigh out the gold and manufacture the ring in the forum at Corduba, while he himself watched from his curule chair. One factor behind Piso's ostentatious demonstration of self-restraint is surely that he wanted to show himself a true son of his father Piso "Frugi."[208] But there obviously had been complaints—after all, at least part of the province was in arms—perhaps even regarding his predecessor C. Marius.

In the event, fighting in Ulterior was serious enough for Piso (as Cicero reports) to be killed in the province. Nothing is known of the activities of the praetor Ser. Galba, who arrived following upon this disaster, reaching Spain in either

112 or 111. It is, however, still another excellent example of the *sors opportuna*: he was son of the Ser. Galba who was *pr.* 151 for Hispania Ulterior (see 7.3.1) and then *cos.* 144. The dispatch of the son of the most notorious commander in Ulterior's history precisely at this time—following upon the death of a praetor in the province, and with Citerior perhaps also in danger, thanks to migrating Germanic tribes[209]— will have been a deliberate gesture on the part of the Senate, meant to send the province a forceful message. From the Senate's perspective, it will have been nicely ironical that he was succeeding the son of the Calpurnius Piso who had established the permanent *quaestio repetundarum* in response to the senior Galba's murderous command (9.2.1). A special arrangement would be particularly understandable if the younger Ser. Galba had to go to Spain for 111, the first year of the war with Jugurtha in not-so-distant Numidia. Perhaps he was praetor in a different *provincia* (city or otherwise), and received Ulterior *ex praetura*, like Marius a few years previously. In short, the fact that a Ser. Galba was available for this command at this time does seem quite unlikely to be a pure accident of the lot.

Galba was back in Rome in time to win the consulship for 108; he must have been at least moderately successful in his fighting in Spain to be elected to the office at this time, with the Jugurthine War of course still raging and the Mamilian *quaestio* setting a harsh political tone at Rome. Galba's successor in Hispania Ulterior was another praetor, Q. Servilius Caepio, the future *cos.* 106. Eutropius implies he was in the *provincia* in the year 109, as we would expect (the absolute upper date is 110). Caepio returned to Rome to triumph over the Lusitani on 28 October 107, and walked right into the consulship.[210] It was the first triumph from Spain since Metellus "Balearicus" in 121, and the first from one of the Spanish *provinciae* proper since Scipio Aemilianus in 132. Yet the province was not fully pacified. By chance, we hear of a major setback in Ulterior just two years (at most) after Caepio's triumph.[211]

Appian[212] provides an odd notice for the period immediately to follow: "When the Cimbri invaded Italy, and Sicily was torn by the second servile war, the Romans were too much preoccupied to send soldiers to Spain, and so sent *legati* to settle the war as well as they could." But a praetorian commander is definitely attested for Hispania Ulterior for 104: a certain L. Caesius did enough fighting to be hailed as "imperator" in or by that year. A recently found inscription from Alcántara—dated by the *coss.* 104 as well as by the title "L. Caesio C.f. imperatore" itself—shows how he granted a *deditio* to a tribe of the province after consultation with his *consilium* on precisely what to exact from them as security.[213] He may have asked for a triumph on his return to Rome, but (if so) was turned down.[214]

Another praetorian commander was soon to follow. Appian says that M. Marius—presumably brother of the seven-time consul—subdued some Lusitanians with the aid of various Celtiberian tribes. The Senate then authorized him to settle those Celtiberian *auxilia* near Colenda (not readily identifiable). There is good reason to date that victory to the year 101, though any time in the period 103–100 is possible.[215] One notes that C. Marius was consul in each of those years. It is hard not to suspect that his influence somehow secured his old *provincia* of Hispania Ulterior for his (putative) brother. If—as is likely—M. Marius received that command while the Cimbri still were threatening north Italy (i.e., in one of the years 103–101), few in the Senate might care to notice the coincidence of two Marii having drawn Ulterior within a dozen or so years.

Almost nothing is known of the arrangements for Hispania Citerior for the last two decades of the second century. We have the milestones of two praetors from this general era, only one of which allows a guess at even an approximate date.[216] For the period 105–101, it is just conceivable (following that odd item in Appian) that a *legatus* held the province in some or even all of these years. A chance notice does hint at administrative neglect. When the Cimbri, Teutones, and their allies crossed the Pyrenees into Spain in 104, the Livian *Periocha* tells us they were routed not by Romans but by Celtiberians.[217] Either there was no proper Roman commander in the province, or there was one and he deliberately (perhaps even on orders from Rome) stayed out of the path of these terrifying tribes.

13.3.2 *The Spanish* Provinciae *in the 90s and 80s*

Both Spanish provinces seem to have had praetorian commanders by around the year 100. C. Coelius Caldus, the future *cos.* 94, apparently recieved Hispania Citerior for 100 or 99.[218] An L. Cornelius Dolabella must have been in Ulterior in 99, and perhaps already in 100, though probably not any earlier (remember M. Marius). He triumphed from Hispania Ulterior on 26 January 98,[219] the second triumph from that *provincia* within a decade.

It is strange that Dolabella never made it to the consulship, the first praetorian *triumphator* in the post-Gracchan period not to have done so.[220] One explanation may be the fact that both Spanish *provinciae* soon once again erupted. The year 98 saw some hard fighting in Spain: Obsequens reports that the Hispani were defeated in "many" battles (but with no indication of province). Other sources attest that one of the consuls of that year, T. Didius, was dispatched to Citerior. Whether Obsequens' notice refers to the consul Didius, or the praetor Coelius Caldus, or the (unknown) successor to L. Dolabella in Ulterior—or some combination of the above—is impossible to tell. For 97, the Senate prorogued T. Didius in Hispania Citerior and declared Ulterior consular as well; it fell to the *cos.* P. Licinius Crassus. Didius and Crassus triumphed over the Celtiberians and Lusitani respectively on 10 and 12 June 93.[221] The years 96–94 are the only years in the period 132–81 in which we can be sure two holders of *imperium* were simultaneously in the Iberian peninsula.

The length of these consular commands begs comment. The fact that T. Didius (*cos.* 98) spent four or (more probably) five years in the *provincia* may in part be due to his military abilities: Citerior seems very much to have needed a capable general, at least at the time of his arrival. Now, the chronology of Didius' command is nearly impossible to work out, since the main account of his campaigning comes from that summary portion of Appian's *Iberica*. Apparently, he scored some early successes (97 and perhaps 96) against the Celtiberians.[222] We also hear of some episodes where his Roman forces were quite at risk of destruction, showing the extent of the military emergency.[223] Appian[224] himself mentions some achievements of T. Didius' long stay in his province: a battle in which he reportedly slew twenty thousand of the Aravaci, his transplantation of the population of Termes from its naturally fortified site, and a successful eight-month siege of Colenda. But he also describes in relative detail an episode which suggests that Didius had finished the real work of his province after just a couple of years or so.

The tale concerns the unnamed town near Colenda which the praetor M. Marius by *senatus consultum* "five years previously" had settled with Celtiberian *auxilia*. Appian says after its establishment it had fallen into poverty and so resorted to banditry. After taking Colenda, Didius had resolved to destroy also this neighboring town, and so "with the concurrence of the ten *legati* who were still present" treacherously slaughtered its entire population. If Appian is correct on the "five years," the date of this massacre is quite possibly 96, and can hardly be later than 95 (see above on the date of M. Marius).

The mention of the "ten *legati*," however, gives pause. Appian seems to equate them with the *legati* he says were sent to administer Spain in the period of the Cimbric War and Sicilian slave revolt. That seems hard to imagine. For a start, Rome sent *decem legati* to serve as a *consilium* to a magistrate in the field (not as a self-standing entity), and in any case a tenure of five or more years for that type of commission is wholly unparalleled. The inclusion of that detail certainly raises a question regarding Appian's general reliability in this passage. It is not impossible, however, that in 96 or 95 the Senate sent *decem legati* to aid T. Didius in making permanent arrangements for a newly pacified Hispania Citerior. In that case, Appian's mistake would be to imagine that his earlier *legati* for Iberia were identical with this later group. The presence of *decem legati* might also help explain Didius' prorogation through 94.

At first glance Didius' action against M. Marius' foundation comes off as an extreme example of triumph hunting.[225] Indeed, the triumph Didius received in 93, Appian alleges, was for this gruesome act. But systematic massacres like this by highranking magistrates are not too often found after the Lusitanian command of the *pr.* Ser. Galba in 151/150.[226] And Didius surely had done enough by this time to earn a triumph.[227] Killing brigands, even en masse, would add little to his military glory.[228] So there may also be a political dimension to his destruction of this town, which after all was populated by recently created *clientes* of the *gens Maria*.

By the 90s, there had developed quite a gap between the number of *provinciae* and the pool of suitable magistrates to staff them (see 11.1.1). That must be another factor behind the *cos.* 98 T. Didius' repeated prorogations in Hispania Citerior. The fact that the *cos.* 97 P. Licinius Crassus (not a famous military man) also had a long tenure in Ulterior confirms it. P. Crassus did enough fighting in his *provincia* to be hailed *imperator* and to triumph on his return *de Lusitaneis* in June 93 (observing propriety, two days after Didius, his senior as *cos.* 98). But Crassus also had enough time to make a purely scientific trip to the not-so-near Cassiterides island group, where he observed some golden-age attributes among its peaceable population.[229] He surely did not need three or four years to earn his triumph: Crassus' multiple prorogations reflect the exigencies, not of his province, but of the wider administrative system.

To be sure, the Spanish *provinciae* always offered unexpected dangers. Obsequens says a "Nasica" in the year 94 punished rebel leaders and destroyed their towns.[230] That man is quite likely to be the P. Cornelius Scipio Nasica who

was (or was soon to be) son-in-law of L. Licinius Crassus (*cos.* 95).[231] The date, however, raises a problem. In the year 94, T. Didius was still in Hispania Citerior and
P. Licinius Crassus in Ulterior. The best explanation is that Nasica saw his service
in Spain as a *legatus*[232] under one of those two consular commanders. His marriage
tie with L. Crassus lends slight support to the idea that he served under the *pro cos.*
P. Crassus (a distant cousin of the *cos.* 95). Praetorian rank might be inferred from
the status of his superior (whichever consular it was) and the semi-independence
of his attested actions. But his family background and connections make it entirely conceivable that he obtained his (putative) legateship as a subpraetorian.[233]

    We do not know exactly how T. Didius and P. Crassus were succeeded when
they left for Rome. The next known commander for Spain is C. Valerius Flaccus,
the consul of 93, who arrived either in or soon after his year of office. It is difficult
to tell, since Appian in that summary portion of his *Iberica* is our only source on
Flaccus' appointment and the initial stage of what was to prove a very long command. Appian says that Flaccus was dispatched in response to another Celtiberian
revolt. (That in itself may imply a date later in 93 or in 92.) He quelled the rebellion, we are told, by killing (once again) twenty thousand, and followed that success by taking police action in Celtiberian Belgida.[234]

    Who was in Ulterior at the time? As it happens, after P. Crassus' departure in
93 there is no firm proof of a separate commander for the *provincia*—indeed, until
the early 70s. C. Flaccus may have been expected to exercise *imperium* in both
Spanish provinces and (at least later) in Gaul as well, though not necessarily all at
the same time: he is attested as *imperator* at Contrebia (i.e., Celtiberia) in 87 and
in Gaul in 83.[235] Flaccus triumphed from Celtiberia and Gaul in 81 or 80, after a
dozen or so years of continuous command.[236] During that span of time, Roman
outlaws found the largely neglected Iberian peninsula a convenient refuge. In 88
or 87, some prominent Marian exiles made their way into Spain and then (when
C. Marius secured his own return to Italy) back out again. Members of the anti-
Marian faction found Spain hospitable, too. M. Licinius Crassus—son of the *cos.*
97 P. Crassus, and a member of his staff in Spain—spent eight months of the year
85 in the peninsula, apparently in his father's old *provincia* of Ulterior. There he
managed to raise a select private army (2,500 men) by making the rounds of the
cities. Crassus allegedly even stormed Malaca before crossing to Africa and thence
to Italy.[237]

    We do not know what the reaction was of the Marian government in Italy to
such escapades. It may have been too preoccupied with the threat of Sulla's
inevitable invasion from the east to care all that much. Or there may have been
arrangements unknown to us. Cicero says that M. Fonteius (a future praetor of the
mid-70s) was in the province of Hispania Ulterior as a *legatus* at the time of Sulla's
arrival in Italy (i.e., in early 83).[238] Fonteius presumably served under someone's
command; he was too junior to hold the *provincia* by himself.

    One notes that even after Sulla's landing the Marians managed to dispatch a
new commander to Spain, namely Q. Sertorius (on whom see 10.5.6). Sertorius'
Spanish *provincia* was apparently Hispania Citerior,[239] which he set out for (after
exploits in Italy) in late 83.[240] But he may have been intended to hold both Citerior
and Ulterior as a combined *provincia*.[241]

Sertorius was a failed candidate for the tribunate of (probably) 88. The precise date of his praetorship seems impossible to ascertain, except (as C. F. Konrad has shown) it is unlikely to be as late as the accepted date of 83. Given the irregularities of the mid-80s, there are clearly a range of possibilities; Konrad has made a reasonable case for a city praetorship in 85 (or perhaps 84), with Citerior as Sertorius' *ex praetura* province.[242] However, it may be relevant for the general chronology that Appian mentions "praetors" who failed to welcome Sertorius in Spain and refused to be superseded, out of partisanship to Sulla, only to find themselves ejected from Iberia.[243] This is puzzling, since Appian also offers an allusion to pro-Marian "praetors" in Spain in 82, who dispatched Celtiberian horse to the consuls of the year.[244] If these notices refer to the same individuals—and it was not Sertorius himself who sent that cavalry—we must assume the "praetors" switched allegiance from the Marians to Sulla during the course of the year 82 (there are plenty of parallels for that).

It indeed would be surprising if Q. Sertorius was the first commander the Marians thought of sending to Spain. For what it is worth, Plutarch implies that Sertorius found Spain not in a state of anarchy, but suffering from the rapacity of Roman commanders (στρατηγοί): he is said to have won native support by remitting taxes and ridding the cities of the burden of billeting.[245] In sum, the picture one gets from our available sources is that Sertorius had praetorian precedessors in Iberia. If true, that would seem to exclude a very early date (i.e., the year 86 and perhaps 85) for his praetorship.

13.4 Spain in the Period after Sulla

Sulla formally outlawed Q. Sertorius on taking power late in the year 82.[246] Other senators proscribed by Sulla were to make their way to Sertorius, including some highranking senators.[247] In time, Sertorius also named his own "senators" and established a "Senate" of 300.[248] Plutarch says that Sertorius, once established, appointed "quaestors" and "praetors," and in general "kept Roman customs." That evidently included the traditional magistrates' insignia, and much else beside.[249] One M. Marius came to Sertorius as a proper Roman senator, served as a "quaestor" in (apparently) early 76, and soon reached the "praetorship" in the renegade government.[250]

Sertorius presided over his "Senate" of *proscripti*, which (like its archetype in Rome) served as a *consilium* to his magistrates and as such issued nonbinding *sententiae*.[251] In other respects, Sertorius apparently took care to appear as a normal Roman provincial governor, as an extended fragment of Livy from a Vatican manuscript goes to show.[252] But the quality of Sertorius' administration is said to have deteriorated over time.[253]

13.4.1 *The Sertorian War: General Chronological Considerations*

Eventually Sertorius was killed by his own officers, an event which our sources variously date to the eighth or tenth year of his rebellion.[254] The chronological confusion on even the major detail of the date of Sertorius' assassination is sadly typi-cal of our sources on this war.[255] Appian purports to give an "annalistic" account, yet what we get is so sketchy that it is impossible to pin down key events such as in what year Pompey arrived to fight the war (77 or 76?), only to be soon routed at the town of Lauro (itself infuriatingly hard to place). Plutarch in the *Sertorius* offers a fair amount of detail, but much of it in generalizing "for instance" passages that cannot be dated. In particular, he reduces Sertorius' early battles to a montage: the result is that the first event that we can truly synchronize with Appian's account is the fighting at Sucro and Segontia some four or five years into the war. Yet Plutarch soon skips to the end of the story, with Sertorius' assassination. In the *Pompey*, he is even more severe in his presentation of datable events. In this *Life*, Plutarch decribes Lauro, Sucro, the threatening letter Pompey wrote to the Senate in winter 75/74—and then the fatal conspiracy. Of Latin sources, that fragment of Livy does provide an invaluable account of Spanish affairs between two (undated) cam-paigning seasons. And the Livian *Periocha* provides a relative chronology of the war full enough to be coordinated with Appian's annalistic narrative. But it is frustrat-ing that overall the *Periocha* mentions just two engagements in this conflict by name (the sieges of Clunia and Calagurris, some years into the war). Even in the tale of Sertorius' death, the epitomator omits the gentilician name of the key con-spirator (offering in *Per.* 96 only "Marcus" for M. Perperna, last mentioned—as "Perperna"—at *Per.* 92). Florus and Orosius mostly corroborate what we find in the *Periocha*, yet not without a twist or two. The remains of Sallust's *Histories* are really only helpful for the initial stages of the war.

Fortunately, the careful recent work of Konrad on the chronology—and indeed all other aspects—of the Sertorian War has made extended discussion of many previously thorny problems unnecessary.[256] Konrad points out that for the later part of the war, the ancient sources tell a relatively coherent story of five years of fighting from the arrival of Pompey to the death of Sertorius, a framework which most scholars have recognized as reliable.[257] Year 1 is marked by Pompeius' defeat at Lauro. Year 2 has three large battles (Valentia, the Sucro, and Segontia) and also the attempted blockade of Sertorius at Clunia. Year 3 sees dissension in Sertorius' ranks (with countermeasures) and unsuccessful sieges of Pallantia and Calagurris by Q. Metellus Pius and Pompey. Year 4 contains no great battles, and in Year 5 a conspiracy led by Perperna results in the assassination of Sertorius.

The trouble is deciding to which five consular years those events belong. Konrad argues in admirable detail for the years 77 through 73, against a traditional view that correlates the five years with 76 through 72. There are, however, a few points in his reconstruction that admit further investigation. For example, it is clear that Metellus Pius and Pompey both returned from Spain to triumph only in late 71.[258] Would the Senate really prorogue each of them twice after Sertorius' death? Sertorius was killed when the campaigning season was still under way. M. Perperna—who had organized the assassination and then taken over his com-mand—saw many Iberians desert to Metellus and Pompey and had trouble instill-ing loyalty among the Sertorian troops. Metellus, in fact, departed for "other [i.e., western] parts of Spain" in the belief that Pompey by himself could handle Perperna. Pompey defeated, captured, and killed Perperna in one battle, thus effectively ending the war, says the Livian *Periocha*, "almost in the tenth year since it began." That same source says that Sertorius was killed in the eighth year of his generalship, suggesting that it took Pompey less than two years to extinguish these last flames of revolt.[259] The rebel cities mostly surrendered to Pompey (and no doubt also Metellus), with the notable exceptions of Uxama and Calagurris. Pompey destroyed the first of those. He then only started the siege of the second before leaving for Italy.[260] These facts suggest that Pompey and Metellus remained in Iberia for about one and a half years (not two and a half years) after Sertorius' death.

13.4.2 *Roman Efforts against Sertorius down to 77*

But let us start near the beginning, in late 82 B.C. Plutarch says that Sertorius, on hearing of Sulla's victory, knew that a new commander from Rome for his *provincia* was inevitable. Accordingly, he sent a deputy with a legion-sized force to hold the Pyrenees against attack. The Sullan general, one C. Annius, should be a praetor of 81. His coinage shows he had two quaestors, which M. Crawford (following Badian) rightly considers to be an indication he was in charge of both Spanish provinces.[261] As it happened, Annius easily crossed into the peninsula and managed to drive Sertorius out of Spain. Sertorius crossed to North Africa (suggesting that the *pro pr.* Pompey had already left by that time to claim his triumph), but the Maurusii there forced him right back to Iberia. Yet Annius effectively secured the Spanish shores against Sertorius. So once again the Marian general ended up in Mauretania. This time, however, Sertorius had a kindlier welcome, since he showed a willingness to involve himself in Mauretanian dynastic disputes. Among his exploits was a decisive victory over a certain "Paccianus," whom Sulla had sent "with a military force" (probably from Spain) to intervene in Mauretania.[262]

It was at this point (probably in early 80) that the Lusitanians invited Sertorius back to Spain to be their leader. As such, Plutarch says he subdued τὴν ἐγγὺς Ἰβηρίαν. That is probably not "Hispania Citerior," as Konrad takes it ("Plutarch is anticipating"), but "neighboring Spain" (sc. to Africa).[263] Indeed, it is southern Spain that will see all of the heavy fighting attested for the next two or so years. In those struggles, we are told that Sertorius had to fight "four Roman *strategoi*" and face a massive show of Roman military might—by Plutarch's count, 120,000 infantry, 6,000 horse, and 2,000 archers and slingers. These huge numbers "derive from a summary of the total of Roman forces engaged in the Sertorian War between 80 and 72," according to Konrad.[264] That seems reasonable. But who are the "four *strategoi*"?

Plutarch combined with some bits of Sallust's *Histories* (especially the Vienna fragment first published in 1979)[265] and a few other sources show a series of battles between Sertorius and Roman forces for what must be the years 80 and 79. First, Sertorius successfully fought a Cotta near Mellaria in the straits. No title is offered, except that he was one of the "antistrategoi" (here, "opposing generals").[266] Next was Fufidius, the governor of Baetica," whom he defeated on the river Baetis. In the battle, Fufidius lost two thousand men (from a force of at least two legions) Fufidius called for help from M. Domitius Calvinus, then evidently *pro consule* in Hispania Citerior. But Domitius was having his own problems with Hirtuleius, a

Sertorian officer who had fortified Consabura.[267] Eventually, Hirtuleius was to defeat Domitius on the Anas river (in Hispania Ulterior), evidently as he was making his way to Fufidius; the Roman commander lost his life in the battle. Around this time—the exact chronology of Domitius' disaster is uncertain—Ulterior was declared consular and allotted to the *cos.* 80 Q. Metellus Pius. For Metellus, things immediately went awry. He sent a "hegemon" Thoranius (or Thorius) with an army, perhaps as an advance force to bail out Domitius. But Sertorius vanquished and killed that man, and then defeated Metellus himself "many times."[268]

This series of events has received expert discussion by Konrad, whose reconstruction I mostly accept—including that Plutarch's "four *strategoi*" are Cotta, Fufidius, Domitius, and Thorius.[269] Cotta (not closely identifiable, but perhaps L. Aurelius Cotta, the future *pr.* 70) must be a *legatus* of L. Fufidius, an intimate of Sulla's[270] who was definitely a praetorian commander in Hispania Ulterior in 80.[271] For M. Domitius Calvinus, the *provincia* of Citerior and rank of *pro consule* are certain.[272] He must be a praetor of 80, losing his life that year or in 79.[273] (We do not hear of any special arrangements for Citerior for 79, suggesting that it had been planned for M. Calvinus to hold the *provincia* for that year.) The only sticking point is the date of L. Fufidius' praetorship. According to Orosius, Fufidius had been merely of centurion status. Even if that last item is an exaggeration,[274] Konrad's idea that he won immediate election as a praetor for 81 seems unlikely.[275] It is very difficult to find room for Fufidius among the praetors for that year, even assuming a college of eight (see 11.1.3).

I suggest Sulla adlected Fufidius into the Senate *inter quaestorios* in 81, and saw to his election[276] as praetor for 80. (If really an ex-*primipilaris*, as Orosius says he was, Fufidius likely will have met the age requirement for the praetorship.) On this interpretation, Fufidius and M. Domitius Calvinus (who must be *pr.* 80) took up armed *provinciae* as *pro consulibus* during the year of their actual magistracy. That is what the praetor C. Annius had done for Spain in 81—and, as we shall see (14.6.1), probably also M. Minucius Thermus for Asia that same year. Our record shows that Sulla, on taking control of the state, had already decided on a system in which commanders normally receive territorial provinces *ex magistratu*. But the emergency posed by Sertorius in Spain from 82 and the necessity—apparently around this same time—of recalling L. Licinius Murena from Asia (14.5.9) forced the dictator to make exceptions from the very start.

As I have noted, for 79 Ulterior was consular while Citerior was supposed to remain as praetorian. Yet the death of M. Calvinus left the latter province without *imperium* for a time, so far as we know. Calvinus' replacement evidently was the *pr.* 79 Q. Calidius. Whether Calidius arrived in his year as praetor or only as a promagistrate in 78, we cannot tell. He probably did not meet with much military success, since he was condemned in a trial before *iudices* on his return.[277]

Before long, the Sertorian War was severe enough to draw in a praetorian commander even from outside Iberia. L. Manlius was a *pro consule* in Gallia Transalpina, who is known to have fled from Aquitania after first losing his army's baggage.[278] He also is said to have crossed into Spain to aid Q. Metellus against Sertorius, but apparently made it not much further than Ilerda in northeast Iberia, having lost all three of his legions in battle with the rebel commander Hirtuleius.

Plutarch tells us that this defeat resulted in the quick (κατὰ τάχος) dispatch to Spain of Cn. Pompeius, that is, as a *privatus cum imperio*.[279]

Konrad regards L. Manlius as "presumably praetor in 79, *pro consule* Gallia Transalpina in 78. He intervened in Spain . . . probably in 78."[280] It does seem reasonable to assume that Manlius was in command of Gallia Transalpina at least in 78, and was defeated while trying to enter Iberia in late 78 or early 77. The Senate must have ordered that move: Manlius can hardly have withdrawn a large army from Transalpine Gaul simply on his own initiative or on Metellus' request. The logical time for the Senate to take such a decision would be later in 78. At that point, M. Aemilius Lepidus (*cos.* 78) had set out for the command of his *provincia* of the two Gauls[281] but had not yet risen against the *res publica*, and Q. Calidius in Hispania Citerior was soon eligible to be superseded. The decision to send Pompey to Spain of course belongs to 77, probably the spring or early summer (11.8.5, 15.2.1). When he moved from Italy against Sertorius, no one seems to have been in Gallia Transalpina.[282]

13.4.3 *Background to the Dispatch of Pompey to Spain*

The year 77 opened without consuls, and thus without praetors (see 11.8.5, 15.2.1). While M. Aemilius Lepidus (*cos.* 78, and now *pro cos.* for the two Gauls) was making threatening gestures in Italy, only so much could be done for the standing *provinciae*. For 77, the Senate prorogued Metellus Pius in Ulterior and no doubt intended for L. Manlius to move permanently out of Transalpina to hold Hispania Citerior. But Manlius' inability to get past Ilerda quashed that plan, and left the *provincia* wholly exposed. Meanwhile, Metellus in Ulterior continued to suffer reverses at the hands of the rebels. Appian even reports contemporary (so it seems) fears that Sertorius would march on Italy.[283]

Those fears would be particularly acute after the defeat and death of Lepidus, once his στρατηγός M. Perperna had found his way to Spain.[284] Perperna, as we have seen (13.1.4), had been a praetor for Sicily under the Marian government. Though Sulla had him proscribed, Perperna apparently retained his praetorian insignia even after abandoning Sicily to Pompey in 82. Perperna is said subsequently to have spent time in Liguria. He shows up in the last phase of Lepidus' revolt, the effort to control Sardinia and starve Rome into submission (11.8.5). On Lepidus' death, Perperna shifted some quite considerable resources (both men and money) to Spain.[285]

Perperna's idea on arrival in Iberia, we are told, was to wage war independently against Metellus Pius. This of course falls into a long tradition of Roman triumph hunting—though no triumph can have been expected in this instance. Perperna may have thought that his birth (he had a consular father and grandfather), wealth, and praetorian status entitled him to his own *provincia*.[285] It was a patently unrealistic plan. There of course was no good reason why Perperna should not acknowledge Sertorius as his superior. At this point, Plutarch says Sertorius "was backed by all the people within the Ebro." In any case, Perperna, as a proscribed ex-praetor of Sicily, was technically inferior to Sertorius, the outlaw *pro consule* for Spain! All the same, Perperna seems to have tried for some time to make his design work.

Plutarch says that Perperna's soldiers forced him to join forces with Sertorius (only) when it was announced that Pompey had crossed the Pyrenees.[287]

It would be good to know for certain the date when Pompey advanced into Spain. Indeed, the chronology of the rest of the Sertorian War wholly depends on it. Konrad summarizes the modern views: "Pompey's arrival in Spain has been variously dated to 77 or 76, but with few exceptions, scholars place in 76 his first clash with Sertorius, at Lauro." For the rest of the war, the traditional chronology has posited "the battles of Valentia, the Sucro, and Segontia in 75, the sieges of Pallantia and Calagurris, and Metellus' return to the interior, in 74," and the death of Sertorius in 72.[288]

Konrad himself offers a powerful argument for placing both Pompey's arrival and the battle of Lauro in fall of 77.[289]

> Lepidus' revolt was short-lived. . . .[There is] no reason to date any of the fighting in Italy later than March. The Senate turned its attention to Spain, and appointed Pompeius, immediately after Lepidus had left Italy—they did not wait until after his death. . . . Pompey's Spanish expeditionary force was ready in forty days or so, perhaps much sooner. . . . Four or five months seems a reasonable estimate for his march from Rome to Spain. To reach Lauro by September he would have to set out in April or May; but there is reason to believe that 77 was intercalary, in which case . . . Pompey's departure may be moved up to as early as March.

Konrad also offers a case for dating the assassination of Sertorius to 72, though one that is much less muscular and which ultimately fails to convince.[290]

This is not the place to take up the vexed question of the chronology of the whole Sertorian War, especially since it was an entirely "consular" affair after the year 77, and as such lies outside the strict scope of this study. Yet it does matter for our study of the praetorship whether Pompey simply passed through Gallia Transalpina in 77 or stayed there through the winter, and whether he was the sole commander in that Gallic *provincia* when he did whatever he did.

Appian offers the first obstacle to Konrad's reconstruction of arrival in Spain already in 77. He says that it was the fear of Sertorius and Perperna joining forces and marching on Italy that prompted the Senate to send "another general [i.e., Pompey] and army" to Spain.[291] Now, we have seen that Plutarch has the two rebels join forces only when Pompey was at the Pyrenees. But the two accounts are not necessarily contradictory. It is safe to assume that the Senate foresaw the possibility of a juncture as soon as Perperna set sail from Sardinia to Spain. It would not know (or perhaps even care) about Perperna's desire for an "independent" command.

Then there is the matter of Pompey's appointment and march to Spain. The process of appointment will not have taken that long (see 11.8.1), but it was hardly instantaneous. True, Pompey, once he was granted this command as *pro consule*, is said to have quickly prepared his army—though within a timespan surely not too much short of the "forty days" Sallust's Pompey claims in the letter (from winter 75/74) in the *Histories*.[292] That letter (unfortunately) is the fullest source on the initial stages of Pompey's Spanish campaign. Sallust has Pompey make four main assertions regarding the early part of his command.[294] He opened up a new Alpine route, which meant driving an enemy that was allegedly poised to attack Italy all the way from the Alps into Spain. (Appian confirms that Pompey created a new pass.)[294] He "took back" Gaul, the Pyrenees, Lacetania (in northeast Iberia), and the Indigetes, and withstood the first attack of Sertorius (who had numerically supe-rior forces). He had his winter camp (we are not told which year or years) in hos-tile territory. Pompey also conducted winter campaigns.

Broughton[295] observed of Pompey's letter that it "admits no interruption in activities from the raising of his army to his settlement in winter quarters (*inter sae-vissimos hostes*) after his first battle with Sertorius." In truth, the letter seems very tendentious. For instance, in it Sallust's Pompey says nothing explicitly of Lauro — just "I weathered the first attack of the victorious Sertorius," which is an artful allu-sion to that defeat, and his subsequent success in not being totally destroyed by Sertorius. That said, Pompey's opening of the Alps and the march through Gaul will have taken some time. We must remember that when Pompey received his Spanish commission, Transalpina was effectively without a commander. That was on account of the disaster of L. Manlius in late 78 or early 77 (who had taken three legions out of Gaul and then lost them) and the revolt of the *cos.* 78 M. Aemilius Lepidus (who was ostensibly *pro cos.* 77 for the two Gauls). So when Pompey is made to say that he "recovered Gaul," perhaps his statement is not pure rhetorical exaggeration. The trophy Pompey set up at the end of the Sertorian War in the Pyrenees (as reported by Pliny) recorded the capture of towns in Gaul, perhaps a large number. And Cicero several times speaks of Pompey's "bellum Trans-alpinum."[296]

13.4.4 *The Praetorian Command of M. Fonteius in Transalpine Gaul*

Another possible obstacle to Konrad's reconstruction is the evidence of Cicero's *Pro Fonteio*. That oration does not figure much in Konrad's chronological studies.[297] Yet the material of this speech seems quite germane to the present investigation. Quaestor in 85 or 84 and afterward a *legatus* in Hispania Ulterior ca. 83 and then Macedonia,[298] M. Fonteius later held a praetorian command in Gallia Transalpina, and was defended by Cicero when he faced *repetundae* charges some-time after 70 B.C. The date of his praetorship is irritatingly problematic, since Cicero offers only a few hazy chronological pointers in his defense speech. He says Fonteius spent a *triennium* in Gallia Transalpina, and was in that *provincia* while Q. Metellus Pius and Pompey were fighting Sertorius. When Fonteius was gover-nor, Pompey's army wintered in Gaul, evidently at its full strength. At some point, Pompey also issued a *decretum* by which hostile parties in Gaul "were forced to withdraw from the lands" ("ex agris . . . decedere sunt coacti"). And Fonteius is said to have been very successful at repeatedly drumming up grain and money for the armies in Spain, as well as supplying cavalry for Rome's wars which at that time were being waged "over the whole world."[299] That last item is especially vague, since Rome had far-flung military commitments in the 70s even before the out-break of the Third Mithridatic War in 73.[300]

Broughton[301] suggests a praetorship for Fonteius in 76 or 75, with the Gallic "triennium" falling in 75–73 or 74–72. Konrad apparently favors the earlier of these two timespans.[302] There is, however, one small piece of evidence that Broughton (and Konrad) have missed, which may turn out to be relevant to this question of chronology. A Titurius helped Fonteius implement his first scheme for raising revenue, one the praetor is said to have thought of while still in Rome: the collection of a transit tax on wine within the Gallic province.[303] Since the name is so rare, he is plausibly to be identified with the moneyer L. Titurius L.f. Sabinus[304] and the *legatus* Titurius whom Pompey placed in charge of a winter camp in Celtiberia in what must be 75/74.[305] Indeed, Titurius is very likely to have been from the start a *legatus* of Pompey. His tax-collecting operations at Tolosa must belong to the period soon after Fonteius arrived in Gaul, and (if the identification with Pompey's *legatus* is accepted) most naturally is placed in the winter in which Fonteius hosted Pompeius' full army.

But when can that have been? Only 75/74 is positively excluded as Pompey's "Fonteian" winter, since that was the occasion (as we know from Sallust's letter) Pompey needed grain so badly that he threatened to march on Rome. But it does seem that Pompey's army is best described as "maximus atque ornatissimus" previous to its hard fighting (and heavy losses) against Sertorius, that is, in 77/76 before that commander entered Spain. Elsewhere in Cicero, the phrase "ornare exercitum" suggests—as we would expect—a newly equipped army.[306] However, Pompey did of course receive substantial reinforcements for 74,[307] so the point is not quite decisive.

Notwithstanding that caveat, I suggest Fonteius was *pr.* 77,[308] and that his "triennium" was in fact a bit of 77, and all 76 and 75, that is, three campaigning seasons.[309] On this interpretation, the Senate sent Fonteius in his year of office to fill in for the unexpected loss of M. Aemilius Lepidus (*cos.* 78), and perhaps to relieve the hapless L. Manlius, who had been defeated in both Aquitania and northeast Spain by early 77.[310] The context of Pompey's *decretum* ordering individuals "to stand out of the way" should be his difficult initial march to his command against the Sertorians, also in 77.[311] I also suggest—as many scholars have postulated[312]— that Pompey wintered in Gaul and only entered Spain in spring 76.

We have seen that Sallust, in the letter he ascribes to Pompey implies he had a hard time getting his army through the Alps and had to "retake" Gaul. There is no telling whether Fonteius was already there when Pompeius first arrived: perhaps not, since it does seem as though Pompey found the whole southern part of the province in chaos. The fact that Fonteius is said to have fought a war against the Vocontii—just about the first tribe one encountered upon entering the *provincia*— suggests that he too worked on safeguarding the passage between Italy and Gaul. That task probably came early in his command, for Cicero claims that Fonteius caused these and other inhabitants of his *provincia* to send grain and money to Iberia "semel atque iterum ac saepius." (Incidentally, Cicero's formulation here is entirely consistent with the "triennium" of 77–75 I have suggested above.) The year 77 is a reasonable date for the collection of the potentially lucrative wine tax by the *legatus* Titurius and others.[313] And Sallust's letter of Pompey relates that Gaul was supplying Metellus with money and food in 76; the year 75, however, saw agricultural disaster in the province, and by year's end Pompey had exhausted both his personal resources and his credit. Plutarch confirms this grim picture when he explicitly states that it was an acute food shortage that caused the Roman armies to separate for winter 75/74.[314]

In short, the possibilities for Fonteius' "triennium" as a praetorian commander in Transalpine Gaul seem limited to either the years 77–75 or 74–72, but the cumulative weight of circumstantial detail favors the earlier of these two periods. I suggest that winter 77/76 saw Metellus in Hispania Ulterior, and Pompey in Gaul near the Pyrenees where (as Sallust's letter attests) he had to do some campaigning. The memory of L. Manlius' disaster in northeast Spain was still fresh. One can understand if Pompey took care in his preparations before descending into Iberia for spring 76.

13.4.5 *Pompey's Arrival in Spain*

On the above interpretation, that Vatican fragment from Livy Book 91 belongs to late 77 and early 76. It corresponds to the summary statement in *Periocha* 91, that "Sertorius stormed some cities and took numerous states under his control" ("Sertorius aliquot urbes expugnavit plurimasque civitates in potestatem suam redegit"). However, against Konrad, it offers not the epilogue to battle at Lauro (which the *Periocha* does not mention), but the dramatic preliminaries to Pompey's arrival, before he has crossed the Pyrenees.

In the actual fragment,[315] we get first the siege (forty-four days) and capture of Contrebia by Sertorius. Next, there is a description of his winter camp at Castra Aelia (location unknown), from which Sertorius orders the manufacture of arms throughout the "provincia," and where he hosts a *conventus* of the friendly Spanish peoples. The rebel arrangements for the spring (i.e., 76) follow. Perperna—now fighting in union with Sertorius—is to protect the eastern coastal regions against Pompey: Sertorius is said to have instructed Perperna on what routes to use against Pompey "to defend the allied cities which Pompey would attack (*quas Pompeius oppugnaret*). Meanwhile, Hirtuleius is to guard against Metellus in the "other province" (i.e., Ulterior). Pompey, it is said, was heading toward Ilercaonia and Contestania, the northeast coastal areas of Citerior allied with Sertorius. There is nothing in this passage so far to exclude the interpretation that Pompey was newly arrived in Spain.

Sertorius' own strategy, we are told by Livy, was to avoid Pompey, whom Sertorius in any case "did not believe would enter into battle" ("neque in aciem descensurum eum credebat"). Konrad, following Maurenbrecher, believes "Sertorius had no basis for such an assumption until after Pompey's disaster at Lauro."[316] Yet the disaster dealt to the last Roman commander to cross into Spain— the praetor for Transalpina, L. Manlius, who had three legions—can just as easily explain Sertorius' confidence at this moment. Sertorius' first targets were the Berones and Autricones, tribes in northern Spain who had hampered his siege of Contrebia. Over the winter, they had summoned Pompey, "sending guides to show the road to the Roman army." Konrad is right that the road in question is "to the Highlands and the upper Ebro Valley," not the passage across the Pyrenees. But it does not necessarily follow that "by implication, Pompeius was already in Spain."[317] These tribes simply wanted Pompey on his arrival in Spain to make them his first priority. One thinks of Plutarch's statement here, that (even) many of Sertorius' cities looked toward Pompey, but changed minds about shifting their allegiance after the disaster at Lauro.[318] Next, Livy states that Sertorius, not knowing which army to turn against, advanced up the river Ebro. There he devastated the territory of several towns, finally encamping at friendly Calagurris. When the Berones learn of Sertorius' arrival, the fragment breaks off.[319]

It was in this campaigning season that Pompey and Sertorius will have had their first military encounter. The catalyst was Sertorius' attack on the town named Lauro. Pompey was unsuccessful in his attempt to protect the place. After twice defeating Pompey, Sertorius, evidently with the aid of Hirtuleius, went on to sack and destroy Lauro, deporting its population to Lusitania.[320] The Sertorian Lauro was evidently a place of some consequence, to judge from the ferocity of fighting for its control. Yet topographical clues to its location are few—precisely two, in fact. Plutarch mentions a prominent hill overlooking the town, which is too vague to be of any real use. Orosius however says that Pompey gathered his army "apud Pallantiam" after his defeat before the town.[321] Most of the various identifications for Lauro which have been offered lie on or near the east coast of Spain.[322] A plausible candidate for the identification is the area near Llerona del Vallès, about thirty kilometers northeast of Barcelona (and so quite close to the Pyrenees), which in this general period had a town that issued numerous coins with the legend "Lauro." Yet Konrad deems "the most attractive candidate" Schulten's solution, that Lauro is identical with La Pedrera, near Puig, about ten kilometers south of Sagunto. As it happens, the geographer Ptolemy mentions a river Pallantia on the east coast, and Palancia is the modern name for the river of Sagunto. Orosius' "apud Palantiam" is odd Latin if Palantia is a river. But he may well have thought that "Palantia" was a town. It is not unlikely that Orosius here was using Livy through an epitome, and was simply relating what he was given.[323] If Lauro was indeed so far south down the east coast of Citerior, it would offer further (slight) support for the year 76 as the date of the battle.

The Vatican fragment of Livy places Metellus Pius in Hispania Ulterior at the beginning of 76. How does he fit into this reconstruction? Orosius gives the only relative chronology of Metellus' movements in this stage of the war. He has Metellus, having been "exhausted by many battles," making a purposely circuitous path to wear out the enemy "until he could join camp with Pompey" ("donec Pompei castris consociaretur"), who meanwhile has been defeated at Lauro. Orosius then mentions a victory of Metellus over Hirtuleius at Italica, which caused Hirtuleius to have to flee into Lusitania. The death of the "Hirtuleii" (there was evidently a brother) comes still later, at an encounter that must be Segontia (one of the "Three Battles" of the year following Lauro). Frontinus confirms Orosius on this last point by placing the death of Hirtuleius at a time when Sertorius was also fighting a battle.

Other sources tell of fighting between Q. Metellus Pius and the Sertorian "quaestor" Hirtuleius. Unfortunately, none of these accounts quite match up. In the *Periocha*, Q. Metellus Pius kills Hirtuleius and defeats his army already in Book

91 (which covers 77 and part of 76). Florus notes a crushing defeat of the Hirtuleii at "Segovia" before he mentions in his narrative the battles at Lauro and the Sucro. Frontinus speaks of preparations for a decisive battle between Metellus and Hirtuleius, and also a conflict between the two (no place named) in "the hottest time of the year." And a fragment of Sallust speaks of a battle in which Hirtuleius was wounded, Metellus almost so.[324]

The narrative of Orosius (supplemented by Frontinus) seems preferable to the implication of the *Periocha* and Florus that Hirtuleius was killed before the year of the "Three Battles." One suspects that in the *Periocha* the epitomator may be collapsing several items. And Konrad persuasively has argued that Florus' "Segovia" is really part of the final conflict between Metellus and Hirtuleius at Segontia. Konrad continues: "[T]hat leaves Italica as the only distinct engagement between Hirtuleius and Metellus; since his victory enabled Metellus to leave his province, Ulterior, and join forces with Pompeius along the East Coast, Italica should be dated to the same year as the 'Three Battles,' that is, Valentia, the Sucro, and Segontia." The remaining passages—Frontinus on the battle preparations and the heat, Sallust on the wounding—should be assigned to Italica as well.[325]

Here Konrad seems right on the attribution of passages and the (relative) chronology of Italica, which must belong to Year 2 of Pompey's command in Spain. Yet Konrad also believes that the first meeting of Metellus and Pompey is "securely dated" to Year 2, after the battle of the Sucro. That, he argues, is what Orosius is alluding to in his notice that Metellus took various byways "donec Pompei castris consociaretur," despite the fact that it is placed immediately before the Lauro incident.[326] Now, Plutarch does describe how Metellus Pius arrived the day after Pompey won a partial victory in the battle at Sucro over Sertorius. Pompey ordered his lictors to lower their *fasces* before Metellus. Yet Metellus, though technically superior, forbade it. Plutarch then describes how the two commanders conducted their joint operations. He is obviously sketching a very general picture here, since the next item mentioned is Pompey's notorious letter of winter 75/74.[327]

What Plutarch does not say is that the incident of the *fasces* was the first occasion Pompey and Metellus had met in Spain. Indeed, the anecdote just as likely describes a change in the relationship between the two men. On this interpretation, Pompey's achievements at Valentia and the Sucro had won Metellus' respect; up to that time, Metellus let Pompey dip his *fasces*.

Orosius, we have seen, prima facie implies a meeting between the two around the time of Lauro. Metellus, he says, took all sorts of byways to effect a juncture. As it happens, a good source may be taken to confirm the hypothesis that the two Roman generals had managed to meet during Pompey's first year fighting Sertorius, and not just after the Sucro in Year 2. Cicero strongly implies that when Pompey arrived in Spain, he had received a quaestor (his own brother-in-law, C. Memmius) from Metellus and used him as his own—including in the difficult battle at the Sucro.[328]

To sum up the reconstruction here offered: In the year 77, Pompey received his commission against Sertorius and did some hard fighting in Transalpine Gaul, wintering with the new commander for the *provincia*, the *pr.* 77 M. Fonteius. One of Pompeius' *legati* even helped Fonteius with tax collecting at Tolosa. In 76

(Year 1), Pompey crossed the Pyrenees into Spain. His first moves may have been against Lacetania and the Indigetes in the northeast. Yet before too long Sertorius handed him a humiliating defeat at Lauro. Metellus, who had trouble moving out of Ulterior, managed to make contact with Pompey only after the battle; it was then that Metellus' quaestor (or rather *pro quaestore*) C. Memmius was transferred to the army of his brother-in-law Pompey. What Metellus and Pompey did for the remainder of this campaigning season is uncertain. But the fact that our sources have no major battles to relate[329] does not mean that either was idle.

We legitimately can doubt Appian's report that, during the winter following Pompey's defeat at Lauro (Year 1) Metellus and Pompey each headed to the Pyrenees, and Sertorius and Perperna to Lusitania.[330] In the next year (Year 2, or 75 on my reckoning), Orosius suggests that Metellus had to fight his way out of Hispania Ulterior by defeating Hirtuleius at Italica. There followed the battles of Valentia (where Pompey scored a victory over Herennius and Perperna), the Sucro (a partial victory for both Pompey and Sertorius, with Metellus arriving a day late), and Segontia (where Metellus killed the two Hirtuleii). The chronology of the rest of the war presents no really significant problems for this particular study. Winter 75/74 had Metellus in Gaul, Pompey in Ulterior; in 74/73 Pompey wintered in Gaul, Metellus in Ulterior. The two subsequent winters apparently saw both commanders in Iberia.[331] Sertorius was assassinated in 72 (see above), and both Metellus and Pompey were to return to Italy to triumph in late 71.

13.4.6 *The Successors of Pompey and Metellus Pius*

It was surely the praetorian commander M. Pupius Piso Calpurnianus who succeeded Q. Metellus Pius in Hispania Ulterior. Pupius' flagrant triumph hunting later was to be criticized by (his relative) L. Piso Caesoninus (*cos.* 58): evidently (and unsurprisingly) there was not all that much fighting to be had in this *provincia* at this point. Yet Pupius Piso got his triumph, in the year 69.[332] So at the least he was in Spain for 70 and (surely) part of 69.

We soon find another praetor in Ulterior, one C.(?) Antistius Vetus. By his time, the province was demonstrably boring. The date of Antistius' praetorship (for which his city activities are unknown) and promagistracy in Hispania Ulterior depends on that of his subordinate C. Caesar's quaestorship, which Broughton assigns with confidence to 69.[333] In truth, the year 68 looks more plausible for that quaestorship. We hear that Antistius delegated some routine legal responsibilities to Caesar in the province. But Caesar, right after what was evidently his first visit to Gades, asked his commander to let him quit Ulterior "as soon as possible" to take part in political events in Rome and left the province before he had a successor. Despite a diversion in Cisalpine Gaul, Caesar made it to Rome in time to support the Gabinian law of early 67.[334] So it seems reasonable to suppose that Antistius at any rate was *pr.* 69, and had Caesar—surely a quaestor of 68—in his *provincia* only for the year 68.

Unless there was a *pr.* 70 who had Ulterior *ex praetura* for just one year, Antistius on his arrival in Spain in 68 will have found Pupius Piso's quaestor or *legatus* holding the province (perhaps for an extended timespan by that point). We cannot tell how long Antistius himself had to stay in the *provincia*. It must have been for more than one year.

Pupius' counterpart in Hispania Citerior apparently had been L. Afranius, the future *cos.* 60. Afranius had fought alongside Pompey in command of one of the wings at the Sucro, a battle that I assign (see above) to the year 75 (Konrad places it in summer 76). Afranius is then not attested again until ca. 71, when he (evidently) picks up the siege of Calagurris on the upper Ebro from Pompey. He later triumphed, apparently from this command.[335]

That Afranius held the praetorship is of course assured by the fact he reached the consulship in 60. And he must have triumphed *ex praetura*. Even with his friend Pompey's support, Afranius could hardly have received the honor as a *privatus*. But a date for these items is hard to find. In Broughton's view, Afranius first came to Spain as a *legatus*, and then sought and won the praetorship not long before the war's end, which brought him back to Hispania Citerior (the *provincia* implied by his presence at Calagurris). For his praetorship Broughton tentatively suggests 71, followed in 70–69 by a provincial command and the triumph. Konrad quite provisionally makes Afranius a legate under Pompey in Spain 77–73, *pr.* 72, *pro cos.* in Hispania Citerior 71–67, with a triumph in 67.[336]

If Afranius went to Spain first as a *legatus,* a good opportunity for his return to Italy for election would be the "quiet year" of the war,[337] Year 3 of Pompey's presence in Spain—on Konrad's reckoning 74, on mine 73. However, any reconstruction involving a return for praetorian elections raises its own problems. Would Afranius have received the province immediately, or after first serving a year in Italy? Through a "lucky" draw of the lot or *extra sortem*? (The assignment obviously cannot be pure coincidence.) One also has to factor in the situation with Spartacus. Alternately, it is at least possible that Afranius was *pr.* 77 or 76, sent by the Senate to rationalize the command of the *privatus* Pompey as *pro consule* (or rather "pro consulibus," according to the quip) For that, the combination of M. Iunius Silanus and P. Africanus in 210 (7.1.3) provides a distant precedent. But one hesitates to posit such a long command in this period. In any case, Afranius will have triumphed from Spain sometime after Pompey (31 December 71) and before he served as legate in the war in the east against Mithridates (where he is attested starting in 66).[338]

13.4.7 *Praetorian Commands in the Spains, 67–60*

For 67, Iberia received two of Pompey's antipirate *legati pro praetore*, one off the coast of each *provincia*.[339] Antistius Vetus probably will have been in Hispania Ulterior at the time (13.4.6). The status of Citerior, however, is uncertain. Indeed, after L. Afranius, no proper praetorian commanders are known for that *provincia* until the early 50s. We do hear of an odd arrangement for the year 65. A number of sources (including one epigraphic text, now lost) report that the Senate dispatched Cn. Calpurnius Piso as a *quaestor pro praetore* to Hispania Citerior. This Cn. Piso is perfectly well known. He was an adherent of Catiline and is widely charged with complicity in the first Catilinarian conspiracy. The Senate, we are told by Sallust, was eager to get this young man out of the way, though some right-thinking individuals thought he might serve as a useful counterbalance to Pompey in the east. Indeed, Crassus is said to have influenced Piso's appointment, out of hostility to Pompey. Once in the *provincia*, Piso was killed by some of his own Spanish cavalry—either because of his cruel behavior in the province, says Sallust, or because they were clients of Pompey's. Whatever the cause, his death (by mid-64) surely will have facilitated those accusations of earlier involvement in a conspiracy (including a plan "to kill the Senate") and of a later scheme to seize both Spanish provinces for Catiline.[340]

It has been suggested that the praetorian commander for Hispania Citerior had died, and Cn. Piso was sent as a replacement.[341] But if so, we might positively expect our (uniformly hostile) sources to blame Piso for such a death. A more recent hypothesis makes Cn. Piso the proper governor of Citerior. "Sometimes a quaestor or ex-quaestor would be sent with praetorian *imperium* to govern a province," states C. Eilers. He adduces the example of Cn. Piso—"who went to govern Nearer Spain as *quaestor pro praetore*"—as one of "the most famous cases." Eilers then seeks to build on it, arguing that this is one way the Romans compensated for the shortage of praetors in their administrative system.[342] That lost inscription did evidently say Piso "quaestor pro pr(aetore) ex S.C. provinciam citeriorem obtinuit." Yet quaestorian *provinciae* are amply attested.[343] And even a quaestor under someone else's command or a *legatus* can be said "obtinere provinciam."[344] Cumulatively, the evidence suggests that Piso's commission in Spain was anything but a routine administrative expedient. Sallust says that Crassus' special influence was needed to push through the appointment, though "the Senate had not given him the province unwillingly." Asconius thinks that Piso went to Spain "per honorem legationis." Suetonius reports that the "provincia Hispania" was given to Piso "ultro extra ordinem."[345]

Cn. Piso will have been quaestor for 65, and the evidence strongly suggests he received the (quaestorian) province of Citerior *extra sortem*. The Senate must have intended him to fulfil some special task, perhaps in addition to normal quaestorian responsibilities.[346] That would explain the special grant of *imperium*. The case of P. Cornelius Lentulus Marcellinus in 75 (11.4), another "extra ordinem" grant of praetorian *imperium*, is a more elaborate instance of the same type of commission. But, specifically what the Senate had charged Piso to do is quite unclear. We hear of disturbances of Spain in 64, though it is evident that Piso himself (at least later) was blamed for causing them.[347]

Perhaps Cn. Piso was meant to hold Hispania Citerior in lieu of a *pr.* 66 who had drawn the province but (for whatever reason) could not take it up immediately. Or perhaps Piso proposed his own project for the *provincia* and requested a significant military force to see to it. The Calpurnii Pisones, after all, had considerable links with Spain.[348] That might explain why Asconius considered Cn. Piso's appointment "per honorem legationis." There is some contemporary evidence to suggest the Senate might acquiesce in such a personal mission. In the year 64, a Campanian *eques* P. Sittius—who will have had a lot less *potentia* than a Calpurnius Piso—set out from Italy and had been able to collect a small army, evidently from Hispania Ulterior, in his effort to reclaim a large debt from the king of Mauretania. As it happens, Sittius too came under suspicion of supporting

Catiline.[349] It is particularly frustrating not to know what praetorian commanders were in charge of Citerior and Ulterior at this time.

It does seem reasonable to assume that throughout the 60s and first half of the 50s both the Spanish *provinciae* came up separately in the praetorian sortition. The evidence of these years even hints at a policy of regular succession. C. Cosconius (*pr.* 63) received Hispania Ulterior for 62, and stayed one year in the *provincia*. He had as his successor C. Iulius Caesar, a former *pro quaestore* (as we have seen) for Ulterior in 68 and a praetor of 62. Caesar's praetorian command provides another striking instance of the *sors opportuna*.[350]

Caesar's actual departure from Rome was not so fortunate. His creditors went so far as to seize his baggage to get him to pay his private debts. One is reminded of the Mamertines, who obstructed the praetor C. Cato in this way (but for a different purpose) almost sixty years earlier (13.1.2). But here we have private citizens hobbling a Roman commander in a domestic setting. It is amazing that neither the Senate nor tribunes seem to have cared. Caesar got back his baggage only when another *privatus*—M. Licinius Crassus—stumped up enough of the money to satisfy the most aggressive creditors.[351] Suetonius says that Caesar then departed for Spain even before the Senate voted him the requisite funds and equipment, either in fear of being brought to trial as a *privatus* (which seems technically impossible), or "to help the allies more quickly who were begging his aid" (which sounds like a pretext).[352] Surely, one of Caesar's main aims will have been to escape further harassment by his creditors. Another was to smuggle a client prince of Numidia out of Rome.[353]

Military operations began immediately after arrival in the province, says Plutarch. Caesar held a supplementary levy and marched on the tribes of the west and (later) extreme northwest of Hispania Ulterior. Apparently, none of these were in open revolt. Caesar could have occupied himself, it is implied, just controlling the regular brigandage in the province. Instead, he embarked on a systematic conquest of all of its independent tribes.[354] It is clear that Caesar above all was looking to make money and to win an imperatorial acclamation, all in preparation for a consular bid.[355] Plutarch reports that he managed to enrich himself and his army, and (in the same breath) notes that those soldiers hailed him as *imperator*.[356] (It would not be surprising if in general there was a material component to the imperatorial acclamation.) Appian reports that Caesar also sent considerable money to the public treasury. That no doubt was to facilitate the Senate's vote of a triumph. Appian also says Caesar had little use for the routine duties of provincial administration.[357] Plutarch, however, gives a different story, with some very specific details on how Caesar attempted by his edict to reconcile the competing claims of creditors and debtors in his *provincia*. Cicero also tells against Appian in his description of Caesar's lawgiving at Gades.[358] But those civil activities probably belong to winter 61/60.

Caesar calculated, says Dio, that after a campaign in Callaecia in early 60 he had done enough for a triumph.[359] He was in a hurry to get back to Italy in time for the consular elections; both Suetonius and Dio explicitly remark that he left the *provincia* without waiting for a successor.[360] Now, it seems to have been unexceptionable for a commander with *imperium* to depart from his *provincia* before his successor was in place.[361] The fact that our sources bother to comment on it in Caesar's case may suggest that no successor was imminent—in other words, Ulterior had not been allotted to a new commander for 60. Cicero shows that Caesar was expected in Rome by June 60,[362] so he must have left quite early in the year, after just a bit of campaigning in Callaecia. There were precedents of well-connected commanders boldly abandoning their province in the hope of a triumph or consulship, without serious repercussions.[363] If no *pr.* 61 had received Ulterior *ex praetura*—see 13.2.6 on the shortage of available commanders precisely at this time—a delegatee of Caesar will have had to hold it for the better part of a year, perhaps even longer.

The epilogue to this story is well known. Seeking to retain his right to triumph, Caesar attempted to get dispensation from a (relatively recent) law that one had to make a *professio* for the consulship in person. Many in the Senate opposed the exemption, in particular Cato, who obstructed Caesar's request up through the last day for declaring one's candidacy. (It is worth suggesting that his early return lost him some potential support.) So Caesar had to enter the city and lose his military *auspicia*. Yet he did, of course, get his consulship.[364]

13.4.8 *The Spanish* Provinciae *in the 50s*

The arrangements for Hispania Ulterior for the next few years are unknown. But we do find P. Cornelius Lentulus Spinther (*pr.* 60) getting Citerior "through Caesar's help" (presumably through cheating in the sortition) for 59. His command should have extended into 58. It was in this year that Spinther definitely returned to Italy and—again, we are told, thanks to Caesar's support—was elected consul for 57.[365]

We do not know what happened immediately next. Lentulus Spinther may have had a successor in Citerior for 58. The alternative—as I have suggested for Caesar as commander for Ulterior—is that he left a quaestor or *legatus* holding the *provincia* for the remainder of 58, and perhaps beyond (the arrangements for 57 are wholly unknown). Soon, trouble is attested for both the Spains. Sex. Quinctilius Varus (*pr.* 57) had Ulterior for 56; during his tenure, rebels at Gades expelled and then slaughtered members of the local senate.[366] That same year, Q. Caecilius Metellus Nepos (*cos.* 57) set out for Citerior, albeit slowly (he stopped at the April conference at Luca on his way to the province). It is unclear whether Nepos was prorogued through 55; but in that year we are told he had to deal with a rising of the Vaccaei, in the west of his province.[367] His command was the first occasion (to our knowledge) that either Spanish *provincia* had been declared consular since the time of the Sertorian War, which shows that the situation in Iberia had become quite serious. Even before the Vaccaei rose up, a tribunician bill (the *lex Trebonia*) had handed the two *provinciae* to the *cos.* II Cn. Pompeius for five years.[368]

There was enough precedent for this type of multiyear command. In this decade, Caesar as *cos.* 59 had taken up as his promagisterial *provincia* the two Gauls and Illyricum for five years (renewed for another five in 55) (15.2.4), and Pompey himself had a five-year grain commission voted to him in 57 (11.8.2). In 55, Pompey's consular colleague Crassus got five years of *imperium* for Syria (11.5.3).

What was unusual about this Spanish command was that Pompey did not like the notion of actually going to Iberia. "His plan was to let *legati* subdue Spain while he took in own hands affairs of Rome and Italy." Thus Dio, adding that the plebeian tribunes tried to obstruct Pompey and Crassus, especially by interfering with their legates and their levies. Pompey is said to have avoided serious interference by sending his two *legati* out early; they arrived in Spain certainly before the end of 55.[369]

One of these legates was L. Afranius—as we have seen, a praetorian *triumphator* from Citerior and later *cos.* 60. Perhaps Afranius returned to his (putative) former *provincia*; however, we are never told the precise arrangements for these *legati*, or what they did in Iberia. The other was M. Petreius, a *pr.* 63 and certifiable *vir militaris* who was widely said to have earned C. Antonius (*cos.* 63) his imperatorial acclamation against the Catilinarians in 62. Pompey evidently also had quaestors go to Spain as his subordinates. In 51, we hear of Pompey mooting some alternate arrangements (government by five *praefecti*, apparently a set for each province). Later in that year, there were reports that he would go to Iberia and take up his joint *provincia* in person. Yet those rumors of course proved empty. Afranius and Petreius remained (it seems) in Spain down through 49 B.C.[370]

It was no doubt a bit disorienting for many to see a full consular commander in Citerior for 56 and then a *legatus* (albeit a senior one) replace him in that same province for 55. Caesar in the *Bellum Civile* sums up his own perceptions in the context of 49. Pompey, he claims, had devised against him commands (*imperia*)[371] of an unprecedented type. He wanted simultaneously to have control of domestic affairs and hold two of the most warlike provinces in absence for a prolonged period. The rights of magistrates had been perverted, to the disadvantage of Caesar; "Men were being sent to provinces not in the regular fashion, namely *ex praetura* and *ex consulatu*, but having been approved and selected by just a few individuals".[372] One notes, however, that those *legati* helped Caesar when he needed it.[373]

In truth, the idea of a commander holding a province *in absentia* was not quite new. C. Calpurnius Piso exercised control over Transalpine Gaul even as *cos.* 67 in Rome. One century earlier, a praetor of 168 may have done the same thing for Sardinia.[374] There were other factors too. Pompey had a long history of letting *legati* do a good part of the work of his ambitious commands. The commission in 67 B.C. against the pirates is just the most outstanding example. There, he secured *imperium* for each of a large number of *legati* (some quite senior in status) and then set them up in independent quasi-*provinciae*. The campaign against Mithridates that followed provides more instances of Pompey's subordinates seeing to some unusually substantial chores. Pompey revived the basic structure of his pirate command for the grain commission of 57, but there we are less well informed on the particulars.[375]

Iberia by now had its own tradition of government for longish spells by *legati*. Appian believed that legates held Spain in the years ca. 105–100; as we have seen (13.3.1), the evidence at least for Ulterior positively contradicts him on this point. But C. Valerius Flaccus (*cos.* 93) must have allowed his subordinates a good deal of independence during his long tenure (a dozen or more years) in the two Spains and Gaul. The same must be true of Q. Metellus Pius, *cos.* 80 and then *pro cos.* in

Ulterior, who de facto was responsible for Citerior after the disaster of L. Manlius (late 78 or early 77) down to Pompey's arrival in early 76. After the Sertorian War, even our patchy evidence suggests that a *legatus* may have held Ulterior for a significant interval between the departure of M. Pupius Piso in 69 and the arrival of Antistius Vetus in 68, and again after the departure of C. Iulius Caesar in early 60; Lentulus Spinther just possibly left Citerior to a subordinate for most of 58. If one looks outside Iberia, many more examples (both possible and certain) of this type of interim arrangement present themselves. In sum, Pompey's notion to govern the Spanish *provinciae* through two senior *legati* strikes one as an exploitation of a variety of preexisiting administrative precedents, some none too salutary, but precedents all the same.

Macedonia, Africa, and Asia, 122–50

14.1 Macedonia in the Pre-Sullan Period

When the commander L. Calpurnius Piso (*cos.* 58) returned from Macedonia to Rome in 55, Cicero tried to convince the Senate that Piso's failure to ask for a triumph was suspicious in itself. "There were some (*aliquot*) with praetorian *imperium*, but no one with consular *imperium* who returned unharmed (*incolumis*) from this province, who did not triumph."[1] Here we can check for accuracy. The provincial *fasti* for Macedonia in the period 122–81 are quite full, and then down to the year 50 almost wholly complete. If we take *incolumis* both literally ("safe and sound") and metaphorically ("unimpaired by prosecution"),[2] Cicero cannot be shown wrong on the consular commanders.[3] For the praetors, however, he badly distorts the picture. After Q. Caecilius Metellus "Macedonicus" in 146, T. Didius is the only praetor known to have triumphed from the *provincia* (probably in the year 100). Even imperatorial acclamations are rarely attested for praetorian commanders in Macedonia.[4] In short, the record suggests that praetors might have long commands in the province, yet when possible the Senate had men of consular rank take on severe fighting. That tendency grows particularly marked in the decades after Sulla.

14.1.1 *Praetorian and Consular Commands in Macedonia down to 101*

The first commander attested for Macedonia in the post-Gracchan period is the praetor Sex. Pompeius, now known to have been in the *provincia* by the twenty-seventh year of its provincial era (121/120).[5] Pompeius was prorogued at least once in Macedonia, since he met his death there apparently a year or two later against the Scordisci. An inscription of Lete in Macedonia (from the month Panemos in Year 29, i.e., July 119) honors Pompeius' quaestor M. Annius P.f., who was still in the *provincia* at that time.[6] This text recounts in detail how Annius took command of the Roman army after Sex. Pompeius had fallen at Argos, near the Epirote border. Annius routed the enemy and recovered the fallen dead (including the praetor). Then, in a second engagement he beat back a combined force of Scordisci and Maedi, without bothering (we are told) the locals of Lete for money or manpower. In return, Lete decided to include an equestrian competition commemorating Annius in the annual games which honored the town's benefactors. The inscription notes also that Annius "has tried to hand over the *provincia* to those who have succeeded him after keeping safe all those in the territory, at peace and in the most settled condition." The reference to individuals "who have succeeded" (in the plural) by the time of this inscription should be to a praetor and quaestor of 119. The death of a praetor in his *provincia* was a serious matter. But the fact that the *cos.* L. Aurelius Cotta had Illyricum for 119 (10.5.4) must have precluded the possibility of declaring also Macedonia consular.

Pompeius' replacement may have been the praetor Cn. Cornelius Sisenna. In any case, Sisenna is known to have adjudicated an ongoing dispute between the managers of the Isthmian games and the Athenian guild of Dionysiac artists in the month Hyperberetaeus of Year 30 of the Macedonian era (August–September 118). The two groups met with the commander at Pella (the head city of the Macedonian district of Bottiaia); on Sisenna's judgement, the Isthmian representatives who were present agreed to pay a fine of ten talents. (The guild, however, later was to rescind that decision, which led to fresh conflict.)[7]

How long Sisenna stayed in the *provincia* is unknown. The next certain incumbent in the province is the *cos.* 114 C. Porcius Cato, a grandson of both the famous censor and L. Aemilius Paullus (and nephew of Scipio Aemilianus).[8] Trouble with the Scordisci had caused Macedonia to be declared consular for that year. Cato suffered a major defeat in Thrace, allegedly losing his entire army to the Scordisci. He was relieved after a single year, and prosecuted *repetundarum* on his return. Yet this Cato escaped with just a minor fine, an outcome that confirms Cicero's description of him as "potentissimus."[9]

Three more consuls would follow in uninterrupted succession into the year 106. C. Caecilius Metellus Caprarius (*cos.* 113) was in the *provincia* for probably just one year. Since he triumphed from Thrace on 15 July 111—on the same day as his brother, a *cos.* 115 for Sardinia (see 13.1.1)—he seems to have spent more time waiting outside Rome to coordinate that impressive display of family power than he did in his military *provincia*. M. Livius Drusus (*cos.* 112) was at least expected to be in Macedonia by mid-June 112. In that year, the prolonged dispute between the Isthmian and Athenian guilds of Dionysiac artists had prompted the city of Athens itself to make a petition to the Roman Senate. As part of its settlement the Senate instructed Drusus to hold a hearing in his *provincia* on the public funds belonging to these groups. And that was despite major problems with Scordisci![10]

Dio tells us that M. Drusus—as a reaction to Cato's disaster, and in his desire for glory—instituted a regime of lighter discipline for his troops. (Perhaps he was trying to pave the way for an imperatorial acclamation.) But he evidently campaigned successfully in Thrace against the Scordisci, eventually (1 May 110) earning a triumph over that people (the name is a reasonable supplement for his entry in the *Fasti*). Ammianus and Rufius Festus report that Drusus "kept the Scordisci from leaving their borders." Florus says Drusus "forbade them to cross the Danube."[11] So one wonders whether M. Drusus—and not (as is often supposed) his successor M. Minucius Rufus (*cos.* 110)—is the commander honored in an epigram from Demetrias: "Having looked at the boundaries of the Ister, you expelled (the) Gaul."[12]

Finally, the consul M. Rufus received Macedonia as his *provincia* for 110. Though Rufus seems to have scored a major victory over "Thracians" by the year 108, he only returned to Italy into the year 106. It was to be the longest proper command in this *provincia* in the period of the free Republic. The background to Rufus' repeated prorogation (four times in all) must be the fact that Rome was simultaneously waging major (i.e., consular) wars in Numidia and against Germanic tribes in Gaul. The first two extensions are not so surprising, especially if Rufus' big victory came only in 108. The Senate certainly had no consuls to spare for Macedonia in 107,[13] and apparently did not want to send any praetors while a substantial military risk remained. M. Minucius Rufus finally triumphed shortly before or on 1 August 106 for his fighting in Thrace against the Scordisci.[14]

M. Minucius Rufus will have been succeeded by a praetor, but precise details are lacking. C. Billienus or C. Cluvius—each attested as *pro cos.* at Delos, Billienus quite probably at this precise time—may have been commanders in Macedonia (the alternative is Asia). However, the first certain incumbent after that string of consuls is C. Memmius (the former *tr. pl.* 111), at an unknown date, but certainly after 107 and before 101 B.C. An inscription from Messenia shows the ἀνθύπατος Memmius—accompanied by the στρατηγός Vibius—honoring in person a secretary of the local *synhedrion*. In this inscription, the two Romans consistently receive those (different) titles. All the same, Broughton suggests that Vibius may have been "a governor of the Macedonian province," succeeding Memmius. Yet it is clear from this epigraphic text that Vibius was just the person most closely working in Messenia, where he supervised the collection of money from the community. He might be simply a quaestor or legate at the head of some troops, holding delegated *imperium* at the most.[15] One can readily imagine how even a minor functionary might make an extraordinary impact in an area like Messenia.[16] Memmius on his return from the province was tried and acquitted on a charge *de repetundis*. He later offered himself as a consular candidate for 99, but was murdered by his rival Glaucia.[17]

14.1.2 *The Command of T. Didius and the* Lex de Provinciis Praetoriis

One of the consuls of the year 98 was T. Didius, a recent praetorian *triumphator* from Macedonia. He had defeated the Scordisci in Thrace; Cicero counts him as one of the great generals who triumphed from Macedonia. (As mentioned above, no praetor since Q. Metellus Macedonicus had done it before, and no praetor would achieve this feat again.) The Livian *Periocha* does not mention Didius' campaign, and the triumphal *Fasti* are lacunose at the relevant point, so the chronology of his command has been hard to pin down.[18] Yet thanks to the discovery of a major inscription from Cnidus (10.1), we are now exceedingly well informed on some of the Senate's arrangements for Macedonia when Didius departed from his *provincia*, in either 101 or 100. The new commander for Macedonia, we are told, is to send to the cities and states in his jurisdiction a copy of the present law—which announces especially the formation of a new praetorian *provincia*, "Cilicia." He is also to proceed to Chersonesus and Kainike (a district of Thrace on the Euxine)— both of which T. Didius has just conquered—and to govern that for a period of at least sixty days. So should subsequent commanders. The primary stated concern is the collection of public revenues, and the protection of "friends and allies" from being driven out of the territory. (The law does not specify by whom.) The commander should also "as soon as possible" set the boundaries of the taxable part of the Chersonesus "just as it seems to him best." In addition, the law provides (evidently) for the discharge of certain veterans in Macedonia, delineates the provisions in case of the commander's or the quaestor's resignation (the powers of each are to remain in force in transit), and spells out some limitations under a praetorian *lex Porcia*—apparently new—on the movements of the commander for Macedonia (or Asia) outside the *provincia*. We also get some elaborate provisions against the nonobservance of this law.[19]

Some provisions, when taken in combination with others in the law, do not quite make logical or practical sense. Chersonesus and Kainike are described as an ἐπαρχεία (*provincia*) that is to be annexed to another ἐπαρχεία, namely, Macedonia.[20] The new commander is ordered by *senatus consultum* to set the administrative boundaries of Kainike as he sees fit: obviously a major responsibility for an individual magistrate, and one that potentially imparts great power. However, the law requires that commander (and the commanders to follow) to remain in the newly annexed districts for two months of each year. (The stipulation seems burdensome, considering the size of "Macedonia," its complex political geography, and the length of its dangerous northern frontier.) Without a *senatus consultum*, the commander is not to lead a military expedition outside his *provincia* (the bounds of which this new magistrate will partly determine). He must prevent members of his staff from doing so, too. Yet even in case of abdication, the commander is empowered, until his return to Rome (and thus outside the *provincia*), "to investigate, to punish, to administer justice, to make (legal) decisions, to assign arbitrators or foreign judges," and to handle sureties, restitution of properties, and manumissions in the same way "just as in his magistracy it was permitted." Apart from the surprising—indeed, paradoxical—point about abdication, this last bit offers a good summary of some of the attributes of *imperium*, and the activities a commander might be expected to perform in his *provincia* and (again, surprisingly) in transit.

It seems hopeless to try to resolve these various contradictions, which we should probably ascribe to the fact that the law contains tralatician elements in addition to some new (or at least partly new) provisions. For example, in this law, the future commander for Macedonia (or Asia) is described as "praetor, *pro praetore*, or *pro consule*," alternately "praetor or *pro consule*," alternately "magistrate or *pro magistratu*."[21] There is no serious doubt that whoever received either of these *provinciae* will have had consular *imperium*. So we are justified in treating the wording here as traditional, taken over from earlier laws on the staffing of territorial provinces. The subelements in the pirate law might contain different strata, too. Consider the praetor M. Porcius Cato and his legislation restricting a commander's movements, probably passed earlier in the same year as our epigraphic law (12.4.3). Quite possibly, he had taken over an old prohibition on a commander marching beyond his *provincia*—the issue had been a burning one already about seventy years earlier, thanks to the aspirations of C. Cassius Longinus (*cos.* 171) to fight a Macedonian war—and simply added a new proviso (e.g. extension of the prohibition to a general's staff) to make his *lex Porcia*.

14.1.3 *The Promagistracy of C. Sentius in Macedonia*

We have no commanders we can posit in the province for the seven or so years after T. Didius, until the arrival of C. Sentius, a *pr. urb.* 94, who was then *ex praetura* in Macedonia from 93 down into 87. Now, it has long been thought that L. Iulius Caesar (the future *cos.* 90) held a praetorian command in Macedonia. An L. Caesar is honored at Samothrace as *pro consule*.[22] And a tetradrachm issue minted by a SVVRA LEG PRO Q.—most naturally taken as Q. Braetius Sura, attested as a *legatus* of Sentius in 88 and 87—continues that of a quaestor AESILLAS of a CAE(sar) PR(aetor).[23] This evidence would seem to suggest that the two commanders were contiguous in this province, with Caesar obviously preceding Sentius. But H. B. Mattingly adduces a powerful numismatic argument for reassigning these sources to the praetorship of this man's son, the L. Caesar who was *cos.* 64. Mattingly persuasively defends D. M. Lewis's identification of SVVRA LEG PRO Q. as L. Caesar's brother-in-law P. Cornelius Lentulus Sura (*cos.* 71, *pr.* II 63), that is, after his expulsion from the Senate by the censors of 70.[24]

   To return to the *pr.* 94 C. Sentius: At some point in his long *ex praetura* command Sentius saw a certain Euphenes proclaim himself "king of the Macedonians" and try to stir up the people who inhabited the old Macedonian royal territory to revolt from Rome. The intervention of a friendly Thracian king made Euphenes abandon his project without fighting. That was fortunate for Sentius, who throughout his command seems to have had his hands full on the province's northern frontier. In 92, "Thracians" dealt Sentius a major defeat. Three or so years later they were still largely unchecked.[25] In 88, Mithridates added considerably to Sentius' woes when he instigated the Thracians to launch a major invasion of Roman Macedonia. Dio says they "overran Epirus and other parts [sc. of the province] as far as Dodona, going even to the point of plundering the temple of Zeus." Cicero speaks of a provincewide revolt against Sentius except for (most notably) the Denseleti.

   Yet Sentius rose to the occasion. Orosius relates how Sentius kept the Thracian king Sothimus out of Macedonia. There is reason to believe that he also beat back Mithridates' son Ariarathes, at least temporarily.[26] And in the south, Sentius' *legatus* Q. Braetius Sura scored some significant successes on both sea and land against some powerful Mithridatic generals. The activities of this individual offer a remarkable illustration of how independently a *legatus* might conduct himself in the field. Braetius defeated the navy of Metrophanes, stormed the enemy treasury on Sciathos (on his own initiative taking some severe punitive measures), and then advanced into Boeotia, where, in a prolonged battle at Chaeronea, he fought to a stalemate with Mithridates' general Archelaus and the Athenian quisling Aristion. After a success against Archelaus in Attica, Braetius eventually headed back to Boeotia, evidently looking for further action. And this despite the fact that the *cos.* 88 L. Cornelius Sulla—now *pro consule*, with the Mithridatic War as his *provincia*—was on his way to Greece. In the event, Sulla's quaestor L. Lucullus had to order the *legatus* to leave Boeotia and return to his superior officer, Sentius. This Braetius immediately did, though (as Plutarch has it) he singlehandedly was on the verge of winning back Greece for the Romans. No source indicates that he held delegated *imperium*, though we cannot exclude that possibility.[27]

We do not know precisely when Sentius returned to Italy, but it was after at least six and a half years of hard fighting in Macedonia, in an *ex praetura* command at that. His example highlights the deep problems that beset Rome's administrative system even before the outbreak of the Social War. It is particularly revealing that in 91 Sentius did not receive a replacement, even after a serious defeat the previous year, in his third year of *imperium*. It is certainly possible that "it was Sentius himself who wished to stay on and avenge the defeat he had suffered."[28] But the important thing is that the Senate now allowed an unsuccessful commander to stay in his *provincia*—other options might not have been available. Sentius managed as best he could. By the time of his departure he even managed to make an enormous profit from a food shortage in the province, apparently by selling his surplus rations at a high price.[29]

14.1.4 *Praetorian Commands in Macedonia during the First Mithridatic War*

In early 87, the *pro cos.* Sulla arrived in western Greece with five legions. His first step was to requisition money and men from Aetolia and Thessaly: no help would be forthcoming from Rome, which by now had outlawed him. Once properly organized, he marched into Boeotia—which crossed back to the Romans, including Thebes—and then into Attica. There he divided his army. Sulla's own troops moved against the Peiraeus, while another part was to lay siege to Athens. The city finally fell on 1 March 86. Both Plutarch and Appian stress that Sulla from the start was in a hurry to get back to Rome. However, Sulla was to campaign a total of more than three years in the east, returning to Italy in spring 83.[30]

There is no need for the purposes of this study to recount the course of Sulla's campaigning in Greece, or the arrangements he made there. Nor do we need to discuss the countermeasures of the Cinnan government: how L. Valerius Flaccus, *cos.* 86, crossed to Asia with Fimbria to fight Mithridates (only to see, while still in transit, some of his troops desert to Sulla), or the massively unsuccessful attempt of the *coss.* 84 Cinna and Carbo to cross to Liburnia on the north coast of Illyria, which led only to a mutiny and Cinna's death.

The only particulars that concern us here have to do with three possible praetors or *praetorii* on Sulla's staff, L. Licinius Murena, L. Hortensius, and a Galba. Their stories are interconnected. Murena appears at the siege of the Peiraeus in 87, where he helps Sulla in an early battle against Archelaus.[31] After Sulla had taken

Athens and burned the Peiraeus in spring 86, Plutarch says his goal was to meet up with L. Hortensius, a στρατηγικὸς ἀνήρ (and apparently elder brother of the orator, Q. Hortensius L.f. Hortalus) who was leading a force southward from Thessaly. This episode of the war had a local interest for Plutarch, for he then proudly relates how a man from his home town of Chaeronea guided Hortensius around hostile forces at Thermopylae.[32] It was near Chaeronea itself that Sulla soon forced a battle with Archelaus. Sulla commanded on the right wing, put Murena in charge of the left, and had Hortensius and a Galba—both termed legates by Plutarch—guard against attacks on the flanks.[33] Quite later, when Sulla in 85 had started campaigning in the Thraceward region while waiting to see if Mithridates would come to terms, Hortensius shows up fighting against Maedi and Dardani. Galba is not heard from again in this war.

Cichorius may be right that Galba is to be identified with the Ser. Sulpicius Galba who was active as a *legatus* (perhaps even as a praetor) in the Social War (10.5.4). Since Hortensius is said to be a "praetorius" (Plutarch seems well informed on this man), Galba—who had similar duties as Hortensius' at Chaeronea—perhaps was one, too. Murena for his part had an important independent command in Asia in the years after 84, with the celebration of his triumph in (probably) 81, after his recall by Sulla. Cicero attests to his praetorship; in any case he cannot have triumphed with merely delegated *imperium*. The date of Murena's actual magistracy must be 88 or 87. So he was a prorogued praetor (or rather considered himself such) during his service in the east.[34]

We may ask whether L. Licinius Murena at the time of his appointment was meant simply to function as an *adiutor* to the *pro cos.* Sulla. After all, Sulla had two senior *legati* on his staff, perhaps both praetorian in status. Is it possible that Murena had received "Macedonia" as his formal *provincia* but never managed to take it up? Now, Badian has suggested that the praetor P. Gabinius (*pr.* 89 or, more probably, 88) relieved C. Sentius in his long Macedonian command.[35] But the hypothesis that Gabinius had an *ex praetura* command in this province has its difficulties. Two events after his praetorship are known from this man's career. First, in the year 76, P. Gabinius was able to head a legation of three XVviri s.f. (the other two were an M. Otacilius and an L. Valerius) which transcribed and brought back to Rome about one thousand verses of the Erythrean Sibyl. Second, Verres' exquaestor Q. Caecilius Niger tried to prosecute Gabinius (apparently) for *repetundae*, but lost out in the *divinatio* to an L. Piso, whom "Achaeans"—evidently the injured party—had chosen as their *patronus*. A trial followed, which led to P. Gabinius' condemnation and exile.[36] That in itself might imply Gabinius once had a command in Macedonia.

One problem is that there is no trace of a praetorian commander in Macedonia in early 86. Mithridates' son Arcathias is said to have invaded and successfully conquered the whole *provincia*, which a "small" Roman force was trying to guard; the general Taxiles may have helped in this. Appian reports Arcathias even appointed satraps to govern Macedonia, but soon died, while marching against Sulla. By all accounts, Taxiles certainly had no trouble marching through the *provincia* to meet Archelaus in spring 86.[37] Moreover, the Cinnan commander L. Cornelius Scipio Asiaticus is found in the *provincia* of Macedonia perhaps later in 86, but certainly by 85. Scipio fought and destroyed a large group of Scordisci, and came to an agreement with the Maedi (who by that point had robbed the sanctuary of Delphi) and Dardani. He may also have captured Philippi as well. It is clear that it was he who recovered the *provincia* of Macedonia for the Romans. But Scipio probably left when Sulla marched with Archelaus toward the Hellespont in 85. There is certainly no sign of him when Sulla initiated his own campaign against the Thracians late that year. At any rate, Scipio returned to Italy by 84, since he fought against Sulla as *cos.* 83.[38]

There is one further argument against the *praetor* P. Gabinius as a commander for Macedonia, especially as the successor to C. Sentius. It is hard to see how the Achaeans—who had sided with Mithridates before Sulla's arrival in Greece[39]—could get a Roman praetor convicted for his conduct around 87 toward them. Though prosecution on such grounds is not inconceivable,[40] the legation to Asia of the year 76 offers a plausible enough context for offences against Achaeans, that is, while P. Gabinius was in transit to or from Erythrae.[41] In modest support of this reconstruction, one notes that we also never hear again of Gabinius' fellow *XVviri s.f.* on that legation, though both *nobiles*: all three *legati* may have been disgraced.[42]

Sulla sailed west to fight for control of Italy in spring 83. But we have no indication what administrative arrangements he made for Macedonia and Greece for the period after his departure. Indeed, each of the years from 83 down through 81 is a blank. This may be where an amazing statement by Cicero in the *De Provinciis Consularibus* (56 B.C.) comes in handy. Cicero remarks that when the province of Macedonia was free of fear from its neighboring tribes, the Romans used to maintain it in peace with only a small garrison force, "through legates without *imperium*" ("sine imperio per legatos"). There is no other period in our (admittedly defective) record that allows this statement so well as the years 83–81. The independent efforts of Scipio Asiaticus and then Sulla had brought peace to the province's northern frontier. And once Sulla had placed Murena in charge of Asia in 84, he had nothing other than *legati* at his disposal for Macedonia. (The government in Rome, of course, could not try to send any praetor to the east in 83 or 82.)

To end with two speculative points. Either the *legatus* L. Hortensius (a certifiable *praetorius*, who now had some experience against Thracians), or the *legatus* Ser. Galba, or both, held Macedonia: one notes that neither of these men show up in the civil warfare that followed Sulla's return to Italy. Further, the interim arrangement I suggest here might be the background to the notorious case of C. Antonius (the future *cos.* 63), who at some point had used cavalry "de exercitu Sullano" to rob Achaeans, for which he was prosecuted in 76.[43]

14.2 Macedonia in the Post-Sullan Period

14.2.1 *The Command of Cn. Dolabella in Macedonia*

It was perhaps natural that the new Sullan government in 81 should declare Macedonia a consular *provincia*. M. Minucius Rufus, the *cos.* 110 who triumphed over the Scordisci in 106, had been the last consular commander to receive the province for its own sake. The Roman administration of Macedonia in the late 90s and all through the 80s was particularly catch-as-catch-can. And during those same years, the province had seen any number of raids from the various tribes to the north as well as a fullscale invasion (and briefly successful takeover) by Mithridatic forces. The new commander was to be the *cos.* 81 Cn. Cornelius Dolabella, attested in the *provincia* for 80. We have no record of what this man was up to during his magistracy in the city, other than that he and his consular colleague are said to have looked insignificant compared to Sulla when the dictator paraded with his twenty-four lictors.[44] It is possible that Dolabella, despite Sulla's apparent ideal of *ex magistratu* provincial commands (11.1.3), set out for Macedonia during his actual consulship. For that, there are good parallels for Spain (13.4.2) and Asia (14.6.1) in the year 81 B.C. Macedonia badly needed a proper commander, especially if (as I have argued) one or more *legati* had been in sole control of it since early 83. What few can have foreseen is that Macedonia would remain a consular *provincia* almost all through the 70s (and for about a third of the two decades to follow).

Cn. Dolabella is attested in Thessalonica in the year 80, meeting with envoys from Thasos, which had remained loyal to Rome in the Mithridatic War. Following this embassy, Dolabella took steps to implement a *senatus consultum* confirming certain rights and privileges Sulla previously had conceded to Thasos, including an expansion of its subject territory.[45] That is all the detailed information we have on what Dolabella did in his *provincia*. But we can assume that quite a bit of Dolabella's time—and perhaps that also of his immediate successors—was spent precisely in this way, seeing to the practical application of the privileges and punishments Sulla had meted out during his command in Greece and Macedonia.[46]

Cicero tells us that M. Fonteius (as we have seen in 13.4.4, a quaestor of 85 or 84, legate ca. 83 in Hispania Ulterior, and a praetor for Transalpine Gaul in the mid-70s) was a *legatus* in Macedonia at a point when the Thracians had entered the province and were threatening its cities. Fonteius, says Cicero (in a quite rhetorical passage), had to save Macedonia "not just by planning but also by might." Broughton dates that legateship to the year 77, under the later Macedonian commander Ap. Claudius Pulcher (*cos.* 79, and arriving in his *provincia* only some time into 77). Münzer took Cicero quite literally, and thought Fonteius had an independent command after Appius' death in 76. But it may be that Fonteius served under Cn. Dolabella. In that case, any time from the year 81 seems possible: perhaps even precisely the year 81, preceding Dolabella in the *provincia* and holding it until his superior's arrival. Dolabella must have done some fighting, too: his triumph on his return, according to Cicero, was "iustitissimus."[47]

The one thing that our sources are interested in telling us about Dolabella is that the young C. Iulius Caesar unsuccessfully prosecuted him for *repetundae* following his Macedonian triumph. Caesar had served under P. Servilius Isauricus (*cos.* 79) in Cilicia in 78. He returned to Rome, as Suetonius has it, following the news of Sulla's death, bringing Dolabella to trial after the revolt of M. Lepidus (*cos.* 78, *pro cos.* 77) had been quelled. The case established Caesar's oratorical reputation, but also generated its share of *invidia*. The specific accusations against Dolabella are not recorded, but Plutarch tells us that many cities of Greece witnessed against him. But it was not easy to bring down a noble who was a consular *triumphator*.[48]

14.2.2 *Consular Commands of the 70s*

Cn. Dolabella may have remained in Macedonia from 81 or (certainly) 80 down into 77. Ap. Claudius Pulcher was supposed to go to the province *ex consulatu* for 78, but fell ill at Tarentum. Pulcher returned to Rome and stayed there that whole year. One would like to know whether he took care to preserve his military auspices by not crossing the *pomerium*. It seems unlikely: as it happens, in the crisis of early 77, Pulcher found himself named *interrex*; he was in that office precisely at the time L. Philippus pushed through the *senatus consultum ultimum* against M. Lepidus. Under the terms of Philippus' motion, Pulcher was to join other holders of *imperium* in taking up the defense of the city.[49] The cumulation of offices—*pro consule* and *interrex*—is noteworthy, and indeed more than a bit confusing. To be elected *interrex* by his fellow patrician senators and then to function in the magistracy, Ap. Pulcher presumably did enter the city. Once he crossed the *pomerium*, he (again, presumably) will have lost his consular military *auspicia*. When Pulcher was ready to set out for Macedonia later in 77, he quite likely needed a fresh grant. The Senate hardly would have refused him, especially since at this very time it had seen fit to give the equestrian Cn. Pompeius consular *imperium* for Spain. The question of Pulcher's technical status in Macedonia, though unanswerable on our evidence, does seem an important one. The possibility that he took up his province a year after his magistracy as (formally) a *privatus* with consular *imperium* would provide a precedent for the measures of 53 and 52 (11.1.7) that institutionalized such an arrangement.

Ap. Pulcher campaigned successfully as *pro consule* in 77 against the Scordisci and in the area of Mt. Rhodope. Our sources (virtually all epitomators) suggest there were a number of battles; Florus says he reached as far as the Sarmatae. Pulcher surely was prorogued in Macedonia for a second year. But he died from illness sometime in 76 in his *provincia*.[50]

The next commander in Macedonia was the *cos*. 76 C. Scribonius Curio, who no doubt had expected to go there only *ex consulatu*. He was active in the city during his magistracy, certainly into the spring or summer. Broughton says that he "proceeded before the end of the year to Macedonia." That may be so, but Broughton's claim rests only on an inference from Frontinus, who describes how "C. Curio consul" quelled a mutiny at Dyrrachium. We need not suppose that Frontinus is trying to be technically accurate here: this author can be spectacularly careless in his substitution of "consul" for "pro consule." For what it is worth, Eutropius has C. Curio go to Macedonia only "post consulatum." But Curio was definitely in place in the *provincia* by the beginning of spring 75. Until his arrival (whether in late 76 or early 75), the Roman province—now said to be in grave danger—must once again have been held for some length of time by a legate or quaestor.[51]

Eutropius lists the highlights of Curio's command, which are enough for our purposes here. He proceeded to Macedonia after his consulship, subjugated the

Dardanians, reached the Danube, and earned a triumph, putting an end to the war after less than three years of campaigning ("intra triennium"). No other source specifies the length of his command. (Though Cicero also mentions Curio's triumph, we cannot assign it to any precise year.)[52] The terminus must be the arrival of the *cos.* 73 M. Terentius Varro Lucullus in Macedonia.

Under the Sullan system, one expects that M. Lucullus would take up Macedonia *ex consulatu*, that is, for 72. But Broughton thinks Lucullus may have gone to the province during his term as consul.[53] His evidence is Cicero's statement that when Dio of Halaesa—whom Verres victimized immediately after his arrival in Sicily as governor in 73 (13.2.3)—appealed to Q. Hortensius in Rome, M. Lucullus, "who was at that time in Macedonia," had a better understanding of Dio's plight than Hortensius did. One should remember, however, that Hortensius was *praetor repetundis* for 72, and it was surely in that capacity that Dio sought him out. So the relative chronology Eutropius provides for Curio's command may be perfectly good; taken by himself, this author implies the *pro consule* fought into late 73. The Livian *Periocha* certainly allows it. Livy apparently narrated Curio's exploits in Books 92 (surely concerned with the year 75) and 95 (apparently later 73). The successes of the "pro consule" M. Lucullus were related in Book 97, which apparently spanned from late 72 through mid-70.[54]

C. Curio will have returned to Rome in 72, when M. Lucullus was set to arrive or had already arrived in Macedonia. Lucullus was to conduct a vigorous campaign that started with a major victory over the Bessi and then continued with further conquests on the shores of the Euxine and as far as the Danube. He even conducted a naval operation against Apollonia in the Euxine itself, though one suspects it was merely to get hold of its colossal statue of Apollo that he hauled away and later dedicated on the Capitol. Some late sources imply that he extended the bounds of the Roman *provincia* to include some Thracian districts. However, the Senate recalled Lucullus—already hailed *imperator*—all the way from Thrace to help put down the slave revolt in Italy. Lucullus reached Brundisium relatively early in 71, while Spartacus was still active. He no doubt had to wait to triumph until after the conclusion of that revolt. The date of his predecessor Curio's triumph cannot be pinned down. It is perfectly conceivable that on arrival in Italy in 72, he first received some military duties in the slave war, then at its height. Whatever the date of his triumph, it should precede that of M. Lucullus over the Thracian Bessi.[55]

14.2.3 *Praetorian Commanders in Macedonia, ca. 71–63*

Once the Senate recalled M. Lucullus, Macedonia became a praetorian *provincia* for a time, perhaps already for 71. Now, Cicero in the *Verrines* alleges that Verres in early 70 tried to arrange the prosecution of a senator who had been active in Achaea in order to postpone his own extortion trial. According to the *Scholia Gronoviana* on the *Verrines*, Verres' target was a certain Oppius, a "praetor" for "Achaea." But another passage, in the pseudo-Asconian *Scholia Sangallensia*, suggests that Oppius was the prosecutor Verres had suborned, not a former governor being prosecuted in 70. Even in antiquity this was evidently a much-discussed

Ciceronian problem, and one can only guess at the solution.[56] If it was an Oppius who was being investigated (rather than doing the investigation), it is just possible that the man in question is P. Oppius, the quaestor of M. Cotta (*cos.* 74) in Bithynia, whom Cicero defended in his *Pro Oppio* sometime after late 70. The charge would have to do with offences committed in Achaea while in transit to or from Bithynia.[57] Yet that is merely a stab in the dark.

After M. Lucullus' departure from Macedonia in 71, the first or one of the first praetorian commanders in the *provincia* may have been L. Iulius Caesar. L. Caesar had served as quaestor (or *pro quaestore*) in Asia probably in 77 and was later *cos.* 64. Mattingly has suggested that this individual "could well have been praetor as early as 70 B.C." and held an *ex praetura* command in Macedonia sometime in the period 69–67 B.C. (but no later, on numismatic grounds) (see 14.1.3). During that time, argues Mattingly, his quaestor Aesillas minted a large number of Roman tetradrachms at Pella and Thessalonica. Caesar's brother-in-law P. Cornelius Lentulus Sura (*cos.* 71, but now freshly expelled from the Senate by the censors of 70) continued that issue at Thessalonica as *legatus pro quaestore*, presumably since Aesillas had died. Mattingly's basic identification of the Macedonian governor L. Caesar as the future *cos.* 64 (against the general view that it was his father, the *cos.* 90), and his explanation of the puzzling tetradrachm seems not just plausible but practically necessary.[58]

The only real problem with Mattingly's reconstruction has to do with the precise dates of Caesar's provincial command. He must have been in Macedonia by 70, with P. Cornelius Sura joining him after receiving his *nota* from the censors of that year.[59] That is because there is really no room in the *fasti* for the years 69–67. Broughton's suggestion, that L. Aurelius Cotta (*pr.* 70, who passed a *lex iudiciaria* late in that year) is to be identified with the "L. Aurelius" who as *pro consule* met a Rhodian embassy at Amphipolis is an excellent guess. If correct, he will have proceeded as *pro consule* to Macedonia in 69.[60] We must also fit in the praetor "Rubrius" under whom the younger (M. Porcius) Cato served as military tribune. Plutarch (our only source on Rubrius and his command) implies that he was already in the *provincia* of Macedonia when he received Cato, apparently in the year 67.[61] If correct, Rubrius' actual praetorship should belong to the year 69 rather than 68, with at least 68 and 67 as the period of his tenure of Macedonia. There is reason to think that he remained in the *provincia* all through 67. Before that year was up, L. Cornelius Sisenna (*pr.* 78)—one of Pompey's *legati pro praetore*, and responsible for ridding the coast of Macedonia and Greece of pirates—could sail off to interfere with the command of Q. Metellus (*cos.* 69) in Crete. Sisenna took his own soldiers with him, never to return.[62]

Before long, Macedonia became once again a consular *provincia*. L. Manlius Torquatus (*cos.* 65) had the province for 64 and at least part of 63. He was back in Rome, in ill health, by autumn of that latter year, having been hailed as *imperator* and perhaps even granted a *supplicatio*. But for whatever reason, he was not able to triumph.[63] C. Antonius Hibrida (*cos.* 63) also received Macedonia *ex consulatu*, as we shall see (14.2.4). Between the commands of these two men, Broughton places as a praetorian governor of Macedonia the στρατηγός Plaetorius, who is epigraphically attested at Delphi "in the archonship of Habromachus."[64] Broughton accepts the common identification of this man with M. Plaetorius Cestianus, a *monetalis* who also issued coins as *aedilis curulis* in (probably) 67, and in 66 held the office of *iudex quaestionis*. Broughton suggests it was probable he was *pr.* 64 and governor of Macedonia in the year after his praetorship. This is a good guess. M. Plaetorius was eligible to hold a praetorship in 64, and, as an ex-curule aedile, it is reasonable to suppose he might have reached the office at the minimum interval. The promagistracy in Macedonia would be a very short command—sandwiched between that of two consulars—but seems conceivable. Yet Broughton's suggestion must remain a hypothesis. For a start, one misses Plaetorius' *praenomen* in the Delphi inscription, which precludes confident identification. Then, there is the fact that one cannot be absolutely sure whether the simple title Plaetorius receives in the inscription really means "praetor."[65] For this whole question, it would obviously be useful to know when Habromachus was archon.[66] In sum, if the Plaetorius who visited Delphi is the same man as M. Cestianus, we cannot disallow the possibility that the inscription refers to a position he held in Greece during the earlier part of his career, at some point in the mid- to late 70s. Or it might be a different Plaetorius altogether.

14.2.4 *C. Antonius and Two Praetorian Successors in Macedonia*

In 63 B.C., the consul C. Antonius obtained Macedonia, apparently *extra sortem*. Before taking up that *provincia*, Antonius—or rather his praetorian legate M. Petreius—first had to quash Catiline and his forces near Faesulae early in 62. For that action, Antonius received the imperatorial acclamation and also the Senate's vote of a *supplicatio*.[67] These honors come as a bit of a surprise. After all, it was a victory over a civil enemy, and Dio reports that there was some doubt whether he had met even the basic technical requirement for number of enemy killed. Antonius' personal influence must have made the difference here. He was obviously eager to preinsure a triumph on his return from Macedonia.

It is easy to see why Antonius—or any commander—might quickly try to get himself named as *imperator*, since no one knew for certain whether there would be any further successful fighting before supersession.[68] But for Antonius to proceed into his territorial province already possessing that title must have irritated many.[69] Once in the province, C. Antonius was badly defeated by the Dardani and (particularly) the Bastarnae. Those setbacks came perhaps already in 62, for there was talk of supersession, indeed even recall by praetorian law, for 61. In the event, Antonius did get his prorogation for that year, and there was no successor until the *novus homo* C. Octavius (*pr.* 61, and father of the future Augustus) set out for Macedonia in 60. Yet even then, Antonius tarried in the province until late 60 or even early 59, infuriating those in Rome who had made preparations for his immediate prosecution (apparently) *de repetundis*.[70] That trial was to come only in mid-April 59. Cicero spoke in his former consular collegue's defense, while M. Caelius Rufus took the role of chief prosecutor. Caelius evidently spent much time on Antonius' alleged links with the Catilinarians. But Antonius' incompetence as a general and rapacity as a governor also came under attack. The jury condemned Antonius, who left Rome for western Greece. His life there as exile in some ways turned out to be no less grandiose than his arrival in Macedonia as *imperator*.[71]

The man sent to succeed Antonius in Macedonia cut a much different figure. C. Octavius' city *provincia* as *pr.* 61 cannot be ascertained, but Cicero says he enjoyed great popularity in Rome for his accessibility and his well-ordered court. But he sometimes exhibited severity, too. Octavius had haled to justice certain ex-magistrates who as private citizens had flouted their own decisions. He also forced certain *Sullani* to return the property which they had stolen "per vim et metum." So when Octavius drew Macedonia as his *ex praetura* province, perhaps some noted the irony that C. Antonius fifteen years previously had stood trial before the peregrine praetor for just this thing, using the might of Sullan horse to prey on provincials in Achaea.[72]

As Suetonius tells us, the Senate also gave C. Octavius a task *extra ordinem*. On the way to his province he was to take police action against some runaway slaves—leftovers from the revolts of Spartacus and Catiline—who had occupied an area around Thurii. The mission cannot have been an easy one, meant to take only a few days. If the slaves really included ex-Spartacans, they obviously were tough or clever enough to have eluded capture the entire previous decade. Octavius, however, crushed these fugitives, and evidently made it to Macedonia by June 60.[73] Antonius for his part might have continued campaigning right up to and indeed after Octavius's arrival. Under Sulla's *maiestas* law, a commander had a full thirty days to leave the *provincia* after succession (11.1.5). Antonius was free, however, to set the pace of his own return to Italy. He may have devised, for instance, a circuitous cultural tour so as to drag his impending trial into the year 59.[74]

Octavius (quite properly) did not get an imperatorial acclamation at Thurii for his operation against the slaves. That came only later, in Thrace in a great battle against the Bessi sometime in 60 or 59.[75] Octavius himself left Macedonia (surely) in early 58. Velleius and Suetonius both say when he departed from the province he aimed "to seek the consulship" (i.e., for 57), but suddenly died before he could formally declare his candidacy. Much later, after the startling rise of this praetor's son—now "Octavianus"—Cicero opines that the Macedonian commander "would have been elected consul, if he had lived."[76] It is interesting that no source says anything about Octavius failing (or even wishing) to triumph. As a praetorian *imperator*, Octavius found himself in the same situation as Caesar did in 60. It is highly likely that he would have to forgo a triumph to make his *professio* on time for 57.

The choice might not have been too difficult a one for Octavius, since in his day triumphs were getting very troublesome to obtain. To be sure, the list of known *imperatores* of the later Republic who do not triumph (or do not seem to triumph) before the Social War is a short one.[77] And as it happens, in our (admittedly defective) record there is no *imperator* who returned to Rome from the time of Sulla's dictatorship down into the mid-60s known to have entered the city without an *ovatio* or triumph. But when Octavius was leaving his *provincia* in 58, he surely noticed that the only commander to have triumphed without obstruction in the previous eight or nine years had been Pompey from his great eastern command, in 61. Several recent *imperatores* were forced to spend years outside the city waiting to be voted a triumph: L. Licinius Lucullus (*cos.* 74, returned ca. 66, triumphed 63),

Q. Marcius Rex (*cos.* 68, who died waiting outside Rome in late 63 or 62), and Q. Caecilius Metellus (*cos.* 69, returned ca. 66, triumphed 62). C. Iulius Caesar, on his return from Spain in 60, just gave up, as did C. Antonius in late 60 or 59 (but for very different reasons).[78] After Octavius' death in 58, no one was to triumph at all for almost another five years. And those that later managed to do so mostly had to wait, namely C. Pomptinus, a *pr.* 63 who returned from Gaul by 58 and triumphed only in 54, and P. Cornelius Lentulus Spinther (*cos.* 57), who returned from his *provincia* of Cilicia in 53 and triumphed in 51. In the meanwhile, there was no shortage of unfulfilled *imperatores*, most of a much higher social status than C. Octavius.[79] All this further undermines Cicero's tendentious observation (14.1.1) on the "ease" of triumphing from Macedonia.[80] Indeed, only one triumph from the 50s seems hassle-free. Interestingly, it is a praetorian one: Q. Caecilius Metellus Pius Scipio (*pr.* 56 or 55, later *cos.* 52) triumphed from a command in an unspecified *provincia* by June 53.[81]

Octavius' direct successor in Macedonia was another non-noble: L. Appuleius, a praetor of 59 said to be the first in his family to reach curule office (though not necessarily the Senate). When Cicero was thrown into exile in 58, he eventually headed to this man's *provincia*. There Appuleius' quaestor (and relative) Cn. Plancius harbored Cicero in his official residence at Thessalonica from at least July through late November 58. When Cicero in 54 defended Plancius on a charge *de sodaliciis* he is tacit about Appuleius' role in all this, except to say that the governor "harbored the same fears as the others" who refused their aid. One automatically thinks here of the praetor C. Vergilius Balbus, who refused Cicero access to his *provincia* of Sicily (13.2.6). Cicero, however, soon had to face a positive danger which forced him to leave Thessalonica for a remote part of Epirus. His enemy, the *cos.* 58 L. Calpurnius Piso, had received Macedonia under a special law of Clodius; Piso was said to have dispatched soldiers to the province as early as November of 58, in anticipation of his own winter crossing.[82]

14.2.5 C. Calpurnius Piso and His Macedonian Command

Piso had received Macedonia under what Cicero terms a "pactio provinciarum."[83] Some background might help. Under the *lex Sempronia* of 123 or 122, the Senate each year, before the consular elections, chose the two *provinciae* that the new consul designates were to receive. These "Sempronian" provinces—unlike praetorian ones—were not liable to tribunician veto (9.3.2). A hallmark of the system was the sortition of the two fixed *provinciae*. In 58, however, the *tr. pl.* Clodius passed a law which rescinded previous arrangements and gave out the consular provinces to be taken up for 57 individually to the two consuls without the lot ("extra ordinem, sine sorte, nominatim"). The *cos.* A. Gabinius was first assigned Cilicia. Yet that was soon made praetorian, and Gabinius received Syria in its stead. Piso's *ex consulatu* province was to be Macedonia. To underline the purely political motivation of the participants in the "pactio," Cicero argues that Macedonia—indeed, all provinces except Gaul—were at peace when Piso arrived there in early 57, and remained so down into 56. (This is the context where Cicero even claims Macedonia was at times held "without *imperium*" by *legati*.)[84]

But that was not all. Clodius, says Cicero in the *De Domo Sua*, granted to these men "infinitum imperium" for their respective provinces. At another point in the speech, he charges Clodius with giving Gabinius the rich province of Syria and "imperium infinitum" to go with it. Broughton takes Cicero's words literally. Now, Cicero refers to "infinitum imperium" elsewhere only in the *Verrines*, in connection with the pirate command of the *pr.* 74 M. Antonius. Long ago, J. Béranger, in a masterly philological and historical study, demonstrated that "pour les romains, un "imperium infinitum" est un non-sens." It was not a technical term, and has nothing to do with the actual quality of the commander's *imperium* or the length of his command. Each of the four times Cicero uses the phrase, it is in a hostile context, flinging it as a barb at political enemies. Béranger, however, might be too hasty in lumping together M. Antonius and the *coss.* 58. When it comes to Gabinius and Piso, Cicero seems to be thinking of something quite definite each of the times he speaks of their "infinitum imperium." One notes that Cicero's comments in the *Verrines* on Antonius' command are quite general and highly acidic: "infinitum *illud* imperium" and "in *isto* infinito imperio." The corresponding notices for Gabinius and Piso, though hostile, lack the derisive modifiers. They are also embedded in a diatribe based on details.[85] The key to the "infinitum imperium" of 58 B.C. must be "boundaries" (*fines*). Cicero in some related passages emphasizes that Clodius' law granted each of the consuls precisely the provincial boundaries he desired. Though the consuls' *provinciae* were not literally boundless, Cicero is determined to show that Clodius had no business letting a magistrate set the *fines* of his own *provincia*.[86] Hence Cicero's decision to recycle here the phrase "infinitum imperium," which he had coined in the *Verrines* to describe a wholly different category of command.

Let us speculate just a bit further. For Gabinius, Clodius may have introduced into his law the formulation, "Syria and the neighboring lands" (see 11.5.3). It is much harder to guess what Clodius did for Piso that could be characterized as "infinitum imperium," since the boundaries of "Macedonia" traditionally had been quite fluid. One possible solution is that Clodius gave Piso special power to conduct some extraterritorial jurisdiction.[87] Whatever the case, the important thing is that L. Calpurnius Piso for his part does not seem to have claimed that he was anything more than "pro consule."[88]

Cicero characterizes Piso's command as a "triennium." But it really consisted of only two campaigning seasons and part of a third, with Piso back in Rome by June 55. Cicero openly attacked him in the Senate in (probably) August of that year, the occasion of the *In Pisonem*.[89] In that speech, Cicero—obviously chagrined that no one had yet prosecuted Piso[90]—is at pains to emphasize the disparity between the commander's reckless ambitions and his limited personal capabilities. He maintains that Piso, despite the substantial resources at his disposal and the rich military possibilities that Macedonia offered, utterly failed to achieve anything creditable, though he had "three years" to do so. Indeed, Piso "lost his army" through defeat and illegal discharge.[91] His most notable campaign was a misguided expedition against the peaceful Denseleti. When the tribe (and apparently others) counterattacked, Piso lost control of the towns in the *provincia*, the Via Egnatia, and indeed had to fortify Thessalonica itself.[92] True, Piso was hailed "imperator" (probably already in 57).[93] But Cicero alleges that was through the efforts of his *legati* L. Valerius Flaccus (*pr.* 63) and Q. Marcius Crispus.[94] Despite some inappropriate celebrations in his *provincia*,[95] Piso never had any of the customary dispatches reach the Senate.[96] When he returned to Rome, he snuck into the city,[97] pretending—for all his earlier triumph hunting—that he disdained a triumph.[98] The one thing Piso did have to show for his "triennium," says Cicero, was the hatred of every constituent element of the province. (Cicero's litany of the commander's victims incidentally constitutes an excellent survey of the scope of Roman Macedonia at that time.)[99]

Elsewhere, Cicero claims that Piso was lucky to have had Macedonia for as long as he did. In 57, the Senate, he says, wanted to "recall" (*deducere, revocare*) both Piso and Gabinius from their provinces, but Clodius and his powerful backers quashed that notion. Cicero is surely dramatizing the procedure. What he means is that there was debate on whether to reallot Syria and Macedonia to new promagistrates in the sortition for 56[100]—the same kind of discussion that a year later prompts Cicero's *De Provinciis Consularibus*, a Senate speech of late spring or early summer 56 on the arrangements for the year 55.

In the deliberations of 56, we learn that four *provinciae* were in serious consideration for the two "consular" slots stipulated by the *lex Sempronia*: the *cos.* 59 Caesar's proconsular provinces of Gallia Cisalpina and Transalpina, and then Macedonia and Syria. At the time, Cicero says the only major fighting to be had was in Gaul.[101] Three main proposals emerged in that debate; I offer here only the baldest of summaries. The first proposal was that Syria and Macedonia should be declared praetorian for 55, so that (barring a veto) Piso and Gabinius be succeeded immediately; the *coss.* 55 should take up the two Gauls.[102] The second was that the *coss.* 55 should receive (respectively) one of the two Gauls, and either Syria or Macedonia. This plan, of course, permits several permutations, and Cicero discusses two of these—each involving Syria—in depth. There was evidently no deep interest in making Macedonia consular; conversely, no one seems to have allowed the possibility that Gallia Cisalpina might be declared praetorian for 55.[103] The third scheme, proposed by P. Servilius (*cos.* 79) and backed by Cicero himself, was that Syria and Macedonia should be declared praetorian for 55, and then consular for 54.[104] In the event, the actual record shows—we do not know the precise outcome of the debate—that Macedonia became praetorian for 55, and Syria consular for 54. So Gabinius continued as *pro consule* for 55 in Syria, unlike Piso in Macedonia, who was superseded—by a praetor.

14.2.6 *Praetorian Commands in Macedonia, 55–50*

The man who was to succeed L. Calpurnius Piso in Macedonia was Q. Ancharius, who opposed Caesar as *tribunus plebis* in 59 and reached the praetorship for 56.[105] He is attested as *pro consule* in the province, but we know almost nothing of his activities, or whether he stayed for one or two years.[106] Piso for his part took the news of supersession (and Gabinius' prorogation) hard indeed, according to

Cicero, especially since it was a praetor that would replace him. Cicero then depicts Piso's departure in the same lurid tones as the rest of his command, and stresses that it is meant to characterize the whole. Among other things, he criticizes the fact that Piso delegated charge of the *provincia* to an ex-quaestor, defying protocol by passing over the aedilicians. We have seen that there was at least one praetorian *legatus* on Piso's staff; he apparently was not interested in staying behind, and probably had left already. (Five years later, when Cicero's term in Cilicia was coming to an end, his praetorian *legati* would act just the same.) Of course, the main thing this talk of delegation shows is that Piso must have left Macedonia before Ancharius' arrival.[107]

It is possible that we might have two more praetorian commanders in Macedonia after the *pr.* 56 Q. Ancharius and before the start of civil warfare in 49. First, an Athenian inscription records honors from the Areopagus, the Boule, and the People to Γαίο[ν —]κώνιον Γαίου υὸν ἀνθύπατον. Broughton convincingly identifies this *pro consule* with the C. Cosconius who was *aed. pl.* 57 and also the *praetorius* Cosconius who was killed by Caesar's troops in 47. The Cosconii were an established praetorian family; that fact, combined with this man's *cursus* and the *Fasti* for Macedonia, fully allow us to postulate a praetorship in 54 with a promagistracy for 53.[108]

The evidence for our second commander is quite a bit murkier. An M. Nonius was evidently (praetorian) commander somewhere in the east in 51; Cicero, writing in February 50, commends his administration, as well as that of Q. Minucius Thermus, who was definitely in Asia in 51. For Nonius' *provincia*, Broughton initially suggested "probably Crete and Cyrene or Macedonia," but later (following Shackleton Bailey) narrowed it to "probably Macedonia."[109] Certainty is impossible on the basis of Cicero's brief notice, but it does seem more probable in any case that someone else had Cyrene and Crete in 51.[110] Nonius' identity and date of praetorship are also a much-discussed problem. It is hard to come up with a single career that would account for the Sufenas whose coin issue commemorated the *pr.* 81 Sex. Nonius' celebration of the first *Ludi Victoriae Sullanae*; the "Struma Nonius" abhorred by Catullus, whose son reached the Senate by 43, when he was proscribed under Antony; the Sufenas acquitted in July 54 of charges (apparently) related to the *tr. pl.* C. Cato's electoral disturbances of 56; the eastern governor M. Nonius of 51–50 who earned the praise of Cicero; and the Sufenas found *cum imperio* in Italy in March 49.[111] At any rate, the last two seem identical. One can readily explain how a provincial commander of 51 could be *cum imperio* in Italy in March 49: he had been hailed as an "imperator" in his *provincia* and on his return was hoping to be voted a triumph. Cicero (*pro cos.* for Cilicia for 51/50) of course had precisely this status at the time. Indeed, even before the start of civil war, Cicero realized that so long as he was *cum imperio* outside the city, he was eligible for another overseas assignment.[112]

If this reconstruction is correct, the likelihood that Nonius held a command in Macedonia rises significantly. That is the province that Cicero in his attack on Piso is so eager to paint as the triumphal province *par excellence*.[113] Earlier in the 50s, the praetorian commander C. Octavius had departed from there as "imperator," followed by Piso himself in 55. As it happens, the sad story Cicero tells of the quaestor T. Antistius—who was stranded in Macedonia at the start of the Civil War[114]—shows that whoever had governed Macedonia in 50 had left already for Italy by early 49.

14.3 Africa in the Pre-Sullan Period

14.3.1 *Commanders for Roman Africa down through the War with Jugurtha*

After the establishment of Roman Africa in 146 B.C., we have to wait almost thirty years before we can name with certainty a single commander for this *provincia*. And that turns out to be a consul. A chance notice in Gellius tells us the *cos.* 118 M. Porcius Cato (grandson of the censor) went to the province during his consulship, and there met his death. Circumstantial evidence strongly suggests that this command should be related to the troubles within Numidia which later led to the Jugurthine War.[115] It is generally agreed that king Micipsa died in that year, after a thirty-year reign, and this led to violence between Jugurtha and his adoptive brothers Hiempsal (whom he soon killed) and Adherbal (whom he dispossessed).[116] Gellius' brief statement on this man need only mean that M. Porcius Cato set out in consular 118. The consul most likely was sent after the news of the violence had reached Rome to keep an eye on the kingdom during its period of transition. There is no indication how long M. Porcius Cato was in the *provincia* before he died. He may have been prorogued—any number of times (see 9.4.3 for some parallels from distant *provinciae* in this period).

Sallust describes how, not long after Micipsa's death and Hiempsal's murder—and so the year 117 or (perhaps) 116—Adherbal and envoys from Jugurtha brought their respective territorial claims to Rome. The Senate sent *decem legati*, headed by L. Opimius (*cos.* 121), to restore Adherbal and divide the Numidian kingdom between its two feuding heirs. Sallust implies that this was an autonomous *legatio*. Indeed, it is its senior member L. Opimius who later received the blame for wrongly favoring Jugurtha.[117]

Yet there are very few examples of sending out a commission of ten in this way down to this time.[118] If M. Porcius Cato was still alive (as *cos.* or *pro cos.*) in "Africa," surely he would be the person to restore Adherbal and settle this contentious frontier, with the *decem legati* serving as his *consilium* (cf. 8.5.3). Most probably Cato was dead, or had died before the *legatio* could complete its work. But it is just possible that it was M. Porcius Cato who in fact brought back Adherbal and then divided the kingdom with the aid of the *legati*, with Sallust ignoring his role (as he does his consulship), since he never made it back to Rome—and so escaped the political prosecutions which came at the beginning of the next decade.[119]

There is no use speculating what arrangements the Senate made for Africa following M. Cato's death, except to say that the volatility of the region doubtless required the presence of a commander in the *provincia* for each of the years down to the start of the Jugurthine War. We have a few hints that the province remained stable. For instance, in 113, one of the consuls in Rome leased tax contracts for Africa, evidently regarded as collectable at that time. In 112, M. Aemilius Scaurus (*cos*. 115), heading a distinguished *legatio* from the Roman Senate, arrived at Utica and urged Jugurtha—who was then besieging Adherbal in Cirta—to come *ad provinciam* (i.e., Roman Africa) for a conference.[120] But the Roman embassy accomplished nothing. Jugurtha forced Adherbal to surrender, and then killed him as well as the Italian traders at Cirta. The Senate decided that the consular *provinciae* for 111 should be "Italia" and a special military *provincia*, "Numidia." The designation "Numidia"—as opposed to "Africa"—made it clear that the conflict with Jugurtha was to be a consular war. And throughout the actual years of fighting (111–105), we continue to find only consuls or prorogued consuls in this special *provincia*. The consular commanders allotted "Numidia" clearly had full powers also in the *provincia* of Africa, which served as the Roman base of operations for this conflict.[121]

Several times we hear of the consular commanders who had "Numidia" delegating their powers to a subordinate. In late 111, Sallust says that the *cos*. L. Calpurnius Bestia left men (no numbers are given) in charge of his army when he returned to Italy to hold the elections. From Sallust's description of the independent conduct of these individuals—which included some military action—it is not impossible that at least one of them had been given *imperium*.[122] That was certainly the case when Bestia's successor, the *cos*. Sp. Postumius Albinus, had to go to Rome to conduct the elections in late 110. He made his brother, the *legatus* Aulus Albinus, *pro praetore* in charge of the Roman camp in Numidia. The appointment implies nothing about the presence of a praetor in Africa in the time. On the face of things, the delegation was perfectly appropriate. Sumner is probably right that A. Albinus was already of praetorian rank when he served as *legatus* under his brother.[123]

The activity of some tribunes delayed the elections for 109, which detained Sp. Albinus in Italy longer than expected. Aulus in turn launched an ambitious expedition against Jugurtha's treasury at Suthul—and ended up leading the Roman army to a thorough defeat. Jugurtha forced the Roman *legatus* into a disgraceful treaty (soon repudiated by the Senate); after making the Roman army pass under the yoke, he had it quit Numidia for the province of Africa. And there the army remained, even after the return of Sp. Albinus, until the *cos*. 109 Q. Metellus came to supersede him. Orosius[125] makes out that at this time, Jugurtha joined to his kingdom "almost the entire" Roman province, which was in revolt. This source is surely exaggerating, since Sallust has Metellus arrive in Africa with no stated difficulty, and then proceed to ravage Numidia. But it is perfectly conceivable that there was trouble in Africa, which would be another reason why it was advisable for the brothers Albinus to stay put.

The defeat prompted the *tr. pl.* 109 C. Mamilius Limetanus to establish his wideranging special *quaestio* in Rome to try those suspected of making accommodations with Jugurtha (10.6.2), in which Sp. Albinus—but not his brother, the legate—was condemned. A. Albinus even reached the consulship, albeit after a bit of a delay, holding the office for 99.[125] The case illustrates vividly the principle—which we have seen in effect almost a century previous (6.1.3), in the episode of Q. Pleminius—that a superior magistrate might be held responsible for the actions of a man to whom he had delegated *imperium*, especially if the delegatee can be shown to have acted according to the superior's "order or consent." Since, in this case, Sp. Albinus had delegated his own brother *imperium*, he may not even have wanted to defend himself by claiming that his subordinate was a renegade. Even if he chose to shift the blame, it might be a hard thing to show that his brother the *legatus* acted without his "order or consent."

We have one further instance of delegation of *imperium* for the Jugurthine War. In late 106, C. Marius (*cos.* 107), when setting off for a minor expedition in Numidia, left his quaestor (or rather *pro quaestore*) L. Cornelius Sulla in charge of the winter camp *pro praetore*. This is very much a chance notice; there must have been any number of similar delegations in the field wherever there were commanders holding consular *imperium* throughout the middle and late Republic. Quaestors like Sulla were a natural choice to receive delegated *imperium*: as magistrates of the Roman People they were fully responsible for their own actions.[126]

In the last stages of the war against Jugurtha, early in the year 105, the *pro cos.* C. Marius summoned to his base at Cirta all Roman senators in North Africa as well as the praetor L. Bellienus, then at Utica. Five legates of king Bocchus of Mauretania had come to Cirta to offer Marius a truce and also get his permission to approach the Senate in Rome for an alliance; Marius wanted to decide on these requests with the most authoritative *consilium* possible. When convened, most members of the *consilium* (including Marius' quaestor Sulla) were in favor of granting the Mauretanians what they wanted. Marius went along with the majority, over the objections of a few fierce dissenters.[127] And that is all we know of the activities of L. Bellienus—the only individual securely attested as praetor for Africa from the establishment of the *provincia* in 146 B.C. down to the Social War.

The presence of the praetor Bellienus at Utica in 105 does not necessarily indicate that both "Africa" and "Numidia" were allotted in each of the years of the conflict. However, it is reasonable to think that the Roman province faced internal and external threats throughout the war. We have seen that Orosius speaks of a large-scale revolt (and actual territorial losses) in Africa for 109. In 107, Jugurtha offered Bocchus a third of Numidia if he could help drive the Romans from Africa, or at least confine them to that *provincia*.[128] On balance, we might suppose that a praetorian commander held the *provincia*, at least in the latter portion (109–105) of the war.

14.3.2 *The Praetorship of M. Aemilius Scaurus*

There is only one slight possibility of salvaging an additional commander for Africa from the wreck of this general era, for the period just before the real ascendancy of Jugurtha. M. Aemilius Scaurus (*cos.* 115) was an unsuccessful consular candidate for 116, and so praetor by 119. The entry in the *De Viris Illustribus* on Scaurus—a relatively detailed and apparently chronologically sequential sketch—says, between notices of his aedileship and consulship, that he was "praetor against Jugurtha (*praetor adversus Iugurtham*), yet was conquered by his money." Broughton, noting that the succession crisis caused by the death of the Numidian king Micipsa came only in 118, considers this statement a mistaken allusion to Scaurus' service as a *legatus* in 112 and 111. Taking the *De Viris Illustribus* at its word is indeed difficult.[129]

It is technically possible that Scaurus was in fact a commander in Africa as praetor in 119, and perhaps into 118, and so was there during the transition in neighboring Numidia. "Praetor" for a prorogued praetor is, of course, common in many authors of all periods. And Scaurus is found in 117 or 116 as the Senate's principal champion of Adherbal, which shows his early interest in Numidian affairs; in 112, Scaurus as legate is said to have been particularly feared by Jugurtha.[130]

However, one problem is that "adversus" in the *De Viris Illustribus* elsewhere has a military sense,[131] and a Roman command "against Jugurtha" of course makes little sense in the context of 119 or even 118, when (as we have seen) the *provincia* of Africa was made consular. That makes even Sumner's solution[132] uncertain, namely that the *De Viris Illustribus* item is a compression of Scaurus' attainment of the praetorship and subsequent resistance to Jugurtha as a senator in Rome.

We do have another possible source for Scaurus' praetorship, but only slightly less vexing. Asconius[133] implies that M. Scaurus held a (praetorian) provincial command in which he extorted enough money from allies to buy himself the consulship, which gave him more *provinciae* to plunder before having to face prosecution. This notice is puzzling, especially since we know that Scaurus was initially defeated for *cos.* 116, and so was exposed to prosecution for abuses committed during a praetorship—even if we suppose a lengthy provincial command—for at least one full year before his successful election as consul.

Here it seems worth suggesting that Scaurus was indeed praetor in a territorial *provincia*—perhaps even Africa—but did not face serious danger of prosecution for *repetundae* on his return. Rather, this charge of "buying the consulship" with money stolen from allies dates precisely to late 116, when P. Rutilius Rufus prosecuted Scaurus (now *cos. designatus*) for *ambitus*.[134] Rutilius—whom Scaurus was to counterprosecute—will have raised the charge of cupidity not just at the trial but also in his political autobiography, which I suggest is how it found its way from this not particularly consequential trial into later tradition. Whether Rutilius as early as 116 can have alleged in addition that Scaurus was "bribed by Jugurtha" (as in the *De Viris Illustribus* notice) is of course entirely uncertain.[135]

14.3.3 *Commanders for Africa of the 90s and 80s*

We can place only two additional regular governors in the *provincia* for the entire pre-Sullan period: P. Sextilius Rufus and C. Fabius Hadrianus, each attested in the context of the Civil War of the 80s, with Q. Metellus Pius (*pr.* 88) appearing as an interloper between these two individuals. First, Sextilius Rufus (through a subordinate) in 88 forbade the exile C. Marius to set foot in his *provincia*. Rufus was perhaps praetor as early as 92, with prorogation down through and beyond the period of the Social War. At any rate, he was in the *provincia* long enough to be a dedicatee of a twenty-volume translation of Mago's agricultural work, which one Cassius Dionysius of Utica had turned from the original Punic into Greek.[136] How long he stayed is anyone's guess. It would be surprising, in view of his treatment of Marius, if he dared to return to Rome once Marius' faction seized total power in 87.

Next, Q. Caecilius Metellus Pius, a praetor (surely) of 88 B.C., who, during the *Bellum Octavianum* of 87, withdrew from Italy to Africa, holding the rank of *pro consule* (10.5.5). Africa was a natural place for Metellus Pius to seek to establish himself, in view of the command his father Q. Metellus Numidicus (*cos.* 109) held there during the Jugurthine War. And perhaps by late 87 P. Sextilius Rufus had simply abandoned the *provincia*. Even if not, Pius had reason to believe that Rufus might allow an opponent of Marius to enter Africa. Whatever the case, there Pius remained, down into the year 84, for most of that time apparently in total control of Africa. That appears from the fact that another refugee, M. Licinius Crassus, even joined Pius there for a time (probably in 85), bringing from Spain a private army of 2,500.[137] The two had a falling out, and Crassus left of his own accord. Not much later—certainly by 84—the Marian praetor C. Fabius Hadrianus had arrived in the province, and successfully drove Metellus Pius himself out of Africa.

By the time Pius quit Italy in 87, he probably had been hailed as *imperator*.[138] Perhaps that status explains why the Cinnans do not appear to have outlawed him as they had Sulla and others in late 87.[139] Even when Pius had been fighting against the government's praetor for Africa in 84, the Senate's response—so the Livian *Periocha* 84 implies—was a *senatus consultum* stipulating "that all armies everywhere be dismissed," passed "through the agency of Carbo and the Marian faction." It is only after the Sullan army started scoring successes in Italy in 83 that the consul Cn. Papirius Carbo managed to push through a vote making Pius a public enemy.[140] Carbo seems not to have had the Senate's support for this measure until then.

The praetor C. Fabius Hadrianus met a grisly end a year or two after his victory over Metellus Pius. He was burned to death in his official residence at Utica in either late 83 (thus Badian) or 82 (Broughton).[141] There was an uprising of some sort at Utica. Accounts vary. Cicero (followed by Valerius Maximus) says that "Roman citizens" who could not stand his *avaritia* took the lead. Diodorus attributes the deed to "Uticans." A Ciceronian scholiast (Ps.-Asconius) speaks of a "slave uprising," that aimed to murder the "principes"—perhaps reflecting an official excuse for the incident. Orosius is the fullest: Hadrianus had a band of slaves that he used for his "regnum," and it was their masters that killed him and his whole *familia*. Whatever the precise cause and whoever the agents, almost all our sources are eager to stress that the Romans took no measures to avenge his death. With the Sullan forces now in Italy, one can fully understand why the Marian government might be too distracted to institute a *quaestio* on the matter. Once Sulla took control of the *res publica*, he hardly will have cared. Hadrianus' fiery end soon became a moral example of justifiable homicide of a provincial governor. But Valerius Maximus' statement that the Senate positively approved of the killing seems to be a dubious extrapolation, perhaps from Cicero's basic account.[142]

The Marians kept their grip on Africa after the murder of Hadrianus and despite their own defeats in Italy. The *cos.* III Cn. Papirius Carbo landed there briefly in 82 before heading to Sicily, where he was to meet his own end at the hands of the *pro pr.* Pompey (13.1.4). And that same year Cinna's son-in-law Cn. Domitius Ahenobarbus—though not known to have held any office at the time—managed to establish himself in the *provincia*, turning it into a haven for the men Sulla was to proscribe. Domitius soon teamed up with Hiertas of Numidia (who had driven off king Hiempsal) and Iarbas of Mauretania, and started planning open war. However, Sulla, by that time firmly in power, cut his scheme short. Sulla transferred Pompey from Sicily to Africa, even taking the step of getting a *senatus consultum* to ratify this addition to his military *provincia*. Pompey "with amazing speed"—in the space of forty days—defeated Domitius, his Marians, and his North African allies, and quashed all movements in Numidia (where he restored Hiempsal) and Mauretania.[143]

The outlines of the rest of the story are perfectly familiar. Sulla's idea was to make Pompey discharge all but one of his (six) legions and wait at Utica for "the στρατηγός who would succeed him." Pompey, however, had his eyes fixed on a triumph. Though only a *privatus*, his troops had acclaimed him *imperator* during the final battle with Domitius, even before his adversary's death. According to Plutarch's uncritical account, they allegedly threatened to mutiny if Pompey obeyed Sulla's order. (Pompey cannot have expected that promised successor anytime soon.) In the end, Pompey forced through what was really his wish, triumphing in all likelihood (as Badian has argued) on 12 March 81, as opposed to that same date in 80 (just possible) or 79 (untenable).[144] The presence of Sertorius in North Africa after his defeat in 81 by the Spanish commander C. Annius (13.4.2) seems to me to provide additional support for Badian's view of an early triumph for Pompey. When a local dynast of Mauretania, hard pressed by Sertorius, sought Sulla's aid in late 81 or early 80, the best the dictator could do was to dispatch the *privatus* "Paccianus" with a small force, probably crossing from Spain.[145] Had Pompey not defied Sulla's order, we can presume he would have had to hold the *provincia* of Africa with one legion for a full year, down into 80. So one of his subordinates must have done it for him.

14.4 Commanders for Africa in the Late Republic

Seven praetorian (and no consular) commanders are attested for Africa in the period following Sulla's dictatorship down to 50 B.C. The evidence for what these individuals did in the *provincia* ranges from slight to nonexistent. However, there is one (slender) common strand: it does seem that in each instance we at least have to allow for the possibility of prorogation in the province. And in no case is the interval between two known commanders so tight as to demand a tenure of just one year by an unknown promagistrate. Cumulatively, the evidence suggests that the Senate did not place a premium on regular succession in the *provincia* of Africa during this era.

The first attested command is that of L. Licinius Lucullus, the future *cos.* 74. Cicero reports that Lucullus was elected, in absence, curule aedile for 79, and then advanced immediately by legal dispensation to the praetorship for 78 ("licebat . . . celerius legis praemio"), followed by a promagistracy in Africa ("praetor . . . post in Africam").[146] Cicero does not say what he did there, but in his summary he places no activities between this promagistracy and his election to the consulship ("inde ad consulatum"), which at least permits us to suppose prorogation in Africa. To return to Lucullus' election to the praetorship: it seems worth suggesting that Lucullus might have owed his acceleration not to his standing as one of the "Sullani,"[147] but to a successful prosecution in the late 90s or early 80s. When

Cicero speaks of "praemia legis," it is invariably in connection with rewards to prosecutors;[148] other Republican sources offer no counterexamples. But there is a snag. The one criminal prosecution reliably attested for L. Lucullus—the famous attack he and his brother made on "Servilius augur"—is said to have ended in an acquittal amidst rioting, and Cicero implies L. Lucullus' prosecutorial career extended no further.[149] So uncertainty remains what *lex* gave Lucullus that *praemium* to hold the aedileship and praetorship back-to-back.

The next known commander for the *provincia* is A. Manlius Torquatus. Under Sulla's dictatorship, there is a quaestor A. Manlius A.f., but the identification of the two cannot be automatically presumed. Manlius proceeded as a praetorian commander to Africa in some year before 68, with the young Cn. Plancius (Cicero's future client) on his staff. Manlius Torquatus himself probably served as a *legatus pro praetore* under Pompey in his pirate command of 67, with special charge of the east coast of Spain and the area of the Balearic islands.[150]

Somewhat better attested is the tenure of L. Sergius Catilina in Africa. Catiline was the nephew of the L. Bellienus who killed Q. Lucretius Afella during his consular bid in 82 (10.5.8) and was condemned for this *inter sicarios* in 64. Alexander identifies this Bellienus (without query) as the praetorian commander found in Africa in 105 (14.3.1). That seems most unlikely: if the praetor were identical with this defendant he would be more than eighty years old when tried![151] (None of our sources on the trial comment on the defendant's status or age.) However, the praetor and the defendant were doubtless related, perhaps father and son; and so it is apparent that Catiline, through the Bellieni, had a preexisting link with his promagisterial *provincia*.

Catiline had reached the praetorship by 68, since he departed from his province of Africa, probably late in 66, to present himself as a consular candidate in (surely) the supplementary elections for 65, to replace a pair of consul designates both spectacularly condemned for *ambitus*. (So he had been prorogued at least once.) Asconius says that Catiline had left Africa specifically to seek the consulship Instead, he found his *professio* refused by the presiding consul—and himself immediately indicted for *repetundae*, with P. Clodius Pulcher as the prosecutor. That cannot have come as a complete surprise. Even before his return, Catiline's conduct had prompted embassies to travel from his *provincia* to protest his exactions. Asconius says many members of the Senate in turn had voiced some prejudicial *sententiae* against the commander.[152] But it is very unlikely Catiline's conduct resulted in an actual *senatus consultum* condemning his actions.[153]

Catiline must have been particularly eager to win the consulship, to shield himself from that prosecution. Yet, as is well known, the *cos*. 66 L. Volcacius Tullus, on the advice of a senatorial *consilium*, refused to accept Catiline's candidacy. The extortion trial came sometime after mid-July of the next year. Senators voted condemnation, but the *equites* and *tribuni aerarii* voted for acquittal, and their verdict set Catiline free to try for the consulship again for 63.[154]

Q. Pompeius Rufus was a *pr*. 63 who is firmly attested as *pro consule* for Africa. The young M. Caelius Rufus was on his staff, and set out with him to the *provincia*. Caelius left from there, says Cicero, to undertake the prosecution of the Macedonian commander C. Antonius (*cos*. 63), who was expected to come to trial in late 60 and was finally prosecuted only in spring 59.[155] So Rufus—who must have been prorogued two or (more probably) three times in Africa—had quite a long command, like several other praetors particularly of the late 60s and early 50s (13.2.6).

Q. Rufus' likely successor was T. Vettius Sabinus. In 59, this man either presided over the extortion trial of L. Valerius Flaccus (*pr.* 63, then *pro cos.* in Asia) or heard it as juror shortly before taking up (so it appears) a promagistracy in Africa. And that is all we can say.[156] The next known governor for Africa arrives in 56: Q. Valerius Orca, a *pr.* 57 who aided in securing Cicero's recall from exile (no city *provincia* is specified in our one source). On behalf of a business associate, Cicero lobbied Orca outside Rome as he left as *pro cos.* for Africa. He addressed further recommendations to him once in the *provincia*.[157] The last two known praetorian commanders for Africa down to 50 are P. Attius Varus and C. Considius Longus. The two cases interrelate. All we know of the tenure of P. Attius Varus is that when he fled from Italy to Africa during the civil warfare of 49 B.C., Caesar notes "a few years previously he had held this province *ex praetura.*"[158] C. Considius came to Africa after P. Attius Varus and before the outbreak of the Civil War. He must have been praetor by 52, since he was a consular candidate for (apparently) the year 49, leaving Africa to his *legatus* Q. Ligarius in order to seek election.[159] In determining the date of Considius' praetorship, one should take into account also the effects of the *lex Pompeia* of 52 that stipulated an interval (allegedly five years) between magistracy and promagistracy. It would help to know when Considius took up Africa. Cicero just possibly can be taken to imply a command of more than one year: the legate Q. Ligarius is said by Cicero to have set out for Africa not with Considius the governor (as a Ciceronian scholiast has it) but while he was governor.[160] At any rate, if Considius was canvassing in 50 for the consulship of 49, he must have had the province at least for both 51 and 50.[161] The command of P. Attius Varus can fall in any of the years 55 through 52. But if Sumner is right that he is to be identified with the juror P. Varus at Milo's trial of 52,[162] that year is excluded.

Eventually, Broughton[163] preferred to make Considius *pr.* 54 and suggested that "he governed Africa from 53 to 50 in succession to P. Attius Varus, and returned in 50 in time to be a candidate for the consulship of 49." That, of course, would insulate C. Considius from those measures of 53 and 52. There is a slight snag. The trial of the Milonian M. Saufeius in 52 took place "apud Considium quaesitorem" under the Plautian law *de vi.*[164] The term *quaesitor* can very well refer to a praetor in office.[165] Despite the doubts of Broughton and others, it is just conceivable— notwithstanding those measures on intervals and the paucity of parallels for a praetor supervising a *vis* trial (11.7.6)—that this is the African commander. The year 52 saw Pompey introduce all sorts of innovations to the conduct of the courts, and it was a *consularis* who presided over Milo's own highly charged trial under the *lex Pompeia de vi*. But two other contemporary Considii seem available.[166]

14.5 Asia in the Pre-Sullan Period

For Roman Asia in the Republic, the praetorian Fasti remain very much in disarray, especially for the early decades of the province. This section and the next (14.6) are concerned solely with the basic and essential problem of the order of commanders and the chronology of their service.

14.5.1 *Three Commanders Attested at Priene*

G. Stumpf has identified our earliest known praetor for Asia: C. Atinius C.f. Labeo Macerio, the *tr. pl.* ca. 130, who (as a praetorian commander) issued a cistophoric coin at Ephesus dated "Year 13" of the provincial era of Roman Asia (24 September 122 to 23 September 121). D. French has brought to light an (undated) gold stater of Ephesus issued by this same praetor.[168] C. Atinius Labeo appears also in an inscription from Priene, where he is first in a series of three στρατηγοί, followed by an L. Piso and M. Hypsaeus, and then a ταμίας M. (Iunius) Silanus Murena.[168] Sumner[169] (who did not connect the inscription to Atinius' coin) had conjectured that the three στρατηγοί were consecutive governors of Asia in either 101–98 or 98–95. However, Stumpf plausibly has suggested that "L. Piso" is L. Calpurnius Piso Caesoninus, the future *cos.* 112 (and thus *pr.* by 115), and that "M. Hypsaeus" is an otherwise unknown son of M. Plautius Hypsaeus, *cos.* 125, and thus praetor ca. 100.[170]

It is reasonable to suppose that C. Atinius Labeo was *pr.* in 122 or 121. His successor may have been Q. Mucius Scaevola, an augur and future *cos.* of 117, who was a governor of Asia probably soon after C. Gracchus' death in 121. He was unsuccessfully prosecuted on his return (119 or early 118) *de repetundis*—the earliest securely attested trial under Gracchus' new-style *quaestio*. It is just possible that a "Valerius Messalla" governed the Asian *provincia* around this general time, and faced trial on the same or a similar charge.[171] Note also Cn. Papirius Carbo, who was honored at Delos (apparently) as *pro consule*. The fact that the dedicator is the Seleucid king Antiochus VIII Grypus (125–96 B.C.) shows that Carbo's *provincia* was almost certainly Asia (as opposed to Macedonia). This man, as consul in 113, fought disastrously against the Cimbri. So the Delos inscription must belong to a praetorian command ca. 116.[172] And we have seen that L. Calpurnius Piso was in Asia as praetor ca. 115 before reaching the consulship for 112. So even on our chance evidence we can place four or five commanders in the *provincia* in the space of a decade. Even if we exclude Messalla, the series of names we have—C. Labeo followed closely by Q. Scaevola, and then Cn. Carbo followed by L. Piso—does seem to hint at a policy of regular succession. And the fact that the praetor Cn. Carbo is attested as "pro consule" suggests that this was the standard rank for governors of Asia from the start. Unfortunately, we cannot trace the story further for this *provincia* for some time. The next Asian commander for whom we can assign even an approximate date is the third of the three στρατηγοί attested at Priene, M. Plautius Hypsaeus, *pr.* ca. 100.

14.5.2 *Three Commanders Attested at Delos*

There are a few more names that one should consider for the early *fasti* of Roman Asia. Three late second-century inscriptions from Delos apply the term στρατηγός ἀνθύπατος to three individuals—doubtless of praetorian rank—whose *provinciae* are unknown. Each of these men could be a governor of either Macedonia or Asia (or Cilicia, after the year 100). One, a certain C. Cluvius L.f., seems quite undatable and hence unassignable.[173] Next is Ser. Cornelius Ser.f. Lentulus, honored by Dionysius son of Nikon, known to be *epimeletes* at Delos in 110/109.[174] This Roman commander is perhaps identical with the "Servius [——] son of Servius" who is second in a senatorial *consilium* from May 112 of at least four, following the *cos.* 115 M. Aemilius Scaurus.[175] If true, he may well have been praetor before 112. F. Papazoglou[176] entertains the possibility Ser. Lentulus had a command in Macedonia. This is certainly conceivable, but one notes the *fasti* for the province are full from 121 through at least 118, and then 114 into 106. Finally, C. Billienus. Here again it is hard to decide whether he was a praetorian commander of Asia or Macedonia.[177] Cicero implies *novitas* and strongly suggests consular candidacy, perhaps more than once, in the period 104–100.[178] If Billienus' *provincia* was Macedonia, he will have been praetor in 106 or later. If Asia, any of the years from, say, 112 on seem possible and are open.

It may be that the C. Rabirius C.f. who is attested *pro consule* at Delos might also belong to this general era.[179] A. Degrassi, in his commentary on this inscription, offers the usual identification of this man with C. Rabirius Postumus, a probable praetor of 48,[180] and assumes a governorship of Asia in 45. However, Syme has argued forcefully against this date and identification.[181] Syme adduces Josephus' notice of a C. Rabirius *pro consule* in Asia during the reign of "Hyrcanus" of Judaea[182] to make a case for assigning this inscription to the period of Hyrcanus I (i.e., 135–104; Hyrcanus II ruled 63–40). Syme continues: "[I]f that were so, the proconsul C. Rabirius might be the maternal grandfather of Rabirius Postumus"—and thus father of the C. Rabirius, *tr. mil.* 89, who took a stand against Saturninus in 100.[183] If we accept Syme's arguments, a date between ca. 120 (but not before) and 110 seems to fit the evidence best.

There are also a few names to be excluded from the *fasti* for Asia of the late second century. An inscription at Delos shows that the Pisidian town of Prostaenna honored M. Antonius M.f. (*cos.* 99) as *quaestor pro praetore*.[184] The date and *provincia* of M. Antonius' quaestorship are known: he set out to Asia in 113.[185] Asia was not declared a consular *provincia* in this year, or in any year (to the best of our knowledge) in the second century after the departure of M.' Aquillius in 126. What we must surmise from this inscription is that a praetor either had left Antonius in charge of the province, or had delegated him *imperium* for some special task. There is no reason to suspect in the case of Antonius that he got his *imperium* through a special *lex*, or still less (as C. Eilers has suggested)[186] that he was the proper commander for Asia, a relatively new (and quite major) province. Before long, another inscription appears that points unequivocally toward delegation of praetorian *imperium*, by a praetor *pro consule* in the east, to his subordinate.[187] The Asian praetor who was Antonius' superior must also have held the province *pro consule*.

14.5.3 *Other Commanders for Asia of the Late Second Century*

With this in mind, let us turn to two inscriptions of the late second or early first century that report a Cn. Aufidius Cn.f. ἀντιστράτηγος.[188] Broughton considered him a governor of Asia, and offered 107 B.C. as a conjectural date for his praetorship.[189] Yet his reported activity—according to one inscription, he adjudicated disputes in Adramyttium—is perfectly proper for a delegatee.[190] This may in fact be the blind *praetorius* whom Cicero saw in his youth, and who adopted the future consul of 71.[191] This inscription would commemorate a position Aufidius held in Asia before his praetorship (quaestor or *legatus*, with delegated *imperium*)—and before his loss of sight. Since Asia was so rarely declared a consular *provincia* before the Civil War of the 80s (just once at most), we confidently can take this as another instance of delegation of *imperium* by a subconsular. The same is true of an unpublished inscription of (perhaps) the late second or early first century, in which a M. Popillius M.f. Laenas was honored as *legatus pro praetore* at Cos.[192]

The Cnidus fragment of the *Lex de provinciis praetoriis* throws some light on the expected activities of the (unnamed) commander for Asia for 100. He is to write letters to a list of allied communities and kings explaining Roman plans for checking piracy, including the creation of Cilicia as a new praetorian *provincia*. The law announces also the further eastward expansion of Roman Asia, with a bald statement that Lycaonia is to be part of that *provincia* (see 9.1.5). In the law the Asian governor is described as a "praetor or *pro consule*."[193] Parallel passages that have to do with the commander for Macedonia (14.1.2) show that the wording here must be traditional, taken over from earlier laws on the staffing of territorial provinces. The evidence so far—notwithstanding the mention of στρατηγοί at Priene and in other contexts[194]—strongly suggests that the praetors who received Asia, like those of Macedonia, were sent out *pro consulibus*. That impression is amply confirmed once we get into the evidence for Asia in the 90s, where we find four or five Asian commanders with the title "pro consule."[195] Let us take our four most closely datable instances first: Q. Mucius Scaevola, C. Valerius Flaccus, L. Gellius, and C. Cassius.

14.5.4 *The Asian Command of Q. Mucius Scaevola*

Scaevola is the first and just about the only governor in this province down to the time of the Mithridatic War for whom we have a detailed report of activities. The date of his command is an extremely difficult problem, and some background is necessary before we can proceed to the central issues.

Scaevola was praetor (possibly 101, but more likely 99 or 98) and then consul in 95. In each of those offices he was a colleague of the orator L. Licinius Crassus.[196] The consulship of Q. Scaevola and L. Crassus fell in a year in which Obsequens says there were no major wars.[197] Their best-known action was the law they carried to reduce Italians who were acting as Roman citizens to the legal status of their own towns. That included the establishment of a *quaestio* to enforce the measure.[198] It would be good to know what *provinciae* they had received under the Sempronian law. One seems to have been Gallia Cisalpina. Crassus managed to campaign there, apparently still as consul, against some undistinguished Alpine tribes.[199] But when he returned to Rome and asked the Senate for a triumph for his achievements, his colleague Scaevola (who evidently had been in or near Rome the entire year) brutally blocked the requisite *senatus consultum* (10.2.1).

Scaevola also was the most famous Republican governor of Asia, and as such is termed ἀνθύπατος Ῥωμαίων, [στρατη]γὸν ἀνθύπατον Ῥωμαίων, and [—— ἀνθύ-]πάτου.[200] He stayed in Asia (by his own decision) only nine months, his *legatus* P. Rutilius Rufus (*pr.* by 118 and *cos.* 105) administering the *provincia* for the rest of the year (and perhaps a bit beyond).[201]

Let us put aside chronological considerations for the moment, and take a brief look at Scaevola's reported administration of the province. Diodorus says that before Scaevola arrived in Asia, his predecessors, "being in partnership with the *publicani*, the very men who sat in judgment on public cases in Rome, had filled the *provincia* with acts of lawlessness." The whole aim of Scaevola's command evidently was to curb these abuses and to set the province aright for the long term.

For a start, Scaevola had spent extra care on his edict, which was notable for its brevity and its fairness. Cicero singles out the provision that Greek cases were to be settled according to Greek law as particularly important.[202] Earlier governors of Asia had been in the habit of exercising their jurisdiction even in extraterritorial parts of the province. That is positively attested in the case of Colophon, in theory a free city, which in the earliest years of the Roman *provincia* at least twice had to defend its autonomy in Rome itself.[203] We also may presume that earlier provincial edicts—in all the *provinciae*—were uncompromisingly Roman in outlook and organization.[204] Perhaps Scaevola—no doubt aided by Rutilius—was the first to draft the bulk of his provincial edict not in Rome (as seems to have been common practice) but on the spot, with the specific needs of the *provincia* in mind. That at any rate is how Scaevola's first known emulator, the praetor L. Sempronius Asellio, composed his edict in Sicily later in the 90s, also with the aid of a senior *legatus* (13.1.4). As we have noted, the Senate was to make Scaevola's edict an official model for governors for Asia. Cicero used it too during his Cilician command of 51/50.[205]

Scaevola, in his own conduct in the *provincia*, self-consciously tried to set an example for those commanders who would follow. He personally paid the expenses for himself and his entourage.[206] And his practical administration of justice put a premium on redressing the financial abuses of the publicans. He also made them stand trial for past criminal conduct.[207]

Diodorus says that Scaevola's actions helped change attitudes in Asia toward Rome.[208] The statement finds ample confirmation. We have a letter in which Scaevola, still *pro consule*, thanked Ephesus for establishing quadrennial games in his honor, elsewhere identified as the Σωτήρια καὶ Μουκίεια. The provincials obviously had tacked a celebration for Mucius Scaevola onto a preexisting festival, the *Soteria*.[209] All the same, these *Mucieia* were "unprecedented, so far as we know, as a provincial honor for a governor."[210] Cicero—who excoriates the Sicilian commander C. Verres for abolishing the *Marcellia* to make way for his own "Verria"—claims that even Mithridates did not disturb Scaevola's games, "though he had occupied this entire province."[211] Within a generation, Scaevola had become a byword for excellence as a provincial governor.[212] But that did not stop the *publicani* from effectively retaliating against this commander: they secured the condemnation of his *legatus* P. Rutilius Rufus for *repetundae* in (surely) the year 92.[213]

The problem is that we cannot ascertain with absolute confidence whether this Asian command should be attached to Scaevola's praetorship or his consulship.

If the latter, it would have to be *ex consulatu*, since (as we have seen) he seems to have spent his year as consul in Italy.[214]

The argument for the earlier date rests entirely on a (corrupt) passage in Asconius, the same one that reports how he quashed Crassus' hope of a triumph. Scaevola, at some point prior to vetoing that vote of a triumph to his consular colleague, for some reason apparently having to do with finances, "had set aside a province in the desire for which many men—even good ones—had committed wrong" ("provinciam, cuius cupiditate plerique etiam boni viri deliquerant, deposuerat ne sumptui esset †oratio†").[215] There are really three possibilities: Scaevola had refused his praetorian *provincia*, or an *ex praetura* command, or his consular *provincia*.

It would be surprising if the *provincia* that Q. Mucius Scaevola had "set aside" was his actual praetorian one. Everything we have seen shows that the refusal of the *provincia* that came to one in the praetorian sortition was a serious business, down to the end of the Republic. It would have been politically risky, even for a well-connected *nobilis*. (The fact that Scaevola held both the praetorship and consulship with L. Licinius Crassus implies that there were no unusual delays in his career.)

A much easier solution is that Scaevola was a city praetor who refused an *ex praetura* command that the Senate gave him. The post-Sullan evidence shows that a city magistrate could extricate himself from a promagisterial *provincia* without too much bother—indeed, simply on general moral grounds. In 67, the praetor L. Lucceius refused to take up a promagisterial command in Sardinia, pointing to the harm that "many individuals" had done to provincials (11.1.6). The notice of Scaevola's refusal of a province in Asconius is not too different ("plerique etiam boni viri").

B. Marshall does make a fair point when he observes, "if Scaevola had declined a province in his consular year, it is easier to understand why he would want to block Crassus' request for a triumph."[216] It is odd that Scaevola was still in Rome at the end of the campaigning season. If he had argued to the Senate that it was a waste of resources (*sumptus*) for him to lead a Roman army to some distant *provincia* (i.e., since there was no real fighting to be had), one can readily understand his annoyance at his colleague's attempt to triumph over some Alpine bandits.[217] Yet if the consular *provinciae* for 95 were Gallia Cisalpina and Italia (cf. 10.6.2 on the consular law and its *quaestio* to investigate Italians illegally acting as Roman citizens), the oddity of Scaevola's presence in the city disappears. The fact Crassus tried to triumph in his actual year of office—always a rare distinction[218]— must have been particularly grating, and is probably enough to explain the fierce reaction of his colleague and (in normal circumstances) political ally Scaevola.

In short, Asconius' implication that by late 95, Q. Mucius Scaevola had turned down a *provincia* on general moral and administrative grounds—not for reasons of *religio* or on oath—suggests that he probably did not hold his command in Asia as praetor or *ex praetura* in the early 90s. On this interpretation, he refused the latter type of commission, with the "moral excuse" he offered on that occasion probably positively enhancing his reputation for probity. The presence of P. Rutilius Rufus as a senior consular *legatus* on Scaevola's staff during his Asian command strongly implies that by that time Scaevola himself had reached the consulship. (No *con-*

sularis is definitely known to have served as the provincial legate of a subconsular in the entire Republican period.)[219] Rutilius' trial of 92 also suggests that he had served under Scaevola in 94, as opposed to some date in the early 90s.

14.5.5 *The Asian Commands of C. Valerius Flaccus, L. Gellius, and C. Cassius*

We can now proceed to the other three commanders who allow at least an approximate date. C. Valerius Flaccus—definitely a *praetor urbanus*, and later *cos.* 93 in Spain—is attested as στρατηγὸς ἀνθύπατος Ῥωμαίων in an inscription from Claros. He will have held Asia *ex praetura* after his urban praetorship.[220] Since Sulla is virtually certain to have been *pr. urb.* 97 (10.1), the date of C. Flaccus' praetorship is very likely 96, but conceivably 98 or earlier.[221] At any rate, Flaccus was a commander in the *provincia* before 95. Secondly, L. Gellius (the future *cos.* 72) was a *praetor inter peregrinos* in 94, and then proceeded to an eastern *provincia* which he held "pro consule ex praetura" (the formulation is Cicero's). The trouble is that his province is just as likely to have been Cilicia as Asia. (The *pr. urb.* 94 C. Sentius took up Macedonia for 93.) Nor do we know how long Gellius stayed in the east, though he certainly was back in Italy by (late) 89.[222]

Finally, there is C. Cassius, termed ἀνθύπατος by Appian. Elsewhere I have discussed in detail this praetor's role in the restoration of Nicomedes of Bithynia and Ariobarzanes of Cappadocia to their respective kingdoms, when he gave military support to the *legati* M.' Aquillius (*cos.* 101) and (apparently) T. Manlius Mancinus (*tr. pl.* 107, and now perhaps a senior praetorian). The Livian *Periocha* lists that action as a foreign affair, clearly of the year 90. Cassius should have been in the *provincia* by that date.[223] When Mithridates drove Ariobarzanes back out, M.' Aquillius, C. Cassius, and now Q. Oppius (*pr.* for Cilicia), without consulting the Senate, tried to restore the Cappadocian king by force. They were soundly defeated, probably in 89. Cassius was forced to flee, eventually (by 88) ending up in Rhodes. He played no discernible part in defending the island when Mithridates tried (unsuccessfully) to besiege it; no doubt the Roman commander had lost most of his troops by that point. Cassius might even have been captured, like the *legatus* Aquillius (whom Mithridates put to death) and Q. Oppius. Though the Senate designated "Asia and the Mithridatic War" as one of the consular *provinciae* for 88, Asia was lost to Rome for some years to come.[224]

There is no real need for the purposes of our study to recount what happened next: the Marian government's dispatch of L. Valerius Flaccus (as *cos. suff.*) to Asia in 86, Flaccus' murder at the hands of Flavius Fimbria, the Peace of Dardanus between Sulla and Mithridates, the details of Fimbria's illegal command and death in 85, Sulla's arrangements in Asia in 85 and 84 (which included the imposition of stiff punitive taxes, amounting to 20,000 talents),[225] his appointment in 84 of L. Licinius Murena to administer the province with Fimbria's two legions, or the events of L. Murena's command in Asia. Some technical questions do present themselves regarding the status of C. Flavius Fimbria and L. Murena, but they are best put off for the moment.

14.5.6 *The Asian Commands of C. Iulius Caesar and L. Lucilius*

Previous to C. Cassius we have to place a pair of sorts, C. Iulius C.f. Caesar (brother-in-law to Marius and father of the dictator) and L. Lucilius, neither of whom permits close dating. Caesar, termed *pro consule* in several inscriptions, was definitely a praetorian commander in Asia in this general era, necessarily before the year 90.[226] But the precise date of this appointment is quite uncertain. The series of events related by the most detailed source for his command, *I. Priene* 111 (unfortunately quite fragmentary),[227] moves from specific embassies to the στρατηγός C. Caesar (lines 14 and 22); to the description of local appeals to an unnamed *pro consule*, perhaps Caesar, against predatory salt-tax collectors (*salinatores*) and *publicani* (lines 112–120); to mention of the relationship of the *publicani* with the province's Roman governors (τοὺ[ς] εἰς Ἀσίαν ἐ[στ]α[λμένους στ]ρα[τ]ηγούς, line 135), over (apparently) the span of three different individuals holding the stephanephorate of Priene. (The stone is quite mutilated here.) The inscription also mentions a continuation of the dispute on salt revenues under the στρατηγός L. Lucilius, and then to other actions by Lucilius. This individual—possibly to be identified with the jurist L. Lucilius Balbus—is likely to be another praetorian commander in Asia.[228] The fact that Lucilius is said to have written a letter to the Senate reporting the third-party adjudication of a dispute between Priene and Miletus "in the stephanophorate of Akrisios" (unfortunately, not independently dated) strengthens this supposition.[229]

The impression one gets is that Caesar was in the *provincia* before Lucilius, and also that one or more praetors possibly held Asia between the commands of these two men.[230] At any rate, both C. Caesar and L. Lucilius are certainly anterior to C. Cassius, who was in the *provincia* by 90 (see above).[231] Sumner placed Caesar in 92 through (at least) early 90 on the basis of *I. Priene* 111. Sumner took that inscription to refer to the terms of three stephanephoroi and to two contemporaneous embassies to Caesar, the last in Lenaion (i.e., January/February) of the year in which the third stephanephoros was eponymous magistrate. At Priene, tenure of the stephanephorate commenced (as Sumner notes) on the first of the month Boedromion, that is, notionally around the autumnal equinox. So, even if we accept the number of three we really need only suppose that C. Caesar was in his *provincia* for the span of two consular years. Most importantly, a date earlier than the very end of the 90s seems positively required. For Lucilius, we cannot accept the precise year Sumner offers, namely 90 and into 89.[232]

14.5.7 *The Asian Command of L. Valerius Flaccus*

At least one more commander has to be squeezed into our record for the 90s: L. Valerius Flaccus, the future *cos. suff.* 86, who replaced C. Marius after his death early that year while *cos.* VII. Broughton[233] summarizes Flaccus' earlier career: "[A]edile in 98 (or 99), he may have become praetor in 95 (or 96?) and then proceeded to his proconsulate in Asia in 94 or 95." The principal evidence for his praetorship—a longish section of the *Pro Flacco*, a speech in which Cicero defends this man's son against an extortion charge from Asia in 59 B.C.—is actually quite sketchy. We hear nothing of an appointment in the city, only of contributions from "the whole of Asia" at some point before the Mithridatic War for a multiday festival in his honor. Once collected, the money was deposited at Tralles, but Cicero says the town lent it out at interest for its own profit, which probably meant that the festival was never performed.[234] It took Flaccus' son (*pr.* 63) during his *ex praetura* command in Asia to recover those sums. From the fact that "the whole of Asia" was financing L. Flaccus *pater*'s commemorative games, we legitimately can infer that he held a praetorian command in that *provincia*, presumably following that of his (elder) brother C. Flaccus, who (as we have seen) must have been *pro consule* in Asia by 95.

Indeed, K. J. Rigsby has hypothesized that Flaccus' games, as well as the "Euergesia" epigraphically attested at Pergamum (in their "fifth celebration"), are just a later incarnation of the quadrennial *Mucieia* established to honor Scaevola.[235] "It may be that these testimonies all concern one festival, not three," argues Rigsby. At some point, the celebration was "stripped of its potentially invidious association with one governor and given the generic name *Euergesia*." This appears at least possible. One notes that when the provincials established the *Mucieia*, they evidently combined it with a preexisting *Soteria*. And when Verres in Sicily tried to set up his own festival, Cicero says he abolished the *Marcellia* and put the *Verria* in their place.[236] In neither case does it seem there was an attempt to make the relevant *provincia* sustain two separate recurring festivals.

If true, Rigsby's conjecture might help with the chronology of Asian commanders in the 90s. As Rigsby fairly points out, "[O]ne implication of this thesis is that a four-year interval separates Scaevola and Flaccus." We might also remember that Cicero says Scaevola's games were celebrated at a time when Mithridates "had occupied this entire province." On a reasonable interpretation, that can refer only to one of the years 88 through 86, before the Peace of Dardanus in 85. If the results of our investigation of Q. Mucius Scaevola's date are accepted, the only sequence possible is that L. Valerius Flaccus had deposited money at Tralles for a festival to be celebrated in 90 B.C., and Asia held a festival (on whatever scale) again in 86, the year when L. Flaccus was to return to the *provincia* as a consular commander against Mithridates.

In any case, a date for L. Flaccus' praetorship in the late 90s, not long before the disorders of the Mithridatic War[237] and the hard financial times that followed for the next decade and a half,[238] makes the most sense. In normal conditions, it is difficult to see how the diversion of funds for a praetor's games would escape the notice of subsequent governors. Of course, once the Sullan government did gain control, it will not have taken any pains to see that this individual received his due, which helps explain why that fund for the Flaccus festival was eventually all but forgotten. Or, L. Flaccus *pater* perhaps pocketed some of the money himself. It appears he too was prosecuted on his return;[239] the question of those missing funds may have come into it, with Flaccus bringing up the cupidity of Tralles as his defense. But we know too little about the incident—our only source is Cicero's defense speech for this man's son when accused *repetundarum* from Asia three decades later—to offer a reconstruction.

14.5.8 *The Praetorian Fasti of Asia down to 90:*
An Overview

So where do we stand? The fact that we can provide the names of six or seven commanders for the Asian *fasti* of the 90s certainly suggests that the Senate aimed at a policy of regular succession in this *provincia* at this time. The order of succession is another question. Broughton initially listed these commanders as follows: Q. Mucius Scaevola, *ex praetura* for 97; possibly L. Gellius, *ex praetura* for 93; L. Valerius Flaccus, *ex praetura* possibly for 92; C. Iulius Caesar, *ex praetura* possibly for 91; L. Lucilius, *ex praetura* possibly for 90; C. Cassius, *ex praetura* for 89.[240] But here Broughton erroneously thought that when an Asian commander shows the title "pro consule," it must refer to a promagistracy. He later corrected that mistake. Following in large part a reconstruction of Sumner's, Broughton in the end chose to make Q. Mucius Scaevola governor in 98 or 97, L. Valerius Flaccus *ex praetura* in 95 or 94, possibly L. Gellius *ex praetura* for 93, C. Iulius Caesar for the years 92 through 90, and L. Lucilius "ca. 90" and perhaps into 89, in which year he places the arrival of C. Cassius.[241] Evidence for the *ex praetura* command of the *cos.* 93 C. Valerius Flaccus had surfaced not long before Broughton offered this revised *fasti*, and managed to escape the author—hence C. Flaccus' absence in both lists.

A reexamination of the *fasti* for Asia in the 90s suggests that C. Iulius Caesar and (perhaps) L. Lucilius belong not at the end of the decade, but near its beginning.[242] The Priene inscription shows that we need two or three years for C. Caesar, and of course at least one for Lucilius. There simply does not appear to be any room for both these men in the latter half of the 90s, if my reconstruction is correct in its essentials: C. Valerius Flaccus, *ex praetura* by 97 or for the year 95; Q. Mucius Scaevola, *ex consulatu* for 94 (with that year seeing the first celebration of a quadrennial festival in his honor); possibly L. Gellius, *ex praetura* for 93; L. Valerius Flaccus for 92 or 91, with some of 90 (the year of the second celebration of the provincewide festival); and C. Cassius in the *provincia* by the year 90. The fact that Priene was hard pressed by the *publicani* during the governorship of both C. Caesar and L. Lucilius offers modest additional support for placing them before Q. Scaevola. It is perhaps best to leave this investigation of the 90s at that for now. A new fact or two might emerge which will necessitate yet another rearrangement of the available pieces of this irritating puzzle.

14.5.9 *Praetorian Commands in Asia during the*
First and Second Mithridatic Wars

There is not much point in trying to disengage general principles from the *fasti* for Asia after the defeat of C. Cassius in 89 down to the end of the 80s. During these years, just three or four individuals in or around Asia are known to have had or claimed praetorian *imperium*. The first two are Q. Minucius Thermus and (quite illegally) C. Flavius Fimbria. When L. Valerius Flaccus (*cos. suff.* 86) had dismissed his subordinate Fimbria at the Hellespont and sent him back to Rome, he put Q. Thermus in his place, leaving him as *pro praetore* in charge of Byzantium. However, Fimbria stirred up the troops at Byzantium to dislodge Thermus, and he took over the delegatee's *fasces*. Fimbria no doubt claimed Thermus' *imperium* as well, until Flaccus returned from Chalcedon in a huff.[243] Fimbria's shortlived appropriation of Thermus' *fasces* was just a first step. After Fimbria had L. Valerius Flaccus put to death at Nicomedia in 85, there is reason to think he represented himself as taking on his superior's consular *imperium*. Now, Lintott has supposed that Fimbria, on murdering Flaccus, took the title *pro quaestore pro praetore*. This seems much too legalistic. Fimbria's behavior at Byzantium (not to mention Nicomedia) shows his attitude toward constitutional propriety. The Livian *Periocha* thinks that Flaccus' *imperium* devolved on Fimbria. And Appian and Strabo are clear that Fimbria henceforth proclaimed himself the head of a consular army. For what it is worth, a late epitomator strongly implies that Fimbria adopted the consular insignia to lead it.[244]

The third (and I would argue last) praetorian commander for this period is L. Licinius Murena. As is well known, Murena—whom Sulla had left in Asia to complete his various administrative arrangements for the *provincia*—conducted a half-hearted campaign against pirates followed by the three-year "Second Mithridatic War," during which he carried hostilities right into Pontus. Murena's activities earned him the title *imperator*, and later a triumph "de Mithridate." But they also had alarmed Sulla enough to order his recall.

Murena's status, though much discussed, poses no great technical difficulty: Cicero quite clearly attests to his praetorship. The date of Murena's actual magistracy must be 88 or—since the *fasti* for that year seem quite full (10.5.5)—87, followed by service in the east. He might have had Macedonia as his formal *provincia*, but never managed to take it up. Rather, he functioned very much as Sulla's subordinate, first in Greece (on which see 14.1.4) and Asia, and then in an independent command in the Roman province. The celebration of that triumph came (probably) in 81, after his recall by Sulla.[245] Yet L. Murena's position certainly seems to have confused Mithridates. When the king formally complained in early 82 that Murena had violated the peace, he did so both to the Senate at Rome, but also to Sulla as his superior.[246] This in turn put the Cinnans in a bind. The Senate responded to Mithridates by sending the *legatus* Calidius to order Murena to back off. However, it took care not to give that envoy an actual *senatus consultum*.[247] Evidently the Senate felt a properly voted decree would imply recognition of Murena's command.

From the (outlawed) *pro cos.* Sulla's perspective, Murena was fighting as a subordinate, yet possessed full *auspicia* (as the grant of a triumph shows). Though Murena's entry in the triumphal *Fasti* is not extant, it seems reasonably secure that he triumphed only *pro praetore*. There is no hint in our sources that he had consular *imperium* in Asia. Sulla is said to have given Murena orders not to fight with Mithridates, and finally recalled him for breaking those orders, all obviously by virtue of *maius imperium*.[248] Quite modest support for the notion that Murena had no more than praetorian *imperium* comes from the status of his own chief subordinate. When Murena went off to campaign in Pontus, he left the *pro quaestore* L. Licinius Lucullus behind to see to Asia proper. And when Murena had to return to Rome, Lucullus may have remained in sole charge of the *provincia* until a proper governor arrived in 81 (see 14.6.1), conducting a major siege of Mytilene in the interim. He then lingered in the *provincia* into the year 80. Yet not one of the (many) dedications to Lucullus extant from this period shows that he had received delegated *imperium*.[249] The same is true of the A. Terentius A.f. Varro who is amply attested as a *legatus* in Asia in the period ca. 85–82.[250] Murena almost certainly was not qualified to confer *imperium* on anyone.

14.6 Asia in the Post-Sullan Period

14.6.1 *Praetorian Commanders in Asia down through 76*

It was a praetor—M. Minucius Thermus—who arrived in Asia to pick up the siege of Mytilene from the *pro quaestore* L. Licinius Lucullus.[251] And when exactly was that? The question is an important one. M. Thermus can only have received the *provincia* subsequent to Sulla's recall order to the renegade commander L. Licinius Murena. Having a terminal date for Murena would illuminate exactly how seriously Sulla took the administration of Asia and the peace with Mithridates.

Broughton[252] rightly regarded Thermus as *pr.* 81, but states equivocally that he was "sent to Asia in or soon after his praetorship." In truth, our evidence points strongly to an early date. We have no record of activities in a city praetorian *provincia* for this man; there is no reason to think he received one. Indeed, Thermus should be the commander for Asia whom a *senatus consultum* (preserved epigraphically) charged to look after the affairs of loyal Stratoniceia in late March of the year 81. The document implies that he was still in the city or in transit to the *provincia* at that time.[253] Murena, by implication, had been recalled and perhaps had already departed from the province. The key point for the chronology of all this is that another praetorian governor, C. Claudius Nero, was in the *provincia* by early 80. Thermus must have left at that time, and the *pro quaestore* Lucullus (elected aedile in absence for 79)[254] apparently went with him.

C. Claudius Nero is postively attested as *pro consule* of Asia.[255] Samos complained to him of the predations of C. Verres, who had beset the island while he was in transit to Cilicia as a *legatus* of its commander Cn. Cornelius Dolabella.[256] So Nero was already in Asia when Verres' superior Dolabella—definitely *pr.* 81 and a promagistrate in 80 (see 15.1.1)—was setting out to his *provincia*, that is, early 80. Nero's city *provincia* is not attested, which allows the possibility he reached the praetorship not in 81 but 80. Though Sulla set up a system in which individuals normally received territorial provinces *ex magistratu*, it was not overly rigid in this requirement (see 11.1.3). At any rate, C. Nero remained in the province of Asia apparently for at least 79. That is the probable date of the murder trial of Philodamus of Lampsacus and his son, charged with murdering a lictor of Verres as that legate passed once again through the province. The Cilician commander Dolabella is said to have attended, leaving his *provincia* for the event to serve in Nero's judicial *consilium*.[257]

Someone was obviously in Asia for the year 78: an inscription of late May of that year instructs the magistrate holding the *provincia* to grant certain honors to some Greek sea captains.[258] But we have no names until the M. Iunius D.f. Silanus attested as *pro consule* in Asia in the year 76.[259]

There is just an outside chance that we might have a praetor for the interim. A late Ciceronian scholiast says that "Terentius Varro," a cousin of Q. Hortensius, was a "defendant from Asia" ("reus ex Asia"). He was accused *de repetundis* before the praetor L. Furius and then (on the same or a different charge?) brought to trial before P. Lentulus Sura (*pr.* 74), only to be scandalously acquitted through Hortensius' agency.[260] There are all sorts of uncertainties here. For a start, we have seen (14.5.9) that an A. Terentius A.f. Varro is found as a Sullan *legatus* in Asia in the period ca. 85–82. If the defendant was A. Terentius Varro, the question remains open whether he faced prosecution for his acts as legate or for a subsequent (unattested) praetorian command in Asia in 78 or 77 (the two available years in the *fasti* for that province). If he was not this A. Varro, one still must wonder whether the "Terentius Varro" of the scholiasts was an ex-praetor.[261] It is technically possible, for instance, that C. Claudius Nero had to stay in Asia through 78 and M. Iunius Silanus arrived in the *provincia* as his direct successor in 77. All we know for certain is that he was in Asia during the year 76.

To continue on a speculative note for the moment: An inscription of Mylasa in Caria[262] might shed some light on Silanus' identification. The document records how one of its citizens travelled to "Asia" and persuaded the στρατηγός M. Iunius D.f. Silanus—termed patron of the city—to visit and act in a "more beneficent manner" toward the Mylasans. This text (especially the mention of patronage) certainly implies that Silanus had been to Mylasa before. It seems just possible that he is the same as the quaestor M. (Iunius) Silanus Murena of *I. Priene* 121, who is found listed after that series of three praetors for Asia of ca. 122–ca. 100 (discussed 14.5.1) in a document which demonstrably includes events down to perhaps the year 95.[263] Now, the name "M. Iunius D.f. Silanus Murena" is impossible for an adoptee, as Shackleton Bailey points out.[264] But there is no technical obstacle to supposing that the Asian commander's father was a Murena adopted into the Iunii Silani, by a D. Iunius Silanus.

At any rate, Eilers, who does not take into consideration the Mylasa decree, is unconvincing in his attempt to split the name to create a M. Silanus ("*pr.* Asia ca. 102") in addition to a quaestorship ca. 100 in Asia for L. Licinius Murena (as we have seen, praetor by 87 before fighting for Sulla in Greece and Asia).[265] The name "M. Silanus Murena" prima facie suggests an adoption, and the Iunii Silani are known to have gone in for that practice even in the mid-second century: the *pr.* 141 D. Silanus Manlianus was born a Manlius Torquatus. There would be nothing incongruous about a Murena born ca. 160 who found himself adopted into the *gens Iunia*—perhaps by the same D. Silanus who saw his son, the *pr.* 141, commit suicide in 140 (9.1.3). On this reconstruction, he himself had a son shortly before ca. 120, who served as quaestor in Asia in the late 90s and reached the praetorship by 77. As Eilers himself mentions,[266] we can see already in the nomenclature of Cn. Aufidius Orestes (*pr.* 77, *cos.* 71) and M. Terentius Varro Lucullus (*pr.* 76, *cos.* 73) an onomastic system where the adoptee's original *cognomen* was simply added unchanged to his new adopted name. And it seems that even in the second century adoptive *cognomina* and *agnomina*, once transferred, could be hereditary.[267] But admittedly, all this is a far stretch.

14.6.2 M. Iunius Iuncus and the Roman Acquisition of Bithynia

Silanus' direct successor in the province was another member of the *gens Iunia*— M. Iunius Iuncus, who received Asia as *pro consule*. By this point, fresh trouble was expected from Mithridates, and the Romans had started making counterpreparations.[268] Iuncus' *provincia* grew only more complicated after the death of king Nicomedes IV and the news that his will left the kingdom of Bithynia to Rome. The Senate decided to add to Iuncus' *provincia* the task of organizing Bithynia.[269] Now, the fact that the recently published *Lex portorii Asiae* shows *publicani* collecting Roman customs revenues in Chalcedon and along the Bosporus in 75 has led some to surmise that Nicomedes was dead and Bithynia had become Roman territory already in that year.[270] The inference is unwarranted. Badian points out that those Hellespontine tolls had been legislated for since (probably) the year 80 and had nothing to do with the death of Nicomedes nor the organization of the new *provincia* of Bithynia. The date of Nicomedes' demise can be placed in either (late) 75 or 74.[271] But there is no reason to suppose that M. Iuncus received his additional commission for Bithynia before early 74.[272]

The details of just a few events from this man's praetorian command have come down to us. During the winter of 75/74 (so it appears), pirates managed to kidnap the young C. Iulius Caesar off Pharmacusa, forcing him to pay a hefty ransom for his freedom. Caesar retaliated—though a *privatus* at the time—by capturing most of these pirates with his own tumultuary fleet. We are told that Caesar then headed to Iunius Iuncus in Bithynia, and asked him to authorize their execution. When Iunius proved slow to send a dispatch on the matter, Caesar took the pirates out of jail at Pergamum and crucified them himself. Suetonius even has Caesar at this time independently raising a force of *auxilia* to drive Mithridatic troops away from cities of the Asian mainland across from Rhodes.[273] M. Iunius Iuncus must have left one of his subordinates in charge of the *provincia* in his absence. Either that deputee was not sufficiently prepared to defend the province or there was trouble in more than one place.[274]

Indeed, the nature of Caesar's activities implies that M. Iuncus was paying scant notice to the administration of Asia after he left for Bithynia. It is not difficult to see how much energy that added assignment might require, not least since Iuncus had to keep Nicomedes' former subjects from revolting while he started turning that old independent kingdom into a Roman *provincia*.[275] Then there was the matter of securing Nicomedes' treasures. The praetor and his staff evidently got their hands on much of the king's wealth: one of Iuncus' (apparent) legates is known to have carted royal furniture to Rome.[276] (It would be surprising if the praetor did not take away even more spectacular items from Nicomedes' estate.) Iuncus also had to take precautions against the possibility that Mithridates might invade Bithynia.

The *coss.* 75 C. Cotta and L. Octavius took up as their promagisterial provinces respectively Cisalpine Gaul and Cilicia,[277] so the threat of Mithridates invading Bithynia was not deemed too acute at the start of 74. Yet open war was just around the corner. The date of the outbreak of the Third Mithridatic War is an old problem, but one that has received renewed attention in the last decade, following the publication of the *Lex portorii Asiae* (though that document surely has no direct relevance to the question). Appian places Mithridates' invasion of Bithynia and rapid defeat of the *cos.* 74 M. Aurelius Cotta in the spring of an unspecified year, and Memnon of Heraclea adds the detail that at the time the *cos.* 74 L. Lucullus already had crossed to the east.[278] The question to be settled is whether the year of that invasion and the first Roman defeat at Chalcedon is 74 or 73, and whether Mithridates' later siege of Cyzicus—a winter operation, which Appian[279] says coincided with the death of Sertorius—belongs to 74/73 or 73/72. The literature is vast on this topic,[280] and I have no desire to attempt a full reexamination of the evidence here—especially since the Third Mithridatic War was a wholly consular affair from the start. However, a brief overview of our basic information on the preliminaries might help us determine the minimum time M. Iunius Iuncus had to stay in the eastern theatre.

Even before the death of Nicomedes, it is said that the Pontic king had made an alliance with Sertorius and received the Sertorian στρατηγός M. Marius to help him win over Asia.[281] Our sources are full of additional details on how carefully Mithridates planned for a new war with Rome.[282] And we are told that in Rome too "many were now stirring up anew the Mithridatic War," with the *cos.* 74 M. Aurelius Cotta leading the van. Cotta claimed that it "had not ended, but rather paused." Obviously he had some noneastern *provincia* but was hoping to go himself to fight Mithridates. His consular colleague L. Licinius Lucullus also had his eyes on a major eastern command, despite having drawn Cisalpine Gaul as his *provincia*. Lucullus' particular fear was that a special command would be created against Mithridates. So he did what he could to keep Pompey—the obvious candidate for such a commission—adequately supplied to keep fighting the Sertorians in Spain.[283]

News of the death of L. Octavius (now *pro cos.*) early in the year set off a lively competition for his *provincia* of Cilicia. As Plutarch tells the story, the real decision was in the hands of the senator (probably a *praetorius*) P. Cornelius Cethegus. Cicero attests to this individual's influence in the Senate, which he says approached that of the consulars. Plutarch implies Cethegus might even have a direct impact on the content of popular legislation. If Pompey were to return in 74 with his army to Italy, says Plutarch, Lucullus realized he was likely to get the Mithridatic command through Cethegus, "who at that time exercised control over political affairs by doing and saying everything with an eye toward winning [popular] favor."[284]

Plutarch states that there were "many" who hoped to get Cilicia.[284] The *provincia*—now suddenly attractive because of its proximity to Cappadocia—had seen only consular commanders since 78 (see 15.1.1), namely, P. Servilius Vatia Isauricus (*cos.* 79) followed (quite briefly) by L. Octavius (*cos.* 75). Now that war with Mithridates was imminent, the Senate was unlikely to declare the province praetorian. What the Senate must have been deliberating was whether to give Cilicia to one of the consuls of 74 or to send a *privatus* with *imperium* instead. Plutarch in fact specifies Pompey and Q. Metellus Pius as Lucullus' chief rivals for the commission.[286]

In the end, the Senate acquiesced in a hybrid solution, one demonstrating that Mithridates' preparations were now that much further advanced than at the time of the *pro cos.* Octavius' death in early 74. Lucullus received Cilicia as his consular *provincia*, almost certainly with Asia attached. Cicero describes his mission as an offensive one, "to proceed against Mithridates." M. Aurelius Cotta—who as we have seen badly wanted the Mithridatic command—"after persistent entreaties to the Senate, was dispatched with ships to guard the Propontis, and to defend Bithynia": thus Plutarch, with Cicero confirming the essentially defensive nature of Cotta's assignment.[287]

All the same, it was indeed a major step (as Cicero notes) to send both consuls to conduct an overseas war.[288] And the consul M. Cotta apparently smoothed the way for other special arrangements. A Ciceronian scholiast says that "through the influence of the consul Cotta and the faction of Cethegus in the Senate,"[289] the *pr.* 74 M. Antonius secured his special commission to fight piracy throughout the Mediterranean area. This, too, might be connected to the eastern war (11.3.1). As noted, had Cotta failed in his attempt to get an eastern *provincia*, he no doubt would have contrived to get this pirate command instead.

This flurry of preparations and the first movements of the war push M. Iunius Iuncus right out of our sources. In brief, M. Aurelius Cotta crossed first to the east and established himself at Chalcedon. Lucullus arrived in Asia only after holding the elections for 73 and raising a legion in Italy. Even then, he did not proceed directly against Mithridates. Plutarch tells us his first task was to retrain the troops he found in Asia, which will have taken some time. When Lucullus did move, he had reached no further than Phrygia when Mithridates invaded Bithynia and shut up Cotta in Chalcedon. Lucullus came to his colleague's rescue, and in the following winter managed also to relieve Cyzicus of Mithridates' siege.[290] Though Cotta and Lucullus might have left Rome to take up these commands during their actual magistracies, it should be clear by now that we have to exclude spring 74 as the date when Mithridates attacked Bithynia. Indeed, if we are to keep Appian's notice that war broke out in the "spring," we have to assign Mithridates' invasion, the actual fighting at Chalcedon, and the start of the siege of Cyzicus all to the year 73.

We may presume that M. Iuncus yielded Bithynia to Cotta as soon as he arrived, and then retired to his proper *provincia* of Asia and stayed there at least until Lucullus touched shore. Iuncus surely had plenty of challenges that kept him busy in the interim. One was gathering the Roman forces and *auxilia* in Asia for Lucullus' arrival, which came no sooner than autumn 74 and conceivably as late as the spring of 73. Iuncus may have seen some fighting in Asia too: as we have noted, the *privatus* Caesar already in 74 had to encounter some Pontic forces in the field.

14.6.3 *The Outbreak of the Third Mithridatic War*

B. C. McGing has effectively addressed most counterarguments in favor of spring 74 as the start of the war.[291] There is just one major piece of evidence that survives his analysis. The *Periocha* of Livy's Book 93, after noting the death and bequest of Nicomedes, Mithridates' alliance with Sertorius, and the king's other preparations for war, mentions the invasion of Bithynia and the defeat of M. Aurelius Cotta "cos." at Chalcedon, then (in a corrupted section) describes the failure of Pompey and Metellus Pius to take Calagurris:

> and exploits by Pompey and Metellus against Sertorius [——] [H]e was equal to all in the arts of war and military service [——] and he forced them, driven from the siege of the town of Calgurris, to head for separate regions, Metellus to Further Spain, Pompey to Gaul.

> resque a Pompeio et Metello adversus Sertorium [——] omnibus belli militiaeque artibus par fuit, [——] et ab obsidione Calagurris oppidi depulsos coegerit diversas regiones petere, Metellum ulteriorem Hispaniam, Pompeium Galliam.

In the *Periocha* Cotta's title "cos." need not be taken literally. It could stand for "pro consule," as often, and so belong to the year 73.[292] But those events in Spain must belong to "Year 3" of Pompey and Metellus' joint fighting against Sertorius, that is, the year 74 (13.4.5).

Keaveney, commenting on the *Periocha's* report of these Sertorian affairs, thinks that "the position of this notice makes the date of 74 virtually certain" for the start of the Mithridatic War.[293] Here he seems too hasty. Scholars apparently have abandoned the text at the end of *Per.* 93 as a lost cause.[294] But for that first lacuna one partial supplement readily presents itself: "resque a Pompeio et Metello adversus Sertorium <gestas continet>" ("and [the book] contains exploits . . . "). Such a formulation—which seems quite inevitable[295]—shows that what we have is a summary statement of the familiar "res praeterea (liber) continet" genre.[296] And that in turn suggests Livy can have related the Calagurris incident and the arrangements Metellus and Pompey took for winter 74/73 anywhere in his Book 93.[297]

The upshot is that the battle at Chalcedon need not have preceded those Sertorian items in Livy's narrative, and so does not necessarily date to the year 74. Nor is there anything further on in the *Periocha* that positively excludes the possibility that Livy in his Book 93 related Chalcedon as an incident of early 73. *Per.* 94 consists of the "cos." L. Lucullus' victories over Pontic cavalry and his quashing of a mutiny, and Deiotarus' success against Mithridates' prefects, followed (in the "praeterea" section) by a notice of Pompey's successes against Sertorius. All that can belong to spring or summer 73. *Periocha* 95 has C. Curio (*cos.* 76) as "pro cos." vanquishing the Dardani (not closely datable), the outbreak of the gladiators' war (demonstrably later 73, as we have seen in 11.8.6), and the "pro cos." Lucullus lifting the siege at Cyzicus. There are independent grounds for dating that event to 73/72, and that is the chronology I assume for what follows below.

14.6.4 *Praetorian Commands in the*
Third Mithridatic War

Other than a few *legati* who might have received delegated *imperium* from M. Cotta or L. Lucullus—and the Sertorian "praetor" M. Marius (see 13.4.1)—no individuals with praetorian *imperium* are explicitly attested in the fighting of the Third Mithridatic War, all the way down to the arrival of Pompey in 66 (and indeed quite a bit beyond). The most probable example of delegation is C. Salluvius C.f. Naso, a *legatus pro praetore* who protected Mysia Abbaetis and Phrygia Epiktetos, no doubt for Lucullus; for this, any date from mid-73 on seems possible. The only reason we hear of this man is that some Mysi Abbaetae set up a bilingual dedication to him, which survived at Nemi. Neither Salluvius nor either of the other two *legati pro praetore* who perhaps belong to this period find their way into literary accounts of this war.[298] Conversely, those literary sources are full of instances where *legati* are fighting in semi-independent commands[299] or are left responsible for substantial towns or territories.[300] Yet one is hard pressed to say which if any of these individuals were *pro praetore*.

In one instance the literary sources do come close to implying delegated *imperium*. Lucullus' chief delegatee in Pontus (occupied in 71) appears to be M. Fabius Hadrianus. Appian says this man "had been left behind by Lucullus to hold a command"; Dio calls him ἄρχων in Pontus.[301] But there are also plenty of apparent counterexamples. P. Rutilius Nudus was possibly of praetorian rank when he served as a *praefectus classis* under M. Aurelius Cotta in Bithynia. Appian tells us he fought semi-independently against Mithridates before Chalcedon in 73, but there is no suggestion in our sources he had *imperium*[302] To take another instance, the *legatus* C. Valerius Triarius probably had held *imperium* in Sardinia before the time of this war (see 13.1.1). From the perspective of the author Memnon, he comes off as almost the equal of the consular commanders Cotta and Lucullus during his long service in the east. Here we do have a number of inscriptions, dating from a visit to Delos to repair fortifications, traditionally (following Phlegon of Tralles) dated ca. 69, but none indicate he had *imperium* at the time.[303] L. Licinius Murena (the future *cos.* 62) also had substantial military responsibilities, but he, too, is never termed anything more than "legatus."[304] One last example: when Lucullus invaded Armenia, he left (apparently in addition to M. Hadrianus) the *legatus* Sornatius in a position of authority in Pontus. Here again we have one, possibly two, epigraphic attestations, but no title more grand than "legatus."[305] It does seem, however, that in this period a *legatus* with *imperium* might be commemorated in a Greek inscription without explicit mention that he was "pro praetore."[306] So a good deal of uncertainty remains.

In sum, the epigraphic evidence—all quite random—suggests that the practice of delegation of *imperium* by consular commanders surely was more common than our surviving literary texts indicate. Still, we have so few ironclad examples of the practice that there is little sense in trying to divine how M. Cotta and L. Lucullus put it to work during their commands in the Third Mithridatic War. Nor is Cn. Pompeius' later command in the east illuminating, for all his wide use of *legati*. We have no explicit instance of the *pro consule* Pompey personally delegating *imperium* to a subordinate in the years 66–62, until he left the *pro quaestore* M. Aemilius Scaurus to hold Syria in early 62 B.C. (11.5.1).

14.6.5 *The "Restoration" of Asia as a Praetorian Provincia*

After reducing Heraclea Pontica by siege—said to be a two-year operation—M. Aurelius Cotta returned to Rome, probably in late 71.[307] Once his consular colleague had departed, Lucullus in 70 turned his attention to the debt-ridden province of Asia, still very much laboring under the fine imposed by Sulla almost a decade and a half previously. He also asked the Senate to send a commission of *decem legati* to organize the territory he had won from Mithridates. The financial reforms Lucullus carried through in Asia, though wildly popular in the *provincia*, are said to have stirred up opposition from *publicani*, who for their part worked on the tribunes in Rome. There were also accusations that Lucullus was intentionally prolonging the war. In 69, right around the fall of Tigranocerta, the Romans (we are not told precisely how) removed Asia from Lucullus' composite *provincia*, "and restored the rule of Asia to the praetors."[308] And that despite a military threat to Asia from Mithridates and the Armenian king Tigranes, which indeed would continue for several years.[309]

Lucullus naturally was not completely shut off from the province of Asia.[310] But to make it once again praetorian was a grave insult to this commander,[311] especially since the decision came at the height of his military success. His *provincia* soon was to shrink to nothing. Lucullus was to lose Cilicia to the *cos.* 68 Q. Marcius Rex, and finally the military *provincia* of Bithynia and Pontus to the *cos.* 67 M.' Acilius Glabrio.[312] The year 67 also saw Cn. Pompeius—*pro cos.* against the pirates under the *lex Gabinia* (11.8.2)—and at least three of his *legati pro praetore* impinge on Asia and the eastern consular military *provinciae*.[313] Finally, in 66 the *tr. pl.* C. Manilius handed over Cilicia, Bithynia, and Pontus entirely to Pompey, who stayed in the east down into late 62 B.C.

But to focus on Asia: The first known commander after the decision of 69 to make this *provincia* praetorian is P. Cornelius Dolabella. This was the individual who, as city praetor, presided over the *sponsio*, known from Cicero's *Pro Caecina*, of A. Caecina versus Sex. Aebutius in 69 or 68. The date of his arrival in Asia as *pro cos.* can be either 68 or 67.[314] We then have four more commanders *ex praetura* to fit into the four or five years down to L. Valerius Flaccus (*pr.* 63) who went to Asia for 62.[315] For none of these four is a city praetorship attested. But the relative order of these four praetors is not hard to divine, thanks especially to some informative passages in the speech Cicero delivered in defense of Flaccus when the latter was prosecuted *repetundarum* in 59. It is also readily apparent that at most one of these predecessors of L. Valerius Flaccus can have been prorogued in the *provincia*. Flaccus himself definitely spent just one year in the *provincia*.[316] So the Senate in the 60s was obviously trying hard to maintain a policy of annual succession for Asia.

The first two commanders for the province after Dolabella were T. Aufidius and P. Varinius. Valerius Maximus makes much of the remarkable coincidence that

T. Aufidius had experience as a *publicanus* in Asia before becoming *pro consule* for the *provincia*; Cicero says in the *Pro Flacco* that he conducted himself "integerrime atque splendidissime" and shows that he directly preceded P. Varinius in that command. Cicero elsewhere mentions Aufidius as a potential candidate for *cos.* 63, which shows he had reached the praetorship by 66.[317] Now, between Aufidius and the arrival of L. Valerius Flaccus in 62, one must fit into the praetorian *fasti* for Asia three individuals. So T. Aufidius was in the *provincia* by 66, perhaps directly succeeding P. Cornelius Dolabella. As for Varinius, Broughton should be right in suggesting that the P. Varinius who shows up as a commander in Asia is identical with the homonymous *pr.* 73 defeated by Spartacus (11.8.6), explaining that he had iterated the praetorship after expulsion from the Senate in 70. The name is exceedingly rare: no other Varinii are known to have held office in the Republic.[318] All we can say is that he had received Asia by 65.

The next two incumbents were P. Orbius and P. Servilius Globulus. In the *Pro Flacco*, Cicero says that each of these men in Asia heard a legal dispute involving the younger Appuleius Decianus (the future prosecutor of L. Valerius Flaccus), but came to two different decisions; Cicero also shows that Globulus directly preceded Flaccus in the *provincia*. P. Orbius (a noted expert in the civil law) then must have held Asia in or before 64. Since P. Globulus was *tr. pl.* 67, the year of his actual praetorship is likely to have been the year 64, as Broughton has it. But the year 65 cannot be absolutely excluded, with a command in Asia for both 64 and 63.[319]

14.6.6 *L. Valerius Flaccus in Asia*

It is another wonderful example of the *sors opportuna* that L. Valerius Flaccus, *pr. urb.* in 63, received Asia in the sortition, where his father had served both as praetor in the late 90s and in an ill-fated consular command of 86–85 (see 14.5.9).[320] As urban praetor, the younger L. Flaccus had played a prominent role in capturing the Allobrogian legates with the letters that exposed the Catilinarians. But he seems to have done very little for the welfare of the province of Asia: Cicero in a letter to his brother reveals that he thought the province a mess at the time Quintus (*pr.* 62) arrived there as Flaccus' successor in 61.[321] The problems evidently included debt and depopulation in the cities, serious urban and rural crime, and actual civil disturbances. There seems to have been an agricultural crisis, too.[322]

Yet when Flaccus later came on trial under the *lex Cornelia de repetundis* in late summer or early autumn 59, Cicero (with Hortensius) defended him all the same. In the *Pro Flacco*, Cicero argued that the trial was not so much about Flaccus' acts as commander in Asia; rather, he was being punished by his enemies for having helped foil Catiline four years earlier. For good measure, Cicero threw in some attacks on the ethnic character of the Asian provincials who had accused Flaccus of wrongdoing, and also some (predictably laudatory) digressions on Flaccus' father and family. The defendant was acquitted after two *actiones*. Despite the success of Cicero's defense, Flaccus was known to Macrobius as one of Cicero's most manifestly guilty clients.[323]

Toward the beginning and conclusion of the *Pro Flacco*, Cicero summarizes L. Flaccus' service in Asia simply as "iuris dictio."[324] A good part of the speech (not entirely extant) is devoted to examining and defending Flaccus' conduct in civil and criminal cases.[325] But he evidently was up to a lot more in the province. By Cicero's own account Flaccus requisitioned money from the cities of Asia to raise a fleet, and then, in coordination with M. Licinius Crassus (*cos.* 70), patrolled the entire coast looking for pirates. One problem was that no praetor before Flaccus had made precisely this type of financial demand on the cities. (The only precedents Cicero can cite are Sulla and Pompey, patently both special cases.) Another problem is that Flaccus never entered those funds into his account books, nor did he do any actual fighting—serious indications of corruption, which Cicero does little to dispel.[326] There were plenty of additional grounds—gleaned even from Cicero's defense speech—for suspecting Flaccus had put a premium on enriching himself while in Asia.[327] "Avaritia" was obviously a central charge that Cicero had to defuse.[328] So it is no doubt a rhetorical ploy that Cicero in his defense speech twice represents Flaccus' main sphere of activity as "iuris dictio." The narrower the range of activity, the more limited might appear the opportunities for abuses.

One notes also that Cicero always calls the defendant simply "praetor," not "pro consule," which was his expected title.[329] In this speech, the only person said to have consular *imperium* in Asia is L. Licinius Lucullus—who was a juror in Flaccus' trial. Cicero probably is trying to downplay Flaccus' powers in his province while simultaneously flattering Lucullus.[330]

In this speech, Cicero has little to say about what L. Flaccus had to show for his administration of Asia. He once terms him "iustissimus praetor," but here he might be thinking just as much of Flaccus' time in the urban province, which (as noted above) he touted loudly because it was so effective against the Catilinarians. Indeed, when searching for positive reasons to acquit his client, Cicero offers the splendor of Flaccus' family, his career up to his promagistracy in Asia, his future prospects—indeed, almost anything but what Flaccus did for Asia. In provincial administration it is difficult to please everyone, offers Cicero: there are plenty of people who hate the whole Roman system; in any case, provincials have no business dictating what Roman commanders should do. In the end, just about the only achievement Cicero registers for Flaccus in Asia is that he frightened the pirates by his manner of naval requisitions. Yet Cicero also plainly says his own brother did not follow Flaccus in this when himself taking up the *provincia*.[331]

Cicero's own correspondence to his brother shows that he had a low opinion of L. Flaccus' tenure of Asia, and it does seem that this attitude colors the *Pro Flacco*. But there may be another reason why Cicero is noticably reticent on the positive aspects of Flaccus' provincial administration. At the time of this speech, his brother Quintus (*pr.* 62) was finishing his third and (as it happened) final year in the *provincia* of Asia. Cicero knew full well that he was liable to prosecution on his arrival in Italy. It was expedient, then, not to let Quintus' predecessor in Asia shine too brightly in the *Pro Flacco*.

14.6.7 *Q. Tullius Cicero in Asia*

Quintus drew Asia as his promagisterial *provincia* definitely after 25 January 61, and probably not long before 15 March 61.[332] Although he expected and in fact wanted only a single year in Asia,[333] he would return from the province only in spring 58, after twice being prorogued. Quintus attempted to bring Atticus with him to Asia as a *legatus*, which shows that (at this time) even nonsenators could hold that post.[334] But Atticus' refusal to serve as a praetor's "attendant" ("assecla," as he put it) resulted in a feud between the two that M. Cicero himself managed to settle only in the next year.[335] It was just the first fire from this provincial command that needed to be put out. For Quintus—by his brother's own account—was quick to anger, and careless, to boot.[336] Those qualities in particular caused Cicero to harbor transparently serious doubts about Quintus' suitability for tenure of a high-profile *provincia* like Asia.[337] At the root of it, he appears to have been worried that Quintus' behavior would reflect poorly on himself.[338]

We are much better informed about the latter stages of Quintus' administration as *pro consule*.[339] Cicero's first extant letter to his brother (*Q. fr.* 1.1), dates to the end of 60 B.C., after the Senate had decided to prorogue this governor for a third year in Asia. That prorogation came despite Cicero's lobbying to the contrary, Quintus' desire to have returned a full year previously, the eagerness of various praetors of 60 to get the province, and the desire of *negotiatores* to turf Quintus out.[340] The picture of Quintus that emerges from this letter and others to follow in 59 is far from flattering.[341] And it is clear that Cicero thought his brother in general all too oblivious to his own public image.[342]

The qualities Quintus showed in the earlier part of his command cannot have been all that different from what we find in this last year. Indeed, Cicero terms his brother's first year the worst for displays of anger (though admitting that the sad state of the province gave Quintus a partial excuse).[343] In his first or second year, Quintus demonstrated questionable judicial severity, too.[344] As for carelessness, it is odd that this praetor delegated a thorny legal case (inherited from Flaccus) to a *legatus*, M. Gratidius, to decide.[345] But from the start, as we have seen, he steered clear of at least one of his predecessor Flaccus' dubious precedents.[346] And Cicero claims he was successful within the space of two years in reversing many of the ills—especially those concerned with public order and unfair taxes—that beset the province on his arrival.[347] We do not learn precisely what attitude Quintus took toward the Asian *publicani*, who had overbid on the taxes for the province and in 60 were pressing hard for a rebate, backed by Crassus and (to an extent) M. Cicero against the strong objections of the *cos.* Q. Caecilius Metellus Celer and the *quaestorius* M. Porcius Cato. Cicero, at the end of 60, says that Quintus had a good reputation with the *publicani*, but one certainly gets the impression that he thought his brother could use greater tact in dealing with this group.[348]

Already in that first letter from the end of 60 we find Cicero voicing strong concerns about the possibility that Quintus would face prosecution on return to Rome from his promagistracy.[349] Indeed, anxiety about possible prosecution motivates a good deal of the practical advice Cicero dispenses in that series of letters from late 60 and 59 to his brother in Asia.[350] As noted, we might count his palpably ambivalent defense of Quintus' predecessor L. Valerius Flaccus in the *Pro Flacco* (August or September 59) as another reflection of that anxiety. The fact that Quintus' successor—T. Ampius Balbus (*pr.* 59 who had drawn the *provincia* before 10 December of that year)—was known to be "very charming" ("perblandus")[351] gave Cicero additional cause for alarm. Comparisons were inevitable.

Quintus left the province at the end of April 58, and had reached Athens by 15 May. Cicero was anxious that he go straight to Rome to prepare against possible legal action and not try to meet him—now in exile—in his abject state at Thessalonica.[352] Cicero's fears for his brother remain prominent in his correspondence for the months that follow.[353] In a way, those fears would reach their most acute point in early September 58, after the sortition of city *provinciae* among the praetors for 57. In a letter to Atticus, Cicero expresses deep concern that Quintus might face prosecution in a quaestio—doubtless repetundarum (11.7.1)—run by the (then praetor designate) Ap. Claudius Pulcher, brother of Clodius.[354] In the event, Quintus probably was never brought to trial.[355]

14.6.8 *Praetorian Commanders in Asia, 58–50*

In the spring of 59, there was some discussion in Rome whether to use cistophoric coinage deposited by Pompey to pay Quintus in his provincial command.[356] As *pro consule* in Asia in 58/57, his successor T. Ampius T.f. Balbus actually minted such coins at Ephesus, Pergamon, Tralles, and Laodiceia. It should be noted that Ampius started producing coin issues at Ephesus by 23 March 58—that is, before Q. Cicero had left (and probably before Ampius had arrived). Ampius' coinage in that province continues through the period 24 January–23 March 57.[357]

The Senate evidently prorogued Ampius for the entire year 57, but with Cilicia—not Asia—now as his *provincia*. The evidence is a chance statement by Cicero that it was Ampius whom P. Lentulus Spinther (*cos.* 57) found in Cilicia when taking it up in 56.[358] The arrangement has caused some confusion.[359] However, Syme adequately explains how the *pro consule* Ampius might find himself transferred from one eastern province to another. He points out that under the Sempronian law, Cilicia was supposed to be consular for 57. When its intended recipient, A. Gabinius (*cos.* 58), managed to have Cilicia declared praetorian and get Syria instead, the Senate put Ampius—for all his charm, not a man of particular *potentia*—in charge of Cilicia until it could come up again in the sortition.[360]

The man who replaced Ampius in Asia for 57 was a C. Fabius M.f., evidently a praetor of 58. As *pro consule* in Asia, he too minted cistophori, at Ephesus, Pergamon, Tralles, Apameia, and Laodiceia. Fabius' Ephesian coins show him in control of the *provincia* from 24 March 57 to perhaps 24 March 56.[361] There are no non-numismatic sources on his command. Some have regarded him as a "Hadrianus"—that is, nephew of the notorious praetor C. Hadrianus burned alive at Utica, and cousin or son of the legate M. Hadrianus active in the Third Mithridatic War—despite the fact that no source offers a *cognomen*.[362] It seems a reasonable guess, since no other senatorial M. Fabii are attested in the previous generation.

Next in the province was C. Septimius T.f. While a praetor in the city in 57 (precise *provincia* unknown), C. Septimius supported Cicero's recall from exile. As *pro consule* for Asia, he minted at Pergamon, Tralles, and Ephesus.[363] His coins are dated by the second of two Ephesian moneyers of "Year 78"—surely 24 March–23 September 56, since at this point these officials seem to have served a six-month term—and under two separate moneyers of "Year 79" of the provincial era.[364] So Septimius was in the province at least until 24 March 55, but probably a bit longer: his successor C. Claudius Ap.f. Pulcher (*pr.* 56) is known to mint at Ephesus only starting in "Year 80" (i.e., after 24 September 55).

As *pr.* 56, C. Claudius had energetically supported another brother—P. Clodius—in Rome,[365] but his city *provincia* is not attested. He issued as *pro consule* for Asia cistophori at Ephesus, Pergamum, and Tralles. C. Pulcher was minting at Ephesus in "Year 80" (i.e., 24 September 55–23 September 54) and "Year 81," with examples of his coins under two separate moneyers for each of these years.[366] So C. Claudius Pulcher remained in this province (supposing a six month term for Ephesian moneyers at this time) at least until 24 March 53. But likely it was somewhat longer, for we know from Cicero he had been prorogued for all that year.[367]

The repeated prorogations do come as a surprise. Though Q. Cicero had three full years in Asia, Claudius' immediate predecessors T. Ampius Balbus, C. Fabius, and C. Septimius, each had to stay in Asia only for one year (though Ampius, of course, found himself prorogued in a different *provincia*). Where we can check, three of the five praetors of 57 who took up a promagistacy found a successor in their *provincia* after a single year.[368] And of Claudius' praetorian colleagues from 56, M. Aemilius Scaurus had just one year in Sardinia, while Q. Ancharius stayed in Macedonia one or at most two years. It certainly seems as though the Senate was taking pains to ensure annual succession where it could in these years (15.3). But for all we know, long prorogations might have been common after 57: as it happens, C. Pulcher, M. Scaurus, and Q. Ancharius are the only praetors from the period 56–53 for whom both the date of magistracy and territorial *provincia* are known. One notes that P. Cornelius Lentulus Spinther (*cos.* 57) was in nearby Cilicia from 56 down into 53, and his successor Ap. Claudius Pulcher (*cos.* 54) from 53 down into 51 (15.1.2), which offer a parallel of sorts for C. Pulcher's three-year command.

Cicero says that before his (second) prorogation, Claudius had hoped to run for the consulship of 53.[369] In the event, the movements of his (presumed) quaestor C. Scribonius Curio (the future *tr. pl.* 50) suggest a return to Rome late in 53 or early in 52.[370] Back in Rome Claudius did not find election to the consulship, but rather condemnation in 51 for *repetundae*, followed by exile.[371]

The last commander to be placed in the Asian *fasti* for this period is Q. Minucius (Q.f) Thermus. He is consistently termed "pro praetore" in Asia, but was definitely of praetorian standing, with charge of the *provincia*.[372] Minucius was at Ephesus in late July 51, and was set to depart from Asia in May of the following year.[373] Broughton suggests he "probably" came to the *provincia* in 52.[374] Yet Minucius' rank—*pro praetore* as opposed to *pro consule*—virtually assures that he received Asia under the *lex Pompeia de provinciis* of 52 (11.1.5), and so quite likely for 51. The arrangements for Asia for 52 remain unknown.

There are other circumstantial details to support this interpretation that Minucius got his province only under the *lex Pompeia*. It is reasonable to suppose that Minucius was son of the *monetalis* Q. (Minucius) Therm(us) M.f., who is probably the same man as the Q. Minuc(ius) M.f. Ter. listed sixth in the *cos.* Cn. Pompeius Strabo's *consilium* at Asculum in 89. The Asian commander himself seems to have reached the Senate as early as 73, and was elected *tribunus plebis* for

62.[375] The date of Minucius' actual praetorship and his activities in the city are not attested. In view of the (probable) details of Minucius' *cursus* and the interval between magistracy and promagistracy stipulated by the *lex Pompeia*, it is reasonable to suggest that his praetorship might have fallen as far back as one of the years 60–58 (all the praetors of 57 are known).[376]

Minucius does seem to have picked up some legal experience before his *ex praetura* Asian command. Cicero personally commends Minucius on his administration of justice, apparently with some sincerity.[377] But all the same, Cicero also gives Minucius some very specific instructions on how to conduct legal affairs in Asia; some of his prescriptions in his letters to this man come off as practically imperious.[378]

15

Cilicia and the Gauls in the Late Republic

So far, our survey of regular praetorian *provinciae* in the later Republic has taken us through the evidence for the city praetorships (10.4, 11.7, 12.1–4) and also the various territorial provinces where praetors served: Sicily and Sardinia (13.1–2), the Spains (13.3–4), Macedonia (14.1–2), Africa (14.3–4), Asia (14.5–6), pre-Sullan Cilicia and the Gauls (10.1–2), and Bithynia/Pontus, Crete, Cyrene, and Syria (11.2–5). In addition, we have examined special praetorian *provinciae* both outside (10.5, 11.8) and inside (10.6, 11.9) the city of Rome. To complete the circuit, it remains to look at praetorian commands in Cilicia (15.1) and the Gauls (15.2) in the period after Sulla. In 15.3 I have added some general remarks on staffing of *provinciae* in the later Republic, meant to complement the discussion in 9.4.1–4 of this same issue in the period down to 122 B.C.

15.1 Roman Cilicia in the Late Republic

15.1.1 *Cn. Cornelius Dolabella (pr. 81) and His Consular Successors*

The first commander to receive the province of Cilicia under Sulla's new system was Cn. Cornelius Dolabella. As praetor, he ruled that the *sponsio* should take place which gave rise to Cicero's *Pro Quinctio* of 81. The date of the speech, and thus Cn. Dolabella's praetorship, is certain (12.1.1). Cn. Dolabella received Cilicia *ex praetura* for 80 and (surely) 79.[1] Dolabella apparently spent quite a bit of time in this province. The fighting in Cilicia was fierce enough for Dolabella's quaestor C. Malleolus to meet his death in battle. It seems unlikely that Dolabella, in the same year in which he lost his quaestor, would let his *legatus* C. Verres (whom he appointed "pro quaestore" in place of the fallen Malleolus) go off on business to Bithynia and Thrace, and then himself take leave of Cilicia and its war to disentangle Verres from troubles at Lampsacus. So more than one year seems required.[2]

His rank raises a more thorny problem. Dolabella is termed "pro consule" (as we would expect) in the scholiasts to the *Verrines*. But when Cicero cites evidence from Dolabella's later trial for extortion (in which he was condemned), it is "from the damages assessed against Dolabella 'pr. et pro pr.'"[3] The title "pro praetore" is very odd for the post-Sullan period, especially in a province where even before Sulla praetorian commanders invariably received enhanced *imperium* (10.1). The designation of Cn. Dolabella as "pro praetore" in his court record may simply reflect the adminstrative perspective of Rome. Strictly speaking, he was a praetor and prorogued praetor, and the fact he held enhanced *imperium* in his *provincia* was perhaps irrelevant in a document of this type. But it is worth suggesting that Dolabella indeed only had the status of *pro praetore*.

Plutarch includes, in a list of instances where Sulla showed jealousy of the supporters who helped him win the Civil War, an attempt to take back a naval command (ναυαρχία) he had given to a "Dolabella."[4] It has been assumed—on the basis of this passage alone—that the elder Cn. Dolabella (i.e., the future *cos.* 81) had command of a fleet in that struggle.[5] However, Plutarch's statement seems better matched to the Cn. Dolabella who was *pr.* 81. Cilicia can plausibly be regarded as a "naval command." There are ample references to the Roman fleet in this *provincia*[6]—as one would expect, since "Cilicia" was specifically set up to combat piracy (see 10.1). And in the two instances where Plutarch elsewhere uses the word ναυαρχία in a Roman context, in both cases it is in reference to Pompey's grand command aginst the pirates under the *lex Gabinia* of 67.[7] It is possible that Sulla for some reason[8] interfered with the younger Dolabella's *ex praetura* command, eventually letting him have Cilicia, but refusing him the same grade of *imperium* that all the other territorial governors in his system had. One notes that the commander for Asia for 80, C. Claudius Nero, was already settled in his *provincia* when Cn. Dolabella was still in transit (see in 14.6.1), which lends modest support to the hypothesis of a quarrel between the dictator and this Dolabella as promagistrate.

After Cn. Cornelius Dolabella, one has to wait about a dozen and a half years before another praetorian commander had a chance to get Cilicia in the sortition. The *cos.* 79 P. Servilius Vatia was in Cilicia probably by early 78. There he remained for a "quinquennium" (as Cicero terms it); more precisely, down into early 74, when he returned to Rome to celebrate a triumph (his second) and assume the *agnomen* "Isauricus."[9] His successor in the province was L. Octavius (*cos.* 75), who died, however, soon after his arrival in Cilicia in 74. By this point, renewed war with Mithridates seemed inevitable. That even prompted talk of creating a special commander to replace Octavius in Cilicia. But L. Licinius Lucullus (*cos.* 74) managed to get the *provincia* decreed to himself, remaining in possession of it for at least five full years. He eventually lost Cilicia to the *cos.* 68 Q. Marcius Rex, who took it up as *pro consule* in 67. After not quite a year in the *provincia* Marcius himself was superseded by the *privatus pro consule* Pompey, under the *lex Manilia* of 66. Pompey held Cilicia as part of his massive eastern *provincia* down to late 62 (on all this, see 14.6.2 and 14.6.5). He even enhanced Roman Cilicia with some new territorial additions in 63. Meanwhile, Marcius—who had been hailed "imperator" in Cilicia—sat outside the walls of Rome at least until late 63, waiting for a triumph that never came.[10]

15.1.2 *Praetorian Commands in Cilicia after 62*

The years 61 through 58 are a blank for Cilicia. It conceivably remained consular (the promagisterial *provinciae* for the *coss.* 62 and 61 are unknown). But in all likelihood, once Pompey completed his organization of Cilicia, it was placed once again in the praetorian sortition. How many times is another question. We know the immediate postpraetorship activities of five or six of the eight members of the college of 62; the only other *provinciae* that admit vacancies for 61 are Sardinia, then Cyrene, Crete (neither of which was ever a high administrative priority), and perhaps Bithynia. Thus there is no technical obstacle to supposing Cilicia was declared praetorian for 61, and allotted to one of the two or three praetors of 62 about whom we are in the dark. In the years 60 through 58, we can account for the *ex praetura* activities of just two or three men each year, but for the governorship of all the standing territorial *provinciae* except for Sardinia, Cyrene, and Crete. So Cilicia can have come up in the sortition for any of these years. But it is even possible that a *pr.* 62 held Cilicia from 61 down through 58. Cilicia by now had a well-established tradition of longish commands, and other *provinciae*—Sicily, Africa, Gallia Transalpina, Asia, Bithynia, Syria—saw prolonged tenures by ex-praetors precisely at this time (13.2.7). Furthermore, if there was just a single commander for Cilicia for this four-year period, it would go some way toward explaining how the administrative arrangements for the province in these years have fallen so completely out of our record.

At the start of 58, it looked as though the *cos.* A. Gabinius would proceed to Cilicia for 57, where his main task would be the annexation and organization of Cyprus. For various reasons, the *tr. pl.* P. Clodius decided to have the *tribunicius* M. Porcius Cato sent *pro quaestore* with praetorian *imperium* to see to that commission instead (11.8.4). But through the agency of Clodius, the consul managed to have Cilicia made praetorian—as it probably had been for the previous four years—and Syria declared consular, to be assigned to himself. As part of this deal, the Senate laterally transferred T. Ampius Balbus (*pr.* 59) *extra ordinem* from his promagisterial command in Asia to Cilicia. Ampius' coins for Asia run up to possibly 23 March 57, but he might have left for Cilicia before or after that point. Ampius then held that *provincia* as his own until it came up again in the sortition for 56. In fact, he waited long enough in Cilicia to meet his successor, the *cos.* 57 P. Cornelius Lentulus Spinther.[11] It was Spinther who in 56 undertook the actual organization of Cyprus, which for the rest of our period was attached to the *provincia* of Cilicia (11.8.4).

Ampius is only the second named praetorian commander we find in charge of this province in the entire period after Sulla's dictatorship. As it happens, he was to be the last before the start of the Civil War in 49. P. Cornelius Lentulus Spinther (*cos.* 57) returned from his *provincia* of Cilicia in 53 and triumphed (after a wait) in 51. During his tenure Phrygia was added to the *provincia* of Cilicia, and with it, Apameia and Laodiceia; the commander for Cilicia now had responsibility also for Cyprus. Lentulus Spinther's direct successor was Ap. Claudius Pulcher (*cos.* 54), who spent more than two full years in the *provincia*. M. Tullius Cicero followed as *pro consule* under the *lex Pompeia*, arriving in the *provincia* 31 July 51 and staying precisely one year to the day.[12]

None of Cicero's immediate predecessors delegated praetorian *imperium* to a subordinate to hold the *provincia* until the arrival of a successor. Indeed, just as T. Ampius Balbus waited for P. Lentulus Spinther, Spinther personally met Ap. Pulcher on his arrival. And when Cicero arrived to supersede Pulcher, he found (to his great annoyance) his predecessor still holding assizes in the province. Ap. Pulcher earlier had claimed he had delegated charge of the *provincia* to a member of his staff, but it seems that was just a ruse.[13] However, Cicero was in a great hurry to quit his provincial command at the first available (legal) opportunity. After much tortured deliberation, on 30 July 50 he left his quaestor C. Coelius Caldus to hold Cilicia until a successor should show up (none was in prospect at the time). Cicero does not say explicitly that he gave Coelius *imperium*. But there is good reason to think the quaestor received it.[14]

The individual who finally took up the *provincia* was P. Sestius L.f. Quaestor 63, he was *tr. pl.* 57, acquitted *de vi* in 56 and also (apparently) on another charge (*de ambitu?*) in 52.[15] He definitely reached the praetorship at some point.[16] Cicero mentions P. Sestius among those *cum imperio* in Italy in March 49[17]—an assorted group that includes Pompey, Q. Metellus Scipio (*cos.* 52, and now *pro cos.* under the *lex Pompeia*), and perhaps even a commander from Macedonia waiting *ad urbem* for a triumph vote (see 14.2.6). In the sortition of provinces that followed, Sestius received Cilicia, where he is found by mid-year.[18] He should have been of praetorian standing by the time of that command,[19] but the date of his actual praetorship is irrecoverable on our present evidence. The years 55, 54, 53, 51, and 50 are each conceivable.[20]

15.2 The Gauls in the Post-Sullan Period

Badian has also comprehensively treated the provincial *fasti* for both Cisalpine and Transalpine Gaul in this period (cf. 10.2.1–3), which removes the need for extended discussion of arrangements for the Gauls in this section.[21] It is clear that Sulla in setting up his new system envisaged these *provinciae* as separate commands: Sulla himself as *cos.* II 80 had Cisalpine Gaul as his promagisterial *provincia*, though he chose not to take it up (11.1.6). In subsequent years, the Senate continued to conceptualize the Gauls as two *provinciae*—at least in principle, that is. It comes as little surprise to find that in this period the Senate several times had to combine the two Gauls and declare them a single (usually consular) *provincia*. We find that certainly for the years 77, 67 through 65, and finally for Caesar in 58 through 50 (joined also with Illyricum). The total accounts for more than one-third of the years of this period. Those instances before Caesar were doubtless in part to compensate for the strain on the system caused by ex-magistrates who followed Sulla's lead and refused their own provincial assignments!

One noteworthy development for the praetorship emerges from this maintenance of Cisalpina and Transalpina as separate provinces. Contrary to long previous practice, after Sulla men of praetorian rank might find themselves assigned a northern command. Despite Sulla's increase in the number of praetors and his integration of ex-consuls into the administrative system, there were still too many territorial *provinciae* relative to the available number of commanders to keep sub-consulars altogether out of the Gauls. Indeed, the first post-Sullan commander we find in Transalpina was of praetorian standing.

15.2.1 *Praetorian Commands in the Gauls of the 70s*

I have argued (13.4.2) that L. Manlius was in command of Gallia Transalpina as *pro consule* at least in 78 and met disaster while trying to enter Iberia in late 78 or early 77. His move was surely fully authorized *ex S.C.* By the time the Senate in 78 sent the consul M. Aemilius Lepidus and his colleague Q. Lutatius Catulus to restore order in Etruria (where the people of Faesulae had attacked Sullan veteran colonies),[22] Lepidus had received both Gauls as his *provincia* under the *lex Sempronia*. Evidently it was he who soon was supposed to succeed L. Manlius in Transalpina.[23]

M. Aemilius Lepidus seems to have operated in Cisalpina already while consul, perhaps aiming to score a triumph over some Alpine tribe.[24] In 77, when Lepidus, now *pro consule*, was causing so much trouble in Italy, we learn that he had left M. Iunius Brutus (*tr. pl.* 83) in charge of that *provincia*. We do not know whether Lepidus dispatched a *legatus* also to Transalpina, now or at a previous time. But the speech in Sallust of the senior consular L. Marcius Philippus—set in early 77 during the *interregnum* that Lepidus caused by his demand for a second consulship—singles out Lepidus' *legati* as a threat in themselves. It would be surprising if Lepidus made no attempt during his consulship or revolutionary promagistracy to assert his authority in the further *provincia*.[25] If he did send a legate there, that would help account for L. Manlius' march with his full forces into Hispania Citerior. What Pompey did to M. Lepidus' legate in Cisalpina, and his elevation to *pro consule* to combat Sertorius later in 77, has already found discussion (11.8.2 and 11.8.5).

To keep to the situation in Transalpina. Manlius' defeat at Ilerda in northeast Spain and Lepidus' insurrection in Italy in 77 left the further *provincia* wholly exposed. If Lepidus had a *legatus* there, he was no longer wanted. To meet the crisis in Transalpina, I have suggested (13.4.4) that the Senate sent M. Fonteius—who should be a *pr.* 77—in his year of office. It is reasonable to think that it was Mam. Aemilius Lepidus who eventually had to hold Cisalpina as consul in 77, perhaps even staying there for a year or two beyond.[26] M. Fonteius, for his part, definitely remained in Transalpina for a "triennium," probably down through the year 75. Fonteius later was prosecuted *repetundarum*, not immediately following his return but sometime after the Aurelian judicial law of the year 70 and previous to the year 67 (discussed shortly below).[27]

Following Fonteius in the *provincia* may have been Cn. Tremelius Scrofa. While holding an appointment in Gallia Transalpina, this man is said to have led a Roman army deep into Gaul, marching toward the Rhine. Scrofa came from a long line of praetors, and himself must have been of praetorian rank at the time of this campaign.[28] Direct succession of Fonteius is not out of the question, but the expedition to the Rhine most naturally dates to a time when the fighting in Spain against Sertorius was no longer acute.

Whether it was precisely Cn. Scrofa who succeeded Fonteius or not, Transalpina should have been praetorian in the years 74 through 72. The proof is that Cisalpina is allotted as a separate consular *provincia* for each of these years. The *provincia* fell to C. Aurelius Cotta (*cos.* 75), who was voted a triumph (albeit on slight grounds) late in 74 or early 73—but died the day before he was to celebrate it.[29] L. Licinius Lucullus (*cos.* 74) had Cisalpina under the *lex Sempronia* for 73, but managed to switch it for Cilicia (14.6.3). And C. Cassius Longinus (*cos.* 73) was killed in the Cisalpine *provincia* fighting in coordination with a praetor (or prorogued praetor) Cn. Manlius against Spartacus' forces in 72 (11.8.7).

This may be a convenient place to point up a vexing puzzle. In a discussion of the cities of Transpadane Italy (i.e., Cisalpine Gaul), Strabo notes that the tribe of the Rhaeti caused damage to the moderate-sized town of Comum, but (Cn.) Pompeius Strabo (*pr.* by 91, *cos.* 89) settled a Roman colony there. "Then C. Scipio added three thousand [sc. colonists], and then the deified Caesar settled it with an additional five thousand," that is, in 59 B.C. Who is this C. Scipio? From the nature of his activity—not to mention the individuals between whom he is grouped—his rank is very possibly praetorian.[30] The *fasti* are open for Cisalpina in 79 (Sulla declined the province, and presumably someone had to fill in), possibly 76–75 (unless Mam. Aemilius Lepidus was there), 71–68 (see below in the next section), and (just conceivably) 60. The year 79 (with Scipio as a praetor for 80, then receiving Gallia Cisalpina *ex praetura*), or 76, or 75 each seems credible. After the fighting in the Civil Wars and the *Bellum Lepidanum*—in which Cisalpine Gaul saw its share of the action, and even some recorded reprisals—Comum might very well need a supplement. However, that is about as far as one can go.

15.2.2 *Praetorian Commands in the Gauls down to 65*

The four years 71 through 68 are a blank, for both Gallic provinces. It has been suggested—with some plausibility—that L. Afranius, as a praetorian commander in Hispania Citerior, had responsibility also for Transalpina for at least part of this time.[31] We do get a glimpse of contemporary conditions in Transalpine Gaul from Cicero's defense of the ex-governor M. Fonteius against a *repetundae* charge in the year 69 or 68. The prosecutors seem to have argued that Fonteius' acquittal would spark a new war in Gaul.[32] Cicero, for his part, in the *Pro Fonteio* (mostly extant) has much to say about the worthlessness of the Gallic witnesses who testified against this commander, the history and character of Gauls in general, and Fonteius' career and family (including a sister who was a Vestal Virgin), suggesting—with amusing hyperbole—that the present trial was a replay of the Gallic sack of 390 B.C.[33] However, Cicero on the whole tries to defend this provincial governor on his record. (His later practice would differ.) Fonteius aided the commanders in Spain with troops, money, and supplies, and administered a provincial levy for wars "all over the world." He carried on some significant military activity in Gaul itself, in the main (apparently) against the Vocontii; he also had his legates improve the Via Domitia.[34] Cicero acknowledges there was no little resistance to the praetor's requisitions. He also admits Gaul was having deep credit problems at the time of Fonteius' praetorship, which did not prevent that governor from thinking up novel taxes.[35] Yet Cicero says that Fonteius had the support of the parties that mattered—the *socii* of Massilia, the people of Narbo, and the Roman citizens in the province.[36]

Unfortunately, we do not know the result of Fonteius' trial. But the prosecution surely had some basis for its claim that Transalpina was troubled. In 67, the *cos.* C. Calpurnius Piso must have received both Gallic *provinciae*. Early in that year, while still in Rome, Piso chose to exercise his authority in Transalpina, refusing (surely through *legati*) to let Pompey's legates hold levies there in preparation for the war with the pirates. Dio tells us that the People, for this, "immediately would have driven Piso out of his ἀρχή"—probably by depriving him of this *provincia*—had not Pompey interceded. (He was evidently still in the city.)[37] Piso managed to keep his command, indeed for two full years beyond his consulship. We know he personally acted in both *provinciae*. At some point he had to subdue a rising of the Allobroges.[38]

In summer 65, Cicero, looking forward to his bid for the consulship, tells Atticus he planned to stay with Piso in Cisalpina from September of that year to January 64, when the law courts in Rome were quiet. We do not know precisely when Piso returned to Rome. When he did (sometime before December 63), he, too, found himself in the *quaestio repetundarum*, prosecuted by Caesar. There the central issue was not conditions in Transalpina, but Piso's punishment of a Transpadane. The Latin colonies in Cisalpina had been clamoring for the Roman citizenship during Piso's entire tenure; as censor in 65, M. Licinius Crassus even had tried to enrol the Transpadanes as Roman citizens, though his colleague Q. Catulus prevented him. The Transpadane issue might explain why the *pro cos.* Piso was spending so much of the year 65 in that *provincia*.[39]

15.2.3 L. Licinius Murena and C. Pomptinus in Transalpine Gaul

From this point, we know the disposition of Gallia Transalpina for each of the years down to the end of our period. The *pr. urb.* 65 L. Licinius Murena definitely succeeded Piso there in 64. Murena held a levy in Umbria while en route to this *provincia*, at the same time taking care to build support among voters in northern Italy for a future consular bid. That came after a year of further prorogation, and efforts to win the goodwill of the *negotiatores* of Transalpine Gaul. By the summer of 63, L. Murena had left his brother and legate Gaius to look after Transalpina while he sought (and won) the consulship in Rome. C. Murena was still there in November 63, when Lucius as consul designate was fighting an *ambitus* prosecution (the occasion of Cicero's *Pro Murena*). In the Catilinarian crisis, the Senate even gave this *legatus* special powers to conduct criminal investigations. The text of Sallust says those took place "'in citeriore Gallia,' the *provincia* he was in charge of as legate." That comes as a surprise, since there is no hint in our sources (including the *Pro Murena*) that L. Licinius Murena had charge of Cisalpine Gaul.

Indeed, Badian has argued for the emendation "in ulteriore Gallia."[40] Let us postpone discussion of this problem for the moment.

The next commander to take up Gallia Transalpina was the *pr.* 63 C. Pomptinus. Pomptinus had already drawn the *provincia* well before the night of 2/3 December 63. That is when Cicero had him aid the *pr. urb.* L. Valerius Flaccus in apprehending two Allobrogian envoys as they headed out of Rome with compromising letters from leading Catilinarians in hand. "Cicero," explains Badian, "in order to impress the Allobroges, will have deliberately assigned the arrest (in part) to the man with whom they knew they would have to get on as their governor in the following year."[41]

The Allobroges seem to have behaved themselves for a spell after Pomptinus arrived in the *provincia*. Yet in 61, Pomptinus had to stand by as Ariovistus, king of the German Suebi, helped the Sequani defeat Rome's allies the Aedui just beyond the northern border of the province. A *senatus consultum* had authorized Pomptinus to protect that Gallic tribe, but he apparently chose not to intervene with his forces (which consisted of a single legion). For that same year, this commander faced also trouble from the Helvetii, who wanted to migrate westwards into the Roman province. And the Allobroges suddenly staged their own rebellion.

We are unusually well informed on Pomptinus' campaign against the Allobroges. The campaigning style reported by Dio for this praetor, where the *legati* do the fighting and the praetor supervises from a central command post, might have been more common than our sources in general suggest. Pomptinus and his legates subdued this people in a series of battles spread over the two years 61 and 60. Still, the military situation with the Helvetii was so acute in mid-March 60 that we find a *senatus consultum* authorizing an immediate sortition of Gallia Cisalpina and Transalpina between the two consuls, who were to conduct a levy—and no doubt proceed straight to their respective *provinciae*. An embassy of three *legati*—headed by Q. Metellus Creticus, *cos.* 69 and *triumphator*, with L. Valerius Flaccus (*pr.* 63) in second position—was to travel north to dissuade Gallic tribes from joining with the Helvetii. There was even to be a sortition among the ex-consuls, apparently for special commands in the field. However, Pomptinus soon put out the fire in Transalpina, removing the need for these emergency arrangements—to the chagrin of the *cos.* Q. Caecilius Metellus Celer, who had drawn that Gallic province, and was hoping for a triumph.[42]

Indeed, Pomptinus' successes apparently made the consul Metellus Celer quickly lose interest in Transalpine Gaul. When the *tr. pl.* L. Flavius (who was trying to push through an agrarian law) threatened to prevent Celer from taking up his allotted *provincia*, the consul professed that he would gladly remain in the city. Q. Metellus Celer was still in Rome in April 59—more than four months after the end of Flavius' tribunate—though he definitely had not renounced Transalpina. Celer soon died, not while in transit to his province but while still acting in the city; just a few days earlier he had been speaking in the Senate and on the Rostra, so Cicero tells us, intimating poison by his wife Clodia.[43] Perhaps already the *cos.* 59 Caesar had received Cisalpine Gaul and Illyricum with three legions for five years under the tribunician *lex Vatinia* (commonly assigned to May of that year). It apparently was Celer's death that prompted the Senate to add Transalpina with a fourth legion. Suetonius tells us the Senate wanted to forestall the People in making that grant; this way, the *provincia* remained notionally subject to the Senate's annual review. Caesar had arrived in Gaul by the end of March 58, and soon started the campaign that took him and his subordinates far beyond the boundaries of the Roman province. Thanks to the arrangements of 59 and a consular law of 55 that gave Caesar his Gallic *provinciae* for five additional years, this *pro consule* was to remain in charge of Cisalpina, Transalpina and Illyricum for just short of nine continuous years.[44]

As for Pomptinus, the Senate at some point in 59 voted him a *supplicatio* for his victories in Transalpina, against the wishes of Caesar and his supporters.[45] We cannot tell precisely when the Senate allowed him that honor, but any time from the start of the year seems possible. Since Pomptinus had every reason to believe in winter 60/59 that Celer would soon proceed to take over Transalpina, he would not wait too far into the year to send his dispatch on the previous campaigning season to the Senate. Cicero himself considered that the best time for a request, and his own letter from Cilicia to Cato in 50 B.C. trying to build support for a *supplicatio* belongs to January of that year. The celebration of the *supplicatio* for Pomptinus' victories need not have followed immediately upon the Senate's vote.[46] All we know is that it took place in 59, simultaneously with the sumptuous funerary banquet Q. Arrius (*pr.* 73) held in honor of his deceased father. Gelzer thought that had taken place by April, before Arrius abandoned hope of winning a consulship for 58. His view is likely to be correct.[47]

C. Pomptinus, on his return, also managed to triumph—but only after a full five years of obstruction. Matters came to a head in 54. Before dawn one morning in (probably) October of that year, a former *legatus* from Pomptinus' Allobrogian campaign—Ser. Sulpicius Galba, now a city praetor—illegally pushed through the vote that allowed Pomptinus *imperium* in the city. Pomptinus planned to stage his triumph on 3 November, and in this he had the support of the *cos.* Ap. Claudius Pulcher as well as some (unnamed) praetors and tribunes. But in steadfast opposition was a formidable group—the praetors M. Porcius Cato and P. Servilius Isauricus (who kept watch for Pomptinus at the *porta triumphalis*) as well as the *tr. pl.* Q. Mucius Scaevola. They vehemently maintained that Pomptinus had not received a legitimate *lex de imperio* (and so could not retain his military auspices to triumph). Pomptinus did get his triumphal procession, but during its course some of the tribunes who missed the chance to veto his *lex* took out their frustration by causing blood to spill.[48]

Sad as it turned out, Pomptinus' triumph was the first Rome had seen in seven years, since Pompey's magnificent display in 61 on his return from the east. And we must remember that no praetorian commander had ever triumphed from "Gallia," however defined, since L. Furius Purpurio in the year 200 (8.3.3). It is a wonder that Pomptinus ever pulled off a triumph at this time specifically from Transalpine Gaul, given the attitude (and political muscle) of Caesar and his friends. As it happens, Pomptinus' Allobrogian war marks the last serious revolt from the Roman *provincia* proper. (Of course, plenty would follow in Gallia Comata and Germania beyond.) We have seen that Pomptinus' success had irritated Q. Metellus Celer, and it must have had even more of that effect on Caesar. One might note that he consistently avoids mentioning Pomptinus by name in the *Bellum Gallicum*.[49]

There is an epilogue of sorts. C. Pomptinus accepted an invitation to serve under Cicero as a *legatus* in Cilicia for the years 51/50 and as such was instrumental in the victory that led to Cicero's imperatorial acclamation in October 51. But Cicero later felt his legate had compromised his chance of a triumph by entering the *pomerium* soon after his return to Italy.[50] Here for once the motivation is clear. Pomptinus surely by this time had had his fill of waiting outside Rome.

15.2.4 *Praetorian Commands in Gallia Transalpina and Gallia Comata under Caesar, 58–50*

A brief comment about the one aspect of Caesar's consular command in the Gallic Wars directly relevant to this study: Caesar made wide use of his *legati* (some quite senior)[51] in his ultra-ambitious campaigns. Many—especially those with smaller armies—had considerable scope for independent action.[52] Often Caesar entrusted two or more legions to a particular *legatus*.[53] And of necessity he routinely must have had to leave subordinates in charge of the individual Roman *provinciae* that made up his command.[54] Yet, curiously, there is just one explicit mention of delegation of praetorian *imperium* in the *Bellum Gallicum*. In describing operations against the Helvetii in 58, Caesar notes that he sent T. Labienus as *pro praetore* with two legions as an advance force.[55] Labienus was a most suitable choice for such an assignment. A *tribunus plebis* of 63, he was certainly of praetorian standing while he served as a *legatus* under Caesar: we are told that Caesar in 50 helped him prepare for a consular bid by giving him charge of Gallia Cisalpina.[56]

The Helvetian campaign of 58 cannot be the only instance in the Gallic Wars in which Caesar made one of his subordinates *pro praetore*. So why the reticence? A clue may lie in a passage of his *Bellum Civile*, in which he sharply criticizes functionaries of the *pro cos.* 49 Q. Scipio. Those subordinates, it is alleged, inappropriately received delegated *imperium* to carry out exactions even in insignificant towns of Asia during the year 48.[57] (Scipio himself was technically *pro cos.* for Syria.) Perhaps Caesar feared his own delegation decisions of the Gallic command might come under scrutiny, and so avoided specifically mentioning grants of *imperium* apart from that one incidental notice near the beginning of the *Bellum Gallicum*. In that work, Caesar does occasionally point out that he gave such and such a subordinate realistic resources for the task at hand—but nothing beyond.[58] In general, he is obviously at pains to communicate his own measured approach to delegating authority and the superb discipline he has imparted to his staff. For instance, Caesar, in the chapter that directly follows the notice of Labienus' delegation, is careful to emphasize that he gave this *legatus* strict orders to wait for him before joining battle with the enemy.[59] There are many similar passages in the *Bellum Gallicum* where Caesar stresses how effective his control was over his subordinates.[60] The reader gets a few negative *exempla* involving subordinates, too, which Caesar clearly introduces to throw the many successful instances of responsible delegation and staff discipline into high relief.[61] And in one instructive passage Caesar describes how the Arvernian chieftain Vercingetorix found himself with a delegation problem all his own.[62]

15.2.5 *Commands in Cisalpine Gaul after 65*

It is time to turn finally to the question of the allotment of Gallia Cisalpina in the years between the tenures of the *cos.* 67 C. Calpurnius Piso—attested in the *provincia* through the end of 65—and the *cos.* 59 C. Iulius Caesar, who held it down through 50. The year 64 is a mystery. Neither of the *coss.* 65 can have had Cisalpina as governor: one was censor in 64, the other *pro consule* in Macedonia. And as Badian has shown, there is no good positive proof that L. Licinius Murena (*pr. urb.* 65) had Cisalpina in addition to his promagisterial *provincia* of Transalpina. So Badian has suggested that the Senate might have prorogued C. Piso in charge of the nearer province alone: "[H]is prosecution by Caesar is not dated, but may well belong to 63. . . . [I]t would make perfect sense to leave such a reliable man there for another year, while relieving him (as soon as manpower allowed) of the troublesome Allobroges."[63] Obviously someone must have been in command of the "Gallicanae legiones" attested in Cisalpine Gaul when the Catilinarian crisis comes up in the next year.[64] Yet there is a snag to Badian's hypothesis. A few years later, Cicero can represent a proposal to take Cisalpina out of Caesar's composite command as a grave insult, a "deminutio provinciae" that one would not inflict even on a man of middling status.[65] It seems hard to believe that Piso would have acquiesced in such an arrangement—but at present we have no better alternative reconstruction.

Under the Sempronian law, the *coss.* 63 were to have Gallia Cisalpina and Macedonia as their provinces. As we have seen (11.1.6, 14.2.4), Cicero struck a deal with his colleague C. Antonius in which he gave him Macedonia in exchange for Cisalpine Gaul. More machinations followed. Sometime after the elections for 62—but before the current praetors had drawn their promagisterial *provinciae*—Cicero called a *contio* in which he announced formally that he would not take up that *provincia*. So Gallia Cisalpina found its way into the sortition of *ex praetura* provinces. The next step (as Cicero explicitly relates) was that C. Antonius and Cicero manipulated the lot so that Cisalpina fell to the *pr.* Q. Caecilius Metellus Celer. (We must allow for the possibility that the consuls also matched other praetors of 63 to specific territorial *provinciae*.) Then, on the same day as the sortition, Cicero saw to the passage of a *senatus consultum* that he characterizes as an outstanding *officium* to Metellus Celer.[66] What was its nature?

To answer that, one should look at what Celer ended up doing the rest of that year. Under the *senatus consultum ultimum* of 21 October, Sallust says two aspiring *triumphatores*—the *cos.* 69 Q. Metellus Creticus and the *cos.* 68 Q. Marcius Rex (both still with *imperium* outside the walls)—took up positions respectively in Apulia and the area around Faesulae in Etruria. Meanwhile, the city praetor Q. Pompeius Rufus was sent to Capua and his colleague Q. Metellus Celer to Picentine territory, each with authority to levy troops to meet the emergency. Cicero confirms Sallust's report, and adds detail. In his Second Catilinarian (9 November), he congratulates himself on the foresight by which he sent Q.

Metellus to the *"ager Gallicus* and *Picenus,"* and predicts the praetor will either crush Catiline or check all his movements. In the same speech, he boasts that Catiline and his forces were no match for the "Gallic legions and the levy which Q. Metellus held in the *ager Picenus* and *Gallicus."*[67]

Metellus appears also to have had special judicial powers from the Senate. Sallust reports that the two Gauls, the *ager Picenus*, Bruttium and Apulia all experienced commotion later in 63. Yet, "[T]he praetor Q. Metellus Celer *ex senatus consulto* threw a good many into chains after examining their case, as did C. Murena *in citeriore Gallia* [thus the MSS.], who was in charge of that *provincia* as legate." Again, Cicero confirms Sallust's report, at least on the praetor. In a letter from January 60 to Metellus, he summarizes that man's role in the Catilinarian affair: "when through my agency you had been set off by the most eminent and honorific distinctions," the task of saving the state was divided in such a way so that "you were to defend Italy both from armed enemies and from hidden conspiracy (*coniuratio*)." Plutarch even goes so far as to say that in the crisis Cicero took charge of affairs in the city and "entrusted matters outside to Q. Metellus."[68] That is obviously an exaggeration. We have seen that the *senatus consultum ultimum* of late October empowered also two consulars who were *cum imperio* and another city praetor to act in the field, and soon also the *legatus* C. Murena is found conducting judicial investigations. Murena must have been in Transalpine Gaul, as Badian suggests; Celer was firmly in possession of Gallia Cisalpina with its (three) legions by early December. Later that month, positioning himself probably just south of Bononia, he effectively blocked Catiline from making his way to the Transalpine province and the Allobroges. Catiline backtracked toward Pistoria, where he met the forces of C. Antonius and was defeated on (very likely) 3 January 62.[69]

On the basis of this evidence, Badian suggests that "the S.C. secured by Cicero's special efforts, and so unusually honorific as regards Celer, gave him consular *imperium* and allowed him to enter his province, as well as giving him the judicial commission that Sallust attests."[70] The first bit seems certain.[71] Yet one notes that in Cicero's letter to Metellus Celer, immediately after mention of that *senatus consultum*, Cicero adds, "in fact, after you set out (*profectus es*) [sc. for your command, as often], please remember what measures I took on your behalf in the Senate, what I said in *contiones*, what letter[s] I sent to you."[72] So Cicero did even more for Metellus Celer after his departure. That might be the occasion when the praetor—and the *legatus* C. Murena—picked up the judicial commission, in Cisalpina and Transalpina respectively.

Celer is clearly attested as *pro consule* in Cisalpina for 62. There, he probably undertook some mopping-up operations against the Catilinarians akin to those we find two city praetors of 62 conducting in the territory of the Paeligni and in Bruttium (11.8.9). While governor in the *provincia*, we happen to know that he received an embassy from Ariovistus, king of the Suebi, that presented him with some Indians who had been shipwrecked and washed up on German shores. The king might have been trying to pave the way for acceptance of his major campaign against the Aedui that came in 61.[73]

Metellus Celer might even have been prorogued into 61. If so, he did not stay in the *provincia* for much of the year. He won election to the consulship for 60—

his tenure in Cisalpina (whatever its length) will have come in handy for that—and by the end of the year was in Rome exerting his authority as *consul designatus*.[74] The alternative is that one of the *coss.* 62 replaced Metellus Celer in Cisalpina: we do not know what L. Licinius Murena did after his consulship, and it appears that his colleague D. Iunius Silanus was positively eager for a military *provincia*.[75] Finally, though detailed evidence is lacking, there is good reason to suspect that the *cos.* 60 L. Afranius took up Cisalpina at some point after he received it in the emergency sortition of March of his consular year. And there he will have remained until the *cos.* 59 C. Iulius Caesar took charge.[76] Of course, Gallia Cisalpina then remained firmly consular down to the end of the decade. In the one real opportunity for a change in that arrangement—the debate of 56 that was the occasion of Cicero's *De Provinciis Consularibus*—we do not see any trace of a suggestion to make it praetorian.[77]

15.3 The Staffing of the Praetorian *Provinciae* after 122

15.3.1 *Decompensation of the Administrative System, 122–82*

In chapters 10 and 12 we explored how after 122 B.C. the Romans set up additional standing courts, each modeled on C. Gracchus' *quaestio repetundarum*. There were at least four such courts in existence by the year 99, and six by 82. And by ca. 100 they created a new (aedilician) quasi magistracy, the *iudex quaestionis*, to preside in the less politically important courts. We first see this officer hearing trials *de veneficiis*; in time it is probable he took over *inter sicarios* and some *peculatus* trials as well. But in this period the other permanent courts (*repetundae, maiestas, ambitus*, and at times *peculatus*) had praetors as presidents. New standing territorial provinces also were instituted, namely, Cilicia ca. 100 and the two Gauls by the mid-90s. All the same, the annual college of praetors stood at six.

One wonders how many senators of the later second and early first centuries thought or cared about the larger questions of imperial administration: it is hard to fathom how they thought the Roman system could take on those extra permanent responsibilities while leaving the number of magistrates untouched. (Compare, e.g., the Senate's meticulous control of succession in the Spains in the latter half of the 140s and early 130s, detailed in 7.3.1.) Indeed, by the 90s, there were twice as many *provinciae* as annual praetors. There was some recognition of the limits of empire. In 96, when the kingdom of Cyrene was bequeathed to the Roman People, the Senate decided to decree that the cities of that kingdom should be "free." All the same, in the early 80s there was an attempt to annex Egypt *ex S.C.*, which a tribune of the plebs had to veto. It is significant that at the time (ca. 87, under the Cinnan government) a majority of senators could not see—or chose not to see— the practical and political problems of such an annexation for themselves.

In the era 122–91, the Senate used prorogation as a panacea for its ailing administrative system. In contrast to the policy of the earlier second century, it now routinely permitted consuls to hold some very long commands—three, four, even five years, in provinces as diverse as Sardinia (a single command spanning 115–111),

Macedonia (110–106), Hispania Citerior (98–early 93) and Ulterior (97–early 93), and the special designation "Numidia" (109–107, then 107–105).[78] Indeed, a fair number of consuls from this period appear to have had three-year commands. But it should be remembered (9.4.3) that if we do not know the actual calendar date of a triumph, a triumph two years after a consulship may mean only one year's prorogation in the *provincia*. For a salutary example, note M. Livius Drusus, *cos.* 112 in Macedonia, who triumphed 1 May 110.[79]

Praetorian commands in the provinces could be lengthy as well. For examples of three-year commands already in the late second century one notes Sex. Pompeius (*pr.* by 121), who probably was prorogued at least twice in Macedonia before he was killed in 119; Q. Servilius Caepio (*pr.* by 109), who celebrated a triumph from Hispania Ulterior in late October 107; the praetor M. Antonius, who was *pro consule* in Cilicia to combat the pirates from 102 to his return to triumph in later 100; and C. Iulius Caesar, praetor in Asia for two or three years in the early 90s. In addition, T. Albucius was *pro praetore* in Sardinia when he demanded a *supplicatio* ca. 107; T. Didius held a command as praetor by 101, and triumphed from Macedonia in 100 or 99. However, two-year commands such as these may be due to mere technical reasons.

There is no use venturing statistics on patterns of prorogation of praetors for the years 122–91. Our evidence is so deficient that the only certain one-year praetorian command in our record for that period is C. Servilius Vatia, who had a troubled time as *pr.* 102 in Sicily. How typical, say, three-year commands were we do not know. At any rate, it clearly was undesirable to prorogue a praetor repeatedly. Asconius, speaking of the future *cos.* 115 M. Aemilius Scaurus, offers one reason why: an unscrupulous praetorian commander was capable of extorting enough money from allies to buy himself the consulship, which gave him another *provincia* to plunder before having to face prosecution (14.3.2).

In this period, the ever widening numerical disparity between *provinciae* that needed *imperium* and the magistrates available to fill them was just one form of pressure on the system. All the city *provinciae* that were praetorian necessarily had to be placed in the sortition each year. And not all the territorial ones received the same treatment. Here the favored province is wealthy Asia. Even on our spotty evidence, we can place four or five commanders in the *provincia* in the years ca. 122–115 (14.5.1), and six or seven for the hard-pressed 90s (14.5.8). But even there, one commander (C. Iulius Caesar, *pr.* ca. 99) had to stay two or three years.

Then there were the accidents. Major wars might upset the system. For instance—to focus just on praetors—three separate praetorian commanders needed to be sent against the rebel slaves of Sicily in the years 104–102, followed by a consul for 101. And from time to time miscellaneous special praetorian *provinciae* had to be declared. In the period 122–82, the Senate seems to have scrupulously avoided setting up commands of this type outside Italy: there is one possible instance in Illyria ca. 120, and then M. Antonius as *pr.* for Cilicia in 102. However, in the crisis years 91–87 we can assume that almost all praetors and recent ex-praetors were needed in Italy for the Social War, which in turn meant that few, if any, of the overseas *provinciae* can have made it into the sortition. Of course, praetorian commanders might die en route to their provinces, or in them. In 119, the fallen Sex. Pompeius immediately had to be replaced in Macedonia. Around 111, L. Calpurnius Piso Frugi was killed in Hispania Ulterior; the Senate did manage to send out an eminently suitable successor (a Ser. Galba) even though the Jugurthine War was raging. The year 91 saw the death of the praetor Q. Servilius at Asculum.

Thus, filling the various *provinciae* each year was a difficult process, subject to all sorts of variables. In the face of all these pressures, it would be a wonder if the Senate did not at least occasionally combine the two Spains in this period. After the year 133, when P. Scipio Aemilianus had reduced Numantia, the military emergency in the peninsula had passed—for a time—and the addition of new praetorian *provinciae* would make separate allotment of Hispania Citerior and Ulterior in the sortition a luxury. It may be relevant that not a single praetorian governor of Citerior can be identified in the years 132–98. At least for the period 105–101, it is possible (following a notice in Appian) that a *legatus* held the province in some or even all of these years (13.3.1).

One administrative expedient that really comes into its own at this time is the use of *ex magistratu* commands. To cover all the *provinciae* which required a commander with *imperium*, the Senate needed increasingly to prorogue city praetors and send them overseas. We know from Plutarch that C. Marius served as a city praetor in 115, and after his praetorship was allotted Hispania Ulterior as a *provincia* (13.3.1). More definite instances come not long after that of Marius. True, L. Licinius Lucullus, city praetor in 104, was prorogued for 103 because he was deemed the most capable commander available to fight a major war in Sicily. But the fact we see at least four city praetors in the four years 97–94 used in this way suggests that by then the expedient had become a necessary part of the system.[80] The most probable disposition of Asia for 94 shows that the Romans had started using *ex consulatu* commands too.

Of course, being assigned a province *ex magistratu* did not preclude further prorogation. Consider Sulla, urban praetor in 97 and then *pro consule* in Cilicia and Cappadocia following his year of office—and for some time beyond. In all, this eastern command lasted perhaps four years. The urban praetor for 94, C. Sentius, had it worse: he returned to Italy after at least six and a half years of hard fighting in Macedonia. In other words, Sentius had been prorogued three times even before the outbreak of the Social War, and that despite a serious defeat in 92. The Senate evidently had a lot less latitude to remove unsuccessful commanders than even a decade earlier.[81] So the system showed real signs of breaking down even before the tumultuous decade 91–82.

It is noteworthy that, despite all the stress on the administrative system, extraordinary votes of *imperium* to nonmagistrates remained rare down until the late 90s. Just one is (apparently) attested in that period, for the city of Rome. In 113, the senior *consularis* L. Cassius Longinus Ravilla received a special appointment by the People to inquire into the case of three Vestals tried on a charge of *incestum* late in the previous year. In this case his *imperium* was just for a special, short-term religious court. He was not meant to take over one of the fixed *quaestiones*.

The extreme crisis of the Social War did necessitate at least a few popular grants of *imperium* for the field. The *legati* C. Marius and Q. Servilius Caepio in

90, and (just possibly) L. Sulla in 89, were voted consular *imperium* to compensate for consuls killed in action. Sex. Iulius Caesar (*cos.* 91) received in late 90 consular *imperium* to take over the siege of Asculum for a time. The emergency practices of this war surely helped change attitudes about the propriety of such extraordinary grants. In 88, the *privatus* Marius was elected to a special Mithridatic command that involved consular *imperium*. (Here one remembers the popular commission P. Cornelius Scipio Aemilianus tried to obtain to fight Aristonicus in 131, the most recent direct precedent.) In late 82, Pompey was dispatched to Sicily with a special grant of praetorian *imperium*; since he triumphed in the next year, it seems likely he received his position through a *lex*, not delegation from the *pro cos.* Sulla.

Several times in this period, we hear of consular commanders delegating their powers to a subordinate. In late 110, when the consul Sp. Postumius Albinus returned from North Africa to Rome to hold the elections, he put his brother Aulus *pro praetore* in charge of his army. In 105, the quaestor L. Sulla was left *pro praetore* in charge of the camp in Africa by the *pro cos.* C. Marius "setting out on an expedition." That latter example shows—against Mommsen—that (at least by this time) a commander did not have to leave his *provincia* to delegate *imperium* (14.3.1). Likewise, in 86, the *legatus* Q. Minucius Thermus was left *pro praetore* at Byzantium by the *cos. suff.* L. Valerius Flaccus (14.5.9). Again, Flaccus did not have to leave his *provincia* (Asia, with the war against Mithridates) to do so.

But those instances from Africa and Asia were meant very much pro tempore. Though precise figures are lacking, the consuls of 90 and 89 who led the Roman effort in the Social War probably delegated *imperium* somewhat freely to the consular and praetorian *legati* who fought under them—and apparently with the intention that those legates have that *imperium* for most, perhaps all, of the year. The legates C. Marius and Q. Servilius Caepio seem to have had praetorian *imperium* at the time their superior P. Rutilius Lupus was killed in 90. The same is true of L. Sulla at the time of the death of his commander, the consul L. Porcius Cato, in 89 (10.5.3–4). It must be emphasized that each of those grants will have come when both general and legate were fighting practically side by side in "Italia." Furthermore, it now appears that in late 87 the *pro consule* Sulla made his *pro quaestore* L. Lucullus *pro praetore* for a far-ranging commission in the eastern Mediterranean that would last through 86. And in 83 the young Cn. Pompeius apparently claimed the title *pro praetore* for himself; it is possible that Sulla confirmed it by delegating him real *imperium*, again to be held for a long period of time (10.5.7).

Balsdon has implied that also praetors with consular *imperium* could always delegate that power. He enunciates the following principle: "[I]f a [proconsular] governor of a province died, his quaestor (or 'pro quaestore') automatically became acting-governor ('pro praetore'), and was attended probably by six fasces, until a replacement arrived; and if a governor left his province before the arrival of his successor, he appointed an acting governor to fill the gap."[82] Balsdon's first hypothesis, the "spontaneous generation" of praetorian *imperium*, cannot be substantiated from our record (such as it is) of the Republic down to 50 B.C. Significantly, it does not appear in the two places where we would expect to find it. The detailed inscription of Lete in Macedonia (discussed in 14.1.1) tells how, in 119, the quaestor M.

Annius P.f. took command of the Roman army in that *provincia* after the death in the field of his praetor, Sex. Pompeius. M. Annius made no claim to praetorian *imperium*. If he acted *pro praetore*, it was de facto, not de jure. By this time, it may have been accepted that a praetor *pro consule* could confer *imperium* on his quaestor, but the praetor Sex. Pompeius died before he got the chance. Nor does (in a later period) C. Cassius Longinus, the quaestor of Crassus, ever seem to have claimed he was acting *pro praetore* after his escape from Carrhae in 53, despite the fact that he took on the entire defense of Syria (11.5.2). It is not until the triumviral era that we find an apparent instance of a *pro quaestore* assuming the title *pro praetore* after his superior has died.[83]

Balsdon's second proposition, that commanders *pro consulibus* (whether of consular or praetorian rank) could delegate their *imperium* to a subordinate, does find some good support already in the second-century record. The earliest datable evidence for the practice of "praetorian delegation" has to do with the orator M. Antonius, epigraphically attested as *quaestor pro praetore* in the *provincia* of Asia in (probably) 113/112 B.C. A praetor *pro consule* either had left him in charge of the province, or had delegated him *imperium* for some special task (11.1.5, 14.5.2). We find additional examples of this form of delegation soon after the case of Antonius.[84] In the Social War, we even see a *privatus* with consular *imperium*— Sex. Iulius Caesar, a former *cos.* 91—making a C. Baebius *pro praetore* to act in his place when he was mortally ill (winter 90/89, discussed in 10.5.3).

Though the quaestor M. Antonius is our first known example of an individual being delegated *imperium* by a praetor, the practice of "praetorian delegation" in fact might go back as far as the very start of the second century. In 11.1.5, I have suggested that the ability to delegate *imperium* in the field helps explain the practice of granting consular *imperium* to regular praetorian commanders for distant provinces (i.e., the Spains, Macedonia, Asia, and Cilicia), as well as Sulla's decision as dictator to standardize the rank of *pro consule* for all commanders who were to take up a territorial province.

The Social and Civil Wars left a number of commanders positively stranded in distant provinces. The praetors affected include C. Norbanus, *pr.* by 90 and in command in Sicily down to perhaps 84; P. Servilius Isauricus, *pr.* perhaps by 92 and (apparently) in Sardinia down through 88 (he triumphed on 21 October in that year); C. Sentius Saturninus, *pr. urb.* 94 and *pro cos.* in Macedonia 93–87; and P. Sextilius Rufus, *pr.* perhaps by 92 and in Africa down to perhaps 87. C. Coelius Caldus (*cos.* 94) had to hold a joint *provincia* (Gallia Transalpina and Cisalpina) over this time, for upwards of eight years. But the unluckiest of all was the *cos.* 93 C. Valerius Flaccus, who had a provincial tenure that was to involve both Spains and Transalpine Gaul (where he succeeded Coelius) for a period of twelve years.

Indeed, in the period 87–82, the Senate seemingly elevates neglect to an adminstrative principle. There is no sign that Gallia Cisalpina had its own governor in the years 87–82. Sicily, Sardinia, and Africa are known to have received commanders in these years (one each), but more as a defense against Sulla than out of concern for administration. The *pr.* Q. Antonius Balbus, who was dispatched to Sardinia in 82, was probably the first governor of any sort the province had seen in six years. When the praetor for Africa, C. Fabius Hadrianus, was burned to death in late 83 during an uprising in Utica, the Senate is said to have taken no measures to avenge his death. However, the Spains probably did get a pair of Marian praetors before Q. Sertorius arrived to take up Citerior in 82.

The praetor M. Perperna Veiento, who took up Sicily in 85 or 84, probably typifies the attitudes of his era. He was the grandson of a successful commander of the First Slave War, and no doubt was chosen to hold Sicily for this very reason, relieving C. Norbanus (the future *cos.* 83) after a tenure of at least six years. Perperna gave little thought to the administration of the island (he apparently wholly neglected his civil law duties), and at one point even threatened to leave it to lift Sulla's siege of Praeneste. However, when Sulla sent Pompey *pro praetore* against this commander, he quickly abandoned the *provincia* altogether.

15.3.2 *The Sullan Reforms and Their Limited Practical Effects*

New challenges faced Sulla upon winning control of the *res publica*. At the start of 81, all ten of the territorial provinces lacked a proper commander: see 11.1.1 on the situation in Sicily, Sardinia, the Spains, Macedonia, Africa, Asia, Cilicia, and Transalpine Gaul. What is more, there were certainly six permanent *quaestiones* in the city (*repetundae, ambitus, maiestas, peculatus, de veneficiis,* and *inter sicarios*) that needed appropriate court presidents. Something significant had to be done. Sulla as dictator decided to retain the basic administrative system as he found it, but to enlarge the praetorian college by two members, for a total of eight. His idea was for praetors normally to remain in Rome during their year of office, to see to the city jurisdictions and permanent *quaestiones*. Then, after their magistracy, they would proceed to an overseas province with consular *imperium*. Consuls and ex-consuls too were to play a role, as commanders in the more important provinces.

As dictator, Sulla did not try to cut back on Rome's basic administrative commitments, either outside or inside Rome. Significantly, he wanted to keep all the permanent *quaestiones*—and the principle of praetorian presidency of those courts—in place. Though the dictator merged the administration of the courts *de veneficiis* and *inter sicarios*, he also introduced at least one additional court (*de testamentis*), which offset that gain and kept the total number (probably) at six. The system of *quaestiones* now covered an extremely broad array of crimes; the establishment of ad hoc courts would become significantly harder to justify (11.9.1). In the city, Sulla retained the institution of the *iudex quaestionis* to aid the praetors, primarily in the superintendancy of the combined court *inter sicarios* and *de veneficiis*. However, when possible Sulla wanted praetors to man even that court (as M. Fannius did in 80—see 11.7.4). Even a decade and a half after Sulla's reforms we find praetors hearing cases *de peculatu* (11.7.5).

Thanks to Sulla's de facto institutionalization of *ex praetura* and *ex consulatu* commands, there were now ten holders of *imperium* available each year to man the ten regular territorial provinces. Henceforth one might reasonably expect that for the various *provinciae*, tenures of one year were to be the norm. But accidents were bound to happen. Special *provinciae* that demanded the diversion of magistrates and ex-magistrates were practically inevitable.[85] Illnesses and deaths of commanders were inevitable, too. The *pr.* 80 M. Domitius Calvinus was killed in Hispania Citerior, probably during the year of his magistracy; he had been expected to hold the province for the year 79 (13.4.2). Ap. Claudius Pulcher, *cos.* 79, fell ill in transit to Macedonia and had to delay his arrival in his *provincia* until 77; he then died there in 76 (14.2.2). In 77, M. Aemilius Lepidus (*cos.* 78) was ejected from the Gauls, which he had as a joint promagisterial province, and soon died in Sardinia (11.8.5). In the 70s alone, three additional holders of *imperium* are known to have died in their military *provinciae*. Two analogous cases are found for the 50s.[86]

Yet the impact that deaths and the declaration of special *provinciae* had on the new administrative system was tiny in comparison to another factor: Sulla's allowance that an ex-consul or ex-praetor could refuse a territorial province, after he had received it in the sortition. Here it was Sulla himself who showed the way, for as *cos.* II 80 he was allotted but never took up Cisalpine Gaul *ex consulatu*. In this, he set an example for many later consuls and (at least starting in the early 60s) praetors (11.1.6). Hard statistics on this phenomenon are impossible to offer. However, the praetorian college of 66—one of our best attested—may not have been wholly atypical. Of the eight praetors that year, at least three declined an *ex praetura* command. One praetor of that year (C. Antonius) apparently even preferred to serve as a *legatus* in Pompey's great eastern *provincia* than to receive one for his own (12.1.3). Other well-attested praetorian colleges (e.g., 63 and 57) seem to have had a higher rate of *ex magistratu* commands. However, only two of the consuls of the years 63 through 59 are definitely known to have reached a territorial *provincia* in the year that followed their magistracy, namely, C. Antonius (*cos.* 63) and C. Iulius Caesar (*cos.* 59). Though the *cos.* 60 L. Afranius probably had Cisalpine Gaul for 59 and his colleague Q. Metellus Celer had planned to go to Transalpina for that same year but died, that still leaves eight noncommanding consuls (two absolutely certain) for just these few years. Of course, the best proof that the refusal of an *ex magistratu* province was a common occurrence in the post-Sullan period is that Pompey, as *cos.* III in 52, introduced a new system of administration that was to be staffed—evidently for five years—solely by those individuals who had previously declined a promagisterial province. Pompey also required that, from this point on, all ex-consuls and ex-praetors should take up a province, after a set interval (11.1.7).

All the same, Sulla's clever reform of the administrative system evidently won the confidence of the Roman Senate. For almost immediately one finds that body taking on further commitments without raising the number of magistrates—a parallel process to the expansionism that followed not long after its institutionalization of prorogation in 146 B.C. In the city, three additional standing criminal courts appear: a *quaestio de vi* (perhaps as early as 78 B.C., but certainly by 63), that of the *lex Papia* (65 B.C.) on claims to citizenship, and another established by the *lex Licinia* (55 B.C.), a measure aimed primarily at the electoral associations known as *sodalitates*. Not just *iudices quaestionis* (as we would expect), but actual praetors are attested as presidents of the new *vis* and *lex Papia* courts. In the *quaestio de sodaliciis*, we invariably find praetors (11.7.6–7). It helped that special *quaestiones* in the city remained rare, with merely two trials known that required a praetor (the processes on *incestum* of 73 and 61 B.C.) down to—and perhaps including—the unusual year 52 B.C., with its spate of extraordinary processes for *vis* and *ambitus* (11.9.1–3).

Within two decades of Sulla's reform, the Senate was to incorporate also four new overseas *provinciae* into Rome's territorial empire: Bithynia/Pontus (organization begun in 74 B.C., with the first regular commander arriving in 61 or 60), Crete (annexed and organized 68–65 B.C.), Cyrene (organized by 63 B.C.), and Syria (annexed and organized 66–62 B.C., and allotted to a praetor for 61). Those accretions brought the total of regular *provincae* to fourteen, which the Senate apparently regarded as an upper limit. So though in 58 it took on responsibility for Cyprus, it did so with the understanding that the island be only a pendant to the province of Cilicia. It was not until after the year 50 that Cyprus received even its first quaestor; in 47 Caesar deannexed the island (11.8.4). Furthermore, the Senate would not exploit its opportunities to annex Egypt, despite some loud agitation (especially in the mid-60s) to take that giant step. Nor did the Senate tamper with Numidia, though interference there too was suggested toward the end of our period (11.6).

15.3.3 *Making the Sullan System Work*

So how did the Senate manage to staff this ever growing system? First, let us turn to the praetorian *provinciae* in the city. Here, the continued acceptance of the device of combination is attested for the immediate post-Sullan period. An epigraphic document of 78 demonstrates that L. Cornelius Sisenna was both *praetor urbanus* and *inter peregrinos* in that year. And that despite the fact there were no major wars under way in Italy or overseas in May 78 (the date of the document), other than the problem of Sertorius in Spain (M. Lepidus' intentions would not be fully known at the time) (12.1.2). Since no individual can be identified as peregrine praetor after the year 76 B.C. (12.2.1), there is reason to suspect that this particular expedient—which of course had an old history (9.4.1)—might have become an increasingly common one in the years down to 50 B.C.

The ambit of the *iudex quaestionis* never expanded to include the major courts *repetundae*, *ambitus*, and *maiestas*. Nor is there good evidence in this era to suggest this quasi magistrate even heard cases *de peculatu* (as he is known to have done in the pre-Sullan era) and under the later charge *de sodaliciis*. His responsibility was restricted to *inter sicarios* and *de veneficiis*, and (once introduced) the courts *de vi* and *lege Papia*. The first two of those quotidian *quaestiones* seem to have been a lot of work. For instance, in 66 B.C., three *iudices* had to split the court *inter sicarios* and *de veneficiis*; the introduction of a Pompeian law *de parricidiis* (probably 55 or 52) no doubt made this court still more labor intensive (11.7.4). *Vis* perhaps necessitated a similar subdivision of tasks among *iudices* (see 11.7.6 on the year 52).

Praetors also occasionally supervised trials in these "minor" courts (e.g., *inter sicarios* in 80 B.C., under the Papian law in 62, *de vi* in 56). But probably few individuals received such *quaestiones* as their main responsibility. What we do find— at least by the 50s—are praetors who have to take on duties in the major permanent courts that went beyond their proper city *provinciae*. In the year 59, two different praetors (apparently) were presiding over trials *de repetundis* (11.7.1). That same year, it seems a would-be prosecutor could approach more than one praetor to indict a consul designate for *ambitus* (11.7.2). In 54, we find a praetor for *maiestas* and another one of his colleagues each hearing cases under the *lex Licinia de sodaliciis* (11.7.1 and 11.7.3, 11.7.6–7). Indeed, the introduction of this new court *de sodaliciis* presupposed that praetors would take on the responsibilities it entailed as an overload.

There was an established tradition of putting praetors who had charge of criminal courts to work simply as needed: see 10.4.2 for the *praetor repetundis* 95 (one of the first we can identify as such) who drafted laws for a Sicilian community, or 11.7.3 on the *praetor maiestatis* 66 who dealt with public grain matters. So it is not all that surprising that by the 50s, praetors who supervised criminal *quaestiones* also occasionally are found as jurors in other courts (11.7.1–2, 12.2.3), or even engaged in activities in the sphere of civil law (11.7.1). Conversely, after Sulla praetors in the "civil" jurisdictions might have to see to cases in the criminal law that went beyond the standing *quaestiones* (12.1.2–3, 12.2.4—certain for 74, perhaps also 58).

The ultimate extension of this principle was to send a praetor into the field during his actual magistracy. Sulla himself sanctioned the continued use of commands *in magistratu*: I have argued that the years 81 and 80 saw perhaps a half-dozen uses of this expedient.[87] Later examples—to name just the praetors—include (just perhaps) an anonymous peregrine praetor of 78 (12.4.1), perhaps the praetor M. Fonteius in Transalpine Gaul in 77 (13.4.4, 15.2.1), certainly the *pr.* 74 M. Antonius in his pirate command (11.3.1, 12.4.1), any number of praetors in the gladiators' war of 73–71, some praetors who were meant to guard Italy against pirates shortly before the year 67, and two city praetors in both of the years 63 and 62, against the Catilinarian conspirators and their supporters (11.8.6–9, 12.4.1). But in those two latter years the praetors spent only a part of their year of office outside the city—in 63 a very small part, a little more than two months. It is to be noted that, as far as our record goes, the Senate never sent more than two city praetors into the field in any given year of the 70s through the 50s. This looks like deliberate policy. In this period, even instances of praetors performing routine nonmilitary tasks outside the city are not that easy to find (12.4.1). But in a crisis, the Senate might be forced to use even recent ex-magistrates. That was certainly the case in the *Bellum Lepidanum* of early 77, which erupted during an *interregnum*, when there were no consuls and praetors in office (11.8.5).

Consider now the handling of the territorial provinces. C. Annius, as *pr.* 81 a member of the first "Sullan" praetorian college, had charge of both Spanish provinces (13.4.2). We do not see the Spains combined again into a single *provincia* until the unusual command of Pompey as *cos.* II 55, who governed both Citerior and Ulterior through legates. Rather, after Sulla it is Cisalpine and Transalpine Gaul that were most commonly collapsed into one. We find that certainly for the years 77, 67 through 65, and finally for Caesar in 58 through 50 (also with Illyricum)—a total of (at least) thirteen years in all, though nine of these are accounted for by Caesar's honorific command (15.2). Combining the two Spains— which evidently happened not all that often in this period—or the two Gauls was a natural expedient. Combinations more exotic than these for praetors do not have good attestation in the sources, though it is possible L. Afranius combined Hispania Citerior with Transalpine Gaul at some point in the years 71–68 (15.2.2). Consular commanders were a different story. L. Licinius Lucullus (*cos.* 74), as *pro consule* against Mithridates, had Asia, Cilicia, and Bithynia/Pontus as a joint *provincia*. So did Cn. Pompeius as a *privatus* with consular *imperium* in the years 66–62.

Of course, from time to time commanders might be asked to take action outside their proper *provinciae*.[88] And occasionally a commander received instructions to leave his territorial *provincia* for one elsewhere. In 79, the Senate (surely) ordered the praetor L. Manlius to move permanently out of his province, Gallia Transalpina, to hold Hispania Citerior, where another praetorian commander had just been killed (13.4.3). And when A. Gabinius (*cos.* 58) contrived to have his province of Cilicia declared praetorian and to receive Syria instead, the Senate put the Asian commander T. Ampius Balbus (*pr.* 59) in charge of Cilicia for the entire year 57 (14.6.8). But transfers of this sort are different from having to govern two regular *provinciae* simultaneously.

Thus far, the Sullan system comes off as relatively healthy. The next indicator to examine is the frequency of prorogation and the length of individual commands beyond the year of magistracy. As noted, since the annual number of magistrates with *imperium* now (once again) equaled that of the territorial *provinciae*, provincial commands should in theory last one or, at most, two years. Yet what we actually find in the post-Sullan record, as early as the 70s, are prolonged tenures that outstrip even those of 122–91 B.C. Some ex-consuls—and (notably) the *privatus* Cn. Pompey—get commands of five years and up, especially to bring major wars to a conclusion. But there are a few instances of repeated prorogation that beg basic administrative questions. In Cilicia, a single (consular) commander—P. Servilius Vatia—from 78 down into 74 fought pirates but also saw to routine administration in that province (15.1.1). L. Afranius, who reached the praetorship at some point in the 70s, was prorogued in Hispania Citerior an indeterminate number of times— conceivably from 76 down into 69 (eight years), or beyond, perhaps eventually with responsibilities also in Gallia Transalpina (13.4.6). So the new system shows signs of stress almost from the time of its introduction.

Starting with the *lex Gabinia* of 67, that gave the *privatus* Pompey a command for three years against the pirates, we occasionally find tenure of such and such a *provincia* guaranteed for a set period of time (by the early 50s, regularly five years). There was in fact an old precedent of sorts for this, the commissions of *IIIviri* with *imperium* for three years active in south Italy in the 190s (8.4.1).[89] In 63, the tribune P. Servilius Rullus must have been thinking of this type of commission—which for all we know might have been common—in his proposal (see 11.8.3) to endow *Xviri* with (praetorian) *imperium* for five years to adjudicate and sell various public lands. In 57, Pompey as a *privatus* received a grain commission that involved *imperium* for five years (11.8.2). In 50, the tribune C. Scribonius Curio floated a purposely provocative proposal for the creation of an elaborate five-year roadbuilding super-intendancy, surely with *imperium*.[90] Yet the crucial development is when the Senate began to allow actual magistrates of the Roman People fixed five-year commands *ex consulatu*, not for major wars but to hold regular provinces that were merely troubled. That is what we see for the two Gauls (with Illyricum) from 58–50, the two Spains for 54–50, and Syria (it was planned) also for 54–50.[91]

Calculating the exact length of overseas commands is difficult in the post-Sullan period, especially since we have precious few triumph dates with which to work. All the same, we have a good number of secure instances of tenures of three (especially) or four years of a wide range of provinces. (If one counts the time some of these commanders spent waiting for a triumph outside Rome, the total span of *imperium militiae* can balloon, in one case—C. Pomptinus, *pr.* 63—to almost a full nine years.) Praetors account for all but six of the sixteen certain or probable cases of these medium-to-long commands.[92] Two-year commands are very common for both ex-consuls and ex-praetors throughout this period, across the range of *provinciae*.[93]

There is a curious "bubble" of prorogation in the general period 62–58, when individual praetorian commanders are repeatedly (twice or thrice) extended in Sicily, Africa, and Transalpine Gaul in the west, and Asia, Bithynia/Pontus, and—just perhaps—Cilicia in the east. The addition of Syria in 61 to the roster of regular *provinciae*, coupled with the reintegration of Bithynia into the normal administrative system about that same time, goes some way toward explaining this phenomenon. It also may be that a lot of ex-magistrates were declining *provinciae* in precisely these years (13.2.6). Yet one also notes that in the years 61–59, no commander was holding more than one province—surely another contributing factor to the "bubble."

In truth, long multiprovince commands quickly became a vital part of the post-Sullan administrative system. Consider the *cos.* 74 L. Licinius Lucullus, who was *pro consule* in Asia in the years 73 through 69, in Cilicia from 73 through 68, and in Bithynia/Pontus from 71 into 67. In crude terms, Lucullus' tenure of those three *provinciae* for those periods of time represents the work of eighteen annual commanders. Pompey's commands in Hispania Citerior (77–71), in Bithynia and Cilicia (66–62), and in the two Spains (54–50) total twenty-seven such "commander years," while Caesar's in the two Gauls (58–50) equal eighteen (twenty-seven if one counts in his service also in the special province of Illyricum). To put it another way: if the Senate in the period 73–50 had wanted to keep to a policy of strict annual succesion, with no combination of *provinciae*, it would need to send out sixty-three (or seventy-two) individual commanders to take on what these three men covered.

I have suggested (9.3.2) that the fact one or both Spains had to be declared consular *provincia* in each of the years 145 to 133 gave the Senate a distorted impression of how well the larger system was functioning at the time, and emboldened it to take on new fixed administrative commitments in the city and abroad. Similarly, the big multiprovince commands of the 70s and 60s created a false impression of efficacy elsewhere in the system, so much so that Rome felt it could afford to add Crete, Cyrene, and Syria, all within a short span, as new permanent *provinciae*. Perhaps the best indication of the importance of megacommands to the efficacy of the late Republican empire is that when there were none in progress—as in the years 61–59—the Senate found itself having to extend praetors for long terms in widely disparate provinces, including Asia, where short commands had been tradi-tional.

No commands of a single year are securely attested for Africa, Cilicia, or Gallia Transalpina in this period down to the *lex Pompeia* of 52 B.C.; the first two of these provinces were probably not administrative priorities in this era. Where we do find one-year commands—and it is almost invariably ex-praetors who get them—is in Sicily (the years 80, 77, 74), Sardinia (56–55), the Spains as a combined *provincia* (81), and individually Hispania Citerior (78, 59) and Ulterior (80, 62–61), Macedonia (70–69, 58, 55), Asia (all or all but one of the years 66–62, then 57–56), Gallia Cisalpina (an ex-consul in 74), and Bithynia/Pontus (57–56).[94] From this list, Sicily (at least at first) and Asia emerge as favored *provinciae*. It also appears that the Senate had the motivation and manpower in the years 58–55 to aim at regular suc-cession across the system. There are two consecutive one-year commands even in Sardinia. Two powerful *nobiles* had received that province for the relevant years; less well-connected individuals might not have been so successful at getting quick supersession. Yet around 55 B.C., the Senate's policy started to unravel. Note P. Cornelius Lentulus Spinther (*cos.* 57), who was in Cilicia from 56 down into 53; C. Claudius Pulcher, *pr.* 56 and *pro cos.* in Asia down through 53 (on whom see 14.6.8); and Ap. Claudius Pulcher (*cos.* 54), who was in Cilicia from 53 down into 51—or consider the situation of Syria, which had no proper commander for the lat-ter half of 53, all of 52, and most of 51. It is a pity our *fasti* of the provinces in the latter half of the 50s are not more complete; as it stands, we cannot trace this par-ticular development in detail.

Yet the neglect of Syria in the years after Crassus' death in 53 raises another point: the ever increasing reliance in this period on *legati* as an administrative expe-dient, not just to play major subordinate roles in large *provinciae* or multiprovince commands (where they were essential), but to fill in gaps between proper com-manders. In this general era, it is not uncommon for quaestors or *legati* to be stuck for some time holding provinces (even some major ones) after the departure or death of a superior. Sometimes those stewardships amounted to a year or (as in the case of Syria after Crassus' death in 53) substantially more.[95] We also see the reverse, that is, a commander having a legate or legates hold a province for him before his arrival. For instance, I have suggested that M. Fonteius as *legatus* pre-ceded Cn. Cornelius Dolabella (*cos.* 81) in Macedonia—which had not seen a real governor in years—and held it until his superior's arrival, for a span of time long enough that he had to take on significant independent action (14.2.1). There were obvious shortcomings to this ploy. For one thing, difficulties might arise when legates were sent to provinces where the *decessor* was still in place and not inter-ested in giving way.[96]

An extreme form of the genre is for someone with *imperium* to command a province wholly in absence. Though a praetor of 167 may have governed Sardinia a full year in this way (6.2.2), there is no sign of such lengthy *in absentia* commands for another hundred years. As *cos.* 67, C. Calpurnius Piso exercised control over Transalpine Gaul through legates while remaining in Rome (15.2.2). However, the outstanding example is the *cos.* II 55 Pompey, who, after receiving the two Spains for five years under the *lex Trebonia*, sent two *legati* to govern his joint province for him. Though Pompey never made it to Spain, his original legates apparently were still there in 49 B.C. (13.4.8).

There is every indication that Pompey—despite his own record—in his reforms as *cos.* III 52, wanted short commands in the territorial provinces to become the norm. Yet even his (ultimately shortlived) scheme presupposed prorogation. On average, the number of available ex-magistrates will have been somewhat less than ten, since at least one or two ex-praetors from each college will have become consuls during the statutory interval between magistracy and promagistracy. Meanwhile, the total of territorial *provinciae* to be staffed stood at fourteen (11.7.1). Pompey's system foundered almost immediately: no praetorian commanders ended up receiving provinces in the year 50 B.C.[97]

To round off our survey of the Roman administrative system after Sulla, we should turn to the commands given to *privati*, both by a special *lex* and through personal delegation of (practorian) *imperium*. In this era, the Senate readily acquiesced in the notion that *privati* and sub-praetorians might hold special or territorial *provinciae*. The most notable instance, of course, is Pompey, granted *ex S.C.* full consular *imperium* in 77 for Hispania Citerior (where he remained down into 71), and then in 67 against the pirates, and again in 66 against Mithridates (triumphing in 61). That last command was envisioned as early as 74, and was forestalled only through some skillful maneuvering on the part of the *cos.* L. Licinius Lucullus (14.6.2). In March 60, a *senatus consultum* apparently provided that ex-consuls take positions in the field to face down a Gallic *tumultus*, but soon proved unnecessary (15.2.3). In Pompey's third consulship of 52, at least two nonmagistrates—a consular and a very senior praetorian—were given *imperium* to preside over special *quaestiones* for *vis* and *ambitus* in the city (11.9.3)

The central issue in instances such as these was competence and authority. Yet we find also the phenomenon of "negative" commands, designed to keep consuls and praetors out of important tasks which they might exploit to their own material and political benefit. In early 75 (11.4), the Senate chose to use a quaestor (probably endowed with *imperium*) to collect money in Cyrene; in 58 (11.8.4), the *tribunicius* M. Porcius Cato was made "pro quaestore pro praetore" to annex wealthy Cyprus. In addition, there were plans afoot in 65 to send a subpraetorian (possibly with *imperium*) to attach Egypt as a tributary province (11.6). There were other miscellaneous schemes, such as the Senate's dispatch of Cn. Calpurnius Piso as a *quaestor pro praetore* to Hispania Citerior for 65 (13.4.7), or Rullus' plan in 63 to create X*viri* with *imperium* for five years, who might simultaneously also hold a magistracy (11.8.3). Overall, the above examples cumulatively go to show that a majority of senators had no objection in principle to extraordinary grants of *imperium*—at least for most of our period. The reaction to a Parthian threat of mid-51 B.C. does suggest an eventual change in attitude. Here the Senate explored a variety of military options (the consuls of the year did not want the task). But, significantly, the dispatch of a *privatus* was not among them.[98]

Personal delegation of *imperium* to nonmagistrates is frequently attested in this period. The evidence is not all that we would like (see 14.6.4), but down to the year 52 we find commanders—mostly consulars but a good number of praetorians *pro consulibus*—giving out *imperium* to subordinates in the western provinces,[99] in the east,[100] and in Italy;[101] *privati* with consular *imperium*, too. Indeed, in the year 67, Pompey had (apparently) twenty-four *legati pro praetore* under him in his special pirate command, including two consulars and three or four known *praetorii*; the Senate might have allowed him a similar setup in his grain commission of 57 (11.8.2). The power to delegate should be one major reason why in certain emergency situations—the Social War, the war with Spartacus, the Catilinarian conspiracy—we see several praetors during their year of office have their *imperium* raised from praetorian to consular. Eventually, that type of enhancement became redundant. The *lex Pompeia de provinciis* of 52 established that ex-praetors proceed to territorial provinces *pro praetore*, and perhaps specifically enabled these praetorian commanders to delegate *imperium*—for the first time in the history of the Republic—at their own level.[102]

One final point: The vexed domestic politics of the 60s and 50s created a surprising new source of manpower—commanders *cum imperio* waiting outside the city for the Senate's vote of a triumph. The precedent was M. Antonius (*pr.* 102, *imperator*, and *cos. des.* 99), who had been asked in a *senatus consultum ultimum* of the year 100 to provide external protection for Rome when Saturninus and his followers had caused a serious disturbance. In the Catilinarian crisis of 63 the Senate, also through a *senatus consultum ultimum*, put to work not outside the city but in Apulia and Etruria the *cos.* 69 Q. Caecilius Metellus and the *cos.* 68 Q. Marcius Rex, each of whom had been waiting before Rome for some years (11.8.9). At the start of 49, it is suggested, the Senate contemplated using the returned eastern governor M. Nonius in the same way, but for service abroad; around this time, Pompey certainly had thought of using the *imperator ex Cilicia* Cicero in this fashion (14.2.6). One wonders whether in the intervening years the Senate gave duties to the *pr.* 63 C. Pomptinus (outside Rome from 58 down until November 54) or the *cos.* 57 P. Cornelius Lentulus Spinther (waiting for a triumph vote from 53 down into 51) (15.1.2, 15.2.3). Men who so badly wanted a triumph no doubt will have eagerly performed anything the Senate asked of them, without a *senatus consultum ultimum*.

16

Conclusions

Its story begins with a woman's jealousy of her sister, married to a patrician who had reached the top of the Roman political pyramid. It involves a struggle so bitter that for five years the Romans descended into anarchy. It owes its genesis to an old war hero who quelled civil strife by suddenly hammering out a brilliant compromise: "The nobility yielded to the Plebs in the matter of the plebeian consul, the Plebs conceded to the nobility a single praetor, elected from the patricians, to administer law in the city." Sad for the historian to say, that is the gist of our fullest account of the creation of the praetorship, that of Livy Book 6. And for the office's subsequent development, we are left on our own.

We can guess the general outlines. Pressures in the areas of domestic policy, warfare, and—in later times—provincial administration must have created, expanded, and shaped the praetorship. Circumstances continually forced the Romans to innovate in their handling of the office. Innovations were remembered and employed when needed. Eventually (and sometimes reluctantly), many of these innovations were institutionalized. And all this had to take place within a complex social framework. The question of how many praetorships there should be, and who should be eligible to hold them, can never have been a purely administrative question. These issues were inextricably connected with basic social and political issues, such as rivalry between patricians and plebeians—later, nobles and nonnobles—as well as issues such as prestige and electoral corruption.

Rome's Earliest Magistrates

Reconstructing the details is the difficult task. For earliest Rome, I accept the view of Mommsen, which is essentially that of Livy and all other ancient writers who treat this era. After the expulsion of the kings from Rome, two magistrates—at least later to be known as consuls—were chosen from among the patricians. Each of the consuls had *imperium*, the full power of the king, but they were limited to one year of office. With *imperium* came the kings' *auspicia*, the right to ascertain the will of Jupiter in certain prescribed ways.

It soon became apparent that two consuls were not enough to look after Rome's ever increasing major administrative and military needs. Yet the Romans were reluctant to give *imperium*, and with it *auspicia*, to too many men. One compromise attempt at a solution was the institution of the so-called "military tribunes with consular *potestas*," a college of up to six magistrates who had the consular right to lead an army, yet who did not have *imperium* and whose auspices were deficient in some way—we know they could not celebrate a triumph. The idea perhaps was to keep plebeians—who were eligible for the office—away from the highest public auspices.

Social conflict between plebeians and patricians, as well as a prolonged military struggle with the Gauls, forced the Romans to abolish the consular tribunate in 367. Instead, under what is known as the Licinian-Sextian legislation, they let plebeians into the consulship, and introduced a new patrician magistrate, the praetor, to serve as a colleague of the consuls. To create this office, the Romans had to put a bold new construction on the regal power. The praetor was to hold the king's *auspicia*, and an *imperium* which was defined as of the same nature as the consuls', but *minus*, "lesser," in relation to theirs. As a magistrate with this type of *imperium* and auspices, the praetor could do all that the consuls could do, save holding elections of major magistrates in the Centuriate Assembly and celebrating the Latin Festival at the beginning of each year. All other activities of the consul were open to the praetor, unless a consul stopped him. But a praetor could not interfere with the consuls.

In sum, the Romans needed more than two regular magistrates who could command an army. But a college of up to six consular tribunes, all with equal *potestas* and thus veto power over each other, did not prove to be a good idea. Witness the dismal military record of the twenty-odd years following the Gallic invasion of 390. The invention of two grades of *imperium*—one *minus* in relation to that of the two chief regular magistrates—solved the problem of excessive conflict in command. It was an artful "dodge."

Prefects, Dictators, Consular Tribunes, and Censors as "Dodges"

It was D. Daube who first articulated the concept of the "dodge" (see 2.1.3). Daube pointed out that all dodges—that is, circumventions of a law—are essentially misinterpretations. He also noted that a dodge may exist for hundreds of years without its nature being fully grasped. Daube was primarily interested in explaining some practices in the Roman civil law, but his observations on the dodge are readily extended to constitutional and religious matters.

A good example of an early dodge is the institution of the Prefect of the City. A king or consul who had to leave Rome would appoint a representative with wide powers to act in his stead, without having to fear that this subordinate would get in the way of his own actions. Now, these prefects cannot have held *imperium*. There is no indication that a Roman king could or would simply delegate his full royal *imperium* to another; and for the Republic, it can be shown that one cannot personally give out *imperium* on one's own level. But the consuls (and later the praetors) presumably inherited with their kingly *imperium* the right to leave a subordinate in a given place to fulfill a specific task, and give him limited public *auspicia*.

The Prefects must have had *auspicia*, especially to judge from their military activities in the field. However, these auspices were not entirely their own. The tenure of the Prefect ended at the discretion of his superior. The Prefecture of the City nicely falls under Daube's definition of a dodge. It was a circumvention of the rule that one needed *imperium* to lead an army and perform certain important civil functions. The king or consul acts through a substitute, with delegated special powers. This clever compromise would serve the Romans for centuries, whenever all holders of *imperium* had to leave the city. But it left at least one thorny question to be answered in the augural sphere. How could two men hold public *auspicia* which were the same yet different? Rather than think too hard about this paradox, the Romans exploited it.

Daube said, "[T]hough dodges assume many forms, they are reducible to very few models." The dictator is like a reverse prefect: a consul names an individual so as to be given orders! The exact nature of the dictator's powers is somewhat of a mystery. It was a primitive office. It embraced full *imperium*, but had a tenure of only six months. To be sure, the standard view is that the dictator, though appointed by a consul, had more powerful *imperium* and *auspicia* than the man who named him. A few ancient texts (most notably Livy) appear to confirm this interpretation. It would seem that the emperor Claudius is the most explicit: in his speech preserved on the Lyons tablet, Claudius states that in military or civil emergencies the old Romans resorted to "the dictator's *imperium*, which was more powerful (*valentius*) than even that of a consul."

But it would be most surprising if the dictator possessed anything qualitatively greater than consular *imperium*. The consul had the *imperium* and *auspicia* of the kings of Rome. Logically, the dictator could have no more. There are one or two fourth-century examples from Livy when a dictator and consul fought and won a victory together, but the consul alone received the triumph. This would be impossible if a consul operating in the same theater of operations as a dictator was fighting not under his own auspices, "alienis auspiciis," as Livy elsewhere implies. Cicero in fact suggests, in the ideal constitution of the *De Legibus*, that the dictator had the same *imperium* as the consuls ("idem iuris").

The dictatorship is a difficult office to comprehend. The dictator had powers which were the same as the consuls', but different. Cicero implies he had as much *imperium* as the two consuls, but no more. However, what about the speech of the emperor Claudius? I would hold that a dictator's *imperium* was indeed *valentius*, "more efficacious," than a consul's—though not *maius* in the technical sense of the word. The Romans of the Republic never accepted the concept of *imperium* which was greater than the regal power.

The dictator (like the consul) had the regal *auspicia*, yet did not have to fear interference from a consul. The dictator's auspices were incommensurable with those of the consul. The dictator should not have been a colleague of the consuls, since he was not created under the same auspices, that is, in the Centuriate Assembly. There are some indications he may not even have been a magistrate of the Roman People. The dictator's primitive, anomalous status, with precedence over all other magistrates, is never adequately explained to us by our ancient sources. By the second century B.C., when people started writing books about *auspicia* and the like, they probably did not quite understand it themselves. One thinks of Daube's observation, "[A] dodge . . . may exist for hundreds of years without its nature being fully grasped."

I offer two brief additional examples of early constitutional dodges. There is the institution of the consular tribunate mentioned above, which was first seen in 444. The bulk of the ancient sources imply that this was a compromise meant to side-step a basic issue of the conflict of the orders. It also was an attempt to supply commanders to fight enemies on multiple fronts. The Romans were to make an ad hoc decision each year whether the chief magistrates in the state be a pair of patrician consuls, or a—theoretically—mixed college of three, four, or six consular tribunes. A top magistracy, and with it, patrician *auspicia*, were for the first time open to the plebeians, yet the patricians still preserved the consulship as their exclusive domain.

There was a twist. The consular tribunes, by virtue of their election in the centuriate assembly, received *auspicia maxima* for the civil sphere, but, in the field, auspices which were somehow less than the regal complement. Their defective military auspices may be precisely why they are called "military tribunes with consular *potestas*." The Romans stopped short of giving the consular tribunes *imperium*, which would imply the full power of the kings—to patricians and plebeians alike. What we see here is a controlled experiment, one which allowed plebeians to handle patrician auspices, within certain limits.

In this case, one dodge necessitated another. The patricians wanted to keep an old regal and consular task, the census and ritual purification, or *lustrum*, out of the hands of the mixed colleges of consular tribunes. To this end, in 443—the year after the appearance of the first consular tribunes—they invented the censorship. This was a specialized patrician collegiate magistracy resembling the consulship in some respects (for example, election in the Centuriate Assembly), but with several important differences.

The patricians designed the new office of the censorship to have enough power to discharge its intended functions, but no more. The censors were to hold *auspicia maxima*. This presumably came with their election in the Centuriate Assembly. But the People chose the censors on a different occasion, and thus under different auspices, than the senior magistrates of the state. The People also followed the election of censors with the passage of a law—not in the Curiate Assembly, as was the practice with new consuls so as to validate their military auspices—but in the Centuriate Assembly, exceptionally of all patrician magistrates. Cicero is probably only guessing when he states the double vote for censors was taken "so that the People might have the power of rescinding its distinction, should it have second thoughts." The procedure of a *lex centuriata* presumably was meant to restrict their powers, to ensure that the censors did not consider themselves colleagues of the consuls, nor think they had military *auspicia*. As M. Valerius Messalla (*cos.* 53) tells us, the augurs in fact deemed the censors' *maxima auspicia* to be of a different grade (*potestas*) than that of the consuls. The consuls could not vitiate the auspices of censors, nor censors those of consuls; these magistrates could interfere only with the *auspicia* of their proper colleagues.

The Creation and Early Development of the Praetorship

The conceptual breakthroughs which came with these dodges paved the way for the invention of *imperium maius* and *minus*. In particular, the relationship of dictator to consul may have partly inspired the consul/praetor arrangement. (The dictator and *magister equitum* combination probably served only as a negative *exemplum*; the master of the horse does not originally seem to have had *imperium*, and his *auspicia* were overly entwined with those of his superior.) We can also view the arrangement of two consuls, one patrician and one plebeian, and a patrician praetor, as a more complex modification of the old system, the mixed colleges of consular tribunes alternating irregularly with patrician consular pairs. The reforms of 367 were not a clean break with the past, as is suggested by the account of Livy, who is taken at his word by many modern scholars, but rather show continuity of development. The system of two consuls and a praetor was more or less a rationalized consular tribunate. But the creation of the praetorship also marked a real innovation. For the first time, the Romans were able to reconcile in a proper magistracy the concept of permanent subordination with what was essentially regal *imperium*. And like a good dodge, some aspects of the praetorship were not completely understood by posterity. For example, no one in the late Republic seems to have been able to explain adequately why a praetor could not hold praetorian elections.

What was this new magistrate supposed to do? Livy's anachronistic explanation, taken over by later authors, that the praetor was created to hear cases at law in the city, is a retrojection from the most familiar function of the praetor in his own day. Livy soon contradicts this by his own narrative; his statement must be rejected. Quite simply, the praetor was to do almost everything that consuls did, unless they were around and wanted to stop him. The sole praetor probably remained in or near the city while the consuls went out on military campaigns. For example, we know that the praetor was not at the famous surrender at the Caudine Forks in 321. And so it came about that the praetor often served as the chief magistrate with *imperium* in Rome. In the absence of the consuls, the praetor looked after the defense of the city, presided over the Senate, held assemblies of the People (including for capital *iudicia*), and regulated the Roman civil law process. But as a holder of *imperium*, the praetor could also exercise a military command when required. The first actual activity we see of the praetor in Livy is in a military capacity, in 350 and 349: the tradition Livy follows for these years did not regard such praetorian commands as anything surprising or exceptional in themselves. It is suggested that the praetor's right to triumph was secured by 283, when the *pr. suffectus* M.' Curius Dentatus scored a victory over the Lucanians, for which he received an *ovatio*. Again, it must be emphasized that the actual evidence for the early development of the office virtually excludes Livy's explanation that the praetor was introduced "qui ius in urbe diceret."

It took thirty years for the praetorship to be opened to plebeians, the last major magistracy to remain so exclusive (a plebeian had reached the dictatorship and even the censorship by the end of the 350s). This development did not come without a struggle. The stipulation that the praetor had to be a patrician was an integral part of the delicate social compromise engineered by the Licinian-Sextian legislation. Even the pioneering C. Marcius Rutilus (*cos.* 357, IV 342), the first plebeian dictator and censor, probably did not sue for the office: a plebeian candidacy for the praetorship would have violently disturbed the uneasy *concordia ordinum* of his time.

However, the senatorial establishment did eventually allow the praetorship to open up, probably to defuse the serious discontent of plebeians whose families had been shut out of the consulship. A series of reforms that started in the late 340s provides the background to this development. In particular, the Genucian plebiscites of 342, that apparently guaranteed one consulship each year to plebeians, also placed a temporary ban on iteration of all magistracies. We should not understand this latter law's stipulation "ne quis eundem magistratum intra decem annos caperet" as "no one might hold the same office twice within ten years"—a provision that is so frequently violated that one scholar not so long ago was driven to suggest that the law is a fake, forged by a reform-minded consul of 198. Rather, the tribune Genucius must have moved "no one might hold the same office twice for the *next* ten years," that is, the decade down to 331, which is what we actually get (at least among plebeians) in the record. In Genucius' measures we have a strong expression of protest directed at the recent domination of the consulship by patricians (who had begun to fill both available places), but especially against members of a few favored plebeian families—like C. Marcius Rutilus, *cos.* IV in the very year of Genucius' plebiscite. So when the patrician consul of 337 refused to accept the candidacy of the plebeian Q. Publilius Philo for the consulship, he did not receive the support he evidently expected from the Senate. Philo won election to the office, and we hear of no further opposition to candidates to the practorship simply because they were plebeians.

The Invention of "Prorogation"

In time, the principle was established that the *imperium* of the consuls and praetors could be extended into the next year (*prorogatio*). Like many aspects of the Roman Republican constitution, prorogation was an ad hoc invention that gradually became more common and was finally institutionalized. The first grant Livy records is for Q. Publilius Philo, who now as *cos.* 327 was besieging the city of Naples. When his year of office was almost up, the Roman Senate, realizing that the city could be taken any day, decided not to recall the man but instead have the tribunes propose a measure, that "on the expiration of his consulship he conduct the campaign *pro consule* (in place of a consul) until the war was concluded." A generation later, because of the prolonged state of military emergency created by the Second and Third Samnite Wars, we find that prorogation—which we can add to our collection of dodges—had passed into regular Roman administrative practice. It allowed the Romans to meet their military needs without increasing the number of magistrates or sacrificing the principle of the annual magistracy.

At first, promagistrates were never used to supplant actual magistrates altogether. This seems clear from a study of the dates of Roman triumphs in the third century, which are preserved in the triumphal *Fasti*. The triumphal dates seem to show that the usual term of prorogation in the period before the war with Hannibal was not a full year, as is generally supposed and indeed was the later regular practice, but only six months—the length of a campaigning season. We have a chance reference to an extension of *imperium* for this term in Livy, in his notice of the arrangements for 296. This must be the standard Roman practice down to the time of the Hannibalic War, even though Livy does not normally bother to mention it. We should also note that, even in the period when individuals were prorogued for a full year, Livy does not use the titles "proconsul" or "propraetor." Neither does Cicero, nor any other Republican source. The Romans obviously never came to terms with recognizing the promagistracy as an actual office.

Livy does not usually give us the details of the process of prorogation, which, though he had found it in his sources, he obviously did not think important. I have suggested that the Romans initially had a two tiered system: *prorogatio*, in which the People would vote (*rogare*) to approve extensions of commands in fixed praetorian *provinciae*, and *propagatio*, for all the other cases, where the Senate alone was competent to make this decision. By the mid-second century, the Senate had usurped the People's powers in this matter: that is why all extensions of *imperium* are eventually called "prorogation."

Introduction of the Peregrine Praetor

The invention of prorogation in 327 allowed the Romans to keep the system of three magistrates with *imperium* for about another ninety years, down to almost the end of the First Punic War. But by the end of that war, Rome had acquired a second praetor, whom we know from Republican documents as the *praetor qui inter peregrinos ius dicit*: "the praetor who administers justice among foreigners." How did this come about?

A late epitomator in Justinian's *Digest* surmised from his title that an influx of foreigners into Rome at the end of the First Punic War made necessary a second praetor to hear law cases that developed between them. Most modern scholars have surprisingly followed this guess. Daube stoutly defended it, and interpretations based on the epitomator's explanation are still being offered. Now, the notion of a praetor specifically created to hear mostly cases in which both litigants were noncitizens (especially at this time) is absurd. On the other hand, if the original jurisdiction of this praetor was to deal with law cases involving conflicts of interest between citizens and noncitizens, one would logically expect a *praetor inter cives et peregrinos*, which was in fact the official titulature under the Empire. But in the mid-third century even that task would hardly have been so onerous that it could not be performed by the urban praetor.

Mommsen, for one, accepted the Digest's view, and conjectured that this magistrate's actual introduction was somehow connected to a crisis of the year 242. A praetor had to be sent to Sicily in place of a patrician consul and *flamen* of Mars, whom the *pontifex maximus* had (unexpectedly) restricted to Italy. Incidentally, this praetor helped score a naval victory in late consular 242 which won the war for Rome, and with it the dominion of Sicily.

At first glance, Mommsen has a good hypothesis for the date. But it is easy to forget that 242 was at least the third time in the First Punic War the praetor had to be in Sicily for an entire year. We also must remember that, in this war, he was normally the only holder of *imperium* for all Italy during the campaigning season—and perhaps beyond. In 248, the praetor needed to ward off a Punic general who was threatening the Italian coast. More Carthaginian raids followed, as Polybius tells us. The Romans took these incursions seriously, to judge from the establishment of citizen maritime colonies in Etruria and the founding of a Latin colony at Brundisium in 244.

More probably, it was the defense needs of Italy in the crisis years of the mid-240s which prompted the Romans to create a second praetor. The Romans realized that they were not properly covered for emergencies, and so added another permanent holder of *imperium*. Even in the later period, the peregrine praetor was marked as a magistrate who could be sent wherever a commander with *imperium* was needed. Livy sometimes reports the allotment "the peregrine province and wherever the Senate has decided," *provincia peregrina et quo senatus censuisset*. The frequent absence of the peregrine praetor from Rome on special missions during (especially) the Hannibalic War helps to confirm this interpretation. I must emphasize that there probably was no legal motive for his introduction, except perhaps that the Romans wanted two praetors instead of one partly to reduce the possibility of frequent suspensions of legal business (*iustitia*) in the city during military crises.

How, then, do we explain the second praetor's titulature, *inter peregrinos*? The preposition *inter* of course can be used to denote the name of a place. For example, in the phrase *inter sicarios*, it also seems to imply competence over a certain group, here, "murderers." A Roman judge was not expected to adjudicate disputes between *sicarii*! Following the treaty with the Carthaginians and the organization of (western) Sicily in 241, the Romans may have sent this praetor literally *inter peregrinos*, that is, as a governor of the newly organized permanent *provincia* "Sicilia" (Rome's first). Like some other Roman titles, such as *pontifex* (literally, "bridge-builder"), the original reason for the designation was forgotten. At some later point in the Republic the peregrine praetor assumed responsibility for hearing law cases involving citizens and noncitizens; but it was only in the Empire that his titulature was changed to reflect his actual sphere of activity.

Indeed, a late summary of Appian's *Sicilian History* reports that, after the war, the Romans "imposed tribute on the Sicilians . . . and sent them an annual praetor." We soon can find confirmation of this notice. In 234, the urban praetor was forced to travel to the recent Roman acquisition of Sardinia to put down a rebellion, even though we know there were no wars at the time other than in the two consular *provinciae* of the year, Liguria and Corsica. That there were no other wars is certain: we are told so by our main literary source for this year, a summary of Dio Cassius. The *praetor inter peregrinos* can have been in no other place than Sicily.

Increase in Praetors to Four

The number of praetors remained stable for little more than a decade. The Romans further raised the number to four in the early 220s. This was an extremely important decision. It increased by fifty percent the number of holders of *imperium*, and, among other things, changed the relationship of the praetorship to the consulship in the career path.

In the days when there was only one praetor, the office, when held, could—and did—either precede or follow the consulship. Sometimes the office was held even in the year directly after one's consulship, as an alternative to prorogation. The choice was between praetorian *imperium* valid both at home and in the field for an entire year, or *imperium* as *pro consule* for six months. Raising the number to two and then four praetors made it almost inevitable that the praetorship would precede the consulship in the normal career pattern. From now on, praetors cannot have expected to reach the consulship automatically, though the men who were successful in the office will have had a better chance at it than nonpraetors.

The increase is traditionally dated to 228 (for 227), which should be right. But the background to this decision must have been the sending of both consuls to Illyria in 229, which exposed the Roman vulnerability in their new overseas provinces. Had there been a serious crisis in, say, Corsica, there was no magistrate who could be dispatched to the island other than the urban praetor (we should remember the incident of 234, when the urban praetor had to be sent to Sardinia). The Romans took a major and unprecedented step to make sure that this situation would not recur. With new overseas responsibilities, even two praetors were not enough, and so two additional ones were created. One of the two new praetors was placed in charge of Sicily, the other had responsibility for Sardinia and Corsica. The peregrine praetor now seems to have shed his earlier role of overseas provincial commander, and was free to be deployed in other capacities. For the sake of convenience, we may call the individuals who received the urban and peregrine *provinciae* "city praetors"—keeping in mind that, especially for the *praetor inter peregrinos*, Rome was only a base. In the 220s and early 210s he can be found in north Italy, fighting (none too successfully, as it happens) against Gallic tribes.

Interrelationship of Praetorian *Provinciae*

The relationship of the two older praetors to each other, and against the "new" ones—including two additional praetors later added for Spain in 197 (see below)—has never been properly sorted out; the topic demands some detailed discussion. The designations as such seem only to mark what they normally did (whatever it was), but each of them could be called upon to do different things. And there is abundant evidence from the entire Republican period that, in a pinch, any praetor—regardless of the *provincia* he received in the sortition—generally could fulfill the functions of any other. The *Ludi Apollinares* are probably the first significant exception. An oracle of 213 attached these games permanently to the urban jurisdiction. But that set-aside came a decade and a half after the introduction of the praetors for Sicily and Sardinia, and is not evidence for some special power inherent in the urban *provincia*. By making this designation, the oracle (or rather its author) simply was trying to guarantee that a praetor was available to celebrate these games each year. After this precedent, it is not surprising that the *praetor urbanus* accrued other fixed religious ceremonies at Rome.

Nevertheless, the urban and peregrine praetorships do show some differences against the Sicilian and Sardinian praetors, and all later ones who were created to command in territorial *provinciae*. There was a legal requirement that the city *provinciae* be placed in the sortition each and every year. The explanation is simple: a prorogued magistrate could not properly exercise his *imperium* within Rome. By 184 we know that the election of a suffect was legally required if either the *praetor urbanus* or *praetor inter peregrinos*—but not an overseas praetor—died in office early in the year. Here the answer is less obvious. This was probably a necessary feature of the earliest praetorship (note the election of a *praetor suffectus* in 283), and so it is strange that it later would be denied to all but the city praetors—especially since praetors in permanent territorial *provinciae* were the more likely to die in office. Perhaps it was felt that a legal stipulation to hold a suffect election for any praetorian place—once there were more than two—would excessively restrict the activities of the consuls of a given year. The city praetors also had precedence over their praetorian colleagues in convening the Senate. In the early first century, we even find a few letters from the Senate to Greek communities in which the names of the consuls of the year as well as those of the urban and peregrine praetor are used to date the document. That seems to confirm that the two old city *provinciae* had at least by now acquired a formal, enhanced status. At this time, the praetors in charge of various standing courts (e.g., *repetundarum*, discussed below) were equally likely to be present at the routine sessions of the Senate where such letters were drafted.

As for the relationship between the *praetor urbanus* and *praetor inter peregrinos*, two main factors seem to have been at play: the chronological seniority of the *provincia urbana*, and the historical mobility of the peregrine praetor. The original and primary role of the peregrine praetor, as we have noted, was to go "quo senatus censuisset." He was in Sicily ca. 240–228, and then available for action, wherever he was needed, in Italy down through the start of the Hannibalic War. In most years of this war, and for a few years beyond, the peregrine praetor was far from Rome, fighting in south Italy (215–213, 211) and later Gaul (210–198). The *praetor urbanus*, as the "original" and sole praetor for more than a century, already had acquired the bulk of the important routine duties in Rome. There was little reason for him to transfer any of these permanently to his far-ranging colleague. Indeed, Livy explicitly tells us a few times in his narrative of the Second Punic War that the urban praetor had to take on the peregrine praetor's *iurisdictio* (we are not told what that was, at this time or any). While the Carthaginians were in Italy, the urban praetor was expected also to defend the city and provide for the protection of the coast near Rome. On occasion, we find him seeing to the provision and enrollment of Rome's armies. Some new responsibilities which the urban praetor accrued in this war (e.g., shipbuilding, formerly a consular task) became permanently attached to his *provincia*. But in the post-Hannibalic period, we see no evidence of the *praetor urbanus* relinquishing any of the traditional responsibilities that dated back to his

days as sole praetor: for instance, in the mid-160s, we find him still supervising viritane land allocation (in Campania).

Development of the Provincia Urbana

So it appears the development of the *provincia urbana* was quite haphazard. The
urban praetor, once he got all the odd jobs piled on to him, seems to have been
tied to Italy—rather like the *flamines*—and then, of course, to Rome, more or less.
Indeed, it is quite startling to see the extent of the urban praetor's routine duties by
the mid-Republic. For a start, during the regular course of the year (when the consuls were off in the field), he can be expected to have chaired meetings of the
Senate. As presiding magistrate, the *praetor urbanus* (or any other praetor to whom
he yielded) had absolute power to frame *relationes*, the setting out of a topic for discussion that often formed the basis of *senatus consulta*. The praetor also moderat-
ed senatorial debate, and put questions to a vote. Numerous other responsibilities
and powers followed from this presidency—too many to list. Of course, a consul
had full power to order a praetor not to convene the Senate, so as to prevent a vote
on a given issue (this in fact happened in 210). However, in the Republican period,
it is significant that a consul never uses his *imperium* to invalidate a praetor's *senatus consultum*, once it was passed. He could, if he chose to, and conflicts over *senatus consulta* did arise; but the maintenance of *concordia* among the governing
class was obviously deemed a much higher priority.

On the whole, the praetor's presidency of the Senate well illustrates his position as colleague of the consuls. We may note that the praetor regularly transmitted the Senate's orders to (often superior) commanders, which, of course, he had
helped to formulate. In a protracted dispute of the late 170s, a plebiscite even gave
an urban praetor precedence over an uncooperative consul in convening the
Senate. That *rogatio* was probably overcompensating: in 169, a simple *senatus consultum* allowed an urban practor (and one for Spain) to take over a consular levy.

This collegiality of consuls and praetors has given rise to at least one myth: that
the urban praetor, like a consul, was able to delegate his *imperium* to a nonmagistrate. There is no good evidence that he had any such special power. But we can
surmise that the Senate on occasion asked the urban praetor to propose a special
rogatio to the People (at least in the Curiate Assembly), so that an individual *privatus* could receive a grant of *imperium*. In 217, it even seems that the urban praetor
passed a measure in the Centuriate Assembly so that Q. Fabius Maximus could act
pro dictatore (until a consul was available to "name" him).

If the praetor engaged in other types of legislative activities in the period down
to 166, we do not know about it. Important bills seem to have been the prerogative
of consuls, or otherwise tribunes; the peregrine praetor who tried to pass a war vote
in 167—when a consul and *praetor urbanus* was in the city—is cited by Livy as an
example of gross constitutional impropriety. The *praetor urbanus* does have the
responsibility of convening the Centuriate Assembly to vote in the final stage of
capital trials. He also regularly conducted elections of minor magistrates and members of special commissions—in (at least) the latter case, even when one or both
consuls are in the city. Precedence in certain matters was readily waived: we find

that the presence of a higher magistrate in no way hindered the urban praetor from performing even some major religious duties.

Though we know little of the urban praetor's supervision of civil procedure in the city down through the mid-Republic, there is no doubt that here his powers will have grown as the rigorous procedural forms of the *legis actiones* gave way to the formulary system. This process seems to have started about 200. Formulae were not prescribed by law; their composition and application rested solely on the praetor's authority. The origins of this new system of procedure (like almost every aspect of Roman civil law in our period) are hotly disputed. I have suggested that wartime conditions and an increase in the praetors' legal (and other) work prompted the *pontifices* to allow that a "formula" could substitute for "certa verba" in a civil suit, thus allowing legal actions to be completed even on *dies nefasti*.

Subsequent developments are not all that easy to trace. We do see the praetor providing remedies outside the existing procedural frameworks by the mid-second century. Not long after 122 B.C., the provisions promulgated by the praetor in his edict started to eclipse popular legislation as the principle vehicle for changing existing civil law rights. In Cicero's day, the praetor undoubtedly could agree to the use of a formula even if it had no basis in the civil law; alternately, he could refuse to assent to a particular formula, even in an area where the civil law provided an action. Professional jurists will have helped in most of these developments: already in the 120s we find one sitting on the praetor's *consilium* during the first part of a civil case.

Development of the Provincia Peregrina

One wonders what was happening with the peregrine praetorship during the second century. Our curiosity should be piqued by the fact that there is separate allotment of the *provincia peregrina* in all but two of the years 197–166. In one case (168, on which see below), there is even an extraordinary arrangement to compensate for the absence of the peregrine praetor when he had to go overseas for the year. A servile insurrection in Latium of 198 may have prompted this new policy of keeping both "old" praetors in or near the city. But what convinced the Romans to keep to this policy for decades to come must have been the growing civil responsibilities of the urban praetor. Around this time (certainly by 190), the *praetor urbanus* even had his lictors reduced from six to two (at least when in the city), showing that the Romans now did not expect him to play a military role. We can suppose that the Senate tried to retain the peregrine praetor in the city to serve as his *adiutor*.

We have only a few glimpses of how the peregrine praetor might help his colleague when in Rome. I must emphasize that the way they divided the tasks should not depend on some special powers inherent in their respective *provinciae*, but can be explained by the urban praetor's "seniority" and the peregrine praetor's traditional mobility. The clearest illustration comes from the Senate's handling of criminal *quaestiones*. The supervision of special *quaestiones* went to the peregrine praetor more often than the *praetor urbanus*. Superintendency appears to have been determined simply by the relative availability of these praetors: for example, in 180, the peregrine praetor saw to poisoning cases in and near Rome (within the tenth milestone), since there were six praetors in that year; the urban praetor took over this same task in 179, because there were (under the *lex Baebia*, discussed below) only four. Provincial praetors also often received *quaestiones* (though always *extra ordinem*), even functioning within the city.

In such instances, the Senate's administrative decisions were informed by practical, not legal, concerns. Confirmation for a "pragmatic" policy comes from other spheres. In granting sessions of the Senate, the urban praetor was responsible for introducing embassies from friendly or allied communities or peoples; the peregrine praetor is found treating with foreign embassies from defeated peoples asking for special treatment, who conceivably might have to be questioned as to their intent before they drew near Rome. Similarly, in a large emergency levy, the *praetor urbanus* appears to have been charged with mustering citizen legions, while the *praetor inter peregrinos* called up soldiers from the Latin League. The rationale in both these cases must be that the peregrine praetor had fewer formal responsibilities, and was more free to move if a task demanded his presence outside Rome.

Cumulatively, these instances help us approach the vexed problem of the peregrine praetor's role in the civil law. As noted, we actually have no good evidence for the Republican period that there existed for the peregrine praetor a discrete *iuris dictio*. In any event, it seems impossible that the peregrine praetor was restricted to hearing cases in which a *peregrinus* was a litigant, or, when it came to procedure, that he was circumscribed in any formal way. Indeed, it can be shown that all praetors had the right (in their own *provinciae*) to hear cases between Roman citizens, or between citizens and peregrines, and in time we know they could even set up a framework for *peregrini* to contest a suit on the Roman citizen model (first attested for the early 80s). The provision of the *lex Plautia Papiria* (of 89 or 88) that a *professio* for citizenship could be made before any praetor—and so the *praetor inter peregrinos*—shows that something of this "collegial" aspect of the praetorship long remained (at least down to Sulla). A good circumstantial case can be made that the peregrine praetor simply was expected to hear cases for which the urban praetor was too busy or considered less important.

Special Grants of Imperium

To move from civil affairs to developments *militiae*: A study of the commands of the Third Samnite War (298–290) and Second Punic War (218–201) amply illustrates exactly how resourceful the Romans could be at finding ways to compromise between institutional principles and military necessities. This latter conflict—which was the longer and obviously more dangerous of the two—forced Rome to make these compromises to an unprecedented extent. Here we find all sorts of dodges to free up manpower, including the combination of two praetorian provinces into one, and the largescale use of prorogation of *imperium* (with repeated extensions particularly common for commanders in special *provinciae*). These practices received their heaviest use in the crisis of the first eight years of the war. But once developed, they were retained throughout our period, and down until the end of the Republic.

One particularly consequential development—which may have got its start well before the Hannibalic period, or even earlier than the Third Samnite War— was the granting of praetorian *imperium* to private citizens, who were usually, but not always, ex-magistrates. This was another dodge to ensure that there were enough men with *imperium* to go around. Yet the Romans seem to have reserved this expedient—in contrast to prorogation—for times of extreme emergency. On the whole, these commands were defensive in nature: the Senate seems to have identified certain tasks that needed *imperium* but not much fighting experience, and then given those to nonmagistrates. Nevertheless, in 215, Ti. Sempronius Longus (*cos.* 218) was active fighting against Hanno in Lucania, probably with a special grant of (praetorian) *imperium*. And some *privati* even received consular *imperium*. M. Claudius Marcellus was probably the first, under special conditions (political and military) in 215. Next came a long series of commanders (starting in 210) who were sent *pro consulibus* to Spain, as well as a commander appointed *pro consule* for Greece in 205. Such grants of consular *imperium* often seem to be large-ly symbolic. It can be shown that enhanced *imperium*—whether that of a praetor or *privatus*—does not necessarily imply a larger army, just a larger task and a more independent position. It did always require a popular vote.

Special grants of *imperium* (at either level) never grew as common as simple prorogation, and, in the period immediately following the Second Punic War, the Senate severely curtailed its use of this expedient for *privati*. There obviously were no more military crises on the scale of Hannibal's invasion of Italy, and after 197 there were (except for a few years) six rather than four praetors on hand. But such grants never disappeared completely. In 133, during the height of a slave war in Sicily, two senior *consulares* received (praetorian) *imperium* to put down a servile uprising at Minturnae and Sinuessa. In 131, Scipio Aemilianus thought he could get such an extraordinary appointment for himself (but at the level of *pro consule*) to fight the pretender Aristonicus in Asia. Yet the Romans who voted on the proposal preferred to ignore a major religious impediment and send the consul and *pontif-ex maximus* P. Licinius Crassus to fight this war (the other consul was a *flamen*, and, as such, no more mobile). In the first century, attitudes changed dramatically, and the practice of giving extraordinary commands to private citizens exploded: Pompey held six such grants in his career, and in many ways paved the way for the Principate.

Limits on Military Initiatives by Praetors in Italy and Gaul

But to return to the Second Punic War: Despite the Senate's ingenuity in exploit-ing the limited number of magistracies, praetorian commanders in Italy rarely were meant to fight significant battles against the Carthaginians, or take on Gallic tribes in the field. Generally, praetors (or *pro praetoribus*) appear in major campaigns only to help a given consular commander. In the dangerous first eight or so years of the war, the Senate did very occasionally allow holders of praetorian *imperium* (mostly already ex-consuls) to initiate battle against these enemies. More often, when we hear of praetors or *pro praetoribus* fighting against Hannibal, it means the Senate simply failed to prevent them from coming into his way.

From 210 on, as the military situation improved—and Rome ran out of experienced *consulares*—the Senate kept praetorian commanders in Italy under extremely tight control. We now hear of very little actual fighting by praetors in the Italian peninsula. This development was partly a consequence of the praetors' *minus imperium* when they served in the same *provincia* as a consul. Then there is the basic fact that praetors often received less experienced troops than consuls and proven consular commanders—and were expected to give up their armies, once seasoned, to their superiors. But a few notable defeats suffered by praetorian commanders in the field—culminating with that of Cn. Fulvius Flaccus, *pr.* 212 in Apulia—also must have conditioned the Senate's willingness to entrust major military responsibilities to men of this rank. In fact, in the entire Second Punic War, only two praetors emerged successful from a major engagement in Italy without consular support: the experienced M. Claudius Marcellus at Nola in 216, and C. Hostilius Tubulus (who probably engaged Hannibal under the Senate's special instructions) in 207.

The main function of praetors and praetorian commanders in Italy in the latter part of the Second Punic War seems to have been simply to maintain order and to prevent defections in problematic districts, especially in the north—well away from Hannibal. Most of their activities concerned members (and former members) of the Italian confederacy. In a few cases they are recorded to have reduced lesser towns, taking disciplinary action as appropriate. Praetorian commanders are wholly absent from south Italy after 210, except for garrison duty at Tarentum and Capua. Following Hannibal's departure from Italy in late 203, praetors would return south to restore order—but only since consuls were not available. There were no praetorian triumphs during the Second Punic War. In fact, only one is known from the Italian peninsula in all the years which follow (that of L. Furius Purpurio in 200, which came not without a dispute), down to Crassus' *ovatio* over Spartacus and his slaves in 71.

Praetors were mostly excluded from the conquest of Gaul and Liguria also in the years after the Hannibalic War. In these campaigns, it was policy for both consuls to proceed to the north. In circumstances when only one consul was available, the Senate preferred to prorogue a consul who was already in the area (multiple times, if need be) or send a sole consul to fight unaided, rather than have one share the main command with a praetor. On the occasions when praetorian commanders do appear, the consuls did not allow them to expand their ancillary role—and disciplined them if they tried. Following the forced dismissal of a praetor in 187, the Senate started making its *mandata* more explicit. This seems to have worked, for a time. Yet soon the practice of sending praetors to the north stops altogether.

After a peregrine praetor of 178 who was prorogued to hold a command (tellingly, *pro consule*) in Liguria, no other praetors are found in northern *provinciae* until one who received Gaul in 146 (perhaps alongside a consul). C. Sempronius Tuditanus, in his ambitious campaign against the Iapydes as *cos.* 129, appears to have used a senior consular (and *triumphator*) as well as a *praetorius* as his *legati*. When the former *triumphator* scored a major success, it was Tuditanus,

as consul, who, despite his own poor performance, received the imperatorial acclamation. This peculiar advantage of fighting with experienced *legati* (as opposed to
praetors possessing their own auspices) cannot have escaped many of the consuls
in our period: note, for instance, the presence of praetorian *legati*, but not praetors,
in the Third Punic War. Praetors had plenty of reason to go triumph hunting for
their own sakes, especially to win a consulship.

On the basis of the actual record, we can assume that many *consulares* in the
Senate of the second century viewed praetors as a danger to Roman lives and reputation, posing too much of a risk to be used on the dangerous northern frontier.
(Livy tells us as much in his narrative of the praetor Purpurio's request for a triumph in 200.) Policy in central and south Italy was a bit different. We find holders
of praetorian *imperium* operating in Magna Graecia from 202 to 199 and then from
193 almost continuously down to 180. But much of their work was police action, or,
in the Syrian War, maintaining defensive positions and preparing expeditionary
forces for the war in Greece. One consequential development does emerge from
Livy's annual lists of provincial allotments. In 190, Etruria as well as Apulia (the latter joined with the "Bruttii") were declared armed praetorian *provinciae*, with prorogation of their commanders into 189 and 188, respectively. For 187 Livy reports
the placement of the *provincia* of Tarentum in the praetorian sortition. The situation in Etruria and south Italy must have been quite serious if the Senate thought
it necessary to keep two praetors there in 190, when the war against Antiochus was
still far from settled, and then to maintain those forces (at least in south Italy), even
after the war was over.

Though Livy does not say so (perhaps intentionally), the special praetorian
assignments in Italy of 190–187 must form the background to the *quaestio de
Bacchanalibus*, assigned *extra ordinem* to the consuls of 186. In each of the six years
that follow, a praetorian commander is found in south Italy. Down through 181,
suppression of the Bacchic cult is said to have been a prime concern. What we
surely do not have here is a genuine spiritual revival (as is often thought). Rather,
rebels in south Italy and Etruria apparently seized upon the Bacchic rituals to give
a religious sanction and organization to their defiance of Rome. It was natural for
the Senate to call upon praetors for the drawn-out task of suppressing them.

More surprising is the choice of a praetor to reduce the rebellious town of
Fregellae in 125. The Senate's selection of L. Opimius may have been ad hominem
(his political sympathies surely recommended him for the task). Alternately, it may
be that neither of the consuls of the year—one of whom was the Gracchan M.
Fulvius Flaccus—wanted the job, and it fell by default to the praetor. An impending Cimbric invasion explains why, in 104, it was the city praetor L. Licinius
Lucullus who had to leave Rome to put down a well-organized slave revolt at Capua.

In 91, with trouble from the Italian allies looming, the Senate stationed a praetor with consular *imperium* in the area of (at least) Picenum. That commander met
his death at Asculum, which led to the dispatch (I suggest) of more praetors of the
year into the field: Cn. Pompeius Strabo to Picenum, probably L. Postumius to
Nola, and perhaps L. Porcius Cato to Etruria. Yet the one possible praetor of 90
known to have served in the war, L. Calpurnius Piso Caesoninus, is said to have
manufactured arms. And Cn. Strabo does not seem to have been prorogued into

90, but made a legate (though probably with *imperium*) of one of the consuls of the year.

Indeed, in the major military emergencies of the post-Gracchan era, the most important subordinate roles generally were filled by *legati*, some quite senior. For instance, in the Cimbric War, the consul L. Cassius Longinus in 107 had a *cos.* 112 as well as a (likely) *praetorius* on his staff, while the consul Cn. Mallius Maximus in 105 had a *cos. suff.* 108 as legate. Likewise, in the dangerous crisis of the Social War, we see that the consuls who held the chief command entrusted much of the serious fighting not to praetors but to experienced *legati* of consular or praetorian rank. Those served as *legati pro praetore*, with *imperium* officially conferred throughout their tenure. In 90 and 89, the Senate even saw fit to raise the rank of certain legates—not praetors—to *pro consule* to compensate for two individual consuls who had fallen in the war. In the latter of these two years, several praetors also had to take on major responsibilities in the southern theater of this conflict.

Yet it is really only in the year 88, when the Italian revolt was on its last legs, that we find praetors in office entrusted with substantial military responsibilities. And in the civil fighting of the years 83 and 82, the Marian government mainly preferred to use consuls and prorogued consuls rather than praetorian commanders, though the latter were often more capable. Sulla, too, organized his force under legates—at least some of whom were of praetorian standing, recent volunteers to his cause—and allowed them the capability to fight independently.

In the decades that followed, certain commanders extended overseas the basic model we find in the Social War. To operate in his massive special *provincia* against the pirates, the *pr.* 74 M. Antonius made wide use of independent *legati* and *praefecti*. Pompey, in his pirate command of 67 under the tribunician *lex Gabinia*, combined the command structure of the Social War and Antonius' huge commission. The Gabinian law entitled Pompey not just to appoint a large number of legates (two dozen or so), but also to delegate each of them praetorian *imperium*. Each of those legates had the responsibility for his own independent quasi *provincia*. Among the thirteen reliably transmitted names, we find two *consulares* and three or four known *praetorii*.

Even after Sulla as dictator increased the number of praetors to eight and provided that they all might hold city *provinciae*, the only instances of city praetors venturing outside Rome on special commissions have to do with military commands, by and large prompted by acute emergencies. In this period, praetors or praetorian commanders only seldom are involved even with a levy in Italy (none are attested between 122 and 72). There are some indications that when the gladiators' revolt of Spartacus first broke in 73, the Senate took pains to spare the city praetors. For 72, the plan was for the two consuls of the year and an ex-consul of the previous year to conduct the major fighting. However, matters for those senior commanders went so badly that the Senate by the fall ordered the consuls not to fight any longer, and allowed M. Licinius Crassus (probably *pr.* 73) to conduct the war with the consuls' legions and surely with their level of *imperium*. As it happens, this praetorian commander had a crisis of confidence in himself: in winter 72/71, Crassus asked the Senate to summon M. Lucullus (*cos.* 73) from Thrace and the *pro cos.* Pompey from Spain to help against the Spartacans. But before either of these men could arrive, Crassus himself went on to win a decisive victory against the gladiators—one of the absolute high points of praetorian generalship in the late Republic.

Independent Commands for Praetors outside Italy

Outside Italy, the Senate allowed holders of praetorian *imperium* much greater latitude. It had not all that much choice, for even in a major war, the Senate was reluctant to let both consuls of a given year go overseas. That happened only twice in the period 218–122. To end the Syrian War, the consuls of 189 received as their *provinciae* Aetolia and Asia. Those were quite separate theaters; the joint command against Carthage which the consuls of 149 managed to secure for themselves was much harder to justify. More telling for normal Roman practice is the fact that the Senate never let both consuls go to the Spains during the serious rebellions of 157 to 150 and then 147 down through 133, though in many of those years there were no significant wars elsewhere.

Wherever a consul could not go, one naturally would expect a praetor to fill his place; but not in a high-profile war (at least ideally). For a decade after 143, the Senate did not allow praetors to do any of the fighting in the Spains. Instead, it aimed at a system where consuls would receive the *provinciae* of Hispania Citerior and Ulterior in alternate years, so long as the emergency should last, even though that meant superseding some successful commanders, and proroguing others who had been defeated. When that emergency policy had to be abandoned (after the recall of a *cos.* 137), the Senate simply sent a string of consuls to Citerior (culminating with Scipio Aemilianus, *cos.* II 134 by special dispensation), and prolonged the *imperium* (for five years) of an effective general in Ulterior, until both *provinciae* were thoroughly pacified, and ready once again for normal praetorian administration.

It is in the Greek east where we best see truly independent commands for holders of praetorian *imperium*. Yet those were developed only gradually. The first praetor we find sent across the Adriatic happens to be a capable *consularis*, M. Valerius Laevinus (*cos.* 220 and *pr.* II 215). As *pro praetore* in Illyria and Greece from 214 down through early 210, Laevinus' role was mainly defensive. He also turns out to be the only praetor to serve in the First Macedonian War. To succeed Laevinus, the Romans prorogued P. Sulpicius Galba (*cos.* 211), keeping him in that theater for five full years. And when it came time to supersede Galba (for 205), the Senate preferred to have the *privatus* P. Sempronius Tuditanus receive a special grant of consular *imperium* than send a praetor or *pro praetore*. By 206, Rome's allies in Greece were quite ready to make peace with Philip. In the delicate political atmosphere, the Senate apparently decided it would be sending the wrong message to replace a *pro consule* with someone possessing (merely) praetorian *imperium*. This principle, which we may call "the persistence of consular *imperium*," can clearly be seen at work later in our period when the Romans started to create permanent praetorian *provinciae* in the east (see below).

In the preliminaries to the Second Macedonian War, the Romans sent Laevinus once again to the east, now as a *privatus* with (praetorian) *imperium*. In 201, Laevinus delivered an expeditionary Roman force to the Illyrian mainland, surely with the understanding that he soon would be replaced. Unlike Laevinus' earlier eastern command, this mission turns out to have set a real precedent for praetors, who are sent to do exactly the same thing at the start of the Syrian as well as the Third Macedonian Wars. All three instances of this practice share the same general features. At the time of each of these expeditionary missions, war had not been formally declared; once a praetor had crossed with an advance force, at the beginning of the next administrative year the war vote would be taken, and a consul (with a proper force) would depart for the east. These praetorian commanders generally maintained a strictly defensive posture up to the time of their supersession (which was never more than a year), though they were fully capable of fighting if the situation demanded. All the same, the Senate must have instructed these commanders to avoid decisive action (and the praetors obeyed), for we hear of no bold initiatives.

Once the actual fighting of the Second Macedonian War commences, we find certain individuals in wideranging naval commissions, serving (so it appears) as *legati pro praetore* of a consular commander. In the first two years of this war, the Senate was trying to maintain annual consular commands; as the consuls were relieved, their appointees sailed home with them. That policy soon changed. T. Quinctius Flamininus went to the east as *cos.* 198, and then stayed as *pro consule* down into 194; the Senate allowed his brother Lucius (*pr.* 199) to be prorogued probably five consecutive times to serve (as a quasi *legatus*) under him.

The success of these men—especially L. Flamininus—facilitated the development of a new category. Starting in the late 190s with the Syrian War, and then again in the Third Macedonian War, praetors regularly went to the east as genuinely independent commanders, especially to conduct naval operations (their *provincia* was a special one, termed the *classis*). In the last year of fighting in the Third Macedonian War (168), the principle was extended and an independent praetorian command was created on land for Illyricum. (This foreshadowed, in a way, the later creation of the praetorian *provincia* "Macedonia".) All these commanders, though tactically subordinate to a consul (or consuls), fought under their own *auspicia* and with their own *imperium*. Indeed, four of these praetors (out of eight)—including the land commander—managed to celebrate a triumph. In these two eastern wars, the Senate adhered rigorously to the principle of annual succession for both praetors and consuls, until the hostilities were settled and peace arrangements had to be made (which, in the case of Illyricum, the praetor worked out himself).

Here, for once, the line of development seems clear. The Senate had noted the usefulness of the *legati pro praetore*, but sought to avoid extended commands such as that of L. Flamininus by placing the "Fleet" in the praetorian sortition each year during actual fighting, replacing even competent naval commanders. (In the Hannibalic War, the tendency had been to keep good admirals on the seas as long as possible.) The pressure to maintain this policy doubtless came from within the governing class, especially from the properly elected magistrates of each year who wanted to have their own chance at military *gloria* in the east.

Otherwise, the Senate obviously did not like praetors as the principal commanders in major conflicts, if it could be helped. In some ways, in the post-

Gracchan era that tendency grew more pronounced. Consider the string of consular commanders (each extended for at least one year and at least one prorogued twice) that undertook major campaigns in the area east of the Rhône in the latter half of the 120s; the prolonged consular commands in Sardinia (one covering the years 126–122, then another 115–111); the whole conduct of the Jugurthine War (consular in each of the years 111–105); and M. Rufus (*cos.* 110), prorogued four times in all in Macedonia before triumphing ca. 1 August 106.

Exceptions are few. I have suggested that in the opening stages of the Second Slave War in 103, the Senate dispatched the modestly experienced L. Licinius Lucullus (*pr.* 104) *ex praetura* as a compromise that spared both the untested new praetors of the year and Marius' consular colleague L. Aurelius Orestes while the Cimbric emergency was ongoing. That slave war eventually had to be declared consular, and given to M.' Aquillius (*cos.* 101). He would be the last consular commander to hold Sicily as a *provincia* in the period down to 49 B.C.; the regular praetorian governors were thought adequate to check occasional dangers from slaves and pirates.

In all, we know only two possible instances of praetorian commands in special *provinciae* outside Italy in the period 122–82 B.C. (perhaps a *pr.* ca. 120 in Illyria, then the *pr.* 102 M. Antonius in Cilicia), and two more from 81 to 50 (the *pr.* II 79 M. Cosconius in Illyria, followed by the *pr.* 74 M. Antonius—son of the aforementioned—in a wideranging pirate command). No individuals with praetorian *imperium* are explicitly attested in the fighting of the Third Mithridatic War from the year 73—when exceptionally both consuls of the previous year began a campaign in the east—all the way down to 63. Granted, in 69, the Romans removed Asia from the *cos.* 74 L. Lucullus' composite *provincia*, "and restored the rule of Asia to the praetors," despite a military threat to the *provincia* from Mithridates and the Armenian king Tigranes. The object here was not primarily military but political, namely, to insult Lucullus.

The triumphal *Fasti* show nicely the Senate's reluctance to expose praetors to dangerous enemies. Consider Macedonia, which Cicero deems the triumphal province par excellence. After Q. Caecilius Metellus "Macedonicus" in 146, T. Didius is the only praetor known to have triumphed from the *provincia* (probably in the year 100). Even imperatorial acclamations are rarely attested for praetorian commanders. In short, the record suggests that praetors might have long commands in the province, yet when possible the Senate had men of consular rank take on severe fighting. That tendency grows particularly marked in the decades after Sulla.

Yet the picture was not the same everywhere. Between the Sertorian War (ended 71 B.C.) and the command of Q. Caecilius Metellus Nepos (*cos.* 57 and *pro cos.* for Citerior in 56), only praetorian commanders received the Spains, and that despite their military possibilities. M. Pupius Piso Calpurnianus (*pr.* by 71) aggressively hunted for a triumph in Ulterior, and was awarded one in 69. L. Afranius, Pupius' counterpart and contemporary in Citerior, also triumphed; C. Iulius Caesar (*pr.* 62) was hailed *imperator* but gave up a near-certain vote of a triumph to make a *professio* for the consulship of 59.

And contrary to long previous practice, after Sulla men of praetorian rank might find themselves assigned a northern command. Indeed, the first post-Sullan commander we find in Transalpina was of praetorian standing. C. Pomptinus (*pr.* 63) even managed to triumph from that province, after years of obstruction, in the year 54—the first praetorian commander ever to triumph from "Gallia," however defined, since L. Furius Purpurio in the year 200.

The explanation must be that after 81, there were still too many territorial *provinciae* relative to the available number of commanders to keep subconsulars altogether out of the Gauls. The Senate was more lenient with Transalpina in this respect than Cisalpina. In the Senate's administrative deliberations of 56 that occasioned Cicero's *De Provinciis Consularibus*, we find that no one seems to have allowed the possibility that Gallia Cisalpina might be declared praetorian for 55. However in the later Republic we occasionally find a reaction against placing consulars in important commands (discussed below).

Restrictions on the Magistrate's Powers in His Provincia

In short, in the post-Livian period, we never see grand commands for holders of *imperium minus* quite like those of the Syrian and Third Macedonian Wars. But some of these individuals were thought to have taken their independence too far. An ex-praetor of 171 chose exile after the People fined him for his excessively stern measures against two Boeotian towns. A prejudicial *senatus consultum* (perhaps more than one) had paved the way for his condemnation. The case is important, for praetors in our period are very rarely successfully prosecuted for offenses committed in the field—otherwise, only for *perduellio*, after major losses of Roman troops (the two known instances are Cn. Flaccus, *pr.* 212, and C. Plautius, *pr.* 145). The incident of 171 is for us an unprecedented example of the Senate's encroachment on the praetor's (originally absolute) powers of *imperium* within his *provincia*. A similar measure soon followed in 169, limiting the requisitions Roman commanders and officers could make from allies. This was a productive development— as the numerous laws on grain requisition that we find a century later in the *Verrines* go to show. However, it is a pity that we lose Livy before we can adequately trace this development further. One thing that is clear is that, despite the growth of central controls from Rome, many commanders went right on behaving as they pleased. We happen to know that the earliest commanders for Roman Asia (i.e., those of the mid-120s) had been in the habit of exercising their jurisdiction even in extraterritorial parts of the province.

We may note that restrictions were also applied to *imperium domi*. The really consequential development here is the law of 122 B.C. in which C. Gracchus introduced his new "praetor repetundis." The praetor, though the presiding magistrate in each trial, was under obligation to choose his panel of *iudices* from a restricted class of individuals, from which senators were excluded. He then was compelled to accept the finding of this body, which the law calls a *consilium* ("advisory council"). This latter detail is particularly remarkable, from a constitutional perspective. Never before, as far as we know, was a magistrate legally required to abide by the decision of his *consilium*. We are perhaps justified in viewing this measure as another encroachment on the (originally near-absolute) *imperium* of the praetor.

Paradoxically, one purpose of this new praetorian *provincia* was to keep other praetors (as well as consuls) in check. Rome's acquisition of Asia must at least partly have prompted Gracchus' reform: it is surely no accident that the earliest securely attested trial under Gracchus' new-style *quaestio* is that of a praetorian governor of Asia, Q. Mucius Scaevola, probably soon after C. Gracchus' death in 121.

By the year 100, we know for a fact that there existed a small forest of regulation concerning administration in the territorial provinces. We owe that knowledge to the discovery of a major inscription from Cnidus (a substantial fragment of a previously known *Lex de piratis*) that dates to the year 101 or 100. Most relevant for our purposes here, it spells out some limitations under a *lex Porcia*—apparently new— on the movements of the commander and his staff outside the *provincia*. It was now law that a commander was liable for the public actions of his *comites*. (That must be one reason why, in the *Verrines*, Cicero is so eager to show that a wide assortment of knaves were members of Verres' official entourage, and as such of his judicial *consilia*.)

Though Sulla is the one who generalized consular *imperium* for the territorial provinces (see below), he also took a keen interest in regulating the behavior of Rome's promagistrates as commanders. To do so, he introduced an elaborate law *de maiestate*, which remained in effect down to the end of the free Republic, even alongside Caesar's extraordinarily comprehensive *lex de repetundis* of 59 B.C.

Like so much else in his reform program, Sulla drafted his *lex de maiestate* partly in response to the irregularities of the tumultuous years 91–82 B.C. But it seems he also had a larger, forward-looking purpose. Here Sulla in a single statute apparently codified not just a whole host of *senatus consulta* and *leges*—some demonstrably containing minute regulations—that had emerged haphazardly over the previous century or so, but also certain restraints previously observed by commanders only *more maiorum*. The provisions of Sulla's *maiestas* law that we know about mostly are concerned with orderly succession in the provinces, crucial if his new administrative system was to work. In this, Sulla's legislation was successful: at any rate, for the late Republic we do not hear of any dangerous conflicts between *decessor* and *successor*.

Sulla's laws of his dictatorship in turn launched a trend. One particularly representative example of the late Republican craze for enshrining *mos maiorum* in statute is the tribunician *lex Cornelia* of 67 B.C., compelling praetors to follow their own edicts. The law surely did not attempt to dictate the actual composition of the individual edicts. Its aim (probably) was only to prevent ad hoc deviations. We find city praetors making plenty of those in our record for the 70s—most notably L. Cornelius Sisenna (*pr. urb. et per.* 78) and C. Verres (*pr. urb.* 74)—prompted by both favoritism and spite. That the *lex Cornelia* also applied to provincial governors— many of whom will have relied on the urban edicts as a model—is conceivable.

All these measures represent significant encroachments on the magistrate's (originally absolute) rights of *imperium*. Yet for all the creep of legislation, Roman commanders were highly skilled at finding the loopholes. Consider C. Verres: Cicero managed to quash this particular commander. Yet the overarching impression we get is that it was no easy thing to call magistrates to account in the late Republic, especially if they were well connected. The Senate was by no means eager to pass an actual *senatus consultum* condemning a given provincial governor's actions.

It is ironic that an era that had such an appetite for legislation on provincial administration might acquit in the extortion court an L. Valerius Flaccus from Asia or an M. Aemilius Scaurus from Sardinia. We have Cicero's defense speech in each case, and can plainly see that he found little in their actual provincial records to commend them. Even more ironic, this general period also saw the creation of a massive *provincia* for the *pr.* 74 M. Antonius in his pirate commission, again for L. Lucullus against Mithridates in the east, and even wider-ranging commands for Pompey and Caesar. There also were special ad hoc (or rather ad hominem) grants of a less spectacular sort, yet that still represented an increase in certain magistrates' powers.

Grants of Consular Imperium to Praetors

But we are getting far ahead of our story. It must be remembered that, with the exception of M. Valerius Laevinus in the First Macedonian War, the only praetors down to 166 who held the eastern theater by themselves were those in charge of crossing expeditionary forces. By the mid-second century, the inhabitants of Macedonia, Greece, and Asia must have expected that consular commanders fight the main campaigns. As chance would have it, the year 149 saw a major rising in Macedonia—after both consuls had fully committed themselves to fighting Carthage. The Romans were forced to assign the rebellion as a praetorian *provincia*; the pretender Andriscus defeated and killed the praetor who was sent (and then prorogued) early the next year. In the emergency, a praetor of 148, Q. Caecilius Metellus, received a grant of higher *imperium* to fight Andriscus (no consul seems to have been available in that year either). Metellus vanquished the pretender, and himself organized the annexation of "Macedonia," winning a triumph and a triumphal *agnomen* (the first and only for an individual qua praetor) on his return home in 146. Epigraphic evidence confirms that consular *imperium* was retained for all subsequent praetorian commanders in this new *provincia*.

The next major eastern war that came along was against Aristonicus in Asia in the years 131–129. Here the Romans gave no fighting to regular praetors. They must have considered the military threat to the region too grave, and the political stakes (ultimately, the organization of another new *provincia*) too high. Instead, we find the war entrusted to a series of consuls, the first of whom (as we have seen) faced a religious impediment. These consuls were subject to strict annual succession—though we do find one instance of a *legatus* who received praetorian *imperium* by (a consul's) delegation in the field. And once "Asia" was properly annexed and organized, the institution of praetorian commanders with consular *imperium* was extended to it as well. The same would be true of "Cilicia," when that was created as a permanent *provincia* ca. 100. Each of these provinces had their military aspects, despite Cicero's famous claim in the *Pro Flacco* (59 B.C.) that an Asian praetor's main sphere of activity was "iuris dictio."

The regular dispatch of praetors *pro consulibus* to provinces such as Asia and Cilicia can be viewed as "persistence of consular *imperium*"—yet another example of the "dodge." The principle can also be seen in the west, though there its application is entirely ad hoc. The Senate took some extraordinary measures to keep Spain consular after the death of the Scipios in 211. True, at first a single praetorian commander was sent to supersede the tumultuary *dux* who had taken emergency charge of the *provincia* (and then started to use the title "pro praetore" for himself). But the military situation in this theater quickly deteriorated, and a special election was held in the *comitia centuriata*, which made the *privatus* P. Cornelius Scipio (the future Africanus) into a *pro consule*. This is how he fought in Spain down into 206, aided by a genuine *pro praetore*. It may be that the two *privati* who were sent to relieve these commanders did so with grants of praetorian *imperium*. But by 204, these same men were certainly *pro consulibus*; Livy can be taken to imply that the People raised their *imperium* after a serious revolt of 205. All subsequent governors sent to Spain—for the rest of the Republican period—also displayed the insignia of a consul (most importantly, attendance by twelve lictors), perhaps to overawe the bellicose Spanish tribes. We find this practice even in Italy: note the peregrine praetor of 178 who was prorogued as *pro consule* against the Ligurians, a traditionally consular *provincia*. In the first century, in certain severe emergency situations—the turbulent year 91, the last stages of the Social War, the first stages of the war with Spartacus, the Catilinarian conspiracy—we see several praetors during their year of office have their *imperium* raised from praetorian to consular. However, in the later Republic such enhancement of *imperium* could not be taken for granted, as the incident of the two praetors and their (combined) "twelve axes" captured by pirates in Italy shortly before 67 B.C. shows.

It is uncertain what grade of *imperium* the pre-Sullan praetorian commanders for the *provincia* of Africa possessed. An African governor might have served *pro consule*: one should keep in mind that consuls in the Second and Third Punic Wars had always done whatever fighting there was on the African mainland, and that (at least) the early praetors for Africa might have occasion to command a large military force.

We hear of consular commanders delegating their powers to a subordinate any number of times down to the end of the period; it is clear (against Mommsen) that they did not have to leave their *provincia* to do so. The quaestor M. Antonius in 113/112 is our first known example of an individual being delegated *imperium* by a *praetor pro consule*. But the practice of praetorian delegation might go back much further, perhaps as far as the very start of the second century. Soon after Antonius, this type of delegation by praetors—and even *privati*—with enhanced (i.e., consular) *imperium* is reasonably well attested, both before and after Sulla took the step of generalizing consular *imperium* for promagistrates in all the territorial provinces.

Indeed, the power to delegate *imperium* may be one of the major factors behind the decision to institutionalize grants of consular *imperium* to praetorian commanders for distant provinces like the Spains, Macedonia, Asia, and Cilicia. There, the seamless succession of proper governors was difficult to achieve, and *legati* might find themselves in sole charge of a large *provincia* for longish stretches. It also may be the main reason why, eventually, Sulla as dictator standardized the rank of *pro consule* for all commanders who had charge of a territorial province. The power to delegate might also explain why, in certain emergencies, the People (surely) raised the *imperium* of various praetors in office for use in Italy.

In time, we find instances of delegation of *imperium* that go beyond short-term stopgaps. Consider the consuls of 90 and 89 who held the chief commands in the Social War. They apparently gave *imperium* to more than a few of the (numerous) consular and praetorian *legati* who fought under (and often in close proximity to) them. The significant thing is that those legates were intended to have their *imperium* for an entire year, or a good part of it. Sulla validated this practice, so it seems, by making similar grants to his subordinates—most notably, to his quaestor L. Lucullus for a prolonged commission in eastern Mediterranean waters in 86, and to the young Cn. Pompeius during the fighting of the Civil War in 83–82. In the year 67, Pompey had (apparently) twenty-four *legati pro praetore* under him in his special pirate command, including two *consulares* and three or four known *praetorii*; the Senate might have allowed him a similar setup in his grain commission of 57. (Below, we shall discuss the situation of delegation after Pompey's reforms of 52.)

Sicily and Sardinia as "Double Provinciae"

Let us turn now to the Senate's policies toward the various standing territorial *provinciae*, especially in the formative middle Republican period. For Sicily, the central administrative issue was different than for most provinces. In times of danger, the island positively required more than one holder of *imperium*. In the first two years of the Hannibalic War, with Hiero's help a single praetor was able to protect the island. However, when the Carthaginians launched a two-pronged attack on Sicily in the crisis year 216, the Romans managed to avert disaster only by sending the urban praetor on a counterraid of the coast of Africa. In 215, upon the news of Hiero's death, the Senate was forced to supplement the regular command on the island by sending a *privatus* to a special praetorian *provincia* ("the fleet"—a handy designation, as we have seen, later to reappear elsewhere).

Sicily was a consular—as well as a praetorian—*provincia* in each of the years 214 through 207, and then in 205 and (surely) 204. After 215, praetors also received the charge of some armies that had disgraced themselves in Italy, now on restricted service. These two factors greatly diminished the possibility that praetors and prorogued praetors in Sicily might have much of an independent role. There was some opportunity for praetors to see action during the siege of Syracuse and the first year after its fall in 211, in both east and west Sicily. A bit later (208), a Sicilian praetor also saw some service in south Italy. Yet the bulk of the campaigns in this theater were conducted by a holder of consular *imperium*, with a praetor acting in tactical subordination. Once the fighting shifted to Africa, the Sicilian praetors remained in place, preparing (not conveying) supplies and defending the coastline against the possibility of a Carthaginian counterattack.

With the end of war, a single praetor once again administered "Sicilia"— though the acquisition of Hiero's kingdom (in 211) had now much enlarged the *provincia*. It was probably in one of the years 210–206 that the Sicilian praetor first received two quaestors, one each for the eastern and western portions of the island.

That is certainly what we find in the late Republic; it may have started as a compromise solution, meant to substitute for the addition of another permanent praetor to the *provincia*.

Yet the need for more than one holder of *imperium* occasionally reappeared. We find the division of the *provincia* between two praetors in the years 191 and 190, when it was feared that Antiochus III might try to use the island as a stepping-stone to Italy. And in the First Slave War, the Romans had to introduce a similar administrative arrangement. The war started in 135, when a praetor was the sole commander in the *provincia*. In each of the years 134 through 132, we find a praetor or *pro praetore* in a western command while a consul fought the main war in the east. In both these theaters, the Senate stuck to a policy of annual succession. Though tactically subordinate to the consuls, these praetorian commanders were fully independent, and fighting under their own *auspicia*. The proof is that M. Perperna, *pr.* 133, was awarded an *ovatio* (probably in 132) for liberating the sanctuary of Demeter at Henna from the rebel slaves.

"Sardinia"—which consisted of the islands of Sardinia and Corsica—was similarly a double *provincia* of sorts. But it was never a major area of conflict during the Hannibalic War, and so we find its praetors were more than twice as likely to be prorogued as their Sicilian counterparts. That changed somewhat in 197–166. The easily rationalized omission of the distant Spains from the sortition in this period meant that Sardinia was left out in only two years (195 and 190), Sicily never.

Yet the sortition lists do not tell the entire story. By late 203, and throughout the decisive year 202, the Romans went so far as to abandon the serious defense of Sardinia, and sent the island's praetorian commanders to Africa to aid P. Cornelius Scipio in the last operations of the war. In these two years, the protection of the *provincia* of Sardinia must have been delegated to a *legatus*. In 200, we find a transferred *pro praetore* serving as the sole commander with *imperium* in this *provincia*. In the mid-180s, the Senate started the habit of asking Sardinian praetors to take on special *quaestiones* in or near Rome, at first (184, 180) for part of the year, but later (177) for the whole. It quite probably used a praetor of 176, who had excused himself from the *provincia*, in the same way (not to forget a Spanish praetor who supervised the first *quaestio repetundarum* in 171). As amazing as it seems, Livy is specific that C. Papirius Carbo (*pr.* 168) had been assigned two *sortes*, Sardinia and the *provincia peregrina*. Carbo ended up staying in Rome, apparently for the entire year. In 167, another Sardinian praetor was retained in Italy, to hear capital cases (and apparently other matters). In these latter two years, the praetors, whatever their exact duties, may have sent *legati* to hold Sardinia (remember the situation of 203–202). Also, the practice of retaining the Sardinian praetor for legal chores (but still placing the *provincia* in the sortition) may have continued to grow after 166, though we have no way to know.

Sardinia and Corsica, of course, occasionally offered possibilities for military *gloria*. Ti. Sempronius Gracchus received the *provincia* as *cos.* 177, and triumphed from there two years later. Gracchus was assisted throughout by a praetor of 178— one of the longest praetorian commands we have for the second century. The Romans were not terribly worried about prorogation in Sardinia; as it happens, we know that this particular praetor could have been replaced in either 177 or 176 (praetors drew "Sardinia" in the sortition in each of those years). This man's first prorogation, when the island was declared consular in 177, is readily explained: as policy, the Senate tried to avoid committing two magistrates in their actual year of office to this *provincia*. And so in perhaps 175, but certainly 174 and 173, a praetor of the year fought in Corsica while the commander of the previous year was prorogued for the island of Sardinia. This contrasts with the practice we have observed during crises in Sicily. That *provincia* was larger, richer, and generally had a higher administrative priority (it is always listed before Sardinia on official lists).

When C. Cicereius, an ex-scribe who was *pr.* 173, decisively ended the unrest on Corsica of the mid-170s, he did not even get a *supplicatio*. But that must have been largely because of his social, not his praetorian or "provincial," status. On his return, Cicereius probably surprised almost everyone by asking for a triumph. When refused, he celebrated one in its quasi-official form on the Alban Mount (much) later in the year, later commemorating it by dedicating a temple on the Alban hill. For an ex-*scriba*, an Alban triumph was a tremendous accomplishment. Indeed, Cicereius was the first (and probably the only) praetor to celebrate this ceremony: we hear of no Alban triumphs after 172. Though it had a distinguished enough pedigree, perhaps the honor was henceforth regarded as so devalued that no would-be *triumphator* considered it as an option. The *patres* may even have decided to put a stop to the practice, partly in the fear that more praetors would go that route to advance their careers (thus subverting the Senate's own authority over the triumph). If so, that would be another example of the Senate's encroachment—attested elsewhere for precisely this time—on the exercise of *imperium*.

Sardinia was declared consular—and entrusted to a single commander—several times in the final decades of our period (163, perhaps 162, and 126). L. Aurelius Orestes (*cos.* 126) spent five years in the *provincia*; there is no sign that he ever had a praetor under him. A bit later, M. Caecilius Metellus (*cos.* 115) served in Sardinia for four and a half years. The length of these Sardinian commands is quite striking, when one notes that other major wars of this general period usually received a regular succession of commanders. From all appearances, the Senate seems to have revived the old practice of the Second Punic War, of making Sardinia the *provincia* of first resort when it needed to make room in the praetorian sortition.

Addition of the Two Spanish Provinciae and Its Effects

We should now focus on Spain. To drive the Carthaginians out of Iberia and prevent its reoccupation, the Senate from 218 on sent out commanders in pairs. As we have seen, at first one and later (after 205 or 204) both these men were endowed with consular *imperium*. The *privatus* P. Scipio held the chief command from 210 down to 206; afterward, the Senate started to entrust the Iberian peninsula to two nonmagistrates. After the conclusion of the Hannibalic War, there must have been strong pressure to devise a more permanent arrangement for Spain. Despite the special grants of consular *imperium*, few men of talent could have been eager to take up an office which lay outside the recognized career path, and go to a distant territory for what often turned out to be quite a long amount of time. We know from Livy that since these men were not proper magistrates of the Roman state, the

Senate (initially) and then—when its resolve gave out—the tribunes tried to debar them from celebrating a triumph.

Those who did go to Spain tried to keep their options open: two different men tried to hold *in absentia* an aedileship in conjunction with their special Spanish commands. Perhaps they thought that holding this magistracy—any magistracy— might get them around the technical restrictions attached to *privati cum imperio* and help their claims to a triumph. From 197, the Senate decided to remove the need for such imaginative dodges and instead entrusted Spain to regular annual magistrates. It added Hispania Citerior and Ulterior to the traditional praetorian provinces of the urban and peregrine jurisdictions, Sicily and Sardinia; it also increased the number of praetors from four to six. The Senate no doubt had seen the necessity for this addition some time before, but the major war with the Macedonian king Philip that started in 200 delayed implementation of this decision.

Like their predecessors, the new praetors went to the Spains with enhanced (i.e., consular) *imperium* right from the start, a development which (as noted) would become applied elsewhere, and throughout the administrative system by the late Republic. It must be emphasized that the rank of *pro consule* had no great relevance to the size of the army these individuals commanded. There were only two legions (or fewer) between the two commanders in Spain in the period 205–188, and then again (probably) from 178 down to the mid-150s. Yet they always retained their enhanced *imperium*. Evidence from outside Spain confirms this finding.

The Spains provide the bulk of the praetorian ovations and triumphs in our period. We know of seven such triumphs and five ovations in the years 197 down to 122; elsewhere, in this same time span, we find attested five triumphs (all from eastern *provinciae*), one Alban triumph (from Sardinia), and one *ovatio* (from Sicily). Iberia was a dangerous theater, and the praetors for the Spains almost invariably fought under their own *auspicia* (only Hispania Citerior in 195 was a consular *provincia* in the period down through 154). It is also just possible that *nobiles* had a better chance of reaching the Spanish *provinciae* in time of war (see Appendix B.9), and thus a better chance of obtaining a triumph or ovation on their return. The Senate appears to have given out *ovationes* quite freely, as a compromise solution in problematic cases. The *pro cos.* L. Cornelius Lentulus (commander in Spain as a *privatus* in 205–200) had set the precedent in 200, followed by another *privatus* in 196. From that point on, when regular praetors from the Spains requested a triumph, they never came away empty-handed—so far as we can tell. Even the obscure M. Helvius (*pr.* 197) got an *ovatio* in 195, when grave doubts arose about his technical eligibility for a triumph. Some successful Spanish commanders do not seem to try for a triumph, if we are correctly informed; but in such cases they are all *nobiles*, who in any case made it to the consulship. For some, perhaps, it did not matter all that much.

Two new praetors for Spain allowed a new administrative attitude toward the city jurisdictions. As we have noted, once the total praetorian college is brought to six, the urban praetor is never again found far from the city on a mission in the period covered by the extant portions of Livy. As far as the peregrine praetor is concerned, he is sometimes sent outside of Rome, but usually on tasks of limited scope, and never as an annual commander in a territorial *provincia,* as in the Hannibalic period. At the time of the Senate's decision to annex the Spanish *provinciae* formally, it seems optimistically to have envisaged a system of annual succession of pairs of praetors. Of course, there were still major foreign wars and various crises in Italy and Gaul that required the presence of a praetor. Within a decade, it was only regular prorogation of the two Spanish praetors that enabled the new system to work: only once in the period 191–181 were the Spains allotted two years in a row (in 188, following the death of the *pr.* 189 for Ulterior).

Six praetors also had significant social and political effects, which (as we shall see below) are quite illuminating for the problem of the decline of the Republic. In the period after the Second Punic War, there was evidently a great deal of confusion as regards the order in which magistracies should be held: the debate on the Roman *cursus honorum,* or career path, spans the 190s and 180s. In 199, the candidacy of T. Quinctius Flamininus for the consulship met with a great deal of opposition by the tribunes, since he was seeking the office without having held the mid-level magistracies of the aedileship or praetorship. The Senate eventually ruled that he could seek the office. The nobles wanted fewer electoral rules, because that meant more opportunity for the use of personal prestige, influence, and wealth — and ultimately, a quicker climb to the top.

But after 196, and down to where Livy breaks off thirty years later, all the consuls except for one can be shown to be ex-praetors. And the exception shows us merely that dispensation was possible, for the right sort of person: namely, the great Scipio Africanus, consul 205 and consul for the second time in 194 — clearly a special case. Astin must be right: a new law came into effect ca. 196 that made the praetorship a prerequisite for consular candidacy.

Another major problem of this general period, beside the vagueness of the career path, was the rise of *ambitus,* "procuring election." The two issues soon became connected. The increase in the number of praetors, and the new stipulation that only ex-praetors could seek the consulship, meant that competition for the highest office soon became fierce. The Romans attempted to settle these issues once and for all with the introduction of two novel laws at the end of the 180s, which are products of the same process of discussion.

The year 181 saw the consul M. Baebius Tamphilus pass a *lex Baebia,* an anti-*ambitus* law that stipulated in one of its provisions that in alternate years, four and six praetors respectively be elected. Mommsen suggested that if there were fewer ex-praetors around, competition for the consulship — and thus bribery — would be less intense. Under the terms of the *lex Baebia,* praetors were sent to the Spains in only even-numbered years: 180, 178, and so on. The two Spains were left out of the sortition in odd-numbered years, when there were just four praetors to go around for six regular provinces. Commanders sent to the Iberian peninsula could thus expect a two-year tenure. Indeed, since 191 this pattern of prorogation had been the de facto situation in the Spains. But now, other *provinciae* could expect to feel the pinch.

It is important to note that at this time the Senate apparently felt the state's administrative needs could be met without routine recourse to special praetorian lots — despite the necessity to declare two such *provinciae* in the very year the

Baebian law was passed. The Senate must have envisaged sending out the *praetor inter peregrinos* (as they did in the Hannibalic era) to meet special administrative needs that might arise in the "Baebian" years. This is good (indirect) evidence that the peregrine praetor's presence in the city was still not regarded as absolutely essential.

Once the number of praetors was set for the moment (in effect, at an average of five per year), in 180 a second law, the *lex Villia Annalis*, was introduced. This law, which evidently kept the praetorship as a prerequisite for the consulship, also stipulated the minimum ages for candidacy for each magistracy. This would have the immediate effect of preventing younger candidates from swelling the ranks of hopefuls for the various curule offices. I also attempt to show from statistics (Appendix B.9) that the Romans made a conscious decision to allow less cheating in the praetorian sortition. In the years down to 180, men of consular and praetorian descent, and men who were elected in first or second place in their colleges, received the attractive urban jurisdiction and the rich *provincia* of Sicily a disproportionately large number of times. After 180, however, the allotment of at least the territorial *provinciae* becomes truly random.

But leaving that aside, the attested reforms of 181 and 180 did what they were supposed to do. Significantly more non-*nobiles* start reaching the praetorship. And ex-praetors, particularly plebeian ex-praetors, begin reaching the consulship at a more swift pace on the whole in the 170s, usually three years after their first praetorship. One perhaps unforeseen result of these new regulations is that in the 170s, a few ex-praetors of sometimes quite advanced age sought a second praetorship—one man twenty-four years after his first incumbency. He must have been looking for a consulship, which—thanks to a well-regulated career path—was easier to obtain than it had been before.

The *lex Baebia* is crucial for the administrative history of the Republic, since it marks the first institutional acceptance of routine prorogation. But the experiment of allotting the Spains only every other year soon floundered. By the mid-170s, six praetors are again being elected every year—over the elder Cato's objections, as we happen to know. He must have put a higher priority on the moral issue of controlled *ambitus* than on the issue of administrative convenience.

Three New Provinciae *between 146 and 122*

Given the nature of our sources, it is not entirely surprising that no ancient author mentions a crucial decision of 146. In that year, the date of the organization of Macedonia and Africa as praetorian provinces, it was decided not to increase the number of praetors. The immediate effect of the Senate's decision was that it became, for the first time since the partial repeal of the Baebian law, impossible for all the provinces to be governed by regular magistrates in their year of office: there were now eight praetorian provinces, counting the two city jurisdictions, but only six praetors. There was no option but to make into actual policy the regular prorogation of overseas governors. The institutional status of prorogation was never again questioned. The year 146, in effect, marked a new system of provincial administration.

The Romans must have been confident in their ability to get by on two consuls, six praetors, and frequent prorogation. In the years that immediately followed their big decision, the fact that hardly any praetors in office went to the Spains (precisely two in the period 145–133) also may have obscured the full consequences of their action. In 133, the Senate decided to acquiesce in the popular passage of a motion brought by Ti. Gracchus, to accept the bequest of Attalus III which left the Pergamene kingdom to Rome; this would soon be organized as the praetorian *provincia* of "Asia." We should note that no actual praetors set foot in this *provincia* until 126 or perhaps 125. The full effects of adding Asia (or, indeed, Macedonia and Africa) may not have been felt when, in 122, yet another *provincia* was created, this time in the city. In that year, C. Gracchus placed a praetor in charge of a permanent court to try cases of provincial extortion (*repetundae*).

The wealth of Attalus' kingdom made the annexation of "Asia" an almost irresistible temptation. We have also seen that, from the mid-180s through the mid-160s (where our detailed record breaks off), the Romans occasionally tried to make three praetors available for tasks near the city. The introduction in 149 of a standing criminal court to try cases of provincial extortion will quickly have given rise to more legal work (as Cicero tells us). However, both the new permanent *provinciae* "Asia" and *repetundarum* were difficult to administer. Asia, which was now the richest Roman *provincia*, virtually required annual sortition. The extortion court absolutely demanded it; as we have seen, one cannot properly prorogue a praetor to serve in a city jurisdiction. All this meant that praetors who received the older territorial *provinciae* could expect significantly longer tenures.

Even the city jurisdictions were affected. Now, occasionally in the "Livian" period, we find that a city praetor is prorogued, and sent *ex praetura* to a special command. This practice is not especially common. There are four known cases of such prorogation to hold a territorial *provincia* in the period down to 166: one peregrine praetor and three urban praetors, distributed quite evenly over the time of Hannibal's Italian campaign (but none later, before Livy fails us). As chance would have it, two instances of *ex praetura* commissions show up right after the big decision of 146. Scipio Aemilianus obtained an *extra ordinem* command in Hispania Citerior for his best friend C. Laelius (a praetor of 145) at the start of 144. In the very next year, the *pr. urb.* 144 Q. Marcius Rex—who had received as praetor a massive project of aqueduct repair and construction—was prorogued in a special *provincia* which allowed him access to the city without losing his *imperium* when crossing the *pomerium*. As noted, no praetors had to go to the Spains in the years 142 through 133, and so the Senate may have been able to place the *ex praetura* expedient on the back shelf. But it is not long after the institution of the *praetor repetundis* that we find a certain instance of an *ex praetura* command: C. Marius, a city praetor in 115 who was sent after his magistracy to hold a different *provincia*, namely, Hispania Ulterior in 114.

The remarkable thing, of course, is that the number of praetorships was not increased. The Senate evidently placed a premium on controlling competition for the consulship, and chose to neglect the rapidly accelerating erosion of a fundamental Republican constitutional principle—the annual magistracy—as well as to ignore the added inconveniences to commanders and possible danger to provincials.

Ti. and C. Gracchus certainly will have known the consequences of their actions on the imperial administrative system. In particular, C. Gracchus had first-hand experience of extended service in an overseas *provincia*, as a quaestor in Sardinia in 126–125; his old commanding officer, L. Aurelius Orestes (*cos.* 126), was still on the island—in his fourth year of *imperium*—even as the new *provincia repetundarum* was being created. The Gracchi brothers simply thought the benefits of their own programs outweighed the advantages of regular succession in the provinces. They could have claimed (and perhaps did have to claim) to be building on precedent, namely, the Senate's decisions of 181 and 146 to remove the numerical correlation of praetors and their *provinciae*.

Whatever the long-term implications of the addition of Asia and the extortion court as praetorian *provinciae*, by and large we can understand why (and, to a certain extent, how) the Gracchi did what they did. What is quite amazing is that, so soon after the introduction of the new system of 146, the Senate seems to have lost its will to control the number of *provinciae* and, with it, the length of provincial commands—a remarkable volte-face from its careful policy of the first half of the second century, when it carefully tried to limit the need for routine prorogation.

Addition of Further Provinciae *between 122 and 82*

Additional standing courts—modeled on C. Gracchus' extortion court—were established after 122 B.C., reaching at least four in number by the year 99 and totaling six by 82. By the start of the first century—perhaps with the introduction of the *quaestio de veneficiis*—a new quasi magistracy for aedilicians was invented, the *iudex quaestionis*. Here is another example of the "dodge." The *iudex* was given all the powers he needed to conduct a criminal trial, and magisterial attributes and *insignia* as well. But he was assigned only the less politically important courts, came under the supervision of the urban praetor, and—unlike an actual magistrate of the Roman People—potentially could be removed from his position and prosecuted during his term of presidency.

The institution of the *iudex quaestionis* gave some relief to the system. But the remaining standing courts (*repetundae, maiestas, ambitus,* and sometimes *peculatus*) were staffed by praetors, and—we can assume—had to be placed in the sortition each year. New standing territorial provinces also were instituted, with Cilicia ca. 100 and the two Gauls by the mid 90s. Nonetheless, the number of praetorships remained at six.

The addition of all those praetorian *provinciae*, with no corresponding increase in magistrates to staff them, suggests that, starting in the last third of the second century, the members of the Senate had lost serious interest in maintaining a workable administrative scheme for Rome's growing empire. By the nineties, the ratio of praetors to praetorian assignments became as skewed as 1:2. Yet it seems the Senate even in that decade gave Asia a succession of annual commanders. And ca. 87, under the Cinnan government, the Senate would have annexed Egypt had not a tribune (or tribunes) prevented it.

In the period 122–82 B.C., the Senate managed to cover its commitments by a number of methods. On the one hand, it seldom allowed praetors to hold special commands outside Italy. It did however use prorogation lavishly. For consuls, we find some significantly long commands—three (common), four, even five years, across the range of western and eastern provinces. That stands in real contrast to the policy of the earlier second century. Praetorian commands in the provinces could be lengthy as well, but none are known to total more than three years in the period down to 91. It clearly was undesirable to prorogue a praetor repeatedly: after a *biennium*, a praetorian commander was entitled to run for the consulship, and from that gain another provincial assignment, all the while free from prosecution by virtue of his magistracy.

Then, there is the device of *ex magistratu* commands, in which the Senate prorogued an individual city praetor and sent him overseas—with the possibility of still further prorogation once in place. We see at least four city praetors proceed to an eastern *provincia* in the four years 97–94. Sulla, who was urban praetor in 97 and sent as promagistrate to Cilicia and Cappadocia following his year of office, then had to stay in the east for quite a long time, perhaps four full years. Another one of these individuals—a *praetor urbanus* for 94—had to stay in his territorial province of Macedonia for at least six and a half years. And it is fairly probable that for the year 94 Asia saw an *ex consulatu* command. So even before the troubled decade 91–82, Rome's imperial system was trying to cope with considerable challenges.

One expedient the Senate did not really use in the period down to the outbreak of the Social War was extraordinary votes of *imperium* to nonmagistrates. There is just one probable instance recorded for the period 122–91—a grant to a senior consular to conduct a *quaestio* regarding charges of *incestum* in 113. The extreme crisis of the Social War changed all that: we find several popular grants of *imperium* for the field in the years 90 and 89. The emergency practices of this war surely helped change attitudes about the propriety of such extraordinary grants. As early as 88 B.C., the *privatus* Marius was elected to a special command to fight Mithridates VI that involved consular *imperium*; in late 82, Pompey was dispatched to Sicily with a special grant of praetorian *imperium*, surely through a *lex*. The 70s saw a number of such grants proposed or realized.

The administrative system received a serious jolt in the crisis years 91–87, when the Social War demanded the presence of praetors and capable *praetorii* for duties within the Italian peninsula. In those years sortition of the overseas *provinciae* must have been rare. At any rate, it is clear that a significant number of commanders (in Sicily, probably Sardinia, the Spains, Macedonia, Africa, and the Gauls) found themselves stranded. The Civil Wars only exacerbated the problems. Most notably, a *cos.* 93 became trapped in a command that ultimately was to involve both Spains and Transalpine Gaul down to the year 81. And the Marian Senate largely abandoned the serious administration of Sicily, Sardinia, and Africa.

By the time Sulla assumed the dictatorship in late 82 or early 81, basically every one of the territorial *provinciae*—then ten in number—was badly in need of a proper commander. But, in addition, there were (apparently) six permanent courts in the city (*repetundae, ambitus, maiestas, peculatus, de veneficiis,* and *inter sicarios*) that needed to be staffed.

Sulla's Reform of the Praetorship and Its Effects

Sulla, in his reforms, chose not to make cuts but rather to shore up the existing system by passing a measure that increased the number of praetors to eight. He meant for praetors to remain in Rome during their year of office (to tend to the city jurisdictions and the various standing courts, where *iudices quaestionis* would also lend a hand), and, on the expiration of their magistracy, to govern an overseas province with consular *imperium* "militiae." (For that last feature there is just one counterexample—Cn. Dolabella, *pr.* 81 and *pro pr.* for Cilicia in 80—but that apparently came about owing to Sulla's own personal pique.) Consuls could be dispatched to important provinces after their year of office to supplement the system. Rome now had notionally ten holders of *imperium* available each year, to match its ten regular territorial provinces.

An immediate effect of increasing the number of praetors was that it lessened the prestige of the office. That was not lost on the ancients: Velleius boasts that an ancestor saw two sons reach the magistracy "when six were still being elected." Other effects followed from the fact that, at all normal times, henceforth there would be at least one holder of *imperium maius* in the city.

Most importantly, the urban praetor was now effectively debarred from serving as Senate president. Nor did the urban praetor (who retained precedence among praetors) and his colleagues stand much of a chance of getting legislation passed if either consuls or tribunes were unwilling. True, we find at least one example of a praetorian law in the period before Sulla passed when a consul or consuls were presumably in the city (the *lex Porcia*, apparently of February 101). And there are some important praetorian laws that date to the post-Sullan era—most notably, the *lex Aurelia iudiciaria* passed toward the end of 70 B.C. Yet we happen to know that this particular measure required a fair bit of groundwork on the part of the promulgator, L. Aurelius Cotta (who was almost certainly not urban praetor).

In general, the ever-present prospect of interference by consuls or tribunes must have had a chilling effect on praetors who hoped to pass bolder initiatives into law. Ambitious praetors often chose to put their main political energy behind pending tribunician bills, probably because they had a greater chance of success. By the year 57 B.C., it appears that a praetor was capable of obnuntiating against a tribune at a plebeian legislative assembly. So by the late Republic, praetors had acquired at least in theory some degree of negative power over the main source of the state's legislation.

Indeed, both before and after Sulla, the disposition and availability of the sitting consuls was important in determining the workload of the individual praetors in a given year. When the consuls were unable or unwilling to see to a particular task, a praetor or praetors might be ordered to step in. For example, in 75 the *pr. urb.* C. Licinius Sacerdos and his praetorian colleague M. Caesius assisted the consuls of the year in the massive task of repairing temples in Rome; the next year, the urban praetor C. Verres and his colleague P. Coelius had to finish the task unaided. In 61, both consuls were available when P. Clodius was brought to trial in a special *quaestio* concerned with profanation of the Bona Dea ceremony, but apparently neither wanted the *invidia* that this trial of a powerful *nobilis* was bound to generate, whatever its outcome. So they let it devolve on a praetor, who had to take the task. Sometimes both the consuls and praetors stepped aside and let a tribune fill the resulting vacuum. In the year 123, apparently no consul or praetor wanted to take responsibility for a *senatus consultum* that overturned an action by a highborn praetorian commander for Spain; so the tribune C. Gracchus ended up convening at least one session of the Senate that dealt with this matter.

Starting in the early 90s, we see urban praetors offering progressively more extravagant Apolline Games: indeed, it was probably L. Cornelius Sulla in 97 who started the trend. The extravagance rose to unprecedented levels in the mid-60s — but it imparted to the office no corresponding increase in prestige. Not long after 78, one notes that the two senior praetors have dropped out of the dating formula in *senatus consulta*, and do not reappear in that context for the rest of the free Republic. The habit of granting consular and praetorian *ornamenta* (first securely attested for the early 60s) went some way toward cheapening the office further.

Then there was the danger factor. By putting so many magistrates in the city, Sulla heightened the danger of future conflict between consuls and praetors, between members of the same praetorian college, and between praetors and lower magistrates. What mitigated this decision is that the whole political system of the Republic was predicated on a basic understanding: its magistrates should restrain themselves from exercising their formidable powers to the fullest extent. That, indeed, most choose to do, to a remarkable degree, right down to the late 50s. The one outstanding exception is found for the year 95, when the consul Q. Mucius Scaevola vetoed the *senatus consultum* that granted his consular colleague L. Licinius Crassus a triumph for fighting some undistinguished tribes in Cisalpine Gaul.

Occasionally, we see consuls using their *maius imperium* against individual praetors. M. Aemilius Scaurus as *cos.* 115 by edict forbade anyone from approaching a certain city praetor to hear cases at law. In 91, the consul L. Marcius Philippus seems to have taken the step of forbidding any praetor from calling the Senate and putting proposals by the *tr. pl.* M. Livius Drusus to a vote. The consul Mam. Aemilius Lepidus in 77 is said to have "abrogated" the jurisdiction of a praetor who granted *possessio bonorum* to a eunuch; a *senatus consultum* followed that backed the consul's decision and (apparently) barred the eunuch from asking other praetors for relief. In late 57, the consul Q. Caecilius Metellus Nepos used his *maius imperium* against the urban praetor L. Caecilius Rufus to save P. Clodius (who was Nepos' half brother) from coming to trial *de vi*. However, on one occasion (the year 67), we find a remarkable show of praetorian solidarity in the face of a distinctly "uncollegial" show of consular power. When the *cos.* M.' Acilius Glabrio smashed a praetor's curule chair for not rising in his presence, this praetor (who demonstrably did not have the urban jurisdiction) and his praetorian colleagues thenceforth gave only judgments *de plano*.

For the later Republic, we do not have a single secure instance of a praetor in the city using his *imperium* to veto a colleague's actions, even in the realm of civil law. Litigants who did not like a praetor's actual decision customarily appealed to a tribune of the Plebs, sometimes a consul. When Cicero says the praetor Piso "intercessit" in Verres' civil law cases, he probably did nothing more than to accept the petitions his colleague had refused. That was indeed a provocative intervention, though Cicero in his description is disingenuous in making it sound like an actual veto. In cases where magistrates fail to show self-restraint, it is the Senate or tribunes which might step in, usually in a reactive way. That sometimes even gave rise to a law circumscribing such and such a behavior. (For a praetor to reverse the ruling of a predecessor was a different matter, and happened with relative frequency — but was still felt to be a blow to one's *dignitas*.)

So far, the evidence suggests that praetors in the city enjoyed no less civilized treatment after Sulla pushed through his reform than before his dictatorship. All the same, it is abundantly clear that the increase in number of praetors and the expectation that they stay in Rome made the city less, not more, safe. That comes across especially in the electoral *comitia*. Sulla surely knew that to introduce two new praetors at once, for a total of eight, would directly cause increased competition in the consular elections. That was the reason why the Senate had let the number of praetors stand at six for so long, and precisely a century earlier even tried reducing the number to four in alternate years. For Sulla suddenly to reduce the odds of a praetor eventually reaching the consulship from one in three to one in four was one of the high costs of his political settlement, only superficially mitigated by his concurrent introduction of new *ambitus* legislation.

An examination of individual careers reveals that Sulla's additions to the number of praetors and reform of the *cursus* created a "winner-takes-all" atmosphere at the curule elections. An ex-praetor had to win the consulship quickly or run a real risk of being shut out permanently. The frequently delayed and disrupted consular elections of the last generation of the Republic, and the steady stream of major *ambitus* laws (each with progressively sharper penalties) show well the now thoroughly overheated atmosphere. In the unusually long *interregnum* of 53 B.C., Dio Cassius tells us all the tribunes even suggested that instead of the election of consuls there should be a reinstitution of the consular tribunes (not seen since 367), "in order that there might be more magistrates."

The heightened intensity of the consular elections in this period seems to have impacted also the praetorian ones — somewhat paradoxically, since Sulla had expanded the college of praetors. The record suggests that ex-tribunes and (especially) ex-aediles had to advance to one of the eight places quickly or face the prospect of losing out altogether. References to prosecutions of praetorian candidates for *ambitus* are frequent enough, and disruptions at praetorian *comitia* could be quite violent (for example, those of 55 B.C.).

Sulla's scheme had another major built-in structural flaw. Oddly, Sulla allowed that an ex-consul or ex-praetor could refuse a territorial province after he had received it in the (requisite) promagisterial sortition. Sulla himself, as *cos.* II 80, drew but never took up Cisalpine Gaul *ex consulatu*, seemingly oblivious to the precedent he was setting. Many consuls and (at least starting in the early 60s) praetors later seem to have followed his lead. By way of example, just two of the consuls of the years 63 through 59 can positively be shown to have reached a territorial *provincia* in the year following their consulship. Indeed, so many individuals in the last two decades of the Republic declined a command that Pompey, as *cos.* III in 52, introduced a new system of administration that (apparently) was meant to run for five years just on the strength of those men. He also made the acceptance of a province (after an interval) mandatory for ex-consuls and ex-praetors.

Post-Sullan Additions and Reforms

One outcome of Sulla's reforms is that they spurred yet another round of expansionism (remember the years following 146 B.C.) by the Senate. Soon after the repairs of 81 to the administrative system, the Senate took on new responsibilities but did not increase the number of higher magistrates. In Rome, it allowed the formation of three new standing courts, namely, a *quaestio de vi* (perhaps as early as 78 but certainly by 63), that of the *lex Papia* (65) on claims to citizenship, and another *quaestio* established by the *lex Licinia* (55) on electoral associations (*sodalitates*). Praetors (as well as *iudices quaestionis*) are attested as presidents for the first two of these courts; for the *quaestio de sodaliciis* we find only praetors. By 62 B.C., the Senate also had added four new territorial *provinciae* that required someone with *imperium*. There is Bithynia/Pontus (organization begun in 74, with the first regular commander taking it up for 61 or 60), Crete (annexed and organized 68–65), Cyrene (a Roman province by 63), and finally Syria (annexed and organized in the years 66–62, and placed in the praetorian sortition for 61).

Yet the Senate in our period went no further than fourteen regular territorial *provinciae*. True, in 58 B.C., the Senate annexed wealthy Cyprus; but from the start it planned that the island be attached to the preexisting province of Cilicia. Though the notion of annexing Egypt had some prominent advocates and a good measure of popular support, it never was allowed to come to pass in this era.

From time to time, we see politicians float various schemes to extend *imperium* past its traditional limits. These seem more like attempts to provoke than genuine reforms. Cicero in 63 implies that Rullus wanted to give his agrarian commission *imperium* both *domi* and *militiae* for five years. At the very beginning of the next year the tribune Q. Metellus Nepos promulgated a bill to allow the *pro consule* Pompey to retain his military *imperium* within the *pomerium* to deal with the Catilinarians. In 57, a tribune proposed that Pompey as grain commissioner hold *imperium* in the provinces which was *maius* against that of their regular governors. To these examples we can add also that tribunician proposal of 53 on the reinstitution of the consular tribunes, "in order that there might be more magistrates."

For genuine attempts at reform, we have to wait almost until the very end of our period. The consuls of 53 set about to remove the protection from prosecution (and opportunity for immediate enrichment) that a promagisterial command had always afforded; they procured a *senatus consultum* that mandated an interval between magistracy and promagistracy for ex-consuls and ex-praetors. It was Pompey who, as *cos*. III 52, implemented that reform. He also got rid of the Sullan loophole that allowed the refusal of consular and praetorian *provinciae*, and scrapped the system of sending both ex-consuls and ex-praetors to territorial provinces with enhanced (i.e., consular) *imperium*. Rather, Pompey made praetorian *imperium* the standard grade for provincial governors. Under his scheme, only ex-consuls were to receive consular *imperium*; ex-praetors got praetorian.

The Sullan System in Practice I

How did the Senate manage to staff this ever-growing system? First, it counted on the innate flexibility of praetors and their *provinciae* in the city. All praetors could hear cases at law—evidently regardless of the citizen status of the litigants—using or (if necessary) adapting existing civil law procedures. There is no reason not to think that, in a pinch, any praetor could fill in for another in a criminal court. For a good demonstration of this "collegial" aspect of the praetorship, note the provision of the *lex Plautia Papiria* (88 B.C.) that a *professio* for citizenship could be made before any praetor.

The Senate did set limits on special *quaestiones* in the city which might require a praetor as president. We know of only two such trials (the *incestum* processes of 73 and 61) down to 52 B.C., a year when Pompey as *cos.* III set up extraordinary courts for *vis* and *ambitus*. Combination of city *provinciae* also helped: we find that for the urban and peregrine jurisdictions as early as 78.

Certainly by the 50s, individual members of a praetorian college are routinely found taking on duties that went beyond their proper city *provinciae*. Consider, for instance, obligations in hearing civil law cases. It seems to have been somewhat common in this era for a petitioner who had been rebuffed at one praetor's tribunal to try his luck at another's; we have notices to that effect for the years 77 and 74. (That in turn is another proof that the urban praetor did not monopolize civil jurisdiction.) Furthermore, for certain years we have chance notices that more than one praetor was hearing cases *de repetundis* (59), *de ambitus* (59), or *de sodaliciis* (54). In that same decade, praetors who had a criminal *quaestio* as their *provincia* sometimes show up as jurors in other standing courts. They are also attested in the civil law sphere; meanwhile, praetors in the "civil" jurisdictions saw to some criminal trials that fell outside the scope of the permanent *quaestiones*. The institution of the *iudex quaestionis* also might have seen an expansion over time in the post-Sullan period: three are attested in just the court *inter sicarios* and *de veneficiis* for 66.

Sulla himself retained the use of commands *in magistratu*. For praetors, the years 81 and 80 alone saw perhaps a half a dozen uses of this expedient, and many more were to follow in the 70s (particularly in the war against Spartacus) and 60s (to guard the coast of Italy against pirates in the early 60s, in the Catilinarian crisis of 63, and against Catiline's alleged sympathizers in 62). For one praetor of 63, Cicero as consul saw to the passage of a *senatus consultum* that led to a bundle of special powers, including enhanced *imperium*, which Cicero implies was a rare distinction for a sitting magistrate. However, no more than two city praetors are found operating outside Rome in any given year of the post-Sullan period; and that may have been deliberate policy. In addition, ex-magistrates might be diverted from their proper *provinciae* in an emergency (as in the *Bellum Lepidanum*), or put to work while in transit to or from their territorial provinces. And we do have a few examples of a permanent lateral transfer of a commander from one *provincia* to another: a *pr.* 79 who moves from Gallia Transalpina to Hispania Citerior, a *pr.* 59 transferred from Asia to Cilicia.

For Italy, in time the Senate even put to work commanders *cum imperio* waiting outside the city for the vote of a triumph. In truth, by the 60s and 50s, triumphs were getting very troublesome to obtain. Here some background will be helpful. In our (admittedly defective) record there is no *imperator* who returned to Rome from the time of Sulla's dictatorship down into the mid-60s known to have entered the city without an *ovatio* or triumph. But after ca. 66 down to the end of our period, the only commander known to have triumphed without obstruction was Pompey from his great eastern command, in 61. Some of the hopeful *imperatores* had to wait for periods that might stretch to five years, while others just gave up. It would be useful to know to what extent the Senate exploited this odd situation and gave these vulnerable commanders chores in Italy. Certainly at the beginning of 49, the Senate takes for granted the service of those *cum imperio* outside the city in the impending conflict with Caesar, even for posting overseas.

But these expedients are overshadowed by three others—the increased use of *legati*, special commands to *privati*, and softening attitudes toward repeated prorogation. On more than a few occasions in the post-Sullan period, we see quaestors or *legati* having to hold down major provinces for considerable stretches of time (up to a year or even more) after the departure or death of a commander. We find this particularly for the Spains at the start of and then following the Sertorian War. Some holders of *imperium* even use *legati* to command a province wholly in absence while in Rome: we see this for the *cos.* 67 C. Calpurnius Piso and Transalpine Gaul, and for the *cos.* II 55 Cn. Pompeius and the two Spains. There may have been an old precedent for this—a praetor of 167 for Sardinia detained for special tasks in the city—but if so, there is little trace of its use in the century that followed.

In the post-Sullan era, the Senate freely allowed the creation of special commands for *privati* and sub-praetorians, even for territorial *provinciae*. Here Pompey takes the prize. With the Senate's approval, in 77 he received consular *imperium* for Hispania Citerior, which he retained until triumphing in late 71. Soon Pompey gained a commission in 67 against the pirates, and then another in 66 (yet mooted as early as 74) to fight Mithridates, over whom he triumphed in 61. In early 60, a *senatus consultum* seems to have empowered ex-consuls to put down a Gallic *tumultus*. There were special grants also for positions in Rome. In 52, Pompey as consul secured *imperium* for at least two nonmagistrates—a consular and a very senior praetorian—to preside over special *quaestiones* for *ambitus* and *vis* in the city—despite the fact that regular courts for these crimes existed and were running.

We find also in some years the phenomenon of "negative" commands. Now, sometimes a *provincia* was made praetorian to keep it away from a dangerous consular. For instance, in 61, Cicero and others had legitimate fears as to what Pompey's protégé, the *cos.* M. Pupius Piso, might get up to if he had Syria as a military arena, and they brought it about that the *provincia* be declared praetorian instead. (The same fears obtained when the *cos.* 58 A. Gabinius wanted the *provincia* for 57, but he could not be stopped.)

This principle could be extended downwards. Sometimes the Senate skipped over the consuls and praetors and used a subpraetorian—or even a junior *privatus*—for an important task, with a special grant of *imperium* to match. The idea was to avoid the the risk of a highranking magistrate exploiting a certain position for his own material and political benefit. We see that ploy used for a money-collecting expedition to Cyrene in 75 and for the annexation of Cyprus in 58. A similar scheme was mooted in 65 for the annexation of Egypt.

Interference by special commanders in overseas praetorian *provinciae* was in fact a hallmark of the age. The trend starts with the special *provincia* of M. Antonius in 74 and continues through Pompey's extraordinary commands of 67 and 66 under the Gabinian and Manilian laws. In 65, the Senate dispatched Cn. Calpurnius Piso as a *quaestor pro praetore* to Hispania Citerior. The land bill the *tr. pl.* P. Servilius Rullus tried to pass at the start of 63 is another example of this phenomenon. In 57, when Pompey received a special grain command *pro consule* for five years, he was voted the right also to appoint (at least) fifteen senatorial *legati* to help him in his task, to be distributed throughout the Mediterranean.

But eventually, there was a backlash against extraordinary commands in general. When faced with a Parthian crisis in the fall of 51, the Senate entertained a range of military solutions—but no one advocated sending a *privatus* to do the job, and that despite the reluctance of the consuls of the year to fight this dangerous enemy.

Then there is prorogation. After Sulla, with ten regular territorial *provinciae* and (in theory) two ex-consuls and eight ex-praetors available for dispatch, one would expect short commands (one, occasionally two years) to be the norm. The reality is that multi-year commands that surpass even those of the period 123–91 B.C. appear immediately in the 70s. Ex-consuls and the *privatus cum imperio* Cn. Pompeius in his various commissions (77–71 in Hispania Citerior, 67 against the pirates, and 66–62 in the east) are responsible for the longest tenures, that is, five years and up, mostly in the context of major wars. Yet the Senate allowed repeated prorogation in other situations: a consular commander for Cilicia who fought from 78 to 74, and a praetorian commander (L. Afranius, apparently *pr.* by 76) for Hispania Citerior prorogued perhaps eight or even more years, maybe eventually with responsibilities also in Gallia Transalpina. We have a good number of secure instances of tenures of three (especially) or four years of a wide range of provinces. Praetors account for all but six of the sixteen certain or probable cases of these medium-to-long commands—another marked departure from the practice of the period down to 91 B.C.

The Senate's handling of each territorial commitment varied in the late Republic. But it is remarkable to see how few territorial *provinciae* show evidence of a sustained policy of annual succession. In the case of Sicily we find one-year commands for the years 80, 77 and 74, but none beyond—despite Rome's experience of Verres and the general political importance of the island as a grain exporter to Rome. There are one-year commands attested for Hispania Citerior for 78 and 59, and Ulterior for 80 and then 62–61. But most of those seem due to exceptional circumstances (military defeats in 80 and 78, premature departures in 61 and 59). For Africa, Cilicia, and Gallia Transalpina, no commands of a single year are securely attested from 80 to 52. Gallia Cisalpina had an ex-consul hold it for one year in 74; other known commanders were prorogued. Asia is the only *provincia* that escapes routine prorogation: we find one year commands in all or all but one of the years 66–62, then 57–56. However, for the mid-50s we can detect an attempt to tighten up the system as a whole (see below).

It is not long after Sulla's dictatorship that the Senate starts positively guaranteeing multi-year commands to certain individuals. Starting with the *lex Gabinia* of 67 that gave the *privatus* Pompey a command for three years against the pirates, we occasionally find tenure of a certain commission or *provincia* guaranteed for stretches of more than one year. One remembers the commissions of *IIIviri* with *imperium* for three years active in south Italy in the 190s. But it was a different matter to allow actual magistrates of the Roman People fixed multi-year commands *ex consulatu*, that is, to hold regular provinces that were merely troubled. Starting in the 50s, we see consular *imperium* handed out in five-year stretches to Caesar, Pompey, and Crassus. The most unusual of these multi-year grants was the Spanish command Pompey received as *cos.* II 55—since he did not like the notion of actually going to Iberia. "His plan," says Dio, "was to let *legati* subdue Spain while he took in own hands affairs of Rome and Italy." And that is what he did, allowing two senior legates to hold Spain down through 49 B.C.

Delegated Authority in the Later Republic

In truth, the idea of a commander holding a province *in absentia* was not quite new. More than a century earlier, as we have seen, a praetor of 167 may have done the same thing for Sardinia. C. Valerius Flaccus (*cos.* 93) must have allowed his subordinates a good deal of independence during his long tenure (a dozen or more years) in the two Spains and Gaul, as we know some other commanders did who held "tandem" provinces such as his. C. Calpurnius Piso exercised control over Transalpine Gaul even as *cos.* 67 in Rome. In sum, Pompey's notion to govern the Spanish *provinciae* through two senior *legati* strikes one merely as an exploitation of a variety of preexisiting administrative precedents.

One can readily understand the general appeal of *legati* to a Roman commander. Even if a legate does all the work for a major victory, his superior gets the imperatorial acclamation. Pompey had a long history of letting *legati* do a good part of the campaigning in his ambitious commands. The commission in 67 B.C. against the pirates is just the most outstanding example. There, he secured *imperium* for each of a large number of legates (here again, some quite senior in status) and then set them up in independent quasi-*provinciae*. The campaign against Mithridates that followed provides more instances of Pompey's subordinates seeing to some unusually substantial chores. In this, he had plenty of precedents, and there is no shortage of subsequent examples, too. Yet it was Pompey's command in Spain in the second half of the 50s that was the pathbreaking one, and the clear source for the system of *legati Augusti pro praetore* under the Empire.

Delegation is one area where over time we can detect a definite broadening of the powers of a magistrate in his *provincia*. By the last third of the second century, it is clear that a consular commander could delegate *imperium* to a subordinate while himself remaining in his military *provincia*. When we get to the point where it is accepted that a commander does not have to step foot in his *provincia* to exercise authority in it, we are getting quite far away from the original conception of the term.

A surprising thing happens after Pompey in 52 modified Sulla's system by completely divorcing the magistracy from the promagistracy and then restoring praetorian *imperium* as the standard grade for praetorian governors. We now find for the first time men who are *pro praetore* delegating *imperium* at their own level. In the late Republic, no one seems to have been able to explain adequately why a praetor could not hold praetorian elections. So perhaps the augurs did not bother to object to this aspect of Pompey's reform. There was a certain logic to it, after all. If a consul could personally give out *imperium* in his *provincia*, why not a praetor who had consular *imperium*? And if a praetor *pro consule* was entitled to do so, why not a praetor—or rather (under Pompey's system) an ex-praetor who was *pro praetore*? (Caesar took Pompey's measure one big step further, by letting two *legati pro praetore* actually celebrate triumphs in the year 45.)

Once a *pro praetore* starts delegating his official power, we are far away from the idea that *imperium* was the full power of the old kings of Rome. The invention of *minus imperium* in the fourth century—followed later by innovations such as prorogation, grants of *imperium* to nonmagistrates, "enhanced" *imperium* for praetors, and the like—made possible Rome's Republican empire. But these circumventions had their own built-in contradictions. Again, rather than think too hard about these paradoxes, the Romans exploited them, particularly so in the last generation of the Republic.

The Sullan System in Practice II

From the Senate's perspective, combination of *provinciae*—especially when combined with prorogation—turns out to be the most important way to make ends meet. Once P. Scipio Aemilianus had taken Numantia in 133, over the next few decades the Romans at times may have felt confident enough to combine the two Spains. Indeed, it is just possible that a *legatus* was the sole commander of Hispania Citerior (so Appian implies) in some or all of the years 105–101 B.C. C. Valerius Flaccus (*cos.* 93) held the two Spains as a combined *provincia* for many years (see above). And C. Annius, as *pr.* 81 a member of the first "Sullan" praetorian college, certainly had charge of both Spanish provinces (in his case for one year only). However, we do not see the Spains combined again into a single *provincia* until the unusual command of Pompey as *cos.* II 55, who governed both Citerior and Ulterior through legates.

In the post-Sullan era, the Senate most readily made the two Gauls into a joint *provincia*. For praetors, more exotic combinations are hard to find, though it is possible the praetorian commander L. Afranius combined Hispania Citerior with Transalpine Gaul at some point in the years 71–68. Consular commanders were given more expansive possibilities. L. Licinius Lucullus (*cos.* 74, then *pro cos.* into 67) against Mithridates at one point had Asia, Cilicia, and Bithynia/Pontus as a joint *provincia*. So did Cn. Pompeius as a *privatus* with consular *imperium* in the years 66–62; remember also his later tenure of the two Spains. C. Caesar had the two Gauls with Illyricum from 58 to 50. These three men served as the functional equivalent of dozens of individual annual commanders.

Extended multiprovince commands certainly offered the Senate a measure of administrative convenience. One of their many troubles, however, is the illusion they gave of efficacy in the larger system. Perhaps that helps explain why Rome in the 60s alone confidently annexed Crete, Cyrene, and Syria. Conversely, when no megacommands were in progress—as in the years 61–59—we see praetors in widely disparate provinces (even Asia) having to serve long terms.

In the years 58–55 the Senate does seem to have aimed at regular succession across the system (so the evidence for Sardinia, Macedonia, and Bithynia/Pontus suggests). But the policy proved impracticable to maintain. We find long commands for Cilicia (two ex-consuls covering the years 56–51) and Asia (where an ex-praetor remained for the years 55–53); Syria was without *imperium* from the latter half of 53 down through most of 51.

Pompey in his reforms as *cos.* III 52 (most importantly, a statutory minimum interval between magistracy and promagistracy) clearly wanted to restore short commands for Rome's provinces. Yet even his scheme implied routine prorogation: the number of magistrates with *imperium* available each year theoretically stood at ten (in practice slightly less), while the total of territorial *provinciae* to be staffed remained at fourteen.

So despite Sulla's far-reaching reforms, signs of stress appear almost immediately in the Roman administrative system, already in the early 70s. By the mid-50s the entire system was again in danger (both from a domestic and provincial perspective), which prompted reforms by the Senate and Pompey in 53–52. In short, the new total of eight praetors—which resulted in increased competition for the consulship, bringing all sorts of concomitant ills (e.g., vastly increased electoral bribery and provincial extortion)—turned out to be an important factor in the dissolution of the Republican political system.

Without going further into the symptoms of the decline of the Republic, I will emphasize that there were men in the mid-second century who could foresee the problems connected with the rise in the number of praetors. The *cos.* 181 M. Baebius Tamphilus, Cato the censorian, and the unnamed magistrates and senators who in 146 brought about the decision not to increase the number of praetors: each had a firm grasp of the social realities of excessive electoral competition at the top. Questions of city and provincial administration aside, the Roman political system could barely tolerate six praetors elected each year. Here is where the radical tribunician proposal of 53 B.C. fits in, that there should be a reinstitution of the consular tribunate. The aim was to remove the bottleneck caused by eight praetors, but only two consuls. Soon after this, Caesar, as dictator, indeed did take steps to increase the number of magistrates—measures that Augustus later made redundant by his reform of the whole system.

Additional Notes

I. *Personal Delegation of* Imperium *in the Period 218–166*

There are four known examples of a consul delegating praetorian *imperium* to a nonmagistrate in the Second Punic War (the earliest period of Roman history for which we have a fully documented and reliable record), the first occurring in 217. In that year, the consul Cn. Servilius Geminus appointed a C. Centenius *pro praetore* in the field to bring a detachment of cavalry to his consular colleague C. Flaminius; Hannibal, however, met and destroyed this man and his force. (On Centenius, see Plb. 3.86.3; Liv. 22.8.1 *pro pr.* ; Zonar. 8.25.9 στρατηγός. App. *Hann.* 9.37 makes him a *privatus*. The grant of *imperium* has been questioned, yet without good reason—see below.)

In the following year, Cn. Servilius Geminus and M. Atilius Regulus, *coss.* 217, remained in command of an army after their term of office had expired. Throughout the spring and early summer of 216, the two ex-consuls were based in Apulia, where they kept an eye on Hannibal. What was their status? Livy (22.34.1) tells us that at the end of 217 "consulibus prorogatum in annum imperium." Polybius (3.106.2) is more detailed: προχειρισθέντες ὑπὸ τῶν περὶ τὸν Αἰμίλιον [i.e., L. Aemilius Paullus, *cos.* 216] ἀντιστράτηγοι καὶ παραλαβόντες τὴν ἐν τοῖς ὑπαίθροις ἐξουσίαν ἐχείριζον κατὰ τὴν ἑαυτῶν γνώμην τὰ κατὰ τὰς δυνάμεις ("They were made *pro prr.* by Aemilius, and, taking command in the field, directed the operations of their forces as they saw fit"). Here οἱ περὶ τὸν Αἰμίλιον is simply a periphrasis for Aemilius himself (cf. *LSJ* s.v. περί C.1.2), as is clear from what immediately follows in 3.106.3, cf. 4. In the other three occurrences of the term ἀντιστράτηγος in this author, it means *pro pr.* at 8.3.1 and 15.4.1, and *pro cos.* at 28.3.1. However, this last passage, from the Constantinian excerpt *De Legat. Gent.*, uses both ἀντιστράτηγος and ἀνθύπατος to describe the status of A. Hostilius Mancinus, *cos.* 170 and *pro cos.* 169 (Plb. 28.3.1 and 5.6; cf. Liv. 43.17.9); F. W. Walbank (*Commentary* III 329) makes a plausible case that the title ἀντιστράτηγος is not the epitomator's wording, but Polybius' own. Nevertheless, Walbank (*Commentary* I 435; cf. II 444) unhesitatingly takes our passage (3.106.2) to mean "the consuls of 217 were appointed proconsuls," and so coordinates it to Livy's notice, thus following the majority view of their status in 216 (see B. Schleussner, *WJA* 4 [1978] 221 n. 27, with earlier bibliography). This cannot be right. The mention of L. Aemilius Paullus appointing these men to their positions (which Walbank ignores) naturally suggests personal delegation of praetorian *imperium*—the only level at which a consul was qualified to make such a grant (see 2.1.2 above). What is more, Polybius (3.106.2–5) shows that the new *pro prr.* were under the consuls' orders. L. Aemilius Paullus is said to have ordered Cn. Servilius to avoid general engagements and to stick to skirmishing, in order to train his inexperienced recruits. We should conclude from Polybius' detailed notice that Livy misreports the nature of the prorogation for the *coss.* 217.

The third example is Q. Pleminius, appointed *pro pr.* in charge of the garrison at Rhegium and then Locri in 205 by the consul P. Cornelius Scipio (Africanus) (Liv. 29.6.9, with 6.1.3 above). (It is possible also that the consul's brother L. Cornelius Scipio received delegated *imperium* that same year to hold Messana— and the Roman forces there—while Publius was away aiding Q. Pleminius at Locri: cf. Liv. 29.7.2.) The last securely recorded instance in this period is L. Baebius, who in 203 was left ἀντιστράτηγος in charge of the Roman camp in Africa by P. Scipio, now *pro cos.* (Plb. 15.4.1).

Mommsen (*St.-R.* I³ 678–685, esp. 678 n. 1; 681 n. 4) refused to believe that a *privatus* who received delegated *imperium* could exercise that command if his superior was also in the field (see further below; cf. ch. 14 n. 126). On this basis, Mommsen reckoned that C. Centenius must have received a special grant of *imperium* from the *pr. urb.* of 217. B. Schleussner (*WJA* 4 [1978] 218–219, strongly supporting Mommsen's view of delegation in the field) went one step further, and altogether dismissed the notices of Centenius' status as a holder of praetorian *imperium*. (On the other hand, W. Kunkel in *Staatsordnung* 285 posited that Centenius already had *imperium* before his special commission—but that only begs the question.) Mommsen (*St.-R.* I³ 678 n. 1 and 681 n. 4) also proposed that Cn. Servilius Geminus and M. Atilius Regulus in 216, and L. Baebius in 203, were only *legati*. A. Giovannini (*Consulare Imperium* 62 n. 14) follows Mommsen's general view, and regards both *coss.* 217 as *legati* in 216.

As for the case of the two consuls of 217, here, surely, actual grants of *imperium* must be meant, as Polybius makes clear in his use of the term ἀντιστράτηγοι, and his explicit description of their competence. Most probably the Senate wanted to make sure their commands were subordinated to the consuls of the year. As *pro coss.*, holding *imperium consulare militiae*, they probably would not be technically subordinate, or might not think so. C. Centenius and L. Baebius do not raise any real difficulty. Their cases are confirmed by the similar command of Q. Pleminius (not mentioned by Mommsen in his discussion of "Stellvertretung"), as well as some certain second century examples, discussed in 9.4.4.

We cannot tell whether delegation of *imperium* to a nonmagistrate by a consul was permissible when both were in the city. It would be useful to know whether the consul P. Aelius Paetus in 201 secured a *lex de imperio* for M. Valerius Laevinus before he set off to Greece (in early consular 200), or delegated praetorian *imperium* to him (Liv. 31.3.2). Mommsen (*St.-R.* I³ 681 n. 1) seems to have envisaged delegation in this case; below I argue that the passage of a *lex de imperio* in this case is more likely.

Let us now move to another thorny problem having to do with delegation. It has long been an article of faith among scholars that the urban praetor—like the consuls—was able to delegate his *imperium*. Mommsen (*St.-R.* I³ 681f, also II³ 652 n. 2) firmly held held that belief; for later adherents to this notion see, for example, W. F. Jashemski, *Origins* 37–39; H. Kloft, *Prorogation* 58 n. 48; A. Keaveney, *Rome and the Unification of Italy* (London 1987) 134; J. S. Richardson, *JRS* 81 (1991) 3; cf. I. Buti, *Index* 19 (1991) 254 (all holders of *imperium* can delegate it).

Mommsen stated the general underlying principle: "[F]requently a command outside the city which has fallen vacant is entrusted to the urban praetor, only so that he—as a commander in chief who is necessarily retained in Rome—might exercise it through a representative ('Stellvertreter')" (*St.-R.* I³ 681f). This in itself might be believed, but it does not follow that the "Stellvertreter" would have *imperium*. I have argued (especially in 2.1.2, and also above) that a consul could not delegate *imperium* at his own level, namely, consular *imperium*; so it would be most surprising if the *pr. urb.* could delegate praetorian *imperium*. Mommsen adduced four passages to support his thesis, to which we shall now turn.

T. Manlius Torquatus in 215   When the praetor for Sardinia, Q. Mucius Scaevola, had fallen ill, "the Senate decreed that Q. Fulvius Flaccus [*pr. urb.* 215] . . . should enlist . . . and see to the transport of a legion to Sardinia at the first available opportunity, and he should send whomever he thought best *cum imperio* to carry on the war until Mucius should recover (*ut . . . mitteret . . . cum imperio quem ipsi videretur, qui rem gereret quoad Mucius convaluisset*)" (Liv. 23.34.13–14). It is difficult to tell from Livy what the actual procedure was by which *imperium* was conferred in this instance. Here the praetor may merely be making a nonbinding designation for the *comitia* formally to appoint. The choice of the *pr. urb.*, T. Manlius Torquatus (*cos.* 235, II 224), received praetorian *imperium*: Livy later (23.40.1) actually calls him *praetor*. After delivering Sardinia from a military emergency, Manlius returned to Rome: "He reported to the Senate that Sardinia was completely subjugated, and turned over the tribute to the quaestors, the grain to the aediles, the captives to the *pr.* Q. Fulvius" (23.41.7). Mommsen sees a legal reason for this last item: Manlius hands the prisoners—namely, the noble Carthaginian officers (cf. 23.41.2)—to Q. Fulvius because he had fought under the urban praetor's *auspicia*. This is not a possible explanation (thus rightly Kunkel, *Staatsordnung* 19 n. 48). T. Manlius Torquatus, on his return, reported directly to the Senate, not to "his superior"; and he clearly delivered each part of what he had brought back to the competent magistrates—again, not everything to "his superior." The urban praetor, as the chief magistrate with *imperium* in Rome in the absence of the consuls, regularly saw (e.g.) to the incarceration of important or dangerous prisoners, just as quaestors looked after money and aediles looked after imported wheat. For this function of the *pr. urb.* see 39.41.7 (184) and 45.42.4–5 (167); cf. ch. 9 n. 36.

M. Valerius Laevinus in 205   "The task was assigned [sc. by the Senate] to the *pr.* [*urb.*] Cn. Servilius [Caepio], if he thought it to the advantage of the state, to order the two urban legions to be brought up from the city, having given *imperium* to whomever he saw fit (*duas urbanas legiones imperio cui videretur dato ex urbe duci iuberet*). M. Valerius Laevinus [*cos.* 220, II 210] led these legions to Arretium" (Liv. 28.46.13). "Imperio . . . dato" seems to show that Livy shared Mommsen's view, that *imperium* was conferred by personal delegation: it also implies that Livy thought this to be the case in the first passage cited above. By now, we have often seen how indifferent Livy is to details of procedure (see in general 1.2.1 above). Here we may have a compressed notice of what actually was a four-part process. First, the decision of the Senate to entrust to the *pr. urb.* the matter of choosing a commander to bring the legions to Arretium; second, the choice of M. Valerius Laevinus by the *pr. urb.*; third, the granting of *imperium* to Laevinus in some unspecified way; and fourth, the orders of the *pr. urb.* to Laevinus.

L. Oppius Salinator in 192   "The Senate . . . decreed . . . that M. Fulvius [Centumalus] the praetor [*urbanus*] should send a fleet of twenty ships to defend the coast of Sicily and that he who led this fleet should be *cum imperio*—L. Oppius Salinator led it, who had been plebeian aedile the previous year" (Liv. 35.23.4 and 6–7). This short notice seems even more compressed: it contains the decision of the Senate that a fleet be prepared, the order to the *pr. urb.* that he fit out these ships (a common task for the city praetors, on which see Additional Note VI), and that the *pr. urb.* also choose a commander who would have *imperium*. How he would have it, we are not told: there is no implication in this passage of a delegation of *imperium*.

Tribuni militum in 171?   "The task was given to the praetor [*urbanus*] C. Sulpicius Galba of levying four city legions . . . and of choosing from the Senate four military tribunes to lead them (*ut . . . iis* [sc. *legionibus*] . . . *quattuor tribunos militum ex senatu legeret, qui praeessent*)" (Liv. 42.35.4). There is no explicit mention of a grant of *imperium* in this item; these men may simply have been military tribunes with special powers *ex S.C.* Cf. Liv. 41.5.8, the dispatch of the *tr. mil.* C. Cassius (surely Longinus, *cos.* 171) to lead a legion to Ariminum in 178 (see Additional Note IX). There, too, we get no mention of a grant of *imperium*.

From these four examples Mommsen (*St.-R.* I 681 n. 6; II 652 n. 2) surmised that five other examples of "delegation" by the *pr. urb.* may be alluded to in Livy. Mommsen's examples are worth citing here.

T. Otacilius Crassus in 215   Livy states that, after T. Otacilius Crassus (*pr.* 217 and *pro pr.* 216) dedicated a temple to Mens on the Capitolium, "he was sent to Sicily with *imperium* to command the fleet" ("in Siciliam cum imperio qui classi praeesset missus") (Liv. 23.32.20). This should not describe prorogation, but rather his dispatch as a *privatus cum imperio* (see 6.1.2 above). T. Otacilius Crassus is nonetheless described as *praetor* (Liv. 23.41.8), just like the *privatus* T. Manlius Torquatus in that same year (see above). But as in the case of T. Manlius, it is by no means clear what the method of appointment was.

M. Centenius Paenula in 212   The centurion M. Centenius Paenula, "having completed his military service, was brought into the Senate by the *pr.* P. Cornelius Sulla and asked the Senate to give him five thousand soldiers. . . . Eight thousand soldiers were given to him, half of them citizens, half allies" (Liv. 25.19.10 and 13). It is unlikely that M. Centenius received *imperium* as well: he is called only "dux" by Livy. Centenius did not ask for *imperium*. If he had in fact received *imperium*, Livy is likely to have pointed up this grant, since it would have reinforced his anecdote (25.19.9–17) on the poor judgment of the Senate (Centenius was soon to be easily defeated by Hannibal). Livy thought the fact Centenius received an army at all incredible (as should we). And on the march, M. Centenius "raised a good number of volunteers from the rural areas," almost doubling the size of his army. The whole episode—a Roman disaster involving the loss of approximately fifteen thousand men under the command of an ex-centurion—has obviously been subject to a good deal of exaggeration. That is, if any of it is to be believed at all (see De Sanctis, *Storia* III 2 370). It is rather strange that two Centenii met disaster in special commands within a few years (see above on the *privatus* C. Centenius in 217); the second of these catastrophes, the defeat of the centurion, may be annalistic fabrication. However, B. Schleussner (*WJA* 4 [1978] 215–222) has argued that the centurion M. Paenula had *imperium* (by "delegation" from the urban praetor, ignored in our sources), whereas C. Centenius in 217 (explicitly termed *pro praetore* and στρατηγός in our sources) did not, suggesting—implausibly—that C. Centenius' status has been confused with that of the later centurion.

C. Terentius Varro in 208   In that year, C. Terentius Varro (*cos.* 216) held *imperium* in Etruria ("cum imperio missus") (Liv. 27.24.1). This is a simple general formulation: no procedure can be divined. Nevertheless, since Varro's (praetorian) *imperium* was then extended into the next year (27.35.2 *pro pr.*), it seems unlikely that his original grant of *imperium* was by delegation. There is no certain case from this general period where a holder of delegated *imperium* is prorogued.

L. Manlius Acidinus in 207   In his report of this year, Livy offers a vague notice concerning L. Manlius Acidinus (*pr. urb.* 210): "A letter then arrived [sc. in Rome], sent by L. Manlius Acidinus from the camp (*ex castris*)" in regard to the Roman victory at the Metaurus (27.50.8, cf. 43.9). Mommsen (followed by *MRR* I 296) supposed he might have held an independent command to guard the Appennine passes against Hasdrubal. No title is preserved, and his status—not to mention his method of appointment—is irrecoverable.

L. Quinctius Flamininus in 198   Livy describes L. Quinctius Flamininus (*pr.* 199) in the year after his praetorship, "to whom the superintendency of the fleet and the *imperium* over the sea-coast had been handed by the Senate" ("cui classis cura maritimaeque orae imperium mandatum ab senatu erat") (32.16.2). This notice may in fact be an instance of prorogation, as is likely from the mention of the Senate (see 8.2.1 above): that is, it is a retrospective summary of his new *provincia*. However, if this was a special grant of *imperium*, the notice refers to only the first step of conferring a command, the initial *S.C.* We have no evidence from the entire free Republic that the Senate could simply "hand" *imperium* to someone; a vote by the People should have been necessary.

Two cases, not found in Mommsen's list, come into Livy's account of the years 173 and 172. When a locust plague hit South Italy in 173, "Cn. Sicinius, pr. designatus, cum imperio <in> Apuliam missus" (42.10.8). As in the similar cases of T. Otacilius Crassus in 215 and C. Terentius Varro in 208 above, no specific procedure is mentioned. The other possibly relevant case is the appointment of A. Atilius Serranus (*pr. urb.* 173) to a special task in 172. After a levy had been conducted by the peregrine praetor, "to receive this force at Brundisium and send it to Macedonia, A. Atilius Serranus was chosen (*deligitur*), who had been praetor the previous year" (42.27.4). This can hardly be prorogation, since it is reported to have taken place well into the consular year. No title is preserved: it is not certain that Atilius held *imperium* for this task. *Imperium* was in fact not necessary for this duty, despite its military aspect. For example, in 212, after the *pr. urb.* sent a C. Servilius (Geminus, the *cos.* 203?) as legate *ex auctoritate patrum* into Etruria to buy grain, this *legatus* went on to relieve the garrison of Tarentum (Liv. 25.15.4–6). *Legati* do not need *imperium*.

Our results have been largely negative, but telling. In not one of the eleven principal passages discussed above do we have a description of the actual delegation of *imperium* in the city, by (for example) the laying on of hands, conferment of a *toga praetexta* (see ch. 11 n. 71) or lictors, or by any other method. The phrase "mittere cum imperio"—found or suggested in three (out of four) of Mommsen's "certain" passages (see on T. Manlius Torquatus in 215, M. Valerius Laevinus in 205, and L. Oppius Salinator in 192, above) and two (out of five) of his "probable" passages (T. Otacilius Crassus in 215 and C. Terentius Varro in 208, above)—tells us nothing, since it is simply a general formulation for the granting of a special command. This is clear, for example, from Livy's account of the process by which C. Claudius Nero (*pr.* 212) was chosen as a replacement for the Spanish commander Cn. Cornelius Scipio in 211. The Senate decided that the tribunes should bring before the Plebs the question "quem cum imperio mitti placeret" (Liv. 26.2.5); Claudius already held *imperium* at the time of his selection (7.1.2 above). On the phrase "cum imperio" in general, which is not used for elected magistrates in their year of office, see *St.-R.* I³ 117 n. 1; cf. *St.-R.* I³ 683 n. 2. On *mittere* = *mandare*, see ch. 4 n. 144.

It appears that an individual could receive *imperium* on the strength of a plebiscite, if he subsequently received a *lex curiata*. We should not assume the cumbersome procedure of (a) the Senate asking the tribunes to (b) procure a *plebiscitum* to (c) have *imperium* granted to the person chosen by the *populus*, and (d) have it confirmed by the *lex curiata*. It seems particularly difficult to believe that (c)—following (b)—was envisaged. After all, a praetor could have been asked to *rogare populum* at once.

One—but only one—passage (M. Valerius Laevinus in 205, "imperio . . . dato") does imply personal delegation by the *praetor urbanus*. Livy may even have thought this was the actual Republican procedure. But the truth must be that Livy did not really know—or care—how *imperium* was granted to *privati* when no consul was present; hence his consistently vague formulations in these contexts.

It should be noted that in the four principal alleged instances of the practice of praetorian delegation (T. Manlius Torquatus in 215, M. Valerius Laevinus in 205, L. Oppius Salinator in 192, and the *tribuni militum* in 171), the *pr. urb.* acts upon instructions of the Senate. This also is true for the one instance in which a consul is employed in the city in a similar manner, in 201: "A full Senate . . . decreed, that the *cos.* P. Aelius (Paetus) should send *cum imperio* whomsoever he saw fit, to take over the fleet . . . brought from Sicily, and then to cross over to Macedonia. M. Valerius Laevinus was sent (*missus*) *pro pr.*" (Liv. 31.3.2–3). A consul, of course, could delegate praetorian *imperium*, and so it had been done *more maiorum*. On the other hand, what we may have in this passage, as well as in all the passages collected above featuring urban praetors, is simply the Senate's use of these magistrates because of their *ius agendi cum populo*—and so their ability to see to the passage of a *lex de imperio*. (It may be relevant that Laevinus was prorogued into the year 200—to be inferred from Liv. 31.5.5 and 7—the year he actually crossed to the east.)

Festus (p. 43 L, *ex Paulo*) points toward the general interpretation offered here in his explanation of the phrase *cum imperio* (found in four of the above passages on the *pr. urb.*—T. Otacilius Crassus and T. Manlius Torquatus in 215, C. Terentius Varro in 208, and L. Oppius Salinator in 192): it was the technical term for an individual to whom the People personally had given *imperium* ("'cum imperio est' dicebatur apud antiquos, cui nominatim a populo dabatur imperium"). A *lex* passed by the People (in accordance with an *S.C.*) must have been the standard way to confer a special command. This is clear from the negative reaction of many senators in 211 on receiving a letter from a de facto commander in Spain, "because he had written '[L. Marcius] *pro praetore* to the Senate,' although *imperium* had not been given to him by order of the People nor by authority of the Senate (*imperio non populi iussu, non ex auctoritate patrum dato*)" (Liv. 26.2.1; here "ex auctoritate patrum" seems to stand for "ex S.C."). Also note M. Claudius Marcellus, *pr.* 216 and *pro cos.* in 215, probably a special command and not prorogation (7.1.3 above), and P. Sempronius Tuditanus, *pro cos.* in Greece in 205 (Additional Note XII).

Another possibility is that the urban praetor was involved only in that he presided over the passing of a *lex curiata* (see 1.3.4 for its military aspects) for the *privatus* in the Curiate Assembly. A *lex curiata* figures in the fullest (and only certifiably authentic) parallel to the procedure needed to confer *imperium* on *privati*, the Rullan rogation of 63. This bill provided for the election of *Xviri* as land commissioners and the granting of *imperium* to them in the *comitia curiata* presided over by a praetor (Cic. *Agr.* 2.26–32, esp. 26, with 11.8.3 and 12.4.3 above). Yet these *Xviri* were magistrates (Cic. *Agr.* 2.26, claiming that the conferment of a magistracy in this way was unprecedented). Livy (34.53.1–2), in his account of the year 194, tells of a plebiscite providing for the establishment of colonies, followed by the urban praetor's presidency of an election on the Capitol (i.e., apparently in the *comitia curiata*) of two sets of *IIIviri coloniis deducendis* who were to hold *imperi-*

um (5.4.7 and 8.4.1 above). *IIIviri* were magistrates of the Roman People (Mommsen, *St.-R.* II³ 624–639).

In sum, there is no strong positive proof that the urban praetor—or any holder of praetorian *imperium*—had the power to delegate his *imperium*. If it were legally possible, it is strange that delegation is never recorded for any holders of praetorian *imperium* in the noncity *provinciae*: surely at least one instance should have come up in Livy's account of the Hannibalic War (noticed by Mommsen, *St.-R.* I³ 681 n. 5). It seems more likely that the urban praetor had responsibility only for the choice of the *privatus* and the securing of a special grant of *imperium* by a *lex*. The *pr. urb.* of course did not always have the choice of who was to be sent to a special command. The Senate left the People, or, more often, the Plebs to decide that. We see selection (not election) of commanders by *plebiscitum* particularly in the special Spanish commands prior to 197 (7.1.1–6).

Finally, it is worth suggesting that a consular commander's order (the verb *iubere* crops up frequently in these contexts) coupled with physical contact in the form of personal investiture of praetorian *insignia* (cf. App. *Mith.* 94.432, of Pompey in 67) may have formed part of the ceremony of delegation of *imperium* in the field. For some illuminating comments on the role of *contactus* in various aspects of Roman religion, see H. Wagenvoort, *Roman Dynamism* (Oxford 1947) 12–51 (but note the criticisms of J. Linderski, ANRW II 16.3 [1986] 2290f); J. Therasse, *CEA* 20 (1987) 29–52; also cf. R. Monier, *Iura* 4 (1953) 96–97 (role of the *sagmina* in the fetial rite).

II. *Laws Restricting Iteration and* Continuatio *in the Mid-Republic*

Was there a legal restriction before the time of the Second Punic War forbidding iteration of the same magistracy within ten years? Two or three passages in Livy might be taken to suggest it. First is Livy's report of the *lex Genucia* on iteration of 342 (7.42.2), which stipulated that "no one should hold the same magistracy within ten years (*intra decem annos*)." This has been the starting point for all discussions of the restriction of iteration in the mid-Republic. However, in 3.3.2 I have argued that we should accept this plebiscite's alleged provision about holding the same magistracy *intra decem annos*, but recognize that this was only a temporary measure that lapsed by 330; as such, it should have no direct bearing on our larger discussion regarding whether there was a ten-year "rule" on iterations in effect before 218.

Second, there is the story of the election of Q. Fabius Maximus Rullianus, *cos.* III 308, to a fourth consulship for 297 (Liv. 10.13.8–13). In this highly dramatized passage, Fabius tries to dissuade the People from making him consul yet again by adducing a law "by which it was prohibited that the same man be reelected as consul within ten years" (13.8: "qua intra decem annos eundem consulem refici non liceret"). As Livy tells it, the tribunes immediately offered to pass a plebiscite granting Fabius a dispensation from the "laws." The People proceeded to a vote, and elected Fabius along with his old consular colleague from 308, P. Decius Mus (who now became *cos*. III). We do not hear whether they received the dispensation that the tribunes offered. Indeed, Livy's anecdote (using his own chronology) makes no sense as it stands. The most plausible explanation is that Livy's source, in an effort to make a good story, ignorantly retrojected the (undoubted) later Republican institution of the ten-year interval for consuls to the beginning of the third century.

A third passage of some relevance is Livy's description of the attempt by a *dictator comitiorum habendorum caussa*, Q. Fulvius Flaccus, to accept his own election as consul for 209 (27.6.2–11). When two tribunes threatened to interpose their veto, Fulvius adduced a recent law, from the year 217 (translation adapted from the 1943 Loeb edition of F. G. Moore):

> In the consulship of Cn. Servilius, when C. Flaminius, the other consul, had fallen at Trasimene, by authority of the Senate it was proposed to the Plebs, and the Plebs had decreed that, so long as the war remained in Italy, the People should have the right to reelect as consuls the men they pleased and as often as they pleased from the number of those who had been consuls (*ex iis qui consules fuissent quos et quotiens vellet reficiendi consules populo ius esset*).

Fulvius also added two precedents (27.6.8): L. Postumius Megellus, who as *interrex* presided over his own election as consul (as *cos*. III for 291), and Q. Fabius Maximus (*cos. suff.* II 215, yet *vitio creatus*; III 214).

Livy's narrative, as so often, is unclear. It appears Q. Fulvius has two points to make. The first is that it is permissable to elect him. There he has a law to support him (the measure passed in 217), which the tribunes must have known. The second is that he may preside over his own election. That was his real difficulty, since there was no law, only *mos maiorum*, which Fulvius duly cites, going back as far as the early third century. To these examples he could have added several other earlier figures (see *St.-R.* I³ 500 n. 1). The tribunes obviously thought the sooner that practice was stopped, the better. But they did not gain their point on this occasion; the Senate, when asked to arbitrate in the dispute, decided in Fulvius' favor. This passage is sometimes taken to refer to the existence of a measure that had placed a prohibition on consular iteration, but that was suspended in mid-217 (e.g., J. Briscoe in *CAH* VIII² [1989] 68; cf. 525; also myself in *Athenaeum* 67 [1989] 467–468). That particular interpretation is impossible. Months before the suspension of this statute, C. Flaminius (*cos*. 223) had already been returned as *cos*. II 217.

Mommsen (*St.-R.* I³ 519 with n. 5) thought a law prohibiting iteration within ten years indeed existed, dating its introduction to 342 or perhaps 330. Mommsen had to suppose that the (many) exceptions to this "rule" in the subsequent consular *fasti* down to ca. 200—when we indeed start to find the regular occurence of a ten-year interval, counting exclusively—were the result of special dispensation in times of military crisis. He pointed out that the exceptions to the ten-year "rule" primarily (though not exclusively) fall in the periods of the Samnite, Pyrrhic, and Punic wars. Mommsen's view has been accepted by most scholars (see, e.g., Develin, *Patterns in Office-Holding* 13–16 and *The Practice of Politics in Rome* 105–118 for an elaborate defense of Mommsen's hypothesis; also K.-J. Hölkeskamp, *Historia* 42 [1993] 24). A few have not been convinced. R. Billows (*Phoenix* 43 [1989] 112–133, esp. 114–118) has emphasized the large number of consuls (more than forty, by his count) who broke this "law" in the period 341–217 by iterating within ten years, several doing so in years of no apparent emergency. Billows argues that, in spite of the literary sources, the actual consular *fasti* have no hint of a ten-year interval for iteration before the end of the Hannibalic War. An independent examination of the basic data (which I cannot set out in detail here, but can be gleaned from *MRR* I) suggests that Billows must be right on this point.

No matter how one reckons the actual count—with or without "dictator years," counting exclusively or inclusively—when "post-Genucian" iterations of the consulship occur in the period 330–218, more than half the time they do so at an interval of under ten years. In all, I find sixty-four certain examples of iteration (and two uncertain cases, which I exclude from consideration—see *MRR* I *sub annis* 328 and 221). Of these sixty-four iterations, if we subtract the dictator years and count exclusively, 63 percent break the ten year "rule"; the number is reduced to 55 percent if we do not not subtract those years. Counting inclusively, the figure is 53 percent whether one subtracts dictator years or not. If iteration within ten years was ever forbidden, there must have been many dispensations—not to be lightly assumed. Though one or two would be acceptable, it is hard to believe the sheer number of ad hoc exceptions which are necessary for defenders of Mommsen's ten-year "rule."

If a ten-year gap were mandated by law, we would expect a significant number of iterations to fall ten to twelve years after a previous consulship (i.e., as close as possible to the legal minimum). To be sure, by any of our modes of reckoning an interval of ten to twelve years is common, comprising about a quarter of our sixty-four examples from 330 to 218 (unless we count inclusively without subtracting "dictator years," in which case it comprises about 19 percent of the total). Yet almost all of these possible iterations at an interval of ten to twelve years are closely framed by exceptions to the supposed ten-year "rule." For instance, it can be argued (if we leave out the possibility that C. Plautius Decianus, *cos.* 329, was II 328) that none of the seven consuls who iterate in the years 329–321 break this "rule." But there is a *cos.* 336 who is II in 330, and all four consuls of 320 and 319 are iterating at short intervals. Or, consider the years 297 and 296, which saw the reelection of the consular pairs of 308 and 307, respectively, while a *cos.* 305 was II 294. However, note M. Valerius Corvus, *cos.* V 300 and VI 299 (albeit in that latter instance as *suffectus*), as well as the years 295 (the reelection of the experienced consuls of 297) and 291 (when the *cos.* II 294 held the office for the third time). In short, it is difficult to recognize from the actual record any standing prohibition on iteration within ten years.

As Mommsen noted, consular iterations at short intervals largely fall in the periods of the major wars. This is natural, since in times of acute crisis the People would be interested in placing the best commanders possible in the field, and members of the ruling class might be less likely to object to a more experienced peer delaying their own advancement. Now, there are a few short stretches in the latter part of the fourth century and in the third century when all repetitions are at least ten years apart or where there are no iterations at all: the years 307–300, 290–279, 269–255, 240–230 (if we count inclusively), and (perhaps) 223–218. But that pattern, such as it is, cannot be due to legislation. In the years 366 to 341, when iteration is undoubtedly unrestricted (and there is continuous hard fighting in central Italy combined with a political struggle over control of the consulship), it does not occur in every year, or even every few years. The same goes for the period 330–218. Here the triumphal *fasti* provide a control of sorts, in showing that the years that show no violation of the ten-year "rule" were hardly quiet. So our conclusion must be that the absence of consular iteration at intervals of less than ten years is partly accident, and partly political reality. There was no special law forbidding it. It is just that few men managed to achieve it (one might distantly compare *consules iterum* under the Empire, apart from Imperial families).

Eventually, iteration of the consulship was restricted in some way. Livy does not tell us the details, nor is there any reason to think he should have. Senatorial issues were (in principle) secret, and this is the type of measure that would be passed by consensus, without a highly visible debate. The Senate probably stipulated a ten-year interval—though it is just possible that they banned consular iteration altogether, except by special dispensation. The exact date for this move is difficult to ascertain. The example of P. Sulpicius Galba, *cos.* 211 and then II 200 (i.e., ten years apart), is probably fortuitous. There was a war against Macedonia afoot in 200, and Galba had experience in that area as a *pro cos.* (Additional Note XII), which amply explains why he reappears precisely in that year. But then we find P. Cornelius Scipio Africanus, *cos.* 205 and II 194, with no counterexamples of iteration at close intervals for decades to come: note M. Aemilius Lepidus, *cos.* 187 and II 175; L. Aemilius Paullus, *cos.* 182 and (after a *repulsa*: Plu. *Aem.* 6.8) II 168; and Ti. Sempronius Gracchus, *cos.* 177 and II 163. When one adds in M. Claudius Marcellus, *cos.* 166 and II 155 (see immediately below), these cases provide a reasonable argument for a ten-year rule.

In the 150s, we find two consuls of 162 who were *vitio creati* iterating in 156 and 155 respectively. We can suppose they won this concession by special permission, when they argued that the augural flaw in their original election should not debar them from reseeking the office before they were too old. In addition, M. Claudius Marcellus, *cos.* 166 and II 155 (a proper interval) became *cos.* III in 152. This has led one scholar (R. L. Calvert, *Athenaeum* 39 [1961] 22–23) to suggest that there was no prohibition on reelection after the second term. Rather, Marcellus, too, must have won the Senate's dispensation, no doubt citing (tendentiously) the *coss.* II of 156 and 155 as precedent and using personal influence to do the rest. But Marcellus' election to a third consulship must have been unpopular with many of his peers. It was probably this which caused consular iteration to be prohibited altogether. The Livian *Periocha* 56 shows that an actual *lex* "that forbade anyone to be made consul a second time" had been passed by 135 (on this, cf. Astin, *Lex Annalis* 19 n. 6).

At all times, multiple consulships were a menace to *concordia* within the senatorial establishment. In times of major overseas wars, they would be particularly resented. Livy is too defective for us to tell whether in the situation of 169/168 there was opposition to L. Paullus' second consulship, and we lose him altogether by the time of Ti. Gracchus' iteration in 163. But in the 150s, it is not difficult to see that many senators might imagine that their political system was breaking down. Not only do we start to see the short intervals, but in the year 155 both consuls were iterating—something which had not been seen since the crisis years of the Hannibalic War (the last case is in 209). The Senate surely considered it necessary to take firm action before initiating hostilities with Carthage. It would be dangerous to let one or two *consulares* monopolize the opportunities for military glory in that war.

A likely date for the introduction of the (putative) ten-year mandatory interval for iteration of the consulship is ca. 196. This is when we know the Senate had turned its attention to regulating access to this office, specifying the praetorship as a prerequisite (7.2.4). Billows (*Phoenix* 43 [1989] 112–133) cannot be correct when he suggests that starting ca. 200 a ten-year interval was required for the iteration of all magistracies (not just the consulship). Except perhaps for the brief "Genucian" decade, praetors at all times—down to the late Republic—seem to have been exempt from restrictions on iteration (T. C. Brennan, *Athenaeum* 67 [1989] 467–487); there is no good reason to suppose that a minimum interval was required before iterating any subpraetorian magistracy, either. The consulship was the real focus of anxiety, as the formulation of the law reported in *Per.* 56 suggests.

We may safely conclude that there was no specified ten-year interval for iteration of the consulship before the early second century. But that is not to say there were no other measures affecting consular iteration previous to that time. In his reported speech at the elections for 209 (Liv. 27.6.7–8, summarized above), Q. Fulvius Flaccus is made to cite a law which he says was passed after the Trasimene disaster, "ut . . . ex iis qui consules fuissent quos et quotiens vellet reficiendi consules populo ius esset." What barriers was this law of 217 meant to eliminate?

Livy's wording raises questions. *Reficere* was the technical term for reelection of a magistrate for a second consecutive year (i.e., *continuatio*); cf. the *rogatio de tribunis reficiendis* of the tribune C. Papirius Carbo in 131 or 130 (*MRR* I 502). This is the meaning of *reficere* in virtually all of its occurrences in an electoral context in Livy: see (e.g.) his description of the elections for 214 (24.9.4). Nevertheless, the bulk of Livy's examples are connected with the same complex of "facts" (the tribunician iterations of the Struggle of the Orders recounted in Books 3–6). And in one passage *reficere* is not synonymous with *continuare*, but must mean simply "to reelect" (10.13.8, the elections for 297, quoted above). This exception shows that we have to consider the wording of the law of 217 independently of Livy's regular usage.

What this law did say, specifically, was that "out of those who had been consuls" (not just the two of the previous year, but clearly a large reservoir of men) the People could *reficere* any it liked as often as it liked. Here *reficere* cannot be taken in its regular technical sense, but must mean "reelect." Now, the case of C. Flaminius (*cos.* 223, II 217), who died at Trasimene, eloquently shows that there was no prohibition on iteration within ten years in effect when the law was passed. What the law must have done was to eliminate other restrictions. It surely allowed *continuatio* of the consulship (cf. Mommsen, *St.-R.* I³ 500 n. 1). Perhaps by extension it was taken to apply to any office involving *imperium* (cf. the dictator Fulvius' bid for election as consul for 209). *Continuatio* of the consulship (on which see *St.-R.* I³ 517 n. 3) is not found from the time of the Pyrrhic War (M.' Dentatus, *cos.* II 275, III 274) until the Hannibalic era. M. Claudius Marcellus was *cos.* II 215 and III 214; Q. Fabius Maximus was III 215 and IV 214 (he is aptly cited as precedent in Q. Flaccus' speech); Flaccus himself was *pr.* 215, II 214. *Continuatio* then disappears until the second through sixth consulships of C. Marius in 104–100. The law of 217 probably also removed a cap on the number of iterations. Nobody, in many decades, has more than one (see the remarks of Cornell, *Beginnings of Rome* 372): the last examples before the Second Punic War (when it is common in the years 215–208) are L. Megellus, *cos.* III 291, and M.' Dentatus, *cos.* III 274. After 208, there is only M. Claudius Marcellus, *cos.* III 152, which caused a stir, and then the extraordinary cases of the later Republic, starting with C. Marius at the end of the first century.

Laws like the measure of 217 may have been traditional in times of extreme emergency. This particular one will not have remained in effect for long. Although technically its terms were to hold good "so long as there was war in Italy," it may have been rescinded soon after the conflict between the dictator Q. Fulvius Flaccus and the tribunes who threatened to veto the consular *comitia* for 209. At some point soon after, it was obviously decided to rationalize the system and allow individuals to iterate the consulship (evidently) at ten-year intervals. The dispensation granted to M. Claudius Marcellus, *cos.* III 152, led to a demand that the rules be tightened even further. But the potential for special legislation like that of 217 probably remained. In the Cimbric War, such a law (with the requisite changes in wording) may have covered C. Marius (*cos.* 107) in his second through fifth consulships of 104–101. Consider also Q. Metellus Numidicus, *cos.* 109 and (as is generally accepted) a consular candidate again for 101 (Broughton, *Candidates Defeated* 9 with n. 14). Marius' sixth consulship of 100 is the puzzling one, for the military crisis had passed—and with it surely any emergency legislation which had suspended electoral restrictions. As it turns out, the sources suggest Marius' sixth consulship was by special dispensation (esp. Vell. 2.12.6 "consulatus veluti praemium ei meritorum datus"). (The petition of C. Servilius Glaucia, *pr.* 100, for election as *cos.* 99—surely inspired by Marius—was considered illegal, and as such was refused: Broughton, *Candidates Defeated* 30.) The outbreak of the Social War seems also to have occasioned emergency legislation lifting the *leges annales*. Either that legislation was not revoked at the war's end or was soon revived, for we see it in effect also during the *regnum Cinnanum* (10.5.8).

III. *Some Possible Praetors of the Years down to 218*

C. *Genucius Clepsina*, ?pr. 273   In 1983, excavations by M. Cristofani in the ancient urban area of Cerveteri uncovered a subterranean complex with the following graffito carved into the wall of its main chamber: C. GENOVCIO(S) CLOVSINO(S) PRAI. For a brief description of this inscription and its archaeological setting (interpreted as a *nymphaeum*, but with no independent date of construction), see M. Cristofani and G. L. Gregori, *Prospettiva* 49 (1987) 2–14, esp. 4; M. G. Marzi, *SE* 52 (1984) 403f (but misrepresenting the reading as CLEVSINO); M. Cristofani, *Archeologia nella Tuscia* 2 (1986) 24–26 and Table XXIV; M. Cristofani in his introduction to G. Proietti, *Cerveteri* (Rome 1988) 8. For a transcription and color photograph of this graffito, see W. V. Harris in M. Cristofani (ed.), *Gli Etruschi: Una nuova immagine* (Florence 1984) 55; see also M. Cristofani (ed.), *Dizionario della civiltà etrusca* (Florence 1985) 123, cf. 49.

The abbreviation of title—whether it be PRAI(TOR) or PRAI(FECTUS)—is unparalleled in Republican Latin inscriptions: PRAE occurs in the Empire for *praefectus* instead of the more normal PR or PRAEF (see *ILS* 2636), but this obviously sheds no light on our isolated inscription, apparently carved centuries earlier. The spelling PRAI is unfortunately no use for the dating (it occurs, at least sporadically, at all times in the Republic, as does OU for U). In addition, the inclusion of the *cognomen* and absence of filiation is most unusual for the mid-Republican period (as far as we can tell). As it happens, eight other graffiti have been found on walls in or just off the main chamber (texts in *Prospettiva* 49 [1987] 4–7), including one with the consular date A.D. 208, which shows exactly how long this space had been in use (though probably not continuously). If Genucius indeed scrawled his name on fresh plaster, as G. L. Gregori maintains (*Prospettiva* 49 [1987] 4), we are probably justified in regarding the Genucius graffito as contemporaneous with the construction of the complex itself. But the variation in the lettering (it looks as if at least two different hands had written it, with the *nomen* and *cognomen* showing not much similarity) makes any present hypothesis uncertain.

All scholars who have discussed the inscription have identified this man with C. Genucius L.f. L.n. Clepsina, cos. 276 and II 270, whose brother L. Clepsina was consul in 271. The *cognomen* "Clusinus" ("from Clusium") is the Latinized version of Etruscan "Clevsina" (which lurks behind the "Clepsina" of the *Fast. Cos. Cap.* in the entries on these two brothers). The *cognomen*—in either Etruscan or Latinized form—is exceedingly rare, with one known occurrence apart from these consular brothers (*TLL Onomasticon* II 492; cf. also *CIE* 5474, from Tarquinii in the third century). Cristofani ventured to offer a date for the inscription as well as a supplement for Clepsina's title: "[H]e was the magistrate who, acting as praetor in 273 B.C., completed the operations, perhaps military, that led to the surrender of Caere, decreeing its definitive incorporation in the Roman state" (*Dizionario della civiltà etrusca* 123). However, we must remember that this Genucius could easily be a later family member (e.g., son, nephew, grandson, or grandnephew) who never made it to the consulship.

Let us suppose for the moment that our Genucius was in fact the two-times consul. Can Cristofani be correct in supposing that he also was praetor in the crucial year 273? Given the nature of this inscription and its context, one can only reexamine the evidence for Caere in the Republic (albeit here only briefly), and then balance the various possibilities. The Caeritans had of course protected the Vestals, priests and sacred implements of the Roman people during the Gallic invasion of 390 (evidence collected in Harris, *Rome in Etruria and Umbria* 45 n. 4). According to Livy (5.50.3) the Romans in turn decided "cum Caeretibus hospitium publice fieret." Gellius (16.13.7) states that the Caeritans received the honor of *civitas sine suffragio* for this deed (no date specified), the first *municipes* to be given this status. Gellius adds that paradoxically this grant was the origin of the term "Caeritan tablets," in which the censors registered those who were marked with a *nota* and were deprived of the right to vote. (For a different interpretation of the same facts, see Strab. 5.2.3 p. 220, cf. Porph. on H. *Ep.* 1.6.62.)

Notwithstanding some tendentious aspects of the Gellius passage (on which see J. Pinsent, *CQ* 7 [1957] 89–97) we should probably believe his statement that

Caere was the first to receive the status of *civitas sine suffragio* (see Badian, *Foreign Clientelae* 17 n. 1). The idea that Caere received the *civitas s.s.* in virtue of its services to Rome during the Gallic invasion (Gellius, Strabo) is not necessarily incompatible with the notion that this status was also *ignominiosum* (Porphyrion, Strabo): whether *civitas s.s.* was an honor or a disgrace may be an anachronistic (later) question. But when did Caere receive its *civitas s.s.*? In 353, the Romans declared war on the Caeritans, who in turn backed off from hostilities. Livy reports that the Caeritans received mild terms, due in part to their protection of the Roman state religion in 390 (7.20.8). Livy makes no mention of a grant of *civitas s.s.* at this time, and it is unlikely that this was the occasion on which it was conferred (on this Harris, *Rome in Etruria and Umbria* 94–95; cf. M. Humbert, *Municipium et civitas sine suffragio* 141–143 and in J. E. Spruit (ed.), *Maior viginti quinque annis* 70–72, who posits the grant ca. 350). In any case, the terminus ante quem for this grant would be 338 (cf. Liv. 8.14.10, three other instances of *civitas s.s.*), if we accept Gellius' assertion that Caere was the first to receive this status.

We hear nothing of official relations between Caere and Rome until ca. 273. At that time, the Romans (for some unknown reason) were at the point of voting for a declaration of war on Caere; hostilities were forestalled when Caeritan ambassadors agreed to a cessation of one-half their land (D.C. 10 F 33 with Zonar. 8.6.10; cf. D.H. 20.15.1 [= 20.5] for the similar case of the Bruttii ca. 271). Within a decade, Rome started planting colonies on this confiscated territory (Harris, *Rome in Etruria and Umbria* 148–149). At some point, Caere itself was made a *praefectura* of the class which received an annual *praefectus* appointed by the *pr. urb.* in Rome (see 5.2.4).

So Cristofani's conjecture—that C. Genucius Clevsina is the *cos.* 276, II 270, and was active in the area of Caere as praetor in 273—is only one of several possibilities. It is true that the combination of Caeritan unrest and the subsequent confiscation of land (the latter reported only by Dio) afforded a good opportunity for a Roman magistrate with *imperium* to be on the spot. Yet it is also possible that C. Genucius—if really the consul—was sent to this Etruscan town as praetor in an earlier period of unrest: note the triumph of Q. Marcius Philippus as *cos.* 281 and that of Ti. Coruncanius as *cos.* 280 for campaigns in Etruria (A. Degrassi, *Inscr. Ital.* XIII 1 72f, 545). An alternative is that he served as one (not even necessarily the first) of the *praefecti* (see 3.2.1 above) sent out every year after the confiscation of Caeritan land. (It is hard to see why anyone would be building an elaborate *nymphaeum* in Caere in the troubled year 273.) Alternately, our C. Genucius is a descendant of the consul of the 270s, to be placed later in (most likely) the third century. Though no Genucii reached the consulship after 270, the *gens* evidently continued in public life for some time: most significantly, in 210 a L. Genucius (doubtless a grandson of one of the two consuls of the 270s) headed a senatorial embassy to Numidia (Liv. 27.4.7–9). Note also the Genucius listed by *MRR* I 219 as *tr. pl.* 241, and the M. Genucius who was killed in Gaul as *tr. mil.* 193 (Liv. 35.5.14). But in purely statistical terms, it is overwhelmingly probable that Genucius—whatever his exact date and identity—was a *praefectus*, not a praetor. As a "Genucius," he may have been well suited for the job: the *cognomen* "Clousinos" probably indicates a deep-rooted

Etruscan connection (cf. A. Naso, *Epigraphica* 48 [1986] 191–198), though he chose to spell it in its fully Latinized form.

M. *Valerius*, pr. *Sardinia ca.* 227   Münzer identified (without a query) the "M. Valerius" of Solin. 5.1 (where he names the first praetor specifically created for Sardinia) as M. Valerius Laevinus, *cos.* 220 (perhaps), *pr.* II 215 (Liv. 23.24.4), *cos.* (II?) 210 in Sicily, and dead in 200 (*RE* s.v. *Valerius* 211 col. 45, followed by Broughton, *MRR* I 229). It is true that the notice of praetorian iteration for 215 will fit, but it is by no means compelling. In the period ca. 227 through 219, about thirty-six men will have held the office of praetor, and more than one man from the *gens Valeria* may have reached the office. A praetorship ca. 227 seems rather early for Laevinus (if indeed he was *cos.* I in 220), an extremely able man whose two sons reached the praetorship in 182 and 179 (i.e., forty-five and forty-eight years later, on this reckoning). C. Flaminius (praetor for Sardinia in the same year as "M. Valerius," i.e., ca. 227) reached the consulship in 223. Though Flaminius' alleged status as a *novus homo* may be questioned (V. Max. 5.4.5 implies his father was a senator), he certainly was no favorite of the Senate (Liv. 21.63.2–3, etc.). Only one patrician iterates as consul in the period 227 through 221 (in 224), so this factor will not have had too severe an impact on Laevinus' chances for the consulship. F. Stella-Maranca (*MAL* [ser. 6] 2 [1927] 296) actually did query this identification of the first praetor for Sardinia, but did not suggest an alternative of his own. Perhaps the first Sardinian praetor is a M.' Valerius (the text of Solinus is very poor), the first-born son of the *cos.* 263. Or he may be a Valerius we never hear of again, because he did not survive to serve (or was not recorded as serving) after 218: for example, a son of the *cos.* 261.

M. *Livius Salinator* (cos. 219), pr. *in the 220s?*   From Nemi comes an intriguing Republican dedication, *CIL* I² 41 = *ILLRP* 76: DIANA | M. LIVIO(S) M. F. | PRAITOR DEDIT. This archaic inscription was found in the grove of Diana at Nemi by L. Boccanera (*NSA* 1887 24f) in roughly the same context as that of the dedicatory inscription of C. Aurelius Cotta, *pr.* II 202 and *cos.* 200 (*CIL* I² 610 = *ILLRP* 75; see T. C. Brennan, *Athenaeum* 67 [1989] 467–487 for discussion). The dative *Diana* (on which see A. Ernout, *Recueil de textes latins archaiques*² [Paris 1957] 28) and the archaic script (similar to that in *CIL* I² 610, which is dateable to 200) suggest a date of the late third or early second century. A. Degrassi (*ILLRP* 76) did not venture an identification: "incertum [est] utrum praetor Aricinus an populi Romani." It is true that non-Roman magistrates made dedications at the grove, a major site for dedications from at least the end of the fourth century down to the beginning of the first (A. E. Gordon, *The Cults of Aricia* [Berkeley 1934] *passim*): see *CIL* I² 40 = *ILLRP* 77, from the same archaeological context as the M. Livius dedication. Yet it is perfectly possible that a Roman praetor in his year of office made a dedication to Diana, as the example of C. Aurelius Cotta demonstrates. No M. Livius M.f. is known to have held the praetorship in the period 218–166, for which our records are almost complete. If the man in question is indeed a Roman magistrate, the only plausible candidates for the identification are M. Livius

Salinator (*cos.* 219, II 207) in some year before 219, or (less likely) his father (known only as X*vir s.f.* in 236—MRR I 223). (For a possible ancestor, cf. also 3.7 on the early third-century "Livius *pro pr.*")

Two Atilii as prr. *218?*　What are we to make of the "C. Atilius Serranus praetor" who made a vow in Rome in the winter of 218 (Liv. 21.62.10, cf. 1), that is, at the same time a "C. Atilius praetor" is said to be wintering at Placentia (21.63.15)? It is just possible that he could be the same praetor, or that Livy (or his annalistic source) is simply mistaken. Yet it should be noted that if L. Manlius Vulso was praetor in 219 (as argued in 4.3.4), there is an open space in the praetorian college for 218. It is possible that in 218 two Atilii held the praetorship, C. Atilius Serranus (consular candidate for 216—Liv. 22.35.2) in the urban jurisdiction, and another C. Atilius as *praetor inter peregrinos* (i.e., *cum Gallia*). If so, it is likely that the peregrine praetor was a Regulus (rather than another Serranus). He would be the eldest son of the consul of 257 and 250, C. Atilius M.f. M.n. Regulus, elder brother of M. Atilius Regulus (*pr.* 213), and cousin of both M. Atilius M.f. M.n. Regulus (*cos.* 227, II 217) and C. Atilius M.f. M.n. Regulus (*cos.* 225). In 216, an M. and a C. Atilius serve as II*viri aed. dedic.* for the dedication of L. Manlius' temple of Concordia (Liv. 23.21.7). The choice of these men may be significant: on my hypothesis, this is the same C. Atilius who, as praetor, brought aid to L. Manlius in 218. What is more, the Atilii Reguli—if that is indeed the family of one or both of these II*viri*—perhaps had a personal link with the Manlii Vulsones. C. Atilius Regulus (*cos.* 257, II 250, and perhaps the father of C. and M. Atilius) and L. Manlius Vulso Longus (*cos.* 256, II 250, presumably the father of our L. Manlius Vulso) had served together as consular colleagues. However, the addition of a "C. Atilius Regulus, *pr.* 218" to our praetorian *fasti* must remain speculative.

IV. Suffectio *of Praetors*

We hear of the election for a suffect praetor only after the death of the urban praetor and the *praetor inter peregrinos*. Livy (39.39.1–15) reports that in 184, after the death of the *pr. urb.* C. Decimius Flavus (early in the year), the regular election ("e lege" 39.39.6; see also 14) to fill his position was scheduled, yet cancelled due to the audacious campaign of the sitting curule aedile Q. Fulvius Flaccus to win the place (see Mommsen, *St.-R.* I³ 513 n. 3). In 180, after the death of the peregrine praetor Ti. Minucius Molliculus (also early in the year), C. Claudius Pulcher was elected suffect in his place (Liv. 40.37.4).

On the two occasions in Livy's record when provincial praetors die—both early in the year—no suffect is elected. In the first case, it is true, practical considerations made a special election near impossible. In 189, L. Baebius Dives was wounded by Ligurians on his way to Hispania Ulterior, and soon died at Massilia (37.57.1–2). In consequence, the *pr. urb.* Sp. Postumius Albinus wrote to P. Iunius Brutus, *pr.* 190 and now *pro pr.* in Etruria, informing him of an S.C. that he should entrust his *provincia* to a *legatus* and leave for Spain at once (37.57.3–4). There was little real alternative: the consuls had already set out for the war against Antiochus III in the east (37.51.7), and could hardly be recalled. However, the second case seems to show that even when a consul was available to hold an election for a fallen provincial praetor, a *suffectus* was not created. The praetor N. Fabius Buteo died on his way to Hispania Citerior in 173, also at Massilia (42.4.1). By the time the news had reached Rome, one of the consuls, L. Postumius Albinus, had set off for his special task of investigating illegal possession of *ager publicus* in Campania (42.1.6) (which responsibility he had in addition to "Liguria"—42.1.1–2), and the other consul, M. Popillius Laenas, was probably already in Liguria. L. Postumius Albinus surely could have been recalled to Rome for the election of a *suffectus*, had there been a legal stipulation that one be elected. Rather, the Senate decreed that the two praetors of the previous year who were in Spain should draw to see which one would be prorogued to replace Fabius in Citerior. Probably not entirely by chance, the praetor who was already in Citerior received the lot to stay (42.4.1–3 "sors opportuna fuit"). When a prorogued praetor died in his *provincia*, no special provisions were made other than to place that lot in the next available sortition (cf. 33.25.8–9, Hispania Citerior in 196) and then to hurry the newly elected praetor out to succeed to this command: cf. the example of the Spains in 39.21.4 (186) and 40.2.5 (182). No permanent *provincia* could be left *sine imperio* for long.

   It would be interesting to know whether a suffect might be elected to replace a *praetor repetundis*—or any of the other praetors in charge of later standing courts—who had died in office. C. Gracchus in his *lex repetundarum* made a provision of some sort for the replacement of praetors who had died or abdicated, but owing to the state of the text, we cannot tell what it was (cf. *CIL* I² 583 lines 72–73). As far as our present information goes, it appears that the original "city" praetors were apparently assimilated to the consuls when it came to *suffectio*, while the later, and "lower," praetors were not. There obviously was a time limit within the year (demonstrable for the consuls) after which suffection did not take place. It is an open question what this limit was (and why it existed): since do not know the cutoff date, we cannot judge, for example, whether Cn. Carbo, as *cos.* II 84, acted improperly in failing to replace his fallen colleague Cinna with a suffect after the summer solstice (App. *BC* 1.78.358–359 with Badian, *Studies* 228 and 233 nn. 12 and 13); see Mommsen, *St.-R.* I³ 29f for other exceptions.

V. *The Defense of Rome in 211*

According to Livy's account of the year 211, the consuls Cn. Fulvius Centumalus and P. Sulpicius Galba, as well as the *pro cos.* Q. Fulvius Flaccus (cos. 212) were called to defend Rome against an expected attack by Hannibal. We are told "lest his *imperium* be annulled were he to come into the city, the Senate decreed that Q. Fulvius shall have equal *imperium* with the consuls" ("cui ne minueretur imperium si in urbem venisset, decernit senatus ut Q. Fulvio par cum consulibus imperium esset"—26.9.10). The notice of Flaccus' recall from Campania has often been doubted (e.g., Münzer, *RE* s.v. *Fulvius* 59 cols. 244–245; De Sanctis, *Storia* III 2 338; cf. *MRR* I 277 n. 5). Yet, even if spurious, the annalist who made it up knew enough to realize that Flaccus as a promagistrate would need a special grant to retain his *imperium* in the city. It is unlikely that an *S.C.* alone (which is all that Livy mentions) was good enough to do this; judging from the procedure adopted for promagistrates who were awarded a triumph, he may have needed at least a *plebiscitum* as well (Liv. 26.21.5–211 and 45.35.4–167; in these cases the Plebs was not making a grant of *imperium*, only extending the bounds in which it could be exercised). What seems amazing, however, is Livy's statement, slightly later in his narrative, that when Hannibal actually came near the walls, all ex-dictators, ex-consuls and ex-censors received a special grant of *imperium* to quash various *tumultus* which had sprung up (26.10.9 "placuit omnes qui dictatores consules censoresve fuissent cum imperio esse, donec recessisset a muris hostis"). If this proposal was actually passed (e.g., J. S. Richardson, *JRS* 81 [1991] 5, fully accepts it), it must have been through a *lex*. Senators had been employed to crush earlier *tumultus*, but no grant of *imperium* is mentioned (22.55.6–8–216). It is particularly strange that censors—who were not holders of *imperium* in their term of office and are invariably ranked below praetors in formal lists (see 2.5.2 above)—should be included in 211, and praetors excluded. Either *censores* is a mistake, possibly Livy's own, for *praetores*, or the word *praetores* was omitted between *consules* and *censoresve*, where it ought to be expected. The homeoteleuton *-ores* makes the latter of these two explanations easier to imagine.

VI. *Praetors and Shipbuilding, 218–166*

In the period 218–166, there appear to have been five major shipbuilding and ship renovation efforts: three during the Hannibalic War, one at the start of the war against Antiochus III, and one at the beginning of the Third Macedonian War. It is uncertain what magistrate or magistrates supervised the first ship construction drive, in early 217, when sixty quinqueremes were built (see Plb. 3.75.4 and J. H. Thiel, *Studies* 48f). It may have been the newly elected consuls, who were still in the city making preparations for their campaign of that year (3.75.5–7). When the Senate ordered one hundred new ships to be built in early 214, we are told explicitly that the consuls had this task in addition to their levy of six new legions (Liv. 24.11.4–6). In 208, there was a rumor of a massive Carthaginian naval invasion (27.22.8). This report (later proved false) prompted a third shipbuilding and renovation program, which the Senate entrusted to the *pr. urb.*, even though the consuls of that year were still in the city (27.22.12; cf. 23.1). Why the involvement of the praetor? This fleet (thirty old ships which were on dry dock at Ostia, and twenty new ships) was supposed to protect the sea coast near the city—part of the urban praetor's defense responsibilities.

The emergency of 208 set a precedent. Henceforth, it was the urban praetor, assisted occasionally by one of his praetorian colleagues, who arranged for the construction or repair of ships and the drafting of personnel to man them, even if one or both consuls were in the city when these orders were given. A list might be helpful. The war against Antiochus required orders of ships for three straight years, 192 through 190. Before the consuls of 192 had set out for their *provinciae*, the Senate ordered the two city praetors to prepare one hundred *quinqueremes*; at the end of the year, when a consul had returned for the elections, the *pr. urb.* had to provide another fifty (Liv. 35.21.1–2; 24.7–8). Early in 191, M. Iunius Brutus, who served as both *pr. urb.* and *pr. per.*, was told to refurbish some old ships stored in the yards, and to draft freedmen ("*socii navales*") to fill them (36.2.15). The consuls were in Rome (cf. 36.3.14; 37.1). In the next year, there was a rumor that Antiochus was increasing the number of ships in his fleet. The *pr. urb.* of 190 saw to the construction of thirty *quinqueremes* and twenty *triremes* (37.4.5); the consuls had probably set out for their *provinciae* by that point (cf. 37.4.2 and 4). We hear no more of such preparations until the start of the war with Perseus. In 172 (when the consuls had left Rome) the urban praetor was ordered to repair all seaworthy *quinqueremes* in the shipyards, as well as to construct fifty new ones; if he was unable to meet this target, the praetor for Sicily was to help him. The urban praetor also was to enrol enough freedmen from the Roman citizen body to fill twenty-five ships (42.27.1–3; cf. Cato *ORF*³ F 190).

So shipbuilding is one specific instance where we can trace how the Senate let a once consular task devolve—permanently—upon the urban praetor. Furthermore, the post-Hannibalic examples show with reasonable clarity how among praetors the Senate entrusted tasks in or near the city to the *praetor urbanus* in the first resort, and brought in others as his (interchangeable) helpmates. Note the aid of the peregrine praetor in 192, but in 172—when the *praetor inter peregrinos* was slated early on to cross to Greece (above, 5.5.1, 8.5.1)—the praetor for Sicily.

VII. *The Case of Pomponius,* Praetor inter Peregrinos *in* 217

In 217, after the Roman disaster at Lake Trasimene, the peregrine praetor M. (?) Pomponius is said to have frankly announced to an assembly of the People the news of the defeat. Widespread consternation, even panic, followed (Plb. 3.85.7–8; Liv. 22.7.7–13; Plu. *Fab.* 3.4.). Broughton (*MRR* I 246 n. 8) is puzzled at Pomponius' action: "[O]rdinarily official announcement of a serious defeat was made, in the absence of the consuls, by the *pr. urbanus.* Since [M.] Aemilius [Regillus] held that position it is reasonable to assume that he could not officiate and that his place was taken by the *pr. peregrinus.*" It should be stated that the actual evidence on this responsibility is ambiguous. I can find no evidence from this period of the *pr. urb.*—or any praetor—announcing a defeat (not that there were that many), and no decisive evidence on which praetor made announcements of victories. In 207, C. Hostilius Cato, *pr. urb. et inter peregrinos,* announced the news of the Metaurus victory (Liv. 27.50.8–11; for the joint *provincia,* see 36.11). In 203 (a year in which the *provincia peregrina* is not reported to have been allotted discretely to an individual), the legate C. Laelius and the *pr. urb.* P. Aelius Paetus ascended the *rostra* together at a *contio* to announce the news of P. Cornelius Scipio's first victory in Africa (30.17.3; cf. 21.10) (i.e., the praetor called a *contio* for the *legatus* to announce it). At Flor. 1.38.20, neither the name nor the *provincia* of the praetor announcing the victory over the Cimbri in 101 B.C. is specified.

The *pr. urb.* 217, M. Aemilius Regillus, was surely in or near the city after the defeat at Trasimene. As *flamen,* he will have been restricted in his movement (24.8.10; cf. 22.9.11, 33.8–9.) The point of the story is that Pomponius tactlessly (though some might think courageously) announced the defeat, perhaps without proper consultation with the Senate as to the form the announcement should take.

The Senate was obviously in continuous session by now, under the *praetor urbanus*. (Note that, immediately following this announcement, "for some days the praetors [the plural posits M. Regillus in the city] kept the Senate in the Curia, from sunrise until sunset"—22.7.14.) When it got late in the day (22.7.8 "haud multo ante solis occasum") and it was felt by the Senate that something simply had to be said to the crowd, the *praetor inter peregrinos* was probably the only man who could do it, since the Senate could not suspend its session. The way Pomponius did it was unfortunate. Although we must assume the praetor called a formal *contio* (on the Senate's instructions), all our sources relate that his blunt statement made the Trasimene disaster seem worse than it actually was, resulting in widespread panic.

In succeeding years, the Senate remained in tight control. After Cannae, the Senate took great pains to ensure that the Forum was cleared out by the magistrates and that anyone with important information from the field be brought before the city praetors (Liv. 22.55.1–56.5). The letter which reported the Metaurus victory in 207 was read first *in senatu* and then *in contione*, even though this time no panic was to be feared (27.50.8–11). Before the public announcement of P. Cornelius Scipio's victory of 203, the *praetor urbanus* consulted the Senate (30.17.3). In 197, when the consuls of the year sent word of their successes in Gaul against various Gallic tribes and the Ligurians, "the *pr. urb.* M. Sergius read aloud these dispatches in the Senate, and then *ex auctoritate patrum* to the People" (32.31.6). And again, on receipt of the news of the victory of T. Quinctius Flamininus in 197, "the *pr.* M. Sergius first read this letter in the the Senate, and then *ex auctoritate patrum* in a *contio*" (33.24.4). The Roman Senate and magistrates had learned from the experience of Pomponius the praetor in 217.

VIII. *The* Magister Equitum *as President of the Senate*

At the very end of the year 216, following the report of the death of the *consul designatus* L. Postumius Albinus in Gaul, it is Ti. Sempronius Gracchus, *mag. eq.* and *cos. des.* 215, who presided over a Senate meeting where the military *provinciae* were reviewed and arrangements for the following year were discussed (Liv. 23.25.2–11, esp. 2 "Ti. Sempronius senatum habuit"). In the light of Livy's explicit statement, Mommsen (*St.-R.* I³ 209 n. 5) is wrong to suppose that a praetor actually may have presided over this session; however, the praetor M. Claudius Marcellus was in Rome at the time, and spoke at this important meeting.

It is very difficult to disentangle the background to this Senate meeting (which finds no discussion in M. Bonnefond-Coudry, *Sénat*). The peregrine praetor Pomponius Matho had summoned the dictator M. Iunius Pera with his *mag. eq.* to hold the elections, and also called the praetor M. Claudius Marcellus to Rome to consult with the Senate (Liv. 23.24.1–2). After the elections, the dictator returned to his legions (23.24.5). What immediately follows in Livy's account is the surprising death of the praetor and *cos. des.* L. Postumius Albinus, which left the remains of the two legions in Gaul without a commander. Pomponius Matho may have been dispatched immediately to Gaul, the *provincia* in which he certainly later served in 215 and 214 (see 5.2.1 above). It is most irregular, however, that in his (presumed) absence, the *mag. eq.* Ti. Gracchus presided over the Senate meeting in late 216, when the praetor M. Claudius Marcellus was available.

How did the *magister equitum* manage to act as president on this occasion? First, *imperium* was not needed for this particular job: in a few years (210) we find that the tribune of the Plebs, who at this time was not a member of the Senate, could perform the task (see 5.4.2 above, also Ateius Capito in Gel. 14.8.2). As far as we know, tribunician presidency of the Senate would not recur for some time in the Republic, though it may have, unrecorded, once the precedent was accepted. (The only Republican parallels down to 50 B.C. are apparently C. Gracchus in 123, then in 91 and late in the year 57: see 12.4.2 above) It also should be mentioned that changes could be made *ad hoc* in the proper order of magistrates qualified to act as president of the Senate: see 5.4.2 for an *S.C.* of 197 and a plebiscite of 172, each privileging praetors over consuls. And one urban praetor in 200 apparently gave over the presidency to his colleague in the peregrine jurisdiction (5.4.1).

But at the end of 216, of course, we have a case of a praetor yielding to a junior magistrate, who may not even have had (at this point, at least) a recognized right of presiding over the Senate. Varro, in the famous *commentarium* on Senate protocol that he originally wrote for Pompey in 70 and revised after 43, skips the *mag. eq.* (as well as the censors) in his apparently comprehensive list of magistrates who had this right (see Gel. 14.7.4–5; Mommsen, *St.-R.* II³ 209 n. 5, even suspected that Varro had an anti-Caesarian motive in this). Cicero in the ideal constitution set out in the *De Legibus* (3.10), does allow the *mag. eq.* the right of presiding over the Senate, but this may be a proposed innovation (see 2.3.2 above).

Of the examples of a *mag. eq.* as president of the Senate collected by Willems (*Sénat* II 129 n. 4), none offers clear confirmation for Ti. Sempronius' case in 216. An alleged instance in 325 (Liv. 8.33.3–4) is particularly problematic, where Livy's formulation ("patre auctore [i.e., the father of the *mag. eq.*, M. Fabius Ambustus, who at the time held no magistracy] . . . vocato extemplo senatu") is (purposely?) vague. Livy may not have known (i.e., his annalistic source did not say) whether the *mag. eq.* actually presided over the Senate in this instance (cf. Mommsen, *St.-R.* I³ 209 n. 5).

Willems also points out that Caesar's *mag. eq.* M. Aemilius Lepidus in 48 is said by Dio to be competent to preside over the Senate, and in this "he exhibited some semblance of the Republic" (42.27.2; cf. the S.C. contained in J. A.J. 14.10.6). It is possible that the *mag. eq.* had by now accrued some special powers not inherent in the original office, which was in abeyance from 202 down to 82/81, and then again until 48. (See 2.3.1, on the lictors of the *mag. eq.*) The master of the horse's constitutional "right" in this regard may be only (pace Dio) a Caesarian innovation. This "right" may have been given to the magistrate by a *lex* (perhaps in the very one mentioned by Dio at 43.48.2, on which see 2.3.1), or it may have been simply arrogated. The dictator Caesar was not over concerned with legal technicalities, especially in 49 and 48 (see 2.3.2 for what he did or allowed in these years). But the most likely explanation is that M. Aemilius Lepidus was seen as acting with derivative power as the dictator's representative (cf. the indisputable power of the *mag. eq.* to command an army), and was accepted as such. By this stage, the *mag. eq.* had received a whole bundle of attributes, and was even claiming a derivative right to remain in office past six months (see 2.3.1). A de facto right to preside over the Senate—which of course is independent of *imperium*—simply may have been assumed.

To return to the problem of 216, where there was probably little precedent to act as a guide. One can only speculate what happened. I would suggest that, after the elections, the dictator M. Iunius Pera ordered the *mag. eq.* Ti. Sempronius Gracchus to act as his representative in the city, forbidding the praetors Pomponius Matho and M. Marcellus to interfere. The statement "the master of the horse was left in Rome to . . . consult the Senate" ("relicto magistro equitum Romae, qui . . . patres consuleret"—Liv. 23.24.5) may in fact allude to Pera's original order. The praetors Matho and Marcellus of course had to bow to the *maius imperium* of the dictator and let the *mag. eq.* preside. (On the *mag. eq.* as "Vertreter" of the dictator, see Mommsen, *St.-R.* II³ 178f; also R. Wittmann in Kunkel, *Staatsordnung* 719, positing that solution for this very incident.) By the standards of 216, a most turbulent year, a *magister equitum* and *consul designatus* as president of the Senate was an acceptable innovation, since it would last only for a few days. The fact that protocol was violated (i.e., an available praetor was supplanted) shows only the extent of the emergency. The dictator M. Iunius Pera must have seen that continuity was of the highest importance.

IX. *The Peregrine Praetor outside of Rome in the 170s*

There are three instances in the 170s when the *praetor inter peregrinos* is known to have left the city. On the first occasion, in 178, it was feared that the Histrians at Aquileia had totally destroyed a consular army under A. Manlius Vulso (Liv. 41.5.3). The Senate ordered Manlius' consular colleague, M. Iunius Brutus, to cross from his *provincia* (the war against the Ligurians) into Gaul; it also instructed the *pr. per.* Ti. Claudius Nero "to defend that *provincia* during the consul's absence." Nero immediately set out to Pisa "paludatus" (see 41.5.5–6 and 8, and cf. C. F. Konrad, *JRA* 7 [1994] 155, on the technical term). M. Titinius, the *pr. urb.*, did not leave the city (Broughton, *MRR* I 395, is wrong in this). He merely ordered that the first legion and an allied force of the same size meet at Ariminum: "Titinius sent C. Cassius, a military tribune, to Ariminum to command the legion, and held a levy at Rome" (Liv. 41.5.7–8). This was late in the year. A decision had already been made to prorogue the consuls of 178 (41.6.2). In addition, the *cos.* M. Iunius Brutus—who never returned to Pisa—boasted at the consular elections that he had not spent more than eleven days in Histria (41.7.6).

The story continues. At the beginning of the next year, 177, Livy states "Ti. Claudius *pro cos.*, who had been praetor in the previous year, was in charge of Pisa (*Pisis praeerat*) with a garrison of one legion" (41.12.1). He stayed in the area of Liguria for all that year (41.14.2), and into 176 (41.14.11; he must have been at Pisa until mid-August—41.17.6). The report of 41.12.1 is puzzling, since we would expect Ti. Claudius to be *pro praetore*. The wording seems to eliminate the possibility of simple scribal error; and we know from practice elsewhere (7.1.4 above) that one's level of *imperium* is not necessarily correlated with army size. If the notice is true (as Mommsen believed—*St.-R.* II³ 649 n. 2), I should think he was prorogued, with the People raising his *imperium*. Note the case of M. Claudius Marcellus, *pr.* 216 and *pro cos.* 215 (8.3.1 above); a similar procedure must have been followed in the case of P. Sempronius Tuditanus, *pro cos.* in Greece in 205 (Additional Note XII). The explanation must be that at the beginning of 177, both of the consuls were needed elsewhere. Ti. Sempronius Gracchus was to serve outside Italy (in Sardinia), and his consular colleague C. Claudius Pulcher was expected to fight a Histrian war. Though Pulcher soon did make it to Liguria (*MRR* I 397–398), Ti. Nero still stayed into 176. The Ligurians for the past seventeen years had seen only men of consular rank in their area: Nero was literally acting pro consule, "in place of a consul," and his *imperium* was enhanced, in keeping with the now-traditional status of the Roman commanders on the Ligurian front (see 8 n. 17).

Our second example is the peregrine praetor of 172, Cn. Sicinius, who crossed to Epirus during his year of office ("priusquam magistratu abiret") to bring a consular army and a fleet into the Macedonian theater (8.5.1). Though Sicinius' actual crossing took place late in the year (mid-February), the *pr. urb.* might have had to see to many of his routine duties (see Additional Note VI). Sicinius stayed in the east well into the next year: before his departure it seems to have been decided that he would be prorogued in Macedonia "donec successor veniret" (42.27.6–8).

The third occasion when a peregrine praetor left the city in this decade is found for 170, when it was decided to send eight ships to the *legatus* C. Furius on the island of Issa, in order to monitor better the activities of the Illyrian king Gentius. "Two thousand soldiers were put aboard these ships, a force that the pr. M. Raecius raised *ex senatus consulto*, in that part of Italy which faced Illyricum" (43.9.6). Later in that consular year (January), when the Senate called back (early) the consul A. Atilius Serranus to Rome to hold the elections for the forthcoming year, M. Raecius was ordered to ensure that all senators returned and remained in the city (43.11.3–5). On the one previous occasion when such a measure was taken—in 191—it was a consul who issued the edict (36.3.2). This seems to have led P. Foucart (*MAI* 37 [1906] 316f) and later Broughton (*MRR* I 423 n. 3) to make M. Raecius *praetor urbanus* and the other city praetor Q. Maenius *praetor inter peregrinos*: most unlikely, in view of Raecius' activities on the Adriatic coast. M. Raecius was chosen to perform the task of recalling senators to Rome precisely because as *praetor inter peregrinos* he was at relative liberty to leave the city and scout out would-be offenders of his edict.

One final note: In 174, the *pr. urb.* may have had to assume the duties (in addition to his own) of the unfortunate *pr. per.* L. Cornelius Scipio. This man, though properly elected, may never have been able to act in his jurisdiction. Scipio allegedly suffered the double indignity of having his family prohibit him from exercising his office (V. Max. 3.5.1; cf. V. Max. 4.5.3, with wrong *praenomen*), and of having the censors eject him from the Senate during his actual year of office (Liv. 41.27.2).

X. The "Two Lictors" of the Urban Praetor

Holders of praetorian *imperium* in the Republic are variously reported to have been attended by six and two lictors. (Praetors who held enhanced, i.e., consular, *imperi-*

um, such as the governors of the Spains, were preceded, like consuls, by twelve lictors—see 7.1.2.) Polybius—who had seen actual praetors in Rome as well as in Greece—makes no reference to two lictors. In fact, for Polybius, "six axes" are synonymous with the praetorship. Polybius calls the magistrate variously στρατηγὸς ἐξαπέλεκυς (3.106.6; 33.1.5), or (more often) simply ἐξαπέλεκυς (2.23.5, 24.6; 3.40.11 and 14), as well as στρατηγός (3.85.8, 118.6; 6.53.7; 7.3.1 ὁ τεταγμένος ἐπὶ Λιλυβαίου στρατηγὸς τῶν 'Ρωμαίων; 21.10.4, 44.3 τὸν ἐπὶ τοῦ ναυτικοῦ στρατηγόν; 23.2.9; 28.16.6 τὸν ἐπὶ τοῦ ναυτικοῦ στρατηγόν; 30.4.4 and 6; 31.23.5; 35.2.5 κατὰ πόλιν ὁ στρατηγός; 36.4.4 and 6; 5.8 ἐπὶ τῆς Σικελίας τετάχθαι στρατηγόν). A prorogued praetor is sometimes designated ἀντιστράτηγος (8.3.1), sometimes simply στρατηγός (8.7.11): both these references refer to the same man, Ap. Claudius Pulcher in 213. Polybius' use of these various designations is not systematic. In his writings, both στρατηγός and ἐξαπέλεκυς can also denote the office in a general sense (στρατηγός—6.53.7; τῶν στρατηγῶν τις—30.4.4; 'Ρωμαῖοι . . . ἐξαπέστειλαν . . . ἕνα δὲ τῶν ἐξαπελέκεων εἰς Τυρρηνίαν—2.23.5) Although he usually terms city praetors στρατηγός (3.85.8; 23.2.9; 31.23.5; 35.2.5 κατὰ πόλιν; 36.4.4 and 6) and praetors in the field στρατηγός or ἐξαπέλεκυς (for the latter, 2.24.6; 3.40.11 and 14), Polybius once uses ἐξαπέλεκυς of a city praetor (33.1.5: A. Postumius Albinus in 155 στρατηγὸς ὢν ἐξαπέλεκυς καὶ βραβεύων τὸ διαβούλιον). A few other authors also allude to "six axes" in reference to both provincial praetors and the praetor in general (Mommsen, *St.-R.* I³ 384 nn. 4–5; of those passages, Cic. *Ver.* 2.5.142 is not relevant—see ch. 13 n. 52).

The original praetor must have had six lictors at the inception of the office, at least when outside of the city. That goes as well for the first provincial governor, the *praetor inter peregrinos*—hence the generalization of this custom for all praetors in the field. A passage in Valerius Maximus (1.1.9) at first glance seems to show that praetors could be accompanied by six lictors in the city. Valerius tells of a praetor L. Furius Bibaculus, "who, when ordered by his own father, the chief of the college of Salii, carried—with his six lictors preceding—the arms and sacred shields, though he had exemption from this duty [i.e., of carrying the *ancilia*] by reason of his magistracy." The location of this (undated) anecdote must be Rome, since that is where the rituals of the Salii took place. The pious Bibaculus may have been a praetor in the period before the Second Punic War, when the complete list of praetors becomes known. (*MRR* I 237 even assigns a tentative date of 219 for his praetorship.) But the period after 166, when Livy's account gives out on us, cannot be excluded (thus Münzer, *RE* s.v. *Furius* 36 col. 320). There is no reason for any preference regarding this praetor's date.

Mommsen (*St.-R.* I³ 384 n. 5), who believed that only praetors receiving a *provincia* outside the city were entitled to six lictors, was convinced that L. Furius Bibaculus must have been a provincial praetor who participated in the procession in the short interval between entering his office and his departure for his *provincia*. This explanation is not necessary. Valerius Maximus' statement that Furius Bibaculus had six lictors probably should be rejected altogether. Lactantius (*Inst. Div.* 1.21), who has this same story and follows the same source as Valerius, does not specify the number of lictors: Valerius may have made up the number himself. In the Empire, praetors do seem to have been accompanied by six lictors in Rome

(Mart. 11.98.15; cf. D.C. 53.13.4). Valerius Maximus may have thought that the same was true for the Republic, or he simply may have ascribed the practice of his own day to Furius Bibaculus for rhetorical effect. Indeed, "Bi-baculus" implies two (see below).

The detail of the *duo lictores* finds confirmation in Plautus' *Epidicus* lines 23–28 (ca. 190 B.C.). Although the setting of the relevant passage is at Athens, the coloring is Roman. The joke is that Epidicus is acting like the urban praetor. Thespio says to him, "at unum a praetura tua, | Epidice, abest | . . . lictores duo, duo ulmei | fasces virgarum."

Cicero speaks of two lictors as the normal number for the *praetor urbanus*. In a (highly rhetorical) section of the *De Lege Agraria* (2.93) on the conduct of certain magistrates in Capua at the time of the Social War, he relates: "These men wished to be called 'praetors', though in other colonies they were called *duoviri* . . . also, lictors walked before them, not with staffs (*bacilli*), but paired, with *fasces*—as they precede urban praetors here (*ut his praetoribus urbanis anteeunt*)." The one detail of this passage that Cicero could hardly exaggerate is the number of lictors, which was certainly known to his audience, the Roman People. A further point: no Latin author uses "praetores urbani" to encompass both praetors at Rome, that is, the urban and peregrine praetor (though cf. "duae urbanae provinciae" at Liv. 43.11.8 and 45.44.2). But one must infer (indirectly) from this passage that the peregrine praetor had two lictors as well. He could hardly have more than the *praetor urbanus*.

A third reference to *duo lictores*, again in connection with the *praetor urbanus*, occurs in a well-known passage in Censorinus (*Natal*. 24.3 = RS II 44):

> In the XII Tables it is written as follows: "The setting of the sun shall be the last part of the day (*suprema tempestas*)." But afterward M. Plaetorius the tribune passed a plebiscite, in which it is written: "praetor urbanus qui nunc est quique post hac fiat duo lictores apud se habeto isque supremam ad solem occasum iusque inter cives dicito."

(The text is that of our oldest manuscript, the eighth-century Coloniensis 166.) The verb *fiat* is certainly strange, and the words "isque . . . inter cives dicito" make no sense as they stand. The text has accordingly often been emended (see the discussion of J. A. Crook, *Athenaeum* 62 [1984] 586–595), but no convincing solution has yet emerged. (The precise extent and nature of the lacuna cannot be known, of course.) But most puzzling of all is the phrase "qui nunc est." This law must be changing an existing function of a current magistrate. In addition to the textual mess, it is doubtful whether Censorinus is quoting accurately. Varro also refers to the *lex Plaetoria*, but differs from our text of Censorinus: *L.* 6.5 "lex Plaetoria (Pretoria, MS.) id quoque tempus esse iubet supremum quo praetor in comitio supremam pronuntiavit populo." The fact that Varro in this passage does not mention the *duo lictores* need not bother us, since his principal interest in this *lex* is its redefinition of the word *suprema*. And the date of the *lex Plaetoria* is likewise irretrievable. Two of the elements in this *lex*—the *duo lictores* and the urban praetor's administration of justice *inter cives*—may not be new measures, but in fact tralatician, thus complicating matters all the more (though the imperatives suggest they are not). However, the redefinition of *suprema* (for which the passage is quoted by Censorinus and Gellius) must definitely be a new feature. The praetor, within limits, was given power to announce it (i.e., he could set his own working hours).

Mommsen believed that the law could not be older than the mid-third century, arguing that the designation *praetor urbanus* assumes the existence of the peregrine praetor (*St.-R.* I³ 384 n. 2). In this he is followed by Münzer, *RE* s.v. *Plaetorius* 10 col. 1947; cf. also F. Millar, *JRS* 79 (1989) 146 ("not earlier than 242"). Though this view has been challenged (see Kunkel, *Staatsordnung* 121 n. 67), it is probably true: we have seen (in 4.2) that the term *praetor urbanus* very likely dates back only to the mid-third century. J. A. Crook (*Athenaeum* 62 [1984] 594) has suggested that the *lex Plaetoria* was occasioned by the creation of the *praetor inter peregrinos*, which he dates ca. 242: "[T]he *lex Plaetoria* was the very statute that set up the new structure of two jurisdictional praetors . . . [T]he creation of the new post would be bound to necessitate a redefinition of the privileges and powers of the original one." Crook's hypothesis makes a fair argument, but is not decisive. As Münzer (*RE* s.v. *Plaetorius* 10 col. 1947) has pointed out, all the known Plaetorii belong to the last 150 years of the Republic, that is, after ca. 200. In addition, the details in the Censorinus passage that Crook considers a "redefinition" of the powers of the *praetor urbanus* may be partly tralatician. It is impossible to ascertain exactly how important or innovative this law actually was.

The evidence of Valerius Maximus, our only authority for a city praetor's six lictors, is too uncertain to use. But it seems practically necessary to suppose that the praetor originally did have six lictors in Rome, a number that at some point was reduced. The *terminus ante quem* for this (presumed) reduction is provided by Plautus (ca. 190). Such a change would not be introduced at random: it should reflect a real innovation in the nature of regular magistrates with *imperium*. If not original to 366, the creation of the *praetor inter peregrinos* in the 240s (and with it, the introduction of the designation "urbanus" for the original praetor) is just one of several possible occasions for the institution of two lictors for the praetor in the city.

The innovations of 227 (4.3.3 above, two additional praetors for Sicily and Sardinia) or (perhaps) 197 (5.3.2 above) can be said to have led to a "redefinition" of the role of the urban and peregrine praetors. Since the function of these offices was planned to change, the insignia of the urban praetor—and probably the peregrine praetor—may have undergone a metamorphosis as well, at least *domi*. (In support of 227 as a terminus post quem see K.-H. Vogel, *ZRG* 67 [1950] 99–104, but with an unacceptable hypothesis that the two lictors represented a minimum requirement for attendance.) Nevertheless, the year 197 itself should probably be excluded as the precise date for a change in the number of the city praetors' lictors. In that year, two new praetors were granted consular *imperium* (i.e., attendance by twelve lictors) to serve as governors of the Spains; it would be surprising if the Romans introduced two (possibly irritating) innovations at the same time.

Two final observations: On the basis of Valerius Maximus' story of L. Bibaculus, Arriat (*Le préteur pérégrin* 11) made the interesting suggestion that praetors were entitled to six lictors on ceremonial occasions, but in their everyday activities used only two. Once the Valerius Maximus "evidence" is taken away, that hypothesis can no longer stand. But Arriat may have a point. There is every reason to think that, at funerals, ex-urban praetors would always be represented by six lictors; at these occasions, other high magistracies seem to have received the grandest insignia to which they were entitled (cf. Plb. 6.53.7–8 with 2.2.2 above). Another possibility is that the two lictors applied to the praetor only in connection with his court of law, which of course was just one of the many tasks he performed. Here one can appeal to Polybius, who uses στρατηγὸς . . . ἑξαπέλεκυς of a praetor acting as Senate president in 155 (33.1.5); but Cicero (Agr. 2.95, on praetors on the move) seems to gainsay him.

XI. *The Praetorian Colleges of 185, 177, and 166*

For the year 185, Livy used mostly Polybius; he did not have (or did not use) a full annalistic source. As Nissen noted, in Livy's report of this year "there is missing the allotment of *provinciae*, the expiation of prodigies, and, especially, all the activities of the consuls in Rome" (*Kritische Untersuchungen* 224). To this list of omissions we should add that Livy's report of the praetorian elections for 185 (39.23.2) is probably mistaken. "Praetores facti P. Cornelius Cethegus A. Postumius Albinus C. Afranius Stellio C. Atilius Serranus L. Postumius Tempsanus M. Claudius Marcellinus." The first and last men on this list are actually non-entities, who have no recorded activities in this year. Münzer (*RE* s.v. *Cornelius* 95, followed by Broughton, *MRR* II 551) identifies Cethegus with P. Cornelius (L.f. P.n.) Cethegus, *aed. cur.* 187, *cos.* 181 (prorogued into 180), and *Xvir agris dandis assignandis* 173. However, we readily can transfer all these offices to a very real character by the same name, who held the praetorship in the next year, P. Cornelius Cethegus (Liv. 39.32.14, 38.2, 39.15). If we excise the otherwise unknown Marcellinus and Cethegus from the praetor list for 185, we have a ready candidate for one of the two vacancies which results: A. Manlius Vulso, *cos.* 178, for whom our sources register no praetorship. (See G. Rögler, *Klio* 40 [1962] 101, who suggests this very solution.) Barring special dispensation, it probably was impossible to reach the consulship without it in this period—especially after the *lex Villia Annalis* of 180 (Liv. 40.44.1). An interval of seven years between praetorship and consulship seems quite representative of the fortunes of the Manlii Vulsones at this time. L. Vulso, *pr.* 197, never reached the consulship, and Cn. Vulso took six years (*pr.* 195 and *cos.* 189). Broughton (*MRR* I 361, with expanded argumentation in III 137) suggested that A. Manlius Vulso was *praetor suffectus* in 189 (presumably to replace L. Baebius Dives, who died on his way to Hispania Ulterior). This cannot be right. *Suffecti* do not seem to be elected when provincial praetors die in office, however early in the year; and Livy tells us exactly how the Romans compensated for this particular mishap (see Additional Note IV).

Cn. Cornelius Scipio and C. Valerius Laevinus served as *prr.* 179 (in the peregrine jurisdiction and Sardinia respectively—Liv. 40.44.2 and 7), but are reported as elected praetors again for 177, with no mention of iteration of office (41.8.1). They are not wanted. If their names are retained, the total of praetors for that year would be six. Under the *lex Baebia* of 181 (Liv. 40.44.2), there should have been only four praetors elected in 177. The law was probably observed: it is suspicious that Livy (41.8.3) reports "Scipio et Laevinus Galliam in duas divisam provincias sortiti sunt," an unparalleled arrangement for this period. And it is difficult to see how, if there were two praetors in Gaul, the Ligurians could launch a surprise attack on Mutina (41.14.1–2). We are told that the consul C. Claudius Pulcher was forced to proceed from Rome to deal with the invaders: there is no mention of Cornelius or Valerius in the field. In addition, one of these two praetors, C. Valerius Laevinus, was elected *cos. suff.* in 176. A consulship in the year following a praetorship is not found for the post-Hannibalic period, and would be particularly strange, now that the *lex Villia Annalis* was in effect. Probably a late annalist thought there ought to be six praetors, and invented two—Cn. Scipio and C. Laevinus—when he found only four.

There is also a problem with the arrangements for 166, the last year for which we have Livy. The exact assignment of *provinciae* to the praetors of this year is unknown; it cannot be based on the supposition that the order of names of praetors at Liv. 45.44.2 is parallel to the order followed in the list of *provinciae* assigned (see D. Wilsdorf, *LSKPh* 1 [1878] 94; cf. Münzer, *RE* s.v. *Licinius* 131 col. 452; H. Gundel, *RE* s.v. *Quinctilius* 13, col. 904; *MRR* I 437 n. 1). Livy employs a similar narrative technique (i.e., a list of praetors elected, followed by a list of the *provinciae* decreed for the sortition) when describing the arrangements for 171 (42.28.5–6), 169 (43.11.7–8), and 168 (44.17.5 and 9). Only for 168 do the two lists match up with what was actually allotted (44.17.10); because of the stress of the war with Macedonia, the sortition might even have been fixed by electoral order (on this, see further Appendix B.9).

XII. *Commands in Greece 214–205: The Principle of "Persistence" of Consular or Praetorian* Imperium

The first eight years of the Second Punic War saw intense fighting in Italy, Sicily, and Spain. Some pressure was released after 211, when Sicily had been rid of the Carthaginians. However, there is no point in the Hannibalic period when the Senate felt it could make a substantial administrative and military commitment to the east.

As we have seen in 8.5.1, the first Roman commander with *imperium* to cross the Adriatic with a military force during this conflict was M. Valerius Laevinus, *pr.* 215, who sailed to Illyria as *pro pr.* in 214, and then had to remain in Greece for a further three years. Laevinus took with him (at most) a Roman legion and fifty ships (Liv. 24.11.3; 40.5 and 8). This, in fact, was larger than the force that his successor, the *pro cos.* P. Sulpicius Galba, was to hold in the years 210–206 (in general, see Brunt, *Italian Manpower* 666, and cf. J. W. Rich, *PCPhS* 30 [1984] 152–155, who thinks the size of Laevinus' force is much exaggerated). After some quick initial military action in 214 that saved Oricum and Apollonia (*MRR* I 260 and 261), Valerius made no move against Philip for the next two years (213 and 212), but instead launched a diplomatic offensive, all in a bid for an alliance with the Aetolian League; the object was to embroil Philip in a Balkanwide war and thus forestall the possibility of him crossing to Italy and joining forces with Hannibal. The Aetolians agreed to a treaty in late summer 211, though its final ratification came only in 210 (Liv. 26.24.1–16, with E. Badian, *Latomus* 17 [1958] 197–206, and cf. F. W. Walbank, *Commentary* II 11–13 and Rich, *PCPhS* 30 [1984] 155–157). For his part, the praetor

Valerius, making good on Rome's end of the bargain, in autumn and early winter 211 effectively debarred Philip's fleet from entering the Corinthian Gulf (26.24.15–26.3). It was at Anticyra in early 210 that M. Valerius Laevinus heard what must have been not entirely unexpected news: "He had been elected consul in his absence, and P. Sulpicius [*cos.* 211] was coming as a successor" (26.26.4). The war had spread beyond a standoff in south Illyria into a major conflict encompassing the entire peninsula, and the Senate had decided that a consular commander should take over the Roman fleet.

Hannibal's presence in Italy meant that P. Sulpicius Galba only made it to Greece as *pro cos.* in early 210. There he remained as the sole Roman commander with *imperium* from 210 through 206 (*MRR* I 287, 292, 296, and 300). Galba was highly competent, yet by autumn 206 the Aetolians were so hard pressed by Philip's raids and so disheartened by Rome's failure to respond to their requests for further military assistance that they decided on making peace with the Macedonians (Plb. 11.7.2–3; Liv. 29.12.1; 32.21.17 and 36.31.11 [both from speeches], with Walbank, *Commentary* II 278–279 for the chronology). The Aetolians had already arranged for peace on Philip's terms—the Peace of Phoenice—by the time long-awaited help came from Italy. P. Sempronius Tuditanus, a *privatus* with consular *imperium*, crossed to Greece in 205 as Sulpicius' successor, bringing ten thousand infantry, one thousand cavalry, and thirty-five additional ships (Liv. 29.12.2). (J. W. Rich, *PCPhS* 30 [1984] 136–151, offers an alternative chronology for these events, with Tuditanus arriving in Greece in 206, but it is far from compelling in its details.)

Livy wholly omits the background and mechanics of P. Sempronius Tuditanus' extraordinary appointment as Galba's successor, forcing us to reconstruct these items for ourselves. Tuditanus, a hero at Cannae (*MRR* I 251), was a man of some experience, having served as *pr.* 213 in Gaul (and *pro pr.* there through 211), as well as censor in 209. His special command is significant in two respects. First, it illustrates the emergence of the principle of what we may call the "persistence" of consular *imperium*. Once a *provincia* had been declared consular, it tended to remain consular for some time, even if a shortage of suitable commanders already holding consular *imperium* meant resorting to a special vote by the People. Similar decisions had been made in 215 (the command of M. Claudius Marcellus to fight against Hannibal in Campania—Liv. 23.30.19 with 8.3.1 above) and in 210 (the special consular command of P. Scipio Africanus, to replace his father in Spain—26.18.4, etc. with 7.1.3 above). I have suggested that the Senate, in the same year as Tuditanus' command (205), had attempted to downgrade the *imperium* of the command in Spain from consular to praetorian (Liv. 28.38.1 with 7.1.4 above), only to reverse the decision when the experiment failed. The *privati* who were to hold the Iberian peninsula received their consular *imperium* by a vote of the People (29.13.7); the Senate retained this development in the new, more permanent arrangements of 197.

A later example of the principle of "persistence" at work is the special consular command of Ti. Claudius Nero, *pr. per.* 178, at Pisa in 177 (see 8.1.1 and Additional Note IX). Again, it must be stressed that the decision to create a special consular command had nothing to do with the size of the army in a particular *provincia* (see 7.1.4). P. Sempronius Tuditanus in Greece in 205 and Ti. Claudius Nero in 178 had in fact only one Roman legion. It appears, rather, that the presence of a consular commander accompanied by twelve lictors in a bellicose *provincia* was perceived to have an important psychological effect on the enemy, which translated into a Roman military advantage. Once the enemy was used to consular commanders, experience showed that it was inadvisable to send praetorian commanders in their stead.

In noncrucial *provinciae*, we can even detect a principle of "persistence of praetorian *imperium*," especially in the maintenance of garrison forces under praetors at Capua and Tarentum, and in Etruria during the Hannibalic War. Occasionally, we can almost glimpse the decision process at work. In 210, there seems to have been a reversal of the decision to hand Gaul to a *legatus*, and rather to continue to treat it as a praetorian *provincia* (Liv. 26.28.5; 27.7.8—see 8.3.2 above). Following the death of Quinctius Claudus Flamininus (*pr.* 208 and *pro pr.* into at least 206) at Tarentum in 206 or 205—roughly the same time as the dispatch of P. Sempronius Tuditanus to Greece—the Romans decided not to return to the policy of 214–210, when Tarentum was governed by a *praefectus*. Instead, the late praetor's putative nephew, T. Quinctius Flamininus, received a special grant of praetorian *imperium* to continue in Claudus' place (inferred from Liv. 29.13.6—204).

There is a second significant feature to the appointment of P. Sempronius Tuditanus to serve as P. Sulpicius Galba's successor in Greece. If Livy's report of the arrangements for 205 is accurate, other options may have been available to solve the problem of succeeding P. Sulpicius Galba in Greece, such as sending L. Veturius Philo, *cos.* 206, who as it happens was not prorogued into the next year (see Liv. 28.45.9–11). L. Philo, like Tuditanus, had served as praetor in Gaul, and, as a *consularis*, would have been just as fully qualified for a command in the east. Moreover, there would be much less constitutional bother, since he need only be prorogued into the next year, as P. Sulpicius Galba (*cos.* 211) had been in 210. In truth, the appointment of Tuditanus seems to have been *ad hominem*, like Pompey's to Spain in 77 "pro consulibus" (11.8.2).

The fact that Tuditanus was sent as a *privatus* to Greece points to 206 as the year the decision was made at Rome. Although Hannibal, holed up in Bruttium, was not all that menacing by now, both consuls of 206 in their actual year of office had to be available to face the Carthaginian general if necessary. (In the event, it did not come to a fight in that year—Liv. 28.10.8; 11.8–12.9.) Meanwhile, the motions of the Aetolian League toward Philip at that time also demanded some action on the Senate's part. The Senate's response was largely symbolic: the appointment (or promise of the appointment) of the *censorius* P. Sempronius Tuditanus to bring reinforcements to Greece and to succeed the *pro cos.* P. Galba. Although Tuditanus and his troops and fleet could not cross until spring 205, the Senate and P. Sulpicius Galba may have adduced (we can imagine) the glorious precedent of the *privatus* P. Cornelius Scipio in Spain (and the like) in the hope of retaining the Aetolians (cf. App. *Mac.* 3.1–3—winter 207/206?—for their truculent mood at this time). As it turned out, P. Sempronius Tuditanus crossed too late. The Roman failure to break the treaty between Philip and Aetolia resulted in Tuditanus negotiating the Peace of Phoenice, and then returning to Rome to serve as consul for 204 (Liv. 29.12.1–16).

Simply put, special considerations affected the creation of P. Sempronius Tuditanus' command—particularly, the pressure exerted by the Aetolian League. But Sempronius' command demonstrates that the Senate, even at this late stage in the war, was still quite willing to invest *privati* with *imperium*. This attitude is confirmed by the case of T. Quinctius Flamininus at Tarentum, who was given a special praetorian command by 205 (8.2.2).

XIII. Praetorii *in the* Consilium *of* RDGE 12 (S.C. de Agro Pergameno)

The *S.C. de agro Pergameno* seems best assigned not to 129 (as had been long supposed) but to 101 B.C.: see the discussion in 9.1.5 with n. 80 and the bibliography there collected, especially E. Badian, *LCM* 11.1 (1986) 16 on C. Coelius C.f., tenth in the *consilium*. Badian presents a strong case for identifying that man with the *tr. pl.* 107 and *cos.* 94 C. Coelius C.f. C.n. Caldus: not only does the rank fit, but his well-attested *novitas* (on which see below) guarantees he had no senatorial antecedents. Assuming the date of 101, how many praetorians can we identify with reasonable certainty?

1. *Q. Caecilius Q.f. Aniensis* First (of 55) in the senatorial *consilium* to RDGE 12. We would expect—given the large size of this *consilium*—that the individual in first position, Q. Caecilius Q.f. of the tribe Aniensis, would be a *consularis*. Mattingly (*AJPh* 93 [1972] 423) makes a good case for Q. Caecilius Q.f. Q.n. Balearicus (*cos.* 123), and that is the solution I adopt here.

2. *C. [——]ius C.f. Menenia* Our second name can be either consular or praetorian: the available possibilities (given the length of the lacuna, which allows a supplement of four letters to the *nomen*) are C. Atilius Serranus (*cos.* 106, filiation unknown), C. Flavius C.f. Fimbria (*cos.* 104), and C. Fannius C.f. (*pr.* by 118) (Mattingly, *AJPh* 93 [1972] 421f). But he may be an otherwise unknown senior *praetorius*.

3. *M. Pupius M.f. Scaptia* From position in this large *consilium*, almost certainly of (senior) praetorian status in 101 B.C. Mattingly (*AJPh* 93 [1972] 421) reasonably equates him with the M. Piso who adopted the future *cos.* 61 at an advanced age (Cic. *Dom.* 35 "summa senectute") but by 91 (*De Orat.* 1.104). Cf. also Badian, *Chiron* 20 (1990) 395, accepting the identification.

4. *C. Cornelius M.f. Stellatina* From position likely to be of praetorian status in 101 B.C. The only Republican Cornelii known to use both the *praenomina* Gaius and Marcus are the patrician Cethegi, and so the identification of this man as a Cethegus (suggested long ago by Willems, *Sénat* I 701) seems relatively secure. Mattingly (*AJPh* 93 [1972] 422) presumes he is son of the *cos.* 160 M. Cornelius C.f. C.n. Cethegus, which seems plausible since the L. Iulius Sex.f. (Caesar), who holds seventh place in the same *consilium* (see below), should be son of the *cos.* 157.

5. *L. Memmius C.f. Menenia*   From position, quite conceivably a *praetorius* in 101 B.C. He is possibly to be identified with either the *monetalis* L. Memmius of *RRC* I 315 no. 304 (dated by Crawford to "109 or 108 B.C."), or the L. Memmius of *P. Teb.* I 33 (112 B.C.), a Roman senator said to be ἐν μίζονι ἀξιώατι κα[ὶ] τιμῆι κείμενος (lines 3–6), who was to receive elaborate entertainment at public expense during his sightseeing tour of the Fayum, or both. Despite the formulation of the Egyptian document, that Memmius need not have been of praetorian standing in the year 112. In Egypt, even a *pro quaestore* might enjoy a lavish reception (see Plu. *Luc.* 2.6–9 on L. Lucullus in 86 B.C.). H. B. Mattingly, in *AJPh* 92 (1972) 421, goes further and regards the identification with the visitor to Egypt as certain.

6. *Q. Valgius M.f. [——]lia*   Probably a junior *praetorius* or (less likely) senior *aedilicius* in 101 B.C. No previous Valgii are known to hold a magistracy in the Republic; on the distribution of the name, see Wiseman, *NM* 269 no. 460.

7. *L. Iulius Sex.f. Falerna*   This man "can surely only be the son of Sex. Iulius Caesar (*cos.* 157 B.C.) and younger brother of the homonymous urban praetor of 123 B.C. In 90 B.C. his own son was consul, so that he was probably born ca. 160 B.C." Thus Mattingly in *AJPh* 93 (1972) 422; Badian (*Chiron* 20 [1990] 389) also makes this L. Iulius fill the generation between the *coss.* 157 and 90. Further, Mattingly (*LCM* 10.8 [1985] 119) and Badian (*LCM* 11.1 [1986] 16) both are inclined to regard this L. Iulius as a senior *praetorius* in 101 B.C. But if Iulius had reached the praetorship ca. 120 or even ca. 115, we would prima facie expect him near the top of this list, not as low as no. 7—especially if Badian (*LCM* 11.1 [1986] 16) is right that no. 10 C. Coelius C.f. represents the grade of *tribunicius*.

As presumptive son of a *cos.* 157 and father of a *cos.* 90, L. Iulius Sex.f. certainly seems much too old to have been a junior praetorian in 101 B.C., just three places above the *tr. pl.* 107 C. Coelius C.f.—whatever the latter man's precise status at this time. So on the basis of Mattingly's reckoning of L. Iulius' age combined with his position in this list of senators, I suggest that Iulius rose no higher in his career than the (curule) aedileship. (As a patrician he obviously cannot have held the plebeian aedileship or tribunate of the Plebs, and the placement of C. Coelius C.f. below this individual disallows the possibility he is a mere *quaestorius*.)

8. *C. Annius C.f. Arnensis*

9. *C. Sempronius C.f. Falerna*

10. *C. Coelius C.f. Aemilia*

11. *P. Albius P.f. Quirina*

12. *M. Cosconius M.f. Teretina*   It is a pity that we can securely identify neither no. 8, C. Annius C.f., nor no. 9, C. Sempronius C.f. This Sempronius may be the

Longus who shows up as a senior *legatus* under a praetor for Sicily in the mid-90s (see 13.1.4), or, as Badian suggests (*LCM* 11.1 [1986] 16), a Tuditanus, namely, son of the *cos.* 129.

C. Coelius, in place no. 10, is somewhat problematic. As noted, he was *tr. pl.* 107 and must have held his praetorian command in Hispania Citerior by 98 (see 13.3.2), but that is all we know for sure of the dates of his earlier *cursus*. Now, the *fasti* for Hispania Citerior are entirely open for some time down to 98, and Caldus technically can have been, for example, *pr.* 103 (note the new man C. Marius, *tr. pl.* in 119 and praetor in 115) and back in Rome as a *praetorius* already in 101 B.C. Yet Coelius' moneyership (*RRC* I 324 no. 318, dated by Crawford to 104) makes such a reconstruction very forced indeed.

P. Albius P.f., listed eleventh, is very probably a *praetorius* by 91 (see Appendix B n. 190), but there is no telling precisely when he reached the office. The last highly-ranked senator in this list who allows identification is no. 12, M. Cosconius M.f., who should be son of the *pr.* ca. 135. Mattingly assumes he is already of praetorian rank (*LCM* 10.8 [1985] 119), but without sufficient warrant; as Badian points out (*LCM* 11.1 [1986] 16), "the son of the praetor may well be born about 140 and is perhaps more plausibly regarded as still too young for praetorian status."

In sum, if no. 7, L. Iulius Sex.f., was really an *aedilicius*, this would mean that C. Annius C.f., C. Sempronius C.f., C. Coelius C.f., and all the other members of the *consilium* below position no. 7 were of subpraetorian status in 101.

XIV. *Verres' Attested Movements in His Sicilian* Provincia, *73–71*

Cicero cites the grievances of over fifty individual Sicilian communities against Verres: for a roster, see L. Havas, *ACD* 5 (1969) 63–75. But Cicero does not offer too many particulars of Verres' personal contact with these towns. A list (however brief) may be instructive: the sheer amount of detail Cicero provides is meant to demonstrate that Verres' rapacity touched every corner of the *provincia*.

At Catina, Verres is said to have visited (and stolen from) its shrine of Ceres (*Ver.* 2.4.100). Verres apparently also personally stole from the town of Henna in the interior (2.4.109–113). Much further west, Verres can be placed at Segesta soon after his arrival in 73 (2.4.76). He also was at Lilybaeum that same year: he overturned his quaestor's decision in an important case that involved a *praefectus* of M. Antonius (*Div. Caec.* 56). It was at Lilybaeum "during the height of the slave war in Italy" that Verres investigated a conspiracy of slaves from the evocative site of Triocala (*Ver.* 2.5.12–14). Indeed, Verres seems to have had a house at Lilybaeum (2.4.32), and perhaps also one at Agrigentum (2.4.94).

On the north coast, Verres is said to have been a "frequent" guest of Sthenius of Thermae (2.2.83), and a dinner guest of Eupolemus of Calacte (2.4.49). Verres travelled also to Haluntium on his assizes, says Cicero, but he was too lazy actually to make the steep ascent to the town, and so had his subordinates rob it for him (2.4.51). Further east (but still on the north coast) at Tyndaris, Verres enjoyed the hospitality of one Dexo (2.5.108); on his first visit to the town the praetor robbed it of its statue of Mercury, which he had shipped to Messana (2.4.85).

Messana was Verres' favorite town in Sicily (2.4.3), says Cicero, and complicit in many of the praetor's predations (see esp. 2.2.13 and 4.23), for which it received a *vacatio* from all of its treaty obligations (2.4.150, 5.58, and *passim* in the speech). Verres entered the province through Messana in 73 (2.2.19); it was there that his unexpected arrival led to the apprehension and crucifixion of P. Gavius in (perhaps) 71 (2.5.160–170). Messana was the home of the festival known as the "Verria" (2.4.24) and the only town to grant the praetor a eulogy at his trial (2.5.57)—with a man Verres had personally stolen from as head of the deputation (2.4.7). Of the other major cities, Tauromenium (a *civitas foederata* on the east coast) does not seem to have suffered too badly (yet see 5.49–50, 56). Verres must have largely respected its status, or at least stayed away. Though he evidently had some friends in the town (5.165), the people of Tauromenium still threw down his statue on departure (2.2.160). Cicero only once (as far as I can tell) states that Verres had never visited a certain place—the distant island of Melita, the furthest point in the province (2.4.103).

XV. Some Possible Praetorian Commands of the Years 50–49

T. Furfanus Postumus, ??pr. *for Sicily before 50*   In late January 49, an S.C. ordained that one L. Postumius should immediately proceed to Sicily to succeed T. Furfanus Postumus (Cic. *Att.* 7.15.2 "Postum<i>us autem, de quo nominatim senatus decrevit ut statim in Siciliam iret Fu<r>fanoque succederet," with Shackleton Bailey, *CEF* II 403 and *Two Studies*[2] 25 on the name Furfanius/ Furfanus), though it seems he was to do so only as a preliminary to the arrival of M. Porcius Cato (*pr.* 54). Cicero (*Att.* 7.15.2) relates that Postumius declined the appointment, and so the Senate chose instead a certain C. Fannius, who received *imperium* for the task. But in early March, Fannius was still *cum imperio* in Italy (*Att.* 8.15.3), and later shows up in Asia (*MRR* II 262). The *praetorius* Cato did make it to his command in Sicily (sources in *MRR* II 263). Broughton had tentatively listed Furfanus as a quaestor in 51, and *pro quaestore* in 50 and early 49 (*MRR* II 241, 250, 262); the rank he suggested is merely an inference from this passage. We do happen to know a bit about this man's career. In Milo's trial of 52, Furfanus evidently had served as one of the jurors (*Mil.* 74–75 "huic T. Furfanio, cui viro . . . tali viro"). Asconius (p. 38 C) says they were drawn from a panel that was especially distinguished ("numquam neque clariores viros neque sanctiores propositos esse"). So Sumner suggested that Furfanus was already of senatorial status and thus quaestorian rank by that year, and indeed had reached the praetorship before taking up his post in Sicily. Shackleton Bailey concurs, as does Broughton: "[I]n view of the decree of 53 setting an interval of five years between city magistracy and provincial command . . . his praetorship would date from 55 at the latest" (*MRR* III 96, giving also citations for Sumner and Shackleton Bailey). But a stipulated interval between magistracy and promagistracy passed into law only in 52 (see 11.1.7). And in the year 52, that panel of jurors—360 in number—also included Velleius Paterculus' grandfather, who rose no higher than *praefectus fabrum* (Vell. 2.76.1), and thus remained an *eques*. It is certainly conceivable that Furfanus had only equestrian status in 52—the way Cicero refers to him in the *Pro Milone* need suggest no more—with election to a quaestorship for 51 or even 50.

That the Senate decreed L. Postumius should "succeed" Furfanus in itself implies nothing about the rank of either individual. Cicero elsewhere speaks of a quaestor "succeeding" a *pro quaestore* in Syria (*Fam.* 2.17.5, the year 50) as well as a quaestor or *pro quaestore* being "succeeded" in Macedonia (see 5.6.1 for supersession by another quaestor, 13.29.4 by a proper commander). But the very fact Furfanus was sitting in Sicily in January 49 waiting for a successor may support the notion he had only quaestorian status. Furfanus prima facie had served his requisite time in Sicily by the end of 50 if the Senate was debating on how to relieve him in early 49. If he really was a praetorian commander, in this era he need not have waited through the winter for the Senate's decision, but can have simply delegated control of the *provincia* to a subordinate and headed home. That, at any rate, is the course of action many commanders whose term expired in 50 chose. At the time of the Senate's decree on Sicily, quaestors were holding the *provinciae* of Syria, Cilicia, Asia, and Macedonia, while a *legatus* had been left in charge of Africa (references in MRR II 249–250, 253). (*Legati* also held the two Spains, the two Gauls, and Illyricum, but under quite different circumstances.)

In 45, Furfanus reappears in Sicily, this time as a *pro cos.* (MRR II 309). Though a praetorship for 46 is not directly attested, it seems a reasonable assumption (see MRR II 295). So his position in January 49 is most likely to have been *pro quaestore* or (just possibly) *legatus*.

L. Postumius, ?pr. before 49   What was the status of the L. Postumius whom the Senate wanted to "succeed immediately" T. Furfanus in Sicily in early 49 (see above in this Additional Note)? The Senate is known to issue directions to all sorts of magistrates as to how or when they should proceed to such and such a *provincia*: see, e.g., *I. Knidos* I 31 Kn. IV lines 5–10 and D. B Lines 27–29 (magistrates with *imperium*, ca. 100 B.C.); *Fam.* 3.3.1 (*pro coss.* in 51); *Fam.* 2.17.5 (a quaestor in 50). So that in itself does not get us very far. But Cicero, when he says that the Senate gave Sicily to Postumius "nominatim," should mean that it gave it to him outside the regular sortition of (praetorian) provinces (cf. *Dom.* 24 "extra ordinem sine sorte nominatim," also 21 and 23). And that grant surely involved *imperium* (cf. *Dom.* 24 "nominatim rei maximae...summum virum...delectum praefecimus"), as we shall see Cicero immediately makes clear in his further discussion of the arrangements for Furfanus' supersession. Yet Postumius demurred, declaring that "he would not go without [M. Porcius] Cato." He also thought, Cicero tells us, that he could best put his energy and *auctoritas* to work in the Senate, namely, in the coming debates on Caesar's term (*Att.* 7.15.2). The mention of this type of *auctoritas* need not imply praetorian status for Postumius. Cicero obviously felt that this man had too high an opinion of himself, as did the author of the pseudo-Sallustian *Epistula ad Caesarem* (2.9.4, supplying also the information that he was not a *nobilis*).

Sumner, Shackleton Bailey, and Broughton (see MRR III 172) all identify this Postumius with the "T. Postumius" of Cic. *Brut.* 269, a pugnacious politician and orator who "bene iuris publici leges atque instituta cognoverat." Perhaps this is so (with emendation of the *Brutus* text). But Sumner's further suggestion that he is to be amalgamated with the moneyer C. Postumius of *RRC* I 407 no. 394 (dated by Crawford to 74) and the "Postumus" who was a candidate for the praetorship of 62 (on whom see Broughton, *Candidates Defeated* 38f), does not convince (thus, rightly, Shackleton Bailey, *Two Studies*[2] 37–38). A more likely possibility is the quaestor L. POS who served in Sicily in this general era (see M. Grant. ap. *MRR* II 479). But, on balance, all that seems secure is that L. Postumius was a *privatus*, possibly but not certainly of praetorian rank when he refused the Senate's Sicilian commission in January of 49.

C. Fannius, ??pr. before 49   When L. Postumius refused in early 49 to go to Sicily (see above in this Additional Note), the Senate's choice fell on one C. Fannius: "is cum imperio in Siciliam praemittitur" (*Att.* 7.15.2). The verb *praemittere* shows that Fannius (and by implication Postumius) merely was meant to precede, and so was in a subordinate position to, the *praetorius* M. Cato. (See, e.g., *Catil.* 2.26, where Cicero uses *praemittere* of himself as consul sending a praetor into the field.) Now, Fannius was a *tr. pl.* of 59 (*MRR* II 189), who in 56 was said to have had good prospects for high curule office (sources and discussion in Broughton, *Candidates Defeated* 36). Broughton once counted him as *pr.* 54 (*MRR* II 222), but that is only a guess based on his (presumed) status in 49. He should have been of praetorian age by 49 (Sumner, *Orators* 145).

In addition to the notice on the Senate's Sicilian deliberations of January 49, Cicero in early March of that year mentions C. Fannius among those *cum imperio* in Italy and thus able to cross to Greece (*Att.* 8.15.3), a group that includes Pompey, Q. Metellus Scipio (*cos.* 52, and now *pro cos.* under the *lex Pompeia*), a possible ex-praetor, and perhaps even a commander waiting *ad urbem* for a triumph vote (see below in this Additional Note) as well as a few men of indeterminate status. It is a very mixed group, and not particularly illuminating for the problem at hand.

As mentioned above (see above in this Additional Note on T. Furfanus Postumus), Fannius soon appears not in Sicily but Asia. Josephus knows of this man, and calls him (apparently) "pro pr." (*AJ* 14.230 ἀντιστρατήγου, though note MSS. ἀρχιστράτηγου) in the context of the year 49, but also (most oddly) has him offer "consul" (14.233 στρατηγὸς ὕπατος) as his title in the prescript of an undated letter to the Coans. Fortunately, we are not totally at the mercy of this source, since Fannius minted coins with the legend C FAN-PONT PR at Apameia, Ephesus, Laodiceia, and Tralles (Stumpf, *Numismatische Studien* nos. 57–67). Of these, the Ephesian issues, two in number (Stumpf nos. 58 and 59), both belong to the "Year 86," that is, between 24 September 49 and 23 September 48. Broughton suggests that "the legend PR may stand for *pr(o praetore)*" (*MRR* III 90, with discussion on whether Fannius was killed in 48 or not). But that abbreviation is hard to parallel: I know of no good example in the epigraphy of the Republican period.

With all due caution, I offer that Fannius was a *privatus*, probably still of sub-praetorian rank, when the Senate decided to grant him *imperium* for Sicily in January 49. He was *pro pr.* in 49 (as Josephus has him at *AJ* 14.230), but for 48 he was "praetor," which is precisely what the legend and date of his coin issue suggest. On this interpretation, he will have received his praetorship at the elections the anti-Caesarian government staged at Thessalonica in the winter of 49/48 (see D.C. 41.43; cf. Caes. *Civ.* 3.82.3).

Fannius was functioning as "praetor" in Asia at least by mid-March of 48, to judge from the fact he is able to mint in conjunction with two separate colleges of Ephesian moneyers in "Year 86" of the *provincia*. Fannius' use of the title of "praetor" on his coins does not preclude the possibility that he held consular *imperium* for 48, as the example of Q. Oppius (*pr.* for Cilicia by 89) shows (see 10.1). Indeed, that might just possibly provide the background to Josephus' confusing notice of his status at *AJ* 14.233. If Fannius wrote that letter to the Coans in 48, it is perfectly possible that he used the title στρατηγὸς ἀνθύπατος, and that the second element in his title was truncated to ὕπατος at some stage in the later transmission of that document. Or the mistake may belong to Josephus' copyists (remember ἀρχιστράτηγου at 14.230 for ἀντιστρατήγου).

Voconius, cum imperio *in 49* Cicero lists a Voconius among those *cum imperio* in Italy in early March 49 (*Att.* 8.15.3). Two holders of this *nomen* are known to be active in the later years of the free Republic. First, a Voconius commanded (or was supposed to command) a fleet under L. Lucullus at Nicomedia in (apparently) 72: Plutarch (*Luc.* 13.1–2) relates how this Voconius' ill-timed decision to be initiated in the Samothracian mysteries allowed Mithridates to sail unobstructed through the Bosporus in flight. Second, there is Q. Voconius Naso, who was presumably (plebeian) aedile in 67, for he was a *iudex quaestionis* in 66 (see *MRR* II 153, also 11.7.4 above). He was an ex-praetor when he served as *iudex* in a private suit in Rome that dates to either the year 60 or 59 (Cic. *Flac.* 50, not listed in Alexander, *Trials*). In view of the rarity of the *nomen*, there is a good chance that he is to be identified with Voconius the fleet commander—and also with the Voconius who was *cum imperio* in Italy in 49. If Q. Naso had not taken up a promagistracy after his praetorship—as certainly seems possible—as a *praetorius* he was liable to receive a *provincia* under the provisions of the *lex Pompeia* of 52.

Table of Commands of Some Imporant *Provinciae,* 219–50

A.1. Location of the *Praetor inter Peregrinos* in His Year of Office, 219–198

(Individuals in parentheses) = not specifically attested by Livy as peregrine praetor.
Location of the *praetor inter peregrinos* when prorogued can be found in the charts in A.3.

	Name	Place	Titulature in Livy; remarks
219	(L. Manlius Vulso)	Gaul	Found in Gaul in early summer 218
218	(C. Atilius ?Regulus)	Gaul	Sent in early summer 218 to Gaul to rescue L. Manlius. Dismissed by *cos.* P. Scipio; returns to Gaul before end of year
217	M.(?) Pomponius	Rome	In the city at the time of the Trasimene disaster
216	M.(?) Pomponius Matho	?Latium	*inter cives Romanos et peregrinos.* Found in city after Cannae, and again at end of year. Departs Rome at very end of 216 to replace L. Postumius Albinus (*pr.* 216), who had fallen in Gaul (see Additional Note III)
215	M. Valerius Laevinus	Luceria	*peregrina sors in iurisdictione.* Said to have set up tribunal with *pr. urb.* at *piscina publica* before leaving city for Apulia
214	(Q. Fabius Maximus)	Apulia	*Provincia* later defined as Luceria
213	M.'(?) Aemilius Lepidus	Luceria	*peregrina sors*
212	P. Cornelius Sulla	Rome	*provincia urbana et peregrina;* other three *provinciae* in this year are all special
211	(M. Cornelius Cethegus)	Apulia	Must be *pr. per.,* despite silence of Livy
210	(C. Laetorius)	Gaul	Must be *pr. per.* Gaul may have been initially given to a *legatus;* C. Laetorius is there by end of year
209	L. Veturius Philo	Gaul	*peregrina cum Gallia*
208	P. Licinius Crassus	?Rome	*peregrina et quo senatus censuisset*
207	(L. Porcius Licinus)	Gaul	Must be *pr. per.*
206	Q. Mamilius Turrinus	Gaul	*(provincia) peregrina*

A.1. (continued)

	Name	Place	Titulature in Livy; remarks
205	(Sp. Lucretius)	Gaul	Must be *pr. per.*
204	L. Scribonius Libo	Gaul	*peregrina et eidem Gallia*
203	(P. Quinctilius Varus)	Gaul	Must be *pr. per.*
202	(M. Sextius Sabinus)	Gaul	
	or (M. Livius Salinator)	?Bruttium	Less likely
201	(M. Valerius Falto)	Bruttium	Must be *pr. per.*; Gaul declared consular this year
200	(L. Furius Purpurio)	Gaul	
	or (Q. Minucius Rufus)	?Bruttium	Less likely
199	(Cn. Baebius Tamphilus)	Gaul	Must be *pr. per.*
198	(C. Helvius)	Gaul	Must be *pr. per.*

A.2. Commanders in Sicily and Sardinia, 218–201

Full references for the commanders in this list can be found in *MRR*. I have added *RE* numbers after the names.

(Parentheses around names) = position not reported in ancient sources.
Praetorian commanders are in normal type, consular commanders are in capitals.
[Single brackets] = prorogued commanders
[[Double brackets]] = special grants of *imperium* from the People
{Curly brackets} = *legati*, quaestors, or *praefecti* who held or may have held *imperium* (only the more important examples are listed)
<Inverted arrows> = not original *provincia*
<<Double inverted arrows>> = never arrived in allotted *provincia*
<–> Extended arrows = complex responsibility (selectively listed)

	West Sicily	Fleet (including permission to raid coast of Africa)	East Sicily/ south Italian coast	West coast of Italy	Sardinia/Corsica
218	M. Aemilius (19, 67) (Lepidus)	TI. SEMPRONIUS (66; LONGUS	?{Sex. Pomponius (14)} (*legatus* of Ti. Longus; "fleet" off Vibo) ?		C. Terentius (83) Varro
217	T. Otacilius (12) Crassus	CN. SERVILIUS (61) GEMINUS			A. Cornelius (257) Mamulla
216	<<M. Claudius (220) Marcellus>> [T. Otacilius (12) Crassus] <–>	<P. Furius (80) Philus> [T. Otacilius (12) Crassus]			[A. Cornelius (257) Mamulla]
215	Ap. Claudius (293) Pulcher	[[T. Otacilius (12) Crassus]]	[[T. Otacilius (12) Crassus]]	[[T. Otacilius (12) Crassus]] (based in Sicily)	Q. Mucius (19) Scaevola (fell ill) [[T. Manlius (82) Torquatus]] (substituted for infirm Mucius) [Q. Mucius (19) Scaevola]
214	P. Cornelius (200) Lentulus	T. Otacilius (12) Crassus (*pr.* II)	M. CLAUDIUS (220) MARCELLUS [Ap. Claudius (293) Pulcher]	T. Otacilius (12) Crassus (based in Sicily)	[Q. Mucius (19) Scaevola]

	West Sicily	Fleet (including permission to raid coast of Africa)	East Sicily/ south Italian coast	West coast of Italy	Sardinia/Corsica
213	[P. Cornelius (200) Lentulus]	[T. Otacilius (12) Crassus]	[M. CLAUDIUS (220) MARCELLUS] [Ap. Claudius (293) Pulcher] {T. Quinctius (38) Crispinus} (replaced Ap. Pulcher in late 213)	[T. Otacilius (12) Crassus] (based in Sicily)	[Q. Mucius (19) Scaevola]
212	[P. Cornelius (200) Lentulus]	[T. Otacilius (12) Crassus]	[M. CLAUDIUS (220) MARCELLUS]	[T. Otacilius (12) Crassus] (based in Sicily)	[Q. Mucius (19) Scaevola]
211	C. Sulpicius (8)	[T. Otacilius (12) Crassus]	[M. CLAUDIUS (220) MARCELLUS] ?{D. Quinctius (7)} (fleet at Rhegium) <M. Cornelius (92) Cethegus> (arrived in Sicily after Marcellus' departure)	[T. Otacilius (12) Crassus] (based in Sicily)	L. Cornelius (187) (Lentulus)
210	L. Cincius (5) Alimentus	{M. Valerius (251) Messalla}	M. VALERIUS (211) LAEVINUS ?[M. Cornelius (92) Cethegus (?prorogued until Laevinus' arrival)		P. Manlius (98) Vulso
209	[M. VALERIUS (211) LAEVINUS]	?{M. Valerius (251) Messalla}	?{D. Quinctius (7)} L. Cincius (5) Alimentus		C. Aurunculeius (1)
208	[M. VALERIUS (211) LAEVINUS] <-> Sex. Iulius (147) Caesar (?returned early from provincia)	[M. VALERIUS (211) LAEVINUS]	L. Cincius (5) Alimentus (active at Locri)	[C. Aurunculeius (1)]<-> (fleet sent from Spain by P. Scipio)	[C. Aurunculeius (1)]

	Sicily		(Bruttium)		
207	[M. VALERIUS (211) LAEVINUS] <-> C. Servilius (60) (Geminus)	[M. VALERIUS (211) LAEVINUS]	C. Mamilius (5) Atellus	A. Hostilius (10) Cato<-> Ti. Claudius (62) Asellus<->	A. Hostilius (10) Cato Ti. Claudius (62) Asellus
206		{C. Laelius (2)}			Cn. Octavius (16)
205	L. Aemilius (109) Papus	{C. Laelius (2)}	P. CORNELIUS (336) SCIPIO (also captured Locri) ?{L. Cornelius (337) Scipio} (?left *pro pr.* in temporary command at Messana) {Q. Pleminius (2)} (garrisoned Rhegium, then Locri as *pro pr.*)	Cn. Octavius (16) <->	Cn. Octavius (16) <->
204	M. Pomponius (19) Matho<-> (received entire *provincia* after Scipio's departure)	[P. CORNELIUS (336) SCIPIO] (permission to invade Africa) {C. Laelius (2)} [L. Cornelius (337) Scipio] [M. Pomponius (19) Matho] (defensive only)	M. Pomponius (19) Matho (investigated Pleminius affair)	[Cn. Octavius (16) (supplied Scipio in Africa)	Ti. Claudius (249) Nero
203	P. Villius (10) Tappulus	[P. Villius (10) Tappulus] (defensive only)		[Cn. Octavius (16) (Sardinian coast; also protected convoys to Africa) <[M. Marcius (86) Ralla]> (Italian coast; also supplied Scipio in Africa)	P. Cornelius (214) Lentulus
202	Cn. Tremelius (4) Flaccus	[P. Villius (10) Tappulus]		[P. Cornelius (214) Lentulus] [Cn. Octavius (16) (both Lentulus and Octavius were active off the African coast) ?{M. Marcius (86) Ralla} (served under Scipio in Africa; termed *legatus*)	?{An unknown *legatus*} (?held command in Sardinia in absence of commanders with *imperium*)
201	P. Aelius (152) Tubero				M. Fabius (54) Buteo

683

A.3. Commanders in the Italian peninsula, 218–176, 91–88

Conventions as in A.2

	Gaul	Picenum	Etruria	Suessula/Capua/ Campania	Luceria/Apulia/ Tarentum	Lucania/Bruttium
218	[L. Manlius (92) Vulso] C. Atilius (11) P. CORNELIUS (330) SCIPIO TI. SEMPRONIUS (66) LONGUS					
217	CN. SERVILIUS (61) GEMINUS C. FLAMINIUS (2) [[C. Centenius (1)]]			Q. FABIUS (116) MAXIMUS dict. M. Minucius (52) Rufus mag. eq.		
216	L. Postumius (40) Albinus			M. IUNIUS (126) PERA dict. Ti. Sempronius (51) Gracchus mag. eq.	C. TERENTIUS (83) VARRO [[Cn. Servilius (61) Geminus]]	
215	[M. Pomponius (18; cf. 20) Matho]	[C. TERENTIUS (83) VARRO]		TI. SEMPRONIUS (51) GRACCHUS Q. FABIUS (116) MAXIMUS [[M. CLAUDIUS (220) MARCELLUS]]	TI. SEMPRONIUS (51) GRACCHUS M. Valerius (211) Laevinus {P. Valerius (181) Flaccus} (coast)	[[Ti. Sempronius (66) Longus]]
214	[M. Pomponius (18; cf. 20) Matho]	[C. TERENTIUS (83) VARRO]		Q. FABIUS (116) MAXIMUS M. CLAUDIUS (220) MARCELLUS (later Sicily)	[TI. SEMPRONIUS (51) GRACCHUS] (later Campania) Q. Fabius (103) Maximus (the son)	

Year						
213	P. Sempronius (96) Tuditanus	[C. TERENTIUS (83) VARRO]		[TI. SEMPRONIUS (51) GRACCHUS] [[? Pomponius (cf. 20)]] (Suessula) Cn. Fulvius (43) Centumalus (Suessula)	[M. Valerius (211) Laevinus] (crosses to Greece) Q. FABIUS (103) MAXIMUS (the son) TI. SEMPRONIUS (51) GRACCHUS M.'(?) Aemilius (cf. 67) Lepidus	TI. SEMPRONIUS (51) GRACCHUS
212	[P. Sempronius (96) Tuditanus]		M. Iunius (167) Silanus	Q. FULVIUS (59) FLACCUS AP. CLAUDIUS (293) PULCHER C. Claudius (246) Nero (Suessula, then Capua)	Cn. Fulvius (54) Flaccus	[TI. SEMPRONIUS (51) GRACCHUS]
211	[P. Sempronius (96) Tuditanus]		[M. Iunius (167) Silanus]	[Q. FULVIUS (59) FLACCUS] [AP. CLAUDIUS (293) PULCHER] [C. Claudius (246) Nero (transferred to Spain)]	CN. FULVIUS (43) CENTUMALUS M. Cornelius (92) Cethegus (later Sicily)	
210	An unknown legatus, then C. Laetorius (2)		[C. Calpurnius (6, cf. 8) Piso] then a legatus	Q. FULVIUS (59) FLACCUS [C. Calpurnius (61) Piso] (temporary transfer from Etruria)	M. CLAUDIUS (220) MARCELLUS [CN. FULVIUS (43) CENTUMALUS]	
209	L. Veturius (20) Philo		[C. Calpurnius (6, cf. 8) Piso]	Q. FULVIUS (59) FLACCUS T. Quinctius (38) Crispinus	Q. FABIUS (116) MAXIMUS [M. CLAUDIUS (220) MARCELLUS]	Q. FULVIUS (59) FLACCUS
208	[L. Veturius (20) Philo]		[C. Hostilius (25) Tubulus] [[C. Terentius (83) Varro]]	[Q. FULVIUS (59) FLACCUS] Quinctius (Claudius 15?) Claudius Flamininus (Tarentum)	M. CLAUDIUS (220) MARCELLUS M. CLAUDIUS (220) MARCELLUS	T. QUINCTIUS (38) CRISPINUS

A.3. (continued)

	Gaul	Picenum	Etruria	Suessula/Capua/Campania	Luceria/Apulia/Tarentum	Lucania/Bruttium
207	M. LIVIUS (33) SALINATOR L. Porcius (22) Licinus [[?L. Manlius (46) Acidinus]]		[C. Hostilius (25) Tubulus] [[C. Terentius (83) Varro]] M. LIVIUS (33) SALINATOR	[C. Hostilius (25) Tubulus]	C. CLAUDIUS (246) NERO (also north Italy) {Q. Catius (3)} left *sine imperio* [Quinctius (Claudius 151) Claudius Flamininus] (Tarentum)	C. CLAUDIUS (246) NERO [Q. FULVIUS (59) FLACCUS]
206	Q. Mamilius (13) Turrinus		[M. LIVIUS (33) SALINATOR]	[C. Hostilius (25) Tubulus]	[Quinctius (Claudius 151) Claudius Flamininus (Tarentum) (?dies)]	L. VETURIUS (20) PHILO Q. CAECILIUS (81) METELLUS
205	[M. LIVIUS (33) SALINATOR] Sp. Lucretius (13) [[?M. Valerius (211) Laevinus]]			[C. Hostilius (25) Tubulus]	[[T. Quinctius (45) Flamininus]] (Tarentum)	P. LICINIUS (69) CRASSUS [Q. CAECILIUS (81) METELLUS]
204	[M. LIVIUS (33) SALINATOR] L. Scribonius (16) Libo [Sp. Lucretius (13)]		M. CORNELIUS (92) CETHEGUS	[C. Hostilius (25) Tubulus]	[[T. Quinctius (45) Flamininus]] (Tarentum)	P. SEMPRONIUS (96) TUDITANUS [P. LICINIUS (69) CRASSUS]
203	[M. CORNELIUS (92) CETHEGUS] P. Quinctilius (12) Varus [Sp. Lucretius (13)]		C. SERVILIUS (60) GEMINUS	?[C. Hostilius (25) Tubulus]	?[[T. Quinctius (45) Flamininus]] ?(Tarentum)	CN. SERVILIUS (44) CAEPIO [P. SEMPRONIUS (96) TUDITANUS]

Year	Gaul	Pisa/Liguria	Etruria	Suessula/Capua/Campania	Luceria/Apulia/Tarentum	Lucania/Bruttium
202	M. Sextius (35) Sabinus [?Sp. Lucretius (13)]		M. SERVILIUS (78) GEMINUS (arrives late)			C. Livius (29) Salinator
201	P. AELIUS (101) PAETUS		[M. SERVILIUS (78) GEMINUS]	M. Valerius (153) Falto (late in year, in "Campania")	?[[T. Quinctius (45) Flamininus]] ?(Tarentum)	M. Valerius (153) Falto (later "Campania")
200	C. AURELIUS (95) COTTA		L. Furius (86) Purpurio (also Gaul)			Q. Minucius (22, 55) Rufus
199	Cn. Baebius (41) Tamphilus (discharged) L. CORNELIUS (188) LENTULUS					[Q. Minucius (22, 55) Rufus]
198	SEX. AELIUS (105) PAETUS C. Helvius (1)					
197	C. CORNELIUS (88) CETHEGUS	Q. MINUCIUS (22, 55) RUFUS				
196	M. CLAUDIUS (222) MARCELLUS	L. FURIUS (86) PURPURIO				
195	L. VALERIUS (173) FLACCUS	P. Porcius (19) Laeca				
194	P. CORNELIUS (336) SCIPIO	TI. SEMPRONIUS (67) LONGUS {L. Cincius (not in RE)} *praefectus* at Pisa				

A.3. (continued)

	Gaul	Pisa/Liguria	Etruria	Suessula/Capua/Campania	Luceria/Apulia/Tarentum	Lucania/Bruttium
193	L. CORNELIUS (270) MERULA [TI. SEMPRONIUS (67) LONGUS]	Q. MINUCIUS (65) THERMUS {L. Cincius} *praefectus* at Pisa				IIIviri cum imperio × 2
192	L. QUINCTIUS (43) FLAMININUS	CN. DOMITIUS (18) AHENOBARBUS (also *quo senatus censuisset*) [Q. MINUCIUS (65) THERMUS]				IIIviri cum imperio × 2 <M. Baebius (44) Tamphilus>
191	P. CORNELIUS (350) SCIPIO NASICA	[Q. MINUCIUS (65) THERMUS]				IIIviri cum imperio × 2 A. Cornelius (258) Mamulla [M. Baebius (44) Tamphilus] (crosses to Greece)
190	C. LAELIUS (2) [P. CORNELIUS (350) SCIPIO NASICA]	[Q. MINUCIUS (65) THERMUS]	P. Iunius (54) Brutus		M. Tuccius (5)	M. Tuccius (5) [A. Cornelius (258) Mamulla] (crosses to Greece)
189	[C. LAELIUS (2)]		[P. Iunius (54) Brutus] (transferred to Spain) An unknown *legatus*		[M. Tuccius (5)]	[M. Tuccius (5)]
188	C. LIVIUS (29) SALINATOR	M. VALERIUS (252) MESSALLA				
187	M. Furius (20, 56) Crassipes (dismissed)	M. AEMILIUS (68) LEPIDUS C. FLAMINIUS (3)	?{P. Cornelius (336) Scipio}		P. Claudius (294) Pulcher (Tarentum)	

186		<<SP. POSTUMIUS (44) ALBINUS>> (detained by Bacch. investigation) Q. MARCIUS (79) PHILIPPUS	?[P. Claudius (294) Pulcher]
185		AP. CLAUDIUS (294) PULCHER M. SEMPRONIUS (95) TUDITANUS	L. Postumius (62) Tempsanus (Tarentum; also in Apulia)
184		P. CLAUDIUS (305) PULCHER L. PORCIUS (23) LICINUS	[L. Postumius (62) Tempsanus] (Tarentum; also in Apulia)
183	L. Iulius (27) (Caesar?)	M. CLAUDIUS (223, 224) MARCELLUS Q. FABIUS (91) LABEO	L. Pupius (5) (Apulia)
182	[M. CLAUDIUS (223, 224) MARCELLUS]	CN. BAEBIUS (41) TAMPHILUS L. AEMILIUS (114) PAULLUS [Q. FABIUS (91) LABEO]	?[L. Pupius (5)]
181	Q. Fabius (32, 58) Buteo	P. CORNELIUS (95) CETHEGUS M. BAEBIUS (16, 44) TAMPHILUS [L. AEMILIUS (114) PAULLUS]	L. Duronius (2) (Apulia and Histria)
180	[Q. Fabius (32, 58) Buteo]	A. POSTUMIUS (46) ALBINUS Q. FULVIUS (60) Cn.f. FLACCUS	[L. Duronius (2)] (Apulia and Histria)

A.3. (continued)

	Gaul	Pisa/Liguria	Etruria	Suessula/Capua/Campania	Luceria/Apulia/Tarentum	Lucania/Bruttium
179		Q. FULVIUS (61) Q.f. FLACCUS L. MANLIUS (47) ACIDINUS FULVIANUS				
178	A. MANLIUS (90) VULSO	M. IUNIUS (48) BRUTUS (also in Gaul) Ti. Claudius (251) Nero (Pisa—late in year)				
177		[[TI. CLAUDIUS (251) NERO]] (imperium raised)				
176	C. CLAUDIUS (300) PULCHER (also Liguria) [C. CLAUDIUS (300) PULCHER]	Q. PETILLIUS (4, 11) SPURINUS (killed in action) C. VALERIUS (208) LAEVINUS				

	North (general)	Picenum	Etruria/Umbria	South (general, including Marsi)	Samnium/Apulia	Lucania/Bruttium
91		Q. Servilius (29) (pro cos.) (killed) {Fonteius (2)} (killed)		??L. Postumius (13)		?Ser. Sulpicius (60) Galba (?pr. 91)

90	P. RUTILIUS (26) LUPUS (killed 11 June) {Cn. Pompeius (45) Strabo} {Q. Servilius (50) Caepio} (pro pr., then pro cos.) {C. Perperna (2)} (removed from command) {C. Marius (14)} (eventually pro cos.) {Valerius (249) Messalla}	Cn. Pompeius (45) Strabo (pr. ?91) {Cn. Pompeius (45) Strabo} (pro pr.) ?{Ser. Sulpicius (60) Galba} [[Sex. Iulius (151) Caesar]] (cos. 91) {C. Baebius (11)} (pro pr.)	L. Porcius (7) Cato (pr. ?91) {A. Plotius (7)} (legatus)	L. IULIUS (142) CAESAR {P. Cornelius (203) Lentulus} {T. Didius (5)} {P. Licinius (61) Crassus} {L. Cornelius (392) Sulla} {M. Claudius (226) Marcellus} L. Postumius (13) (killed)	{M. Claudius (226) Marcellus}	{P. Licinius (61) Crassus}
89	CN. POMPEIUS (45) STRABO {L. Gellius (17)} {Cn. Octavius (21)} {M. (Caecilius) (44) Cornutus} {Ser. Sulpicius (60) Galba}	{C. Baebius (11)} (pro pr.) CN. POMPEIUS (45) STRABO		L. PORCIUS (7) CATO (killed) {T. Didius (5)} (killed) {L. Cornelius (392) Sulla} {A. Postumius (32, 33, 34) Albinus} {A. Gabinius (9, cf. 8)} {Ser. Sulpicius (60) Galba} {Q. Caecilius (98) Metellus Pius}	C. Cosconius (3)	Cn. Papirius (38) Carbo {A. Gabinius (9, cf. 8)} (killed late in year)

A.3: (continued)

	North (general)	Picenum	Etruria/Umbria	South (general, including Marsi)	Samnium/Apulia	Lucania/Bruttium
88	[CN. POMPEIUS (45) STRABO] {Ser. Sulpicius (60) Galba} ?{(M.) Caecilius (44) (Cornutus)}			L. CORNELIUS (392) SULLA P. Gabinius (13) Q. Caecilius (98) Metellus Pius ?Ap. Claudius (296) Pulcher {L. Cornelius (106) Cinna}	[C. Cosconius (3)] Q. Caecilius (98) Metellus Pius ?{Mam. Aemilius (80) Lepidus (Livianus)}	

A.4 Commanders in overseas *provinciae*, 218–150

Conventions as in A.2. Praetorian commanders in the Spains will have held consular *imperium* (except as noted)

	Sicily	Sardinia	Spain Command A	Spain Command B	South Illyrial/Macedonia/Greece	Asia Minor
218	See A.2	See A.2	P. CORNELIUS (330) SCIPIO	{Cn. Cornelius (345) Scipio Calvus}		
217–215	See on 218	See on 218	[P. CORNELIUS (330) SCIPIO]	[[Cn. Cornelius (345) Scipio Calvus]] (?*pro pr.*)		

214	See on 218	See on 218	[P. CORNELIUS (330) SCIPIO]	[[Cn. Cornelius (345) Scipio Calvus]] (?*pro pr.*)	[M. Valerius (211) Laevinus] (*pr.* II 215)
213	See on 218	See on 218	[P. CORNELIUS (330) SCIPIO]	[[Cn. Cornelius (345) Scipio Calvus]] (?*pro pr.*)	[M. Valerius (211) Laevinus]
212	See on 218	See on 218	[P. CORNELIUS (330) SCIPIO]	[[Cn. Cornelius (345) Scipio Calvus]] (?*pro pr.*)	[M. Valerius (211) Laevinus]
211	See on 218	See on 218	[P. CORNELIUS (330) SCIPIO]	[[Cn. Cornelius (345) Scipio Calvus]] (?*pro pr.*) <[C. Claudius (246) Nero]>	[M. Valerius (211) Laevinus]
210	See on 218	See on 218	[[P. Cornelius (336) Scipio (Africanus)]] (*pro cos.*)	<[M. Iunius (167) Silanus]>	<[P. SULPICIUS (64) GALBA]>
209–207	See on 218	See on 218	[[P. Cornelius (336) Scipio (Africanus)]] (*pro cos.*)	[M. Iunius (167) Silanus]	[P. SULPICIUS (64) GALBA]
206	See on 218	See on 218	[[L. Cornelius (188) Lentulus]] (*pro pr.*)	[[L. Manlius (46) Acidinus]] (*pro pr.*)	[P. SULPICIUS (64) GALBA]
205	See on 218	See on 218	[[L. Cornelius (188) Lentulus]] (*pro pr.*)	[[L. Manlius (46) Acidinus]] (*pro pr.*)	[[P. SEMPRONIUS (96) TUDITANUS]]
204–202	See on 218	See on 218	[[L. Cornelius (188) Lentulus]] (*pro cos.*)	[[L. Manlius (46) Acidinus]] (*pro cos.*)	
201	See on 218	See on 218			[[M. Valerius (211) Laevinus]]

A4 (continued)

	Sicily	Sardinia	Spain Command A	Spain Command B	South Illyria/ Macedonia/Greece	Asia Minor
200	Q. Fulvius (69) Gillo	<[M. Valerius (153) Falto]>	[[C. Cornelius (88) Cethegus]] (pro cos.)	[[L. Manlius (46) Acidinus]] (pro cos.)	[[M. Valerius (211) Laevinus]] (part of year) P. SULPICIUS (64) GALBA [[L. Apustius (2 and 5) Fullo]] (fleet) {C. Claudius (105) Centho} (legatus)	
199	L. Valerius (173) Flaccus	L. Villius (9) Tappulus	[[Cn. Cornelius (74) Blasio]] (pro cos.)	[[L. Stertinius (5]] (pro cos.)	P. SULPICIUS (64) GALBA] (part of year) [[L. Apustius (2 and 5) Fullo]] (fleet) (part of year) {C. Claudius (105) Centho} (legatus) (part of year) P. VILLIUS (10) TAPPULUS [[(C.) Livius (29) (Salinator)]] (fleet)	
198	M. Claudius (222) Marcellus	M. Porcius (9) Cato	[[Cn. Cornelius (74) Blasio]] (pro cos.)	[[L. Stertinius (5]] (pro cos.)	T. QUINCTIUS (45) FLAMININUS <[L. Quinctius (43) Flamininus]> (fleet)	

	Sicily	Sardinia	Hispania Citerior	Hispania Ulterior	South Illyrial Macedonia/Greece	Asia Minor
197	L. Manlius (93) Vulso	L. Acilius (Acilius 7 = Atilius 16)	C. Sempronius (90) Tuditanus (killed) [[Cn. Cornelius (74) Blasic]]	M. Helvius (4) [[L. Stertinius (5)]]	[T. QUINCTIUS (45) FLAMININUS] [L. Quinctius (43) Flamininus] (fleet)	
196	C. Laelius (2)	Ti. Sempronius (67) Longus	Q. Minucius (65) Thermus	Q. Fabius (57) Buteo [M. Helvius (4) (fell ill)]	[T. QUINCTIUS (45) FLAMININUS] [L. Quinctius (43) Flamininus] (fleet)	
195	Cn. Manlius (91) Vulso	[Ti. Sempronius (67) Longus]	M. PORCIUS (9) CATO P. Manlius (31) (?pro pr.)	Ap. Claudius (245) Nero [M. Helvius (4)] (only part of year)	[T. QUINCTIUS (45) FLAMININUS] [L. Quinctius (43) Flamininus] (fleet)	
194	Cn. Cornelius (74) Blasio	Cn. Cornelius (265) Merenda	Sex. Digitius (2)	P. Cornelius (350) Scipio Nasica	[T. QUINCTIUS (45) FLAMININUS] [L. Quinctius (43) Flamininus] (fleet)	
193	L. Cornelius (337) Scipio	L. Porcius (23) Licinus	C. Flaminius (3)	M. Fulvius (91) Nobilior	<M. Baebius (44) Tamphilus>	
192	L. Valerius (350) Tappo [[L. Oppius (32) Salinator]] (pro pr. to deliver ships; elected pr. 191)	Q. Salonius (not in RE) Sarra	<<M. Baebius (44) Tamphilus>> (sors changed to "Bruttii") [C. Flaminius (3)]	<<A. Atilius (60) Serranus>> (sors changed to "fleet") [M. Fulvius (91) Nobilior]	<A. Atilius (60) Serranus> ("fleet")	
191	M. Aemilius (68) Lepidus [L. Valerius (350) Tappo] (guarded eastern shore with small "fleet")	L. Oppius (32) Salinator	[C. Flaminius (3)]	L. Aemilius (114) Paullus	M.' ACILIUS (35) GLABRIO [M. Baebius (44) Tamphilus] C. Livius (29) Salinator ("fleet")	

A.4 (continued)

	Sicily	Sardinia	Hispania Citerior	Hispania Ulterior	South Illyrian/ Macedonia/Greece	Asia Minor
190	C. Atinius (9) Labeo [M. Aemilius (68) Lepidus] (probably in east Sicily; deserted *provincia*)	[L. Oppius (32) Salinator]	[C. Flaminius (3)]	[L. Aemilius (114) Paullus]	L. CORNELIUS (337) SCIPIO <–> L. Aemilius (127) Regillus ("fleet") <–>	L. CORNELIUS (337) SCIPIO L. Aemilius (127) Regillus
189	M. Sempronius (95) Tuditanus	<<Q. Fabius (127) Pictor>> (transferred to *provincia peregrina*) [L. Oppius (32) Salinator]	L. Plautius (19) Hypsaeus	<<L. Baebius (25)>> (died en route) <[P. Iunius (54) Brutus]>	M. FULVIUS (91) NOBILIOR	CN. MANLIUS (91) VULSO Q. Fabius (91) Labeo ("fleet")
188	Q. Marcius (79) Philippus	C. Stertinius (4)	L. Manlius (47) Acidinus Fulvianus	C. Atinius (2, cf. 1)	[M. FULVIUS (91) NOBILIOR]	[CN. MANLIUS (91) VULSO] [Q. Fabius (91) Labeo]
187	L. Terentius (58) Massaliota	Q. Fulvius (60) Flaccus	[L. Manlius (47) Acidinus Fulvianus]	[C. Atinius (2, cf. 1)]	[M. FULVIUS (91) NOBILIOR] (part of year)	[CN. MANLIUS (91) VULSO] (part of year)
186	P. Cornelius (384) Sulla	C. Aurelius (213) Scaurus	L. Quinctius (37) Crispinus	C. Calpurnius (62) Piso		
185		Unknown	[L. Quinctius (37) Crispinus]	[C. Calpurnius (62) Piso]		
184	C. Sempronius (30) Blaesus	Q. Naevius (4, 16) Matho (saw to *quaestio* for four months nr. Rome) ?[Unknown *pr.* 185] (?forced to await arrival of Q. Matho)	A. Terentius (80) Varro	P. Sempronius (65) Longus		

183	Sp. Postumius (49) Albinus	Cn. Sicinius (8)	A. Terentius (80) Varro]	[P. Sempronius (65) Longus]
182	L. Caecilius (49) Denter	C. Terentius (51) Istra	Q. Fulvius (61) Flaccus]	P. Manlius (31) (pr. II)
181	Ti. Claudius (250) Nero	M. Pinarius (21) Rusca (Corsica, then Sardinia) ?[C. Terentius (51) Istra] (?held Sardinia until arrival of M. Rusca from Corsica)	[Q. Fulvius (61) Flaccus]	[P. Manlius (31)]
180	P. Cornelius (260) Mamulla	C. Maenius (10) (detained in Italy to hold special *quaestio*) ?[M. Pinarius (21) Rusca] (?prorogued until arrival of C. Maenius)	Ti. Sempronius (53) Gracchus	L. Postumius (41) Albinus
179	Q. Mucius (20) Scaevola	C. Valerius (208)	[Ti. Sempronius (53) Gracchus]*	[L. Postumius (41) Albinus]*
178	Unknown	T. Aebutius (10) (Parrus)	M. Titinius (20) Curvus	?T(i). Fonteius (26) Capito
177	C. Numisius (2)	TI. SEMPRONIUS (53) GRACCHUS <<L. Mummius (7)>> (conducted special *quaestio* in Rome) [T. Aebutius (10) (Parrus)]	[M. Titinius (20) Curvus]*	[?T(i). Fonteius (26) Capito]*
176	L. Aquillius (24) Gallus	[TI. SEMPRONIUS (53) GRACCHUS] <<M. Popillius (24) Laenas>> (refused *provincia*) [T. Aebutius (10) (Parrus)]	<<P. Licinius (60) Crassus>> (refused *provincia*) [M. Titinius (20) Curvus]	<<M. Cornelius (348) Scipio Maluginensis>> (refused *provincia*) [?T(i). Fonteius (26) Capito]

	Sicily	Sardinia	Hispania Citerior	Hispania Ulterior	South Illyria/ Macedonia/Greece	Asia Minor
175	Unknown	[TI. SEMPRONIUS (53) GRACCHUS] (Sardinia) (Ser.) Cornelius (2, 388) (Sulla) (?Corsica) ?[T. Aebutius (10) (Parrus)] (?Sardinia)	Ap. Claudius (103) Centho	Unknown		
174	L. Claudius (22)	M. Atilius (21, 68) (?Serranus) (Corsica) [(Ser.) Cornelius (2, 388) (Sulla)] (Sardinia)	P. Furius (82) Philus	Cn. Servilius (45) Caepio		
173	M. Furius (56) Crassipes	C. Cicereius (1) (Corsica)	<<N. Fabius (56) Buteo>> (died en route) [P. Furius (82) Philus]	C. Matienus (2)		
172	C. Memmius (4)	Sp. Cluvius (8)	M. Iunius (122) Pennus	Sp. Lucretius (14)	Cn. Sicinius (8)	
171	C. Caninius (8) Rebilus	L. Furius (77) Philus	L. Canuleius (12, cf. 6) Dives (both provinciae)		[Cn. Sicinius (8)] (part of year) P. LICINIUS (60) CRASSUS C. Lucretius (23) Gallus ("fleet")	

Year					
170	Unknown	Unknown	[L. Canuleius (12, cf. 6) Dives (both *provinciae*)		A. HOSTILIUS (16) MANCINUS {Ap. Claudius (103) Centho} (Illyria) L. Hortensius (4) ("fleet")
169	Ser. Cornelius (208a) Lentulus	P. Fonteius (24) Capito	P. Fonteius (24) Capito		Q. MARCIUS (79) PHILIPPUS {Ap. Claudius (103) Centho} (Illyria) C. Marcius (61) Figulus ("fleet")
168	M. Aebutius (13) Helva	<<C. Papirius (32) Carbo>> (assigned *provincia peregrina* in addition to Sardinia after departure of L. Anicius to east) ??[P. Fonteius (24) Capito] or ??{An unknown *legatus*} (??held *provincia* in presumed absence of C. Carbo)	M. Claudius (225) Marcellus (both *provinciae*)	P. Fonteius (24) Balbus (both *provinciae*)	L. AEMILIUS (114) PAULLUS L. Anicius (15) Gallus (Illyria) Cn. Octavius (17) ("fleet")
167	Ti. Claudius (252) Nero	<<A. Manlius (73) Torquatus>> (conducted special *quaestio* in Italy) ??[P. Fonteius (24) Capito] or ??{An unknown *legatus*} (??held *provincia* in presumed absence of A. Torquatus)	Cn. Fulvius (13)	C. Licinius (133) Nerva	[L. Anicius (15) Gallus] (Illyria) [Cn. Octavius (17)]

A.4 (continued)

	Sicily	Sardinia	Hispania Citerior	Hispania Ulterior	South Illyria/ Macedonia/Greece	Asia Minor
166	Unknown	Unknown	Unknown	Unknown		
165						
164						
163	Unknown	M.' IUVENTIUS THALNA (30) (fought in Corsica; died late in year) TI. SEMPRONIUS (53) GRACCHUS (arrived in *provincia* after holding elections for 162)				
162	Unknown	?[TI. SEMPRONIUS (53) GRACCHUS]				
161						
160						
159						
158						
157			Unknown	M.' Manilius (12) (possibly already prorogued)		

	Sicily	Sardinia	Hispania Citerior	Hispania Ulterior	Dalmatia	Asia Minor Dalmatia
156	Unknown		Unknown	L. Calpurnius (87) Piso Caesoninus	C. MARCIUS (61) FIGULUS	
155	Unknown		Unknown	L. Mummius (7a)	P. CORNELIUS (353) SCIPIO NASICA	

	Hispania Citerior	Hispania Ulterior
154	Unknown	[L. Mummius (7a)]
153	Q. FULVIUS (95) NOBILIOR	M. Atilius (22) (Serranus)
152	M. CLAUDIUS (225) MARCELLUS (cos. III)	[M. Atilius (22) (Serranus)]
151	L. LICINIUS (102) LUCULLUS	Ser. Sulpicius (58) Galba
150	[L. LICINIUS (102) LUCULLUS]	[Ser. Sulpicius (58) Galba]

A.5. Commanders in Sicily, the Spains, Macedonia, and Africa, 149–50

Conventions as in A.2. Praetorian commanders in the Spains and Macedonia will have held consular *imperium* (except as noted), as will all provincial commanders sent out in the years 81–53.

	Sicily	Sardinia	Hispania Citerior	Hispania Ulterior	Macedonia	Africa
149	Q. Fabius (109) Maximus Aemilianus		Unknown	Unknown	P. Iuventius (31) (Thalna)	
148			Unknown	Unknown	[P. Iuventius (31) (Thalna)] (killed) Q. Caecilius (94) Metellus	
147			Unknown	C. Vetilius (1)	[Q. Caecilius (94) Metellus] (*pro cos.*)	

A.5 (continued)

	Sicily	Sardinia	Hispania Citerior	Hispania Ulterior	Macedonia	Africa
146			Unknown	C. Plautius (9)	L. MUMMIUS (7a)	
145			Claudius (376) Unimanus	Q. FABIUS (109) MAXIMUS AEMILIANUS	[L. MUMMIUS (7a)] Q. Fabius (115) Maximus Servilianus	
144			<[[C. Laelius (3)]]>	[Q. FABIUS (109) MAXIMUS AEMILIANUS]	[Q. Fabius (115) Maximus Servilianus]	
143			Q. CAECILIUS (94) METELLUS MACEDONICUS	Quinctius (2) (Crispinus or Flamininus)	Cn. Egnatius (cf. 1)	
142			[Q. CAECILIUS (94) METELLUS MACEDONICUS]	Q. FABIUS (115) MAXIMUS SERVILIANUS	Licinius (130) Nerva	
141			Q. POMPEIUS (12)	[Q. FABIUS (115) MAXIMUS SERVILIANUS]	?[Cn. Egnatius (cf. 1)] D. Iunius (161) Silanus (Manlianus)	
140			[Q. POMPEIUS (12)]	Q. SERVILIUS (48) CAEPIO		
139			M. POPILLIUS (22) LAENAS	[Q. SERVILIUS (48) CAEPIO]		
138			[M. POPILLIUS (22) LAENAS]	D. IUNIUS (57) BRUTUS		
137			C. HOSTILIUS (18) MANCINUS (recalled) <M. AEMILIUS (83) LEPIDUS PORCINA>	[D. IUNIUS (57) BRUTUS]		

Year				
136	?(L.) Cornelius (172, 192) Lentulus	L. FURIUS (78) PHILUS [M. AEMILIUS (83) LEPIDUS PORCINA]	[D. IUNIUS (57) BRUTUS]	SER. FULVIUS (64) FLACCUS (Illyria) M. Cosconius (8)
135	?[(L.) Cornelius (172, 192) Lentulus] L. Plautius (20) Hypsaeus	Q. CALPURNIUS (86) PISO	[D. IUNIUS (57) BRUTUS]	[M. Cosconius (8)]
134	T. Manlius (2, cf. 74) C. FULVIUS (53) FLACCUS (arrives in mid-year)	P. CORNELIUS (335) SCIPIO AEMILIANUS (cos. II)	[D. IUNIUS (57) BRUTUS]	[M. Cosconius (8)]
133	L. CALPURNIUS (96) PISO FRUGI M. Perperna (4) ?[T. Manlius (2, cf. 74)]	[P. CORNELIUS (335) SCIPIO AEMILIANUS]	[D. IUNIUS (57) BRUTUS]	?[M. Cosconius (8)]
132	P. RUPILIUS (5) [M. Perperna (4)] (ovatio in this year)	[P. CORNELIUS (335) SCIPIO AEMILIANUS]		
131	<T. Annius (78) Rufus> (south Italy, perhaps prorogued)			
130	?[T. Annius (78) Rufus] (see 131)			
129				
128				
127	T. Quinctius (47) Flamininus			??P. Cornelius (202a) Lentulus (date approx.)
126	L. AURELIUS (181) ORESTES			
125	[L. AURELIUS (181) ORESTES]			

A.5 (continued)

	Sicily	Sardinia	Hispania Citerior	Hispania Ulterior	Macedonia	Africa
124		[L. AURELIUS (181) ORESTES]	Q. Fabius (110) Maximus (possibly prorogued, exact *provincia* unknown)	See Hispania Citerior		
123		[L. AURELIUS (181) ORESTES]	[Q. Fabius (110) Maximus] (see 124) ?Q. CAECILIUS (82) METELLUS (BALEARICUS)	See Hispania Citerior		
122		[L. AURELIUS (181) ORESTES (triumph 8 Dec.)]	[?Q. CAECILIUS (82) METELLUS (BALEARICUS)]			
121			[?Q. CAECILIUS (82) METELLUS (BALEARICUS)]		Sex. Pompeius (17) (possibly prorogued)	
120					[Sex. Pompeius (17)]	??M. Aemilius (140) Scaurus
119					[Sex. Pompeius (17)] (killed)	
118					{M. Annius (not in *RE*) P.f.} (quaestor, no *imperium*) Unnamed praetor and quaestor Cn. Cornelius (373) Sisenna (possibly prorogued; see 119)	
117	C. Porcius (5) Cato (latest possible date)					M. PORCIUS (10) CATO (dies in province)

Year				
116	M. CAECILIUS (77) METELLUS		?C. Servilius (91, cf. 14) (M.f.) Vatia (not certain, latest possible date)	
115	[M. CAECILIUS (77) METELLUS]		C. PORCIUS (5) CATO	
114	[M. CAECILIUS (77) METELLUS]	?M. Papirius (39) Carbo (not certain, date quite approximate); [C. Marius (14)] (city pr. 115)		
113	[M. CAECILIUS (77) METELLUS]		C. CAECILIUS (84) METELLUS CAPRARIUS	
112	[M. CAECILIUS (77) METELLUS]		?[C. CAECILIUS (84) METELLUS CAPRARIUS] (triumph 15 July 111); M. LIVIUS (17) DRUSUS	
111	[M. CAECILIUS (77) METELLUS] (triumph 15 July)	L. Hortensius (2 or 5) (only probable); L. Calpurnius (97) Piso Frugi (killed) (latest possible date); Ser. Sulpicius (59) Galba (latest possible date)	[M. LIVIUS (17) DRUSUS]	L. CALPURNIUS (23) BESTIA (Numidia)
110			[M. LIVIUS (17) DRUSUS] (triumph 1 May); M. MINUCIUS (54) RUFUS	SP. POSTUMIUS (45, cf. 23) ALBINUS (Numidia); {A. Postumius (33 = 32) Albinus} (leg. pro pr.)
109		Q. Servilius (49) Caepio (latest possible date)	[M. MINUCIUS (54) RUFUS]	Q. CAECILIUS (97) METELLUS (NUMIDICUS) (Numidia)
108		[Q. Servilius (49) Caepio]	[M. MINUCIUS (54) RUFUS]	[Q. CAECILIUS (97) METELLUS (NUMIDICUS)]

	Sicily	Sardinia	Hispania Citerior	Hispania Ulterior	Macedonia	Africa
107		T. Albucius (2) (date only approximate)		[Q. Servilius (49) Caepio] (triumph 28 October)	[M. MINUCIUS (54) RUFUS]	[Q. CAECILIUS (97) METELLUS (NUMIDICUS)] {P. Rutilius (34) Rufus} {A. Manlius (12)} C. MARIUS (14) (all Numidia)
106		[T. Albucius] (2) (date only approximate)			[M. MINUCIUS (54) RUFUS] (triumph ca. 1 Aug.)	[C. MARIUS (14)] {L. Cornelius (392) Sulla} (q., also pro pr.) [C. MARIUS (14)] (Numidia) L. Bellienus (5) (Africa, possibly prorogued)
105			?{legatus}			
104	P. Licinius (135) Nerva (possibly prorogued)		See 105	L. Caesius (see RE 4)		
103	[L. Licinius (103) Lucullus] (city pr. 104)		See 105			
102	C. Servilius (see 12, cf. 11) (Vatia)		See 105	?M. Marius (22)	??C. Billienus (4, cf. 3) (not certain, latest possible date; cf. also Asia) ?C. Memmius (3 = 5) (latest possible date)	
101	M.' AQUILLIUS (11)		See 105	M. Marius (22) (possibly prorogued)	T. Didius (5)	

100	[M'. AQUILLIUS (11)]		?C. Coelius (12) Caldus (date only approximate)		?L. Cornelius (138) Dolabella	?[T. Didius (5)]	
99	?[M'. AQUILLIUS (11)] (ovatio in this year)		?[C. Coelius (12) Caldus] (see above)		[L. Cornelius (138) Dolabella] (triumph 26 Jan. 98)	?[T. Didius (5)]	
98				T. DIDIUS (5)			
97	L. Domitius (26) Ahenobarbus (latest possible date)			[T. DIDIUS (5)]	P. LICINIUS (61) CRASSUS		
96				[T. DIDIUS (5)]	[P. LICINIUS (61) CRASSUS]		
95				[T. DIDIUS (5)]	[?P. LICINIUS (61) CRASSUS]		
94				[T. DIDIUS (5)]	?P. LICINIUS (61) CRASSUS ?{P. Cornelius (351) Scipio Nasica}	??L. Iulius (142) L.f. Caesar (not certain, latest possible date)	
93	L. (Sempronius) (?18) Asellio (date only approximate)			[T. DIDIUS (5)] (triumph II 10 June) ?C. VALERIUS (168) FLACCUS	P. LICINIUS (61) CRASSUS (triumph 12 June)	[C. Sentius (3) Saturninus] (pr. urb. 94)	
92	?P. Servilius (93) Vatia (Isauricus) (province only likely)		[C. VALERIUS (168) FLACCUS]<->	[C. VALERIUS (168) FLACCUS]		[C. Sentius (3) Saturninus]	??P. Sextilius (12) (?Rufus)
91	?[P. Servilius (93) Vatia] (Isauricus) (see 92)		[C. VALERIUS (168) FLACCUS]<->	[C. VALERIUS (168) FLACCUS]		[C. Sentius (3) Saturninus]	??P. Sextilius (12) (?Rufus)
90	?[P. Servilius (93) Vatia] (Isauricus) (see 92)	C. Norbanus (5) (quite possibly prorogued)	[C. VALERIUS (168) FLACCUS]<->	[C. VALERIUS (168) FLACCUS]		[C. Sentius (3) Saturninus]	??P. Sextilius (12) (?Rufus)
89	?[P. Servilius (93) Vatia] (Isauricus) (see 92)	[C. Norbanus (5)]	[C. VALERIUS (168) FLACCUS]<->	[C. VALERIUS (168) FLACCUS]		[C. Sentius (3) Saturninus]	P. Sextilius (12) (?Rufus) (quite possibly prorogued)

A.5 (continued)

	Sicily	Sardinia	Hispania Citerior	Hispania Ulterior	Macedonia	Africa
88	[C. Norbanus (5)]	?[P. Servilius (93) Vatia] [Isauricus] (triumph 21 Oct., see 92)	[C. VALERIUS (168) FLACCUS]<~>	[C. VALERIUS (168) FLACCUS]	[C. Sentius (3) Saturninus]	[P. Sextilius (12) (?Rufus)]
87	[C. Norbanus (5)]		[C. VALERIUS (168) FLACCUS]<~>	[C. VALERIUS (168) FLACCUS]	[C. Sentius (3) Saturninus] [L. CORNELIUS SULLA (cos. 88)] L. Licinius (122) Murena	??[P. Sextilius (12) (?Rufus)]
86	[C. Norbanus (5)]		?[C. VALERIUS (168) FLACCUS]<~>	?[C. VALERIUS (168) FLACCUS]	L. CORNELIUS (392) [SULLA] [L. Licinius (122) Murena] ?L. Cornelius (338) Scipio Asiaticus	[Q. Caecilius (98) Metellus Pius] (pr. 88, now pro cos.) (de facto control)
85	[C. Norbanus (5)] or ?M. Perperna (6) Veiento		?[C. VALERIUS (168) FLACCUS]<~>	?[C. VALERIUS (168) FLACCUS]	[L. CORNELIUS (392) SULLA] [L. Licinius (122) Murena] [L. Cornelius (338) Scipio Asiaticus]	[Q. Caecilius (98) Metellus Pius] (see 86)
84	[C. Norbanus (5)] or ?M. Perperna (6) Veiento		?[C. VALERIUS (168) FLACCUS]<~>	?[C. VALERIUS (168) FLACCUS]	[L. CORNELIUS (392) SULLA]	[Q. Caecilius (98) Metellus Pius] (see 86; ejected) C. Fabius (82) Hadrianus
83	M. Perperna (6) Veiento (probably)		?[C. VALERIUS (168) FLACCUS]<~> ?Unnamed praetor	?[C. VALERIUS (168) FLACCUS]. ?Unnamed praetor	??[legati]	C. Fabius (82) Hadrianus [Hadrianus] killed

Year						
82	[M. Perperna (6) Veiento] [[Cn. Pompeius (31) Magnus]] (pro pr., dispatched to Africa) {C.(?) Memmius (7)} {C.(?) Memmius (7)}	Q. Antonius (4) Balbus (killed) {L. Marcius (75) Philippus}	?[C. VALERIUS (168) FLACCUS]<-> ?Unnamed praetor [Q. Sertorius (3)] (pr. by 83) (soon outlawed)	?[C. VALERIUS (168) FLACCUS] ?Unnamed praetor	??{legati}	CN. PAPIRIUS (38) CARBO III (briefly) {Cn. Domitius (22) Ahenobarbus} [[Cn. Pompeius (31) Magnus]]
81		?{L. Marcius (75) Philippus}	C. Annius (9)<->	C. Annius (9)	??{legati} ??CN. CORNELIUS (134) P.f. DOLABELLA	{Cn. Domitius (22) Ahenobarbus} (killed) [[Cn. Pompeius (31) Magnus]] (pro pr.) [Q. Sertorius (3)] (pr. by 83) (visits Mauretania)
80	[M. Aemilius (72) Lepidus] (pr. 81)		M. Domitius (44) Calvinus (see 79)	L. Fufidius (4) {Aurelius (cf. 102) Cotta}	[CN. CORNELIUS (134) P.f. DOLABELLA]	
79	[C. Claudius (214) Marcellus] (pr. 80)		?[M. Domitius (44) Calvinus] (killed in 80 or 79)	[Q. CAECILIUS (98) METELLUS PIUS] (cos. 80) {Thoranius}	[CN. CORNELIUS (134) P.f. DOLABELLA]	
78	?[C. Claudius (214) Marcellus]		[Q. Calidius (5;] (pr. 79)	[Q. CAECILIUS (98) METELLUS PIUS]	<<[AP. CLAUDIUS (296) PULCHER]>> [CN. CORNELIUS (134) P.f. DOLABELLA]	[L. Licinius (104) Lucullus] (pr. 78)
77	{C. Valerius (363, 366) Triarius} (leg., probably pro pr.)		?<[Q. Calidius]> (5) [L. Manlius (30)] (?pr. 79, transferred in late 78/early 77 from GT [[Cn. Pompeius (31) Magnus]] dispatched, pro cos.)	[Q. CAECILIUS (98) METELLUS PIUS]	[CN. CORNELIUS (134) P.f. DOLABELLA] [AP. CLAUDIUS (296) PULCHER]	
76	[Sex. Peducaeus (5)] (pr. 77)		[[Cn. Pompeius (31) Magnus]] (see 77)	[Q. CAECILIUS (98) METELLUS PIUS]	[AP. CLAUDIUS (296) PULCHER] (died) ?{legatus or quaestor} ??C. SCRIBONIUS (10) CURIO (cos. 76)	

	Sicily	Sardinia	Hispania Citerior	Hispania Ulterior	Macedonia	Africa
75	[Sex. Peducaeus (5)]		[[Cn. Pompeius (31) Magnus]] (see 77)	[Q. CAECILIUS (98) METELLUS PIUS]	[C. SCRIBONIUS (10) CURIO]	
74	[C. Licinius (154) Sacerdos] (pr. 75) M. Antonius (29) (Creticus) (visits)		[[Cn. Pompeius (31) Magnus]] (see 77)	[Q. CAECILIUS (98) METELLUS PIUS]	[C. SCRIBONIUS (10) CURIO]	
73	[C. Verres (1)] (pr. 74)		[[Cn. Pompeius (31) Magnus]] (see 77) [M. Antonius (29) (Creticus)] (pr. 74) (visits)	[Q. CAECILIUS (98) METELLUS PIUS]	[C. SCRIBONIUS (10) CURIO] (triumph, probably in 72)	
72	<<[Q. Arrius (7 = 8)]>> [C. Verres (1)]		[[Cn. Pompeius (31) Magnus]] (see 77)	[Q. CAECILIUS (98) METELLUS PIUS]	[M. TERENTIUS (Licinius 109) VARRO LUCULLUS (cos. 73)]	
71	[C. Verres (1)]		[[Cn. Pompeius (31) Magnus]] (see 77; triumph 31 Dec.) ?[L. Afranius (6)] (pr. by ?76)	[Q. CAECILIUS (98) METELLUS PIUS] (triumph before 31 Dec.) ?[M. Pupius (10) Piso Frugi Calpurnianus] (pr. by ?72)	[M. TERENTIUS (Licinius 109) VARRO LUCULLUS] (triumph)	
70	[L. Caecilius (74) Metellus] (pr. 71)		?[L. Afranius (6)]	[M. Pupius (10) Piso Frugi Calpurnianus]	??["Oppius" (9, cf. 17)] ?[L. Iulius (143) Caesar] (pr. ?71)	
69			?[L. Afranius (6)] (triumph at some point)	[M. Pupius (10) Piso Frugi Calpurnianus] (triumph) ??[legatus]	[L. Aurelius (102) Cotta] (pr. 70)	
68				[C. (?) Antistius (46) Vetus] (pr. ?69)	?[Rubrius (4)] (pr. by 68)	[A. Manlius (70) Torquatus] (pr. by 69, latest possible date)

Year						
67	{A. Plautius or Plotius (8)} {M. Terentius (84, Supb. 6) Varro} (*legg. pro pr.* under Pompey)	{P. Atilius} (23) (*leg. pro pr.* under Pompey)	?A.(?) Manlius (76, cf. 70? Torquatus) (*leg. pro pr.* under Pompey)	?[C.(?) Antistius (46) Vetus] {Ti. Claudius (253) Nero} (*leg. pro pr.* under Pompey)	[Rubrius (4)] {L. Cornelius (374) Sisenna} (*leg. pro pr.* under Pompey)	[L. Sergius (23) Catilina] (*pr.* by 68, possibly prorogued)
66						[L. Sergius (23) Catilina] (returns)
65			[[Cn. Calpurnius (69) Piso]] (*q. pro pr. ex S.C.*)			{P. Sittius (3)}
64			[[Cn. Calpurnius (69) Piso]] (see 65, killed)		[L. MANLIUS (79) TORQUATUS] (*cos.* 65)	
63					?[L. MANLIUS (79) TORQUATUS]; ??[M. Plaetorius (16) Cestianus] (??*pr.* 64)	
62	[C. Vergilius (2, 3) Balbus] (*pr.* 62)			[C. Cosconius (4)] (*pr.* 63); [C. Iulius (131) Caesar] (*pr.* 62); ??{*legatus*}	[C. ANTONIUS (19)] (*cos.* 63)	[Q. Pompeius (42) Rufus] (*pr.* 63)
61	[C. Vergilius (2, 3) Balbus]				[C. ANTONIUS (19)]	[Q. Pompeius (42) Rufus]
60	[C. Vergilius (2, 3) Balbus]				[C. Octavius (15)] (*pr.* 61)	[Q. Pompeius (42) Rufus]
59	[C. Vergilius (2, 3) Balbus]	[P. Cornelius (238) Lentulus Spinther] (*pr.* 60) ??{*legatus*}			[C. ANTONIUS (19)] (in transit); [C. Octavius (15)]	?[Q. Pompeius (42) Rufus]
58	?[C. Vergilius (2, 3) Balbus]				[L. Appuleius (30) Saturninus] (*pr.* 59); L. CALPURNIUS (90) PISO CAESONINUS (crosses late in year)	[T. Vettius (9a and 14) Sabinus] (*pr.* 59)

A.5 (continued)

	Sicily	Sardinia	Hispania Citerior	Hispania Ulterior	Macedonia	Africa
57	{Q. Tullius (31) Cicero} (legatus under Pompey)				[L. CALPURNIUS (90) PISO CAESONINUS]	
56	?[L. Caecilius (110) Rufus] (pr. 57) (not certain, cf. Crete, Cyrene) [[Cn. Pompeius (31) Magnus]] (pro cos.) (visits)	[Ap. Claudius (297) Pulcher] (pr. 57) {Q. Tullius (31) Cicero} (legatus under Pompey; leaves June) [[Cn. Pompeius (31) Magnus]] (pro cos.) (visits)	?[Q. CAECILIUS (96) METELLUS NEPOS] (cos. 57)	[Sex. Quinctilius (4) (pr. 57) Varus]	[L. CALPURNIUS (90) PISO CAESONINUS]	[Q. Valerius (280) Orca] (pr. 57) [[Cn. Pompeius (31) Magnus]] (pro cos.) (visits)
55	[M. Aemilius (141) Scaurus] (pr. 56)		[Q. CAECILIUS (96) METELLUS NEPOS] {L. Afranius (6)} (leg. pro pr. of cos. II 55 Pompey; exact Spanish provincia uncertain)	?[Sex. Quinctilius (4) Varus] {M. Petreius (3)} (leg. pro pr. of cos. II 55 Pompey; exact Spanish provincia uncertain)	[L. CALPURNIUS (90) PISO CAESONINUS] (in Rome in June) [Q. Ancharius (3)] (pr. 56)	
54			{L. Afranius (6)} (see on 55)	{M. Petreius (3)} (see on 55)		
53			{L. Afranius (6)} (see on 55)	{M. Petreius (3)} (see on 55)	[C. Cosconius (5)] (?pr. 54; command probable)	
52			?{L. Afranius (6)} (see on 55)	?{M. Petreius (3)} (see on 55)	?[M. Nonius (52) (?Sufenas)] (pr. by 52)	?[P. Attius (32) Varus] (latest likely date)
51	??[T. Furfanius (1) Postumus] (probably quaestor)		?{L. Afranius (6)} (see on 55)	?{M. Petreius (3)} (see on 55)		[C. Considius (11) Longus]

50	??[T. Furfanius (1) Postumus] {probably quaestor}	?[L. Afranius (6) (see on 55)	?[M. Petreius (3) (see on 55)	?[M. Nonius (52) (?Sufenas)]	[C. Considius (11) Longus] {Q. Ligarius (4)} (leg.)
49	{M. Aurelius (109) Cotta}			{T. Antistius (22)} (quaestor)	

A.6. Commanders in Asia, Cilicia, and the Gauls, 131–50

Conventions as in A.2. Commanders in Asia and Cilicia will have held consular *imperium* (except as noted), as will all provincial commanders sent out in the years 81–53.

	Asia	*Cilicia*	*Gallia Transalpina*	*Gallia Cisalpina*
131	P. LICINIUS (72) CRASSUS MUCIANUS			
130	Cn. Octavius (18) (fleet) M. PERPERNA (4)			
129	M'. AQUILLIUS (10) {Cn. Domitius (20) Ahenobarbus} (*pro pr.*)			
128	{Q. Servilius (49) Caepio} (?*pro pr.*) [M'. AQUILLIUS (10)]			
127	[M'. AQUILLIUS (10)]			
126	[M'. AQUILLIUS (10)]			
125			M. FULVIUS (58) FLACCUS	
124			[M. FULVIUS (58) FLACCUS] C. SEXTIUS (20) CALVINUS	

A.6 (continued)

	Asia	Cilicia	Gallia Transalpina	Gallia Cisalpina
123			[M. FULVIUS (58) FLACCUS] (triumph this year)	
122	C. Atinius (10) Labeo Macerio (but possibly *pr.* 121)		[C. SEXTIUS (20) CALVINUS] [C. SEXTIUS (20) CALVINUS] (triumph this year)	
121	??M'. (or M.) Valerius (248) Messalla (not certain, date approximate)		CN. DOMITIUS (20) AHENOBARBUS [CN. DOMITIUS (20) AHENOBARBUS] Q. FABIUS (110) MAXIMUS (ALLOBROGICUS)	
120	Q. Mucius (21) Scaevola (latest possible date)		[CN. DOMITIUS (20) AHENOBARBUS] (triumph, prob. in this year) [Q. FABIUS (110) MAXIMUS (ALLOBROGICUS)] (triumph, prob. in this year)	
119				
118				
117				Q. MARCIUS (91) REX [Q. MARCIUS (91) REX] (triumph 3 Dec.)
116		Cn. Papirius (37) Carbo (latest likely date)		??L. CAECILIUS (93) METELLUS DIADEMATUS
115		L. (Calpurnius) (88) Piso (Caesoninus) (latest likely date)		??[L. CAECILIUS (93) METELLUS DIADEMATUS]
114				M. AEMILIUS (140) SCAURUS (triumph after 27 Nov.)
113		Unnamed praetor {M. Antonius (28)} (quaestor, also *pro pr.*)	CN. PAPIRIUS (37) CARBO (in Noricum)	

Year					
112	M. IUNIUS (169) SILANUS [M. IUNIUS (169) SILANUS]		?Ser. Cornelius (208b) Ser.f. Lentulus (not certain, date quite approximate)		
111					
110			??C. Rabirius (see 6) C.f. (not certain, date quite approximate)		
109			Praetor		
108			{Cn. Aufidius (6, 7) Cn.f.} (*pro pr.*, date quite approximate)		
107	L. CASSIUS (62) LONGINUS (killed)				
106	Q. SERVILIUS (49) CAEPIO				
105	[Q. SERVILIUS (49) CAEPIO] (*imperium abrogated*) CN. MALLIUS (13) MAXIMUS				
104	C. MARIUS (14) II {M.' Aquillius (11)} (*leg.*)				
103	C. MARIUS (14) III		??C. Billienus (4, cf. 3) (not certain, latest possible date; cf. also Macedonia)	M. Antonius (28)	
102	C. MARIUS (14) IV Q. LUTATIUS (7) CATULUS			[M. Antonius (28)]	
101	C. MARIUS (14) V [Q. LUTATIUS (7) CATULUS]			[M. Antonius (28)]	
100			M. (Plautius) (22) Hypsaeus (date quite approximate)		
99			C. Iulius (130) Caesar (date quite approximate)		
98			[C. Iulius (130) Caesar] (see on 99)		
97					
96			L. Lucilius (8) (date quite approximate)		[L. Cornelius (392) Sulla] (*pr. urb.* 97)
95	L. LICINIUS (55) CRASSUS		[C. Valerius (168) Flaccus] (*pr. urb.* ?96) (latest possible date)		[L. Cornelius (392) Sulla]

A.6 (continued)

	Asia	Cilicia	Gallia Transalpina	Gallia Cisalpina
94	?[Q. MUCIUS (22) SCAEVOLA] (cos. 95)	?[L. Cornelius (392) Sulla]	See Gallia Cisalpina	?[L. LICINIUS (55) CRASSUS] (command not certain, Gallic province unspecified)
93	?[L. Gellius (17)] (pr. per. 94) (not certain; cf. also Cilicia)	?[L. Cornelius (392) Sulla] or L. Gellius (17) (pr. per. 94; cf. also Asia)	?[C. COELIUS (12) CALDUS] (cos. 94) (command not certain, Gallic province unspecified)	See Gallia Transalpina
92			?[C. COELIUS (12) CALDUS] (see on 93)	See Gallia Transalpina
91	L. Valerius (178) Flaccus (latest possible date) ?C. Cassius (10)		?[C. COELIUS (12) CALDUS] (see on 93)	See Gallia Transalpina
90	C. Cassius (10) (possibly prorogued)		?[C. COELIUS (12) CALDUS] (see on 93)	See Gallia Transalpina
89	[C. Cassius (10)]	Q. Oppius (20) (pr. by 89) (possibly prorogued)	??[C. COELIUS (12) CALDUS] (see on 93)	See Gallia Transalpina
88	[C. Cassius (10)]	[Q. Oppius (20)]	??[C. COELIUS (12) CALDUS] (see on 93)	See Gallia Transalpina
87	[L. CORNELIUS (392) SULLA] (cos. 88)	[Q. Oppius (20)] (in captivity)	??[C. COELIUS (12) CALDUS] (see on 93) ??[C. VALERIUS (168) FLACCUS] (cos. 93) (also Spains)	See Gallia Transalpina {P. Coelius (Caelius 13)} [CN. POMPEIUS (45) STRABO] (cos. 89) (command in Bellum Octavianum)
86	[L. CORNELIUS (392) SULLA] {L. Licinius (104) Lucullus} (pro q. pro. pr.) L. VALERIUS (178) FLACCUS	[Q. Oppius (20)] (in captivity)	??[C. VALERIUS (168) FLACCUS] (see on 87)	
85	[L. CORNELIUS (392) SULLA] [L. VALERIUS (178) FLACCUS] (killed)	[Q. Oppius (20)] ?[L. Cornelius (194, 195) Lentulus] (pr. ?88)	?[C. VALERIUS (168) FLACCUS] (see on 87)	

84	[L. CORNELIUS (392) SULLA]	?[L. Cornelius (194, 195) Lentulus]	?[C. VALERIUS (168) FLACCUS (see on 87)	CN. PAPIRIUS (38) CARBO II
83	[L. Licinius (122) Murena]	?[L. Cornelius (194, 195) Lentulus]	[C. VALERIUS (168) FLACCUS (see on 87)	[CN. PAPIRIUS (38) CARBO]
82	[L. Licinius (122) Murena]	??[L. Cornelius (194, 195) Lentulus]	?[C. VALERIUS (168) FLACCUS (see on 87)	CN. PAPIRIUS (38) CARBO III [C. NORBANUS (5)] (cos. 83) ?P. Albinovanus (2) ?C. (Coelius) (6) Antipater ?Flavius (86) Fimbria ?Quinctius (3)
81	[L. Licinius (122) Murena (recalled, triumph)] M. Minucius (64) Thermus		[C. VALERIUS (168) FLACCUS (triumph)	
80	C. Claudius (247) Nero (pr. 81 or 80)	[Cn. Cornelius (135) Dolabella] (pr. 81) (as pro pr.)		<<[L. CORNELIUS (392) SULLA]>> (cos. II 80) (declined province) ??[C(n.) (Cornelius) (see S.I col. 326 Scipio] (??pr. 80) (entirely uncertain) ?M. AEMILIUS (72) LEPIDUS (cos. 78)
79	[C. Claudius (247) Nero]	[Cn. Cornelius (135) Dolabella] (as pro pr.)		
78		P. SERVILIUS (93) VATIA (ISAURICUS)] (cos. 79)	[L. Manlius] (30) (pr. ?79; transferred to Hispania Citerior in late 78/early 77)	[M. AEMILIUS (72) LEPIDUS] (cos. 78) (ejected) {M. Iunius (52) Brutus} (leg., killed) ?MAM. AEMILIUS (80) LEPIDUS ?[MAM. AEMILIUS (80) LEPIDUS]
77	??[Terentius (see 82) Varro] (not certain, date approximate)	[P. SERVILIUS (93)' VATIA (ISAURICUS)]	[M. AEMILIUS (72) LEPIDUS] (cos. 78) (ejected) ??{legatus} (of Lepidus) M. Fonteius (12) (?pr. 77)	
76	[M. Iunius (170) Silanus (?Murena)] (pr. by 77) (latest possible date)	[P. SERVILIUS (93) VATIA (ISAURICUS)]	?[M. Fonteius (12)]	??[MAM. AEMILIUS (80) LEPIDUS]
75	[M. Iunius (84) Iuncus] (pr. 76)	[P. SERVILIUS (93) VATIA (ISAURICUS)] '(triumph II in 74)	?[M. Fonteius (12)]	??[MAM. AEMILIUS (80) LEPIDUS]
74	[M. Iunius (84) Iuncus] (also Bithynia) <-> ?L. LICINIUS (104) LUCULLUS	[L. OCTAVIUS (26)] (cos. 75) (died)	?[Cn. Tremelius (5) Scrofa] (pr. ?75)	[C. AURELIUS (96) COTTA] (cos. 75) (death precludes triumph)

A.6 (continued)

	Asia	Cilicia	Gallia Transalpina	Gallia Cisalpina
73	[L. LICINIUS (104) LUCULLUS]	[L. LICINIUS (104) LUCULLUS] (cos. 74)	?[Cn. Tremelius (5) Scrofa]	<<[L. LICINIUS (104) LUCULLUS]>> (cos. 74) (switches for Cilicia)
72	[L. LICINIUS (104) LUCULLUS]	[L. LICINIUS (104) LUCULLUS]	?[Cn. Tremelius (5) Scrofa]	[C. CASSIUS (58) LONGINUS] (cos. 73) (killed?)
71	[L. LICINIUS (104) LUCULLUS]	[L. LICINIUS (104) LUCULLUS]	??[L. Afranius (6)] (pr. by ?76) (?with Hispania Citerior)	
70	[L. LICINIUS (104) LUCULLUS]	[L. LICINIUS (104) LUCULLUS]	??[L. Afranius (6)] (see 71)	
69	[L. LICINIUS (104) LUCULLUS]	[L. LICINIUS (104) LUCULLUS]	??[L. Afranius (6)] (see 71)	
68	Unnamed praetor	[L. LICINIUS (104) LUCULLUS] (province withdrawn)		
67	[P. Cornelius (140) Dolabella] (pr. by 68) (latest possible date) At least four of Pompey's legati pro praetore ??M.' ACILIUS (38) GLABRIO	Q. MARCIUS (92) REX (cos. 68) [[Cn. Pompeius (31) Magnus]] (pro cos.) {Q. Caecilius (96) Metellus Nepos} (legatus pro pr. under Pompey)	C. CALPURNIUS (63) PISO<-> (through legati)	C. CALPURNIUS (63) PISO (see Gallia Transalpina)
66	[T. Aufidius] (pr. by 67) (latest possible date)	Q. MARCIUS (92) REX (superseded) [[Cn. Pompeius (31) Magnus]]	[C. CALPURNIUS (63) PISO]<->	[C. CALPURNIUS (63) PISO]
65	[P. Varinius (1)] (pr. II by 66) (latest possible date)	[[Cn. Pompeius (31) Magnus]]	[C. CALPURNIUS (63) PISO]<->	[C. CALPURNIUS (63) PISO]
64	[P. Orbius (3)] (pr. by 65) (latest possible date)	[[Cn. Pompeius (31) Magnus]]	L. Licinius (123) Murena] (pr. 65)	??[C. CALPURNIUS (63) PISO]
63	[P. Servilius (66) Globulus] (pr. by 64) (latest possible date)	[[Cn. Pompeius (31) Magnus]]	L. Licinius (123) Murena] (leaves in summer) {C. Licinius (119) Murena} (granted special powers late in year) [C. Pomptinus (1)] (pr. 63)	Q. Caecilius (86) Metellus Celer (pr. 63) (by mid-December) (pro cos.)
62	[L. Valerius (179) Flaccus] (pr. 63)	[[Cn. Pompeius (31) Magnus]]		<<[C. ANTONIUS (19)]>> (cos. 63) (substituted Macedonia) [Q. Caecilius (86) Metellus Celer]

61	[Q. Tullius (31) Cicero] (pr. 62)				
60	[Q. Tullius (31) Cicero]		[C. Pomptinus (1)]	<<Q. CAECILIUS (86) METELLUS CELER>>	?<<L. AFRANIUS (6)>>
59	[Q. Tullius (31) Cicero]		[C. Pomptinus (1)]	?[C. Pomptinus (1)] (triumph Nov. 54) <<[Q. CAECILIUS (86) METELLUS CELER]>>[cos. 60] (dies in April or May in Rome)	?[L. AFRANIUS (6)]
58	[T. Ampius (1) Balbus] (pr. 59) (transferred to Cilicia for 57)	[[M. Porcius (16) Cato]] (pro pr.) (annexation of Cyprus)		[C. IULIUS (131) CAESAR] (cos. 59) (with Illyria)	[C. IULIUS (131) CAESAR] (cos. 59) (see Gallia Transalpina)
57	[C. Fabius (17) (?Hadrianus)] (pr. 58)	<<[A. GABINIUS (11)]>> (cos. 58) (exchanged province for Syria) <[T. Ampius (1) Balbus]> (pr. 59; pro cos. 58 Asia) [[M. Porcius (16) Cato]] (pro pr.) (Cyprus)		[C. IULIUS (131) CAESAR] (see 58)	[C. IULIUS (131) CAESAR] (see 58)
56	[C. Septimius (7)] (pr. 57)	P. CORNELIUS (238) LENTULUS SPINTHER] (cos. 57)		[C. IULIUS (131) CAESAR] (see 58)	[C. IULIUS (131) CAESAR] (see 58)
55	[C. Claudius (303) Pulcher] (pr. 56) ?(arriving late)	P. CORNELIUS (238) LENTULUS SPINTHER]		[C. IULIUS (131) CAESAR] (see 58)	[C. IULIUS (131) CAESAR] (see 58)
54	[C. Claudius (303) Pulcher]	P. CORNELIUS (238) LENTULUS SPINTHER]		[C. IULIUS (131) CAESAR] (see 58)	[C. IULIUS (131) CAESAR] (see 58)
53	[C. Claudius (303) Pulcher]	?[P. CORNELIUS (238) LENTULUS SPINTHER] (triumph in 51) [AP. CLAUDIUS (297) PULCHER] (cos. 54) (arrived late)		[C. IULIUS (131) CAESAR] (see 58)	[C. IULIUS (131) CAESAR] (see 58)
52		[AP. CLAUDIUS (297) PULCHER]		[C. IULIUS (131) CAESAR] (see 58)	[C. IULIUS (131) CAESAR] (see 58)
51	[Q. Minucius (67) Thermus] (pr. by ?58)	[AP. CLAUDIUS (297) PULCHER] (superseded 31 July) ??[Q. Mucius (23) Scaevola] [M. TULLIUS (29) CICERO]		[C. IULIUS (131) CAESAR] (see 58)	[C. IULIUS (131) CAESAR] (see 58)

A.6 (continued)

	Asia	Cilicia	Gallia Transalpina	Gallia Cisalpina
50	{L. Antonius (23)} (quaestor, pro pr.) {C. Coelius (14) Caldus} (quaestor)	[M. TULLIUS (29) CICERO]	[C. IULIUS (131) CAESAR] (see 58) {T. Labienus (6)} (leg.)	[C. IULIUS (131) CAESAR] (see 58)
49		[P. Sestius (6)]		

A.7. Commanders in Bithynia/Pontus, Crete, Cyrene, and Syria, 75–50

Conventions as in A.2. All provincial commanders sent out down to the year 53 will have held consular *imperium*.

	Bithynia/Pontus	Crete	Cyrene	Syria
75			[[P. Cornelius (231, cf. 238) Lentulus Marcellinus]] (quaestor *pro pr.*) [[P. Cornelius (231, cf. 238) Lentulus Marcellinus]]	
74	[M. Iunius (84) Iuncus] (*pr.* 76) (with Asia) ?M. AURELIUS (107) COTTA	M. Antonius (29) (Creticus)		
73	[M. AURELIUS (107) COTTA] [L. LICINIUS (104) LUCULLUS] (*cos.* 74)	[M. Antonius (29) (Creticus)]	??[[P. Cornelius (231, cf. 238) Lentulus Marcellinus]]	
72	[M. AURELIUS (107) COTTA] [L. LICINIUS (104) LUCULLUS]	[M. Antonius (29) (Creticus)]		
71	[M. AURELIUS (107) COTTA] [L. LICINIUS (104) LUCULLUS]	[M. Antonius (29) (Creticus)]		
70	[L. LICINIUS (104) LUCULLUS]	[M. Antonius (29) (dies)]		

69	[L. LICINIUS (104) LUCULLUS]	[Q. CAECILIUS (87) METELLUS CRETICUS]		{Q. Caecilius (96) Metellus Nepos} (leg. pro pr. under Pompey)
68	[L. LICINIUS (104) LUCULLUS]	[Q. CAECILIUS (87) METELLUS CRETICUS]		
67	[L. LICINIUS (104) LUCULLUS] (province withdrawn) M.' ACILIUS (38) GLABRIO	{L. Octavius (27)} {L. Cornelius (374) Sisenna} (leg. pro pr. under Pompey) [Q. CAECILIUS (87) METELLUS CRETICUS]	{Cn. Cornelius (228) Lentulus Marcellinus} (leg. pro pr. under Pompey)	
66	[M.' ACILIUS (38) GLABRIO] [[Cn. Pompeius (31) Magnus]] (pro cos.)	[Q. CAECILIUS (87) METELLUS CRETICUS]		?{M. Aemilius (141) Scaurus} (pro q.)
65	[[Cn. Pompeius (31) Magnus]] (see 66)			[[Cn. Pompeius (31) Magnus]] ?{M. Aemilius (141) Scaurus} (see 66)
64	[[Cn. Pompeius (31) Magnus]] (see 66)			[[Cn. Pompeius (31) Magnus]] {M. Aemilius (141) Scaurus} (see 66)
63	[[Cn. Pompeius (31) Magnus]] (see 66)		Unnamed praetor (?) {M. Iuventius (16) Laterensis} (pro q.; date approximate)	[[Cn. Pompeius (31) Magnus]] {M. Aemilius (141) Scaurus} (see 66)
62	[[Cn. Pompeius (31) Magnus]] (see 66; triumph in 61)			{M. Aemilius (141) Scaurus} (see 66; pro pr.)
61	?[C. Papirius (35) Carbo] (pr. 61)			[L. Marcius (76) Philippus] (pr. 62)
60	[C. Papirius (35) Carbo]			[L. Marcius (76) Philippus]
59	[C. Papirius (35) Carbo]			[Cn. Cornelius (228) Lentulus Marcellinus] (pr. 60)
58	[C. Papirius (35) Carbo]			[Cn. Cornelius (228) Lentulus Marcellinus]
57	[C. Memmius (8)] (pr. 58)	??[L. Caecilius (110) Rufus] (pr. 57) (not certain, cf. Cyrene, Sicily)	?[L. Caecilius (110) Rufus] (pr. 57) (not certain, cf. Crete, Sicily)	A. GABINIUS (11) (departure late in year)
56	[C. Caecilius (43) Cornutus] (pr. 57)			[A. GABINIUS (11)] [A. GABINIUS (11)]
55				[A. GABINIUS (11)] M. LICINIUS (68) CRASSUS (departure late in year)

A.7 (continued)

	Bithynia/Pontus	Crete	Cyrene	Syria
54				[M. LICINIUS (68) CRASSUS]
53				[M. LICINIUS (68) CRASSUS] (killed) {C. Cassius (59) Longinus} (pro q.)
52				{C. Cassius (59) Longinus} (see 53)
51	[P. Silius (8)] (pr. by 52) (pro pr.)		?[Cn. Tremelius (5) Scrofa]	{C. Cassius (59) Longinus} (see 53) [M. CALPURNIUS (28) BIBULUS] (cos. 59)
50	?[A. Plautius (8)] (pr. 51)			[M. CALPURNIUS (28) BIBULUS] {Veiento (Fabricius 14)}

Fasti Praetorii

Symbols and Abbreviations

Dates: >120 = "previous to 120"; ≥120 = "previous to, or in, 120"; 2c = "2nd century."

A question mark before a date indicates that it is uncertain; two question marks, that it is very uncertain.

Names: *RE* number (where available) follows *nomen*; suff.= *praetor suffectus*; des.= *praetor designatus*.

A question mark before a name indicates that the praetorship itself is uncertain; two question marks that it is very uncertain. A question mark following *praenomen, nomen,* or *cognomen* indicates that this element of the name is uncertain.

Provinciae (pv): U = *praetor urbanus*; ip = *inter peregrinos*; C = city (U, ip, or both); amb = *ambitus*; mai = *maiestas*; pec = *peculatus*; rep = *repetundae*; sic = *inter sicarios*; ven = *de veneficiis*; vis = *de vi*.

A = Asia; Af = Africa; Ap = Apulia; Bi = Bithynia/Pontus; Ci = Cilicia; Cy = Cyrene; Etr = Etruria; Fl = fleet; G = Gallia; GC = Gallia Cisalpina; GT = Gallia Transalpina; H = Hispania; HC = Hispania Citerior; HU = Hispania Ulterior; Il = Illyria; Ist = (H)istria; Lig = Liguria; Luc = Lucania; M = Macedonia/Achaea; Pi = Pisa; qe = quaestio extraordinaria; qsc = quo senatus censuisset; Sd = Sardinia; Si = Sicilia; Su = Suessula; Sy = Syria; T = Tarentum; Z = provincia declined

Si>Sd = "Sicily allotted in the sortition, but changed to Sardinia." C/HU = "served as city praetor in actual year of praetorship, and sent as a promagistrate to Hispania Ulterior in following year." C/Z/HU = "served as city praetor; declined promagisterial *provincia*; but after interval assigned Hispania Ulterior" (i.e., under the *lex Pompeia*).

Ancestry is indicated as follows (adapted from E. Badian, "The Consuls, 179-49 B.C.," *Chiron* 20 [1990] 371–413, as are the actual individual attributions, where relevant):

c = consular; p = praetorian; sp = senatorian subpraetorian; na = not attested or recoverable

P = Patrician; (P) = Patrician descent displayed in name; N = *novus homo*, attested or implied; N? = probably *novus homo*.

In cases where descent can be further specified: (<cos. 200) = "son of consul 200"; (<<cos. 200) = "grandson of consul 200"; (~cos. 100) = "related through male line to consul 200" (including direct descent beyond the past two generations).

X indicates what is practically certain.

(X) Parentheses around an X in the consul or praetor columns marks descent from a holder of that office, yet not father or grandfather (but also uncles).

[X] Square brackets round an X in the c column mark consular descent claimed and/or perceived, whether or not historical.

? A question mark preceding a P, X, or (X) indicates that placement in this column is uncertain but considered probable or possible.

B.1. 366 to 219

Date	Name	pv	c	p	sp	na
366	Sp. Furius (48) M.f. L.n. Camillus		PX (<dict. V 367)			
350	P. Valerius (300) P.f. L.n. Poplicola		PX (cos. 352); <tr.mil.c.p. 386, VI 367)			
349	L. Pinarius (18) (?Natta)[1]		P(X) (~cos. 489 or 472)			
341	T.(?) Aemilius (100) (?Mamercinus)[2]		P(X) (~cos. I 470)			
340	L. Papirius (45) L.f. L.n. Crassus		PX or (X) (cf. cos. 436, tr.mil.c.p. I 382)			
336	Q. Publilius (11) Q.f. Q.n. Philo		X (cos. 339; cf. trr.mil.c.p. 400 and 399)			
332	L. Papirius (16, cf. 46 and 52)[3]		P(X) (cf. pr. 340)			
322	L. Plautius (33 or 34) (L.f. L.n. Venno)		X (cos. 330, or <cos. 330)			
318	L. Furius (14)		P?(X)			
>308	M. Valerius (137) M.f. M.n. Maximus Corvus		PX (cos. 348, VI 299; <tr.mil.c.p. I 398)			
>308	M. Valerius (137) M.f. M.n. Maximus Corvus II		PX			
>308	M. Valerius (137) M.f. M.n. Maximus Corvus III		PX			
308	M. Valerius (137) M.f. M.n. Maximus Corvus IV[4]		PX			
296	P. Sempronius (85) P.f. C.n. Sophus		X (cos. 304)			X
295	Ap. Claudius (91) C.f. Ap.n. Caecus (?II)[5]		PX (cos. 307, II 296; <<dict. 362, cos. 349)			
293	M. Atilius (50) M.f. M.n. Regulus		X (cos. 294; prob. <cos. 335)			
292	L. Papirius (53) L.f. Sp.n. Cursor		PX (cos. 293)			
283	L. Caecilius (92) Metellus Denter[6]		X (cos. 284)			X
283	M'. Curius (9) M.f. M'.n. Dentatus (suff.)[6]		X (cos. 290)			
?280	Q. Marcius (78) Q.f. Q.n. Philippus[7]		X (cos. 281) (?cf. cos. 357, IV 342)		X	
?273	C. Genucius (17) L.f. L.n. Clepsina[8]		X (cos. I 276)			
270	(Minucius?) (2)[9]		X			
?≥268	??M. Livius (12, 13) Drusus[10]		?X (cf. mag.eq. 324)			
257	A. Atilius (36) A.f. C.n. Calatinus		X (cos. 258, II 254)			X

B.1 (continued)

Date	Name	pv	c	p	sp	na
253	L. Postumius (56) L.f. L.n. Megellus[11]		PX (< or <<cos. I 305)			
242	Q. Valerius (157) Q.f. P.n. Falto	U	P			X
234	P. Cornelius (42)	U	P			N?
227	C. Flaminius (2) C.f. L.n.[12]	Si				X
227	M. Valerius (see 211)[8]	Sd	P			X
?>220	M. Livius (33) M.f. M.n. Salinator[8]					
219	L. Manlius (92) (Vulso)[13]	G	PX (<cos. 256, II 250)			
>218	M. Claudius (220) M.f. M.n. Marcellus		X (<<cos.287)			
>218	L. Postumius (40) A.f. A.n. Albinus		PX (<cos. 242)			X
>218	M.(?) Pomponius (18) Matho		?X			
>218	P. Furius (80) Sp.f. M.n. Philus		P			
>218	M. Valerius (211) P.f. P.n. Laevinus		PX (<<cos. 280)			
>218	C. Aurelius (95, cf. 15) C.f. C.n. Cotta[14]		(X) (~cos. 252, II 248)			
>218	Q. Terentius (30)[15]					X
?>218	C.? Aelius (103, cf. 148, 149) Tubero[16]	U				X
?>218	C. Servilius (59) (Geminus)[17]		X (<cos. I 252)		?X (<aed. cur. ca. 290)	
?>218	C. Papirius (58) L.f. Maso[17]		P			
?>218	M. Annius (15)[17]					X
?>218	M.? Acilius (9)[17]					X
?>218	C. (Baebius??) (not in RE) Herennius[17]					X
?>218	Q. Baebius (45) (Cn.f.) Tamphilus[18]					X
?>218	Q. Aelius (103) Paetus[19]		(X) (~cos. 337)			
?>218	P. Cornelius (266) Merenda[19]		PX (<cos. 274)			
??>218	K. Quinctius (41) Flamininus[20]		PX (<cos. 271)			

B.2. 218 to 200

Date	Name	pv	c	p	sp	na
218	M. Aemilius (19, 67) (Lepidus)[21]	Si	PX (<cos. 232)			
218	C. Terentius (83) C.f. M.n. Varro[22]	?Sd				N

218	C. Atilius (62) Serranus[23]	?U	(X)	
?218	C. Atilius (11) (?Regulus)	?ip	?X (<cos. 261)	
217	T. Otacilius (12) Crassus	Si	X (<cos. 261)	
217	M.(?) Pomponius (20, cf. 18)[24]	ip	?X (<cos. 233 or 231?)	
217	M. Aemilius (20, 128) (Regillus)[25]	U	P	X
217	A. Cornelius (257) Mamula[26]	Sd	P	X
216	M. Claudius (220) M.f. M.n. Marcellus II	Si	X (cos. 222; <<cos.287)	
216	L. Postumius (40) A.f. A.n. Albinus II	G	PX (cos. 234; <cos. 242)	X
216	M.(?) Pomponius Matho (18, cf. 20) II	ip	X (?=cos. 231)	
216	P. Furius (80) Sp.f. M.n. Philus II	U	P (cos. 223)	
215	M. Valerius (211) P.f. P.n. Laevinus II	ip	PX (cos. I 220; <<cos. 280)	
215	Ap. Claudius (293) P.f. Ap.n. Pulcher	Si	PX (<cos. 249)	
215	Q. Fulvius (59) M.f. Q.n. Flaccus	U	X (cos. 237; <cos. 264)	X
215	Q. Mucius (19) P.f. ?n. Scaevola	Sd	(= cos. 220)	
214	Q. Fulvius (59) M.f. Q.n. Flaccus II	U	X (cf. 215)	
214	T. Otacilius (12) Crassus II	Fl	X (cf. 217)	
214	Q. Fabius (103) Q.f. Q.n. Maximus	Ap	PX (<cos. I 223)	
214	P. Cornelius (200) Lentulus[27]	Si	P(X) (?<cos. 237 or 236)	
213	P. Sempronius (96) C.f. C.n. Tuditanus	G	(X) (<cos. 240)	
213	Cn. Fulvius (43) Cn.f. Cn.n. Centumalus	Su	X (<cos. 229)	
213	M. Atilius (53, cf. 20) (?Regulus)	U+ip	?X (<cos. 225)	
213	M.'(?) Aemilius (cf. 67) Lepidus[28]	ip+L	P(X) (~cos. 285)	
212	Cn. Fulvius (54) Flaccus	Ap	X (<cos. 264)	
212	C. Claudius (246) Ti.f. Ti.n. Nero	Su	P(X) (~cos. I 307)	
212	M. Iunius (167) Silanus	Etr		
212	P. Cornelius (383) Sulla	U+ip	PX (<<cos. 290)	X
211	L. Cornelius (187) (Lentulus)	Sd	P(X) (cf. 214)	
211	M. Cornelius (92) M.f. M.n. Cethegus[29]	Ap	P	X
211	C. Sulpicius (8) (?Galus)[30]	Si	PPX (<cos. 243)	
211	C. Calpurnius (61, cf. 8) Piso	U		X
210	P. Manlius (98) Vulso	Sd	PX (<cos. 256)	
210	L. Manlius (46) (L.f.) Acidinus	U	P	
210	C. Laetorius (2)[31]	?ip	?X	?X

B.2 (continued)

Date	Name	pv	c	p	sp	na
210	L. Cincius (5) Alimentus	Si				X
209	L. Veturius (20) L.f. L.n. Philo	ip+G	X (<cos. 220)			
209	T. Quinctius (38) L.f. L.n. Crispinus	Cap	P(X) (~cos. 271)			
209	C. Hostilius (25) Tubulus	U				X
209	C. Aurunculeius (1)	Sd				X
208	P. Licinius (69) P.f. P.n. Crassus Dives[32]	ip	(X) (~cos. 236)			
208	P. Licinius (175) Varus	U	X (<cos. 236)			
208	Sex. Iulius (147) Caesar	Si	P(X) (~Iulii Iulli)			
208	Quinctius (Claudius 151) Claudus Flamininus, K.[33]	T	?X (<<cos. 271)			
207	L. Porcius (22) (M.f.) Licinus	G				X
207	C. Mamilius (5) (Atellus)	Si	X (<cos. 239)			X
207	C. Hostilius (12) Cato	U+ip				X
207	A. Hostilius (10) Cato	Sd				
206	C. Servilius (60) C.f. P.n. (Geminus)	Si	X (<<cos. 252)	X (<pr. pre 218)		
206	M. Caecilius (76, cf. 73) Metellus[34]	U+ip	X (<cos. 251)			X
206	Ti. Claudius (62, cf. 61) Asellus	Sd	X (cf. 207)			
206	Q. Mamilius (13) Turrinus	ip+G				X
205	Sp. Lucretius (13)	G				
205	Cn. Octavius (16)[35]	Sd			?X	
205	Cn. Servilius (44) Cn.f. Cn.n. Caepio	U	PX (<< cos. 253)	?X		
205	L. Aemilius (109) (L.f.) Papus[36]	Si	PX (<cos. 225)			
204	Ti. Claudius (249) P.f. Ti.n. Nero	Sd	P(X) (~cos. I 307)			
204	M. Marcius (86) Ralla	U	?(X) (~cos. 281?)			
204	L. Scribonius (16) Libo	ip+G				X
204	M. Pomponius (19) Matho	Si	?X (<cos. 233 or 231?)			
203	P. Cornelius (214) Lentulus Caudinus	Sd	PX (<cos. 237)			
203	P. Quinctilius (12) Varus[37]	G	P(X) or [X] (~tr.mil.c.p. 403)			
203	P. Aelius (101) Q.f. P.n. Paetus[38]	U	(X) (~cos. 337)	?X		

203	P. Villius (10) Ti.f. Ti.n. Tappulus	Si			X
202	M. Sextius (35) Sabinus	G	[?X] (cf. cos. 366)		X
202	Cn. Tremelius (4) Flaccus[39]	Si		X	
202	C. Livius (29) M.f. M.n. Salinator	Br	X (<cos. 219)		
202	C. Aurelius (95, cf. 15) C.f. C.n. Cotta II	U	(X) (~cos. 252)		
201	M. Iunius (121) (M.f.) Pennus	U			X
201	M. Valerius (153) Falto	Br	PX (<cos. 239 or 238)		
201	M. Fabius (54) Buteo[40]	Sd	PX (<< cos. 245)		
201	P. Aelius (152) Tubero[41]	Si	(?X)	?X	
200	Q. Minucius (22, 55) C.f. C.n. Rufus[42]	Br	(X) (~cos. 221)		
200	L. Furius (86) Sp.f. Sp.n. Purpurio	G	P(X) (~cos. 223)		
200	Q. Fulvius (69) Gillo	Si			X
200	C. Sergius (36) Plautus[43]	U	?P		X

B.3. 199 to the *lex Villia Annalis* (180)

199	L. Quinctius (43) T.f. L.n. Flamininus	U	P(X) (~cos. 271)		
199	L. Valerius (173) P.f. L.n. Flaccus	Si	PX (<cos. 227)		
199	L. Villius (9) (Ti.f. Ti.n.) Tappulus[44]	Sd			X
199	Cn. Baebius (41) Q.f. Cn.n. Tamphilus	G		?X (<?pr. pre-218)	
198	L. Cornelius (270) L.f. ?.n. Merula	U	P		X
198	M. Claudius (222) M.f. M.n. Marcellus	Si	X (<cos. 222)		
198	M. Porcius (9) M.f. Cato	Sd			N
198	C. Helvius (1)	G			X
197	L. Manlius (93) (Cn.f. L.n.) Vulso[45]	Si	PX (<<cos. 256)	X (<pr. ?219)	X
197	C. Sempronius (90) Tuditanus	HC	(X) (~cos. 240)		
197	M. Sergius (40) Silus	U	P(X) (~Sergii Fidenates)		
197	M. Helvius (4)	HU			X
197	M. Minucius (53) Rufus	ip	X (<cos. 221)		
197	L. Acilius (Atilius 16 = Acilius 7) K.f. (Sapiens)[46]	Sd			X

B.3 (continued)

Date	Name	pv	c	p	sp	na
196	Q. Fabius (31, 57) Buteo	HU	PX (<<cos. 247 or 245?; cf. pr. 201)			N?
196	Ti. Sempronius (67) Ti.f. C.n. Longus	Sd	X (<cos. 218)			
196	Q. Minucius (65) Q.f. L.n. Thermus	HC	?(X) (~Minucii Rufi; ?cf. pr. 197)			X
196	M' Acilius (35) C.f. L.n. Glabrio[47]	ip				
196	L. Apustius (5) Fullo	U	X (< cos. 226)			
196	C. Laelius (2) C.f. C.n.	Si				
195	Cn. Manlius (91) Cn.f. L.n. Vulso	Si	PX (cf. pr. 197)			
195	Ap. Claudius (245) Nero	HU	P(X) (~cos. 307; cf. pr. 204)			X
195	P. Porcius (19) Laeca	Pi				
195	C. Fabricius (10) Luscinus	U				
195	C. Atinius (8) Labeo[48]	ip	?X (?<<cos. I 282)			X
195	P. Manlius (31)	HC	?P?X	?X (<pr. 210)		
194	P. Cornelius (350) Cn.f. L.n. Scipio Nasica	HU	PX (<cos. 222)			
194	Cn. Cornelius (265) Merenda	Sd	P(X) (~cos. 274)			
194	Cn. Cornelius (74) Blasio[49]	Si	PX (<<cos. 270)			
194	Cn. Domitius (18) L.f. L.n. Ahenobarbus	U	?(X) (~cos. 283)			
194	Sex. Digitius (2)[50]	HC				N
194	T. Iuventius (32) (T.f.) Thalna[51]	ip				X
193	L. Cornelius (337) P.f. L.n. Scipio (Asiaticus)	Si	PX (<cos. 218)			
193	M. Fulvius (91) M.f. Ser.n. Nobilior	HU	X (<<cos. 255)			X
193	C. Scribonius (8) (Curio)	U				
193	M. Valerius (252) M.f. M.'n. Messalla	ip	PX (<cos. 226)			
193	L. Porcius (23) L.f. M.n. Licinus	Sd		X (<pr. 207)		
193	C. Flaminius (3) C.f. C.n.	HC	X (<cos. 223)			
192[52]	L. Scribonius (17) Libo	ip+qsc		X (<pr. 204)		
192	M. Fulvius (44) Centumalus	U	X (<cos. 211)			

192	A. Atilius (60) C.f. C.n. Serranus	HU>Fl	?X (?<<cos. 245)	X (<pr. 218)		X
192	M. Baebius (44) Q.f. Cn.n. Tamphilus	HC>Br		?X (cf. pr. 199)		X
192	L. Valerius (350) C.f. Tappo	Si				
192	Q. Salonius (not in *RE*) Sarra	Sd				
191	L. Aemilius (114) L.f. M.n. Paullus	HU	PX (<cos. I 219)	X (<pr. 218)		
191	M. Aemilius (68) M.f. M.n. Lepidus	Si	PX (<<cos. 232)			
191	M. Iunius (48) M.f. L.n. Brutus[53]	U	[(X)] (~cos. 509)			
191	A. Cornelius (258) Mamulla	Br	P			
191	L. Livius (29) M.f. M.n. Salinator II	Fl	X (see 202)	X (<pr. 217)		
191	L. Oppius (32) Salinator[54]	Sd				
190	M. Tuccius (5)[55]	Ap				?X
190	L. Aurunculeius (4)[56]	U				X
190	Cn. Fulvius (12)[57]	ip	?X (<<cos. 264)	?X (<pr. 212)		X
190	L. Aemilius (127) M.f. Regillus[58]	Fl	P	X (<pr. 217)		X
190	P. Iunius (54) Brutus	Etr	[X] (cf. pr. 191)			X
190	C. Atinius (9) Labeo[48]	Si				X
189	Q. Fabius (91) Q.f. Q.n. Labeo[59]	Fl	P			X
189	Q. Fabius (127) Pictor[60]	Sd>ip	P(X)			
189	M. Sempronius (95) M.f. C.n. Tuditanus	Si	X or (X) (cf. cos. 240)		?X	
189	Sp. Postumius (44) L.f. A.n. Albinus[61]	U+ip>U	PX (<<cos. 242)			
189	L. Plautius (19) Hypsaeus[62]	HC	[?X] (~cos. 329)			
189	L. Baebius (25, cf. 14) Dives	HU	P			X
188	Q. Marcius (79) L.f. Q.n. Philippus[63]	Si	(X) (~cos. 281)			
188	M. Claudius (223 = 224) M.f. M.n. Marcellus	U	X			
188	C. Stertinius (4)[64]	Sd				X
188	C. Atinius (2, cf. 1)[48]	HU				X
188	Ap. Claudius (305) Ap.f. P.n. Pulcher	ip	PX (<cos. 212)			
188	L. Manlius (47) L.f. L.n. Acidinus Fulvianus	HC	PX (<cos. 237)			
187	P. Claudius (294) Ap.f. P.n. Pulcher	T	PX (<cos. 212)			
187	Ser. Sulpicius (57) Galba	U	PX or (X) (cf. cos. 211)			X
187	Q. Terentius (43) Culleo[65]	ip				
187	L. Terentius (58) Massiliota	Si				

B.3 (continued)

Date	Name	pv	c	p	sp	na
187	Q. Fulvius (60) Cn.f. M.n. Flaccus	Sd	X (<cos. 264)	X (<pr. 212)		
187	M. Furius (20, 56) (C.f.?) Crassipes	G	P?(X) (~Furii Pacili?)			
186	T. Maenius (15)	U	(X) (~cos. 338)			
186	P. Cornelius (384) Sulla	Si	P(X)	X (<pr. 212)		
186	C. Calpurnius (62) C.f. C.n. Piso	HU		X (<pr. 211)		X
186	M. Licinius (108) (M.f.) Lucullus[66]	ip				X
186	C. Aurelius (213) Scaurus	Sd	PX (<cos. 208)			
186	L. Quinctius (37) Crispinus	HC	PX (<<cos. 242)			
185[67]	A. Postumius (46) A.f. A.n. Albinus (Luscus)	?				N?
185	C. Afranius (15) Stello[68]	?	(X)	X (<pr. 218)		
185	C. Atilius (63) Serranus	?	?P	X		
185	L. Postumius (62) (Tempsanus)	T				
?185	A. Manlius (90) Cn.f. L.n. Vulso[69]	?	PX (<<cos. 256)			X
184	C. Decimius (9) Flavus	U	?X			
184	P. Sempronius (65) Longus[70]	HU	P[(X)]			
184	P. Cornelius (95 = 96) L.f. P.n. Cethegus[71]	U+ip			X	
184	Q. Naevius (4, 16) Matho	Sd+qe			?X (<tr. pl. 211)	
184	C. Sempronius (30) Blaesus	Si	?X (<<cos. 253)			
184	A. Terentius (80) Varro	HC	X (<cos. 216)			
183	C. Valerius (166) (P.f. L.n.) Flaccus[72]	ip	PX (<cos. 227)			
183	Sp. Postumius (49) A.f. A.n. Albinus Paullulus	Si	PX (cf. pr. 185)			
183	P. Cornelius (375) Sisenna	U	?P			
183	L. Pupius (5)[73]	Ap	P(X) (~Iulii Iulli; cf. pr. 208)		?X	X
183	L. Iulius (27) (Caesar?)	G	?[X] (~cos. 487?)			
183	Cn. Sicinius (8) S	d	X (<cos. 237)			
182	Q. Fulvius (61) Q.f. M.n. Flaccus	HC	PX (<cos. 210)			
182	M. Valerius (210) Laevinus	ip				
182	P. Manlius (31) II	HU	?P?X	?X (cf. 195)		

182	M. Ogulnius (4) Gallus	U	(X) (~cos. 269)		
182	L. Caecilius (49) Denter	Si	?(X) (~cos. 284?)		X
182	C. Terentius (51) Istra	Sd			
181	Q. Fabius (105) Maximus[74]	ip	P?X (?<<cos. I 223)		
181	Q. Fabius (32, 58) Buteo[75]	G	P(X) (~cos. 247 or 245?)		
181	Ti. Claudius (250) Nero[76]	Si	P(X) (~cos. 207?)		
181	Q. Petillius (4, 11) C.f. Q.n. Spurinus	U			X
181	M. Pinarius (21) Rusca	Sd			X
181	L. Duronius (2)	Ap+Ist	?P		X
180	Ti. Sempronius (53) P.f. Ti.n. Gracchus	HC	X (<<cos. 238)		
180	L. Postumius (41) A.f. A.n. Albinus	HU	PX (cf. pr. 185)		
180	P. Cornelius (260) Mamulla	Si		X (<pr. 217)	
180	Ti. Minucius (43) Molliculus[77]	ip	(X) (~Minucii Augurini)		X
180	A. Hostilius (16) L.f. A.n. Mancinus[78]	U	(X) (cf. pr. 186)		
180	C. Maenius (10)	Sd	PX (<cos. 212)		
180	C. Claudius (300) Ap.f. P.n. Pulcher (suff.)	ip	PX (<cos. 212)		

B.4. 179 to the end of Livy (166)

179	Cn. Cornelius (346) Cn.f. L.n. Scipio Hispallus	ip	PX (<cos. 222)		
179	C. Valerius (208) M.f. P.n. Laevinus	Sd	PX (cf. pr. 182)		
179	P. Mucius (16) Q.f. P.n. Scaevola	U	X (<cos. 220)		
179	Q. Mucius (20) Q.f. P.n. Scaevola	Si	X (<cos. 220)		
178	T. Aebutius (10) (Parrus)[79]	Sd			X
178	M. Titinius (13)[79]	U			X
178	UNKNOWN[79]	?Si			
178	M. Titinius (20) Curvus[80]	HC			X
178	Ti. Claudius (251) Nero[81]	ip+qsc	P?X (<cos. 207 or 202?)		
178	T.<i> (?) Fonteius (26) Capito[82]	HU			X
177[67]	P. Aelius (152) Tubero II	U	(?X)	?X (cf. 201)	

B.4 (continued)

Date	Name	pv	c	p	sp	na
177	K. Quinctius (40) Flamininus[83]	ip	P(X)	?X (?<pr. 208)		X
177	C. Numisius (2, cf. 10) (Tarquiniensis?)	Si				X
177	L. Mummius (7)	Sd			X (<leg. 210)	
176	M. Popillius (24) P.f. P.n. Laenas[84]	Sd	(X) (~cos. I 359)			
176	P. Licinius (60) C.f. P.n. Crassus	HC	?(X) (~cos. 205)			
176	M. Cornelius (348) Scipio Maluginensis	HU	P(X)			
176	L. Papirius (62) Maso[85]	U	P(X)	?X		
176	M. Aburius (2)	ip	(?X)			X
176	L. Aquillius (24) Gallus[86]	Si	P(X)			
175-87	(Ser.) Cornelius (2, 388) (Sulla)[88]	Sd	PX (<<cos. 240)	X (<pr. 212)		X
175	Ap. Claudius (103) (C.f.) Centho	HC				
?175	P. Aelius (84) P.f. P.n. Ligus[87, 89]	?	(X) (cf. pr. 176)			
?175	C. Popillius (18) P.f. P.n. Laenas[87]	?	X (<<cos. 241)			
?175	Cn. Lutatius (11) Cerco[90]	?				
?175	Q. Baebius (40) Sulca[90]					
174	M. Atilius (68) Serranus	Sd	(X)	X (<pr. 218)		X
174	Cn. Servilius (45) Cn.f. Cn.n. Caepio	HU	PX (<cos. 203)			
174	P. Furius (82) Philus	HC	PX (<<cos. 223)			
174	L. Claudius (22)[91]	Si	?P			X
174	L. Cornelius (325) Scipio	ip	PX (<cos. I 205)			
?174	C. Cassius (55) C.f. C.n. Longinus[92]	?U	[X] (cf. cos. 502)			X
173	N. Fabius (56) Buteo	HC	P(X) (~cos. 245; cf. pr. 201)			
173	C. Matienus (2)	HU				X
173	C. Cicereius (1)	Sd				N
173	M. Furius (20, 56) Crassipes II	Si	P (cf. 187)			
173	A. Atilius (60) Serranus II	U		X (cf. 192)		X
173	C. Cluvius (14) Saxula	ip				
173	C. Licinius (51) C.f. P.n. Crassus	U	?(X) (cf. 176)			
172	M. Iunius (122) M.f. M.n. Pennus	HC		X (<pr. 201)		

Year	Name					
172	Sp. Lucretius (14)	HU		X (<pr. 205)		X
172	Sp. Cluvius (8)	Sd				
172	Cn. Sicinius (8) II	ip+qsc	?[X] (cf. 183)			
172	C. Memmius (4)[93]	Si			?X	
171	C. Sulpicius (50) Galba	U	PX (<cos. I 211)			
171	L. Furius (77) Philus	Sd	PX (cf. pr. 174)			
171	L. Canuleius (12, cf. 6) Dives	H				X
171	C. Lucretius (23) Gallus	Fl				X
171	C. Caninius (8) Rebilus	Si				X
171	L. Villius (5) Annalis	ip	?(X) (~cos. 199?)		?X	
170	Q. Maenius (14) (T.f.)[94]	U	?(X)		?X	
170	M. Raecius (3)[95]	ip				
170	L. Hortensius (4)	Fl	?[X] (~dict. 287?)			
?170	Q. Aelius (104) P.f. Q.n. Paetus[96]	?	X (<cos. 201)			
?170	T. Manlius (83) A.f. T.n. Torquatus[96]	?	PX (<<cos. 235)			
?170	Cn. Domitius (19) Cn.f. L.n. Ahenobarbus[96]	?	X (<cos. 192)			
169	C. Decimius (1)	ip		X (<pr. 184)		
169	M. Claudius (225) M.f. M.n. Marcellus	H	X (<cos. I 222)			
169	C. Sulpicius (66) C.f. C.n. Galus[97]	U	PX (<<cos. 243)	?X (<pr. 211)		
169	C. Marcius (61) C.f. Q.n. Figulus[98]	Fl	?(X) (~cos. 281) (cf. pr. 188)			
169	Ser. Cornelius (208a) Lentulus[99]	Si	P(X)			X
169	P. Fonteius (24) Capito[99]	Sd				
168	Cn. Baebius (42, cf. 43) Tamphilus	U	X (<cos. 182)			X
168	L. Anicius (15) L.f. L.n. Gallus[100]	ip>qsc			?X (cf. aed. cur. 304)	
168	Cn. Octavius (17) Cn.f. Cn.n.[101]	Fl	P[?X] (cf. coss. 499, 463, 442) [X]	X (<pr. 205)		
168	P. Fonteius (17) Balbus	H	X (brother = cos. 171)			
168	M. Aebutius (13, cf. 7) Helva	Si				X
168	C. Papirius (32) Carbo	Sd>ip				
167	Q. Cassius (69) L.f. Q.n. (Longinus)	U				
167	M.' Iuventius (30) T.f. T.n. Thalna	ip	P?X (cos. 207 or 202)	X (<pr. 194)		X
167	Ti. Claudius (252) Nero	Si	?(X) (?<<cos. 264)			
167	Cn. Fulvius (13)	HC		?X (?<pr. 190)		

B.4 (continued)

Date	Name	pv	c	p	sp	na
167	C. Licinius (133) Nerva	HU	PX (cf. pr. 170)			X
167	A. Manlius (73) A.f. T.n. Torquatus	Sd>qe	P(X)	?X (?<pr. 208)		
166[67]	L. Iulius (28, cf. 127) (Caesar)[102]	?	P(X)			
166	L. Appuleius (28) Saturninus	?				X
166	A. Licinius (131) Nerva[103]	?				X
166	P. Rutilius (12) Calvus	?				X
166	P. Quinctilius (13) Varus	?	P[X]			
166	M. Fonteius (11) (?Capito)[99]	?		?X (?<pr. 203)		X

B.5. 165 to ca. 120

B.5.1. Praetorships Inferred from Consulship, Consular Candidacy, or High-ranking Legateship[104]

Date	Name	pv	c	p	sp	na
≥165	P. Cornelius (353) P.f. Cn.n. Scipio Nasica (Corculum) (cos. 162)		PX (<cos. 191)			
≥164	C. Fannius (20) C.f. C.n. Strabo[105] (cos. 161)			?X		
≥164	M. Valerius (253) M.f. M.n. Messalla (cos. 161)		PX (<cos. 188)			
≥163	M. Cornelius (93) C.f. C.n. Cethegus[106] (cos. 160)		P?(X)			
≥162	M. Fulvius (93) M.f. M.n. Nobilior[107]		X (<cos. 189)			
162	Cn. Cornelius (132) Cn.f. Cn.n. Dolabella[108] (cos. 159)		P(X) (~cos. 283)			
≥161	M. Aemilius (70) M.f. M.'n. Lepidus[109] (cos. 158)		P?(X) (?~cos. 232)	?X		
≥160	L. Aurelius (179) L.f. L.n. Orestes (cos. 157)		X			

736

Year	Name			
≥160	Sex. Iulius (148, 149) Sex.f. L.n. Caesar (cos. 157)	X	P(X)	X (<pr. 208)
≥157	M.' Acilius (36) M.f. C.n. Glabrio (cos. suff. 154)		X (<cos. 191)	
≥157	Q. Opimius (10) Q.f. Q.n. (cos. 154)		X	
≥157	L. Postumius (42) Sp.f. L.n. Albinus (cos. 154)		PX (<cos. 186)	
≥156	T. Annius (63, 64) T.f. ?n. Luscus (cos. 153)			
≥156	Q. Fulvius (95) M.f. M.n. Nobilior (cos. 153)		X (<cos. 189)	
?>155	L. Oppius (10)[110]			?X (<pr. 192)
≥155	L. Valerius (174) L.f. P.n. Flaccus (cos. 152)		PX (<cos. 195)	?X (<pr. 186)
≥154	L. Licinius (102) ?f. ?n. Lucullus (cos. 151)			X (<pr. 197)
≥153	M.' Acilius (25) L.f. K.n. Balbus (cos. 150)			
≥153	T. Quinctius (46) ?f. T.n. Flamininus (cos. 150)		PX (<cos. 198 or 192)	
≥152	L. Marcius (46) C.f. C.n. Censorinus (cos. 149)		P(X) (~cos. 310)	
≥151	Sp. Postumius (47, cf. 23) Sp.f. Sp.n. Albinus Magnus (cos. 148)		P(X) (?~cos. 242)	
≥150	C. Livius (14) M. Aemiliani f. M.n. Drusus (cos. 147)		(P)X (<<cos. 219)	
>149	M. Licinius (22)[111]			?X (<pr. 186)
≥149	Cn. Cornelius (175, 177) ?f. ?n. Lentulus (cos. 146)		P?X or (X) (~cos. 201)	
≥148	L. Hostilius (20) L.f. L.n. Mancinus (cos. 145)		(X) (?~cos. 170)	
≥147	L. Aurelius (98) ?f. ?C.n. Cotta (cos. 144)		(X) (~cos. I 252; cf. cos. 200)	
??>146	C. Sempronius (91) Tuditanus[112]		(X)	?X (?<pr. 197)
≥146	Ap. Claudius (295) C.f. Ap.n. Pulcher (cos. 143)		PX (<cos. 177)	
≥145	L. Caecilius (83) Q.f. ?L.n. Metellus Calvus (cos. 142)		X (<cos. 206)	

B.5.1 (continued)

Date	Name	pv	c	p	sp	na
≥144	Cn. Servilius (46) Cn.f. Cn.n. Caepio (cos. 141)		PX (<cos. 169)			N
?≥144	Q. Pompeius (12) A.f. ?n.[113] (cos. 141)[114]			X (<pr. 177)		
≥144	Sp. Mummius (13) (L.f. L.n.)[114]					
≥143	Q. Servilius (48) Cn.f. Cn.n. Caepio (cos. 140)		PX (<cos. 169)			
≥142	Cn. Calpurnius (73) ?C.f. C.n. Piso (cos. 139)		?X (?<cos. 180)			
≥141	P. Cornelius (354) P.f. P.n. Scipio Nasica (Serapio) (cos. 138)		PX (<cos. 162)			
≥141	D. Iunius (57) M.f. M.n. Brutus Callaicus (cos. 138)		X (<cos. 178)			
≥139	Sex. Atilius (69) M.f. C.n. Serranus (cos. 136)		(X) (–cos. 170)	X (<pr. 174)		
≥139	L. Furius (78) ?.f. ?P.n. Philus (cos. 136)		P?X (cf. cos. 223)	?X (cf. prr. 174 and 171)		
≥138	Ser. Fulvius (64) Q.f. ?n. Flaccus (cos. 135)		X (<cos. 180 or 179)			
≥137	C. Fulvius (53) Q.f. Cn.n. Flaccus (cos. 134)		X (<cos. 180)			
≥136	L. Calpurnius (96) L.f. ?Cn. or ?C.n. Piso Frugi[115] (cos. 133)		?X	X (<pr. c. 159)		
>135	L. Tremelius (6) Cn.f. Scrofa[116]					
≥135	P. Rupilius (5) P.f. P.n. (cos. 132)				?X	X
≥135	P. Popillius (28) C.f. P.n. Laenas[117] (cos. 132)		X (<cos. 172)			
≥134	P. Licinius (72) P.f. P.n. Crassus Dives Mucianus[118] (cos. 131)		X (<cos. 175)			
≥134	L. Valerius (175) ?L.f. ?L.n. Flaccus[119] (cos. 131)		P?X (?<cos. 152)			
≥133	Ap. Claudius (11) ?Ti.f. ?n. ?Nero (cos. suff. 130)		PX or (X)			

≥133	L. Rupilius (4) (P.f. P.n.)[120]	X (<cos. 162)			X
?ca. 133	C. Marcius (62) Figulus[121]	?(X) (?~cos. 259)			
≥132	M.' Aquillius (10) M'.f. M'.n. (cos. 129)			?X	
?>130	Ti. Latinius (6) Pandusa[122]				N?
≥130	L. Cassius (72) ?f. ?n. Longinus Ravilla[123] (cos. 127)	X (<cos. 171 or 164)			
≥130	L. Cornelius (105) L.f. ?n. Cinna (cos. 127)	P(X)			
≥129	M. Aemilius (71) ?f. ?n. Lepidus[124] (cos. 126)	P(X) (?<cos. 158)			X
≥129	L. Aurelius (180) L.f. L.n. Orestes (cos. 126)	X (<cos. 157)			
≥128	M. Fulvius (58) M.f. Q.n. Flaccus (cos. 125)	X (<<cos. 180 or 179)			X
≥128	M. Plautius (21) ?f. ?n. Hypsaeus[125] (cos. 125)	[?X]			X
≥127	C. Cassius (56) ?f. ?n. Longinus (cos. 124)	[X] (cf. cos. 127)	?X (?<<pr. 189; cf. prr. 146, 135)		
≥ca. 126	L. Manlius (Mallius 6) L.f.[126]	?P			
≥?ca. 126	C. Sempronius (5) ?Cn.f.[126]				
≥126	Q. Caecilius (82) Q.f. Q.n. Metellus (Baliaricus) (cos. 123)	X (<cos. 143)			
≥125	Cn. Domitius (20) Cn.f. Cn.n. Ahenobarbus (cos. 122)	X (<cos. 162)			
≥123	P. Manilius (14) ?f. ?P.n. (cos. 120)	X or (X) (~cos. 149)			
≥123	C. Papirius (33) C.f. ?n. Carbo[127] (cos. 120)	[X]	X (<pr. 168)		
≥122	L. Caecilius (91) L.f. Q.n. Metellus (Delmaticus) (cos. 119)	X (<cos. 142)			
≥121	Q. Marcius (91) Q.f. Q.n. Rex[128] (cos. 118)	P?[X]	X (<pr. 144)		
≥121	M. Porcius (10) M.f. M.n. Cato (cos. 118)	X (<<cos. 195)	X (<pr. des. 152)		

B.5.2 Attested praetorships

165	P. Cornelius (202) L.f. L.n. Lentulus	U	PX (<cos. 199)
ca. 164	Q. Minucius (24) Q.f.	C	X (<cos. 197 or 193)

B.5.2 (continued)

Date	Name	pv	c	p	sp	na
161	M. Pomponius (9)	U	?(X) (~Mathones?)	?X		
ca. 159	Cn. Tremelius (2)					
ca. 159	L. Cornelius (224) Cn.f. L.n. Lentulus Lupus	U	PX (<cos. 201)			
ca. 157	M.' Manilius (12) P.f. P.n.[129]	HU	X (<cos. 180)			X
ca. 156	L. Calpurnius (87) C.f. C.n. Piso Caesoninus[129]	HU				
155	A. Postumius (31) A.f. A.n. Albinus[129]	U	PX (<cos. 180)			
155	L. Mummius (7a) L.f. L.n.[129]	HU		X (<pr. 177)		
ca. 153	M. Atilius (22) (Serranus?)[130]	HU	?(X) (cf. cos. 170)	?X (?<pr. 174)		
152	M. Porcius (14) Cato Licinianus (des.)		X (<cos. 195)			
151	Ser. Sulpicius (58) ?Ser.f. ?n. Galba[131]	HU	P?X (cf. cos. I 211)			
149	Q. Fabius (109) Q.f.? Q.n. Maximus Aemilianus[132]	Si	PX (<cos. 182)	?X (?<pr. 187)		
149	P. Iuventius (31) (Thalna)	M	?(X) (~cos. 163)			X
148	Q. Caecilius (94) Q.f.? L.n. Metellus (Macedonicus)[133]	M	X (?<cos. 206)			X
147	C. Vetilius (1)[134]	HU	[?X] (see pr. 189)			
?>146	L. Licinius (120) Murena[135]	HU				
146	C. Plautius (9) (Hypsaeus)[134]	G				X
146	Oppius (2)	HC	?P			X
145	Claudius (376) Unimanus[136]	?C/HU				
145	C. Laelius (3) C.f. C.n. (Sapiens)[137]		X (<cos. 190)			
145	Q. Fabius (115) Q.f. ?Q.n. Maximus Servilianus[138]	M	PX (<cos. 169)			
144	Q. Marcius (90) Rex	U	P?[X]			X
ca. 143	Cn. Egnatius (cf. 1) C.f.	M				X
143	Quinctius (2) (?Flamininus)[139]	HU	?P			X
ca. 142	Licinius (130) Nerva[140]	M			?X (cf. prr. 167, 166)	

Year	Name	Cat.					
142	L. Hostilius (26) Tubulus[141]	qe	X (<cos. 173)				X (<pr. 209)
?≥142	M. Popillius (22) M.f. P.n. Laenas[142]	qe	(P)X (<cos. 165)				
141	D. Iunius (161) Silanus (Manlianus)[140]	M	P(?X)				?X (<pr. 194?)
ca. 140	P. Cornelius (76) Blasio[143]	U	X (<cos. 170)				
ca. 140	C. Hostilius (18) A.f. L.n. Mancinus	U					
ca. 140	M. Aemilius (83) M.f. M.n. Lepidus Porcina[144]	U	PX (<cos. 187)				
ca. 140	M. Iunius (49) Brutus	ip	X (<cos. 178)				
139	Cn. Cornelius (347) Scipio Hispanus	C	PX (<cos. 176)				
≥138	Q. Calpurnius (86) C.f. C.n. Piso[145]		X (<cos. 180)				
137	M. Claudius (26) (Marcellus?)		?[X]				
136	P. Mucius (17) P.f. Q.n. Scaevola[146]	?Si	X (<cos. 175)				
?ca. 136	L. Cornelius (192) ?f. ?. Lentulus[147]	Si	P?X or (X) (??<cos. 162)				
135	L. Plautius (20) Hypsaeus[148]	M	?[X]				
ca. 135	M. Cosconius (8) C.f.[149]	Si		?X			
134	T. Manlius (2, cf. 37 and 74)[150]	Si			X		
ca. 134	C. Hostilius (18) A.f. L.n. Mancinus II[151]		P?X (<cos. 165)				
133	M. Perperna (4) M.f. ?L.n.[152]	Si	X (cos. 137)				
132	C. Sempronius (92) C.f. C.n. Tuditanus	Si	(X) (~cos. 240)			X (<leg. 168)	
ca. 131	T. Annius (78) T.f. ?n. Rufus[153]	?Fl	X (<cos. 153)				
131	Cn. Octavius (18) Cn.f. Cn.n.[154]	?M	X (<cos. 165)				
ca. 128	P. Cornelius (202a) P.f. Lentulus[155]		PX (<cos. 162)				
≥127	C. Sextius (20) C.f. C.n. Calvinus[156]	C	X (<cos. 171)				
ca. 127	M. Licinius (57) Crassus (Agelastus)[157]	Si	PX (?<cos. 150)		X		
≥126	T. Quinctius (47) ?T.f. ?T.n. Flamininus[158]	?U					
?ca. 126	C. Fannius (7) M.f. ?C.n.[159]	qsc	X (<cos. 154)				
125	L. Opimius (4) Q.f. Q.n.	H	PX (<cos. 145)				
>123	Q. Fabius (110) Q. Aemiliani f. Q.n. Maximus (Allobrogicus)						
123	Sex. Iulius (150) Caesar	U	PX (<cos. 157)				
>122	L. Aurelius (99) ?f. ?n. Cotta[160]		?X or (X) (cf. cos. 144)				
>122	?(Livius or Oppius?) (RE I A2 col. 1903) Salinator[160]		?X				

Date	Name	pv	c	p	sp	na
?>121	C. Servilius (91, cf. 14) (M.f.) Vatia[161]	?M	(X) (–cos. I 252)	X (<pr. 190)		
≥121	C. Atinius (10) Labeo Macerio[162]	A				
≥121	Sex. Pompeius (17) (Cn.f.)[163]	M				X
≥120	L. Caecilius (93) Q.f. Q.n. Metellus (Diadematus)[164]	??Ill	X (<cos. 143)			
120	Q. Mucius (21) Q.f. Q.n. Scaevola	A	X (<cos. 174)			
?ca. 120	C. Licinius (88) P.f. ?.n. Getha[165]	?U			?X	X
?ca. 120	M.? Valerius (248) Messalla[166]	??A	PX (?<cos. 161)			

B.6. ca. 120 to ca. 82

B.6.1. Praetorships inferred from consulship, consular candidacy, or high-ranking legateship[104]

Date	Name	pv	c	p	sp	na
≥118	C. Fannius (7) C.f.[167]		X (<cos. 161)			
≥118	M. Caecilius (77) Q.f. Q.n. Metellus (cos. 115)		X (<cos. 143)			
≥118	P. Rutilius (34) P.f. ?.n. Rufus[168] (cos. 105)			?X (?<pr. 166)		
?≥117	C. Scribonius (9) Curio[169]			X (cf. pr. 193)		
≥117	M.' Acilius (26) M.f. L.n. Balbus (cos. 114)		X (<cos. 150)			
≥114	L. Calpurnius (23) ?f. ?n. Bestia[170] (cos. 111)		?X or ?(X)			
≥114	P. Cornelius (355) P.f. P.n. Scipio Nasica Serapio (cos. 111)		PX (<cos. 138)			
≥113	M. Minucius (54) Q.f. ?.n. Rufus (cos. 110)		(X) (cf. coss. 221, 197)			
≥113	Sp. Postumius (45, cf. 23) ?Sp.f. ?Sp.n. Albinus (cos. 110)		PX (cf. coss. 154, 151, 148)			
??>112	Ser. [——] (not in RE) Ser.f.[171]					X
??>112	L. Memmius (11)[172]					
≥112	M. Iunius (169) ?D.f. ?D.n. Silanus[173] (cos. 109)		?X or ?[X]	?X (cf. pr. 172)		

≥111	M. Aurelius (215) ?f. ?C.n. Scaurus (cos. suff. 108)		X (<pr. 186)	PX (<cos. 144)
≥?110	C. Sulpicius (51) (Ser.f.) Galba[174]			PX (cf. coss. 154, 151, and esp. 148)
>?110	A. Postumius (33 = 32) ?Sp.f. ?Sp.n. Albinus (cos. 99)[175]			
??>110	Q. Minucius (56) Q.f. Rufus[176]			(X) (cf. coss. 221, 197)
≥109	C. Atilius (64) ?f. ?n. Serranus (cos. 106)	N		X (cf. coss. 170, 136)
≥108	Cn. Mallius (13) Cn.f. M. (or M.')n. (?Maximus)[177] (cos. 105)	N		
?>107	C. Popillius (19) P.f. Laenas[178]			X (<cos. 132)
≥107	C. Flavius (87) C.f. ?n. Fimbria (cos. 104)[179]			X (<<cos. 157, cf. cos. 126)
≥106	L. Aurelius (181) ?L.f. L.n. Orestes			X (<cos. 129)
≥104	M.' Aquillius (11) ?M.f. ?M.'n.[180] (cos. 101)			
≥103	L. Valerius (176) L.f. L.n. Flaccus (cos. 100)[181] <cos. 152>			PX (<<cos. 152, <cos. 131 or <cos. 152)
??>101	C. [——]ius C.f.[182]	X	X or (X) (cf. pr. 183)	
>101	M. Pupius (7) M.f.[182]	X	X (cf. pr. 172)	
>101	C. Cornelius (17) M.f. (Cethegus)[182]			PX (<cos. 160)
>101	L. Memmius (cf. 12) C.f.[182]			
?>101	Q. Valgius (not in RE) M.f.[182]			
??>101	L. Iulius (141) Sex.f. (Caesar)[182]			PX (<cos. 157)
≥101	Q. Caecilius (95) Q.f. Q.n. Metellus Nepos (cos. 98)			X (<cos. 123, <<cos. 143)
?>100	Q. Marcius (81) Philippus[183]			X or (X) (~cos. 186)
?>100	Cn. Cornelius (133) Dolabella[184]			PX (<cos. 159)
≥100	Cn. Cornelius (178) Cn.f Cn.n. Lentulus (cos. 97)			PX (<< or < cos. 146)
≥100	P. Licinius (61) M.f. P.n. Crassus (cos. 97)		X (<pr. ca. 127)	X (<<cos. 171)
≥99	C. Cassius (57) L.f. ?n. Longinus (cos. 96)			X (?<cos. 127)
≥99	Cn. Domitius (21) Cn.f. Cn.n. Ahenobarbus (cos. 96)			X (<cos. 122)
≥98	L. Licinius (55) L.f. C.n. Crassus (cos. 95)[185]			X (<<cos. 168)
≥96	M. Herennius (10) M.f. ?n.[186] (cos. 93)		?X	(X) (~cos. 186)
≥96	L. Marcius (75) Q.f. Q.n. Philippus[187] (cos. 91)			

B.6.1 (continued)

Date	Name	pv	c	p	sp	na
≥95	M. Perperna (5) M.f. M.n. (cos. 92)		X (<cos. 130)			
??>94	P. Cornelius (351) Scipio Nasica[188]		PX (<cos. 111)			
?>94	C. (Sempronius) (64) Longus[189]		(X) (cf. coss. 218, 194)			
≥94	Sex. Iulius (151) C.f. ?n. Caesar (cos. 91)		P?X (?<cos. 157) or (X) (?<<pr. 166)			
≥93	P. Rutilius (26) L.f. L.n. Lupus (cos. 90)		X			
?>91	P. Albius P.f. (not in *RE*)[190]				?X (<q. 120)	
?≥91	Ser. Sulpicius (60) Galba[191]		PX or (X)			
>90?	D. Iunius (46) D.f. M.n. Brutus (cos. 77)[192]		X (<cos. 138)			
?>90	Q. Servilius (50) Caepio[193]		PX (<cos. 106)			
?>90	C. Perperna (2)[194]		?X or ?(X) (cf. cos. 130)			
?>90	?Cn. Octavius (21 = 82) Q.f. (Ruso)[195]					X
?>90	A. Gabinius (9, cf. 8)[196]		X or (X) (cf. cos. I 166)		X (cf. tr.pl. 139)	
??>90	M. Claudius (226) Marcellus[197]		PX or (X) (cf. cos. 161)			
??>90	M. or M.' Valerius (249 or 248) Messalla[198]		P?X or ?(X) (cf. coss. 162, 130)			
??>90	P. Cornelius (203) Lentulus[199]		P(X) (~cos. 193)			
≥90	L. Cornelius (272) ?f.?n. Merula (cos. suff. 87)		?X or ?(X)			
≥90	Cn. Octavius (20) ?Q.f. ?n. (cos. 87)[200]		X (<pr. by 121)			
??≥90	Sex. Pompeius (18) (Sex.f. Cn.n.)[201]		(X) (~ cos. I 252)			
??≥87	M. Servilius (19, cf. 4) C.f.[202]			?X (<?pr. pre-120)		X
≥84	M. Tullius (34) M.f. A.n. Decula (cos. 81)		P(X) (~cos. 283)			
≥84	Cn. Cornelius (134) P.f. L.n. Dolabella[203] (cos. 81)		P(X) (~cos. 181)			
?≥83	P. Cornelius (97) Cethegus[204]					
??83	T. Cloulius (Cloelius 5)[205]				X	
?≥82	?P. Albinovanus (2, cf. 3)[206]					X
?≥82	?C. (Coelius) (6) Antipater[206]					X
?≥82	?Flavius (86) Fimbria[206]		X (<cos. 104)			
?≥82	C. Fannius (8) C.f.[207]		X or (X) (cf. coss. 161, 122)			

744

??82	A. Postumius (35) Sp.f. Albinus[208]		PX (<cos. 110)	?X (<?pr. by 117) or (X) (~pr. 193)
?≥81	C. Scribonius (10) C.f.? C.n. Curio (cos. 76)[209]			

B.6.2. Attested praetorships

Date	Name	Class	Cos	Pr	Leg	Far
≥119	M. Aemilius (140) M.f. L.n. Scaurus[210]	??Af	P(X) (cf. Aemilii Barbulae)			
119	Q. Fabius (111) Q. Serviliani f. Q.n. Maximus (Eburnus)[211]	?rep	PX (<cos. 142)			
118	Cn. Cornelius (373) Sisenna[212]	M	?P	?(X) (cf. pr. 183)		
≥117	C. Porcius (5) M.f. M.n. Cato[213]	Si	X (<cos. 195)	X (<pr. des. 152)		
ca. 117?	L. Licinius (121) Murena[214]			X (<pr. by 147)		
≥116	C. Caecilius (84) Q.f. Q.n. Metellus Caprarius[215]	?U	X (<cos. 143)			
≥116	Cn. Papirius (37) C.f. ?n. Carbo[216]	A	[X]			
?<ca. 115	Q. Fabius (cf. 92) Q.f. Labeo[217]	HC	PX (<cos. 183)			
?<ca. 115	M.' Sergius (17) M'.f[218]	HC	P(X) (~Sergii Fidenates)		X (?<leg. 164)	
≥115	L. Calpurnius (88) L.f. C.n. Piso Caesoninus[219]	?A	X (<cos. 148)			
≥115	M. Livius (17) C.f. M.(Aemiliani) n. Drusus[220]	U	?(P)X (<cos. 447)			
115	C. Marius (14, Supb. 6) C.f. C.n.[221]	C/HU				N
115	P. Decius (9) Subulo[222]	C				
?ca. 114	M. Papirius (39) (C.f. ?n.) Carbo[223]	Si	[X]	X (<pr. 168)		
ca. 113	M. Porcius (15) Cato (Salonianus)[224]	?	X (<cos. 195)			
≥112	Q. Caecilius (97) L.f. Q.n. Metellus (Numidicus)[225]		X (<cos. 142)			X (<leg. 168)
>111	L. Calpurnius (97) L.f. L.f. Piso Frugi[226]	HU	X (<cos. 133)			
≥111	Ser. Sulpicius (59) Ser.f. ?n. Galba[227]	?HU	PX (<< or <cos. 144)			
?ca. 111	L. Hortensius (2 or 5)[228]	Si	?(X)			
111	L. Cassius (62) ?L.f. ?n. Longinus[229]	C	?X (?<cos. 127)			
ca. ?110	Ser. Cornelius (208b) Ser.f Lentulus[230]	?A	P(X) (cf. cos. 303)			
≥109	Q. Servilius (49) C.f. Cn.n. Caepio[231]	HU	PX (<cos. 141)	X (<<pr. 169)		

B.6.2 (continued)

Date	Name	pv	c	p	sp	na
≥109	Q. Lutatius (7) Q.f. ?n. Catulus[232]	?	(X) (~cos. 242)			X
>?107	A. Manlius (12)[233]		?P?X (cf. coss. 178 or 165, 164)			
ca. 107	T. Albucius (2)[234]	Sd				X
≥105	L. Bellienus (5)[235]	Af				N?
??ca. 105	Tremelius (not in RE) Scrofa[236]			X (<pr. by 135)		
105	L. [——]onius L.f.[237]	U				X
105	[——] P.f.[238]	ip				X
≥104	C. Billienus (4, cf. 3) C.f.[239]	M or A				N
≥104	L. Caesius (see 4) C.f.[240]	HU				X
≥104	P. Licinius (135) Nerva[241]	Si		?X (cf. pr 142)		
104	L. Licinius (103) (L.f.) Lucullus[242]	C+qsc/Si	X (<cos. 151)			
≥102	C. Memmius (3 = 5)[243]	M		X (cf. pr. 172)		
102	C. Servilius (see 12, cf. 11) (Vatia)	Si	(X) (~ cos. I 252)	?X (<?pr. by 120)		
102	M. Antonius (28) M.f. M.n.[243]	qsc		?X (cf. tr.pl. 167)		
≥101	T. Didius (5) T.f. Sex.n.[244]	M				
101	M. Porcius (11) Cato[245]	?C	X (<cos. 118)			N?
?>100	Cn. Cornelius (321) (Cn.f) Scipio[246]	H	PX (<<cos. 176)			
>ca. 100	M. Plautius (22) Hypsaeus[247]	A	X (<cos. 125)			
100	C. Servilius (65) Glaucia[248]	C		X (<pr.139)		
>99	M. Marius (22)[249]	HU	(X) (~cos. 107, etc.)			
≥?99	C. Iulius (130) C.f. Caesar[250]	A	P(X)			
≥99	L. Cornelius (138) P.f. L.n. Dolabella[251]	HU	P(X) (~cos. 283)			
>?98	C. Coelius (12) C.f. C.n. Caldus[252]	?HC				N
≥98	Q. Mucius (22) P.f. P.n. Scaevola[253]	??A	X (<cos. 133)			
≥97	L. Domitius (26) Cn.f Cn.n. Ahenobarbus[254]	Si	X (<cos. 122)			
97	L. Cornelius (392) L.f. P.n. Sulla (Felix)[255]	U/Ci	P(X)			
≥?96	L. Lucilius (8, cf. 19) L.f.[256]	A	PX (<<cos. 152)		?X	X
?96	C. Valerius (168) C.f. L.n. Flaccus[257]	U/A	X (<cos. 119)			
ca. 95	L. Aurelius (100) Cotta[258]					

	Name					
95	C. Claudius (302) Ap.f. C.n. Pulcher	rep	PX (<cos. 143)			
?≥94	L. Iulius (142) L.f. Sex.n. Caesar[259]	?M	PX (<<cos. 157)			
94	C. Sentius (3) C.f. Saturninus[260]	U/M		?X		
94	L. Gellius (17) L.f.?.n.[261]	ip?A or Ci		?X		
94	L. Sentius (6) C.f. (Saturninus)[262]	C		?X		
<94	L. (Sempronius) (18) Asellio[263]	Si		X		
≥91	Cn. Pompeius (45) Sex.f. Cn.n Strabo[264]	?qsc	X (<<cos. 195)		X (<pr. by 121)	
≥91	L. Porcius (7) M.f. M.n. Cato[265]	?qsc	PX (<cos. 127)		X (<pr. ca. 113)	
≥91	L. Cornelius (106) L.f. L.n. Cinna[266]					
≥91	M. Caecilius (44) Cornutus[267]					X
91	Q. Pompeius (39) Q.f. ?A.n. Rufus[268]	U	X (<cos. 141)			
91	Q. Servilius (29)[269]	qsc	?P?X or ?(X) (cf. cos. 140)			N
91	C. Norbanus (5)[270]	S₁				
>90	P. Servilius (93) C.f. M.n. Vatia (Isauricus)[271]	?Sd	(X) (~ cos. I 252)	?X (<?pr. pre-120)		
>90	L. Valerius (178) C.f. L.n. Flaccus[272]	A	PX (<<cos. 152)			X
≥90	C. Cassius (10)[273]	A	?X (~Cassii Longini)			X
≥90	L. Postumius (13)[274] (Albinus?)	qsc	?P?X or ?(X) (?~Postumii Albini)			
??90	??L. Calpurnius (89) Piso Caesoninus[275]		X (<cos. 112)			
≥89	Q. Oppius (20) Q.f.[276]	Ci				
≥89	P. Sextilius (12) (?Rufus)[277]	Af	?[X] (cf. tr.mil.c.p. 379)	?X		
89	A. Sempronius (17) Asellio[278]	U		X		
89	C. Cosconius (3)[279]	qsc		?(X) (cf. pr. 135)		
89	Cn. Papirius (38) Cn.f. C.n. Carbo[280]	qsc	X (<cos. 113)			
88	Q. Caecilius (98) Q.f. L.n. Metellus Pius[281]	C+qsc	X (<cos. 109)			
88	P. Gabinius (13)[282]	C/??M			X (cf. tr.pl. 139)	
88	Ap. Claudius (296) Ap.f. C.n. Pulcher[283]	C	PX (cos. 143)			
88	M.(?) Iunius (51) Brutus[284]	C	?X or ?(X)			
88	Servilius (3)[284]	C				X
?88	L. Cornelius (194, 195) (L.f.) Lentulus[285]	C/??Ci	P?X (?<<cos. 130) or (X)			
≥87	L. Licinius (122) L.f. Murena[286]	??/A		X		
>87	L. Hortensius (6)[287]		?X or (X) (~cos. 108)			
?87	Q. Ancharius (2)[288]					
?86	L. Cornelius (338) L.f. L.n. Scipio (Asiaticus)[289]	M or ?/M	P(X) (~cos. 190)			N?

B.6.2 (continued)

Date	Name	pv	c	p	sp	na
?85	M. Marius (42) Gratidianus[290]	C	(X) (~cos. 107, etc.)	X (<pr. before 99)		X
≥84	C. Fabius (82) (?C.f. ?Q.n.) Hadrianus[291]	Af				N
>83	Q. Sertorius (3)[292]	HC				
≥83	M. Perperna (6) (M.f. M.n.) Veiento[293]	Si	X (<cos. 92)			N?
83	P. Burrenus (Burrienus 1)[294]	C				
>82	C. Papirius (40) C.f. Carbo (Arvina)[295]		X (<cos. 120)			X
≥82	Q. Lucretius (25) Afella[296]					
82	L. Iunius (58) Brutus Damasippus[297]	U+qsc	?(X)			
82	Q. Antonius (41) Balbus[298]	Sd			?X	X
82	C. Carrinas (1)[299]	qsc				N?
82	M. Marius (42) Gratidianus II[290]		(X) (~cos. 107, etc.)	X (= pr. ?85)		X
>81	C. Papirius (34) (Cn.f.) Carbo[300]		X (<cos. 113)			
>81	P. Sextius (9)[301] (des.)					
>81	P. Magius (10, see 8) Min.f.[302]					
>81	?M. Magius (see 8) Min.f. (?Sarus)[302]					

B.7. 81 to 50

B.7.1. Praetorships inferred from consulship, consular candidacy, or high-ranking legateship[104]

Date	Name	pv	c	p	sp	na
≥81	Q. Lutatius (8) Q.f. Q.n. Catulus[303] (cos. 78)		X (<cos. 102)			X
≥80	Mam. Aemilius (80) ?Mam.f. ?n. Lepidus Livianus (cos. 77)[304]		PX (?<cos. 112)			
≥79	Cn. Octavius (22) M.f. Cn.n.[305] (cos. 76)		X (<<cos. 128)			
?>78	L. Faberius (2) L.f.[306]					
≥78	C. Aurelius (96) M.f. ?n. Cotta[307]		(X) or ?X (cf. cos. 144)			
≥78	L. Octavius (26) Cn.f. Cn.n. (cos. 75)		X (< or <<cos. 128)			

Date	Name	?GC	Notation		
≥77	M. Aurelius (107) M.f. ?n. Cotta (cos. 74)		(X) or ?X (cf. cos. 144)		
≥76	C. Cassius (58) L.f. ?L.n. Longinus[308] (cos. 73)		X (<cos. 107)		?X (<?pr. by 90)
≥75	M. Claudius (227) M.f. Marcellus[309]		(X)	X	
≥75	C. Claudius (see 165) C.f. Glaber[310]		PX (<cos. 97)		
≥75	Cn. Cornelius (216) Cn.f. Cn.n. Lentulus Clodianus[311] (cos. 72)				
>74	C. Valerius (366) Triarius[312]		?(X) (cf. cos. 105)	X	
?>74	P. Rutilius (30) P.f. Nudus[313]		PX (<< or <cos. 118)	X	
>?73	L. Cossinius (2)[314]		?(X)		
≥71	Q. Marcius (92) Q.f. Q.n. Rex (cos. 68)		P?X or (X)	X	
??ca. 70	Q. Pompeius (25) A.f. Bithynicus[315]				
≥69	M.' Aemilius (62) ?M.'f. ?n. Lepidus[316] (cos. 66)			X	
≥69	L. Volcacius (8) ?f. ?n. Tullus[317] (cos. 66)			X	
69	M. Lollius (21) Palicanus[318]			N?	
?≥68	C(n). (Cornelius) (not in RE) Scipio[319]	?GC	PX or (X)	X	
≥68	P. Autronius (7) L.f. ?n. Paetus (cos. des. 65)				
≥68	P. Cornelius (386) ?f. ?n. Sulla[320] (cos. des. 65)		(X) (~cos. 88, II 80)	N?	
≥68	L. Manlius (79) L.f. ?n. Torquatus[321]		P(X) (~Manlii Capitolini)		
??>67	L. Lollius (6) (Palicanus)[322]				
≥67	M. Marcius (63) C.f. ?C.n. Figulus (cos. 64)		(X) (~cos. I 162)		
≥67	?(A.) (Minucius) (60) Thermus[323]		(X) (~cos. 193)		
??≥67	Q. Curius (1)[324]				
67	D. Iunius (163) M.f. ?n. Silanus[325] (cos. 62)		?X or ?(X) (?cf. cos. 109)	X	
66	M. Caesonius (1)[326]			X	
≥66	Q. Cornificius (7)[327]			X	
>63	Ti. Claudius (253) (Ti.f. Ap.n.) Nero[328]		P(X) (~cos. 202)	N?	
≥61	L. Cornelius (234) Lentulus Niger[329]		PX or (X)		
61	A. Gabinius (10 = 11) A.f. ?A.n.[330] (cos. 58)				
≥59	T. Labienus (6)[331]				
>58	Q. Fabius (143) (Maximus) Sanga[332]		PX (<cos. 121)	N?	
?>55	T. Manlius (85) T.f. Torquatus[333]		P(X) (~cos. 165)		
≥55	(Gutta?) (RE VII 2 col. 1952)[334]				
?55	P. Plautius (23) (P.f.) Hypsaeus[335]		(X) (cf. cos. 125)	N?	

B.7.1 (continued)

Date	Name	pv	c	p	sp	na
≥54	M. Claudius (229) M.f. M.n. Marcellus[336] (cos. 51)		(X) (~cos. I 166)			
≥53	C. Claudius (216) C.f. M.n. Marcellus[336] (cos. 50)		(X) (~cos. I 166)			
≥52	C. Claudius (217) M.f. M.n. Marcellus[336] (cos. 49)		(X) (~cos. I 166)			
??>52	T. Fadius (9)[337]					N
??>50	T. Furfanus (1) Postumus[338]					N?
?>49	L. Postumius (15, cf. 26)[339]					X
?>49	Q. Fabius (108) Q.f. Q.n. Maximus (?Sanga)[340] (cos. suff. 45)		P(X) (cf. cos. 121)			
??>49	C. Fannius (9) C.f.[341]		X or (X) (cf. coss. 161, 122)	?X (<?pr. by 82)		
??>49	Q. Marcius (52) Crispus[342]				?X	X
??>49	L. Scribonius (34) L.f. Libo (cos. 34)[343]			X (cf. pr. 203)		

B.7.2. Attested praetorships[344]

Date	Name	pv	c	p	sp	na
81	Cn. Cornelius (135) (Cn.f. Cn.n.) Dolabella[345]	C/Ci	P(X) (~cos. 159)			
81	M. Aemilius (72) Q.f. M.n. Lepidus[346]	?/Si	P(X) (cf. cos. I 187) or ?X (?<<cos. 158)			
81	C. Annius (9) T.f. T.n.[347]	H	X (<cos. 128)			
81	M. Minucius (64) Thermus[348]	A	(X) (cf. pr. 196)		X	
81	Sex. Nonius (53) Sufenas[349]	C				
?81	C. Claudius (247) P.f. Nero[350]	?/A	P(X) (cf. coss. 207, 202)			
80	C. Claudius (214) (M.f.) Marcellus[351]	?/Si	(X) (cf. cos. I 166)			X

Year	Name	Code				
80	M. Fannius (15)[352]	sic	?X	?X (cf. coss. 161, 122)		X
80	L. Fufidius (4)[353]	HU				
80	M. Domitius (44) (M.f.) Calvinus[354]	HC		(X) (~cos. 283)	X	
79	Q. Calidius (5)[355]	?/HC	(= pr. 89)			
?79	C. Cosconius (3) II[356]	?/Ill				
?79	L. Manlius (30)[357]	?/GT>HC		?P?(X)		
78	L. Cornelius (374) Sisenna[358]	U+ip/?Si	?(X) (cf. prr. 183, 118)	?P		
78	L. Licinius (104) L.f. L.n. Lucullus[359]	C/Af		X (<<cos. 151)		
?>77	Terentius (see 82) Varro[360]	?/??A				
≥77	M. Iunius (170) (?D.f.) Silanus (?Murena)[361]	?/A	?(X) (cf. pr. 184)	(X) (cf. cos. 109)		
77	Cn. Aufidius (32) Cn.f. Cn.n. Orestes[362]	U	?X (<<pr. 141)	X (<cos. 103)		
77	Sex. Peducaeus (5) Sex.f.[363]	?/Si				
?77	M. Fonteius (12)[364]	??/GT	X or (X) (cf. pr. 166)		X (<tr. pl.113)	
76	M. Terentius (Licinius 109) M.f. ?n. Varro Lucullus[365]	ip		X (<<cos. 151)		X
76	M. Iunius (84 = Iuncus 4) Iuncus[366]	?/A	X			
?≥75	Cn. Tremelius (5) Scrofa[367]	?/GT			X	
75	C. Licinius (154) C.f. Sacerdos[368]	U/Si	X		X	
75	M. Caesius (9) (?M.f.)[369]	C	(X) (cf. pr. by 104)			X
≥74	L. Furius (18, cf. 2) or Turius (2)[370]	rep				N?
74	C. Verres (1) (C.f.)[371]	U/Si	??X		X	
74	P. Cornelius (240) ?f. P.n. Lentulus Sura[372]	?rep	X (<pr. before 111)	PX (<<cos. 162)		
74	L. Calpurnius (98) L.f. L.n. Piso Frugi[373]	C		X (<<cos. 133)	X	
74	P. Coelius (2)[374]	C		(X) (~cos. 94)		X
74	M. Antonius (29) (M.f.) ("Creticus")[375]	qsc		X (<cos. 99)		
73	Claudius (165) (C.f.) Glaber[376]	qsc	?X or (X)			X
73	P. Varinius (1)[377]	qsc				X
73	Q. Arrius (7 = 8)[378]	?/Si >qsc				
?73	M. Licinius (68) P.f. M.n. Crassus[379]	?/qsc		X (<cos. 97)	N	
≥72	Q. Caecilius (87) C.f. Q.n. Metellus (Creticus)[380]	U		X (<cos. 113)		

B.7.2 (continued)

Date	Name	pv	c	p	sp	na
≥72	Cn. Manlius (21)[381]	qsc	?P?(X)			X
72	Q. Hortensius (13) L.f. ?n. Hortalus[382]	rep	?X or (X) (cf. cos. 108)			
>71	L. Afranius (6) A.f. ?n.[383]	?/?HC		?(X) (cf. pr. 185)		?N
≥71	M. Pupius (10) M.f. M.n. Piso Frugi Calpurnianus[384]	?C/HU	X (<<cos. 133)	X		
?71	C. Calpurnius (63) ?f. ?Cn. or Q.n. Piso[385]	U/?Z	X (?<<cos. 139 or 135)			
?71	L. Iulius (143) L.f. L.n. Caesar[386]	?/?M	PX (<cos. 90)			
71	L. Caecilius (74) C.f. Q.n. Metellus[387]	C/Si	X (<cos. 113)			
>70?	L. Titius (14)[388]	C			?X	
70	M. Mummius (9)[389]	?U	?(X) (cf. cos. 146)			
70	M.' Acilius (38) M.f. M.n. Glabrio[390]	rep	X (<<cos. suff. 154)			
70	L. Aurelius (102) M.f. ?n. Cotta[391]	C/?M	(X) (~cos. I 252) or ?X (<<cos. 144)			
≥69	A. Manlius (70, 76) Torquatus[392]	?/Af	P(X) (cf. coss. 165, 164)			
69	M. Caecilius (78) (C.f. Q.n.) Metellus[393]	rep	X (<cos. 113)		X	
69	C.(?) Antistius (46) Vetus[394]	?/HU	?(X) (cf. tr.mil.c.p. 379)		?X	
≥68	Rubrius (4, cf. 17)[395]	?/M				X
≥68	P. Cornelius (140) Dolabella[396]	C/A	P(X)	X (<pr. by 100)		
≥68	L. Sergius (23) L.f. Catilina[397]	?/Af	P(X) (~Sergii Fidenates)	(X) (cf. pr. 197)		
>67	C. Licinius (112) L.f. Macer[398]	??	[X] (cf. cos. 364)			X
>67	M. Terentius (84, Supb. 6) Varro[399]	??	(X) (~cos. 216)			
≥67	Bellienus (1)[400]	qsc		?X (cf. pr. by 105)		
≥67	Sextilius (3)[400]	qsc		?X or ?(X) (cf. pr. ?2c, pr. by 88)		
≥67	T. Aufidius (12)[401]	?/A		?X	?X	X
67	M. Iunius (25, cf. 23)[402]	U	?(X)			X
67	Q. Publicius (13) (Q.f.)[403]	C	?(X) or ?[X] (cf. cos. 232)			X
67	L. Lucceius (6, cf. Licinius 105) (?Q.f.)[404]	C/Z			?X	N
?67	L. Quinctius (12)[405]	C				

≥66	P. Varinius (1) II[406]	?/A	PX or (X) (~cos. I 211)		X (= pr. I 73)	
≥66	P. Sulpicius (55, cf. 48) Galba[407]	?U/Z	X (<cos. 99)			
66	C. Antonius (19) M.f. M.n. (?Hibrida)[408]	rep/Z	(X) (?~cos. 164)			
66	M. Tullius (29) M.f. M.n. Cicero[409]	ambZ			(X) (cf. pr. 176)	N
66	C. Aquillius (23) Gallus[410]	mai/?Z				
66	L. Cassius (64) (Q.f.) Longinus[411]	pec/?X				N?
66	C. Orchivius (Orcivius 1)[412]	?/A				N?
≥65	P. Orbius (3)[413]					
65	L. Licinius (122) L.f. L.n. Murena[414]	U/GT (?+ GC)			X (<pr. by 87)	
65	Ser. Sulpicius (95) Q.f. ?n. Rufus[415]	pec/Z	P(X) (~tr.mil.c.p. I 388)			X
65	Q. Gallius (6)[416]	mai/Z				X
65	C. Attius (not in RE) Celsus[416]	C				X
??64	M. Plaetorius (16) M.f. Cestianus[418]	??/?M		?X		X
≥64	P. Servilius (66) Globulus[419]	?/A				
≥64	M. Petreius (3)[420]	?C/?				N?
??64	M. Valerius (266) M.f. M'n. Messalla (Niger)[421]	U	P(X) (~cos. 263, etc.)			
63	L. Valerius (179) L.f. (C.n.) Flaccus[422]	U/A	PX (<cos. suff. 86)			
63	Q. Pompeius (42) (Q.f.) Rufus[423]	C>qsc/Af	X (<cos. 88)			
63	C. Cosconius (4, cf. 12) (Calidianus?)[424]	C/HU				
63	Q. Caecilius (86) Q.f. ?L.n. Metellus Celer[425]	C>qsc/GC	X (?<<cos. 117)		X (cf. pr. c. 135)	
63	C. Pomptinus (1)[426]	C/GT				N?
??63	P. Cornelius (240) ?f. P.n. Lentulus Sura II[427]	C	PX (= cos. 71)	?X		
63	C. Sulpicius (10)[428]	C	?P?(X) (?~Sulpicii Galbae)	?X		X
??63	??L. Roscius (22) Otho[429]	??C				X
?62	M. Valerius (268) M.f. M.n. Messalla (Rufus)[430]	?U/HU	P(X) (~cos. 263, etc.)			
62	C. Iulius (131) C.f. C.n. Caesar[431]	C/Si	P(X)		X (<pr. c. 91)	
62	C. Vergilius (2, 3) C.f. Balbus[432]	C+qsc/A				
62	Q. Tullius (31) M.f. (M.n.) Cicero[433]	C+qsc	(X) (~cos. 63)			X
62	M. Calpurnius (28) C.f. ?n. Bibulus[434]	?/Sy	?(X)			
62	L. Marcius (76) L.f. Q.n. Philippus[435]	?/Bi	X (<cos. 91)			X
≥61	C. Papirius (35) Carbo[436]	?/Bi	X or (X) (<~coss. 120 or 113)			
61	L. Calpurnius (90) L.f. L.n. Piso Caesoninus[437]	?	X (<<cos. 112)		?X (?<pr. pre-82)	

B.7.2 (continued)

Date	Name	pv	c	p	sp	na
61	C. Octavius (15) C.f. C.n.[438]	C/M				N
?≥61	C. Toranius (4)[439]	?/Ill				N?
≥60	L. Culleolus (1)[440]	?/Z/?				X
≥60	Q. Voconius (3, cf. 1 and 2) Naso[441]	?/Z/?			X	
60	P. Cornelius (238) P.f. ?L.n. Lentulus Spinther[442]	U/HC	P?X or ?(X) (?<<cos. 130)			
60	Q. Caecilius (96) Q.f. Q.n. Metellus Nepos[443]	C/?	X (<cos. 98)			
60	Cn. Cornelius (228) P.f. P.n. Lentulus Marcellinus[444]	?/Sy	P(X)			
>59	M. Atius (11) Balbus[445]	C/Af				N
59	T. Vettius (9a and 14) Sabinus[446]	rep			X	
59	Cn. Cornelius (217) Lentulus Clodianus[447]	C	PX (<cos. 72)			
59	Q. Fufius (10) Q.f. C.n. Calenus[448]	?/M				N?
59	L. Appuleius (30)[449]	?/A, then Ci				N?
59	T. Ampius (1) T.f. Balbus[450]	C/Bi				N?
58	C. Memmius (8) (L.f.)[451]	C		X or (X) (cf. prr. 172, by 102)	X	
58	L. Cornelius (218) P.f. ?L.n. Lentulus Crus[452]	C/?Z	P?X or (X) (?<<cos. 130)			X
58	L. Domitius (27) Cn.f. Cn.n. Ahenobarbus[453]	C	X (<cos. 96)			X
58	L. Flavius (17)[454]	?/A				X
58	C. Fabius (17) M.f. (?Hadrianus)[455]	U/?			?X	
58	P. Nigidius (3) Figulus[456]	C/HU			?X	
>57	L. Villius (7) L.f. Annalis[457]	rep/Sd		(X) (~pr. 171)		
57	L. Caecilius (110) L.f. Rufus[458]	C/Af	P[X] (see prr. 203, 166)			
57	Sex. Quinctilius (4) Varus	C/A	PX (<cos. 79)			
57	Ap. Claudius (297) Ap.f. Ap.n. Pulcher[459]	C/Bi				X
57	Q. Valerius (280) Q.f. Orca[460]	C			?X	
57	C. Septimius (7) T.f.[461]	C/A				X
57	C. Caecilius (43) Cornutus[462]	C/Bi		?X	X	X
57	M. Calidius (4) (Q.f.)[463]	C		X (<pr. 79)		

Date	Name				
57	P. (Licinius) (71) Crassus Dives[464]	C	X (-cos. 131)		
56	M. Aemilius (141) (M.f. M.n.) Scaurus[465]	?vis/Sd	PX (<cos. 115)		
56	Q. Ancharius (3) Q.f.[466]	C/M		X (<pr. by 87)	
56	C. Claudius (303) Ap.f. (Ap.n.) Pulcher[467]	C/A	PX (<cos. 79)		
56	Cn. Domitius (43) M.f. M.n. Calvinus[468]	amb/?Z	(X) (<cos. 283)		
≥55	P. Attius (32) Varus[469]	C/A?			?X
≥55	Q. Caecilius (99) Q.f. Q.n. Metellus Pius Scipio[470]	??	X (<cos. 8c)		
55	P. Vatinius (3) P.f.[471]	?Z	(X) (cf. coss. 153, 128)		N
55	T. Annius (67) (T.f.) Milo (Papianus)[472]	?Z		X (<pr. c. 113)	
≥54	C. Considius (11) C.f. Longus[473]	?A?			X
54	Fonteius (not in RE)[474]	?U	?X		
54	M. Porcius (16) (M.f.M.n.) Cato (Uticensis)[475]	rep/Z/Si	(X) (-cos. 195)	X (<pr. c. 113)	N?
54	C. Alfius (7) Flavus[476]	mai			
54	P. Servilius (67) P.f. C.n. (Vatia) Isauricus[477]	C	X (-cos. 79)		
54	Ser. Sulpicius (61) Galba[478]	C	PX (< or <<cos. 108)		
?54	C. Cosconius (5) C.f.[479]	?/M		X (<pr. 79)	
53	L. Aemilius (81) M.f. Q.n. (Lepidus) Paullus[480]	C?Z	PX (<cos. 78)		
>51	Q. Minucius (67) (Q.f) Thermus[481]	??Z/A	(X) (cf. cos. 193)	X or (X) (<pr. 81)	
>51	M. Nonius (52) (Sufenas?)[482]	??Z/?M			
>51	Cn. Tremelius (see 5) Scrofa[483]	??Z/?Cy			X
>51	P. Silius (8)[484]	??Z/Bi			X
51	A. Plautius (8) (or Plotius)[485]	?U/?Bi			X (cf. leg. 90)
51	M. Iuventius (16) Laterensis[486]	rep	(X) (-cos. 163)		X
?>50	?M. Aurelius (109) Cotta[487]	?Sd	X (cf. coss. 75, 74, 65)		X
50	C. Titius (37) L.f. Rufus[488]	U			?X
50	M. Curtius (23 = 8) Peducaeus[489]	C	(P)X (~Claudii Pulchri)	X (<pr. 77)	
50	?M. Livius (19) Drusus Claudianus[490]	?C			
50	P. Sestius (6) L.f.[491]	?/Ci		X (<tr. pl.91)	
>49	M. Considius (13) Nonianus[492]		?X (?-pr. 81)	X (<tr.pl. 91)	
?>49	L. Livineius (2) Regulus[493]				
??>49	L. Furius (55) L.f. Crassipes[494]	??M	P	(X) (~pr. I 187)	X

Date	Name	pv	c	sp	p	na
?≥49	M. Favonius (1)[495]	Af				N
?≥49	L. Aelius (150) Tubero[496]				(X)	

B.8 Praetors of Uncertain Date

Date	Name	pv	c	sp	p	na
?4/3c	Genucius (16, RE III 2 col. 2565) Cipus[497]		P			X
?4/3c	P. Claudius (27)[498]					X
?3c	?[—]ilius M.f. (Aemilius 18)[499]					X
?3c	C. An(n)ius (8)[499]					X
?3 or 2c	?Domitius (40) Calvinus[500]	??G	X or (X) (cf. cos. 332)			
3 or 2c	L. Furius (36) Bibaculus[501]		?P			
??2c	A. Manlius (74) (Torquatus?)[502]		P?X (cf. coss. 165, 164)			
?2c	?Octavius (7 = ?17) Cn.f.[503]	?U	?X (<cos. 165)			
?2c	P. Sextilius[504]	C				X
?2c	C. Rabirius (see 6) C.f.[505]	A				N?
2c	??Aelius (1)[506]					X
2c	??Fufius (1)[506]	U				X
2c	P. Atilius L.f.[507]	U				X
2c	M. Marcius (cf. 23)[508]	C	?P			
2c	L. Furius L.f.[509]	Si	P			
2c	(Cornelius) Scipio[510]	?Si				X
2c	Cn. Aufidius T.f.[511]	??HU				
2c	??(Cornelius) Sulla[512]					
??2/1c	[—]us[513]					
?2/1c	C. Aelius (149) Tubero[514]				X or (X)	X
?2/1c	Calpurnius (see 97)[515]					X

?2/1c	L. Fufidius (3)[516]			X
2/1c	C. Cluvius (2) L.f.[517]	A or M		?(X) (cf. prr. 173, 172)
2/1c	C. Caninius (Supb. 3.232f) C.f. (Rebilus)[518]	U		X (~pr. 171)
2/1c	C. Megabocchus (RE XVI 1 col. 121)[519]	Sd		N?
1c	??C. Coelius (13) Caldus[520]		X (<cos. 94)	
1c	L. Quinctius (52) L.f. Rufus[521]		??P	X
1c	?(Terresius?)[522]			
?1c	Fabius (144) Senator[523]			X
?1c	Furius (cf. 62, Fulvius 108) Leptinus[524]			X
??1c	?Procilius[525]			

B.9 Analysis of the Praetorian *Fasti*

For the later Republic (179–49 B.C.), Badian has demonstrated that the number of first consuls who can show a certain or probable consular background remains remarkably steady. Now, in the years from the *lex Villia Annalis* (7.2.5) to the election of the first pair of plebeian consuls (179–173) fully thirteen of the fourteen first consuls have direct (eleven) or more distant (two) consular antecedents. After 172, the proportion of *nobiles* in the consulship falls significantly. But it never dips below 70 percent, with the norm somewhere in the area of 80 per cent (above that number in the last twenty years of the Republic).[526]

For the praetorship, it will come as no surprise to find that, for the entire period for which we can glean statistics from relatively complete praetor lists (218–166), *nobiles* were at all times much more likely to reach the praetorship than non-*nobiles*. In the years 218–198, roughly 65–71 percent of praetors were *nobiles* (and only 29–35 percent non-*nobiles*). Only one or two non-*nobiles* from these years can be shown to have been of praetorian descent (not enough to bother factoring in), but there may have been more. It is significant that, even after the creation of six praetors in 197 down to the passage of the *lex Villia Annalis*, the proportion of *nobiles* to non-*nobiles* falls only slightly. In the period 197–180, 61 to 66 percent were *nobiles*; up to 72 percent of praetors show either *nobilitas* or praetorian descent.

The praetorship loosens up quite a bit (to the advantage of non-*nobiles*) after the *lex Villia Annalis*. In the years 179 through 166, the percentage of *nobiles* to reach the praetorship falls to 52–59 percent, and that of *non-nobiles* rises to 41–48 percent. If we leave out of account the years in which the *lex Baebia* was in effect, the percentage of praetors who were *nobiles* is even (slightly) lower, a range of 51–57 percent. *Nobiles* and men of praetorian descent added together make up (at most) 66 percent of the praetors in the subperiod 179–166. The minimum age for candidature to the praetorship set by the *lex Villia Annalis* (whatever it was at this time) will have helped in this demographic shift. Thus far, it is clear that *nobiles* did not dominate the praetorship at the rates they did the consulship. When it comes to the individual praetorian colleges of 165–82 B.C., our information is poor. Overall, a little more than 40 per cent of the names (209 out of a possible 504) for this period are lost to us. The situation improves somewhat for the last generation of the Republic, with the number of missing names falling to 24 percent (62 out of a possible 256) for the years 81–50 B.C. (1.2.4).

With those caveats in mind, if one takes stock of the praetors in this period—leaving aside the highly irregular years 86 through 82—the proportions of *nobiles* for the pre-Sullan years appear high, somewhat akin to what we have seen for the two decades preceding the *lex Villia Annalis*: a range of 62–77 percent for the years 165–120 B.C. (67–86 per cent adding in those of praetorian descent), and 60–64 percent for 119–87 B.C. (62–74 per cent with the praetorians). The number remains steady for the years 81–79 B.C., when Sulla controlled elections. In these years, there will have been twenty-four praetorian slots (cf. 11.1.1): as it stands, thirteen of these praetors are attested with reasonable certainty, another three inferred from subsequent consulships. So we have two-thirds of the names. Of these sixteen individuals, nine to eleven (56–69 per cent) are *nobiles*; of the remaining number, one is an iterating praetor, and the other one or two from praetorian families. That leaves Sex. Nonius Sufenas, *pr.* 81 (probably Sulla's nephew) and Q. Calidius, *pr.* 79 (certainly of senatorial descent). Then after Sulla's domination (78–50 B.C.) our numbers drop significantly, with just 41–52 percent of attested or inferred praetors showing *nobilitas*. If we count in addition to the *nobiles* individuals of praetorian descent or iterating praetors, the numbers rise somewhat, overall for the period 81–50 B.C. to a range of 49–66 per cent (just about the same if the years of Sullan control are excluded).

It seems perfectly reasonable that Sulla's expansion in 81 of the annual college of praetors to eight would give nonnobles a much better chance of reaching the office than under the old system of six. Indeed, Velleius Paterculus for one goes so far as to imply that this reform of Sulla's lessened the prestige of the office (11.1.1). The trouble for this hypothesis is that for the years 165–87 B.C. almost half of the names of praetors we have are inferred from the list of consuls for the corresponding period, while for the years 81–50 B.C. just a little over 12 percent of our named praetors are known to us in this way. This source problem surely distorts our picture. Since *nobiles* are quite likely overrepresented in our praetorian lists for the earlier of these two periods, the apparent "leap" in number of non-*nobiles* winning the praetorship after Sulla may be illusory. An alternative hypothesis—based on the two major eras for which we have good evidence, namely, the last third of the second century and then the late 80s through 50s—is that the percentage of *nobiles* winning praetorian places remained at (very roughly) 50 percent from 180 B.C. down to the end of the Republic.

The latter hypothesis seems the sounder one to follow. In fact, Gruen, noticing from *MRR* and his own prosopographical work that "close to half of the known praetors in the Ciceronian age [through 49 B.C.] derived from consular families," considered that number remarkably high—given the availability of eight places each year. His general conclusion that "the voting populace had not altered its tastes or its habits" (sc. from praetorian elections in previous eras) seems the right one.[527]

So it seems beyond dispute that at all times (but especially before 180), *nobilitas* was a tremendous advantage for candidates for the praetorship. What is interesting is that *nobilitas* or unusual ability also may have brought advantages once an individual gained the office. Not all praetorian *provinciae* were equally desirable, as a number of sources make clear (see 12.1.3). Nor at any given time were all equally vital. In particular, in the extreme military emergency of the Hannibalic War, praetorian *provinciae* would not always be allotted randomly. The fact that T. Otacilius Crassus in 214 received the fleet based in Sicily—his *provincia* as pro *praetore* in the previous year—is sufficient presumptive proof of at least occasional use of the fixed lot in this period. For the later Republic, Cicero provides proof of manipulation of the sortition, for the benefit of the *pr.* 63 Q. Caecilius Metellus Celer, who received Cisalpine Gaul (15.2.5). Similarly, P. Cornelius Lentulus Spinther (*pr.* 60) is said to have received Hispania Citerior "through Caesar's help" (13.4.8). L.R. Taylor has demonstrated how Romans physically might have made the sortition work out.[528]

In a recent study, N. Rosenstein[529] has argued that "although manipulation of the lot was always possible, it nevertheless remained rare in practice." In Rosenstein's view, the inherent fairness of the Republican Roman process of sortition is an outstanding example of how, "out of motives usually self-interested but occasionally altruistic a group of highly partisan individuals could nevertheless agree to reach decisions on some matters in a way that avoided politics altogether."

However, there appears to be some evidence for even the nonemergency period 197–166 (where the list of praetors is largely complete) that there was a correlation between the social background of praetors and the *provinciae* they received in the sortition. Men of talent who were not of consular descent may also have been favored in the sortition. Rosenstein in his study does not take account of the social background of the individuals who drew specific *provinciae*, nor the fact that in many years we can detect the actual order in which praetors were elected (1.2.2). It appears that men who placed first or second in the elections for a praetorian college often received a more prestigious *provincia* than those at the bottom of the list.

It is revealing to look at the statistics of praetors and the *provinciae* they received in the first third of the second century, where our evidence is unusually complete. It will immediately be apparent that the sample for this study is too small to admit technical statistical significance; other miscellaneous difficulties intrude, such as the fact that one must omit the atypical "Baebian" years, 179 and 177. So whatever figures are produced must stand on their own merit. But this is not to say that some instructive trends cannot be discerned—patterns that seem to vitiate Rosenstein's thesis for the one period where we can check.[530]

In 197–180, the proportion of *nobiles* among urban praetors (56–61 percent) is roughly the same as that among peregrine praetors (60 percent), and both jurisdictions were regularly held by men who placed in the top half of their college. A few more ex-urban praetors reach the consulship than ex-peregrine praetors (six versus four), but the difference is not all that great. In 178 and 176–166, the gap between urban and peregrine praetors grows. Ninety percent of urban praetors are of consular or praetorian descent, compared to 40 percent of peregrine praetors. Three first-place winners in the praetorian elections receive the urban jurisdiction, one the peregrine jurisdiction. Over 70 percent of the urban praetors of this period had finished in the top half of their college; less than 30 percent of the peregrine praetors. In the seven years when both *provinciae* were placed in the sortition, the urban praetorship was six times allotted to a man who had obtained the higher electoral position. Five ex-urban praetors from the period 178 and 176–166 go on to the consulship, two ex-peregrine praetors.

Next let us turn to the elite *provincia* of Sicily and less glamorous Sardinia. In the period of the Hannibalic War Sicily was a challenging province to administer, even when Rome's ally Hiero was still alive and Roman responsibilities were (theoretically) limited to Messana and the western portion of the island. Two-thirds to three-quarters of the men sent to this *provincia* can be classed as *nobiles*, somewhat higher than the number of *nobiles* sent to the less desirable Sardinia during this same period (a little over 40 percent of Sardinian praetors). This trend grew more pronounced after the war in the period 197–180. Almost twice as many *nobiles* received Sicily as their *provincia* in these years (76 percent) as did Sardinia (33 to 47 percent). Although three men who were returned in first position in their praetorian elections in the period 197–180 (and one in the period 178 and 176–166) received Sicily in the sortition, no first-place winner in a praetorian election after 204 receives Sardinia. In fact, almost 50 percent of the praetors who served as governors of Sicily in 197–180 finished in the first half of their praetorian college; only 18 percent of Sardinian praetors in the same period could boast this distinction. And in the years 197–180, when both Sicily and Sardinia were placed in the sortition, of the men in each year who received these *provinciae*, the praetor allotted Sicily almost invariably had been returned in the higher electoral position (nine out of eleven instances). And former Sicilian praetors from this period outperformed ex-Sardinian praetors—and every other type of ex-praetor—in consular elections. Seven praetors who had served in Sicily in 197–180 went on to capture consulships (nine from the period 199–180), rivaled only by the six ex-urban praetors from this period (eight from 199–180) who reached the highest office. Three ex-Sardinian praetors from 197–180 were returned as consuls (four in 199–180).

In the period 178 and 176–166, the gulf between the Sicilian and Sardinian praetors becomes less marked. This may be partly an effect of the *lex Villia Annalis* of 180, which regularized the *cursus*, to the advantage of men who were not from consular families. More than half the governors of each of these *provinciae* are *nobiles*: 50 to 75 percent in the case of Sicily, 60 percent for Sardinia. In the years in which Sicily and Sardinia are both placed in the sortition, of the two men who receive these lots, Sicily and Sardinia fall equally to a praetor elected in a higher electoral position. Only one Sicilian praetor from this whole period finishes in the top half of his college, and that in first place (176). In fact, the three instances in which Sardinia falls to the higher-placed praetor are all consecutive (173, 172, and 171). Was this arranged? The fighting in that *provincia*—almost but not quite quelled—may have made it a more attractive assignment. Or it may be the fact that Sardinia had just produced two consuls: C. Valerius Laevinus, *pr.* 179 and *cos. suff.* 176, and M. Popillius Laenas, *pr.* 176 then *cos.* 173 (note the short intervals). It should be mentioned that Sardinian ex-governors from 178 and 176–166 outperform their Sicilian counterparts from those same years in the consular elections two to none. On the whole, although more Sicilian than Sardinian ex-praetors from the period 197–166 reach the consulship (seven as opposed to five), the Sardinian ex-praetors reach the office faster. Only two ex-Sicilian governors reach the consulship within two or three years of their praetorship, as opposed to three ex-Sardinian praetors. The remaining five ex-Sicilian praetors take four or more years to reach the office; only two ex-Sardinian governors are that slow. But they are very slow: L. Porcius Licinus, *pr.* 193 and consul in 184 (nine years); and Q. Fulvius Flaccus, *pr.* 187 and finally elected consul suffect in 180—his fourth attempt at the office.[531]

It is difficult to generalize, but it may be said that Sicily—once obtained—at any time offered no special electoral advantage in itself at the consular *comitia*, such as did the high-profile urban praetorship. Rather, it seems that it was often allotted to men who would have reached the consulship anyway. The praetors who received Sardinia, on the other hand, did no worse than the men who received the peregrine praetorship. The allotment of the *provincia* involved no particular career disadvantage other than the fact that one had to live there for one or (regularly) more years.

It is also difficult to make blanket statements about the Spains. Not quite 60 percent of the praetors who received a Spanish *provincia* in the years 197–166 were *nobiles*, that is, somewhat less than the overall percentage of praetors who were *nobiles* in this same period (approximately 65 percent). Of the two Spanish *provinciae*, slightly more *nobiles* go to Citerior. In the years 197–166, close to 70 percent of the commanders in Citerior are *nobiles*, whereas in Ulterior for these same years less than 50 percent can boast that status (the proportions are not that much different before and after 180). If one includes praetorian status, however, the gap is not so marked (just under 70 percent for each *provincia*). Both Hispania Citerior and Hispania Ulterior generate about the same number of future consuls (seven and six respectively). This is quite a high number considering that only sixteen men are known to have returned from Citerior alive, and fifteen from Ulterior; three men returned from the joint *provincia* Hispania. Konrad[532] rightly points out that the ex-Spanish praetors who do reach the office are mostly *nobiles* who would have won the office in any case. But the constant fighting in the Spains previous to 178, and the many triumphs and *ovationes* that followed from this action, will have helped.

Finally, the special praetorian *provinciae*: The demographics of the men who received these assignments in the period 197–180 are very close to what we have observed is the "norm" for the praetorship as a whole in this period. Nine of the fourteen praetors in the special *provinciae* were *nobiles* (64 percent), not far short of the standard. Nevertheless, these praetors were usually returned fourth, fifth, or sixth in their colleges (only two out of fifteen men were placed in the top three), and did not do very well in the consular elections (the worst record of any *provincia*). After 180, a special *provincia* was declared only four times: the fleet, in each of the years 171 through 168. This number is too small to admit of scrutiny or comparison with the somewhat surprising results from the previous period.

It is time to venture some tentative overall conclusions for the "Livian" period. In a purely random sortition, we would expect an even distribution of *nobiles* and non-*nobiles* in each of the praetorian *provinciae* throughout the time span for which Livy provides a full record: before 180, approximately 65 percent of the commanders in each *provincia* should theoretically be *nobiles*; after 180, we should expect about 55 percent to be *nobiles*. In addition, in a random sortition, there should be no difference over the years between the *provinciae* allotted to the men who were returned first and those returned last in their colleges: whether first or last, the chance of an individual praetor drawing any particular *sors* in this era should be one in six.

The actual results of our study are much different. A confluence of data from several different perspectives reveals some trends which may be more than coincidence. In the years 197–180, men of consular and praetorian descent, and men who were returned at or near the top of their colleges received the attractive urban jurisdiction and the economically advanced *provincia* of Sicily a disproportionately large number of times. There is, of course, quite a bit of overlap between these two groups: only two men who were returned first in their colleges (in the twenty-one years when we can ascertain an order) in this period are not known to have consular or praetorian ascendants (M. Tuccius, *pr.* 190; C. Decimius Flavus, *pr.* 184). On the other hand, newly elected praetors of less illustrious background, as well as those who placed lower in the electoral order, received the less glamorous peregrine jurisdiction and Sardinia, which was then a malaria-ridden backwater.

An examination of the sortition after 180 reveals a difference: the sortition of the extra-city *provinciae* seems totally random. The *provincia urbana*, however, still falls to *nobiles* a disproportionate number of times. There may have been a conscious decision around 180 to check widespread fixing of the lot in the sortition process. Such a reform, of course, would be instituted quietly, and would never have been reported in an ancient source — perhaps not even discussed openly in the Senate.[533] Men from lesser families may have been tired not only of the difficulty of attaining the top magistracies at reasonable intervals (a situation that was remedied in part by the *lex Villia Annalis*), but also of having to settle consistently for the less desirable praetorian *provinciae*. At least in the late Republic, there was a perception that the *provincia* impacted one's future career (see 12.1.3).

For the whole period after 166 B.C., we must give up on generating statistics on the phenomenon of cheating. Yet here we find a good number of "coincidences" of praetors receiving a *provincia* where they have a preexisting family or personal connection, with a surprisingly large proportion of the examples clustered in the years 63–59. So we are justified in suspecting continued — at times even increased — acquiescence on the part of the governing class in manipulation of the lot, for both the city[534] and the more desirable or important territorial[535] *provinciae*.

Notes to Volume II

1. *ILLRP* 342 line 3, *IGRP* IV 1116 lines 4–5, Cic. *de Orat.* 1.82. On his *imperium*, see T. R. S. Broughton, *MRR* III 119, recanting an earlier view in *MRR* I 569 n. 2 and 573 n. 3. The date of M. Antonius' praetorship is merely an inference from the order of events in *Per.* 68 with 67 (implying it fell in the fourth consulship of C. Marius, i.e., 102), but a reasonably secure one (Antonius was *cos.* 99).

2. Cic. *de Orat.* 1.82 with *ILLRP* 342 line 6.

3. Obseq. 44 (102 B.C.) "piratae in Cilicia a Romanis deleti"; cf. *Per.* 68, Trogus *Prol.* 39.

4. See *MRR* I 569 n. 2, 576, III 19; also E. Badian, *Chiron* 14 (1984) 102–107, 123f (waiting outside the city for his triumph by Oct. 100). See further 11.8.9.

5. See *I. Knidos* I 31 = *RS* I 12 (with commentary on pp. 261f, suggesting that that Cilicia was to be a province "only for the coming year"). Announcement of formation of "Cilicia": Kn. III lines 35–37 with 28–35; also D. B lines 7–8 with 5–6. Cilicia, of course, was virtually synonomous with piracy in antiquity: on this see H. Mattingly in M. J. Fontana, M. T. Piraino, and F. P. Rizzo (eds.), Φιλίας Χάριν, *Miscellanea di studi classici in onore di Eugenio Manni* IV (Rome 1979) 1496 with n. 19; C. F. Konrad, *Plutarch's Sertorius: A Historical Commentary* (Chapel hill, N.C., 1994) 103.

6. See Strab. 14.6.6 p. 685 (who uses ἐπαρχεία στρατηγική to mean "provincia praetoria" in discussing the annexation of Cyprus in 58) with further discussion by T. C. Brennan, *Chiron* 22 (1992) 104 n. 4.

7. *GRBS* 19 (1978) 216.

8. See 9.1.2 and 9.1.5. Granted, the praetor M. Antonius was *pro cos.* from 102 to the time of his triumph in 100, but that was to fight a pirate war, not to serve as a routine commander.

9. Sources in *MRR* II 18 (under the year 92), of which see esp. *Vir. ill.* 75.4. On the date of his praetorship and the extent of his promagistracy, see T. C. Brennan, *Chiron* 22 (1992) 103–158 (with references to earlier literature); cf. A. Keaveney, *Historia* 44 (1995) 29–36, effectively refuting a recent attempt to downdate the command on the dubious evidence of Sidonius Apollinaris *Carm.* 7.79–82. The Delian dedications of Sulla (*ILLRP* 349 and 350), where he is termed *pro cos.*, probably date from this Cilician command, since the title *imperator* (first earned at Chaeronea?) is not mentioned; see, however, Crawford on *RRC* I

373–374 no. 359 (84–83 B.C.) L. SVLLA IMPER. ITERVM. A late literary source, Rufius Festus (*Brev.* 15), terms Sulla *pro cos.* in connection with this command.

10. Cic. *Leg.* 1.53.

11. App. *Mith.* 17.59–60.

12. App. *Mith.* 20.78. On the title (year 88), see J. M. Reynolds, *Aphrodisias and Rome* (London 1982) Document 2, esp. lines 1, 3–4, 6–7 (στρατηγὸς ἀνθύπατος); also E. Badian, *AJAH* 1 (1976) 109–111 (with corresponding notes) on the chronology. See also n. 14 below.

13. Laodiceia surrenders Oppius: App. *Mith.* 20.78–79. Oppius paraded as prisoner: *Per.* 78 (with title "pro cos."), App. *Mith.* 20.79, 112.544, Posidon. ap. Ath. 5.213A. Released to Sulla: Gran. Lic. 35.75 C; App. *Mith.* 112.544.

14. Reynolds, *Aphrodisias and Rome* Document 3 lines 1–3 (ἀνθύπατος Ῥωμαίων στρατηγός).

15. *ANSMusN* 29 (1984) 99–102.

16. M. Crawford, *RRC* I 545–546, no. 550; E. Badian, *ANSMusN* 29 (1984) 99–102.

17. Cic. *Arch.* 9.

18. *SIG*³ 745 lines 3–4 with P. Foucart, *RPh* 23 (1899) 267. T. Reinach (*Hermes* 34 [1899] 159–160) also makes him commander in Cilicia (suggesting the period 83–81 as the approximate date), and plausibly connects him with the "Cornelius Lentulus" who bought Alexander Polyhistor of Miletus as a prisoner of war, and kept him at Rome in the Sullan era (Suid. I 104 A); in this he is followed by W. F. Jashemski, *The Origins and History of the Proconsular and Propraetorian Imperium down to 27 B.C.* (Chicago 1950) 147. (Münzer, *RE* s.v. *Cornelius* 194, 195 cols. 1371, is skeptical.) Note also the later L. Lentulus whose patronage of Thyateira in Lydia is said to be hereditary (*SIG*³ 745 n. 2). Our commander had occasion to find himself in both Roman Asia and Cilicia (see in text immediately below).

19. *MRR* II 68.

20. Against reconstructions such as that of P. Freeman in P. Freeman and D. Kennedy (eds.), *The Defence of the Roman and Byzantine East* (Oxford 1986) 253–275 (a massive *argumentum ex silentio*, based on "supposed irregularities in the *fasti*" for Cilicia [260]), see now also L. Lucullus' letter of 86 as *quaestor pro praetore* to Mopsuestia in Cicilia (*AE* 1994, 1755), where he refers to οἱ π[ρ]ὸ ἡμῶν αὐ[τοκρά]||τορες — more evidence for a series of regular Roman commanders.

21. Q. Marcius Rex: Degrassi, *Inscr. Ital.* XIII 1 82f with *Per.* 62, Oros. 5.14.1–5 (providing the quote). L. Diadematus: see *ILLRP* 476 with *MRR* III 38; on the (possible) road-building activities of the *cos.* 117 in Italy, see *ILLRP* 459 (found in Picenum, and difficult to interpret) with T.P. Wiseman, *PBSR* 38 (1970) 134–136. M. Scaurus: *Inscr. Ital.* XIII 1 84f with *Vir. ill.* 72.7; cf. M. C. Alexander, *Trials in the Late Roman Republic* (Toronto 1990) no. 37.

22. For the possibility that L. Calpurnius Piso Caesoninus (*cos.* 112) served in Cisalpina, see *MRR* III 36–47 with Alexander, *Trials* no. 48. The matter depends on whether "ille Gallus" (Cic. *de Orat.* 2.265) who witnessed against him was an actual Gaul or a Roman with the cognomen "Gallus" (I should think the latter; contra, D. R. Shackleton Bailey, *Onomasticon to Cicero's Treatises* [Stuttgart 1996] 21–22).

23. Request for triumph: Cic. *Inv.* 2.111 ("consul . . . in citeriore Gallia"). Veto: *Pis.* 62, and Asc. pp. 14–15 C.

24. V. Max. 4.5.4.

25. *St.-R.* I³ 282 n. 5.

26. See V. Max. 3.7.6 "cum ex consulatu prouinciam Galliam obtineret" with *MRR* II 113 (prorogation for Cisalpina); E. Badian, *Studies in Greek and Roman History* (Oxford 1964) 92, 103 n. 146 and *Mélanges d'archéologie et d'histoire offerts a André Piganiol* II (Paris 1966) 901–918, at 907 (both Gauls).

27. "Gallia" = "Gallia Cisalpina": see, e.g., Cic. *Ver.* 2.1.34 (the year 83), Oros. 5.24.16 (77), Cic. *Brut.* 318 (74), *Att.* 1.1.2 (65), Sal. *Cat.* 58.6 (62), Nepos ap. Mela 3.45, and Plin. *Nat.* 2.170 (apparently 62). "Gallia" = "Gallia Transalpina": see, e.g., Cic. *Flac.* 100 (the year 85), *Quinct.* 24 and 28 (83), Oros. 5.23.4 (apparently 78), Sal. *Hist.* 2.98.5 (77), Cic. *Font.* 11–12, 16, 19, 27, 32, 36, 45 (77–75, I would argue), Sal. *Hist.* 2.98.9 (76), Cic. *Mur.* 42 and *Har.* 42 (64/63), Sal. *Cat.* 57.3 (63), Cic. *Att.* 1.19.2 (60), and *Att.* 1.20.5 (also 60). The usage seems to have found its way into official administrative language: see Caes. *Gal.* 1.35.4 (an S.C. of 61, where "Gallia" stands for the Transalpine province), and Cic. *Att.* 1.19.2 (report of an S.C. of the year 60, mentioning the "duae Galliae").

28. On the possibility this is a slip, note, e.g., the *lemma* in Asc. p. 17 C "L. Opimius . . . qui et post praeturam et consul," where the scribe misquotes Cic. *Pis.* 95 ("qui praetor et consul").

29. *Inscr. Ital.* XIII 1 82f. For discussion of the military aspects of this campaign, see C. Ebel, *Transalpine Gaul: The Emergence of a Roman Province* (Leiden 1976) 64–70; A. L. F. Rivet, *Gallia Narbonensis* (London 1988) 39–40.

30. Sources for the activities of the *coss.* 125 and 124 in Gaul can be found in *MRR* I 510, 511, 515f, 518.

31. E.g., J. F. Drinkwater *OCD*³ s.v. *Gaul (Transalpine)* 626 (presenting a date of 121 B.C. as fact); cf. also E. Hermon, *Ktèma* 4 (1979) 256–258, *CEA* 24 (1990) 389–396, and *CEA* 26 (1991) 197–214.

32. *Mélanges Piganiol* II 901–908. Caes. *Gal.* 1.45.2, discussed at length by Ebel, *Transalpine Gaul* 78–82, implies nothing about the formation of a new permanent territorial province at this time: thus rightly, Rivet, *Gallia Narbonensis* 41f. But Rivet (ibid. 48) still allows for "at least a possibility that a province of a smaller size had originally been created and that it was only expanded eastward after the experience of Marius".

33. Preliminary foundation at Narbo: *ILLRP* 460a (a milestone from the *via Domitia* with mileage numbered from Narbo) with *MRR* III 82. Discussion of the date for the Roman colony at Narbo (trad. 118, on the basis of Vell. 1.14.5) can be found in *MRR* III 118. On Rome's early garrisons in Transalpine Gaul, see Badian, *Mélanges Piganiol* II 903f.

34. For Domitius' major victory (at Vindalium) see references in *MRR* I 516 with ch. 13 n. 4 below. His imperatorial acclamation: *ILLRP* 460a. His triumphlike display: Suet. *Nero* 2.1–2 with Oros. 5.13.2, cf. Flor. 1.37.4 (showing that it followed Vindalium). Complete sources for Gaul in the years 122–120 are collected in *MRR* I 516, 520f, 522, 524.

35. Fabius as "successor" to Domitius: V. Max. 9.6.3. On Fabius' great victory, see *MRR* I 520–521. Domitius' capture of Bituitus: V. Max. 9.6.3, cf. *Per.* 61 and Jer. *Chr.* ad ann. 127 p. 146 H.

36. *Inscr. Ital.* XIII 1 82f.

37. See 8.5.3 for the discussion of the triumphs of the *pro pr.* L. Aemilius Regillus and the *pro cos.* L. Cornelius Scipio in 189. To take some illustrative instances of this aspect of triumph etiquette just from this general period: note M. Caecilius Metellus (*cos.* 115) and his brother C. Caecilius Metellus Caprarius (*cos.* 113), who triumphed in that order on the same day in July 111, though the *cos.* 113 had been relieved in Macedonia a full year earlier (13.1.1 and 14.1.1); T. Didius (*cos.* 98) and P. Licinius Crassus (*cos.* 97), who triumphed from Spain on 29 May and 12 June 93 respectively (13.3.2); and Q. Metellus Pius (*cos.* 80, *pro cos.* into 71) and Cn. Pompeius (*privatus pro cos.* 77–71), who celebrated triumphs in that order, though Pompey reached the city well before Metellus (App. *BC* 1.121.561).

38. See Ebel, *Transalpine Gaul* 81–84 and 93 (allowing a return to Rome for both commanders as late as 117) with 72–73 for older discussions of this unexpected order.

39. Sources in *MRR* I 535 with Alexander, *Trials* no. 47.

40. Sal. *Jug.* 27.3–5, 28.2–3 (111) and 35.3 (110).

41. See Badian, *Mélanges Piganiol* II 903 with Rivet, *Gallia Narbonensis* 45 and sources in 52 nn. 53–54.

42. The quote is from *Mélanges Piganiol* II 903.

43. In the disastrous Roman defeat at the hands of the Tigurini in 107, the *legatus* C. Laenas was evidently third in command after the *cos.* L. Longinus and the consular legate L. Piso Caesoninus (both killed in battle), and so may well have been a *praetorius*. *MRR* I 552 collects the sources, of which see esp. Oros. 5.15.24 (but giving the name as "C. Publius") and Cic. *Inv.* 2.72 ("quidam imperator"). On Aurelius Scaurus in 105 B.C., see *MRR* I 557.

44. Plu. *Mar.* 14.11. Sumner (*Orators* 91f) suggests M. Claudius Marcellus—no doubt a *praetorius* by 90 (see ch. 10 n. 156 below) was already of praetorian status when he served under Marius at Aquae Sextiae in 102 (sources in *MRR* I 569). Sumner rightly points out that Marcellus played an important role in this battle, but it does not follow that Marcellus' formal position was also an important one. Our sources are unanimous that Marius gave him charge of a small force (Frontinus) of three thousand soldiers (Plutarch, Polyaenus) to create a diversion. Marcellus need have been no more than a military tribune at the time, albeit a particularly trusted and capable one. Note, e.g., Fron. *Str.* 2.4.7, or 2.5.34 (from Livy) with Plu. *Crass.* 11.4, where in the war against Spartacus the *pro cos.* M. Licinius Crassus twice sends out officers of middling status with similarly sized forces on missions of this type. In the Cimbric War L. Sulla also had some significant responsibilities as military tribune and *legatus* (*MRR* I 564, 569, 573), though no more than quaestorian in standing.

45. See E. Badian, *Foreign Clientelae (264–70 B.C.)* (Oxford 1958) 203–212; also in *Mélanges Piganiol* II 901–918. Cf. Ebel, *Transalpine Gaul* 75–105, who credits its organization to Pompey in 77/76. Ebel surely places this development too late; already by the mid-90s we can detect a policy, at least in principle, of regular succession for this area, and thus an annual vote on administrative arrangements—so, like Cilicia, an organized *provincia*.

46. See Badian, *Studies* 90–96, cf. Ebel, *Transalpine Gaul* 94–95, Rivet, *Gallia Narbonensis* 54–55 (accepting the basic identification).

47. Many have placed the date of the establishment of Cisalpina considerably lower, at the time of Sulla's dictatorship (as Mommsen did) or even later, though in the latter case for no compelling reasons: see U. Laffi, *Athenaeum* 80 [70] (1992) 12–14 for a roster of views, with Laffi himself venturing an absolute terminus of 75 B.C.

48. Celtiberia in 87: *CIL* I² 2951a line 14, on which see 13.3.2. Gaul in 83: Cic. *Quinct.* 24 and 28. Flaccus' nephew was in Gaul already in 85: see Cic. *Flac.* 63 with Rivet, *Gallia Narbonensis* 55.

49. See Gran. Lic. 36.5 C with *Inscr. Ital.* XIII 1 563. .

50. Badian, *Mélanges Piganiol* II 908 n. 2.

51. *Per.* 70. See S. I. Oost, *CPh* 58 (1963) 11–25, esp. p. 15 on the definition of "free." Full sources for the bequest and the Senate's decision of 96 can be found in Oost's article, p. 22 n. 3. In general on Cyrene in this period, see A. Laronde, *Cyrène et la Libye hellénistique* (Paris 1987) 455–485.

52. L. Gasperini, *QAL* 5 (1967) 53–57; cf. *AE* 1967, no. 532 Cyrene, with further embellishment, on which see the remarks of E. Badian, *Roman Imperialism in the Late Republic*² (Oxford 1968) 99f n. 1 and *Phoenix* 25 (1971) 134–136. C. Pulcher as *cos.* 92 is attested in Rome early in the year (Cic. *Leg.* 3.42 with *MRR* II 19 n. 5), but that is all.

53. Badian, *Phoenix* 25 (1971) 136.

54. *I. Délos* 4.1.1700.

55. Plu. *Luc.* 2.4–5 with J. *AJ* 14.114. Cf. also Plu. *Mor.* 255E–257E.

56. Cic. *Agr.* 1.1, 2.41–42. For the date of the testament and the division of opinion at Rome whether to annex Egypt, see Badian, *RhM* 90 (1967) 178–192, esp. 180f and (for the

precedents available to Ptolemy X) 186–187; cf. also *Roman Imperialism*[2] 31 and 73. See also G. Hölbl, *Geschichte des Ptolemäerreiches* (Darmstadt 1994) 191, following Badian. For a different (and unconvincing) view, see D. C. Braund, *PBSR* 54 (1983) 16–57.

57. This must be the sense of the *senatus auctoritas* reported in Cic. *Agr.* 2.41–42. Sources on the events that led to the death of Ptolemy X are collected in Hölbl, *Geschichte des Ptolemäerreiches* 191.

58. See Cic. *Agr.* 2.41 with E. Badian, *RhM* 110 (1967) 187–188, also *Roman Imperialism*[2] 31 and 73.

59. Cic. *Brut.* 106. Here I cannot attempt to discuss the various *leges iudiciariae* (contemplated and realized) on the composition of juries in the later Republic, or the modes by which jurors were selected. For excellent general sketches, see Greenidge, *The Legal Procedure of Cicero's Time* (Oxford 1901) 433–456 (technical aspects) and P. A. Brunt, *The Fall of the Roman Republic and Related Essays* (Oxford 1988) 194–239; cf. also E. Badian, *Historia* 11 (1962) 206–209 (stressing that Q. Servilius Caepio, *cos.* 106, followed by M. Livius Drusus, *tr. pl.* 91 B.C., were the first to attempt to equip the various permanent courts with a uniform jury type).

60. See, e.g., Cicero's criticism of "vis tribunicia" in the trials of P. Popillius in 123 (= Alexander, *Trials* no. 25, probably a *quaestio extraordinaria*) and Q. Metellus Numidicus in 100 (= no. 77) at *Clu.* 95; also *Brut.* 135 (public *invidia* in the condemnation of the *cos.* 106 Q. Servilius Caepio [= no. 66]); no. 79 (the defendant P. Furius lynched by a mob before the verdict in his trial of [probably] 99). For the post-Sullan period, see Cic. *Clu.* 93, 96, 103 and 108 (the problems of a public *iudicium* revealed in the prosecution of C. Iunius in 74 [= no. 153]) and the sources in no. 266 (Milo's prosecution *de vi* in 56). For a detailed description of the course of various popular *iudicia* in the relevant period, see E. S. Gruen, *Roman Politics and the Criminal Courts, 149–78 B.C.* (Cambridge, Mass., 1968) 106–214 passim.

61. Evidence on the titulature of the praetor who had this *provincia* is not all that plentiful and certainly not consistent. In addition to the (vague) mentions of the office in the Gracchan extortion law (*CIL* I[2] 583) collected in ch. 9 n. 116, one notes esp. *Inscr. Ital.* XIII 3 70b (*elogium* of C. Claudius Pulcher) *pr. repetundis* (i.e., in 95 B.C.) and Asc. p. 19 C (C. Cato in the year 54) "postulatus <est> apud M. Catonem praetorem repetundarum, ut in Actis scriptum est." But those two examples—each different from the other—demonstrably contain shortened forms of the title. It is Cic. *Ver.* 1.21 (on the praetorian sortition for 69) that seems to preserve the full name of the actual lot: "M. Metello obtigisset ut is de pecuniis repetundis quaereret"; cf. *Rab. Post.* 9 (Cicero as *pr.* 66) "de pecuniis repetundis . . . praetor quaesivi." "Praetor repetundis" or "repetundarum" are probably popular designations that by reason of convenience crept into semi-official use. Other Republican references: *Ver.* 1.27 (M. Caecilius Metellus, *pr.* 69) "quaesiturum de pecuniis repetundis"; *Clu.* 147 (Cicero as *pr.* 66) "mea [i.e., quaestio] de pecuniis repetundis"; perhaps cf. *Ver.* 1.38 (on the year 72) "Q. Hortensio praetore de pecuniis repetundis" and *Corn.* 1 F 7 Crawford[2] "postulatur a<pud> me praetore<m> primum de pecuniis repetundis." The Ciceronian scholiasts (see Ps.-Asc. pp. 186, 193, 214, 215 and *Schol. Gron.* p. 350 St.) are not far off Cicero's own usage in this respect, but offer nothing of independent value.

62. There are about half a dozen cases known for the period 123–100, with half those cases clustered in the last years of the second century. The defendant C. Papirius Carbo (*cos.* 120) committed suicide when accused in a praetorian *quaestio* in 119; the charge is uncertain but probably *de repetundis* (Alexander, *Trials* no. 30). His younger brother M. Papirius Carbo was condemned for (apparently) *repetundae* or *peculatus* after service in Sicily, possibly as praetor, probably sometime ca. 114 (*Trials* no. 46 with 13.1.2 below). C. Porcius Cato (*cos.* 114) was condemned *de repetundis* and penalized by a (light) fine in 113 B.C. on his return from Macedonia (*Trials* no. 45). T. Albucius (*pr.* ca. 107) was brought to trial (proba-

bly in 105) after a praetorian command in Sardinia, convicted (surely) *de repetundis*, and took up exile (*Trials* no. 67 with 13.1.1 below). The commanders L. Lucullus (*pr.* 104) and C. Servilius (*pr.* 102) were each condemned for their failures in the Second Sicilian Slave War (*Trials* nos. 69 and 70), probably both *de repetundis* (13.1.3). On the acquittal of P. Decius Subulo in what is possibly a trial *repetundarum* shortly after his tribunate of 120, see no. 31 with n. 75 below.

63. On the institution of various new *quaestiones perpetuae* in this era, see in general E. Gruen, *Roman Politics* 258–262.

64. Amazingly, there is no good evidence from any point in our period on the formal name of this praetorian *provincia* or the magistrate who held it. The closest we get is Cic. *Clu.* 147 (66 B.C.) "[quaestio] C. Aquili apud quem nunc de ambitu causa dicitur"; also Q. *fr.* 2.3.6 (56 B.C.) "dixi pro Bestia de ambitu apud praetorem Cn. Domitium."

65. See Alexander, *Trials* nos. 36 (the *pr. des.* C. Marius as defendant), and 34 and 35 (the counterprosecutions of P. Rutilius Rufus and M. Aemilius Scaurus, for which see 14.3.2 below).

66. See Alexander, *Trials* nos. 58 (the *cos. des.* 108 Hortensius possibly prosecuted on this charge in 109 B.C.), 83 (M. Antonius hauled into the *ambitus* court in 97 or 96 for offences in the censorian elections for 97), 95 (L. Marcius Philippus as *cos. des.* 91 said by Florus—but no other source—to have been prosecuted for *ambitus*), and 107 (a P. Sextius elected to the praetorship, but condemned for *ambitus* before he could assume the office). The date for that last trial depends on that of the prosecutor, the *tribunicius* T. Iunius L.f. (see Cic. *Brut.* 180, our sole source for the trial), which itself is uncertain ("likely to have been tribune between ca. 95 and ca. 85," according to Sumner, *Orators* 108f). See in general Gruen, *Roman Politics* 299f (conjecturing the *cognomen* Brutus); and on the date, P. Nadig, *Ardet Ambitus: Untersuchungen zum Phänomen der Wahlbestechungen in der römischen Republik* (Frankfurt a. M. 1997) 182 (provisionally accepting ca. 90–89).

67. See Alexander, *Trials* nos. 86 (C. Norbanus prosecuted in 96 for conduct as *tr. pl.* 103) and 88 (Q. Servilius Caepio charged in 95 with offences as *quaestor urbanus* 100); also probably no. 80 (the condemnation of the *tr. pl.* 99 Sex. Titius in 98, where no plausible alternative presents itself). The precise formal name of the *provincia* in the years down to 50 cannot be divined from our sources.

68. The fact that the central issue in our first two certain *maiestas* trials—that of C. Norbanus and Q. Servilius Caepio (see n. 67 above)—was precisely what "maiestas" under the *lex Appuleia* meant (Cic. *de Orat.* 2.107 and 109, cf. *Part.* 104–105 on Norbanus, *Rhet. Herr.* 2.17 and 4.35 for Caepio) shows how novel the concept was as a legal charge. Indeed, its very generality helped lead to acquittals in both those trials: see the remarks of E. Badian, *Historia* 18 (1969) 450. Cic. *Fam.* 3.11.2 shows that even in the late 50s, "maiestas" remained an ambiguous term, in spite of Sulla's efforts to restrict the scope of prosecution on this charge; *Ver.* 2.4.88 (admittedly rhetorical) alleges that one of Verres' acts might fall under the categories of *repetundae*, *peculatus*, and *maiestas*—and then complicates things further by adducing some decidedly nontechnical accusations. For the hodgepodge of charges that might actually come up in a *maiestas* case, see *Clu.* 97, 99–100.

69. Cf. T. C. Brennan, *Emerita* 63 (1995) 62 n. 53, for Diodorus' notion (33.2) that the *pr.* 146 C. Plautius had been condemned on this charge for his defeat against Viriathus.

70. Asc. p. 21 C. (At issue was the proper celebration of the rites of the Penates at Lavinium.) For general sources on this prosecution (unsuccessful), see Alexander, *Trials* no. 68. See B. A. Marshall, *A Historical Commentary on Asconius* (Columbia, Mo., 1985) 277–278, on the date.

71. Alexander, *Trials* no. 59, with Cic. *Leg.* 3.36 for the charge. Orosius (5.15.24) has the fullest account of the procedure but (as often) an erroneous name ("C. Publius"). Cicero

(*Inv.* 2.72) says that C. Popillius Laenas in this trial "accusatur maiestatis," cf. also the speaker in *Rhet. Herr.* 1.25 But Cicero in the *De Inventione* passage also refers to C. Laenas as "quidam imperator," which shows that here he is not taking pains to be technically accurate.

72. Alexander, *Trials* no. 63 (only two of the thirty-five tribes voted to condemn).

73. *Roman Politics* 167–168. The temporary court is that of 109, on which see 10.6.2. The cases referred to are Alexander, *Trials* nos. 66 and 64.

74. C. Claudius Pulcher (*aed. cur.* 99) is attested as "iudex q(uaestionis) veneficiis" in (surely) 98 (*Inscr. Ital.* XIII 3 70b). Trials "inter sicarios" came before M. Fannius, *aed. pl.* in 86 (see *MRR* III 90), as *iudex quaestionis* in (probably) 85 (Cic. *S. Rosc.* 11, commenting that then there were no such trials for a "long interval" prior to the year 80, i.e., the killers in the *Bellum Sullanum* and the civil war were never tried). The venue for the *parricidium* trial of Publicius Malleolus attested for 101 (Alexander, *Trials* no. 75) was no doubt a *iudicium populi* (as Alexander tentatively suggests), to judge from the traditional nature of the penalty applied (i.e., the sack). But the trial of the brothers Cloelii (= Cloulii) of Tarraco on that charge (probably) in the 90s (no. 367) was definitely before *iudices* (V. Max. 8.1 abs. 13), and thus in the *quaestio inter sicarios*, the competent body for *parricidium* cases by the year 80 (as Cic. *S. Rosc.* shows). See also Cic. *Inv.* 2.59–60 (written in the early 80s) with D. Cloud, *CAH* IX^2 521. Full title of court in the pre-Sullan era: *S. Rosc.* 90 "qui inter sicarios et de veneficiis accusabant." As supervised by ex-aediles: see *Inscr. Ital.* XIII 3 70b cited above; also Cic. *Clu.* 147 (66 B.C.) "[quaestio] M. Plaetori et C. Flamini inter sicarios"; Suet. *Iul.* 11 (C. Iulius Caesar in 64) "in exercenda de sicaris quaestione." Note also Cic. *Fin.* 2.54 (L. Tubulus) "cum praetor [i.e., in 142] quaestionem inter sicarios exercuisset" (but in this case a special court, on which see 8.6.2 above). Post-Sullan terminology: see 11.7.4 below, on Ulpian's quotation from the *lex Cornelia* that reorganized this *quaestio*.

75. For an idea of the scope of the charge, cf. *Dig.* 48.13.1 with Mommsen, *Strafrecht* 760–772 (esp. 768 on the penalty), also the short discussion of W. Kunkel, *RE* s.v. *quaestio* col. 745. For examples of *peculatus* trials in this era, see perhaps Alexander, *Trials* no. 120 (the young Cn. Pompeius as defendant in a δίκη κλοπῆς ca. 85 before the *iudex quaestionis* P. Antistius, in which some booty from his father's sack of Asculum came up as an issue). I. Shatzman, *Historia* 21 (1972) 195, rejects the notion that appropriation of booty can have been the central charge in this case; but note Cic. *Ver.* 2.4.88 (admittedly post-Sullan). *Trials* no. 123 (suit against C. Curtius *de peculatu* in 83, with Cic. *Rab. Perd.* 8 recording the charge) is our first definite case of *peculatus*; cf. perhaps also no. 122 (83 or soon after). There is no good evidence for the existence of this court prior to the mid-80s. P. Decius Subulo (*tr. pl.* 120) was a defendant at some point (probably soon after his tribunate and prosecution of the *cos.* 121 L. Opimius) for taking money "contra leges." But there is no reason to think it was *de peculatu*—or even took place in a *quaestio*. Alexander, *Trials* no. 31, collects sources and bibliography and suggests (following Badian) *de repetundis* or (as Gruen holds) the Gracchan *lex ne quis iudicio circumveniretur*. If the latter, it went before the *comitia*. Nor is there any compelling reason to think (as Gruen, *Roman Politics* 177, has suggested) that the trial of the elder L. Lucullus for κλοπή ca. 102 (*Trials* no. 69 with 13.1.3 below) took place in a permanent *peculatus* court. Once established, evidence on the official name of this *provincia* is (yet again) sparse: Cic. *Clu.* 147 (66 B.C.) "[quaestio] C. Orchivi peculatus; *Mur.* 42 (of a *pr.* 65 B.C.) "tua sors . . . quaestio peculatus."

76. See Cic. *Brut.* 304–305 and cf. Asc. p. 73 C with the detailed discussion of E. Badian, *Historia* 18 (1969) 452–460.

77. As it happens, jurors are explicitly mentioned for almost half the attested *quaestio* trials for this period. See Alexander, *Trials* nos. 30 [119 B.C.] (Cic. *Brut.* 103 and *de Orat.* 121), 36 [116 B.C.] (V. Max. 6.9.14), 48 [possibly ca. 110 B.C., but date quite uncertain] (V. Max. 8.1. abs. 6), 51 [probably 106 B.C.] (Cic. *Att.* 1.16.4, *Balb.* 11, V. Max. 2.10 praef.), 60 [between 104

and 102 B.C.] and 61 [103 B.C.] (Cic. *Font.* 24–25), 70 [?101 B.C.] (*Div. Caec.* 63), 80 [98 B.C.] (*Rab. Perd.* 24), 84 [97 B.C.] (*Ver.* 2.5.3, etc.), 87 [later 90s B.C.] (V. Max. 8.5.3), 90 = 359 [by 91 B.C.] (Cic. *de Orat.* 2.245), 94 [92 B.C.] (*de Orat.* 1.229, etc.), 98 [90s B.C.] (*Clu.* 140), 96 [?92 B.C.] (Asc. p. 21 C), 367 [90s B.C. (V. Max. 8.1. abs. 13), 120 [85 B.C.] (Plu. *Pomp.* 4.3), perhaps 123 [83 B.C.] (*Rab. Perd.* 8 "iudicio clarissimo"), 356 [date uncertain, but definitely pre-81 B.C.] (V. Max. 8.1. abs. 8).

78. Cic. *S. Rosc.* 11–12, 85.

79. Explicitly, sixty-seven times in Cic. *S. Rosc.* On this feature and on the advocate's flattery of the *consilium* in general (but in the context of private suits) see B. W. Frier, *The Rise of the Roman Jurists: Studies in Cicero's Pro Caecina* (Princeton 1985) 197–199.

80. The praetor's many duties as court president are set out in Greenidge, *Legal Procedure* 456–516. A praetor's absence (Asc. p. 59–60 C, 66 B.C.) or illness (Cic. *Q. fr.* 3.1.15 and *Att.* 4.18.4, 54 B.C.) would postpone the trial. When a praetor is away, chaos might break loose in a *quaestio*: see Asc. pp. 59–60 C.

81. Personal connections of defendant and president matter: Plu. *Pomp.* 4.1–4 (a *iudex quaestionis* of ca. 85 B.C.), Cic. *Ver.* 1.26 (of a *pr. des.* 69), cf. *Att.* 3.17.1 (enmity of a *pr. des.* 57 toward defendant) and Cael. *Fam.* 8.8.1 (showing the disparities of quality of criminal justice from year to year). Or those of a prosecutor and president: Asc. p. 19 C. For the *advocatus* making an appeal on personal grounds to the court president, see Cic. *Planc.* 104 (54 B.C.). The president was thought worth bribing: Cic. *Ver.* 1.41, 52 (70 B.C.), *Planc.* 43 "sine ulla cupiditatis suspicione," Asc. p. 19 and cf. D.C. 39.55.4 (all 54 B.C.). Toward the end of our period, we even find a *pr. de repetundis* who acquits a defendant in ignorance of the relevant law and then (in effect) disregards the vote of his *consilium* by not officially recording its verdict: see Cael. *Fam.* 8.8.3 (51 B.C.) with D. R. Shackleton Bailey, *Cicero, Epistulae ad Familiares* I (Cambridge 1977) 399f (a legal mess).

82. See Cic. *de Orat.* 1.121 — the trial took place before a "consilium," i.e., of *iudices* (cf. also *Brut.* 103) — with the sources and discussion in Alexander, *Trials* no. 30 (who rightly dates this prosecution precisely to 119). For the praetor's power of suddenly adjourning a *quaestio*, see also Cic. *Ver.* 2.5.163 (70 B.C.). Gruen's suggestion (*Roman Politics* 108 n. 9) that *de Orat.* 1.121 does not belong to this famous and dramatic trial is unconvincing.

83. V. Max. 6.5.6.

84. *Trials* p. 16.

85. For Cicero's belief in his guilt, see *Q. fr.* 2.3.3; *Fam.* 9.21.3. Issue raised at trial: *de Orat.* 2.170.

86. For the trial, Alexander, *Trials* no. 69. Metellus Numidicus' refusal to testify: *Vir. ill.* 62.4 "quod is [sc. Lucullus] olim iudicium contra leges detrectaret." Broughton considers Lucullus "Pr. Urbanus or Peregrinus" (*MRR* I 559, following Münzer, *RE* s.v. *Licinius* 103 col. 375).

87. For the allotment of the *provincia peregrina* for 105 (i.e., the year previous to Lucullus' praetorship), see *RDGE* 16 A lines 17–18.

88. See Cic. *Ver.* 2.2.122 with *Inscr. Ital.* XIII 3 70b "q(uaestor), IIIvir a(ere) a(rgento) a(uro) f(lando) f(eriundo), aed(ilis) cur(ulis), iudex q(uaestionis) veneficis, pr(aetor) repetundis, curator vis sternundis, cos. cum M. Perperna."

89. *Inscr. Ital.* XIII 3 70b, cited in n. 61 above. The title "aed. cur(ulis) iudex q(uaestionis) veneficiis" is usually taken to be a sequence, since cumulation ought to be noted (e.g., *idem* or *simul*). On the title "iudex (quaestionis)," see already in the Gracchan *repetundae* law — but of a praetor (ch. 9 n. 116).

90. See nn. 74–75 above on P. Antistius (with Vell. 2.26.2 on his murder) and also M. Fannius. The standard pattern was for a man to be *iudex quaestionis* after his aedileship (Mommsen, *St.-R.* II³ 587 n. 3 and 589 n. 3), probably in the year directly following the office

(see Cic. *Clu.* 147 with *MRR* II 150 n. 3). For the date of 85 see J. Seidel, *"Fasti aedilicii* von der Einrichtung der plebejischen Adilität bis zum Tode Caesars"* (diss. Breslau 1908) 49–50; Sumner, *Orators* 111.

91. In general, see *St.-R.* II³ 589, also Greenidge, *Legal Procedure* 432–433; see esp. Cic. *Clu.* 4, 91 (the oath) and 147, cf. Ps.-Asc. p. 256 St. on his lictors and the power of enforcing the attendance of jurors in his *quaestio*.

92. The *pr. urb.* C. Verres is represented as supervising the *iudex quaestionis* C. Iunius in 74: Cic. *Clu.* 91, *Ver.* 2.1.157–158, Ps.-Asc. pp. 216, 219, and 255 St. Liability of the *iudex quaestionis* to prosecution: Cic. *Clu.* 89 (on C. Iunius in 74) "tum est condemnatus cum esset iudex quaestionis" (though arguing that it was illegal for him to be prosecuted as he was, with a case still in progress—see n. 95 below); perhaps also Suet. *Jul.* 17.1–2 (the "quaestor" Novius Niger, surely a "quaesitor"—as E. S. Gruen, *The Last Generation of the Roman Republic* [Berkeley and Los Angeles 1974] 286, has it against Mommsen, *St.-R.* II³ 584 n. 1 and (most recently) F. X. Ryan, *C&M* 46 [1995] 151–156—in charge of the *quaestio de vi*). On the magistrates who were protected from criminal prosecution in the Republic, see in general E. J. Weinrib, *Phoenix* 22 (1968) 32–56 and also 25 (1971) 145–150 (esp. 147–148 for a succinct formulation of some principles).

93. *St.-R.* II³ 590.

94. *Legal Procedure* 433, citing Suet. *Jul.* 11 for the ability of the *iudex* to accept or refuse his own cases.

95. On this, see Cic. *Clu.* 89 (the prosecution of C. Iunius in 74) "quo tempore illum a quaestione ad nullum aliud rei publicae munus abduci licebat, eo tempore ad quaestionem ipse abreptus est." But Cicero's "quo tempore" here might not refer to the entire year, just the time when an individual trial in a *quaestio* was in progress. If so, that leaves open the possibility that the *iudex quaestionis* might have been shifted between particular courts as needed. Cf. possibly *Inscr. Ital.* XIII 3 75b (Augustan date), an *elogium* of C. Octavius (*pr.* 61, and father of the future Augustus) that records his position of plebeian aedile followed by "iudex quaestionum." Since the other items of the *elogium* seem careful in regard to titulature, it may be that C. Octavius presided over more than one *quaestio* as *iudex*, if only the constituent units of the amagamated *quaestio de sicariis et veneficiis*. (F. X. Ryan, *RhM* 139 [1996] 251–253, notes the plural, but interprets it to mean "at least two terms as *iudex quaestionis*." But in that case would we not expect rather the simple *bis*?) In addition to C. Octavius, the precise court (or courts) of two men of the post-Sullan period who had this office are unknown: Q. Curtius, who held the post in 70 (Cic. *Ver.* 2.1.158), and C. Visellius Varro, who died in office (possibly) in 67 or 66 (see Alexander, *Trials* no. 254, and *MRR* III 222). See further in 11.7 below.

96. Cic. *de Orat.* 2.245.

97. *Iudex quaestionis:* Cic. *Clu.* 55. Special court president: e.g. Asc. pp. 38–39, 54 C. Praetor: note *Schol. Gron.* p. 330 St. "praetori qui praeerat iudicio aliquando, quaesitori" and Ps.-Asc. p. 215 St., confirmed by Cicero's usage at *Ver.* 1.29; cf. also *Font.* 21 (surely it was not a *iudex quaestionis* in charge of that *repetundae* trial) and *Rab. Post.* 9 ("de pecuniis repetundis . . . praetor quaesivi"). See further J. Linderski, *Roman Questions: Selected Papers* (Stuttgart 1995) 238 n. 26.

98. Sources and discussion in *Trials* no. 90 (cf. no. 359, not coordinated), with Cic. *de Orat.* 2.220 for the taunt at Catulus. Philippus' praetorian *provincia* will not have been the urban jurisdiction: see Cic. *Off.* 2.59 on his not having given games.

99. See *Fam.* 9.21.3 on the M. Carbo "condemnatus, fur magnus, ex Sicilia" with 13.1.2 below.

100. See, e.g., Cic. *Font.* 5, implying that the offices of *monetalis* and quaestor routinely excited suspicion of this type.

101. Flor. 2.5.5 = Alexander, *Trials* no. 95.

102. Cic. *de Orat.* 3.229.

103. Rutilius: Alexander, *Trials* no. 94 with Oros. 5.17.12. Sosius: *Trials* no. 122, with Cic. N.D. 3.74 for the praetor and *Rab. Perd.* 8 for the technical charge.

104. As is generally recognized: see the lists compiled in A. H. M. Jones, *The Criminal Courts of the Roman Republic and Principate* (Oxford 1972) 128 nn. 86 and 87 (no *iudex quaestionis* is known to have supervised any of these three courts, or *peculatus*). Further discussion follows in 11.7.

105. Sources in Alexander, *Trials* no. 71, of which see esp. Plu. *Luc.* 1.3 with E. Badian, *Klio* 66 (1984) 301–303. For later Republican examples, see ch. 11 n. 430.

106. For *iudicia populi* between 137 and 88, see Alexander, *Trials* nos. 12 (ca. 136 B.C.), 20 (131 B.C.), 24 (124 B.C.), 27 (120 B.C.), possibly 31 (?119 B.C.) and 47 (112 B.C.), 59 (106 B.C.), 62, 63, and 68 (104 B.C.), 64 and 66 (103 B.C.), possibly 75 (101 B.C.), 77 (100 B.C.), 78 and 79 (both probably 99 B.C.), possibly 81 (98 or 97 B.C.), and possibly 371 (perhaps 90 B.C.); add also the trial for "perduellio" for which the tribune Licinius asked the praetor M. Marcius to set a day (ca. 125–110, discussed in 5.6.1). Of those listed in Alexander, there was a capital penalty at stake at least in (probably) nos. 47, 59, 62 and (probably) 63, 64 and 66, 75 and 81 (but this was possibly a *quaestio*). See n. 108 below for the *iudicia populi* of 87 and 86.

107. See Alexander, *Trials* nos. 23 and 355 (125 or 124 B.C.), (possibly) 29 (?ca. 120 B.C.), 28 and 30 (119 B.C.), (possibly) 37 (115 B.C. or after), (possibly) 48 (?ca. 114 B.C.) and 46 (?113 B.C.), 45 (113 B.C.), 51 (106 B.C.), 60 (between 104 and 102), 67 (104 B.C.), 61 (103 B.C.), (probably) 69 (102 B.C.) and 70 (?101 B.C.), 84 (97 B.C.), (probably) 87 (between 95 and 91 B.C.), (perhaps) 90 (95 B.C.), 94 (92 B.C.), 96 (?92 B.C.), (perhaps) 71 (?ca. 91 B.C.) and 91 (91 B.C.) and 357 and 358 (probably 90s B.C.), 356 (?ca. 88 B.C.), and (just perhaps) 120 (85 B.C.). That gives sixteen certain or probable trials *de repetundis* for this period, and ten less certain instances. Yet virtually all of these trials (the exceptions are nos. 37, 46, 357 and 358) at least are securely attested as *quaestio* procedures, even if the exact charge is hazy.

108. See in general E. J. Weinrib, *Phoenix* 22 (1968) 43. On the trials of 87 in particular, see Alexander, *Trials* no. 113 (attempted tribunician prosecution of Sulla) and 114 (a tribune summoned the prorogued praetor Ap. Claudius Pulcher, now stripped of his army, to a trial before the People; when he refused to appear, a tribunician bill abrogated his *imperium*). Trials that might belong to either late 87 or 86: see no. 115 for the tribune M. Marius Gratidianus' prosecution of Q. Lutatius Catulus (*cos.* 102) on a capital offence (D.S. 39.4.2); also no. 116 for L. Cornelius Merula (*cos. suff.* 87) as defendant on an unspecified charge, but definitely before a popular court (App. *BC* 1.74.341–342 is explicit on the procedure); and 117 (two former tribunes of 87 prosecuted by the *tr. pl.* 86 P. Popillius Laenas). In 86, C. Flavius Fimbria (as quaestor?) dropped his prosecution of the *cos.* 95 Q. Mucius Scaevola (no. 119).

109. On the general character of the legal system in the years 87–83, see Cic. *Brut.* 227 "sine iure fuit et sine ulla dignitate res publica," *Dom.* 83 "iniquitatem illius Cinnani temporis."

110. Alexander, *Trials* nos. 83 (Duronius), 181 (C. Licinius Macer, who was *tr. pl.* 73). Whatever its date, the latter trial—despite the suggestion of Alexander—was not before the People (Cic. *Rab. Perd.* 7 "aequi et iurati iudices iudicarint").

111. Alexander, *Trials* no. 187 (with fuller discussion by this author at *CPh* 80 [1985] 25), cf. no. 244 (Carbo's own conviction on return from Bithynia) with 11.2 below. Against Alexander, the charge was probably not *peculatus*. See D.C. 36.40.3 ἐπί τε δώροις καὶ ἐπὶ ὑποψίᾳ ἐπιβουλῆς and esp. Quint. *Inst.* 5.13.17 "obicitur Oppio . . . quod is uoluerit exercitum largiendo corrumpere." The trial was definitely before *iudices* (partly equestrian): *Inst.* 5.13.21. On Carbo's reward for prosecution—the first certain case we have of this type of

grant—and subsequent examples of *praemia legis* see H. E. Russell, "Insignia of Office as Rewards in the Roman Republic: Advancement in Rank for the Soldier and the Public Prosecutor" (diss. Bryn Mawr 1950) 66–82.

112. In 66, an unnamed tribune tried to bring Faustus Cornelius Sulla before the *peculatus* court, but we are told the jurors refused to take the case (Cic. *Clu.* 94 with Alexander, *Trials* no. 196, cf. Mommsen, *Strafrecht* 372 n. 2 suggesting a *divinatio* as the context); Cicero implies—tendentiously—that for a tribune in office to prosecute in that way did not make for a fair fight. In 66 or 65, the *tr. pl.* C. Memmius unsuccessfully prosecuted M. Terentius Varro Lucullus (*cos.* 73) and then (in a separate action) L. Licinius Lucullus (*cos.* 74), but it is not certain whether those were in a *quaestio* (nos. 204, 206; in the latter case, Plu. *Cat. Mi.* 29.5 may imply a *iudicium populi*). In 59, the *tr. pl.* P. Vatinius prosecuted under the *lex Plautia de vi* the *eques* L. Vettius, who died in prison (no. 242). In 58, the *tr. pl.* Aelius Ligus started and then dropped a prosecution of Sex. Propertius, possibly *inter sicarios* (no. 253). In 57, the tribune T. Milo prosecuted P. Clodius Pulcher *de vi*, but the trial was obstructed (no. 261). See further text above. In 54 the *tr. pl.* C. Memmius successfully prosecuted A. Gabinius (*cos.* 58) *de repetundis* (no. 303), and also brought C. Rabirius Postumus into the same court (no. 305, outcome uncertain). And it is at least possible that this tribune (and not the *pr.* 58) was the "C. Memmius" who brought Cn. Domitius Calvinus (the future *cos.* 53) into the *ambitus* court that same year (no. 301).

113. For example, in the case of 57, the *tr. pl.* T. Annius Milo made P. Clodius a defendant in the *quaestio de vi*. But in the next year when P. Clodius (now curule aedile) counterprosecuted Milo on a *vis* charge, it was not in a *quaestio* but before the People, as Alexander (*Trials* no. 266) rightly has it, against Gruen, *Last Generation* 298 n. 139. In support, note the technical expression "diem dicere" at Cic. *Sest.* 95, *Vat.* 41, and Schol. Bob. p. 122 St.

114. Instances of popular *iudicia* for this period: Alexander, *Trials* nos. 180 (an aedicilian prosecution, lightly threatened for 69), 206 (a *tr. pl.* of 66 or 65 drops his prosecution of L. Lucullus), 204 (the same *tr. pl.* unsuccessfully prosecutes M. Lucullus), 221 (a *tr. pl.* 63 prosecutes C. Rabirius, probably after his notorious trial *perduellionis*, but the proceedings are stopped), 257 (a tribune's attempt to try Caesar in early 56—thus Badian ap. *Trials* 257 n. 2 blocked by another *tr. pl.*), 266 (see n. 113 above), and perhaps V. Max. 8.1 abs. 3 (a tribune's prosecution of A. Gabinius in 54, stopped by one of his colleagues—not in Alexander as such). On this last case, see E. Fantham, *Historia* 24 (1975) 434, suggesting that the tribune wanted "a device to provoke popular indignation and support his prosecution in the regular *quaestio*." Cf. perhaps also no. 371 (the condemnation of a Cn. Sergius Silus to a fine, but not certainly from this era).

115. *Ill.* 10.30.

116. Broughton, *MRR* I 525. L. Delmaticus against the Dalmatians: see esp. App. *Ill.* 11.33 and *Per.* 62.

117. See Oros. 5.23.23, Eutrop. 6.4 with 11.8.1 below.

118. M. G. Morgan, *Athenaeum* 49 (1971) 271–301. Triumph: *Inscr. Ital.* XIII 1 82f, before Dec. 117.

119. As Broughton seems willing to entertain in *MRR* III 38.

120. L. Cornelius Scipio Asiaticus had not "Illyria" but "Macedonia" as his *provincia* (by 84): see 14.1.4.

121. He was still alive in mid-September: see Cic. *de Orat.* 1.24.

122. "Praetor": Vell. 2.15.1, D.S. 37.13.2, Oros. 5.18.8 (with wrong name). Enhanced *imperium*: *Per.* 72 *pro cos.*; App. *BC* 1.38.171. For his station in Picenum, cf. D.S. 37.13.2 with App. *BC* 1.38.173. Chronology: Konrad, *Plutarch's Sertorius* 54f ("end of October, perhaps later"). Full sources in Broughton, *MRR* II 20; see Obseq. 54 for the date. For a roster of the Roman commanders in the Social War in tabular form, see Appendix A.3.

123. See *BC* 1.38.171–172. The closest parallels for this type of command are M. Claudius Marcellus (*pr.* 216), who was prorogued into 215 and had his *imperium* raised to the consular level (8.3.1 above); and Ti. Claudius Nero (*pr. per.* 178), who held a command *pro cos.* at Pisa in 177 (8.3.5 above, also Additional Note IX). But both these men were promagistrates when they received consular *imperium*.

124. See Cic. *Mur.* 42 (L. Murena's leisurely *dilectus* in Umbria en route to his praetorian province of Gaul in 64), Suet. *Aug.* 3.1 (the Senate's special orders to C. Octavius in transit to an *ex praetura* Macedonian command in 60), and possibly Jul. Exup. 8.50 (extra orders given to Q. Sertorius as praetor for Hispania Citerior in 83).

125. Plu. *Sull.* 6.1–2 with T. C. Brennan, *Chiron* 22 (1992) 156.

126. App. *BC* 1.38.170 with Flor. 2.5.9 and Oros. 5.18.8.

127. *BC* 1.38.172.

128. *MRR* II 24 n. 6; see in addition A. Keaveney, *Rome and the Unification of Italy* (London 1987) 117 (venturing to place also three other praetors in the field that year, making a total of five in all).

129. *BC* 1.38.170–171.

130. See *Per.* 73, with MS. reading "Sex. Sul"; but also *MRR* II 31 n. 11.

131. *Per.* 73.

132. *RE* s.v. *Postumius* 13 cols. 897–898; cf. A. Keaveney, *Rome and the Unification of Italy* 118, 134 (making him a *pr.* 90).

133. Oros. 5.18.10. See E. Badian, *Klio* 66 (1984) 306–309 for Cn. Pompeius Strabo's early career (quaestor ca. 106, *tr. pl.* 104); there is no good evidence for a praetorian command in Macedonia (*contra* Broughton, *MRR* III 166).

134. *BC* 1.47.204.

135. App. *BC* 1.40.179; full sources in *MRR* II 29.

136. *Per.* 74, Oros. 5.18.17.

137. *Per.* 74, Oros. 5.18.17; cf. Flor. 2.6.13. The *legatus* A. Plotius who simultaneously fought against the Umbrians (*Per.*, Oros.) might have been a subordinate of L. Porcius Cato.

138. App. *BC* 1.39.177, Flor. 2.6.10.

139. D.S. 37.2.4–5, 7. Cf. also Strab. 5.4.2 p. 241 C, Vell. 2.16.4 and Flor. 2.6.7 on Corfinium.

140. D.S. 37.2.6–7. For lists of the most important Italian generals, see esp. App. *BC* 1.40.181 (with E. Gabba, *Appiani Bellorum Civilium Liber Primus: Introduzione, testo critico e commento* [Florence 1958] ad loc.), Vell. 2.16.1, Flor. 2.6.5, Eutrop. 5.3.2. For confirmation of the title "praetor" for the subordinate officers, see *ILLRP* 1089 (*glandes* of T. Lafrenius *pr.*). Later, after the surrender of the Marsi in 89, the Italians reorganized, abandoning Corfinium and setting up Bovianum in its place. The rebel forces were unified under Q. Poppedius Silo, one of five "praetors" who was appointed supreme commander (D.S. 37.2.8–9, cf. App. *BC* 1.51.224). For general discussion (properly stressing the military nature of the Italian "government"), see H. Meyer, *Historia* 7 (1958) 74–79.

141. Cic. *Brut.* 304 and Asc. pp. 73–74 C with Badian, *Studies* 177 n. 67; *Historia* 18 (1969) 460.

142. In 125, L. Opimius (the future *cos.* 121) destroyed the rebellious town of Fregellae (8.6.2). Praetors in their year of office were sent to quell the slave revolt in Italy in 73 and 72 (11.8.6–7); and praetors were sent against the Catilinarian conspirators and their sympathizers in 63 and 62 (11.8.9).

143. See *Per.* 73, where the phrase "saga posita" should imply resumption of forensic business. Also *Per.* 74 "Cn. Pompeius Picentes proelio fudit et obsedit," etc.

144. See in particular App. *BC* 1.54.235–239, esp. 235 (Asellio allowed the dispute between debtors and creditors to go ἐς τοὺς δικαστάς); cf. *Per.* 74; V. Max. 9.7.4. See also E.

Badian, *Historia* 18 (1969) 452ff (on the Varian court) and 475ff (on Asellio, *inter alia* giving a date in late Jan. for the praetor's death, discussed in 12.1.1).

145. Cf. esp. Cic. *Font.* 43 with the discussion of Badian, *Studies* 52–56 (demonstrating that in both 90 and 89 the staffs of each of the consuls divide along political lines).

146. See Cic. *Font.* 43 for each of these individuals, specifying that the last three were praetorian; for Marius and Sulla see also Vell. 2.15.3 and 2.16.4, Plu. *Sull.* 6.2 and *Mar.* 33.1, Eutrop. 5.3.3–4; cf. D.S. 37.2.8 (Sulla in 89). Cic. *Font.* 43 has simply "M. Cornutum"; for the *nomen* cf. the *prr.* 57, 43. Cornutus' name is often supplied for the lacuna at the third place in the *consilium* of the *cos.* 89 Cn. Pompeius Strabo at Asculum (*ILLRP* 515); see above all C. Cichorius, *Römische Studien* (Leipzig 1922) 140–141. L. Cornelius Cinna is the *cos.* 87, IV 84.

147. Cic. *Pis.* 87. Quaestor in 103 or 100 (*MRR* III 47), R. Syme (*Roman Papers* I [Oxford 1979] 277) identifies him with the L. Calpurnius Piso who in 90 (*MRR* III 48) introduced a bill to add two new tribes and also a law that granted citizenship to soldiers *virtutis causa* (Sis. *HRR* I² FF 17, 119, 120). Broughton in *MRR* II 33f offers the standard interpretation that this was tribunician legislation and that the man in question is L. Frugi, the future *pr.* 74. However, in *MRR* III 47 he accepts Syme's view, making L. Caesoninus "*pr.* 90" without query—while simultaneously holding onto the standard view at III 48. On balance, Syme's basic suggestion seems reasonable—esp. if M. Crawford (*RRC* I 340–344 no. 340) is right that L. Frugi was a *monetalis* in 90—yet it hardly allows for certainty.

148. See above in text on Cn. Pompeius Strabo. C. Perperna was perhaps a younger brother of the *cos.* 92 M. Perperna; for his likely praetorian status, see *MRR* II 29. For Q. Caepio as *praetorius*, see Badian, *Studies* 42f. Broughton (*MRR* II 24 n. 5) makes a good circumstantial case for a praetorship precisely in 91. Caepio was quaestor (*MRR* I 576) in 103 (cf. Badian, *Studies* 35 with n. 9) or possibly 100; Sumner (*Orators* 116f) is over skeptical on his praetorian status. The noble Valerius Messalla served as a *legatus* in 90 "almost certainly as a *praetorius*": thus Broughton in *MRR* II 630; see also II 30, where he implausibly interprets Gel. 15.14.1 as a reference to this Messalla. But once the Gellius evidence is removed from consideration (see R. Syme ap. *MRR* III 213), we have no additional information on this individual.

149. *BC* 1.41.183.

150. Ov. *Fast.* 6.563–566.

151. Thus *MRR* II 28.

152. *Per.* 73 "aequatum ei cum C. Mario esset imperium," cf. App. *BC* 1.44.196.

153. See App. *BC* 1.48.210 ἀνθύπατος ὑπὸ τῆς βουλῆς αἱρεθείς with the interpretation of Münzer, *RE* s.v. *Iulius* 151 col. 477; see also *MRR* II 31 n. 11. This C. Baebius will not have been the same man who (as *tr. pl.* 111) was bribed by Jugurtha to impede the king's questioning by C. Memmius (Sal. *Jug.* 33.2–34.2).

154. See *Per.* 74, App. *BC* 1.50.216 (Marsi); also *Per.* 75, *BC* 1.52.227 (Marsi, Marrucini, Vestini).

155. App. *BC* 1.40.179; on Didius and Sulla cf. also Cic. *Font.* 43.

156. According to Appian (*BC* 1.40.179), P. Lentulus served as *legatus* under the *cos.* "Sex." (i.e., L.) Iulius Caesar—"his own brother." For an explanation of this (erroneous) statement, see Badian, *Studies* 52, against Münzer, *RE* s.v. *Cornelius* 203 col. 1375. The existence of this Lentulus has been doubted (*MRR* II 31 n. 16), though without good reason. He was certainly a *nobilis*, perhaps (if Appian is accurate) also through the *gens Iulia*. Praetorian status, however, is just a guess, despite the fact that Appian lists him first of the consul's *legati*. For M. Marcellus, see *MRR* III 55. He was prosecuted at some point, but certainly by 91 in a permanent *quaestio* (Alexander, *Trials* no. 87), perhaps *de repetundis* (thus Badian, *Studies* 44 and 53), with L. Licinius Crassus (*cos.* 95) as a hostile witness who failed to make

his testimony stick. That trial in itself may imply a praetorian command. At any rate, Marcellus was very likely a *praetorius* in 90 (cf., in addition to Appian, *Per.* 73 with Badian, *Studies* 52f, 281). Sumner (*Orators* 91f) goes further and suggests Marcellus was already of praetorian status when he served under Marius at Aquae Sextiae in 102 (sources in MRR I 569). But that is unlikely to be correct (n. 44 above).

157. According to Appian (*BC* 1.46.201–202); *Per.* 73 and Oros. 5.18.5 give Marius the sole credit. For the reliability of Appian on this incident, see T. C. Brennan, *Chiron* 22 (1992) 157 n. 157.

158. Eutrop. 5.3.2. Sources for Sulla as *legatus* in 90 are gathered in MRR II 29.

159. See *ILLRP* 515 with the masterful exposition of C. Cichorius, *Römische Studien* 130–185.

160. For Cn. Piso, see Sal. *Jug.* 104.3; E. Badian (*Chiron* 20 [1990] 406) discusses the identification with the *cos.* 87 Cn. Octavius.

161. *Römische Studien* 137–139; see MRR II 31 n. 18 and III 201f for further discussion. H. B. Mattingly (*Athenaeum* 53 [1975] 264–266) less convincingly supplements the lacuna as [P. Sulpi]cius, i.e., the *tr. pl.* 88. Though that man was a *legatus* in probably both 90 and 89 (Cic. *Brut.* 304), within a few weeks after the Asculum *consilium* he is attested back in Rome, necessarily entering office on 10 Dec. 89.

162. Plu. *Sull.* 17.7 for title; see also App. *Mith.* 43.166.

163. Thus Sumner, *Orators* 74 (accepting Cichorius' restoration of the name to Ser. Sulpicius C.f.).

164. App. *BC* 1.51.217 (giving the chronology as "winter" 89).

165. For the title *legatus*, see *Per.* 75; *Nat.* 22.12 (from Sulla's autobiography). Sulla claimed no title for himself in his three inscriptions of that year found at Pompeii (*ILLRP* 346–348).

166. MRR II 37. On his status, see *Per.* 75 (termed *legatus*) and Oros. 5.18.22 *vir consularis* against Plu. *Sull.* 6.9 στρατηγικὸν ἄνδρα πρεσβευτήν (followed by Polyaen. 8.9.1). Albinus was killed by his own troops because of his *superbia* (Oros. 5.18.22), or a charge of *proditio* (*Per.* 75, with Gronovius' emendation for MS. *perditiones*)—the divergence is a bit odd, since both should be from Livy. Sulla did not even grant a military trial to air charges, and then ignored the breakdown in military discipline, allegedly because he was looking toward his candidacy for *cos.* 88 (Plu. *Sull.* 6.9). Full sources for Sulla in this year can be found in MRR II 36.

167. V. Max. 1.6.4 with Cic. *Div.* 1.72 (at Nola the *haruspex* Postumius interprets a portent, said to be described in Sulla's "*historia*" = autobiography, verified by Q. Cicero's eyewitness account); cf. 2.65.

168. Oros. 5.18.23 "Sylla consul [before Orosius reports the death of L. Porcius Cato!] civilem cruorem non nisi hostili sanguine expiari posse testatus est." This may have come (at second or third hand) from Sulla's *Memoirs* (cf. "testatus"); we know that Sulla spoke of his military activities in ritual terms (T. C. Brennan, *Chiron* 22 [1992] 108 n. 8). Nevertheless, it seems certain that Sulla would not call himself consul (as Orosius calls him), or even *pro cos.*, in relating the anecdote.

169. E. T. Salmon, *Samnium and the Samnites* (Cambridge 1967) 364.

170. Ov. *Fast.* 6.567f.

171. MRR II 38 n. 7.

172. App. *BC* 1.52.227 and D.S. 37.2.8 σταλέντος εἰς Ἰαπυγίαν στρατηγοῦ: cf. *BC* 1.53.230 στρατηγία and *Per.* 75.

173. Sources in MRR II 36, III 77.

174. *Per.* 75. See further MRR II 37 with 39 n. 24 on that man's name, and T. P. Wiseman, *NM* 238 no. 232 for discussion and bibliography. The *Periocha* reports that

"Cosconius et Lucanus [Gronovius has "Lucceius"] Samnites acie vicerunt, Marium Egnatium . . . occiderunt compluraque eorum oppida in deditionem acceperunt." Appian, who certainly knows of Egnatius (*BC* 1.40.181; 41.183; 45.199), represents (*BC* 1.52.229) the praetor Cosconius alone engaging Trebatius on a river. Egnatius' death is nowhere found in Appian's full description of the battle, nor anywhere else for that matter: his silence on "Lucanus" thus does not necessarily mean that this Roman was an unimportant figure. Münzer (*RE* s.v. *Lucanius* cols. 1552–1553), following Cichorius, *Römische Studien* 1715, suggests this man was a member of the *gens Lucania*, a name found in the *consilium* of Cn. Pompeius Strabo at Asculum in 89 (*ILLRP* 515). He could alternatively be a Terentius Lucanus: the family was senatorial by ca. 170 (*MRR* III 204). His rank must remain uncertain. See also Münzer, *RE* s.v. *Cosconius* 3 col. 1667 (accepting the date of 89 for the praetorship).

175. Thus, rightly, *MRR* II 39 n. 21, following a suggestion of Münzer. But identification with the egregiously guilty C. Cosconius who found himself unexpectedly acquitted in a trial before *iudices* under a *lex Servilia* (*de repetundis*, and hence after 106?) seems dubious (see V. Max. 8.1. abs. 8 for the story) The details are hard to imagine for the mid- to late 80s, and the post-Sullan era (when the statute would be a *lex Cornelia*) seems impossible. Perhaps it was the praetor's father.

176. See Flor. 2.6.13 with *MRR* II 33. For his tribunate, see *MRR* II 18. His cousin Carbo Arvina (*pr.* before 82) is a less likely candidate for the command reported by Florus, since he surely was not yet of praetorian rank. Konrad (*Plutarch's Sertorius* 78) offers the attractive hypothesis that when he collaborated with the *cos.* L. Cinna during the siege of Rome in 87 "he may still have been with *imperium* (*pro praetore* or even *pro consule*)."

177. *IGRP* IV 1116 line 5 ταμίας; *MRR* I 573 n. 3 is wrong to date this inscription to 101 solely on the basis of Antonius' title στρατηγὸς ἀνθύπατος = "pro cos."

178. Command against Marsi: Flor. 2.6.13. Falls in Lucania: *Per.* 76, Oros. 5.18.25, both with title *legatus*. Possible praetorian status: Münzer, *RE* s.v. *Gabinius* 9 col. 424; cf. *MRR* II 36, also III 97.

179. *Per.* 76, preceding notice of the fall of Asculum.

180. Cic. *Arch.* 9.

181. Cic. *Arch.* 7 and 9, cf. 31.

182. Badian, *Studies* 75–80; T. R. S. Broughton, *MRR* III 98 (favoring rather 89), and cf. *Candidates Defeated in Roman Elections: Some Ancient Roman "Also-Rans"* (Philadelphia 1991) 40 (dating the praetorship of Ap. Pulcher to 89, without query).

183. Cf. the confusing notice of *Vir. ill.* 63.3 "adolescens in petitione praeturae et pontificatus consularibus viris praelatus est."

184. See 14.1.4 on his phantom Macedonian command. For his earlier career, see Badian ap. *MRR* III 97.

185. App. *BC* 1.53.230 ἐπελθὼν ἐπὶ τὴν στρατηγίαν διάδοχος.

186. Orosius (5.18.25) attributes the victory to the *legatus* "Sulpicius" (= Cn. Strabo's *legatus* Ser. Sulpicius Galba, on whom see text above). Meanwhile, the Livian *Periocha* (*Per.* 76) and Diodorus (37.2.10) ascribe it to a "Mam. Aemilius," termed *legatus* (*Per.*, cf. D.S. Μαμέρκου στρατηγοῦντος αὐτῶν, sc. Romans). This Mam. Aemilius should be the *cos.* 77 (as Badian, *Studies* 217, has it), so definitely praetor by 80. Whether Mamercus was a *praetorius* by that time is anyone's guess. In Diodorus' version, Metellus was responsible just for the capture of Venusia. On the early career of Mam. Lepidus, see further A. Keaveney, *Klio* 66 (1984) 138.

187. *Per.* 79, cf. Vell. 2.20.4 and App. *BC* 1.65.298.

188. *MRR* II 48.

189. Cic. *Dom.* 83.

190. Plu. *Sull.* 9.2. For a suggested identification of this Servilius with the "Servilius Augur" who prosecuted the elder L. Lucullus (*pr.* 104) and in turn was brought to trial by that man's son (the later *cos.* 74), see E. Badian, *Klio* 66 (1984) 304–305.

191. *BC* 1.60.271 with Badian, *Klio* 66 (1984) 305 n. 58; cf. also *Per.* 77 on the number twelve.

192. Gran. Lic. 35.7 C.

193. *Per.* 89 with *MRR* II 40, 44 n. 2; cf. Münzer, *RE* s.v. *Iunius* 51 col. 972.

194. E.g., the list of the seven most prominent in App. *BC* 1.60.271, where we might positively expect this Servilius. E. Badian (*Klio* 66 [1984] 305 n. 58) notices the omission and suggests Appian should have included him, but simply did not have the praetor's name in his source.

195. App. *BC* 1.68.309, D.C. 30–35 F 102.6–7; cf. *Per.* 80.

196. Sources in *MRR* II 47f, 58; see also Gabba, *Commento* p. 214 for his departure from Italy, and 14.3.3 below. The chaotic events of the *Bellum Octavianum* of 87 offer no real material for this study of the praetorship. We do find notice of one attempted delegation of *imperium*. Plutarch (*Mar.* 41.5) reports that L. Cinna—after he had been deposed from his consulship in 87—offered to make C. Marius (on his return to Italy from exile) a *pro cos.* and sent him the appropriate *insignia*. Marius declined the offer—perhaps because he knew that Cinna was unqualified to delegate consular *imperium*! (Indeed doubly so, if one recognized his deposition as valid.) On the principle Cinna ignored, see 2.1.2 and 3.6.2.

197. App. *BC* 1.80.365, 81.370.

198. Gran. Lic. 35.23 C, App. *BC* 1.68.309.

199. See *ILLRP* 366 (Tibur) with discussion in 14.3.3.

200. Cf. App. *BC* 1.95.441 for the participation of Marian praetors, quaestors and *tribuni militum* in this civil war; see also n. 204 below on Plu. *Sull.* 27.3. For discussion of the date of the the the arrival of the praetorian commander M. Perperna Veiento in Sicily (probably 85 or 84, but just possibly 82), see 13.1.4 below.

201. Eutropius (5.9.1) and Orosius (5.22.4) claim that six (Oros.) or seven (Eutrop.) *praetorii* died in the Social and Civil Wars. This is certainly conceivable (even low), although their other figures are manifestly exaggerated (24 *consulares*, 60 *aedilicii*, and 200 senators), even if one takes into account natural deaths. Livy should have been the common source for the figures.

202. Praetorship: *BC* 1.86.392 ἐκ πολλοῦ στρατηγεῖν ἡρημένος Ἰβηρίας; cf. *BC* 1.108.505 ("fighting with Carbo") and *Hisp.* 101.438. Warned L. Scipio of treachery at Teanum Sidicinum: Plu. *Sert.* 6.3. Sertorius takes Suessa: App. *BC* 1.85.384–385, cf. 108.505 (Sulla's reaction). He was still in Italy at the time of the younger Marius' election to the consulship: Plu. *Sert.* 6.1. Leaves for Spain, partly motivated by disgust for "superiors": *Sert.* 6.1 and 5. *Pro cos.*: *Sert.* 6.6. See further 13.3.2.

203. *Pomp.* 7.1–2 with D.S. 38/39.9.

204. See Plu. *Sull.* 27.3, where Sulla in his *Memoirs* claimed to have advanced in 83 "against fifteen στρατηγοὶ πολέμιοι."

205. See, e.g., *Sull.* 28.8; *Luc.* 26.5, 28.9, and cf. *Pomp.* 29.2 (στρατηγοῦντες = *legati*).

206. *MRR* II 65, 67 with Oros. 5.21.10 "Carrinatem praetorem Sylla iugulavit," and Appendix B n. 299 on the *praenomen*. Münzer (*RE* s.v. *Carrinas* 1 col. 1612) dates his praetorship to 82. G. V. Sumner (*Phoenix* 25 [1971] 267) allows for a praetorship in any one of the years 84 through 82.

207. See the passages collected in *MRR* II 67, esp. App. *BC* 1.92.425 on the legion.

208. Appian calls Carrinas a "στρατηγός of Carbo" early in that year (*BC* 1.87.395) and counts him among the στρατηγοί (some Italian) who fought at the Colline Gate (1.93.431, listing also Telesinus, Albinus, Lamponius and Marcius [Censorinus]. At App. *BC* 1.90.413,

again in the narrative of 82 B.C., Καρρίναν τὸν ἀντιστρατηγοῦντα does not mean "pro pr." but merely "opposing general" (as at *BC* 1.44.197).

209. See *RRC* I 331 no. 332 with Wiseman, *NM* 224 no. 122, cf. *CR* 17 (1967) 263–264.

210. See C. Tuplin, *Chiron* 9 (1979) 137–145.

211. *Per.* 86 "praetor . . . cum senatum contraxisset," Oros. 5.20.4 "praetor . . . in curiam quasi ad consultandum vocatos . . . occidit," App. *BC* 1.88.403. In general on this individual, see F. Hinard, *Les proscriptions de la Rome républicaine* (Rome 1985) 363–364 (terming him "pr. urbanus"); Münzer, *RE* s.v. *Iunius* 58 col. 1025 (also accepting "urbanus").

212. *CPh* 56 (1961) 22–23.

213. *BC* 2.2.7 and 112.466 are particularly instructive, as is 3.14.49.

214. See App. *BC* 1.92.423 (his desperate and unsuccessful march on Praeneste to relieve Marius), 425, and 427 (an eleventh-hour attempt to join with the Samnites, themselves trying to break through to Praeneste).

215. See esp. Asc. p. 84 C, V. Max. 9.2.1 and Firm. Mat. 1.3, with text below.

216. App. *BC* 1.91.420–421, cf. *BC* 1.60.271 for his relationship to the elder Marius. Fimbria was brother of the renegade (App. *BC* 1.91.421), on whom see 14.5.9 below.

217. See *BC* 1.108.508, *Mith.* 88.400.

218. Compare *Mith.* 15.50, 19.70 with 11.36 and 54.222.

219. Who (I suggest) perhaps included the "Quintius" of Oros. 5.20.8.

220. Ps.-Asc. p. 234 St. On Albinovanus' (apparent) later career, see *MRR* III 14; Hinard, *Proscriptions* 123.

221. Censorinus defeated by Pompey near Sena: App. *BC* 1.88.401. The cos. Carbo sends Censorinus with "eight legions" in an attempt to relieve his colleague Marius at Praeneste: *BC* 1.90.414–415 (στρατηγός). Late in 82 he seems to have had a legion: App. *BC* 1.92.425. Final movements and battle at Colline Gate: App. *BC* 1.92.427 and 93.431, 433, where "Marcius" and "Albinus" are listed among στρατηγοί. On this list see n. 208 above.

222. See *RRC* I 333–335 no. 335 (A. S[P.].F. ALBINVS), 1.357–361 no. 346 (C. CENSORI). Gabba (*Commento* p. 249) considered identification of the Marian Albinus with this moneyer possible, even reckoning from a date of 89 B.C. On the career of C. Marcius Censorinus, see *MRR* III 138 with T. C. Brennan, *Chiron* 22 (1992) 154–156.

223. See esp. App. *BC* 1.80.365 and 81.370, cf. *Per.* 87 (where Sulla's subordinates are called "legati"), Plu. *Sull.* 28.8 (στρατηγοί, discussed in text below) and Plu. *Pomp.* 9.1 (ἡγεμόνες καὶ στρατηγοί). Sulla's general policy toward subordinates: D.C. 30–35 F 108.1.

224. *Pomp.* 6.3 ὑπ᾽ οὐδενὸς δὲ ἀνθρώπων ἀποδεδειγμένος στρατηγός, αὐτὸς ἑαυτῷ δοὺς τὸ ἄρχειν.

225. Activities in Picenum: Plu. *Pomp.* 6.3–4, also Vell. 2.29.1, D.S. 38/39.9, D.C. 30–35 F 107.1. Dispatches: D.S. 38/39.10

226. *Pomp.* 8.2, cf. *Crass.* 6.5. Other signs of honor at this time: V. Max. 5.2.9, Plu. *Pomp.* 8.3, App. *BC* 1.80.366.

227. *Sull.* 28.8. This "Servilius" is generally taken as P. Servilius Vatia: an ex-praetor (by 90), *triumphator* and the future cos. 79 "Isauricus." Velleius refers to "duo Servilii" who fought an important battle for Sulla at Clusium in 82 (2.28.1 with *MRR* II 74 n. 10). The other Servilius is presumably his (elder) brother, M. Servilius C.f., a moneyer dated by M. Crawford to 100 B.C. (*RRC* I 329–329, no. 327). Even if the identification of Velleius' "Servilii" is correct, one can just guess whether M. Servilius was of praetorian status at the time.

228. *Nobilis*: cf. Cic. *Clu.* 69 with 84–85. He was perhaps son of the moneyer CETEGVS (*RRC* I 302–303 no. 288, dated by Crawford to 115 or 114 B.C.). Exile in 88: App. *BC* 1.60.271, cf. 62.280; Plu. *Mar.* 40.4.

229. Crosses to Sulla: App. *BC* 1.80.369. Service at Praeneste: V. Max. 9.2.1. Praetorian status seems assured: see further Appendix B n. 204.

230. Vell. 2.27.6. See discussion in 10.5.8 below.

231. On this, see in general A. Keaveney, *Klio* 66 (1984) 142–143 (offering a list of names).

232. Garrisons: App. *BC* 1.95.440. *Quaestiones*: *BC* 1.96.445–446. Punishment: *BC* 1.96.447, cf. 448 on the role of his veteran colonies in keeping control.

233. Gran. Lic. 36.8 C, cf. *Per.* 89 for the capture of Volaterrae.

234. See *MRR* II 30 n. 8. For doubts, see D. R. Shackleton Bailey, *CEF* II 328f (suggesting rather he was son of the M. Carbo [*RE* 39] condemned for actions in Sicily ca. 114).

235. *MRR* II 76.

236. App. *BC* 1.40.179.

237. At least in the late Republic, a *privatus* who had received from the Senate the status of *legatus pro praetore* was supposed to have less than six lictors (ch. 2 n. 157). The idea (surely) was to prevent conflict with actual praetors in office.

238. See Additional Note II.

239. Evidence, discussion, and bibliography collected in Broughton, *Candidates Defeated* 25–26. See esp. E. Badian, *Historia* 18 (1969) 481–490 on the date, and Marshall, *Asconius* 144–145, for an overview of counterarguments against Badian (none compelling) for Strabo standing in 88 for the consulship of 87. The elections for 88 were held very late in 89. The one competent magistrate—the *cos.* Cn. Pompeius Strabo—was still at Asculum in mid-November. That Caesar Strabo had an *S.C.* follows from Cic. *Phil.* 11.11; *Brut.* 226 strongly implies that one of the earliest acts of the tribunes of 88 (who had taken office on 10 Dec. 89) was to oppose Strabo's petition. And Diodorus (37.2.12) is explicit that Caesar Strabo was aiming at the Mithridatic command.

240. Vell. 2.21.2 (in the context of a summary of Strabo's career) "frustratus spe continuandi consulatus." If we take Velleius literally—who elsewhere always uses *continuare/continuatio* in its strict technical sense—that would mean Pompeius Strabo wanted a consulship for 88.

241. Plu. *Sull.* 45.1–2 with *Per.* 80.

242. For that last item, see Plu. *Sert.* 6.1 (Sertorius' opposition) with Vell. 2.26.1, *Per.* 86, App. *BC* 1.87.394.

243. Cf. App. *BC* 1.78.358–359, where the tribunes in the year 84 insist on the election of a suffect consul (to no effect, as it happens).

244. Tribunate: see *MRR* II 47 and 52 n. 2 (the year 87), III 140f (86). Twice praetor: Asc. 84 p. C. His murder: many sources, but see esp. V. Max. 9.2.1 "praetore" and Firm. Mat. 1.3 "praetorio viro, minori scilicet Mario" (i.e., confusing him with the *cos.* 82).

245. Sumner, *Orators* 119; he is followed by C. Konrad, "Notes on Roman Also-Rans," in J. Linderski (ed.), *Imperium Sine Fine: T. Robert S. Broughton and the Roman Republic* (Stuttgart 1996) 104. It was in this praetorship that Gratidianus' edict on the testing of coinage for forgery and debasement is said to have anticipated a joint declaration of the tribunes and his *collegium praetorium* on that matter (Cic. *Off.* 3.80–81 with full sources on this popular act in *MRR* II 57).

246. *Orators* 118f, dismissing the evidence of Firmicus Maternus in n. 244 above. See further Konrad, *Imperium sine fine* 104 (accepting this year for Gratidianus as *pr.* II).

247. *Per.* 89; full sources in *MRR* II 72, with E. Badian, *JRS* 57 (1967) 227f on his name (on which see also D. R. Shackleton Bailey, *Onomasticon to Cicero's Speeches* [Norman, Okla., 1988] 63, *MRR* III 130) and status. He was probably not of senatorial descent (cf. D.C. 30–35 F 108.1).

248. Sumner, *Orators* 106f, on Vell. 2.27.6 and App. *BC* 1.101.471.

249. Reported in *BC* 1.100.466 (text cited in ch. 11 n. 26). Indeed, throughout this general section of the *Bellum Civile* Appian seems particularly keen to comment on the Republican institutions he finds familiar: note *BC* 1.97.452 (Appian's autopsy of a Sullan

S.C.); 98.459 (Sulla the first dictator in "400 years"); 100.467 (Appian's speculation whether Sulla was responsible for attaching the tribunate to the Senate, "as it is now"); 103.479 (another false parallel from his own day, this time regarding the consulship); cf. 38.172 (an anachronistic interpretation of ἀνθύπατοι in Italy).

250. *Brut.* 178 "Afella contionibus aptior quam iudiciis."

251. Note Alexander, *Trials* nos. 5 (141 B.C., the *cos.* Cn. Servilius Caepio), 10 (138 B.C., the *coss.* P. Cornelius Scipio Nasica Serapio and D. Iunius Brutus), and 15–17, cf. 19 (132 B.C., the *coss.* P. Popillius Laenas, P. Rupilius), and W. Kunkel, *Staatsordnung und Staatspraxis der römischen Republik: Die Magistratur* (Munich 1995) 236 with n. 472 on the *quaestiones* conducted by the *cos.* L. Opimius in 121. For an exception, see no. 25 (123 B.C., the *tr. pl.* C. Gracchus' prosecution of the *cos.* 132 for the extraordinary *quaestiones* of his consulship).

252. The Vestal Aemilia was condemned on 18 Dec.; Marcia and Licinia were acquitted, the latter on 20 Dec.. See Alexander, *Trials* nos. 38–40, for the sources for the trial of 114, esp. Macr. 1.10.5 for the calendar dates. Sources for L. Cassius Longinus Ravilla and his *quaestio* in 113 can be found in *Trials* nos. 41–43.

253. Asc. pp. 45–46 C (also providing a general framework for what follows below).

254. *N.D.* 3.74.

255. See D.C. 26 F 87.1; also V. Max. 3.7.9 (M. Antonius) "quaestor proficiscens in Asiam . . . litteris certior incesti se postulatum apud L. Cassium praetorem . . . cum id uitare beneficio legis Memmiae liceret . . . in urbem tamen recurrit" with 6.8.1 (for the *iudices*), cf. Oros. 5.15.22. There is the disturbing possibility that Valerius may be doubly anachronistic: in 111 there is not only a C. Memmius as tribune (see *MRR* I 537 n. 4) but an L. Cassius Longinus as praetor in the city (Sal. *Jug.* 32–33). However, Valerius Maximus brings in L. Cassius Longinus Ravilla elsewhere to demonstrate *severitas* (8.1 *damn.* 7), and so I accept his report on the president and the law. One wonders why the quaestor P. Clodius Pulcher could not plead protection under the Memmian law in 61 when he was prosecuted "non aliter quam de incestu" (*Schol. Bob.* p. 89 St.) for violating the Bona Dea ceremony (discussed in 11.9.2); probably the law establishing that latter *quaestio* removed all such exemptions. On the prosecution of M. Antonius while a quaestor in office, see E. J. Weinrib, *Phoenix* 22 (1968) 37–38; cf. E. S. Gruen, *RhM* 111 (1968) 61, who steers around the difficulty by suggesting Antonius was quaestor 114, and set out for Asia *pro quaestore* in 113. On the equestrian *iudices*, see Gruen, *Roman Politics* 131f with the bibliography in 131 n. 145. For the possible prosecution of a Ser. Fulvius Flaccus (the *cos.* 135?) in this *quaestio* (Alexander, *Trials* no. 44) see *Roman Politics* 130 n. 41; also Shackleton Bailey, *Onomasticon to Cicero's Treatises* 33 (doubting identification with the consular).

256. See Cic. *S. Rosc.* 85, *Ver.* 2.3.137 and 146; cf. Sen. *Ep.* 97.6 ("iudices Clodiani," in the Bona Dea trial of 61 B.C.).

257. V. Max. 3.7.9 (cited in n. 255 above); Münzer, *RE* s.v. *Cassius* 72 col. 1742.

258. See Alexander, *Trials* no. 49, esp. Sal. *Jug.* 32.1 and 5. Sumner (*Orators* 49–50) adduces the latter of these passages and other points to support the possibility that this praetor's father was *cos.* 127. E. Badian, *Chiron* 20 (1990) 386 adds "immediate consular descent is not unlikely, but cannot be proved."

259. *Roman Politics* 141.

260. See Alexander, *Trials* nos. 52–57. For the three *quaesitores*, who included M. Scaurus: Sal. *Jug.* 40.4; cf. Cic. *de Orat.* 2.283 (Scaurus defends the *cos.* L. Calpurnius Bestia in another court). Voting by *iudices*: *Brut.* 128 ("Gracchani iudices," probably here as a political term, not necessarily *equites*), *Planc.* 70 (equating these *iudices* with "parricidae patriae"). For a full study of this *quaestio* (with previous bibliography), see G. Farney, *MAAR* 42 (1998) 83–97.

261. Cf. Cic. *Brut.* 128.

262. *Brut.* 127.

263. *Imperium Sine Fine* 107. By 109 he might have reached the requisite age for the consulship: see the observations of Sumner, *Orators* 72–74 ("born between 153 and 150," with a firm terminus of 149).

264. *MAAR* 42 (1998) 83–97, emphasizing Sal. *Jug.* 65.5 "ea tempestate plebs nobilitate fusa per legem Mamiliam novos extollebat."

265. See *Brut.* 236, and also 3, 307, 324, 328, 332. (I thank Prof. John Morgan for this observation.)

266. To judge from the terminus for his date of birth and Cicero's formulation at *Brut.* 128 (see nn. 262–263 above).

267. Sources in Alexander, *Trials* no. 65, of which see esp. Cic. *N.D.* 3.74 (fame), Oros. 5.15.25 "magna quaestio . . . Romae acta est," D.C. 26 F 90, cf. *Vir. ill.* 73.5 (convictions).

268. See D.S. 36.15.1–3 (esp. 15.1 τοῦ . . . ἀγῶνος . . . δημοσίου καὶ μεγάλου) with Alexander, *Trials* no. 74.

269. For sources on this *lex*, see *MRR* II 11 (but omit Cic. *Sest.* 30). For the scope of the law, see E. Badian, *JRS* 63 (1973) 127–128. On Alexander, *Trials* no. 89 (the prosecution of T. Matrinius of Spoletium, commonly but erroneously thought to be a trial under the *lex Licinia Mucia*), see Badian, *Historia* 18 (1969) 490–491, *DArch* 4–5 (1970–1971) 406–407.

270. See Alexander, *Trials* 100–108 (first phase) and 109–110 (second phase), with the study of E. Badian, *Historia* 18 (1969) 446–491. For the charge, see esp. Asc. p. 22 C. Equestrian *iudices* in 90: App. *BC* 1.37.165. Only *iudicium* operating when Cicero came to the forum in 90: Cic. *Brut.* 304. Reconstitution under the *lex Plotia*: Cic. *Corn.* I F 53 Crawford[2] with Asc. p. 79. On the question of what form the *quaestio* took, see Alexander, *Trials* p. 53. Alexander is unconvincing in his view that it was *apud populum* until the *lex Plotia*. All the evidence suggesting the involvement in the People in this process comes from the case of M. Aemilius Scaurus (*Trials* no. 100), and there each of the relevant passages (Asc. p. 22 C, V. Max. 3.7.8, *Vir. ill.* 72.11) fits better the circumstances of a *contio* (i.e., as the run-up to a prosecution) than an actual trial. *Contiones* are often described in language reminiscent of a trial (see, e.g., Cic. *Off.* 3.79) The item (Asc. p. 22 C) that M. Scaurus' *consilium* of friends advised him not to expose himself to the "invidia populi" is just one of several indications in our sources that Varius had summoned him merely to a *contio*. Another is that for no other "trial" under the *lex Varia* can Alexander list Q. Varius as prosecutor.

271. Three successful prosecutions are recorded under the *lex Varia* for the year 90 B.C.: Alexander, *Trials* no. 104 (the cos. 111 L. Calpurnius Bestia), 105 (the orator C. Aurelius Cotta), 102 (a Mummius Achaicus, on whom see E. Badian, *Historia* 18 [1969] 469 n. 65). Asconius (p. 73 C) says that "many" were unfairly condemned.

Notes to Chapter 11

1. Sources in *MRR* II 66–67, 74, of which see esp. App. *BC* 1.98.456–99.462 for the circumstances of Sulla's appointment as dictator; Degrassi, *Inscr. Ital.* XIII 1 84f with 637 on the triumph; ch. 2 n. 107 above on the *magister equitum*; and 2.2.2 on the lictors (App. *BC* 1.100.465 with 104.484 shows that as dictator Sulla also had a bodyguard). There soon followed the triumphs of L. Licinius Murena—whom Sulla had recalled from Asia (14.5.9)—and Pompey from Africa, the latter on 12 Mar. 81 (14.3.3). C. Valerius Flaccus, who had *imperium* continuously from his consulship of 93, must have triumphed from Celtiberia and Gaul in this year as well (see *Inscr. Ital.* XIII 1 563 for sources and discussion). For a brief overview (with sources) of Sulla's reforms see W. Kunkel, *Staatsordnung und Staatspraxis der römischen Republik: Die Magistratur* (Munich 1995) 702–711; on the general tendencies, see, above, all E. Badian, *Lucius Sulla: The Deadly Reformer* (Sydney 1970) 20–27.

T. Hantos, *Res Publica Constituta: Die Verfassung des Dictators Sulla* (Stuttgart 1988) is a detailed study that also carefully collects the most important earlier views.

2. MRR II 73 notes 1–2 discuss what chronological pointers we have. Appian has the consular election notice immediately follow Sulla's invitation of athletes to Italy (*BC* 1.99.464)—for his *ludi Sullani* of 26 Oct.–1 Nov. 81 (thus rightly E. Gabba, *Appiani Bellorum Civilium Liber Primus: Introduzione, testo critico e commento* ([Florence 1958] ad loc.)—and indicates that it was as dictator that Sulla held the *comitia* (1.100.465, on which basis Gabba dates the elections to Dec. 82). But that is all we have to go on; and no source mentions elections of the other magistrates (F. Hurlet, *La dictature de Sylla* [Rome 1993] 160 with n. 123). On the dictator's relation to the consuls M. Tullius Decula and Cn. Cornelius Dolabella, see App. *BC* 1.100.465.

3. *Quinct.* 30, with Gel. 15.28.3 dating the *sponsio* that followed (Alexander, *Trials* no. 126) by the names of the *coss.* 81.

4. See RDGE 18 line 90 (the *S.C. de Stratonicensibus*) with the explanation of P. Viereck cited on p. 110 n. 3 ("magistratus militaris et extraordinarius"). Cf. also T. E. Kinsey, *M. Tulli Ciceronis: Pro P. Quinctio oratio* (Sydney 1971) 94f, who is at a loss to explain why P. Quinctius was inactive against his adversary Naevius for that full eighteen-month period.

5. See CIL I² 587 = RS I 14 (year 81) lines 10, 22, 26, etc. with J. Keil, WS 24 (1902) 548–551.

6. On the *quaestores urbani*, see the exposition of Mommsen, *St.-R.* II³ 535–557. If this hypothesis is accepted, it would provide a precedent for Caesar's dictatorship of 45 (on which see Kunkel, *Staatsordnung* 276), in which he appointed *praefecti* to do the work of the lower magistrates, delaying the elections—for significantly enhanced colleges (MRR II 305–306)—until his return from his Spanish campaign.

7. On Mam. Lepidus, see Cic. *Off.* 2.58 with T. R. S. Broughton, *Candidates Defeated in Roman Elections: Some Ancient Roman "Also-Rans"* (Philadelphia 1991) 6. In general on the individuals who must be fitted into the praetorian *fasti* by 80, see C. F. Konrad, *CPh* 84 (1989) 124f.

8. For a full study of the effects of the Social and Civil wars on Rome's administration of her territorial *provinciae*, see E. Badian, *PACA* 1 (1958) 1–18 = *Studies in Greek and Roman History* (Oxford 1964) 71–104.

9. Vell. Pat. 2.89.3. Ten praetors were introduced for 46 (D.C. 42.51.3), fourteen for 45 (43.47.2); and sixteen for 44 (43.49.1, cf. 51.4). Caesar must have been aiming for sixteen all along. The most remarkable increase is the jump from ten to fourteen, the first time to date that the number of praetors was not increased by a single pair.

10. The praetorships of A.D. 15: Vell. 2.124.4. Julius Caesar in 47 B.C.: D.C. 42.51.3 ὑπὲρ τὸ νενομισμένον.

11. *Dig.* 1.2.2.32 "Cornelius Sulla quaestiones publicas constituit, veluti de falso, de parricidio, de sicariis, et praetores quattuor adiecit. deinde C. Iulius Caesar duos praetores . . . constituit. ita duodecim praetores . . . creati." On Sulla's expansion of the college of praetors to eight see Mommsen, *St.-R.* II³ 200 n. 2.

12. Cicero says that seven of the eight praetors of 57 supported his recall from exile: see *Mil.* 39 with *Att.* 4.1.6, *Pis.* 35, *Sest.* 87, and Asc. 11 C.

13. Pace J. D. Cloud, *LCM* 13.5 (1988) 69, who suggests as a possibility that "there had to be a minimum of eight praetors, but the Senate could permit up to ten to stand for office when need arose." It is most unlikely that Sulla would have introduced such a measure. Unlike his other administrative reforms (discussed below), this would have had absolutely no direct precedent. See also below in text on *ambitus*.

14. Vell. 2.16.2–3. The date must be prior to 81: leaving aside other considerations, there is no room for either Magius in the college of that year. See also Appendix B n. 302.

15. As Prof. Badian has suggested to me. For the pre-Sullan electoral calendar, see Mommsen, *St.-R.* I³ 583 n. 2 (noting the shortage of direct evidence). Unfortunately, in this period triumph dates (such as Degrassi, *Inscr. Ital.* XIII 1 84f under the years 107 and 88, where we have late October triumphs respectively for a returned consul and a probable consular candidate for the following years) cannot be brought to bear (cf. the remarks of J. Linderski, *Roman Questions: Selected Papers* [Stuttgart 1995] 94 on place of election), though it stands to reason that an *imperator* who wanted a consulship would celebrate his triumph before the elections rather than afterward. Some evidence (mostly from years when major wars were in progress) tends to support Mommsen's suggestion of November. For consular elections late in the year see Sal. *Jug.* 29.7 (in 111 for 110) and App. *BC* 1.51.226 (elections in winter 89 for 88). But Plu. *Mar.* 5.5 speaks of praetorian elections for 116 being held in the heat; see also Sal. *Jug.* 44.3 (those for 108 early enough to impinge on the campaigning season in Numidia); App. *BC* 1.32.148 (said to be held on 9 Dec. 100 for 99, but see Gabba, *Commento* ad. loc. and E. Badian, *Chiron* 14 (1984) 102–107, 123f). The evidence for post-Sullan elections (much fuller and more coherent) is assembled at *St.-R.* I³ 584 n. 5.

16. In the one instance in this period where we can check—the consular elections for 63 B.C.—there were in the end seven candidates for the two consular places, including two patricians, two plebeian *nobiles*—and a praetor of the year 75 (obviously not his first try at the higher office). See Asc. p. 82 C with Broughton, *Candidates Defeated* 2–3.

17. *Schol. Bob.* p. 78 St. The existence of this law has been doubted; but see the discussions of Linderski, *Roman Questions* 112; E. Bauerle, "Procuring an Election: *Ambitus* in the Roman Republic 432–49 B.C." (diss. Univ. of Michigan, Ann Arbor, 1990) 47–49; P. Nadig, *Ardet Ambitus: Untersuchungen zum Phänomen der Wahlbestechungen in der römischen Republik* (Frankfurt a. M. 1997) 31–33.

18. But the sample is skewed by a rash of prosecutions for electoral offences in the last years of our period. See M. C. Alexander, *Trials in the Late Roman Republic* (Toronto 1990) nos. 190 (68 B.C., aborted); 200 and 201 (66 B.C., condemnation); 224 (63 B.C., acquittal); 248 (59 B.C., dismissed); 298, 299, 300, 301, and 304 (54 B.C., all of uncertain outcome except the last, which was dropped); eight separate trials in the years 52–51, many under a special court (nos. 310, 319 [a dubious prosecution of M. Scaurus—see G. S. Bucher, *Historia* 44 [1995] 396–421], 320–322, 329, 330, 333), and no. 345 (50 B.C.); cf. also the trials *de sodaliciis* nos. 311 (52 B.C.) and 331 (51 B.C.). For a suggestion that the census of 70–69—which enrolled almost twice as many new citizens as that of 86—marked a turning point in the history of *ambitus*, see T. Wallinga, *RIDA* 41 (1994) 435–438, esp. 437 ("suddenly, a large number of new voters without any ties of loyalty became available to candidates").

19. See Cic. *Q. fr.* 3.1.16 (Sept. 54), *Mil.* 42, and many other instances.

20. To take only the reasonably certain cases, see Alexander, *Trials* nos. 143 (75 B.C., dropped); 214 (64 B.C., defendant evidently acquitted); 274 (56, apparently dropped); 268 and 269 (56 B.C., acquittal in second trial); 323 (52 B.C., eventually condemned); cf. also no. 292 (a trial *de sodaliciis* of an ex-praetor in 54 B.C., resulting in acquittal). Trials of candidates for subpraetorian offices are scattered throughout this period: see the chart in Nadig, *Ardet Ambitus* 210–211. The example of C. Iulius Caesar (*pr.* 62), though an extreme case, shows that a politician might incur substantial debts even by the time of the praetorship: see Suet. *Jul.* 11.8, Plu. *Caes.* 11.1 and *Crass.* 7.6, App. *BC* 2.8.26 for Caesar's situation in early 61. Cf. also Cicero's attack on C. Verres at *Ver.* 2.1.101 and 4.45 with Nadig, *Ardet Ambitus* 188–189. I should note that we find prosecutions for *ambitus* in the praetorian elections also before Sulla: see Alexander, *Trials* nos. 36 (C. Marius in 116 B.C.) and 107 (condemnation of a *pr. des.* P. Sextius by 81 B.C., on which see ch. 10 n. 66 above). Those of a few consular candidates (*Trials* no. 34–35, 116 B.C.; perhaps nos. 58, 109 B.C., and 95, 92 B.C.) and a sitting censor (no. 83, 97 B.C.) constitute the rest of the known pre-Sullan *ambitus* cases.

21. See Nadig, *Ardet Ambitus* 33–71, 76–80, 214–218 for evidence on the *lex Antia sumptuaria* (ca. 71–68 B.C.), a law ca. 67 banning the use of *nomenclatores*, the consular *lex Calpurnia de ambitu* of 67, the *lex Fabia de numero sectatorum* of ca. 67–64, the consular *lex Tullia de ambitu* of 63, the consular *lex Licinia de sodaliciis* of 55, and the consular *lex Pompeia de ambitu* of 52, as well as additional proposals from the 60s and 50s not enacted into law. For an excellent short general sketch, see Linderski, *Roman Questions* 112–114.

22. See E. S. Gruen, *The Last Generation of the Roman Republic* (Berkeley 1974) 160–161 for a roster.

23. Cic. *Q. fr.* 2.8(7).3, reporting a defeated rider to an *S.C. de ambitu* moved by the consular L. Afranius; see also Plu. *Cat. Mi.* 42.2–7 for a description of the praetorian *comitia* of that year (though erroneously placing the repudiation of the rider before the elections). For discussion, see F. X. Ryan, *Athenaeum* 82 [72] (1992) 511; Nadig, *Ardet Ambitus* 89f (with 89 n. 320 reporting views on the chronology) and 186; cf. Broughton, *Candidates Defeated* 37. Gruen (*Last Generation* 167) argues from the lack of evidence relative to the consular contests of this period that generally "praetorian elections were untroubled by tumult or political clash."

24. Contra G. Rotondi, *Leges Publicae Populi Romani* (Milan 1912) 351 (providing sources on this *cursus* law, but placing it at the beginning of Sulla's dictatorship).

25. See Cic. *Planc.* 52, cited by E. Badian, *JRS* 58 (1968) 246. Badian's suggestion that Sulla allowed patricians to advance to the praetorship at a somewhat quicker rate than plebeians (*Studies* 140–156) offers a good solution to some thorny prosopographical problems, but falls short of definite proof: see the remarks of G. V. Sumner, *The Orators in Cicero's Brutus: Prosopography and Chronology* (Toronto 1973) 134–138.

26. *BC* 1.100.466 καὶ στρατηγεῖν ἀπεῖπε, πρὶν ταμιεῦσαι, καὶ ὑπατεύειν, πρὶν στρατηγῆσαι, καὶ τὴν ἀρχὴν τὴν αὐτὴν αὖθις ἄρχειν ἐκώλυσε, πρὶν ἔτη δέκα διαγενέσθαι. A good summary of the Sullan *cursus* legislation can be found in Sumner, *Orators* 7–10, which removes the need for extended discussion here.

27. A C. Cosconius was *pr.* 89 and II 79 or 78—an apparent example of the ten-year "rule" (especially if one counts inclusively). But see the discussion in 11.8.1, and note P. Varinius, *pr.* 73 and II 66. If Varinius was expelled from the Senate in 70 (see 11.8.6 for his disastrous first praetorship), this may have constituted an exemption.

28. Cf. 10.5.8 with *Per.* 89 for the *contio* Sulla needed to call after the murder.

29. See M. Palicanus (*tr. pl.* 71, *pr.* 69), Q. Cornificius (*tr. pl.* 69 and *pr.* by 66), C. Antonius (*tr. pl.* 68—surely—and *pr.* 66), P. Globulus (*tr. pl.* 67, *pr.* 64), perhaps T. Labienus (*tr. pl.* 63, *pr.* by 59), then Q. Metellus Nepos (*tr. pl.* 62, *pr.* 60), Q. Calenus (*tr. pl.* 61, *pr.* 59), L. Flavius (*tr. pl.* 60, *pr.* 58), Q. Ancharius (*tr. pl.* 59, *pr.* 56), Cn. Calvinus (*tr. pl.* 59, *pr.* 56), T. Milo (*tr. pl.* 57, *pr.* 55), and P. Sestius (*tr. pl.* 57, *pr.* 55). These were the lucky ones, as Cic. *Sest.* 113 makes clear—noting in 56 B.C. that just two of the ten tribunes of the year 59 thus far had reached the praetorship (though eventually at least five were to do so). On the consular law of 75 that permitted tribunes to stand for higher office, see *MRR* II 96.

30. C. Cosconius (*tr. pl.* 59, *aed.* 57, *pr.* perhaps 54) and A. Plautius (*tr. pl.* 56, *aed. cur.* 54, *pr.* 51).

31. For longer intervals see L. Quinctius (*tr. pl.* 74, *pr.* 67), C. Macer (*tr. pl.* 73, *pr.* before 67), A. Gabinius (*tr. pl.* 67, *leg.* in the east, then *pr.* 61), C. Memmius (*tr. pl.* 66, *pr.* 58), T. Balbus (*tr. pl.* 63, *pr.* 58), L. Rufus (*tr. pl.* 63, *pr.* 57), L. Bestia (*tr. pl.* 62, *aed.* probably 58, and *pr. cand.* for 56—Broughton, *MRR* II 189, *Candidates Defeated* 35–36; F. X. Ryan, *Athenaeum* 85 [75] [1997] 258), M. Cato (*tr. pl.* 62, *pr. cand.* for 55 *suo anno*, and *pr.* 54, on whom see Broughton, *Candidates Defeated* 37), C. Cornutus (*tr. pl.* 61, *pr.* 57), P. Vatinius (*tr. pl.* 59, *pr.* 55), P. Pulcher (*tr. pl.* 58, *aed.* 56, *pr. cand.* for 52, just a year later than

suus annus), M. Peducaenus (*tr. pl.* 57, *pr.* 50), P. Lupus (*tr. pl.* 56, *pr.* 49), L. Fabatus (*tr. pl.* 55, *pr.* 49), and A. Allienus (*tr. pl.* 55, *pr.* 49).

32. Note, e.g., C. Labeo Macerio (*tr. pl.* 131 or 130, *pr.* 122), M. Pennus (*tr. pl.* 126, *pr. cand.* ca. 116/5, on whom see F. X. Ryan ap. C. Konrad, "Notes on Roman Also-Rans," in J. Linderski [ed.], *Imperium Sine Fine: T. Robert S. Broughton and the Roman Republic* [Stuttgart 1996] 106f), C. Norbanus (*tr. pl.* 103, *pr.* by 91), Q. Rufus (surely *tr. pl.* 100, and then *pr.* 91). The praetorship in 79 of Q. Calidius (*tr. pl.* 99, or just possibly 98) is due to special circumstances: see Cic. *Planc.* 69, V. Max. 5.2.7.

33. Ex-curule aediles: L. Lucullus, *aed.* 79, *pr.* 78; M. Varro Lucullus, *aed.* 79, *pr.* 76; M. Cestianus, *aed.* 67, perhaps *pr.* 64; M. Bibulus, *aed.* 65, *pr.* 62; C. Caesar, *aed.* 65, *pr.* 62; P. Lentulus Spinther, *aed.* 63, *pr.* 60; L. Ahenobarbus, *aed.* 61, *pr.* 58; M. Scaurus, *aed.* 58, *pr.* 56; P. Hypsaeus, *aed.* 58, *pr.* perhaps 55. The career of Q. Maximus (*aed. cur.* 57) was retarded, only reaching the praetorship of 48 under Caesar. Ex-plebeian aediles: M. Cicero, *aed.* 69, *pr.* 66; M. Caesonius, *aed.* 69, *pr.* 66; Q. Gallius, *aed.* 67, *pr.* 65; Q. Cicero, *aed.* 65, *pr.* 62; C. Balbus, *aed.* 65, *pr.* 62; P. Crassus Dives, *aed.* 60, *pr.* 57. Q. Naso (*aed.* 67) reached the praetorship by 60, but the precise interval is lacking. Note also Q. Hortalus, *aed.* (plebeian or curule) 75, *pr.* 72; and M. Favonius, *aed.* 53 or 52, *?pr. cand.* for 50.

34. See Appendix B n. 232.

35. On the special conditions in the consular elections for the years 172–158, 103–99, and 86–79 see E. Badian, *Chiron* 20 (1990) 409–413, esp. the chart at 410.

36. Three years: Q. Maximus Servilianus (*cos.* 142), P. Scaevola (*cos.* 133), M. Perperna (*cos.* 130), Cn. Octavius (*cos.* 128), Q. Scaevola (*cos.* 117), Q. Maximus Eburnus (*cos.* 116), M. Antonius (*cos.* 99), probably C. Flaccus (*cos.* 93), then C. Pulcher (*cos.* 92), L. Cato and Cn. Strabo (*coss.* 89, perhaps in less than a *biennium* after praetorship), Q. Rufus (*cos.* 88). Four years: A. Albinus (*cos.* 151), Q. Maximus Aemilianus (*cos.* 145), L. Opimius (*cos.* 121, after a *repulsa*, on which see Broughton, *Candidates Defeated* 15), probably M. Scaurus (*cos.* 115, on whom see *Candidates Defeated* 7), then L. Longinus (*cos.* 111). Ser. Galba was elected *cos.* 108 three or four years after his praetorship.

37. M.' Manilius (*pr.* ca. 157, *cos.* 149—ca. eight years), L. Piso Caesoninus (*pr.* ca. 156, *cos.* 148—ca. eight), L. Mummius (perhaps *pr.* 155, *cos.* 146—nine), Ser. Galba (*pr.* 151, *cos.* 144—seven), Q. Metellus Macedonicus (*pr.* 148, *cos.* 143—five years, after two *repulsae*, on which see Broughton, *Candidates Defeated* 8–9), C. Laelius (*pr.* 145, *cos.* 140—five years, on which see *Candidates Defeated* 12), L. Lentulus (*pr.* ca. 136, *cos.* 130—ca. six), C. Marius (*pr.* 115, *cos.* I 107—eight), L. Sulla (*pr.* 97, *cos.* I 88—nine years). C. Caldus (*cos.* 94) and L. Cinna (*cos.* 87) each had an interval of at least four years between praetorship and consulship.

38. Three years: M. Lepidus (*cos.* 78), M. Lucullus (*cos.* 73), P. Lentulus Sura (*cos.* 71), M. Crassus (certainly *pr.* no earlier than 73, then *cos.* 70), Q. Hortensius (*cos.* 69), L. Metellus (*cos.* 68), M.' Glabrio (*cos.* 67), both *coss.* 63, L. Murena (*cos.* 62), probably M. Messalla Niger (*cos.* 61), Q. Metellus Celer (*cos.* 60), both *coss.* 59, L. Piso Caesoninus (*cos.* 58), both *coss.* 57, Ap. Pulcher (*cos.* 54), Cn. Calvinus (*cos.* 53), L. Paullus (*cos.* 50). Four years: L. Lucullus (*cos.* 74), probably C. Piso (*cos.* 67), then Cn. Lentulus Marcellinus (*cos.* 56), L. Ahenobarbus (*cos.* 54, on whom see Broughton, *Candidates Defeated* 25 on his exclusion for 55 by the iterating *coss.* 70). Q. Metellus Creticus (*cos.* 69) shows three or four years.

39. Cn. Orestes (*pr.* 77, *cos.* 71), L. Cotta (*pr.* 70, elected *cos.* in a supplementary election for 65, on which see Broughton, *Candidates Defeated* 7–8), L. Iulius Caesar (probably *pr.* ca. 70, *cos.* 64), L. Philippus (*pr.* 62, *cos.* 56).

40. See also M. Pupius Piso Calpurnianus (*pr.* by 71, *cos.* 61), L. Afranius (*pr.* before—probably well before—71, and *cos.* 60), M. Messalla Rufus (perhaps *pr.* 62, *cos.* 53, on whom see F. X. Ryan ap. Konrad in *Imperium Sine Fine* 1–6), and L. Lentulus Crus (*pr.* 58, *cos.* 49).

For superannuated consular candidates who never gain the office, see C. Sacerdos, *pr.* 75 and *cos. cand.* for 63 (Broughton, *Candidates Defeated* 12); L. Turius, perhaps *pr.* 75 or 74 and *cos. cand.* for 64 (*ibid.* 19); Q. Arrius, *pr.* 73 and potential *cos. cand.* for 58 (*ibid.* 23); L. Lucceius, *pr.* 67 and *cos. cand.* for 59 (*ibid.* 13); C. Memmius, *pr.* 58 and *cos. cand.* for 53 (*ibid.* 28); and M. Calidius, *pr.* 57 and *cos. cand.* for 50 and probably also 49 (*ibid.* 10). Note also L. Catilina, *pr.* 68 and *cos. cand.* for 63 and 62 (*ibid.* 16–17).

41. Clear, e.g., from Cic. *Balb.* 61 (56 B.C.), where the Senate is said to have decided already not to supersede Caesar under the *lex Sempronia* in the year 54: see N. J. Woodhead, "A Study of the *Lex Sempronia De Provinciis Consularibus* with Reference to the Roman Constitution and Roman Politics from 123 to 48 B.C." (diss. State University of New York at Albany 1972) 38f.

42. "A Study of the *Lex Sempronia*" 39f; on this point see also J. P. V. D. Balsdon, *JRS* 52 (1962) 139.

43. For an instructive example of how an ex-consul might dally in Rome well into the spring before setting off for his province, see Cic. *Att.* 2.5.2 with *Cael.* 59 (the activities of a *cos.* 60 in Rome up through Apr. 59). Contrast Cic. *Prov.* 36–38 (a theoretical argument predicated on the assumption that ex-consuls were in their provinces by 1 Mar. of the year following their magistracy). On early departures (i.e., before the year of office had elapsed) see J. P. V. D. Balsdon, *JRS* 29 (1939) 61–63.

44. On the timing, see Cic. *Ver.* 2.1.104 (sortition of urban *provincia* in 75 for 74); *Ver.* 1.21 (sortition of praetorian city provinces a few days after consular elections in 70 for 69); *Att.* 3.17.1 (praetorian *provinciae* already drawn well before Sept. 58 for 57).

45. L. Caecilius Metellus (*pr.* 71) already had the *provincia* of Sicily in his year of office (cf. Cic. *Ver.* 2.3.45), and the praetors of 63 also drew their territorial *provinciae* while still magistrates (*Fam.* 5.2.3–4). Yet the praetors of 62 drew their lots not long before 15 Mar. 61 (*Att.* 1.15.1, cf. 1.13.5—here the Bona Dea affair was largely to blame for the delay) and the praetors of 60 had their sortition in the year 59 (*Fam.* 1.9.13 with Caes. *Civ.* 1.22.4). Note also that as of 6 Feb. 56 the praetors of 57 had neither been assigned their quaestors nor received the military resources they would have in their territorial provinces (Cic. *Q. fr.* 2.3.1). For sortition among promagistrates, cf. perhaps also Oros. 5.23.23 "Cosconius [pr. II probably in 79] pro consule sortitus Illyricum"; Vell. 2.59.2 (C. Octavius, pr. 61) "ex eo honore sortitus Macedoniam." But it is improbable that these latter two sources are trying to be technically accurate.

46. *Mar.* 6.2 μετὰ δὲ τὴν στρατηγίαν κλήρῳ λαβὼν τὴν ἐκτὸς Ἰβηρίαν.

47. L. Lucullus, *pr.* 104, then prorogued for Sicily (13.1.3); L. Sulla, *pr. urb.* 97 then *pro cos.* in Cilicia (10.1); C. Flaccus, *pr. urb.* (probably) in 96 then *pro cos.* in Asia (14.5.5); C. Saturninus, *pr. urb.* 94 then *pro cos.* in Macedonia (14.1.3); and L. Gellius, *pr. per.* 94 then *pro cos.* in Asia or Cilicia (14.5.5).

48. It appears that the *cos.* 95 L. Licinius Crassus retained one of the Gauls and his colleague Q. Mucius Scaevola received Asia, each *ex consulatu*: see 10.2.3 and 14.5.4.

49. Whether Sulla's contemporaries realized that the promagistracy had been fully institutionalized is another matter. For the continued omission of promagistracies in *elogia*, note, e.g., *Inscr. Ital.* XIII 3 84 "L. Licinius L.f. Lucullus, cos., pr., aed. cur., q., tr. militum, aug(ur)." Lucullus (*pr.* 78, *cos.* 74) had an *ex praetura* command in Africa in addition to his consular major command against Mithridates (14.4, 14.6.3–4). On the phantom Cornelian law retaining consuls and praetors in Rome during their magistracy, see H. F. Pelham, *Outlines of Roman History* (New York 1900) 238 n. 3, also *Essays on Roman History* (Oxford 1911) 67 n. 4.

50. Aedilician prosecution for capital offences was obviously conceivable in 70 (Cic. *Ver.* 1.51, 2.1.13–14, 5.151, 173, 183).

51. Cf. Cic. *Ver.* 1.38 with Mommsen, *St.-R.* II 326 (arguing that Sulla did away with all tribunician criminal jurisdiction). Among the numerous general statements on Sulla's curtailment of the power of tribunes (collected in *MRR* II 75), see esp. Sal. *Hist.* 1.55.23 M (speech of the *cos.* 78 M. Aemilius Lepidus to the People) "tribuniciam potestatem . . . per arma . . . utique iura et iudicia sibimet extorquerent" and 24 (Sulla's reconstitution of law courts) "ius iudiciumque omnium rerum penes se, quod populi Romani fuit"; cf. Cic. *Ver.* 1.44 (agitation for restoration of tribunician power really a demand for *vera iudicia* in disguise). E. S. Gruen (*Roman Politics and the Criminal Courts, 149–78* B.C. [Cambridge, Mass., 1968] 260) envisages only indirect limits to the judicial powers of tribunes.

52. See Alexander, *Trials* nos. 153 (prosecution of C. Iunius for acts as *iudex quaestionis*) and 154 (prosecution of the ex-juror C. Fiduculanius Falcula).

53. On the *lex Aurelia* of 75, see Asc. p. 67 C.

54. Plutarch (*Pomp.* 47.3, cf. *Caes.* 14.1) explicitly criticizes the consulship of C. Iulius Caesar on this score; see also the remarks of Cicero (*Clu.* 110) on the praetorship of L. Quinctius (*tr. pl.* 74 and then *pr.* probably in 67).

55. All the same, the urban jurisdiction remained the most sought-after *provincia* among praetors: see 12.1.3.

56. For a consul's open use of *maius imperium* against a praetor in this era, see 12.1.2 (77), 12.2.2 (67), 12.2.4 (57). But a particularly obnoxious example is attested already for 115 (12.2.2), an affront to the principle that a praetor was the colleague of the consuls.

57. See esp. 12.1.2 on the year 74 (but stopping short of a veto), also 12.2.4 (the years 70 and 57), and immediately below in text.

58. See 12.2.2 for an instance (difficult to interpret) of a highly visible clash between a tribune and a praetor already in 100 B.C. On tribunes' intervention in the praetors' administration of civil and criminal law in the post-Sullan period, see ch. 12 n. 45 and 12.2.4. For an example of a personal conflict between praetor and tribune, see Asc. p. 47 with D.C. 38.30.1–2 (the *pr.* 58 L. Flavius and the *tr. pl.* P. Clodius fight over custody of Tigranes of Armenia).

59. See Cic. *Off.* 3.80 with 12.3.1 below on the edict of the *pr.* I 85 M. Marius Gratidianus.

60. Cf. Cic. *Planc.* 95 on the *prr.* 62 Q. Cicero and C. Vergilius Balbus, showing praetorian collegiality to be a special bond with practical significance. Note also Caes. *Civ.* 3.16.3, asserting with reference to that same praetorian college Bibulus "inimicitias . . . habebat . . . privatas cum Caesare ex aedilitate et praetura conceptas"—no doubt meant to cast a particularly negative light on Bibulus.

61. Most remarkably in 67 B.C. (D.C. 36.41.1–2), a praetors' work "slowdown" protesting a consul's action, on which see 12.2.2. Cicero (*Q. fr.* 1.2) says that he and "the praetors" of 60 had worked to forestall his brother's prorogation in Asia for a third year. Each of those that helped was probably interested in a vacancy in Asia on his own account, as D. R. Shackleton Bailey (*CEQF* 148) points out. On joint praetorian legislation (promulgated in the agitation for Cicero's recall in 57) see 12.4.3.

62. See, e.g., 12.4.2 on the *prr.* 58 L. Domitius Ahenobarbus and C. Memmius and their attack on Caesar's *acta*; Cic. *Q. fr.* 1.4.4 for Cicero's remarks on the attitude of the praetors of 58 to his exile; also *Att.* 6.8.1 on the political attitude of the praetors for 49. Cf. *Mil.* 24 (Clodius' hypothetical thought process on a colleague he wanted to avoid as praetor).

63. See 12.2.3 with ch. 12 n. 146.

64. Cf. Cic. *Fam.* 1.4.3 (mention in Jan. 56 of the "imbecillitas magistratuum" in the face of violence).

65. Expulsion from the Senate, allegedly for expensive living: Plu. *Cic.* 17.2–3. Iteration of praetorship: see Plu. *Cic.* 17.1 and D.C. 37.30.4 with T. C. Brennan, *Athenaeum* 67 (1989) 481 with n. 68. Full sources on his praetorship of 63 are collected in *MRR* II 166.

66. Cic. *Catil.* 3.6 and 16. In Sallust even Catiline himself is made to complain of Lentulus' idleness (*Cat.* 58.4).

67. See, e.g., Cic. *Sul.* 16, 75–76; *Per.* 102; App. *BC* 2.2.7 (but erroneously considering the conspirator C. Cornelius Cethegus also "a praetor of the city"); Plu. *Cic.* 24.2; Flor. 2.12.3 and 5–6; D.C. 37.30.4; cf. also Luc. 2.541–543.

68. See Cic. *Catil.* 3.15 (explicitly comparing the situtations of Glaucia and Lentulus) with App. *BC* 1.32.145; cf. *Schol. Grov.* p. 284 St. The occasion of Glaucia's (and Saturninus') death was an attempt to pass a plebiscite to overturn the consul C. Marius' decision, taken on the advice of his *consilium*, to disallow this praetor's extraordinary *professio* for the consulship of 99: see E. Badian, *Chiron* 14 (1984) 101–147, esp. 106–121. On Lentulus' status and the difficulties it caused, cf. esp. Sal. *Cat.* 52.13 and 55.6, Vell. 2.34.4 "consularis et praetor iterum"; Plu. *Cic.* 19.6; cf. *Schol. Gron.* p. 284 St. (Cicero) "timet invidiam Lentuli praetoris."

69. Sal. *Cat.* 46.3–6. On the self-incriminating testimony Lentulus and other conspirators produced in this Senate meeting, see esp. Cic. *Catil.* 3.7–12.

70. Cic. *Catil.* 3.13–15, esp. 14 "ut P. Lentulus, cum se praetura abdicasset, in custodiam traderetur" and 15 "magistratu se abdicavit" with *Schol. Gron.* p. 284 St., *Catil.* 4.5 "P. Lentulum se abdicare praetura coegistis"; Sal. *Cat.* 47.3 "senatus decernit, uti abdicato magistratu" ; Plu. *Cic.* 19.1–4; D.C. 37.34.2; cf. App. *BC* 2.5.16. On this expedient in general in the Republic, see E. J. Weinrib, *Phoenix* 22 (1968) 46–47. See also n. 71 below.

71. For the mechanics of the abdication of 63, see esp. Plu. *Cic.* 19.2 and cf. D.C. 37.34.2 ὁ Λέντουλος ἀπειπεῖν τὴν στρατηγίαν ὑπὸ τῆς γερουσίας ἀναγκασθείς. On the oath, cf. *I. Knidos* I 31 Kn. IV lines 31–39. For the laying down of *fasces*, see App. *BC* 1.65.298 (87 B.C.) and 1.104.484 (Sulla's return to private life), and esp. Suet. *Jul.* 16.1 (the praetor Caesar in 62) "dimissis lictoribus abiectaque praetexta" (his abdication was soon reversed). As for the *praetexta*, note that when Pompey created his *legati pro praetore*, he is said to have personally invested them with the requisite insignia (App. *Mith.* 94.432).

72. Sal. *Cat.* 47.3.

73. After his indictment *de vi*, Catiline voluntarily took up residence—for a time—at the house of the *pr.* Q. Metellus Celer (D.C. 37.31.2 and 4). Once the Senate decided to punish the conspiracy in earnest, the city praetors were responsible for putting the other prominent Catilinarians into custody and bringing them to the place of execution: Sal. *Cat.* 55.2, Plu. *Cic.* 19.4, 22.1, App. *BC* 2.5.16–17, cf. 6.22.

74. On this proposal, moved by the *pr. des.* C. Iulius Caesar, see esp. (for Lentulus) Cic. *Catil.* 4.10, Sal. *Cat.* 51.7, Vell. 2.35.3, Suet. *Jul.* 13.1–2.

75. Cic. *Sul.* 30 and 33, Vell. 2.34.3–4, D.C. 38.14.5.

76. Cic. *Catil.* 3.15, cf. 16.

77. Sal. *Cat.* 55.1–6, cf. 57.1; Plu. *Cic.* 22.3; App. *BC* 2.6.22; cf. Juv. 10.286–288.

78. Cic. *Cat.* 3.14 (provocatively in his thanks privileging the praetors over his consular colleague C. Antonius), *Sul.* 82,

79. Explicit in D.C. 38.14.5–6.

80. Sicily: Cic. *Ver.* 2.3.212 with 13.2.2 below for C. Marcellus (*pr.* 80), perhaps *ILLRP* 391 = *CIL* I² 761 for L. Rufus (*pr.* 57). Sardinia: *ILLRP* 393 with 13.2.8 below on M. Scaurus (*pr.* 56). Africa: see Cic. *Cael.* 73 on Q. Rufus (*pr.* 63), and *Fam.* 13.6 prescript for Q. Orca (*pr.* 57). Gallia Transalpina: Caes. *Gal.* 3.20.1, *Per.* 90, and Oros. 5.23.4 for L. Manlius (*pr.* 79). Gallia Cisalpina: Cic. *Fam.* 5.1 and 2 prescripts for Q. Metellus Celer (*pr.* 63), also Nepos ap. Plin. *Nat.* 2.170 and Mela 3.45. Illyricum: Oros. 5.23.23 and Eutrop. 6.4 for C. Cosconius (*pr.* II 79 or 78); Cic. *Fam.* 13.42 prescript for L. Culleolus (*pr.* by 59). It is in fact generally accepted that provincial governors after Sulla, whether *praetorii* or *consulares*, regularly held consular *imperium*: see A. J. Marshall, *ANRW* I 1 (1972) 903.

81. See 15.1.1 on the *pr.* 81 Cn. Cornelius Dolabella and his *ex praetura* command as "pro pr." in Cilica. *ILLRP* 474, which reveals that M. Terentius Varro Lucullus (*pr.* 76 and *cos.* 73) restored Gracchan *termini* as "pro pr(aetore) . . . ex s(enatus) consulto)," has nothing to do with a provincial command. He must have received this duty as a special commission with a grant of *imperium* to match, either before his praetorship or afterward (no promagisterial *provincia* following his peregrine praetorship is known). Similarly the Cn. Egnatius C.f. who had the title *pr(o) pr(aetore)* (*AE* 1988, 555, from Lucus Feroniae) probably had some special commission in Italy, dating sometime to the 70s. He plausibly can be identified with the Cn. Egnatius expelled in (at least) middle age from the Senate in 70: see Cic. *Clu.* 135 with R. Syme, *Roman Papers* I, ed. E. Badian (Oxford 1979) 280–281, and *AE* note ad loc.

82. See *I. Délos* IV 1 1603, honors from the Pisidian town of Prostaenna. That Antonius served under a praetor and not a consul can be inferred from the fact that the consular provinces for 113 and 112 include Macedonia in each year; both consuls would not be in the east.

83. Sources in *MRR* II 175, and cf. 188 for the *lex Iulia de repetundis.*

84. Cic. *Pis.* 50 (translation adapted from that of N. H. Watts, Loeb edition 1931).

85. For these provisions, see Cic. *Fam.* 3.6.3 and 5–6; 12.4.

86. See ch. 5 n. 91.

87. For *testimonia* and discussion, see *RS* II 55.

88. Gran. Lic. 36.11 C.

89. For lists of consuls who did not go to territorial provinces, see J. P. V. D. Balsdon, *JRS* 29 (1939) 63 n. 45; Badian, *Lucius Sulla* 30 n. 81 (fifteen assured cases—including two because of death in office—and eight uncertain). Q. Metellus Celer in 60 threatened it: D.C. 37.50.4–5. *Coss.* of 51 terrified (late in the year) that they will have to fight in Syria (notwithstanding the provisions of the *lex Pompeia* of 52): Cael. *Fam.* 8.10.2.

90. L. Lucceius in 67 (Sardinia): D.C. 36.41.1–2. M. Tullius Cicero in 66: Cic. *Mur.* 42, *Flac.* 87. C. Aquillius in 66: *Att.* 1.1.1. C. Antonius in 66: Q. Cic. *Pet.* 8. Ser. Rufus, *pr.* 65: Cic. *Mur.* 42. Q. Gallius, *pr.* 65: Alexander, *Trials* no. 214 (prosecution in latter half of 64). P. Vatinius, *pr.* 55: cf. *Trials* no. 292 (prosecuted August 54). T. Annius Milo, *pr.* 55: see E. Klebs, *RE* s.v. col. 2273 (in Rome, Sept. 54). M. Porcius Cato, *pr.* 54: Plu. *Cat. Mi.* 45.5. Several more cases can be inferred with some confidence. See Appendix B on C. Calpurnius Piso (*pr.* ?71), C. Orchivius (*pr.* 66), L. Cassius Longinus (*pr.* 66), Q. Voconius Naso (*pr.* by 60), L. Domitius Ahenobarbus (*pr.* 58), Cn. Domitius Calvinus (*pr.* 56), L. Aemilius Paullus (*pr.* 53); and Q. Minucius Thermus, M. Nonius Sufenas, Cn. Tremelius Scrofa, and P. Silius (all *prr.* before 51). See also V. Max. 6.3.3b with Appendix B n. 246 on the *pr.* Cn. Cornelius Scipio who was debarred from Spain, probably ca. 109 (on an entirely different matter).

91. I am leaving the difficult case of Q. Mucius Scaevola (*cos.* 95) out of consideration here: see the discussion at 14.5.4.

92. See Liv. 41.15.6–10 and 42.32.2–3 with 6.2.2 and 7.2.6 above.

93. For the issues involved, see perhaps Cic. *Ver.* 2.1.37, on M. Piso, quaestor to the *cos.* 83 L. Cornelius Scipio Asiaticus, who even in the context of the Civil War did not go so far as to refuse his quaestorian *provincia* formally, but only in practical terms. Cf. also *Ver.* 2.1.38, on the chaos that will result "si nullam religionem sors habebit."

94. See Badian, *Lucius Sulla* 31 n. 82, on the formal background ("presumably by the first century each praetor had already had a *provincia* in the city and could claim that he was not liable to serve again *ex praetura*").

95. It is not that "some praetors did not want a province, and abstained from the lot with the tacit approval of the Senate" (thus J. M. Cobban, *Senate and Provinces, 78–49 B.C.* [Cambridge 1935] 73, reflecting a common view).

96. Rejection of *provincia* as a sign of integrity: Vell. 2.31.1 (Pompey's oath, "cum consul perquam laudabiliter iurasset se in nullam prouinciam ex eo magistratu iturum idque seruasset"), Cic. *Fam.* 2.12.2 (referring to his own decision as *cos.* 63), cf. D.C. 36.41.1–2 (L. Lucceius, a particularly self-serving example, on which see below in text) and Cael. *Fam.* 8.10.2 "sub hac temperantiae existimatione, nolle provinciam." Lightness of decision, based in part on a conviction that provincial achievement is irrelevant: Cic. *Mur.* 42, *Planc.* 66, and cf. (for the general mindset) *Planc.* 13, 63–67 passim and esp. *Fam.* 2.12.2. Refusal of promagisterial *provincia* as self-liberation from external political pressures during one's magistracy: Cic. *Agr.* 2.25–26. Some ambiguity remained on the correctness of this act, as can be seen from the various formulations used to describe these acts: see Cic. *Mur.* 42 "provincias contemni," *Flac.* 87 "in praetermittendis provinciis," *Fam.* 2.12.2 "ex contemnenda . . . ex conservata provincia," 5.2.3 "praetermisisse provinciam," *Fam.* 15.4.13 "provinciam ornatam . . . neglexi." The record (see n. 90 above) suggests that for an ex-praetor to refuse a *provincia* imparted no compelling advantage when running for the consulship. Of our twenty possible instances, only two of the certain examples (M. Cicero and C. Antonius in 66) and four of the dubious cases (C. Piso, *pr.* ?71; L. Ahenobarbus, *pr.* 58; Cn. Calvinus, *pr.* 56; and L. Paullus, *pr.* 50) made it to the higher office.

97. As apparently happened to C. Orchivius (*pr.* 66), Q. Gallius (*pr.* 65), and P. Vatinius (*pr.* 55): see Appendix B nn. 412, 416, 471.

98. Full sources for what follows can be found in W. Drumann and P. Groebe, *Geschichte Roms* (Leipzig 1899–1929) V 452 and 462f. For Cicero as *cos.* 63 exchanging Macedonia for Gallia Cisalpina, and then turning that down see esp. Cic. *Agr.* 1.25–26, *Fam.* 5.2.3, Plu. *Cic.* 12.4, D.C. 37.33.4, cf. Cic. *Att.* 2.1.3 (implying that he did refuse the *provincia* at the very beginning of the year), *Mur.* 42, *Flac.* 87, *Pis.* 5, *Fam.* 2.12.3, 5.5.2, and 15.4.13.

99. Cic. *Agr.* 1.26 (translation adapted from that of J. H. Freese in the Loeb edition of 1930).

100. Cic. *Pis.* 5, *Fam.* 15.4.13, *Phil.* 11.23. Cicero had agreed on the switch already by the time of his second speech *contra Rullum* (i.e., the very start of 63): see *Agr.* 2.103 with W. Allen, Jr., *TAPhA* 83 (1952) 235.

101. Cicero's later *contio*: Cic. *Att.* 2.1.3 "cum provinciam in contione deposui," *Pis.* 5 "provinciam Galliam . . . in contione deposui," cf. *Fam.* 5.2.3 "me . . . praetermisisse provinciam." The date of Cicero's speech in the *contio* cannot be closely determined. But it is clear that it came after the squabble regarding the sons of the proscribed who wanted to stand in the elections for 62 (see *Att.* 2.1.3 with *Pis.* 4), and shortly before the praetorian sortition for 62 (*Fam.* 5.2.3). It was certainly previous to his First Catilinarian of 8 Nov. 63 (see *Att.* 2.1.3).

102. As the *tr. pl.* L. Flavius threatened to do to the *cos.* Q. Metellus Celer in 60: see D.C. 37.50.4.

103. D.C. 36.41.1.

104. For this and what follows, see D.C. 40.45.4–5. On the length of the *interregnum*, see Linderski, *Roman Questions* 233 n. 9.

105. Revival of the office of dictator was obviously a real fear of the post-Sullan era. Already in 65 B.C. we hear of rumors that Crassus was to be dictator and C. Iulius Caesar his *magister equitum* (Suet. *Jul.* 9.1–2, citing sources, some contemporary). Leaving aside D.C. 36.33 (a speech given to Q. Lutatius Catulus against the *lex Gabinia* in 67) and Cic. *Q. fr.* 1.2.15 (Pompey publicly called a "privatus dictator" in 59), we find the notion that Pompey might be named dictator considered a real possibility starting in fall of the year 54 (E. Fantham, *Historia* 24 [1975] 442 n. 41, providing references). See in general Drumann and Groebe, *Geschichte Roms* IV 531–533.

106. Cf. Plu. *Pomp.* 54.2 for his motives; also Obseq. 63 (53 B.C.) "propter dictaturam Pompeii ingens seditio in urbe fuit."

107. D.C. 40.46.1–3, cf. also 40.30.1.

108. See Cic. *Fam.* 2.15.4 "senatum eos voluisse provinciis praeesse qui antea non prae-fuissent" and *Att.* 6.6.3 with n. 96 above. Pace G. V. Sumner (*Phoenix* 25 [1971] 268 n. 41) and others (see Additional Note XV, on T. Furfanus Postumus), there is no good reason to think that this measure (which was merely an *S.C.*, not a *lex*) kept praetors of 53 from taking up territorial provinces *ex praetura*. The consuls of 54 had attempted to carry a SC of some sort dealing with the (territorial) provinces (Cic. *Att.* 4.16.5), which Cobban, *Senate and Provinces* 82, plausibly took as part of this same reform movement.

109. On this law see in general the careful study of A. J. Marshall, ANRW I 1 (1972) 887–921, esp. 891–892 for a summary of modern views on Pompey's motives (going beyond administrative concerns) and 901 n. 56 for the short lifespan of his law.

110. Reliable evidence on the precise length is lacking. D.C. 40.30.1 speaks of a five-year interval for both ex-praetors and ex-consuls—but in a passage where he says M. Bibulus (*cos.* 59) by going to Syria in 51 violated it! That there was an interval for ex-consuls can be inferred from Cael. *Fam.* 8.10.3 (17 Nov. 51), cf. *Att.* 6.1.7 (24 Feb. 50), where it is suspected that L. Aemilius Paullus (*cos.* 50) might break it by proceeding immediately to a province. Broughton at first suggested (*MRR* II 240 n. 1) that the Pompeian law did not apply to the magistrates of 52, but then (III 96 and 148–149) changed his mind. Since it was primarily an anti-*ambitus* measure, immediate application seems most likely, but the fact that we cannot name a single praetor for 52 prevents certainty.

111. See Cic. *Fam.* 3.2.1–2 "ex senatus consulto provinciam esse habendam" and the "senatus auctoritas" of Sept. 51 (making provisions for summer 50) reported by Cael. *Fam.* 8.8.8 with Badian, *Lucius Sulla* 31 n. 83 ("Pompey's law . . . seems to have avoided compulsion; but the Senate expressed strong views, which could not reasonably be resisted").

112. We have no information on Cn. Cornelius Lentulus Marcellinus (*cos.* 56). Certain are L. Marcius Philippus (*cos.* 56), L. Domitius Ahenobarbus (*cos.* 54) (on these cf. Caes. *Civ.* 1.6), and the *coss.* 53 Cn. Domitius Calvinus and M. Valerius Messalla Rufus.

113. See Appendix B on Cn. Domitius Calvinus (*pr.* 56), P. Vatinius and T. Annius Milo (*prr.* 55), M. Porcius Cato (*pr.* 54), and L. Aemilius Lepidus Paullus (*pr.* 53).

114. Cf. Cael. *Fam.* 8.8.8 (with numerous mentions of sortition). This passage shows that for 50, the consular *provinciae* were Cilicia and Syria while the praetorian *provinciae* were (evidently) Sicily, Sardinia, Macedonia, Africa, Asia, Bithynia, Crete, and Cyrene; at the time Pompey had the Spains and Caesar the Gauls. For the lot, see also Plu. *Cic.* 36.1 (used in 51), Caes. *Civ.* 1.6.5 (not used for consular *provinciae* in 49).

115. See Additional Note XV on Voconius. On the selection of specifically Cicero and Bibulus, see A. J. Marshall, ANRW I 1 (1972) 888 n. 4.

116. Inferred from Cael. *Fam.* 8.8.8, the provisions for finding a pool of ex-praetors equivalent in number to the territorial *provinciae* that had to be filled for 50.

117. See esp. Caes. *Civ.* 1.6.6 (the year 49) "praetores mittuntur . . . neque exspectant—quod superioribus annis acciderat—ut de eorum imperio ad populum feratur paludatique votis nuncupatis exeant." In general, see the discussion of A. J. Marshall, ANRW I 1 (1972) 894–895, esp. 894 n. 27 on the Caesar passage.

118. Abundantly clear in general from Cael. *Fam.* 8.8.8, and in particular from the status of Q. Minucius Thermus in Asia (Cic. *Fam.* 13.53–57 prescripts) and P. Silius in Bithynia/Pontus (*Fam.* 13.61–65), both *pro praetore* in 51/50.

119. *IGRP* IV 401 (Pergamum) Λεύκιον Ἀντώνιον Μαάρκου υἱὸν ταμίαν καὶ ἀντι-στράτηγον and J. *AJ* 14.235 Λούκιος Ἀντώνιος Μάρκου υἱὸς ἀντιταμίας καὶ ἀντιστράτηγος. This *quaestor/pro quaestore pro praetore* is the future *cos.* 41; for his service in Asia, see further D. Magie, *Roman Rule in Asia Minor* (Princeton 1950) II 1256 n. 76. His superior was Q. Minucius Thermus, definitely "pro pr." in Asia (see n. 118 above) in 51/50. On his gover-

norship see 14.6.8. Minucius was at Ephesus in late July 51 (Cic. *Att.* 5.13.2), and was set to depart from Asia in May of the following year (*Fam.* 2.18), on which occasion Cicero candidly advised him to leave his quaestor "C." Antonius in charge of province (*Fam.* 2.18.2–3). But here Lucius and not Gaius is meant: see D. R. Shackleton Bailey, *CEF* I 455.

120. As argued by A. J. Marshall, ANRW I 1 (1972) 891, 895–901, 910–912 (e.g., 912 "a uniform requirement which did not allow a decision based on assessment of the needs of those provinces"). The case of C. Considius Longus, who is said to have left Africa not in compliance of the *lex Pompeia* but to run for consul 49 (discussed in 14.4), does not support Marshall's hypothesis.

121. For the S.C. of 51 that pressed Cicero into service, see A. J. Marshall, ANRW I 1 (1972) 892–893. On the "one-year" provision, contrast the increasing shrillness of Cic. *Fam.* 15.9.2 (early Sep. 51), 15.14.5 (ca. 14 Oct. 51, "hanc provinciam, quam et senatus et populus annuam esse voluit"), 2.12.1 (after early May 50), *Att.* 6.5.3 (26 June 50, "mihi . . . a. d. iii Kal. Sext. de provincia decedendum est," the first letter from Cilicia in which the one-year "rule" appears as a mandate, and then only in a parenthetical statement), and 6.6.3 (Rhodes, ca. 10 Aug. 50) with *Att.* 7.3.1 (Trebula, 9 Dec. 50). Full references on Cicero's "necessity" to leave his province after a year are collected in Marshall, ANRW I 1 (1972) 899 nn. 46 and 48, 900 n. 50. As in previous practice, a "Pompeian" commander's *imperium* remained valid until he entered the *pomerium*: see, e.g., *Att.* 7.7.4 with Marshall, ANRW I 1 (1972) 897f.

122. See, however, 14.6.4 for a list of possible delegatees of praetorian *imperium* in this theater during the Third Mithridatic War; also, further, 14.6.2 for M. Iuncus.

123. See Plu. *Pomp.* 38.2, D.C. 37.7a. Departure for Syria: Plu. *Pomp.* 39.1; Flor. 1.40.29.

124. Return to Pontus: Plu. *Pomp.* 42.1; cf. D.C. 37.20.1. Formation of new *provincia* of Bithynia/Pontus: *Per.* 102 "Cn. Pompeius in provinciae formam Pontum redigit," App. *Mith.* 118.579 with 581, Cic. *Prov.* 31; cf. D.S. 40.4 (Pompey's claim to have "rescued Bithynia"); see also Kunkel, *Staatsordnung* 360 n. 210 for references to the "lex Pompeia" for the province (but perversely assigning it to Q. Pompeius Bithynicus—on whom see Appendix B n. 315—and the year 75). On the name of the *provincia*, see Cic. *Red. Sen.* 38 (Cicero's son-in-law C. Calpurnius Piso Frugi, who in 58 or 57 "Pontum et Bithyniam quaestor . . . neglexit"); cf. (for nontechnical usage) Catul. 10.7 "Bithynia".

125. Embarkation of force: App. *Mith.* 116.565–566. Pompey stopped at Athens en route to Brundisium (Plu. *Pomp.* 42.5).

126. D.C. 36.40.3–4. For the prosecution of P. Oppius (the occasion of Cicero's lost *Pro Oppio*), see Alexander, *Trials* no. 185 with n. 304 below.

127. G. R. Stumpf, *Numismatische Studien zur Chronologie der römischen Statthalter in Kleinasien* (122 v. Chr.–163 n. Chr.) (Saarbrücken 1991) 56–69 nos. 94–130.

128. See Stumpf, *Numismatische Studien* pp. 66f

129. On this see Appendix B n. 155.

130. *MRR* II 173, 181; cf. III 154.

131. See Stumpf, *Numismatische Studien* p. 68

132. See D.C. 36.40.4 and V. Max. 5.4.4 (the latter with mistaken *praenomen*) with Alexander, *Trials* no. 244 (dated to "?59"). His prosecutor was M. Cotta's young son.

133. See *MRR* II 153.

134. *MRR* II 203, esp. Catul. 10.9–13 for a graphic comment in verse on Memmius' perceived attitude toward his staff.

135. For his title "imperator," see *RRC* I 451–452 no. 427 (issued by his nephew, C. Memmius C.f., a future *tr. pl.* 54), dated by Crawford to 56 B.C. On the phenomenon of acclamation early in one's command, see ch. 14 n. 68. Presumably Memmius went looking (in the mountainous regions of eastern Pontus?) for an enemy to fight: for this time-honored Roman tradition cf. Cic. *Inv.* 2.111 and *Pis.* 62 (Cisalpine Gaul, 95 and 74 B.C.); D.C.

37.52.3–4 (Hispania Ulterior 60 B.C.). Sumner (*Orators* 89f), however, is deeply skeptical, and instead assigns the acclamation here commemorated to the C. Memmius attested as commander in Macedonia sometime in the period 107–101 (14.1.1 below).

136. Memmius later turns up as a candidate in 54 (backed by Caesar) for the consulship of 53. For his fate (conviction for *ambitus* in 52, followed by exile), see Broughton, *Candidates Defeated* 28–29, Alexander, *Trials* nos. 298 (an apparently unsuccessful prosecution for *ambitus* in 53), 320.

137. Cic. *Red. Sen.* 22–23.

138. Stumpf, *Numismatische Studien* 69–70 no. 131.

139. Title: see prescripts of Cic. *Fam.* 13.61–65; for his praetorian status see also *Fam.* 13.63.2, 64.2, 65.2; cf. *Att.* 6.1.13 (evidence also he was still in the *provincia* in early 50). *Fam.* 13.64–65 show Cicero thought Silius had influence in Asia too, beyond his own *provincia*.

140. Cic. *Att.* 7.1.8.

141. *MRR* III 158 (aedileship in 55), cf. II 223 (placing it in 54).

142. *Att.* 5.15.1 (3 Aug. 51).

143. *MRR* II 241, with no query. Cf. D. R. Shackleton Bailey, *CEF* I 479, pointing out that *praetor inter peregrinos* is also conceivable.

144. *Flac.* 6 "Romae ius dixerat," cf. 100 "urbana iuris dictio"; *Mur.* 41 "sors . . . iuris dicundi," all of the *provincia urbana*.

145. Note Asc. p. 29 C "in forum . . . descendebat iusque dicebat," of the *pr. repetundis* for 54, M. Porcius Cato.

146. Cic. *Fam.* 13.29.4.

147. That Antonius was praetor in 74 seems quite secure: see Cic. *Ver.* 2.3.215, cf. Vell. 2.31.3 (cited in n. 151 below).

148. On this see the remarks of R. Kallet-Marx, *Hegemony to Empire: The Development of the Roman Imperium in the East from 148 to 62 B.C.* (Berkeley 1995) 304–306.

149. See Plu. *Sert.* 21.7 with Konrad, *Plutarch's Sertorius* 177–178, also 199–200 (adventurously suggesting that there were Pontic ships helping the Sertorians in Spain already by spring 74).

150. See *AJAH* 2 (1977) 33, citing App. *Mith.* 9.63.

151. *Schol. Bob.* p. 96 St., Ps.-Asc. p. 202, p. 239, p. 259 St. "curationem infinitam nactus totius orae maritimae," Vell. 2.31.3 (Pompey's pirate command of 67) "paene totius terrarum orbis imperium . . . idem hoc ante †biennium† in M. Antonii praetura decretum erat." Cf. Lact. *Inst. Div.* 1.11.32 (even more rhetorical).

152. See T. Reinach, *REG* 17 (1904) 210 no. 2 [Rhodes] ([Μά‹ρκου Ἀντωνίου στραταγοῦ ἀνθυπά[του] with E. Maróti, *AAntHung* 19 (1971) 263 n. 31 for further bibliography (yet wrongly thinking that this title shows prorogation).

153. Cic. *Ver.* 2.2.8 "M. Antoni infinitum illud imperium," 2.3.213 "in isto infinito imperio."

154. Note M. Antonius' *legatus* "Manius" in the west at Sal. *Hist.* 3.6 M, cf. 3.5 (another subordinate "Mamercus"). For the trouble one of Antonius' *praefecti* (unnamed) stirred up in Sicily in 74, see Cic. *Div. Caec.* 55. For Antonius' subordinates in the east (including at least three *legati*) see esp. *SIG³* 748 (the Gytheum inscription), with P. Foucart, *Journal des savants* n.s. 4 (1906) 569–581, esp. 576–581 for the chronological pointers in the inscription; also M. Hatzfeld, *Les trafiquants italiens dans l'Orient hellénique* (Paris 1919) 80–82. It refers to at least six separate years. Antonius' legate L. Marcilius (lines 11, 16) was in Gytheum during the magistracies of Phleinos (?74/73) and Biadas (?73/72). Other subordinates (see lines 16, 22–23) — incuding Antonius' brother-in-law C. Iulius Caesar, the future dictator (see Plu. *Ant.* 2.1 with T. R. S. Broughton, *TAPhA* 79 [1948] 63–67; contra, e.g., Sumner, *Orators*

138)—are placed in the year of Biadas (?73/72). Antonius himself (line 32) arrives in the year of Timocrates (?72/1). For Q. Ancharius, see *SIG*³ 748 line 26 with *I. Olymp.* 328 (Ancharius as "pro quaestore"). *IG* IV² 1 66 lines 23–25 with 30–33 suggest that Antonius had troops quartered at Epidaurus from July 72 down to June 71: see Foucart, *Journal des savants* n.s. 4 (1906) 577–578.

155. Full sources for what follows can be found in MRR II 123 with 101, 111, 117, and 123. See Linderski, *Roman Questions* 436–443, for an important discussion of Antonius' pirate command, which forms the basis for the reconstruction in this section. Ancient testimony for the *agnomen* "Creticus" is slim (just App. *Sic.* 6.1–2 and Plu. *Ant.* 1.1); Linderski demonstrates "it was an *appellatio privata*, never acknowledged by the senate" (*Roman Questions* 443).

156. App. *Sic.* 6.1–2 with Memn. (*FGrH* II B 434) 29.5, 33.1; Flor. 1.42.1.

157. Flor. 1.42.2–3 (making much of Antonius' unrealistic expectations of military success, and implying he did not use his full capabilities), *Per.* 97 (for the date); cf. App. *Sic.* 6.4 for the involvement of Lasthenes and D.S. 40.3 for that of Panares.

158. See D.S. 40.1 with the explication of Linderski, *Roman Questions* 442..

159. Place of death: Ps.-Asc. pp. 202 and 239 St.; the former passage is very likely based on information derived from Sallust's *Histories*: see Linderski, *Roman Questions* 441 with n. 31. Terminus for death: Cic. *Ver.* 2.3.213, cf. *Per.* 97 (implying, perhaps misleadingly, a date of 71 for both defeat and death). See also *Schol. Bob.* p. 96 St. "rebus nondum confectis morte praeventus est" (implying he was to be prorogued for 70?).

160. *IG* IV² 1 66 line 25 Μάρκου Ἀντωνίου τοῦ ἐπὶ Κρητῶν στραταγοῦ. On the nature of this inscription, see Linderski, *Roman Questions* 436 n. 2.

161. Cic. *Ver.* 2.2.8, 3.213–216; cf. *Div. in Caec.* 55 (abuses by one of Antonius' *praefecti*).

162. As Plu. *Pomp.* 29.1 points out.

163. See Kallet-Marx, *Hegemony to Empire* 307–308, and also 11.4 below.

164. Sources in MRR II 131, esp. *Schol. Bob.* p. 96 St. for Hortensius' refusal of the *provincia*, with the narrative of Kallet-Marx, *Hegemony to Empire* 309–311.

165. His first reported military action, a naval battle against Lasthenes off Cydonia followed by a siege of that town (App. *Sic.* 6.5), was as *pro cos.* (*Per.* 98).

166. He took along C. Licinius Sacerdos (*pr.* 75) as his senior *legatus* (Cic. *Planc.* 27); we know his staff members (like those of Antonius before him) made wideranging requisitions on the Greek mainland. The *legatus* L. Valerius Flaccus (the future *pr. urb.* 63), was active certainly in Achaea, Boeotia, and Thessaly (Cic. *Flac.* 63), and perhaps elsewhere on the mainland (cf. 6, 100) as well as in Crete itself (6, 30, 100, *Planc.* 27; cf. Solin. 1.90–91 pp. 22–24 M.). Metellus had at least two legions: Vell. 2.34.1 ("Roman armies" in the plural); cf. Phleg. F 12 in *FHG* III 606 ("thirty legions"). Metellus' conquest of the "whole of Crete" is pointed up a number of our sources (App. *Sic.* 6.7, D.C. 36.17a (Xiph.) and 19.2, Eutrop. 6.11.2, etc.) and it was obviously his aim from the start.

167. Vell. 2.34.1 "per triennium," Eutrop. 6.11.2 "intra triennium," cf. Oros. 6.4.2 "per biennium."

168. See, e.g., V. Max. 7.6 ext. 1 on some Cretans he reduced to the bitterest necessity.

169. Plu. *Pomp.* 29.1–2, cf. also App. *Sic.* 6.6, Flor. 1.42.5. For the terms of the *lex Gabinia*, see 11.8.2 below.

170. *Per.* 99, Plu. *Pomp.* 29.2, Flor. 1.42.6 (calling the *legatus* "Antonius" but getting the detail "aliena provincia" right), App. *Sic.* 6.7 and D.C. 36.18.1 (Metellus attacks the Cretans who came to terms with Pompey), cf. Vell. 2.34.2.

171. Plu. *Pomp.* 29.2 with *Per.* 99 ("suus legatus"). Sources on this *legatus* can be found in MRR II 147.

172. Sisenna's death: D.C. 36.18.1 with 19.1–2 for his army (which L. Octavius prompt-ly took over on his death, to no avail against Metellus). For Pompey's attitude, see D.C. 36.45.1–2.

173. Vell. 2.34.1, Ruf. Fest. *Brev.* 7.1 (particularly explicit), Oros. 6.4.2; cf. (with erro-neous chronology) Just. 39.5.3. Law giving: *Per.* 100, Oros. 6.4.2. Cf. also Cic. *Flac.* 30 (59 B.C.) "Cretam Metelli virtute esse nostram" and 100 "provinciam Cretam."

174. Hailed as *imperator* in Crete: see sources in *MRR* II 145, to which add Cic. *Flac.* 6; the unreliable Phlegon of Tralles (F 12 in *FHG* III 606) says it came "after the victory over Lasthenes," i.e., 68, which is perfectly possible (ch. 14 n. 68). Waiting for triumph: Sal. *Cat.* 30.3–4 (outside city *cum imperio* in late October 63, on which see 11.8.9). Metellus' triumph: see esp. Vell. 2.34.2 (popularity of triumph) and D.C. 36.19.3, each noting Pompey's inter-ference. Sources for the *agnomen* "Creticus" can be found in *MRR* II 176.

175. See Cael. *Fam.* 8.8.8 with G. Perl, *Klio* 52 (1970) 330–332 (esp. 331 on Cic. *Planc.* 85 and the nature of M. Iuventius Laterensis' visit to the island), 353–354, and *Klio* 53 (1971) 371–373.

176. Sal. *Hist.* 2.43 M, with text of G. Perl, *Klio* 52 (1970) 321 n. 3 (accepted by L.D. Reynolds in the *OCT*): "P(ublius)que Lentulus Marcel<linus> eodem auctore quaest<or> in novam provinci<am> Curenas missus est, c<um> ea mortui regis Apio<nis> testamento nobis d<ata> prudentiore quam <adu>lescentis et minus q[uam] ille avide imperio co<nti>nenda fuit." The date of 75 seems certain from the position of this fragmentary notice in the original manuscript—just ca. ten lines after *Hist.* 2.42 M (the start of the year 75) and ca. ten lines previous to *Hist.* 2.45 M (buildup to the elections for 74). For a recon-struction of these items in the Fleury MS., see H. Bloch in S. Prete (ed.), *Didascaliae: Studies in Honor of A. M. Albareda* (New York 1961) 59–60.

177. See Kallet-Marx, *Hegemony to Empire* 364–367. Kallet-Marx goes one step further. He reasonably dates this event to early 75, but identifies the "adulescens" as Ptolemy of Cyprus, and "ille" as Ptolemy Auletes, hypothesizing that these two rival kings were each in an audience with the Senate laying claim to Cyrene—despite the will of 96 B.C. that had ceded it to Rome. Yet the expansive way Sallust identifies this "new *provincia*" in the frag-ment suggests that he has not mentioned it previously or at least for some time in his text— and also that he did not know quite what he was talking about (see E. Badian, *JRS* 55 [1965] 119 n. 66; App. *BC* 1.111.517 actually dates Apion's will to 74). In the fragment Sallust should be using "adulescens" as an equivalent for "a man of quaestorian age," with the implication (as often) that such an individual was too young to be doing what he was. Parallels are not hard to find: see Asc. p. 28 C (Faustus Sulla as quaestor 54), Cic. *Fam.* 2.15.4 (C. Coelius as quaestor 50), cf. Asc. p. 92 C and Suet. *Jul.* 9.3 (Cn. Piso just before appointment as *quaestor pro pr.* 65). And the most natural antecedent of "ille" is P. Cornelius Lentulus Marcellinus himself, as opposed to an individual named even earlier than Marcellinus (and Apion) in a portion of the text now lost.

178. See E. Badian, *JRS* 55 (1965) 120, also *Roman Imperialism in the Late Republic*[2] (Oxford 1968) 35–37.

179. It was surely Marcellinus' return from his fundraising activity that made possible the purchase of Sicilian grain in 73 under the *lex Terentia Cassia*: see Badian, *JRS* 55 (1965) 120.

180. *Legatus* under Pompey: see App. *Mith.* 95.434 (with responsibility for "Libya, Sardinia, and nearby islands"), Flor. 1.41.9 (the Libyan sea). *Legatus pro praetore* in Cyrene: see the dossier of eight inscriptions assembled in J. M. Reynolds, *JRS* 52 (1962) 97–103, at 97–101, esp. no. 4 (Marcellinus' name perhaps used as a date) and no. 6 = *RDGE* 50 (arbi-tration between the cities of Apollonia and Cyrene), with Reynolds' interpretation at 101–103.

181. *JRS* 52 (1962) 101f.

182. *JRS* 55 (1965) 119f, also *Roman Imperialism*[2] 36–37.

183. Cf. D.S. 40.4 (Pompey's summary tablet in 61 B.C. of his accomplishments) ὑποτάξας . . . Κυρηναϊκὴν ἐπαρχίαν.

184. See Cic. *Planc.* 13 and (showing the presence of *publicani*) 63 with Badian, *JRS* 55 (1965) 120.

185. This man's date and city *provincia* (for which see Asc. p. 48 C, a grain riot during his *Ludi Apollinares*) are certain. L. Rufus evidently held an overseas *provincia* (*ILLRP* 391, "pro cos."), certainly for 56, since his rank under the *lex Pompeia* of 52 would be "pro pr." The possibilities for 56 are limited to Sicily or Cyrene (cf. *MRR* II 210, but not realizing that the rank of *pro cos.* was generalized for praetorian governors in this period).

186. Cael. *Fam.* 8.8.8 with Badian, *JRS* 55 (1965) 120 n. 73

187. Family: Var. *R.* 2.4.2. Quaestorship: Plu. *Crass.* 11.6. Senatorial status: Cic. *Ver.* 1.30.

188. Cic. *Att.* 5.4.2.

189. Cic. *Att.* 6.1.13, 7.1.7.

190. *MRR* III 208.

191. *MRR* II 242 with 251, then III 149; cf. 208; also D. R. Shackleton Bailey, *Cicero's Letters to Atticus* (Cambridge 1965–1970) III 246. Contra G. Perl, *Klio* 52 (1970) 333 (arguing that he was actually in Rome and not a provincial governor in mid-October 50).

192. Sources and discussion in E. Schürer, G. Vermes, and F. Millar, *The History of the Jewish People in the Age of Jesus Christ (175 B.C.–A.D. 135)* I² (Edinburgh 1973) 133–136, also (more fully) A. R. Bellinger in *Transactions of the Connecticut Academy of Arts and Sciences* 38 (1949) 51–102; G. Downey, *A History of Antioch in Syria* (Princeton 1961) 126–142. On the date of Tigranes' occupation of Syria (perhaps as early as 87/6), see T. Liebmann-Frankfort, *La frontière orientale dans la politique extérieure de la République romaine* (Brussels 1969) 192–195. Antiochus XIII as *amicus et socius populi Romani*: Cic. *Ver.* 2.4.67–68.

193. For the *legati pro praetore* in 67, see App. *Mith.* 95.436 (Q. Metellus Nepos and L. Lollius) with Flor. 1.41.10 (implausibly assigning Metellus also the Pontic coast). Arrangements for early 66: Plu. *Pomp.* 32.1.

194. Scaurus supersedes Metellus and Lollius at Damascus: J. *AJ* 14.29, *BJ* 1.127. Dispatch of Gabinius: J. *AJ* 14.37. L. Afranius at Amanus: Plu. *Pomp.* 39.2.

195. See esp. App. *Syr.* 49.250–50.251 and 70, *Mith.* 106.500 and *BC* 5.10.40, Vell. 2.37.5. For general narrative and discussion of Pompey's motives, see Liebmann-Frankfort, *La frontière orientale* 288–293, also Badian, *Roman Imperialism*² 74–75. New era: see H. Seyrig, *Syria* 27 (1950) 11–14. Rationale for annexation: Just. 40.2.4–5, cf. Plu. *Pomp.* 39.2 (specifying Seleucid dynastic troubles). On the involved series of events that led to this annexation, see G. Downey, *TAPhA* 81 (1951) 149–163, Schürer, Vermes, and Millar, *History of the Jewish People* I² 236–242. A detailed narrative can be found in H. Koehler, *Die Nachfloge in der Seleukidenherrschaft und die parthische Haltung im römisch-pontischen Konflikt* (Bochum 1978), esp. 31–75 (background), 75–82 (Pompey's organization). Piracy in Syria: explicit in Cic. *Flac.* 30, cf. D.C. 39.56.1 and 5 (still flourishing there ca. 55 B.C.), 59.1–2.

196. Plu. *Pomp.* 38.2–3, App. *Mith.* 106.498, D.C. 37.15.1, Flor. 1.40.29.

197. Title: *IGRP* III 1102 (Tyre) ἀντιτάμιαν ἀντιστράτηγον. For the appointment, see also App. *Syr.* 51.255 and *BC* 5.10.40, J. *AJ* 17.74 and 79, *BJ* 1.155 and 157.

198. J. *AJ* 14.80–81, *BJ* 1.159.

199. *Syr.* 51.255–256.

200. Appian (*Syr.* 51.257) indeed notes his command as the terminus of the four years of praetorian administration. For the basic facts (with sources) on what follows below, see Schürer, Vermes, and Millar, *History of the Jewish People* I² 245–246 (Gabinius), 246 (M. Crassus), 247 (C. Cassius Longinus and M. Calpurnius Bibulus).

201. That is the title Cicero uses to address Cassius in Sept. 51 B.C. (*Fam.* 15.14 pre-script)—a powerful argument against the doctrine of "spontaneous generation" of *imperium*

(for which see 15.3.1). C. Cassius Longinus is likely to have reached the quaestorship in 55, and certainly by 54: see G. V. Sumner, *Phoenix* 25 (1971) 365.

202. For this attitude, cf. esp. Cael. *Fam.* 8.10.1–2 (17 Nov. 51), discussing proposals to create an extraordinary command—for an existing commander—to deal with the Parthian situation. For Cassius in Syria, see the sources in *MRR* II 229, 237.

203. Cic. *Att.* 7.3.5.

204. Cic. *Dom.* 23 "illam opimam fertilemque Syriam."

205. The sortition of praetorian promagisterial *provinciae* for 61 was delayed until the first half of March of that year: see Cic. *Att.* 1.15.1, cf. 13.5 with 14.6.7 below.

206. App. *Syr.* 51.256; Cic. *Prov.* 9 and *Sest.* 71. *Dom.* 23, in its reference to the "pacatissimae gentes" of Syria, is disingenuous; contrast *Prov.* 15 (of A. Gabinius' campaigns of 57). One must also factor in the endemic troubles in Judaea, on which see J. *AJ* 14.82–83, *BJ* 1.160–161 (the situation in 57).

207. App. *Syr.* 51.257 (called off in 56 B.C.); J. *AJ* 14.103, *BJ* 1.178 (successful campaign of spring 55).

208. Cic. *Att.* 1.16.8 with Shackleton Bailey, *CLA* I 318. For the chronology, see *Clod.* F 8 Crawford[2] for the boast of P. Clodius, quaestor-designate 61, "Syriam sibi nos extra ordinem polliceri" with *Schol. Bob.* p. 87 on his hopes for self-enrichment. It must have been Pupius as consul designate who raised Clodius' hopes of being appointed his *quaestor extra sortem* (L. A. Thompson, *PACA* 5 [1962] 21–22); the two were political allies in 61 (see n. 420 below). On the unlikelihood that the Senate in either 62 or 61 would have declared Syria consular under the *lex Sempronia*, see J. P. V. D. Balsdon, *JRS* 52 (1962) 140; cf. P. Moreau, *Clodiana Religio* (Paris 1982) 230. Syme's conjecture (*Roman Papers* I 301) that Pupius received Cilicia or Hispania Citerior as a "consolation prize" does not convince.

209. See, e.g., the references in n. 420 below.

210. App. *Mith.* 95.436 (with a certain emendation of the name). He was honored as a *legatus* at Samos (*IGRP* IV 1709 lines 2–3) and Miletus (*Milet.* I 3 393 no. 173), in both cases probably post 67 B.C. but still during his service under Pompey: see F. Münzer, *Römische Adelsparteien und Adelsfamilien* (Stuttgart 1920) 334 n. 1. Siege of Jerusalem: Hegesipp. 1.16. Elections for 61 B.C.: Plu. *Pomp.* 44.1 (request denied), D.C. 37.44.3 (request granted).

211. For the suggestion (and his career in general), see Sumner, *Orators* 133–134.

212. The *coss.* 59 were (initially) saddled with a trivial province, "silvae callesque" (Suet. *Jul.* 19.1–2). See J. W. Rich, *Latomus* 45 (1986) 505–521, attractively conjecturing (519) that the Senate wanted this device specifically for the year 59, "to challenge Caesar's right to remain in Rome throughout his year of office".

213. Cic. *Q. fr.* 1.2.7 (between 25 Oct. and 10 Dec. 59).

214. *RRC* I 544–545 no. 549 (with legend CN. LENTVL).

215. See 14.2.5.

216. Appointment as *legatus* in 66 B.C.: cf. Cic. *Man.* 57–58. Gabinius' semi-independent campaigning leads to the renewal of an alliance (autumn 65) with the Parthian king Phraatres III: D.C. 37.5.2–4. Gabinius' early presence (by autumn 64) in Judaea, where his bribe-taking prompts Aristobulus to complain before Pompey: J. *AJ* 14.37, and cf. 29. Pompey in spring 63 sends Gabinius to take over Jerusalem (and receive more cash from Aristobulus), but he is shut out of city: *AJ* 14.55–56, *BJ* 1.139–140, Oros. 6.6.1.

217. Gabinius' provincial edict, prejudicial to the *publicani*: Cic. *Prov.* 9–12, 14, cf. *Pis.* 58 for his alleged self-enrichment at their expense. Losses against Arabs: see n. 206 above. For Alexander's attempt to raise the wall of Jerusalem that Pompey had destroyed, and Gabinius' military response, see Jos. *AJ* 14.82–86, *BJ* 1.160–165. Gabinius rebuilds cities in Judaea: *AJ* 14.87–88, *BJ* 1.165–167. Installs Hyrcanus in Jerusalem: *AJ* 14.89–90, *BJ* 1.167–169. His administrative reorganization of Judaea: *AJ* 14.91, *BJ* 1.169–170. *Supplicatio* denied: Cic.

Q. fr. 2.8.1 (mid-May 56), *Phil.* 14.24. Gabinius' dispatches not believed: *Pis.* 41, 44–45, *Prov.* 14–15, 25.

218. Cic. *Prov.* 13 and passim, cf. *Pis.* 88 and Asc. pp. 1–2 C.

219. D.C. 39.56.1.

220. For Gabinius' Parthian campaign, see App. *Syr.* 51.257, cf. Just. 42.4 (role of Mithridates); Strab. 12.3.34 p. 558 and 17.1.11 p. 795 (implying a lengthy planning stage); J. *AJ* 14.98, *BJ* 1.175 (mentioning the Euphrates).

221. Pompey allegedly behind the restoration: D.C. 39.55.1–6, cf. 42.2.1. Ptolemy approaches Gabinius, with a letter from Pompey and promises of large amounts of money: D.C. 39.56.3. Anti-piracy measures as pretext for the expedition: Cic. *Rab. Post.* 19–20. The bribe: *Rab. Post.* 21, 30–31, 48, Plu. *Ant.* 3.4. Delegation of province: D.C. 39.56.5. Move from province strictly illegal (under *lex Cornelia de maiestate* and *lex Iulia de repetundis*) and in contravention of an *S.C.* of 59, that Ptolemy was not to be restored with an army: D.C. 39.56.4–5, Cic. *Pis.* 49–50, cf. App. *BC* 2.24.90. After Gabinius' return to Rome in 54 he was acquitted *de maiestate* (23 Oct.), but condemned *de repetundis* (Alexander, *Trials* nos. 296, 303, cf. no. 304, a prosecution for *ambitus*).

222. The tribune C. Trebonius' proposal: D.C. 39.33.1–2, also App. *BC* 2.18.65. Ostentatious sortition: Plu. *Crass.* 15.7 and 16.1–2 with D.C. 40.12.1 (noting that in the *S.C.* defining the mission there was no mention of Parthian War); cf. (inaccurately) *Per.* 105 "Crasso Syria et Parthicum bellum," Oros. 6.13.1 and (most inaccurately) Ruf. Fest. *Brev.* 17.1 "adversum rebellantes Parthos." Obstruction: App. *BC* 2.18.66 (specifically mentioning tribunician opposition to Parthian War), D.C. 39.39.6–7 (more than one tribune), Plu. *Crass.* 16.6–7, and Flor. 1.46.3 (extreme measures of Ateius), cf. D.H. 2.6.4. C. Ateius was later blamed for Crassus' disaster: Cic. *Div.* 1.29–30. Crassus' one recorded action in Roman Syria in 54 was to seize Jewish temple treasures to fund his Parthian campaign: J. *AJ* 14.104–109, *BJ* 1.179, Oros. 6.13.1. His idle winter of 54/53 in the province: Plu. *Crass.* 17.7–9, cf. D.C. 40.13.3–4.

223. Sources collected in G. Hölbl, *Geschichte des Ptolemäerreiches* (Darmstadt 1994) 193–194 (of which see esp. App. *BC* 1.102.476 for the appointment by Sulla).

224. *Roman Imperialism*[2] 31.

225. See Hölbl, *Geschichte des Ptolemäerreiches* 195 with 325 n. 1.

226. Catulus opposes his censorial colleague Crassus in his attempt to annex Egypt: Plu. *Crass.* 13.1–2. Termed (in 63) a "straight grasp": Cic. *Agr.* 1.1, 2.44. The plebiscite: Suet. *Jul.* 11. Optimates opposed: Suet. *Jul.* 11, Cic. *Agr.* 1.1. This is likely to have been the occasion of Cicero's speech "De rege Alexandrino": see E. Badian, *RhM* 110 (1967) 185 n. 26.

227. Cic. *Agr.* 1.1, 2.41–44, esp. 2.43–44 on the danger that Rullus would adjudicate Egypt to king Auletes.

228. Cavalry: Plin. *Nat.* 33.136. Invitation to Egypt: App. *Mith.* 114.556–557. On the Egyptian fear of annexation at this time, see E. Bevan, *A History of Egypt under the Ptolemaic Dynasty* (London 1927) 350–352.

229. For sources on this and what follows below in text, see Hölbl, *Geschichte des Ptolemäerreiches* 199–203.

230. Caes. *Civ.* 3.4.4 and 110.2, cf. *B. Alex.* 3.3; V. Max. 4.1.15 with Sen. *Dial.* 6.14.2 (on the *pro cos.* Bibulus' absolute refusal to apply his jurisdiction outside his province of Cilicia to the "Gabiniani" in Egypt); D.C. 42.5.4; cf. App. *BC* 2.84.356.

231. In February of 50 B.C., C. Scribonius Curio as *tr. pl.* made a serious attempt to strip Juba of his kingdom of Numidia and confiscate his lands for the Roman People, not to make a new *provincia* (as H. W. Ritter, *Rom und Numidien* [Lüneburg 1987] 127–128 and others have it) but as part of an agrarian scheme: see Caes. *Civ.* 2.25 and D.C. 41.41.3, against Luc. 4.688–692 with *Schol. Bern.* p. 146 U. The bill came to nothing.

232. For an excellent short survey of Sulla's general reorganization of the system of *quaestiones*, see Gruen, *Roman Politics* 258–265; also Hantos, *Res Publica Constituta* 61–68.

233. Sources on L. Furius in *MRR* II 97 under the year 75. If the *nomen* is indeed "Turius" (as the scholia on Hor. *Sat.* 2.1.49 have it, against Ps.-Asc. p. 193 St. "L. Furius"), he is the L. Turius who was consular candidate for 64 (Cic. *Att.* 1.1.2) and perhaps other years as well (cf. *Brut.* 237 "multo labore," also giving the *praenomen*). He was no doubt "a *novus homo* or of a recently senatorial family," as Broughton believes (*Candidates Defeated* 19). P. Cornelius Lentulus Sura was definitely *pr.* 74 (Ps.-Asc. p. 193 St. with Cic. *Clu.* 130) in charge of a *quaestio* (full sources in *MRR* II 102)—but again not necessarily *repetundarum*. See also n. 376 below on the *legatus* Furius in 73 B.C. Hortensius: *MRR* II 116.

234. See *MRR* II 127 for M.' Acilius Glabrio's *provincia* and date (both certain); for M. Metellus, see Cic. *Ver.* 1.21–32.

235. For the "quaesitor," see Cic. *Font.* 21. The jury was partly composed of *equites*: see esp. *Font.* 11, 12, 46. On "quaesitor," see 10.4.2 with ch. 10 n. 97. Full sources on the prosecution of Fonteius can be found in Alexander, *Trials* no. 186; see also 13.4.4 and 15.2.1 below.

236. The date is amply attested (full sources in *MRR* II 152) as is the *provincia* (see esp. Cic. *Clu.* 147, *Corn.* 1 F 7 Crawford², *Rab. Post.* 9, and the sources in Alexander, *Trials* no. 195, cf. no. 205).

237. Full sources on Cicero's praetorship in *MRR* II 152; see esp. Asc. p. 73 C with Alexander, *Trials* no. 196 (the trial de peculatu), also no. 198 (that de veneficiis); Cicero himself boasts to have been as praetor an open partisan of Pompey (*Fam.* 1.9.11). The exchange between the praetor Cicero and P. Vatinius related in Plu. *Cic.* 9.3, with Vatinius engaged in συνηγορία, probably belongs to the *repetundae* court (it finds no listing in Alexander, *Trials*). Elsewhere in the *Cicero* (3.6, 7.3, 9.7, 25.1), συνηγορία is used of advocacy in a criminal trial.

238. See Cic. *Vat.* 27 "C. Antonius reus fieret apud Cn. Lentulum Clodianum," with full sources in Alexander, *Trials* no. 241. Time of trial: see ch. 14 n. 71. Despite Alexander's doubts (*Trials* p. 119), the formal charge Antonius faced was apparently *repetundarum* (Schol. Bob. p. 94 St.). Pace T. J. Cadoux ap. *MRR* III 147, there is no reason to think that P. Nigidius Figulus (*pr.* 58) had any formal connection with administration of this trial: see Cic. *Att.* 2.2.3 with Badian, *Studies* 143, D. R. Shackleton Bailey, *CLA* I 354.

239. Cic. *Flac.* 85 with Alexander, *Trials* no. 247 and 14.5.7 below on the promagistracy (the *Pro Flacco* passage is the only evidence). The Flaccus trial came perhaps in August (Cic. *Att.* 2.25.1 with L. R. Taylor, *Historia* 1 [1950] 48), but certainly after the condemnation of C. Antonius (*Flac.* 95).

240. Suggested by E. S. Gruen, *Latomus* 32 (1973) 308 n. 40, offering as an alternative that there were two praetors de repetundis in 59. For what it is worth, Cicero seems to suggest that for the case of Antonius the choice of president was not automatic (*Vat.* 28 "quaesitore consilioque delecto").

241. Vacatio: Cic. *Ver.* 1.29–30. Possibly lifted: see Plu. *Cat. Mi.* 16.9 on the quaestor L. Lollius. There was probably never any restriction on a magistrate serving as a *iudex* in a civil trial: see Alexander, *Trials* no. 76, on C. Marius, *cos.* VI in 100 (but incorrectly terming him "juror").

242. Cic. *Vat.* 16 with *Schol. Bob.* p. 146 St.

243. *Att.* 3.17.1 (4 Sept. 58).

244. Most notably, *Q. fr.* 1.1.41 (end of 60), *Att.* 3.8.2–4 (29 May 58) and 3.9.1 (13 June 58), *Q. fr.* 1.3.5 and 8 (13 June 58) and 1.4.2 and 4–5 (early Aug. 58), *Att.* 3.13.2 (5 Aug. 58), cf. *Dom.* 59 and *Sest.* 68.

245. Candidacy for *pr.* 55: Broughton, *Candidates Defeated* 37. *Pr. repetundis* 54: Asc. p. 19 C, cf. Cic. *Q. fr.* 3.1.15. Trial of Scaurus: Alexander, *Trials* no. 295; for the *calumnia*

trial, see Asc. p. 29 C (not listed in Alexander's collection). Trial of Gabinius: see Cic. *Q. fr.* 3.1.15 and 3.2.1 with Alexander, *Trials* no. 303.

246. See Asc. p. 29 C "Cato praetor iudicium . . . sine tunica exercuit campestri sub toga cinctus. In forum quoque sic descendebat iusque dicebat," and cf. possibly Plu. *Cat. Mi.* 44.4 on his tribunal. See further 12.2.3 below.

247. Alexander, *Trials* no. 296.

248. Cic. *Q. fr.* 3.4.1.

249. Linderski, *Roman Questions* 121–123; Broughton, *MRR* III 169f. On a praestorship immediately following a tribunate, Linderski (*Roman Questions* 122) can offer no better than his own reconstruction of the career of the ill-attested M. Nonius Sufenas, on whom see 14.2.6. D. R. Shackleton Bailey (*Cicero, Epistulae ad Quintum Fratrem et M. Brutum* [Cambridge 1980] 215) sees merit in Linderski's conjecture, but also has suggested emendation, either to "Cotta," "Otho" (*PCPhS* 7 [1961] 3), or (later) "Gutta" (*Two Studies in Roman Nomenclature*[2] [Atlanta, Ga., 1991] 27).

250. For instances of the adjective *praetorius* in a loose sense, note *Mur.* 57 where Cicero uses "praetorius candidatus" of someone seeking the praetorship, or *Att.* 12.21.1 where in Dec. 63 C. Caesar (*pr.* 62) is said to have spoken "praetorio loco" in the debate on how to punish the Catilinarians.

251. *Roman Questions* 122.

252. Cic. *Q. fr.* 3.1.15.

253. Cf. Cic. *Att.* 4.16.5 on C. Cato's acquittal under the *lex Iunia et Licinia* in 54: "Fufia [sc. lege] ego tibi nuntio absolutum iri." (M. Cato will have forecast to Pompey the opposite result.)

254. Cic. *Q. fr.* 3.4.1, followed by the process of Alexander, *Trials* no. 303.

255. Cael. *Fam.* 8.8.2–3 with Alexander, *Trials* nos. 336–339, cf. 340. In no. 338, Laterensis, despite the (equal) vote of the jurors, refused to acquit the defendant (ch. 10 n. 81)—the only instance known of a praetor in a post-Gracchan standing court ignoring his *consilium*.

256. See Alexander, *Trials* nos. 131 (79 B.C., probably *repetundarum*, but dropped), (probably) 135 (78 B.C. or later), (probably) 139 (77 B.C.), 140 (77 B.C.), 174 (mid-70s B.C.), 170 (73 B.C.), 212 (65 B.C.), 225 (63 B.C.), (perhaps) 240 (59 B.C.), 244 (57 B.C. or later—see 11.2 on the date), 305 (54 B.C.), and 340 (51 B.C., but presumably here the president is the *pr.* M. Iuventius Laterensis, on whom see n. 255 above). *Trials* no. 192 (M. Aurelius Cotta, *cos.* 74 as "defendant") is probably not a *quaestio* procedure: see ch. 14 n. 307.

257. Conveniently listed in P. Nadig, *Ardet Ambitus* 210–211, cf. 212 (five threatened prosecutions), with cross-references in each case to Alexander, *Trials*. More than two-thirds of the *ambitus* prosecutions known to make it to trial date to the years 56–50 B.C.

258. *Clu.* 147 with Alexander, *Trials* no. 199.

259. See Alexander, *Trials* nos. 200, 201, and (possibly) 202. Despite the absence of evidence, Alexander supplies C. Gallus' name for nos. 200 and 202. On the date of that latter trial, see Nadig, *Ardet Ambitus* 184–185 ("66?–62?").

260. Cic. N.D. 3.74 "iudicium de dolo malo . . . protulit," *Off.* 3.60 "protulerat de dolo malo formulas," cf. 61.

261. See *Ver.* 2.3.16 The fact that Cicero (*pr.* 66) calls Aquillius "collega et familiaris meus" at *Off.* 3.60 counts for little, as *Top.* 32 shows.

262. We know how much trouble Cicero took avoiding anachronism even for a dialogue set in the middle of the second century: cf. E. Badian, "Cicero and the Commission of 146 B.C.," in J. Bibauw (ed.), *Hommages à M. Renard* I (Brussels 1969) 54–65 and (on the N.D. passage in particular) *RS* I p. 316. F. Wieacker, in *Römische Rechtsgeschichte* I: *Einleitung, Quellenkunde, Frühzeit und Republik* (Munich 1988) 452 n. 37, accepts that

Gallus came up with his *actio de dolo* as a jurist, as have most others; M. Kaser, *Das römisches Privatrecht* I² (Munich 1971) 246 n. 39 lists some dissenting views.

263. V. Max. 8.2.2 with Alexander, *Trials* no. 391. Valerius' treatment of the role of the *iudex* is quite rhetorical, especially the statement that Aquillius "adulterii crimen publicae quaestioni uindicandum reliquit"—obviously anachronistic for the Republic. Alexander is wrong to take Valerius to mean that the charge was dismissed, and then to surmise that "given [Aquillius'] power to dismiss the case, he may have been the magistrate."

264. V. Max. 4.2.5, cf. Schol. Bob. p. 89 St., giving the three Lentuli (apparently) as L. Cornelius Lentulus Niger (*pr.* by 61), Cn. Cornelius Lentulus Marcellinus (*pr.* 60, *cos.* 56), and (with wrong *praenomen*) L. Cornelius Lentulus Crus (*pr.* 58, *cos.* 49). See Alexander, *Trials* no. 237, who notes the trial, but misses the charge. For discussion, see Nadig, *Ardet Ambitus* 159 (with date "between 61 and 54").

265. See Cic. *Q. fr.* 1.2.15 (C. Cato) "cum Gabinium de ambitu vellet postulare neque praetores [the Loeb edition translates as singular!] diebus aliquot adiri possent vel potestatem sui facerent" with Shackleton Bailey, *CEQF* 165; cf. *Sest.* 18 (claiming that Gabinius also used violence to stave off prosecution). This episode is Alexander, *Trials* no. 248. In this connection, note that the Gracchan *repetundae* law—and thus surely all subsequent laws that set up permanent *quaestiones*—provided for the replacement of the praetor by another in certain circumstances (*CIL* I² 583 lines 72–73, 79–80).

266. Cic. *Q. fr.* 2.3.6.

267. Cic. *Cael.* 32.

268. For a dramatic instance, cf. Cic. *Att.* 4.17.5 and 4.18.3 (Oct. 54) for the indictment of all the candidates in the buildup to the consular *comitia* for 53; as it happened, there were to be no curule elections until July 53.

269. See Alexander, *Trials* 190 (68 B.C.), 200 and 201 (66 B.C.), 224 (63 B.C.), 238 (60 B.C.), 248 (59 B.C.), 269, 270, and 274 (56 B.C.).

270. See Alexander, *Trials* no. 214, on the prosecution of the *pr.* 65 Q. Gallius in the latter part of 64 (Asc. p. 88 C, dating it after the *In Toga Candida*; cf. Q. Cic. *Pet.* 19 with the discussion of Nadig, *Ardet Ambitus* 164–165) and no. 304 for A. Gabinius (*cos.* 58 and then *pro cos.* in Syria) as a defendant for *ambitus* in 54. In an *ambitus* case it appears that all previous offices might come in for retrospective scrutiny (Cic. *Fam.* 3.11.2).

271. *Trials* nos. 268 and 282.

272. Cic. *Q. fr.* 2.13.2; this passage is the sole piece of evidence for Caelius' second prosecution. For what Cicero means here by "the requisite number of jurors," see *Clu.* 74.

273. *MRR* III 81; also D. R. Shackleton Bailey, *CEQF* 195. F. X. Ryan, *Hermes* 123 (1995) 85 n. 13, provides a list of modern advocates for one of these positions or the other.

274. As W. G. Williams in the Loeb edition ad *Q. fr.* 2.13.2 rightly surmises.

275. *Fam.* 8.12.2.

276. Cael. *Fam.* 8.1.4, 11.2, 14.1 "mihi est Domitius inimicissimus"; cf. 15.2.

277. Alexander, *Trials* no. 310. For a list of special *quaesitores* attested for 52, see B. A. Marshall, *A Historical Commentary on Asconius* (Columbia, Mo., 1985) 185–186. The election of L. Domitius Ahenobarbus as "quaesitor" is reported by Asc. p. 38 C; see further 11.9.3. On Annius' prosecution for *ambitus* in connection with his consular bid for 52, see Nadig, *Ardet Ambitus* 147–149.

278. See Alexander, *Trials* nos. 159 (the quaestor 77 C. Aelius Paetus Staienus, tried and condemned in the latter half of the 70s), 160 (M. Atilius Bulbus, convicted for offenses in Illyria by 70 B.C.), and (possibly) 185 (the defendant P. Oppius, in all likelihood condemned, shortly after 70 B.C.). Cf. *Trials* 179 (70 B.C., merely threatened by Cicero for rhetorical purposes against C. Verres). See immediately below in text on the three *maiestas* trials (contemplated or realized) of the years 66–65.

279. Asc. pp. 59–60 C, with *praenomen* "P."; cf., however, "L. Cassium Longinum" at p. 82 C.

280. Deemed a possible consular candidate for 63 (Asc. p. 82 C, Q. Cic. *Pet.* 7, both commenting on his *nobilitas*), Cassius did not run himself for 62 but supported Catiline instead (*AE* 1979, no. 63). Indeed, he backed Catiline's program so enthusiastically that he was to be executed among the Catilinarian conspirators.

281. Asc. p. 62 C, full sources in Alexander, *Trials* no. 209.

282. Cic. *Corn.* 1 F 16 Crawford[2] (cited in n. 285 below) with Asc. p. 65 C. Full sources can be found in Alexander, *Trials* no. 210.

283. *Trials* p. 105, with no query. This notice has introduced no end of confusion into modern interpretations: see, e.g., Marshall, *Asconius* 234.

284. See. e.g.. *Fam.* 1.9.4, 13.66.1, and more generally Q. *fr.* 3.4.1 and *Att.* 4.18.1, and *Fam.* 7.2.2.

285. Cicero at the *contio*: cf. Q. Cic. *Pet.* 51. On the question whether Cicero spoke at the trial, see Alexander, *Trials* 106 n. 1. J. T. Ramsey tries to make 66 the year of C. Attius Celsus' praetorship (*Phoenix* 34 [1980] 332–336); cf. also A. M. Ward, *TAPhA* 101 (1970) 549 n. 15. One argument to the contrary: at Cic. *Corn.* 1 F 16 Crawford[2] instead of "petivit . . . a me praetor [sc. C. Celsus] maxima contentione ut causam Manili defenderem," we might expect "petivit . . . collega." Note *Clu.* 94 (Cicero speaking of C. Orchivius, *pr.* 66); *Off.* 3.60 and *Top.* 32 (of C. Aquillius Gallus, *pr.* 66).

286. Asc. p. 60 C. with Marshall, *Asconius* 226.

287. Trial of Cn. Plancius: Alexander, *Trials* no. 293. Edict summoning Gabinius: Cic. Q. *fr.* 3.1.24. Presidency of *quaestio*: see Q. *fr.* 3.3.3 with *Trials,* no. 296. "Quaesitor": *Planc.* 43, Q. *fr.* 3.3.3. On the basis of these notices, Mommsen (*St.-R.* II[3] 201 n. 4) denied he can have been praetor in 54.

288. *Tr. pl.* 59: Broughton, *MRR* II 189. Candidate for *pr.* 56: *Candidates Defeated* 35 (see esp. Cic. *Vat.* 38), to which add *Sest.* 113–114 and *Schol. Bob.* pp. 135 and 151 St.

289. Alexander, *Trials* no. 344.

290. See Cic. *S. Rosc.* 90 for the full name. On the unification of the courts *inter sicarios* and *de veneficiis* see Ulp. *Coll.* 1.3.1 with Kunkel, *RE* s.v. *quaestio* col. 741, cf. 746.

291. The quotation is from Cic. *S. Rosc.* 11. For a detailed description of the classes of crimes that fell under the *lex Cornelia de sicariis,* see Mommsen, *Strafrecht* 629–650.

292. Mundanity: see (on Sulla's law) Cic. *N.D.* 3.74 "haec quotidiana sicae, veneni, peculatus, testamentorum etiam lege nova quaestiones." Rank of victim immaterial: Cic. *Mil.* 17. Flimsiness: Cic. *Dom.* 49 offers one such example (not pursued beyond the *nominis delatio* stage). For creative embellishment in such prosecutions, see, e.g., *Clu.* 125 for a summary of the charges Cicero alleges against Oppianicus in his *veneficium* case of 66 B.C.

293. Ulp. *Coll.* 1.3.1, on which see A. H. J. Greenidge, *The Legal Procedure of Cicero's Time* (Oxford 1901) 431 n. 6; cf. Cic. *Clu.* 148 (another direct quotation from the law, also showing that it allowed for the *iudex quaestionis*). It is conceivable that the wording in the *lex Cornelia* for each individual *quaestio* gave the alternative "praetor iudexve quaestionis," just as in the *Lex de provinciis praetoriis* of 101 B.C. the future commander for Macedonia or Asia (who will have had consular *imperium*) is described as "praetor, *pro praetore* or *pro consule*," "praetor or *pro consule*," or "magistrate or *pro magistratu*" (14.1.2).

294. *Provincia*: Cic. *S. Rosc.* 11, cf. 8 and 90. Presidency: *S. Rosc.* 11–12, cf. 85. The date is certain (Gel. 15.28.3 = Fen. *HRR* II F 17).

295. For all this, see Cic. *S. Rosc.* 11. *MRR* III 90 and also 10.4.3 discuss the date of Fannius' service as *iudex quaestionis.*

296. See Alexander, *Trials* 147–149 and (for the *tr. pl.* L. Quinctius' successful prosecution of Iunius) 153 with 10.4.5 above.

297. See Cic. *Clu.* 147–148 with Alexander, *Trials* no. 198 for the prosecution of A. Cluentius Habitus *de veneficiis* under the presidency (not noted by Alexander) of Q. Voconius Naso. Mommsen, *Strafrecht* 648 n. 3, conjectured that a praetor also was functioning alongside these *iudices quaestionis*. Perhaps the division of labor was along geographical lines, as in the praetorian *quaestiones de veneficiis* we see in the 180s and 170s (5.6.2). The actual Sullan law certainly seems to suggest it: see *RS* I p. 753.

298. See Alexander, *Trials* nos. 215–217. Contra Gruen, who argues on the basis of Cic. *Lig.* 12 and *Schol. Gronov.* p. 293 St. (*Last Generation* 76 n. 124) that Caesar was merely an *accusator* in those trials. Yet Suet. *Jul.* 11 "in exercenda de sicaris quaestione" should be decisive: on the phrase, cf. Mommsen, *Strafrecht* 208 n. 1 and *RS* II p. 323. For additional trials on this charge where the president is not mentioned, see Alexander, *Trials* nos. 368 (80 or early 70s B.C.), and (probably) 253 (58 B.C., dropped for fear of *calumnia*) and 284 (54 B.C.). Cf. perhaps *Trials* no. 390 (definitely a *quaestio*, but date hard to ascertain and crime not specified).

299. Evidence on the Pompeian law—most importantly *Dig.* 48.9.1, specifying that it took over a provision from the *lex Cornelia de sicariis*—is collected in Rotondi, *Leges Publicae Populi Romani* 406–407 (exclusively Imperial). For discussion of the introduction and scope of the law, see Mommsen, *Strafrecht* 643–646 (dating it as early as 70), Gruen, *Last Generation* 246–247 (opting for 55); cf. J. D. Cloud, ZRG 88 (1971) 47–66 (discussion of penalty). The epitomator of Pomponius (*Dig.* 1.2.2.32) speaks of a Republican *quaestio de parricidio*, yet wrongly attributes it to Sulla. That Pompey's law established a (subpraetorian) *quaestio* for this crime, alongside the divisions *inter sicarios* and *de veneficiis*, seems perfectly conceivable.

300. Cic. N.D. 3.74 (cited in n. 292 above), *Mur.* 42 ("Quid ta sors? tristis, atrox, quaestio peculatus . . .").

301. See ch. 10 n. 103 with text.

302. C. Orchivius: date of praetorship and his *quaestio* attested by Cic. *Clu.* 94 and 147; for speculation on his activities as court president, see further E. S. Gruen, *Athenaeum* 49 (1971) 56–58, and F. X. Ryan, *Hermes* 123 (1995) 296–297. Ser. Rufus: the date of his praetorship and *provincia* are certain (*Mur.* 35, 41–43).

303. RE s.v. *quaestio* col. 745.

304. See Alexander, *Trials* nos. 162 and 175 (both by 70 B.C.) and 178 (70 B.C., only threatened). Plu. *Cat. Mi.* 16.6–9, the quaestor M. Porcius Cato's prosecution of a (quaestorian) *scriba* for defrauding the Treasury (not in Alexander) seems quite likely to be a *peculatus* trial; cf. Cic. *Mur.* 42 (on the *quaestio peculatus* court) "scriba damnatus, ordo totus alienus" (referring to this precise case?). Note perhaps also Alexander, *Trials* no. 171, the undated prosecution of C. Rabirius (apparently on a charge involving *sacrilegium*) by C. Licinius Macer (*tr. pl.* 73, *pr.* by 68), which was definitely a *quaestio* trial (Cic. *Rab. Perd.* 7); for the connection of *sacrilegium* and *peculatus*, cf. Mommsen, *Strafrecht* 760–761. However, Alexander, *Trials* no. 185 (P. Oppius as defendant, shortly after 70 B.C.) seems closer to *maiestas* than *peculatus* (Alexander suggests the latter), especially since it involved a charge of mutiny and earned the prosecutor a grant of consular *ornamenta* (D.C. 36.40.3–4). *Trials* no. 192 (M. Aurelius Cotta, *cos.* 74 "as defendant" *de repetundis* or *de peculatu*) is unlikely to be a trial (see ch. 14 n. 307). The process in *Trials* nos. 240 (by 59 B.C.) and 244 (57 or later) is unknown (the former is perhaps not even a *quaestio*), but is more likely to be *de repetundis* than anything.

305. See Mommsen, *Strafrecht* 669–670 and Kunkel, *RE* s.v. *quaestio* col. 742, for the evidence on the existence of this court in this period, which is mentioned only in passing in Cic. N.D. 3.74 (dramatic date 77 or 76) and *Ver.* 2.1.108f. Alexander (*Trials* no. 136) detects

a reference to an actual *lex testamentaria* case in Cic. *N.D.* 3.74, the L. Alenus who forged the signatures of the six senior public scribes. Cicero here strongly implies that a praetor presided in that trial, so there is something to recommend Alexander's suggestion.

306. *Lex Lutatia* and *lex Plautia*: see Mommsen, *Strafrecht* 652–660, esp. 654 n. 1. For an excellent short sketch of laws dealing with public *vis* in this era, see Gruen, *Last Generation* 224–227, esp. 226 n. 68 for the terminus ante quem. For an overview of the range of offenses covered by the *lex Plautia de vi* (and the added information that this court never took a holiday), see esp. Cic. *Cael.* 1. Earliest known prosecutions *de vi*: Alexander, *Trials* nos. 223 (63 B.C.), and 227, 229–234, cf. 228 (all 62 B.C.). *Lex Plautia* not entirely superseded: see Cael. *Fam.* 8.8.1 (Oct. 51) = Alexander, *Trials* no. 335. Cf. Kunkel, *RE* s.v. *quaestio* cols. 747–748, who argues against the notion that a *quaestio perpetua* was established to hear charges *de vi*. But Kunkel's attempt to support his view with *Schol. Bob.* p. 150 St. (= Alexander, *Trials* no. 255) does not convince: see 12.1.3.

307. See Alexander, *Trials* nos. 227 (62 B.C., with Novius Niger as "quaesitor," on whom see 10.4.2), and 242 (59 B.C., P. Licinius Crassus Dives [the future *pr.* 57] as *iudex quaestionis*).

308. No presidency is registered for Alexander, *Trials* nos. 381–382 (late 60s or early 50s), 261–262 (57 B.C., with P. Clodius Pulcher as defendant), or 267 (early 56 B.C.). See 10.4.5 for the *iudicium populi* "de vi" (*Trials* no. 266, with Cic. *Sest.* 95 for the charge) that P. Clodius Pulcher hatched against the ex-tribune T. Annius Milo as *aed. cur.* in 56.

309. Scaurus' presidency is inferred from Cic. *Sest.* 101 and 116. Full sources for the prosecution of P. Sestius are collected in Alexander, *Trials* no. 271. The date of Scaurus' praetorship is secure, the city *provincia* not independently attested. Against the notion that Scaurus—or any praetor—presided in the *quaestio de vi*, see Mommsen, *St.-R.* II³ 584 with n. 3.

310. Cic. *Vat.* 16, cf. *Schol. Bob.* p. 146 St. with 11.7.1 above.

311. See Cic. *Cael.* 32 with 11.7.2 above.

312. See Alexander, *Trials* nos. 309 (the special *quaestio de vi*) with 310 (*de ambitu*), 311 (*de sodaliciis*), 312 (prosecution *de vi* before L. Fabius) and 313–314 (trials of M. Saufeius). For discussion of the status of M. Favonius (aedile 53 or 52), see J. Linderski, *Roman Questions* 231–250 (esp. 238 n. 26) with 651–652. Asc. p. 55 C (Milo) "repetitus . . . apud <C.> Considium quaesitorem est lege Plautia de vi" is the one passage in our sources for the later Republic that seems most closely to reflect the official terminology for a presiding magistrate in a *vis* trial. Cf. Cic. *Att.* 2.24.4 (59 B.C.) "reus erat apud Crassum Divitem Vettius de vi"; Asc. p. 54 C (Milo) "apud L. Fabium quaesitorem . . . damnatus est de vi."

313. See the discussion of Marshall, *Asconius* 186, rightly arguing against the assumption that there would only be one *quaesitor* for the Plautian court that year. In addition to those listed in n. 312 above, see *Trials* nos. 315 (perhaps *lex Pompeia*, 52 B.C.), 327 (*lex Pompeia*, late 52 or early 51), 328 (*lex Pompeia*, by May 51), (perhaps) 316 (precise *quaestio* and date uncertain, but before June 51), 334 and 335 (probably both under the *lex Plautia*, by mid-October 51), and 341 (*de vi*, law uncertain, later 51); note also no. 349 (50 B.C.). For none of these prosecutions is the presiding magistrate specified.

314. For the chronology of the praetorian elections for 52 B.C. (by the first half of March of that year), see Linderski, *Roman Questions* 245–247, esp. 245 n. 59 (older views on Considius) with Marshall, *Asconius* 182. The date of the trial in which the *quaesitor* Considius presided is "on or after ca. 18 April" (Alexander, *Trials* no. 314). On the identity and rank of Considius see also 14.3.3.

315. See Alexander, *Trials* nos. 235 (Archias), 385 (M. Cassius, known only from a statement *obiter* in Cic. *Balb.* 52), 276 (Balbus), and 297 (Gabinius Antiochus, for whose trial the sole source is *Att.* 4.18.4). (V. Max. 3.4.5 is wildly anachronistic.) Scope of law: see esp. Cic.

Balb. 5 (summary of typical charges), cf. *Schol. Bob.* p. 175 St. with E. Badian, *JRS* 63 (1973) 128–129. *Lex Papia* characterized (with some exaggeration?) as an expulsion act: Cic. *Agr.* 1.13, *Off.* 3.47, also D.C. 37.9.3–5 (alleging it was especially aimed at Transpadanes). Establishment of *quaestio*: see Cic. *Arch.* 3 "in quaestione legitima et in iudicio publico . . . apud praetorem populi Romani . . . praetore exercente iudicium."

316. *Schol. Bob.* p. 175 St.; cf. Cic. *Arch.* 3 and 32. Even if true, there is no reason to believe Quintus was *pr. urbanus* (as tentatively suggested by *MRR* II 173); his colleague C. Iulius Caesar seems a better candidate for that position (see *MRR* III 106).

317. *Balb.* 52 "iudicum qui huic quaestioni praefuerunt."

318. Legislation (passed or mooted) against electoral *divisores* in the 60s B.C.: Linderski, *Roman Questions* 112–113. S.C. of 64 B.C. suppressing *collegia*: Asc. p. 7 C. An abortive proposal against electoral *divisores* of 61 B.C.: Cic. *Att.* 1.16.13. *Lex Clodia* of 58 B.C.: sources in *MRR* II 196. For the S.C. of Feb. 56, see esp. Cic. *Q. fr.* 2.3.5, *Cael.* 16, and *Planc.* 37 with the discussion of Linderski, *Roman Questions* 328–335, also 213–217. Consular elections for 55: Linderski, *Roman Questions* 120 n. 32. On the *lex Licinia de sodaliciis* and its more general background, see sources in *MRR* II 215 (usefully arranged in tabular form in Nadig, *Ardet Ambitus* 216–217) with Linderski, *Roman Questions* 113–114, 165–203, 204–217, cf. 647–649 and 657–659; see also the overview of Gruen, *Last Generation* 228–233.

319. For 54 B.C., see Alexander, *Trials* nos. 289 (C. Messius, with Sen. *Con.* 7.4.8 for the previous acquittals), 292 (P. Vatinius, a trial of late August), 293 (Cn. Plancius, late August or early September). For the date of Plancius' aedileship, see L. R. Taylor, *Athenaeum* 42 (1964) 12–28; J. Linderski, *Roman Questions* 118–121. For Milo in 52, see Alexander, *Trials* no. 311, and for M. Messalla in 51, nos. 329 (*lex Pompeia de ambitu*) and 331 (*de sodaliciis*).

320. Cic. *Att.* 4.15.9 with Alexander, *Trials* no. 289. For some parallels for the procedure, see Asc. p. 59 C on the *maiestas* case of *Trials* no. 203 (the year 66), and Cic. *Q. fr.* 3.1.24 with 3.3.3 for the *maiestas* prosecution listed as *Trials* no. 296 (from P. Servilius' praetorship year of 54). But a procedure of 58 B.C. offers a cautionary counterexample. There, the praetor issuing the edict of summons (as it happens, to another *legatus* in Gaul) plans merely to supervise the selection by lot of a *quaesitor* for the defendant's trial under (apparently) the *lex Licinia et Iunia*: see Cic. *Vat.* 33 with *Trials* no. 255 (58 B.C.) and the discussion of 12.1.3. Unfortunately, nothing else is known of P. Servilius' legal activities as praetor.

321. See Cic. *Planc.* 43 (presidency of Plancius trial) with text above on his praetorship.

322. Asc. p. 54 C "Milo apud M. Favonium quaesitorem de sodaliciis damnatus est." If the "de sodaliciis" goes with "damnatus est" (as seems necessary, not least from associated passages in this section of Asconius), we have no further precise references to the titulature of the individuals who administered this *quaestio*.

323. Kunkel (*RE* s.v. *quaestio* col. 748, cf. 746) doubted whether the *quaestio de sodaliciis* was a standing court. Mommsen (*St.-R.* II³ 583–585) accepted it as a permanent *quaestio*, but dismissed the idea that a praetor ever presided in trials *de sodaliciis*. For additional arguments against Mommsen's view on the president, see Linderski, *Roman Questions* 238 n. 26.

324. Oros. 5.23.23, Eutrop. 6.4, each with title "pro cos."; cf. Cic. *Clu.* 97 for confirmation of the *provincia*. For the military background to this commission, see P. Culham, *ClAnt* 12 (1993) 61–62, with references to previous studies.

325. *MRR* II 39 n. 21. Cf. also Münzer, *RE* s.v. *Cosconius* 3 col. 1668 (placing him in Illyria "ca. 78–76").

326. M. Atilius Bulbus as juror: Cic. *Clu.* 97, cf. 71–73. Condemnation: *Clu.* 97 with *Ver.* 1.39.

327. App. *BC* 1.100.466.

328. App. *BC* 1.103.480; cf. Plu. *Sull.* 34.3 (Sulla on abdication "puts consular elections back in the hands of the People").

329. On praetorian iteration in general in this period, see T. C. Brennan, *Athenaeum* 67 (1989) 479–481.

330. *Fam.* 13.42, cf. 41.

331. Caes. *Gal.* 1.10.3. Information on Illyria is largely lacking in the period between C. Cosconius' command in the early 70s and Caesar's proconsulship: see G. Zippel, *Die römische Herrschaft in Illyrien bis auf Augustus* (Leipzig 1877) 175–179. Yet the Romans must have had some continued involvement in the interim, as is shown by Badian, *Roman Imperialism*[2] 68f. On the probable nature of the threat from the Illyrians ca. 59, see Hirt. *Gal.* 8.24.3, who attests to Illyrian raids on northeast Italy in 53 and 52. For the suggestion that Culleolus was governor of Cisalpine Gaul or Macedonia, see Shackleton Bailey, *CEF* I 353. Neither of these alternatives seems likely. The *fasti* for Macedonia in the relevant period seem to leave no room between 64 and 59. And Cisalpine Gaul (where the *fasti* admittedly are more open) has just one known commander of praetorian status in the years 80–50, the *pr.* 63 Q. Caecilius Metellus—whose attested duties did not take him near the border between Cisalpina and Illyria (15.2.5). Note also that Caesar received Gallia Cisalpina and Illyricum as two separate *provinciae*.

332. Shackleton Bailey, *CLA* III 263 (also adducing Cic. *Div.* 1.4 to suggest that he may have been a "Cornelius Culleolus"); see in addition G. R. Stanton and B. A. Marshall, *Historia* 24 (1975) 216.

333. Consuls positively refuse command: Cic. *Phil.* 11.18, cf. D.C. 36.25.3 (from a composed speech). *S.C.* to appoint Pompey on motion of L. Philippus: Plu. *Pomp.* 17.3. Debate in Senate regarding what grade of *imperium* Pompey should receive (with Philippus' jibe that he should be sent "pro consulibus"): Cic. *Man.* 62 (showing that the opposition argued "non oportere mitti hominem privatum pro console"), *Phil.* 11.18, cf. Plu. *Pomp.* 17.4, Oros. 5.23.8, *Vir. ill.* 77.4 (all reporting the "pro consulibus" joke, though one doubts whether the last source understood it) and *Per.* 91 "cum imperio proconsulari." It is abundantly clear that Pompey was granted consular *imperium* to fight Sertorius in Spain. Valerius Maximus (8.15.8) may reflect what was surely a central issue in the debate, i.e., what Pompey's relationship to Metellus Pius was to be. Metellus still seems technically to have had precedence: see Plu. *Pomp.* 19.5; also 13.4.5 below. On Hispania Citerior as Pompey's province, see Plin. *Nat.* 3.18 (quite clear) and cf. Sal. *Hist.* 2.98.9 M.

334. Members of Pompey's staff include—or would include—C. Cornelius (*tr. pl.* 67) as quaestor (Asc. p. 57 C), Cassius Longinus as quaestor (D.C. 41.24.2), a D. Laelius *legatus* who saw some portents and (later) fell at Lauro (Obseq. 58, dated to 77 B.C., but only the portents and not his death need belong to that year), and M. Terentius Varro (R 3.12.7).

335. Vell. 2.31.3.

336. The sources vary on the precise details. The law granted Pompey *legati* to the number of fifteen (D.C. 36.37.1) or, as Appian has it, twenty-five of senatorial rank (*Mith.* 94.431). Most detailed (and credible) is Plutarch, who says originally there were fifteen *legati* of senatorial rank, and then the number was raised to 24 ("who had held command or served as praetors"), with two quaestors thrown in as well (*Pomp.* 25.3, 26.1). Velleius (2.32.4) is vague. Their *imperium* came personally from Pompey: App. *Mith.* 94.432.

337. App. *Mith.* 95.434–436 and Flor. 1.41.9–10 offer lists of Pompey's *legati*, on which see esp. L. P. D. Breglia, *AFLN* 13 (1970–1971) 47–66 (mainly *Quellenforschung*, but also collecting all the relevant earlier bibliography). The *consulares* are L. Gellius (*pr.* 94 and *cos.* 72) and Cn. Cornelius Lentulus Clodianus (*cos.* 72). Consular legates rarely appear in military campaigns of the later Republic (see J. P. V. D. Balsdon, *JRS* 55 [1965] 231); Pompey was giving this pair a chance to remove the blot of their massive failure against Spartacus in 72 (on which see 11.8.7). *Praetorii*: L. Cornelius Sisenna (*pr.* 78), M. Pupius Piso Frugi Calpurnianus (*pr.* by 71, and a *triumphator*), (surely) M. Terentius Varro, and quite possibly

A. Manlius Torquatus (*pr.* ca. 70). Ti. Claudius Nero was possibly a *praetorius* in 63 (Sal. *Cat.* 50.4 with *MRR* II 463) and so perhaps already at the time of the *lex Gabinia*.

338. Each *legatus* had his own district (Plu. *Pomp.* 25.3), thirteen in all (26.1), and had both land and sea forces (App. *Mith.* 94.432). Limited to assigned stations: *Mith.* 94.432–433, 95.437–438, 440, cf. D.C. 37.37.3. P. Groebe, in his fundamental discussion of Pompey's *legati pro praetore* (*Klio* 10 [1910] 374–389), offers a map of districts (between pp. 388 and 389).

339. D.C. 36.37.2, Plu. *Pomp.* 27.1–2 (fierce opposition in Rome to efforts by the *cos.* C. Calpurnius Piso to keep these *legati* out of his assigned *provincia* of Gallia Transalpina).

340. *Pomp.* 27.4.

341. Plu. *Pomp.* 32.1 (probable use of some of these *legati* in 66).

342. Cf. Plin. *Nat.* 37.16 (rewards in 61 "legatis et quaestoribus, qui oras maris defendissent"), and Cic. *Red. Pop.* 17, the naval detachment which L. Gellius is said to have protected against Catiline (*MRR* II 156 n. 4).

343. Scope of command: Cic. *Att.* 4.1.7 (Sept. 57) "per quinquennium omnis potestas rei frumentariae toto orbe terrarum" (see also this passage on the tribune C. Messius' extravagant proposal on Pompey's powers, discussed in 2.2.2), *Dom.* 25 (Pompey) "extra ordinem rei frumentariae praeficiendus . . . fuit," *Per.* 104 "per quinquennium annonae cura mandata est," Plu. *Pomp.* 49.4, also D.C. 39.9.3 (specifying consular *imperium*, and pirate command as model). According to Cic. *Att.* 4.1.7, Pompey asked for fifteen *legati*, including the *consularis* M. Tullius Cicero; cf. App. *BC* 2.18.67 (twenty senatorial "assistants," again citing the pirate command as precedent). Pompey's travel to (i.e., interference in) praetorian provinces: Cic. *Fam.* 1.9.9, Plu. *Pomp.* 50.1, *Moralia* 204 C.

344. J. P. V. D. Balsdon, *JRS* 52 (1962) 137–139 argues that when Caesar in 56 asked the Senate to send him "decem legati" in Gaul, the request was for ten *legati pro praetore*. But that could hardly be characterized as "unprecedented" (cf. Cic. *Prov.* 28) after the example of 67 and (perhaps) 57. Rather, Caesar must have been seeking to undercut the established procedure of the Senate's "Commission of Ten" (formally known as the "decem legati"), all with an eye toward pushing through the ratification of his own *acta* in Gaul. Dio (39.25.1) confuses the ten *legati* of 56 B.C. with that old institution, which (one suspects) would have delighted Caesar.

345. Contradictions: *Agr.* 2.26, 29–30. Rullus' care: see esp. 2.31–32 (reference to *pullarii*) with T. C. Brennan, *AJPh* 118 (1997) 145.

346. See *MRR* II 168. Cf. Cic. *Att.* 2.1.3 for the publication of the speeches in 59 B.C.

347. Cic. *Agr.* 2.26–28, 31–32, 45, also 1.9, 2.34 and 2.99 "summum imperium." The *lex curiata* for the *Xviri* was to be passed by a praetor, determined by electoral order, not *provincia*: 2.26.

348. Cic. *Agr.* 2.33–34, 45.

349. Plu. *Cic.* 12.2–4.

350. See D. J. Gargola, *Lands, Laws and Gods: Magistrates and Ceremony in the Regulation of Public Lands in Republican Rome* (Chapel Hill, N.C., 1995) 179. An even more elaborate variation was soon to follow in 59 B.C., i.e., the board of twenty created to assign land under Caesar's agrarian laws, and alongside it a board of five (with overlapping members) that also had judicial powers (see Gargola, ibid. 179–180, 185).

351. Cic. *Agr.* 2.30–31.

352. Cic. *Agr.* 2.34–35, 45.

353. Cic. *Agr.* 2.34 "cum velint, Romae esse, cum commodum sit, quacumque velint summo cum imperio iudicioque rerum omnium vagari ut liceat conceditur."

354. For this technical expression, see, e.g., Cic. *Att.* 7.5.3, *Fam.* 3.8.1 and 16.11.2, Caes. *Gal.* 6.1.2, *Civ.* 1.5.3, and in general Ps.-Asc. p. 260 St.

355. *JRS* 55 (1965) 110–121.

356. Sources for this and what follows are collected in *MRR* II 195f and 198, of which see *Schol. Bob.* p. 133 St. on the possible pretext.

357. Lobbying: Plu. *Cat. Min.* 34.3–4. Cato's traditional opposition to such commands: Cic. *Dom.* 21–22, *Sest.* 60.

358. For the title see Vell. 2.45.4, *Vir. ill.* 80.2. Staff: Vell. 2.45.4, Plu. *Cat. Mi.* 34.6. Military capability: Cic. *Dom.* 20, cf. Plu. *Pomp.* 48.6 (προφάσει στρατηγίας). Pace F. X. Ryan, *C&M* 46 (1995) 149, this grant of a quaestor to a *pro quaestore* was clearly exceptional.

359. Sources (many) on this commission are gathered in *MRR* II 198.

360. Procession: Plu. *Cat. Mi.* 39.1–3, cf. Flor. 1.44.5, D.C. 39.22.4 and 39.23.1. Plutarch characterizes Cato's return as rude, snubbing consuls and praetors: Plu. *Cat. Mi.* 39.1–2. For a more charitable interpretation: Vell. 2.45.5, cf. V. Max. 8.15.10.

361. V. Max. 4.1.4, Plu. *Cat. Mi.* 39.3–4, D.C. 39.23.1 and 4 (reporting it was on the motion of both consuls). One of the consuls was Cato's father-in-law, L. Marcius Philippus (see Plu. *Cat. Min.* 39.5).

362. Mommsen, *St.-R.* I² 570 n. 2; cf. Linderski, *Roman Questions* 120 n. 32, on the date of the elections for 55. Cato still had not returned from Cyprus at the time of Luca in Apr. 56 (Plu. *Caes.* 21.8).

363. H. E. Russell, "Insignia of Office as Rewards in the Roman republic: Advancement in Rank for the Soldier and the Public Prosecutor" (diss. Bryn Mawr 1950) 44–45. Russell considers the Senate's vote (as reported by Plutarch and Dio) as a form of the *dona militaria*, and adduces (not entirely convincingly) the *toga praetexta* granted to the centurion Cn. Petreius Atratinus in the Cimbrian War (Plin. *Nat.* 22.11) as a precedent.

364. Strab. 14.6.6 pp. 684–685, cf. also Vell. 2.38.6, *Per.* 104, and cf. App. *BC* 2.23.86 (with erroneous date of 52).

365. Cyprus joined to mainland *provincia*: Cic. *Fam.* 1.7.4 (to Spinther, end of Aug. 56) "qui Ciliciam Cyprumque teneas." Spinther's administrative arrangements in Cyprus: *Fam.* 13.48, which mentions a *lex Cornelia* (as well as some *constituta* that Cicero as *pro cos.* for Cilicia in 51/50 gave the island). Affair of M. Scaptius: Cic. *Att.* 6.1.4–7, 2.7–9, 3.5. Cicero delegates litigation to his *praefectus* Q. Volusius: *Att.* 5.21.6. Cicero's other references to Cyprus in connection with his command are slim: *Att.* 5.21.7 (Cyprus pays 200 talents to avoid Roman winter camp in 51/50), cf. *Fam.* 15.4.15 (mention). First quaestor: Cic. *Fam.* 13.48 with E. Badian, *JRS* 55 (1965) 114–115, on the suggested date and explanation of his presence. For the end of Roman rule of the island, see D.C. 42.35.5 and cf. A. J. Marshall, *Phoenix* 18 (1964) 207–208 (suggesting it came perhaps later than 47 B.C.).

366. Sal. *Hist.* 1.77.22 M with Kunkel, *Staatsordnung* 233, cf. App. *BC* 1.107.503 and 11.8.5.

367. See Plu. *Pomp.* 16.2 ἀπεδείχθη στρατεύματος ἡγεμών ἐπὶ τὸν Λέπιδον with *MRR* II 90 ("probably *pro praetore*").

368. See Criniti ap. *MRR* III 161–162, to be preferred to the suggestion of B. Twyman (*MRR* III 161–162, apparently endorsed by Broughton) that Pompey's *imperium* came from the *interrex* Ap. Claudius Pulcher. Two main battles in war: Oros. 5.22.16. Battle near Rome: Flor. 2.11.6–7, cf. App. *BC* 1.107.504. Lengthy siege at Mutina: Plu. *Pomp.* 16.3; full sources in *MRR* II 90. Pompey assists Catulus by cutting down fugitives from Cosa: Jul. Exup. 6.39 "Pompeius de Gallia rediens" (this source is well informed on the Lepidan revolt), cf. *Vir. ill.* 77.3. Pompey's later actions at Alba against Lepidus' son: Oros. 5.22.17, cf. 24.16. Pompey said to capitalize on Catulus' success: Plu. *Pomp.* 31.7 (reported speech). Order from Catulus to disband troops: *Pomp.* 17.3. I should think Pompey's massacre of the senate of Mediolanum to forestall a *tumultus* (Fron. *Str.* 1.9.3) is to be attached not to this legateship but to his transit to Spain as *pro cos.* later in 77.

369. Fron. *Str.* 1.5.21.

370. Sources collected in *MRR* II 109. For the chronology, see Sal. *Hist.* 3.96 and 98 M (defeats of later commander Varinius dated to summer and autumn).

371. *Per.* 95, Flor. 2.8.4, Oros. 5.24.1, Plu. *Crass.* 9.2, App. *BC* 1.116.541. On Appian's mistake, see the discussion in *MRR* II 115 n. 1.

372. See *RDGE* 23 with *MRR* II 109, III 54.

373. Thus F. X. Ryan, *Klio* 78 (1996) 377–378.

374. Subsequent to Claudius Glaber: Plu. *Crass.* 9.5. Enhanced *imperium*: Fron. *Str.* 1.5.22 "L. Varinio proconsule." F. X. Ryan, who wants to deny Varinius a praetorship in 73 — solely on the grounds that this same man was praetor in 67 or 66 — dismisses the evidence of the Frontinus passage out of hand (*Klio* 78 [1996] 374 n. 2).

375. For which see *MRR* II 110.

376. Status of Furius: Plu. *Crass.* 9.5 ὑποστράτηγος. Other subordinates: note the quaestor C. Thoranius (Flor. 2.8.5 with Sal. *Hist.* 3.96 M), and just possibly the *legatus* "Claudius Pulcher" of *Per.* 95.

377. *Crass.* 9.5 σύμβουλον αὐτῷ καὶ συνάρχοντα; cf. Sal. *Hist.* 3.94 M.

378. *Legatus*: cf. *MRR* III 77, and now F. X. Ryan, *Klio* 78 (1996) 376. *MRR* II 110 tentatively has him as a praetor in 73, following a suggestion of Münzer (*RE* s.v. *Cossinius* 2 col. 1671).

379. Plu. *Crass.* 9.7, App. *BC* 1.116.541, Flor. 2.8.5. See Sal. *Hist.* 3.96, 98 M for the chronology.

380. *MRR* II 115 n. 1, 119; also H. Gundel, *RE* s.v. *Varinius* 1 col. 384. As noted above (11.8.1), he seems to have made a comeback as *pr.* II in the mid-60s, even receiving Asia as his promagisterial *provincia*: see 14.6.5.

381. Q. Arrius was definitely *pr.* 73 (*MRR* II 109), though nothing is known of his city activities; see *MRR* II 117 for sources on the modification of his promagisterial *provincia*, esp. Cic. *Ver.* 2.2.37, 2.4.42 on the lateness of the decision to keep Arrius in Italy. *Per.* 96 gives his title for 72 as "praetor." *Schol. Gron.* p. 324 St. thinks that the reason Verres was prorogued was that Arrius had died in transit! This is surely a pure conjecture: see Sumner, *Orators* 130.

382. Victory: Oros. 5.24.4, App. 1.117.542–543; cf. Plu. *Crass.* 9.9. Defeat: compare *Per.* 96 with Oros. 5.24.4 and App. *BC* 1.117.544. On Q. Arrius' further career—which included a tentative candidacy for the consulship of 58—see the references in Broughton, *MRR* II 161 (here following Klebs's mistaken notion in *RE* s.v. *Arrius* 7 and 8 coll. 1252–1254 that there were two praetorian Q. Arrii active at this time) with *MRR* III 25 and *Candidates Defeated* 23 (rightly combining *RE* nos. 7 and 8). For a fuller (and not entirely satisfactory) study, see B. A. Marshall and R. J. Baker, *Historia* 24 (1975) 220–231 (incidentally, at p. 226 letting his great victory of 72 pass without notice). H. Mattingly, "M. Antonius, C. Verres, and the Sack of Delos by the Pirates," in M. J. Fontana, M. T. Piraino, and F. P. Rizzo (eds.), in Φιλίας Χάριν: *Miscellenea di studi classici in onore di Eugenio Manni* IV (Rome 1979) 1508, is more appreciative.

383. *Per.* 96.

384. See Plu. *Cat. Mi.* 8.2; cf. Cic. *Ver.* 2.5.2 "imperatorum peniuriam."

385. *Per.* 96; full sources in *MRR* II 116–118.

386. Defeat of *cos.* Clodianus: *Per.* 96. His *legati*: Plu. *Crass.* 9.9. Appennines: Flor. 2.8.10. Spartacus' victory: *Per.* 96 (Gellius and Arrius), Oros. 5.24.4 (both consuls); App. *BC* 1.117.544 has Spartacus defeat each consul in turn.

387. *Per.* 96; Oros. 5.24.4.

388. *BC* 1.117.546.

389. Plu. *Crass.* 10.1, Oros. 5.24.5.

390. As Prof. Christopher Mackay has suggested to me.

391. Starting at *BC* 1.118.550.

392. See *MRR* II 121 n. 2 for the chronology. Sources for Crassus' activities in 72 and 71 can be found in *MRR* II 118 and 123.

393. Plu. *Crass.* 11.3, cf. Cic. *Man.* 30, Plu. *Pomp.* 21.1 and App. *BC* 1.119.554, 120.555.

394. Though Pompey certainly tried: Plu. *Crass.* 11.10, *Pomp.* 21.2, Jul. *Caes.* 322 D. For the role of M. Terentius Varro Lucullus in the last stage of this conflict, see App. *BC* 1.120.557 with 14.2.2. On the vote, see App. *BC* 1.119.554–555 with H. T. Wallinga, *Athenaeum* 70 (1992) 40f.

395. App. *BC* 1.121.560 ὁ μὲν ἐστρατηγηκὼς κατὰ τὸν νόμον Σύλλα with *MRR* III 120.

396. Eutrop. 6.7.2.

397. See App. *BC* 1.121.560, and cf. 1.100.466 with 10.5.7 above on Q. Lucretius Afella.

398. See Cic. *Pis.* 58 and Gel. 5.6.23 (explicit on the role of Crassus' *gratia* in obtaining the requisite *S.C.*). One last note on the chronology: The (undated) prosecution of Crassus for *incestum* with the Vestal Virgin Licinia (sources in Alexander, *Trials* no. 169, cf. 168) should almost certainly be attached to the famous trial of the Vestals Fabia and Licinia in 73 (Cic. *Brut.* 236, *Catil.* 3.9, with full sources in *Trials* no. 167): see Marshall, *Asconius* 310. If true, the trial does not exclude 73 as the possible date of Crassus' praetorship. The case of the quaestor P. Clodius in 61 B.C. (see ch. 10 n. 255 and 11.9.2 below) shows that—in this age at least—magistrates in office might be subject to prosecution for religious offences.

399. On the initial Roman response to the increased pirate activity in these years, see D.C. 36.23.2; cf. Cic. *Leg. Man.* 53.

400. *Man.* 33.

401. App. *Mith.* 93.423; cf. D.C. 36.23.2.

402. See Cic. *Man.* 33 with App. *Mith.* 93.427, Plu. *Pomp.* 24.6.

403. *Pomp.* 24.6; the form "Bellinus" is unparalleled.

404. *Man.* 53 with 32, App. *Mith.* 93.427.

405. Cic. *Rab. Perd.* 26 with T. R. S. Broughton, *TAPhA* 77 (1946) 36–37.

406. D.C. 37.41.1 (the source of the quotation) with Oros. 6.6.7. On contemporary conditions in these regions, see R. Stewart, *Latomus* 54 (1995) 73f.

407. *Schol. Bob.* p. 175 St.; cf. Cic. *Arch.* 3 and 32 with 11.7.7.

408. That Quintus held the urban *provincia* is tentatively suggested by *MRR* II 173; see, however, *MRR* III 106.

409. See Caesar's comments in *Civ.* 3.16.3, noting Bibulus' opposition as his colleague in both the (curule) aedileship (of 65) and praetorship. Both men, of course, would be colleagues again in the consulship of 59.

410. Cic. *Clu.* 136–137 (not in Alexander, *Trials* as such); cf. *Trials* no. 153 (the *iudicium populi*).

411. Cic. *Att.* 1.17.8 (5 Dec. 61); cf. Alexander, *Trials* no. 236 (not separating it from Clodius' main trial).

412. Cic. *Vat.* 26 (not in Alexander, *Trials*, as such).

413. Alexander (*Trials* no. 264) cites Cic. *Att.* 4.3.3 and *Q. fr.* 2.1.2 as evidence of a mooted *quaestio extraordinaria* to try Clodius for violence against Cicero in late 57 B.C., but the passages only vaguely support this assumption. By mid-Feb. 56, the *tr. pl.* C. Porcius Cato had promulgated a *rogatio* of some sort against T. Annius Milo (an ex-tribune of 57) which Cicero was eager to see stopped, by violence if need be (*Q. fr.* 2.3.4); it is possible that it provided for a special *quaestio*.

414. Explicit in Cic. *Mil.* 13.

415. Full sources with discussion in Alexander, *Trials* nos. 167–169. General references to trials of "virgines": Cic. *Catil.* 3.9 (providing date), *Brut.* 236. Prosecution of Fabia and (perhaps) Catiline for *incestum*: Asc. p. 91 C, Oros. 6.3.1 and cf. Sal. *Cat.* 15.1, Q. Cic. *Pet.*

10, *Schol. Gron.* p. 287 St. with E. S. Gruen, *Athenaeum* 49 (1971) 61 n. 28 and Marshall, *Asconius* 310; see also Plu. *Cat. Mi.* 19.5 (often taken as evidence for P. Clodius as prosecutor, but almost certainly not to be assigned to the year 73—see Alexander, *Trials* p. 83 n. 3). Prosecution of Licinia: Plu. *Crass.* 1.4. Trial of Crassus: Plu. *Crass.* 1.4–5 (his defense before the *iudices*), also *Moralia* 89 E; contra D. R. Shackleton Bailey (*CLA* I 319), who argues Crassus (like Catiline) "was never formally accused." On the "secularization" of *incestum* trials, see E. Rawson, *Roman Culture and Society: Collected Papers* (Oxford 1991) 163f (but suggesting that "Peducaeus' bill, or a subsequent one, was generally framed," i.e., set up a regular procedure).

416. Cic. *Att.* 1.13.3. Sources can be found in Alexander, *Trials* no. 236 (omitting to note the nature of the court president), to which add Cic. *Att.* 1.14. For a general study of the trial, see P. Moreau, *Clodiana Religio*, esp. 51–141 on Clodius' offense and the reaction, and 151–222 for his reconstruction of the procedure. On the religious aspect, see esp. J. Scheid in *Le délit religieux dans la cité antique* (Rome 1981) 130–133. For an illuminating exposition of the procedural debate, see W. K. Lacey, *Antichthon* 8 (1974) 85–92. On the surprising fact that Clodius had no immunity from prosecution by virtue of his magistracy, see ch. 10 n. 255.

417. For the S.C., see Asc. p. 53 C "decretum . . . <ut> extra ordinem <de ea re> iudicium fieret," also Sen. *Ep.* 97.7 "in ea ipsa quaestione quae extra ordinem senatus consulto exercebatur," and esp. Cic. *Att.* 1.13.3, 14.1, 16.2 and *Schol. Bob.* p. 89 St. "non aliter quam de incestu quaereretur." (On that last item, see Stangl's note ad loc., pointing out that the scholiast seems particularly well informed on this trial.) On the apparently unique method of selecting the jury, see the comments of Mommsen, *Strafrecht* 211–212 with 198 n. 3; J. L. Strachan-Davidson, *Problems of the Roman Criminal Law* II (Oxford 1912) 102.

418. *Legal Procedure* 387, followed by P. Moreau, *Clodiana Religio* 98. Strachan-Davidson (*Problems of the Roman Criminal Law* II 102) is more cautious: "choice of the one method or the other was the issue vital to the success of the prosecution."

419. On the agitation of the *tr. pl.* Q. Fufius Calenus which led to the adoption of his *rogatio*, see Cic. *Att.* 1.14.1–2 and 5–6; 16.2; Asc. p. 44 C, *Schol. Bob.* p. 85 St., cf. Cic. *Mil.* 13 and *Parad.* 32 (that last passage showing that exile was to be the definitive punishment if Clodius was found guilty). Fufius' bill at least provided for a challenging of jurors: *Att.* 1.16.3.

420. For the *invidia* arising from this trial, see e.g. Cic. *Att.* 1.13.3, 14.5 ("Piso autem consul, lator rogationis, idem erat dissuasor"), 16.2 (Cicero's view that the trial was better threatened than implemented); this point is somewhat lost on Moreau, *Clodiana Religio* 97, who sees the involvement of the ("urban") praetor as natural. Of the consuls, Piso was friendly to Clodius and supportive of Fufius (Cic. *Att.* 1.13.3, 14.1 and 5–6), while Messalla proved a stalwart advocate of the S.C. in its original form (*Att.* 1.13.3, 14.2 and 5), but obviously did not want to pique his colleague by pressing to preside himself. Necessity of Senate's resolution (vetoed by Fufius) that consuls persuade the People of utility of *rogatio* in original terms: *Att.* 1.14.5. Clodius' opposition to prosecution: Cic. *Att.* 1.14.5 (use of *sodalitates*—see Linderski, *Roman Questions* 210—gangs, and fiery *contiones*) with *Schol. Bob.* p. 85 St.

421. Cic. *Att.* 1.16.4 (not specifically identifying a praetor as the presiding magistrate). For speculation as to his identity, see Moreau, *Clodiana Religio* 132f.

422. Cic. *Att.* 1.16.5, Sen. *Ep.* 97.6 ("iudices Clodiani"), Plu. *Cic.* 29.6, *Schol. Bob.* p. 85 St.

423. Cic. *Att.* 1.17.8 (5 Dec. 61).

424. On the date of the passage of the two (Asc. p. 36 C) *leges Pompeiae* (quite uncertain, but probably by 25 Mar.), see Linderski, *Roman Questions* 246 n. 63, cf. Marshall, *Asconius* 184 (with 177 for the date of Pompey's entry into office).

425. See the exposition of Gruen, *Last Generation* 233–239 (with full documentation), rightly differentiating the nature of the two laws, esp. 236–237 for what is known of the provisions. The decisive case for Gruen's thesis is the prosecution of Ap. Claudius Pulcher for *ambitus* in 50 B.C. (Alexander, *Trials* no. 345), which was definitely under the *lex Pompeia* (Cic. *Brut.* 324). See also Greenidge, *Legal Procedure* 391–393 (but with a different general interpretation) and cf. (for a useful summation of the evidence on *ambitus*) Nadig, *Ardet Ambitus* 217–218. There were to be heavier penalties for both *vis* and *ambitus* (Asc. p. 36 C); for those convicted of the latter crime, that included (apparently) exile for life, with enhanced rewards for the successful prosecutors (see Nadig, *Ardet Ambitus* 218).

426. D.C. 40.52.3 and Tac. *Dial.* 38 with Gruen, *Last Generation* 237f; contra A. C. Clark, *M. Tulli Ciceronis Pro T. Annio Milone* (Oxford 1895) 101. On the "five days," see Marshall, *Asconius* 159–160.

427. See Caes. *Civ.* 3.1.4 with discussion by Greenidge, *Legal Procedure* 394–395, Strachan-Davidson, *Problems of the Roman Criminal Law* II 110–111, Gruen, *Last Generation* 238 n. 116, Marshall, *Asconius* 187. Precisely how the board of *iudices* of the first four days related to that of the fifth—for that apparently was the scheme—remains an open question. However conceptually this is not too far removed from Pompeius' anti-*ambitus* measures of 52 B.C., the full dissociation of magistracy in the city from promagistracy in a territorial province (11.1.7).

428. Asc. pp. 40–41 C.

429. General notices of extension to other trials: Plu. *Cic.* 35.1, App. *BC* 2.24.89, D.C. 40.54.1, cf. Cic. *Brut.* 324, Caes. *Civ.* 3.1, Tac. *Ann.* 3.28. Armed guards at the Milo trial (Alexander, *Trials* no. 309) (a selection): Cic. *Mil.* 1–3, 11, 70–71, 101, 105 with *Fam.* 3.10.10 (giving it a positive spin), also Asc. pp. 40–42 C, Quint. *Inst.* 4.1.20 and 4.2.25, Plu. *Cic.* 35.1–5, D.C. 40.53.1–3 and 54.1–2, *Schol. Bob.* p. 112 St. At the (alleged) trial of M. Scaurus *de ambitu* in 52 (*Trials* no. 319): App. *BC* 2.24.91. At the trial of T. Munatius Plancus Bursa in the special *quaestio de vi* (*Trials*, no. 327): D.C. 40.55.4. G. S. Bucher (*Historia* 44 [1995] 396–421) goes so far as to reject the "praesidium" as a formal feature of the trials of 52.

430. For disruption of judicial proceedings in a permanent *quaestio* through violence, see in addition to Alexander, *Trials* no. 71 (the prosecution of Servilius Augur ca. 91 B.C.), e.g., nos. 200 (P. Autronius defendant *de ambitu* in 66), 203 (C. Cornelius *de maiestate* in 66), 205 (C. Manilius *de repetundis* in 66), 210 (C. Manilius *de maiestate* in 65), 248 (threatened prosecution of A. Gabinius *de ambitu* in 59, with Cic. *Sest.* 18 for the alleged violence), 261 (P. Clodius *de vi* in 57), 295 (M. Aemilius Scaurus *de repetundis* in 54, with violence looming both before and after the proceedings—Asc. pp. 20 and 29 C), 296 (A. Gabinius *de maiestate* in 54, with esp. D.C. 39.62.2 and 63.1–2 on the atmosphere), and cf. no. 255 (P. Vatinius charged with violating the *lex Iunia Licinia* in 58).

431. Asc. p. 60 C (both consuls provide protection at the trial of C. Manilius *de maiestate* in 65); and see above in text on the bodyguard for the jurors at the *quaestio extra ordinem* that tried P. Clodius in 61.

432. Cic. *Mil.* 22, Asc. p. 38 C with Marshall, *Asconius* 184. It would be interesting to know whether any in the long series of *interreges* of the year 53 (see 11.1.7) got *quaesitores* appointed in this way—thus providing a direct precedent for Pompey. As it happens, we do not have positive evidence for any trials in that year, either before or after the curule magistrates finally took office in July or August. It seems difficult to believe, however, that no criminal justice was administered in the year 53 from 1 Jan. until after the time of the elections. Litigation in civil law was difficult though apparently not technically impossible in this *interregnum*: see Cic. *Fam.* 7.11.1 with A. W. Lintott, *JRS* 64 (1974) 67 and 71. On the source problem for this period, see G. S. Bucher, *Historia* 44 (1995) 402–404.

433. See Alexander, *Trials* nos. 309–312 with 11.7.2, 11.7.6, and 11.7.7 on the individual *quaesitores*.

434. Pompey will have held the praetorian elections for 52 B.C. by the first half of March: see n. 314 above. See also 11.7.2, 11.7.6, and 11.7.7 for the details of what follows immediately below, on the administration of the courts *de sodaliciis*, *de vi*, and *de ambitu*.

435. Trial of M. Saufeius (Alexander, *Trials* no. 313, "on or after ca. 12 April"), probably that of Sex. Cloelius (no. 315, "after 22 April") and other (unnamed) defendants, mostly Clodians (Asc. p. 56 C, not in Alexander as such). Next, two tribunes of 52, Q. Pompeius Rufus (no. 328) and T. Munatius Plancus Bursa: Plancus was tried after Rufus (D.C. 40.55.3, contra Alexander) between 10 Dec. 52 and the end of Jan. 51 (no. 327), probably after 31 Dec. (see Gruen, *Last Generation* 346 n. 172).

436. Trial of M. Saufeius (Alexander, *Trials* no. 314), with Considius as "quaesitor".

437. Probably C. Memmius (Alexander, *Trials* no. 320), and allegedly M. Aemilius Scaurus (no. 319), in each case—according to Appian—for offenses connected with the consular elections for 53 B.C. (see App. *BC* 2.24.90–93 on the form of each trial, and n. 18 above on the historicity of that of Scaurus). Then Q. Caecilius Metellus Pius Scipio Nasica (no. 321, with App. *BC* 2.24.93 and Plu. *Pomp.* 55.4 indicating the operative law), for his consular candidacy for 52 B.C. Finally, P. Plautius Hypsaeus (no. 322), consular candidate for 52 B.C., whose trial—almost certainly under the Pompeian law—followed that of Plancus *de vi* (Plu. *Pomp.* 55.6 with n. 435 above), and so came no earlier than late 52 B.C.

438. Trial of P. Sestius, *tr. pl.* 57 (Alexander, *Trials* no. 323), perhaps *de ambitu*—but for what elections is unknown. See further 15.1.2 (he was probably praetor by 49 B.C.).

439. Trial of T. Fadius (Alexander, *Trials* no. 318). Cf. nos. 316 and 317 (two prosecutions of P. Cornelius Dolabella, sometime before spring 51 B.C.).

440. We hear of prosecutions under the *lex Plautia* also in Sept. 51 B.C. See Alexander, *Trials* no. 331 (M. Tuccius as defendant, with Cael. *Fam.* 8.8.1 for the charge); cf. no. 341 (prosecution of Ap. Claudius Pulcher under an unspecified *lex de vi*—not the Pompeian one, as Alexander has it).

441. Tac. *Dial.* 38 implies as much.

442. *Ambitus* in 51 B.C.: see Alexander, *Trials* nos. 329 (M. Valerius Messalla Rufus, *cos. cand.* for 53), 330 (M. Calidius, *cos. cand.* for 51), 332 ("Servaeus," *tr. pl. cand.* 50), 333 (C. Claudius Marcellus, *cos. cand.* 50). *De sodaliciis*: no. 331 (M. Valerius Messalla Rufus, *cos. cand.* for 53). *Vis*: nos. 335 (M. Tuccius), 341 (Ap. Claudius Pulcher). *Ambitus* in 50 B.C.: no. 345 (Ap. Claudius Pulcher prosecuted for his conduct—apparently, though Gruen, *Last Generation* 352 n. 194, is dubious—in the censorial elections for 50), a trial specifically said to have been under the Pompeian law (n. 425 above); so we can assume the four *ambitus* trials of 51 B.C. were as well. Yet it is strange—given the severity of the *leges Pompeiae*—that when M. Valerius Messalla Rufus escaped condemnation for *ambitus* in 51 B.C., Caelius opined to Cicero that in his upcoming prosecution under the *lex Licinia de sodaliciis* he faced a more serious danger (*Fam.* 8.2.1).

443. *Trials* nos. 336–339.

Notes to Chapter 12

1. The one identifiable praetor to have conducted these games is Sex. Nonius Sufenas, on whom see Appendix B n. 349.

2. The *locus classicus* on the volume of praetorian legal business (both civil and criminal) is Cic. *N.D.* 3.74. See also *Caec.* 36 (on praetorian interdicts) "qui dies totos aut vim

fieri vetat aut restitui factam iubet, qui de fossis, de cloacis, de minimis aquarum itinerumque controversiis interdicit," cf. 74. For the (urban) praetor's clientele—which included litigants also from the various *municipia*—see esp. *Ver.* 2.1.127, 137–138, cf. 2.5.34. For an attempt to quantify the urban praetor's workload, see B. W. Frier, *The Rise of the Roman Jurists: Studies in Cicero's Pro Caecina* (Princeton 1985) 278 n. 14.

3. Known from *ILLRP* 479 (four *cippi* found at Ostia), "C. Caninius C.f. | pr. urb. | de sen(atus) sent(entia) | poplic(um) ioudic(avit)"; "probably before the period of Sulla" (*MRR* II 463). The abbreviation "de sen(atus) sent(entia)" (on which see ch. 5 n. 212) suggests a date after ca. 120; it is likely he was grandfather—though possibly father—of the *cos. suff.* 45. If so, the urban praetor's *cognomen* will have been Rebilus. On this individual, see Appendix B n. 518.

4. C. Getha: *cos.* 116, and so definitely reached the praetorship. See *RDGE* 13 lines 6–7 with T. Drew-Bear, *Historia* 21 (1972) 84f, for his presidency, possibly as praetor, of the Senate meeting which determined administrative arrangements for Phrygia (reclaimed some time after the death of Mithridates V of Pontus in 120); *contra* Münzer, *RE* s.v. Licinius 88 col. 375. C. Metellus Caprarius: *praetorius* at the time of his father Macedonicus' death in (early) 115 (Cic. *Fin.* 5.82, *Phil.* 8.14; Plin. *Nat.* 7.142; V. Max. 7.1.1; Vell. 1.11.7 "candidatus consulatus, quem honorem adeptus est"; cf. Plu. *Moralia* 318 B.C. "consular"), he reached the consulship in 113. T. R. S. Broughton (*MRR* I 530 n.2, cf. *Candidates Defeated in Roman Elections: Some Ancient Roman "Also-Rans"* [Philadelphia 1991] 9) suggests on the basis of the Velleius passage that Caprarius "must have held the praetorship not later than 117, and was defeated for the consulship of 114." But Velleius' formulation hardly gives confidence that he had exact information on this man. On the possible praetorian *provincia* see C. Cichorius, *Untersuchungen zu Lucilius* (Berlin 1908) 87; *MRR* I 530 n. 2.

5. *Rhet. Herr.* 2.19 (specifying *provincia*), cf. Cic. *Att.* 7.2.8 (a "Drusus praetor" cleverly rescinds a manumission). On the *Rhet. Herr.* passage, see esp. *Dig.* 17.1.34.1 for the legal point at issue and the bibliography in ch. 5 n. 272.

6. See *RDGE* 16 A lines 16–17 for this urban praetor (not "pr. urbanus or peregrinus" as *MRR* I 556 has it) and lines 17–18 for his counterpart in what must be the peregrine jurisdiction.

7. See sources in *MRR* I 14–15 (but under the year 93 B.C.), esp. Plu. *Sull.* 5.2 for C. Iulius Caesar Strabo's taunt that Sulla had "bought" the praetorship, *Vir. ill.* 75.3 for the *provinciae*, and Plin. *Nat.* 8.53 and Sen. *Dial.* 10.13.6 for the games. The *venatio* remained a staple of the *Ludi Apollinares* down to the end of our period: see Cic. *Att.* 4.15.6 (54 B.C.). On Sulla's praetorship and promagistracy, see T. C. Brennan, *Chiron* 22 (1992) 103–158. Cic. *Off.* 2.57 suggests that aedilician games had become consistently more sumptuous just shortly before Sulla's praetorship; for a detailed examination of the aediles mentioned in this passage, see F. X. Ryan, *Klio* 78 (1996) 68–86.

8. C. Valerius Flaccus: see 14.5.5. C. Sentius Saturninus: see *SIG*[3] 732 for urban praetorship of 94, and 14.1.3 below for promagistracy. On his praetorship add also to the sources in *MRR* (collected in II 15, 35, 42f, and 49 with III 191) Plin. *Nat.* 14.96 (from Varro).

9. Suit for debt: Cic. *de Orat.* 1.168 (indicating that it came shortly before Crassus' death on 20 Sept. 91). For an exposition of the legal issue, see A. H. J. Greenidge, *The Legal Procedure of Cicero's Time* (Oxford 1901) 176–177, also M. Kaser, *Das römische Zivilprozeßrecht* (Munich 1966) 567. On the city praetor's *consilium* for civil proceedings (references are sparse), see Greenidge, *Legal Procedure* 133–134, F. Wieacker, *Römische Rechtsgeschichte* I: *Einleitung, Quellenkunde, Frühzeit und Republik* (Munich 1988) 556 n. 19; W. Kunkel, *Staatsordnung und Staatspraxis der römischen Republik: Die Magistratur* (Munich 1995) 136 n. 138. The reluctance of consulars to serve as the *legati* of praetorian commanders is discussed in 14.5.4 below.

10. V. Max. 3.5.2; cf. *RS* II 40 *Tab.* V, 7h with commentary on p. 645.

11. See App. *BC* 1.54.232–239 and also V. Max. 9.7.4 and *Per.* 74 with the reconstruction of E. Badian, *Historia* 18 (1969) 475–481 (esp. 479 n. 98 suggesting the point on the *exceptio* as "the most reasonable possibility"), which I have followed closely here.

12. P. Burrenus: see D. R. Shackleton Bailey, *CEQF* 192–193, *Two Studies in Roman Nomenclature*[2] (Atlanta, Ga., 1991) 13. and *Onomasticon to Cicero's Speeches* (Norman, Okla., 1988) 24 for name and references to his praetorship of 83 (the date is certain). Burrenus and the *nobiles*: Cic. *Q. fr.* 2.11(10).3, with Wiseman's conjecture "qui Burrenum," on which see Shackleton Bailey, *Onomasticon to Cicero's Letters* (Stuttgart 1995) 23. His relationship with Sex. Naevius: *Quinct.* 69–70. Grants *missio*: *Quinct.* 26, 33, 48, cf. 26, 30, 45, 48, 83–85 on his edict and 63, 65 on Burrenus' use of praetorian powers. L. Iunius Damasippus: see the discussion in 10.5.6. Cn. Cornelius Dolabella forces *sponsio* between Quinctius and Sex. Naevius: *Quinct.* 30, 33, 71, 96; cf. 9–10 and 84. *Sponsio* as bad innovation: *Quinct.* 30, cf. 9–10, 30 on relationship to his edict. Edictal provisions inappropriate to Quinctius' situation: see (esp.) *Quinct.* 36, 48, 54, 60, 82–84. The date of the speech, and thus Cn. Dolabella's praetorship, is certain (ch. 11 n. 3).

13. Burrenus: *MRR* II 62, III 35. Dolabella: II 76, III 65.

14. Cic. *Corn.* I F 36 Crawford[2] in Asc. p. 74 C = M. C. Alexander, *Trials in the Late Roman Republic* (Toronto 1990) no. 127 (Dolabella's arbitrary treatment of a C. Volcacius).

15. See B. W. Frier, *TAPhA* 113 (1983) 222 n. 3 and 232–233 with *Rise of the Roman Jurists* 93: but that involves an unlikely interpretation of Cic. *Q. fr.* 1.1.21, on which see n. 84 below. Another alternative has been to attach the *formula Octaviana* (for which see Cic. *Ver.* 2.3.152) to L. Octavius, in a praetorship before he reached the consulship for 75: see Münzer, *RE* s.v. *Octavius* 26 col. 1819.

16. See 12.2.1 below on the edictal innovations of M. Terentius Varro Lucullus as *pr. per.* in 76 and perhaps also 11.7.2 on C. Aquillius Gallus as *pr. de ambitu* in 66. At *TAPhA* 113 (1983) 221–241 and *Rise of the Roman Jurists* 92–94, Frier offers three other highly conjectural candidates for the urban *provincia*: an L. Scribonius Libo as *pr.* 80 (guessing that the urban praetor's tribunal was moved from the *comitium* to a spot near the *puteal Libonis* precisely at this time); a Salvius (inferring his existence from the *interdictum Salvianum*, on pledges by *coloni*) as *pr. urb.* 76; and (very) tentatively, the *pr.* 67 Q. Publicius (because of the *actio Publiciana*). That last suggestion seems very dubious (see n. 69 below), while the others are so speculative that inclusion in the *fasti* set out in Appendix B would serve only to mislead.

17. For the joint jurisdiction, see *RDGE* 22 lines 2–3 (22 May 78, cited in ch. 5 n. 17).

18. Thus C. Damon and C. S. Mackay, *Historia* 44 (1995) 52 n. 65, reviving an old suggestion of M. Voigt, *Römische Rechtsgeschichte* I (Leipzig 1892) 721 with n. 18.

19. Gran. Lic. 36.36–38 C, cf. Sal. *Hist.* 1.66 M.

20. Cic. *Corn.* I F 37 Crawford[2] in Asc. p. 74 C with A. W. Lintott, *CQ* 27 (1977) 184–186, esp. 185 for the quotes. Alexander, *Trials* no. 134, cites (only) Lintott but misinterprets the anecdote by having P. Scipio receive *possessio bonorum*.

21. Date and *provincia* are certain from V. Max. 7.7.6 "praetore urbis" (i.e., "urbanus," as 7.7.5 and esp. 7.7.7 make clear); see probably also Cic. *Off.* 2.58 with R. E. A. Palmer ap. F. X. Ryan, *SIFC* 13 (1995) 248 n. 11 (Orestes' disposition of a tithe for *prandia*, to be connected with the cult of Hercules at the Ara Maxima, which the urban praetor supervised).

22. For the actual abrogation of *imperium*, a vote of the People or Plebs was required (Mommsen, *St.-R.* I[3] 629 n. 4). For *abrogare* in a nonliteral sense, see V. Max. 7.7.3 and 8.5.1. But cf. perhaps Cic. *Ver.* 2.2.140.

23. Sources: *MRR* II 97 (Broughton does not bother to query Sacerdos as "pr. urbanus"). Predecessor of Verres in civil law activities: cf. Cic. *Ver.* 2.1.104, 121 (particularly clear), and 125 with Ps.-Asc. p. 251 St. (his *edictum*). Predecessor in temple repair: *Ver.* 2.1.130.

24. For C. Verres, see (for an indication of the range of formulations) Cic. *Ver.* 1.12 "praetura urbana," 1.39 "praetore urbano," 2.1.104 "sortem nactus est urbanae provinciae," 2.1.112 "ex urbano edicto decernere," 2.1.127 "praetorem urbanum," 2.2.39 "in urbana iuris dictione," 2.3.78 "in . . . praetura . . . urbana," 2.5.34 "iura . . . praetoris urbani," 2.5.38 "cum tibi sorte obtigisset uti ius diceres."

25. Abuses in public contracts as a major category: *Ver.* 1.12, 2.1.103, 127.

26. Cic. *Ver.* 2.1.154, cf. 2.5.186.

27. Cic. *Ver.* 2.1.11.

28. Cic. *Ver.* 2.1.130–154, esp. 130 "qua potestate . . . permissa." On Verres and the temple contract, see the brief discussion of S. D. Martin, *The Roman Jurists and the Organization of Private Building in the Late Republic and Early Empire* (Brussels 1989) 74 and 103–104.

29. Cic. *Ver.* 2.5.184–186. Cicero suggests some other reasons for outrage at Verres' treatment of the temple at 2.1.129.

30. See Cic. *Ver.* 2.1.148–149, cf. 147 (describing the necessary repair as a simple task, undermining the assertion that the deadline Verres set was "unreasonably" tight). Verres applied unwanted innovations to the censors' contract: *Ver.* 2.1.143. The crooked setting of bidding times and the flouting of censorial law are attributes that Verres shows again in Sicily: see *Ver.* 2.3.16–17, 51 (continuity between city and provincial practice explicit). Evidence for praetors setting contracts for the remainder of our period is largely lacking. M. Pupius Piso Frugi Calpurnianus as city praetor (by 71) was engaged in building activities: see *ILLRP* 377 with Degrassi *ad loc.* (yet note that no title is preserved); also E. Badian, "M. Calpurnius M.F. Frugi," in *Acta of the Fifth International Congress of Greek and Latin Epigraphy, Cambridge 1967* (Oxford 1971) 209–214, esp. 212 (conjecturing that the building in question was a granary).

31. Cic. *Ver.* 1.39, 2.1.157 with Ps.-Asc. pp. 219 and 255 St., cf. also *Clu.* 121 (adding the detail that urban praetors assembled those jury lists under oath). In general on these passages, see Greenidge, *Legal Procedure* 437–439. By the early 50s, it appears that the city quaestors aided the urban praetor in this task: see D.C. 39.7.4 with Cic. *Q. fr.* 2.1.2, and the discussion of Mommsen, *St.-R.* II³ 585 and n. 5. Perhaps the quaestors were an original feature of the system of jury allotment for permanent criminal *quaestiones*. But it seems possible that they came into the process only some time after the year 74 B.C., the object being to relieve the urban praetor of some of his workload. For a review of the evidence on dividing jurors for private courts, see Frier, *Rise of the Roman Jurists* 200–201, esp. 200 n. 12.

32. See Cic. *Ver.* 2.1.155–157 (esp. 157 "cum praetor iudicio eius praefuisset"), and cf. Ps.-Asc. p. 255 and *Schol. Gronov.* p. 341 St. with Alexander, *Trials* no. 157.

33. Cic. *Ver.* 2.1.122.

34. Cic. *Ver.* 2.1.103 "et iuris dicendi et sartorum tectorum exigendorum."

35. Cic. *Ver.* 2.3.16.

36. Alexander, *Trials* nos. 151 and 156 (Verres alleged to have applied retrospective conditions to wills that had gone uncontested in 75 B.C.); 152 (Verres granted the goods of a deceased Minucius to a man who claimed to be heir, rather than to the *gens Minucia*); also (not in Alexander) *Ver.* 2.1.123–124 (Verres forbade a freedman to enter into an inheritance because he took an oath, prescribed under the terms of the will, that was technically illegal). For a description of these cases, with the legal points at issue, see F. H. Cowles, *Gaius Verres: An Historical Study* (Ithaca, N.Y., 1917) 17–21.

37. Cic. *Ver.* 2.1.105, 119.

38. Conflict with statutory law: Cic. *Ver.* 2.1.109. Broke with precedent: 2.1.104, cf. 115. Rulings inconsistent with city edict: 2.1.119, cf. 2.3.6 "varietatem libidinemque decretorum tuorum." Decisions ad hominem in nature: 2.1.105, 116. Accepted bribes for legal decisions: 2.1.116, 125, 127, 137. Provincial edict dropped city innovations: 2.1.112, 117–118 (but see Greenidge, *Legal Procedure* 128). Innovations not followed by subsequent praetors: 2.1.111–112, 117–118 with Frier, *The Rise of the Roman Jurists* 49–50

39. See Cic. *Ver.* 2.1.119 and 124. When relating Verres' activities in the territorial provinces, the specter of choice is the African praetor C. Fabius Hadrianus, burned to death in his own *praetorium* (14.3.3): see *Ver.* 2.1.69–70, 78, 2.5.94.

40. See *Ver.* 2.1.119 (Piso's responsibilities as *pr.* 74 in the civil law) and cf. 2.4.56, which sets out Piso's ancestry in fulsome terms.

41. See Ps.-Asc. p. 250 St. "intercedere, ut vides, etiam praetor praetori solet . . . appellatione causae ad collegam facta"; also, e.g., Frier, *Rise of the Roman Jurists* 73; Kunkel, *Staatsordnung* 10 and 190 n. 335 (offering also at p. 202 that praetorian collegial vetoes might have been relatively common).

42. As in *TLL* s.v. *intercedo* col. 2156 I B 2b.

43. See *TLL* s.v. *intercedo* col. 2155 I B 1a ii.

44. Nicely seen in two letters of 50 B.C. from Cilicia where the *pro cos.* Cicero intercedes—in nearly identical terms—with the *pr. urb.* C. Titius Rufus on behalf of L. Custidius of Arpinum, and for M. Fabius (Gallus) with another city praetor of the year, M. Curtius Peducaenus (*Fam.* 13.58 and 59).

45. See esp. V. Max. 9.7.4 on the riot the *tr. pl.* L. Cassius helped foment against the *pr. urb.* A. Sempronius Asellio; also, e.g., Cic. *Quinct.* 63–65 on the year 83, *Tul.* 38 on the year 71, and cf. Plu. *Caes.* 4.1, a confused account of an appeal to tribunes against a peregrine praetor in 76. The *appellatio* to tribunes in civil law cases came commonly after the praetor chose the wording of the formula. In general, see Cic. *Luc.* 97 with Greenidge, *Legal Procedure* 232 and n. 5; also C. Damon and C. S. Mackay, *Historia* 44 (1995) 47–55, esp. 48 n. 47; Kunkel, *Staatsordnung* 210–213, esp. 210 n. 385.

46. Cic. *Ver.* 2.2.62–63, 138–140.

47. See, e.g., *Flac.* 49, 79 and 91 on the series of praetors who received Asia in the mid-60s, or *Fam.* 15.4.2 and *Att.* 6.1.1–2 on Cicero's reversals of the enactments of his predecessor Appius in Cicilia.

48. Cic. *Ver.* 2.2.140, *Att.* 6.1.2.

49. See Asc. p. 84 C "cum Lucullus id quod Graeci postulabant decrevisset," cf. *Rhet. Herr.* 2.19.

50. V. Max. 7.7.6

51. Explicit at Cic. *Ver.* 2.2.119, 2.3.17, 41.

52. Cic. *Ver.* 2.1.104 and 2.5.38 (sortition as *pr. des.*); 2.2.17 (*ex praetura* sortition). At 2.1.104 Cicero introduces the notion that Verres "auspicato a Chelidone surrexisset" to draw the urban *sors*; for the widespread belief that a certain prostitute might bring good fortune, see the discussion of J. Linderski, *RhM* 140 (1997) 162–167 (not citing this passage).

53. Cic. *Ver.* 1.23, 2.1.100–101, 2.4.45.

54. Influence of Chelido: *Ver.* 2.1.104, 106, 120 (Chelido as jurisconsult), 136, 140; 2.2.39, 48; 2.3.78; 2.4.7, 71; 2.5.34, 38. Her successors in Sicily: *Ver.* 2.3.78; 2.4.136; 2.5.31, 40, 81–82.

55. Note *Ver.* 2.2.127, where Cicero specifically points up the powerlessness of Verres to influence the sortition for a Syracusan priesthood (which he manages to do anyway, but through a legal dodge).

56. V. Max. 7.7.7. The date of his praetorship is difficult. Both consuls of 75 had backed Metellus when he sought a praetorship for 74 (Sal. *Hist.* 2.45 M), but he cannot have won

the office, since C. Verres was of course *pr. urb.* for that year. The date of Metellus' consulship secures his praetorship for either 73 or 72.

57. V. Max. 7.7.5. Almost certainly not the *pr. urb.* 211 C. Calpurnius Piso, since the passage in question is followed by *exempla* featuring the urban praetors Cn. Aufidius Orestes (*pr.* 77) and Q. Caecilius Metellus (*pr.* 73 or 72).

58. See Cic. *Ver.* 2.3.123 with *MRR* III 46.

59. *MRR* III 46.

60. Cic. *Tul.*, especially 39.

61. Cic. *Tul.* 39–40 with 7–8; cf. Asc. 84 C and (most comprehensively on the legal aspects) M. Balzarini, *Studi in onore di Giuseppe Grosso* I (Turin 1968) 323–382; L. Solidoro, *AAN* 92 (1981) 197–229 (the free *dominus* was also held responsible for acts committed by the slaves of his *familia*); Frier, *Rise of the Roman Jurists* 52–53. See also below, 12.2.1.

62. *Ver.* 2.3.152.

63. When L. Quinctius (prosecutor in the case) might not be needed against the Spartacans: see *MRR* II 125; also III 46; Alexander, *Trials* 86.

64. *MRR* III 65, citing Cic. *Caec.* 23. For discussions of the date of the *Pro Caecina*, see Alexander, *Trials* p. 96 n. 1. There is no compelling reason to favor one of the two available years over the other.

65. Cic. *Clu.* 126 (Alexander, *Trials* no. 193).

66. *Clu.* 147.

67. *MRR* II 150 n. 3, *RRC* I 436–437 no. 409.

68. Plin. *Nat.* 35.100.

69. The identification (already in Münzer, *RE* s.v. Iunius 25 col. 964, cf. W. Drumann and P. Groebe, *Geschichte Roms* V [Leipzig 1912] 357 n. 7) indeed seems likely. The only other available candidate is the M. Iunius Brutus who was hobbled as praetor in 88 (10.5.5). In 44 M. Iunius Brutus, though *pr. urb.*, did not manage to celebrate the Apolline games (see *MRR* II 319, on C. Antonius). If the *provincia* is correct, that eliminates the tentative suggestion of B. W. Frier (*TAPhA* 113 [1983] 228–229) that Q. Publicius was *pr. urb.* 67.

70. For an exposition of what is known of the organization of *scribae* at Rome, see E. Badian, *Klio* 71 (1989) 598–603, with 600 on D. Matrinius himself. For Mommsen's view, see *St.-R.* I³ 337 n. 5 and 339 n. 5, followed by Drumann and Groebe, *Geschichte Roms* V 357–358 n. 7.

71. Asc. p. 59 C "legem Cornelius, etsi nemo repugnare ausus est, multis tamen invitis tulit"; cf. D.C. 36.40.1–2 οἱ στρατηγοὶ πάντες τὰ δίκαια καθ' ἅ δικάσειν ἔμελλον, αὐτοὶ συγγράφοντες ἐξετίθεσαν.

72. Frier, *Rise of the Roman Jurists* 73–76 (following A. Metro, *La "Denegatio Actionis"* [Milan 1972] 145–150); cf. also N. Palazzolo in L. Amirante et al. (eds.), *Sodalitas: Scritti in onore di A. Guarino* V (Naples 1984) 2427–2448.

73. The extreme example is P. Pinna Parpaglia (*Per una interpretazione della Lex Cornelia de Edictis Praetorum del 67 a.C.* [Sassari 1987]), who takes it narrowly as a law compelling the praetor to protect debtors against excessive demands by their creditors; against this, see the objections of G. Provera, *SDHI* 54 (1988) 454–456.

74. *Clu.* 147 mentions Cicero's own court and identifies the praetors who had *ambitus* and *peculatus*, and gives the arrangement for the *quaestio inter sicarios et de veneficiis*. Asc. pp. 59–60 C gives the name of the praetor for *maiestas*. See the discussion in 11.7.1–5 above, passim.

75. For the date, see *Tog.* F 5 with F 26. There Cicero claims it was he who especially helped Antonius rise "from last place to third" in the praetorian *comitia* for 66, an election in which Antonius thought himself entitled to first position—perhaps on the strength of his *nobilitas* alone.

76. See Q. Cic. *Pet.* 8.

77. See V. Max. 2.4.6, Plin. *Nat.* 33.53 and Cic. *Mur.* 40 with *MRR* II 151f.

78. Expulsion: Asc. p. 84 C, Q. Cic. *Pet.* 8. Tribunate: see *CIL* I² 744 with J. L. Ferrary, *Athenaeum* 73 (1985) 419–457 on the date. In an unpublished paper, I offer further arguments for placing Antonius' tribunate (and also that of a L. Volscius) in 68 B.C. Cicero's concern about Antonius' games: *Mur.* 40.

79. Plin. *Nat.* 33.53 "C. Antonius ludos scaena argentea fecit, item L. Murena." For the expensive games of Murena's praetorship, see Cic. *Mur.* 37–40, with 41 for the *provincia*.

80. See Q. Cic. *Pet.* 8 with *MRR* II 161 n. 4 on the reading "Cappadoces" for MS. *caupodoces*. If *caupones* is to be preferred, that too might suggest Antonius turned down a territorial *provincia*: see R. O. Jolliffe, *Phases of Corruption in Roman Administration in the Last Half-Century of the Roman Republic* (Menasha, Wis., 1919) 83 with n. 37 (hypothesizing he used a *legatio libera* "to plunder the innkeepers along the route of electioneering journeys").

81. Cic. *Mur.* 41.

82. Complexity: Cic. *Ver.* 2.5.38, cf. *Flac.* 6 and 100. For further emphasis on the advantages that accrued from the giving of games, see *Mur.* 37 and 53.

83. Cic. *Flac.* 6.

84. What pertained to the urban praetor clearly applied also to other city praetors: compare, e.g., Cic. *Fam.* 13.59 with 58 (both 50 B.C.), where Cicero separately asks the city praetor M. Curtius Peducaenus and his colleague in the urban *provincia* C. Titius to exhibit the identical "praetorian" qualities. And the positive city attributes extended to promagistrates when they administered law in the territorial provinces: see, e.g., Cic. Q. *fr.* 1.1.21 (the civil court of C. Octavius, *pr.* 61—not specifically attested as urban praetor—urged as a model to Q. Cicero in Asia). On ideal praetorian qualities, see the remarks of Frier, *Rise of the Roman Jurists* 72–73; cf. Kunkel, *Staatsordnung* 105–110 (magisterial qualities in general).

85. For *aequitas* and related qualities, see Cic. *Fam.* 13.58 and 59, cf. *Ver.* 2.1.116 and 119, Sal. *Cat.* 33.5 ("iniquitas praetoris"); and (in the provincial sphere) *Ver.* 2.3.87 and 196, 2.4.146 (ironic), 2.5.27, Q. *fr.* 1.1.20 and 1.2.9. For a praetor presiding in a criminal *quaestio* as *aequus*, see *Att.* 1.4.2. A praetor as *iustissimus*: Cic. *Flac.* 8, *Mil.* 38.

86. *Sapientia*: cf. Cic. *Ver.* 2.4.146 (ironic, of Verres' Sicilian command). Praetorian *prudentia*: *Ver.* 2.1.119, cf. *Flac.* 76 (provincial). Cf. *Ver.* 2.3.87 (provincial, ironic).

87. *Lenitas, clementia*, and related concepts: Cic. Q. *fr.* 1.1.21 (*lenitas, humanitas*). Provincial examples: *Fam.* 2.18.1 and 13.55.2 (*clementia*), cf. *Att.* 6.2.4 (*clemens*, of the *pro cos.* Cicero); Q. *fr.* 1.1.25 (*clementia, manseutudo, humanitas*), *Fam.* 13.6 (*humanitas*).

88. *Integritas*: cf. Cic. *Fam.* 2.18.1, 13.55.2, V. Max. 6.9.7 (all provincial). *Innocentia*: cf. Plu. *Cic.* 9.1, also (provincial) Cic. *Ver.* 1.12, *Flac.* 76. *Fides*: *Fam.* 13.58 and 59; also (provincial) *Fam.* 13.61.

89. *Facilitas*: Cic. Q. *fr.* 1.1.21, *Fam.* 13.58 and 59, also (provincial) Q. *fr.* 1.1.25, cf. *Att.* 6.2.4 (of Cicero himself as *pro cos.*).

90. For Cicero's views on the attributes of a good provincial governor, see A. H. Mamoojee, *EMC* 13 (1994) 33–35.

91. *Gravitas*: Cic. *Ver.* 2.1.106 (ironic), *Fam.* 13.55.2. *Diligentia*: Q. *fr.* 1.1.21; also (provincial) Q. *fr.* 1.1.4 and 20, *Cael.* 73. Importance of precedent: *Ver.* 2.1.116 (many other examples). Correct *severitas*: Q. *fr.* 1.1.21, also (provincial) Q. *fr.* 1.1.20.

92. Open favoritism: Cic. *Ver.* 2.1.116, also Q. *fr.* 1.2.10 (provincial). Arbitrariness: Cic. *Ver.* 2.1.120, also (provincial) *Ver.* 2.3.6. Cruelty: cf. Sal. *Cat.* 33.3 ("saevitia . . . praetoris"), also (provincial) Cic. *Ver.* 2.3.28, Q. *fr.* 1.1.25.

93. Cic. *Mur.* 53 "praetura probata in iure," cf. *Ver.* 2.1.121 (jokes about "ius verrinum," and comparison of Verres with his predecessor in the urban *provincia*).

94. Cic. *Ver.* 2.1.106 (ironic), cf. *Att.* 6.2.4 (provincial, of Cicero himself as *pro cos.*) "iuris dictio nec imperita."

95. Cic. *Mur.* 23; but note (contra) *Orat.* 142. In general, for the view that technical specialists not needed for magistracies: Cic. *Planc.* 62, cf. Plu. *Cat. Mi.* 16.1 (Cato's "professional" approach to candidacy for the quaestorship, with the clear implication that this was rare).

96. On these men, see esp. Cic. *Caec.* 78 (praise of C. Aquillius), *Brut.* 178 (P. Orbius). In general on nonexperts administering the law see Frier, *Rise of the Roman Jurists* 47f .

97. Cic. *Q. fr.* 2.14(13).3.

98. C. Getha (*pr. ?urb.* ca. 120, *cos.* 116), C. Metellus Caprarius (*pr. ?urb.* by 116, *cos.* 113), M. Drusus (*pr. urb.* by 115, *cos.* 112), L. Sulla (*pr. urb.* 97, *pro cos.* Cilicia, and eventually elected *cos.* for 88), C. Flaccus (*pr. urb.* by 96, *pro cos.* Asia, *cos.* 93), Q. Rufus (*pr. urb.* 91, *cos.* 88), Cn. Orestes (*pr. urb.* 77, *cos.* 71), Q. Metellus (*pr. urb.* by 72, *cos.* 69), C. Piso (*pr. urb.* by 71, *cos.* 67), C. Antonius (very likely *pr. urb.* 66, *cos.* 63), L. Murena (*pr. urb.* 65, *cos.* 62).

99. Owing to the conditions of the Social War, C. Saturninus (*pr. urb.* 94) had to stay as *pro cos.* in Macedonia at least into 87. A. Asellio (*pr. urb.* 89) was killed in office, as was L. Brutus Damasippus (*pr. ?urb.* 82); P. Burrenus (*pr. ?urb.* 83) had no chance of further office after Sulla's victory. Had C. Verres (*pr. urb.* 74) not been condemned in 70, he might very well have won a consulship: see 13.2.4. Remaining cases: C. Caninius (*pr. urb.*, date unknown); L. [———]onius L.f. (*pr. urb.* 105 — here C. Marius' repeated consulships of 104–100 will have had their impact); L. Sisenna (*pr. urb. et per.* 78, then apparently *pro cos.* Sicily); C. Sacerdos (*pr. urb.* 75, then *pro cos.* Sicily); M. Mummius (*pr. ?urb.* 70); P. Dolabella (*pr. ?urb.* 69 or 68), and M. Iunius (*pr. urb.* 67).

100. See the discussion of G. V. Sumner, *The Orators in Cicero's Brutus: Prosopography and Chronology* (Toronto 1973) 131. If he is to be identified with the M. Valerius Messalla who received a censorial *nota* only to go on to reach the office himself (V. Max. 2.9.9), the details of his *elogium* (*Inscr. Ital.* XIII 3 77) do not hint at such a setback.

101. For the city *provincia*, see MRR III 37 and 212 citing Cic. *Flac.* 6 and 100. It seems he and a colleague (whose name is lost) as aediles contracted a temple for Aesculapius on the Tiber Island and approved it as practors: see *ILLRP* 39 (now long lost) with D. Degrassi, *Athenaeum* 65 (1987) 521–527, esp. 527 n. 29 (adducing Liv. 34.53.4 as a nice parallel for an urban praetor of 193 making an analogous dedication). Ordered by Cicero to assist Pomptinus in the arrest of the Allobrogian envoys: Cic. *Catil.* 3.5–6, 14; Sal. *Cat.* 45.1. Brought in dossier of letters on decisive 3 December Senate meeting, chaired by the consul Cicero: Sal. *Cat.* 46.5–6. Cicero's general praise of Flaccus for his actions against the Catilinarians: Cic. *Flac.* 1, 5, 94, 102, cf. *Pis.* 54 (noting also his legateship in Macedonia). In the *Pro Flacco* Cicero does not say much else about the particulars of his client's urban praetorship, probably because his fellow advocate Q. Hortensius covered it in his own defense speech (*Att.* 2.25.1). On the promagistracy and *repetundae* trial, see 14.6.6.

102. In the pre-Sullan period only one ex-praetor is definitely known to survive prosecution in the *repetundae* court and then go on to win a consulship: see Alexander, *Trials* no. 32 (Q. Mucius Scaevola, acquitted *repetundarum* in 119 and then *cos.* 117). Related instances: perhaps nos. 48 (if this is L. Calpurnius Caesoninus, *cos.* 112), 90 (a highly uncertain case involving L. Marcius Philippus, before he was *cos.* 91), and (probably) 91 (trial of Asian commander L. Valerius Flaccus, later *cos. suff.* under special circumstances in 86); cf. also nos. 60 (C. Memmius, acquitted before ca. 102 and consular candidate for 99, but killed) and 92 (aborted prosecution, perhaps in the extortion court, of L. Sulla, future *cos.* I 88). After Sulla the only known ex-praetor who (apparently) was prosecuted for *repetundae* and then reached the consulship is M. Aemilius Lepidus (*pr.* 81, *pro cos.* in Sicily, and then *cos.* 78): see no. 131 with 13.2.2 below (prosecution dropped after initial proceedings).

103. Cf. Cic. *Flac.* 105–106, where it is implied that Flaccus' prospects for the consulship were still realistic at the time of the trial.

104. Cicero's house in 63: Plu. *Cic.* 19.4–5 and 20.1–2, D.C. 37.35.3–4. For that of Caesar in 62, see especially Cic. *Att.* 1.13.3, *Schol. Bob.* p. 85 St.

105. *CLA* I 299, accepted by Broughton in *MRR* III 106.

106. See Cic. *Har.* 37 "fit in ea domo quae est in imperio." Cf. Plu. *Caes.* 9.7, D.C. 37.45.1 (held at the house of a consul or praetor).

107. Suet. *Jul.* 16.1.

108. See Cic. *Q. fr.* 1.1.21 for Octavius' legal activities. R. Stewart, *Latomus* 54 (1995) 75f, suggests this incident belongs to C. Octavius' promagistracy, when he stamped out some brigands in south Italy while in transit to his province of Macedonia. Yet that police action seems an unlikely opportunity for displaying the *facilitas* and *lenitas* Cicero praises in this passage. With equal implausibility, F. X. Ryan (*RhM* 139 [1996] 251–253) speculates that the Cicero passage might refer to Octavius' service as a *iudex quaestionis*. Frier (*Rise of the Roman Jurists* 51) thinks that the Octavius in question is the *pr.* 79. Against that notion, see Shackleon Bailey, *CEQF* ad loc.

109. Praetorship: Plin. *Nat.* 19.23, his *Ludi Apollinares*. Promagistracy: see Cic. *Fam.* 1.9.13 with Caes. *Civ.* 1.22.4.

110. Cic. *Vat.* 33, with further sources in *MRR* II 194. On the *lex Licinia Iunia*, see *Schol. Bob.* p. 140 St.; note also the discussion of E. Badian in H. D. Evjen (ed.), *Mnemai: Classical Studies in Memory of Karl K. Hulley* (Chico, Calif., 1984) 101f.

111. On the trial of Q. Opimius, see Cic. *Ver.* 2.1.155–157. E. Gruen (*Athenaeum* 49 [1971] 66), discussing the case of Vatinius in 59, states confidently that "a praetor would not regularly have been assigned to hear those rare cases that came under the *lex Licinia Iunia*." But the truth is that we simply do not know the regular procedure.

112. Suet. *Jul.* 23.1; cf. Cic. *Sest.* 40.

113. This man's date and city *provincia* (for which see Asc. p. 48 C, a grain riot during his *Ludi Apollinares*) are certain. B. A. Marshall, *A Historical Commentary on Asconius* (Columbia, Mo., 1985) 200 implausibly dismisses Asconius' account and confines rioting to the *Ludi Romani* of September; against Marshall, see F. X. Ryan, *SIFC* 13 (1995) 245–248. Overseas *provincia*: *ILLRP* 391 (his sepulchral inscription, found at Alba), "pro cos." The date of his promagistracy is certainly 56, since his rank under the *lex Pompeia* of 52 would be "pro pr."

114. See Broughton, *MRR* II 221, citing Cic. *Att.* 4.15.6 "redii Romam Fontei causa a. d. vii Id. Quint. veni spectatum," i.e., 9 July, and so during the period of the *Ludi Apollinares* (cf. 5.2.2). Contra Crawford, *RRC* I 453 ("not necessarily a praetor"), who suggests that the Fonteius in question is the moneyer (no. 429) P. Fonteius P.f. Capito (whom he dates to 55 B.C.). But in truth, our Fonteius is not easily identified with any of the known Fonteii of this general period.

115. D.C. 40.45.3.

116. See Cic. *Fam.* 13.58 prescript, with Shackleton Bailey, *CEF* I 479 for the date.

117. See *RDGE* 16 A lines 17–18 ([——] P.f.).

118. Peregrine praetorship: *SIG*³ 732 line 4 (giving date and *provincia*) with *CIL* I² 2978, a milestone from the road Canusium–Butunum–Barium, with mileage (LII) measured from Canusium. On the *ex praetura* command, see 10.1, 14.5.5.

119. Asc. p. 84 C; further sources collected in *MRR* II 93. F. X. Ryan, *Klio* 78 (1996) 81–82 argues that 77 is an equally valid date for this praetorship, but does not grapple with Asconius' precise chronological reference. On this civil trial, see above all the careful reconstruction of C. Damon and C. S. Mackay, *Historia* 44 (1995) 37–55. In Plutarch's version (Plu. *Caes.* 4.1–4) the trial actually takes place in Greece, resulting in a very confused nar-

rative. The mistake may be ascribed to Plutarch's general knowledge (see *Crass.* 11.3) of M. Lucullus as a (consular) governor of Macedonia.

120. Cic. *Tul.* 7–12.

121. See especially *Tul.* 8 "qui summa aequitate et sapientia ius dixit" and compare with, e.g., *Ver.* 2.5.38, where "ius dicere" is equivalent to "the urban *provincia.*" C. Damon and C. S. Mackay, *Historia* 44 (1995) 52, even suggest that "perhaps Lucullus held both the urban and peregrine praetorships."

122. See *Vir. ill.* 72.6 (our one source on his praetorship) with the perceptive comments of Kunkel, *Staatsordnung* 202; on the political background, see E. Badian, *JRS* 46 (1956) 94–95. ·

123. *Vir. ill.* 73.2 "Glauciae praetori, quod is . . . ius dicendo partem populi avocasset, sellam concidit, ut magis popularis videretur." Full sources on Glaucia's praetorship can be found in *MRR* I 574f.

124. *MRR* I 563.

125. See, e.g., that of Sulla (75.7), Q. Metellus Pius (63.1–3), and Cato the younger (80.2).

126. See *ILLRP* 485 (a *terminatio*) with full discussion by J. Bodel, *AJAH* 11 (1986) [1994] 38–54, 110–114. This praetor must be the moneyer L. SENTI C.F. of *RRC* I 327 110. 325 (dated by Crawford 101 B.C.), and as such is presumably younger brother of the *pr.* 94. He is commonly given the title "urbanus" in modern scholarship: see, e.g., Münzer, *RE* s.v. *Sentius* 6 col. 1511.

127. On the date, cf. Bodel, *AJAH* 11 (1986) [1994] 110 n. 169. He is listed first among the witnesses to *RDGE* 19, an *S.C.* of 80 B.C. (from Cormi in Lycia), and so was by then surely of praetorian standing; the *fasti* of praetors for the year 81 seem full, so that year must be excluded.

128. On Peducaenus' name and identity, see especially Cic. *Flac.* 30 and (attesting descent) *Red. Sen.* 21 with *MRR* III 79. For the suggestion he was peregrine praetor, see Shackleton Bailey, *CEF* I 480. Civil suit: Alexander, *Trials* no. 343. Edict: Cic. *Fam.* 13.59.

129. D.C. 36.41.1–2.

130. *MRR* II 143; see also the sources in Broughton, *Candidates Defeated* 13, and cf. *MRR* III 127f. W. C. McDermott (*Hermes* 97 [1969] 233–246) was wrong to consider this individual *pr. urb.* in 67 (p. 241) and to dissociate him from the consular candidate for 59. But McDermott must be correct on the basic point that the L. Lucceius in question here was probably Q.f. the historian (*RE* no. 6) as opposed to M.f. the businessman (*RE* no. 5): see D. R. Shackleton Bailey, *CEF* I 319.

131. M. Dondin and J. M. David, *MEFRA* 92 (1980) 199–213; see further Dondin in her book *Exercice du pouvoir et continuité gentilice: les Acilii Glabriones* (Rome 1993) 235. F. X. Ryan (*C&M* 45 (1994) 186–192) proposes to keep "Lucius Lucullus" at D.C. 36.41.1–2 but to emend the name of the consul from "Acilius" to "Aemilius" (i.e., M. Aemilius Lepidus, *cos.* 78). This suggestion of course faces the same obstacle as that of Dondin and David: L. Lucullus did not refuse a province *ex praetura.*

132. Plu. *Luc.* 1.

133. Greenidge, *Legal Procedure* 135.

134. *MRR* II 582, perhaps a slip.

135. There are three *repetundae* trials known for 54 B.C. (Alexander, *Trials* nos. 295, 303, and 305) and five for 51 B.C. (nos. 336–340). A glance at the charts in P. Nadig, *Ardet Ambitus: Untersuchungen zum Phänomen der Wahlbestechungen in der römischen Republik* (Frankfurt a. M. 1997) 210–211, suggests that busy years in the *ambitus* court were certainly 116 (three trials), 66 (three or four trials), 56 (three or four), and 54 (nine). Note also the years 52 (eight) and 51 (five); but many of those *ambitus* prosecutions were in the special courts set up by the

consul Pompey in 52 B.C. The most *maiestas* trials attested for a given year are two, in the year 65 B.C. (*Trials* nos. 209–210). On the difficulty of estimating forensic activity from our available sources see M. C. Alexander, *Phoenix* 47 (1993) 250.

136. Cic. *Clu.* 147. See Alexander, *Trials* no. 198 with the discussion of the arrangements for this *quaestio* in 66 B.C. in 11.7.4.

137. For simultaneous *quaestiones*, see also Cic. *Vat.* 34 (violence in the court for *lex Licinia Iunia* disturbed more than one adjoining *iudex quaestionis* in 58); *Q. fr.* 2.4.6 (Mar. 56) "cottidianae damnationes inimicorum . . . ceteri conciduntur"; *Att.* 4.15.4 (three individuals all prosecuted on different criminal charges on 4 July 54, certainly one *inter sicarios*); *Q. fr.* 2.16.3 (in late Aug. 54, Cicero set to defend P. Vatinius on charge *de sodaliciis* on same day as hearing of acquittal of another client in an unknown court); *Att.* 4.18.4 (concurrent trials for *maiestas* and under the *lex Papia* in Oct. 54). Pompey's sole consulship of 52 and its new judicial laws occasioned a large number of trials, some demonstrably simultaneous: see esp. Asc. p. 39 C on the various prosecutions of Milo, and cf. Cic. *Brut.* 324 and *Fam.* 7.2.4. Frequency of a single court: cf. Cic. *Clu.* 116 on the *quaestio repetundarum* (exaggerated). In general, see Cic. *N.D.* 3.74 and *Ver.* 2.5.143 (bulk of criminal and civil activity in Rome).

138. Cic. *Att.* 1.1.2 (July 65), naming those months as the time "cum Romae a iudiciis forum refrixerit."

139. See the discussion of Greenidge, *Legal Procedure* 467–472.

140. *Legal Procedure* 456–504, cf. 504–516.

141. On the minimum interval, see Plu. *Cic.* 9.5 with Greenidge, *Legal Procedure* 466–467.

142. See Alexander, *Trials* nos. 271 (P. Sestius as defendant), 295 (M. Scaurus, with Cic. *Scaur.* 24, 28 and Asc. p. 18 C on the nature of the prosecution, and Asc. pp. 19–20 on the interval), and 296 (A. Gabinius).

143. On this, see Greenidge, *Legal Procedure* 499–502.

144. *CIL* I² 583 line 7, cf. 9.

145. See, e.g., Cic. *Ver.* 1.6 and 2.1.30 with A. H. M. Jones, *The Criminal Courts of the Roman Republic and Principate* (Oxford 1972) 25, 65–66, 76–77 (esp. 77 n. 215), 80.

146. His last-minute decision to cancel a bid for the curule aedileship and run for the praetorship instead: Cic. *Dom.* 111–112 (alleging election by fraud). On the *provincia* (definitely a *quaestio*), see *Att.* 3.17.1 with 11.7.1 above. As praetor (or augur?) he threatened to obnuntiate at a tribune's assembly, but in fact introduced gangs (already on 23 Jan.) against Clodius' enemies, all in an attempt to forestall legislation prejudicial to his brother: *Sest.* 75–78 with D.C. 39.7.2–3 and 12.4.3 below. Helped impede the *tr. pl.* Milo from prosecuting Clodius under the *lex Plautia de vi*: Cic. *Sest.* 89, cf. 95. Opposed his seven colleagues in recalling Cicero from exile, and even in allowing him to speak to the People in a *contio* on his return: *Att.* 4.1.6 and *Pis.* 35 with Asc. p. 11 C. For Appius' various *contiones*—more are recorded for this individual than any other praetor—see esp. n. 245 below; he also filibustered in the Senate on Clodius' behalf (*Att.* 4.3.3). Cicero flatly charges Ap. Claudius with dereliction of his praetorian duties: see *Sest.* 126 with *Schol. Bob.* p. 138 St. The family tradition continued. In 56, another brother, C. Claudius Pulcher, as praetor aided Clodius (now curule aedile) in trying to prevent the removal of the inscribed tribunician *acta* on the Capitol that included the law that led to Cicero's exile (D.C. 39.21.1–4, cf. Plu. *Cic.* 34.1–3).

147. See Asc. p. 29 C "in forum quoque . . . descendebat iusque dicebat" with 11.7.1. References and arguments for what follows below is gathered in that section.

148. See ch. 10 n. 61.

149. Verres in 70 B.C.: Plu. *Cic.* 7.5 τῶν . . . στρατηγῶν τῷ Βέρρῃ χαριζομένων. Ap. Pulcher: Cic. *Sest.* 89, cf. 85 ("gladiatores ex praetoris comitatu"), 95 and *Att.* 4.3.3. For the two instances from 66 B.C., see 11.7.1 above.

150. See D.C. 37.27.3. Responsibility for the Janiculum flag must have been a fossilized prerogative of holders of *imperium*.

151. E.g., Cicero as consul in 63 appeared as an advocate in both the *ambitus* and *repetundae* courts: see Alexander, *Trials* no. 224 (especially *Mur.* 2–3, 5, where Cicero has to defend the appropriateness of taking on a client accused under his own consular *ambitus* law) and 225.

152. Cic. *Sest.* 135 with *Schol. Bob.* p. 140 St., *Vat.* 33–34.

153. See, e.g., Cic. *Clu.* 74 (the *tr. pl.* L. Quinctius' energetic defense of his client in a trial *de veneficiis* in 74); Plu. *Cic.* 9.6 and D.C. 36.44.2 (tribunes drag Cicero as *pr. rep.* 66 before a *contio* and denounce him); Cic. *Sest.* 89 and 95 (tribunes helped prevent Milo prosecute Clodius *de vi*); *Att.* 4.17.3 (prospective jurors for a special *quaestio* in fall 54 appeal to tribunes so as not to serve); cf. *Q. fr.* 3.2.3 (more obstruction of cases being brought to trial in Oct. 54).

154. See Cic. *Q. fr.* 2.1.1–3 with D.C. 39.7.4 (though not mentioning the praetor by name), and cf. *Sest.* 89 with D. R. Shackleton Bailey, *CEQF* 172. On the Senate session, see E. Badian, *CQ* 19 (1969) 203f; L. Thommen, *Das Volkstribunat der späten römischen Republik* (Stuttgart 1988) 204; and 12.4.2 below. For the political attitude of L. Caecilius Rufus in his praetorship, see Cic. *Red. Sen.* 22 (personal and official measures while praetor on behalf of Cicero in exile), *Mil.* 38 with Asc. p. 48 C (alleged attack on his house by Clodius' forces in the tussle over Cicero's recall), and in general Marshall, *Asconius* 200.

155. *I. Knidos* I 31 D. C lines 28–31.

156. Sources in *MRR* II 184 (tribunate), 194 (praetorship).

157. Asc. pp. 46–47 C, with G. V. Sumner, *Hermes* 93 (1965) 135–136 for text of p. 46 C, line 26 to p. 47 C, line 4

158. Nor does Marshall, in his *Asconius* 198, venture a guess.

159. See Cael. *Fam.* 8.14.4 "curre . . . et quam primum haec risum veni, legis Scantin<ia>e iudicium apud Drusum fieri," cf. 8.12.3 "postulandum . . . lege Scantinia." On the law as establishing a (non-permanent) criminal court, see W. Kunkel, *Untersuchungen zur Entwicklung des römischen Kriminalverfahrens in vorsullanischer Zeit* (Munich 1962) 72–73. So Drusus presumably received the cases listed in Alexander, *Trials* nos. 347 and 348.

160. Münzer, *RE* s.v. *Livius* 19 col. 883; *MRR* II 248; Alexander, *Trials* p. 168. F. X. Ryan, *CPh* 89 (1994) 159–162 (esp. 160), argues that "Drusus might have been a *iudex* appointed by the urban praetor" (i.e., in a civil procedure), but does not give Republican parallels for how he is proposing to take "iudicium apud Drusum fieri." (Against Ryan's implication that preliminary civil proceedings could not be termed "apud praetorem," see Cic. *Q. fr.* 1.1.21, also V. Max. 8.3.2.)

161. For proceedings in a non-permanent criminal court "apud praetorem," see Cic. *Arch.* 3 (trial under *lex Papia*); cf. also *Clu.* 126, and probably *Vat.* 27.

162. For full sources on this man see *PIR*² II 291 no. 210.

163. See D.S. 36.2.5 with 12.4.1 below on the *pr.* L. Licinius Lucullus. But we do not know what time of the year L. Lucullus was called on to crush the slave revolt at Capua.

164. See Cic. *Rab. Perd.* 20, the *S.C.U.* mobilizing the "<praetores> praeter Glauciam," and 21 "omnes praetores." By "omnes praetores," Cicero must mean simply all others than Glaucia who were available.

165. Cic. *Arch.* 7 and 9, cf. 31. The purpose of Lentulus' *quaestio* presumably was to hear challenges to citizenship; Alexander (*Trials* no. 369) finds it only approximately datable ("perhaps by 83"). But the wideranging activities of Metellus Pius, *pro cos.* in the years 87 through 82 (see 10.5.5, 14.3.3), make 88 B.C. the only real possibility; it also appears that L. Lentulus saw service under Sulla in the east after 88, ending up (probably) as governor of Cilicia, where he was replaced only in 80 B.C. (10.1).

166. Cic. *Off.* 3.80–81, with additional sources on the enthusiastic popular reception of this act in *MRR* II 57 (see esp. Plin. *Nat.* 33.132, calling it inaccurately a "lex"). For discussion of this measure, see C. M. Bulst, *Historia* 13 (1964) 335f.

167. No praetors are attested in the city for the years 79, perhaps 68, and 52. Only one of the eight annual praetors can be placed in Rome for the years 80, 78, 77, 76, 64, 61, 55, and 53 B.C. Two of eight praetors can be posited there for the years 75, perhaps 72, 71, and 69, then 60, 51, and 50 B.C.

168. Cic. *Att.* 4.15.7–8 and *Q. fr.* 2.15(14).4 (27 July 54), also (on the backlash) Plu. *Cat. Min.* 44.7–11; cf. Plin. *Nat.* praef. 9.

169. *CIL* I² 583 lines 31, 35, 39, 76, 78, cf. 19 and 83 with A. W. Lintott, *Judicial Reform* 118. Cicero is quite insistent in the *Verrines* that the purpose of the *repetundae* court was to protect Rome's allies: see *Div. Caec.* 11, 17–19 with 65; *Ver.* 1.41–42, 2.1.59, 2.2.15, 2.3.127 and 218. On the *praetor repetundis*, see 9.2.2, 10.4.2, 11.7.1.

170. Cic. *Arch.* 7 "si sexaginta diebus apud praetorem essent professi"; see also *Schol Bob.* p. 175 St. E. Badian (*Studies in Greek and Roman History* [Oxford 1964] 75–79, with corresponding notes, esp. n. 37; cf. *JRS* 63 [1973] 128 n. 43) emphasizes (against A. N. Sherwin-White, *Roman Citizenship*¹ [Oxford 1939] 151–152) that here "apud praetorem" does not mean "before the praetor (i.e. the *praetor urbanus*) at Rome," but "before a praetor" (anywhere), as is clear from *Arch.* 9. Broughton wholly accepts this point (*MRR* III 159); G. Luraschi in his study of the *lex Plautia Papiria* (*SDHI* 44 [1978] 321–370, at 347) is more tentative—indeed, it is very much at variance with his own idea of a quite restrictive scope of the law.

171. *CIL* I² 592 = *RS* I 16 ch. XX lines 24–25 and 34–35; cf. XXII 42–43, 45, 48, 50. On this law, see U. Laffi, *Athenaeum* 64 (1986) 5–44 (dating the law to the year 41), esp. 24–38 for an attempt to determine the exact extent of the praetor's jurisdiction (civil cases involving more than 15,000 sesterces were to be referred to Rome, but the praetor reserved competence even in some lesser cases); cf. also Laffi in *Athenaeum* 78 [68] (1990) 167–175 and 85 (1997) 119–138. In this study, I tentatively accept Laffi's identification of the Este fragment (*RS* I 16) as forming part of this law.

172. *CIL* I² 593 lines 7–9 and 10–12 (relevant text in ch. 5 n. 20; on the uncertain purpose of these *professiones*, see G. Rickman, *The Corn Supply of Ancient Rome* (Oxford 1980) 241–243.

173. *CIL* X 4842 (Augustus' edict de aquaeducto Venafro, from the year 11) line 65; in Fron. *Aq.* 2.129.5 (the *lex Quinctia de aquaeductibus*, from the year 9), the peregrine praetor is to exercise jurisdiction when no *curator aquarum* is available.

174. Gai. *Inst.* 4.31; F. Wieacker (*Römische Rechtsgeschichte* I 439 n. 6) finds this astounding.

175. *Law Making in the Later Roman Republic* (Oxford 1974) 80–82; cf. 64–67 and 72–75.

176. Watson, *Law Making* 76–80, citing especially *Lex de Gallia Cisalpina* (*CIL* I² 592) ch. XX (see n. 171 above); Gai. *Inst.* 1.6 "amplissimum ius est in edictis duorum praetorum, urbani et peregrini"; Boethius *ad top. Ciceronis* 5.28 "edicta magistratuum sunt, quae praetores urbani vel peregrini vel aediles curules iura dixere"; cf. Ulpian in *Dig.* 4.3.9.4a, citing Labeo's thirtieth book *praetoris peregrini* (a number that few scholars, including Watson, accept as possible).

177. See 5.6.3.

178. E.g., Frier, *Rise of the Roman Jurists* 52 n. 38: "it seems doubtful that, as some scholars have supposed, the peregrine praetor had jurisdiction over suits between Roman citizens."

179. See 5.6; and in general for the overseas praetors, R. J. Hoffman, *IJ* 11 (1976) 355–374.

180. Cf. Caes. *Civ.* 3.20.1–4 (a threat not actually realized). Watson (*Law Making* 81) very much exaggerates in stating "praetors did not hesitate to use" their right of *intercessio* against one another; see in general 5.4.2. *Par potestas* was sometimes used as a threat, but surely only very rarely as a weapon.

181. On the latter, see Greenidge, *Legal Procedure* 119–129; W. W. Buckland, RD (ser. 4) 13 (1934) 81–96 (still fundamental, stressing that the provincial edicts were an extension of the city ones, aimed primarily at the protection of Roman citizens in the provinces); A. J. Marshall, *AJPh* 85 (1964) 185–191; L. Peppé, *Labeo* 37 (1991) 14–93 (emphasizing the originality of Cicero's *compositio*—though we have practically nothing for comparison). Cf. B.D. Hoyos, *Antichthon* 7 (1973) 47–53, arguing unconvincingly that the "*lex provinciae*" was simply a particularly authoritative edict; a good formulation of the standard view on the "lex provinciae" is provided by H. Galsterer in M. Crawford (ed.), *L'impero romano e le strutture economiche e sociali delle province* (Como 1986) 15–17.

182. D.C. 36.40.1 (cited in n. 71).

183. *Law Making* 32 n. 2, 74f, and 82 n. 2.

184. *Att.* 6.1.15.

185. See esp. Cic. *Tul.* 7 with J. M. Kelly, *Roman Litigation* (Oxford 1966) 15–16; Watson, *Law Making* 31 n. 6 and 65–67; Frier, *Rise of the Roman Jurists* 52–57.

186. V. Max. 8.15.6 with Cic. *Att.* 6.1.15. On Scaevola, see 14.5.4 below.

187. Gai. *Inst.* 1.6, quoted in n. 176 above.

188. On the transferability of provisions in urban edicts to provincial ones, see, e.g., Cic. *Ver.* 2.1.112, 117–118; 2.3.152.

189. See n. 176 above.

190. As judges for the *perduellio* trial of C. Rabirius in 63 (Alexander, *Trials* no. 220), a praetor (probably but not certainly the *pr. urb.* L. Valerius Flaccus) personally—and improperly, we are told—chose the *duumviri* L. Caesar (*cos.* 64) and C. Caesar (*aed. cur.* 65). The praetor was supposed to put the choice before the People (D.C. 37.27.3) but did not bother to do so.

191. On Lucullus' date and his actions as praetor (departing from the city with six hundred troops, and on his march south raising a tumultuary force amounting almost to the strength of a legion), see D.S. 36.2.1–6 with Obseq. 43 (registering troubles from slaves in south Italy in 104); cf. *MRR* I 562 n. 2.

192. On this cf. perhaps App. *BC* 1.40.178 (defense of gates and walls by οἱ ὑπόλοιποι).

193. App. *BC* 1.116.541.

194. Cic. *Catil.* 3.5, Sal. *Cat.* 45.1 (*pr. urb.* L. Flaccus and C. Pomptinus at the Mulvian Bridge); Sal. *Cat.* 46.6 (C. Flaccus at the Senate meeting of 3 Dec.); Cic. *Catil.* 3.8 (C. Sulpicius ordered to confiscate weapons at house of Cethegus); D.C. 37.35.4 (Cicero orders "praetors" to give a *sacramentum* to people in the city); Cic. *Sul.* 42 (the *pr.* C. Cosconius takes notes in the Senate); cf. Cic. *Catil.* 2.26, Plu. *Cic.* 16.1, D.C. 37.33.4 (Q. Metellus, sent ultimately by Cicero's orders to the *ager Gallicus* and *Picenus*). Cicero given charge of city in 63: see, e.g., Cic. *Catil.* 2.26, Plu. *Cic.* 16.1. That was by now a traditional measure; an S.C.U. entrusted the city to the consuls once again in the disturbances caused by the *tr. pl.* Q. Caecilius Metellus Nepos in early 62 (D.C. 37.43.3).

195. Cic. *Phil.* 2.31 "cur M. Brutus [pr. urb. 44 B.C.] referente te legibus est solutus, si ab urbe plus quam decem dies afuisset?"

196. See Kunkel, *Staatsordnung* 296 n. 6.

197. In 58 B.C. we find a city praetor making an unofficial visit to Pompey at Alba (ca. 100 km from Rome): Cic. *Pis.* 77. W. Kunkel (*Staatsordnung* 210) plausibly connects the rise in extraordinary commands in the post-Sullan era with the localization of the consuls in the city. One wonders whether a restriction on the movement of praetors in this general era—

either de iure or de facto—necessitated more special commissions in Italy *pro praetore* (on which see ch. 11 n. 81, two examples probably from the 70s).

198. M. Licinius Crassus: Plu. *Crass.* 10.1, Oros. 5.24.5. L. Licinius Murena: Cic. *Mur.* 64. Q. Pompeius Rufus and Q. Metellus Celer: Cic. *Catil.* 2.5–6 and Sal. *Cat.* 30.5. On the unofficial "levy" of Pompey in 83 B.C. in Picenum, see 10.5.7.

199. D.C. 37.35.3–4 with Kunkel, *Staatsordnung* 336 (taking this measure quite seriously).

200. See, e.g., Sal. *Jug.* 39.2 (110 B.C.), 43.1–5 (109 B.C.), 86.1 and 95.1 (107 B.C.), App. *BC* 1.66.303 and 86.393 (87 and 83 B.C., levies in Italy and Cisalpine Gaul), App. *BC* 1.77.353 (84 B.C.), Plu. *Luc.* 7.1 (late 74 or early 73 B.C.), App. *Mith.* 94.429–430 with Plu. *Pomp.* 27.1 (the *pro cos.* Pompey in 67), Cic. *Att.* 1.19.2 (60 B.C.), *Pis.* 57 with 5 and 37 (57 B.C.), Asc. p. 33 C (the *pro cos.* Pompey in the long *interregnum* of 52), and Cic. *Fam.* 3.3.1 (blocked by a *cos.* 51). Cf. also the levies in Cisalpine Gaul reported at Plu. *Sert.* 4.2 (91 B.C., a quaestor, surely acting under a consul's orders), Suet. *Jul.* 8 (67 B.C.), D.C. 39.39.1–2 (55 B.C.); also D.C. 36.37.2 (67 B.C., Transalpine Gaul). In general on the levy in this period, see Liebenam, *RE* s.v. *dilectus* cols. 609–615.

201. See, e.g., Cic. *Font.* 13, on Fonteius in Transalpine Gaul in the mid-70s, said to have collected cavalry for Rome's wars "throughout the world".

202. See Suet. *Jul.* 4.1, Vell. 2.42.2 (C. Iulius Caesar in Asia ca. 74 B.C.) with Suet. *Jul.* 2 (his previous experience in this *provincia*).

203. At the very least, both consuls were away from the city for the bulk of the years 119 (see 10.5.1), 118, 115, 113, 111–109, 107, (perhaps) 105 and 104, 102–101, then 90–89, and for much of 85–82. Even there, we naturally have reports of Senate meetings convened by consuls, at least early in the year: see Sal. *Jug.* 28.2 (111 B.C.), 39.2 (110 B.C.), D.S. 36.13 (102 B.C., both consuls), *I. Knidos* I 31 D. B lines 14–15 (envisaging a consul as Senate president sometime after mid-February 101 B.C.).

204. Evidence collected by J. P. V. D. Balsdon, *JRS* 29 (1939) 61–62. The *coss.* 78 were still in Rome as of 22 May (*RDGE* 22); on the *coss.* 74, see 14.6.3; the *coss.* 72 were back in the city probably by October (Cic. *Ver.* 2.2.95). Of the consuls of 57 B.C., at least Q. Caecilius Metellus Nepos (pace Baldson) was still in Rome in December (D.C. 39.7.4 with 12.2.4).

205. See Gel. 14.7.4 (Varro's handbook on Senate procedure, composed in 70 B.C. and then revised in the Triumviral period), cited in Additional Note VIII; cf. Cic. *Leg.* 3.10. See also the passages in Mommsen, *St.-R.* II³ 129 n. 2.

206. Contrast *RDGE* 16 A–B lines 15–18 (S.C. and treaty with island of Astypalaea, 105 B.C.), *SIG*³ 732 lines 2–4 (treaty with Thyrrheum in 94 B.C.) and *RDGE* 22 lines 2–3 (*S.C. de Asclepiade*, 78 B.C.) with *RDGE* 23 (73 B.C.) lines 3–4, cf. 53–54; *RDGE* 24 (56 B.C.) A lines 1–3; *RDGE* 26b (47–46 B.C.) line 37; *RDGE* 27 (39 B.C.) lines 3–4; *RDGE* 29 (35 B.C.) line 1. Cf. perhaps in this connection Cic. *Ver.* 2.3.123, a Sicilian governor's letter of 70 B.C., addressed to the consuls, the urban praetor (apparently), and the urban quaestors.

207. See Cic. *de Orat.* 3.2 and V. Max. 9.5.2 (mentioning the consul's imprisonment) with L. Thommen, *Das Volkstribunat* 203. On Philippus' (negative) attitude toward the Senate in September 91, see P. A. Brunt, *The Fall of the Roman Republic and Related Essays* (Oxford 1988) 209.

208. See *RDGE* 13 lines 6–7 with n. 4 above; *RDGE* 8 lines 1–2; cf. 5.

209. See, e.g., Cic. *Sul.* 65 (1 Jan. 65 B.C.), *Att.* 4.3.3 (a praetor's filibuster), cf. *Att.* 4.18.4 (54 B.C.). Against the old notion that magistrates in office were not asked for *sententiae* (see F. X. Ryan, *AJPh* 115 [1994] 587, with authorities collected in his n. 4; also *Hermes* 123 [1995] 83 n. 9), see E. Badian, *AJAH* 13 1988 [1997] 108–109.

210. E.g., Cic. *Q. fr.* 1.2, on which see ch. 11 n. 61.

211. The evidence is collected and discussed by P. Willems, *Le Sénat de la république romaine: Sa composition et ses attributions* II (Louvain 1883) 134–137.

212. See Cic. *Man.* 58 with R. Seager, *Pompey: A Political Biography* (Oxford 1979) 43 and n. 138, for the background. Gabinius apparently got his legateship.

213. Suet. *Jul.* 23.1 with 24.1 and Cic. *Att.* 3.15.6; cf. Suet. *Nero* 2.2, Cic. *Sest.* 40 and *Schol. Bob.* pp. 130 and 146 St.

214. Plu. *Cat. Mi.* 44.3–5.

215. Collected (with earlier examples) by Thommen, *Volkstribunat* 202–205.

216. See Willems, *Sénat* II 135, followed by Thommen, *Volkstribunat* 201 n. 56. On the volume of routine legislation in this period, see the remarks of E. Badian, "*Tribuni Plebis* and *Res Publica*," in J. Linderski (ed.), *Imperium Sine Fine: T. Robert S. Broughton and the Roman Republic* (Stuttgart 1996) 208 n. 33 (on tribunician *relationes*).

217. D.C. 55.3.6, accepted at face value by R. J. A. Talbert, *The Senate of Imperial Rome* (Princeton 1984) 235. For an attempted (and implausible) rationalization of Dio's account, see Willems, *Sénat* II 136 n. 7 (interpreting Dio to mean that Augustus gave the praetors the same freedom the tribunes had from consular interference), followed by F. X. Ryan, *AJPh* 115 (1994) 590 n. 4.

218. See Mommsen, *St.-R.* I³ 192 with n. 7.

219. See, e.g., the *S.C.* of September 51 B.C. regarding the contentious question of the consular *provinciae* for the year 49, which provides that a consul, praetor, or tribune can bring legislation on the matter before the People or Plebs (Cael. *Fam.* 8.8.5).

220. Prestige: cf. Cic. *Sest.* 135 "consularem legem." Heading off unwelcome legislation: D.C. 36.38.1–4 (67 B.C.); Cic. *Att.* 4.1.6–7 (Sept. 57). Cf. also the various competing measures on the recall of Cicero from exile in 57 B.C. (discussed below in text).

221. On the praetor M. Porcius Cato, see Gel. 13.20.12 (explaining descent and noting a curule aedileship, a praetorship, and his death in Narbonensis), and *I. Knidos* 31 Kn. III lines 1–9 for his actual activities as praetor. The Gellius passage alone provides no firm basis for assuming a Gallic command (thus, rightly, Broughton in *MRR* III 170, recanting an earlier view in II 22). For a different reconstruction of the passage in the *Lex* (with the reading "third day before the Feralia," i.e., 19 Feb.) that identifies this Cato with the future *cos.* 118, see J. Ferrary ap. *RS* I 12 p. 260.

222. Cic. *Balb.* 55.

223. Sis. *HRR* I² F 17, 119, 120 with ch. 10 n. 147.

224. Sources collected in *MRR* I 127, to which add Cic. *Flac.* 12 (Aurelian *iudices* liable to service in criminal or civil *iudicia*). For discussion, see Brunt, *Fall of the Roman Republic* 210–214, 232, and 237.

225. Stricter courts: Cic. *Div. Caec.* 8, *Ver.* 2.2.174. Problem of corruption: *Ver.* 1.38–39, 2.3.224, also *Clu.* 130.

226. Cic. *Ver.* 2.2.174, 5.177–178.

227. See esp. Cic. *Div. Caec.* 8 and *Ver.* 2.2.174.

228. Cic. *Ver.* 2.3.223. For "templum tenere" cf. Cic. *Vat.* 5. On auspicated *contiones*, see G. W. Botsford, *The Roman Assemblies* (New York 1909) 111 with 144f.

229. See Plu. *Pomp.* 22.3 with P. A. Brunt, *Chiron* 10 (1980) 285f for Pompey's nonrole. On the attitude of the tribunes, cf. *Schol. Gron.* p. 328 St. (confused). That same year it is possible that L. Aurelius Cotta also carried a *lex de ambitu* (content unknown): see Cic. *Q. fr.* 1.3.8 with the discussion of E. Bauerle, "Procuring an Election: *Ambitus* in the Roman Republic, 432–49 B.C." (diss. Univ. of Michigan, Ann Arbor, 1990); also Nadig, *Ardet Ambitus* 223–224 (each tentatively accepting it as a praetorian law of 70 B.C.).

230. Tribunate: *MRR* II 103. *Novitas* and demeanor as praetor: Cic. *Clu.* 111.

231. Sal. *Hist.* 4.71 M, cf. *Schol. Gron.* p. 321 St; Plu. *Luc.* 33.5–6 ὑφ' οὗ [sc. Quinctius] μάλιστα πεισθέντες ἐψηφίσαντο πέμπειν διαδόχους, and cf. 33.1 for the chronology.

232. At *MRR* II 144, Broughton cites *Luc.* 33.5 (L. Quinctius urges "successors" for Lucullus) under the evidence for the Gabinian law; on his date of 69 or 68 for Quinctius, see *MRR* II 138 with 141 n. 6, III 180.

233. See App. *Mith.* 90.411. If correct, he is unlikely to be identified with the L. Quinctius L.f. Rufus attested as ἀνθύπατος at Tenos (see *IG* XII 5 924 with *MRR* III 180, offering the caveat that this inscription "may be dated as late as Augustus"). There is no room in two of the three possibly relevant provincial *fasti* for an *ex praetura* command in the year 66 (Asia and Cilicia are closed, distant Macedonia is open). Cicero anyhow implies Quinctius had died by that date, at age 50 (*Clu.* 110).

234. Cic. *Agr.* 2.26 and 28.

235. See, e.g., *I. Knidos* I 31 Kn. III lines 28–35 and D. B lines 5–8, 10–12, cf. 16–19.

236. First place enjoyed by Cicero for 66 B.C.: Cic. *Man.* 2, *Tog.* FF 5 and 26 in Asc. pp. 85 and 92–93 C, *Pis.* 2, *Brut.* 321, Plu. *Cic.* 9.1. See also Vell. 2.59.2 (C. Octavius for 61 B.C.) and cf. Cic. *Mur.* 18 and 35 (claiming for a particular rhetorical purpose that such order was not so important). Ignominy of last place: V. Max. 6.9.14 (C. Marius as *pr.* 115 "supremo in loco adhaesit"), Cic. *Tog.* F 5 in Asc. p. 85 C (C. Antonius ran the risk of that for 66 B.C.).

237. Cic. *Agr.* 2.30 "consulibus legem curiatam ferentibus a tribunis plebis saepe est intercessum."

238. Bill on Jupiter Optimus Maximus: Suet. *Jul.* 15, D.C. 37.44.1–2, cf. Cic. *Att.* 2.24.3 (a preliminary *contio* on the measure?). Nepos' bills: *Schol. Bob.* p. 134 St., Plu. *Cat. Mi.* 26.2–5 (including the detail on Pompey's *imperium*), cf. Plu. *Cic.* 23.4 (ὅ τε Καῖσαρ οἵ τε δήμαρχοι). Caesar and Nepos disregard tribunician vetoes, leading to S.C.U.: Cic. *Sest.* 62, Suet. *Jul.* 16.1, Plu. *Cat. Mi.* 27.1–28.6, D.C. 37.43.1–3. Suspension from office (which causes Metellus to flee to Pompey): Suet. *Jul.* 16.1, Plu. *Cat. Mi.* 29.1–4, cf. Cic. *Fam.* 5.1 and 2. Caesar abdicates office, but is reinstated: Suet. *Jul.* 16.1–2.

239. See Cic. *Att.* 1.12.1 (1 Jan. 61), and cf. 13.5 (25 Jan. 61) and 15.1 (15 Mar. 61) on the sortition of the overseas praetorian *provinciae*.

240. D.C. 37.51.3–4. On the effects of this law, see E. S. Gruen, *The Last Generation of the Roman Republic* (Berkeley 1974) 432–433.

241. Sources in *MRR* II 118f, of which see especially D.C. 38.8.1.

242. Of these, Cicero singles out the *pr.* 57 M. Calidius for special efforts in securing his recall from exile (*Red. Sen.* 22–23). Calidius was a leading orator of his day (Cic. *Brut.* 274–278, cf. Jer. *Chron.* ad ann. 57 p. 154 H), who already as *designatus* for 57 voiced his *sententia* (i.e., in the Senate) in support of Cicero's recall from exile (Cic. *Red. Sen.* 22). (The date of his praetorship has been doubted, yet without good reason: see Sumner, *Orators* 147f.) Evidently as praetor he delivered his own speech "de domo Ciceronis" (Quint. *Inst.* 10.1.23).

243. Cic. *Sest.* 126.

244. Cic. *Red. Sen.* 22 (for L. Rufus' bill) with (for the six other praetors) *Pis.* 35 and *Mil.* 39, cf. D.C. 39.6.1. For an explication (with sources) of the various measures to recall Cicero see G. Rotondi, *Leges Publicae Populi Romanae* (Milan 1912) 400–403.

245. Cic. *Att.* 2.24.3 (C. Iulius Caesar in Jan. 62 B.C.). For *contiones* where a praetor discusses proposed legislation, see above in the text on the *pr.* 70 L. Cotta and his judiciary bill, and the anti-Ciceronian *contiones* of Ap. Pulcher in 57. For other types of praetorian *contiones* cf. Asc. p. 73 C (the *pr. repetundarum* M. Tullius Cicero in 66, speaking on a case pending in another *quaestio*), Suet. *Jul.* 17.2 (C. Iulius Caesar in 62, on his own accusation *de vi*), *Att.* 4.1.6 (the praetors and tribunes who supported Cicero's recall "give" a *contio* for him in Sept. 57), also 4.2.2–3 (the *pr. repetundarum* Ap. Claudius Pulcher holds a *contio* on

the legal status of Cicero's house in late Sept. 57), and 4.3.4 (Ap. Pulcher in 57 joins a consul and tribune designate in pressing for immediate aedilician elections, in which his brother was a candidate). Cicero (*Fin.* 2.74, addressed to a praetor designate for 49) implies that it was normal for a praetor on entering office to announce in a *contio* what principles he was to follow in administering law.

246. The first and only apparent notice of this capability is Cic. *Sest.* 78, of the *pr.* Ap. Claudius Pulcher who threatened to obnuntiate against the *tr. pl.* Q. Fabricius, but used armed gangs instead. On this item, and the *auspicia* of the plebeian assembly, see Badian in *Imperium Sine Fine* 201. But it is possible—despite Cicero's wording in the *Pro Sestio* passage—that Appius had threatened to obnuntiate against the tribune, not as praetor, but as augur, a priesthood he had held at least since 63 (*MRR* II 171): see G. V. Sumner, *AJPh* 84 (1963) 353–354.

247. On Clodius' withdrawal of candidacy for *pr.* 53 and transfer to that of 52, see Cic. *Mil.* 24–25 with Broughton, *Candidates Defeated* 37f. One of Clodius' alleged considerations, says Cicero, was whom he might have as a praetorian colleague in 53 (24). And he, of course, feared the prospect of Milo having *maius imperium* in 52 (25, 34). His plans to ensure the cooperation of Milo's competitors for the consulship: 25, 32, cf. 89. Clodius' praetorship to be feared: 34, 43, 91. Senate to be powerless against him: 88. Legislation to be the main instrument of Clodius' praetorship: 33. The *libertini*: 87, 89, also *Aer. Al. Mil.* FF 17–18 Crawford[2] with Asc. p. 52 C. Posthumous fate of laws: *Mil.* 33. In general on Clodius' "praetorship," see the perceptive comments of A. C. Clark in his commentary, *M. Tullius Ciceronis Pro T. Annio Milone* (Oxford 1895) 28–29, 78–79, 115.

248. The same goes for the alleged fears—as reported by Plutarch—of Pompey and Crassus regarding Cato's praetorian candidacy for 55, that "he would make the praetorship a match for the consulship" (*Cat. Mi.* 42.2, cf. D.C. 39.32.2).

Notes to Chapter 13

1. M. Metellus' command: *CIL* X 7852 lines 7–8 (evidence for routine administration, in this case adjudication of boundary dispute involving the Patulcenses of Corsica) with *Inscr. Ital.* XIII 1 84f, Vell. 2.8.2, and Eutrop. 4.25.1 on the triumph. Caprarius waiting outside Rome: *RDGE* 15 = *SIG*[3] 705 lines 2f with line 62 shows that the *cos.* 112 M. Livius Drusus was in Macedonia or at least expected in the *provincia* by mid-June of that year.

2. *Prov.* 15 for this and what follows immediately below.

3. The *supplicatio* did not give the commander the presumptive right to a triumph (famously, Cato *Fam.* 15.5.2–3), but certainly was thought to have helped any request (Cic. *Fam.* 2.15.1 and *Att.* 7.1.5); the absence of one was probably fatal to a vote of the honor. *Fam.* 3.9.4 offers a useful late Republican view on the proper time for asking for a *supplicatio*, i.e., after the completion of one's summer campaign. That the imperatorial acclamation precedes the request for *supplicatio* is implied most notably by V. Max. 2.8.7; the relationship between the two emerges quite clearly from D.C. 37.40.2 (on C. Antonius in 62). Incidentally, when Cicero sought Cato's support for a *supplicatio* in Jan. 50, he had already been hailed as *imperator* in Cilicia some two months earlier (13 Oct. 51, as seen from *Att.* 5.20.3), but (purposely) omits mention of the acclamation in his letter (see *Fam.* 15.4.9). Passages such as this throw the tactlessness of Albucius' provincial display into high relief. In general on the link between *supplicatio* and triumph, see T. C. Brennan, "Triumphus in Monte Albano," in E. Harris and R. Wallace (eds.), *Transitions to Empire: Essays in Greco-Roman History, 360–146 B.C., in Honor of E. Badian* (Norman, Okla., 1996) 318 and 325 with 331 n. 16.

4. The only sources on Albucius' actual command are Cic. *Prov.* 15 with *Pis.* 92 (both passages referring to his celebration in Sardinia as a "triumph"). On his prosecution, see the passages collected in Alexander, *Trials* no. 67, but with E. Badian, *Klio* 66 (1984) 306–309 on the (approximate) date (not ca. 103, as Alexander has it). For brief discussion and a precedent of sorts for Albucius' provincial "triumph"—the *pro cos.* Cn. Domitius Ahenobarbus in 121 (10.2.2)—see Brennan in *Transitions to Empire* 329 with 337 n. 86 (but like *MRR* I 560, erroneously suggesting that Albucius' "triumph" came after the *supplicatio* was refused).

5. Cicero compares the Macedonian commander L. Calpurnius Piso Caesoninus (*cos.* 58) to Albucius, though Piso seems to have done little more than to set up trophies (*Pis.* 92, cf. 97), which was a conventional form of expression by the victorious Roman general. Florus (1.37.6) claims it was a novelty in the year 121; perhaps so, but at least starting with Sulla (see, e.g., App. *Mith.* 45.176, Plu. *Sull.* 19.5, Paus. 9.40.7 with ch. 14 n. 33) it grew to be commonplace (cf. D.C. 37.21.2 on Pompey's trophy mania). Various individuals drew upon triumphal imagery during celebrations in the city (see Plu. *Cic.* 22.1 and 5–7 on Cicero in 63, or *Cat. Min.* 39.3 with D.C. 39.23.1 on Cato in 56), but no one would mistake these demonstrations for the real thing.

6. *Inscr. Ital.* XIII 1 84f.

7. For the date see E. Badian, *Studies in Greek and Roman History* (Oxford 1964) 82–84. We have no evidence that Servilius as praetor first held a city *provincia*, as *MRR* III 197 seems to imply. And to dispose of an old suggestion: Servilius cannot have triumphed as praetor from Cilicia (see *MRR* I 26 and 30 n. 5) for in that case his rank would be *pro cos.* A "Servaeus" failed of election to a political office for 87 though supported by Sulla (Plu. *Sull.* 10.3); if he is identical with this Servilius (and assuming that the office in question was the consulship) that would imply a praetorship at least by 90.

8. *Ver.* 2.2.155.

9. C. Cato: see Cic. *Ver.* 2.4.22 with the explication of E. Badian, *Historia* 42 (1993) 203–210; also ch. 14 n. 119 for the possibility that he served as a *legatus* in Africa ca. 117 (and so in this way escaped prosecution?). M. Carbo: Cic. *Fam.* 9.21.3 "condemnatus, fur magnus, ex Sicilia" (= Alexander, *Trials* no. 46) with E. S. Gruen, *Roman Politics and the Criminal Courts, 149–78 B.C.* (Cambridge, Mass., 1968) 132. For the (entirely conjectural) date of "ca. 114" see *MRR* I 534 n. 2. He was (by M. Crawford's dating, *RRC* I 295 no. 276) *monetalis* in 122.

10. See Sal. *Jug.* 28.6 and also Appendix B n. 228 for the suggestion that L. Hortensius (*cos. des.* for 108) held a command on the island precisely in the year 111.

11. D.S. 36.1.1 (providing the chronology of the outbreak and explicit notice of the manpower crisis that resulted for Sicily); cf. App. *Hisp.* 99.430 (no troops available for Spain). On the involvement of freedmen in the revolt, see D.S. 36.6.1.

12. Sources for what follows are D.S. 36.3–6; D.C. 27 F 93. For the special reliability of Diodorus on the Sicilian slave revolts, see T. C. Brennan, *RFIC* 121 (1993) 155 n. 1.

13. Cf. D.S. 36.7.1.

14. D.S. 36.4.1–7.4 and Flor. 2.7.10–11; on the officer M. Titinius who was Nerva's officer at Henna, cf. also *MRR* III 206.

15. D.S. 36.8.1–4.

16. Clearly implied by D.S. 36.8.1, and expected in any case.

17. Plu. *Mar.* 14.11.

18. D.S. 36.8.5 and 9.2; Flor. 2.7.11.

19. D.S. 36.9.1 and 10.1–3; Flor. 2.7.10–11.

20. Sources for Aquillius in *MRR* I 571, 577, II 2; see esp. D.S. 36.10.1–3 (details of fighting and description of games at his *ovatio*), Flor. 2.7.11–12 (Perperna, Aquillius, and the technique of starvation), Cic. *Agr.* 2.83 (loan of grain to cities), *Vir. ill.* 73.5 (veteran colonies).

On the possibility Aquillius asked for a triumph see T. C. Brennan, *RFIC* 121 (1993) 172 n. 1; cf. *Transitions to Empire* 334 n. 58.

21. In the mid-130s, note the prosecution of the Spanish commanders Q. Pompeius (*cos.* 141) (Alexander, *Trials* no. 8, a *quaestio* before *iudices*) and M. Aemilius Lepidus Porcina (*cos.* 137) (no. 12, a *iudicium populi*); the *quaestio extraordinaria* under the *lex Mamilia* in 109 aimed at Roman conduct of the Jugurthine War (nos. 52–57); and the prosecutions that came out of the fighting against Gauls and Germans in the period 106–103 (nos. 59 and 63, *iudicia populi* of 106 and 104 respectively; no. 65, a *quaestio extraordinaria* of 103; and nos. 64 and 66, two *iudicia populi* of 103). The trials of the Macedonian commanders C. Porcius Cato (*cos.* 114) ca. the year 113 (no. 45, *de repetundis*) and Cn. Papirius Carbo (*cos.* 113) (no. 47, process unknown) in 112 arose from quite different circumstances and were of less gravity.

22. One might add that Lucullus' treatment of his successor C. Servilius probably brought on his prosecution by the augur Servilius in the first place. Sources and bibliography in Alexander, *Trials* no. 69, of which see esp. Plu. *Luc.* 1.1 on the charge (ὁ . . . πατὴρ ἑάλω κλοπῆς), *Vir. ill.* 62.4 on Numidicus' refusal to serve as a character witness, and D.S. 36.8.3 for the importance of Triocala in Lucullus' prosecution; also E. Badian, *Klio* 66 (1984) 301–306, on the identity of the prosecutor and importance of the case. Lucullus' exile: I. Shatzman, *Senatorial Wealth and Roman Politics* (Brussels 1975) 275 no. 56. Lucullus' sons later famously counterprosecuted the augur: see *Trials* no. 71.

23. Alexander, *Trials* no. 70 with Badian, *Klio* 66 (1984) 291–296 and 301–306 (identifying the quaestor as L. Sempronius Pithio).

24. It is not until the late 50s that we find firm evidence for a *divinatio* of prosecutors where the charge is not *repetundae*: see Alexander, *Trials* nos. 304 and 310 (*ambitus* cases of 54 and 52 respectively). For *divinatio* in extortion trials, see nos. 67 (104 B.C.), 91 (ca. 91 B.C., only possibly *repetundae*), 140 (77 BC, only possibly a *divinatio*), 174 (shortly before 70 B.C.), 177 (70 B.C.), 303 (54 B.C.), 338 and 339 (both 51 B.C.). For a possible *divinatio* in a *peculatus* trial of 66, see ch. 10 n. 112.

25. Cic. *Flac.* 98 (charges and reaction of *iudices*) with *Brut.* 222 and *Off.* 2.50 on the prosecution. For full ancient sources and bibliography, see Alexander, *Trials* no. 84 (wrongly suggesting on p. 44 that the *Periocha* "gives" a date of 98 for the trial).

26. Stable conditions on island: Cic. *Ver.* 2.5.5, cf. 3.125. Restrictions on weapons in all praetorian edicts of this era: *Ver.* 2.5.7. Ahenobarbus and the *pastor*: *Ver.* 2.5.7, retold by V. Max. 6.3.5 (from the section "de severitate") and Quint. *Inst.* 4.2.17.

27. Asking the commander who is present for laws: Plu. *Luc.* 2.4 and J. *AJ* 14.114 (Cyrene and L. Lucullus in 86); Cic. *Balb.* 43 (Gades and C. Caesar in 61/60). The case of Halaesa: Cic. *Ver.* 2.2.122. But appeal to patrons, particularly in instances of prolonged strife, was also traditional: see T. C. Brennan, *RFIC* 121 (1993) 178–183 on the "leges Scipionis" of 131/130 (not to be dated to the late third or early second century, as is generally supposed), and Cic. *Sull.* 60 on Pompeii in the 60s. For the Sicilian conections of the Claudii Pulchri, see E. Badian, *Phoenix* 25 (1971) 136–137.

28. For this and what follows on the praetor Asellio, see D.S. 37.8.1–4 with Münzer, *RE* s.v. *Sempronius* 18 col. 1364 (emulation of Q. Scaevola). On the identity and family of this praetor, see E. Badian, *PACA* 11 (1968) [1970] 1–6.

29. That at any rate was what Cicero did for Cilicia in 51 (*Fam.* 3.8.4, admitting a few ad hoc additions while in transit); cf. *Font.* 19 (Fonteius faulted for devising a "portorium vini" before setting out for Gaul in the mid-70s). The provincial edict seems to have been set up very soon after a commander's arrival in his *provincia*, as we would expect: see Cic. *Ver.* 2.3.152 (clearly within the first month of L. Metellus' Silician command in 70).

30. Cf. Cic. *Att.* 6.1.15 (Cicero's own practice in his Cilician edict of 51).

31. Contrast Cic. *Fam.* 13.55 and 56.3 (to Q. Minucius Thermus in Asia) with *Fam.* 3.7.3.

32. In general on this man's command see Badian, *Studies* 84–86. Norbanus' quaestorship: E. Badian, *AJPh* 104 (1983) 171. Norbanus' service in Sicily during Social War: Cic. *Ver.* 2.5.8 "cum bello sociorum tota Italia arderet." Sicily as supplier of Roman armies in that war: *Ver.* 2.2.5, cf. 2.3.117. Norbanus "easily" keeps Sicily free of disturbances: *Ver.* 2.5.8. His quaestor in western Sicily attacks Marius and entourage at Erycina: Plu. *Mar.* 40.2–3 (not in *MRR*). Norbanus' energetic measures at Rhegium in 87 (incidently revealing Cicero's remarks on Norbanus' "easy" peace as tendentious): D.S. 37.2.13–14, cf. *SEG* I 418 with F. Münzer, *Hermes* 67 (1932) 233–235. See in addition *SIG*³ 715 (the praetor Cn. Aufidius T.f.) with Appendix B n. 511 for the close relationship between Rhegium and the *provincia* of Sicily in this general era; cf. also Cic. *Ver.* 2.5.44 and 47 (Verres requisitions timber from Rhegium) with R. O. Jolliffe, "Phases of Corruption in Roman Administration in the Last Half-Century of the Roman Republic" (diss. Chicago 1919) 45. Road improvement activities in eastern Sicily before departure, delegating *imperium* to his quaestor Q. Anicius to help in the task: *CIL* I² 2951. Opportunity for return in 85: App. *BC* 1.76.349. Broughton in *MRR* III 149 suggests Norbanus stayed into 84.

33. Sources on his praetorship are collected in *MRR* II 67f and 73 n. 4, under the year 82, the date offered by Münzer (*RE* s.v. col. 897). Sulla's offer to him is reported by D.S. 38.14.

34. See *Per.* 86 with Appendix B n. 298. Badian (*Studies* 86) allows for the possibility that there may have been a commander in Sicily between Norbanus and Perperna, while stressing "there would almost certainly not be *more* than one."

35. On Perperna's rule and then abandonment of Sicily see Plu. *Pomp.* 10.1–2 and 6. The detail that Sulla sent Pompey to Sicily when the proscriptions were already under way is provided by *Pomp.* 10.1 (mentioning also his force); cf. *Vir. ill.* 77.1 "Siciliam sine bello a proscriptis recepit" (sc. Pompey). Appian (*BC* 1.95.440) has Sulla dispatch Pompey just before announcing the proscriptions. For Pompey's *imperium* see *Per.* 89 (explicit), Plu. *Moralia* 203 C (στρατηγός) and cf. Cic. *Man.* 61 ("Siciliam permitti") with 10.5.7 above. His advance force surprises Carbo's fleet and captures the Marian consul: *Per.* 89 and App. *BC* 1.96.449.

36. D.S. 38.20.

37. D.S. 38.20; Cic. *Ver.* 2.3.42 (tithes) and 45 (envoys); Plu. *Pomp.* 10.2 (Pompey and the cities, including Messana) and 10.7 with *Moralia* 203 C (control of subordinates).

38. Pompey's general policy toward Sulla's enemies: Plu. *Pomp.* 10.4–5. On Carbo, see App. *BC* 1.96.449 (Carbo's execution contrasted with that of other *Mariani*) and Plu. *Pomp.* 10.3; cf. V. Max. 5.3.5 and 9.13.2 with A. Keaveney, *AC* 51 (1982) 122 for the chronology (Carbo killed while still consul, and so in the year 82). On the possibility that Pompey was the *"praetor"* who put the tribune or *tribunicius* Q. Valerius Soranus to death on order of the Senate (thus Serv. A. 1.277), see *MRR* II 68; also Keaveney, *AC* 51 (1982) 128.

39. Plu. *Pomp.* 10.6 ("Sthenis"); Cic. *Ver.* 2.2.113 "sensisse contra rem publicam." Cf. also *Ver.* 2.2.110 (Sthenius as a *hospes* of Pompey).

40. Plu. *Pomp.* 11.1–2. On C. Memmius (who later served as a quaestor in Spain against Sertorius), see C. F. Konrad, *Plutarch's Sertorius: A Historical Commentary* (Chapel Hill, N.C., 1994) 175. Perhaps it was he who built the *via Pompeia* in eastern Sicily (on which see W. Kunkel, *Staatsordnung und Staatspraxis der römischen Republik: Die Magistratur* [Munich 1995] 365 n. 221); for a parallel note *CIL* I² 2951 with n. 32 above.

41. See above in text on the year 87 and Plu. *Crass.* 10.6–7 for 72 (quite explicit).

42. Admissions of circumstantiality: see, e.g., Cic. *Ver.* 2.3.146, 178, 200–201; 5.22 and 65. Verres blamed underlings: e.g., *Ver.* 2.2.49. Not deemed an appropriate defense: e.g., *Ver.*

2.3.175 (on some offenses by *mancipes*, i.e., members of trading firms) "nihil haec ad te pertinere?" Vicarious responsibility: *Ver.* 2.3.65, 91, 153, 156, 175.

43. See, above all, *I. Knidos* I 31 Kn. III lines 9–15 (the commander's legal responsibility for his *comites* outside his province; he was obviously liable for them in the *provincia* as well); also Cic. *Q. fr.* 1.1.10–11 for the general principle. Magistrates (such as quaestors) were liable for their own behavior (quite explicit at *Fam.* 2.18.2–3), though Cicero fudges that principle when it serves his purpose (as at *Div. Caec.* 35). A key passage for Cicero's argument is *Ver.* 2.3.156, where he stresses that Verres should be held responsible for the crimes of the *decumanus* Apronius, the *accensus* Timarchides and the lictor Sextius (for which Cicero offers an abundance of details throughout the speech). On the continued resistance in the later Republic to making subordinates themselves subject to the *lex de repetundis*, see C. Damon and C. S. Mackay, *Historia* 44 (1995) 43–46. C. J. Classen, *Ciceroniana* 4 (1980) 93–114, collects all the subordinates mentioned in the *Verrines*—so many as to be almost stupefying, but of whom only a few come off as members of Verres' "inner circle" (pp. 109–110).

44. See esp. *Ver.* 2.3.23 on the *decumanus* Apronius, said by Cicero to have sat *in tribunali proximus* to Verres, i.e., implying he was the senior member of the praetor's *consilium* (on this position see e.g. V. Max. 3.7.6). For the low-status individuals in Verres' judicial *consilia*, see 2.2.75; 2.3.28, 30, 54, 69, 137, cf. 138 (*medicus* given as civil *iudex*). For Verres' inappropriate general use of his *cohors* as his *consilium*, see 2.2.71; 2.3.28, 68, 136, cf. 2.2.66 and perhaps 2.5.54. So it comes almost as a surprise when Cicero in an aside (2.5.114, regarding an incident from Verres' last year of command) implies that some reputable senior members of Verres' staff were regular members of his judicial *consilia*.

45. "Go-betweens": see esp. Cic. *Ver.* 2.3.61 and 65, 91, 149, 156; cf. 2.2.26–27, 46, 49 (use of *cohors* for predations). Their cases prejudicial: *Ver.* 2.3.153. The praetor's innovations suspicious: *Ver.* 2.3.51 and 142 (edict); 3.183 (an innovation involving his scribes). Also judicial reversals: *Ver.* 2.5.19. And composition of *consilia*: *Ver.* 2.3.138 with n. 44 above. Failure to keep records: *Ver.* 2.3.112, 165–166; 4.36. Also personal enemies: *Ver.* 2.3.52. Cicero's caricature: cf. *Scaur.* 26, where the orator states his concern for vivid description in his prosecution of Verres. Cicero's grudging admission: *Ver.* 2.2.146 ("fere omnia"). For some aspects of Cicero's techniques of distortion in the *Verrines*, see (a sample) F. de Visscher, *REL* 33 (1955) 136–139; A. J. Marshall, *CQ* 17 (1967) 408–413; W. C. McDermott, *RhM* 120 (1977) 74f; G. Martorana, *Kokalos* 25 (1979) 73–103 (esp. 98f); O. A. W. Dilke, *Ciceroniana* 4 (1980) 43–51. On the political background to Cicero's prosecution of Verres, see the survey of opinions (with references) collected in B. A. Marshall, *Philologus* 120 (1976) 86f.

46. Cic. *Ver.* 2.2.8 with 2.3.212.

47. Cic. *Ver.* 2.2.8, cf. 2.3.212 (he did not demand grain for his *cella*).

48. Ps.-Asc. pp. 187 and 259 St. It has been thought (see Alexander, *Trials* no. 131) that the charge was *de repetundis*, but that in fact is nowhere stated in our (admittedly slim) sources, and Cic. *Ver.* 2.2.8 implies that there was no attempt on the part of Sicilians to have Lepidus punished. There are other possibilities, such as an accusation of *ambitus* connected with his earlier bid for that praetorship.

49. Cic. *Ver.* 2.3.212; cf. 2.2.8. For 80 as the date of Marcellus' praetorship, see Appendix B n. 351.

50. Cic. *Ver.* 2.3.212.

51. For Sulla's control of consular elections for 79, see 11.8.1.

52. Note instead for the period of his time in Sicily Cic. *Ver.* 2.2.11 "praetor"; 2.17 "praetura"; 5.40 "cum penes te praetorium imperium ac nomen esset." But twice (2.2.14, 2.5.134) Verres is said to have "summum imperium." At *Ver.* 2.5.142, Cicero speaks of "sex lictores" of Verres surrounding one of the praetor's hapless victims. But that need only refer to those who

were doing the punishing in this instance. More lictors—to be precise, another six—will have remained around Verres.

53. See Cic. *Ver.* 2.3.212 (addressed, and said to be "hoc ipso ex consilio").

54. Cic. *Ver.* 2.3.42, citing L. Hortensius (*pr.* ca. 111) and Cn. Pompeius (*pro pr.* 82) as other examples of fairness in this type of tithe. Cf. Cic. *Ver.* 2.4.86–87 (equestrian statues in Marcellus' honor at Tyndaris and elsewhere) and J. B. Rives, *CPh* 88 (1993) 32–35 (his inclusion in the festival of the *Marcellia*, founded in honor of his ancestor M. Marcellus after the sack of Syracuse in 211 B.C.).

55. E. Badian, *Gnomon* 39 (1967) 94 n. 1 on *ILLRP* 320; see further *MRR* III 71.

56. Cic. *Ver.* 2.2.110 and 4.43–44.

57. Cf. Cic. *Ver.* 2.4.33–34.

58. *Ver.* 2.3.216 "fortissimo atque innocentissimo viro . . . ad hoc tempus innocentissimam omnium diligentissimamque praeturam"; cf. 2.2.138 "viro fortissimo atque innocentissimo." Cicero says he was correct in his dealings with Sicilian farmers (2.3.216—but see below in text) and the city of Messana (2.5.55), as well as the holding of local elections (2.3.156), and the provincewide census (2.2.138–139).

59. And so had an interest in protecting this praetor—and himself: see E. Fallu, *CEA* 2 (1973) 31–53 (inter alia, describing precisely what Cicero's administrative responsibilities will have been as quaestor at Lilybaeum).

60. Cic. *Ver.* 2.4.142 "ei negotium facessitum" and 143 "Peducaeus eorum laudatione iam non uteretur."

61. For *negotium* in the sense of "legal case," see Cic. *de Orat.* 2.274; *Clu.* 43, 77, and 92; *Cael.* 74; *Q. fr.* 3.2.1; Cael. *Fam.* 8.6.2; cf. possibly Cic. *Fam.* 2.14.

62. Several times used of P. Rutilius (*cos.* 105 and condemned in 92): Cic. *Font.* 38; *Brut.* 115; *N.D.* 3.80; cf. Vell. 2.13.1. See also Cic. *S. Rosc.* 14, and cf. *Planc.* 12 (M. Pupius Piso depicted as *innocentissimus* in contrast with a man who had lost his equestrian standing).

63. Sal. *Hist.* 2.44–48 M.

64. Peducaeus, the grain prices of 76 and 75, and his profits *ex cibariis*: Cic. *Ver.* 2.3.216–217, cf. *Planc.* 64–65 for Cicero's description of his own role in the shortage. Debate on tithes—extending to Sicilian wine, oil and minor crops—with S.C. and vote of People entrusting final decision to the *coss.* 75, who convene a large *consilium* on the matter: *Ver.* 2.3.18–19. Peducaeus is not listed as a possible defendant in Alexander, *Trials.* If he indeed did face prosecution for his profiting from the grain crisis, his troubles cannot have failed to affect also his quaestor Cicero (see Cic. *Div. Caec.* 31–32 for the general principle). For Cicero's continued loyalty to his superior Peducaeus (which included cultivation of his son M. Curtius Peducaenus, *pr.* 50), see *Red. Sen.* 21; *Att.* 13.1.3.

65. On the respective *aestimationes* of Sacerdos, Antonius and Verres, see Cic. *Ver.* 2.3.214–216; cf. 2.5.55 (Sacerdos quite properly included Messana in his requisitions), and also 2.2.8 (more on the impact of Antonius' brief visit to the province). For a good short description of the practice in general, see G. H. Stevenson, *Roman Provincial Administration till the Age of the Antonines* (Oxford 1939) 89.

66. For this fear, see Cic. *Ver.* 2.2.142, 2.3.43, 219–220.

67. Cic. *Ver.* 2.3.119.

68. See Cic. *Ver.* 2.2.68–75 (a capital case involving Sopater of Halicyae), with esp. 2.70 and 81 on the overlap in their *consilia.*

69. Cicero's formulation is consistent in each of three mentions of Turpio's condemnation: note *Ver.* 2.2.22 "C. Sacerdote praetore condemnatus iniuriarum," 3.90 "iniuriarum Sacerdote praetore damnatus est," 2.5.108 "C. Sacerdote praetore iniuriarum damnatus est"; contrast 2.2.68 on Sopater ("ab inimicis suis apud C. Sacerdotem praetorem rei capitalis

cum accusatus esset"). The first three references merely "date" the condemnation of Naevius Turpio to Sacerdos' praetorian command; there is no implication that he personally heard the case.

70. Cic. *Ver.* 2.1.27 and 2.21 (inheritances that came safely to the intended recipients during Sacerdos' promagistracy in 74, which Verres later disturbed).

71. Cic. *Ver.* 2.3.49 and 119; see also 2.3.40, 43 (explicit on consular bid), 103 (expected grain delivered in all three years), 148, 151.

72. Cicero argues that there was no precedent for the way Verres drove up profits from the sale of grain tithes (*Ver.* 2.3.42, 48, 51, 117, 147). Indeed, it was not really a profit to sell "tithes" that were not 10 percent but really 30–50 percent of the crop (2.3.40, 42, 117, 119). The motive, says Cicero, was really Verres' personal profit (2.3.43, 49–51). Verres' heavy-handed innovations in this sphere resulted only in the desertion of *ager decumanus* (2.3.43, 119–120).

73. Cic. *Ver.* 2.3.163, 173, 5.52 (the grain was to be bought in Sicily) with Sal. *Hist.* 1.55 M and Asc. p. 8 C.

74. Cic. *Ver.* 2.3.204. For an admission that grain matters can be boring, see *Ver.* 2.3.10.

75. Cf. Cic. *Ver.* 2.3.10 (explicit in this regard).

76. He is listed fourth (apparently) in the senatorial *consilium* to RDGE 23 (16 Oct. 73).

77. Cf. *Ver.* 2.2.17.

78. Cicero mentions his *triennium* of service frequently: see, e.g., *Div. Caec.* 3 and 11, *Ver.* 1.40, 2.2.49. See also *Ver.* 2.3.103 (Roman people evidently got expected grain in all three years), 118 (his satellite Apronius active in all three years), 216 (Verres practiced *commutatio*, i.e., the acceptance of cash in lieu of grain, in all three years), 4.23 and 5.51 (general remission of Messana's obligations *per triennium*), 4.136 (Verres under the influence of Syracuse's women in all three years).

79. *Div. Caec.* 38.

80. N. Marinone, *AAT* 100 (1965–1966) 219–252. For a summary of previous views (through Broughton in *MRR* II) on the order of Verres' quaestors and legates—one important guide to the chronology—see H. Habermehl, *RE* s.v. *Verres* 1 col. 1580. Habermehl's 1958 article (cols. 1561–1633) offers a valuable detailed summary of the events of Verres' promagistracy, yet it is arranged by category of crime and disengages only the more obvious dates. The same goes for F. H. Cowles, *Gaius Verres: A Historical Study* (Ithaca, N.Y., 1917). Indeed, Cowles (p. 27) considers it "a manifest impossibility to separate this mass of evidence [sc. pertaining to Verres' Sicilian command] and arrange it with any strict regard to chronological sequence." For a still earlier narrative (following quite closely Cicero's own sequence in the *Verrines*), see A. Holm, *Geschichte Siciliens im Alterthum* III (Leipzig 1898) 134–179.

81. Cic. *Ver.* 2.2.39. Hence, e.g., the relatively detailed description of Verres' crimes as urban praetor, which are meant to further substantiate the Sicilian charges: see *Ver.* 2.2.119, 2.3.17 and 41 where Cicero spells out his purpose in introducing this material.

82. Cic. *Ver.* 2.2.17–18, 21.

83. Cic. *Ver.* 1.40.

84. As urban praetor in 74, Verres had let a contract on 13 Sept. for 1 Dec. completion. Cicero says that was considered a short time; Verres in fact left for Sicily before the work was done (*Ver.* 2.1.148 with 149 and 5.39). He is said to have presented the certificate of *probatio* for the work only a full four years later (2.1.149).

85. Cic. *Ver.* 2.5.34, cf. 2.2.24.

86. Clear esp. from Cic. *Ver.* 2.5.1–4 (cf. 33), on which see the discussion of Cowles, *Gaius Verres* 136–142.

87. Albeit always in deeply ironical passages, e.g., *Ver.* 2.5.25 "habetis hominis consilia, diligentiam, vigilantiam, custodiam defensionemque provinciae." Consider also the terms of

the eulogy for Verres that was extorted from the Syracusan senate in 70, as reported by Cicero: "quod vigilanter provinciam administrasset . . . quod praedones procul ab insula Sicilia prohibuisset" (2.4.144). See also 2.5.42.

88. Cic. *Ver.* 2.2.19–24. "Ad urbem": see 2.2.21, misunderstood by L. H. G. Greenwood in the Loeb translation; cf. Ps.-Asc. p. 260 St. for a good explanation of the phrase. Eagerness to investigate upon landing: chronological pointers in *Ver.* 2.1.27 and 2.19 (Verres' "first day in Sicily"). In 72, the heir appealed against Verres to both Q. Hortensius in Rome in his capacity as *pr. repetundis* and M. Terentius Varro Lucullus (*cos.* 73) when *pro cos.* in Macedonia (2.2.24, and on Hortensius cf. 1.38).

89. Cic. *Ver.* 2.4.74 with 76 for the chronology.

90. Cic. *Ver.* 2.4.38–42, with 40 and 42 establishing the chronology.

91. Cic. *Ver.* 2.3.75 (in connection with Herbita). But Cicero also favorably compares the agricultural situation of several Sicilian towns in 73 with that of 71: Leontini (2.3.120, cf. 97), Mutyca (2.3.120), Herbita (2.3.75, 120), and Agyrium (2.3.120). For Sicilian farming in 73, see also *Ver.* 2.3.86 on the Tissenses and perhaps 3.88 on the Amestratini (the year 73 or 72, as is clear from 3.89).

92. Cic. *Ver.* 2.2.35–49, 62–63, esp. 35 on Heraclius' personal situation. For the chronology see 2.2.37, 47–49, and 62; see also 44 on this incident as Verres' only Syracusan trial.

93. Cic. *Ver.* 2.2.53–63, with 53–54 for the chronology; cf. 62.

94. Cic. *Ver.* 2.2.49. Those departing will have included the quaestor M. Postumius (2.2.44, based at Syracuse) and also the Lilybaeum quaestor Q. Caecilius Niger (who in 70 sought to prosecute Verres). Caecilius' one attested action as quaestor is his ruling against the wealthy freedwoman Agonis in her dispute with an unnamed *praefectus* of M. Antonius (*pr.* 74). Verres overturned the quaestor's decision in this doubtless diplomatically sensitive case (*Div. Caec.* 55–58). N. Marinone, *AAT* 100 (1965–1966) 238–252, interprets *Ver.* 2.2.49 overliterally, and takes it to mean (quite implausibly) that P. Tadius also left after 73—only to return to serve Verres for 71.

95. Broughton holds that the quaestor T. Vettius was "in Sicily in 72 and probably 71" (*MRR* III 219, following N. Marinone, *AAT* 100 [1965–1966] 219–252, esp. 229–232, who places him in Syracuse); cf. also E. Badian, *AJPh* 104 (1983) 166 n. 32. However, we are told nothing of substance about Vettius other than that he was the brother of Verres' wife (2.3.168) and that Verres should have "summoned" him to his *consilium* when hearing the major capital case of the Sicilian naval commanders at Syracuse (2.5.114). And that trial should belong to 71 (see below in text). The quaestor P. Caesetius surely belongs to the latter part of Verres' tenure: see 2.4.146 for his presence on the island after Verres' departure in 70. Broughton (*MRR* III 43, cf. 231, again following Marinone) places him at Lilybaeum in 72 and 71. But there is no certain attestation for 72, only 71 (2.5.63) and 70 (2.4.146). And both those passages suggest that Caesetius served at Syracuse. That means the quaestor T. Vettius must have been based in the west in 71 (2.5.114 in no way disallows it). Finally, the *legatus* P. Cervius. He is mentioned only at 2.5.114, in connection with T. Vettius and the trial of the *nauarchoi.* Marinone has him only in the year 72: but that is based in large part on his misguided reconstruction of the movements of P. Tadius (see n. 94 above), and the apparent belief (*AAT* 100 [1965–1966] 250–251) that Verres had just one legate at a time.

96. Cic. *Ver.* 2.2.25–26 (specifying that this case started two years before the trial of Verres).

97. See Cic. *Ver.* 2.5.16–24, esp. 21 on the chronology.

98. For this and what follows, see Cic. *Ver.* 2.5.26–33 (general rhythm of Verres' service in *provincia*, including mode of transport); 5.26 and 30, cf. 2.48, 4.61–62 (residence in Syracuse); 4.54 (workshop in residence at Syracuse); 5.86 (never commanded a fleet); 5.63 and 80 (traditional summer naval activities eschewed by Verres and instead delegated to sub-

ordinates). *Ver.* 2.4.76 offers another minor slip (assizes "circum omnia provinciae fora"), as does perhaps 2.3.193 (Verres orders grain to be brought to him in remotest corners of *provincia*); cf. 2.4.118 (other praetors base selves at Hiero's *regia*). On that last item, Syracuse was the most important administrative center of Sicily, a fact that emerges from even some of the less tendentious passages of the *Verrines*. It was the site of Verres' court of law: 2.3.27, 68, 78, cf. 149 (tithes for all Sicily sold here).

99. Cic. *Ver.* 2.4.40 (indicating that it was subsequent to and much more significant than the case of Diodorus of Melita). On the character of Sthenius see *Ver.* 2.2.83, 110–111, 113 (acquittal by Pompey in 82), 117 (Cicero's ties with Sthenius); 2.3.18 (in 75 Sthenius vociferously had opposed in Rome the *publicani* over a proposed innovation in the *locatio* for Sicily); 5.109 (*hospes* of Verres and previous commanders).

100. Cic. *Ver.* 2.2.83–118. On the chronology see 2.91 ("hiems") with 94–95 and 97.

101. Cic. *Ver.* 2.2.95–97, 102–103.

102. Notices for Herbita (*Ver.* 2.3.76), the Tissenses (2.3.86), and the Amestratini (2.3.88–89—one of the two years mentioned must be 72).

103. Cic. *Ver.* 2.5.160. Verres claimed he was a Sertorian refugee (2.5.161), i.e., after the deaths of Sertorius and his successor M. Perperna in Spain (see 2.5.146 and esp. 153 for the relative chronology). In general for the problem (real or alleged) of Sertorian refugees in Sicily, see 2.5.72, 146, 151, 153–155. I argue in 13.4.3 that Sertorius was killed in 72 and Perperna in (very probably) 71.

104. Cic. *Ver.* 2.5.63 and (for the date) 76. Though the *legatus* P. Tadius served under Verres for all three years of his command (2.2.49), the quaestor P. Caesetius belongs only to the latter part of Verres' tenure: see n. 95 above. Against the chronology of Habermehl, *RE* s.v. *Verres* 1 col. 1619 (summer 72), see N. Marinone, *AAT* 100 (1965–1966) 224–229 (but who tries to place this incident precisely in Sept. 71).

105. Cic. *Ver.* 2.2.131–140, esp. 131 (portrayed by Verres as an anti-*ambitus* measure) and 138–139 (character of these new censors and their census). Sex. Peducaeus conducted the last one for Sicily as promagistrate in 76; Cicero asserts that L. Metellus in 70 had to disregard Verres' census and hold another one himself (2.2.131–140).

106. See Cic. *Ver.* 2.3.101 (the stipulation that certain Sicilian communities should deliver grain to a different *conventus* than their own).

107. Contribution of Sicilian censors: Cic. *Ver.* 2.2.137. Of the farmers: *Ver.* 2.2.150, 167–168.

108. Cicero, of course, offers no such sinister interpretation of, e.g., the monument set up by the juror P. Servilius Isauricus (*cos.* 79) after his own consular command in Cilicia (*Ver.* 2.4.82).

109. Such as a planned reception by a company of *publicani* for his arrival in Italy, arranged already in 71 (Cic. *Ver.* 2.2.172).

110. Cic. *Ver.* 2.3.36 and 51 (each of Verres' three edicts is said to have been motivated by his satellite Apronius).

111. Cic. *Ver.* 2.3.104.

112. See n. 91 above on the relative position of Leontini, Mutyca, Herbita and Agyrium in 71 as compared to two years earlier, and n. 102 on the Amestratini (an incident of 72 or 71). Cicero has to draw on the experience of Leontini (2.3.110–117, 147–151) to make a central point—that Verres generated no profit for the Roman People—though the town did not aid Cicero in his investigations in 70 and did not testify against Verres at his trial (2.3.109–110). (Cicero's explanation for this is that virtually no citizen land owners of this *civitas* remained after Verres' tenure as governor.)

113. See, e.g., Cic. *Ver.* 2.3.105–108, esp. 105 where it is implied Apronius played the part of an imperious praetor; also 2.3.77–80 for the *decumanus* Aeschrio (represented as an

eastern-style "Rex Siculorum") and his entourage. Cf. also *Ver.* 2.3.86 on the bonuses an individual public slave of Venus of Eryx extorted from the Tissenses in 71.

114. On this, see Cowles, *Gaius Verres* 59–94.

115. Cic. *Ver.* 2.3.130–142, a charge finally "confirmed" by a document Cicero adduces at 3.157. Requisitioned grain was a more straightforward matter: see the direct charges of corruption at 2.3.225 and 3.163.

116. Apronius is attested at Aetna (*Ver.* 2.3.105), Agyrium (3.67–74) and Imachara (3.100), each of which Cicero visited (2.3.47) in his investigative tour of 70. In general, Cicero seems to have concentrated on the agricultural towns in the interior of the eastern part of the island, where "agents" such as Apronius will have had their greatest impact. Yet *Scaur.* 25 (mention of a visit to Agrigentum) shows that the roster of towns he lists in the *Verrines* (see esp. 2.3.47, 109–110, 200; 4.110 and 112, 136–139) is not exhaustive.

117. Cic. *Ver.* 2.3.45 (appeal to patrons, including the *cos. des.* for 70, Pompey); 2.3.72 (appeal to patrons and consuls); cf. 2.2.10 (request for Metellus' immediate succession).

118. Cic. *Ver.* 2.3.44, cf. 121.

119. Cic. *Ver.* 2.5.5, cf. Sal. *Hist.* 4.30–31 M.

120. Verres' claim to have staved off slave revolt: Cic. *Ver.* 2.5.5 and 42. The slaves pose a genuine threat: 2.5.14 and 18. Verres accused of inadequate measures at Messana: *Ver.* 2.5.5, cf. Sal. *Hist.* 4.30–31 M. Sallust's report: *Hist.* 4.32 M "C. Verres litora Italiae propinqua firmavit." Since we have no context, it is of course fully possible that this refers only to belated action on Verres' part.

121. *Crass.* 10.6–9, where the slaves voluntarily move to the sea and (later) break out of a circumvallation Crassus threw up at Rhegium while it was still winter; cf. App. *BC* 1.118.551 (slaves actually driven to sea and try to cross to Italy).

122. Cic. *Ver.* 2.5.9–14.

123. Cic. *Ver.* 2.5.15. The classic example of that latter method is the case of Apollonius of Panhormus (5.16–24, on which see immediately below in text).

124. D.C. 27 F 93.1, on the praetor P. Licinius Nerva in 104. Prosecution of the rich on a false charge is a standard method of greedy praetors: see Cic. *Q. fr.* 1.1.25 for a general statement on the topic, and D.S. 38/39.8.3 (Fimbria at Cyzicus in 85) for a good specific example.

125. Cic. *Ver.* 2.5.86 (Verres never boarded a ship as commander during his time in Sicily); cf. perhaps also in this connection Sal. *Hist.* 4.53 M.

126. Verres neglects naval duties: Cic. *Ver.* 2.5.80, 86, 136–137. His "summer camp": *Ver.* 2.5.80–81, 131, 136–137. Use of Sicilian Cleomenes as legate: *Ver.* 2.5.82, 104 "cui [sc. Cleomenes] potestatem imperiumque permisi [sc. Verres]," 111, 131, 136–137; cf. 83 on the inappropriateness of the delegation of authority from the Roman perspective, and 83–86 for the Sicilian view on the same; also 2.5.87–90, 136–137 on his rout at Odyssea. Self-defense of Syracuse: 2.5.92–95. Pirates' mock triumph in harbor: 2.5.96–100, 136, and 138. Roman military decorations: 2.3.185–186. Trial of the sea captains and outrages of post-sentencing phase: 2.5.101–120, 123–125, 133–134, 136, 138. On Verres' abuse of the naval contingents in his *provincia* see Jolliffe, "Phases of Corruption" 38–46. The naval disaster and the trial of the sea captains belongs to the period when Verres had (or was supposed to have had) in his *consilium* the quaestor T. Vettius and the *legatus* P. Cervius (2.5.114, cf. also 2.3.168 on Vettius), neither of whom can have been part of Verres' original staff of 73 (see nn. 94–95 above). N. Marinone, *AAT* 100 (1965–1966) 232–235, makes a weak case assigning this incident to 72. Vettius seems to have been quaestor at Lilybaeum, which seems adequately to explain his absence from Verres' *consilium* at this trial.

127. Testimony of two captains: *Ver.* 2.5.121–122, cf. 128 (some relatives also present) and 129 (others prevented from testifying). Variant with Pyrganio: Oros. 6.3.5.

128. *Ver.* 2.1.113.

129. *Ver.* 2.2.12 (some overlap with Metellus' staff, resulting in four quaestors at one time in Sicily); cf. 2.4.146. That Verres delegated at least one of them *imperium* seems not unlikely, both from general administrative practice in the later Republic (see 15.3.4) and from the chance notices provided by *CIL* I² 2951 (see n. 32 above) and *ILLRP* 446 that L. Caecilius Metellus, son of the Sicilian commander of 70 (Münzer, *RE* s.v. *Caecilius* 75 col. 1205) and a quaestor evidently at Lilybaeum in 52, held delegated *imperium* when (doubtless among other things) he was in charge of a minor military detachment stationed at Mt. Eryx (on which see D.S. 4.83.7 and *IGRP* I 507). Another dedication to this L. Metellus (*IGRP* I 501) mentions that he was quaestor but not (in contrast to *ILLRP* 446) that he was *quaestor pro praetore*, which shows how spotty notices of official status can be.

130. Timarchides: *Ver.* 2.3.154 and 157. Tasks on return to Italy: 2.5.39 with 41 (Tempsa) and 40 (Valentia). Hope of triumph: 2.5.40 and 67. Verres and the *societas*: 2.2.172 with 165–166 (records showing nonpayment of *portoria* in Sicilian harbors). Deposit of accounts: 2.1.99 (Verres' request for permission to wait until the arrival of a quaestor, citing the example of his former superior Cn. Cornelius Dolabella [*pr.* 81] after his promagistracy in Cilicia).

131. Cicero as *patronus* of Sicily: Cic. *Div. Caec.* 2, *Ver.* 2.4.138, cf. *Scaur.* 26, and in general P. A. Brunt, *CQ* 10 (1980) 288–289. Doubts regarding Sicily's initiative: *Div. Caec.* 12–13. Rivalry with Hortensius: *Brut.* 320–323. The praetorian speaking place: L. R. Taylor, *Party Politics in the Age of Caesar* (Berkeley 1949) 113–115. Links with Sthenius: *Ver.* 2.2.117–118.

132. No business of quaestor to prosecute superior: Cic. *Div. Caec.* 46, 60–65. Impact on Sicilian testimony: 28–35, 58. Caecilius' abilities: 39, 71; cf. Plu. *Cic.* 7.6 (material not in the published *Divinatio*).

133. Cicero spells out his fears in *Ver.* 1.21–23, 26–32. Cf. Ps.-Asc. pp. 185, 213–215, 217, 260 St.; *Schol. Gron.* pp. 337, 350 St.

134. Cic. *Ver.* 1.6 (Cicero covered the whole of Sicily in 50 days), cf. 8–9 and 2.1.30 (Cicero had asked for 110 days to gather evidence).

135. The bribery agent: Cic. *Ver.* 1.16. Plots against Cicero: 1.3–4. Shameless also in city: 2.4.33 (late summer 70). Kept pirates: 2.1.12, 5.136 (providing the date).

136. See, e.g., Cic. *Font.* 38 on wild accusations flung at respectable defendants in some famous extortion trials.

137. A small sampling: Cic. *Div. Caec.* 3 ("every type of outrage," including the theft of Sicily's gods in the form of their *simulacra*); *Div. Caec.* 11 (depopulation and thefts); *Ver.* 1.12 (long-term damage to province that will need many years and *innocentes praetores* to heal); 2.3.66 (abuses to farmers worse than a slave war); 1.13 and 2.3.17 (suspension of all forms of law and justice); 2.3.143 (inequity and extortions); 2.3.6 and 2.4.116 (physical cruelty and executions).

138. For the list that follows, see Cic. *Ver.* 1.13–14.

139. Abuses regarding appointments in local senates: Cic. *Ver.* 2.2.120–121 with 123–124 (Agrigentum), 125 (Heraclea), and 122 (Halaesa). Abuses regarding local *censores* (2.2.131–139), priesthoods (2.2.126–128), and even intercalation (2.2.129–130). Verres' statues of self and family: see 2.2.141–153, esp. 141 for a general statement. His festival, the *Verria*: 2.2.51–52, 114, 154; 4.89 and 151. Avoids *portoria*: 2.2.169–190. Unfair sales: 2.4.8, 14. Total profit from predations: 1.56, 2.1.27. For an overview of Verres' modes of self-enrichment in Sicily, see Shatzman, *Senatorial Wealth* 429–437 no. 218, esp. 431–436.

140. Evidence on the details of the actual trial is collected in Alexander, *Trials* no. 177, of which see esp. Plu. *Cic.* 7.3–8.2, esp. 7.5 (Verres supported by "the praetors"—including the *pr. repetundis* M.' Acilius Glabrio?—in Rome) and 8.1 (the rumor that Cicero had been bribed to acquiesce in a low fine).

141. *Ver.* 2.2.63.

142. Cic. *Ver.* 2.2.62–63, 138–140.

143. Cic. *Ver.* 2.4.90 (Tyndaris); 2.2.160–162 (edict and the response of Centuripa).

144. Provincewide effort to revive farming: Cic. *Ver.* 2.3.46 and 125. Requisitions from Messana: 2.5.55 "statim L. Metellus ut isti [sc. Verres] successit." Metellus' letter to Rome's magistrates: 2.3.122–128, 144. "Reinstatement" of Hieronic law: 2.2.63. Desertion of fields: 2.3.43 and 124. Attempted prosecution of Apronius: 2.3.152–153, with 152 "adventu L. Metelli praetoris" for the chronology.

145. Cic. *Ver.* 2.2.64, 140, 148. On Cicero's visit to the *provincia* (still in winter), see esp. *Scaur.* 25–26.

146. General statement: Cic. *Ver.* 2.2.156, cf. *Div. Caec.* 22. Cicero boasts of his visits to the homes of ordinary farmers (*Scaur.* 25) and his inspection of the fields in diverse communities (*Ver.* 2.3.47). But a good part of Cicero's investigation seems to have been going to local senates and listening to speeches. Cicero was given an audience—with his cousin L. Tullius Cicero—in senates at Halaesa (2.3.170), Entella (2.3.200), and Syracuse (2.4.137–139 and 147, criticized by Metellus).

147. Cic. *Ver.* 2.2.11.

148. Cic. *Ver.* 2.2.187–190 (the *publicanus* Carpinatius), cf. 2.4.137; 2.3.112 (Apronius).

149. Cic. *Ver.* 2.4.140–149, esp. 146 (Verres' ex-quaestor P. Caesetius prevails on Metellus to stop the vote of the Syracusan senate to rescind its earlier eulogy of Verres) and 147–149 (a good description of a meeting before a praetor in his court). The attitude of the city was hardly unified: cf. 138–139 (evidence of support in Syracusan senate) but also 151 (the *Verria* rescinded).

150. Cic. *Ver.* 2.4.137 (help from *equites* deciphering some prejudicial financial accounts) and 149 (Theomnastus gives Cicero a list of Verres' thefts in Syracuse).

151. Cic. *Ver.* 2.3.122 (general), 2.2.65 (retention of Heraclius and Epicrates), 5.129 (female relatives of sea captains executed by Verres).

152. *Per.* 98 (Metellus' success against the pirates placed between events *domi* of 70 and 69); Oros. 6.3.5.

153. App. *Mith.* 93.423; Flor. 1.41.6.

154. *IGRP* I 508 = *IG* XIV 356 (honors from Halaesa to Balbus as *pro quaestore*). On the date, see *MRR* III 218, cf. II 155.

155. The *legati* were A. Plotius (Flor. 1.41.9 with App. *Mith.* 95.435, offering the *cognomen* "Varus") and also the *praetorius* M. Terentius Varro (Flor. 1.41.9, App. *Mith.* 95.435 with Appendix B n. 399). Appian (*Mith.* 95.435) says that their territory was Sicily and the Adriatic as far as Acarnania; Varro himself terms it "between Sicily and Delos" (*R.* 2 proem. 6). There are no actions attested for Plotius; those known for Varro have to do with Epirus (*R.* 2 proem. 6; Plin. *Nat.* 3.101).

156. References to Clodius' quaestorship are collected in *MRR* II 180; see Cic. *Att.* 2.1.5 for the date of return.

157. Cic. *Planc.* 95–96 (Balbus allegedly feared his own exile at the hands of his ex-quaestor Clodius, now *tr. pl.* 58); cf. *Q. fr.* 1.2.7 (between 25 Oct. and 10 Dec. 59) on Balbus' good general reputation as governor.

158. L. Caecilius Rufus (*pr. urb.* 57) is not unlikely to have received Sicily for the year 56 (see Appendix B n. 458). If so, there is no telling how long he stayed, since we have no names of praetors for the rest of the decade. On the L. Caecilius Metellus attested as *quaestor pro praetore* at Mt. Eryx in 52, see n. 129 above. The T. Furfanus who is found holding Sicily in Jan. 49 is most likely to have been *pro quaestore* or (just possibly) *legatus*: see Additional Note XV. Whoever commanded the *provincia* in 50 had already left by that time.

159. Career of Triarius: Asc. p. 19 C. Rank of "pro praetore" in Sardinia: Jul. Exup. 6.40, emending "contrario" to "cum Triario," with MSS. A and V. *Praenomen* (and identification with eastern *legatus*): see *MRR* II 113, etc.

160. See *MRR* III 214–215, revising the earlier view of *MRR* II 86 and 81. For the urban quaestor, see Cic. *Ver.* 2.1.37, reading with D. R. Shackleton Bailey (*Two Studies in Roman Nomenclature*[2] [Atlanta, Ga., 1991] 45) "C." instead of "L." for the *praenomen*.

161. *Per.* 90, Jul. Exup. 6.39; cf. Sal. *Hist.* 1.83 M.

162. Cic. *Scaur.* 29 "qui patris tui beneficio civitate donatus," addressed to P. Triarius; on this passage, note the case of Q. Lutatius Diodorus, a Sicilian "qui Q. Catuli beneficio ab L. Sulla civis Romanus factus est" (*Ver.* 2.4.37).

163. *Mith.* 95.434; see also Flor. 1.41.9, who reports merely that Atilius "Ligusticum sinum . . . obsedit."

164. D.C. 36.41.1–2 with 12.2.2 for the identification; see also 11.1.4 on the refusal of *provinciae*.

165. See Cic. *Scaur.* 39 "rei <fr>u<mentariae> Cn. Pompei missu praefuisset" (this passage constitutes the best source on the formal aspect of Quintus' legateship!); of the other sources collected in *MRR* II 205, see esp. Q. *fr.* 2.3.7 (the unhealthiness of Sardinia), 2.5.4–5 (Pisa as departure point for Sardinia, and even mid-April weather tricky for sailing), *Fam.* 1.9.9 (short sailing time to Sardinia).

166. Plu. *Caes.* 21.5 (presence of Ἄππιος ὁ τῆς Σαρδόνος ἡγεμών at Luca); cf. Cic. Q. *fr.* 2.4.6 (implying that he did not go to the *provincia* straight after the conference).

167. On his background, see Appendix B n. 465. Sources (many) on the aedileship are collected in *MRR* II 195, of which see esp. Asc. p. 18 C on the debts it caused him; also Shatzman, *Senatorial Wealth* 290f no. 81. C. Henderson, *CJ* 53 (1957–1958) 194–206, provides a good biographical sketch of the younger Scaurus' career.

168. See Appendix B n. 465.

169. See Asc. pp. 18–19 C on both Corsica (the prosecution planned to investigate there for his trial of 54) and Scaurus' character in his province.

170. V. Max. 8.1. abs. 10.

171. Asc. p. 18 C.

172. Alexander, *Trials* no. 286 (trial for offences against the *lex Fufia*, with acquittal on 4 July 54). C. Cato did not forget Scaurus' efforts on his behalf: he was to appear as a *supplicator* at his extortion trial when the jury took its vote (Asc. p. 28 C).

173. Full sources on Scaurus' actual trial are collected in Alexander, *Trials* no. 295; of secondary discussions, B. A. Marshall, *A Historical Commentary on Asconius* (Columbia, Mo.) 119–158 is particularly valuable. For the politics, see E. S. Gruen, *The Last Generation of the Roman Republic* (Berkeley 1974) 331–337.

174. For an attempt at an explanation of this allusion, see 14.3.2.

175. Asc. p. 19 C.

176. Asc. pp. 19–20 C.

177. Cic. *Att.* 4.16.6 (June or July 54).

178. Cic. *Att.* 4.15.9 (written 27 July 54, the day before the consular elections for 53).

179. See Cic. Q. *fr.* 2.16.3 for the start and Asc. p. 18 C on the finish.

180. Asc. pp. 27–28 C.

181. See Asc. p. 20 C (Faustus assembles a bodyguard of three hundred), probably (cf. p. 19 C) based on the *acta senatus*.

182. *Scaur.* 21–22, esp. 22 "horribile et formidolosum frumentarium crimen" (ironic).

183. See *Scaur.* 1–13, with 15 and 17. Cicero's view on Sardinians seems to have been genuinely bigoted (see *Fam.* 7.24). For a discussion of Carthaginian mendacity (for

which Cicero advances an explanation based on "environmental determinism"), see *Agr.* 2.95.

184. *Scaur.* 19–20, cf. 21, 38–39.

185. *Scaur.* 40–41.

186. See *Scaur.* 42–44 with, e.g., 46 "sordidissimae, vanissimae, levissimae genti ac prope dicam pellitis testibus."

187. *Scaur.* 28–30.

188. After Appius had left his consular province of Cilicia to Cicero in 51, Cicero claimed—quite disingenuously—that he wanted none of the usual comparison-drawing between the two (*Fam.* 3.8.7—to Appius, *Att.* 6.1.1, *Fam.* 2.13.2—to Caelius).

189. For an extreme case, see above in 13.1.3 on L. Lucullus in 102 (D.S. 9.6.2). At *Fam.* 3.3.1 (late May 51), Cicero begs Appius to make the transition as easy as possible. But the *successor* could also undermine the *decessor*. The obvious example is Pompey's supersession of Lucullus in the command against Mithridates in 66 (Plu. *Pomp.* 31.1 and *Luc.* 36.1 and 4–7, D.C. 36.46.2).

190. See *Scaur.* 31–36, esp. 33 for Appius as Scaurus' successor. Of course there was just one patrician consular place open each year: see the comments of Marshall, *Asconius* 123f, on this case.

191. Asc. p. 28 C.

192. Asc. p. 29 C., not listed as a separate action in Alexander, *Trials*. On the charge, see A. H. J. Greenidge, *The Legal Procedure of Cicero's Time* (Oxford 1901) 468–470.

193. See Alexander, *Trials* no. 300 (process starting in Oct. 54) and cf. no. 319 (successful prosecution by a "C." Valerius Triarius under the *lex Pompeia de ambitu*, traditionally dated to 52) with G. S. Bucher, *Historia* 44 (1995) 396–421 on the date of condemnation.

194. *MRR* I 250, cf. 260.

195. Caes. *Civ.* 1.30.2; cf. App. *BC* 2.40.161–162.

196. *Civ.* 1.31.1; cf. D.C. 41.18.1, also noting the withdrawal of the Pompeian ἄρχοντες.

197. See 1.85.8 (the two *legati* who administered, "against precedent," Cn. Pompeius' consular *provincia* of the Spains for years in his absence); 3.32.3–4 (Q. Scipio's functionaries in Asia who inappropriately had received delegated *imperium*); and 3.82.3 (offices sought illegally, in Caesar's view, by members of the Pompeian camp before Pharsalus).

198. *Q. fr.* 3.6.6.

199. *Epistolae ad Q. fratrem* (Heidelberg 1843) ad loc.

200. Plu. *Mar.* 6.2 with *MRR* I 532, 534, and 535 n. 3; III 140. For the date (which is certain), see Cic. *Off.* 3.79. Plutarch's notice was rejected outright by A. Passerini (*Athenaeum* 12 [1934] 17); even G. V. Sumner found it hard to believe (*The Orators in Cicero's Brutus: Prosopography and Chronology* [Toronto 1973] 72). Yet Plutarch is specific: μετὰ δὲ τὴν στρατηγίαν κλήρῳ λαβὼν τὴν ἐκτὸς Ἰβηρίαν. κτλ.

201. See E. Badian, *Gnomon* 46 (1974) 422.

202. In this year, Macedonia and Sardinia were entrusted to a consul and prorogued consul respectively; arrangements for the city provinces, Sicily, Hispania Citerior, Africa, and Asia are unknown, as well as whether any commander was in Gaul. T. F. Carney (*AClass* 2 [1959] 76) implausibly argued that Marius' promagistracy was "a reward for his cooperation through inactivity" in his city praetorship, and served as a precedent for further "promotions" of other ex-praetors.

203. Plu. *Mar.* 6.2–3. Marius' *elogium* (*Inscr. Ital.* XIII 3 83) mentions his praetorship but not this promagistracy.

204. Cic. *Ver.* 2.3.209.

205. Cic. *Ver.* 2.4.56 provides evidence for descent, rank and *provincia* (he is attested at Corduba, hence the assignment to Hispania Ulterior), stating he was killed in Spain while

praetor. Sumner (*Orators* 72) suggests that, like Marius, L. Calpurnius Piso took up his Spanish province *ex praetura*—and then assumes the same of Piso's next two successors (on whom see below).

206. *Hisp.* 99.430 διαδέξατο. I have not found any instance in Appian where διαδέχεσθαι—a verb the author uses almost twenty times—does not denote direct succession.

207. *Hisp.* 99.430.

208. Cicero points up this heritage after narrating this anecdote at *Ver.* 2.4.56: "filius enim L. Pisonis erat, eius qui primus de pecuniis repetundis legem tulit." The *pr.* ca. 112 was the fourth member of the Calpurnii Pisones to hold *imperium* in one of the Spains (and the third in Ulterior) in the second century: see the list in E. Badian, *Foreign Clientelae (264–70 B.C.)* (Oxford 1958) 312.

209. Cf. Flor. 1.38.2 with App. *Ill.* 4.10 for the (unsuccessful) attempt of the Cimbri, Teutones, and Tigurini to enter Spain sometime before the year 109.

210. Eutrop. 4.27.3; *Inscr. Ital.* XIII 1 84f. Cf. V. Max. 6.9.13 (mention of praetorship and triumph).

211. Obseq. 42 (105 BC) "a Lusitanis exercitus Romanus caesus" (no commander named).

212. *Hisp.* 99.430 (translation adapted from the 1932 Loeb edition of H. White).

213. AE 1984, 495. For a full study (emphasizing legal aspects relating to *deditio*) see D. Nörr, *Aspekte des römischen Völkerrechts. Die Bronzetafel von Alcántara* (Munich 1989). On the identification of L. Caesius, see Appendix B n. 239.

214. The record of the *Fasti triumphales* for 103–99 has been lost, but there were probably no Spanish triumphs in these years. There is a lacuna of ten lines available to cover these years, and four triumphs and one *ovatio* known from the literary sources which must be fitted in (Degrassi, *Inscr. Ital.* XIII 1 561–562).

215. See App. *Hisp.* 100.433 with Appendix B n. 249.

216. See Appendix B nn. 217, 218 on Q. Fabius Q.f. Labeo (a *monetalis* of 124) and M.' Sergius M'.f.

217. *Per.* 67; cf. Obseq. 43 (104 B.C.) and Plu. *Mar.* 14.1.

218. The identification of Hispania Citerior as this man's praetorian *provincia* rests merely on an inference from the iconography of a descendant's coin issue (RRC I 457–458 no. 437, "51 B.C."), but is generally accepted. If the *provincia* is right, Coelius' praetorship must fall before 98 (MRR II 3 n. 2) and after the year 101, when—we may now assert with confidence—he is attested in Rome (he is listed in tenth place, as *tribunicius*, in the *consilium* of RDGE 12). Münzer (*RE* s.v. col. 196) placed his praetorship precisely in 99. See, further, Additional Note XIII.

219. *Inscr. Ital.* XIII 1 84f.; cf. also Obseq. 46 (99 B.C.) "Lusitani rebellantes subacti . . . in Lusitania prospere a Romanis pugnatum."

220. Note Q. Caepio, *pr.* by 109, triumphed 28 Oct. 107 from Hispania Ulterior (*Inscr. Ital.* XIII 1 84f), and *cos.* 106; M. Antonius, *pr.* 102, triumphed (probably) 100 from Cilicia (cf. Degrassi, ibid. 561), and *cos.* 99; T. Didius, *pr.* by 101, triumphed (probably) 100 from Macedonia (see ibid. 562), and *cos.* 98. Starting with Dolabella, praetorian *triumphatores* seem to have more difficulty reaching the consulship. P. Vatia triumphed *pro praetore* from an unknown *provincia* on 21 Oct. 88 (*Inscr. Ital.* XIII 1 84f) and reached the consulship for 79. The civil fighting that intervened adequately explains the delay; but he may have been defeated for the consulship immediately upon his return (see n. 7). L. Murena (*pr.* by 87 and triumphed 81, for which see ibid. 84f) never reached the consulship. Two unusual cases follow: Cn. Pompeius, triumphed 81 and again in 71, in each case as a *privatus* (the first one ever to be awarded a full triumph), and then *cos.* 70; also M. Crassus (*pr.* 73) who (somewhat improperly) celebrated an *ovatio* over the slaves in (probably) 71 and held the consulship for

70. No subsequent commander quite equaled Crassus' quick success. M. Piso Calpurnianus (*pr.* by 71) triumphed from Spain in the year 69, as did L. Afranius (*pr.* by 72) sometime in the period 70–67 (see on both, Degrassi, *Inscr. Ital.* XIII 1 565); each reached the consulship only after a significant interval, for 61 and 60 respectively. C. Caesar (*pr.* 62) waived his right to a triumph from Ulterior to be elected *cos.* 59. C. Pomptinus (*pr.* 63), who triumphed from Gallia Transalpina in 54 after long obstruction (*Inscr. Ital.* XIII 1 84f), never reached the consulship (he probably knew better than to try).

221. See *Inscr. Ital.* XIII 1 84f for both Didius ("ex Hispania de Celtibereis") and Crassus ("de Lusitaneis"). *MRR* II 7 and 10 provides full sources for what follows on these two commanders.

222. Obseq. 48 (97 BC) "Celtiberi . . . subacti"; *Per.* 70 (97 or 96 B.C.) "T. Didius pro cos. adversus Celtiberos feliciter pugnavit."

223. See Fron. *Str.* 1.8.5 and 2.10.1. Cf. also the various anecdotes told of Q. Sertorius (who served as a *tr. mil.* under Didius) at Plu. *Sert.* 3.5–4.1, cf. Sal. *Hist.* 1.88 M (notice of service), and Plin. *Nat.* 22.12 (Sertorius awarded the grass crown). From Plutarch, one gets the impression that the Roman military camps in Ulterior faced constant risk of attack. See, further, the discussion of Plutarch's narrative in Konrad, *Plutarch's Sertorius* 48–51, esp. 50 (Sertorius' brutality as *tr. mil.* mirrors that of his superior).

224. App. *Hisp.* 99.431–100.437.

225. For the mindset, see App. *Ill.* 11.33 (war declared on peaceful Dalmatians in 135 in hope of a triumph), *Gall.* 13.3–4 (though not provoked, the *cos.* Cn. Carbo attacked the Teutones in 113), Cic. *Pis.* 84 (the *cos.* 58 Piso allegedly attacked the peaceful Denseleti in Macedonia). Attacks on peoples who had come to terms are amply attested: see, e.g., V. Max. 9.6.3 (Cn. Domitius in Gaul in 121), D.C. 36.18.1 (Metellus in Crete in 67), Suet. *Jul.* 54.1 (Julius Caesar as praetor in Lusitania in 61). See also ch. 11 n. 135 on C. Memmius' triumph hunting in Pontus.

226. See the list in W. V. Harris, *War and Imperialism in Republican Rome, 327–70 B.C.* (Oxford 1979) 52 n. 3.

227. D.C. 37.53.4 (Julius Caesar, as praetorian commander in Spain for the year 60, confidently stops working for triumph); Cael. *Fam.* 8.5.1 (Caelius advises Cicero in 51 to take a minimalist view toward winning a triumph) with 2.10.2 (Cicero acts on that advice); cf. *Fam.* 15.4.14 (Cicero to Cato on the low military standard of some triumphs).

228. As is clear from Cic. *Inv.* 2.111 (L. Licinius Crassus, *cos.* 95 in Gallia Citerior); D.C. 37.52.1 (Caesar's *ex praetura* command in Spain for 61).

229. Strab. 3.5.11 p. 176; cf. on his foundation of "Castra Liciniana" (in the vicinity of Emerita) Ptol. *Geog.* 2.5.6 and *Itin. Ant.* p. 428, 3 M.

230. Obseq. 51 (94 B.C.) "per Nasicam Hispaniae principes qui rebellabant supplicio consumpti, urbibus dirutis."

231. Cic. *de Orat.* 3.134, *Brut.* 211.

232. See Sumner, *Orators* 74. Contra Konrad, *Plutarch's Sertorius* 88f, making Nasica governor of Ulterior in 93 ("Obsequens frequently misdates events to the preceding consular year: so at 57, 63–66"). But see n. 254 below.

233. Indeed, generational intervals—Nasica was grandson of the *cos.* 138, son of the *cos.* 111, and biological father (D.C. 40.51.3) of the *cos.* 52—suggest that he was too young to have reached the praetorship by the mid-90s. But subsequent tenure of the office is of course possible, and perhaps even likely.

234. App. *Hisp.* 100.436.

235. Contrebia: *CIL* I² 2951a line 14, from 15 May 87 (a *iudicium* in a land dispute between the Salluienses and Allavonenses, with Flaccus' formulation manifestly in the former tribe's favor). Gaul in 83: Cic. *Quinct.* 24 and 28. J. S. Richardson (*Hispaniae: Spain*

and the Development of Roman Imperialism, 218–82 B.C. [Cambridge 1986] 159 n. 14) states for 93 that "Flaccus was in Citerior (App. *Hisp.* 100.436–7), so Nasica [whom he makes *pr.* 93] must have been in Ulterior." But Appian reports only that C. Flaccus fought in Celtiberia; it is wrong to infer from this notice alone that each of the two Spanish *provinciae* received its own commander.

236. See Degrassi, *Inscr. Ital.* XIII 1 563 and (especially) the discussion of Badian, *Studies* 88–90, 94–96.

237. Exiles of 88/87: Gran. Lic. 35.7 C. M. Crassus in Spain: Plu. *Crass.* 6.1.

238. Cic. *Font.* 6 with 45. The attempt of F. X. Ryan, *Hermes* 124 (1996) 250–253, to use *Font.* 1 (highly rhetorical) to make Fonteius quaestor in 83 does not convince.

239. Jul. Exup. 8.50; cf. App. *BC* 1.108.506, Sertorius' early recruitment of Celtiberians.

240. Cf. Plu. *Sert.* 6.1 and 5.

241. See Badian, *Studies* 88–96; Konrad, *Plutarch's Sertorius* 88f.

242. Evidence and discussion in *Plutarch's Sertorius* 74–76, cf. 85–87 for a reconstruction of the strategic and political background (i.e., the face-saving supersession of C. Valerius Flaccus, *cos.* 93, in one of his several *provinciae*). The one close parallel Appian offers to the phrase ἐκ πολλοῦ . . . ἠρημένος in *BC* 1.86.392 (in reference to Sertorius' status in 83) denotes a span of almost five years (*BC* 1.80.365; cf. also *BC* 1.35.156 with E. Gabba *Appiani Bellorum Civilium Liber Primus: Introduzione, testo critico e commento* [Florence 1958] ad loc.). Other sources offer little help on this problem. Plutarch alludes to the praetorship only retrospectively in his *Life*, in his description of Sertorius' transit to Spain (*Sert.* 6.6), which incidentally shows that his rank was *pro cos.*, as we would expect. (The title is confirmed by five separate sling bullets from Spain bearing the name Q. Sertorius and inscribed "pro cos.," for which see Konrad, *Plutarch's Sertorius* 87f.) Iulius Exuperantius (7.43–48, 8.49–50) makes Sertorius a "dux" for 83 (7.44) and places his Spanish commission in the consulship of "Marius VII and Carbo," i.e., 82. But Exuperantius' confusion here of the elder and younger Marius hardly lends confidence to the other details of his report.

243. "Praetors" fail to welcome Sertorius: *BC* 1.86.392 τῶν προτέρων στρατηγῶν οὐ δεχομένων; themselves ejected from Iberia: *BC* 1.108.506, esp. τούς . . . πρὸ ἑαυτοῦ στρατηγούς, οὐ παραδιδόντας οἳ τὴν ἀρχὴν ἐς χάριν Σύλλα. Konrad, *Plutarch's Sertorius* 89 (following Gabba), dismisses the problem as Appian's mistake.

244. *BC* 1.89.409.

245. Plu. *Sert.* 6.6–8, esp. 7.

246. Flor. 2.10.1, cf. 10.2. His rhetorical statement is, of course, more than a bit reductionist: see Konrad, *Plutarch's Sertorius* 96–98, on the role of the Hispanienses of Italic ancestry in this struggle.

247. See, e.g., Plu. *Sert.* 22.5 and 11, cf. 25.1 (the *praetorius* Perperna stirs up discontent among "senators and peers") and Sal. *Hist.* 3.83 M (Sertorius had harbored "L. Fabius Hispaniensis senator ex proscriptis").

248. See App. *BC* 1.108.507 (giving the number 300) and *Mith.* 68.286, Plu. *Sert.* 22.5; cf. App. *Hisp.* 101.439 (implying that the formation of the "Senate" came by 77). What these passages describe must have taken some years to develop. For a deeply—and I think excessively—skeptical interpretation of the detailed sources on Sertorius' "Senate" and (especially) "praetors," see Konrad, *Plutarch's Sertorius* 184–187 (though allowing that Sertorius just might have formally constituted a "Senate" at a late stage in the war, perhaps only the year 77).

249. In general, see Plu. *Sert.* 22.5; cf. 24.4 on the insignia (the rods and axes of a Sertorian "praetor"). Plutarch alludes (less specifically) to Sertorius' subordinate ἡγεμόνες and στρατηγοί (*Sert.* 11.8, 19.1, 26.1 and 5), and the fact that he selected Romans as *strategoi* and *archontes* to command Iberian troops (*Sert.* 22.6). Our sources also speak of Sertorian

legati (Fron. *Str.* 1.5.8, on Hirtuleius, on whom see, however, n. 250 below), *praefecti equitum* (Liv. 91 F 22 W, on C. Insteius), and *scribae* (Sal. *Hist.* 3.83 M).

250. See Liv. 91 F 22 W (quaestorship), Plu. *Sert.* 24.4 (attesting to previous senatorial status and Sertorian "praetorship"). Cf. also Plu. *Sert.* 12.4 (Sertorius' "quaestor" Hirtuleius); *Sert.* 24.3 and App. *Mith.* 68.288 (Sertorian "praetors").

251. On the presidency, see App. *Mith.* 68.288 (Sertorius introduces legates to his "Senate") and Plu. *Sert.* 23.5 (the latter passage also showing the purely advisory function of the "Senate"). The "Senate," however, was deemed competent to draft treaties (App. *Mith.* 68.288 and Plu. *Sert.* 24.3).

252. See Liv. 91 F 22 W for the *conventus* of allied Spanish towns and tribes Sertorius called in his winter camp and the military orders he issued by edict. In a reported speech in this fragment Sertorius talks of "Hispania prouincia," and perhaps he really did think of Iberia as "one province." For routine administration, see also D.S. 37.22a (exercise of criminal jurisdiction).

253. See D.S. 37.22a (in later years, Sertorius is said to have judged capital cases without a *consilium*, and in general alienated his senior officers).

254. Sertorius' rebellion is said to last "eight years" in App. *BC* 1.108.505; cf. App. *Mith.* 72 (news of death of Sertorius synchronized with the siege of Cyzicus, itself datable to either 74/73 or 73/72). The Livian *Per.* 96 has Sertorius killed in the eighth year of his command, with the whole war lasting "almost ten" years before Pompey brought it to a close. Eutropius (6.1.3) supports the *Periocha* in its statement that Sertorius in the eighth year was killed by his own men. Yet Orosius—whose account one would suppose also derives from Livy— places Sertorius' assassination in his tenth year of fighting (5.23.13).

255. Collected in *MRR* II sub ann. 81–71 passim. For an overview (with references) of where our sources agree on the events of the later years of the war, see C. F. Konrad, *Athenaeum* 83 [73] (1995) 158–159.

256. C. F. Konrad, *Athenaeum* 83 [73] (1995) 157–187, with his *Plutarch's Sertorius* passim, esp. xxx–lvi for a thorough discussion of the various sources on this war. See also Konrad in *CPh* 84 (1989) 119–129, and *Historia* 43 (1994) 440–453.

257. *Athenaeum* 83 [73] (1995) 158–159.

258. See Degrassi, *Inscr. Ital.* XIII 1 565 for evidence and discussion. In Pompey's case, the date is attested: 31 Dec. 71 (Vell. 2.30.2).

259. *Per.* 96. Sertorius killed during campaigning season: Plu. *Sert.* 26.5. On the desertions from Perperna: Plu. *Sert.* 27.1; cf. App. *BC* 1.114.529, 532–533 for the shaky allegiance of his soldiers. Metellus leaves Pompey to handle Perperna: App. *BC* 1.115.534, cf. Sal. *Hist.* 3.44–45. M. Perperna easily defeated: App. *BC* 1.115.534–537, cf. esp. *Hisp.* 101.441 (saying that this marked the end of the war), Plu. *Sert.* 27.1–6 and *Pomp.* 20.2–4.

260. Resistance of Uxama and Calagurris: Oros. 5.23.14. In general, on this last phase of the war, see Flor. 2.10.9 (a list of major cities forced to surrender, probably reliable), Jul. Exup. 8.56 (mistakenly giving Pompey credit for Calagurris), Plu. *Pomp.* 21.1 (explicitly noting that Pompey remained in Spain only long enough to quell the "greatest" disturbances); cf. Eutrop. 6.1.3, Jer. *Chr.* ad ann. 72 p. 152 H, Isidor. *Orig.* 9.2.108, and in general Konrad, *Plutarch's Sertorius* 216f. For Pompey's destruction of Uxama, see Oros. 5.23.14. The early siege of Calagurris: V. Max. 7.6 ext. 3, cf. Sal. *Hist.* 3.86–87. Foundations in Spain: see Plin. *Nat.* 3.18 and cf. 7.96, Ath. 14.75 p. 657 F (from Strabo), Isid. *Orig.* 9.2.108. Admittedly, Pompey did claim a lot of activity in his trophy on the Pyrenees: Plin. *Nat.* 3.18 and 7.96 (866 or 876 towns subdued "ab Alpibus ad fines Hispaniae ulterioris"). But we see that included towns he had taken on his march through Gaul to Spain (on which more below).

261. See Plu. *Sert.* 7.1–2 with Badian, *Studies* 96 and 104 n. 65; also *RRC* I 381–386 no. 366 (dated by Crawford to "82–81 B.C."), which preserves filiation and his (expected) rank of

pro cos. That title oddly led Broughton to imply he went to Spain as a promagistrate (*MRR* III 15 "perhaps praetor in 83 or 82").

262. Arrival and early success of Annius: Plu. *Sert.* 7.1–3, cf. Sal. *Hist.* 1.95–97 and 99. M. Sertorius' first crossing to Africa: Plu. *Sert.* 7.3. Annius effectively prohibits him from relanding in Spain: *Sert.* 7.5–6, cf. 8.1–9.1, Flor. 2.102, Sal. *Hist.* 1.100–103. M. Sertorius returns to Mauretania: Plu. *Sert.* 9.2–6 and 11, esp. 9.5 with Konrad's commentary on "Paccianus" (p. 112 "it is safe to see in Sertorius' opponent a Vibius Pac(c)iaecus," i.e., identical to or a relative of the man said in *Crass.* 4.2 to have sheltered the young M. Crassus in Ulterior in the year 85).

263. Invitation from Lusitanians: Plu. *Sert.* 10.1 and 11.1. Ensuing conquests: Plu. *Sert.* 11.1–2 with Konrad, *Plutarch's Sertorius* 123, cf. Flor. 2.102, Jul. Exup. 8.51 and 53, Sal. *Hist.* 1.104–105 M.

264. See Plu. *Sert.* 12.1–2 with Konrad, *Plutarch's Sertorius* 127.

265. B. Bischoff and H. Bloch, WS 13 (1979) 116–129.

266. Thus, rightly, Konrad, *Plutarch's Sertorius* 128.

267. Cotta near Mellaria: Plu. *Sert.* 12.3. Fufidius on river Baetis: *Sert.* 12.4 with Sal. *Hist.* 1.108 M ("Fufidius . . . cum legionibus"). Fufidius' call to M. Domitius Calvinus: Sal. *Hist.* 1.111 M. On Hirtuleius' semi-independent command, see Fron. *Str.* 1.5.8 ("legatus") and 4.5.19. On Domitius' name (variously reported in our sources), see Konrad, *Plutarch's Sertorius* 130.

268. For the dispatch of Metellus Pius (*cos.* 80) to Spain, see esp. App. *Hisp.* 101.430 (noting it was "with a large army"), also (singling out Domitius and Metellus as the two important commanders for this stage of the war) Eutrop. 6.1.2 ("L. Domitius praetor") and Oros. 5.23.3. On Hirtuleius' defeat of Domitius, see Plu. *Sert.* 12.4, Oros. 5.23.3, and Flor. 2.10.6–7 (implying that Domitius and Thorius were killed at about the same time, but also — mistakenly — that both were *legati*), but esp. Sal. *Hist.* 1.107 and 136 M with the "Vienna fragment" *Cod. P. Vindob. Lat.* 117 A + B (showing that Sallust desctibed the death of Domitius' legatus Septimius and then Domitius himself). For the death of Thorius/Thoranius, Plu. *Sert.* 12.4 and Flor. 2.10.6–7, perhaps identical with the moneyer L. Thorius Balbus of *RRC* I 323 no. 316 (dated by Crawford to 105 B.C.), an Epicurean who is described in Cic. *Fin.* 2.63–64 (but with no hint of a violent end). Metellus' "many" defeats: Plu. *Sert.* 12.5; cf. Flor. 2.10.6, Eutrop. 6.1.2.

269. *Plutarch's Sertorius* 127.

270. Plu. *Sull.* 31.3, Flor. 2.9.25, cf. Sal. *Hist.* 1.55.22.

271. Plu. *Sert.* 12.4 with Konrad, *Plutarch's Sertorius* 127–131.

272. Sal. *Hist.* 1.111 "Domitium pro cos. ex citeriore Hispania"; also Plu. *Sert.* 12.4; cf. Eutrop. 6.1.2 "L. Domitius praetor."

273. See Konrad, *Plutarch's Sertorius* 130–131, against *MRR* III 84.

274. See Oros. 5.21.3 "L. Fursidio primipilari" with Appendix B n. 353 on the question of his descent.

275. *Plutarch's Sertorius* 129; see also *MRR* III 93.

276. Indeed implied by Sal. *Hist.* 1.55.22.

277. Date of praetorship certain from Cic. *Planc.* 69 (see also V. Max. 5.2.7). The only evidence on his Spanish command is Ps.-Asc. p. 219 St. "Q. Calidius . . . ex praetura Hispaniensi accusatus," on which see Alexander, *Trials* no. 139 (suggesting 77 as the date of his condemnation). Calidius surely received Hispania Citerior, for Q. Metellus Pius (*cos.* 80) was in Ulterior at the time.

278. Caes. *Gal.* 3.20.1 with Plu. *Sert.* 12.5 and Oros. 5.23.4.

279. Stopped at Ilerda: Oros. 5.23.4, Plu. *Sert.* 12.5 and *Per.* 90. Loss of legions: Oros. 5.23.4. Prompted dispatch of Pompey: Plu. *Sert.* 12.5.

280. *Plutarch's Sertorius* 134.

281. See App. *BC* 1.107.502 (Lepidus' allotment of Gallia Transalpina in 78) with 15.2.1 below.

282. Cf. Sal. *Hist.* 2.98.4 M "hostis . . . in cervicibus iam Italiae agentis ab Alpibus in Hispaniam submovi."

283. Reverses of (probably) the period 79–77: Plu. *Sert.* 13.7–12 with Konrad, *Plutarch's Sertorius* 137–140. Fear of Sertorius marching on Italy: App. *Hisp.* 101.440.

284. Explicit in App. *BC* 1.108.508.

285. Perperna proscribed: Vell. 2.30.1. Retained insignia: V. Max. 6.2.8 (admittedly rhetorical). Presence in Liguria: Oros. 5.24.16. *Strategos* of Lepidus: App. *BC* 1.108.508. Transfers Lepidan resources from Sardinia to Spain: Jul. Exup. 7.42.

286. See Plu. *Sert.* 15.2 on Perperna's ambition to take on Metellus separately (with explicit mention of his pretensions of birth and wealth). There is no shortage of examples from the later Republic where commanders refuse to coordinate their efforts fully. For a good firsthand instance, see Cic. *Fam.* 2.17.6 (from July 50 B.C.), where Cicero in Cilicia complains that the Syrian commander Bibulus was deliberately failing to coordinate efforts for a possible Parthian War.

287. Plu. *Sert.* 15.3–16.1. It seems worth suggesting that Perperna's campaign in the far west of Spain, in Gallaecia (attested by Sal. *Hist.* 3.43 M), just possibly belongs to 77—the period of his "independent" campaign—rather than to the final stage of the war after Sertorius' assassination. Plu. *Sert.* 16.1 shows that in 77 Sertorius' attentions were centered on eastern Iberia. On Perperna's technical inferiority, see Konrad, *Plutarch's Sertorius* 148.

288. Quotations from *Athenaeum* 83 [73] (1995) 161 and 182.

289. *Athenaeum* 83 [73] (1995) 182–186. The citation that follows is from pp. 184–185 (omitting the ancient references, which Konrad duly cites). See also *MRR* III 162–165 for a summary of other views on the chronology of this phase of the Sertorian War.

290. *Athenaeum* 83 [73] (1995) 160–162. Konrad's argument depends on the sources (*Per.*, Eutrop.) that speak of Sertorius being killed in the "eighth year" or (Appian) fighting a war "lasting eight years" (see n. 254 above); "counting from 80," he maintains, "we are led to 73 as the year of the assassination." But the fact remains that *Per.* 96 places the notice of the death (and the aftermath) firmly between two *res militiae* of the year 72, the disasters of the *coss.* 72 against the slaves, and the defeat of C. Cassius Longinus, *pro cos.* in Gallia Cisalpina against that same enemy, which resulted in Crassus' special command.

291. App. *BC* 1.108.508, cf. *Hisp.* 101.440 (no mention of Perperna, but again the threat of Sertorius invading Italy). Other sources also focus on the "sole" commander Metellus, with Pompey making a "second" leader: see Flor. 2.10.6, Eutrop. 6.1.2, cf. Jul. Exup. 8.54. This also tells against the view of G. V. Sumner (*JRS* 54 [1964] 46), that in 77 the Senate contemplated recalling Metellus altogether and sending out another sole commander to hold both Spains.

292. Sal. *Hist.* 2.98 M.

293. For what follows, see Sal. *Hist.* 2.98.5–6 M.

294. App. *BC* 1.109.509.

295. *MRR* III 162.

296. See Cic. *Man.* 28 and 30, discussed by Konrad, *Plutarch's Sertorius* (holding that in his references to an actual "bellum" "undoubtedly Cicero exaggerated"). On the trophy, see n. 260 above.

297. For instance it is never cited in his major chronological article in *Athenaeum* 83 [73] (1995) 157–187.

298. Quaestorship: *MRR* II 60 and 62 n. 2. Legateship in Spain: Cic. *Font.* 6 "Hispaniensis legatio . . . cum adventu L. Sullae maximi exercitus in Italiam cives vi dis-

siderent" with 45 "ex altera parte ulterior Hispania." Service in Macedonia: *Font.* 44 with 14.2.1 below, arguing that his superior can very well have been Cn. Cornelius Dolabella (*cos.* 81), which would allow any of the years 81 through 77 for his legateship. Münzer conjectured that Fonteius was a legate of the *pr.* C. Annius in Hispania Ulterior in 81 (*RE* s.v. *Fonteius* 12 col. 2844, followed by *MRR* II 78). The guess is a natural one (note *Font.* 18–19 for the presence of a C. Annius Bellienus on Fonteius' staff in Transalpina), but *Font.* 6 plainly shows that Fonteius was in Spain a year or two prior to Sulla's victory.

299. Fonteius' *triennium*: *Font.* 32. Presence in Transalpina during Sertorian War: *Font.* 16. Pompey wintered with army at full strength: *Font.* 16 "exercitus . . . maximus atque ornatissimus." Pompey's *decretum*: *Font.* 14. Grain and money for Spain: *Font.* 13, 26. Supplies cavalry: *Font.* 13.

300. See, e.g., Sal. *Hist.* 2.47.7 M, a speech of early 75. On the outbreak of the War, see 14.6.2–3 below.

301. *MRR* II 109 n. 6; III 93.

302. Cf. *Plutarch's Sertorius* 147.

303. See Cic. *Font.* 19 for Titurius' activities for Fonteius at Tolosa, with no title; he is not listed in this connection by *MRR*. On the other (far less significant) places where Fonteius' various subordinates tried to collect the wine tax, see E. Hermon, *REA* 97 (1995) 571–573.

304. *RRC* I 352–356 no. 344, dated by Crawford to 89 B.C.

305. Sal. *Hist.* 2.94 M.

306. Cf. *Man.* 9, *Agr.* 2.90, *Pis.* 5, *Fam.* 2.10.2 and 12.10.2.

307. Cf. Sal. *Hist.* 2.98.10 M with App. *BC* 1.111.519.

308. See already B. Maurenbrecher, *C. Sallusti Crispi Historiarum reliquiae* (Leipzig 1891–1893) 277f; also J. M. Cobban, *Senate and Provinces, 78–49 B.C.* (Cambridge 1935) 77 (suggesting that Fonteius left for Gaul in the year of his praetorship).

309. For precisely this use of *triennium*, see Sal. *Hist.* 2.98.2 M (Sallust's letter of Pompey of late 75); also Cic. *Pis.* 55 and 86 with 97.

310. One notes that in the extant portions of the *Pro Fonteio*, Cicero has nothing to say about Fonteius' activities as praetor in the city, though again this is not decisive—cf. the (also lacunose) *Pro Scauro.*

311. Konrad (*Plutarch's Sertorius* 147) thinks it alludes to "certain territorial disputes in Transalpina".

312. See *MRR* III 162.

313. The Vocontii: Cic. *Font.* 20; on the tribe see Caes. *Gal.* 1.10. Gallic tribes repeatedly send grain to Spain: *Font.* 26. The lucrative wine tax: *Font.* 20.

314. Pompey exhausts credit: Sal. *Hist.* 2.98.9 M. Armies separate for 75/74: Plu. *Sert.* 21.7.

315. Liv. 91 F 22 W.

316. *Athenaeum* 83 [73] (1995) 183 with n. 90.

317. Konrad, *Athenaeum* 83 [73] (1995) 184.

318. Plu. *Sert.* 18.2.

319. Liv. 91 F 22 W.

320. That Lauro was the first battle between Sertorius and Pompey is explicitly stated in Fron. *Str.* 2.5.31, from Livy. On the fighting, see esp. that Frontinus passage (fullest description of the action, with notice that Pompey lost "ten thousand" men); Plu. *Sert.* 18.4–9, App. *BC* 1.109.510 (loss of one legion), Flor. 2.10.7 (mention of battle). On the death of Pompey's *legatus* D. Laelius at Lauro, at the hands of Hirtuleius' troops, see Sal. *Hist.* 2.31 M, cf. Fron. *Str.* 2.5.31 and Obseq. 58. See also Konrad, *Athenaeum* 83 [73] (1995) 182–183, for a demonstration that Hirtuleius was "practically certain" to have fought at Lauro. Destruction of Lauro and deportation of its people: App. *BC* 1.109.510–511, Plu. *Sert.* 18.10

and *Pomp.* 18.3, Oros. 5.23.7 and 8 (noting the relative strength of forces at time of Lauro, with Pompey outnumbered more than twofold).

321. Plu. *Sert.* 18.3; Oros. 5.23.6 "Pompeius contracto apud Palantiam exercitu."

322. On these identifications (and other less likely ones), see Konrad, *Plutarch's Sertorius* 156–159. The river Pallantia: Ptol. *Geog.* 2.6.15. For Orosius' ignorance of Spanish geography, see 6.16.7 "apud Mundam flumen," cited by Konrad, *Plutarch's Sertorius* 157.

323. Konrad, *Plutarch's Sertorius* 157 and 159.

324. The sources are *Per.* 91, Flor. 2.10.7 ("Segovia"), Oros. 5.23.6 (juncture "apud Palantiam"), 10 (Italica), and 12 (death of "Hirtulei" at what must be Segontia); Fron. *Str.* 2.1.2 (battle in heat), 2.3.5 (arrangements for the decisive battle in which Metellus defeated Hirtuleius) and 2.7.5 (the death of Hirtuleius). Cf. (on Segontia) *Vir. ill.* 63.2 (Metellus Pius) "in Hispania Herculeios fratres oppressit."

325. See *Historia* 43 (1994) 440–445; the quotation is from *Athenaeum* 83 [73] (1995) 159 n. 4.

326. Sucro as "first meeting": Konrad, *Historia* 43 (1994) 441, citing Plu. *Pomp.* 19.6–8 and *Sert.* 19.11. Oros. 5.23.5 "summarizes the activities of Metellus" before Sucro: *Plutarch's Sertorius* 157f.

327. Plu. *Pomp.* 19.5–8, cf. 20.1.

328. Oros. 5.23.5; Cic. *Balb.* 5 (on Balbus' service in the Sertorian War) "hunc in Hispania durissimo bello cum Q. Metello, cum C. Memmio . . . ut Pompeius in Hispaniam venerit Memmiumque habere quaestorem coeperit, numquam a Memmio discessisse." For an explication of the battles Cicero then goes on to list in this passage, see Konrad, *Historia* 43 (1994) 451–453. Konrad (ibid. 452, cf. *Plutarch's Sertorius* 175) has C. Memmius serve under Metellus "for some time between 79 and 77 . . . presumably as Tribune or Prefect. . . . [I]n 76, Memmius returned to Spain as Pompey's Quaestor." But if "quaestor" in the *Balb.* passage means "pro quaestore," as often (see, e.g., *Arch.* 11, Sal. *Jug.* 103.7 and 113.5, etc.), we avoid the difficulty of having Memmius travel from Spain to Italy and then back again. Indeed, Cicero's wording prima facie suggests that upon Pompey's arrival Memmius was already there as quaestor. Memmius was killed at Segontia: Plu. *Sert.* 21.2 (implying he had considerable military service), Oros. 5.23.12 "quaestor Pompei idemque vir sororis eius."

329. Cf. Konrad, *Athenaeum* 83 [73] (1995) 182: "[I]f all of 76 was available and Pompeius arrived in the spring of that year . . . one might legitimately expect further events—Pompeius did not wage the war passively, even under adverse circumstances, as the next two years clearly show."

330. App. *BC* 1.110.512, on which see Konrad, *Historia* 43 (1994) 441 with n. 4: "Appian cannot be trusted here . . . virtually all attested warfare involving Sertorius from 77 B.C. onward indubitably occurred in Citerior, and nothing suggests that he ever returned to Lusitania after the conquest of Hither Spain in 78–77." Yet Lusitania is where we are told Sertorius transplanted the population of Lauro. Someone (though perhaps not Sertorius himself) had to take them to that part of Spain.

331. Arrangements of 75/74: Plu. *Sert.* 21.7, confirmed by Sal. *Hist.* 2.93 M against App. *BC* 1.111.519. For 74/73, see *Per.* 93.

332. Triumph hunting: Cic. *Pis.* 62. His triumph: Asc. p. 15 C "triumphavit pro cos. de Hispania" (with consular date). Cf. *MRR* III 177 on the *provincia*. The date of his praetorship is unknown, but is likely to have been 71. It is possible that as city praetor—like those of 75 and 74—Pupius was engaged in building activities: see ch. 12 n. 30.

333. *MRR* III 105–106, duly reporting but rightly ignoring a more adventurous suggestion by Cadoux. Caesar is said to have pronounced a funeral oration over both his aunt and wife as quaestor (according to Suetonius) before setting out to Ulterior with Antistius Vetus: Suet. *Jul.* 6.1 and 7.1 "quaestori ulterior Hispania obuenit" with Plu. *Caes.* 5.2–6 ταμίας εἰς Ἰβηρίαν ἐνὶ τῶν στρατηγῶν Βέτερι συνεξῆλθεν. Other sources: Vell. 2.43.4 "praetura quaes-

turaque . . . in Hispania . . . quaestor sub Vetere Antistio"; D.C. 37.52.2 and 41.24.2. See also Caesar's reported speech at *B. Hisp.* 42.1.

334. First visit to Gades: Suet. *Jul.* 7.1 (mentioning that it was in the course of conducting assizes) and D.C. 37.52.2. Caesar takes leave of province: *Jul.* 7.1 and 8.1, with Cic. *Ver.* 2.3.44 for the technical meaning of *ante tempus*. Diversion in Cisalpine Gaul: Suet. *Jul.* 8.1, where the "consules" who made him tarry must be those of 67. Support of Gabinian law: Plu. *Pomp.* 25.3–4.

335. Afranius at the Sucro: Plu. *Sert.* 19.5–9. His siege of Calagurris: Oros. 5.23.14 with V. Max. 7.6 ext. 3 against Jul. Exup. 8.56. Afranius' triumph: Cic. *Pis.* 58; cf. M. Malavolta, *MGR* 5 (1977) 258–261, reporting modern hypotheses.

336. See *MRR* III 13; Konrad, *Plutarch's Sertorius* 168.

337. App. *BC* 1.113.525–526.

338. *MRR* II 156. A good part of 67 may be excluded, since Pompey presumably was in the city when the triumph was voted.

339. See App. *Mith.* 95.434 and Flor. 1.41.9 on the *legati* A(?). Manlius Torquatus (the *pr.* ca. 70?), apparently in the east (with responsibility for the Balearic islands) and Ti. Claudius Nero in the south off Gades. No activities are attested.

340. Appointment: *ILLRP* 378 "Cn. Calpurnius Cn.f. Piso quaestor pro pr(aetore) ex SC provinciam citeriorem obtinuit"; Sal. *Cat.* 19.1–2, esp. 1 "postea Piso in citeriorem Hispaniam quaestor pro praetore missus est adnitente Crasso," and 21.3 (Catiline counts him and the *eques* P. Sittius in Mauretania as followers in June 64); Suet. *Jul.* 9.3 "prouincia Hispania ultro extra ordinem data sit," Asc. 92 C "in Hispaniam missus a senatu per honorem legationis"; D.C. 36.44.5 (the Senate "in fear" sent away Piso, using as a pretext ὡς καὶ ἐπὶ ἀρχήν τινα). Enemy of Pompey: see the discussion of R. Seager, *Historia* 13 (1964) 346; E. S. Gruen, *CPh* 64 (1969) 23f; E .J. Phillips, *RhM* 116 (1973) 353–357. Adherent of Catiline: Asc. p. 66 C "adulescens potens et turbulentus." Party to "First Catilinarian Conspiracy": Cic. *Mur.* 81 "a L. Catilina et Cn. Pisone initum consilium senatus interficiendi"; *Sul.* 67–68, Asc. pp. 83 and 92 C; D.C. 36.44.4. Catiline planned for him to seize both Spanish provinces: Sal. *Cat.* 18.5. Death in province: *Cat.* 19.3–5 (marking it as last episode in the "First Conspiracy"); Asc. pp. 92–92 C, esp. p. 92 C (noting death by time of Cicero's *In Toga Candida* of 64). Piso had seen some previous service in the east, apparently in the province of Macedonia: see *IG* VII 268 (patron of Oropus), cf. 305 (revealing that he was old enough at the time to have a daughter). For a good discussion of various views on the background to this commission, see Marshall, *Asconius* 312–314.

341. R. Seager, *Historia* 13 (1964) 346.

342. C. Eilers, *CQ* 46 (1996) 181 with n. 38. Two other instances are cited: P. Cornelius Lentulus Marcellinus, "who was sent in 75 or 74 BC to organize the new province of Cyrene. . . . [A]lso noteworthy is M. Antonius (*cos.* 99 B.C.) in 113 B.C." On Marcellinus (not a regular provincial governor) see 11.4. M. Antonius, quaestor 113 (V. Max. 3.7.9 with 10 n. 255) is attested as *quaestor pro pr.* in the *provincia* of Asia (*I. Délos* IV 1 1603). But surely he was not sole commander for Asia (see 14.5.2 below). One notes that Antonius' coin issues (for which see G. R. Stumpf, *Numismatische Studien zur Chronologie der römischen Statthalter in Kleinasien (122 v. Chr.–163 n. Chr.)* [Saarbrücken 1991] nos. 2 and 3) show only the title "Q(uaestor)." What Antonius' example does show is that even in the second century, a praetor *pro consule* (the standard rank at all times for governors of Asia) was entitled to delegate *imperium* (see 11.1.5 with n. 82). We can thus dismiss Eiler's additional argument (*CQ* 46 [1996] 181–182) that the quaestor "Murena" of *I. Priene* 121 (14.5.1 below) may have been allotted Asia as his own province to govern *pro praetore*.

343. E.g., Cic. *Div. Caec.* 4, cf. *Ver.* 2.2.11–12 (quaestors who had "Verres" as their province); *Mur.* 18; *Q. fr.* 2.3.1 "de provinciis quaestorum."

344. Quaestor: Cic. *Vat.* 25, *Fam.* 13.29.3. *Legatus*: *Per.* 90 (M. Iunius Brutus) "qui Cisalpinam Galliam obtinebat." Nor does *obtinere provinciam* necessarily imply one's presence in a province for an entire year: see Cic. *Cael.* 10 (the *pr.* 68 Catiline in Africa in 66).

345. Sal. *Cat.* 19.1–2, Asc. p. 92 C, Suet. *Jul.* 9.3.

346. See Suet. *Jul.* 9.3 and compare Suetonius' usage at *Aug.* 3.1 (C. Octavius, *pr.* 62) "ex praetura Macedoniam sortitus . . . negotio [sc. in Italy] sibi in senatu extra ordinem dato."

347. Cic. *Sul.* 57, cf. Suet. *Jul.* 9.3 for his "unrealized plans" of revolution.

348. See Badian, *Foreign Clientelae* 312, cf. 278f. The most recent example (13.3.1) was the *pr.* L. Piso Frugi, who made his ostentatious display of justice in Ulterior ca. 112.

349. Cic. *Sul.* 56–58, Sal. *Cat.* 21.2.

350. Sortition and *provincia*: Suet. *Jul.* 18.1 "ex praetura ulteriorem sortitus Hispaniam," cf. 54.1 "in Hispania pro consule." See also D.C. 37.52.1 (accurate on *provincia*, and the *ex praetura* command); Plu. *Caes.* 11.1 (also noting *ex praetura*); and *Vir. ill.* 78.4 (less accurately) "praetor Lusitanam . . . subegit"; cf. App. *Hisp.* 102.442 (a summary passage, dating Caesar's Spanish command "after the death of Sulla"). Caesar had been *pontifex maximus* since 63, but we hear of no objections to his leading an army outside Italy, no doubt thanks to the precedent of 131 (for which see 9.1.5).

351. Plu. *Caes.* 11.1–2 and *Crass.* 7.6 (noting involvement of Crassus); App. *BC* 2.8.26–27; Suet. *Jul.* 18.1. On Caesar's debts at this time, see Shatzman, *Senatorial Wealth* 346–356 no. 152, at 347.

352. Suet. *Jul.* 18.1. Caesar may have alleged that Cosconius (or his staff, which included Vatinius, a *quaestor* of 63 and now a *legatus*—see Cic. *Vat.* 12) had caused some trouble for his old quaestorian province. For provincials requesting early succession, see Cic. *Ver.* 2.2.10 (formal *legationes* to Rome in Verres' third year in Sicily); cf. *Flac.* 87 and *Q. fr.* 1.1.15 for a critique of provincial attitudes toward the outgoing praetor. The actual transit to Spain was entirely by foot (Plu. *Caes.* 11.3) which shows that he was not in too much of a hurry.

353. Suet. *Jul.* 71.

354. Plu. *Caes.* 12.1; cf. App. *BC* 2.8.27, App. *Hisp.* 102.442, *Vir. ill.* 78.4, Jer. *Chr.* ad ann. 60 p. 154 H.

355. In general, see D.C. 37.52.1 (Caesar's ambitious quest for military glory and desire for consulship); cf. Suet. *Jul.* 55.4 (his publication of a military harangue from this command, no doubt meant for domestic consumption in Rome). Our sources draw a less than flattering picture of his actions in Ulterior. Caesar extorts money from allied cities to pay personal debts: Suet. *Jul.* 54.1. Provokes pacific tribe to war: D.C. 37.52.3. Attacked towns that had accepted terms: Suet. *Jul.* 54.1, cf. D.C. 44.41.1 (from a speech, where Antony claims Caesar found Spain "secretly disloyal").

356. Plu. *Caes.* 12.4.

357. App. *BC* 2.8.27.

358. Plu. *Caes.* 12.2–3 (favorable to Caesar); Cic. *Balb.* 43. Yet at *Att.* 5.21.13, Cicero (at this point *pro cos.* in Cilicia) brings up as an old example ("olim") C. Iulius' irresponsible leniency to debtors. That fits well with Plutarch's account of Caesar's Spanish command. At this point, Caesar surely had no little empathy toward those who had to fight off creditors.

359. D.C. 37.53.4, cf. *Per.* 103 and esp. Obseq. 62 (60 B.C.), which establish the chronology.

360. Suet. *Jul.* 18.1 "non expectato successore"; D.C. 37.54.1 πρὶν τὸν διάδοχον ἐλθεῖν.

361. For routine cases, see 13.2.2–3, 13.2.5 on the Sicilian praetors of the 70s (none of these praetors is known to have waited for his successor, including Verres—who is not criticized for it); also Cic. *Lig.* 2 and 5 with *Schol. Gron.* p. 291 St. (a praetor leaves Africa late in the year 50 to canvass for the consulship before his successor arrives). It apparently was expected for the *decessor*, if still in the *provincia*, to meet his *successor*: Cic. *Fam.* 3.7.5, cf.

Plu. *Mar.* 10.2 (Metellus arrogantly, it is implied, returned from Numidia without meeting Marius). But actually delaying one's return specifically for that purpose was considered a signal compliment: Cic. *Fam.* 3.4.2.

362. Cic. *Att.* 2.1.6.

363. A notorious instance is the *pro pr.* Pompey in 81 (Plu. *Pomp.* 13.1). See also 6.2.1 above for the Sicilian *pro pr.* M. Aemilius Lepidus in 190.

364. On the request to stand *in absentia* see esp. Suet. *Jul.* 18.2. See also App. *BC* 2.8.29 (stating that there were precedents for an exemption), Plu. *Caes.* 13.1, *Cat. Mi.* 31.3–5 (probably overemphasizing Cato's antagonistic role), D.C. 37.54.2–3 and (from a speech) 44.41.3–4, cf. Plu. *Crass.* 14.1.

365. See Cic. *Fam.* 1.9.13 "cum tu Hispaniam citeriorem cum imperio obtineres" (followed by mention of the *coss.* 58); Caes. *Civ.* 1.22.4 (Lentulus Spinther in 49 recounting his favors from Caesar) "quod provinciam Hispaniam ex praetura habuerat, quod in petitione consulatus erat sublevatus." R. Syme (*Roman Papers* I [Oxford 1979] 303–304) has suggested that Spinther's predecessor in the *provincia* was L. Calpurnius Piso Caesoninus (i.e., the future *cos.* 58). But for that there is no compelling evidence.

366. Cic. *Fam.* 10.32.2.

367. Stopped at Luca on way to province: Plu. *Caes.* 21.5. Rising of the Vaccaei in 55 (after the Spains had already been allotted to Pompey): D.C. 39.54.1–2 (Nepos defeated at Clunia and afterward quiescent).

368. *MRR* II 215.

369. D.C. 39.39.1–4.

370. On Afranius and Petreius, see Vell. 2.48.1 (but claiming the original idea was that Pompey would hold Spain through legates *per triennium*) with *Per.* 110. Note also the quaestor Q. Cassius Longinus, sent to Spain *sine sorte* (*MRR* II 236, III 52), in a year before 51 (J. Linderski, *Roman Questions: Selected Papers* [Stuttgart 1995] 282–283). The *praefecti*: Cic. *Att.* 5.4.3 (12 May 51, five prefects, apparently for each of Spains), cf. *Att.* 5.7 (20 May). Pompey allegedly going to Spain: *Att.* 5.11.3 (6 July) and *Fam.* 3.8.10 (8 Oct. 51). Afranius and Petreius were perhaps joined by M. Terentius Varro as *legatus* before the year 49 (Caes. *Civ.* 2.17.1 "M. Varro in ulteriore Hispania," *Per.* 110, and in general *MRR* II 69).

371. See 13.2.8 for Caesar's derogative use of this word in the plural.

372. Caes. *Civ.* 1.85.8. For a more charitable view, see *Gal.* 6.1.2.

373. Cf. Caes. *Gal.* 7.55.1 (Caesar had received Spanish horse by 52).

374. C. Piso in 67 B.C.: D.C. 36.37.2 with 15.2.2 below. C. Papirius Carbo, a *pr.* 168 who perhaps governed Sardinia *in absentia*: see 5.3.2 and 6.2.2 above. For the view that Pompey, as *cos.* 55 and then *pro cos.*, was the first to govern a *provincia* through *legati*, see Kunkel, *Staatsordnung* 376.

375. See in general 11.8.2. The point does not require extensive demonstration. Pompey campaigns in Crete through a legate in 67: *Per.* 99. Use of Afranius in semi-independent commands in the year 65 against Mithridates: Plu. *Pomp.* 36.1, D.C. 37.5.4–5 (65 B.C.). At the end of the war, Plutarch tells us Pompey set up trophies corresponding to the number of his own victories "and those of his *legati*" (*Pomp.* 45.4). Pompey, of course, was not alone in this. Occasionally we find explicit observations on the independence of certain *legati*, e.g., Marius under Metellus against Jugurtha (Sal. *Jug.* 55.4–7), Sulla under Catulus in the Cimbric War (Plu. *Sull.* 4.2–3), or Murena as *legatus* of Lucullus against Mithridates (Cic. *Mur.* 20), and the legates under the praetor C. Pomptinus in Gaul in 61 B.C. (D.C. 37.47.1, on which see 15.2.3 below). For a useful observation on Caesar and his legates, see Plu. *Caes.* 18.2 and App. *Gall.* 15.2–3 with Caes. *Gal.* 1.12.6 (Labienus really responsible for a victory over Tigurini, though Caesar credits it to himself); cf. D.C. 39.5 and 40.31 (realizing that *legati* responsible in large part for Caesar's successes), and in general see 15.2.4 below.

Notes to Chapter 14

1. Cic. *Pis.* 38. Any praetor who took up Macedonia had enhanced *imperium* (9.1.3). For "praetorium imperium" in the same loose sense as in this passage, see *Ver.* 2.5.40 with 13.2.1 above (C. Verres *pro cos.* in Sicily), cf. *Schol. Amb.* p. 275 St. "C. Claudius qui Asiam tenebat praetorio imperio" with G. R. Stumpf, *Numismatische Studien zur Chronologie der römischen Statthalter in Kleinasien (122 v. Chr.–163 n. Chr.)* (Saarbrücken 1991) nos. 43–56 (each of these issues showing title "pro cos."). Piso had been hailed as "imperator": Cic. *Har.* 35 (before the murder of Plator of Orestis), *Pis.* 38–39, 44, 54–55, 97, *Q. fr.* 3.1.24 (Sept. 54), also *I. Samothrace* 18 B (probably from the year 55—cf. *Pis.* 89). The acclamation came definitely before the time of the *Prov.* of late spring/early summer 56, and so probably in the first year of his command. But Cicero alleges that none of the field dispatches expected from him reached the Senate (*Prov.* 14–15, 25; *Pis.* 38–41, 44, 97), and that Piso claimed on his return to have no wish for a triumph (*Pis.* 56–63, 97, cf. 90).

2. The physical sense of *incolumitas* is of course common: e.g., Cic. *Ver.* 2.1.12, *Font.* 14 and 17, *Fam.* 6.6.13. *Incolumis* metaphorically in a legal sense: *Font.* 32, *Clu.* 77, *Balb.* 28, *de Orat.* 3.9. R. G. M. Nisbet in his commentary on this passage (*M. Tulli Ciceronis in L. Calpurnium Pisonem Oratio* [Oxford 1961] 100) takes the adjective in the latter way.

3. The one questionable individual—L. Manlius Torquatus (*cos.* 65, *pro cos.* in Macedonia, and then back in Rome by autumn 63)—does not seem to have triumphed. Torquatus was ill during the Catilinarian conspiracy in 63 (*Sul.* 34), and so perhaps did not return from Macedonia "incolumis." Cicero at *Pis.* 44 does note that he was named "imperator" by the Senate. But that seems to be a tactful circumlocution which probably implies that he got no further than a *supplicatio.* (The phrase finds no closer parallel than Cic. *de Orat.* 2.195, on M.' Aquillius, *cos.* 101, "consulem . . . imperatorem ornatum a senatu, ovantem") Nor does there appear to be room in the epigraphical record. Degrassi (*Inscr. Ital.* XIII 1 565) provides an ample number of triumphs much better attested in literary sources (about a dozen) to fill the large lacuna (ca. 20 lines) in the triumphal *Fasti* between 81 and 62.

4. I have found just one explicit instance: C. Octavius (*pr.* 61) who was hailed as "imperator" in Macedonia but died on his return home in 58 (Vell. 2.59.2 and *Inscr. Ital.* XIII 3 75b).

5. See *AE* 1993, 1385 (Beroia) lines 2–3 στρατηγοῦντος Σέξστου | Πονπηίου. I thank Prof. J. D. Morgan for first bringing this inscription to my attention.

6. *SIG³* 700, discussed briefly also in 15.3.4. The quotation from the text is from line 32. On the significance of the games, see K. J. Rigsby, *TAPhA* 118 (1988) 147 n. 97 ("this seems rather less than cult, and is not a new festival named for Annius").

7. See *SIG³* 705 = *RDGE* 15, with 9 n. 57 on Sisenna's titulature in this inscription, and *SIG³* 705 K¹ line 1 for the date ([ἔτους] . . . τρ[ι]ακοστοῦ), and *SIG³* 704 I³ + I⁴ Column IV l lines 3–4 for Pella as the location of the decision. See also *SIG³* 826 n. 1 for a full list of all possible mentions (some more probable than others) of the praetor Sisenna in Macedonia. H. Mattingly, *RAN* 5 (1972) 10, discusses the technical possibility of reading τρ[ίτου καὶ τρι]ακοστοῦ ("the thirty-third") for the year, i.e., 115 B.C. I do not see, however, any plausibility to Mattingly's suggestion that this praetor should be identified with the moneyer of the Narbo coinage Cn. Cornelius L.f. Sisenna (*RRC* I 318–319, no. 310).

8. See Appendix B n. 161 on the possibility that C. Servilius Vatia, the father of the *cos.* 79, was a praetorian commander in Macedonia ca. 115 B.C.; and also 14.5.2 below that the *pro cos.* Ser. Cornelius Ser.f. Lentulus honored in *I. Délos* IV 1 1845 served in Macedonia at this time.

9. *Per.* 63, Flor. 1.39.4 "totus interceptus exercitus," Ruf. Fest. *Brev.* 9.1. His trial: Cic. *Ver.* 2.3.184 and 4.22 (also offering family background), cf. Vell. 2.8.1 with M. C. Alexander,

Trials in the Late Roman Republic (Toronto 1990) no. 45. He later was condemned by the Mamilian inquisition, which led to his exile at Tarraco: Alexander, *Trials* no. 55.

10. See *RDGE* 15 = *SIG*³ 705 lines 2f (date) with 61–64 (the *cos.* M. Livius Drusus to hold a hearing in his province). Drusus also may well be the author of one or both partially preserved letters to a group of Dionysiac artists (*RDGE* 44, from Thebes). In line 10 (the start of the second letter), the writer terms himself στρατηγὸς ὕπατος, a title which Sherk takes as an indication of a date earlier than Drusus, claiming its "last known occurrence is 112–111," in *I. Cret.* III 4 9 line 11 and 10 lines 59–60, 62f, 69–70 (*RDGE* p. 252 n. 6). But *I. Délos* IV 1 1700 (which must postdate the year 97) has the title, as does a more recent find from Cyrene (*AE* 1967, no. 532), which strengthens the case for Drusus.

11. *Inscr. Ital.* XIII 1 84f "[pro cos. de Scordist]eis Macedonibusq(ue)"; also Ammian. Marc. 27.4.10–11 "has gentes [i.e., those of Thrace—Scordisci, Odrysae] . . . Drusus intra fines continuit proprios"; Ruf. Fest. *Brev.* 9.2 (the Scordisci) "Marcus Drusus intra fines proprios continuit"; Flor. 1.39.5 (Scordisci) "Drusus ulterius egit [i.e., than Didius, who *intra suam reppulit Thraciam*] et vetuit transire Danuvium."

12. *IG* IX 2 1135 with L. Robert, *Bull. épig.* 1954 no. 152 (suggesting M. Minucius Rufus, Sulla or M. Lucullus), *Bull. épig.* 1955, no. 136a (M. Rufus). The Scordisci are sometimes known in our sources as "Gauls" (*SIG*³ 700 lines 10–11 and line 21, cf. *Per.* 63 (on this very commander), though at other times they are associated but differentiated, e.g., at *SIG*³ 710 A (to M. Minucius Rufus [*cos.* 110]), or *Bull. épig.* 1934 p. 230 (to an unknown general).

13. The *coss.* 109 received Numidia and Gaul as their *provinciae*; arrangements for the *cos.* and *cos. suff.* 108 are unknown; the *coss.* 107 had Numidia (C. Marius) and Gaul (where L. Cassius Longinus was killed in battle). In 106, the *cos.* Q. Servilius Caepio had Gaul; in the crisis, his colleague C. Atilius Serranus must have stayed in Italy.

14. Sources (both certain and possible) for his campaigning are collected in *MRR* I 543 and III 144, of which see especially *Per.* 65 (major victory over "Thracae" by 108, perhaps to be associated with the famous battle at the frozen river Hebrus recounted in Flor. 1.39.5, Ammian. Marc. 27.4.10–11, and Ruf. Fest. *Brev.* 9.2 "vagantes Thracas . . . Minucius in Hebri fluminis glacie vastavit"), *ILLRP* 337 (Rufus attested as *imperator* at Delphi), and (for his triumph) *Inscr. Ital.* XIII 1 84f with Vell. 2.8.3 "ex Scordiscis triumphus fuit." His (elder) brother Q. Minucius Rufus as senior *legatus*: see Appendix B n. 171.

15. The Messenian inscription is *IG* V 1 1432. There Vibius is repeatedly referred to as ὁ στρατηγός (lines 6, 10, 11, 17, 36f), but Memmius is termed ὁ ἀνθύπατος (lines 36f). In his fundamental study of this inscription, A. Wilhelm (*JOEAI* 17 [1914] 1–120, at 37 and 95) properly notes the apparent difference in rank; see also M. Holleaux, ΣΤΡΑΤΗΓΟΣ ΥΠΑΤΟΣ (Paris 1918) 163f. Each correctly interpreted ἀνθύπατος to signify a holder of consular *imperium*, but took στρατηγός to mean that Vibius was an actual praetor attached to Memmius. For the suggestion that Vibius too was a governor, see *MRR* III 220.

16. The impact of lower Roman officers on more remote provincials emerges nicely from the honors of Lete to the quaestor M. Annius (*SIG*³ 700) discussed above. A sample of other glimpses into local perceptions: *I. Priene* 121 lines 21–24 (mention of embassies to Roman "στρατηγοί for Asia," a list which includes a quaestor—see 14.5.1); *Bull. épig.* 1952 p. 156f no. 87 lines 1–6 (honors from Mesambria, on the Pontic coast of Thrace, to a subordinate of the *pro cos.* M. Terentius Lucullus, probably 72/71); Colin, *FD* III 4 69 no. 45 (the στρατηγός "Plaetorius," not certainly a governor of Macedonia); cf. J. *AJ* 14.114 (Lucullus' visit to Cyrene, from the provincial viewpoint).

17. Memmius' trial: Cic. *Font.* 24, V. Max. 8.5.2 with Alexander, *Trials* no. 60. The date of that trial is uncertain (Alexander offers 106, without query) but Cicero and Valerius Maximus associate it (especially the latter, "eadem lege") with the prosecution of the *cos.* 104 C. Flavius Fimbria (*Trials* no. 61). A reasonable guess places Memmius' trial between 104

(the most plausible date for the reinstitution of *equites* in jury under C. Glaucia's *lex Servilia*, the operative law in Fimbria's trial) and 102 (death of M. Gratidius, prosecutor of Fimbria); however note the caveats of G. V. Sumner, *The Orators of Cicero's Brutus: Prosopography and Chronology* (Toronto 1973) 85–86. On Memmius, see also T. R. S. Broughton, *MRR* I 562 n. 4 and III 141; *Candidates Defeated in Roman Elections: Some Ancient Roman "Also-Rans"* (Philadelphia 1991) 28; cf. ch. 11 n. 135 on Sumner's suggestion that he received an imperatorial acclamation in Macedonia.

18. Victory over Scordisci: Flor. 1.39.5, Ammian. Marc. 27.4.10–11, Ruf. Fest. *Brev.* 9.1, cf. Jer. *Chr.* ad ann. 100 p. 149 H "Thraces a Romanis victi"; also *I. Knidos* I 31 = *RS* I 12 Kn. IV 5–10 with D. B lines 27–29. Didius' triumph: Cic. *Pis.* 61.

19. Letter to cities and states: *I. Knidos* I 31 D. B lines 22–27, Kn. IV 1–4 with 10.1 above on the formation of "Cilicia." Mandated visit for present and future commanders to Chersonese and Kainike: Kn. IV 5–10 with D. B lines 27–29, Kn. IV lines 11–21 with D. B lines 29–33, with commentary at *RS* I 12 p. 264. New commander to set boundaries of taxable (so suggests a new reading by W. Blümel in *I. Knidos* I 31) Chersonese: Kn. IV lines 24–30. The consuls of the year are to waive the routine procedure for sending troops to Macedonia: Kn. II Lines 12–31. Limits on the commander's movements: Kn. III lines 1–15, esp. lines 4–6 on the praetorian law passed by one M. Porcius Cato "on the fifth day before the Feralia" (thus Blümel's new reading). Provisions in case of commander's resignation: Kn. IV lines 31–39, D. C lines 1–3. Quaestor's resignation: Kn. IV lines 40–42 with D. C lines 4–8. Oath to uphold provisions: D. C lines 8–15. Provisions against breaking law: D. C lines 15–23, cf. D. C lines 23–31 and (unfortunately in places quite lacunose) Kn. col. V lines 1–46.

20. *I. Knidos* I 31 Kn. IV lines 11f with lines 25–26.

21. "Praetor, *pro praetore* or *pro consule*": *I. Knidos* I 31 Kn. II lines 13–15, Kn. IV lines 5–8 and D. B lines 27–28. "Praetor or *pro consule*": Kn. IV lines 24–26, D. C line 8. "Magistrate or *pro magistratu*": Kn. III line 9, cf. D. C line 7. "Quaestor or *pro quaestore*": Kn. IV lines 40–41, D. C lines 3–4. At one point the future governor of Macedonia or Asia is simply called "praetor" (Kn. IV lines 31–32); cf. Kn. IV line 38 for a hypothetical provincial commander as simply "pro cos.".

22. *IG* XII 8 241 (Samothrace), cf. 232 (with *praenomen* "Gaius"); see Broughton, *MRR* II 13 and 14 n. 3 (erroneously implying that L. Caesar can have governed Macedonia only as a promagistrate), also III 109–110, 264.

23. H. Gäbler, *Die antiken Münzen Nordgriechenlands* III 1 (Berlin 1906) 9 and 73 nos. 224 and 225. The name of Sentius' legate appears as "Braitios" in *IG* IX 2 613 (from Larisa); Plutarch calls him Βρέττιος Σούρρας (*Sull.* 11.4–5), while Appian has "Bruttios" (*Mith.* 29.113–115).

24. *Chiron* 9 (1979) 147–167, emphasizing especially that a coin of Aesillas was overstruck on an Athenian tetradrachm that is demonstrably post-Sullan. See further R. A. Bauslaugh, *ANSMusN* 32 (1987) 11–21, offering additional numismatic evidence (but opting all the same for Aesillas' traditional date). Broughton, in *MRR* III 264, cites but does not grapple with Mattingly's challenge to this traditional identification; cf. also *Candidates Defeated* 41. Broughton (*MRR* III 166) tries to squeeze also a praetorship for Cn. Pompeius Strabo (*cos.* 89) into the Macedonian *fasti* of this period, on the basis of *IG* II/III² 4101, honors from the Athenian *demos* to "Sextus Pompeius." The absence of a title does not exclude the possibility that he was a praetorian commander (see *SIG*³ 704 B and C, Appendix B n. 155). Indeed, the most natural identification is that of Dittenberger (ap. *SIG*³ 701 n.), who considers him the homonymous father of the *cos.* 89, i.e., the praetor for Macedonia who was killed in the *provincia* by 119 (on whom see above in text). That Sex. Pompeius was in Macedonia by 121/120 (n. 5), and so had been prorogued at least once in his command—leaving plenty of time for honors.

25. Euphenes, son of Execestus, and his incipient revolt: D.S. 37.5a. Sentius' defeat in 92: *Per.* 70 and Obseq. 53 (92 B.C., with a necessary emendation), with T. C. Brennan, *Chiron* 22 (1992) 143. In the *Periocha*, the news of Sentius' defeat directly follows the mention of the trial of P. Rutilius Rufus (traditionally and rightly dated to 92), and precedes the report of the tribunate of M. Livius Drusus in 91 B.C. R. Kallet-Marx has dated Rutilius' trial to "ca. 94" (*Phoenix* 44 [1990] 122–139). The year 93, however, should be excluded, for both the trial and Sentius' defeat: see Obseq. 52 "totus annus domi forisque tranquillus fuit." Raids on Macedonia ca. 89: see *Per.* 74 (but in the "praeterea" section—and thus not closely datable—with no explicit mention of Sentius).

26. Mithridates instigates raids: D.C. 30–35 F 101.2 (just possibly to be identified with the "incursiones Thracum in Macedoniam populationesque" of *Per.* 74?). The virtually province-wide revolt: Cic. *Pis.* 84, cf. Gran. Lic. 35.81 C (implying that the Denseleti did revolt by 85/84). Sothimus: Oros. 5.18.30. Ariarathes: see Plu. *Sull.* 11.2 with T.C. Brennan, *Chiron* 22 (1992) 127–128.

27. Braetius as "legatus": *IG* IX 2 613 (Larissa), Plu. *Sull.* 11.4. Braetius versus Metrophanes, and at Sciathus: App. *Mith.* 29.113–114. Battle at Chaeronea: Plu. *Sull.* 11.3 and 4, *Mith.* 29.114. Braetius defeats Archelaus and drives him into the Peiraeus: Paus. 1.20.5, cf. *Mith.* 29.114–115 with E. Badian, *Lucius Sulla: The Deadly Reformer* (Sydney 1970) 17 n. 46. Lucullus orders Braetius out of Boeotia: Plu. *Sull.* 11.5 (including praise of his achievements). For Lucullus' activities at Chaeronea, see Plu. *Cim.* 1–2 with J. Ma, *PCPhS* 40 (1994) 60–69.

28. E. Badian, *Studies in Greek and Roman History* (Oxford 1964) 74.

29. Cic. *Ver.* 2.3.217.

30. Full sources on this campaign can be found in *MRR* II 48, 55, 58, 61, and 63. First steps: App. *Mith.* 30.116, Plu. *Sull.* 12.1, Memn. 22.10–11. Arrival in Attica: App. *Mith.* 30.118, Plu. *Sull.* 12.1–2. On Sulla's haste, see Plu. *Sull.* 12.2, App. *Mith.* 54.217 (both relating to the year 87).

31. App. *Mith.* 32.127.

32. Plu. *Sull.* 15.3, also Memn. 22.13, giving *praenomen* (L. Hortensius is said to have brought six thousand troops from Italy).

33. Sources on these legates are collected in *MRR* II 56. For a remarkable find (a trophy) associated with this battle, see J. Camp, M. Ierardi, J. McInerney, K. Morgan, and G. Umholtz, *AJA* 96 (1992) 443–455.

34. On Galba, see 10.5.2 and 10.5.4. Hortensius in the north: Gran. Lic. 35.79 C "Ac dum de condicionibus disceptatur [i.e., between Archelaus and Mithridates], M<a>edos et Dardanos, qui socios vexabant, Hortensius <l>e<gatus> fugaverat." Hortensius in general: A. Keaveney, *Klio* 66 (1984) 122. On Murena's command in Asia, see esp. App. *Mith.* 64.265, and 14.5.9 below.

35. *Studies* 74–82; cf. *MRR* III 98. The year in which P. Gabinius functioned in the city as a praetorian colleague of Q. Metellus Pius (future *cos.* 80) and Ap. Claudius Pulcher (*cos.* 79) (Cic. *Arch.* 9), is less likely to be 89 than 88: see Badian, *Studies* 75–80 and 10.5.5 above. (Broughton himself at *MRR* III 98 is convinced of the earlier date.) Against Badian's suggestion that Gabinius succeeded Sentius in Macedonia, cf. (unpersuasively) A. Keaveney, *Klio* 66 (1984) 118 n. 30 ("his governorship could with equal plausibility be fitted into 81").

36. Legation of three *XVviri s.f.* to Asia: Fen. *HRR* II F 18 = Lact. *Div. Inst.* 1.6.14. The *divinatio* to Gabinius' extortion trial: Cic. *Div. Caec.* 64, noting that the *divinatio* was "nuper" in relation to 70 B.C.; cf. *Div. Caec.* 65 for the charge. Gabinius' exile: *Arch.* 9.

37. App. *Mith.* 35.137 (Arcathias, on whom cf. T. C. Brennan, *Chiron* 22 [1992] 127–128), also Memn. 22.12 (Macedonia revolts to Taxiles). Taxiles, marching through Thrace

and Macedonia with a huge force, tries to join with Archelaus: Plu. *Sull.* 15.1, Memn. 22.13, Pausan. 1.20.6.

38. In general, see Badian, *Studies* 80–81. Sack of Delphi: MRR II 58 and 59 n. 2. Scipio's campaign: App. *Ill.* 5.13–14 with MRR II 58 and 59 n. 2; III 71; cf. also Gran. Lic. 35.70 (a Mithridatic force abandons Abdera on the news of the "capture of Philippi"). Crawford dates his moneyership (*RRC* I 319 no. 311) to 106 B.C. There is no guarantee — given the electoral irregularities of the *regnum Cinnanum* — that Scipio had filled the proper interval between praetorship and consulship stipulated by the *leges annales*, and thus was *pr.* in or by 86. For Sulla's campaign in the Thraceward region while waiting for Mithridates' response to Archelaus, see MRR II 58.

39. App. *Mith.* 29.112 and 115.

40. See the case of C. Antonius in Asc. p. 84 C (discussed in text below), for which some Greeks prosecuted him in 76 — yet not in a *quaestio* (as in the case of Gabinius) but before the peregrine praetor.

41. Cf. Cic. *Ver.* 2.1.44–45 and 60–61 with *Div. Caec.* 6 for Verres' predations in Achaea en route to Cilicia; also *Att.* 5.11.5, which Cicero wrote from Athens on 6 July 51 as *pro cos.* in transit to Cilicia, expressing relief at the self-restraint of his staff on the "iter per Graeciam."

42. Alexander rightly dates the prosecution of Gabinius "between 76 and 70" (*Trials* no. 174). Yet most of the year 73 is excluded, since Q. Niger was then quaestor under Verres in Sicily.

43. Asc. p. 84 C = Cic. *Tog.* F 2; full sources in Alexander, *Trials* no. 141. C. Damon and C. S. Mackay, *Historia* 44 (1995) 38, accept the conventional dating "between 87 and 83." Cf. also 12.2.1.

44. App. *BC* 1.100.465.

45. *RDGE* 21. See also *RDGE* 20, an S.C. and letter of Sulla to Thasos, dated to 80 B.C. (col. I A line 2); col. III E Lines 13ff, though quite fragmentary, show that the S.C. is a confirmation of territorial grants Sulla had made in the field.

46. On the advice of his *consilium*, as Sulla's documents are careful to note. See especially *RDGE* 23 lines 38f and 55f (Sulla's grant of privileges to Oropus in Boeotia, still a matter of contention in 73 B.C., the date of this decree). From Asia, note the "field" decisions mentioned in *RDGE* 49 B lines 1–3 (ca. 84 B.C.), and cf. *RDGE* 17 (S.C. of 81 or 80 B.C. confirming privileges to Tabae) lines 9–10, *RDGE* 18 (an S.C. of 27 Mar. 81 B.C. confirming privileges to Stratoniceia) col. III lines 95f. If Dolabella was in the *provincia* still in 78 (as seems likely — see below in text), he will have had to put into effect the S.C. of May of that year on honors to certain Greek sea captains: see *RDGE* 22 lines 28–31 of the Greek text, 15–16 of the Latin, stipulating the dispatch of letters "ad magistratus nostros, quei Asiam, Macedoniam provincias optinent."

47. Fonteius in Macedonia: Cic. *Font.* 44 "Macedonia . . . non solum consilio sed etiam manu M. Fontei . . . a Thraecum adventu ac depopulatione defensa <est>" (from the peroration of this speech). On the date of 77, see MRR II 91 and (in basic agreement) E. Badian, "Notes on *Provincia Gallia* in the Late Republic," in R. Chevallier (ed.), *Mélanges d'archéologie et d'histoire offerts à André Piganiol* II (Paris 1966) 911, against Münzer, *RE* s.v. *Fonteius* 12 col. 2844. Dolabella's triumph: Cic. *Pis.* 44, cf. Suet. *Jul.* 4.1.

48. This last point is explicit in Suet. *Jul.* 4.1 and Vell. 2.43.3. Full sources and discussion in Alexander, *Trials* no. 140, of which see esp. Suet. *Jul.* 3 and 4.1 for the chronology, and 55.1 on Caesar's fame from this trial; also Plu. *Caes.* 4.1 for the Greek cities as hostile witnesses.

49. Illness at Tarentum: Sal. *Hist.* 1.127 M. Named *interrex* in early 77: *Hist.* 1.77.22 M (speech of Philippus in Senate).

50. Sources in *MRR* II 89; see esp. *Per.* 91 (implying the date of 77 for his main campaigning), Flor. 1.39.6 (Sarmatae).

51. The Broughton quotation is from *MRR* II 93, see also 99, 104, and 112 for sources on C. Curio's Macedonian command. Curio still in Rome in 76 while the weather was warm: Cic. *Brut.* 217, Quint. *Inst.* 11.3.129. Curio as "consul" at Dyrrachium, where he faced down a mutiny in one of his five legions: see Fron. *Str.* 4.1.43, and cf. 44 (an excellent example of Frontinus' indifference to the technical use of *consul*). Campaign *post consulatum*: Eutrop. 6.2.2. Direct successor to Ap. Pulcher: Sal. *Hist.* 2.80 M, Eutrop. 6.2.1–2, Oros. 5.23.20. Ready to campaign against the Dardani in spring 75: Sal. *Hist.* 2.80 M. Macedonia "full of enemies": Sal. *Hist.* 2.47.7 (speech of *cos.* Cotta at the beginning of 75).

52. Summary of campaigning: Eutrop. 6.2.2. Notice of triumph: Cic. *Pis.* 44 (termed "iustissimus") and 58, Eutrop. 6.5.2, none too helpfully grouping it ("uno tempore") with those of Servilius Isauricus (triumphed probably in 74), and Metellus Pius and Pompey (both in 71).

53. Cf. Ps.-Asc. p. 261 St. for the basic fact of M. Lucullus' succession of Curio, terming Lucullus "consul." For the suggestion that M. Lucullus did arrive as *cos.* 73, see *MRR* II 109.

54. To judge not so much from the contents of *Per.* 97 (which mentions only events of 71 and 70), but from the cutoff point of *Per.* 96 (Crassus receives command against the slaves in mid-72); cf. *Per.* 98 (which contains some *res domi* of 70). On the chronology offered here, see also *Per.* 92 (following the notice of the blockade of Sertorius at Clunia, which must be 75 [13.4.5 above]) "praeterea [thus anywhere in Book 92!] res ab Curione procos. in Thracia gestas adversus Dardanos . . . continet"; *Per.* 95 "C. Curio pro cos. Dardanos in Thracia domuit" (followed by Spartacus' initial revolt in 73); *Per.* 97 (following the death of M. Antonius in his pirate command) "M. Lucullus pro cos. Thracas subegit." Eutropius is useless on absolute dates: for instance, at 6.7.1 he has Curio's successor, the *cos.* 73 M. Terentius Varro Lucullus, fighting in Macedonia already in 74.

55. M. Lucullus summoned from Thrace: Plu. *Crass.* 11.3 with App. *BC* 1.120.557 (but the latter passage confusing him with his brother, the *cos.* 74). The sources for M. Lucullus' campaign are collected in *MRR* II 118–119; for the triumph see II 124, esp. *Bull. épig.* 1952 p. 156f no. 87 (acclamation by winter 72/71) and Cic. *Pis.* 44 (55 B.C., implying that Curio triumphed before M. Lucullus, as we would expect). M. Lucullus was in the city of Rome in autumn 70 to witness against another commander with a penchant for monumental statues, C. Verres (Cic. *Ver.* 2.2.23). Said to have added new districts to the Roman *provincia*: Ammian. Marc. 27.4.11, Ruf. Fest. *Brev.* 9.3. For the Senate putting would-be *triumphatores* to work in the field, see Cic. *Rab. Perd.* 26 (M. Antonius, *pr.* 102, in the Saturninus crisis of 100 B.C.); also Sal. *Cat.* 30.3–4, cf. 33.1 (the *imperatores* Q. Caecilius Metellus Creticus and Q. Marcius Rex active against the Catilinarians in Oct. 63); cf. Cic. *Att.* 7.7.4 (mid-Dec. 50, on Pompey's plan to send Cicero to Sicily while he still has *imperium*). See also below in 14.2.6 on M. Nonius Sufenas.

56. For a full collection of sources on the incident, see Alexander, *Trials* no. 181; see also B. A. Marshall, *Philologus* 120 (1976) 83–89, who collects the most important modern views. Basic texts: Cic. *Ver.* 1.6 with Ps.-Asc. p. 232 St., also *Ver.* 1.9. Oppius as governor: *Schol. Gron.* p. 332 St. "Oppium [Opium MS. C; Opimium Bn] significat ex praetore [expraetorem Sz] Achaiae, cuius accusatorem subditum esse dixit <a> Verre," cf. *Schol. Gron.* p. 331 St. "Praetor 'Achaicus' Oppius [Opimius MS. C v] dictus est." Oppius as the suborned prosecutor: Ps.-Asc. p. 207 St.

57. For sources on P. Oppius' trial, see Alexander, *Trials* no. 185, to which add Quint. *Inst.* 5.10.76. For depredations in transit through Greece, see 14.1.4 with n. 41.

58. For Mattingly's reidentification, see 14.1.3. The quotation is from *Chiron* 9 (1979) 156, where Mattingly also sets out the argument for excluding 66/65 as a possible date for this

command. An L. Iulius L.f. Caesar shows up as ταμίας in *OGIS* 444 (Ilium), dated to the "ninth year" of either the Roman province of Asia (and thus 125) or (more likely, to judge from the content of this inscription) a new Sullan era, and so probably 77. For ταμίας as "pro quaestore," see *SIG*³ 700 (Lete) lines 16 and 37 on M. Annius P.f. in 119 (his superior was *pr.* by 121), and *SIG*³ 743, which honors L. Licinius Lucullus (*q.* 88) sometime in the period 87–80 B.C. We do not know what the arrangements were for the *provincia* of Asia in 78 and 77, and thus (assuming that the Ilium inscription is post-Sullan) when L. Caesar was likely to have arrived there.

59. The censors will have compiled the senatorial album as one of their first acts: see T. C. Brennan, *Athenaeum* 67 (1989) 486–487.

60. See *MRR* III 30, on C. Dunant and J. Pouilloux, *Études thasiennes* V 2 (Paris 1958) 26–35 no. 172, with lettering dated by the editors to the late second or early first century. Sources on L. Aurelius' city *provincia* are collected in *MRR* I 127.

61. See *Cat. Mi.* 9.1 εἰς Μακεδονίαν ἐπέμπετο πρὸς Ῥούβριον τὸν στρατηγόν with 9.5, and (on the date of 67) *MRR* II 147. On Cato's service in the east as military tribune, see J. Bellemore, *Historia* 44 (1995) 376–379.

62. He fell ill and died on the island. See App. *Mith.* 95.435 (scope of Sisenna's assignment); D.C. 36.18.1 and (for the fate of Sisenna and his army on Crete) 19.1. Since these *legati* were supposed to stay put in their districts (App. *Mith.* 94.433, cf. 95.437), Pompey must have given Sisenna the command to move to Crete.

63. See n. 3.

64. *Monetalis*: *RRC* I 414–418 no. 405 (dated by M. Crawford to 69 B.C., but see Appendix B n. 418). Coins as aedile: *RRC* I 436–437 no. 409, which supplies filiation. *Iudex quaestionis*: *MRR* II 143, 152f, III 216. Visit to Delphi: *FD* III 4 68 no. 45. His putative praetorship: *MRR* II 161f and 169.

65. Note *IG* V 1 1432 (Messenia, ca. 104, discussed in 14.1.1), where a certain Vibius who supervises the collection of money from the community, is repeatedly referred to as ὁ στρατηγός (lines 6, 10, 11, 17, 36f), but is clearly not a praetorian commander (see lines 36f, the mention of Memmius ὁ ἀνθύπατος).

66. *FD* III 4 70 no. 46, honors for a C. Orconius C.f., belongs also to a Habromachus' year, but despite attempts, the archonship cannot be closely dated (see Colin ad loc.).

67. Special deal for Macedonia: Plu. *Cic.* 12.4 (mentioning a vote). Victory over Catiline and acclamation: *MRR* II 175 has full sources, but see esp. Cic. *Fam.* 5.5 (to Antonius in Jan. 61, with title "imperator"), D.C. 37.40.2 (claim that Antonius failed to meet requisite number killed, and notice of the vote of "sacrifices," i.e., a *supplicatio*), and Obseq. 61a (62 B.C.) "laureatos fasces in provinciam tulit."

68. Acclamation in the first year of fighting is attested, e.g., for M. Lucullus (*cos.* 73) in 72 (*Bull. épig.* 1952 p. 156f no. 87); Q. Metellus "Creticus" (*cos.* 69) in 68 (thus Phleg. F 12 in *FHG* III 606, but also saying he had "thirty legions"); L. Piso (*cos.* 58) in 57 (Cic. *Har.* 35); C. Memmius (*pr.* 58) in Bithynia in 57 (11.2 above); and M. Crassus (*cos.* II 55) as *pro cos.* for Syria in 54 (Plu. *Crass.* 17.6). One suspects it was the norm, especially to judge from the coinage of the consular commanders for Cilicia in the 50s. P. Lentulus Spinther (*cos.* 57) has "imperator" on all but the first of his coins minted at Laodiceia (see Stumpf, *Numismatische Studien* no. 75 "pro cos.," then 76–79 "imp."), and on all his issues from Apameia, including the first (Stumpf nos. 71–74). For Ap. Pulcher (*cos.* 54), only the first of his issues from Apameia and Laodiceia have "pro cos.," the rest "imp." (Stumpf no. 80, then nos. 81–83 [Apameia]; no. 84, then nos. 85–88 [Laodiceia]). M. Cicero, who was commander for Cilicia in 51, has "pro cos." on his sole Apameia and first two Laodiceia issues (Stumpf nos. 89–91), and then afterward "imp." (nos. 92–93). But in his case we know he had received the acclamation after a victory of 13 Oct. 51 (Cic. *Att.* 5.20.3).

69. As Obseq. 61a (cited in n. 67 above) seems to realize. Pompey's supersession of Lucullus in 66 is another example (Plu. *Luc.* 36.3, *Pomp.* 31.2), but at least in that case he had gotten his acclamation outside Italy, for fighting against the pirates in 67. Perhaps it was Antonius' example that prompted the tribunician legislation of 62 that tightened the rules for a triumph (V. Max. 2.8.1).

70. Sources on C. Antonius' command are collected in *MRR* II 175f and 180; for the trial, see Alexander, *Trials* no. 241, esp. (against the doubts of Alexander p. 119) *Schol. Bob.* p. 94 St. for the formal charge and 11.7.1 above on the presiding magistrate Cn. Cornelius Lentulus Clodianus. Possibility of supersession for 61: Cic. *Fam.* 5.6.3 (perhaps), *Att.* 1.12.1 with 12.4.3 above. Cf. also *Fam.* 5.6.1, the strenuous efforts of Antonius' *pro quaestore* P. Sestius to be replaced for 61, and then his wholly unexpected change of mind. (Had his superior convinced him it would weaken his own position?) Antonius (unexpectedly) had not returned to Rome as 1 Jan. 59 approached: Cic. *Att.* 2.2.3.

71. In general, see E. S. Gruen, *The Last Generation of the Roman Republic* (Berkeley 1974) 288f. Time of trial: Cic. *Att.* 2.12.1, *Dom.* 41, cf. Suet. *Jul.* 20.4. Caelius' alleged links with Catilinarians: Cic. *Cael.* 15, 74, 78, Asc. p. 86 C, *Schol. Bob.* pp. 94 and 126 St. Military aspects of promagistracy assailed: Quint. *Inst.* 4.2.123–124, cf. 9.3.58; D.C. 38.10.1 and 3. Dio (38.10.1 and 3) thought that Antonius was formally on trial for complicity with the Catilinarians, which must be a misunderstanding of Caelius' wideranging accusations and Cicero's equally discursive defense (on which see D.C. 38.10.4 with esp. *Flac.* 5 and 95). Exile at Cephallenia (including activities as city founder): Strab. 10.2.13 p. 455. He was restored in 44 B.C.

72. Octavius in the city: Cic. *Q. fr.* 1.1.21 (the general description certainly suggests activities in a civil law court rather than a permanent *quaestio*). Receives Macedonia: Vell. 2.59.1 "praetor . . . ex eo honore sortitus Macedoniam"; Suet. *Aug.* 3.1 "ex praetura Macedoniam sortitus." On the trial of Antonius, see 14.1.4 above.

73. Suet. *Aug.* 3.1, cf. Cic. *Att.* 2.1.12 on the chronology.

74. *Per.* 103 reports as an item clearly under the year 59 "C. Antonius pro cos. in Thracia parum prospere rem gessit." But Livy must have narrated this as a "flashback" in connection with Antonius' trial in that year; it is the only time the epitomator mentions this command. For an egregious case of a superseded commander tarrying in a *provincia*, see V. Max. 9.6.3 (the *pro cos.* Cn. Domitius Ahenobarbus in Gaul in 121). Even after the *lex Cornelia*, a stubborn commander could effectively delay his supersession: see D.C. 39.60.4, where the Syrian commander A. Gabinius refuses to yield to his successor Crassus' *legatus* in 54. Slow transit home: see D.C. 39.62.1 (Gabinius departing Syria in 54), also Cic. *Att.* 7.3.5 (Bibulus' slow return from Syria in 50 predicted). Cicero, whose year-long command in Cilicia was up on 30 July 50, was just departing from Ephesus a full two months later (*Att.* 6.8.4), arrived in Athens 14 Oct. (*Att.* 6.9.1, 7.1.1, *Fam.* 14.5.1), and reached Brundisium only on 24 Nov. 50 (Cic. *Att.* 7.2.1).

75. C. Octavius active in remote areas of Thrace: Suet. *Aug.* 94.5. Victory over the Bessi, for which he was saluted as "imperator": Suet. *Aug.* 3.2, and esp. (stating Macedonia as location of acclamation) *Inscr. Ital.* XIII 3 75b (*elogium*), Vell. 2.59.2.

76. Cic. *Phil.* 3.15. Consular intentions but sudden death: Vell. 2.59.2, Suet. *Aug.* 4.1. Presence in *provincia* still in late 59: Cic. *Q. fr.* 1.2.7 (termed "tuus vicinus" to Quintus in Asia between 25 Oct. and 10 Dec. 59), which runs counter to C. F. Konrad's belief ("Notes on Roman Also-Rans," in J. Linderski [ed.], *Imperium Sine Fine: T. Robert S. Broughton and the Roman Republic* [Stuttgart 1996] 105) that Octavius died in 59 and sought the consulship for 58.

77. On the Senate's refusal of triumphs in the well-attested period 218–166 (rare), see T. C. Brennan, "Triumphus in Monte Albano," in E. Harris and R. Wallace (eds.),

Transitions to Empire: Essays in Greco-Roman History, 360–146 B.C., in Honor of E. Badian (Norman, Okla., 1996) 315–337 passim, esp. 327 with 336 nn. 72–74. For the later Republic, note L. Opimius, *pr.* 125 in Italy (acclamation attested in V. Max. 2.8.4, cf. Amm. Marc. 25.9.10), who was refused the honor; L. Caesius, *pr.* ca. 104 in Hispania Ulterior (*AE* 1984, 495), who conceivably might have triumphed (the relevant *fasti* are not extant); and possibly L. Sulla, *pr.* 97, then *pro cos.* in Cilicia (*RRC* I 373 no. 359 with Crawford commentary). The turmoil of the Social and Civil Wars perhaps is enough to explain some instances of the late 90s and 80s: C. Caldus, *cos.* 94 then *pro cos.* in Gaul (*RRC* I 457–458 no. 437); L. Caesar, *cos.* 90 in Italy (Oros. 5.18.14), who was killed in action; Q. Metellus Pius, *pr.* 88, then *pro cos.* in Italy and indeed probably hailed *imperator* twice during the Social and Civil Wars, to judge from *ILLRP* 366. (Perhaps Sulla bought off Metellus' claim to a triumph by making him *cos.* 80.) Note also the *privatus* C. Flavius Fimbria in Asia, improperly acclaimed *imperator* ca. 85 (Vell. 2.24.1), and then soon to die.

78. For Q. Marcius Rex (*cos.* 68 and then *pro cos.* in Cilicia) as *imperator*, see Sal. *Cat.* 30.3–4, 33.1. C. Iulius Caesar, *pr.* 62 and then *pro cos.* in Hispania Ulterior (Plu. *Caes.* 12.4, etc.), preferred to be a candidate for *cos.* 59 (13.4.7 above); C. Antonius, *cos.* 63 and then *pro cos.* for Macedonia (Cic. *Fam.* 5.5 prescript, etc.), probably realized he had no hope of a triumph, and so entered the city—to find himself promptly condemned (see text above).

79. We get (in very rough order) C. Memmius, *pr.* 58, *pro cos.* in Bithynia (*RRC* I 451–452 no. 427); L. Piso, *cos.* 58 and then *pro cos.* for Macedonia, who did not bother to ask for a triumph in 55 (n. 1); his consular colleague A. Gabinius (Cic. *Pis.* 44, Q. *fr.* 3.2.2, etc.), who gave up on a triumph request, entered the city, and was condemned in 54; M. Crassus, *cos.* II 55 and *pro cos.* in Syria (Plu. *Crass.* 17.6), who was killed in his *provincia* in 53; and the Cilician commander Ap. Pulcher (*cos.* 54) (on whose acclamation see n. 68 above), who abandoned his claim to a triumph and unexpectedly entered the city in an attempt to stymie his prosecutor in 50 (Cael. *Fam.* 8.6.1). Finally, the civil war with Caesar dashed the aspirations of the *imperatores* M. Cicero, who was *pro cos.* 51 in Cilicia (n. 1), M. Bibulus, *pro cos.* Syria for 51 (Cic. *Phil.* 11.34), and (as I argue in 14.2.6 below) M. Nonius Sufenas in 49 (*Att.* 8.15.3).

80. Note also in this connection Cic. *Fam.* 15.4.13 (a letter requesting Cato's support for *supplicatio* vote, Jan. 50) "et provinciam ornatam [i.e., Macedonia, which in 63 he let his consular colleague Antonius have] et spem non dubiam triumphi neglexi."

81. See Var. *R.* 3.2.16 with Appendix B n. 470.

82. On the command of L. Appuleius and the aid his quaestor Cn. Plancius offered to Cicero from his "quaestorium" at Thessalonica, see the sources collected in *MRR* II 197, esp. Cic. *Planc.* 98 and *Red. Sen.* 35 (mentioning Plancius' "lictores" and "provincialia ornamenta," suggesting possible delegation of *imperium* from his superior). Cicero blames the *coss.* 58 for his exile: *Prov.* 15, 24, 30, 32, 76 (a small sample). Troops arrive: *Att.* 3.22.1 and 4, *Fam.* 14.1.3 (both 25 Nov. 58). Winter crossing: *Pis.* 57. As it happens, C. Vergilius Balbus just possibly was on Piso's staff: see Cic. *Prov.* 7 on "C. Vergilius legatus" with *MRR* III 218 (the *pr.* 62 was *pro cos.* in Sicily down into 58). One certain *praetorius* under Piso was L. Valerius Flaccus (*pr.* 63, and then *pro cos.* in Asia) (*Pis.* 54).

83. *Pis.* 28.

84. The *lex Sempronia* vitiated by Clodius' law: Cic. *Dom.* 23–24. Macedonia at peace when Piso received it: *Prov.* 4–5, 30–31, cf. 5 on the *legati*.

85. See *MRR* II 202–203 (Piso and Gabinius granted "unlimited *imperium*") with J. Béranger in *Mélanges de philologie, de littérature et d'histoire anciennes offerts à J. Marouzeau* (Paris 1948) 19–27; the quotation is from p. 24. The command of M. Antonius: Cic. *Ver.* 2.2.8 and 3.213. The phrase seems to have made an impression: see Lact. *Inst. Div.* 1.11.32 "Marci Antoni . . . infinitum illud imperium," and cf. Ps.-Asc. p. 259 St. (on *Ver.* 2.2.8)

"M. Antonius qui . . . curationem infinitam nactus totius orae maritimae." The alleged grant of "infinitum imperium" in 58: Cic. *Dom.* 23 and 55 (see n. 86 below).

86. Cicero's argument against the provincial arrangments for the *coss.* 58 has to be pieced together. Clodius gave "infinitum imperium" to Gabinius when he assigned him Syria (*Dom.* 23). Indeed, both Gabinius and Piso received "infinitum imperium" with their respective provinces (*Dom.* 55). Piso had specified what boundaries he wanted for Macedonia (*Pis.* 57, also 37). So did Gabinius, but even then he could not keep himself in his *provincia* (*Pis.* 49).

87. See *Dom.* 23, also *Pis.* 37 with *Prov.* 8, where Cicero complains that Piso "through bribery" obtained from Clodius the right to exercise jurisdiction over the loans that citizens of free states made to their fellow citizens or to Romans. In various speeches, Cicero extrapolates from this finite grant to make some fiery attacks on Piso's flagrant disregard for the principle of civic "freedom" (*Dom.* 6, *Prov.* 6 and 8, *Pis.* 90). Cf. *Prov.* 5, where Piso is said to have appropriated the local custom dues of (free) Dyrrachium.

88. See *I. Délos* 4.1.1737.

89. *Pis.* 55, 86, cf. 97 "ex trinis aestivis" (suggesting that Piso did some fighting in 55) with *MRR* II 220 n. 3 and III 47 on the date of return in 55.

90. Cf. *Pis.* 82, 94–96, 99.

91. Cicero alleged that as early as late spring/early summer 56: see *Prov.* 5 and 8, and then *Pis.* 40, 46 (with Cicero gleeful, despite the Roman loss of life!), 47–48, 92, cf. *Sest.* 71.

92. Cic. *Pis.* 84 with 40 and 92; also *Prov.* 4. In that last passage Cicero claims Piso sold peace to the Thracians and Dardani, who then raided the province to repay themselves (there is an even more damning version of this allegation in *Sest.* 94).

93. See n. 1.

94. Cic. *Pis.* 54.

95. Cic. *Pis.* 92, cf. 90, where Piso is said to have "contemplated" breaking a provision of the *lex Iulia de repetundis*.

96. Cic. *Pis.* 38–41, 44, 97; cf. *Prov.* 14–15, 25.

97. Cic. *Pis.* 53–55, 61, 74, 97. Cf. Asc. pp. 1–2 and 15–16 C on the chronology of his return (definitely in 55).

98. Cic. *Pis.* 56–63, 97.

99. *Pis.* 86, 96, 98. Piso's alleged modes of extortion are outlined in I. Shatzman, *Senatorial Wealth and Roman Politics* (Brussels 1975) 314–317 no. 107. His special targets for thefts were the Achaeans, Thessalians, and (free) Dyrrachium and Byzantium (*Pis.* 90, cf. 38 and 40, *Prov.* 5–7 and 8, *Sest.* 94).

100. Cic. *Prov.* 13, at 29 indeed clarifying what a "recall" means.

101. Cic. *Prov.* 3. Cf. (on the two "slots") 3 "decernendae nobis sunt lege Sempronia duae." Peace outside Gaul: 30

102. First proposal: Cic. *Prov.* 17. Second proposal: 17 and 36, with 36 for the idea of making Gallia Transalpina and Syria consular for the year 54, and 36–38 for declaring Gallia Cisalpina and Syria consular.

103. Cf. Cic. *Prov.* 39 (envisaging that after the *coss.* 55 someone might receive the *provincia* through an extraordinary command).

104. Cic. *Prov.* 1, 17, cf. 18.

105. His city *provincia* is not known, but during his magistracy he sat as a juror in the trial of P. Sestius *de vi*: see Cic. *Vat.* 16 with *Schol. Bob.* p. 146 St. with 11.7.1 above.

106. Cic. *Pis.* 88–89; cf. Asc. pp. 1–2 C (Piso blamed Cicero's speech *De Provinciis Consularibus* for his supersession). See also G. Daux, *Delphes au IIe et au Ier siècle* (Paris 1936) 598 no. 10 (the *koinon* of the Amphictyons dedicates a statue to Ancharius); Cic. *Fam.* 13.40 prescript.

107. Mode of transit helps characterize commander: Cic. *Pis.* 97, cf. *Ver.* 2.1.113 for the same idea. Ex-quaestor placed in charge of the province: *Pis.* 88, 92. The *praetorius* L. Valerius Flaccus—and other *legati*—return to Rome before Piso: 53–54. Soldiers burn Piso's *praetorium* at Dyrrachium: *Pis.* 93, with overt allusions to a notorious praetor who actually was burned alive in his *praetorium* (14.3.3). When it was time for Cicero to leave his province of Cilicia in August 50, he faced his own delegation problem; in the end he could not use either of his two praetorian legates (see especially *Fam.* 2.15.4).

108. *IG* II/III² 4106 with *MRR* II 233 n. 1, III 77. For the *praetorius*, see Plu. *Caes.* 51.2. For bibliography of earlier views on the identity of this man, see Wiseman, *NM* 247 no. 297. Broughton's view is questioned on slender grounds by F. X. Ryan, *AAntHung* 36 (1995) 73–76.

109. Evidence for M. Nonius: Cic. *Att.* 6.1.13. Date of Q. Thermus: *Att.* 5.13.2. For Broughton's views, see *MRR* II 242, III 149; cf. D. R. Shackleton Bailey, *CLA* III 246 ("clearly" Macedonia "by process of elimination"). The suggestion of Macedonia is an old one (cf., e.g., M. Hölzl, "Fasti Praetorii ab A.U. DCLXXXVII usque ad A.U. DCCX" [diss. Leipzig 1876] 70).

110. See 11.4 on Cn. Tremelius Scrofa.

111. See *MRR* III 148–149 for a summary of major views; add now also F. X. Ryan, *Eranos* 93 (1995) 113–121 (somewhat heavy handed, esp. at p. 120, in its use of Catullus as a source). Sufenas the moneyer: *RRC* I 445–446 no. 421, dated by Crawford to 59 B.C. "Struma Nonius": Catul. 52 lines 2–3 "sella in curuli Struma Nonius sedet | per consulatum perierat Vatinius" and Plin. *Nat.* 37.81 with (esp.) L. R. Taylor, *Athenaeum* 42 (1964) 12–28, at 18–20. The Sufenas acquitted in 54: Cic. *Att.* 4.15.4 (highly critical). The Sufenas *cum imperio* in 49: *Att.* 8.15.3.

112. *Att.* 7.7.3–4, mid-December 50 (Pompey had plans to send him to Sicily). On Nonius, see Münzer, *RE* s.v. Nonius 52 col. 901, also F. X. Ryan, *Eranos* 93 (1995) 116–117 (adumbrating the view developed here); contra G. Perl, *Klio* 52 (1970) 332 (arguing that in Mar. 49 Nonius had "ein neues Imperium").

113. Macedonia as military *provincia*: *Pis.* 44 "ea provincia . . . ex omnibus una maxime triumphalis," also 61 (famous Macedonian *triumphatores*) and 97 "ex illo fonte et seminario triumphorum." Of the prosopographical items in n. 111 above, the moneyership is the easiest to attach to this governor's career, the trial in 54 (or more exactly, the circumstances that led to it) the hardest. In general, Broughton (*MRR* III 149) seems right to suppose that more than one Nonius was active in the 50s. Yet Broughton goes too far in suggesting that "Struma Nonius" "must" have held the praetorship. In this era not just curule but also plebeian aediles had curule chairs (cf. Cic. *Ver.* 2.5.36), as Broughton himself realizes (*MRR* III 148).

114. Cic. *Fam.* 13.29.3.

115. Gel. 13.20.10 "in . . . eo consulatu in Africam profectus in ea provincia mortem obit." Scholars generally agree that the dynastic dispute in Numidia provides the context for this command: see S. Gsell, *Histoire ancienne de l'Afrique du Nord* VII (Paris 1928) 21 and 142 (but cf. 66); Broughton, *MRR* I 527; I. M. Barton, *MusAfr* 1 (1972) 52. Barton misinterprets Gellius' Latin here ("M. Porcius Cato . . . who is stated to have died in Africa during his consulate in 118 B.C.")—a common presumption (also in Gsell, *Histoire ancienne* 66) but quite unwarranted. On this, see immediately below in text.

116. For Micipsa's death and the events that followed, see Sal. *Jug.* 11.2–16.5 with *Per.* 62. The *Periocha* places the king's demise between two *res militiae*: the victory of Q. Marcius Rex (*cos.* 118) over the Ligurian Stoeni (for which he was to triumph in Dec. 117) and the subjugation of the Delmatae by L. Caecilius Metellus (*cos.* 119, with triumph also in 117, before Marcius'—*Fast. Triumph.*). The *Periocha* does not allow us to decide whether Micipsa succumbed in 118 or 117; but the consular *provincia* of M. Porcius Cato seems to

support the earlier of these dates. The violence over the succession (and the Senate's response) is mentioned directly after Metellus' success, but before a *res domi* of 115, which gives us 117 and 116 as possibilities.

117. See Sal. *Jug.* 11.2–16.5, esp. 16.2–5 ("decretum fit, uti decem legati regnum . . . dividerent") and 20.1 for the *legatio*; also Alexander, *Trials* no. 53 who collects sources on Opimius' conviction under the *lex Mamilia* in 109. Gsell (*Histoire ancienne* VII 147) had favored 117 for this commission; Broughton (*MRR* I 531) places it under the year 116, but noting that it merely "is the latest possible date." There is nothing in Sallust's narrative (our only continuous source) that helps us to decide, though 118 should probably be excluded.

118. B. Schleussner, *Legaten* 94–96, comes up with only two plausible parallels, the embassy sent in 155/154 to end the fighting between Pergamum and Bithynia (Plb. 33.7.3–4; 12–13), and another—often challenged, as Schleussner notes—to North Africa before the Third Punic War (*Per.* 48). The commission of five *legati* sent to Asia in 132 in the midst of the Aristonicus revolt (Strab. 14.1.38 p. 646, cf. Plu. *TG* 20.5–6 for the chronology) were not there to organize the *provincia* (pace W. V. Harris, *War and Imperialism in Republican Rome, 327–70 B.C.* [Oxford 1979] 148–149), but rather to drum up support for the impending Roman expedition from the allied kings and Greek cities in the area: thus P. D. Lackie, "The Revolt of Aristonicus and the Roman Annexation of Asia" (M.A. thesis, Bryn Mawr 1993) 52–58, adducing other embassies of five *legati*, especially one of 172 that fulfilled a similar role at the outset of the Third Macedonian War (*MRR* I 413).

119. His younger brother C. Porcius Cato (*cos.* 114) however was convicted under the Mamilian *quaestio* (Cic. *Brut.* 128; cf. *Balb.* 28), though no direct connection with Africa is known. Broughton (*MRR* I 544) lists him as a possible *legatus* to Africa in 111; but if we need to place him on a *legatio*, better the one of ca. 117, where there are nine unknown places.

120. Taxes of 113: *CIL* I² 585. *Legatio* of 112: Sal. *Jug.* 25.5. Consular *provinciae* for 111 under the Sempronian law: *Jug.* 27.3–5.

121. "Numidia" as consular *provincia*: Sal. *Jug.* 27.3–5 (111), 35.2 (110), 43.1 (109), 62.10 (108), 73.7, 82.2, and 84.4 (107, where a popular vote handing the *provincia* to the *cos.* C. Marius overrides the Senate's previous prorogation of Metellus). Africa as base of operations: Sal. *Jug.* 28.6 (early 111, cf. 27.5), 39.2 (winter quarters in 110/109), 44.1 and 4 (early 109), 61.2 (winter 109/108), 64.5 (108), 86.4 (early 107), 103.3 (late 106).

122. Sal. *Jug.* 32.4f.

123. *Orators* 83–84. Sources for the incident of the *legatus* A. Postumius Albinus are collected in *MRR* I 544.

124. Oros. 5.15.6.

125. See Alexander, *Trials* nos. 56 (Sp. Albinus) and 57 (discussion of question whether A. Albinus faced prosecution, rightly deciding against Münzer that he was not legally disgraced and is identical with the *cos.* 99); cf. *MRR* III 173 (also favoring the identification).

126. The principle is explicit in Cic. *Fam.* 2.18.2–3, cf. *Att.* 6.6.4. For Sulla made *pro praetore*, see Sal. *Jug.* 103.4. Mommsen is not convincing when he attempts to use this passage to support his view that a consul could not delegate *imperium* to a "Stellvertreter," unless he planned to leave his military *provincia* (*St.-R.* I³ 681 with n. 5). Sallust does not tell us where C. Marius went. Since as *pro cos.* he had surely been assigned "Numidia," it would be most difficult for him to leave this *provincia*. His *expeditio* (we can assume) was related to the war at hand.

127. Sal. *Jug.* 104.1. In 109, the *cos.* Q. Metellus had called a similar high-ranking *consilium* when Jugurtha made an offer of peace (*Jug.* 62.4–5, but no mention that a praetor was in attendance). The year 111 had seen the *cos.* L. Calpurnius Bestia grant a *deditio* to Jugurtha without proper consultation of his *consilium* (*Jug.* 29.5–6), a deal that led to his later condemnation by the Mamilian inquisition.

128. Sal. *Jug.* 97.2.

129. Defeat in consular elections for 116: Cic. *Mur.* 36, who calls that defeat surprising. Notice of Scaurus' praetorship "adversus Iugurtham": *Vir. ill.* 72.4 with *MRR* III 10.

130. "Praetor" for "pro praetore": see *Vir. ill.* 63.1–2 (where also "consul" means "pro cos."), in addition to 74.1, 75.4 (particularly revealing of this author's practice), and 78.1. Scaurus champions Adherbal in 117 or 116: Sal. *Jug.* 15.3–4, cf. *MRR* II 530f. Legate in 112: *Jug.* 25.10.

131. See *Vir. ill.* 74.4 [L. Lucullus] "adversus Mithridatem missus."

132. *Orators* 69.

133. Asc. p. 19 C.

134. Nonprosecution for *repetundae*: cf. Cic. *Mur.* 36 (his defeat for the consulship considered one of the great electoral upsets). Scaurus prosecuted for *ambitus*: Cic. *Brut.* 113 with Alexander, *Trials* no. 34.

135. B. A. Marshall (*A Historical Commentary on Asconius* [Columbia, Mo., 1985] 124–125) explains the Asconius passage (p. 19 C) by suggesting that M. Iunius Brutus brought Scaurus to trial for extortion (Cic. *Font.* 38 with Scaurus, *ORF*[3] FF 6 and 7), not after his consulship (as is generally supposed), but after his praetorship while a candidate for *cos.* 116 or 115. But this reconstruction fails to account for Asconius' implication that Scaurus entered the consulship "ante quam de eo [sc. his corrupt provincial command] iudicari posset." On the inconsequentiality of the *ambitus* counterprosecutions of 116, see Badian, *Studies* 107.

136. Sources in *MRR* II 41, to which add Sen. *Con.* 7.2.6. On the possibility that he had been prorogued a number of times by 88, see Badian, *Studies* 71–72. If correct, that would virtually guarantee that the province P. Servilius Vatia (Isauricus) triumphed from *pro praetore* in 88 was Sardinia (see 13.1.1). The identification of the praetor for Africa with the P. Sextilius Rufus who asked and then ignored the advice of his friends on an inheritance issue (Cic. *Fin.* 2.55) remains uncertain. If they are the same man, E. Badian (*JRS* 55 [1965] 113) and Broughton (*MRR* III 198) are unlikely to be right in thinking that the incident belongs to Sextilius' praetorship, since Cicero (born 106) says he himself was a member of the *consilium* (*Fin.* 2.55 ; cf. *OLD* s.v. *adsum* 7b—the use extends beyond the Senate).

137. Plu. *Crass.* 6.2.

138. See *ILLRP* 366 (Tibur) "[Q. Caeci]lius Q.f. | [L.n. Mete]llus Pius | [imp.] iter(um)." The second acclamation will have come in the civil warfare of 83 or 82.

139. Cf. App. *BC* 1.81.370 with 1.73.339. Contra Broughton in *MRR* II 57 n. 4, who thinks "the Marians doubtless had abrogated" Pius' *imperium* in 87.

140. App. *BC* 1.86.390.

141. The sources for the death of C. Fabius Hadrianus are numerous: see *MRR* II 69, but especially Cic. *Ver.* 2.1.70 with Ps. Asc. p. 241 St. He very likely held the praetorship in either the year 85 or 84 (cf. Oros. 5.20.3 "cui imperium pro pr. erat"—for 82). *Per.* 84 implies that he was in his *provincia* of Africa by 84; Münzer, *RE* s.v. col. 1771, places his praetorship exactly in that year. Date of death: Badian, *Studies* 72 and 98 n. 15.

142. For the basic event, see Cic. *Ver.* 2.1.70, D.S. 38/39.11.1, Ps.-Asc. p. 241 St., Oros. 5.20.3 (alone in not specifying the Roman reaction), and especially V. Max. 9.10.2, probably exaggerating *Ver.* 2.1.70. Perhaps Hadrianus had not implemented the system of abatements to *publicani* the quaestor Hirtuleius ca. 85 had instituted for Africa and other *provinciae* (Cic. *Font.* 2). Hadrianus as *exemplum*: H. Usener, *RhM* 56 (1901) 2 n. 1 (collecting Cic. *Ver.* passages). Burning a commander's *praetorium* may have been a traditional form of revenge (see Plu. *Pomp.* 3.1; Cic. *Pis.* 93), no doubt because it could be portrayed as a camp accident.

143. Full sources are collected in *MRR* II 77. The quotation is from *B. Afr.* 22.1–3 (a speech).

144. See the evidence gathered in *MRR* II 81 (esp. Plu. *Pomp.* 13.1 on the order to await a successor), 84, cf. III 161. For the date of 81, see the detailed discussion of E. Badian, *Hermes* 83 (1955) 107–118 (esp. 112–116 for the chronology of Pompey's campaign in Africa); 89 (1961) 254–256.

145. See 13.4.2.

146. *Luc.* 1. See also 12.2.2.

147. See Badian, *Studies* 141 with Sumner, *Orators* 114.

148. See *Balb.* 54 (the year 95), *Clu.* 98 (by 70), *Balb.* 57 (by 57) and cf. Asc. p. 54 C (two instances from 52); cf. H. E. Russell, "Insignia of Office as Rewards in the Roman Republic: Advancement in Rank for the Soldier and the Public Prosecutor" (diss. Bryn Mawr 1950) 75.

149. For this prosecution, see Alexander, *Trials* no. 71. Acquittal: Plu. *Luc.* 1.3. No further prosecutions for L. Lucullus after ca. 91: see Cic. *Luc.* 1 with Badian, *Klio* 66 (1984) 303f. Yet note Ps.-Asc. p. 222 St.—the prosecution by L. and M. Lucullus of a "Cotta"—with E. S. Gruen, *Athenaeum* 49 (1971) 54–55, suggesting the defendant was L. Cotta, *tr. pl.* 103 and *pr.* at some point in the 90s.

150. The quaestor A. Manlius A.f.: see M. Crawford on *RRC* I 397 no. 381, "80 B.C.,"; also the contrasting views of Mitchell and Mattingly ap. *MRR* III 135. *Ex praetura* command: inferred from Cic. *Planc.* 27 (no title), with date fixed by Cicero's statement (ibid.) that Plancius later served in Crete under Q. Metellus (*cos.* 69). Legateship under Pompey: App. *Mith.* 95.434 and Flor. 1.41.9.

151. See Asc. p. 91 C with Alexander, *Trials* no. 215. G. M. Paul (*A Historical Commentary on Sallust's Bellum Jugurthinum* [Liverpool 1984] 249) is slightly more dubious.

152. In general, see *MRR* II 147, 155; for an (unpersuasive) attempt to make Catiline a candidate for the regular elections in 66, see F. X. Ryan, *MH* 52 (1995) 45–48. *Ex praetura* command in Africa: Asc. pp. 66, 85 C, cf. Cic. *Cael.* 10 (presence in *provincia* in 66). Embassies to Senate in protest: Asc. pp. 85 "multae . . . graves sententiae," 89 C. Departs *provincia* to seek consulship: Asc. p. 89 C. On the details of Catiline's unsuccessful bid for the consulship in this year, see Marshall, *Asconius* 302–305.

153. For the Senate as the appropriate forum for *socii* who had complaints against Roman officials, see (in general) Cic. *Ver.* 2.1.50, Mcmn. 27.6. Specific examples are not hard to find in the later Republic: see, e.g., Plu. *CG* 2.2–3 (Sardinians in 126 B.C.), Gel. 15.14.1 (the complaints of unspecified *socii* against a Valerius Messala, perhaps ca. 120—see Appendix B n. 166), Cic. *Ver.* 2.2.146–147 (Sicilian complaints against C. Verres), D.S. 40.1–2 (a well-organized *legatio* of Cretans ca. 70 B.C.), Cic. *Flac.* 79 (provincials from Asia in 63). We have seen prejudicial *senatus consulta* against commanders in the Third Macedonian War (8.5.3), but they seem to have been rare in the later Republic. Cicero (*Ver.* 2.2.95–96) says that one was almost passed against Verres, but failed to be ratified.

154. The *cos.* Volcacius rejects Catiline's candidacy: Asc. pp. 89, 92 C. Trial: Alexander, *Trials* no. 212. On Catiline's consular bids in general, see Broughton, *Candidates Defeated* 29f, also 16–17.

155. As *pr.* 63 Q. Pompeius Rufus was active in the area of Capua against the Catilinarians (12.4.1). The sole source on his African command is Cic. *Cael.* 73–74. For the trial of C. Antonius, see 14.2.3.

156. Cic. *Flac.* 85 with Broughton, *MRR* III 219. It is more likely that Vettius served as *pr. repetundis* in the Flaccus case than juror, but either is possible (11.7.1).

157. Praetorship: Cic. *Red. Sen.* 23. Promagistracy: *Fam.* 13.6 (with Orca's title) and 13.6a.

158. Caes. *Civ.* 1.31.2 with *MRR* III 29.

159. See Cic. *Lig.* 2 and 5 and *Schol. Gron.* p. 291 St. with F. X. Ryan ap. Konrad in *Imperium Sine Fine* 106.

160. See Cic. *Lig.* 2 against *Schol. Gron.* p. 291 St.

161. Thus rightly Broughton in *MRR* II 242. On Considius' successor L. Aelius Tubero (who arrived after a delay in 49), see Appendix B n. 496.

162. See Cic. *Mil.* 74 with G. V. Sumner, *Phoenix* 25 (1971) 268 n. 41.

163. *MRR* III 61.

164. Asc. p. 55 C. = Alexander, *Trials* no. 314. See 11.7.6 and 11.9.3 for discussion.

165. See 10.4.2 with n. 97 above.

166. See in general the discussion of Marshall, *Asconius* 186 and 210, with 11.9.3. For doubts whether the *quaesitor* is the African commander, see *MRR* III 61. Other Considii: *MRR* II 240 n. 3. Possible praetorian presidency of *vis* trial: see 11.7.6 on the year 56 B.C. (one probable and one possible instance).

167. G. R. Stumpf, *ZPE* 61 (1985) 186–190, and also *Numismatische Studien* 6–12; D. French in C. S. Lightfoot (ed.), *Recent Turkish Coin Hoards and Numismatic Studies* (Oxford 1991) 201–203. K. Rigsby, *TAPhA* 118 (1988) 137–141, has made a good case that Ephesus—and not Pergamum (as Dessau and others have argued)—was, from the start, the capital of the Roman *provincia* of Asia.

168. *I. Priene* 121 lines 21–23.

169. *GRBS* 19 (1978) 147–153, esp. 150.

170. See *MRR* III 27–28; Stumpf, *Numismatische Studien* 6–12. C. Eilers (*CQ* 46 [1996] 175–182) follows Stumpf's basic view, but (p. 175f) pushes back the date of M. Hypsaeus to make room for his own conjectural identification of the quaestor M. Silanus Murena as really two individuals, a M. (Iunius) Silanus, "*pr.* c. 102," and (L. Licinius) Murena, "*quaest.* Asia c. 100" and later *pr.* 88. "Since Hypsaeus *pater* was a *novus homo* and so may have been a late consul, Hypsaeus *filius* may have become praetor slightly earlier than the date c. 100. . . . [A] date as early as c. 105 should not be excluded." On the unlikelihood of Eiler's hypothesis that the quaestor should be split into two, see text below.

171. On Q. Scaevola's praetorian command, the main evidence is Cic. *de Orat.* 2.269 (providing chronology); for his prosecution by T. Albucius, the later *pr.* ca. 107 for Sardinia, see the sources in Alexander, *Trials* no. 28. On Valerius Messalla, see Appendix B n. 166.

172. *I. Délos* IV 1 1550, reasonably supplemented στρατη[γὸν ἀνθύπατον 'Ρωμαίω]ν.

173. *I. Délos* IV 1 1679. Münzer (*RE* s.v. *Cluvius* 2 col. 119) guesses "between 134 and 104."

174. *I. Délos* IV 1 1845, cf. 1551 for Dionysius' career.

175. *RDGE* 15 lines 2–6.

176. *ANRW* II 7.1 (1979) 310–311.

177. *ILLRP* 358 = *I. Délos* IV 1 1854, which gives filiation; cf. also *I. Délos* IV 1 1710, reflecting service in the east on a different occasion as a *legatus*.

178. *Brut.* 175; cf. Broughton, *Candidates Defeated* 8, somewhat overcautious on this individual.

179. *ILLRP* 399.

180. See the discussion of *MRR* III 181.

181. *Roman Papers* II 639–640; cf. also (following Syme) E. Champlin, *CPh* 84 (1989) 54.

182. J. *AJ* 14.10.20.

183. Sources in *MRR* II 35, 38 n. 15, 495, and III 180; listed as *novus* in Wiseman, *NM* 255 no. 353.

184. *I. Délos* IV 1 1603.

185. V. Max. 3.7.9 and 6.8.1 with *MRR* I 537 n. 4; cf. M. Holleaux, *REA* 19 (1917) 92.

186. *CQ* 46 (1996) 181 n. 38.

187. See *ILLRP* 342, showing that as the *pr.* 102 for Cilicia, M. Antonius (10.1 above) could delegate his (enhanced) *imperium* to his subordinate Hirrus while still in transit to the *provincia*.

188. *IG* XII 5 722 lines 6–7; *IG* IX 2 613 (Andros) lines 6f and 33.

189. *MRR* II 551, 552 n. 2, 553; on this man see also W. Kunkel, *Staatsordnung und Staatspraxis der römischen Republik: Die Magistratur* (Munich 1995) 362 (accepting Broughton's identification of office and approximate date).

190. See for Asia Cic. *Flac.* 49, cf. *Q. fr.* 1.1.20.

191. Blind *praetorius*: Cic. *Fin.* 5.54, *Tusc.* 5.112. Adoption: *Dom.* 35 with H. B. Mattingly, *AJPh* 93 (1972) 421 n. 38.

192. See *MRR* III 168, with prosopographical speculation. Note also the "Marcus" who was honored at Delos as *quaestor pro praetore* by an Athenian known to be active in the last quarter of the second century (*I. Délos* IV 1 1843); and the late-second- or first-century Cornelius L.f. Lentulus who shows up as *legatus pro praetore* in Samothrace (*I. Samothrace* 28a). But in these latter two cases, any of the eastern *provinciae* are (at least theoretically) possible, and either or both of these men may have had a consul as a superior. See further 15.3.1 on "praetorian delegation."

193. *I. Knidos* I 31. For the titulature, see Kn. III lines 22f (with the comments of Badian in the *apparatus* to Blümel's text), also D. B lines 20f. Instructions to the prospective governor of Asia: D. B lines 20–22, cf. 22–27. Lycaonia: Kn. III lines 22–27, D. B lines 1–4, cf. D. A line 6. Phrygia: *RDGE* 13 (119 or 116 B.C.), cf. App. *Mith.* 15.51, 57.231–232 (speeches).

194. E.g., the unnamed στρατηγοί who improperly exercised jurisdiction in cases involving free Colophon in (probably) the 120s: L. and J. Robert, *Claros* I: *Décrets hellénistiques* (Paris 1989) p. 13 (decree honoring Polemaios of Colophon, active in the late 130s and 120s) col. II lines 51, 55; p. 64 (decree honoring Menippos of Colophon, active in the same era as Polemaios) col. II line 5. For an excellent exposition of the central issues that emerge from these documents, see also J.-L. Ferrary, *CRAI* 1991 557–577; moreover A. W. Lintott, *Imperium Romanum: Politics and Administration* (London 1993) 62–63 and (on the Menippos decree) S. Ager, *Interstate Arbitrations in the Greek World, 337–90 B.C.* (Berkeley 1996) no. 162.

195. See perhaps also *AE* 1993, 457 (Rhodes), a badly mutilated stone ("peut-être fin de l'époque hellénistique") that preserves the title [ἀν]|θύπατον. What follows below supersedes earlier arguments I offered in *Chiron* 22 (1992) 142 n. 113.

196. See Cic. *Brut.* 161 with E. Badian, *Athenaeum* 34 (1956) 105 n. 4 on the date; cf. V. Max. 4.5.4 for the relation by marriage.

197. Cf. Obseq. 50.

198. For their presence in the city as *coss.* 95, see esp. Cic. *de Orat.* 3.229, *Brut.* 229 and the references to the *lex Licinia Mucia* collected in *MRR* II 11, with ch. 10 n. 269 on the scope of the law.

199. See Cic. *Inv.* 2.111 ("consul . . . in citeriore Gallia"), *Pis.* 62. For the possibility that Crassus was prorogued in one or both of the Gauls, see 10.2.3 above.

200. *OGIS* 437 = *RDGE* 47 I A line 2 (also II B line 2 ἀνθύπατος Ῥω[μαίων]); *OGIS* 439 lines 6 and 7; G. Patriarca, *Bull. del. Mus. Imp. Rom.* 3 (1932) 7 no. 4; cf. also *Per.* 70 ("pro cos."). The inscription from Oenoanda alluding to this man's Asian command— recently published by C. F. Eilers and N. P. Milner in *AS* 45 (1995) 73–89—gives no title.

201. Cic. *Att.* 5.17.5 (length of service); D.S. 37.5.1 (with translation adapted from that of F. R. Walton in the 1967 Loeb edition). For a basic discussion of P. Rutilius Rufus, see D. Magie, *Roman Rule in Asia Minor* (Princeton 1950) II 1065 n. 49.

202. Cic. *Att.* 6.1.15. On this feature see Kunkel, *Staatsordnung* 360f.

203. See L. and J. Robert, *Claros* I p. 63 (Menippos decree) col. I lines 29ff; p. 13 (Polemaios decree) col. II lines 51ff. *RDGE* 70 (80 B.C., an *S.C.* guaranteeing the right of Chios to conduct its own legal affairs) shows that the question was not definitively resolved even after Scaevola.

204. Of course, we would expect provincial edicts to contain some provisions conditioned by local conditions: see J. M. Cobban, *Senate and Provinces, 78–49 B.C.* (Cambridge 1935) 161 on the slave law M.' Aquillius (*cos.* 101) instituted for Sicily, adopted by every subsequent commander in the province.

205. V. Max. 8.15.6; also Cic. *Att.* 6.1.15.

206. D.S. 37.5.1 and 4. Though apparently not all the expenses: Cicero says he requisitioned grain from the province (*Ver.* 2.3.209).

207. D.S. 37.5.2–3 with D.C. 28 F 97.1, cf. V. Max. 8.15.6, *Per.* 70, Ps.-Asc. p. 202 St. (but that last passage calling Rutilius Rufus the "quaestor" of Scaevola).

208. D.S. 37.5.1 and 6.

209. Thus, rightly, F. Pfister, *RE* s.v. *Soteria* col. 1229; see further Magie, *Roman Rule* II 1064f. On these games, see above all Scaevola's letter in *RDGE* 47 = *OGIS* 437 II B lines 28–31. Other evidence: *OGIS* 439 = *I. Olympia* 327 line 4, *OGIS* 438 = *IGRP* IV 188 line 5 (each providing the full name of the festival), Ps-Asc. pp. 202 and 262 St., cf. D.S. 37.5.6. For discussion, see K. J. Rigsby, *TAPhA* 118 (1988) 141–149. Rigsby, among other things, makes a good case for dissociating Scaevola from the arbitration agreement between Ephesus and Sardis found in *OGIS* 437 I A and III C (= S. Ager, *Interstate Arbitrations* no. 170).

210. K. J. Rigsby, *TAPhA* 118 (1988) 147 n. 97.

211. *Ver.* 2.2.51.

212. See the passages collected in A. H. Mamoojee, *EMC* 13 (1994) 36 n. 33.

213. Sources in Alexander, *Trials* no. 94. In the Livian *Periocha* 70, the trial is mentioned between *res militiae* of 96 or 95 (Sulla in Cappadocia) and 92 (the defeat of C. Sentius in Macedonia), but it must come just before the *tr. pl.* M. Drusus' attempted judicial reforms of 91. On this see esp. Cic. *Scaur.* F 4 in Asc. p. 21 C, which links this trial and a (difficult to place) prosecution of the *cos.* 115 M. Aemilius Scaurus "ob legationis Asiaticae invidiam" with Drusus' reforms. See also *Brut.* 115 "quo iudicio convolsam penitus scimus esse rem publicam," V. Max. 6.4.4 "magis ordinum dissensione"; Vell. 2.13.2, Flor. 2.5.3, cf. *Per.* 70.

214. Basic discussions: J. P. V. D. Balsdon, *CR* 51 (1937) 8–10 (arguing for praetorship); E. Badian, *Athenaeum* 34 (1956) 104–123 (a command *ex consulatu*); B. A. Marshall, *Athenaeum* 54 (1976) 117–130 (a praetorian command); R. Kallet-Marx, *CPh* 84 (1989) 305–312 (*ex praetura*); Kunkel, *Staatsordnung* 372–374 (*ex consulatu*). Kallet-Marx (p. 307) is wrong in thinking that "Scaevola was in Asia after completing whatever magistracy he had held, for he is given the title *proconsul* (ἀνθύπατος) in inscriptions"; see also G. V. Sumner, *GRBS* 19 (1978) 147, for the same mistake.

215. Asc. pp. 14–15 C. R. Kallet-Marx (*CPh* 84 [1989] 309) rightly argues that in this passage, *cupiditas provinciae* "must concern the mere act of holding a province." In addition to the passages specifically concerning triumph hunting that Kallet-Marx adduces, cf. Cic. *Ver.* 2.3.44 (of Sicily) and *Man.* 67. For *sumptus* as "finances for a campaign," see, e.g., *Pis.* 97. Balsdon (*CR* 51 [1937] 8, suggesting the emendation *ornatio* for the obelized word in Asconius' text) argued that *deponere provinciam* was "a technical term for 'resigning a province on appointment'." But a closer examination (11.1.6) suggests that though the phrase plainly means to refuse a province in some way (through exchange or outright rejection), it was not part of Rome's formal administrative vocabulary.

216. Asconius 110.

217. It is just possible that Scaevola originally had received Gallia Cisalpina, and exchanged it with Crassus—we have seen (11.1.6) that Cicero uses *deponere provinciam* in

this connection—for Italia, or turned it down flat, with Crassus—whose influence in the Senate is said to have been enormous (Asc. pp. 14–15 C)—getting the *provincia* decreed to himself once Scaevola refused it.

218. Four known instances in the previous four decades: C. Sempronius Tuditanus, *cos.* 129 "de Iapudibus"; M. Aemilius Scaurus, *cos.* 115 "de Galleis Karneis"; and then the special case of C. Marius as *cos.* II 104 for the Jugurthine War and as *cos.* V 101 over the Cimbri and Teutones.

219. The only related exception is the A. Postumius Albinus who served as a *legatus* under Sulla in 89 during the Social War, quite possibly to be identified with the *cos.* 99 (see *MRR* II 37, III 173 for references and discussion). For a list of consular *legati* between 189 and the Social Wars (only seven known), see E. Badian, *Historia* 42 (1993) 205 n. 6; for the years 70 down to the end of our period, Kunkel, *Staatsordnung* 374 n. 251.

220. Cic. *Balb.* 55 ("praetorem urbanum") and K. Tuchelt, *Frühe Denkmäler Roms in Kleinasien: Beiträge zur archäologischen Überlieferung aus der Zeit der Republik und des Augustus* I (Tübigen 1979) 160, cf. F. Coarelli in S. Panciera (ed.), *Atti del colloquio internazionale AIECL su epigrafia e ordine senatorio* I (Rome 1982) 435–451.

221. Though not too much earlier: Cicero in *Balb.* 55 says it was "proxime . . . ante civitatem Veliensibus datam," i.e., 90 B.C. Badian (*Studies* 94–95 with 103–104 n. 159), before the Claros inscription had come to light, had suggested that C. Flaccus was one of the two "nobilissimi" who competed against C. Coelius Caldus for *cos.* 94 (Q. Cic. *Pet.* 11). But that is doubtful if Flaccus was really *pr.* 96 and *ex praetura* for 95.

222. Peregrine praetorship: 12.2.1. His promagistracy: Cic. *Leg.* 1.53. Against Broughton in *MRR* III 99 ("Cilicia was not yet a regularly organized province"), see 10.1 above. Return to Italy: see *ILLRP* 515, where he is listed first in the *consilium* of Cn. Pompeius Strabo at Asculum.

223. Pace Münzer, *RE* s.v. *Cassius* 10 col. 1680 (dating his praetorship to 90). Cassius joins in initial restoration of kings, and in inciting them to invade Mithridates' territory: App. *Mith.* 11.33–35 (and cf. 56.233), *Per.* 74.

224. Cassius defeated by Mithridates in his counterattack: App. *Mith.* 17.59–61, cf. 19.72. Cassius retreats from Apameia to Pergamum: *Mith.* 19.74–75, cf. *RDGE* 48, esp. lines 1–4. "Asia" part of Sulla's consular *provincia* for 88: *Mith.* 22.84, cf. 60.246. Retreats to Rhodes: *Mith.* 24.94 (with title, ὁ τῆς Ἀσίας ἀνθύπατος), cf. 24.95–98. Cassius appears among the prisoners surrendered by Mithridates to Sulla: *Mith.* 112.544, cf. *MRR* II 45 n. 7 (doubting report).

225. On these fines, see App. *Mith.* 63.260–261 (with effects), Plu. *Sull.* 25.2 (details of billeting) and *Luc.* 4.1 (the *pro quaestore* Lucullus' role in collecting), Cic. *Flac.* 32 (amount allotted proportionately among cities of Asia).

226. C. Caesar's filiation and status as a governor of Asia are amply attested, best by *I. Priene* 111 line 22 (but here simply [στρ]ατηγοῦ) and *ILLRP* 344–345 (Delos); cf. *I. Délos* IV 1 1701, *IGRP* IV 970 (Samos) (neither with title) and *Inscr. Ital.* XIII 3 75a (an *elogium*) "q., pr., [——] cos. in Asia." See *MRR* III 104–105 for suggested supplements to the lacuna in that last item, some quite hard to swallow. He is [σ]τρατη[γὸν ἀ]νθ[ύπ]ατόν at *IG* XII 8 241—yet with wrong *praenomen*; ἀνθύπατος in *I. Priene* 117 lines 17 with 49. This Caesar participated in an agrarian commission to settle "coloni," apparently Marian veterans under Saturninus' tribunician legislation of 103 or (less likely) 100 (*MRR* III 104–105 with 21): see *Inscr. Ital.* XIII 3 7, another *elogium*. In this fragmentary inscription the position is listed after the praetorship, quaestorship, and (military) tribunate. Yet the fact that it is an extraordinary office leaves open the possibility that the entire series is not in strict descending chronological order, with the colonial commission coming to Caesar before he reached the Senate. He died a *praetorius* in the year 85 at Pisa (Plin. *Nat.* 7.181 with Suet. *Jul.* 1.1).

227. For discussion of the content of this Priene inscription, see Ager, *Interstate Arbitrations* no. 170 (but with no contribution toward the chronological issues).

228. Lucilius is termed στρατηγός in *I. Priene* 111 line 136; cf. 142 and 147. On the title, see *I. Priene* 111 line 119, where στρατηγός clearly denotes a *pro cos.*, and also line 135, "the στρατηγοί dispatched to Asia," a routine phrase in both epigraphical and literary texts for Roman praetors for this *provincia*.

229. *I. Priene* 111 line 147f.

230. At *I. Priene* 111 lines 21–22, the phrase τ[ούς τε ἀπεσταλμέν]ους εἰς τὴν | Ἀσίαν ὑπὸ Ῥωμαίων στρατηγοὺς encompasses three praetors representing a span of probably twenty years!

231. The Cn. Octavius Cn.f. στρατηγὸς Ῥωμαίων of *I. Délos* IV 1 1782 is surely not the *cos.* 87, and can safely be left out of the reckoning of the Asian *fasti* for this era: see 9.1.5 with n. 85 above.

232. *GRBS* 19 (1978) 148–150, with *I. Priene* 113 line 53 (and Sumner, *Orators* 149 n. 10) on the start of the Stephanophorate.

233. *MRR* III 212.

234. See Cic. *Flac.* 55–59 passim. Contributions: *Flac.* 56, cf. 59 for the chronology. Tralles lends dedicated money at interest: *Flac.* 56, cf. (for some Hellenistic and Imperial attempts to legislate against this type of diversion) C. P. Jones, *JRS* 73 (1983) 121–122. Festival never performed: *Flac.* 59 "(pecunia) ad eius honores conlata, ex quibus nihil ipse capiebat." But see K. J. Rigsby, *TAPhA* 118 (1988) 149 ("perhaps this celebration did occur . . . Tralles using its own money").

235. *IGRP* IV 291 with Rigsby, *TAPhA* 118 (1988) 148–149, for the quotes below.

236. See esp. Cic. *Ver.* 2.2.51 (cf. 2.4.151) with 2.2.114, 154.

237. For the impact on Tralles, see App. *Mith.* 23.90.

238. See esp. App. *Mith.* 63.261 and Plu. *Luc.* 20.1–4.

239. Cicero speaks of a M. Aurelius Scaurus, a quaestor for Asia (*Ver.* 2.1.85 and *ILLRP* 373 [Delos]), failing at the *divinatio* stage in his attempt to prosecute his superior L. Flaccus: see *Div. Caec.* 63 (cf. Ps.-Asc. p. 203 St.) with Broughton, *MRR* III 32 and 212. Broughton (ibid., following a view E. Badian set forth in *Klio* 66 [1984] 298–301) rightly recognizes that Flaccus should be the same individual as our putative praetor, while Scaurus presumably is the son of the *cos. suff.* 108.

240. Q. Scaevola: *MRR* II 7 with 9 n. 2. L. Gellius: II 15 and 16 n. 4. L. Flaccus: II 18–19. C. Caesar: II 20. L. Lucilius: II 27. C. Cassius: II 34.

241. Q. Scaevola: *MRR* III 145–146. L. Flaccus: III 212. L. Gellius: III 99. C. Caesar: III 105. L. Lucilius and C. Cassius: III 128.

242. Indeed, T. Frank (*AJPh* 58 [1937] 90–93) had suggested the date of 98, and in this has been followed by a number of authorities: see E. Gabba, *Gnomon* 24 (1952) 289.

243. See App. *Mith.* 52.208, cf. D.C. 30–35 F 104.3–5. Q. Minucius Thermus should be identical with the *monetalis* of *RRC* I 324 no. 319 (dated by Crawford to 103 B.C.), and was perhaps of quaestorian rank at the time of this incident (*MRR* III 144f).

244. The tradition on Fimbria's status in 86 could hardly be more diverse, with one source (Dio) even reporting two different titles. He was a senator at the time, who accompanied Flaccus merely as a *comes*: App. *Mith.* 51.205, 52.209. Or as a quaestor: Strab. 13.1.27 p. 594, D.C. 30–35 F 104.4. *Legatus*: Oros. 6.2.9, *Vir. ill.* 70.1, cf. D.C. 30–35 F 104.1 ὁ ὑποστράτηγος Φλάκκου. *Praefectus equitum*: Vell. 2.24.1. Appian seems the best informed on this man, and his view that he was a *privatus* seems the most worthy of credence. For confirmation, note *Mith.* 52.207, which relates how Fimbria and Flaccus' quaestor disputed about lodgings; the dispute came about precisely because Fimbria's position was so ambigu-

ous. For Lintott's argument, see *Historia* 20 (1971) 696–701, esp. 701, deducing C. Flavius Fimbria's title largely on the basis of Strab. 13.1.27 p. 594 and App. *Mith.* 52.208 (the tale how Fimbria assumed the *legatus* Q. Thermus' praetorian insignia at Byzantium); Sumner (*Orators* 124) and C. F. Konrad (*Plutarch's Sertorius: A Historical Commentary* [Chapel Hill, N.C., 1994] 86) endorse it. Yet see *Vir. ill.* 70.2, where Fimbria "ipse correptis imperii insignibus [surely those of Flaccus, now dead] provinciam ingressus." For Fimbria's pretensions as the independent commander of a consular army, see App. *Mith.* 52.210, Strab. 13.1.27, p. 594, also Vell. 2.24.1 "imperator appellatus." On Fimbria's possible claim to consular *imperium*, see *Per.* 82 "L. Valerius Flaccus cos . . . .occisus est et imperium ad Fimbriam translatum"; cf. perhaps also Memn. 24.3–4 who says that the Roman Senate made Fimbria consul (!), and later terms him ὁ τῶν Ῥωμαίων στρατηγός. Many of our sources strongly imply that Fimbria presented himself in Asia as the practical equivalent of the *pro cos.* Sulla (see, e.g., App. *Mith.* 59.241).

245. Praetorship: *Mur.* 15 "cum . . . ex praetura triumphasset." For the nature of Murena's appointment in Asia (and ambition for a triumph), see especially App. *Mith.* 64.265, cf. Memn. 26.1 (erroneously reporting that the Senate had put him in charge of the war!). Length of "Second Mithridatic War": App. *Mith.* 66.281; it follows that Murena spent more than three years in Asia. Acclaimed "imperator": *SIG³* 745 lies 5–6, Tuchelt, *Frühe Denkmäler* I 153–154 lines 2–3. Recall: Cic. *Man.* 8, App. *Mith.* 66.279–280. Triumph: Cic. *Mur.* 15, *Man.* 8. For sources on Murena's eastern command in general, see *MRR* II 61 with 62 n. 4 (84 B.C.), 64 (83 B.C.), 70 (82 B.C.), 77 (81 B.C.). See also the discussion in *MRR* III 123, with further references; D. G. Glew, *Chiron* 11 (1981) 110–120 provides a fully documented narrative of Murena's aggressive campaigning. A. Keaveney, *Klio* 66 (1984) 118–119, suggested that Murena on first leaving Italy had been assigned Cilicia as his *provincia*: against this, see 10.1 above.

246. App. *Mith.* 65.270.

247. See App. *Mith.* 65.272–273 with A. Keaveney, *Klio* 65 (1983) 185 n. 4, on the possible identifications of the Senate's legate, and D. G. Glew, *Chiron* 11 (1981) 115–116, on the context for this mission.

248. App. *Mith.* 64.265 (initial appointment and commission to finish Sulla's administrative arrangements), 66.279, Cic. *Man.* 8 (recall).

249. Had charge of Asia while Murena campaigned: Cic. *Luc.* 1 (incidentally revealing that he had not returned to Rome in time for the aedilician elections of 80 for 79). Siege of Mytilene: Plu. *Luc.* 4.2–4. Honors in the east as *pro quaestore*: see the list in L. and J. Robert, *Bull. Epig.* 1970 no. 441. Contrast *AE* 1994, 1755, where Lucullus as *quaestor pro praetore* confirms privileges to the temple of Isis and Sarapis at Mopsuestia in Cicilia—but clearly while traversing the eastern Mediterranean in service of Sulla in 86 (on which see *MRR* II 55–56).

250. See *SIG³* 745, *IGRP* I 843, *ILS* 8773, and cf. *I. Délos* IV 1 1698 = *ILLRP* 369 with E. Badian, *JRS* 58 (1968) 245–246. (All inscriptions show filiation.) On the *pro cos.* L. Cornelius L.f. Lentulus of *SIG³* 745 lines 3–4 (surely a commander in Cilicia rather than in Asia at this time), see 10.1 above.

251. See 14.5.9 above. For M. Thermus' praetorian rank and his *provincia* of Asia, see Suet. *Jul.* 2 and *Vir. ill.* 78.1 (the young C. Iulius Caesar was his *contubernalis*). Finishes siege of Mytilene: Plu. *Luc.* 4.2–3 with Suet. *Jul.* 2; see however Magie, *Roman Rule* I 245–246 and II 1124f, arguing that it was Lucullus who brought the city to terms.

252. *MRR* II 76, also 81.

253. See *RDGE* 18 (27 Mar. 81) lines 60–61, and cf. lines 114f.

254. See 14.4.

255. *IGRP* IV 196 = *OGIS* 443, describing how he ordered the Poemaneni of Mysia to provide a garrison for Ilium (probably as a precaution against pirate attacks), gives title and filiation: on this inscription see Magie, *Roman Rule* II 1120 n. 25.

256. Cic. *Ver.* 2.1.50.

257. See esp. Cic. *Ver.* 2.1.71–76 with 15.1.1 below.

258. See 14.2.1 n. 46.

259. Plin. *Nat.* 2.100.

260. Ps.-Asc. p. 193 St. with *MRR* II 97. There, Broughton collects other sources specifically naming this Varro, unfortunately all scholiasts. Magie, *Roman Rule* II 1125 n. 42, provides a detailed discussion (tentatively dating this Varro's command in Asia to 77/76).

261. The precise date of the first of these trials might also be open to question. L. Furius need not have been *pr.* 75, as Broughton (*MRR* II 97) supposes: see 11.7.1.

262. *I. Mylasa* I 109.

263. See *I. Priene* 121 line 23 Μᾶρκον Ὑψαῖον κ<αὶ Μ>ᾶρκον Σιλανὸν Μυρέναν ταμίαν (also line 32 for the lower date of the events mentioned) with Magie, *Roman Rule* II 1126 n. 43. Subsequent views are collected in *MRR* III 114.

264. D. R. Shackleton Bailey, *Two Studies in Roman Nomenclature*[2] (Atlanta, Ga., 1991) 76f: "the adoptive father of an M. Silanus Murena must also have been an M. Silanus."

265. For discussion of the Priene inscription, see most recently C. Eilers, *CQ* 46 (1996) 175–182.

266. *CQ* 46 (1996) 176f.

267. See Shackleton Bailey, *Two Studies*[2] 79 on the generations of Plaetorii Cestiani, starting perhaps already in the mid-second century. Later evidence is ample: see pp. 67 (C. Appuleius Decianus [*tr. pl.* 99] and his son C. Decianus), 81 (M. Pupius Piso Frugi, *cos.* 61, and his son), 84f (A. Terentius Varro Murena and son); and perhaps 72f (the *cos.* 72 Cn. Cornelius Lentulus Clodianus and his homonymous son).

268. Sal. *Hist.* 2.47.7 M (speech of *cos.* 75 C. Cotta) "exercitus in Asia Ciliciaque ob nimias opes Mithridatis aluntur."

269. Title: Vell. 2.42.1 and Plu. *Caes.* 2.6. Asia with Bithynia: Vell. 2.42.3, cf. *Per.* 93 "Nicomedes . . . regnumque eius in provinciae formam redactum est." For the praetor's name, date ("75/4"), and details of his command in the east, see A. M. Ward, *AJAH* 2 (1977) 26–36 (esp. the timeline on p. 31), cf. A. Keaveney, *Lucullus: A Life* (London 1992) 201–202. Roman *publicani* active on south shore of Euxine before the outbreak of the Third Mithridatic War: Memn. 27.5–6 (their encroachment on free Heraclea).

270. See, e.g., C. F. Konrad, *Athenaeum* 83 [73] (1995) 171, on lines 7–26 of the *Lex portorii Asiae* published by H. Engelmann and D. Knibbe, *EA* 14 (1989) 1–206; cf. also R. Merkelbach, *ZPE* 81 (1990) 97–100.

271. E. Badian, *Zöllner und Sünder*, trans. W. Will and S. Cox (Darmstadt 1997) 219–231, esp. 227–230 (a revised and expanded version of *Publicans and Sinners: Private Enterprise in the Service of the Roman Republic* [1972, rev. ed. Ithaca, N.Y., 1983]). See also H. Engelmann and D. Knibbe, *EA* 14 (1989) 161.

272. The date offered by Eutrop. 6.1.1, cf. *Per.* 93. A royal tetradrachm dated to year 224 of the Bithynian era, i.e., after October 74 (see W. H. Bennett, *Historia* 10 [1961] 459–472), need not have been minted while Nicomedes IV was still alive: see B. C. McGing, *Phoenix* 38 (1984) 14–15, cf. A. M. Ward, *AJAH* 2 (1977) 32–33, Keaveney, *Lucullus* 191.

273. Caesar, the pirates, and the praetor Iunius Iuncus: Vell. 2.41.3–42.3 (fullest account) with Plu. *Caes.* 1.7–2.7 (stressing the venality of "the praetor," but not mentioning Iuncus by name and confusing the date), cf. Suet. *Iul.* 4.1–2. Caesar expels a Mithridatic force: Suet. *Iul.* 4.2 with M. Gelzer, *Caesar: Politician and Statesman*, trans. P. Needham (Oxford 1969) 24.

274. Once in Asia, Lucullus found the troops—including two legions of Fimbriani—in a sorry state (Plu. *Luc.* 7.1–2, cf. 34.1–3; App. *Mith.* 72.305). Yet the allied fleet must have been adequate (Plu. *Luc.* 13.4).

275. Caesar delivered a speech *pro Bithyniis*, in which he addressed Iuncus (occasion unknown): see Gel. 5.13.6, also Caes. *ORF*³ 45. Perhaps the Bithynians had asked Caesar to represent them at the time Iuncus set his hand to the organization of the Roman province (thus A. M. Ward, *AJAH* 2 [1977] 30–31), or M. Iuncus was prosecuted *de repetundis* on his return to Rome with C. Iulius Caesar speaking *pro Bithyniis* (H. Dahlmann, *Hermes* 73 [1938] 341–346).

276. Iuncus probably had on his staff Q. Pompeius "Bithynicus" and his brothers A. Pompeius (on whom cf. *ILLRP* 364) and Sex. Pompeius: see *SIG*³ 1125 (Eleusis, "aetate Augusti") with Fest. p. 320 L on "Pompeius Bithynicus," and in general *MRR* III 161.

277. Sal. *Hist.* 2.98 M (implying their presence in the city at the beginning of 74).

278. App. *Mith.* 70.295 with 71.299, cf. perhaps 70.297 (Mithridates' pre-invasion speech, where he counts the slave war in Italy as one of the troubles facing Rome); Memn. 27.2 and 4 (Lucullus already in Asia at time of invasion).

279. *Mith.* 72.308. Yet see on this synchronism (and on Appian's synchronisms in general) C. F. Konrad, *Athenaeum* 83 [73] (1995) 175–177 ("terminally useless").

280. Broughton, *MRR* II 106–108 (arguing for the earlier date), also III 121–122 (reversing his position); and for the later date Magie, *Roman Rule* II 1204–1205 n. 5. The best recent assessment of the evidence seems to me that of B. C. McGing, *Phoenix* 38 (1984) 12–18, whose reconstruction I largely follow here. See also (for the "early" date) R. Merkelbach, *ZPE* 81 (1990) 97–100, P. McGushin, *Sallust: The Histories* I (Oxford 1992) 248–249, and Keaveney, *Lucullus* 188–205, esp. 204f (implausibly suggesting that Mithridates invaded not Bithynia but Paphlagonia in spring 74).

281. Mithridates makes an alliance with Sertorius: *Per.* 93, cf. Flor. 2.10.4 (inaccurately stating that Sertorius sent Mithridates a fleet); also App. *Mith.* 68.286–288, Plu. *Sert.* 23.1–24.3 (each dating the alliance before the outbreak of the Third Mithridatic War, and Plutarch at 23.6 indeed placing it before news of the death of Nicomedes). Quick arrival (within three months) of Sertorians to Mithridates: Sal. *Hist.* 2.79 M. Mithridates begins Third War with assistance of Sertorian commander: App. *Mith.* 68.289; see also 13.4.1 above, and H. B. Mattingly, "M. Antonius, C. Verres, and the Sack of Delos by the Pirates," in M. J. Fontana, M. T. Piraino, and F. P. Rizzo (eds.), Φιλίας Χάριν: *Miscellenea di studi classici in onore di Eugenio Manni* IV (Rome 1979) 1504–1506.

282. *Per.* 93 "apparatus dein regiarum copiarum pedestrium navaliumque"; Plu. *Luc.* 7.4–6; Memn. 27.2–3.

283. See Plu. *Luc.* 5.1–3 with Sal. *Hist.* 2.98.10 M on the *provinciae* allotted to the *coss.* 75 for 74.

284. On Cethegus, see Appendix B n. 204. His popularity: Plu. *Luc.* 5.4, cf. also 6.3. Influence in Senate: Cic. *Brut.* 178.

285. *Luc.* 6.1.

286. Plu. *Luc.* 6.5, cf. 5.2.

287. Cicero on the *provinciae* of the *coss.* 74: *Mur.* 33, cf. *Luc.* 1. L. Lucullus received Cilicia (Plu. *Luc.* 6.5) and Asia (Cic. *Flac.* 85, Vell. 2.33.1, Memn. 27.1, cf. D.C. 36.2.2 for the later "restoration" of Asia as a praetorian *provincia*). M. Cotta given Bithynia: Plu. *Luc.* 6.6, also Memn. 27.1.

288. Cic. *Mur.* 33, also Eutrop. 6.6.2.

289. Ps.-Asc. p. 259 St.

290. For Lucullus' presence in the city in July/August 74, see Cic. *Clu.* 136–137 with Keaveney, *Lucullus* 188f. Levy: Plu. *Luc.* 7.1, App. *Mith.* 72.305. Training: Plu. *Luc.* 7.1–3.

Cotta moves into Chalcedon, where on Lucullus' "orders" he establishes the Roman naval base: Memn. 27.4. Mithridates, on the move, receives market privileges at Heracleia: Memn. 27.5. Cotta goes triumph hunting against Mithridates while Lucullus still in Phrygia: Plu. *Luc.* 8.1. Mithridates invades Bithynia and drives Cotta back into Chalcedon: Plu. *Luc.* 7.6, App. *Mith.* 71.299. Mithridates hems Cotta in the town: *Per.* 93, Oros. 6.2.13, App. *Mith.* 71.300–304, Memn. 28.7, Plu. *Luc.* 8.2, cf. Sal. *Hist.* 4.69.13 M (letter of Mithridates).

291. *Phoenix* 38 (1984) 12–14, supplemented by ZPE 109 (1995) 283–288.

292. In fairness, this epitomator obviously makes an attempt to be precise with his titles: see, e.g., *Per.* 77 (on the year 88) "Q. Pompeius cos. ad accipiendum a Cn. Pompeio pro cos. exercitum profectus." Yet for some clear instances of "consul" standing for "pro consule," see *Per.* 26 (Q. Fulvius Flaccus and Ap. Claudius Pulcher, *coss.* 212, in 211, the former called "consul" *bis*); *Per.* 54 (Q. Pompeius, *cos.* 141, in 139); *Per.* 82 (L. Valerius Flaccus, *cos.* 86, in 85). Sometimes we even get "pro consule" for "consul": *Per.* 76 (Cn. Pompeius, *cos.* 89, clearly still in 89); cf. perhaps *Per.* 61 "Cn. Domitius pro cos. adversus Allobrogas . . . pugnavit" (prior to a *res domi* of 121).

293. *Lucullus* 256 n. 45.

294. See, for instance, the supplements to *Per.* 93 offered *exempli gratia* by R. Merkelbach in ZPE 81 (1990) 99.

295. See *Per.* 108 "praeterea . . . resque a M. Bibulo in Syria gestas continet," the only other clause in the entire *Periocha* that contains "resque." For the vexed passage in *Per.* 93 the (15th-century) MS. Guelferbytanus 175 in fact offers "Metello gestas continet adversus Sertorium quibus omnibus." The reading is obviously corrupt, but perhaps less so than some of the other variations we get, best seen in the apparatus to P. Jal's Budé edition, *Abrégés des livres de l'histoire romaine de Tite-Live* II (Paris 1984) p. 24. After <res continet>, one can envisage repetition of the proper name *Sertorius* (cf. *Per.* 32)—which would help explain how a lacuna developed in the first place—alternately *is* or *qui* (cf. *Per.* 26, 39, 46). No other additions to this lacuna at *Per.* 93 are needed for the clause that follows to make sense. "Omnibus . . . par" ("the equal of any"), though not Livian, finds a parallel at Flor. 1.34.1; the adjective *artibus* (ablative of respect) needs no modifier (see *Per.* 39 "M. Porcio Catone et belli et pacis artibus maximo").

296. The formulae "res praeterea adversus" or "contra [such and such a foe] prospere gestas continet" are exceedingly common in this epitomator. See the formulae at *Per.* 2, 4, 6, 11, 24, 26 (cf.), 27, 34, 36, 39, 41–42, 46, 58, 60, 87, 90, 92, 99, 107, 109, 112 (with *adversus*); also *Per.* 3, 7–8, 10–11, 13–14, 16, 40, 84 (with *contra*). He sometimes offers summary statements without *praeterea*: *Per.* 40, 43, 109; cf. *Per.* 6 (*init.*). But since we cannot tell the length of the lacuna (cf. O. Rossbach, *T. Livi Periochae omnium librorum* [Leipzig 1910] p. xxiv) it is just possible that the word *praeterea* has fallen out of our passage as well.

297. On this well-known feature of the *Periocha*, see the general comments of Jal, *Abrégés* I p. lxxviii (offering in n. 7 some clear examples of chronological displacement).

298. On C. Salluvius Naso, see *CIL* I² 743 with *MRR* II 105 and Magie, *Roman Rule* II 1208 n. 15. Note also *AE* 1983, 920 (Ephesus), for Q. Publicius Q.f. *pro quaestore pro praetore*, reasonably to be dated prior to 67 (*MRR* III 176). Cf. perhaps also B. E. Thomasson, ZPE 68 (1987) 275–276, with Tuchelt, *Frühe Denkmäler* I 187, on the L. Manlius L.f. Torquatus attested as πρεσβευτὴς καὶ ἀντιστράτηγος (not "legatus pro consule," as had long been thought) at Miletus; he might have seen service in Asia in the late 70s or early 60s. There is now no evidence that he was a regular governor of the province (as entertained by *MRR* II 142 n. 9, 151 n. 16). He is most probably to be identified with the future *cos.* 65; but note just possibly the senator "L. Mallius" killed in 73 at Chalcedon (App. *Mith.* 71.304).

299. E.g., Barba (*MRR* II 112, cf. III 199f), M. Pompeius (*MRR* II 120), or "Sextilius" (II 134). See also immediately below in text.

300. For Lucullus' practice of placing *legati* over foreign districts as he conquered them, see D.C. 36.8.1, Eutrop. 6.9.2, and (in addition to the instances cited immediately below) the sources on L. Fannius in *MRR* II 140.

301. Full sources on this man in *MRR* II 119, 140. For the assignment in Pontus, see App. *Mith.* 88.398 τῷ . . . ἐκ Λουκούλλου στρατηγεῖν ὑπολελειμμένῳ and 88.400, where he is said to have had τήν . . . ἀρχήν . . . καὶ τὸ ἀξίωμα in Pontus; also D.C. 36.9.2.

302. Sources in *MRR* II 105. Possible praetorian standing: see the discussion of Münzer in *RE* s.v. *Rutilius* 30 col. 1268 (also suggesting he was somehow related to the *cos.* 105), Badian in *Gnomon* 33 (1961) 492–493, and Broughton in *MRR* III 183. Appian (*Mith.* 71.300) gives his title only as ὁ ναύαρχος of Cotta.

303. Sources in *MRR* II 113, 120, 125, 134, 141, 148. For Memnon's view, see particularly 29.1 αὐτόκλητος ὁ Τριάριος, 29.5 Λεύκολλος δὲ καὶ Κόττας καὶ ὁ Τριάριος οἱ Ῥωμαίων αὐτοκράτορες στρατηγοί, yet cf. 34.5 and 35.6 (showing that this author fully realizes he was formally a subordinate of M. Cotta). For an indication of Triarius' independence, see, e.g., App. *Mith.* 77.333, 88.400 μετ᾽ οἰκείου στρατοῦ, and esp. his actions at Gaziura in 67 (D.C. 36.12.1, App. *Mith.* 89.402, Plu. *Luc.* 35.1). The Delian inscriptions are listed in *MRR* II 134; on these see H. B. Mattingly, Φιλίας Χάριν IV 1491–1493 (suggesting a redating to 73 B.C.).

304. L. Murena as *legatus*: Cic. *Mur.* 20 "hic multas res et magnas sine imperatore gesserit," 89, cf. also Plu. *Luc.* 19.9 (a frank assessment); full sources collected in *MRR* II 119, 134. In winter 72/71, Lucullus left him in charge of the siege of Amisus with two legions: Phleg. F 12 in *FHG* III 606, cf. Plu. *Luc.* 15.1. He was apparently left to besiege Tigranocerta in 69: Plu. *Luc.* 27.1; but see *MRR* II 129 with 131 n. 6.

305. Position in Pontus: Plu. *Luc.* 30.3 τοῖς περὶ Σωρνάτιον ἡγεμόσιν. Title: *I. Pergamum* 431, cf. perhaps *MAMA* VI 260 (no title). For full sources and discussion, see *MRR* II 120, 134, 140, with III 199f.

306. See n. 313 below on M. Pupius Piso Frugi Calpurnianus as *legatus pro praetore* under Pompey in 67.

307. Memn. 35.7 and 36, cf. App. *Mith.* 82.369 (erroneously crediting Lucullus with the siege of Heracleia). Alexander (*Trials* no. 192) posits a condemnation for M. Cotta *de peculatu* or *de repetundis* in the early 60s, with C. Papirius Carbo (a future praetorian commander for Bithynia ca. 61) as the prosecutor, receiving "consular insignia as a reward." Yet, despite V. Max. 5.4.4—who says that Cotta "damnatus fuerat" and for this his son later prosecuted Carbo—the notion that the *cos.* 74 ever went on trial for his actions in Bithynia seems quite dubious. Dio says that C. Carbo won those *insignia* for his prosecution of Cotta's quaestor Oppius, and implies that was what caused Cotta's son to launch a counterprosecution (36.40.3–4). The main thing Carbo seems to have done to M. Cotta himself was to express a *sententia* that led to this consular's expulsion from Senate: see Memn. 39.3.

308. *Decem legati*: *MRR* II 129. Reforms: App. *Mith.* 83.376 (Lucullus' expectation that the war was over), Plu. *Luc.* 20.1–3, Cic. *Luc.* 3. Opposition in Rome: Plu. *Luc.* 20.4–5. Asia declared praetorian: D.C. 36.2.2 (alleging Lucullus' footdragging as reason). Assessments of precisely how large a role the *publicani* played in all this vary: see Keaveney, *Lucullus* 95–98 (the reforms themselves), 114–115 with 236 n. 31 (removal of Asia).

309. Plu. *Luc.* 23.7, also Cic. *Man.* 12.

310. In 68, Lucullus' *legatus* C. Valerius Triarius at least passed through Asia with an army on his way from Delos to Pontus: D.C. 36.10.1, cf. App. *Mith.* 88.400 and *I. Délos* IV 1 1621, 1855–1858.

311. Cf. Cic. *Prov.* 38 "quod multari imperatorem deminutione provinciae contumeliosum est."

312. Q. Marcius Rex set out for the east only in 67 (see Sal. *Hist.* 5.14 M), and was "relieved before his time of command had expired" (D.C. 36.43.1) by Pompey in 66 (see

immediately below in text). So he had less than a full year of command in Cilicia. In 67, Appian (*Mith.* 90.411) tells us that ὁ τῆς Ἀσίας στρατηγός sent heralds to order the dismissal of Lucullus' troops. This is obviously not an actual praetor for Asia, but the *cos.* M.' Acilius Glabrio (cf. Cic. *Man.* 26 and *Schol. Gron.* p. 321 St.), whom Appian never mentions by name. For further discussion of the error see Keaveney, *Lucullus* 238 n. 43. Acilius, too, had less than a full year in the east (D.C. 36.43.1).

313. Pompey's *legatus* L. Lollius had the eastern Aegean and Hellespont (App. *Mith.* 95.436). M. Pupius Piso Frugi Calpurnianus (the future *cos.* 61) is said to have had charge of the Propontis and the Bosporus (App. *Mith.* 95.436), but he is attested at Samos (*IGRP* IV 1709) and Miletus (*Milet.* I 3 393 no. 173), in the latter case certainly as just "legatus" with no indication of *imperium* (though he must have had it). And Q. Caecilius Metellus Nepos (the future *cos.* 60) received as his territory "Lycia, Pamphylia, Cyprus, Phoenicia," according to Appian (*Mith.* 95.436), but "Aegean, Pontic, and Pamphylian" waters, by Florus' account (1.41.10)—obviously somewhat different. On some of Florus' other dubious assertions connected with Pompey's subordinates in his pirate command, see *MRR* II 149, III 160. On the possibility that L. Manlius Torquatus (*cos.* 65) was a *legatus* against the pirates see *MRR* II 151 n. 16 with n. 298 above.

314. On the city praetorship, see 12.1.2. For Dolabella's *ex praetura* command in Asia, see esp. *IGRP* IV 422 (honored as *pro cos.* at Pergamum) and cf. V. Max. 8.1 amb. 2 (legal activities as *pro cos.* at Smyrna). Magie, *Roman Rule* II 1127 n. 47, assigns his arrival in Asia to 68. For further references and discussion see *MRR* II 139 with 142 n. 9.

315. Broughton (*MRR* II 142 n. 9 with III 215), in discussing the order of commanders for Asia in the mid-60s, need not have taken into consideration L. Manlius Torquatus (*pr.* by 68 and *cos.* 65)—see n. 298 above.

316. Explicit in Cic. *Flac.* 100.

317. See V. Max. 6.9.7 (former *publicanus*), Cic. *Flac.* 45 (directly preceded Varinius); cf. *Att.* 1.1.1 on his consular candidacy.

318. See Broughton in *MRR* II 142 n. 9. On the phenomenon of praetorian iteration in general, see T. C. Brennan, *Athenaeum* 67 (1989) 467–487, esp. 480f on P. Cornelius Lentulus Sura (*pr.* 74, *cos.* 71, *pr.* II 63), who provides a good parallel for what Broughton has postulated.

319. Orbius and Globulus each make decisions at law concerning Decianus: Cic. *Flac.* 76 and esp. 79 (showing, as if proof were needed, that each preceded Flaccus in Asia). On Orbius, see Cic. *Brut.* 178 with 179 "P. Orbius meus fere aequalis." Globulus as direct predecessor of Flaccus: *Flac.* 85 with *Schol. Bob.* p. 107 St. (the latter terming him Flaccus' *decessor*), cf. *Flac.* 91. For Globulus' tribunate, see *MRR* II 145, and praetorship, II 162. (An interval of a single year between tribunate and praetorship was perfectly common in this period: ch. 11 n. 29.) Command in Asia: II 170. There is no compelling reason to identify P. Globulus with the *pro cos.* P. Servilius P.f. "Galka" of J. *AJ* 14.244 (see Broughton, *MRR* II 172 n. 2, though not realizing that ἀνθύπατος indeed would be the expected title for a governor of Asia; also Münzer, *RE* s.v. col. 1798). The fact that Globulus and "Galka" each is said to have been active at Tralles (Cic. *Flac.* 91, J. *AJ* 14.245) is hardly surprising, given that it was a regular stop on the legal circuit of praetors for Asia (cf. Cic. *Flac.* 71, Q. *fr.* 1.1.17).

320. For the city *provincia*, see *MRR* III 37 and 212 citing Cic. *Flac.* 6 and 100. Filiation positively attested in Tuchelt, *Frühe Denkmäler* I 164 (Claros) (on which see *MRR* III 212), and *I. Magn.* 144–146 (definitely to be attributed to this praetor, despite Broughton's hesitation in *MRR* II 178 n. 2).

321. Cic. *Q. fr.* 1.1.40.

322. See *Q. fr.* 1.1.25 (a summary of Quintus Cicero's achievements in province); *Flac.* 17 (famine).

323. Macr. 2.1.13. Full sources on the trial (and discussion of date) are collected in Alexander, *Trials* no. 247. Trial's lateness due to political factors: S.I. Oost, *AJPh* 77 (1956) 28. Flaccus' family: see esp. *Flac.* 25, 40, 81 "nobilissima familia natum," 106. Flaccus a hero as *pr. urb.* 63 in the Catilinarian affair: *Flac.* 1, 4–6, 94–96, 98–99, 101, 103–104. Sinister domestic forces behind prosecution: 13–15. Unreliability of the Asian witnesses: 3, 7–12, 16–20, 51, 60–61 (a scathing attack on Asia's conduct during the First Mithridatic War), 64–65, 100, cf. 62–63 (superiority of testimony by respectable Greeks from Old Greece and Massilia); see also the comment of *Schol. Bob.* p. 94 St., how Cicero purposely avoids "Asiam provinciam" in speech, but instead substitutes "Lydos . . . Mysos . . . Frygas" (best seen at *Flac.* 3, 65, and 100). Cicero in his speech also alleges improprieties in the present legal procedure (21–23) and even the possibility that Flaccus' condemnation will wreck the *cursus honorum* (105–106). One suspects Cicero might have offered even more on Flaccus' urban praetorship of 63, but Hortensius in his defense speech seems to have concentrated on that (ch. 12 n. 101).

324. Cic. *Flac.* 6 "is qui anno ante Romae ius dixerat anno post in Asia ius dixerit"; also 100 "Asiaticae iuris dictioni urbana iuris dictio respondebit."

325. Criminal justice at Cyme (*Flac.* 17), Temnos (45–49 and probably 43), and against various freedmen (88); a civil decision (reversing those of his predecessor P. Globulus) against Appuleius Decianus (70–83); and his own entrance into the inheritance of a Valeria (84–89 with *Schol. Bob.* p. 107 St.). On that last item, see C. Macdonald in the Loeb edition p. xxxviii on *Flac.* 86, for Cicero's previous (contrary) views on the propriety of a Roman official conducting his own business in his province.

326. See Cic. *Flac.* 27–33 and *Schol. Bob.* p. 100 St., which set out the central issues, with the exegesis of R. O. Jolliffe, "Phases of Corruption in Roman Administration in the Last Half-Century of the Roman Republic" (diss. Chicago 1919) 35–37; also Shatzman, *Senatorial Wealth* 427f no. 213. On M. Crassus' presence in the east, see Plu. *Pomp.* 43.2.

327. He forbade by edict the Jews of his province from exporting the poll tax of two drachmas to the Temple in Jerusalem, and seized gold at several major towns in Asia: *Flac.* 66–69 with Magie, *Roman Rule* II 1244 n. 10. He recovered—apparently for his own purse—common funds deposited at Tralles (52–59 with 14.5.7 above). He allegedly extorted fifty talents from a *publicanus* for the right to collect the revenues of that city (90–93). He allegedly accepted bribes from Dorylaeum in north Phrygia (39–41) and Temnos (42–44, where Cicero offers a particularly halfhearted defense). He exerted pressure on Acmona to give him a forged *laudatio*: *Flac.* 34–38 (which Cicero tries to disprove on forensic grounds!).

328. *Flac.* 7, 41, 83, 85 (cf.), 89, 98 (cf.), and (confirming the accuracy of the charge) *Q. fr.* 1.1.40 (end of 60). However, the prosecution no doubt put forward a wider range of allegations in its own speeches, including murder, it seems (cf. *Flac.* 41), and—at the time of the trial itself— corruption of witnesses (81–83).

329. Flaccus as "praetor": Cic. *Flac.* 6, 31, 43 (and cf. also Caes. *Civ.* 3.53), but also *Flac.* 18 "qui nuper summo cum imperio fuerit." For his title *pro cos.*, see Tuchelt, *Frühe Denkmäler* I 164 (from Claros; the reference to ancestral benefits [διὰ προγόνων] surely signals an honor not to the *cos. suff.* 86 but to his son); *I. Magn.* 144–146. The surface discrepancy between the literary and epigraphic testimony on Flaccus' status in Asia confused Broughton: see *MRR* II 178 n. 2 (in the inscriptions from Magnesia, "the title may be an error"), cf. III 212.

330. Cic. *Flac.* 85 "L. Luculle, qui de L. Flacco sententiam laturus es . . . cum Asiam provinciam consulari imperio obtineres." On this mode of flattery, see 13.2.2 on C. Claudius Marcellus, *pr.* 80 and afterwards *pro cos.* for Sicily, as juror in Verres' trial of 70 B.C.

331. Cicero's reticence about the Asian command even in extended passages of praise is well illustrated by *Flac.* 8 (which contains the phrase "iustissimus praetor") and 101. In this

oration there is precisely one (passing) reference to Flaccus' *innocentia* (64). Difficulty of popularity in province: *Flac.* 87 with 18–19. Not for Greeks to say whether Flaccus had abused his *imperium*: 27. Flaccus terrified (but did not fight) the pirates: 31. Q. Cicero reverses Flaccus: 33 with *Schol. Bob.* p. 100.

332. Cic. *Att.* 1.15.1. For a detailed exposition of this command (with full citation of the evidence, literary and epigraphic), see A. H. Mamoojee, *EMC* 13 (1994) 23–50; cf. also E. Fallu, *REL* 48 (1970) 180–204, esp. 182–188.

333. Cic. Q. *fr.* 1.1.2.

334. Thus, rightly, *MRR* III 115.

335. On the quip, see Nep. *Att.* 6.4. For the feud (defused by Quintus' apology), see Cic. *Att.* 1.17.1–2 (5 Dec. 61); 1.19.11 (15 Mar. 60).

336. Well attested from any number of Cicero's *Letters*. To take an instance simply from a provincial context, see Cic. *Att.* 6.6.4 with *Fam.* 2.15.4 (from his Cilician command in 50).

337. Anger: Cic. Q. *fr.* 1.1.37–40. News from Asia travels quickly: 1.1.9, 42. Cf. 1.1.4–7, 27, where Cicero explains that Asia is a peaceful *provincia*, filled not with warlike barbarians but with civilized peoples (not-so-subtly hinting that Quintus should act accordingly).

338. See particularly Cic. Q. *fr.* 1.1.43–44.

339. On the title, a dedication of Colophon to Q. Cicero as *pro cos.* in Asia (see *Bull. épig.* 1958 no. 390; M. Mellink, *AJA* 62 [1958] 98f) gives his filiation (obviously not in doubt). For Quintus as *pro cos.*, see also Cic. *Div.* 1.58, Suet. *Aug.* 3.2. M. Cicero himself dispenses with a title in the letters which he addresses to his brother during his Asian command (see Q. *fr.* 1.1–4 prescripts).

340. Cic. Q. *fr.* 1.1.1–2, cf. 3 (unlikely possibility of a fourth year), 19, 30, 46. The thesis of E. Fallu (*REL* 48 [1970] 180–204), that M. Cicero composed Q. *fr.* 1.1 in response to specific provisions expected in the *cos.* 59 Caesar's impending legislation *de repetundis*, seems dubious, especially in the subsequent light of *I. Knidos* I 31 Kn. III lines 9–15 (provisions regarding a magistrate's *comites*), on which see ch. 13 n. 43.

341. Open favoritism in giving law (Q. *fr.* 1.2.10–11). Exceedingly harsh letters threatening criminal prosecution, sometimes not even taking the care to write them personally (Q. *fr.* 1.2.6–8, 13). Brutal judicial decisions (see esp. 1.2.4–5 for his punishment of parricides at Smyrna). For an enumeration of Quintus' enemies (many) in the province, see A. H. Mamoojee, *EMC* 13 (1994) 40–46. On the importance of perceptions in the last year in one's *provincia*, see 1.1.12, 46; and in general, see Hirt. *Gal.* 8.49.2–3.

342. He has to remind Quintus there were dangers inherent in assuming honors (albeit legitimate) that might be perceived as excessive (see Q. *fr.* 1.1.26 and 31, and cf. Macr. 2.3.4, also *Bull. épig.* 1958 no. 390). Quintus for his part was vigilant in blocking honors to others (Q. *fr.* 1.2.14). Cicero also considered his brother's *libertus* Statius an all-too-influential member of his staff (1.2.1–3, cf. 8). Most seriously, Cicero points out that by late 59, Quintus had created a massive "paper trail" in his province (which he urges him to destroy as best he can) (1.2.8–9). He carelessly sent some inappropriate documents to Rome, too (*Att.* 2.16.4, May 59).

343. Cic. Q. *fr.* 1.1.40.

344. To 61 or 60 belong Quintus' trials of Paconius and Tuscenius—who went on to complain at Rome (Q. *fr.* 1.1.19).

345. Cic. *Flac.* 49 (a new trial for Heracleides of Temnos); cf. Q. *fr.* 1.1.10 on Gratitidus.

346. Cic. *Flac.* 33 with *Schol. Bob.* p. 100 St. (Quintus decides on a "just-in-time" policy for collecting an allied fleet).

347. Cic. Q. *fr.* 1.1.25–26.

348. Sources on the Asian "rebate" are collected in *MRR* II 183 (the year 60) and 188 (Caesar as *cos.* 59 grants the *publicani* a remission of one-third of their bid). Cicero in his extant correspondence to his brother goes no further than to describe the difficulty the Asian *publicani* had turning a profit from the province by late 60 (*Q. fr.* 1.1.33). For Cicero's more general advice on this topic, see 1.1.6–7, 32 (pointing up complexity), 34–35, also 36 (Quintus' satisfactory reputation). Quintus backed Terentia in dispute with *publicani*: *Att.* 2.15.4 (Apr. 59). Cicero in late 59 strongly criticized Quintus for a vehement letter he wrote regarding the *publicanus* Licinius (*Q. fr.* 1.2.6).

349. See *Q. fr.* 1.1.41.

350. Possibilities of corruption: *Q. fr.* 1.1.8, 19. General qualities of praetor in hearing law, of which accessibility and impartiality are especially important: 1.1.20–24 (esp. 1.21, citing C. Octavius in Macedonia as a paradigm). Vicarious liability for junior officers and staff: 1.1.10–14, 17. How to deal with *publicani*: see references in n. 348 above. Dangers from private individuals—citizen and noncitizen—in province: 1.1.15–16.

351. Cic. *Q. fr.* 1.2.8.

352. Cic. *Att.* 3.8.1 with 2–4 (29 May 58), 3.9.1 (13 June 58), *Q. fr.* 1.3.1, 4–5, and 8 (13 June 58).

353. *Q. fr.* 1.4.2 and 4–5 (early Aug. 58), *Att.* 3.13.2 (5 Aug. 58), cf. *Dom.* 59 and *Sest.* 68.

354. *Att.* 3.17.1 (4 Sept. 58). One assumes Ap. Pulcher had received the *repetundae* court, but Cicero, for all his worrying, never spells out the precise charge he feared his brother might face.

355. See the discussion in Alexander, *Trials* no. 263. For his later consular ambitions (first detected for the elections for 53), see T. P. Wiseman, *JRS* 56 (1966) 108–115.

356. Cic. *Att.* 2.6.2 (Apr. 59), 16.4 (May 59).

357. Ampius' coins: Stumpf, *Numismatische Studien* 17–23 nos. 4–20, all of which give his filiation. Chronology of first issue: see Cic. *Att.* 3.9.1 (indicating a departure date for Quintus in late Apr. 58) with Stumpf p. 22 (dating Ampius' nos. 4–5 to "24 January–23 March 58"). Terminus: see Stumpf p. 22 on Ampius' no. 11.

358. *Fam.* 3.7.5, confirmed by 1.3.2.

359. See, e.g., Broughton, *MRR* II 197 and cf. 202, where he omits Ampius from the list of promagistrates for 57.

360. See Cic. *Dom.* 23–24 with R. Syme, *CPh* 50 (1955) 130, an explanation tentatively accepted in *MRR* III 15. For Ampius' lack of real influence, cf. *Schol. Bob.* p. 156 St. on Cic. *Planc.* 25 (he was a luckless candidate for *cos.* 54, despite Pompey's backing). On this transfer, see further 15.1.2. Pompey and Cicero supported Ampius when he was prosecuted at some point after his promagistracy (sources in Alexander, *Trials* no. 281), perhaps in 55 (for *ambitus?*). But the date and details of the charge are actually quite uncertain.

361. Fabius' coins: Stumpf, *Numismatische Studien* 23–28 nos. 21–33, which give the filiation; his Ephesian issues are nos. 23–25. Chronology of command: see Stumpf no. 25 (dated to "Year 78" of the provincial era, i.e., after 24 Sept. 57) with no. 34, a coin his successor C. Septimius issued in the latter six months of "Year 78" (see n. 364 with text below).

362. See Stumpf, *Numismatische Studien* 26 n. 61.

363. City praetorship: Cic. *Red. Sen.* 22–23. Coins: Stumpf, *Numismatische Studien* 28–31 nos. 34–42, which give filiation.

364. Stumpf, *Numismatische Studien* nos. 34–36; on the Ephesian colleges of moneyers at this time, see p. 27 with 31, and cf. p. 22.

365. D.C. 39.21.2.

366. Stumpf, *Numismatische Studien* 31–35 nos. 43–56; his Ephesus issues are nos. 44–47 (showing filiation).

367. Cic. *Scaur.* 35, where he says Claudius was prorogued a second time "by the prayers of all the province." On his first prorogation (i.e., through 54) cf. *Att.* 4.15.2. For honors to Claudius (with no title) at Pergamum that surely date to this command, see *IGRP* IV 417 = Tuchelt, *Frühe Denkmäler* I 200, and cf. *MRR* III 232 (with faulty reference).

368. Supersession after one year: Ap. Claudius Pulcher (Sardinia), C. Septimius (Asia), and probably Sex. Quinctilius Varus (Hispania Ulterior). We cannot determine the length of command for Q. Valerius Orca (Africa), and C. Caecilius Cornutus (Bithynia).

369. Cic. *Scaur.* 31–36 *passim.*

370. See Cic. *Fam.* 2.6.1 (Curio's presence in Asia in 53) and *Phil.* 2.4 (not yet returned by the date of Cicero's election to the augurate) with extensive discussion by J. Linderski, *Roman Questions: Selected Papers* (Stuttgart 1995) 231–250, esp. 234–235 for the (putative) quaestorship.

371. Alexander, *Trials* no. 336 (over by October 51).

372. Title "pro pr.": Cic. *Fam.* 13.53, 54, 55, 56, 57 prescripts. Praetorian status: clear especially from *Fam.* 13.55.2. Charge of the *provincia*: see *Fam.* 13.56.1, and all of *Fam.* 2.18.

373. Cic. *Att.* 5.13.2, *Fam.* 2.18. See 11.1.7 above for his arrangements on departure.

374. *MRR* II 238.

375. *Monetalis*: *RRC* I 324 no. 319, dated by M. Crawford to 103 B.C. The *consilium*: *ILLRP* 515. Senator by 73: note the Q. Minucius Q.f. Ter. Thermus in twelfth position in the senatorial *consilium* of *RDGE* 23 (four places below M. Tullius Cicero, *q.* 75). Tribunate of 62: *MRR* II 174. F. X. Ryan, in *ZPE* 108 (1995) 307–308, seeks to dissociate the *consilium* member and tribune: but on that see n. 376 immediately below.

376. F. X. Ryan, in *AJPh* 115 (1994) 595–599, argues that Q. Thermus was sent to govern Asia while still a *tribunicius*, and reached the praetorship only for 49 B.C. (on the strength of Caes. *Civ.* 1.12.1 "Iguvium Thermum praetorem . . . tenere"). Elsewhere (*AClass* 65 [1996] 241 n. 7), he seeks to build on this hypothesis, arguing that in the late 50s the Romans employed as provincial governors "men of less than praetorian rank." But the Thermus at Iguvium can very well be a (younger) brother of the Asian commander, or a more distant relation: cf. Cic. *Flac.* 98 (delivered 59 B.C.) with Appendix B n. 323 for the existence of a prominent A. Thermus in this era. It seems quite unlikely that Q. Thermus (who after all was from an established noble *gens*) will have taken thirteen years to advance from tribunate to praetorship—and have held a major territorial *provincia* in the meantime.

377. Cic. *Fam.* 13.55.2, cf. his remarks at *Att.* 6.1.13.

378. *Fam.* 13.53.2, 54, 55.1, 56.3.

Notes to Chapter 15

1. Sources in *MRR* II 80, 84 (accepting prorogation for this man into 79). On his career ("an ex-Marian" and "a late converter" to the Sullan side), see E. S. Gruen, *AJPh* 87 (1966) 389–399.

2. Death of quaestor: Cic. *Ver.* 2.1.41. Verres appointed *pro quaestore* in his place: 2.1.41, 77 with Ps.-Asc. pp. 208 and 234 St., *Schol. Gron.* p. 333 St. Verres in Bithynia and Thrace: *Ver.* 2.1.63. Dolabella absents *provincia* for Asia: 2.1.73.

3. See Ps.-Asc. p. 208, *Schol. Gron.* pp. 325 and 333 St. against Cic. *Ver.* 2.1.99; cf. 96. On his prosecution, see the sources in M. C. Alexander, *Trials in the Late Roman Republic* (Toronto 1990) no. 135; the *litis aestimatio* was 3 million sesterces (2.1.95, a passage that also nicely describes the geographical stretch of Roman Cilicia at this time). We have no date for the trial, but it was probably soon after his return, to judge from Cicero's statement (2.1.77) that Verres—a hostile witness at the trial—wanted his superior in exile before his own accounts were examined. Dolabella later appears in Juvenal as a byword for corruption

(8.105–7, obviously drawing on the *Verrines*). Cicero says an unscrupulous commander could make much money from requisitions in Cilicia at this time (2.3.211 "innumerabilem pecuniam"). But Dolabella was charged with stealing while in transit too (2.1.45, thefts at Athens).

4. *Comp. Lys. and Sulla* 2.4.

5. Thus E. S. Gruen, *AJPh* 87 (1966) 386 n. 4.

6. In rough chronological order of events, Flor. 1.41.4–5; D.C. 36.17.2; Cic. *Fam.* 1.7.4, 3.5.3, 9.25.1; and *Att.* 5.11.4, 6.8.4.

7. *Pomp.* 25.2 and *Moralia* 779 A.

8. On the several grounds for *inimicitia* between the younger Cn. Dolabella and Sulla—existing well before the Civil War—see E. S. Gruen, *AJPh* 87 (1966) 389–398; cf. E. Badian, *PBSR* 33 (1965) 49.

9. It was definitely a command *ex consulatu* (Eutrop. 6.3, Oros. 5.23.21, Ruf. Fest. *Brev.* 11.1 and 12.2, cf. *Per.* 90); see Suet. *Jul.* 3 with Sal. *Hist.* 1.127 M for the chronology of Servilius' arrival. For the "quinquennium," see Cic. *Ver.* 2.3.211; cf. Oros. 5.23.22 (inaccurately referring to a *triennium*). For his triumph (probably in 74), see Degrassi, *Inscr. Ital.* XIII 1 564. In addition to his military activities, Servilius found time to hold routine assizes in the *provincia* (cf. Cic. *Att.* 6.1.16).

10. Pompey's additions: App. *Mith.* 106.499. For Marcius, cf. 11.8.9 (he must have died soon after his activities *cum imperio* at Faesulae in late 63).

11. On all this, see 14.6.8, esp. ch. 14 n. 357 on Ampius' coin issues in Asia. For the lateral transfer, see Cic. *Dom.* 23 (to Clodius) "mutasti pactionem et Ciliciam ad praetorem item extra ordinem transtulisti." Contra the doubts of E. Badian (*JRS* 55 [1965] 118 with n. 61, arguing that "'praetor' . . . in this context . . . must refer to a praetor of 58"), see D. R. Shackleton Bailey, *CEF* I 372 (at *Dom.* 23 "praetorem" stands for a prorogued praetor). We have for Ampius just one attested action in Cilicia before supersession (*Fam.* 1.3.2—he issued a *decretum* favorable to the *negotiator* A. Trebonius). For a commander to meet his successor was considered a special compliment: see ch. 13 n. 361.

12. Phrygia: G. R. Stumpf, *Numismatische Studien zur Chronologie der römischen Statthalter in Kleinasien (122 v. Chr.–163 n. Chr.)* (Saarbrücken 1991) p. 49. Cyprus: Cic. *Fam.* 1.7.4. The numismatic evidence for Lentulus' tenure is collected by Stumpf, *Numismatische Studien* 46–51 nos. 71–79 (itself suggesting a command from 57/56 to late 54). For the coins of Ap. Pulcher, see Stumpf nos. 80–88, and for Cicero, nos. 89–93. Cicero's date of entry and departure: see esp. *Att.* 5.21.9, 6.2.6, and (now representing 30 July 50 as a mandate!) 6.3.1. All these ex-consuls received imperatorial acclamations soon after their arrival in Cilicia: see ch. 14 n. 68. For Appius' self-enrichment in the province, see I. Shatzman, *Senatorial Wealth and Roman Politics* (Brussels 1975) 321–323 no. 115; for Cicero's, ibid. p. 413. Appius upon his return had to give up his claim to a triumph (Cic. *Fam.* 3.10.1); for his unsuccessful prosecution in 50 for *maiestas* and *ambitus* by P. Cornelius Dolabella (now Cicero's son-in-law), see Alexander, *Trials* nos. 344 and 345.

13. See Cic. *Fam.* 3.7.5 (Ampius, Lentulus Spinther, and Ap. Pulcher); also (for Cicero and Ap. Pulcher) *Att.* 5.16.4, 5.17.6, *Fam.* 3.6.3–5. For Appius' false claim of delegation to Q. Mucius Scaevola, see *Fam.* 3.5.5 (27 July 51).

14. See Cic. *Fam.* 2.15.4, *Att.* 6.6.3–4, 7.1.6; for the likelihood he had *imperium*, cf. *Att.* 6.4.1 (soon after 5 June 50) "de Coelio nihil audiebamus. rectissimum videbatur Quintum fratrem cum imperio relinquere." For an extended and detailed discussion of Cicero's deliberations on this matter, see A. J. Marshall, *ANRW* I 1 (1972) 887–921.

15. For that last item, see Cic. *Att.* 13.49.1 with ch. 11 n. 438; there is no reason to associate this man with the "Sextus" of App. *BC* 2.24.90 who was condemned and had to go into exile in 52.

16. In *RDGE* 27, the *S.C. de Panamara* of 39 B.C. (which provides filiation), he is listed second in the *consilium*, i.e., in a position consistent with that of a *praetorius*.

17. Cic. *Att.* 8.15.3.

18. Plu. *Brut.* 4.3; Cic. *Fam.* 5.20.5.

19. See Caes. *Civ.* 1.6.5–6.

20. On this, see in general E. Badian, *ZPE* 55 (1984) 106 with n. 10 (pointing out that as quaestor in 63, Sestius must have been born by 94). Our praetorian *fasti* for none of these years are completely full.

21. E. Badian, "Notes on *Provincia Gallia* in the Late Republic," in R. Chevallier (ed.), *Mélanges d'archéologie et d'histoire offerts à André Piganiol* II (Paris 1966) 909–917. For an overview of Cisalpina Gaul as a *provincia* in this period, see U. Laffi, *Athenaeum* 80 [70] (1992) 5–14.

22. Gran. Lic. 36.38, Sal. *Hist.* 1.66 M.

23. Lepidus allotted Transalpina as *cos.* 78: App. *BC* 1.107.502. Lepidus' control of Cisalpina attested for 77: Plu. *Pomp.* 16.2, *Per.* 90.

24. For Lepidus' expedition "in <m>ontes," see Gran. Lic. 36.39 C, cf. 40–41 C (unfortunately quite corrupt). Ready parallels for Cisalpine triumph hunting are provided by L. Licinius Crassus as *cos.* 95 (Cic. *Inv.* 2.111, *Pis.* 62), and C. Aurelius Cotta (*cos.* 75) in 74 (*Pis.* 62).

25. On M. Iunius Brutus, who held Cisalpine Gaul for M. Lepidus in 77 (Plu. *Pomp.* 16.2, *Per.* 90 "qui Cisalpinam Galliam obtinebat"), Broughton (*MRR* III 112) offers that the *Periocha* passage "might suggest an independent command." But *obtinere* can be used of a subordinate: see 13.4.7 above. For other *legati* under Lepidus in 77, see Sal. *Hist.* 1.77.7 M (Philippus' speech) "nunc est pro consule cum imperio . . . cum legatis adhuc iure parentibus."

26. See Cic. *Clu.* 99 with Badian, *Mélanges Piganiol* II 912–913, esp. 913 n. 3.

27. See Alexander, *Trials* no. 186, and (for the *equites*) Cic. *Font.* 11, 12, 46. The terminus ante quem comes from the fact that Pompey was a witness for the defendant; see also Cic. *Att.* 1.6.1 (if the reading "M. Fonteius" is correct, the passage suggests that his trial was resolved by 27 Nov. 68). In support of the year 69 for the *Pro Fonteio*, see F. X. Ryan, *Philologus* 140 (1996) 351–352.

28. Var. *R* 1.7.8; cf. 1.3.1 with P. A. Brunt, *CR* 22 (1972) 304–305 (the passage suggests Scrofa was born ca. 120–117). See the views of G. Perl, *AJAH* 5 (1980) 97–109, on Cn. Scrofa's identity, descent, and general date. As summarized by Broughton in *MRR* III 207f, he was "praetor ca. 77, or perhaps 72, dates which would allow his command in Transalpine Gaul to be dated either before or after M. Fonteius." But on my reconstruction he can only be dated before Fonteius if he preceded Cn. Manlius as well, and so if he was *pr.* in 80 (there is no room for him in the *fasti* for 81).

29. Cic. *Pis.* 62, Asc. p. 14 C.

30. See Strab. 5.1.6 p. 213. I owe thanks to Prof. J. D. Morgan for bringing this passage to my attention, and suggesting (*per litteras*) that C. Scipio is "a missing praetor," rightly doubting the *praenomen* as transmitted ("presumably this is an error for 'Cnaeus Scipio'"). A glance at the relevant indices in *MRR* II (pp. 555–556) shows there are any number of possibilities for descent; in this connection, one should remember also the (Cornelius) Scipio who was a praetor in Sicily sometime before 91 (Cic. *de Orat.* 2.280). For Caesar's colony at Comum, see E. G. Hardy, *Some Problems in Roman History* (Oxford 1924) 126–149.

31. See 13.4.6 with Badian, *Mélanges Piganiol* II 913 n. 4.

32. Cic. *Font.* 33. On the political background to the trial, see the basic bibliography gathered in C. Ebel, *Phoenix* 29 (1975) 367 n. 38.

33. Gallic witnesses: *Font.* 21, 27, 33, 36. Cicero on Gauls in general: see esp. *Font.* 30–31. Fonteius' (praetorian) family: *Font.* 41, 46–47, 49. Cicero evokes sack: *Font.* 49.

34. Levies and requisitions: *Font.* 13, 16. Campaigns: *Font.* 12–13 (resulting in confiscations of land), 20, 26, 36, 46, 49; there is much in these passages on the military dangers of the *provincia.* Roadbuilding: *Font.* 17–18. See further 13.4.4.

35. Resistance to requisitions: *Font.* 17, 26–27. Credit problems: *Font.* 11–12, and see 19–20 on the *portorium vini,* perhaps a special war tax associated with the Sertorian War, to judge from the involvement of Pompey's legate Titurius in its collection (13.4.4).

36. Massilia and Narbo: *Font.* 13, 14, 45–46. Roman citizens: *Font.* 15, 46; on this group, see the comments of Badian, *Mélanges Piganiol* II 909.

37. D.C. 36.37.2 εὐθύς γ᾽ ἂν αὐτὸν ἐκ τῆς ἀρχῆς ἐξήλασαν. The word ἀρχή in the sense of a territorial *provincia* is common enough in Dio: see 36.2.2, 39.55.5 and 56.5, 40.51.2; cf. also 38.10.2 ἐκ . . . τῆς χώρας . . . ἐξήλασαν and 16.4 ἐκ τῆς πόλεως ἐξήλασε.

38. Cic. *Att.* 1.13.2.

39. Cicero visits Piso in Cisalpina: *Att.* 1.1.2 (July 65), and cf. Suet. *Jul.* 8 (Transpadane agitation in early 67) with D.C. 37.9.3 (the censors of 65). Prosecution: Alexander, *Trials* no. 225 (he was acquitted).

40. For L. Murena's *ex praetura* province, see especially Cic. *Mur.* 89 (explicit, and attesting the presence of his brother there in Nov. 63). Levy in Umbria and attention to *negotiatores* in Gaul: *Mur.* 42; cf., however, *Har.* 42 for the alleged actions of P. Clodius while on the staff of this governor (his brother-in-law). C. Murena's criminal jurisdiction: Sal. *Cat.* 42.1 with the discussion of Badian, *Mélanges Piganiol* II 914–916, esp. 916; the emendation is accepted by (among others) A. L. F. Rivet, *Gallia Narbonensis* (London 1988) 71 n. 62.

41. See Cic. *Catil.* 3.5–6 and 14, *Flac.* 102 and Sal. *Cat.* 45.1–4 (adding that Pomptinus was an acquaintance of the conspirator Volturcius) with Badian, *Mélanges Piganiol* II 917 n. 1.

42. Pomptinus' single legion: cf. Caes. *Gal.* 1.7.1. Defeat of the Aedui: Caes. *Gal.* 1.35.4 (special orders to Pomptinus, not mentioned by name here), 44.9. Movement of Helvetii: Caes. *Gal.* 1.2.1–5 (esp. 2.1 for date of Helvetian revolt). Defeat of Allobroges: Caes. *Gal.* 1.6.2, 44.9, 7.64.7; also Cic. *Prov.* 32, D.C. 37.47.1–48.2 (esp. 48.1 for the apparent independence of Pomptinus' *legati*), *Per.* 103. On the geography of this campaign, see Rivet, *Gallia Narbonensis* 61–63. S.C. of March 60: Cic. *Att.* 1.19.2–3. Metellus Celer's reaction: *Att.* 1.20.5 (May 60).

43. Flavius' threat: D.C. 37.50.4. Celer's departure still expected in April 59: Cic. *Att.* 2.5.2. His death: *Cael.* 59, *Sest.* 131.

44. The sources for the *lex Vatinia* (by July—see Cic. *Att.* 2.18) and the S.C. (on Pompey's motion) that added Transalpine Gaul to Caesar's *provincia* in 59 are collected in *MRR* II 188 and 190. For sources on the extension of 55 B.C., see *MRR* II 215.

45. Pomptinus' *supplicatio:* Cic. *Vat.* 30 with *Schol. Bob.* pp. 149–150 St.

46. See *Fam.* 3.9.4 and 15.4 for Cicero's *supplicatio* strategy. On the delay of *supplicationes,* cf. Cael. *Fam.* 8.11.1 (discussion in Apr. 50 of pushing off Cicero's *supplicatio* into next year).

47. M. Gelzer, *Caesar: Politician and Statesman,* trans. P. Needham (Oxford 1969) 85f. On Arrius' tentative candidacy for the consulship of 58, see ch. 11 n. 382.

48. On Pomptinus and his triumph, see Cic. *Pis.* 58 (mentioned while outside the walls in late summer 55), and in particular D.C. 39.65.1–2, Cic. *Att.* 4.18.4 (with D. R. Shackleton Bailey, *CLA* II 223), and *Q. fr.* 3.4.6.

49. The war of 61–60 as the last serious revolt: Rivet, *Gallia Narbonensis* 63. See n. 42 above for Caesar's references to the events of Pomptinus' command (but not the commander himself).

50. After causing Cicero much anxiety and some delay in late May and June 51 (Cic. *Att.* 5.1.5, 4.2, 5.1, 6.1, *Fam.* 3.3.2, *Att.* 5.10.1), Pomptinus finally joined the *pro cos.* at Athens in early July (*Att.* 5.11.4). Pomptinus' importance at the crucial battle at Amanus comes over clearly in *Att.* 5.20.3; cf. *Fam.* 15.4.8–9. Pomptinus was to leave Cilicia quite early, by early May 50 (*Fam.* 3.10.3). For his entry in the city, see *Att.* 7.7.3 (written between 18 and 21 Dec. 50). Pomptinus plainly knew the value of his presence as a praetorian and *triumphator* on Cicero's staff.

51. There is one *consularis*, his distant cousin L. Iulius Caesar (*Gal.* 7.65.1), who shows up in charge of Gallia Transalpina in 52. *Praetorii*: T. Labienus, a *pr.* by 59 (see text below) and *legatus* in the years 58–50; Q. Tullius Cicero (*pr.* 62, and *legatus* in Gaul 54–52); and two *legati* attested for 51, Q. Fufius Calenus (*pr.* 59) and P. Vatinius (*pr.* 55).

52. A selective list: Caes. *Gal.* 2.34 (P. Crassus' subjection of the maritime states of Gaul with a single legion), cf. 8.46.1; 3.1.1–3 and 6.4–5 (Ser. Galba with one legion ordered to open up the route over the Alps); 3.23 (P. Crassus on advice of *consilium* decides on instant action against the Vocates and Tarusates); 7.5.1–7 (*legati* give independent advice to the Aedui); and Hirt. *Gal.* 8.26.1–4 and 36.1–6 (the movements of C. Caninius, albeit with a small force). Instances of initiative or independent decisions by T. Labienus are common: see *Gal.* 5.57.1–4, 6.7.1–2, 6.8.8 (promoting Cingetorix to the leadership of the Treveri), 7.59.1–6, and esp. Hirt. *Gal.* 8.23.1–6 (an episode of 52/51 omitted by Caesar in his narrative of that year). Our Greek sources are alert to the importance of Caesar's *legati* for his success: see esp. Plu. *Caes.* 18.2 and App. *Gall* 15.2–3 (and compare Caes. *Gal.* 1.12.6) for his campaign of 58; also D.C. 39.5.1 (57 B.C.) and 40.31.1 (53 B.C.).

53. For instances of a *legatus* in charge of two legions, see, e.g., Caes. *Gal.* 1.21.2 (T. Labienus), 7.40.3 (C. Fabius), 7.83.3 (C. Antistius Reginus with C. Caninius Rebilus), 8.24.2 (C. Fabius), 8.39.4 (Q. Calenus). Three legions: Caes. *Gal.* 2.11.3 (T. Labienus), 3.11.4 (Q. Titurius Sabinus), 5.8.1 (T. Labienus—but with especially broad responsibilities), 5.17.2 (C. Trebonius), 6.33.1 (T. Labienus), 6.33.2 (C. Trebonius). Toward the end of Caesar's command he gave *legati* charge of even four legions: Caes. *Gal.* 7.57.1 (T. Labienus), 8.54.4 (to both C. Trebonius and C. Fabius).

54. Though Caesar himself explicitly notes it only once, for Transalpina in 52 (*Gal.* 7.65.1—see n. 51 above). On T. Labienus holding Cisalpina in 50 (reported by Hirtius), see text immediately below.

55. Caes. *Gal.* 1.21.2 "[Caesar] legatum pro praetore . . . iubet." On this passage, see J. P. V. D. Balsdon, *JRS* 52 (1962) 138 with n. 34; W. Kunkel, *Staatsordnung und Staatspraxis der römischen Republik: Die Magistratur* (Munich 1995) 286 n. 47.

56. Tribunate: *MRR* II 167f. Delegated authority for Gallia Cisalpina: Hirt. *Gal.* 8.52.2–3, with the discussion of R. Syme, *Roman Papers* I (Oxford 1979) 71–74. and T. R. S. Broughton, *Candidates Defeated in Roman Elections: Some Ancient Roman "Also-Rans"* (Philadelphia 1991) 26f.

57. *Civ.* 3.32.3–4.

58. E.g., *Gal.* 4.22.3 and 6, 5.11.3.

59. *Gal.* 1.22.3.

60. Caes. *Gal.* 3.11.1–2 (specific orders to T. Labienus); 3.17.5–7 (Titurius Sabinus here the very *exemplum* of a well-disciplined subordinate); 5.8.1 (more specific orders to Labienus); 5.28.3–7 (Sabinus' military *consilium* offers appropriate advice); 5.40.1–6 (Q. Cicero appropriately communicates with Caesar); 7.1.7–8 (discipline of Caesar's subordinates in winter quarters); 7.86.2 with 87.3 (a good example of standard orders to a subordinate, in this case Labienus, who acts responsibly).

61. Most notably, the whole story of the destruction of the *legati* Q. Titurius Sabinus and L. Aurunculeius in 54 at the hands of the Eburones (*Gal.* 5.24–37), for which Caesar

squarely blames Sabinus (clear also from 5.39.1, 5.52.6, 5.53.4, 6.2.4, cf. 6.37.8). Caesar is obviously very defensive about this incident, hence, e.g., his careful description (5.24–25) of how his *legati* set up their winter camps (precisely the type of thing that might be questioned in a court case, as Cic. *Font.* 20 shows), not to mention the fact he tells the tale of the disaster at such length. Cf. also 6.42.1, where Caesar holds up Q. Cicero as somewhat of a negative *exemplum*; his personal letter to Quintus' brother (ap. Charisius I p. 160 B) apparently pulled no such punches. In general on this feature of the *Gal.*, see W. B. Tyrrell, *Historia* 21 (1972) 426–427.

62. *Gal.* 7.20.1–5.

63. *Mélanges Piganiol* II 916.

64. Cic. *Catil.* 2.5.

65. Cic. *Prov.* 38.

66. Cic. *Fam.* 5.2.3–4, esp. 3 "nihil dico de sortitione vestra."

67. The *S.C.U.* of 21 Oct.: Sal. *Cat.* 30.3 and 5; Cic. *Catil.* 2.5–6 and 26.

68. Sal. *Cat.* 42.1 and 3; Cic. *Fam.* 5.2.1 "cum tu a me rebus amplissimis atque honorificentissimis ornatus esses"; Plu. *Cic.* 16.1. For a brief discussion of contemporary conditions in the *ager Picenus* and *Gallicus* (with ample bibliography), see R. Stewart, *Latomus* 54 (1995) 72–73.

69. On all this, see the careful chronological study of G. V. Sumner, *CPh* 58 (1963) 215–219. For Metellus' movements, see esp. Sal. *Cat.* 57.2–3 and cf. 58.6 (Catiline's harangue); also Cic. *Fam.* 5.2.5 for Metellus' brief return to the vicinity of Rome to support his brother Nepos (*tr. pl.* for 62) some time shortly after 5 December. Sumner (*CPh* 58 [1963] 218 n. 10) suggests he was back with his army before 20 December. Against D.C. 37.39.2, Celer probably was still at Bononia at the time of the final battle: see Sumner, *CPh* 58 (1963) 219 n. 17, for an explanation.

70. *Mélanges Piganiol* II 916.

71. Thus J. Spielvogel, *Hermes* 121 (1993) 245–246 (but improperly using this incident also as evidence for attitudes toward grants of enhanced *imperium* in the middle Republic).

72. Cic. *Fam.* 5.2.4.

73. See Met. Cel. *Fam.* 5.1 (Jan. 62, after the battle of Pistoria) prescript (for title) and 5.1.2 "qui provinciae, qui exercitui praesum, qui bellum gero" for his possible police activities in early 62. Gift of the king of the Suebi (not explicitly named): Nepos *HRR* II F 7 = Plin. *Nat.* 2.170, cf. Mela 3.45 "a rege Botorum" (yet each with title *pro cos.*) with T. R. S. Broughton, *TAPhA* 79 (1948) 75–76. On Ariovistus' campaign of 61 (and subsequent recognition in 59 as "Friend of the Roman People"), see esp. Caes. *Gal.* 1.31–53 passim.

74. See Münzer, *RE* s.v. *Caecilius* 86 col. 1209 with B. A. Marshall, *A Historical Comentary on Asconius* (Columbia, Mo., 1985) 96 for the chronology.

75. Cf. Cic. *Pis.* 56.

76. Badian, *Mélanges Piganiol* II 917 with n. 4.

77. Cf. *Prov.* 38–39.

78. Note M. Caecilius Metellus, *cos.* 115 (four and a half years of *imperium* in Sardinia); M. Minucius Rufus, *cos.* 110 (*imperium* for four and a half years in Macedonia); T. Didius, *cos.* 98 (five years in Hispania Citerior); P. Licinius Crassus, *cos.* 97 (four years in Hispania Ulterior). In the war against Jugurtha, Q. Caecilius Metellus Numidicus, *cos.* 109, was *pro cos.* into 106 (at least three years of *imperium*), while C. Marius (*cos.* 107) was prorogued into 105 (three years of *imperium*, and then elected as *cos.* II for 104).

79. E.g., for Spain, note Q. Caecilius Metellus Balearicus, *cos.* 123, *tr.* 121; for Gaul, M. Fulvius Flaccus, *cos.* 125, triumphed 123; C. Sextius Calvinus, *cos.* 124, triumphed 122, Cn. Domitius Ahenobarbus, *cos.* 122, triumphed 120; for Sicily, M.' Aquillius, *cos.* 101, *ovatio* in 99. C. Caecilius Metellus Caprarius, *cos.* 113 who triumphed 15 July 111 from Macedonia, is

a particularly deceptive case: he apparently spent a good part of 112 and the first half of 111 outside Rome (13.1.1).

80. L. Cornelius Sulla, *pr. urb.* 97 then served *pro cos.* in Cilicia; C. Valerius Flaccus, *pr. urb.* (probably) in 96 was *pro cos.* in Asia; and two of the city praetors of 94, namely, the *pr. urb.* C. Sentius, who took up Macedonia and the peregrine praetor L. Gellius, who went *pro cos.* to Asia or Cilicia.

81. Note the rapid replacement of (unsuccessful) praetorian commanders in the Second Slave War in Sicily: P. Licinius Nerva (*pr.* by 104), L. Licinius Lucullus (*pr.* 104, then *pro pr.* 103), C. Servilius (*pr.* 102), followed by M.' Aquillius (*cos.* 101). That was certainly the predominant practice in major consular wars in this general era. In Macedonia, C. Porcius Cato, *cos.* 114, who suffered an overwhelming defeat at the hands of the Scordisci, was succeeded by C. Caecilius Metellus Caprarius, *cos.* 113. In the war against Jugurtha, note the series L. Calpurnius Bestia, *cos.* 111; Sp. Postumius Albinus, *cos.* 110 (left late in year); Q. Caecilius Metellus Numidicus, *cos.* 109 (who was prorogued into 106 by the Senate); and then C. Marius (*cos.* 107), prorogued into 105. In the Cimbric wars, L. Cassius Longinus, *cos.* 107 (killed); Q. Servilius Caepio, *cos.* 106; Cn. Mallius Maximus, *cos.* 105 (disaster); and then C. Marius, consul in each of the years 104–101. Yet occasionally unsuccessful commanders were prorogued: see the discussion in N. Rosenstein, *Imperatores Victi* (Berkeley 1990) 32–33.

82. *JRS* 52 (1962) 134; cf. also Kunkel, *Staatsordnung* 287, implying as much.

83. See Cic. *Fam.* 12.15 prescript (P. Cornelius Lentulus in 43 B.C.) with J. M. Cobban, *Senate and Provinces, 78–49 B.C.* (Cambridge 1935) 82.

84. See esp. *ILLRP* 342, the praetor *pro cos.* M. Antonius delegating *imperium* to his subordinate Hirrus *en route* to Cilicia in 102 B.C. (10.1, 14.5.2), and the cases (late second or early first century) of Cn. Aufidius Cn.f. and M. Popillius M.f. Laenas (both *pro praetore* in Asia) discussed in 14.5.3. Note perhaps also the στρατηγός Vibius who accompanied the *pro cos.* C. Memmius in Macedonia ca. 103 (14.1.1). For the pre-Sullan era we have also a few instances where the delegatee can just as easily have served under a consul as praetor. A Macedonian inscription of the second century (T. Sarikakis, Ῥωμαῖοι ἄρχοντες τῆς ἐπαρχίας Μακεδονίας [Thessaloniki 1971] 173) preserves the fragmentary name and title: "Pos[——]us [——] ταμίας καὶ ἀντιστράτηγος" (reported by F. Papazoglou in ANRW II 7.1 [1979] 310). Note also the *quaestor pro praetore* "Marcus" who was honored at Delos, and the *legatus pro praetore* Cornelius L.f. Lentulus who shows up as *legatus pro praetore* in Samothrace, discussed in ch. 14 n. 192.

85. See 11.3 and 11.8 on the special *provinciae* necessitated in this period, especially by the *Bellum Lepidanum* (77), trouble in Illyria (early 70s), the activities of pirates (74–67), the war against Spartacus (73–71), and the Catilinarian conspiracy (63–62).

86. M. Antonius (*pr.* 74, then *pro cos.* in a special pirate command) in (probably) 70 (11.3.1); L. Octavius (*cos.* 75) in Cilicia in early 74 (15.1.1); perhaps C. Longinus (*cos.* 73) against Spartacus in 72 (11.8.7). Note also Q. Metellus Celer (*cos.* 60), who died in early 59 before he could reach Gallia Transalpina (15.2.3); and M. Crassus (*cos.* II 55), who was killed in Syria in 53 (11.5.3). Examples of a commander dying after leaving his province but before entering the city are C. Cotta (*cos.* 75, *pro cos.* Gallia Cisalpina) in 74, after a triumph vote (15.2.1); also C. Octavius (*pr.* 61) in 58 (14.2.4).

87. Certainly C. Annius, *pr.* 81 in both Spanish *provinciae*, followed (surely) by L. Fufidius and M. Calvinus (*prr.* 80) in Citerior and Ulterior respectively (13.4.2); also M. Thermus, *pr.* 81 in Asia (14.6.1), and (possibly) C. Nero (*pr.* 81 or 80) in that same province. In 14.2.1, I have suggested that the *cos.* 81 Cn. Dolabella set out for Macedonia during his magistracy.

88. Such as M. Iunius Iuncus, *pr.* 76 and then *pro cos.* for Asia, who in early 74 left his *provincia* for some time to annex and organize Bithynia/Pontus (14.6.2). Note also—to look just at praetors—the military action C. Verres (*pr.* 74) had to take *ex S.C.* in Italy, when returning from Sicily in 70, or that of C. Octavius (*pr.* 61) in south Italy in early 60, while en route to his proper province of Macedonia (11.8.7, 13.2.3, 14.2.4)

89. For commands of a fixed term longer than one year in the late Republic, see in general, F. Hurlet, *CCCG* 5 (1994) 256–258 (but missing the precedent of the 190s).

90. See App. *BC* 2.27.102 with Cael. *Fam.* 8.6.5 "legem . . . viariam non dissimilem agrariae Rulli."

91. For commands of five years and up, note (in addition to the *pr.* [?] 76 L. Afranius) Q. Metellus Pius (*cos.* 80), in Hispania Ulterior as *pro cos.* 79–71 (nine years); P. Vatia Isauricus, *cos.* 79, *pro cos.* in Cilicia for a "quinquennium," returning to triumph in 74 (almost five years); Cn. Pompeius, *pro cos.* for Hispania Citerior 77, triumphed 31 Dec. 71 (seven years); L. Lucullus, *cos.* 74 and *pro cos.* in Asia (73 through 69), Cilicia (73 through 68), Bithynia/Pontus (71 into 67) (seven years); Cn. Pompeius, *pro cos.* 67–62 under the *lex Gabinia* (67, guaranteeing a three-year command) and *lex Manilia* (66–62); C. Caesar, *cos.* 59, and then *pro cos.* in the two Gauls and Illyricum for five years (the term granted by the *lex Vatinia*), with another five added by a consular law in 55 B.C. (nine years served); Cn. Pompeius, in a special grain commission with powers for five years (starting 57), then *cos.* II 55, for both Spanish provinces (under the *lex Trebonia*) for five years; M. Crassus, *cos.* II 55, and *pro cos.* in Syria for five years through the *lex Trebonia* (but killed in 53).

92. Four years: Cn. Dolabella, *cos.* 81 (with transit to province in magistracy?), *pro cos.* in Macedonia into 77; M. Antonius, *pr.* 74 and *pro cos.* in a special pirate command into 71. Three or four years: Q. Metellus Creticus, *cos.* 69 and *pro cos.* in Crete into (probably) 65; then Q. Rufus, *pr.* 63 and *pro cos.* in Africa through 60 and perhaps into 59; C. Pomptinus, *pr.* 63, and *pro cos.* in Transalpina perhaps through 59; C. Balbus, *pr.* 62, then *pro cos.* in Sicily through 59 and perhaps into 58; C. Carbo (*pr.* 62 or 61), *pro cos.* in Bithynia/Pontus through 58. (See also 15.1.2 on the possibility that a single praetorian commander was in Cilicia 61–58.) Three years: M. Fonteius, *pr.* 77, *pro cos.* in Transalpina for a "triennium" (probably through 75); C. Curio (*cos.* 76), *pro cos.* in Macedonia probably into 72; M. Cotta, *cos.* 74, *pro cos.* in Bithynia and Pontus 73 into 71; C. Verres, *pr.* 74, *pro cos.* in Sicily 73–71 (it was planned that he serve for only one year—13.2.2); Q. Cicero, *pr.* 62, and *pro cos.* in Asia through 59; L. Piso Caesoninus (*cos.* 58), and *pro cos.* in Macedonia into 55. P. Lentulus Spinther, *cos.* 57, and then *pro cos.* in Cilicia into 53 (relieved in late summer); C. Pulcher, *pr.* 56, and *pro cos.* in Asia 55–53. Two or three years: M. Piso Calpurnianus, *pr.* 72 or 71, *pro cos.* in Ulterior into 69.

93. Two years: C. Nero, *pr.* 81 or 80, *pro cos.* in Asia through 79; Cn. Dolabella, *pr.* 81, and *pro pr.* (*sic*) in Cilicia through 79; L. Manlius (*pr.* 80 or 79), *pro cos.* into 77 (defeated); Ap. Pulcher, *cos.* 79, then *pro cos.* in Macedonia 77–76 (died); Sex. Peducaeus, *pr.* 77, then *pro cos.* Sicily 76–75; M. Iuncus, *pr.* 76, *pro cos.* in Asia down through 74; M. Lucullus, *cos.* 73, then *pro cos.* in Macedonia into 71, triumphing that year after further service in Italy; M. Crassus, *pr.* 73 (probably), and prorogued into 71 in Italy; C. Piso, *cos.* 67, and *pro cos.* in both Gallic provinces (at least) 66–65; L. Murena, *pr.* 65, and *pro cos.* in Hispania Citerior through 63 (though leaving early); C. Antonius, *cos.* 63, *pro cos.* in Macedonia, who was relieved in 60 (though returning only in 59); L. Philippus, *pr.* 62, and *pro cos.* in Syria through 60; Cn. Lentulus Marcellinus, *pr.* 60, and *pro cos.* in Syria through 58; T. Balbus, *pr.* 59, and *pro cos.* in Asia (58) then Cilicia (57); A. Gabinius, *cos.* 58, *pro cos.* in Syria into 55; Ap. Pulcher, *cos.* 54, and *pro cos.* in Cilicia into 51. (See also 14.4 on the possibility of regular two-year commands in Africa in the 50s.) One or two years: C. Marcellus, *pr.* 80, *pro*

cos. Sicily 79 and (probably) 78; Antistius Vetus, *pr.* (?) 69, and *pro cos.* in Hispania Ulterior (perhaps) into 67; Rubrius, *pr.* by 68, then *pro cos.* in Macedonia down through 67; Q. Metellus Nepos, *cos.* 57, and *pro cos.* in Hispania Citerior into 55; Sex. Varus (*pr.* 57), *pro cos.* in Hispania Ulterior into 55; C. Longus, *pro pr.* in Africa 51 and 50.

94. See C. Annius, *pr.* 81 in the two Spains; M. Thermus, *pr.* 81 in Asia; M. Lepidus, *pr.* 81, *pro cos.* Sicily 80; L. Fufidius, *pr.* 80 in Hispania Ulterior. Then Q. Calidius, *pr.* 79 and *pro cos.* 78 in Hispania Citerior; L. Sisenna, *pr.* 78 and *pro cos.* in Sicily 77 (probable); C. Cotta, *cos.* 75 and *pro cos.* in Cisalpine Gaul 74; C. Sacerdos, *pr.* 75 and *pro cos.* in Sicily 74; probably L. Caesar (*pr.* ?71), *pro cos.* 70, then L. Cotta, *pr.* 70 and *pro cos.* 69, both in Macedonia. Note also T. Aufidius, *pr.* by 67, P. Varinius, *pr.* II by 66, P. Orbius, *pr.* 65, P. Globulus, *pr.* by 64, all *pro coss.* in Asia (though one of these men might have been pro-rogued a single time—14.6.5), then L. Flaccus, *pr.* 63, *pro cos.* Asia 62; C. Cosconius, *pr.* 63 and *pro cos.* 62, then (perhaps) C. Caesar, *pr.* 62 and *pro cos.* 61 in Ulterior (if he did not return early); perhaps P. Lentulus Spinther, *pr.* 60, and *pro cos.* 59 in Citerior (again leaving early?). Also L. Saturninus, *pr.* 59 and *pro cos.* Macedonia 58; C. Fabius, *pr.* 58 and *pro cos.* 57, then C. Septimius, *pr.* 57 and *pro cos.* 56, both in Asia; C. Memmius, *pr.* 58 and *pro cos.* 57, then C. Cornutus, *pr.* 57 and *pro cos.* 56, both in Bithynia/Pontus; Ap. Pulcher, *pr.* 57 and *pro cos.* Sardinia 56; M. Scaurus, *pr.* 56 and *pro cos.* Sardinia 55; Q. Ancharius, *pr.* 56 and *pro cos.* Macedonia 55; M. Cicero, *cos.* 63 and *pro cos.* in Cilicia under the *lex Pompeia* 51/50; also M. Bibulus, *cos.* 59 and *pro cos.* in Syria under that same law, 51/50.

95. See 14.3.3 on Africa in 80, 15.2.1 on Cisalpine Gaul in 77, 14.2.2 for Macedonia in 76, 14.6.2 on Asia in 75/74, 14.6.4 on the significant responsibilities of *legati* in the Third Macedonian War, 13.4.6 on Hispania Ulterior in 69/68, and 13.4.7 for that same *provincia* in 60, 13.4.8 for Hispania Citerior in 58, and 11.5.2 for Syria 53–51.

96. See ch. 14 n. 74.

97. See Cael. *Fam.* 8.8.8 and 13.2 and *Att.* 6.2.6 with G. V. Sumner, *Phoenix* 25 (1971) 268.

98. Cael. *Fam.* 8.10.2 (17 Nov. 51 B.C.).

99. Sicily: the quaestor L. Caecilius Metellus in 52 (ch. 13 n. 129). Sardinia: probably C. Valerius Triarius in 77 (13.2.7). Africa: perhaps L. Vehilius, attested as "q(uaestor) pro pr(aetore)" at Hippo Regius (AE 1955, no. 148). Gallia Comata: T. Labienus leading an advance force against the Helvetii in 58 (15.2.4). See also 11.8.2 for Pompey's *legati pro praetore* of 67 B.C.

100. Macedonia: perhaps the quaestor Cn. Plancius in 58 (ch. 14 n. 82); perhaps belonging to this period is also C. Quinctius C.f. Trogus, honored at Megara as *pro praetore* (*Bull. épigr.* 1979, 205). Asia: see 14.6.4 on the *legatus pro praetore* C. Salluvius C.f. Naso, Q. Publicius Q.f. *pro quaestore pro praetore*, and the *legatus pro praetore* L. Manlius L.f. Torquatus (all probably belonging to the late 70s or early 60s, in the war against Mithridates); note also [——]cius Balbus, *legatus pro praetore* at Cos (AE 1934, no. 85, with a date after 74 B.C. suggested). Syria: the *pro quaestore* M. Aemilius Scaurus in 62 B.C. (11.5.1). See also 11.8.2 for Pompey's *legati pro praetore* of 67 B.C.

101. Probably Cn. Pompeius in the *Bellum Lepidanum* of 77 (15.2.1), also L. Cossinius in the early stages of the war against Spartacus in 73 (11.8.6); cf. also (in the early 70s?) M. Terentius Varro Lucullus as well as Cn. Egnatius C.f. (11 n. 81).

102. See 11.1.7 with n. 119 on L. Antonius, *pro quaestore pro praetore* in Asia 50/49.

Notes to Appendix B

1. See Münzer, *RE* s.v. col. 1402 for the possible *cognomen*.
2. On the *praenomen*, see *MRR* I 135 n. 2.
3. On this man's identity, see *MRR* I 142 n. 2.

4. Liv. 9.41.1 "quartum creatus"; cf. Plin. *Nat.* 7.157. The dates of his three previous praetorships are unknown.

5. Claudius Caecus was *praetor bis*, according to his *elogium* (*Inscr. Ital.* XIII 3 79).

6. See T. C. Brennan, *Historia* 43 (1994) 423–439.

7. See *MRR* I 191 with 192 n. 3; cf. also the discussions of E. Gabba, *RFIC* 103 (1975) 153–154; O. Skutsch, *The "Annals" of Q. Ennius* (Oxford 1985) 337f.

8. See Additional Note III.

9. No name can be readily supplied for the praetor of 270 who, according to Fron. *Aq.* 1.6.2, consulted the Senate regarding the completion of the Anio aqueduct: "†referente —— nocumi —— praetor<e>." F. Stella-Maranca, *MAL* 6 [ser. 2] (1927) 363, guessed "Minucius" (he misdates the Frontinus passage to 262); "Genucius" (cf. the *cos.* 276 and II 270, and also *cos.* 271) seems paleographically as plausible.

10. See Suet. *Tib.* 3.2 with 3.7.

11. This man was also censor in this same year (4.1.3). On his descent see Münzer, *RE* s.v. col. 941.

12. The father of this man (see V. Max. 5.4.5, with Münzer, *RE* s.v. *Flaminius* 1 col. 2497) may have held a political office of some sort.

13. See Liv. 22.35.1 (*cognomen*) with 4.3.4 above (date of praetorship).

14. See *ILLRP* 75 ("praitor iterum") with R. Develin, *The Practice of Politics in Rome, 366–167 B.C.* (Brussels 1985) 122, and T. C. Brennan, *Athenaeum* 67 (1989) 467–476.

15. Praetorian status inferred from a combination of Liv. 21.63.12 and V. Max. 5.2.5. See Münzer, *RE* s.v. cols. 597–598.

16. V. Max. 5.6.4 ("Aelius praetor"); Fron. *Str.* 4.5.14 (C. Aelius, or "Caelius"); Plin. *Nat.* 10.41 ("Aelius Tubero"). A woodpecker perched itself on the head of this "praetor urbanus" (Fron., Plin.) when he was engaged in hearing cases at law; Aelius unhesitatingly killed the bird when the *haruspices* (Fron., V. Max.; Plin. "vates") asserted this act would portend the survival of the *res publica* (Plin., V. Max.) or a Roman victory over an enemy (Fron.), though the destruction of the praetor (Plin.) or his "domus" (V. Max.) or both (Fron.). Frontinus states that fifteen Aelii (including this man) died in a battle that ensued; Valerius Maximus asserts he lost seventeen members of his family at Cannae; Pliny (who makes this portent strictly personal, and not extended to the *gens*) says only that the praetor soon was dead. Valerius Maximus, the only source to suggest a date, implies this man was still alive in 216; Pliny and perhaps Frontinus seem to think not much time elapsed between the portent and its fulfillment. The destruction of a large number of Aelii best fits the circumstances of the Hannibalic War—hence the conjectural date I have offered. However, the date of this man—if he existed—must remain quite uncertain, especially since none of our three sources tell the story, once the woodpecker lands, the same way.

17. See *MRR* I 240 and 241 n. 12 on C. Servilius, C. Papirius Maso, M. Annius, M.' Acilius, and C. Herennius, each of whom shows up in one or another of our variant lists of the colonial commissioners for Placentia and Cremona (founded 218). Two of these four men (we cannot tell which) should have been praetors (cf. Plb. 3.40.9). The last two names are rejected by B. L. Twyman in C. Deroux (ed.), *Studies in Latin Literature and Roman History* IV (Brussels 1986) 109–121; D. J. Gargola (*Athenaeum* 78 [68] [1990] 465–473) offers a reconstruction which includes them all. Neither of these recent attempts to solve this old problem is convincing (see 4.3.4 with ch. 4 n. 135); indeed, the tradition on the founding of Placentia and Cremona was hopeless even by Livy's time (cf. 21.25.4).

18. Q. Baebius Tamphilus, the father of Cn. and M. Tamphilus (*prr.* 199 and 192), may have been praetorian in rank, as can be seen from his participation in two important embassies at the start of the conflict with Hannibal, in the years 219 (*MRR* I 237) and 218 (*MRR* I 239—the only nonconsular on an embassy of five).

19. Q. Aelius Paetus and P. Cornelius Merenda were consular candidates for 216 (Liv. 22.35.1–2), and may have been ex-praetors (see T. R. S. Broughton, *Candidates Defeated in Roman Elections: Some Ancient Roman "Also-Rans"* [Philadelphia 1991] 20 and 24f).

20. See Liv. 22.33.7–8 with E. Badian, *JRS* 61 (1971) 105–106, for the possibility that K. Quinctius Flamininus, who served as a II*vir aed. loc.* in 217, was of praetorian rank. One might add his colleague in this commission, C. Pupius.

21. For the praetor's cognomen see Liv. 22.35.1. For a stemma of the Aemilii Lepidi, see G. V. Sumner, *The Orators in Cicero's Brutus: Prosopography and Chronology* (Toronto 1973) 66 (quite speculative).

22. See Liv. 22.34.7 ("homo novus").

23. The Serrani were an offshoot of the Reguli (V. Max. 4.4.6 with 4.5); cf. C. Atilius M.f. M.n. Regulus, *cos.* 257 (listed in Cassiod. *Chron.* as "C. Atilius Erranus"), II 250. C. Atilius Serranus should be distinguished from the C. Atilius who is found at Placentia at the end of 218 (see Additional Note III).

24. He should be a different man from the M.(?) Pomponius Matho who as praetor held the same *provincia* in 216 (see Additional Note VII).

25. For the *cognomen*, see Liv. 24.8.10; 29.38.6.

26. For the spelling of the *cognomen*, see *CIL* I² 1444 with P. Castrén, *Arctos* 14 (1980) 5–13.

27. P. Cornelius Lentulus was a cousin of the *cos.* 201 (App. *Pun.* 62.272, from a speech), and thus perhaps a nephew of L. Cornelius Lentulus Caudinus (*cos.* 237) or P. Cornelius Lentulus Caudinus (*cos.* 236).

28. Should be the X*vir s.f.* M.' Aemilius Lepidus who died in 211 (Liv. 26.23.7 "M. Aemilius Lepidus" with Sumner, *Orators* 47, 64–66 for emendation of the *praenomen*): see T. C. Brennan, *Athenaeum* 67 (1989) 474–475.

29. Note cousin C. Cornelius L.f. M.n. Cethegus, *cos.* 197.

30. Direct descent from the *cos.* 243 is probable: see Münzer, *RE* s.v. col. 734, cf. s.v. *Sulpicius* 66 col. 808.

31. Note M. Laetorius M.f. M.n. Plancianus, *mag. eq.* 257.

32. See Liv. 30.1.5 ("nobilis").

33. See E. Badian, *JRS* 61 (1971) 107–109. The name "Q. Claudius Flamen" (Liv. 27.22.3) is defended by R. E. A. Palmer in "The Deconstruction of Mommsen on Festus 462/464 L," in J. Linderski (ed.), *Imperium Sine Fine: T. Robert S. Broughton and the Roman Republic* (Stuttgart 1996) 75–101, esp. 83–90.

34. Presumably M. Caecilius Metellus is the younger brother of Q. Caecilius L.f. Metellus (*cos.* 206), and thus son of the *cos.* I 251.

35. His grandfather (so it seems) was C. Octavius Rufus, who reached the quaestorship (but perhaps not the Senate): see Suet. *Aug.* 2.1–2 with Münzer, *RE* s.v. *Octavius* 79 col. 1853. The praetor's father may have reached a curule magistracy. For discussion, see L. Pietilä-Castrén, *Arctos* 18 (1984) 75–77.

36. See *ILLRP* 251 "L. Aimilius L.f. praitor"; the stone may alternatively refer to L. Aemilius L.f. M.n. Paullus, *pr.* 191 (as Degrassi suggests in his commentary ad loc.).

37. The (eldest?) son of P. Quinctilius Varus was given the praenomen M. (Liv. 30.18.5), perhaps a conscious attempt to link the family to the consular tribune of 403, M. Quinctilius Varus; of course, genuine descent is not out of the question. Cf. also P. Quinctilius Varus, *pr.* 166, almost certainly another son (for the exact interval, note the Cn. Octavii who were *prr.* 205 and 168).

38. See n. 19 above on the possibility that P. Paetus' father, Q. Paetus, was a praetor.

39. Münzer (*RE* s.v. *Tremellius* 4 col. 2287) considers this man the third in the series of (seven) Tremelii who reached the praetorship (see Var. *R.* 2.4.2). For the spelling of the *nomen*, see G. Perl, *AJAH* 5 (1980) [1983] 105 n. 1.

40. M. Fabius Buteo conceivably could be a son of the *cos.* 245; cf. also *prr.* 196.

41. See P. Aelius Paetus, *cos.* 337; also P. Aelius Q.f. Paetus, *cos.* in this year (201).

42. Q. Minucius Rufus is a younger brother—or possibly nephew—of the the *cos.* 221, M. Minucius C.f. C.n. Rufus. Cf. *pr.* 197.

43. On the name, see E. Badian, *ZPE* 55 (1984) 104.

44. A brother of the *cos.* 199.

45. See Münzer, *RE* s.v. col. 1223 for descent. His brother was *pr.* 195 (and *cos.* 189).

46. On the *nomen*, see E. Badian in N. Horsfall (ed.), *Vir bonus discendi peritus* (Festschrift O. Skutsch), *BICS* Suppl. 51 (1988) 11–12. For the filiation, cf. *cos.* 150.

47. *Novus homo* (Liv. 37.57.10–12). Note, however, the M.' Acilius who may have held a praetorship prior to 218 (n. 17 above); also the senator M.' Acilius found as a *legatus* in 210 (Liv. 27.4.10; cf. 25.2).

48. Livy reports the activities of a *tr. pl.* C. Atinius in 197, and a C. Atinius Labeo *tr. pl.* in 196. Neither of these men (if they are indeed two individuals, and not one, as Broughton accepts) is likely to be identical with the *pr.* 195 (thus *MRR* I 336 with 339 n. 3, cf. II 535). Note the C. Atinii who are *prr.* in 190 and 188; on the Atinii of this generation, see A. E. Astin, "The Atinii," in J. Bibauw (ed.), *Hommages à M. Renard* II (Brussels 1969) 35–37.

49. Cn. Cornelius Blasio as a *privatus* had a command *pro cos.* in Spain 199–197 (7.1.6).

50. See Liv. 26.48.6–13 for his father, a *praefectus socium* in 210 under P. Cornelius Scipio (*cos.* 205, II 194) in Spain.

51. See Liv. 33.22.8 with Münzer, *RE* s.v. col. 1372 on his putative father, killed as *tr. mil.* 197. But this makes for an amazingly short generational interval.

52. This year marks the first known all-plebeian praetorian college of two or more. The next will fall in the year 172 (also notable for its landmark pair of plebeian consuls). For the proportions of patricians and plebeians in praetorian colleges of this era, see R. F. Vishnia, *Athenaeum* 84 [74] (1996) 434 with n. 8.

53. Cf. Iunii Bubulci, Perae, Pulli, Scavae. A claim to descent from the tyrannicide is first attested in the first century (Crawford, *RRC* I 455 no. 433).

54. Just possibly a natural brother of C. Livius Salinator (*cos.* 188).

55. Note Tuccia, vestal virgin perhaps ca. 230 (*MRR* I 227 with n. 2).

56. Cf. *pr.* 209.

57. On his possible descent, see Münzer, *RE* s.v. col. 230.

58. Liv. 40.52.5 provides filiation.

59. Filiation from *Inscr. Ital.* XIII 1 80f.

60. See the *coss.* of 269 and 266; also see *MRR* I 251 on the historian and senator (Plb. 3.9.4) Q. Fabius Pictor, who was sent to consult the Delphic oracle after Cannae (and thus a member of the Senate already at this time?).

61. See Münzer, *RE* s.v. col. 921 on his descent.

62. Descent of the Hypsaei from C. Plautius Decianus (*cos.* 329) explicitly claimed by the year 60: see Crawford, *RRC* I 444f no. 420 and 446f no. 422.

63. Presumably great-grandson of Q. Marcius Philippus, *cos.* 281 (E. Badian, *Chiron* 20 [1990] 375–376). See Münzer, *RE* s.v. *Marcius* 79 col. 1573; also s.v. *Marcius* 61 col. 1557 (C. Marcius C.f. Q.n. Figulus, *cos.* 162).

64. Cf. L. Stertinius, the *privatus* who was *pro cos.* in Spain 199–197 (7.1.6).

65. For this man's praetorian descent, see V. Max. 5.2.5 with Münzer, *RE* s.v. col. 652; also n. 15 above.

66. Note L. Lucullus, *aed. cur.* 202, and C. Lucullus, *tr. pl.* 196.

67. On Livy's defective notice on the praetorian college of this year (as well as 177 and 166), see Additional Note XI.

68. Considered *novus* by C. Nicolet, *L'ordre équestre à l'époque républicaine (312–43 av. J.-C.)* II (Paris 1974) 768.

69. See Additional Note XI for this man's praetorship; the date is practically required.

70. This man could be the son of the *cos.* 218, or a nephew of the *cos.* 218, and cousin of the *cos.* 194.

71. Note that relatives held the consulship in 204 and 197.

72. See Münzer, *RE* s.v. col. 5 for descent.

73. Note C. Pupius, *IIvir aed. loc.* 217 (n. 20 above).

74. Münzer, *RE* s.v. col. 1790 discusses descent.

75. Cf. *pr.* 196. Indeed, J. D. Morgan ("The Fabii Buteones," unpublished) goes so far as to identify the two, and considers the praetorship of 181 an iteration, unrecorded by Livy.

76. It is difficult to sort out the three different Ti. Nerones who held the praetorship in this general period (in 181, 178, and 167). One branch of the family seems to be descended from a Ti. Nero (born ca. 270); the other from a P. Nero (born ca. 265).

77. See Münzer, *RE* s.v. *Minucius* 30 and 43 (cols. 1945 and 1955–1956). The *praenomen* Ti. is found only among the Minucii Augurini; Münzer suggests that Molliculus may be a nickname.

78. Note L. Hostilius Mancinus, a junior officer under the dictator Q. Fabius Maximus in 217 (Liv. 22.15.4–10 — killed in action).

79. Only the names of the last three praetors returned for 178 are given at Liv. 40.59.5 (M. Titinius Curvus, Ti. Claudius Nero, "T." Fonteius Capito), with no mention of their *provinciae*. Livy does not take the trouble to explain why he could not report the full election. For T. Aebutius and M. Titinius as *prr.* 178, see *MRR* I 395 with corresponding notes.

80. An L. Titinius L.f. M.'n. Pansa Saccus was *tr. mil. c. p.* in 400 and 396; also note the M. Titinius C.f. C.n. who served as *mag. eq.* in 302.

81. J. D. Morgan ("The Praetors of 179–165 B.C.," unpublished) points out that our two earliest sources for the text of Liv. 40.59.5 (i.e., the elections for 178), the Mainz edition of 1519 and the first Froben edition (Basel 1531), give the *praenomen* "T." for this man; T<i>. Claudius Nero is Pighius' emendation. Morgan suggests that the *praenomen* may well be "C."

82. J. D. Morgan ("The Praetors of 179–165 B.C.") notes that the *praenomen* "T." (unparalleled among Fonteii who hold Republican magistracies) is first offered as a supplement in the 1531 Froben edition of Livy (at 40.59.5, also 41.15.11); Morgan goes on to suggest that this man should be a C. Fonteius Capito. The *praenomen* "C." is found in this *gens* by the end of the second century (note *RRC* I 304–305 no. 290, a moneyer dated by Crawford to 114 or 113, and the C. Fonteius C.f. Capito who was *cos. suff.* 33). However, I would hold that "Ti." is entirely possible (perhaps even probable, at this time): note Ti. Fonteius, found as a prominent *legatus* in Spain in 211 (*MRR* I 275).

83. See E. Badian, *JRS* 61 (1971) 106, for the *praenomen*.

84. See Liv. 27.4.7–9 for the man who must be his father, P. Popillius (Laenas), who was sent as a *legatus* to king Syphax in Numidia in 210 (and therefore probably of senatorial rank).

85. See C. Papirius C.f. L.n. Maso, *cos.* 231; also C. Papirius L.f. Maso, perhaps *pr.* pre-218 (see n. 17).

86. Note C. Aquillius M.f. C.n. Florus, *cos.* 259; also C. Aquillius, *cos.* 487; L. Aquillius Corvus, *tr. mil. c.p.* 388.

87. It is uncertain whether four or six praetors were elected in this year (though probably the latter — see 7.2.6). Only two names are certain ("Cornelius" and Ap. Claudius Centho), the rest conjectural. P. Aelius Ligus and C. Popillius Laenas were *coss.* in 172, and therefore must have held the praetorship in or before 175 under the terms of the *lex Villia*

Annalis. One praetorian place is open for 178, and two or four for the year 175 (as well as one for 174, not relevant in these particular cases).

88. On the *praenomen* and *cognomen*, see *MRR* I 402. However, J. D. Morgan ("The Praetors of 179–165 B.C."), rightly notes that Ser. Sulla appears in second place (not "immediately," as reported in *MRR* I 402) after the *consulares* in the list of *decem legati* sent to Macedonia in 167 (Liv. 45.17.3), and so need not be a *praetorius* identical with the Cornelius who was *pr.* 175. Morgan thus suggests, as an alternate identification for this "Cornelius," M. Cornelius Mamulla, sent as a *legatus* to the east in 173 (42.6.4–5), observing that P. Cornelius Mamulla was *pr.* 180 and A. Mamulla in 191, and that all three could be sons of A. Cornelius Mamulla, *pr.* 217. But in Livy's list of *legati* for 173, M. Mamulla is fourth of five, after two individuals whose status as *praetorii* is merely possible, not certain (see n. 90 below).

89. P. Aelius Ligus may have had a connection with the Aelii Paeti, but note the different *praenomina* (as well as *cognomina*).

90. See *MRR* I 402 on Cn. Lutatius Cerco and Q. Baebius Sulca, who seem to have held the praetorship before 173. For the available openings in praetorian colleges previous to that date, see ii. 87 above.

91. See Suet. *Tib.* 1.2, claiming that the *gens Claudia* abolished use of the *praenomen* "Lucius" after one L. Claudius was condemned for *latrocinium* and another for murder. If so, it can only have been the plebeian Claudii: note L. Claudius, attested as *rex sacrorum* (and thus a patrician—Cic. *Dom.* 38) in 57 (*Dom.* 127 with *Har.* 12), and cf. L. Claudius L.f. in a senatorial *consilium* of 73 (*RDGE* 23 lines 15–16). On these latter two men see Taylor, *VDRR* 203.

92. Since C. Longinus was *cos.* in 171, he must have held the praetorship in 178, 175 or 174 (the three years in which there are spaces available in the college of praetors—see n. 87 above). The Cassii Longini may have claimed descent from Sp. Cassius Vicellinus, *cos.* 502, III 486.

93. See Crawford, *RRC* I 451 no. 427, for the moneyer C. Memmius C.f. (the year 56), claiming descent from the aedile Memmius who (he indicates) first celebrated the Cerealia, tentatively assigned by Broughton (*MRR* I 273) to 211.

94. Cf. *pr.* 186, possibly this man's father (thus Münzer, *RE* s.v. col. 251); alternately, a brother or cousin.

95. An M. Raccius was sent (by the Senate, one must assume) as a *legatus* to Massilia in 208 (Liv. 27.36.3).

96. The names of only three praetors are certain for this year. The praetorships of Q. Aelius Paetus (*cos.* 167), T. Manlius Torquatus (*cos.* 165), and Cn. Domitius Ahenobarbus (*cos. suff.* 162) are inferred from their consulships. Other possible dates are 178, 175, and 174. For Domitius, see *MRR* I 422.

97. For the (good) possibility the *pr.* 211 C. Sulpicius was his father, see Münzer, *RE* s.v. col. 808, cf. s.v. *Sulpicius* 8 col. 734.

98. See Ser. Cornelius Cn.f. Cn.n. Lentulus, *cos.* 303; also the *aed. cur.* Ser. Lentulus of 207. The latter should be this man's father.

99. Perhaps a brother of ?T<i>. Capito, *pr.* 178. Cf. also M. Fonteius, *pr.* 166 (for the praenomen M. among the Fonteii Capitones, see *CIL* VI 18515).

100. See Q. Anicius Praenestinus, *aed. cur.* 304.

101. Though son of a praetor, called *novus homo* by Cicero (*Off.* 1.138; cf. *Phil.* 9.4)—an excellent demonstration of Gelzer's definition of *nobilitas* in the late Republic (1.5.2). On this case, see D. R. Shackleton Bailey, *AJPh* 107 (1986) 259f.

102. J. D. Morgan ("The Praetors of 179–165 B.C.") suggests this man might be the *pr.* (Iulius) Caesar said to have suddenly died in Rome (Plin. *Nat.* 7.181, with no date, but probably second century).

103. Cf. C. Nerva, *pr.* 167; also the *legatus* C. Nerva active in Thrace and Illyria in that same year (Liv. 45.42.11; cf. 26.2–3). Münzer (*RE* ad. loc. col. 452) suggests a link with the Licinii Crassi (*coss.* 171 and 168).

104. I have ordered individuals in this list whose praetorship is inferred from consulship or consular candidacy according to latest date permissable under the *lex Villia Annalis* (i.e., supposing a minimum of a *biennium* between praetorship and candidacy for the consulship).

105. Cf. C. Fannius, who shows up as *tr. pl.* in the story of the Petillian rogation (Liv. 38.60.3, under the year 187).

106. Note three relatives as *coss.* in the last generation: M. Cornelius M.f. M.n. Cethegus in 204, C. Cornelius L.f. M.n. Cethegus in 197, and P. Cornelius L.f. P.n. Cethegus in 181.

107. M. Fulvius Nobilior and Cn. Cornelius Dolabella, who were consular colleagues in 159, were *aed. cur.* in 166 and 165 respectively. Supposing a mandatory *biennium* at this time between curule aedileship and praetorship (A. E. Astin, *The Lex Annalis before Sulla* [Brussels 1958] 13–14), Dolabella must have been *pr.* 162, and Nobilior *pr.* 163 or 162 (but not later).

108. See E. Badian, *PBSR* 33 (1965) 48 on descent (almost certainly son of a *rex sacrorum* who died in 180).

109. Cf. (with caution) the stemma in Sumner, *Orators* 66.

110. In second place on a high-ranking embassy to the east of 154 (Plb. 33.13.4–10), above A. Postumius Albinus, *pr.* 155, and so very likely a *praetorius*. See Münzer, *RE* s.v. *Oppius* 10 cols. 736–737 on his inferred praetorship and possible descent.

111. Praetorian status is virtually assured by the fact that he led an important eastern embassy in 149 (Plb. 37.6.1–2); see Münzer, *RE* s.v. *Licinius* 22 col. 220. Son of *pr.* 186, or grandson or son of *aed.* 202.

112. Father of *pr.* 132 and *cos.* 129. If he assisted L. Mummius as a *legatus* in Greece in 146 (see Münzer, *RE* s.v. *Sempronius* 91 cols. 1440–1441), he was possibly of praetorian status. But his attendance on this embassy is wholly uncertain: see E. Badian, "Cicero and the Commission of 146 B.C.," in J. Bibauw (ed.), *Hommages à M. Renard* I (Brussels 1969) 54–65.

113. See Cic. *Ver.* 2.5.181 for his *novitas* ("humili atque obscuro loco natus").

114. Brother of the *cos.* 146, and probably of praetorian rank by 144/143, when he was sent as a member of a high-ranking embassy to the east with P. Cornelius Scipio Aemilianus, *cos.* 147, and L. Caecilius Metellus Calvus, *cos.* 142 (*MRR* I 481 with n. 2). On the date of this embassy, see H. B. Mattingly, *CQ* 36 (1986) 491–495, persuasively arguing against the traditional date of 140/139 (for which see *MRR* I 481). Sp. Mummius was probably praetor ca. 145, for he is said to have been an *aequalis* of C. Laelius (*pr.* 145 and *cos.* 140) and P. Scipio Aemilianus (*cos.* 147 at thirty-seven or thirty-eight, under the legal age) (Cic. *Amic.* 101; cf. Sumner, *Orators* 45).

115. Exact descent is difficult to ascertain: see E. Badian, *Chiron* 20 (1990) 399 n. 5. Against the notion that he served as praetor in Sicily, see T. C. Brennan, *RFIC* 121 (1993) 166–167.

116. See *RDGE* 10 B line 3 (the year 135), where he is the senior member of the senatorial *consilium*, and thus must be a *praetorius*. For the praetorian status of his family, see n. 39 above. This man was a quaestor in 143 or 142 (9.1.3); cf. G. Perl, *AJAH* 5 (1980) [1983] 98–99.

117. There is no compelling evidence to suggest that this man served as praetor in Sicily: see the references collected in *MRR* III 169 with 16f, esp. T. P. Wiseman, *PBSR* 32 (1964) 21–37 = *Roman Studies, Literary and Historical* (Liverpool 1987) 99–115. See ch. 9 n. 80 for this man's presidency of the Senate as *cos.* 132 for the passage of *RDGE* 11—not a *pr. urb.* "C. Popillius".

118. See Cic. *Brut.* 98 with *Luc.* 13 for descent.

119. See 5.4.5 with ch. 5 n. 169.

120. A consular candidate before 129 (Broughton, *MRR* I 493 and *Candidates Defeated* 16), quite possibly for 130: T. C. Brennan, *RFIC* 121 (1993) 173 n. 1.

121. Defeated candidate for the consulship: see V. Max. 9.3.2 with Broughton, *Candidates Defeated* 14.

122. See *NM* 237 no. 224, where Wiseman (following *MRR* I 504) designates this man as "*pr.* Mac[edonia] 129." But he is much more likely to have fought against the Cisalpine Iapydes in 129 as a *legatus* of praetorian rank: see 8.6.1.

123. *Nobilis* (Cic. *Leg.* 3.35). On the Cassii Longini see Sumner, *Orators* 48–51 (with some caution).

124. Probably son of M. Lepidus, *cos.* 158: see Sumner, *Orators* 64–66 with (speculative) *stemma* on 66.

125. See *prr.* 189, 146, 135.

126. L. Manlius and C. Sempronius are listed first and second in the *consilium* to the S.C. reported at J. *AJ* 13.260, a session at which C. Fannius presided. See *MRR* I 509 n. 2 on the date "ca. 126"; but see 5.4.5 on the possibility that this S.C. might date to 122. L. Manlius is certainly not a *consularis*, and should be a praetorian; the status of C. Sempronius is of course unknown. For discussion of these individuals, see Taylor, *VDRR* 230 (L. Manlius) and 252f (C. Sempronius, suggesting he is a Longus).

127. See Cic. *de Orat.* 3.74 ("nobilissimum") with M. Gelzer, *The Roman Nobility*, trans. R. Seager (Oxford 1969) 31.

128. Undoubtedly patrician, though not recognized as such in *MRR*: see E. Badian, *Chiron* 20 (1990) 402 n. 13, noting that the Marcii Reges at some stage (we cannot tell when) evidently claimed descent from Ancus Marcius (Plin. *Nat.* 31.41; also Plu. *Cor.* 1.1).

129. See T. C. Brennan, *Emerita* 63 (1995) 50–60; also 7.3.1.

130. Possibly son of M. Atilius Serranus, *pr.* 174, and brother of Sex. Atilius M.f. C.n. Serranus (*cos.* 136): see T. C. Brennan, *Emerita* 63 (1995) 52 n. 17 (also outlining other options). For the date of his praetorship, see *Emerita* 63 (1995) 52 and 59, and 7.3.1 above.

131. For the possibilities regarding this man's descent, see E. Badian, *Chiron* 20 (1990) 400 n. 6. His praetorship is discussed in 7.3.1.

132. Adopted by *pr.* 181.

133. On his father, see Plin. *Nat.* 7.142 with E. Badian, *Chiron* 20 (1990) 400 n. 7.

134. See T. C. Brennan, *Emerita* 63 (1995) 60–69; also 7.3.1.

135. See Cic. *Mur.* 15 with Crawford, *RRC* I 237 no. 186, on this man's praetorship; the date is inferred from his presence on the embassy sent to assist L. Mummius in Greece in 146 (see Münzer, *RE* s.v. *Licinius* 120 col. 444).

136. Cf. the epitomator of Pompon. *Dig.* 1.2.2.36 (Ap. Claudius Caecus, *cos.* 307, II 296) "hic Centemmanus appellatus est." "Unimanus" may have been a (derogatory) nickname attached to this unsuccessful praetor; cf. Münzer, *RE* s.v. *Claudius* 376 col. 2885. Alternately, he indeed might have had only one arm. See T. C. Brennan, *Emerita* 63 (1995) 63–65 and 7.3.1 above.

137. On the *provinciae*, see T. C. Brennan, *Emerita* 63 (1995) 65–69, and 7.3.1 above.

138. Adopted by *pr.* 181. On the date and *provincia* of his praetorship, see 9.1.3.

139. See T. C. Brennan, *Emerita* 63 (1995) 69–72, 73–76; also 7.3.1.

140. For date, see 9.1.3. On descent and name, see D. R. Shackleton Bailey, *Onomasticon to Cicero's Treatises* (Stuttgart 1996) 36.

141. Note *pr.* 209; also C. Hostilius, senatorial envoy in 168 (*MRR* I 430).

142. See V. Max. 8.1 amb. 1, with 6.2.2 and 9.2.1 above; the date of the incident in this passage may be either 176 or ca. 142. In any event, this M. Popillius Laenas was *cos.* 139, so his praetorship is assured.

143. For the date, see *RDGE* 4 with H. B. Mattingly, *NC*[7] 9 (1969) 103–104; Crawford, *RRC* I 239–241 no. 189.

144. See *RDGE* 7 with H. B. Mattingly, *NC*[7] 9 (1969) 103–104. He was *cos.* 137.

145. See *SIG*[3] 683 lines 42–43 and 50 for Q. Calpurnius' praetorship, which must fall after the year 145 (cf. lines 53–55 and 64–65 of this document) and 138 (he was *cos.* 135).

146. We know from Cicero (*Att.* 12.5b) that P. Mucius Scaevola (*cos.* 133) was praetor in 136; he also was in Rome to pronounce his opinion on the question of the citizen status of C. Hostilius Mancinus (*cos.* 137), who had been extradited after his consulship to Numantia—and rejected. But Mancinus' return, and the attempt of the *tr. pl.* P. Rutilius to keep him out of the Senate, may have come only in 135 (for the chronology, see T. C. Brennan, *Athenaeum* 67 [1989] 486–487). None of the sources collected on P. Mucius Scaevola in *MRR* I 487 say that he argued as praetor against Mancinus' right to be a citizen (though that position is usually assumed without discussion—e.g., R. Seguin, *REA* 72 [1970] 101). P. Scaevola's activities as praetor as well as his *provincia* must remain wholly unknown.

147. That the *cos.* 130 was *pr.* in Sicily—and identical with the "Lentulus" defeated just before the start of the First Slave War (Flor. 2.7.7)—is possible, but not probable or certain: see T. C. Brennan, *RFIC* 121 (1993) 166 n. 1; cf. 6.3.1 above. But this L. Lentulus reached the praetorship in any case.

148. See *pr.* 189. For the date, see T. C. Brennan, *RFIC* 121 (1993) 174–177, esp. 176, and 6.3.1 above.

149. See 9.1.3 with ch. 9 n. 52 for the filiation.

150. For the date and identification, see T. C. Brennan, *RFIC* 121 (1993) 165, 178–183, and cf. 6.3.1.

151. For the date, see T. C. Brennan, *Athenaeum* 67 (1989) 486–487.

152. For the date, see T.C. Brennan, *RFIC* 121 (1993) 167–174, 177. On his descent, cf. E. Badian, *Chiron* 22 (1990) 381.

153. Praetorship (and filiation) directly attested by *ILLRP* 454a, on which see *MRR* III 16f. He was *cos.* 128.

154. See 9.1.5 n. 85. On the "Octavius Cn.f." of *RDGE* 1, see below in B.8.

155. See *MRR* I 507 n. 1 for a discussion of status and date. The evidence comes from a dossier of inscriptions from Delphi, *SIG*[3] 704 B and C (honors to a P. Cornelius P.f. Lentulus, no title of office), and esp. 705 (= *RDGE* 15, ca. 112 B.C.) col. II line 21, which refers to an S.C. of some years previous stipulating joint meetings of Dionysiac artists passed "in the time of P. Cornelius" (ἐπὶ Ποπ[λίου Κορ]νηλίο[υ]), with no title given. Broughton makes P. Lentulus a praetor for the relevant *provincia*, i.e., Macedonia. A dating formula with ἐπί is found later in this same inscription (*RDGE* 15 lines 32–33 and 59–60), where events are placed "in the time of" Cn. Cornelius Sisenna, explicitly called praetor for Macedonia (on his date 118/117, see 14.1.1); *SIG*[3] 704 K[1] line 1 again dates by this *pro cos.* for the province. See also *SIG*[3] 748 line 11, where an inscription of Gytheum recounts an event "in the time of [L.] Marcilius"—who though no more than a legate of the *pr.* 74 M. Antonius Creticus (cf. line 16), was then in charge of the area, preparing for Antonius' arrival. However, Prof. Badian has offered (*per litteras*) a powerful counterinterpretation of *SIG*[3] 705 col. II line 21, that ἐπί with an S.C. means (as usual) "under the presidency of," and so P. Cornelius Lentulus must be a city praetor.

156. See *ILLRP* 291 with 5.5.2. On the basis of this inscription Broughton (*MRR* II 18, III 199) assigns a praetorship to his son the orator C. Sextius Calvinus (on whom see Cic. *Brut.* 130, *de Orat.* 2.246 and 249, each passage mentioning his poor physical state). The evidence for that of course disappears if the stone belongs instead to the father, as it seems it must.

157. For the date, see Cic. *de Orat.* 1.166–167, where Cn. Octavius (*cos.* 128)—though not M. Plautius Hypsaeus (*cos.* 125)—is *consularis* at the time of this man's praetorship.

158. On this man's descent, see the detailed discussion of E. Badian, *Chiron* 20 (1990) 398 n. 3. The moneyer TQ (*RRC* I 291 no. 267, dated by Crawford to 126 B.C.) should be his son; but see Sumner, *Orators* 68.

159. Definitely reached the praetorship (he was *cos.* 122). Yet direct attestation disappears if J. *AJ* 13.260—a Senate meeting at which C. Fannius presided as στρατηγός—indeed belongs to his consulship (as suggested in 5.4.5).

160. See App. *BC* 1.22.92 with 9.2.2 above. L. Cotta was *cos.* 119. For the possible descent of Salinator, cf. the *cos.* 188, also the *pr.* 191.

161. Father of P. Servilius C.f. M.n. Vatia Isauricus (*cos.* 79), born ca. 134 (C. Cichorius, *Untersuchungen zu Lucilius* [Berlin 1908] 156 n. 1 and Münzer, *RE* s.v. *Servilius* 93 coll. 1812 and 1816, citing Cic. *Phil.* 2.12 and Suid. s.v. Ἀπίκιος Μάρκος I 1 pp. 287–288 A) and *pr.* perhaps by 93 (13.1.1). Cic. *Ver.* 2.3.211 clearly implies that the consul's father held a command in an armed *provincia* (and so as praetor?)—perhaps Macedonia, if (as likely) he is identical with the C. Servilius Vatia who dedicated a statue at Olympia (see *I. Olymp.* 329 with *MRR* II 465). The date is difficult, especially since Badian (*PBSR* 52 [1984] 52–55) has cast doubt on whether he should be identified with either the C. Servilius M.f. who was (on Crawford's dating) a moneyer ca. 136 (*RRC* I 270–271, no. 239) or—as Crawford had argued—the C. Servilius whom he makes a moneyer ca. 127 (*RRC* I 289, no. 264). (See further the remarks of C. A. Hersh, *NC*[7] 17 [1977] 24–27, questioning Crawford's basic arrangement of the coinage of the mid-130s through mid-120s.) Lucilius (801 M, from Book 28), plays with the name "Vatia," which should show that the father was active by ca. 129: see Cichorius, *Untersuchungen zu Lucilius* 154–157, and E. Badian, *PBSR* 39 (1984) 52. But that does not get us much further in determining the details of his career. If this man's command does not belong to a year or years before 121, the Macedonian *fasti* hardly allow any alternate date other than one ca. 115. Just before this book went to press, Prof. Badian brought to my attention a recently discovered pavement inscription from the temple of Jupiter or Veiovis on the Tiber Island. It commemorates a dedication by C. Servilius M.f. pr(aetor) and at least two sons whose *praenomina* are lost. (The text is to appear as *CIL* VI 40896a, with commentary by G. Alföldy.) This praetor may be our Vatia (i.e., acting in the city before setting off for his province); he indeed had multiple male issue, to judge from the nomenclature of the *cos.* 79. But viable alternatives are the aforementioned *monetales* of ca. 136 or ca. 127 (assuming that each is to be dissociated from C. Vatia), or another later second/early first century C. Servilius M.f. otherwise unknown to us.

162. See *MRR* III 27–28 with 12.5.1 above for date, and Plin. *Nat.* 7.142 for the *agnomen*.

163. See 14.1.1 for date.

164. *Cos.* 117, so praetor by 120 under the *leges annales*; see E. Badian, *Chiron* 20 (1990) 384, for descent. The praetorian *provincia* suggested here is highly conjectural (10.5.1).

165. *Cos.* 116, and so definitely reached the praetorship. See *RDGE* 13 lines 6–7 with ch. 12 n. 4 for his presidency of a Senate meeting, very possibly as praetor.

166. Q. Caecilius Metellus (Numidicus, the future *cos.* 109) prosecuted this man for improperly exacting money from *socii* (Gel. 15.14.1), i.e. on a charge de repetundis or peculatus. R. Syme (*Roman Papers* I [Oxford 1979] 265–266 and 290–291), noting that *OGIS* 460 (from Magnesia ad Sipylum, honoring Potitus Valerius Messalla, the *cos. suff.* 29) implies a hereditary link of the Valerii Messallae with Asia, argues that Gellius' "Valerius Messalla" is the grandfather of the *cos.* 61, M. Valerius M.f. M.'n. Messalla, and father of Valerius Messalla, *legatus* 90 in the Social War (App. *BC* 1.40.179), and thus *pr.* ca. 120 in Asia. For further literature, see M. C. Alexander, *Trials in the Late Roman Republic* (Toronto 1990)

no. 29 (with date "ca. 119?"). From the fact that Q. Metellus' speech *In Valerium Messalam* stretched to at least three books (Gel.), the accused does seem likely to have been a praetor. But his precise date and even *provincia* must remain uncertain.

167. Second place (of five) on a high-ranking legation to Crete of 113 (H. Van Effenterre, *REA* 44 [1942] 36 document D lines 63–65), above P. Rutilius P.f. (Rufus), *pr.* by 118 (and later *cos.* 105). Broughton (*MRR* I 536 with 537 n. 5, III 89) is surely right to suppose he was then a *praetorius*, with his praetorship falling in or before 118. On the difficult problems surrounding the identity and career of this man, see above all Sumner, *Orators* 53–55 and 171–175, esp. 54 where he suggests that this C. Fannius C.f. was "born ca. 170" and "praetor between ca. 130 and ca. 119 (probably in the period ca. 130–124, aged about 39–45)." Perhaps he is to be identified with the C. [——]ius C.f. who has second position in the senatorial *consilium* to *RDGE* 12, best dated to 101 B.C. (Additional Note XIII).

168. Unsuccessful consular candidate for 115 (Broughton, *Candidates Defeated* 16), only reaching the office in 105. See E. Badian, *Chiron* 20 (1990) 387 on his descent ("probably" son of *pr.* 166, P. Rutilius Calvus).

169. Cic. *Brut.* 124 implies this man reached the praetorship (see *MRR* I 521 and 522 n. 2); Sumner (*Orators* 68–69), accepting this interpretation, suggests a date between 121 and 117. For his descent, note C. Scribonius, *pr.* 193 ("probably his grandfather," according to Sumner, *Orators* 68). Badian (*Chiron* 20 [1990] 391) adds, "there may be a *pr.* (after 167) in the generation between them, perhaps identical with the moneyer *RRC* 201, put by Crawford in 154."

170. *Cos.* 111; see Badian, *Chiron* 20 (1990) 385 for discussion of descent.

171. This individual appears in second position—following the *cos.* 115 M. Aemilius Scaurus—in a senatorial *consilium* of at least four members, securely dated to May 112 (*RDGE* 15 lines 2–6. This Ser [——] Ser.f. is possibly though not certainly to be identified with a contemporary Ser. Cornelius Ser.f. Lentulus (14.5.2, and also text corresponding to n. 230 below).

172. See *P. Teb.* I 33 lines 3–6 with Additional Note XIII.

173. See E. Badian, *Chiron* 20 (1990) 386, for discussion of identification (possibly *tr. pl.* 124) and descent, and also M. Crawford on the moneyer M. Silan(us) in *RRC* I 300–301 no. 285 (which Crawford dates to 116 or 115 B.C.). The moneyer and the *cos.* 109 are unlikely to be identical, though it is not unknown for men to hold the position of *monetalis* after a quaestorship (cf. *RRC* I 313 no. 300, 414 no. 404, 414–418 no. 405, and possibly 316 no. 306) or a tribunate (324 no. 318). The supposition that M. Silanus held a praetorian command in Spain (for which see *MRR* I 535 and 537 n. 2) seems highly dubious (7.3.2).

174. See 10.6.2.

175. Discussed in 14.3.1. For identification and descent see E. Badian, *Chiron* 20 (1990) 388 and 404 n. 19.

176. *Monetalis* (*RRC* I 296 no. 277, dated by Crawford to 122 B.C.) and by 117 a senator (*CIL* I² 584). Possibly of praetorian status when he served in Macedonia for all or part of the years 110 to mid-106 on the staff of his brother M. Minucius Rufus (*cos.* 110) (Fron. *Str.* 2.4.3) as *legatus* (confirmed by *SIG*³ 710 D = *CIL* I² 693 [Delphi], also offering filiation).

177. For discussion of name and social rank, see E. Badian, *Chiron* 20 (1990) 387 and 403f n. 17, cf. Wiseman, *NM* 239 no. 243.

178. See ch. 10 n. 43. *Praenomen* in Cic. *Brut.* 95; on his descent (merely probable) see Sumner, *Orators* 46.

179. Cic. *Ver.* 2.5.181 and *Planc.* 52 may imply that this *novus homo* (cf. *Planc.* 12 with Wiseman, *NM* 231 no. 180) did not proceed to the consulship quickly (thus, rightly, *MRR* I 552 n. 4). His prosecution for *repetundae* is just as plausibly attached to a consular command as a praetorian one (see Alexander, *Trials* no. 61 with p. 31 n. 1, also *MRR* III 92). Among oth-

ers, he is a candidate for identification with the C. [——]ius C.f. who has second position in the senatorial *consilium* to RDGE 12, best dated to 101 B.C. (see Additional Note XIII).

180. Attested as a (senior) *legatus* in Gaul under Marius in 103 (ch. 10 n. 44). If he was with Marius also in 104, his praetorship probably belongs earlier than that year (cf. *MRR* I 561 n. 1).

181. The *cos.* 100 is a priori identical with the *monetalis* L. VALERI FLACCI of *RRC* I 316 no. 306 (dated by Crawford to 108 or 107 B.C.). If so—and if Crawford is right on the date of that issue—this would be another likely instance of an individual holding the office of moneyer after a quaestorship (see n. 173 above). Badian once suggested (*Studies* 86–87, also *Gnomon* 33 [1961] 498) that this man is the (praetorian) commander L. Flaccus who saw his quaestor M. Aurelius Scaurus attempt to prosecute him but fail in the *divinatio* (Cic. *Div. Caec.* 63, cf. Ps.-Asc. p. 203 St.). But Badian's subsequent identification of this commander with the L. Valerius Flaccus who governed Asia before 90 and later was *cos. suff.* 86 seems preferable: see ch. 14 n. 239.

182. See Additional Note XIII. On the family of L. Memmius, see Sumner, *Orators* 85–90.

183. Cicero at *Balb.* 28 lists three Roman exiles who took up citizenship at Nuceria: Q. (Fabius) Maximus (*cos.* 116, exile probably 104—Alexander, *Trials* no. 32), C. (Popillius) Laenas (a senior, perhaps praetorian [see n. 178 above] *legatus* in 107, with exile in that year or 106—*Trials* no. 59), and Q. (Marcius) Philippus. He then brings up three consular exiles who became citizens elsewhere: at Tarraco, C. (Porcius) Cato (*cos.* 114, exile 110—*Trials* no. 55), and at Smyrna, Q. (Servilius) Caepio (*cos.* 106, exile 103—*Trials* no. 66) and P. Rutilius (Rufus) (*cos.* 105, exile [surely] 92—*Trials* no. 94). It seems reasonable to suppose—given the status and general date of the other men on this list—that Q. Philippus had reached the praetorship sometime in the late second century. (The Social War, when Nuceria itself gained Roman citizenship, provides a terminus.) He will have been the father (thus G. V. Sumner, *Phoenix* 25 [1971] 253 n. 22) or elder brother of the *cos.* 91 L. Marcius Q.f. Philippus. Note the moneyer Q. Philippus of *RRC* I 284–285 no. 259, which is dated by Crawford to 129 B.C. If accepted, this man could be father or even possibly brother of the *cos.* 91 (who was a *monetalis* on Crawford's dating as early as 113 or 112 [*RRC* I 307–308 no. 293]). But Crawford's dating of his no. 259 may be too late: see C. A. Hersh, *NC*[7] 17 (1977) 24–27.

184. See E. Badian, *PBSR* 20 (1965) 49f for the suggestion.

185. Cicero (*Brut.* 161) relates that L. Crassus was colleague of Q. Mucius Scaevola in all his magistracies except the tribunate (107 B.C.) and censorship (92 B.C.). Unfortunately, we do not have a date for the praetorship of either man; see further on Scaevola in 14.5.4.

186. See E. Badian, *Chiron* 20 (1990) 389 with 405 n. 21 for discussion of descent.

187. Candidate for *cos.* 93 (Broughton, *Candidates Defeated* 15), he finally reached the office two years later; see E. Badian, *Chiron* 20 (1990) 389, for discussion of his descent. Philippus' praetorian *provincia* will not have been the urban jurisdiction: see Cic. *Off.* 2.59 on his not having given games. (In this passage, "sine ullo munere" is interpreted to mean "without any gladiatorial show" by F. X. Ryan, *AClass* 38 [1995] 98–99: implausibly, as, e.g., *Dom.* 111–112 shows.) On the supposition that he was prosecuted *de repetundis* following a praetorian command, see 10.4.4.

188. See 13.3.2 for discussion.

189. Possibly of praetorian standing. Longus was senior *legatus* of the *pr.* L. Sempronius Asellio in Sicily in the mid- to late 90s, in which capacity he gave advice on the drafting of the praetor's edict (D.S. 37.8.1–3), obviously playing the role of "Rutilius" to Asellio's "Scaevola" (13.1.4 above). He is perhaps to be identified with C. Sempronius C.f. Fal., listed ninth (as *aedilicius* or *tribunicius*) in the *consilium* of RDGE 12, the S.C. *de agro Pergameno* of (surely) 101 (see Additional Note XIII). See further *MRR* III 187f for this man's possible

family. The Sempronii Longi had an old connection to Sicily (see *MRR* I 238 on the *cos.* 218).

190. Eleventh (probably as *tribunicius*) in the senatorial *consilium* of *RDGE* 12 of 101 B.C. (see Additional Note XIII), and perhaps to be identified with the P. Al[——] who is listed second in an inscription from Vibo widely regarded as a list of land commissioners under Drusus' law of 91 (*CIL* X 44 and p. 1003; C. Cichorius, *Römische Studien* 116–125; but cf. Badian, *Gnomon* 33 [1961] 494–495 on this particular supplement). If accepted, his position between [?L. L]icinius L.f. Crassus (apparently the *cos.* 95) and [Sempronius As]ellio (i.e., either the *pr.* ca. 93 or *pr. urb.* 89) suggests that he was certainly of praetorian rank by the year 91. He was perhaps son of the *quaestorius* Albius (*RE* 2), on whom see *MRR* III 14.

191. See 10.5.2 and 10.5.4.

192. See Sumner, *Orators* 103, for the suggestion that his career was delayed by the wars, speculating that he "probably held the praetorship between 94 and 90 (at the latest)."

193. For descent, see Münzer, *RE* s.v. col. 1786. Quaestor in 103 (but possibly 100), Q. Caepio had probably reached the praetorship by the time he saw service in the Social War in 90 as a *legatus* of the consul P. Rutilius Lupus (see App. *BC* 1.40.179, *Per.* 73 for title, cf. Eutrop. 5.3.2 "nobilis iuvenis"): see 10.5.3 with esp. ch. 10 n. 148. Sumner, *Orators* 116–117 (assuming a quaestorship in 100) is dubious.

194. Served in the Social War as a *legatus* under the *cos.* 90 P. Rutilius Lupus (App. *BC* 1.40.179). Broughton (*MRR* II 29) is likely to be correct that Perperna was already praetorian in status by the year 90: see 10.5.3. Perhaps a younger brother of M. Perperna M.f., *cos.* 92 (thus Münzer, *RE* s.v. *Perperna* 2 col. 893, suggesting C. Perperna was precisely *pr.* 92).

195. In the *cos.* Cn. Pompeius Strabo's *consilium* at Asculum in 89 (*ILLRP* 515), a Cn. Octavius Q.f. is listed second after L. Gellius (*pr.* 94)—and so probably is also a *praetorius*. He is generally identified with the Cn. Octavius Ruso who served as quaestor in 105 in the war against Jugurtha (Sal. *Jug.* 104.3). See, however, E. Badian, *Chiron* 20 (1990) 405f n. 22, who argues that this individual is Cn. Octavius, *cos.* 87 (see further n. 200 below). The *praenomen* "Quintus" is not found among the noble Octavii, making descent from the *cos.* 165 unlikely.

196. See 10.5.4. On descent, see the *stemma* of the Gabinii of the later Republic at E. Badian, *Philologus* 103 (1959) 97; also C. Nicolet, *Insula sacra: La loi Gabinia-Calpurnia de Délos* (58 av. J.-C.) (Rome 1980) 50f.

197. His son was M. Claudius Marcellus Aeserninus, whose own homonymous son was *cos.* 22 B.C.: see Sumner, *Orators* 91–93. But against Sumner's argument that our putative praetor had reached the office by 103, see ch. 10 nn. 44 and 156.

198. See ch. 10 n. 148.

199. See ch. 10 n. 156. Sumner in his stemma of the Cornelii Lentuli (*Orators* 143) makes this man son of the *cos.* 130.

200. This man was once defeated for an aedileship (Broughton, *Candidates Defeated* 42, offering the date "ca. 95" on the basis of his presumed praetorship). See E. Badian, *Chiron* 20 (1990) 390 with 405f n. 22, for discussion of name and descent, also arguing convincingly against attributing *I. Délos* IV 1 1782 to this man. See further ch. 9 n. 85 and (for his possible service at Asculum in 89) n. 195 above.

201. See Sumner, *AJAH* 2 (1977) 18, for the suggestion that the brother of Cn. Pompeius Strabo (*cos.* 89) may have reached the praetorship.

202. See ch. 10 n. 227. On the possibility of praetorian descent see Münzer, *RE* s.v. col. 1766.

203. See n. 251 below on L. Dolabella (a praetorian *triumphator* of 98) for descent.

204. Probably reached the praetorship under the Marian government: see 10.5.7 with ch. 10 nn. 228–229. On Cethegus' further career, see *MRR* III 64 (with sources), correctly

noting he was "very influential in the Senate and in the political intrigues of the decade of the 70s"; A. Keaveney, *Lucullus: A Life* (London 1992) 67–71 with 222, offers a good sketch of the details. Cicero (*Brut.* 178), discussing Cethegus as an orator, makes him an *aequalis* of C. Iulius Caesar Strabo (born at the latest ca. 127) and says that his deep practical knowledge of the *res publica* gave him an impact equal to that of the *consulares* in the Senate (i.e., when he was called upon to give his *sententia*). And so Sumner (*Orators* 106) reasonably suggests "it appears highly probable that he reached praetorian rank. . . . [I]t could be conjectured that he returned with the Marian victory in 87, and held the praetorship—for which he was actually qualified by age—in one of the immediately following years." Cethegus' patrician family background (see ch. 10 n. 228) makes Sumner's reconstruction all the more plausible. Contra F. X. Ryan, *Mnemosyne* 47 (1994) 681–685, a useful but ultimately unconvincing discussion that attempts to make Cethegus a subpraetorian solely on the basis of the loose parallel passage Cic. *Vat.* 16 (an ex-tribune said to have gained "consularem auctoritatem").

205. He was presumably son of the *monetalis* T. Clouli(us) (*RRC* I 285 no. 260): see Wiseman, *NM* 224 nos. 122 and 123. For possible praetorian status, see 10.5.6.

206. See 10.5.6.

207. First in the senatorial *consilium* to RDGE 18 (81 B.C.).

208. See 10.5.6.

209. A candidate for the consulship of 77 (see Sal. *Hist.* 1.86 M with Broughton, *Candidates Defeated* 29), he withdrew from competition but reached the office for the next year. Curio is listed first in the *consilium* to RDGE 20 (col. I A lines 5–6, on which see also Taylor, *VDRR* 268–269), and so was very likely an ex-praetor by 80, not (as F. X. Ryan, *AClass* 38 [1995] 99 has it) *pr.* 80. Whatever the year of his praetorship, he was not *pr. urbanus*: see Cic. *Off.* 2.59 on his lack of games. See E. Badian, *Chiron* 20 (1990) 391, for name and discussion of descent.

210. For descent, see Badian, *Chiron* 20 (1990) 384, citing Asc. p. 23 C "patricius . . . neque pater neque avus neque etiam proavus . . . honores adepti sunt." See also Sal. *Jug.* 15.4 ("nobilis"). For speculation on his praetorship, see 14.3.2 above.

211. His praetorship is discussed in 10.4.2. See Badian, *Chiron* 20 (1990) 384, for name and descent.

212. See ch. 14 n. 7 on the date.

213. Cic. *Ver.* 2.4.22 (cf. 2.3.184) with 13.1.2 above and E. Badian, *Historia* 42 (1993) 203–210. Not actually called "praetor," but on Badian's demonstration, almost certain to have been a governor of Sicily.

214. See Cic. *Mur.* 15, with *SIG*[3] 745 line 5 for name. The date is very approximate: he was son of a *praetorius* by 146 and father of a *pr.* 88 or 87.

215. See ch. 12 n. 4.

216. See 14.5.1. For discussion of descent, see E. Badian, *Chiron* 20 (1990) 385 with 402 n. 12.

217. Attested by *ILLRP* 461, a milestone found at Ilerda (hence Hispania Citerior), showing Fabius' rank as *pro cos.* For the descent see Degrassi ad loc., who reasonably suggests identifying this Spanish commander with the moneyer Q. Fabi(us) Labeo, dated by Crawford to 124 (*RRC* I 294 no. 173). Broughton is perhaps not too far off in his quite approximate date of ca. 110 (*MRR* I 543f; I suggest that his command can fall pretty much anywhere in the decade or so after ca. 115. (There is not a single known commander for Hispania Citerior in the period ca. 120–ca. 100.)

218. Known from *ILLRP* 462, a milestone found near Barcino (hence Hispania Citerior) showing Sergius as *pro cos.* Probably from the last third of the second century (cf. *MRR* I 543f, which tentatively assigns to this praetor a date very approximately ca. 110), and

perhaps from the same program of roadbuilding that produced *ILLRP* 461 (see n. 217 above).

219. The praetor for Asia "L. Piso" of *I. Priene* 121 line 22 should be identical with the future *cos.* 112: see 14.5.1. So L. Piso Caesoninus' service in Cisalpine Gaul (on which see *MRR* III 46–47) will have been as a consular commander. E. Badian, *Chiron* 20 (1990) 385, discusses descent.

220. See E. Badian, *Chiron* 20 (1990) 112, for name and descent. He was *cos.* 112, and so *pr.* by 115; the *provincia* is certain (12.1.1).

221. Wiseman, *NM* 240 no. 248.

222. *Provincia* not specified in *Vir. ill.* 72.6—our one source on his praetorship—but it entailed responsibilities in civil law (12.2.2).

223. See 13.1.2 for questions of identity, status and (approximate) date. Likely—but not certain—to have been praetor.

224. A son of the elder Cato by his second wife; he died in his praetorship. See Plu. *Cat. Ma.* 27.9 with F. Miltner, *RE* s.v. col. 168 (with strong arguments for a birthdate ca. 152); cf. also A. E. Astin, *Cato the Censor* (Oxford 1978) 105 (but suggesting a birth date of 154, and hence praetor "ca. 115"). M. Szymanski, *Hermes* 125 (1997) 384–386, tries to emend Salonianus out of a praetorship (offering also an absurd supplement for Plutarch's text).

225. Possibly the *monetalis* Q. Met(ellus) of *RRC* I 300 no. 284 (dated by Crawford to 117 or 116). *Cos.* 109, and so praetor by 112, evidently with service—if not in his magistracy then as promagistrate—in a territorial *provincia* (see Cic. *Ver.* 2.3.209). But Metellus' trial in which the equestrian jury refused to examine his account books (Alexander, *Trials* no. 51) should have followed his consular command in Numidia: see E. Badian, *Roman Imperialism in the Late Republic*² (Oxford 1968) 103 n. 19.

226. Cic. *Ver.* 2.4.56 provides evidence for descent, rank and *provincia*: see the discussion at 13.3.1 above.

227. *Cos.* 108, and thus *pr.* by 111. Appian (*Hisp.* 99.430) provides evidence of his Spanish command, and implies an absolute upper date of 112: see 13.3.1 above.

228. Either the future *cos. des.* 108 or his brother; at any rate, father of the orator (Cic. *Ver.* 2.3.42). Cicero in this passage does not explicitly call L. Hortensius "praetor," but the office seems certain: he lists him with Cn. Pompeius (in command of Sicily *pro pr.* in 82) and C. Marcellus (*ex praetura* in Sicily ca. 79) as men who, unlike C. Verres (*pr.* 74), "ab aequitate, ab lege, ab institutis non recesserunt" in their handling of emergency Sicilian grain tithes. C. Cichorius (*Untersuchungen zu Lucilius* 339) suggests a date between ca. 110 and 105 (preferring precisely the year 105); Broughton lists this putative praetor under 111 for convenience's sake, realizing that he may not be the *cos. des.* 108 (*MRR* I 540 with 541 n. 2). In (slight) support of Broughton's date, one notes that Hortensius had to collect an extra tithe (which Cicero later claims was a rare expedient before his own day—*Ver.* 2.3.227): one explanation for this unusual step is that Hortensius had to supply Roman troops staging in Sicily in 111 for the war against Jugurtha (see Sal. *Jug.* 28.6). On the question of the ancestry of the Hortensii of this era, see E. Badian, *Chiron* 20 (1990) 386.

229. See 10.6.2 with ch. 10 n. 258.

230. See 14.5.2.

231. See 13.3.1 on the date.

232. Apparently held a praetorian command in a territorial *provincia* (Cic. *Ver.* 2.3.209); Münzer, *RE* s.v. col. 2074 suggested Sicily, but there is no evidence. Before reaching the consulship for 102, Catulus had been defeated three times for the office, first for 106 (Broughton, *Candidates Defeated* 13f).

233. Reached the praetorship (Plin. *Nat.* 33.21 = Fen. *HRR* II F 12), probably before 107 when he crossed to Numidia as the consul C. Marius' principal *legatus* (*MRR* I 552). He was

certainly senior to Marius' quaestor L. Sulla in age (Sal. *Jug.* 102.4), and surely in rank, too (as is clear from Appian's version of their embassy to Bocchus at *Num.* 4.1–3). He was perhaps a patrician Torquatus or (just conceivably) Vulso. But Crawford may be right that he is to be identified with the moneyer A. MANLI(us) Q.F. SER (*RRC* I 318, no. 309, dated to 118–117 B.C.), in which case patrician status would not be guaranteed: see Taylor, *VDRR* 229–230, and note Q. Manlius (*RE* 34), *tr. pl.* 69.

234. Wiseman, *NM* 210 no. 16. For this praetor's approximate date, see Badian ap. *MRR* III 165f. Cicero (*Prov.* 15) terms T. Albucius "pro pr." at the time he scored a minor victory in Sardinia (see 13.1.1). Therefore his command in Sardinia lasted more than one year, or (just possibly) he was a city praetor sent *ex praetura* to that *provincia*.

235. See Wiseman, *NM* 217 no. 66; also D. R. Shackleton Bailey, *CEF* I 489f, and Broughton, *MRR* III 34 (on the name). Klebs (*RE* s.v. col. 253) dates his praetorship precisely to 107, without foundation: see 14.3.1.

236. For the existence of this praetor, see Var. *R.* 2.4.2 with *MRR* III 208. The date I supply here is quite conjectural, essentially splitting the difference between his father (a quaestor in 142, but apparently a *praetorius* by 135) and his son, whom I tentatively assign to a praetorship in or after 75 (see 15.2.1).

237. See 12.1.1.

238. Wiseman, *NM* 217 no. 69. See 14.5.2.

239. Known only from *AE* 1984, 495 (the *tabula Alcantarensis*), which provides name, date, status—Caesius bears the title "imperator"—and (to judge from find spot) *provincia* (13.3.1). Note the moneyer L. CAESI (*RRC* I 312 no. 298), dated by Crawford to 112–111 B.C. E. Champlin, *CPh* 84 (1989) 54, offers that the "praetor is presumably father of the *monetalis*." But if Crawford's date is approximately correct, they could very well be identical, as the career of another non-*nobilis*, C. Coelius Caldus (*mon.* ca. 104 and *pr.* before 98), goes to show. J. S. Richardson, *Hispaniae: Spain and the Development of Roman Imperialism, 218–82 B.C.* (Cambridge 1986) 199, accepts this identification as probable.

240. Found in 104 as *pr.* or possibly *pro pr.* in Sicily (*MRR* I 559 and 562 n. 3; cf. Münzer, *RE* s.v. col. 453 with date for his praetorship of 105). See further 13.1.3.

241. Plu. *Luc.* 1.1 provides descent. See 10.4.2 and 13.1.3 on his praetorship.

242. *Tr. pl.* 111, evidently *pro cos.* in Macedonia in some year after 107 (see 14.1.1), acquitted on a charge de repetundis (Cic. *Font.* 24, V. Max. 8.5.2), and consular candidate for 99. See Broughton, *MRR* I 562 n. 4 and III 141, also *Candidates Defeated* 28; cf. Münzer, *RE* s.v. col. 604 (with date of 103). His family: Sumner, *Orators* 85–90.

243. E. Badian, *Chiron* 20 (1990) 388 discusses descent. On the praetorship, see 10.1.

244. Wiseman, *NM* 229 no. 156. See E. Badian, *Chiron* 20 (1990) 388 and 404f n. 20, for discussion of descent, and 14.1.2 above for praetorship.

245. See 12.4.3 with ch. 12 n. 221 on descent and praetorship.

246. Son of Scipio "Hispalus," who, according to Valerius Maximus (6.3.3b), received "Hispania" in the (apparently praetorian though possibly quaestorian) sortition; the Senate then formally pronounced that he could not go to the province, offering as its reason "quod recte facere nesciret" (a vague rationale, even colloquial in its expression, for which Cic. *Ver.* 2.3.62 offers the only close parallel). For this, Valerius tells us that, despite his lack of provincial service, he was "as good as" ("tantum non") condemned for *repetundae*—clearly an exaggeration (cf. V. Max. 1.8.10 and 8.15.9). Mommsen (*St.-R.* III 1226 n. 4) had no parallel or ready explanation to offer for this incident. Münzer in *RE* reasonably considered this man to be a praetor—son of the Cn. Scipio Hispanus who was *pr. per.* 139—and suggested a date ca. 109, which Broughton follows (*MRR* I 546). The epitaph of the *pr.* 139 (*ILLRP* 316) certifies that he had at least one son (line 5 "progenies"), as Prof. Badian has pointed out to me.

247. See *I. Priene* 121 lines 21–23 with the discussion of Stumpf, *Numismatische Studien* 11–12 for status, likely descent and date ("ca. 100"); also 14.5.1 above. Stumpf (11-12) rightly dissociates this M. Hypsaeus from the "M. Plautius" of V. Max. 4.6.3, who was probably a *praefectus classis* (as *MRR* II 484 has it).

248. He obviously held a city *provincia* during his tumultuous year as praetor (sources in *MRR* I 574f): see 12.2.2, and on his fatal attempt to stand for a consulship for 99, E. Badian, *Chiron* 14 (1984) 106–121.

249. Presumably brother of *cos.* 107, etc. and adoptive father of their nephew M. Marius Gratidianus (Cic. *Brut.* 168, *Leg.* 3.36, *Schol. Bern.* on Luc. 2.173 p. 62 U): see, e.g., Münzer, *RE* s.v. col. 1818; Wiseman, *NM* 240 no. 249; D. R. Shackleton Bailey, *Two Studies in Roman Nomenclature*[2] (Atlanta, Ga., 1991) 78. On the date of M. Marius' tenure of Ulterior, see 13.3.1.

250. Father of the dictator. See 14.5.6 on his praetorship.

251. Triumphed from Hispania Ulterior on 26 January 98 (*Inscr. Ital.* XIII 1 84f, providing filiation), and so naturally in the *provincia* in 99, though probably not any earlier: see 13.3.1. Descent: E. Badian, *PBSR* 33 (1965) 49 (older brother of *cos.* 81).

252. *Cos.* 94, and certainly the same man as the C. Caldus who was *tr. pl.* 107 (*MRR* I 551), the moneyer "C. Coil(ius) Cald(us)" (*RRC* I 324 no. 318, dated by Crawford to 104), and the "C. Coelius C.f. Aem." who is listed in tenth place (as *tribunicius*) in the *consilium* of *RDGE* 12 (late June of what must be the year 101). See Additional Note XIII. On his *novitas*, see Wiseman, *NM* 225 no. 127. Evidence for praetorship is discussed in 13.3.2 (with ch. 13 n. 218).

253. See 14.5.4 on Scaevola's famous tenure of Asia (where I argue that it came *ex consulatu* in 94).

254. Discussed in 13.1.4. *MRR* II 8 n. 2 entertains the possibility that L. Domitius went to Sicily *ex praetura.* But there is nothing in our record for this particular man that suggests it.

255. On his praetorship and promagistracy, see T. C. Brennan, *Chiron* 22 (1992) 103–158. There is no firm basis for considering that his father held the praetorship: see J. A. Madden and A. Keaveney, *CPh* 88 (1993) 138–141.

256. Discussed in 14.5.6. This Asian praetor is possibly to be identified with the jurist L. Lucilius (19) Balbus; if so, he then was definitely of senatorial descent (see Syme, *Roman Papers* I 283f; *MRR* III 128 with 129).

257. For the *provinciae*, see Cic. *Balb.* 55 ("praetorem urbanum") and K. Tuchelt, *Frühe Denkmäler: Roms in Kleinasien. Beiträge zur archäologischen Überlieferung aus der Zeit der Republik und des Augustus* (Tübingen 1979) I 160 (from Claros) with 12.4.3 and 14.5.5. On his descent see E. Badian, *Chiron* 20 (1990) 389.

258. *Praetorius* (Cic. *Brut.* 137), perhaps even reaching the office in the first half of the 90s: he was *monetalis* 105 (thus Crawford, *RRC* I 321f no. 314) and *tr. pl.* (probably) in 103 (*MRR* I 563 with II 12 n.1). For discussion of descent and age, see Sumner, *Orators* 93; cf. E. Badian, *Studies in Greek and Roman History* (Oxford 1964) 64.

259. *Cos.* 90; see E. Badian, *Chiron* 20 (1990) 389, for descent; also Additional Note XIII. On the praetor L. Caesar who was *pro cos.* in Macedonia, see 14.1.3 and 14.2.3.

260. Wiseman, *NM* 260 no. 387. See *SIG*[3] 732 for urban praetorship of 94 and filiation; Cic. *Planc.* 19 with *MRR* III 191 for *cognomen* and descent; *MRR* II 15, 35, 42f, and 49, with III 191, for promagistracy. On his praetorship, add also Plin. *Nat.* 14.96 (from Varro) to the sources in *MRR*, and see in general 14.1.3. Cicero (*Planc.* 19) says Sentius' aedileship and praetorship made him the first curule magistrate in his family and of his town of Atina; that he was the first in his family to enter the Senate is unlikely, given Cicero's wording.

261. See E. Badian, *Chiron* 20 (1990) 392 for discussion of name and descent; also 12.2.1 and 14.5.5 on his praetorship and promagistracy.

262. Wiseman, *NM* 260 no. 388. For his city praetorship, see 12.2.2.

263. His praetorship is dated by *MRR* II 9 to "?96." At any rate, it must fall after the governorship of Q. Scaevola in Asia (probably 94—14.5.4), which he emulated (D.S. 37.8.1), and before the tribunate of M. Livius Drusus in 91: see E. Badian, *PACA* 11 (1968) [1970] 1–6, with 13.1.4 above. Asellio's father was a *quaestorius* (D.S. 37.8.1), perhaps to be identified with the historian of that name (C. Cichorius, *Römische Studien* [Leipzig 1922] 119).

264. *Cos.* 89. See E. Badian, *Chiron* 20 (1990) 389, for descent and ap. *MRR* III 165f for his early career (quaestor ca. 106, tr. pl. 104); there is no good evidence for a praetorian command in Macedonia (contra Broughton, *MRR* III 166). For the (conjectural) possibility that he was praetor as late as 91, see 10.5.2.

265. *Cos.* 89, and so under the *leges annales* should have reached the praetorship by 92. See, however, 10.5.2. For his descent, see Gel. 13.20.13 with E. Badian, *Chiron* 20 (1990) 389; R. Helm, *RE* s.v. *Porcius* 7 col. 107.

266. *Cos.* 87, IV 84; already of praetorian standing when he served as a *legatus* in the Social War: see 10.5.3. E. Badian, *Chiron* 29 (1990) 390, gives descent.

267. He had reached the praetorship by the time of his service as *legatus* in the Social War (Cic. *Font.* 43 "M. Cornutum"; for the *nomen* cf. the *prr.*, 57, 43): see 10.5.3 above. His name is often supplied for the (empty) third place in the *consilium* of the *cos.* 89 Cn. Pompeius Strabo at Asculum (*ILLRP* 515) (cf. 10.5.4).

268. See E. Badian, *Chiron* 20 (1990) 389, for name and descent. The date and *provincia* are certain (12.1.1).

269. Discussed in 10.5.2. For discussion of descent, see Münzer, *RE* s.v. cols. 1767f.

270. On descent, see Wiseman, *NM* 245 no. 278; E. Badian, *Chiron* 20 (1990) 390. On the dates of his Sicilian command, see 13.1.4.

271. On his descent, see E. Badian, *Chiron* 20 (1990) 391. For his praetorship (perhaps as early as 93) and praetorian *provincia*, see 13.1.1.

272. *Cos. suff.* 86, replacing C. Marius after his death early that year; see E. Badian, *Chiron* 20 (1990) 390, for descent. On Flaccus' praetorship, see 14.5.7.

273. See 14.5.5 on the date. Descent unknown, but to judge from the *praenomen*, perhaps a Cassius Longinus. For a speculative reconstruction of that family's *stemma*, see Sumner, *Orators* 50. His chart at least shows the range of possibilities: e.g., descent from C. Longinus, *cos.* 124 (to whom Sumner assigns no offspring).

274. See 10.5.2; also Münzer, *RE* s.v. col. 897 for possible descent.

275. See 10.5.3 with ch. 10 n. 147.

276. Filiation preserved in J. M. Reynolds, *Aphrodisias and Rome* (London 1982) Document 3 lines 1–2. For discussion, see 10.1 above.

277. Likely to be descended from the city praetor P. Sextilius of *RDGE* 8 line 1 (mid-second century): see E. Badian, *AJPh* 101 (1980) 478. See 14.3.3 on his praetorship.

278. Should be descended from A. Sempronius (*RE* 3) A.f., listed third and last in the *consilium* to *RDGE* 9 (lines 13–14), and thus a senator by ca. 140: see E. Badian, *PACA* 11 (1968) [1970] 1–2. Likely to be the brother of L. Asellio, *pr.* for Sicily ca. 94; if so, his father had reached only quaestorian rank (D.S. 37.8.1). On his praetorship, see 12.1.1 above.

279. For identification and (first) praetorship, see 10.5.4. For a (speculative) *stemma* of the senatorial Cosconii, see H. Mattingly, *RAN* 5 (1972) 15 (making this man grandson of the *pr.* 135).

280. *Cos.* 85, III 82; for his descent, see E. Badian, *Chiron* 20 (1990) 390. Carbo was *tr. pl.* in 92 (*MRR* II 18) and almost certainly praetor in 89, as *MRR* II 33 suggests. See 10.5.4.

281. See 10.5.5 and 14.3.3.

282. Discussed in 10.5.5 and 14.1.4. On descent, see n. 196 above.

283. See E. Badian, *Chiron* 20 (1990) 391 with 389, for descent. Ultimately Broughton (*Candidates Defeated* 40) dated his praetorship to 89, without query. Yet the year 88 seems much more probable (10.5.5).

284. On their identifications and praetorships, see 10.5.5.

285. See 10.1 and 10.5.5.

286. Filiation is preserved in *SIG*³ 745 line 5. Cic. *Mur.* 15 attests to his praetorship ("cum . . . ex praetura triumphasset") and shows that his father and grandfather also reached the office. The date of Murena's actual magistracy must be 88 or 87, followed by service in the east—first under Sulla (14.1.4) and then in an independent command in Asia (14.5.9).

287. Apparently an ex-praetor by the time of his service as a *legatus* under Sulla in the First Mithridatic War: see 14.1.4. Should be the elder brother of Q. Hortensius L.f. Hortalus, *cos.* 69.

288. See Wiseman, *NM* 212 no. 25, for discussion of descent and family. He was a *praetorius* when Marius ordered his death in 87 (Plu. *Mar.* 43.5; cf. App. *BC* 1.73.337 and Flor. 2.9.16).

289. Date of praetorship probably 86, but possibly 85: see 14.1.4. For descent, see E. Badian, *Chiron* 20 (1990) 390. The name Asiaticus is not attested under the Republic, as Prof. Badian has pointed out to me.

290. See Wiseman, *NM* 240 no. 250 with no. 249 and n. 249 above, for descent. See 10.5.8 on his career and cf. 12.3.1 on his first praetorship.

291. Probably to be identified with the *monetalis* C. Fabius C.f. of *RRC* I 326–327 no. 322 (dated by Crawford to 102), and thus the (C. Fabius) C.f. Q.n. Hadrianus of *ILLRP* 363 (Delos). See also Wiseman, *NM* 230 no. 166; cf. Taylor, *VDRR* 212. *Per.* 84 implies that he was in his *provincia* of Africa by 84: see 14.3.3.

292. Wiseman, *NM* 394 no. 260. See 10.5.6 and 13.3.2.

293. Sources on his praetorship are collected in *MRR* II 67f and 73 n. 4, under the year 82. For discussion of the date, see 13.1.4. Spelling of *cognomen*: see D. R. Shackleton Bailey, *Onomasticon to Cicero's Speeches* (Norman, Okla., 1988) 75. For the suggestion that he is perhaps nephew rather than son of the *cos.* 92, see C. F. Konrad, *Plutarch's Sertorius: A Historical Commentary* (Chapel Hill, N.C., 1994) 146.

294. Wiseman, *NM* 217 no. 71. On his name and his praetorship of 83 (the date at least is certain), see 12.1.1.

295. *Tr. pl.* 90 (see *MRR* II 26, esp. Cic. *Orat.* 213, providing filiation) and *praetorius* at the time of his murder by Damasippus in 82 (Vell. 2.26.2, mistakenly regarding him as brother of the *cos.* III 82). On his identity, see *MRR* II 30 n. 8; cf. Sumner, *Orators* 113.

296. On name and status see 10.5.8.

297. See 10.5.6.

298. Date is only probable, from a combination of *RRC* I 379, no. 364, the anti-Sullan coin of Q. ANTO BALB PR. (dated by Crawford to "83–82 B.C."), and V. Max. 7.6.4, an S.C. of 82 which apparently provides the background to that emergency issue (Rome's temples were to provide precious metal for minting, to pay government troops). Q. Balbus is the only praetor in the period covered by this study known to have minted a coin in Rome. Perhaps it was thought that an unusually high-ranking moneyer was needed to smooth the way for acceptance of this extraordinary issue. Balbus was driven from Sardinia and killed in 82 (13.1.1). His descent is unknown: note, however, Q. Antonius (*RE* 33), likely of senatorial status in 190 (see Liv. 37.32.8). The praenomen is otherwise unattested for the Antonii of the middle and later Republic.

299. See Wiseman, *NM* 222 no. 105, for discussion of Carrinas' background; his *praenomen* is not directly attested save in the filiation of his son (D.C. 51.21.6), the *cos. suff.* 43 C. Carrinas C.f. His praetorship is discussed in 10.5.6.

300. See 10.5.7 for discussion.

301. See ch. 10 n. 66.

302. See Vell. 2.16.1–3 (two sons of Minatius Magius of Aeclanum elected as praetors *cum seni adhuc crearentur*, but after the year 89), with Wiseman, *NM* 239 nos. 240–242, G. V. Sumner, *HSPh* 74 (1970) 259f. Even if there were six praetors elected for the year 81 (as Sumner, *Orators* 107, holds), that college does not readily have room for either Magius; an earlier date for both seems required. One of these men is almost certainly the P. Magius who was *tr. pl.* 87 (Cic. *Brut.* 179). If the other is not the M. Magius Min.f. Sarus who held a local magistracy at Aeclanum in this period (*ILLRP* 523), he is that man's brother.

303. Born in or shortly before 121, and of senatorial status by 87: see Sumner, *Orators* 116; cf. *JRS* 54 (1964) 44, suggesting he was *pr.* precisely in 81.

304. He is quite likely to be identified with the "Mam. Aemilius *legatus*" who, according to one tradition, in the year 88 inflicted the final defeat on the Marsic general Poppaedius Silo: see ch. 10 n. 186. For descent, see E. Badian, *Chiron* 20 (1990) 391: "presumably grandson (by birth) of *cos.* 147, perhaps son of *cos.* 112." For his career, see G. V. Sumner, *JRS* 54 (1964) 41–46 (conjecturing at p. 44 that he was *pr.* 81).

305. On the possibility that he introduced the *formula Octaviana* as praetor (which would be potentially relevant to his *provincia*), see 12.1.2.

306. Listed first in the senatorial *consilium* of witnesses to *RDGE* 22 = *ILLRP* 513 (78 B.C.).

307. See E. Badian, *Chiron* 20 (1990) 392, for his family ("descent from *cos.* I 252 certain"). He was seeking the tribunate of the Plebs in 91 (Cic. *de Orat.* 1.25), and found himself exiled after conviction under the *lex Varia* ca. 90 (*Brut.* 205, 305), only to be restored later by Sulla (*Brut.* 311). Cotta will not have been a *pr. urb.* (see *Off.* 2.59 on his lack of games). Sumner (*Orators* 110) suggests a praetorship in precisely 81; but that is prompted by the mistaken belief that the Cotta who fought against Sertorius in 80 did so as a praetorian commander (see Konrad, *Plutarch's Sertorius* 127–131).

308. For his (presumed) descent, see E. Badian, *Chiron* 20 (1990) 392; he is likely identical with the *monetalis* C. Cassius of *RRC* I 370–371 no. 355 (put by Crawford in 84).

309. Listed first in the *consilium* of *RDGE* 23 (73 B.C.), three positions (see Badian, *Historia* 12 [1963] 134–136) above C. Licinius Sacerdos (*pr.* 75). He was probably curule aedile in 91 (Cic. *de Orat.* 1.57 with *MRR* II 24 n. 7 and III 55; Sumner, *Orators* 83, considering the identification certain), and so likely to be of quite senior praetorian standing by the year 73.

310. Listed second in the *consilium* of *RDGE* 23 (73 B.C.), two positions above C. Licinius Sacerdos (*pr.* 75). See further in 11.8.6.

311. Probably the *monetalis* Cn. Lentul(us) of *RRC* I 356–357 (dated by Crawford to 88 B.C.). See E. Badian, *Chiron* 20 (1990) 392, for name and (presumed) descent.

312. Discussed in 13.2.7.

313. See 14.6.4 for possible descent and status.

314. Wiseman, *NM* 227 no. 140. He was possibly himself of praetorian status when he served as (apparently) a *legatus* under the *pr.* P. Varinius against Spartacus' forces in 73 (11.8.6). Against the identification of this man with the L. Cossinius of Cic. *Balb.* 53, see Shackleton Bailey, *Onomasticon to Cicero's Speeches* 42.

315. Thus P. Willems, *Le Sénat de la république romaine: Sa composition et ses attributions* I (Louvain 1878) 457 no. 62, on the basis of possible service with his brother A. Pompeius under Pompey as *legati pro praetore* in 67, endorsed by E. S. Gruen, *The Last*

Generation of the Roman Republic (Berkeley 1974) 165 with n. 5 (discussing also descent). The relevant passage (Flor. 1.41.9–10) speaks only of "Pompeii iuvenes"—hardly suggesting praetorian status (notwithstanding Flor. 2.9.20, "Marius iuvenis et Carbo consules," i.e., in the extraordinary year 82). On this man's attested career, see *MRR* III 161 and II 100 (he was apparently still a subpraetorian in 75/74). W. Kunkel (*Staatsordnung und Staatspraxis der römischen Republik: Die Magistratur* [Munich 1995] 360 n. 210) implausibly gives him a major special praetorian command in Bithynia for 75 (analogous to that of M. Cato for Cyprus in 58), assigning to him also the "lex Pompeia" for the province.

316. See Badian, *Chiron* 20 (1990) 393, for discussion of name.

317. Volcacius' descent is unknown, but he evidently was not the first in his family to reach the Senate: see Cic. *Agr.* 2.3 with *MRR* III 223. At some point, Volcacius had been defeated for the aedileship (*Planc.* 51), but it seems most unlikely that he was *tr. pl.* 68, as Broughton (*MRR* III 223, following Syme and Sumner) has it. In the damaged first line of *CIL* I² 744, the partially preserved name of the tribune L.V[——]C[——] should be supplemented "L. V[ols]c[ius]," as I plan to demonstrate in a projected publication.

318. *Tr. pl.* 71 (sources in *MRR* II 122) and unsuccessful candidate in the consular elections for 66 (see Broughton, *Candidates Defeated* 27)—and perhaps later ones as well (cf. Cic. *Att.* 1.1.1 with Shackleton Bailey, *CLA* I 291). See Wiseman, *NM* 237 no. 231. Sal. *Hist.* 4.43 M ("humili loco Picens") would seem to exclude close connection with the M. Lollius Q.f. Men. who is listed in forty-eighth place in the *consilium* to *RDGE* 12 (surely 101 B.C.). Though his praetorship is not in itself attested, the date seems reasonably certain from the known facts of his *cursus*.

319. See 15.2.1 for discussion.

320. See E. Badian, *Chiron* 20 (1990) 394, for descent (nephew of the dictator).

321. For descent, see Badian, *Chiron* 20 (1990) 394. On his earlier service as a *legatus pro praetore* (not "legatus pro consule") in Asia, see ch. 14 n. 298.

322. See n. 318 above on descent. L. Lollius served under Pompey in 67 as a *legatus pro pr.* against the pirates (*MRR* II 148), and shows up in 64 as one of his *legati* in Syria (*MRR* II 164, cf. 160), taking Damascus with Q. Caecilius Metellus Nepos (*pr.* 60, *cos.* 57) (11.5.1). Broughton (*MRR* II 164) assumes Lollius held a praetorship at some point. Even if true, the status of his fellow *legatus* Metellus Nepos shows that he need not have reached the office by the date suggested here. The *pro quaestore* M. Aemilius Scaurus seems from Josephus' account (*BJ* 1.127, cf. *AJ* 14.29) to have been technically superior to both these men.

323. Praetorship conjectured from Cic. *Att.* 1.1.2, which mentions a "Thermus" who was *curator* of the Flaminian way in 65 and a consular candidate for 64. For his possible identity, see *Flac.* 98 "omnibus rebus ornatus . . . A. Thermus," a man whom Cicero, as consul in 63, twice successfully defended on criminal charges. That Thermus was quite possibly of praetorian status, since Cicero mentions him alongside two high-ranking defendants—M.' Aquillius, *cos.* 101 and L. Murena, *cos. des.* 62. However, D. R. Shackleton Bailey, *Two Studies*² 34f, points out that the *praenomen* "Aulus" is open to suspicion on paleographic grounds, and at any rate is not found among the Minucii; he identifies the defendant in question as Q. Minucius Thermus, *tr. pl.* 62. Shackleton Bailey also revives the old idea— set out in W. Drumann and P. Groebe, *Geschichte Roms* V (Leipzig 1912) 431 n. 3—that the "Thermus" of *Att.* 1.1.2 is identical with the *cos.* 64 C. Marcius Figulus (see Shackleton Bailey, *Two Studies*² 34f, also *CLA* I 292 and *Onomasticon to Cicero's Speeches* 66 for an explication). But that seems hard to swallow. See E. Badian, *Chiron* 20 (1990) 403 n. 17, gathering some consular "names" in the Chronographer of 354 just as inexplicable as the entry that prompted Drumann to adopt that conjecture, its "Caesare et Turmo" for the consuls of the year 64. Shackleton Bailey (*Onomasticon* 66) downplays these oddities, and regards "the case for identifying Thermus with Figulus" as "almost irresistible."

324. Expelled from the Senate in 70, he regained his rank by the time he joined Catiline's conspiracy: MRR II 122, cf. 149 n. 1. A praetorship has been inferred from Cic. Att. 1.1.2, which mentions a "Curius" who was candidate for the consulship of 64. But see (persuasively) D. R. Shackleton Bailey, CLA I 292–293, emending to "Turius"; also B. A. Marshall, A Historical Commentary on Asconius (Columbia, Mo., 1985) 316f (excellent on the career of Q. Curius), and n. 370 below.

325. See E. Badian, Chiron 20 (1990) 395, for name and discussion of descent. He was a candidate for the consulship of 64 (Cic. Att. 1.1.2), but reached the office only two years later. See Sumner, Orators 129, and F. X. Ryan, Klio 78 (1996) 73, on the date of praetorship.

326. Wiseman (NM 219 no. 87) regards him as novus. Like Cicero, he was aed. pl. 69 (MRR II 132) and consular candidate for 63: see Cic. Att. 1.1.1 with Broughton, Candidates Defeated 24. A praetorship in 66 seems virtually certain (thus, rightly, Münzer, RE s.v. col. 1317).

327. Tr. pl. 69 (MRR II 132) and consular candidate for 63: see Cic. Att. 1.1.1 with Broughton, Candidates Defeated 11. Asconius (p. 82 C) says he was one of two competitors for that year who were "tantum non primi" in their family to win a magistracy, and so Shackleton Bailey (CLA I 290) and Wiseman (CQ 14 [1964] 123) rightly regard this Cornificius to be of senatorial descent. He was father of the poet of the same name.

328. Monetalis (by Crawford's dating) in 79 (RRC I 398 no. 383, providing filiation), a legatus pro pr. under Pompey against the pirates in 67 (MRR II 148), and probably a praetorius by 63 (Sal. Cat. 50.4 with MRR II 463).

329. A flamen Martialis who was candidate for the consulship of 58 (Broughton, Candidates Defeated 10). Clearly nobilis, though details on his descent are lacking: Münzer in RE s.v. col. 1391 does not even venture a guess; cf. Sumner's (adventurous) stemma of the Cornelii Lentuli (Orators 143), making him a descendant of the cos. 156 L. Lentulus Lupus. He was in the city in 61 (Münzer, RE s.v. col. 1391).

330. E. Badian, Chiron 20 (1990) 395, discusses descent. For his (delayed) career, see MRR III 97f, where Broughton plausibly attributes the lex Gabinia (reserving February for the Senate's reception of foreign embassies) to his tribunate of 67 rather than a praetorship. Gabinius was in the east with Pompey until at least 63, and so it is highly probable that the year for which he reached the praetorship was 61 (Münzer, RE s.v. col. 426; MRR II 170, 182 n. 3).

331. For discussion of descent, see Wiseman, NM 236 no. 220; for speculation on his birth date, see Münzer, RE s.v. col. 260 (but the evidence adduced does not permit an accurate guess). T. Labienus was tr. pl. 63 (MRR II 167f), and certainly of praetorian standing while he served as a legatus under Caesar in Gaul from 58 to 50, for we are told that in 50, Caesar helped him prepare for a consular bid (Hirtius, BG 8.52.2 with Syme, Roman Papers I 71–74). See the further discussion in Broughton, Candidates Defeated 26f. Labienus is the only figure in the Bellum Gallicum for whom Caesar explicitly notes the delegation of praetorian imperium (see BG 1.21.2 with 15.2.4 above).

332. Quite possibly a praetorius by 58, as F. X. Ryan (C&M 47 [1996] 210–211) has posited, arguing that Cic. Pis. 77—Sanga listed between a pr. of 58 and two senior consulares—reflects ascending order of rank.

333. See Cic. Brut. 245 "T. Torquatus T.f. . . . si vita suppeditavisset, sublato ambitu consul factus esset." Since Cicero considered this man a possibility for the consulship, "he presumably reached the praetorship, but died before the consular elections at which he was entitled to stand" (Sumner, Orators 130f). I. Délos IV 1 1660 records his service in the east as an officer, also with filiation. Though there is a lacuna after Torquatus' name, the rank to be supplemented is surely pro quaestore—see IV 1 1659, a twin dedication to the pro q. M.' Aemilius M.'f. Lepidus. These two inscriptions are dated to the term of Nicanor son of

Nicanor Leukoneus as *epimeletes* of Delos. Traditionally this Nicanor has been assigned to the period 84–78 (F. Münzer, *Römische Adelsparteien und Adelsfamilien* [Stuttgart 1920] 318f; *MRR* II 493), but see the arguments of H. B. Mattingly (*Chiron* 9 [1979] 167) for 65/64. The terminus I have suggested for his (possible) praetorship is based on Mattingly's date for his (presumed) proquaestorship.

334. See Cic. *Q. fr.* 3.6(8).6 with the discussion in Shackleton Bailey, *Two Studies*[2] 26f, Broughton, *MRR* III 100, and also Wiseman, *NM* 281 no. 537, on this possible candidate for the consulship of 52. The name seems perfectly possible (note the Ti. Gutta of Cic. *Clu.* 127); at any rate, it should not be emended to yield (M. Aurelius) (*RE* 109) "Cotta" (see 13.2.8). Shackleton Bailey also entertains the notion that "Gutta" might be a nickname for one of Milo's competitors for the consulship of 52 (*CEQF* 223).

335. Curule aedile in 58 (Broughton, *MRR* II 195, III 159) and consular candidate for 52 (*Candidates Defeated* 29); see Marshall, *Asconius* 160, for his career. He probably was praetor in 55, to judge from the known details of his *cursus*. Cf. *ILLRP* 386, which, if it belongs to this Plautius Hypsaeus, may refer to his praetorship.

336. See E. Badian, *Chiron* 20 (1990) 397, on the names and descent of the three Claudii Marcelli who reached the consulship in the years 51–49, and cf. Cic. *Att.* 4.3.5 ("Marcellus") with Broughton, *MRR* II 208 and *Candidates Defeated* 44, for the possible candidacy of one of these men for the curule aedileship of 56.

337. Quaestor 63, *tr. pl.* 57, and perhaps elected aedile or (just possibly) praetor before a judicial condemnation in 52. See Cic. *Fam.* 5.18 (attesting to *novitas*) with Wiseman, *NM* 230 no. 169 and Shackleton Bailey, *CEF* I 350; cf. Alexander, *Trials* no. 318.

338. In all likelihood he was *novus*: see Wiseman, *NM* 233 no. 188. On his name and possible praetorship, see Additional Note XV.

339. See Additional Note XV. He was just possibly son of the praetor or *legatus pro pr.* L. Postumius (13), active in the early stages of the Social War.

340. *Aed. cur.* (probably) in 57, and *cos. suff.* 45, on whom see Broughton, *MRR* III 87. Broughton adopts Sumner's basic suggestion that he held a "praetorship well before 48"; but see Sumner's own caveat at *Phoenix* 25 (1971) 357.

341. Filiation is provided by J. *AJ* 14.233 (but with the impossible title στρατηγὸς ὕπατος). He was very likely son of the senator (and *praetorius?*) C. Fannius C.f., who is first in the *consilium* to *RDGE* 18 (81 B.C.) (cf. Münzer s.v. *Fannius* 8 col. 1991). See further Additional Note XV.

342. Caesar appointed him *pro cos.* for Bithynia and Pontus for 45 (*MRR* II 309). That he reached aedilician status by the year 57 seems possible (cf. Cic. *Pis.* 54 with 88), but is quite uncertain. Broughton's suggestion (*MRR* III 138) that "he might have been a praetor as early as 54" is only a guess. His father may be Crassus' *legatus* in 71 (Fron. *Str.* 2.4.7) Q. Marcius Rufus (like "Crispus," a *cognomen* from hair).

343. On the date of his praetorship (probably not by 49), see the discussion in *MRR* III 187.

344. Starting in the year 81, I assume that each praetorian commander found in a territorial *provincia* outside Italy first will have spent the year of his actual magistracy in a city *provincia*, as expected under Sulla's system. (Attested exceptions are duly noted.)

345. See E. Badian, *PBSR* 33 (1965) 48–51 (esp. 49), on his (probable) filiation. Broughton (*MRR* II 76) tentatively suggests he was "pr. urbanus," but there is no positive attestation of his city *provincia*: see 12.1.1. For his promagistracy in Cilicia (with unexpected rank "pro praetore"): 15.1.1.

346. For discussion of Aemilius' descent, see E. Badian, *Chiron* 20 (1990) 391 with 406f n. 23. On his praetorship, see 13.2.2.

347. Should be *pr.* 81 in charge of both Spanish provinces, with enhanced *imperium* (13.4.2). I do not see why the title "pro cos." on Annius' coins should have confused Konrad

(*Plutarch's Sertorius* 100 "he must have held a praetorship with his *imperium* prorogued through 81"), since Konrad in general has an excellent grasp of Roman titulature (*Plutarch's Sertorius* 88) and realizes that even after Sulla's victory praetors did not invariably stay in Rome during their year of office (p. 131). On Annius' descent, see E. Badian, *Chiron* 20 (1990) 382; Konrad, *Plutarch's Sertorius* 100; cf. Taylor, *VDRR* 191.

348. Perhaps son of the moneyer Q. (Minucius) Therm(us) M.f. of *RRC* I 324 no. 319, dated by Crawford to 103 B.C., and by H. B. Mattingly (*NC*[7] 17 [1977] 206 n. 35) to "c. 100 B.C., not any earlier." The date of Thermus' praetorship and Asian command must be 81 (14.6.1).

349. Wiseman, *NM* 245 no. 277. His praetorship is known only from the coin issue of M. Nonius Sufenas (*RRC* I 445–446 no. 421), which Crawford dates to 59 B.C., convincingly supplementing the legend as SEX. NONI(us) PR(aetor) L(udos) V(ictoriae) P(rimus) F(ecit). (See *MRR* III 73 and 149 for H. B. Mattingly's implausible reading of PR as PR[aeneste] in *NC*[6] 16 [1956] 189–203.) Nonius' celebration of those first games should date to (at a minimum) 1 November in the year 81, marking the anniversary of Sulla's success at the Colline Gate. For the evidence on these *ludi*, see Mattingly, *NC*[6] 16 (1956) 191f; also A. Keaveney, *Klio* 65 (1983) 189–191; Marshall, *Asconius* 302. The praetor should be the same man as the "Nonius"—a nephew of Sulla—who unsuccessfully stood for some political office in 88 for 87 (Plu. *Sulla* 10.3 with Broughton, *Candidates Defeated* 46). His kinship with Sulla helps explain his presidency of those first games (he was definitely not *pr. urb.*). What principle guided the allotment of these games in subsequent years is unknown. After Sulla's death—and especially after the progressive dismemberment of his settlement in the latter half of the 70s—the duty might have devolved upon some lower magistracy than the praetorship.

350. See 14.6.1.

351. For name and descent, see E. Badian, *Chiron* 20 (1990) 397 (on the *cos.* 50, who should be son of this praetor). On the praetorship, see 13.2.2.

352. Discussed in 11.7.4. He was possibly son of the *monetalis* M. Fannius C.f. (*RRC* I 295 no. 275, dated by Crawford to 123 B.C.) and grandson of C. Fannius Strabo (*cos.* 161); but direct descent from the *cos.* 122 C. Fannius M.f. is also perfectly conceivable.

353. Wiseman, *NM* 232 no. 182. An intimate of Sulla (Plu. *Sull.* 31.3, Flor. 2.9.25, cf. Sal. *Hist.* 1.55.22 M) who was definitely a praetorian commander in Hispania Ulterior in 80 (13.4.2)—having been, according to Orosius, of merely centurion status as recently as late 82 (see Oros. 5.21.3 "L. Fursidio primipilari"). Fufidius' origins are a puzzle. An L. Fufidius gained fame as the addressee of the autobiography of M. Aemilius Scaurus (*cos.* 115, who died ca. 89, and whose widow Sulla then married) and also for wearing an iron *anulus* long after his praetorship (see Plin. *Nat.* 33.21 with 20, a discussion of senatorial ring-wearing habits at the time of the Social War). Broughton (*MRR* III 93) entertains and dismisses the possibility that Scaurus dedicated his work to the praetor for Spain, and instead makes him that man's father. However, C. F. Konrad, *CPh* 84 (1989) 125–128 makes a strong case for just one prominent Fufidius, a solution I here tentatively accept.

354. The *provincia* (and rank of *pro cos.*) is certain, and the date virtually so (13.4.2). For descent from the *cos.* 283 and filiation, see E. Badian, *Chiron* 20 (1990) 396, on Domitius' son, the *cos.* I 53. The M. Domitius P.f. who is found as the junior member of a senatorial legation to Crete ca. 113 (*MRR* I 536f) should be father of the *pr.* 80 and grandfather of the consul.

355. Wiseman, *NM* 220 no. 92. But he should be son of the moneyer M. Calid(ius) (*RRC* I 300 no. 284, whom Crawford dates to 117 or 116 B.C.). See 13.4.2 on his praetorship.

356. See 11.8.1; cf. F. X. Ryan, *AAntHung* 36 (1995) 73–75 (suggesting the death of this man fell in 59).

357. See 13.4.2 with 15.2.1. L. Manlius' identity and thus descent are not readily ascertainable. He is perhaps the same as the L. Manlius *pro quaestore* who issued gold and silver coins under Sulla (*RRC* I 386–387 no. 367), whom Crawford dates to 82 and believes went on to reach the consulship in 65 (followed by Broughton, *MRR* III 136). What is hard to imagine is that the Sullan quaestor, this praetor—a failure in two major *provinciae*—and L. Torquatus (*cos.* 65) are all identical. Of course, even if we dissociate our L. Manlius from the *cos.* 65, the possibility is open that he was a patrician. If so, he is likely to be a Torquatus (to judge from the *praenomen*), in which case consular descent would be certain, ultimately from the Manlii Capitolini (cf. E. Badian, *Chiron* 20 [1990] 394, on the *cos.* 65). But caution is necessary, since there were other, humbler Manlii active in this period who show *praenomina* not unknown to the patrician *gens*: see L. R. Taylor ap. *MRR* III 136 and above (n. 233) on A. Manlius, *pr.* by (?)107.

358. See 12.1.2 (joint jurisdiction in the city) and 13.2.2 (probable Sicilian command).

359. See E. Badian, *Chiron* 20 (1990) 392, for descent (citing Plu. *Luc.* 1.1) and *MRR* II 88 n. 2 with III 121 for date. See further 14.4.

360. See 11.7.1, 14.5.9, and esp. 14.6.1 for discussion of the possible connection between A. Terentius A.f. Varro (a Sullan *legatus* in Asia in the period ca. 85–82) and the Terentius Varro (a cousin of Q. Hortensius) who, as a "reus ex Asia," was accused *de repetundis*.

361. Discussion in 14.6.1.

362. See Cic. *Dom.* 35 with E. Badian, *Chiron* 20 (1990) 392, for descent. On his date and *provincia* see 12.1.2.

363. Filiation in Cic. *Fin.* 2.58. His descent seems certain (thus Gruen, *Last Generation* 171).

364. Fonteius' descent was definitely praetorian (Cic. *Font.* 41 "continuae praeturae"), but the date of his own praetorship is a vexed problem: see 13.4.4.

365. See E. Badian, *Chiron* 20 (1990) 392, for descent. His date and *provincia* are certain (12.2.1).

366. For the praetor's name and date of his command in the east, see 14.6.2. For speculation on his descent (suggesting he might even have been a Iunius Brutus or Silanus), see Gruen, *Last Generation* 172.

367. See 15.2.1.

368. For Sacerdos' descent (senatorial, but only barely so), see Asc. p. 82 C; filiation is provided by *RDGE* 23 (Oct. 73), where he is listed (probably) fourth in the *consilium*. For his praetorship and promagistracy, see 12.1.2 and 13.2.2.

369. In 75, the *pr. urb.* C. Licinius Sacerdos and the praetor M. Caesius assisted the consuls of the year in the massive task of repairing temples in Rome, but apparently did not have enough time to inspect all those in need of maintenance (12.1.2). E. Badian (*Historia* 12 [1963] 135–136) suggested that this Caesius is the same as the M. Ca<e>sius M.f. Pom. who appears in third place in the *consilium* to *RDGE* 23 (73 B.C.), one position above Sacerdos. (Contra J. M. Cody, *CPh* 64 [1969] 177–178, who takes the *consilium* member to be a M. Cassius Longinus, otherwise unattested.) His descent is uncertain, but M. Caesius was not the first member of his *gens* to reach high office in the Republic: note the praetor (and "imperator") by 104, L. Caesius C.f.

370. Wiseman, *NM* 267 no. 448 (opting for "L. Turius"). Sources on this individual in *MRR* II 97 are under the year 75, but he was quite possibly *pr. repetundis* for 74: see 11.7.1 with ch. 11 n. 233 (discussing descent), and 14.6.1.

371. During Verres' command in Sicily, his father was active in the Senate (Cic. *Ver.* 2.2.95–97, 102, etc.) and evidently possessed some influence with other members of that body (2.2.95–96, 2.5.136), but there is no real indication of rank. Cicero does not give us his name, but it was also C. Verres (H. Habermehl in *RE* s.v. *Verres* 1 col. 1562, citing Ps.-Asc. p. 185 St.;

see also *Ver.* 2.2.187 on the praetor's pseudonym "C. Verrucius C.f."). For the *nomen* Verres, see Syme, *Roman Papers* I 291.

372. See E. Badian, *Chiron* 20 (1990) 392, for descent. He was definitely *pr.* 74 (Ps.-Asc. p. 193 St. with Cic. *Clu.* 130) in charge of a *quaestio* (full sources in *MRR* II 102), but not necessarily *repetundarum*, as Broughton has it: see 11.7.1 and 14.6.1 above.

373. Cic. *Ver.* 2.4.56 sets out his ancestry in fulsome terms—he was a juror in the trial. Piso's coins as *monetalis* (*RRC* I 340–344 no. 340, a massive issue dated by Crawford to 90 B.C.) give his filiation. On his city praetorship, see 12.1.2.

374. Should be son of the aged senator P. Coelius Caldus (see Badian, *Studies* 90–96), who met his death at Placentia in 87.

375. Filiation assured from that of his son (Plu. *Ant.* 2.1, App. *Sic.* 6.1), the *cos.* 44 M. Antonius M.f. M.n. (sources in *MRR* II 315).

376. See 11.8.6 for identity, name, and title.

377. Wiseman, *NM* 270 no. 462. See further 11.8.6.

378. Wiseman, *NM* 214 no. 37; also I. Shatzman, *Senatorial Wealth and Roman Politics* (Brussels 1975) 305 no. 92. See esp. Cic. *Brut.* 243 "infimo loco natus," providing also the information that he lived past the year 52. On his praetorship, promagistracy and further career, see 11.8.7.

379. On Crassus' descent, see E. Badian, *Chiron* 20 (1990) 393. For discussion of the date of his praetorship, see 11.8.7.

380. On his urban praetorship, see 12.1.2 (either 73 or 72). He may be the praetor "Metellus" who granted the action "damnum vi hominibus armatis coactisve datum" in a dispute over possession of some land near Thurii (Cic. *Tul.*, especially 39). The alternative is that the "Metellus" in question is the *pr.* 71 L. Metellus, Verres' successor in Sicily and the future *cos.* 68, which I am inclined to favor (12.1.2).

381. Termed "praetor" when he was defeated by Spartacus in (apparently) Gallia Cisalpina in 72 (*Per.* 96), and so praetor in 73 or 72: see 11.8.7. Münzer (*RE* s.v. cols. 1157f) doubts patrician ancestry; contra Gruen, *Last Generation* 166.

382. For name and descent, see the discussion of E. Badian, *Chiron* 20 (1990) 393. *Provincia* and date secured by Cic. *Ver.* 1.38 with 2.2.24.

383. Wiseman, *NM* 210 no. 9. E. Badian, *Chiron* 20 (1990) 395, also discusses descent, doubting *novitas*. Despite much speculation (see *MRR* III 13), Afranius' triumph (for which see Cic. *Pis.* 58), and thus his praetorship, remain a mystery: see 13.4.6 for discussion.

384. E. Badian, *Chiron* 20 (1990) 395, discusses descent. See Syme, *Roman Papers* II 501, for the suggestion that he was a younger brother of L. Piso Frugi, *pr.* 74 (endorsed by Sumner, *Orators* 127). It is possible that as city praetor—like those of 75 and 74—he was engaged in building activities: see ch. 12 n. 30. Calpurnianus surely succeeded Q. Metellus Pius (*cos.* 80, *pro cos.* 79–71) in Hispania Ulterior (13.4.6).

385. *Cos.* 67; for name and descent see E. Badian, *Chiron* 20 (1990) 393 and 407 n. 25. On his praetorship (72 or more likely 71), see 12.1.2. He was in Rome in the year 69 (Cic. *Caec.* 34–41 with Münzer, *RE* s.v. col. 1376), which just possibly suggests he did not take up a territorial province.

386. *Cos.* 64, and so presumably praetor by 67. See 14.2.3 on Mattingly's suggestion that this individual held an *ex praetura* command in Macedonia ca. 70.

387. For descent, see E. Badian, *Chiron* 20 (1990) 393. He—and not the *pr. urb.* of 73 or 72 Q. Metellus—may very well have been the "Metellus" who was praetor in the case for which Cicero wrote his *Pro Tullio* (12.1.2).

388. He presided as praetor over the *quaestio* in which Maesia of Sentinum successfully spoke in her own defense before a large crowd, a performance that earned her the nickname "Androgynes" (V. Max. 8.3.1). Alexander (*Trials* no. 384) is properly cautious on the

date, suggesting "sometime between 80 and 50." Yet the trial seems best placed in a year earlier in that range. Valerius (8.3.2) follows his story of Maesia with an exceedingly harsh assessment of the long (it is implied) forensic career of C. Afrania, who died in 48 — clearly no popular favorite. Maesia should have preceded Afrania: the nickname "Androgynes" suggests that at the time of her trial female orators were still very much a novelty in Rome. If so, L. Titius is very possibly father of the *pr. urb.* 50 C. Titius L.f. Rufus (on whom see n. 488 below). Some Titii had apparently reached the Senate by 81: see the roster of names in *MRR* II 626 with III 206.

389. Probably *pr. urb.*: see Cic. *Ver.* 2.3.123 with *MRR* III 46 and 12.1.2 above. Gruen (*Last Generation* 176) doubted whether he had even senatorial ancestry, but see Shackleton Bailey, *Onomasticon to Cicero's Speeches* 70.

390. See *MRR* II 127 for *provincia* and date (both certain); E. Badian, *Chiron* 20 (1990) 393, on descent.

391. On descent, see E. Badian, *Chiron* 20 (1990) 394 with 392; also E. Klebs, *RE* s.v. col. 256. I discuss the city praetorship in 12.4.3. On his possible promagisterial province, see 14.2.3.

392. See 14.4.

393. Brother of Q. Metellus (Creticus), *cos.* 69: see Cic. *Ver.* 1.27; cf. Münzer in *RE* s.v. *Caecilius* 78 col. 1206. All the same, Crawford identified him with the M. (Caecilius) Q.f. Metellus of *RRC* I 387–388 no. 369 (assigned to "82–80" B.C.), making him "the son of a cousin" (thus Crawford) of the *cos.* 115 M. Caecilius Q.f. Q.n. Metellus. The *provincia* and date of this praetor are certain (Cic. *Ver.* 1.21–32).

394. Presumably son of the senator L. Antistius C.f. Men., who occupies twenty-second place in the *consilium* of *RDGE* 12 (surely 101 B.C.), and grandson of the moneyer C. ANTESTI(us) (*RRC* I 257 no. 219, dated by Crawford to 146 B.C.). On the date of Antistius' praetorship and promagistracy in Hispania Ulterior, see 13.4.6. On the family (later pretensions), see Taylor, *VDRR* 192.

395. On the date of Rubrius' actual praetorship, see 14.2.3. Plutarch (our only source on Rubrius and his command) omits his *praenomen*, allowing only broad speculation on his descent. Two members of the *gens* Rubria are known to have reached the office of *tr. pl.* in the Gracchan era (see *MRR* I 493 and 517, III 182), and there is a C. Rubrius C.f. in fifteenth place in the senatorial *consilium* of *RDGE* 12 (surely 101 B.C.). Note also the moneyer L. Rubri(us) Dossenus (*RRC* I 362–363 no. 348, "87 B.C."), conceivably the same man as the praetor. Precise identity or even family line cannot be established. However, the M. Rubrius who saw service as a junior officer under Cato at Utica in 46 (*Cat. Mi.* 62.4, 63.1) may well be the Macedonian praetor's son. (For this type of intergenerational bond between an ex-subordinate and his commander's family, see, e.g., Plu. *Caes.* 5.6 with *MRR* III 17.)

396. See 12.1.2 (city praetorship, not necessarily in the urban jurisdiction) and 14.6.5 (promagistracy). On his (probable) descent, see E. Badian, *PBSR* 20 (1965) 50.

397. Filiation from *ILLRP* 515. For descent from the Sergii Sili, see M. Gelzer, *RE* s.v. col. 1693.

398. The historian; see Münzer, *RE* s.v. col. 419f, for the claims of descent. Macer was *tr. pl.* 73 (*MRR* II 110) and by the time of his suicide in the first half of 66 had reached the praetorship (V. Max. 9.12.7 "vir praetorius"). He took his life while a defendant in the praetor Cicero's *repetundae* court (sources in Alexander, *Trials* no. 195). It is reasonable to surmise that Macer was on trial for extortion charges connected with a provincial appointment: hence praetor at least by 68, to allow time for an *ex praetura* command and return to Rome. Macer's coin issue as *monetalis* (*RRC* I 370 no. 354, dated by Crawford to 84 B.C.) shows filiation.

399. For descent, see Varro ap. Serv. A. 11.743 with H. Dahlmann, *RE Supb.* 6 s.v. *Terentius* 84 col. 1173. The evidence for Varro's praetorship is surprisingly late and inciden-

tal (App. *BC* 4.47.202 and Them. *Or.* 34.34 [= 34.8 p. 453 D]), with no details other than the fact that he reached the office. On the date—quite uncertain, but probably soon after 75—see E. Badian, *Chiron* 27 (1997) 4, cf. *Studies* 230. Quaestor very likely in 85 and then *tr. pl.* (see Badian, ibid.), he seems to have served as a *legatus* under Pompey in the Sertorian War (*MRR* II 100) before taking up a post as *legatus pro praetore* against the pirates in 67 (*MRR* II 148). I have given here merely the latest likely terminus for his holding of the praetorship. In this capacity (surely) he had a *praefectus fabrum* (Var. *R.* 1.2.7, Marcius Libo, on whom see Badian, *Chiron* 27 [1997] 3f, esp. 4 n. 3), which may imply a provincial command.

400. Discussion in 11.8.8. Gruen (*Last Generation* 169) considers both these men to have direct praetorian ancestry.

401. See 14.6.5. An *eques* before his praetorship, but quite possibly (ultimately) of senatorial descent: note the senator ca. 140 T. Ofidius M.f. who is second in the *consilium* to *RDGE* 4 (on which see n. 143 above for the date); note also, in B.8 below, the Sicilian praetor of unknown date (but probably late second or early first century) Cn. Aufidius T.f. Gruen (*Last Generation* 169) seems to consider senatorial descent likely. For his career, see D. R. Shackleton Bailey, *CLA* I 291; Shatzman, *Senatorial Wealth* 306 no. 95.

402. See 12.1.2 on his praetorship (the *provincia* is reasonably secure). Without a *cognomen*, speculation as to which branch of the *gens Iunia* the *pr.* 67 belonged seems pointless. But the odds are favorable that he was a *nobilis*: see the index of Iunii at *MRR* II 576–577.

403. For the filiation (and his earlier service in Asia), see *MRR* III 176: he is attested as *pro quaestore pro praetore* at Ephesus. He should be brother of the *monetalis* C. Publicius Q.f. (*RRC* I 396 no. 380), dated by Crawford to 80 B.C. The (consular) Publicii Malleoli are known to have used the *praenomina* Quintus and Gaius: see *RRC* I 298–299 no. 282; cf. Gruen, *Last Generation* 166. But a glance at the roster of Publicii assembled in *MRR* (II 609, III 175f) shows that there is no guarantee they were closely related to our praetor's family (which all the same, pace Wiseman, *NM* 255 no. 347, was probably senatorial). For the date of Q. Publicius' praetorship, see 12.1.2.

404. See 12.2.2 on identity and praetorship: he drew Sardinia as his promagisterial *provincia*, but then turned it down. His *gens* was quite possibly senatorial: see *ILLRP* 210 for an L. Lucceius M.f. attested in the year 92 (apparently) as *legatus* in Macedonia.

405. A *novus homo* (Cic. *Clu.* 111 with Wiseman, *NM* 255 no. 351), he was *tr. pl.* in 74 (*MRR* II 103). See 12.4.3 on the date of his praetorship (esp. n. 233, dissociating him from the L. Quinctius L.f. Rufus attested as ἀνθύπατος at Tenos).

406. Discussion in 14.6.5.

407. A *praetorius* "Galba" was killed by Caesar's mutinous troops in 47 (Plu. *Caes.* 51.2). It is quite likely he is to be identified with the ex-curule aedile P. Galba (*RRC* I 418 no. 406), who was an eager candidate for the consulship of 63 (sources in Broughton, *Candidates Defeated* 17f), and so definitely a praetor by 66: see D. R. Shackleton Bailey, *CLA* I 289; F. X. Ryan, *Athenaeum* 84 [74] (1996) 555–556.

408. For name and descent, see E. Badian, *Chiron* 20 (1990) 394. See 12.1.3 on his praetorship and refusal of a promagisterial *provincia*.

409. Wiseman, *NM* 267 no. 446. The date is amply attested (full sources in *MRR* II 152), as is the *provincia* (see esp. Cic. *Clu.* 147, *Corn.* 1 F 3, *Rab. Post.* 9, and the sources in Alexander, *Trials* no. 195, cf. no. 205). Cicero refused a promagisterial *provincia* (*Mur.* 42), and in July 65 started his campaign for the consulship of 63 (*Att.* 1.1.1).

410. A famous jurist. Cic. *Clu.* 147 gives the date of his praetorship and *provincia* (on which see 11.7.2). Aquillius apparently turned down a promagisterial *provincia*, perhaps alleging health concerns (cf. *Att.* 1.1.1 with B. W. Frier, *The Rise of the Roman Jurists: Studies in Cicero's pro Caecina* (Princeton 1985) 148 on his reluctance to run for *cos.* 63). Possible

(distant) praetorian descent: Plin. *Nat.* 17.2 (calling him an *eques Romanus*) with Gruen, *Last Generation* 169; cf. Shackleton Bailey, *CLA* I 290 (considering it probable).

411. Should be identified with the *monetalis* L. CASSI Q.F. (*RRC* I 403 no. 386, dated by Crawford to ca. 78–76). Shackleton Bailey (*Two Studies*[2] 16) identified him also with the L. Cassius who served as a (senatorial) juror in the cases of Oppianicus in 74 (Cic. *Clu.* 107) and Verres in 70 (*Ver.* 1.30), and as a *tribunus militum* in 69 (*Ver.* ibid.). Contra G. V. Sumner, *CPh* 73 (1978) 160; also cf. his reconstruction of the *stemma* of the Cassii Longini at *Orators* 52. On Cassius' praetorship of 66, consular candidacy (in 64 for 63), and further (ignominious) career, see 11.7.3.

412. Wiseman, *NM* 247 no. 296; cf. Taylor, *VDRR* 240, and P. Harvey, *Athenaeum* 53 (1975) 53 n. 56 on the Orchivii of Praeneste. On the name Orc(h)ivius, see Shackleton Bailey, *Two Studies*[2] 35f. The date of praetorship and *quaestio* are attested by Cic. *Clu.* 94 and 147. The fact that Orchivius himself stood trial in 65 or 64 (Q. Cic. *Pet.* 19 with Münzer, *RE* s.v. cols. 907–908, charge unknown) suggests that he did not hold a promagistracy, but does not absolutely exclude the possibility (thus, rightly, J. T. Ramsey, *Historia* 29 [1980] 405).

413. Wiseman, *NM* 247 no. 245.

414. See Badian, *Chiron* 20 (1990) 395, for his filiation and descent, and 12.1.3 with 15.2.3 for his praetorship and promagistracy.

415. A famous jurisconsult, from a family of obscure nobility: see the references in E. Badian, *Chiron* 20 (1990) 397. The date of his praetorship and his *provincia* are certain (Cic. *Mur.* 35, 41–43). Rufus turned down an *ex praetura* command (*Mur.* 42–43) and ran for the consulship at the first opportunity (i.e. in 63 for 62), for which he was defeated (Cic. *Mur.* passim). In general on his consular ambitions—he won the office only for the year 51—see Broughton, *Candidates Defeated* 18–19. He was paternal grandfather of the poet Sulpicia (D. R. Shackleton Bailey, *CLA* I 361).

416. Wiseman, *NM* 233 no. 192. He presided at the trial of C. Cornelius (*tr. pl.* 67) for *maiestas* in 65 (Asc. p. 62 C., full sources in Alexander, *Trials* no. 209; see 11.7.3). Gallius' candidacy for his praetorship later gave rise to a trial for *ambitus* in the latter part of 64: see *Trials* no. 214, with the date derived from a combination of Asc. p. 88 C (after the *In Toga Candida*) and Q. Cic. *Pet.* 19 (implying acquittal in 64); also Gruen, *Last Generation* 270 n. 33. So Gallius must not have taken up a promagisterial *provincia*: see J. P. V. D. Balsdon, *CQ* 13 (1963) 248–249. No previous senatorial Gallii are known except the possible case of the C. Gallius who visited Gytheum (*SIG*[3] 748 line 26, no title), almost certainly as a subordinate of M. Antonius (*pr.* 74).

417. Wiseman, *NM* 216 no. 58. On his praetorship and city *provincia* (not *maiestas*, as is commonly supposed), see 11.7.3.

418. Wiseman, *NM* 251 no. 320. Plaetorius was prima facie a *monetalis* (*RRC* I 414–418 no. 405, dated by Crawford to 69 B.C.); issued coins again as *aed. cur.* in (probably) 67 (see *RRC* I 436–437 no. 409, which supplies filiation); and in 66 held the office of *iudex quaestionis* (*MRR* II 143, 152f, III 216). But see C. Hersh and A. Walker, *ANSMusN* 29 (1984) 132 and 133, arguing on the basis of the Mesagne hoard that Cestianus minted *RRC* I no. 405 only ca. 57, "under senatorial authority, acting as a pro-praetor perhaps, rather than as a regular moneyer." His descent is uncertain, since he cannot be son of the senator M. Plaetorius who was killed in the proscriptions of 82 (F. Hinard, *Les proscriptions de la Rome républicaine* [Rome 1985] 393f). For a discussion of attested Plaetorii Cestiani, see Shackleton Bailey, *Two Studies*[2] 79. On this man's possible Macedonian command, see 14.2.3.

419. No city *provincia* is attested, and his command in Asia (for which see *MRR* II 170) is dated solely on the relative order of praetors for that province in the mid-60s: see 14.6.5 (esp. n. 319 on his identity).

420. He was a *praetorius* by the year 62 (Sal. *Cat.* 59.6). Sallust (ibid.) speaks of Petreius' long military career, specifying more than thirty years of distinguished service as military tribune, *praefectus*, *legatus*, and praetor. If that last item is literally true, we should assume Petreius held a command *ex praetura*. A praetorship in any of the years 70 through 64 is conceivable, since (to judge from Sallust's report of his career) he must have been around forty-seven years of age in early 62. Valerius Maximus (2.4.6) reports that Petreius gave lavish games, but he does not specify whether he did so as aedile or praetor (in which case they might have been either the *Ludi Apollinares* or *Victoriae Sullanae*); see further Münzer, *RE* s.v. col. 1183 (arguing strongly for an urban praetorship), *MRR* II 164 n. 1. Wiseman is surely right to regard him as *novus* (*NM* 250 no. 314).

421. Cos. 61 and later censor in 55. The date of the praetorship is not attested, but is quite likely to have been 64: see 12.1.3.

422. For the city *provincia*, see *MRR* III 37 and 212, citing Cic. *Flac.* 6 and 100; also 12.1.3. His filiation is positively attested in Tuchelt, *Frühe Denkmäler* I 164 (Claros) (on which see *MRR* III 212), and *I. Magn.* 144–146 (definitely to be attributed to this praetor, despite Broughton's hesitation in *MRR* II 178 n. 2). On the promagistracy, see 14.6.6.

423. Filiation from *RDGE* 23 (73 B.C.), where he occupies tenth position in the *consil ium* of fifteen senators, two below M. Tullius Cicero (quaestor in 75). Direct consular descent seems certain, given the paucity of "Q. Pompeii" available. Now, the cos. 88 Q. Pompeius Rufus witnessed the murder of a son in the riots of that year (*Per.* 77, App. *BC* 1.56.247, Plu. *Mar.* 35.2 and *Sull.* 8.3). The first two of these sources note that he was Sulla's son-in-law, but none report this young victim's *praenomen*. (Sigonius emended the text of *Per.* 77 to read "occiso Q. Pompeio," but that is just his guess.) F. Miltner (*RE* s.v. col. 2253) tentatively accepts T. Mommsen's suggestion (*Gesammelte Schriften* [Berlin 1905–1913] V 510) that the praetor of 63 was an adoptive son of the consul. But it is conceivable he was a natural son, born at the latest by ca. 105. It seems unlikely that the cos. 88 adopted anyone to replace his slain son, since he himself was killed before his year of office was up (sources in Miltner, *RE* s.v. *Pompeius* 39 col. 2251).

424. "Generally assumed" (E. Champlin, *CPh* 84 [1989] 57) that this man is to be identified with the orator C. Cosconius (*RE* 12) Calidianus of Cic. *Brut.* 242. If true—Münzer (*RE* s.v. col. 1670) entertains it and Sumner (*Orators* 25) accepts it—his natural father might have been the rich and well-connected *eques* Cn. Calidius of Cic. *Ver.* 2.4.42–45, if not one of the senatorial Calidii (see *MRR* II 541 and III 45 for a roster). Contra F. X. Ryan (*SIFC* 90 [1997] 81–84), who tries to make the (iterated) praetor of 79 the orator, not grappling (84 n. 11) with the considerable evidence for that man's first praetorship in 89: he really was almost a full generation older than the orators Cicero discusses in the relevant *Brutus* passage, and as such should be ruled out. In 63, as praetor, C. Cosconius helped transcribe the proceedings against the Catilinarian conspirators (Cic. *Sull* 42). Cosconius' city *provincia* is unrecorded, but as promagistrate he definitely went to Hispania Ulterior (Cic. *Vat.* 12 "pro consule").

425. See Sumner, *Orators* 132, and E. Badian, *Chiron* 20 (1990) 395, for descent ("presumably adoptive grandson of cos. 117").

426. Wiseman, *NM* 253 no. 334.

427. On Sura's iteration of the praetorship, see T. C. Brennan, *Athenaeum* 67 (1989) 480–481.

428. Possibly son of the moneyer C. Sulpici(us) C.f. (*RRC* I 320 no. 312, dated by Crawford to 106 B.C.): see Shackleton Bailey, *Onomasticon to Cicero's Speeches* 90.

429. Wiseman, *NM* 253, 256 no. 359. Descent is uncertain, but he was perhaps son or grandson of the moneyer L. R(oscius?) of *RRC* I 299–300 no. 283 (dated by Crawford to 118 or 117 B.C.). One notes also the slain legate L. Roscius of 438 B.C., who was honored with a

statue on the Rostra (*MRR* II 58). As *tr. pl.* 67, L. Roscius Otho passed the "lex theatralis" that (again) reserved the first fourteen rows for the *equites* (*MRR* II 145). Early in 63, his presence in the theater set off a tumult that culminated in a heated exchange between knights and Plebs (full sources in V. Mühll, *RE* s.v. col. 1126, of which see esp. Cic. *Att.* 2.1.3 for the chronology). Plutarch—our fullest source on this near riot—seems to think that "M." Otho passed his law in 63 as praetor (*Cic.* 13.2 στρατηγῶν). That is obviously a mistake. But it does seem reasonable to suppose that L. Otho was wearing the insignia of some office in the theater that day. Otherwise the Plebs' strong response on spying him is hard to understand (at this point its seats had been segregated from those of the *equites* for more than three years). That he was praetor (as *MRR* II 167 suggests, and as, e.g., Gruen, *Last Generation* 174, takes as fact) is one possibility (though not—as F. X. Ryan, *Hermes* 125 [1997] 236–240, offers—in the urban jurisdiction, where L. Flaccus seems securely attested). But given Plutarch's inaccuracy throughout this passage, aedile is another possibility: one curule and both plebeian aediles for that year are unknown. Perhaps the event in question was the *Megalesia* (4–10 Apr.), the first major festival of the year to feature theatrical performances, with Roscius (as *aed. cur.*) in charge: for the splendid garb of aediles at their games, see Kunkel, *Staatsordnung* 122 n. 72. In that case, the one surviving fragment we have of Cicero's conciliatory speech for Otho (Crawford[2] F 1) is enumerating "coming attractions" ("Cerealia, Floralia ludosque Apollinares").

430. See E. Badian, *Chiron* 20 (1990) 396, for the name. Cic. *Sull.* 42 reports that at the time the suspected Catilinarian conspirators were giving their evidence in the Senate, M. Messalla was a candidate for the praetorship of 62, which we can reasonably assume he won. (It would be perverse for Cicero in this highly laudatory passage to bring up a past *repulsa* for an intermediate office.) A tentative candidate for the consulship of 54 (*Att.* 4.9.1), he reached the office for 53.

431. See D. R. Shackleton Bailey, *CLA* I 299f for the suggested city *provincia*; also 12.1.3. Whether urban praetor or not, he is said in this year to *ius dicere* (Suet. *Jul.* 16.1).

432. Filiation and cognomen from *IGRP* I 508 = *IG* XIV 356 (Halaesa, honors for Vergilius during previous service in Sicily as *pro quaestore*). The date of his praetorship is certain (see Cic. *Planc.* 95, *Schol. Bob.* p. 87 St., with 13.2.6), though his city *provincia*—he must have held one—is unknown. See also Gruen, *Last Generation* 171 with n. 30, on the possibility his family was senatorial.

433. Wiseman, *NM* 267 no. 447. On his praetorship see 11.7.7, 11.8.9, and 12.4.1 (there is no reason to believe Quintus was *pr. urb.*, as tentatively suggested by *MRR* II 173); for his promagistracy, see 14.6.7, with ch. 14 n. 339 on attestation of filiation.

434. See E. Badian, *Chiron* 20 (1990) 395, on name and discussion of descent ("seems to be treated and to behave as a *nobilis*; but we have no information"). On his praetorship, see 11.7.7 and 11.8.9.

435. There is no record of a city praetorship for this man (the later *cos.* 56), but he should be *pr.* 62 (11.5.2). See E. Badian, *Chiron* 20 (1990) 396, for Philippus' descent; cf. also *Phoenix* 25 (1971) 142–144.

436. Discussion of activities in 11.2. Descent: cf. Cic. *Fam.* 9.21.3, on which see D. R. Shackleton Bailey, *CEF* II 329 (making him C.f. C.n., i.e., grandson of the *cos.* 120, and tentatively son of the *praetorius* C. Carbo Arvina).

437. Piso in his career advanced without a defeat, according to Cicero, up through his consulship of 58 (*Pis.* 2, explicitly including his praetorship). That he was *pr.* 61 is thus probable, though not absolutely certain, since "sine repulsa" is of course a different thing than "suo anno." There is no compelling reason to follow Münzer (*RE* s.v. col. 1387) in identifying him with the L. Piso who owed his acquittal for *repetundae* to a cloudburst (V. Max. 8.1. abs. 6, on which see also Syme, *Roman Papers* I 303). There is no evidence that Piso held a

territorial *provincia*, though Syme (*Roman Papers* I 303–304) suggested that he held Hispania Citerior in 60/59. See E. Badian, *Chiron* 20 (1990) 395, for descent.

438. Wiseman, *NM* 246 no. 287. He was father of Octavian; see Vell. 2.59.2 for descent (equestrian), but with an ancestor who was *tr. mil.* 205 (Suet. *Aug.* 2.2). *Inscr. Ital.* XIII 3 75b offers filiation. See 12.1.3 and 14.2.4 on the city and promagisterial *provinciae*.

439. Quaestor 73 (*MRR* II 110), plebeian aedile ca. 64 with C. Octavius (the future *pr.* 61) as his colleague (II 162), and said to be an old ex-praetor when he was proscribed in 43 (V. Max. 9.11.5, Oros. 6.18.9, App. *BC* 4.18.71, cf. 4.12.47). For full discussion, see F. Hinard, *Proscriptions* 534–536 (against *MRR* III 207, which identifies him with C. Turranius, *pr.* 44). Wiseman (*NM* 267 no. 439) regards C. Toranius as *novus*.

440. On his identity and praetorship, see 11.8.1.

441. This man's family was surely senatorial: note Q. Voconius Saxa, *tr. pl.* 169, with Gruen, *Last Generation* 171. The Voconius who commanded (or was supposed to command) a fleet under L. Lucullus at Nicomedia in (apparently) 72 is probably identical with our Q. Voconius Naso: see Additional Note XV on his identification and career.

442. E. Badian, *Chiron* 20 (1990) 396 for filiation and descent: he is "presumably identical" with the *quaestor urbanus* and moneyer P. LENT P.F. L.N. (*RRC* I 409 no. 397 ["74 B.C."]). The date of Spinther's praetorship, and the *provinciae* of his magistracy (12.1.3) and promagistracy (13.4.8), are certain.

443. On his city praetorship, see 12.4.3. He planned to take up a promagistracy in an unrecorded *provincia* (Cic. *Att.* 2.5.2, cf. *MRR* III 40 for a list of the possibilities). There is no good reason to think from *Att.* 2.12.2 he was still in Rome in April 59 (contra Münzer, *RE* s.v. col. 1217). E. Badian, *Chiron* 20 (1990) 396, gives name and descent.

444. See E. Badian, *Chiron* 20 (1990) 396, on his descent (details unclear), and 11.5.2 on the (probable) date of his praetorship.

445. For discussion of name and descent, see Wiseman, *NM* 216 no. 56; *MRR* III 28. He was praetor before 59, when he served as one of the XXviri who divided Campanian land under the *lex Iulia agraria* (Suet. *Aug.* 4.1, confirmed on the detail of the praetorship by Cic. *Phil.* 3.16): see D. R. Shackleton Bailey, *CLA* I 374f. There is no evidence on a promagistracy.

446. In 59, he either presided over the extortion trial of L. Valerius Flaccus (*pr.* 63, then *pro cos.* in Asia) or heard it as juror (11.7.1) shortly before taking up a promagistracy in Africa (14.4). For his family, note the quaestor P. (Vettius) Sabinus (*RRC* I 331 no. 331, dated by Crawford to 99 B.C.). He is perhaps identical with the T. Vettius who was C. Verres' brother-in-law, serving under him as quaestor in 71 (ch. 13 n. 95): see Shackleton Bailey, *Onomasticon to Cicero's Speeches* 99.

447. See Sumner, *Orators* 124–125, and Shackleton Bailey, *Two Studies*[2] 72f on descent (his *agnomen* may have come to him by adoption rather than birth); 11.7.1 on the *provincia*.

448. Quite possibly *novus* (Wiseman, *NM* 232 no. 185), he was a *monetalis* ca. 70 B.C. (*RRC* I 413 no. 403) and *tr. pl.* in 61 (*MRR* II 180); Gruen however floats the possibility of distant senatorial ancestry (*Last Generation* 171, on the basis of the mid-second-century *lex Fufia*). On his praetorship, see 12.4.3. He reached the consulship for 47.

449. First in his family to reach curule office (Cic. *Planc.* 19), though not necessarily the Senate. See 14.2.4 on the promagistracy and Syme, *Roman Papers* II 600–601 and 606–607, on the name (not a Saturninus); cf. also D. R. Shackleton Bailey, *CEF* I 431.

450. Wiseman, *NM* 212 no. 23. A C. Ampius was killed while serving as a *praefectus socium* under the *cos.* 201 P. Aelius Paetus (Liv. 31.2.5–9), but no Ampii before the *pr.* 59 are known to have reached the Senate. On the *provinciae* of his promagistracy, see 14.6.8 and cf. 15.1.2.

451. The patron of Lucretius. Cic. *Brut.* 247 provides the filiation (confirmed by that of his son, *cos. suff.* 34); Sumner, *Orators* 85–90, discusses descent and offers a stemma of his family. See 12.1.3 on Memmius' city praetorship (possibly in the urban jurisdiction) and 11.2

on the promagistracy. For a summation of his "erratic" career, see D. R. Shackleton Bailey, *CLA* I 331.

452. For discussion of descent, see E. Badian, *Chiron* 20 (1990) 397 and 407 n. 26, backing Sumner's suggestion that he is the younger brother of the *pr.* 60 and *cos.* 57 P. Cornelius Lentulus Spinther. That he held a praetorship in the city this year is certain (Cic. *Pis.* 77, cf. *Q. fr.* 1.2.16), but the *provincia* is unknown.

453. See Badian, *Chiron* 20 (1990) 396, for descent. Domitius was apparently in Rome in spring 56 B.C. (Münzer, *RE* s.v. col. 1336), and so perhaps did not take up a promagisterial province.

454. Discussion in 12.2.4.

455. See 14.6.8 for possible descent and his promagistracy.

456. Not necessarily anything more than a *privatus* in 60 (11.7.1, pace *MRR* III 147), Nigidius is attested as *pr. designatus* for 58 (Cic. *Q. fr.* 2.1.16). The *legatus* (not praetor) of 145 C. Nigidius (7.3.1) may be an ascendant, as Shackleton Bailey has suggested: see the discussion in Wiseman, *NM* 244 no. 271.

457. See Cic. *Fam.* 8.8.5–6 for filiation and status (he is listed third and a *pr.* 57 fourth in the *consilium* to two *senatus consulta* of 50) with *MRR* II 246f on the lower date (all the other praetors of 57 are known). His praetorian standing (just barely) receives direct attestation in App. *BC* 4.18.69, on which see Cadoux ap. *MRR* III 221.

458. He was half-brother of P. Cornelius Sulla (*cos. des.* 65), himself the nephew of the dictator Sulla (D.C. 36.44.3 with Münzer, *RE* s.v. col. 1232). This man's date and city *provincia* (for which see 12.1.3 and cf. 12.4.3) are certain. L. Rufus evidently held an overseas *provincia* (*ILLRP* 391, providing filiation and giving title "pro cos."), certainly for 56, since his rank under the *lex Pompeia* of 52 would be "pro pr." The possibilities for 56 are limited to Sicily or Cyrene with Crete (cf. *MRR* II 210, but not realizing that the rank of *pro cos.* was generalized for praetorian governors in this period).

459. On the city *provincia* (merely inferred), see 11.7.1; for the promagisterial *provincia*, see 13.2.8.

460. Filiation from Cic. *Fam.* 13.6 prescript. As praetor, he supported Cicero's recall from exile (Cic. *Red. Sen.* 22–23 and cf. 12.4.3); see 14.4 above for the promagistracy. Taylor (*VDRR* 261) makes him son of Q. Valerius Soranus (*tr. pl.* by 82); see further A. Keaveney, *AC* 51 (1982) 128.

461. Wiseman, *NM* 260 no. 389. While a praetor in the city (precise *provincia* unknown) C. Septimius supported Cicero's recall (Cic. *Red. Sen.* 22–23 and cf. 12.4.3). For his tenure as *pro cos.* for Asia, see 14.6.8.

462. Definitely *pr.* 57, in which capacity he aided in securing Cicero's recall from exile (Cic. *Red. Sen.* 22–23 and cf. 12.4.3). On the promagistracy, see 11.2. Cf. also F. X. Ryan, *Mnemosyne* 49 (1996) 185–186 (suggesting that he is the anonymous praetor designate of Cic. *Vat.* 38 whose election vexed Caesar).

463. The *monetalis* M. Calid(ius) of *RRC* I 300 no. 234 (dated by Crawford to 117 or 116 B.C.) should be this man's grandfather. His father is said to have been Q. Calidius, *pr.* 79 (Ps.-Asc. p. 219 St. with Münzer, *RE* s.v. col. 1353). For his activities as praetor, see ch. 12 n. 242. Further details on career: D. R. Shackleton Bailey, *CLA* III 314; Marshall, *Asconius* 128. On his unsuccessful consular bids for 50 and perhaps 49, see Broughton, *Candidates Defeated* 10. His relationship to the senator "Calidius," who in 82 warned L. Licinius Murena not to make war on Mithridates (App. *Mith.* 65.272–273), is unknown: see *MRR* III 45 for some guesses as to this legate's identification.

464. For the name, see Cic. *Att.* 2.13.2 (he was *iudex quaestionis* in a case *de vi* of the year 59) with *P. Red. in Sen.* 22 (the sole attestation of his praetorship). On this man, see D. R. Shackleton Bailey, *CLA* I 379; B. A. Marshall, *Historia* 22 (1973) 463–464, with the

stemma at p. 466. Shackleton Bailey (*Onomasticon to Cicero's Letters* [Stuttgart 1995] 62) makes him grandson of the *cos.* 131 P. Crassus Mucianus.

465. He was son of the famous *princeps senatus* and Caecilia Metella, the future wife of Sulla (Cic. *Sest.* 101, Asc. 18 C). For a useful stemma of his family, see E. Courtney, *Philologus* 104 (1960) 152–153. The date of Scaurus' praetorship is secure, the city *provincia* less so (11.7.6). *CIL* I² 811 ([Aemilius] SCAVRVS PR. PRO COS BAS[ilicam])—which surely belongs to this Scaurus—confirms what we would expect, that he set out *ex praetura* to his province of Sardinia (Asc. 18 C with 13.2.8) with consular *imperium*.

466. City *provincia* not known, but while praetor he sat as a juror in the trial of P. Sestius *de vi* (11.7.6). Ancharius' filiation is attested by Daux, *Delphes* 598 no. 10 = H. Pomtow, *Klio* 15 (1918) 70, no. 99; Cic. *Fam.* 13.40 prescript. Direct praetorian descent seems reasonably certain (the name is quite rare).

467. For descent, see E. Badian, *Chiron* 20 (1990) 396, on Ap. Claudius Pulcher (*cos.* 54), brother of this praetor (Cic. *Scaur.* 33). As *pr.* 56, C. Claudius energetically supported another brother—P. Clodius—in Rome (ch. 12 n. 146), but his city *provincia* is not attested. On his Asian command, see 14.6.8.

468. See E. Badian, *Chiron* 20 (1990) 396, for name and descent. Cic. *Q. fr.* 2.3.6 gives Domitius' city *provincia*, on which see 11.7.2 above. He is positively attested in the city in Oct. 54 (Cic. *Q. fr.* 3.4.1), serving as a juror in the *maiestas* court. His presence on the roll of jurors that year perhaps suggests he did not go to a province *ex praetura*. In 54, he was a candidate—ultimately successful—in the massively delayed elections for *cos.* 53 (cf. Münzer, *RE* s.v. col. 1420).

469. On the date, see Caes. *Civ.* 1.31.2 with *MRR* III 29 and also 14.4 above. For his possible descent, see P. Attius P.f. Ouf., listed seventh in the *cos.* Cn. Pompeius Strabo's *consilium* at Asculum (*ILLRP* 515) of 89 B.C.

470. Triumphed from a praetorian command in an unspecified *provincia* (Var. *R.* 3.2.16) in 54 or before June of 53 (see E. Badian, *Athenaeum* 48 [1970] 4–6, and J. Linderski, *Roman Questions: Selected Papers* [Stuttgart 1995] 100–106), and was *cos.* 52, so should be praetor at the latest by 55. Metellus Scipio is generally assumed to have held the curule aedileship in 57 (*MRR* II 201, 207 n. 1, cf. III 41f), but the evidence is exceptionally thin: see the discussion of C. F. Konrad, "Notes on Roman Also-Rans," in J. Linderski (ed.), *Imperium Sine Fine: T. Robert S. Broughton and the Roman Republic* (Stuttgart 1996) 134–141 (esp. p. 140, rightly suggesting "praetor in 56 or 55"). On the name and his descent, see E. Badian, *Chiron* 20 (1990) 396, but esp. J. Linderski, "Q. Scipio Imperator," in *Imperium Sine Fine* 145–185.

471. See Taylor, *VDRR* 263, and Wiseman, *NM* 270 no. 467, on his name and descent. Our sources have plenty to say about Vatinius' contentious election to the praetorship of 55 (*MRR* II 216), but nothing about his city *provincia* or (surprisingly) his activities once he entered the magistracy. He was prosecuted in late August 54 (Alexander, *Trials* no. 292), and so did not go to a territorial *provincia*.

472. See Wiseman, *NM* 213 no. 30; contra Shackleton Bailey, *Onomasticon to Cicero's Speeches* 15. See also Shackleton Bailey, *Two Studies²* 66, on his adoption and name; Shatzman, *Senatorial Wealth* 293 no. 86. Milo was *tr. pl.* 57 (Broughton, *MRR* II 201) and a competitor for the consulship of 52 (*Candidates Defeated* 22f); we are told that Pompey supported his candidacy for the praetorship (*Mil.* 68), which by process of elimination, should be that of 55. No details of his tenure of the office are known. He is attested in the city in November 54 (Klebs, *RE* s.v. col. 2273) and so did not have a promagisterial province.

473. See 14.4 for discussion. His filiation is shown in *ILLRP* 394 (later service in Africa as *legatus pro praetore* during the Civil War).

474. Not easily identified with any of the known Fonteii of this general period, but reasonably regarded as *pr. urb.* by Broughton (*MRR* II 221): see 12.1.3. The fact that we have no

praenomen for this man precludes real discussion of descent; but see Gruen, *Last Generation* 168 with n. 19 (surely from the established praetorian family).

475. See Gel. 13.20.13–14 and cf. Cic. *Off.* 3.66 for name and descent. He was an unsuccessful candidate for *pr.* 55 (Broughton, *Candidates Defeated* 37). See esp. 11.7.1 on his city praetorian *provincia*. M. Cato did not take up a command *ex praetura* (see esp. Plu. *Pomp.* 54.2–3 for his activities in the city in 53) until 49 (*MRR* II 263).

476. Wiseman, *NM* 211 no. 20. See 11.7.3 for his career and praetorship (in which he presided over trials both *de maiestate* and *de sodaliciis*); cf. also 11.7.7.

477. On his praetorship, see 11.7.7 (apparently presiding over a trial *de sodaliciis*) and 15.2.3 (his opposition to C. Pomptinus' triumph).

478. See Suet. *Gal.* 3.2 (identifying him as "nepos" of the *cos.* 144) with Münzer, *RE* s.v. col. 769.

479. Name and date highly probable (14.2.6). His direct descent from the *pr.* 79 is likely.

480. See E. Badian, *Chiron* 20 (1990) 397, on name and descent, and *MRR* III 9 for discussion of his career. Cic. *Mil.* 24 strongly implies that he held the praetorship in 53; the date is guaranteed by the fact he reached the consulship for 50. He was elected to that higher office in July 51 (Klebs, *RE* s.v. col. 564), and so perhaps had no *ex praetura* province.

481. Minucius' rank in Asia—*pro pr.* as opposed to *pro cos.*—strongly implies that he received Asia under the *lex Pompeia de provinciis* of 52, and so quite likely for 51. See 14.6.8 for his probable descent, praetorship (quite possibly one of the years 60–58, as Münzer, *RE* s.v. col. 1972 suggested), and praetorian command.

482. Discussion in 14.2.6. For his descent, see Taylor, *VDRR* 237–238.

483. See 11.4 for family, career, and praetorian command.

484. See 11.2 for his Bithynian command (under the *lex Pompeia*). The date of his actual praetorship, however, is wholly uncertain. On his descent, note the P. Silius L.f. Gal. listed twenty-fourth in the senatorial *consilium* of *RDGE* 12 (almost certainly 101 B.C.), who was perhaps his grandfather—or even his father.

485. Wiseman, *NM* 252 no. 324; also L. R. Taylor, *MAAR* 24 (1956) 25–26, on probable descent. See 11.2 on his praetorship (quite possibly in the urban *provincia*) and circumstances of his later Bithynian command.

486. Definitely *pr. repetundis* (11.7.1). His family traced descent to the Iuventii Thalnae: see esp. Cic. *Planc.* 15 and 18 with additional references gathered in Münzer, *RE* s.v. col. 1365f. The status of M. Laterensis' father is not certain. Cicero refers to that man (*Planc.* 19) as "ornatissimus atque optimus vir." Yet he applies this precise formulation to *equites* at *Sest.* 29 and *Balb.* 53; cf. also *Planc.* 19, of a praetor's son for whom no position is known higher than "miles" (see *Planc.* 27 with Shackleton Bailey, *Two Studies*[2] 10). Crawford suggests that the father is to be identified with the moneyer LATERENS(is) of *RRC* I 372 no. 358 ("83 B.C.")—which seems reasonable—but perhaps also with the Μάνιος (Iuventius) Λατερήνσιος Λευκίου υἱὸς στρατηγός who restored four statue bases *ex S.C.* on Calymna (*AE* 1940, no. 129 = *ASAA* 22/23 [1952] 158ff nos. 130 A, Cb, Da, and E). The latter identification does not convince, since one of the Calymna bases has below the (restored) name of M.' Laterensis also a dedication (no. 130 Dc) by the ἀνθύπατος P. Servilius P.f. Isauricus (i.e., the *cos.* I 48, *pro cos.* in Asia 46–44). Syme (*Roman Papers* I 283) noted that "M.' Laterensis might be several years, or a whole generation, earlier: conceivably a governor of Asia c. 77." Yet in that case we would expect Laterensis to use in the inscriptions he set up, not the title στρατηγός, but ἀνθύπατος, the standard rank for governors from the formation of the *provincia* down to 52 B.C. In addition, I can find no exact parallel in magistrates' inscriptions from the east or west in the period down to 50 B.C. for the nomenclature style Laterensis uses here (*praenomen* + *cognomen* + filiation), except of course on coins, where space was short (see E. Badian, "M. Calpurnius M.f. Frugi," in *Acta of the Fifth International Conference of*

Greek and Latin Epigraphy, Cambridge 1967 [Oxford 1971] 211). That, too, suggests M.' Laterensis should be more closely associated in time with P. Servilius Isauricus. It is perfectly possible that this Laterensis is the (younger) brother or first cousin of the *pr. rep.* 51.

487. See 13.2.8 on his supposed praetorian command in Sardinia.

488. For name and *provincia*, see Cic. *Fam.* 13.58 prescript with 12.1.3. Very possibly son—though conceivably brother—of the city praetor L. Titius of V. Max. 8.3.1 (see n. 388 above), he is the only individual by that name known to reach office in the relevant period of the Republic: cf. Gruen, *Last Generation* 171 n. 30 (suggesting also that the family of these Titii was senatorial by the early first century). The *cos. suff.* 31 M. Titius (18) L.f. was perhaps a nephew of the *pr.* 50.

489. On his name and identity, see esp. Cic. *Flac.* 30 and (attesting descent) *Red. Sen.* 21 with Münzer, *RE* s.v. col. 1869, Broughton, *MRR* III 79, and Shackleton Bailey, *Two Studies*[2] 21. Not *pr. urb.* (see n. 488 on C. Titius Rufus above), and not necessarily *pr. per.* either (12.2.2).

490. See 12.2.4 for discussion.

491. Descent assured by Cic. *Sest.* 6. On his Cilician command, see 15.1.2.

492. Almost certainly an ex-praetor when he received Cisalpine Gaul *pro praetore* for 49 in succession to Caesar (*MRR* II 261). Broughton suggests "*pr.* 54? or 50?" but precision is impossible. See Shackleton Bailey, *Two Studies*[2] 70f for speculation on his descent.

493. Wiseman, *NM* 237 no. 228. Praetor (*RRC* I no. 494 nos. 26a to 31), quite possibly before 49: see Broughton's discussion in *MRR* III 125f. He was exiled at some point after Sept. 58 (Cic. *Att.* 3.17.1 with *Fam.* 13.60.1), though not necessarily soon after, as Alexander (*Trials* no. 258) tentatively suggests.

494. Just possibly a praetorian commander in Macedonia in the later Republic: see the evidence collected in *MRR* II 464 (but neither inscription listed offers an actual title).

495. Wiseman, *NM* 231 no. 173. *Praetorius* by 48 (Vell. 2.43.1), after some *repulsa* for 50 (Cael. *Fam.* 8.9.5), having been *aed. pl.* in 53 or 52 (*MRR* II 235, 240 n. 2; C. Konrad in J. Linderski [ed.], *Imperium Sine Fine* 141–143). F. X. Ryan (ultimately) dismisses a praetorship for 51 or 50, but also 49, since he spoke in the Senate that year (*AJPh* 115 [1994] 587–601); however, cf. Badian, *AJAH* 13 (1988) [1997] 108–112.

496. For the evidence on this man's African command for 49 see *MRR* III 4 with F. X. Ryan, *AClass* 65 (1996) 239–242. Caes. *Civ.* 1.6.5 strongly suggests that L. Tubero was a praetor of 49 who was sent to Africa *in magistratu*; contra Ryan (who aims to make Tubero a *pr.* by 55), the evidence of Quint. *Inst.* 11.1.80—a tendentious claim from a law case of 46 delivered in Caesar's presence—hardly gainsays it.

497. Allegedly a praetor who sprouted horns as he exited through a city gate for the field *paludatus* (V. Max. 5.6.3). The tale of Genucius was obviously well known: cf. Plin. *Nat.* 11.123 and (for a free adaptation) Ov. *Met.* 15.565–621. As Valerius Maximus tells it, the horns were interpreted as portending Genucius would become king if he returned to the city; instead, the praetor went into self-imposed exile, and the grateful city affixed a bronze likeness of his head (evidently horns and all) to the gate, henceforth called the "porta Rauduscula" ("nam olim aera raudera dicebantur"). This is just one of several etymologies (though by far the most elaborate) offered for the name of this gate, which lay on the eastern part of the Aventine (S. B. Platner and T. Ashby, *A Topographical Dictionary of Ancient Rome* [Oxford 1929] 414): see also Var. *L.* 5.163; Fest. (and Paulus) pp. 338–339 L. This Genucius, if he existed at all and was indeed a praetor (we can join Pliny in rejecting the detail of the horns), is doubtless early, i.e., when the Genucii were still an important family.

498. As Valerius Maximus (6.5.1) tells it, this individual captured and sold the "Camerini" (*codd.* also "Amerinos," "Camarinos") "ductu atque auspiciis suis," taking also their territory which "neighbored" that of Rome; the Roman People, however, decided that

the "imperator" had violated *fides*, and searched out and bought back these prisoners, and settled them on the Aventine. This notice makes for a real puzzle. Old Latin Cameria was razed in 502 (D.H. 5.49.3–5 and 51.1; cf. Plin. *Nat.* 3.68); however, it is just possible that there was a later refounding. Cato (*ORF*³ F 56—ca. 192) had occasion to mention the prosperity of the town of the Camerini, "cives nostri," "who straightaway lodged as guests with their own friends when they used to come to Rome"; the reference to citizenship can hardly apply to the status of Cameria prior to 502. Umbrian Camerinum is an implausible alternative for the vanquished town, on both historical and linguistic grounds (see V. Max. 5.2.8, properly calling its inhabitants "Camertes"). Broughton considers P. Claudius an early praetor (*MRR* I 463). P. Conole (*Antichthon* 15 [1981] 129–140) is unconvincing in his attempt to argue that Ameria rose at the same time as Fregellae in 125, and that it was crushed by a *pr.* P. Claudius Nero (father of C. Claudius P.f. Nero, *pr.* 81) (ch. 8 n. 283).

499. *CIL* I² 20 = *ILLRP* 184 for both this [——]ilius M.f. and C. An(n)ius, "[?prai]toris pro po[plod |Tonan]ti Diove dede[re]" (for the text, see K. Latte, *Römische Religionsgeschichte* (Munich 1960) 81 n. 1, offering by far the most plausible supplement yet for the major lacuna). Scholars unhesitatingly (and rightly) assign this archaic inscription to the third century; if these individuals are actually Roman praetors—and not quaestors (see *MRR* II 462, 474), or, as Degrassi cautioned ad loc. and II p. 467, magistrates of another town—a date between 241 and 219 seems required. [Aem]ilius is just one possible supplement of the *nomen* of the first; cf. the reverse index in H. Solin and O. Salomies, *Repertorium nominum gentilium et cognominum Latinorum* (Hildesheim 1984) 237–240. He may even be an "Aurilius" (for this spelling see *ILLRP* 75, the year 200).

500. Held a command in Liguria at some point, perhaps as praetor: see Fron. *Str.* 3.2.1 with *MRR* II 560.

501. See Additional Note X.

502. Fron. *Str.* 3.5.3. He besieged a "Greek city"; no title has been preserved. Sicily should not be ruled out as a possibility for his theater of operations: note that at *Strat.* 4.7.22 Frontinus calls the inhabitants of Henna "Graeci."

503. *RDGE* 1 C lines 1–2, on which see ch. 5 n. 155 (most likely Cn. Octavius, *cos.* 165, in his consulship).

504. *RDGE* 8 line 1. He was a praetor who drafted the cover letter of a *senatus consultum* concerning the town of Triccala in Thessaly. See also n. 277 above.

505. See 14.5.2 for discussion.

506. L. R. Taylor (*JRS* 52 [1962] 23) has suggested that the Aelius who introduced the *lex Aelia* on *obnuntiatio* toward the middle of the second century B.C. and the Fufius who passed a related law on legislative procedure did so as praetors: see the discussion in *MRR* III 3–4, cf. 94.

507. *ILLRP* 340, on which see ch. 8 n. 272.

508. *Pr. urb.* ca. 125–110. See 5.6.1.

509. *RDGE* 1 D line 1, on which see ch. 5 n. 155 (possibly the *cos.* 136, L. Furius Philus, as praetor or consul).

510. Praetor (Cic. *de Orat.* 2.280), evidently in Sicily; period not ascertainable but before 91. He is perhaps identifiable with the *pr.* 193 for Sicily, L. Cornelius (337) Scipio (Asiaticus). But note also the Scipiones who were *coss.* 165 and 141 (whose praetorian *provinciae* are unknown); there are obviously other possibilities.

511. For his praetorship, see *SIG*³ 715, a proxeny decree from Rhegium. Probably (late) second century: for the date, see Dittenberger *SIG*³ ad loc.; *MRR* III 29; O. Wikander, *ORom* 15 (1985) 157 with n. 14 (providing further bibliography). If so, he may be the father of the Cn. Auf[idius] in the *S.C. de agro Pergameno* of (surely) 101 (see *RDGE* 12, line 45, no. 51 of a *consilium* of 55). However, both men must be distinguished from the Cn. Aufidius

Cn.f. who was active as a *legatus pro praetore* (so I would hold) in Asia at the end of the first century (14.5.3).

512. See Ruf. Fest. *Brev.* 5.1 with 7.3.2 above.

513. See *AE* 1991, 426a (Setia) "[——]us pr(aetor) de s(enatus) s(ententia) refec(it) de m[——]." He was possibly not a praetor of Rome, and the date in any case is quite uncertain.

514. A *praetorius* of the Republic. M. Valerius Messalla (*cos.* 53) "and many others" reported he had been carried to safety when he revived on his funeral pyre (Plin. *Nat.* 7.173); he need not be early.

515. Fenestella (ap. Plin. *Nat.* 33.21 = *HRR* II F 12) cited "Calpurnius" and (A.) Manlius (*pr.* by 107) as examples of *praetorii* who lived to old age still wearing an iron ring. Broughton (*MRR* III 45, following Syme) infers from Pliny's context that Calpurnius was a "senator and praetorius of the period of the Social War." Maybe so, but even the approximate date of his praetorship remains quite uncertain.

516. Wiseman, *NM* 232 no. 182. He was the addressee of the political autobiography of M. Aemilius Scaurus (*cos.* 115), who reached the praetorship, and despite his status, apparently lived to old age still wearing an iron ring (Plin. *Nat.* 33.21). He is very possibly identical with the *pr.* 80 of this name, rather than his father: see 11. 353 above.

517. *I. Délos* IV 1 1679 (*pro cos.*) with 14.5.2.

518. Known from *ILLRP* 479 (Ostia), "C. Caninius C.f. | pr. urb. | de sen(atus) sent(entia) | poplic(um) ioudic(avit)"; "probably before the period of Sulla" (*MRR* II 463). He should be a direct descendant of C. Caninius Rebilus (*pr.* Sicily 171) and ascendant of the *cos. suff.* 45 C. Caninius C.f. C.n. Rebilus. The abbreviation "de sen(atus) sent(entia)" (on which see ch. 5 n. 212) suggests a date after ca. 120. It is likely (as Münzer, *RE* s.v. col. 232f holds) he was grandfather—though possibly father—of the *cos. suff.* 45. See 12.1.1, and cf. 12.4.1, for brief discussion.

519. Wiseman, *NM* 281 no. 542. Cic. *Scaur.* 40 (54 B.C.) "damnatus est T. Albucius, C. Megaboccus ex Sardinia non nullis etiam laudantibus Sardis." Albucius was praetor for Sardinia (ca. 107—see 13.1.1), and Megabocchus probably had the same status as well. There is no use guessing at a date, but he should be father or grandfather of the officer Megabocchus who met his death with the younger Crassus at Carrhae in 53 (*MRR* II 230).

520. From *RRC* I 457–468 no. 437 2a-4b (dated by Crawford to 51 B.C., with legend IMP A X), it has been thought that there existed a son of the *cos.* 94 C. Coelius Caldus who was hailed as "imperator" (i.e., from a praetorian command in an armed *provincia*) and also reached the positions of *Xvir s.f.* (before 80) and augur (before 61): see *MRR* II 285, III 60, with G. Radke in *RE* s.v. *quindecemviri* col. 1142 on the college of *Xviri s.f.* (raised to 15 probably by Sulla). Yet it seems hard to believe that an (otherwise unknown) individual simultaneously might hold two major Roman priesthoods, always a rare distinction in the Republic (cf. E. Badian, *Arethusa* 1 [1968] 39f). Furthermore, it strains credulity to think that this simple "X" can stand for "Xvir s.f." when this same coin issue shows also the legends IIIVIR and VIIVIR EPVL(onum). In sum, the interpretation of this legend seems too uncertain to postulate the existence of a son of the *cos.* 94 who was a praetorian *imperator*. (See now E. Badian, *Arctos* 32 [1998] 45–60, rejecting this conjectural praetorian altogether.)

521. Pro cos. in the east at an unknown date in the first century (perhaps well after our period). See *IG* XII 5 924 (Tenos) with discussion in ch. 12 n. 233. The *cognomen* "Rufus" evokes the hair *cognomina* of the patrician Quinctii. But actual descent seems unlikely.

522. Termed στρατηγός in *Milet.* I 2 118 no. 14 (the reading of the name is very dubious, and the *nomen* itself is impossible). See *MRR* III 225 for discussion.

523. A praetor of unknown date: see Plin. *Nat.* 7.44 (a very miscellaneous list of deaths from trivial causes) with *MRR* II 464.

524. See *MRR* III 97. A Furius Leptinus said to be "of praetorian descent" ("stirpe praetoria") appeared as a gladiator in Caesar's triumphal games in 46 (Suet. *Jul.* 39.1); Dio (43.23.5) mentions that a son of an ex-praetor fought on that occasion. If we are justified in combining these notices, it seems there was a Furius Leptinus who reached the praetorship in the first half of the first century.

525. See *Schol. Gron.* p. 321 St. for a summary statement on the provincial extortions of a "†Procaelius quidam Romanus imperator." If he is a real person and the name is not too far distorted, he is best placed in the later Republic. (No members of the *gens* Procilia or Precilia are known to hold office in the pre-Sullan period.)

526. *Chiron* 20 (1990) 409–413, esp. 410 for a table setting out the figures for the period under question. Badian for his study usefully divides the years 179–49 into nine subperiods, to take into account various technical factors that affected the consulship (elections of pairs of plebeians starting in 172, the end of iteration after 151—neither applicable to the praetorship) and extraordinary circumstances when elections were not free. I, too, exclude the years 86–82 B.C. from consideration (though unfortunately also 49 B.C., since I have not treated the complex events—and difficult prosopographical issues—of that year in this study), but leave in the period of Marius' ascendancy (103–99, for which very few praetors are known). On the social background of the praetors in the three years when Sulla controlled elections (81–79), see below in text.

527. *Last Generation* 163–177 (an important detailed discussion), esp. pp. 164 and 166 for the quotes. Less certain is Gruen's parallel contention that men of consular stock rarely failed in their quest for the praetorship. We have precious little information on failed praetorian candidacies in this period, as a glance at Broughton, *Candidates Defeated* 35–39, will now show. See esp. *MRR* II 108 n. 3 on Q. Caecilius Metellus (the future *cos.* 69, Creticus) as an (unsuccessful?) candidate for the praetorship of 74; and *Candidates Defeated* 35f on the frustrated ambitions of L. Calpurnius Bestia (*aed.* ca. 59). On the limits of *nobilitas* in this era, see the general remarks of Marshall, *Asconius* 138–139.

528. *Roman Voting Assemblies* 73f; on the "sors opportuna" in general, cf. the remarks of E. Badian, *Titus Quinctius Flamininus: Philhellenism and Realpolitik* (Cincinnati 1970) 30–32.

529. *AJPh* 116 (1995) 43–75. The quotations which follow are from 69–70.

530. I have omitted specific references here. The requisite data can be gleaned from the list of praetors in sections B.2–4 in this Appendix (with *MRR* I for subsequent careers).

531. See Liv. 40.37.6.

532. *CJ* 84 (1988) 63.

533. For Cicero's public reticence about cheating in not just the praetorian sortition but in fact in any sortition, see 12.1.2 n. 55.

534. See 11.7.4 on M. Fannius, *pr. inter sicarios* 80, a former *iudex quaestionis* in that very *provincia*.

535. See 13.3.1 on Ser. Galba, *pr.* by 110 in Hispania Ulterior, and M. Marius, *pr.* by 101 in that same province; 13.2.2 on M. Lepidus (*pr.* 81) and C. Marcellus (*pr.* 80) as *pro coss.* for Sicily in 80 and 79 respectively; 14.6.1 on M. Silanus (*pr.* by 77) as *pro cos.* by 76 in Asia; 12.1.2 on the series of three ex-urban praetors who received Sicily in the years 77–73; 14.4 for L. Catilina (*pr.* by 68) and Africa; 14.6.5 on T. Aufidius (*pr.* by 67) as *pro cos.* in Asia; 14.6.6 on L. Flaccus (*pr.* 63) as *pro cos.* 62 for Asia; 15.2.5 on Q. Metellus Celer (*pr.* 63), *pro cos.* 62 for Cisalpine Gaul; 13.2.6 on C. Balbus (*pr.* 62) as *pro cos.* for Sicily; 13.4.7 on C. Caesar (*pr.* 62) as *pro cos.* 61 for Ulterior; 11.2 on C. Carbo (*pr.* by 61) as *pro cos.* in the newly reintegrated Bithynia/Pontus; and 13.4.8 for P. Lentulus Spinther (*pr.* 60), *pro cos.* 59 for Hispania Citerior.

Select Bibliography

This bibliography omits repeated references to works found in *Conventions and Abbreviations*; and does not (on the whole) include works cited in just one chapter.

Ager, S. *Interstate Arbitrations in the Greek World, 337–90 B.C.* (Berkeley 1996).

Alexander, M. C. *Trials in the Late Roman Republic* (Toronto 1990).

Amat-Seguin, B. "Ariminum et Flaminius," *RSA* 16 (1986) 79–109.

Arriat, D. *Le préteur pérégrin* (Paris 1955).

Astin, A. E. *The Lex Annalis before Sulla* (Brussels 1958).

——. *Scipio Aemilianus* (Oxford 1967).

——. *Cato the Censor* (Oxford 1978).

——. "The Censorship of the Roman Republic: Frequency and Regularity," *Historia* 31 (1982) 174–187.

Badian, E. "The Early Career of A. Gabinius (*cos.* 58 B.C.)," *Philologus* 103 (1959) 87–99.

——. *Foreign Clientelae (264–70 B.C.)* (Oxford 1958).

——. Review of T. R. S. Broughton, *Supplement to The Magistrates of the Roman Republic*, in *Gnomon* 33 (1961) 492–498.

——. *Studies in Greek and Roman History* (Oxford 1964).

——. "M. Porcius Cato and the Annexation and Early Administration of Cyprus," *JRS* 55 (1965) 110–121.

——. "The Dolabellae of the Republic," *PBSR* 20 (1965) 48–51.

——. "Notes on *Provincia Gallia* in the Late Republic," in R. Chevallier (ed.), *Mélanges d'archéologie et d'histoire offerts à André Piganiol* II (Paris 1966) 901–918.

——. "The Testament of Ptolemy Alexander," *RhM* 110 (1967) 178–192.

——. *Roman Imperialism in the Late Republic*[2] (Oxford 1968).

——. Review of A. Degrassi (ed.), *CIL. Auctarium. Inscriptiones Latinae Liberae Rei Publicae: Imagines*, in *JRS* 58 (1968) 240–249.

——. "Cicero and the Commission of 146 B.C.," in J. Bibauw (ed.), *Hommages à M. Renard* I (Brussels 1969) 54–65.

——. "Quaestiones Variae," *Historia* 18 (1969) 447–491.

——. *Titus Quinctius Flamininus: Philhellenism and Realpolitik* (Cincinnati 1970).

——. *Lucius Sulla: The Deadly Reformer* (Sydney 1970).

——. "The Sempronii Aselliones," *PACA* 11 (1968) [1970] 1–6.

——. "Roman Politics and the Italians (133–91 B.C.)," *DArch* 4–5 (1970–1971) 373–409.

——. "The Family and Early Career of T. Quinctius Flamininus," *JRS* 61 (1971) 102–111.

——. "M. Calpurnius M. f. Frugi," in *Acta of the 5th International Congress of Greek and Latin Epigraphy, Cambridge 1967* (Oxford 1971) 209–214.

——. "Two More Roman Non-Entities," *Phoenix* 25 (1971) 134–144.

——. *Publicans and Sinners: Private Enterprise in the Service of the Roman Republic* (1972, rev. ed. Ithaca, N.Y., 1983). Trans. into German (with revisions) as *Zöllner und Sünder*, trans. W. Will and S. Cox (Darmstadt 1997).

——. "Tiberius Gracchus and the Beginning of the Roman Revolution," *ANRW* I 1 (1972) 668–731.

——. "Marius' Villas: The Evidence of the Slave and the Knave," *JRS* 63 (1973) 121–132.

——. Review of H. Kloft, *Prorogation und außerordentliche Imperien 326–81 v. Chr.*, in *Gnomon* 51 (1979) 792–794.

——. "The Silence of Norbanus: A Note on Provincial Quaestors under the Republic," *AJPh* 104 (1983) 156–171.

——. "The Death of Saturninus: Studies in Chronology and Prosopography," *Chiron* 14 (1984) 101–147.

——. "Three Non-Trials in Cicero: Notes on the Text, Prosopography and Chronology of *Divinatio in Caecilium* 63," *Klio* 66 (1984) 291–309.

——. "Two Notes on *Senatus Consulta* concerning Pergamum," *LCM* 11 (1986) 14–16.

——. "The *Scribae* of the Roman Republic," *Klio* 71 (1989) 582–603.

——. "Magistratur und Gesellschaft," in W. Eder (ed.), *Staat und Staatlichkeit in der frühen römischen Republik* (Stuttgart 1990) 458–475.

——. "The Consuls, 179–49 B.C.," *Chiron* 20 (1990) 371–413.

——. "The Legend of the Legate who Lost his Luggage," *Historia* 42 (1993) 203–210.

——. "*Tribuni Plebis* and *Res Publica*," in J. Linderski (ed.), *Imperium Sine Fine: T. Robert S. Broughton and the Roman Republic* (Stuttgart 1996) 187–213.

Balsdon, J. P. V. D. "Consular Provinces under the Late Republic," *JRS* 29 (1939) 57–73, 167–183.

——. "Roman History, 65–50 B.C.: Five Problems," *JRS* 52 (1962) 134–141.

Bandelli, G. "La frontiera settentrionale: l'ondata celtica e il nuovo sistema di alleanze," in A. Momigliano and A. Schiavone (eds.), *Storia di Roma* I (Turin 1988) 505–525.

Barigazzi, A. "Liguri Friniati e Apuani in Livio," *Prometheus* 17 (1991) 55–74.

Bauerle, E. "Procuring An Election: Ambitus in the Roman Republic, 432–49 B.C." (diss. Univ. Michigan, Ann Arbor, 1990).

Bauman, R. A. *Lawyers in Roman Republican Politics: A Study of the Roman Jurists in Their Political Setting, 316–82 B.C.* (Munich 1983).

Billows, R. "Legal Fiction and Political Reform at Rome in the Early Second Century B.C.," *Phoenix* 43 (1989) 112–133.

Bleicken, J. "Kollisionen zwischen Sacrum und Publicum. Eine Studie zum Verfall der altrömischen Religion," *Hermes* 85 (1957) 446–480.

Bodel, J. *Graveyards and Groves: A Study of the Lex Lucerina* (Cambridge, Mass., 1994).

Bonnefond-Coudry, M. *Le sénat de la république romaine de la guerre d'Hannibal à Auguste* (Rome 1989).

Brennan, T. C. "C. Aurelius Cotta, *Praetor Iterum* (CIL I² 610)," *Athenaeum* 67 (1989) 467–487.

——. "Sulla's Career in the Nineties: Some Reconsiderations," *Chiron* 22 (1992) 103–158.

——. "The Commanders in the First Sicilian Slave War," *RFIC* 121 (1993) 153–184.

——. "M.' Curius Dentatus and the Praetor's Right to Triumph," *Historia* 43 (1994) 423–439.

——. "*Triumphus in Monte Albano*," in E. Harris and R. Wallace (eds.), *Transitions to Empire: Essays in Greco-Roman History, 360–146 B.C., in Honor of E. Badian* (Norman, Okla., 1996) 315–337.

Briscoe, J. *A Commentary on Livy, Books XXXI–XXXIII* (Oxford 1973).

——. *A Commentary on Livy, Books XXXIV–XXXVII* (Oxford 1981).

Broughton, T. R. S. "More Notes on Roman Magistrates," *TAPhA* 79 (1948) 63–78.

——. *Candidates Defeated in Roman Elections: Some Ancient Roman "Also-Rans"* (Philadelphia 1991).

Brunt, P. A. Review of W. Kunkel, *Untersuchungen zur Entwicklung des römischen Kriminalverfahrens*, in *RHD* 32 (1964) 440–449.

——. *Italian Manpower, 225 B.C.–A.D. 14* (Oxford 1971).

——. *The Fall of the Roman Republic and Related Essays* (Oxford 1988).

Bucher, G. "Appian *BC* 2, 24 and the Trial *De Ambitu* of M. Aemilius Scaurus," *Historia* 44 (1995) 396–421.

Buti, I. "Appunti in tema di *prorogatio imperii*," *Index* 19 (1991) 245–267 and *Index* 20 (1992) 435–472.

Castrén, P. "I Cornelii Mamullae: Storia di una famiglia," *Arctos* 14 (1980) 5–13.

Catalano, P. *Contributi allo studio del diritto augurale* I (Turin 1960).

Champlin, E. Review of T. R. S. Broughton, *Magistrates of the Roman Republic* III, in *CPh* 84 (1989) 51–59.

Cichorius, C. *Römische Studien* (Leipzig 1922).

——. *Untersuchungen zu Lucilius* (Berlin 1908).

Clark, A. C. *M. Tulli Ciceronis Pro T. Annio Milone* (Oxford 1895).

Cloud, D. "The Constitution and Public Criminal Law," in *CAH* IX² (1994) 491–530.

Cobban, J. M. *Senate and Provinces, 78–49 B.C.* (Cambridge 1935).

Coli, U. *Scritti di diritto romano* I–II (Milan 1973).

Combès, R. *Imperator: Recherches sur l'emploi et la signification du titre d'imperator dans la Rome républicaine* (Paris 1966).

Cornell, T. J. "The Failure of the Plebs," in E. Gabba (ed.), *Tria Corda: Scritti in onore di A. Momigliano* (Como 1983) 101–120.

——. *The Beginnings of Rome: Italy and Rome from the Bronze Age to the Punic Wars (c. 1000–264 B.C.)* (London 1995).

Dahlheim, W. *Gewalt und Herrschaft. Das provinziale Herrschaftssystem der römischen Republik* (Berlin 1977).

Damon, C., and C. S. Mackay. "On the Prosecution of C. Antonius in 76 B.C.," *Historia* 44 (1995) 37–55.

Daube, D. "The Peregrine Praetor," *JRS* 41 (1951) 66–70.

——. *Collected Studies in Roman Law*, ed. D. Cohen and D. Simon (Frankfurt a. M. 1991).

Develin, R. "*Lex Curiata* and the Competence of Magistrates," *Mnemosyne* 30 (1977) 49–65.

——. *Patterns in Office-Holding 366—49 B.C.* (Brussels 1979).

——. "The Roman Command Structure and Spain, 218–190 B.C.," *Klio* 62 (1980) 355–367.

——. *The Practice of Politics in Rome, 366–167 B.C.* (Brussels 1985).

——. "The Integration of the Plebeians after 366 B.C.," in K.A. Raaflaub (ed.), *Social Struggles in Archaic Rome* (Berkeley 1986) 327–352.

Drumann, W., and P. Groebe. *Geschichte Roms* I–VI (Leipzig 1899–1929).

Dyson, S. L. "Native Revolt Patterns in the Roman Empire," *ANRW* II 3 (1975) 138–175.

Earl, D. C. "Calpurnii Pisones in the Second Century B.C.," *Athenaeum* 38 (1960) 283–298.

Ebel, C. *Transalpine Gaul: The Emergence of a Roman Province* (Leiden 1976).

Eckstein, A. M. *Senate and General: Individual Decision Making and Roman Foreign Relations, 264–194 B.C.* (Berkeley 1987).

Edelstein, L., and I. G. Kidd. *Posidonius* I²–II² (Cambridge 1988–1989).

Eder, W. *Das vorsullanische Repetundenverfahren* (Munich 1969).

Eilers, C. "Silanus <and> Murena," *CQ* 46 (1996) 175–182.

Evans, J. K. "Resistance at Home: The Evasion of Military Service in Italy during the Second Century B.C.," in T. Yuge and M. Doi (eds.), *Forms of Control and Subordination in Antiquity* (Leiden 1988) 121–140.

Fantham, E. "The Trials of Gabinius in 54 B.C.," *Historia* 24 (1975) 425–443.

Ferrary, J.-L. *Philhéllenisme et impérialisme: Aspects idéologiques de la conquête romaine du monde hellénistique, de la seconde guerre de Macédoine à la guerre contre Mithridate* (Rome 1988).

Flach, D. *Die Gesetze der frühen römischen Republik: Text und Kommentar* (Darmstadt 1994).

Forsythe, G. *The Historian L. Calpurnius Piso Frugi and the Roman Annalistic Tradition* (Lanham, Md., 1994).

Foucart, P. "ΣΤΡΑΤΗΓΟΣ ΥΠΑΤΟΣ. ΣΤΡΑΤΗΓΟΣ ΑΝΘΥΠΑΤΟΣ," *RPh* 23 (1899) 254–269.

——. "Les campagnes de M. Antonius Creticus contre les pirates, 74–71," *Journal des Savants* n.s. 4 (1906) 569–581.

Fraccaro, P. *Opuscula* I-IV (Pavia 1956–1975).

Frier, B. W. "Urban Praetors and Rural Violence: The Legal Background of Cicero's *pro Caecina*," *TAPhA* 113 (1983) 221–241.

——. *The Rise of the Roman Jurists: Studies in Cicero's pro Caecina* (Princeton 1985).

Gabba, E. *Appiani Bellorum Civilium Liber Primus: Introduzione, testo critico e commento* (Florence 1958).

——. "Istituzioni militari e colonizzazione in Roma medio-repubblicana (IV–III sec. a. C.)," *RFIC* 103 (1975) 144–154.

——. *Le rivolte militari romane* (Florence 1975).

Gargola, D. J. "The Colonial Commissioners of 218 B.C. and the Foundation of Cremona and Placentia," *Athenaeum* 68 (1990) 465–473.

Gelzer, M. *Kleine Schriften* I–III (Wiesbaden 1962–1964).

——. *The Roman Nobility*, trans. R. Seager (Oxford 1969).

——. *Caesar: Politician and Statesman*, trans. P. Needham (Oxford 1969).

Gilbert, R. L. "The Origin and History of the Peregrine Praetorship, 242–166 B.C.," *Res Judicatae* 2 (1939) 50–58.

Giovannini, A. *Consulare imperium* (Basel 1983).

Girardet, K. M. "*Imperium* und *provinciae* des Pompeius seit 67 v. Chr.," CCGG 3 (1992) 177–188.

——. "Zur Diskussion um das *imperium consulare militiae* im Jh. v. Chr.," CCGG 3 (1992) 213–220.

Greenidge, A. H. J. *The Legal Procedure of Cicero's Time* (Oxford 1901).

Gruen, E. S. *Roman Politics and the Criminal Courts, 149–78 B.C.* (Cambridge, Mass., 1968).

——. "Some Criminal Trials of the Late Republic: Political and Prosopographical Problems," *Athenaeum* 49 (1971) 54–69.

——. *The Last Generation of the Roman Republic* (Berkeley 1974).

——. *The Hellenistic World and the Coming of Rome* I–II (Berkeley 1984).

——. "The Exercise of Power in the Roman Republic," in A. Mohlo, K. A. Raaflaub, and J. Emlen (eds.), *City States in Classical Antiquity and Medieval Italy* (Stuttgart 1991) 251–267.

Gsell, S. *Histoire ancienne de l'Afrique du Nord* I-VIII (Paris 1913–1928).

Hackl, U. *Senat und Magistratur in Rom von der Mitte des 2. Jahrhunderts v. Chr. bis zur Diktatur Sullas* (Kallmünz 1982).

Halpérin, J.-L. "Tribunat de la plèbe et haute plèbe (493–218 av. J.-C.)," RD 62 (1984) 161–181.

Hanell, K. *Das altrömische eponyme Amt* (Lund 1946).

Hantos, T. *Res Publica Constituta: Die Verfassung des Dictators Sulla* (Stuttgart 1988).

Harris, W. V. *Rome in Etruria and Umbria* (Oxford 1971).

——. "The Development of the Quaestorship, 267–81 B.C.," CQ 26 (1976) 92–106.

——. *War and Imperialism in Republican Rome, 327–70 B.C.* (Oxford 1979).

——. "Roman Warfare in the Economic and Social Context," in W. Eder (ed.), *Staat und Staatlichkeit* (Stuttgart 1990) 494–510.

Hartfield, M. E. "The Roman Dictatorship: Its Character and its Evolution" (diss. Univ. California, Berkeley 1982).

Hersh, C. A. "Notes on the Chronology and the Interpretation of the Roman Republican Coinage," NC (ser. 7) 17 (1977) 19–36.

Heuss, A. *Gedanken und Vermutungen zur frühen römischen Regierungsgewalt* (Göttingen 1982).

Hinard, F. *Les proscriptions de la Rome républicaine* (Rome 1985).

Hölbl, G. *Geschichte des Ptolemäerreiches* (Darmstadt 1994).

Hölkeskamp, K.-J. *Die Entstehung der Nobilität: Studien zur sozialen und politischen Geschichte der römischen Republik im 4. Jhdt. v. Chr.* (Stuttgart 1987).

——. "Conquest, Competition and Consensus: Roman Expansion in Italy and the Rise of the *nobilitas*," *Historia* 42 (1993) 12–39.

Holleaux, M. "Textes greco-romaines," REA 19 (1917) 77–97.

——. ΣΤΡΑΤΗΓΟΣ ΥΠΑΤΟΣ (Paris 1918).

——. *Études d' épigraphie et d'histoire grècques* I–VI (Paris 1938–1968).

Hölzl, M. "Fasti praetorii ab A.U. DCLXXXVII usque ad A.U. DCCX" (diss. Univ. Leipzig 1876).

Hoyos, B. D. "Lex Provinciae and Governor's Edict," *Antichthon* 7 (1973) 47–53.

——. "Roman Strategy in Cisalpina, 224–222 and 203–191 B.C.," *Antichthon* 10 (1976) 44–55.

Humbert, M. *Municipium et civitas sine suffragio: L'organisation de la conquête jusqu'à la guerre sociale* (Rome 1978).

——. "L'organisation de l'Italie romaine avant la guerre sociale," in J. E. Spruit (ed.), *Maior viginti quinque annis: Essays in Commemoration of the Sixth Lustrum of the Institute for Legal History of the University of Utrecht* (Assen 1979) 66–84.

Jahn, J. *Interregnum und Wahldiktatur* (Kallmünz 1970).

Jashemski, W. F. *The Origins and History of the Proconsular and Propraetorian Imperium down to 27 B.C.* (Chicago 1950).

Jolliffe, R. O. "Phases of Corruption in Roman Administration in the Last Half-Century of the Roman Republic" (diss. Univ. Chicago 1919).

Jones, A. H. M. *The Criminal Courts of the Roman Republic and Principate* (Oxford 1972).

Kallet-Marx, R. *Hegemony to Empire: The Development of the Roman Imperium in the East from 148 to 62 B.C.* (Berkeley 1995).

Kaser, M. *Das römisches Privatrecht* I²–II² (Munich 1971–1975).

——. "'Ius Honorarium' und 'Ius Civile'," ZRG 101 (1984) 1–114.

Keaveney, A. "Studies in the *Dominatio Sullae*" *Klio* 65 (1983) 185–208.

——. "Who Were the Sullani?" *Klio* 66 (1984) 114–150.

——. *Rome and the Unification of Italy* (London 1987).

——. *Lucullus: A Life* (London 1992).

Kloft, H. *Prorogation und außerordentliche Imperien 326–81 v. Chr: Untersuchungen zur Verfassung der römischen Republik* (Meisenheim a. Glan 1977).

Knapp, R. C. "Festus 262L and *Praefecturae* in Italy," *Athenaeum* 58 (1980) 14–38.

Konrad, C. F. Review of J. S. Richardson, *Hispaniae*, *CJ* 84 (1988) 61–63.

——. "Cotta off Mellaria and the Identities of Fufidius," *CPh* 84 (1989) 119–129.

——. *Plutarch's Sertorius: A Historical Commentary* (Chapel Hill, N.C., 1994).

——. "Segovia and Segontia," *Historia* 43 (1994) 440–453.

——. "A New Chronology of the Sertorian War," *Athenaeum* 83 (1995) 157–187.

——. "Notes on Roman Also-Rans," in J. Linderski (ed.), *Imperium Sine Fine: T. Robert S. Broughton and the Roman Republic* (Stuttgart 1996) 103–143.

Kukofka, D.-A. *Süditalien im Zweiten Punischen Krieg* (Frankfurt a. M. 1990).

Kunkel, W. *Untersuchungen zur Entwicklung des römischen Kriminalverfahrens in vorsullanischer Zeit* (Munich 1962).

——. *Staatsordnung und Staatspraxis der römischen Republik: Die Magistratur* (Munich 1995).

Laffi, U. "La lex Rubria de Gallia Cisalpina," *Athenaeum* 64 (1986) 5–44.

——. "Di nuovo sulla datazione del *fragmentum Atestinum*," *Athenaeum* 78 [68] (1990) 167–175.

——. "La provincia della Gallia Cisalpina," *Athenaeum* 80 [70] (1992) 5–24.

Last, H. "*Imperium Maius*: A Note," *JRS* 37 (1947) 157–164.

Leifer, F. *Die Einheit des Gewaltgedankens im römischen Staatsrecht* (Munich 1914).

Linderski, J. "The Augural Law," *ANRW* II 16.3 (1986) 2146–2312.

——. *Roman Questions: Selected Papers* (Stuttgart 1995).

Lintott, A. W. "Provocatio. From the Struggle of the Orders to the Principate," *ANRW* I 2 (1972) 226–267.

——. "What Was the 'Imperium Romanum'?," *G&R* 28 (1981) 53–67.

——. "The *Leges de Repetundis* and Associative Measures under the Republic," *ZRG* 98 (1981) 162–212.

——. "Democracy in the Middle Republic," *ZRG* 104 (1987) 34–52.

——. *Judicial Reform and Land Reform in the Roman Republic* (Cambridge 1992).

——. *Imperium Romanum: Politics and Administration* (London 1993).

Lübtow, U. von. *Das Römische Volk. Sein Staat und sein Recht* (Frankfurt a. M. 1955).

——. "Die Aufgaben des römischen Praetors auf dem Gebiet der Zivilrechtspflege," *Studi in onore di A. Biscardi* IV (Milan 1983) 349–412.

Luzzatto, G. I. *Storia di Roma*, XVII: 1, *Roma e le province: Organizzazione, economia, società* (Bologna 1985).

Mackay, C. "The Judicial Legislation of C. Sempronius Gracchus" (diss. Harvard 1994).

Magie, D. *Roman Rule in Asia Minor* I–II (Princeton 1950).

Mamoojee, A. H. "Le proconsulat de Q. Cicéron en Asie," *EMC* 13 (1994) 23–50.

Marino, R. *La Sicilia dal 241 al 210 a. C.* (Rome 1988).

Marshall, A. J. "The *Lex Pompeia de provinciis* (52 B.C.) and Cicero's *Imperium* in 51–50 B.C.: Constitutional Aspects," *ANRW* I 1 (1972) 887–921.

Marshall, B. A. "The Case of Metellus Nepos v. Curio: A Discussion of Cicero, *Verr.* I 6 and 9 and the Scholiasts," *Philologus* 121 (1977) 83–89.

——. *A Historical Commentary on Asconius* (Columbia, Mo., 1985).

Martin, P. M. *L'idée de royauté à Rome I: De la Rome royale au consensus républicain* (Clermont-Ferrand 1982).

Martino, F. De "Intorno all'origine della repubblica romana e delle magistrature," *ANRW* I 1 (1972) 217–249.

——. *Storia della Costituzione Romana* I²–VI² (Naples 1972–1990).

Mattingly, H. B. "Notes on Some Roman Republican Moneyers," *NC* (ser. 7) 9 (1969) 95–105.

——. "The Date of the Senatus Consultum 'De Agro Pergameno'," *AJPh* 93 (1972) 412–423.

——. "Coinage and the Roman State," *NC* (ser. 7) 17 (1977) 199–215.

——. "The Numismatic Evidence and the Founding of Narbo Martius," *RAN* 5 (1972) 1–19.

——. "L. Julius Caesar, Governor of Macedonia," *Chiron* 9 (1979) 147–167.

——. "M. Antonius, C. Verres, and the Sack of Delos by the Pirates," in M. J. Fontana, M. T. Piraino, and F. P. Rizzo (eds.), Φιλίας Χάριν: *Miscellanea di studi classici in onore di Eugenio Manni* IV (Rome 1979) 1491–1515.

Maxis, E. "Die Praetoren Roms von 367–167 v. Chr." (diss. Univ. Breslau 1911).

McGing, B.C. "The Date of the Outbreak of the Third Mithridatic War," *Phoenix* 38 (1984) 12–18.

McGushin, P. *Sallust: The Histories* I–II (Oxford 1992–1994).

Meloni, P. *La Sardegna romana* (Sassari 1975).

Meyer, E. *Kleine Schriften* I–II (Halle 1910–1924).

Michels, A. *The Calendar of the Roman Republic* (Princeton 1967).

Millar, F. "Political Power in Mid-Republican Rome: Curia or Comitium?," *JRS* 79 (1989) 138–150.

Mitchell, R. E. *Patricians and Plebeians: The Origin of the Roman State* (Ithaca, N.Y., 1990).

Mócsy, A. "Die Vorgeschichte Obermösiens im hellenistisch–römischen Zeitalter," *AAHung* 14 (1966) 87–112.

——. *Pannonia and Upper Moesia* (London 1974).

Mommsen, T. *Die römische Chronologie bis auf Cäsar*² (Berlin 1859).

——. *Römisches Strafrecht* (Leipzig 1899).

Morgan, M. G. "The Introduction of the Aqua Marcia into Rome, 144–140 B.C.," *Philologus* 122 (1978) 25–58.

Müller-Seidel, I. "Q. Fabius Cunctator und die Konsulwahlen der Jahre 215 und 214 v. Chr: Ein Beitrag zur religiosen Situation Roms im zweitem punischen Krieg," *RhM* 96 (1953) 241–281.

Münzer, F. *Römische Adelsparteien und Adelsfamilien* (Stuttgart 1920).

Nadig, P. *Ardet Ambitus: Untersuchungen zum Phänomen der Wahlbestechungen in der römischen Republik* (Frankfurt a. M. 1997).

Nissen, H. *Kritische Untersuchungen über die Quellen der vierten und fünften Dekade des Livius* (Berlin 1863).

Oakley, S. P. *A Commentary on Livy Books VI–X*, I: *Introduction and Book VI*. II: *Books VII–VIII* (Oxford 1997–1998).

Ogilvie, R. M. *A Commentary on Livy Books 1–5* (Oxford 1965).

Oost, S. I. "Cyrene, 96–74 B.C.," *CPh* 58 (1963) 11–25.

Pailler, J. M. *Bacchanalia. La répression de 186 av. J.-C. à Rome et en Italie: vestiges, images, tradition* (Paris 1988).

Palazzolo, N. "La proposito in albo degli *edicta perpetua* e il *plebiscitum Cornelium* del 67 a. C.," in L. Amirante et al. (eds.), *Sodalitas: Scritti in onore di Antonio Guarino* V (Naples 1984) 2427–2448.

Palmer, R. E. A. *The Archaic Community of the Romans* (Cambridge 1970).

Papazoglou, F. "Quelques aspects de l'histoire de la province de Macédoine," *ANRW* II 7.1 (1979) 302–369.

Passerini, A. "C. Mario come uomo politico," *Athenaeum* 12 (1934) 10–44, 109–143, 257–297, 348–380.

Paul, G. M. *A Historical Commentary on Sallust's Bellum Jugurthinum* (Liverpool 1984).

Perl, G. "Die römischen Provinzbeamten in Cyrenae und Creta zur Zeit der Republik," *Klio* 52 (1970) 319–354; 53 (1971) 369–379.

Pietilä-Castrén, L. "The Ancestry and Career of Cn. Octavius, cos. 165 B.C.," *Arctos* 18 (1984) 75–92.

———. *Magnificentia Publica: The Victory Monuments of the Roman Generals in the Era of the Punic Wars* (Helsinki 1987).

Pinna Parpaglia, P. "Sulla *rogatio Metilia de aequando magistri equitum et dictatoris iure*," *SDHI* 35 (1969) 215–248.

Pinsent, J. *Military Tribunes and Plebeian Consuls: The Fasti from 444 V to 342 V* (Wiesbaden 1975).

Rawson, E. *Roman Culture and Society: Collected Papers* (Oxford 1991).

Reynolds, J. M. *Aphrodisias and Rome* (London 1982).

Rich, J. W. "Roman Aims in the First Macedonian War," *PCPhS* 30 (1984) 126–180.

Richard, J.-C. *Les origines de la plèbe romaine: Essai sur la formation du dualisme patricio-plébéien* (Rome 1978).

———. "Sur le Plébiscite *ut liceret consules ambos plebeios creari* (Tite-Live VII, 42, 2)," *Historia* 28 (1979) 65–75.

———. "*Praetor collega consulis est*: Contribution à l'histoire de la préture," *RPh* 56 (1982) 19–31.

Richardson, J. S. *Hispaniae: Spain and the Development of Roman Imperialism, 218–82 B.C.* (Cambridge 1986).

——. "Les *peregrini* et l'idée d' 'empire' sous la République romaine," *RD* 68 (1990) 147–155.

——. "*Imperium Romanum*: Empire and the Language of Power," *JRS* 81 (1991) 1–9.

Rickman, G. *The Corn Supply of Ancient Rome* (Oxford 1980).

Ridley, R. T. "The Extraordinary Commands of the Late Republic. A Matter of Definition," *Historia* 30 (1981) 280–297.

Rigsby, K. "*Provincia Asia*," *TAPhA* 118 (1988) 123–153.

Rivet, A. L. F. *Gallia Narbonensis* (London 1988).

Rosenberger, V. *Bella et expeditiones: Die antike Terminologie der Kriege Roms* (Stuttgart 1992).

Rosenstein, N. *Imperatores Victi* (Berkeley 1990).

——. "Sorting Out the Lot in Republican Rome," *AJPh* 116 (1995) 43–75.

Rotondi, G. *Leges Publicae Populi Romani* (Milan 1912).

Rudolph, H. "Das Imperium der römischen Magistrate," *NJAB* 114 (1939) 145–164.

Russell, H. E. "Insignia of Office As Rewards in the Roman Republic: Advancement in Rank for the Soldier and the Public Prosecutor" (diss. Bryn Mawr 1950).

Ryan, F. X. "The Praetorship of Favonius," *AJPh* 115 (1994) 587–601.

——. "The *Lex Scantinia* and the Prosecution of Censors and Aediles," *CPh* 89 (1994) 159–162.

——. "L. Novius Niger," *C&M* 46 (1995) 151–156.

——. "Senate Intervenants in 61 B.C., and the Aedileship of L. Domitius Ahenobarbarus," *Hermes* 123 (1995) 82–90.

——. "Ten Ill-starred Aediles," *Klio* 78 (1996) 68–86.

——. "The Quaestorship and Aedileship of C. Octavius," *RhM* 139 (1996) 251–253.

Salmon, E. T. *Roman Colonization under the Republic* (Ithaca, N.Y., 1970).

Sanctis, G. De. *Storia dei Romani* I–IV: 1 (Turin 1907–1923); IV: 3 (Florence 1964).

Schleussner, B. *Die Legaten der römischen Republik: Decem legati und ständige Hilfs-gesandte* (Munich 1978).

——. "M. Centenius Pacnula und C. Centenius," *WJA* 4 (1978) 215–222.

Serrao, F. *La 'iurisdictio' del pretore peregrino* (Milan 1954).

Shackleton Bailey, D. R. "Nobiles and novi Reconsidered," *AJPh* 107 (1986) 255–260.

——. *Onomasticon to Cicero's Speeches* (Norman, Okla., 1988).

——. *Two Studies in Roman Nomenclature*[2] (Atlanta, Ga., 1991).

——. *Onomasticon to Cicero's Letters* (Stuttgart 1995).

——. *Onomasticon to Cicero's Treatises* (Stuttgart 1996).

Shatzman, I. *Senatorial Wealth and Roman Politics* (Brussels 1975).

Sherwin-White, A. N. *Roman Citizenship*[2] (Oxford 1973; 1st ed. 1939).

——. *Roman Foreign Policy in the East* (Norman, Okla., 1984).

Sohlberg, D. "Militärtribunen und verwandte Probleme der frühen römischen Republik," *Historia* 40 (1991) 257–274.

——. "Dictateurs et tribuns de la plèbe: Problèmes de la république romaine à ses débuts," *CCGG* 4 (1993) 247–258.

Starr, C. G. *The Beginnings of Imperial Rome: Rome in the Mid-Republic* (Ann Arbor, Mi., 1980).

Staveley, E. S. "The *Fasces* and *Imperium Maius*," *Historia* 12 (1963) 458–484.

Stella Maranca, F. "Fasti Praetorii I: Dal 366 al 44 av. Cristo," in *MAL* (ser. 6) 2 (1927) 277–376.

Stewart, R. "Catiline and the Crisis of 63–60 B.C.: The Italian Perspective," *Latomus* 54 (1995) 62–78.

Strachan-Davidson, J. L. *Problems of the Roman Criminal Law* I–II (Oxford 1912).

Stumpf, G. R. *Numismatische Studien zur Chronologie der römischen Statthalter in Kleinasien (122 v. Chr.–163 n. Chr.)* (Saarbrücken 1991).

Sumner, G. V. "The Lex Annalis under Caesar," *Phoenix* 25 (1971) 246–271, 357–371.

———. *The Orators in Cicero's Brutus: Prosopography and Chronology* (Toronto 1973).

———. "Governors of Asia in the Nineties B.C.," *GRBS* 19 (1978) 147–153.

Syme, R. *Roman Papers* I–II, ed. E. Badian (Oxford 1979).

Taylor, L. R. "Magistrates of 55 B.C. in Cicero's *Pro Plancio* and Catullus 52," *Athenaeum* 42 (1964) 12–28.

———. *Roman Voting Assemblies from the Hannibalic War to the Dictatorship of Caesar* (Ann Arbor, Mi., 1966).

Thiel, J. H. *Studies on the History of Roman Sea-Power in Republican Times* (Amsterdam 1946).

———. *A History of Roman Sea-Power before the Second Punic War* (Amsterdam 1954).

Thommen, L. *Das Volkstribunat der späten römischen Republik* (Stuttgart 1989).

Toynbee, A. J. *Hannibal's Legacy: The Hannibalic War's Effects on Roman Life* I–II (Oxford 1965).

Tuchelt, K. *Frühe Denkmäler Roms in Kleinasien: Beiträge zur archäologischen Uberlieferung aus der Zeit der Republik und des Augustus* I (Tübigen 1979).

Valditara, G. *Studi sul magister populi, dagli ausiliari militari del rex ai primi magistrati repubblicani* (Milan 1989).

Versnel, H. *Triumphus: An Inquiry into the Origin, Development and Meaning of the Roman Triumph* (Leiden 1970).

Walbank, F. W. *A Historical Commentary on Polybius* I–III (Oxford 1957–1979).

Watson, A. *Law Making in the Later Roman Republic* (Oxford 1974).

———. *Roman Private Law around 200 B.C.* (Edinburgh 1971).

Weinrib, E. J. "The Prosecution of Roman Magistrates," *Phoenix* 22 (1968) 32–56.

Werner, R. *Der Beginn der römischen Republik: Historisch-chronologische Untersuchungen über die Anfangszeit der libera res publica* (Munich and Vienna 1963).

Wieacker, F. *Vom römischen Recht: Zehn Versuche*[2] (Stuttgart 1961).

———. "Altrömische Priesterjurisprudenz," in *Iuris professio: Festgabe für M. Kaser zum 80. Geburtstag* (Vienna 1986) 347–370.

———. *Römische Rechtsgeschichte*, I: *Einleitung, Quellenkunde, Frühzeit und Republik* (Munich 1988).

Wilkes, J. *The Illyrians* (Oxford 1992).

Willems, P. *Le Sénat de la république romaine: Sa composition et ses attributions* I–II (Louvain 1878–1883).

Wiseman, T.P. *Roman Studies, Literary and Historical* (Liverpool 1987).

Wulff Alonso, F. *Romanos e Itálicos en la Baja República: Estudios sobre sus relaciones entre la Segunda Guerra Púnica y la Guerra Social (201–91 a. C.)* (Brussels 1991).

Ziólkowski, A. "The Plundering of Epirus in 167 B.C.: Economic Considerations," *PBSR* 54 (1986) 69–80.

Zippel, G. *Die römische Herrschaft in Illyrien bis auf Augustus* (Leipzig 1877).

Select Index of Roman Names

The list below collects references to the Roman officials of most importance to the main arguments of this book, ordered by *nomina* followed by *RE* numbers (except for emperors, who are presented simply in anglicized form), and, after each full name, representative magistracies or commissions. In a few instances, I have altered the *RE* sequence of names within a given *gens* to clarify family relationships. Parentheses surrounding a page number indicate that there the person appears without name; specific footnote numbers are added to page locators only where otherwise there would be ambiguity. On the whole, I have excluded from this index (a) early Republican non-praetors and Imperial figures mentioned incidentally, e.g., in prosopographical discussions; (b) praetors (attested and inferred) who appear only in Appendix B; (c) sub-praetorians not of direct relevance to the central issues of this study.

Acilius (25) Balbus, M.' (pr. ≥153, cos. 150), (174–175), 737

Acilius (35) Glabrio, M.' (pr. 196, cos. 191), 109, 124, 206–207, 301, 695, 730

Acilius (38) Glabrio, M.' (pr. 70, cos. 67), 404, 416, 455, 459, 472–473, 491, 564, 631, 718, 721, 752, (772 n. 81), 788, (790 n. 56)

Acilius (Atilius 16 = Acilius 7) (Sapiens), L. (pr. 197), 695, 729

Aebutius (2) (?tr. pl. 2c), introduces *lex* on civil procedure, 132, 134

Aebutius (10) (Parrus), T. (pr. 178), 147–148, 353, (622–623), 697–698, 733

Aebutius (13, cf. 7) Helva, M. (pr. 168), 699, 735

Aelius (84) Ligus, P. (pr. ?175, cos. 172), 114, (122), 734

Aelius (100) Paetus, P. (cos. 337), 68, 274, 897

Aelius (101) Paetus, P. (pr. 203, cos. 201), (116), 197, 206, 208, 261, (293 nn. 135 and 143), 296, (298 n. 208), 641–642, 646, 659–660, 687, 728, 897, 925

Aelius (103) Paetus, Q. (pr. ?>218), 726, 896

Aelius (104) Paetus, Q. (pr. ?170, cos. 167), (124), 735

Aelius (105) Paetus Catus, Sex. (cos. 198), 60, 108, 200, 273, 319, (602), 687

Aelius (150) Tubero, L. (pr. ?≥49), 756, 872

Aelius (152) Tubero, P. (pr. 201, II 177), 138–139, 170–171, 290, (626), 683, 729

"Aemilius, M." (spurious pr. 216), 287

Aemilius (cf. 67) Lepidus, M.'(?) (pr. 213), (107), 323, 679, 685, 727

Aemilius (62) Lepidus, M.' (pr. ≥69, cos. 66), 749, 915

Aemilius (19, 67) (Lepidus), M. (pr. 218), (137), 483, 681, 726

Aemilius (68) Lepidus, M. (pr. 191, cos. 187, II 175), (99), 145–146, 199, 201–202, 310, 339, (353 n. 146), 483, 650, 688, 695–696, 731, 857

Aemilius (70) Lepidus, M. (pr. ≥161, cos. 158), 295, 736, 901

Aemilius (72) Lepidus, M. (pr. 81, cos. 78), 389, 394–395, 430–431, 446, 483–484, 486, 494, 507, 509–510, 575–576, 589–591, 709, 717, 750, 788, 790, 823, 830, 894, 932; generally, in the *Bellum Lepidanum*, 425, 466, 481, 496, 529–530, 634

Aemilius (73) Lepidus, M. (pr. 49, cos. 46, II 42), 46, 121, 252, 266, 661–662

Aemilius (80) Lepidus Livianus, Mam. (pr. ≥80, cos. 77), 389, 446, 450, 459, 575–576, 631, 692, 717, 748, 779, (790 n. 56)

Aemilius (81) (Lepidus) Paullus, L. (pr. 53, cos. 50), 755, 788, 792, 793, 794 nn. 110 and 113

Cicereius (1), C. (pr. 173), 148, 623, 698, 734

Cincius (5) Alimentus, L. (pr. 210), 193, 247, 312, 682, 728

Claudius (emperor), 39, 41, 51–53, 218–219, 599

Claudius (22), L. (pr. 174), 698, 734

Claudius (62, cf. 61) Asellus, Ti. (pr. 206), 683, 728

Claudius (91) Caecus, Ap. (pr. ?II 295, cos. 307, II 296), 56, 76, 82, 649, 725, 901

Claudius (103) Centho, Ap. (pr. 175), 109, 172, 174, 211–212, 214, 317, 320, 698–699, 734

Claudius (122) Crassus Inregillensis, Ap. (cos. 349), 71, (273 n. 47)

Claudius (165) Glaber (pr. 73), 431, 751

Claudius (see 165) Glaber, C. (pr. ≥75), 431, 467, 749

Claudius (166) Glicia, M. (dict. 249), 283

Claudius (214) Marcellus, C. (pr. 80), 483–484, 709, 750, 791, 816, 883, 893–894, 908, 932

Claudius (218) Marcellus, M. (cos. 331), 274, (292 n. 127)

Claudius (220) Marcellus, M. (pr. II 216, cos. 222, V 208), 94, 252, 681–682, 684–685, 727; in 216 and (as pro cos.) 215 against Hannibal, 102, 139–140, 157, 186, 191–192, 277, 301, 313, 324, 340, 610–611, 646, 660–663, 669, 776; in other years of Second Punic War, 113–114, 138, 141, 144–145, 148, 156–157, 196, 292, (301 n. 245), 310, 334, 651, (658), 838; honored in Sicily by "Marcellia" festival, 550, 554, 838

Claudius (222) Marcellus, M. (pr. 198, cos. 196), 687, 729

Claudius (223 = 224) Marcellus, M. (pr. 188, cos. 183), 116, (170), 201, (293 n. 145), 294, 298, 353, 689, 694, 731

Claudius (see 223, 224) Marcellinus, M. (spurious pr. 185), 667

Claudius (225) Marcellus, M. (pr. 169, cos. 166, III 152), 123, 174, 298 nn. 205 and 206, (607), 650, 652, 699, 701, 735

Claudius (226) Marcellus, M. (pr. ??>90), 375, 691, 744, 768

Claudius (229) Marcellus, M. (pr. ≥54, cos. 51), 595, (636), 750, (792 n. 89)

Claudius (245) Nero, Ap. (pr. 195), 166–167, 695, 730

Claudius (246) Nero, C. (pr. 212, cos. 207), 155–157, 192–195, (324 n. 14), (620), 645, 685–686, 693, 727

Claudius (247) Nero, C. (pr. ?81), 389, 394, 557, 572, 717, 750, 892, 893, 930

Claudius (249) Nero, Ti. (pr. 204, cos. 202), 683, 728

Claudius (250) Nero, Ti. (pr. 181), 697, 733

Claudius (251) Nero, Ti. (pr. 178), 201, 230, 243, 291, (297 n. 196), 315, 324, (611), (620), 662–663, 669–670, 690, 733, 776

Claudius (252) Nero, Ti. (pr. 167), 699, 735

Claudius (253) Nero, Ti. (pr. >63), 711, 749, 810, 855

Claudius (293) Pulcher, Ap. (pr. 215, cos. 212), 116, 139, 145–146, 187, 308, 310, 312, 334, 664, 681–682, 685, 727, 880

Claudius (294) Pulcher, P. (pr. 187, cos. 185), (124), 203, 333, 688–689, 731

Claudius (295) Pulcher, Ap. (pr. ≥146, cos. 143), 177, 219, 737

Claudius (296) Pulcher, Ap. (pr. 88, cos. 79), 377–378, 383, 403, 460, 466, 529–530, 589, 692, 709, 747, 774, 861, 893

Claudius (297) Pulcher, Ap. (pr. 57, cos. 54), 712, 719, 754; in 57 and (*ex praetura*) in 56, 397, 417, 457–458, 474, 495, 568, (594), (630), (772 n. 81), 894; subsequent career, 18, 402, 420, 430, 497, 569, 573–574, 579, 594, 788, (794 n. 108), 815, 816 nn. 440 and 442, 820, 846 nn. 188 and 189, 864, 887, 893, 927

Claudius (300) Pulcher, C. (pr. suff. 180, cos. 177), (128)–129, (147), 203, 309, 333, 368, 656, 663, 668, 690, 733

Claudius (302) Pulcher, C. (pr. 95, cos. 92), 237, 368, 480, 591, 747, 769, 771, 788

Claudius (303) Pulcher, C. (pr. 56), 397, 497, 569, 594, (639), 719, 755, 826, 893

Claudius (304) Pulcher, P. (cos. 249), 85

Claudius (305) Pulcher, Ap. (pr. 188, cos. 184), 689, (612), 731

Claudius (376) Unimanus (pr. 145), 176, 702, 740

Clodius (48) Pulcher, P. (tr. pl. 58, pr. cand. 52), 397, 413, 418, 423, 428, 459, 467, 535, 545, 568–569, 573, 787–788, 889; in Bona Dea affair, 436–437, 493, 631, 783, 800, 813, 815; passes tribunician law for coss. 58 on their provinces, 395, 535; moves law to annex Cyprus, 428–430; after tribunate, 18, 422, 438, 457–458, 470, 474–475, 631, 775, 790 nn. 58 and 62, 807, 815, 826, 827, 927; and "iudices Clodiani," 783

Cloulius (Cloelius 5), T. (pr. ??83), 379–380, 744, 907

Cluvius (2), C. (pr. 2/1c), 523, 548, 757

Cluvius (8), Sp. (pr. 172), 698, 735

Coelius (2), P. (pr. 74), 445–446, 630, 751

Coelius (6) Antipater, C. (?pr. ?≥82), 363–364, 380–381, 717, 744

Coelius (12) Caldus, C. (pr. >98, cos. 94), (99), 348, 363, 366, 500, 587, 671–673, 707, 716, 746, 788, 875, 909

Coelius (14) Caldus, C. (q. ?pro pr. 50), 574, 720, 798

Considius (3) (quaesitor 52), 422, 439

Considius (11) Longus, C. (pr. ≥54), 546, 712–713, 755, 795, 856, 894

Cornelius (not in *RE*) (pr?), defeated by Pannonians, 229

Cornelius (18), C. (tr. pl. 67), 419, 809, 815, 922; passes law on praetors' edicts, 133, 449–450, 463–464, 618

Cornelius (42), P. (pr. 234), (89), 90–91, (604–605), 726

Cornelius (69) Balbus, L. (cos. suff. 40), 423, 854

General Index

The analysis in this index is largely confined to Roman wars, institutions, and concepts. Where non-Roman peoples and territories appear as military *provinciae*, the reader should consult also the Select Index of Roman Names (hereafter, Name Index) under the relevant commanders. Specific footnote numbers on individual pages are listed only as necessary.